24th Conference on Computational Natural Language Learning (CoNLL 2020)

Online
19 - 20 November 2020

ISBN: 978-1-7138-1992-9

CoNLL 2020

The 24th Conference on Computational Natural Language Learning (CoNLL)

Proceedings of the Conference

November 19-20, 2020
Online

Introduction

Welcome to the the 24th Conference on Computational Natural Language Learning (CoNLL). This year, CoNLL, like many conferences, is taking place online, due to the impact of the COVID-19 pandemic. In a major shift from previous editions of the conference, CoNLL 2020 focuses on theoretically, cognitively and scientifically motivated approaches to computational linguistics, rather than on work driven by particular engineering applications. This shift was indicated in the call for papers, and was reflected in the instructions given to the reviewers and area chairs.

We received 255 submissions, of which 227 were sent out for review (the remaining submissions were desk rejected or withdrawn by the authors). We accepted 53 of the submissions that were sent out for review (23.3% acceptance rate). CoNLL 2019 features two invited speakers, Emmanuel Dupoux (Ecole des Hautes Etudes en Sciences Sociales and Facebook AI Research, Paris, France) and Kristina Toutanova (Google, Seattle, USA).

We are extremely grateful to all our reviewers (too many to list), and our dedicated area chairs: Aida Nematzadeh, Alvin Grisom II, Andrew Caines, Arianna Bisazza, Barry Devereux, Colin Bannard, Daniel Cer, David Schlangen, Erik Velldal, Greg Durrett, Grzegorz Chrupala, Jacob Andreas, Kevin Duh, Kyle Gorman, Leon Bergen, Marten van Schijndel, Michael Roth, Raffaella Bernardi, Roi Reichert, Sam Bowman, Stella Frank, Tim O'Donnell, Vivek Srikumar, Yevgeni Berzak, Yonatan Belinkov and Yulia Tsvetkov. We are also grateful to Google for generously supporting the conference.

We would also like to thank Julia Hockenmaier and Afra Alishahi and the members of the SIGNLL board for entrusting to us the task of organizing the conference, and Mohit Bansal and Aline Villavicencio, the organizers of CoNLL 2019, for their patient advice.

Raquel Fernández and Tal Linzen
CoNLL 2020 conference co-chairs

Organizers:

Tal Linzen, New York University
Raquel Fernandez, University of Amsterdam

Area Chairs:

Aida Nematzadeh
Alvin Grisom II
Andrew Caines
Arianna Bisazza
Barry Devereux
Colin Bannard
Daniel Cer
David Schlangen
Erik Velldal
Greg Durrett
Grzegorz Chrupala
Jacob Andreas
Kevin Duh
Kyle Gorman
Leon Bergen
Marten van Schijndel
Michael Roth
Raffaella Bernardi
Roi Reichert
Sam Bowman
Stella Frank
Tim O'Donnell
Vivek Srikumar
Yevgeni Berzak
Yonatan Belinkov
Yulia Tsvetkov

Invited Speakers:

Emmanuel Dupoux (Ecole des Hautes Etudes en Sciences Sociales and Facebook AI Research,
Paris, France)
Kristina Toutanova (Google, Seattle, USA)

Table of Contents

Conference Program

Enriching Word Embeddings with Temporal and Spatial Information

Hongyu Gong   Suma Bhat   Pramod Viswanath
University of Illinois at Urbana-Champaign
`{hgong6,spbhat2,pramodv}@illinois.edu`

Abstract

The meaning of a word is closely linked to sociocultural factors that can change over time and location, resulting in corresponding meaning changes. Taking a global view of words and their meanings in a widely used language, such as English, may require us to capture more refined semantics for use in time-specific or location-aware situations, such as the study of cultural trends or language use. However, popular vector representations for words do not adequately include temporal or spatial information. In this work, we present a model for learning word representation conditioned on time and location. In addition to capturing meaning changes over time and location, we require that the resulting word embeddings retain salient semantic and geometric properties. We train our model on time- and location-stamped corpora, and show using both quantitative and qualitative evaluations that it can capture semantics across time and locations. We note that our model compares favorably with the state-of-the-art for time-specific embedding, and serves as a new benchmark for location-specific embeddings.

1   Introduction

The use of word embeddings as a form of lexical representation has transformed the use of natural language processing for many applications such as machine translation (Qi et al., 2018) and language understanding (Peters et al., 2018). The changing of word meaning over the course of time and space, termed *semantic drift*, has been the subject of long standing research in diachronic linguistics (Ullmann, 1979; Blank, 1999). Additionally, the emergence of distinct geographically-qualified English varieties (e.g., South African English) has given rise to salient lexical variation giving several English words different meanings depending on the geographic location of their use, as documented in studies on World Englishes (Kachru et al., 2006; Mesthrie and Bhatt, 2008). Considering the multiplicity of meanings that a word can take over the span of time and space owing to inevitable linguistic, and sociocultural factors among others, a static representation of a word as a single word embedding seems rather limited. Take the word *apple* as an example. Its early to near-recent mentions in written documents referred only to a fruit, but in the recent times it is also the name of a large technology company. Another example is the title for the head of government, which is "president" in the USA, and is "prime minister" in Canada.

Naturally, we expect that one word should have different representations conditioned on the time or location. In this paper, we study how word embeddings can be enriched to encode their semantic drift in time and space. Extending a recent line of research on time-specific embeddings, including the works by Bamler and Mandt and Yao et al., we propose a model to capture varying lexical semantics across different conditions—of time and location.

A key technical challenge of learning conditioned embeddings is to put the embeddings (derived from different time periods or geographical locations) in the same vector space and preserve their geometry within and across different instances of the conditions. Traditional approaches involve a two-step mechanism of first learning the sets of embeddings separately under the different conditions, and then aligning them via appropriate transformations (Kulkarni et al., 2015; Hamilton et al., 2016; Zhang et al., 2016). A primary limitation of these methods is their inadequate representation of word semantics, as we show in our comparative evaluation. Another approach to conditioned embedding uses a loss function with regularizers over word embeddings across conditions for their smooth trajectory in the vector space (Yao et al.,

Proceedings of the 24th Conference on Computational Natural Language Learning, pages 1–11
Online, November 19-20, 2020. ©2020 Association for Computational Linguistics
https://doi.org/10.18653/v1/P17

2018). However, its scope is limited to modeling semantic drift over only time.

We propose a model for general conditioned embeddings, with the novelty that it explicitly preserves embedding geometry under different conditions and captures different degrees of word semantic changes. We summarize our contributions below.

1. We propose an unsupervised model to learn condition-specific embeddings including time-specific and location-specific embeddings;

2. Using benchmark datasets we demonstrate the state-of-the-art performance of the proposed model in accurately capturing word semantics across time periods and geographical regions;

3. We provide the first dataset[1] to evaluate word embeddings across locations to foster research in this direction.

2   Related Work

Time-specific embeddings. The evolution of word meaning with time has been a widely studied problem in sociolinguistics (Ullmann, 1979; Tang, 2018). Early computational approaches to uncovering these trends have relied on frequency-based models, which have used frequency changes to trace semantic shift over time (Lijffijt et al., 2012; Choi and Varian, 2012; Michel et al., 2011). More recent works have sought to study these phenomena using distributional models (Kutuzov et al., 2018; Huang and Paul, 2019; Schlechtweg et al., 2020).

Recent approaches on time-specific embeddings can be divided into three broad categories: aligning independently trained embeddings across time, joint training of time-dependent embeddings and using contextualized vectors from pre-trained models. Approaches of the first kind include the works by Kulkarni et al., Hamilton et al. and Zhang et al.. They rely on pre-training multiple sets of embeddings for different times independently, and then aligning one set of embeddings with another set so that two sets of embeddings are comparable.

The second approach—joint training—aims to guarantee the alignment of embeddings in the same vectors space so that they are directly comparable. Compared with the previous category of approaches, the joint learning of time-stamped embeddings has shown improved abilities to capture semantic changes across time. Bamler and Mandt used a probabilistic model to learn time-specific embeddings (Bamler and Mandt, 2017). They make a parametric assumption (Gaussian) on the evolution of embeddings to guarantee the embedding alignment. Yao et al. learned embeddings by the factorization of a positive pointwise mutual information (PPMI) matrix. They imposed L2 constraints on embeddings from neighboring time periods for embedding alignment (Yao et al., 2018). Rosenfeld and Erk proposed a neural model to first encode time and word information respectively and then to learn time-specific embeddings (Rosenfeld and Erk, 2018). Dubossarsky et al. aligned word embeddings by sharing their context embeddings at different times (Dubossarsky et al., 2019).

Some recent works fall in the third category, retrieving contextualized representations from pre-trained models such as BERT (Devlin et al., 2018) as time-specific sense embeddings of words (Hu et al., 2019; Giulianelli et al., 2020). These pre-trained embeddings are limited to the scope of local contexts, while we learn the global representation of words in a given time or location.

The underlying mathematical models of these previous works on temporal embeddings are discussed in the supplementary material. Our model belongs to the second category of joint embedding training. Different from previous works, our embedding is based on a model that explicitly takes into account the important semantic properties of time-specific embeddings.

Embedding with spatial information. Lexical semantics is also sensitive to spatial factors. For example, the word denoting the head of government of a nation may be used differently depending on the region. For instance, the words can range from *president* to *prime minister* or *king* depending on the region. Language variation across regional contexts has been analyzed in sociolinguistics and dialectology studies (e.g.,(Silva-Corvalán, 2006; Kulkarni et al., 2016)). It is also understood that a deeper understanding of semantics enhanced with location information is critical to location-sensitive applications such as content localization of global search engines (Brandon Jr, 2001).

Some approaches towards this have included, a latent variable model proposed for geographical linguistic variation (Eisenstein et al., 2010) and a

---

skip-gram model for geographically situated language (Bamman et al., 2014). The current study is most similar to (Bamman et al., 2014) with the overlap in our intents to learn location-specific embeddings for measuring semantic drift. Most studies on location-dependent language resort to a qualitative evaluation, whereas (Bamman et al., 2014) resorts to a quantitative analysis for entity similarity. However, it is limited to a given region without exploring semantic equivalence of words across different geographic regions. To the extent we are aware, this is the first study to present a quantitative evaluation of word representations across geographical regions with the use of a dataset constructed for the purpose.

3 Model

We now introduce the model on which the condition-specific embedding training is based in this section. We assume access to a corpus divided into sub-corpora based on their conditions (*time* or *location*), and texts in the same condition (e.g., same time period) are gathered in each sub-corpus. For each condition, the co-occurrence counts of word pairs gathered from its sub-corpus are the corpus statistics we use for the embedding training. We note that because these sub-corpora vary in size, we scale the word co-occurrences of every condition so that all sub-corpora have the same total number of word pairs. We term the scaled value of word co-occurrences of word w_i and w_j in condition c as $\mathbf{X}_{i,j,c}$.

A static model (without regard to the temporal or spatial conditions) proposed by Arora et al. provides the unifying theme for the seemingly different embedding approaches of word2vec and GloVe. In particular, It reveals that corpus statistics such as word co-occurrences could be estimated from embeddings. Inspired by this, we proposed a model for conditioned embeddings, and characterize such a model by its ability to capture the lexical semantic properties across different conditions.

3.1 Properties of Conditioned Embeddings

Before exploring the details of our model for condition-specific embeddings, we discuss some desired semantic properties of these embeddings. We expect the embeddings to capture time- and location-sensitive lexical semantics. We denote by c the condition we use to refine word embeddings, which can be a specific time period or a location. We then have temporal embeddings if the condition is *time period*, and spatial embeddings if the condition is *location*. For a word w, the condition-specific word embedding for condition c is denoted as $\mathbf{v}_{w,c}$. The key semantic properties of the condition-specific word embedding, which we consider in our model are:

(1) **Preservation of geometry**. One geometric property of static embeddings is that the difference vector encodes word relations, i.e., $\mathbf{v}_{\text{bigger}} - \mathbf{v}_{\text{big}} \approx \mathbf{v}_{\text{greater}} - \mathbf{v}_{\text{great}}$ (Mikolov et al., 2013). Analogously, for the condition-specific embedding of semantically stable words across conditions, given word pairs (w_1, w_2) and (w_3, w_4) with the same underlying lexical relation, we expect the following equation to hold in any condition c.

$$\mathbf{v}_{w_1,c} - \mathbf{v}_{w_2,c} \approx \mathbf{v}_{w_3,c} - \mathbf{v}_{w_4,c}. \tag{1}$$

This property is implicitly preserved in approaches aligning independently trained embeddings with linear transformations (Kulkarni et al., 2015).

(2) **Consistency over conditions**. Most word meanings change slowly over a given condition, i.e., their condition-specific word embeddings should be highly correlated (Hamilton et al., 2016). When the condition is time period, for example, c_1 is the year 2000, and c_2 is the year 2001, we expect that for a given word, $\mathbf{v}_{w,c_1}$ and $\mathbf{v}_{w,c_2}$ have high similarity given their temporal proximity. The consistency property is preserved in models which jointly train embeddings across conditions (e.g., (Yao et al., 2018)).

(3) **Different degrees of word change**. Although word meanings change over time, not all words undergo this change to the same degree; some words change dramatically while others stay relatively stable across conditions (Blank, 1999). In our formulation, we require the representation to capture the different degrees of word meaning change. This property is unexplored in prior studies.

We incorporate these semantic properties as explicit constraints into our model for condition-specific embeddings, which we formulate as an optimization problem.

3.2 Model

We propose a model that generates embeddings satisfying the semantic properties as discussed above. Writing the embedding $\mathbf{v}_{w,c}$ of word w in condition c as a function of its condition-independent representation $\mathbf{v}_w$, condition representation vector

$\mathbf{q}_c$ and deviation embedding $\mathbf{d}_{w,c}$:

$$\mathbf{v}_{w,c} = \mathbf{v}_w \odot \mathbf{q}_c + \mathbf{d}_{w,c}, \qquad (2)$$

where $\odot$ is Hadamard product (i.e., elementwise multiplication). We decompose the conditioned representation into three component embeddings. This novel representation is motivated by the intuition that a word w usually carries its basic meaning $\mathbf{v}_w$ and its meaning is influenced by different conditions represented by $\mathbf{q}_c$. Moreover, words have different degrees of meaning variation, which is captured by the deviation embedding $\mathbf{d}_{w,c}$.

We begin with a model proposed by Arora et al. for static word embeddings regardless of the temporal or spatial conditions (Arora et al., 2016). Let $\mathbf{v}_w$ be the static representation of word w. For a pair of words w_1 and w_2, the static model assumes that

$$\log \mathbb{P}(w_1, w_2) \approx \frac{1}{2} \|\mathbf{v}_{w_1} + \mathbf{v}_{w_2}\|^2, \qquad (3)$$

where $\mathbb{P}(w_1, w_2)$ is the co-occurrence probability of these two words in the training corpus.

Let $\mathbb{P}_c(w_1, w_2)$ be the co-occurrence probability of word pair (w_1, w_2) in the condition c. Based on the static model in Eq. (3), for a condition c we have

$$\log \mathbb{P}_c(w_1, w_2) \approx \frac{1}{2} \|\mathbf{v}_{w_1,c} + \mathbf{u}_{w_2,c}\|^2. \qquad (4)$$

Here, borrowing ideas from previous embedding algorithms including word2vec (Mikolov et al., 2013) and GloVe (Pennington et al., 2014), we use two sets of word embeddings $\{\mathbf{v}_{w,c}\}$ and $\{\mathbf{u}_{w,c}\}$ for a word w_1 and its context word w_2 respectively in condition c. Accordingly, we have two sets of condition-independent embeddings $\{\mathbf{v}_w\}$ and $\{\mathbf{u}_w\}$, and two sets of deviation vectors $\{\mathbf{d}_{w,c}\}$ and $\{\mathbf{d}'_{w,c}\}$. The condition-specific embeddings in Eq. (2) can be written as:

$$\begin{cases} \mathbf{v}_{w_1,c} &= \mathbf{v}_{w_1} \odot \mathbf{q}_c + \mathbf{d}_{w_1,c} \\ \mathbf{u}_{w_2,c} &= \mathbf{u}_{w_2} \odot \mathbf{q}_c + \mathbf{d}'_{w_2,c} \end{cases} \qquad (5)$$

By combining Eq. (4) and (5), we derive the model for condition-specific embeddings:

$$\log \mathbb{P}_c(w_1, w_2) \approx \frac{1}{2} \|(\mathbf{v}_{w_1} \odot \mathbf{q}_c + \mathbf{d}_{w_1,c})$$
$$+ (\mathbf{u}_{w_2} \odot \mathbf{q}_c + \mathbf{d}'_{w_2,c})\|^2. \qquad (6)$$

This model can be simplified as

$$\log \mathbb{P}_c(w_1, w_2) \approx b_{w_1,c} + b'_{w_2,c} +$$
$$(\mathbf{v}_{w_1} \odot \mathbf{q}_c + \mathbf{d}_{w_1,c})^T (\mathbf{u}_{w_2} \odot \mathbf{q}_c + \mathbf{d}'_{w_2,c}), \qquad (7)$$

where $b_{w_1,c}$ and $b'_{w_2,c}$ are bias terms introduced to replace the terms $\|\mathbf{v}_{w_1,c}\|^2$ and $\|\mathbf{u}_{w_2,c}\|^2$ respectively. We document the derivation details of Eq. (7) in the supplementary material.

Optimization problem. This model enables us to use the conditioned embeddings to estimate the word co-occurrence probabilities in a specific condition. Conversely, we can formulate an optimization problem to train the conditioned embeddings from the word co-occurrences based on our model.

We count the co-occurrences of all word pairs (w_1, w_2) in different conditions based on the respective sub-corpora. For example, we count word co-occurrences over different time periods to incorporate temporal information into word embeddings, and we count word pairs in different locations to learn spatially sensitive word representations.

Recall that $\mathbf{X}_{i,j,c}$ is the scaled co-occurrence counts of w_i and w_j in condition c. Denote by W the total vocabulary and by C the number of conditions, where C is the number of time bins for the temporal condition or the number of locations for the location condition. Suppose that $\mathbf{V}$ is an $(m \times |W|)$ condition-independent word embedding matrix, where each column corresponds to an m-dimension word vector $\mathbf{v}_w$. Matrix $\mathbf{U}$ is an $(m \times |W|)$ basic context embedding matrix with each column as a context word vector $\mathbf{u}_w$. Matrix $\mathbf{Q}$ is an $(m \times C)$ matrix, where each column is a condition vector $\mathbf{q}_c$. As for deviation matrices, $\mathbf{D}_{m \times |W| \times C}$ and $\mathbf{D}'_{m \times |W| \times C}$ consist of m-dimension deviation vectors $\mathbf{d}_{w,c}$ and $\mathbf{d}'_{w,c}$ respectively for word w in condition c.

Our goal is to learn embeddings $\mathbf{U}$, $\mathbf{Q}$ and $\mathbf{D}$ so as to approximate the word co-occurrence counts based on the model in Eq.(7). Here, we design a loss function to be the approximation error of the embeddings, which is the mean square error between the condition-specific co-occurrences counted from the respective sub-corpora and their estimates from the embeddings.

To satisfy the property 2 of condition-specific embeddings, we impose L_2 constraints $\|\mathbf{q}_a - \mathbf{q}_b\|^2$ on the embeddings of condition a and b to guarantee the consistency over conditions. For time-specific embeddings, the constraints are for adjacent time bins. As for location-sensitive embeddings, the constraints are for all pairs of location embeddings.

Furthermore, to account for the slow change in meaning of most words across conditions (as in time periods or locations) listed as property 3 of conditioned embeddings, we also include L_2 constraints $\|\mathbf{D}\|^2$ and $\|\mathbf{D}'\|^2$ on the deviation terms to penalize big changes.

Putting together the approximation error, constraints on condition embeddings and deviations, we have the following loss function:

$$L = \sum_{c=1}^{C} \sum_{i=1}^{|W|} \sum_{j=1}^{|W|} \left((\mathbf{V}_i \odot \mathbf{Q}_c + \mathbf{D}_{i,c})^T (\mathbf{U}_j \odot \mathbf{Q}_c + \mathbf{D}'_{j,c}) \right.$$
$$\left. + \mathbf{b}_{i,c} + \mathbf{b}'_{j,c} - \log(\mathbf{X}_{i,j,c}) \right)^2$$
$$+ \frac{\alpha}{2} \sum_{a,b} \|\mathbf{Q}_a - \mathbf{Q}_b\|^2 + \frac{\beta}{2} (\|\mathbf{D}\|^2 + \|\mathbf{D}'\|^2). \quad (8)$$

In addition to ensuring a smooth trajectory of the embeddings, the penalization on the deviations $\mathbf{D}$ and $\mathbf{D}'$ is necessary to avoid the degenerate case that $\mathbf{Q}_c = \mathbf{0}, \forall c$.

We note that, for the constraint on condition embeddings in the loss function L, for time-specific embeddings we use $\sum_{c=1}^{C-1} \|\mathbf{Q}_{c+1} - \mathbf{Q}_c\|^2$, whereas for location-specific embeddings, the constraint becomes $\sum_{a=1}^{C-1} \sum_{b=a+1}^{C} \|\mathbf{Q}_a - \mathbf{Q}_b\|^2$.

Model Properties. We have presented our approach to learning conditioned embeddings. Now we will show that the proposed model satisfies the aforementioned key properties in Section 3.1. We start with the property of geometry preservation. For a set of semantically stable words $S = \{w_1, w_2, w_3, w_4\}$, it is known that $d_{w,c} \approx 0$ for $w \in S$. Suppose that the relation between w_1 and w_2 is the same as the relation between w_3 and w_4, i.e., $\mathbf{v}_{w_1} - \mathbf{v}_{w_2} = \mathbf{v}_{w_3} - \mathbf{v}_{w_4}$. Given Eq. (2) for any condition c, it holds that

$$\mathbf{v}_{w_1,c} - \mathbf{v}_{w_2,c} \approx (\mathbf{v}_{w_1} - \mathbf{v}_{w_2}) \odot q_c$$
$$\approx (\mathbf{v}_{w_3} - \mathbf{v}_{w_4}) \odot q_c \approx \mathbf{v}_{w_3,c} - \mathbf{v}_{w_4,c}. \quad (9)$$

As for the second property of consistency over conditions, we again consider a stable word w. Its conditioned embedding $v_{w,c}$ in condition c can be written as $\mathbf{v}_{w,c} = \mathbf{v}_w \odot q_c$. As is shown in Eq. (8), the L_2 constraint $\|q_a - q_b\|^2$ is put on different condition embeddings. The difference between word embeddings of w under two conditions a and b are:

$$\|\mathbf{v}_{w,a} - \mathbf{v}_{w,b}\|^2 = \|\mathbf{v}_w \odot (\mathbf{q}_a - \mathbf{q}_b)\|^2$$
$$\leq \frac{1}{2} \|\mathbf{v}_w\|^2 \cdot \|\mathbf{q}_a - \mathbf{q}_b\|^2. \quad (10)$$

According to Cauchy-Schwartz inequality, the L_2 constraint on condition vectors $\mathbf{q}_a - \mathbf{q}_b$ also acts as a constraint on word embeddings. With a large coefficient α, it prevents the embedding from differing too much across conditions, and guarantees the smooth trajectory of words.

Lastly we show that our model captures the degree of word changes. The deviation vector $\mathbf{d}_{w,c}$ we introduce in the model captures such changes. The L_2 constraint on $\|\mathbf{d}_{w,c}\|$ shown in Eq. (8) forces small deviation on most words which are smoothly changing across conditions. We assign a small coefficient β to this constraint to allow sudden meaning changes in some words. The hyperparameter setting is discussed below.

Embedding training. We have hyperparameters α and β as weights on the word consistency and the deviation constraints. We set $\alpha = 1.5$ and $\beta = 0.2$ in time-specific embeddings, and $\alpha = 1.0$ and $\beta = 0.2$ in location-specific embeddings.

At each training step, we randomly select a nonzero element $x_{i,j,c}$ from the co-occurrence tensor $\mathbf{X}$. Stochastic gradient descent with adaptive learning rate is applied to update $\mathbf{V}$, $\mathbf{U}$, $\mathbf{Q}$, $\mathbf{D}$, $\mathbf{D}'$, $\mathbf{d}$ and $\mathbf{d}'$, which are relevant to $x_{i,j,c}$ to minimize the loss L. The complexity of each step is $O(m)$, where m is the embedding dimension. In each epoch, we traverse all nonzero elements of $\mathbf{X}$. Thus we have $\text{nnz}(\mathbf{X})$ steps where $\text{nnz}(\cdot)$ is the number of nonzero elements. Although $\mathbf{X}$ contains $O(|W|^2)$ elements, $\mathbf{X}$ is very sparse since many words do not co-occur, so $\text{nnz}(\mathbf{X}) \ll |W|^2$. The time complexity of our model is $O(E \cdot m \cdot \text{nnz}(\mathbf{X}))$ for $E-$epoch training. We set $E = 40$ in training both temporal and spatial word embeddings.

Postprocessing. We note that embeddings under the same condition are not centered, i.e., the word vectors are distributed around some non-zero point. We center these vectors by removing the mean vector of all embeddings in the same condition. The centered embedding $\tilde{\mathbf{v}}_{w,c}$ of word w under condition c is:

$$\tilde{\mathbf{v}}_{w,c} = \mathbf{v}_{w,c} - \frac{1}{|W|} \sum_{\bar{w} \in W} \mathbf{v}_{\bar{w},c}. \quad (11)$$

The similarity between words across conditions is measured by the cosine similarity of their centered embeddings $\{\tilde{\mathbf{v}}_{w,c}\}$.

4 Experiments

In this section, we compare our condition-specific word embedding models with corresponding state-

Across time	the, in, to, a, of, it, by, with, at, was, are, and, on, who, for, not, they, but, he, is, from, have, as, has, their, about, her, been, there, or, will, this, said, would
Across regions	in, from, at, could, its, which, out, but, on, all, has, so, is, are, had, he, been, by, an, it, as, for, was, this, his, be, they, we, her, that, and, with, a, of, the

Table 1: Stable Words across Time and Locations

of-the-art models combined with temporal or spatial information. The dimension of all vectors is set as 50. We have the following baselines:

(1) **Basic word2vec** (BW2V). It is word2vec CBOW model, which is trained on the entire corpus without considering any temporal or spatial partition (Mikolov et al., 2013);

(2) **Transformed word2vec** (TW2V). Multiple sets of embeddings are trained separately for each condition. Two sets of embeddings are then aligned via a linear transformation (Kulkarni et al., 2015).

(3) **Aligned word2vec** (AW2V): Similar to TW2V, sets of embeddings are first trained independently and then aligned via orthonormal transformations (Hamilton et al., 2016).

(4) **Dynamic word embedding** (DW2V): This approach proposes a joint training of word embeddings at different times with alignment constraints on temporally adjacent sets of embeddings (Yao et al., 2018). We modify this baseline for location based embeddings by putting its alignment constraints on every two sets of embeddings.

4.1   Training Data

We used two corpora as training data–the time-stamped news corpus of the New York Times collected by (Yao et al., 2018) to train time-specific embeddings and a collection of location-specific texts in English, provided by the International Corpus of English project (ICE, 2019) for location-specific embeddings.

New York Times corpus. The news dataset from New York Times consists of $99,872$ articles from 1990 to 2016. We use time bins of size one-year, and divide the corpus into 27 time bins.

International Corpus of English (ICE). The ICE project collected written and spoken material in English (one million words each) from different regions of the world after 1989. We used the written portions collected from Canada, East Africa, Hong Kong, India, Ireland, Jamaica, the Philippines, Singapore and the United States of America.

Deviating from previous works, which remove both stop words and infrequent words from the vocabulary (Yao et al., 2018), we only remove words with observed frequency count less than a threshold. We keep the stop words to show that the trained embedding is able to identify them as being semantically stable. The frequency threshold is set to 200 (the same as (Yao et al., 2018)) for the New York Times corpus, and to 5 for the ICE corpus given that the smaller size of ICE corpus results in lower word frequency than the news corpus.

We evaluate the enriched word embeddings for the following aspects:

1. **Degree of semantic change**. As mentioned in the list of desired properties of conditioned embeddings, words undergo semantic change to different degrees. We check whether our embeddings can identify words whose meanings are relatively stable across conditions. These stable words will be discussed as part of the qualitative evaluation.

2. **Discovery of semantic change**. Besides stable words, we also study words whose meaning changes drastically over conditions. Since a word's neighbors in the embedding space can reflect its meaning, we find the neighbors in different conditions to demonstrate how the word meaning changes. The discovery of semantic changes will be discussed as part of our qualitative evaluation.

3. **Semantic equivalence across conditions**. All condition-specific embeddings are expected to be in the same vector space, i.e., the cosine similarity between a pair of embeddings reflects their lexical similarity even though they are from different condition values. Finding semantic equivalents with the derived embeddings will be discussed in the quantitative evaluation.

4.2   Qualitative Evaluation

We first identify words that are semantically stable across time and locations respectively. Cosine similarity of embeddings reflects the semantic similarity of words. The embeddings of stable words

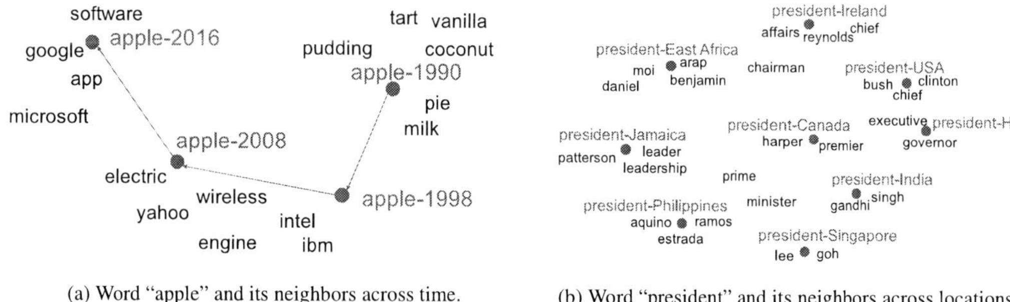

(a) Word "apple" and its neighbors across time.　　　　(b) Word "president" and its neighbors across locations.

Figure 1: The trajectory of word embeddings over time and locations.

should have high similarity across conditions since their semantics do not change much with conditions. Therefore, we average the cosine similarity of words between different time durations or locations as the measure of word stability, and rank the words in terms of their stability. The most stable words are listed in Table 1. We notice that a vast majority of these stable words are frequent words such as function words. It may be interpreted based on the fact that these are words that encode structure (Gong et al., 2017, 2018), and that the structure of well-edited English text has not changed much across time or locations (Poirier, 2014). It is also in line with our general linguistic knowledge; function words are those with high frequency in corpora, and are semantically relatively stable (Hamilton et al., 2016).

Next we focus on the words whose meaning varies with time or location. We first evaluate the semantic changes of embeddings trained on time-stamped news corpus, and choose the word *apple* as an example (more examples are included in the supplementary material). We plot the trajectory of the embeddings of *apple* and its semantic neighbors over time in Fig. 1(a). These word vectors are projected to a two-dimensional space using the locally linear embedding approach (Roweis and Saul, 2000). We notice that the word *apple* usually referred to a fruit in 1990 given that its neighbors are food items such as *pie* and *pudding*. In recent years, the word has taken on the sense of the technology company Apple, which can be seen from the fact that *apple* is close to words denoting technology companies such as *google* and *microsoft* after 1998.

We also evaluate the location-specific word embeddings trained on the ICE corpus on the task of semantic change discovery. Take the word *president* as an example. We list its neighbors in different locations in Fig. 1(b). It is close to names

of the regional leaders. The neighbors are president names such as *bush* and *clinton* in USA, and prime minister names such as *harper* in Canada and *gandhi* in India. This suggests that the embeddings are qualitatively shown to capture semantic changes across different conditions.

4.3 Quantitative Evaluation

We also perform a quantitative evaluation of the condition-specific embeddings on the task of semantic equivalence across condition values. The joint embedding training is to bring the time- or location-specific embeddings to the same vector space so that they are comparable. Therefore, one key aspect of embeddings that we can evaluate is their semantic equivalence over time and locations. Two datasets with temporally- and spatially- equivalent word pairs were used for this part.

4.3.1 Dataset

Temporal dataset. Yao et al. created two temporal testsets to examine the ability of the derived word embeddings to identify lexical equivalents over time (Yao et al., 2018). For example, the word *Clinton-1998* is semantically equivalent to the word *Obama-2012*, since Clinton was the US president in 1998 and Obama took office in 2012.

The first temporal testset was built on the basis of public knowledge about famous roles at different times such as the U.S. presidents in history. It consists of $11,028$ word pairs which are semantically equivalent across time. For a given word in specific time, we find the closest neighbors of the time-dependent embedding in a target year. The neighbors are taken as its equivalents at the target time.

The second testset is about technologies and historical events. Annotators generated 445 conceptually equivalent word-time pairs such as twitter-

Dataset	Temporal testset 1					Temporal testset 2				
Metric	MRR	MP@1	MP@3	MP@5	MP@10	MRR	MP@1	MP@3	MP@5	MP@10
BW2V	0.36	0.27	0.42	0.48	0.56	0.05	0.00	0.08	0.08	0.20
TW2V	0.09	0.05	0.12	0.15	0.19	0.07	0.04	0.08	0.10	0.14
AW2V	0.16	0.11	0.18	0.22	0.30	0.05	0.02	0.05	0.08	0.14
DW2V	0.42	0.33	0.49	**0.55**	**0.62**	**0.14**	**0.08**	**0.16**	**0.22**	**0.38**
CW2V	**0.43**	**0.34**	**0.51**	**0.55**	**0.62**	0.13	**0.08**	**0.16**	0.19	0.27

Table 2: Ranking Results on Temporal Testsets

Metric	MRR	MP@1	MP@3	MP@5	MP@10
BW2V	0.25	0.20	0.27	0.29	0.35
TW2V	0.00	0.00	0.00	0.00	0.00
AW2V	0.17	0.11	0.18	0.24	0.33
DW2V	0.12	0.11	0.11	0.13	0.14
CW2V	**0.31**	**0.24**	**0.35**	**0.39**	**0.46**

Table 3: Ranking Results on Spatial Testset

2012 and newspaper-1990. Here the equivalence is functional considering that Twitter played the role of an information dissemination platform in 2012 just as the newspaper did in 1990.

Spatial dataset. To evaluate the quality of location-specific embeddings, we created a dataset of 714 semantically equivalent word pairs in different locations based on public knowledge. For example, the capitals of different countries have a semantic correspondence, resulting in the word *Ottawa-Canada* that refers to the word *Ottawa* for Canada to be equivalent to the word *Dublin-Ireland* that refers to the word *Dublin* used for Ireland. Two annotators chose a set of categories such as capitals and governors and independently came up with equivalent word pairs in different regions. Later they went through the word pairs together and decided the one to include. We will release this dataset upon acceptance.

4.3.2 Evaluation metric

In line with prior work (Yao et al., 2018), we use two evaluation metrics—mean reciprocal rank (MRR) and mean precision@k (MP@K)—to evaluate semantic equivalence on both temporal and spatial datasets.

MRR. For each query word, we rank all neighboring words in terms of their cosine similarity to the query word in a given condition, and identify the rank of the correct equivalent word. We define r_i as the rank of the correct word of the i-th query,

and MRR for N queries is defined as

$$\text{MRR} = \frac{1}{N} \sum_{i=1}^{N} \frac{1}{r_i}.$$

Note that we only consider the top 10 words, and the inverse rank $1/r_i$ of the correct word is set as 0 if it does not appear among the top 10 neighbors.

MP@K. For each query, we consider the top-K words closest to the word in terms of cosine similarity in a given condition. If the correct word is included, we define the precision of the i-th query P@K_i as 1, otherwise, $\text{P@K}_i = 0$. MP@K for N queries is defined as

$$\text{MP@K} = \frac{1}{N} \sum_{i=1}^{N} P@K_i.$$

4.3.3 Results

Temporal testset. We report the ranking results on the two temporal testsets in Table 2, and report results on the spatial testset in Table 3. Our condition-specific word embedding is denoted as CW2V in the tables. In the temporal testset 1, our model is consistently better than the three baselines BW2V, TW2V and AW2V, and is comparable to DW2V in all metrics.

In the temporal tesetset 2, CW2V outperforms BW2V, TW2V and AW2V in all metrics and is comparable to DW2V with respect to precision in the top 1 and top 3 words, but falls behind DW2V in MP@5 and MP@10. This lower performance may actually be a misrepresentation of its actual performance, since the word pairs in testset 2 are generated based on human knowledge and is potentially more subjective than testset 1.

As an illustration, consider the case of *website-2014* in testset 2. Our embeddings show *abc, nbc, cbs* and *magazine* as semantically similar words in 1990. These words are reasonable results since a website acts as a news platform just like TV broadcasting companies and magazines. The ground truth neighbor of *website-2014* is the word *address*. Another example is *bitcoin-2015*. The semantic neighbors of our embeddings are *currency*, *monetary* and *stocks* in 1992. These words are semantically similar to *bitcoin* in the sense that *bitcoin* is cryptocurrency and a form of electronic cash. However, the ground truth is *investment* in the testset.

Spatial testset. Considering the evaluation on the spatial testset in Table 3, our condition-specific embedding achieves the best performance in finding semantic equivalents across regions. We note that the approaches which align independently trained embeddings such as TW2V and AW2V have poor performance. Due to the disparity in word distributions across regions in the ICE corpus, words with high frequency in one region may seldom be seen in another region. These infrequent words tend to have low-quality embeddings. It hurts the accurate alignment between locations and further degrades the performance of location-specific embeddings.

DW2V, the jointly trained embedding, does not perform well on the spatial testset. It puts alignment constraints on word embeddings between two regions to prevent major changes of word embeddings across regions. This may lead to an interference between regional embeddings especially in cases where there is a frequency disparity of the same word in different regional corpora. In such cases, the embedding of the frequent word in one region will be affected by the weak embedding of the same word occurring infrequently in another region. Our model decomposes a word embedding into three components: a condition-independent component, a condition vector, and a deviation vector. The condition vector for each region takes care of the regional disparity, while the condition-independent vectors are not affected. Therefore, our model is more robust to such disparity in learning conditioned embeddings.

5   Conclusion

We studied a model to enrich word embeddings with temporal and spatial information and showed how it explicitly encodes lexical semantic properties into the geometry of the embedding. We then empirically demonstrated how the model captures language evolution across time and location. We leave it to future work to explore concrete downstream applications, where these time- and location-sensitive embeddings can be fruitfully used.

Acknowledgments

This work was supported by the IBM-ILLINOIS Center for Cognitive Computing Systems Research (C3SR)—a research collaboration as part of the IBM AI Horizons Network. We would like to thank the anonymous reviewers for their constructive comments and suggestions. We also thank Daniel Polyakov and Yuchen Li for the data annotations.

References

2019. International corpus of english. `http://ice-corpora.net/ice/`. Accessed: 2019-03-12.

Sanjeev Arora, Yuanzhi Li, Yingyu Liang, Tengyu Ma, and Andrej Risteski. 2016. A latent variable model approach to pmi-based word embeddings. *Transactions of the Association for Computational Linguistics*, 4:385–399.

Robert Bamler and Stephan Mandt. 2017. Dynamic word embeddings. In *International Conference on Machine Learning*, pages 380–389.

David Bamman, Chris Dyer, and Noah A Smith. 2014. Distributed representations of geographically situated language. In *Proceedings of the 52nd Annual Meeting of the Association for Computational Linguistics*, volume 2, pages 828–834.

Andreas Blank. 1999. Why do new meanings occur? a cognitive typology of the motivations for lexical semantic change. *Historical semantics and cognition*, 13:6.

Daniel Brandon Jr. 2001. Localization of web content. *Journal of Computing Sciences in Colleges*, 17(2):345–358.

Hyunyoung Choi and Hal Varian. 2012. Predicting the present with google trends. *Economic Record*, 88:2–9.

Jacob Devlin, Ming-Wei Chang, Kenton Lee, and Kristina Toutanova. 2018. Bert: Pre-training of deep bidirectional transformers for language understanding. *arXiv preprint arXiv:1810.04805*.

Haim Dubossarsky, Simon Hengchen, Nina Tahmasebi, Dominik Schlechtweg, et al. 2019. Time-out: Temporal referencing for robust modeling of lexical semantic change. In *The 57th Annual Meeting of the Association for Computational Linguistics (ACL2019) Proceedings of the Conference*. ACL.

Jacob Eisenstein, Brendan O'Connor, Noah A Smith, and Eric P Xing. 2010. A latent variable model for geographic lexical variation. In *Proceedings of the 2010 conference on empirical methods in natural language processing*, pages 1277–1287.

Mario Giulianelli, Marco Del Tredici, and Raquel Fernández. 2020. Analysing lexical semantic change with contextualised word representations. In *Proceedings of the 58th Annual Meeting of the Association for Computational Linguistics, ACL 2020, Online, July 5-10, 2020*, pages 3960–3973. Association for Computational Linguistics.

Hongyu Gong, Suma Bhat, and Pramod Viswanath. 2018. Embedding syntax and semantics of prepositions via tensor decomposition. In *Proceedings of the 2018 Conference of the North American Chapter of the Association for Computational Linguistics: Human Language Technologies, Volume 1 (Long Papers)*, pages 896–906.

Hongyu Gong, Jiaqi Mu, Suma Bhat, and Pramod Viswanath. 2017. Prepositions in context. *arXiv preprint arXiv:1702.01466*.

William L Hamilton, Jure Leskovec, and Dan Jurafsky. 2016. Diachronic word embeddings reveal statistical laws of semantic change. In *Proceedings of the 54th Annual Meeting of the Association for Computational Linguistics*, pages 1489–1501.

Renfen Hu, Shen Li, and Shichen Liang. 2019. Diachronic sense modeling with deep contextualized word embeddings: An ecological view. In *Proceedings of the 57th Annual Meeting of the Association for Computational Linguistics*, pages 3899–3908.

Xiaolei Huang and Michael Paul. 2019. Neural temporality adaptation for document classification: Diachronic word embeddings and domain adaptation models. In *Proceedings of the 57th Annual Meeting of the Association for Computational Linguistics*, pages 4113–4123.

Braj B Kachru, Yamuna Kachru, Cecil L Nelson, Daniel R Davis, and Zoya G Proshina. 2006. *The handbook of world Englishes*. Wiley Online Library.

Vivek Kulkarni, Rami Al-Rfou, Bryan Perozzi, and Steven Skiena. 2015. Statistically significant detection of linguistic change. In *Proceedings of the 24th International Conference on World Wide Web*, pages 625–635.

Vivek Kulkarni, Bryan Perozzi, and Steven Skiena. 2016. Freshman or fresher? quantifying the geographic variation of language in online social media. In *Tenth International AAAI Conference on Web and Social Media*.

Andrey Kutuzov, Lilja Øvrelid, Terrence Szymanski, and Erik Velldal. 2018. Diachronic word embeddings and semantic shifts: a survey. In *Proceedings of the 27th International Conference on Computational Linguistics*, pages 1384–1397.

Jefrey Lijffijt, Tanja Säily, and Terttu Nevalainen. 2012. Ceecing the baseline: Lexical stability and significant change in a historical corpus. In *Studies in Variation, Contacts and Change in English*, volume 10.

Rajend Mesthrie and Rakesh M Bhatt. 2008. *World Englishes: The study of new linguistic varieties*. Cambridge University Press.

Jean-Baptiste Michel, Yuan Kui Shen, Aviva Presser Aiden, Adrian Veres, Matthew K Gray, Joseph P Pickett, Dale Hoiberg, Dan Clancy, Peter Norvig, Jon Orwant, et al. 2011. Quantitative analysis of culture using millions of digitized books. *science*, 331(6014):176–182.

Tomas Mikolov, Ilya Sutskever, Kai Chen, Greg S Corrado, and Jeff Dean. 2013. Distributed representations of words and phrases and their compositionality. In *Advances in neural information processing systems*, pages 3111–3119.

Jeffrey Pennington, Richard Socher, and Christopher Manning. 2014. Glove: Global vectors for word representation. In *Proceedings of the 2014 conference on empirical methods in natural language processing (EMNLP)*, pages 1532–1543.

Matthew Peters, Mark Neumann, Mohit Iyyer, Matt Gardner, Christopher Clark, Kenton Lee, and Luke Zettlemoyer. 2018. Deep contextualized word representations. In *NAACL 2018*, volume 1, pages 2227–2237.

Éric André Poirier. 2014. A method for automatic detection and manual localization of content-based translation errors and shifts. *Journal of Innovation in Digital Ecosystems*, 1(1-2):38–46.

Ye Qi, Devendra Sachan, Matthieu Felix, Sarguna Padmanabhan, and Graham Neubig. 2018. When and why are pre-trained word embeddings useful for neural machine translation? In *NAACL 2018*, volume 2, pages 529–535.

Alex Rosenfeld and Katrin Erk. 2018. Deep neural models of semantic shift. In *Proceedings of the 2018 Conference of the North American Chapter of the Association for Computational Linguistics: Human Language Technologies*, pages 474–484.

Sam T Roweis and Lawrence K Saul. 2000. Nonlinear dimensionality reduction by locally linear embedding. *science*, 290(5500):2323–2326.

Dominik Schlechtweg, Barbara McGillivray, Simon Hengchen, Haim Dubossarsky, and Nina Tahmasebi. 2020. Semeval-2020 task 1: Unsupervised lexical semantic change detection. *arXiv preprint arXiv:2007.11464*.

Carmen Silva-Corvalán. 2006. Analyzing linguistic variation: Statistical models and methods. *Journal of Linguistic Anthropology*, 16(2):295–296.

Xuri Tang. 2018. A state-of-the-art of semantic change computation. *Natural Language Engineering*, 24(5):649–676.

Stephen Ullmann. 1979. Semantics: an introduction to the science of meaning.

Zijun Yao, Yifan Sun, Weicong Ding, Nikhil Rao, and
Hui Xiong. 2018. Dynamic word embeddings for
evolving semantic discovery. In *Proceedings of
the Eleventh ACM International Conference on Web
Search and Data Mining*, pages 673–681. ACM.

Yating Zhang, Adam Jatowt, Sourav S Bhowmick,
and Katsumi Tanaka. 2016. The past is not a for-
eign country: Detecting semantically similar terms
across time. *IEEE Transactions on Knowledge and
Data Engineering*, 28(10):2793–2807.

Interpreting Attention Models with Human Visual Attention in Machine Reading Comprehension

Ekta Sood[1], **Simon Tannert**[2], **Diego Frassinelli**[3], **Andreas Bulling**[1], **Ngoc Thang Vu**[2]
[1]University of Stuttgart, Institute for Visualization and Interactive Systems (VIS), Germany
[2]University of Stuttgart, Institute for Natural Language Processing (IMS), Germany
[3]University of Konstanz, Department of Linguistics, Germany
`{ekta.sood,andreas.bulling}@vis.uni-stuttgart.de`
`{simon.tannert,thang.vu}@ims.uni-stuttgart.de`
`diego.frassinelli@uni-konstanz.de`

Abstract

While neural networks with attention mechanisms have achieved superior performance on many natural language processing tasks, it remains unclear to which extent learned attention resembles human visual attention. In this paper, we propose a new method that leverages eye-tracking data to investigate the relationship between human visual attention and neural attention in machine reading comprehension. To this end, we introduce a novel 23 participant eye tracking dataset - MQA-RC, in which participants read movie plots and answered pre-defined questions. We compare state of the art networks based on long short-term memory (LSTM), convolutional neural models (CNN) and XLNet Transformer architectures. We find that higher similarity to human attention and performance significantly correlates to the LSTM and CNN models. However, we show this relationship does not hold true for the XLNet models – despite the fact that the XLNet performs best on this challenging task. Our results suggest that different architectures seem to learn rather different neural attention strategies and similarity of neural to human attention does not guarantee best performance.

1 Introduction

Due to the high ambiguity of natural language, humans have to detect the most salient information in a given text and allocate a higher level of attention to specific regions to successfully process and comprehend it (Schneider and Shiffrin, 1977; Shiffrin and Schneider, 1977; Poesio, 1994). Eye tracking studies have been extensively used in various reading comprehension tasks to capture and investigate these attentive strategies (Rayner, 2009) and have, as such, helped to interpret cognitive processes and behaviors during reading.

Attention mechanisms in neural networks have been inspired by human visual attention (Bahdanau et al., 2014; Hassabis et al., 2017). Similar to humans, they allow networks to focus and allocate more weight to different parts of the input sequence (Mnih et al., 2014; Chorowski et al., 2015; Xu et al., 2015; Vaswani et al., 2017; Jain and Wallace, 2019). As such, neural attention can be viewed as a model of visual saliency that makes predictions over the elements in the network's input – whether a region in an image or a word in a sentence (Frintrop et al., 2010). Attention mechanisms have recently gained significant popularity and have boosted performance in natural language processing tasks and computer vision (Ma and Zhang, 2003; Sun and Fisher, 2003; Seo et al., 2016; Veličković et al., 2017; Sood et al., 2020).

Although attention mechanisms can significantly improve performance for different NLP tasks, performance degrades when models are exposed to inherent properties of natural language, such as semantic ambiguity, inferring information, or out of domain data (Blohm et al., 2018; Niven and Kao, 2019). These findings encourage work towards enhancing network's generalizability, deterring reliance on the closed-world assumption (Reiter, 1981). In machine reading comprehension (MRC), it has been proposed that the more similar systems are to human behavior, the more suitable they become for such a task (Trischler et al., 2017; Luo et al., 2019; Zheng et al., 2019). As a result, much recent work aims to build machines which read and understand text, mimicking specific aspects of human behavior (Hermann et al., 2015; Nguyen et al., 2016; Rajpurkar et al., 2016;

Proceedings of the 24th Conference on Computational Natural Language Learning, pages 12–25
Online, November 19-20, 2020. ©2020 Association for Computational Linguistics
https://doi.org/10.18653/v1/P17

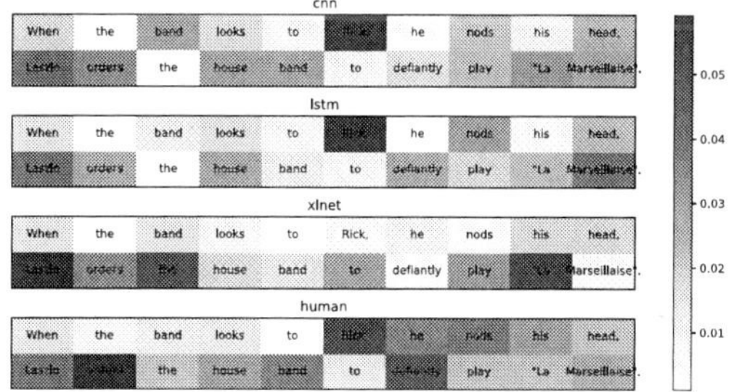

Figure 1: Example attention distributions of neural models (cnn, lstm, xlnet) and humans.

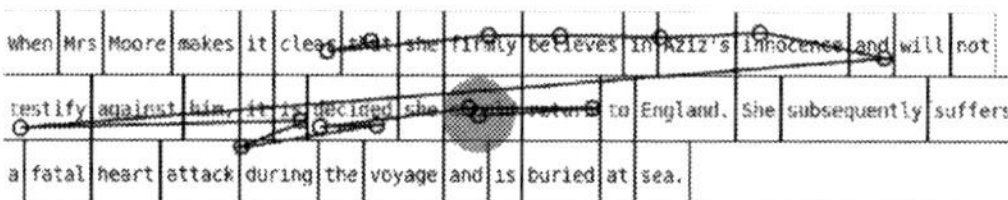

Figure 2: An exemplary scan path shows a reading pattern. The red circle corresponds to the location of the current fixation. Its size is proportional to the duration of the fixation.

Blohm et al., 2018). To that end, by employing self-attention, researchers attempt to enhance comprehension by building models which better capture deep contextual and salient information (Vaswani et al., 2017; Devlin et al., 2019; Shen et al., 2018; Yu et al., 2018; Zhang et al., 2019).

As neural attention allows us to "peek" inside neural networks, it can help us to better understand how models make predictions (see Figure 1). Similarly, human visual attention (which is captured by physiological data such as eye tracking), allows us to quantify the relative importance of items within the visual field when reading texts (see Figure 2).

In this work, we propose a novel method that leverages human eye tracking data to investigate the relationship between neural performance and human attention strategies. Concretely, by interpreting and comparing the relationship between neural attention distributions of three state of the art MRC models to human visual attention, our research for the first time addresses the following questions: (i) What is the correlation between a particular network behavior and the human visual attention? (ii) Is the emulation of the human attention system the reason why neural models with attention mechanisms achieve state of the art results on machine reading comprehension tasks?

To answer these questions, we first extend the MovieQA dataset (Tapaswi et al., 2016) with eye tracking data. In addition, we present a novel visualization tool to qualitatively compare the differences in attentive behaviors between neural models and humans by showing their patterns over time in a split screen mode. Second, as widely suggested in the cognitive science literature, we quantify human attention in terms of the word-level gaze duration recorded in our eye tracking dataset (Rouse and Morris, 1986; Milosavljevic and Cerf, 2008; Van Hooft and Born, 2012; Lipton, 2018; Wiegreffe and Pinter, 2019). Third, we interpret the relationship between human attention and three state of the art systems based on CNN, LSTM, and XLNet (Hochreiter and Schmidhuber, 1997; Yang et al., 2019) using Kullback-Leibler divergence (Kullback and Leibler, 1951). By doing so, we are able to compare, evaluate and better understand neural attention distributions on text across these attention models. To the best of our knowledge, we are the first to propose a systematic approach for comparing neural attention to human gaze data in machine reading comprehension.

The main findings of our work are two-fold: First, we show that there is a statistically significant correlation between the CNNs and LSTMs model performances and similarity to human attention. Second, we show that the behavior of LSTM models is significantly more similar to humans than the XLNet ones even though the latter perform best on the MovieQA dataset.

2 Related Work

2.1 Eye-tracking for Attention and Comprehension

Eye tracking studies have been extensively used in cognitive science research to investigate human attention over time (Rayner, 1998; Wojciulik et al., 1998; Tsai et al., 2012; Eckstein et al., 2017). Importantly, it has been demonstrated that attention and saccadic movements are strongly intertwined (Hoffman and Subramaniam, 1995; Deubel et al., 2000; Kristjansson, 2011). Eye movement behaviors which are evoked from intricate information processing tasks, such as reading, can be used to identify visual attentional allocation (Posner et al., 1980; Posner, 1980; Henderson, 1992).

As indicated in the *Reading Model* (Just and Carpenter, 1980), we assume a strong relationship between eye fixations, attention, and reading comprehension. In their eye tracking study, Just and Carpenter (1980) measured cognitive processing load using fixation duration. Specifically, they found that participants look longer or more often at items that are cognitively more complex, in order to successfully process them. Cognitive load increases when readers are "accessing infrequent words, integrating information from important clauses and making inferences at the ends of sentences".

2.2 Attention Mechanisms

In the attention-based encoder-decoder architecture, rather than ignoring the internal encoder states, the attention mechanism takes advantage of these weights to generate a context vector, which is used by the decoder at various time steps (Bahdanau et al., 2014; Luong et al., 2015; Chorowski et al., 2015; Wang and Jiang; Yang et al., 2016; Dzendzik et al., 2017).

In Transformer networks, the main differences to previous attentive models are that these networks are purely based on attention where LSTM or GRU units are not used, and attention is applied via self-attention and multi-headed attention (Vaswani et al., 2017) without any order constraint. Since the introduction of pre-trained Transformer networks, we have observed, on the one hand, a rise in state of the art performance across a multitude of tasks in NLP (Devlin et al., 2019; Radford et al., 2018; Yang et al., 2019). On the other hand, much effort is needed to interpret these highly complex models (e.g. in Vig and Belinkov (2019)).

2.3 Question Answering and Machine Comprehension

We use question answering (QA) tasks to compare human and machine attention. Although such tasks have been widely explored with neural attention models, creating systems to comprehend semantically diverse text documents and answer related questions remains challenging (Qiu et al., 2019). These models tend to fail when faced with adversarial attacks: the type of noise humans can easily resolve (Jia and Liang, 2017; Blohm et al., 2018; Yuan et al., 2019). These studies uncovered the limitations of QA systems, indicating that models might process text in a different manner than humans: they rely on pattern matching in lieu of human-like decision making processes which are required in comprehension tasks (Just and Carpenter, 1980; Posner et al., 1980; Blohm et al., 2018).

2.3.1 Eye Tracking and Neural Networks

In the past years, researchers have started leveraging human gaze data for attentive neural modeling tasks. For example, Hahn and Keller (2016, 2018) presented a neural QA network that combined both a task and attention module to predict and simulate human reading strategies. The authors proposed the *trade-off hypothesis:* human reading behaviors are task-specific and therefore evoke various specific strategies for each of these tasks. To validate their hypothesis, they used eye tracking data as the gold standard and compare model predictions of zero or one (fixated or not). In another work, Das et al. (2017) investigated the differences between neural and human attention over image regions in a visual question answering task. Their method focused on correlation ranking and visualizations. Note that comparisons of human and neural attention distributions over text have not been explored so far. When the goal is to purely improve performance, several papers proposed integrating gaze data into neural attention as an additional variable in the equation or as a regularization method (Sugano and Bulling, 2016; Barrett et al., 2018; Qiao et al., 2018; Sood et al., 2020).

2.4 Neural Interpretability

In order to further understand the behavior of neural networks, research in neural interpretability has grown dramatically in the recent years (Lipton, 2018; Gilpin et al., 2018; Hooker et al., 2019). Such methods include: introducing adversarial examples, error class analysis, modeling techniques (e.g. self-explaining networks), and post-hoc analysis of attention distributions (Lipton, 2018; Alvarez-Melis and Jaakkola, 2018; Rudin, 2019; Sen et al., 2020).

To shed light on the decisions taken by these networks, multiple interpretability studies have investigated their outputs and predictions (Alvarez-Melis and Jaakkola, 2018; Blohm et al., 2018; Gilpin et al., 2018), and analyzed their behavior through loss visualization from various architectures (Ribeiro et al., 2016).

Nevertheless, a real understanding of the internal processes of these black boxes is still rather limited (Gilpin et al., 2018). Although these interpretations might explain predictions, there is still a lack of explanation regarding the mechanisms by which models work as well as limited insight regarding the relationship between machine and human visual attention (Lipton, 2018).

3 Resources

3.1 MovieQA Dataset

The MovieQA dataset (Tapaswi et al., 2016) is used in all experiments conducted in this work. The dataset was comprised of a variety of available sources, however for the tasks in this work we only use the plot synopses. The plots vary between 1 to 20 paragraphs in size, and are checked by annotators to ensure they consist of movie relevant events and character relationships. There are a total of almost 15,000 human generated questions in this dataset corresponding to 408 movie plots. Of the 5 answer candidates denoted for each question, there is only one with a correct answer and the rest are deceptive incorrect answers. The data used for training all our models consists of plots with their corresponding questions: 9,848 training, 1,958 development and 3,138 test questions, respectively.

3.2 Reading Comprehension with Eye Tracking Dataset

We present a novel reading comprehension eye tracking dataset[1] - MQA-RC - which allows researchers to observe changes in reading behavior in three comprehension tasks and to potentially induce processing strategies evoked by humans. This new extension provides a gold standard to compare and synchronize model versus human visual attention in comprehension tasks. To the best of our knowledge there are no available eye tracking datasets which use machine learning corpora as stimuli. Therefore, we build and use our reading comprehension gaze dataset as the gold standard. In addition, we provide coreference chains labeled by two human annotators[2]. Based on the lower fixation durations observed in the eye tracking data, we find that humans can easily resolve pronouns in the MQA-RC dataset (cf. Figure 6), where fixation durations are used to measure information processing load (Arnold et al., 2000; Rahman and Ng, 2012; Cinkara and Cabaroğlu, 2015). The figure also shows saliency over the proper nouns compared to their mentions in the chains.

Data collection Our dataset is based on two studies: in Study 1 we randomly selected a set of 16 documents on which the majority of both LSTMs and CNNs models failed to correctly answer the questions; in Study 2 we selected a different set of 16 documents on which the majority of models succeeded in predicting the correct answers.

In total, our dataset contains gaze data from 23 English native speakers who were recorded while reading 32 documents (around 200-250 words each) in three different comprehension tasks. We used a Tobii 600Hz head-mount eye-tracker. In total, each session lasted 45 minutes including the time required for calibration and 5-minutes breaks every 15 minutes.

Study 1 For each of the 16 documents we designed three experimental conditions: 1) regular QA where the participants have access to the plot, the question, and five answer candidates; 2) open-ended answer generation where the participants see the plot and the question but have to generate their own responses; and 3) QA by memory where the participants can first read the plot and then answer to the question (5 possible answers) without having the plot available. In condition 3, participants have to recover information from memory in order to answer the question. To guarantee a balanced design, we divided the 48 experimental items in three schemes containing each document only once: 5-5-6 items (for condition 1-2-3) in schema A, 5-6-5 in schema B, and 6-5-5 in schema C. We randomly assigned each participant to one of these schemes where the order of the conditions followed a Latin Squared Design (Bradley, 1958).

Study 2 We conducted a follow up study in which we took only the plots for which the majority of CNN and LSTM models predicted correctly. We hypothesized that such items that are, on average, easier for the models are also easier for the humans (higher correlation score). In this study, we only collected data for the regular QA task (condition 1). The experiment was performed by five new participants. Each participant saw all the 16 plots in a randomized order. [3]

Data analysis Table 1 shows the distribution of data, inter-annotator agreement, and accuracy observed on our MQA-RC dataset. We show across both studies that humans agree on selected answers for the given questions and are highly accurate. It is important to note that we only use data from

---

[1] The dataset is available at https://perceptualui.org/publications/sood20_conll/

[2] See appendix material for further information on coreference annotation

[3] In order to maintain the same amount of data samples for both study 1 and 2, we randomly selected a subset participants data from study 1. Instead of using the full 18 participants from study 1, we used 15 participants.

Study	Schema	No. Doc	No. Participants	IAA	Acc
Study1	A	5	1-6	83.3%	93%
Study1	B	5	6-12	100%	100%
Study1	C	6	12-18	100%	100%
Study2	No-Schema	16	5	89.0%	95%

Table 1: Distribution in MovieQA with eye tracking. We show the two different studies and the number of documents seen in each schema iteration. For study 1, there are three schema iterations (A, B, C) and for study 2 there are no schema iterations (as this is only for answer by selection). We also show the number of participants for each schema iteration, and the corresponding inter-annotator agreement (agreement on answer selected). Lastly, we show the accuracy of the participants for correctly answering each question in the respective study and schema iteration.

the regular QA task (condition 1) so that we can compare attention and performance for difficult vs. easy cases.

Visualization tool   We developed a web interface tool[4] to visualize the eye tracking data (cf. Figure 5a). This tool is simple, easy to use and can visualize any eye tracking data where text is used as the stimulus (see an example in Figure 2). Inputs to the tool are two files – one with eye tracking data and another with the corresponding text stimulus. The eye tracking data consists of the x and y on-screen gaze coordinates, fixation duration for each word, and word IDs (cf. Figure 5b). Our tool then maps the coordinates to the stimulus and provides real time scanpaths visualization. In addition, our tool can compare neural and human visual attention via linear visualization (left to right) with a split screen (e.g., left side model, right side human). This functionality allows users to observe, in real time, the dynamic network and human visual attention distributions.

4   Neural Models

4.1   Two Staged Attention Models

We re-implement both the CNN and LSTM QA ensemble models with two staged attention from Blohm et al. (2018) that provides state of the art results on the MovieQA dataset (Tapaswi et al., 2016). This is a multiple choice QA task in which each datapoint contains the plot of a movie as well as its corresponding question and five potential answer candidates. The models are based

on the compare-aggregate framework. Concretely, the models compare the plot to the respective question and aggregates this comparison into one vector representation to obtain a confidence score after applying the softmax, for each answer candidate. The best results were obtained from the majority vote of the nine best performing models.

The two-staged attention is performed at the word and at sentence level, where the plot is weighted with respect to the question or a possible answer candidate.

$$G = \mathrm{softmax}\left(X^T P\right) \qquad (1)$$
$$H = XG \qquad (2)$$

The word level X indicates the answer candidate (5 total) or the question. Subsequently, when computing sentence level attention, the question or answer candidate are represented as such. Blohm et al. (2018) apply the dot-product computation for the attention mechanism. The two variations of this model with CNN and LSTM models provided state of the art results on the MovieQA dataset with an average of 84.5% on the validation set and an average of 85% on the test set.

The authors performed a case study to further investigate the comprehension limitations of the models compared to human inference. In their analysis, they compared both networks against human performance in order to infer processing strategies which human possess but are not shown by the models. They investigated the most difficult cases, where the majority of both nine best models failed to correctly answer the question. This motivates why we used the difficult and easy documents for the CNN and LSTM models (Blohm et al., 2018), as they are the only paper to date which both obtain SOTA results and offered qualitative analysis on the gap between human and model performance. When the majority of the models fail to correctly answer the question, we classify these documents as *difficult* cases for the two networks; vice versa for the *easy* documents.

4.2   XLNet Models

We used the pre-trained XLNet model and fine-tuned it for the QA task (Tapaswi et al., 2016; Yang et al., 2019). We opted for XLNet given that it is a recent Transformer network for language understanding that outperformed BERT and other large-scale pre-trained language models on a variety of

---

[4]The tool is also available at `https://perceptualui.org/publications/sood20_conll/`

NLP tasks (Yang et al., 2019). It was trained on large corpora with training objectives which are compatible with unsupervised learning and can be fine-tuned to new tasks and datasets.

XLNet is based on an auto-regressive approach in which the model uses observations from previous time steps in order to predict the weight for the next time step. Advancing from the traditional auto-regressive approach, such as a Bidirectional LSTM, the authors also combine their network with an auto-encoding approach seen with the BERT model (Devlin et al., 2019). By combining both approaches, XLNet introduces permutations on both sides. Moreover, the self-attention network (Vaswani et al., 2017) uses three components, queries, keys and values, all of which are calculated from their respective embeddings. The output is a weighted sum of the values, in which the values are weighted with a score calculated as the dot product of the respective queries and keys. It is important to note that the queries are related to the output and the keys are related to the given input. During fine-tuning, however, the model is essentially the Transformer-XL (Vaswani et al., 2017; Dai et al., 2019; Yang et al., 2019). The auto-regressive language model estimates the joint probability over the input elements (in XLNet this x is language agnostic, i.e it is a subtoken).

$$P(X) = \prod_t P(x_t|X_{<t}) \qquad (3)$$

The input sequence is the concatenation of each x in the plot with the question and a potential answer candidate (there are five possible answer candidates and one correct answer).

When fine-tuning on the question answering task, the model objective is multi-label classification given an input sequence. Note, the permutation language model is the component which helps XLNet capture longer dependencies between elements in a given input sequence (Yang et al., 2019). In our method, we fine-tune the XLNet with 24 attention layers and 16 attention heads (Yang et al., 2019). The fine-tuned model makes a prediction by applying the argmax over the softmax, selecting the potential y-label, or answer candidate, with the highest confidence scores. The fine-tuned XLNet outperforms all other results on the validation set, obtaining the new highest accuracy of 91%.

5 Analysis Method

5.1 Human Gaze-Attention Extraction

We obtain token level gaze counts (frequency counts) by mapping the x, y coordinates to bounding boxes set around each word of the stimuli. We convert the raw gaze counts into a probability distribution over the document by dividing each gaze count by the sum of all gaze counts. These token level frequency counts obtained in the hit testing method, reflecting gaze duration: the more often a token of the text is attended to, the more important it is for humans to answer the question (Just and Carpenter, 1980).

We extract word level attention weights and average them over documents, thereby comparing the word attention at document level. Since for humans, the task is to read the entire short document and then answer the question given the entire context, all items within the context are interconnected. Therefore, it is misleading to only analyze attention over one sentence or one part of the document. Furthermore, it is not cognitively plausible to limit comparison to attention distribution over specific sentences or only part of the documents.

5.2 Extracting LSTM and CNN Word Level Attention

The sentence level attention for the CNN and LSTM models have very low entropy, where essentially almost all of the attention is distributed to one sentence and the rest of the sentence attention weights are almost zero. This is a property of the two-staged attention, which XLNet does not have. Therefore, we leverage word level attention to compare model attention versus human visual attention. During evaluation, we extract token attention weights for each of the nine best models. We then ensemble the neural attention weights. Figure 7a and 7b in the Appendix show the word level attention distribution of CNN and LSTM models.

5.3 Extracting XLNet Word Level Attention

We extracted the attention weights from the nine best XLNet models by leveraging the output of the last attention layer. It contains token level weights for each plot-answer candidate pairing. More specifically, the output of the last attention layer is a matrix of 1024 x 1024, which contains a vector of attention weights vectors for each respective token. We did so because in Transformers, attention computations happen simultaneously, while for LSTMs and CNNs they happen last. In order to compare XLNet to the LSTM and CNN models, we therefore only take the final output of the self-attention layer. Furthermore, to make these weights comparable to human gaze attention we take the maximum value in each token vector (Htut et al., 2019) and normalize them by the sum of the weights.

5.4 Attention Comparison Metrics

KL divergence In order to compare the human and neural attention distributions, we computed the Kullback-Leibler divergence (Kullback and Leibler, 1951). Concretely in this paper, we calculate the KL divergence for average-human to average-model along the word level attention distributions. This method is used to compare two probability distributions, akin to relative entropy. The output will reflect an understanding of the differences between the two probability distributions (cf. Equation 4).

$$D_{\mathrm{KL}}(H \parallel M) = \sum_{x \in \mathcal{X}} P(x) \log \left(\frac{H(x)}{M(x)} \right). \quad (4)$$

where H stands for the human attention distribution and M for the model attention distribution.

Spearman's rank correlation Spearman's rank correlation coefficient is used to discover the relationship between two variables (Zar, 1972). We use the standard Spearman's rank correlation coefficients implementation from SciKit-Learn (Kokoska and Zwillinger, 2000; Pedregosa et al., 2011), to measure if there is a correlation between model performance and the KL divergence between models and humans attention distributions. Model performance refers to the number of models that provide correct answers in the ensemble setting. Because KL divergence reflects the differences between distribution, i.e. lower divergence means high similarity to human visual attention, a negative Spearman's rank correlation indicates that higher performance means high similarity to human visual attention. The p-value indicates the significance and the likelihood that the null hypothesis will be rejected. With p-values below 0.01, we can reject the null hypothesis and thus accept that there is a statistically significant correlation between divergence and accuracy.

6 Analysis Results

6.1 Models vs. Humans

In order to explore the relationship of model performance and similarity between model attention and human visual attention, we plot in Figures 3a and 3b the nine best LSTM and XLNet models performances for each document, sorted by the sum of divergence scores and number of correct models. Similar comparison between CNN and XLNet models can be found in the Appendix, Figure 4a and 4b. Performance, i.e. correctness, refers to the number of models within the ensemble that provided correct answer. The y-axis represents the KL divergence on the left, while the x-axis represents the documents (32 in total), and the legend indicates which models the datapoints refer to. The documents presented on the left of the figure are part of the easier ones and the divergence scales up as document difficulty increases. When models are faced with difficult questions, we observe performance drops and this seems to be at a specific KL threshold. We suppose that this behavior aligns with the observations reported in the case study from (Blohm et al., 2018), where human annotators required several strategies to solve difficult questions. Moreover, our plots show a correlation between attentive LSTM and CNN model performance and similarity to human visual attention.

Nine Best	Val Accuracy	Spearman	p−value
LSTM	84.37%	**-0.73**	**< 0.001**
CNN	82.58%	**-0.72**	**< 0.001**
XLNet	91.00%	-0.16	0.381

Table 2: Spearman's rank correlation coefficients between the number of models which correctly answered a given question on each document and the KL divergence between models and human visual attention. Bold numbers indicate statistically significant correlation scores, where p-value < 0.001.

To quantify the correlation between system performance and dissimilarity between model and human visual attention, we report in Table 2 the majority vote ensemble accuracy scores for each of the nine best models, Spearman's rank correlation coefficients between the KL divergence scores and the number of models that correctly answered questions, and the corresponding p-values. As observed in Figure 3a (and Figure 4a in the Appendix), there are two **statistically significant negative correla-**

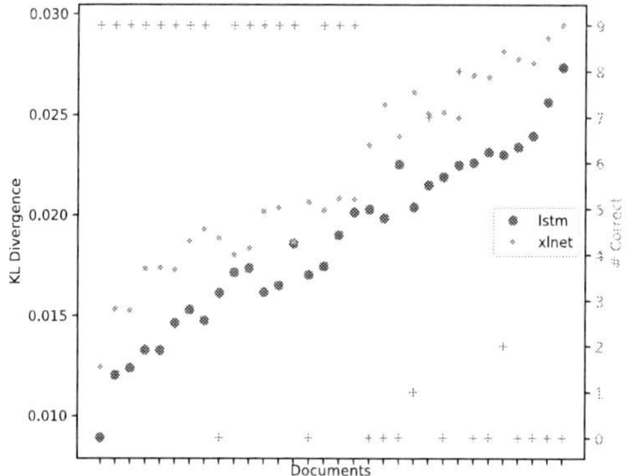 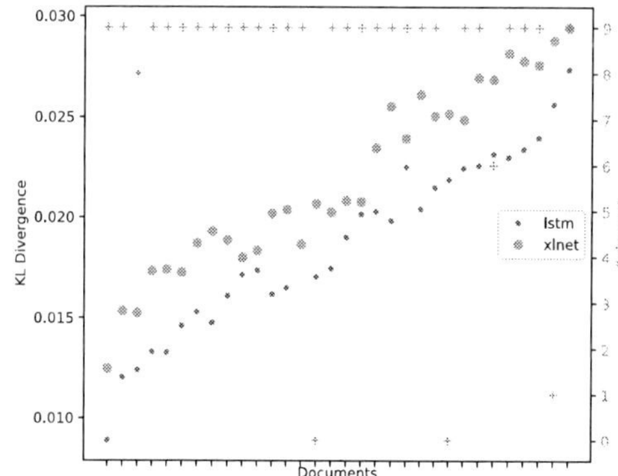

(a) LSTM versus humans — KL divergence and number of correct models per document.

(b) XLNet versus humans — KL divergence and number of correct models per document.

Figure 3: Models attention vs. human visual attention. On the x-axis we show each of the 32 documents with the corresponding KL divergence score on the left y-axis. We plot performance of LSTM (cf. Figure 3a) and XLNet (cf. Figure 3b) models for each document with green plus signs as the number of correct models indicated on the right y-axis. In Figure 3a, the larger blue dots show the LSTM divergence score for each document, while the smaller orange dots show the divergence score of XLNet models. Vice-Versa, in Figure 3b, the larger orange dots show the XLNet score for each document, while the smaller blue dots show the divergence score of the LSTM models. The documents are ordered by ascending divergence score.

tions from the attentive **LSTM (-0.73) and CNN (-0.72) models**. These correlation scores indicate that for either LSTM or CNN, as the number of models that correctly answered a question related to a document increases, the KL divergence of these model types to human visual attention decreases. We conclude that there is a correlation between task performance and similarity between neural attention when leveraging LSTM or CNN and human visual attention distributions.

However in contrast, behavior from XLNet models show weak negative correlation of -0.16 and p = 0.381 (cf. Table 2, cf. Figure 3b). Most XLNet models correctly answer the questions, although the KL divergence increases (cf. Figure 3b), i.e. there is no significant correlation between performance and similarity to human visual attention. All the nine XLNet models always provide correct answers. One potential reason could be that we chose documents that are difficult to answer based on an analysis of CNN and LSTM models.

6.2 Models vs. Models

In Table 3, we perform a pairwise comparison of the average KL divergence for the three neural models using a linear regression model with Tukey's alpha adjustment method (Sinclair et al., 2013). Interestingly, there is a **statistically significant** difference between the KL divergence of **LSTMs** compared to **XLNets** ($\beta = -0.003, p < 0.01$). Even though the performance of the XLNets are better with respect to accuracy, LSTMs are significantly more similar to human visual attention.

This observation suggests that even though aiming to interpret the black box by comparing it to human performance provides insight, we should not force all model types to emulate human visual attention while performing the same task.

7 Conclusion and Future Work

Our core contribution is a new method for comparing human visual attention versus neural attention distributions in machine reading comprehension. To the best of our knowledge, we are the first to do so with gaze data. Our findings show that CNNs and LSTMs have a statistically significant correlation between similarity to human visual attention distributions and system performance. Interestingly, the same is not true for XLNets. Moreover, the attention weights of the LSTMs are significantly different compared to the XLNets. Although these pre-trained Transformer networks are less similar to human visual attention, our fine-tuned model obtains the new SOTA on the MovieQA benchmark dataset with 91% accuracy on the validation set. In addition, we extend the MovieQA dataset with eye tracking data, release this as open source and present an attentive reading visualiza-

Nine Best	Avg KL	Combo	Estimate	Std. Error	t-value	p-value
LSTM	0.018	LSTM vs. XLNet	-0.003	0.001	-2.835	**< 0.01**
CNN	0.020	LSTM vs. CNN	-0.001	0.001	-1.098	0.27
XLNet	0.022	CNN vs. XLNet	-0.001	0.001	-1.736	0.17

Table 3: Pairwise comparison of the average KL divergence for the three models. Here we show the comparison of each model against each other (LSTM vs. CNN, LSTM vs. XLNET, and CNN vs. XLNet). We compare the models to show if the differences in attention distributions between models is of statistical significance; the significantly different model type (LSTM) can be seen in bold, where p-value < 0.01.

tion tool that supports users to gain insights when comparing human versus neural attention.

In future work we plan to extend our understanding of these large-scale pre-trained language models. It would be interesting to investigate whether the observed increase in performance but lack of similarity to humans in the XLNet models is because they are pre-trained on large external corpora or whether this is due to inherent properties in architecture, when compared to other pre-trained models (such as BERT). Lastly, to further disentangle token level saliency versus cognitive load of processing, additional analyses and metrics could be considered.

8 Acknowledgements

E. Sood was funded by the Deutsche Forschungsgemeinschaft (DFG, German Research Foundation) under Germany's Excellence Strategy - EXC 2075 – 390740016; A. Bulling was funded by the European Research Council (ERC; grant agreement 801708); S. Tannert was supported by IBM Research AI through the IBM AI Horizons Network; N.T. Vu was funded by the Carl Zeiss Foundation. We would like to especially thank Manuel Mager for his valuable feedback and guidance. And to Pavel Denisov and Sean Papay for their helpful insights and suggestions. We would also like to thank Glorianna Jagfeld for her contributions on the dataset, and Fabian Kögel for his contributions on the visualization tool. Lastly, we would like to thank the anonymous reviewers for their useful feedback.

References

David Alvarez-Melis and Tommi S Jaakkola. 2018. Towards robust interpretability with self-explaining neural networks. In *Proceedings of the 32nd International Conference on Neural Information Processing Systems*, pages 7786–7795. Curran Associates Inc.

Jennifer E Arnold, Janet G Eisenband, Sarah Brown-Schmidt, and John C Trueswell. 2000. The rapid use of gender information: Evidence of the time course of pronoun resolution from eyetracking. *Cognition*, 76(1):B13–B26.

Dzmitry Bahdanau, Kyunghyun Cho, and Yoshua Bengio. 2014. Neural machine translation by jointly learning to align and translate. *arXiv preprint arXiv:1409.0473*.

Maria Barrett, Joachim Bingel, Nora Hollenstein, Marek Rei, and Anders Søgaard. 2018. Sequence classification with human attention. In *Proceedings of the 22nd Conference on Computational Natural Language Learning*, pages 302–312.

Matthias Blohm, Glorianna Jagfeld, Ekta Sood, Xiang Yu, and Ngoc Thang Vu. 2018. Comparing attention-based convolutional and recurrent neural networks: Success and limitations in machine reading comprehension. In *Proceedings of the 22nd Conference on Computational Natural Language Learning*, pages 108–118.

James V Bradley. 1958. Complete counterbalancing of immediate sequential effects in a latin square design. *Journal of the American Statistical Association*, 53(282):525–528.

Richard Eckart de Castilho, Éva Mújdricza-Maydt, Seid Muhie Yimam, Silvana Hartmann, Iryna Gurevych, Anette Frank, and Chris Biemann. 2016. A web-based tool for the integrated annotation of semantic and syntactic structures. In *Proceedings of the Workshop on Language Technology Resources and Tools for Digital Humanities (LT4DH)*, pages 76–84, Osaka, Japan. The COLING 2016 Organizing Committee.

Jan K Chorowski, Dzmitry Bahdanau, Dmitriy Serdyuk, Kyunghyun Cho, and Yoshua Bengio. 2015. Attention-based models for speech recognition. In *Advances in neural information processing systems*, pages 577–585.

Emrah Cinkara and Neşe Cabaroğlu. 2015. Parallel functioning hypothesis to explain pronoun resolution and processing load: Evidence from eye-tracking. *Journal of Quantitative Linguistics*, 22(2):119–134.

Zihang Dai, Zhilin Yang, Yiming Yang, Jaime G Carbonell, Quoc Le, and Ruslan Salakhutdinov. 2019. Transformer-xl: Attentive language models beyond a fixed-length context. In *Proceedings of the 57th Annual Meeting of the Association for Computational Linguistics*, pages 2978–2988.

Abhishek Das, Harsh Agrawal, Larry Zitnick, Devi Parikh, and Dhruv Batra. 2017. Human attention in visual question answering: Do humans and deep networks look at the same regions? *Computer Vision and Image Understanding*, 163:90–100.

Heiner Deubel, K O'Regan, Ralph Radach, et al. 2000. Attention, information processing and eye movement control. *Reading as a perceptual process*, pages 355–374.

Jacob Devlin, Ming-Wei Chang, Kenton Lee, and Kristina Toutanova. 2019. Bert: Pre-training of deep bidirectional transformers for language understanding. In *NAACL-HLT*.

Daria Dzendzik, Carl Vogel, and Qun Liu. 2017. Who framed roger rabbit? multiple choice questions answering about movie plot.

Maria K Eckstein, Belén Guerra-Carrillo, Alison T Miller Singley, and Silvia A Bunge. 2017. Beyond eye gaze: What else can eyetracking reveal about cognition and cognitive development? *Developmental cognitive neuroscience*, 25:69–91.

Simone Frintrop, Erich Rome, and Henrik I Christensen. 2010. Computational visual attention systems and their cognitive foundations: A survey. *ACM Transactions on Applied Perception (TAP)*, 7(1):6.

Leilani H Gilpin, David Bau, Ben Z Yuan, Ayesha Bajwa, Michael Specter, and Lalana Kagal. 2018. Explaining explanations: An overview of interpretability of machine learning. In *2018 IEEE 5th International Conference on data science and advanced analytics (DSAA)*, pages 80–89. IEEE.

Michael Hahn and Frank Keller. 2016. Modeling human reading with neural attention. In *Proceedings of the 2016 Conference on Empirical Methods in Natural Language Processing*, pages 85–95, Austin, Texas. Association for Computational Linguistics.

Michael Hahn and Frank Keller. 2018. Modeling task effects in human reading with neural attention. *arXiv preprint arXiv:1808.00054*.

Demis Hassabis, Dharshan Kumaran, Christopher Summerfield, and Matthew Botvinick. 2017. Neuroscience-inspired artificial intelligence. *Neuron*, 95(2):245–258.

John M Henderson. 1992. Visual attention and eye movement control during reading and picture viewing. In *Eye movements and visual cognition*, pages 260–283. Springer.

Karl Moritz Hermann, Tomas Kocisky, Edward Grefenstette, Lasse Espeholt, Will Kay, Mustafa Suleyman, and Phil Blunsom. 2015. Teaching machines to read and comprehend. In *Advances in neural information processing systems*, pages 1693–1701.

Sepp Hochreiter and Jürgen Schmidhuber. 1997. Long Short-Term Memory. *Neural Computation*, 9(8).

James E Hoffman and Baskaran Subramaniam. 1995. The role of visual attention in saccadic eye movements. *Perception & psychophysics*, 57(6):787–795.

Sara Hooker, Dumitru Erhan, Pieter-Jan Kindermans, and Been Kim. 2019. A benchmark for interpretability methods in deep neural networks. In *Advances in Neural Information Processing Systems*, pages 9737–9748.

Phu Mon Htut, Jason Phang, Shikha Bordia, and Samuel R Bowman. 2019. Do attention heads in bert track syntactic dependencies? *arXiv preprint arXiv:1911.12246*.

Sarthak Jain and Byron C. Wallace. 2019. Attention is not explanation.

Robin Jia and Percy Liang. 2017. Adversarial examples for evaluating reading comprehension systems. In *Proceedings of the 2017 Conference on Empirical Methods in Natural Language Processing*, pages 2021–2031.

Marcel A Just and Patricia A Carpenter. 1980. A theory of reading: From eye fixations to comprehension. *Psychological review*, 87(4):329.

Stephen Kokoska and Daniel Zwillinger. 2000. *CRC standard probability and statistics tables and formulae*. Crc Press.

Ami Kristjansson. 2011. The intriguing interactive relationship between visual attention and saccadic eye movements. *The Oxford handbook of eye movements*, pages 455–470.

Solomon Kullback and Richard A Leibler. 1951. On information and sufficiency. *The annals of mathematical statistics*, 22(1):79–86.

Kenton Lee, Luheng He, and Luke Zettlemoyer. 2018. Higher-order coreference resolution with coarse-to-fine inference. *arXiv preprint arXiv:1804.05392*.

Zachary C Lipton. 2018. The mythos of model interpretability. *Queue*, 16(3):31–57.

Ling Luo, Xiang Ao, Yan Song, Feiyang Pan, Min Yang, and Qing He. 2019. Reading like HER: Human reading inspired extractive summarization. In *Proceedings of the 2019 Conference on Empirical Methods in Natural Language Processing and the 9th International Joint Conference on Natural Language Processing (EMNLP-IJCNLP)*, pages 3031–3041.

Thang Luong, Hieu Pham, and Christopher D. Manning. 2015. Effective approaches to attention-based neural machine translation. In *Proceedings of the 2015 Conference on Empirical Methods in Natural Language Processing, EMNLP 2015, Lisbon, Portugal, September 17-21, 2015*, pages 1412–1421.

Yu-Fei Ma and Hong-Jiang Zhang. 2003. Contrast-based image attention analysis by using fuzzy growing. In *Proceedings of the eleventh ACM international conference on Multimedia*, pages 374–381. ACM.

Milica Milosavljevic and Moran Cerf. 2008. First attention then intention: Insights from computational neuroscience of vision. *International Journal of advertising*, 27(3):381–398.

Volodymyr Mnih, Nicolas Heess, Alex Graves, et al. 2014. Recurrent models of visual attention. In *Advances in neural information processing systems*, pages 2204–2212.

Tri Nguyen, Mir Rosenberg, Xia Song, Jianfeng Gao, Saurabh Tiwary, Rangan Majumder, and Li Deng. 2016. Ms marco: A human-generated machine reading comprehension dataset.

Timothy Niven and Hung-Yu Kao. 2019. Probing neural network comprehension of natural language arguments. In *Proceedings of the 57th Annual Meeting of the Association for Computational Linguistics*, pages 4658–4664.

F. Pedregosa, G. Varoquaux, A. Gramfort, V. Michel, B. Thirion, O. Grisel, M. Blondel, P. Prettenhofer, R. Weiss, V. Dubourg, J. Vanderplas, A. Passos, D. Cournapeau, M. Brucher, M. Perrot, and E. Duchesnay. 2011. Scikit-learn: Machine learning in Python. *Journal of Machine Learning Research*, 12:2825–2830.

Massimo Poesio. 1994. Semantic ambiguity and perceived ambiguity. In *Semantic Ambiguity and Underspecification*, pages 159–201. CSLI Publications.

Michael I Posner. 1980. Orienting of attention. *Quarterly journal of experimental psychology*, 32(1):3–25.

Michael I Posner, Charles R Snyder, and Brian J Davidson. 1980. Attention and the detection of signals. *Journal of experimental psychology: General*, 109(2):160.

Sameer Pradhan, Alessandro Moschitti, Nianwen Xue, Olga Uryupina, and Yuchen Zhang. 2012. Conll-2012 shared task: Modeling multilingual unrestricted coreference in ontonotes. In *Joint Conference on EMNLP and CoNLL-Shared Task*, pages 1–40.

Tingting Qiao, Jianfeng Dong, and Duanqing Xu. 2018. Exploring human-like attention supervision in visual question answering. In *Thirty-Second AAAI Conference on Artificial Intelligence*.

Boyu Qiu, Xu Chen, Jungang Xu, and Yingfei Sun. 2019. A survey on neural machine reading comprehension. *arXiv preprint arXiv:1906.03824*.

Alec Radford, Karthik Narasimhan, Tim Salimans, and Ilya Sutskever. 2018. Improving language understanding by generative pre-training.

Altaf Rahman and Vincent Ng. 2012. Resolving complex cases of definite pronouns: the winograd schema challenge. In *Proceedings of the 2012 Joint Conference on Empirical Methods in Natural Language Processing and Computational Natural Language Learning*, pages 777–789. Association for Computational Linguistics.

Pranav Rajpurkar, Jian Zhang, Konstantin Lopyrev, and Percy Liang. 2016. Squad: 100, 000+ questions for machine comprehension of text. *ArXiv*, abs/1606.05250.

Keith Rayner. 1998. Eye movements in reading and information processing: 20 years of research. *Psychological bulletin*, 124(3):372.

Keith Rayner. 2009. Eye movements and attention in reading, scene perception, and visual search. *The quarterly journal of experimental psychology*, 62(8):1457–1506.

Raymond Reiter. 1981. On closed world data bases. In *Readings in artificial intelligence*, pages 119–140. Elsevier.

Marco Tulio Ribeiro, Sameer Singh, and Carlos Guestrin. 2016. Why should i trust you?: Explaining the predictions of any classifier. In *Proceedings of the 22nd ACM SIGKDD international conference on knowledge discovery and data mining*, pages 1135–1144. ACM.

William B Rouse and Nancy M Morris. 1986. On looking into the black box: Prospects and limits in the search for mental models. *Psychological bulletin*, 100(3):349.

Cynthia Rudin. 2019. Stop explaining black box machine learning models for high stakes decisions and use interpretable models instead. *Nature Machine Intelligence*, 1(5):206–215.

Walter Schneider and Richard M Shiffrin. 1977. Controlled and automatic human information processing: I. detection, search, and attention. *Psychological review*, 84(1):1.

Cansu Sen, Thomas Hartvigsen, Biao Yin, Xiangnan Kong, and Elke Rundensteiner. 2020. Human attention maps for text classification: Do humans and neural networks focus on the same words? In *Proceedings of the 58th Annual Meeting of the Association for Computational Linguistics*, pages 4596–4608, Online. Association for Computational Linguistics.

Minjoon Seo, Aniruddha Kembhavi, Ali Farhadi, and Hannaneh Hajishirzi. 2016. Bidirectional attention flow for machine comprehension. *arXiv preprint arXiv:1611.01603.*

Tao Shen, Tianyi Zhou, Guodong Long, Jing Jiang, Shirui Pan, and Chengqi Zhang. 2018. Disan: Directional self-attention network for rnn/cnn-free language understanding. In *Thirty-Second AAAI Conference on Artificial Intelligence.*

Richard M Shiffrin and Walter Schneider. 1977. Controlled and automatic human information processing: Ii. perceptual learning, automatic attending and a general theory. *Psychological review*, 84(2):127.

J Sinclair, Paul J Taylor, and Sarah Jane Hobbs. 2013. Alpha level adjustments for multiple dependent variable analyses and their applicability–a review. *Int J Sports Sci Eng*, 7(1):17–20.

Ekta Sood, Simon Tannert, Philipp Müller, and Andreas Bulling. 2020. Improving natural language processing tasks with human gaze-guided neural attention. In *Advances in Neural Information Processing Systems (NeurIPS).*

Yusuke Sugano and Andreas Bulling. 2016. Seeing with humans: Gaze-assisted neural image captioning. *arXiv preprint arXiv:1608.05203.*

Yaoru Sun and Robert Fisher. 2003. Object-based visual attention for computer vision. *Artificial intelligence*, 146(1):77–123.

Makarand Tapaswi, Yukun Zhu, Rainer Stiefelhagen, Antonio Torralba, Raquel Urtasun, and Sanja Fidler. 2016. Movieqa: Understanding stories in movies through question-answering. In *Proceedings of the IEEE Conference on Computer Vision and Pattern Recognition*, pages 4631–4640.

Adam Trischler, Tong Wang, Xingdi Yuan, Justin Harris, Alessandro Sordoni, Philip Bachman, and Kaheer Suleman. 2017. Newsqa: A machine comprehension dataset. In *Rep4NLP@ACL.*

Meng-Jung Tsai, Huei-Tse Hou, Meng-Lung Lai, Wan-Yi Liu, and Fang-Ying Yang. 2012. Visual attention for solving multiple-choice science problem: An eye-tracking analysis. *Computers & Education*, 58(1):375–385.

Edwin AJ Van Hooft and Marise Ph Born. 2012. Intentional response distortion on personality tests: Using eye-tracking to understand response processes when faking. *Journal of Applied Psychology*, 97(2):301.

Ashish Vaswani, Noam Shazeer, Niki Parmar, Jakob Uszkoreit, Llion Jones, Aidan N Gomez, Łukasz Kaiser, and Illia Polosukhin. 2017. Attention is all you need. In *Advances in neural information processing systems*, pages 5998–6008.

Petar Veličković, Guillem Cucurull, Arantxa Casanova, Adriana Romero, Pietro Lio, and Yoshua Bengio. 2017. Graph attention networks. *arXiv preprint arXiv:1710.10903.*

Jesse Vig and Yonatan Belinkov. 2019. Analyzing the structure of attention in a transformer language model. In *Proceedings of the 2019 ACL Workshop BlackboxNLP: Analyzing and Interpreting Neural Networks for NLP*, pages 63–76.

Shuohang Wang and Jing Jiang. A compare-aggregate model for matching text sequences.(2017). In *ICLR 2017: International Conference on Learning Representations, Toulon, France, April 24-26: Proceedings*, pages 1–15.

Sarah Wiegreffe and Yuval Pinter. 2019. Attention is not not explanation. In *Proceedings of the 2019 Conference on Empirical Methods in Natural Language Processing and the 9th International Joint Conference on Natural Language Processing (EMNLP-IJCNLP)*, pages 11–20.

Ewa Wojciulik, Nancy Kanwisher, and Jon Driver. 1998. Covert visual attention modulates face-specific activity in the human fusiform gyrus: fmri study. *Journal of neurophysiology*, 79(3):1574–1578.

Kelvin Xu, Jimmy Ba, Ryan Kiros, Kyunghyun Cho, Aaron Courville, Ruslan Salakhudinov, Rich Zemel, and Yoshua Bengio. 2015. Show, attend and tell: Neural image caption generation with visual attention. In *International conference on machine learning*, pages 2048–2057.

Zhilin Yang, Zihang Dai, Yiming Yang, Jaime G. Carbonell, Ruslan Salakhutdinov, and Quoc V. Le. 2019. Xlnet: Generalized autoregressive pretraining for language understanding. In *NeurIPS.*

Zichao Yang, Diyi Yang, Chris Dyer, Xiaodong He, Alexander J. Smola, and Eduard H. Hovy. 2016. Hierarchical Attention Networks for Document Classification. In *HLT-NAACL.*

Adams Wei Yu, David Dohan, Minh-Thang Luong, Rui Zhao, Kai Chen, Mohammad Norouzi, and Quoc V Le. 2018. Qanet: Combining local convolution with global self-attention for reading comprehension. *arXiv preprint arXiv:1804.09541.*

Xiaoyong Yuan, Pan He, Qile Zhu, and Xiaolin Li. 2019. Adversarial examples: Attacks and defenses for deep learning. *IEEE transactions on neural networks and learning systems.*

Jerrold H Zar. 1972. Significance testing of the spearman rank correlation coefficient. *Journal of the American Statistical Association*, 67(339):578–580.

Han Zhang, Ian Goodfellow, Dimitris Metaxas, and Augustus Odena. 2019. Self-attention generative adversarial networks. In *International Conference on Machine Learning*, pages 7354–7363.

Yukun Zheng, Jiaxin Mao, Yiqun Liu, Zixin Ye, Min Zhang, and Shaoping Ma. 2019. Human behavior in-spired machine reading comprehension. In *Proceedings of the 42nd International ACM SIGIR Conference on Research and Development in Information Retrieval*, pages 425–434. ACM.

A Appendix

A.1 Analysis Results – Models vs. Humans

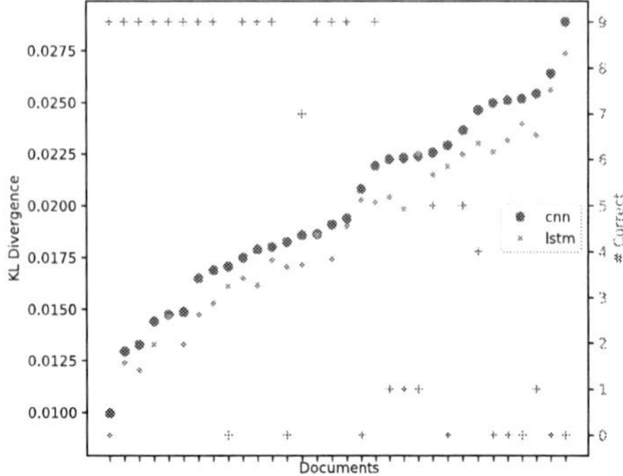

(a) CNN and LSTM versus humans — KL divergence and number of correct CNN models per document.

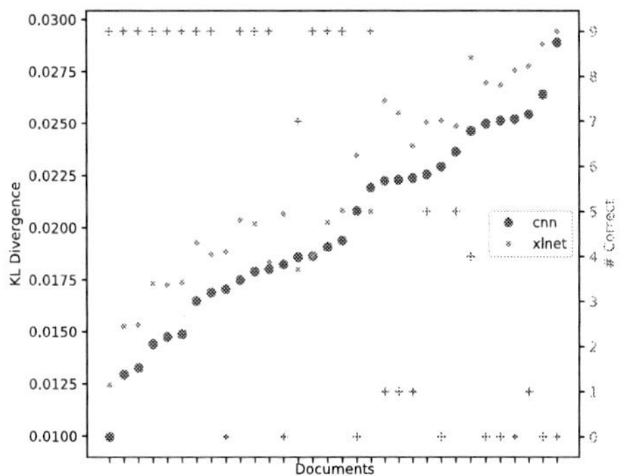

(b) CNN and XLNet versus humans — KL divergence and number of correct CNN models per document.

Figure 4: In this Figure we show the KL divergence to human attention of CNN and the LSTM models (cf. Figure 4a as well as of CNN and the XLNet models (cf. Figure 4b) to point out the differences between models. The CNN model divergences are highlighted in the large blue dots, and LSTM and XLNet models are indicated in smaller orange dots. The correctness (in red) indicated on the right y-axis, shows the number correct CNN models per document.

A.2 Visualization Tool

A.3 Coreference Resolution

The coreference annotation We used the off-the-shelf high performing coreference model (Lee et al., 2018) (following the implementation from `https:`

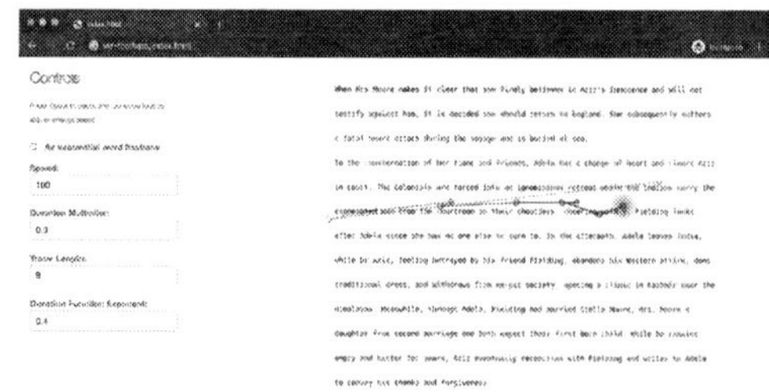

(a) Interface for visualization tool and example of visualization scan path.

```
x        y        dur    word_id word
945.0    540.0    950    150     women
928.0    458.0    108    129     created
705.0    151.0    67     33      Ronny
639.0    85.0     342    16      independence
727.0    79.0     147    4       in
698.0    82.0     195    17      movement
798.0    76.0     253    6       1920s
853.0    78.0     225    7       during
916.0    76.0     207    9       period
940.0    75.0     288    9       period
916.0    71.0     187    9       period
1000.0   72.0     290    11      growing
958.0    70.0     183    9       period
940.0    73.0     207    9       period
1016.0   71.0     172    11      growing
1067.0   74.0     228    12      influence
1150.0   72.0     163    13      of
1198.0   71.0     98     15      Indian
687.0    106.0    142    16      independence
629.0    119.0    220    16      independence
738.0    114.0    252    17      movement
817.0    113.0    293    19      the
888.0    118.0    128    21      Raj.
```

(b) Eye tracking data file required for visualization tool

Figure 5: Figure 5a shows the control options (left side) that allow users to pause the visualization with the space bar, change the speed, duration variables, and length of the scan path. Figure 5a, on the right side, shows an example txt stimuli file and the simulated scan path. The red dot indicates fixation duration and expands given the duration length (what we extract as human attention weights). In Figure 5b we show an example of the gaze data txt file required for visualization tool.

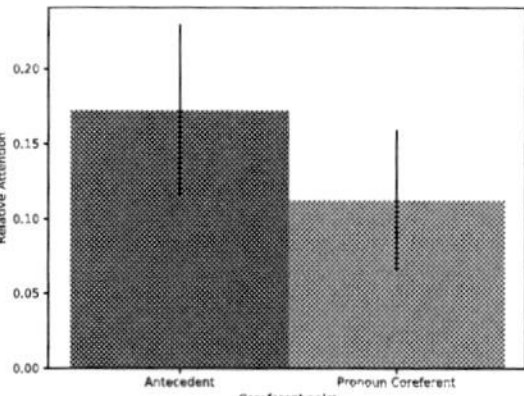

Figure 6: Here we compute the relative importance of coreference chains observed in the human data, where we use fixation durations to denote saliency. We show the agreement in our MQA-RC dataset, between humans, that antecedents are more salient compared to pronoun co-reference chains.

`//github.com/kentonl/e2e-coref`), in order to obtain coreference chains over our MQA-RC dataset. We train the model on the same data as reported in (Lee et al., 2018), reproducing reported results over the OntoNotes data, that is, the CoNLL 2012 version of it; thus the model predictions are based on the annotation schema defined in (Pradhan et al., 2012). We then test the model on the MQA-RC dataset to obtain our coreference chains. We prepared the data with the automatically generated coreference chain predictions (antecedents and their corresponding pronouns coreference chains), into a web-based annotation tool, WebAnno3 (Eckart de Castilho et al., 2016). At this point, two experienced annotators (one English native speaker, and the other near-native) checked and corrected the automatically generated annotations. The annotators obtained 100% agreement; we suppose this is due to the small amount of documents, short length of sentences in the documents, and the documents contain easy to resolve pronouns (as seen in Figure 6). We then merge the corrected annotations between annotators, and present this as our coreference annotation over the 32 documents.

A.4 Extracting LSTM and CNN Word Level Attention

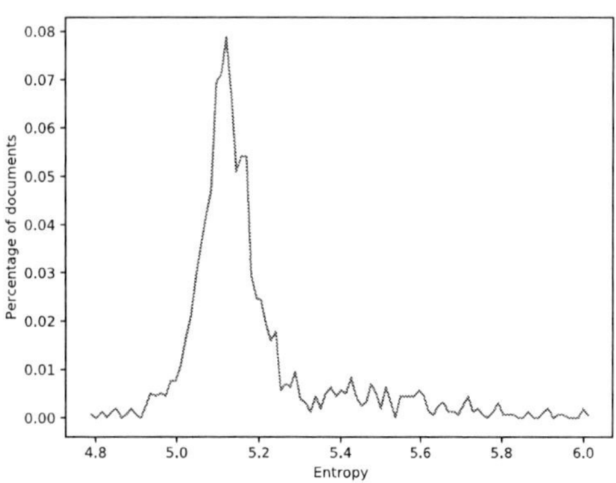

(a) CNN word level attention distribution

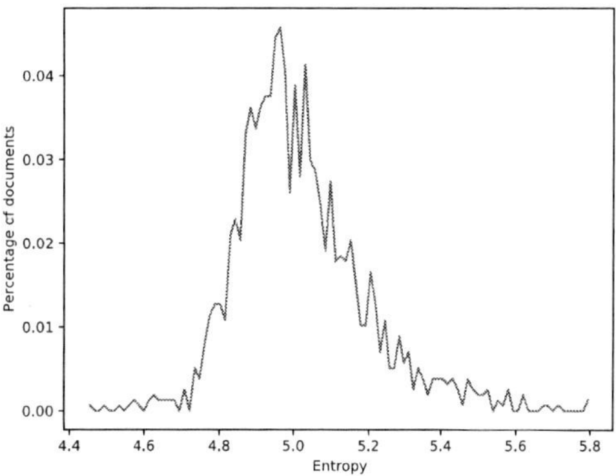

(b) LSTM word level attention distribution

Figure 7: We show the word level attention distributions for both CNN 7a and LSTM 7b. The word level attention distribution has high entropy, and thus provide a suitable option to compare to human attention.

Neural Proof Nets

Konstantinos Kogkalidis[♭] and **Michael Moortgat**[♭] and **Richard Moot**[♮]

[♭] Utrecht Institute of Linguistics OTS, Utrecht University

[♮] LIRMM, Université de Montpellier, CNRS

`{k.kogkalidis,m.j.moortgat}@uu.nl, richard.moot@lirmm.fr`

Abstract

Linear logic and the linear λ-calculus have a long standing tradition in the study of natural language form and meaning. Among the proof calculi of linear logic, proof nets are of particular interest, offering an attractive geometric representation of derivations that is unburdened by the bureaucratic complications of conventional prooftheoretic formats. Building on recent advances in set-theoretic learning, we propose a neural variant of proof nets based on Sinkhorn networks, which allows us to translate parsing as the problem of extracting syntactic primitives and permuting them into alignment. Our methodology induces a batch-efficient, end-to-end differentiable architecture that actualizes a formally grounded yet highly efficient neuro-symbolic parser. We test our approach on Æthel, a dataset of typelogical derivations for written Dutch, where it manages to correctly transcribe raw text sentences into proofs and terms of the linear λ-calculus with an accuracy of as high as 70%.

1 Introduction

There is a broad consensus among grammar formalisms that the composition of form and meaning in natural language is a resource-sensitive process, with the words making up a phrase contributing exactly once to the resulting whole. The sentence "the Mad Hatter offered" is ill-formed because of a *lack* of grammatical material, "offer" being a ditransitive verb; "the Cheshire Cat grinned Alice a cup of tea" on the other hand is ill-formed because of an *excess* of material, which the intransitive verb "grin" cannot accommodate.

Given the resource-sensitive nature of language, it comes as no surprise that Linear Logic (Girard, 1987), in particular its intuitionistic version ILL, plays a central role in current logic-based grammar formalisms. Abstract Categorial Grammars and Lambda Grammars (de Groote, 2001;

Muskens, 2001) use ILL "as-is" to characterize an abstract level of grammatical structure from which surface form and semantic interpretation are obtained by means of compositional translations. Modern typelogical grammars in the tradition of the Lambek Calculus (Lambek, 1958), e.g. Multimodal TLG (Moortgat, 1996), Displacement Calculus (Morrill, 2014), Hybrid TLG (Kubota and Levine, 2020), refine the type language to account for syntactic aspects of word order and constituency; ILL here is the target logic for semantic interpretation, reached by a homomorphism relating types and derivations of the syntactic calculus to their semantic counterparts.

A common feature of the aforementioned formalisms is their adoption of the *parsing-as-deduction* method: determining whether a phrase is syntactically well-formed is seen as the outcome of a process of logical deduction. This logical deduction automatically gives rise to a program for meaning composition, thanks to the remarkable correspondence between logical proof and computation known as the Curry-Howard isomorphism (Sørensen and Urzyczyn, 2006), a natural manifestation of the syntax-semantics interface. The Curry-Howard λ-terms associated with derivations are neutral with respect to the particular semantic theory one wants to adopt, accommodating both the truth-conditional view of formal semantics and the vector-based distributional view (Muskens and Sadrzadeh, 2018), among others.

Despite their formal appeal, grammars based on variants of linear logic have fallen out of favour within the NLP community, owing to a scarcity of large-scale datasets, but also due to difficulties in aligning them with the established high-performance neural toolkit. Seeking to bridge the gap between formal theory and applied practice, we focus on the *proof nets* of linear logic, a lean graphical calculus that does away with the bureau-

Proceedings of the 24th Conference on Computational Natural Language Learning, pages 26–40

Online, November 19-20, 2020. ©2020 Association for Computational Linguistics

https://doi.org/10.18653/v1/P17

cratic symbol-manipulation overhead characteristic of conventional prooftheoretic presentations (§2). Integrating proof nets with recent advances in neural processing, we propose a novel approach to linear logic proof search that eliminates issues commonly associated with higher-order types and hypothetical reasoning, while greatly reducing the computational costs of structure manipulation, backtracking and iterative processing that burden standard parsing techniques (§3).

Our proposed methodology relies on two key components. The first is an encoder/decoder-based supertagger that converts raw text sentences into linear logic judgements by dynamically constructing contextual type assignments, one primitive symbol at a time. The second is a bi-modal encoder that contextualizes the generated judgement in conjunction with the input sentence. The contextualized representations are fed into a Sinkhorn layer, tasked with finding the valid permutation that brings primitive symbol occurrences into alignment. The architecture induced is trained on labeled data, and assumes the role of a formally grounded yet highly accurate parser, which transforms raw text sentences into linear logic proofs and computational terms of the simply typed linear λ-calculus, further decorated with dependency annotations that allow reconstruction of the underlying dependency graph (§4).

2 Background

We briefly summarize the logical background we are assuming, starting with $\text{ILL}_{\multimap}$, the implication-only fragment of ILL, then moving on to the dependency-enhanced version $\text{ILL}_{\multimap,\diamond,\square}$ which we employ in our experimental setup.

2.1 $\text{ILL}_{\multimap}$

Formulas (or *types*) of $\text{ILL}_{\multimap}$ are inductively defined according to the grammar below:

$$\mathcal{T} ::= A \mid T_1 \multimap T_2$$

Formula A is taken from a finite set of atomic formulas $\mathcal{A} \subset \mathcal{T}$; a complex formula $T_1 \multimap T_2$ is the type signature of a transformation that applies on $T_1 \in \mathcal{T}$ and produces $T_2 \in \mathcal{T}$, consuming the argument in the process. This view of formulas as non-renewable resources makes $\text{ILL}_{\multimap}$ the logic of *linear* functions.[1]

---

[1] We refer to Wadler (1993) for a gentle introduction.

We can present the inference rules of $\text{ILL}_{\multimap}$ together with the associated linear λ-terms in Natural Deduction format. Judgements are sequents of the form $x_1 : T_1, \ldots, x_n : T_n \vdash M : C$. The antecedent left of the turnstile is a *typing environment* (or *context*), a sequence of variables x_i, each given a type declaration T_i. These variables serve as the *parameters* of a program M of type C that corresponds to the proof of the sequent.

Proofs are built from axioms $x : T \vdash x : T$ with the aid of two rules of inference:

$$\frac{\Gamma \vdash M : T_1 \multimap T_2 \quad \Delta \vdash N : T_1}{\Gamma, \Delta \vdash (M\,N) : T_2} \; {\multimap} E \quad (1)$$

$$\frac{\Gamma, x : T_1 \vdash M : T_2}{\Gamma \vdash \lambda x.M : T_1 \multimap T_2} \; {\multimap} I \quad (2)$$

(1) is the elimination of the implication and models *function application*; it proposes that if from some context Γ one can derive a program M of type $T_1 \multimap T_2$, and from context Δ one can derive a program N of type T_1, then from the multiset union Γ, Δ one can derive a term $(M\,N)$ of type T_2.

(2) is the introduction of the implication and models *function abstraction*; it proposes that if from a context Γ together with a type declaration $x : T_1$ one can derive a program term M of type T_2, then from Γ alone one can derive the abstraction $\lambda x.M$, denoting a linear function of type $T_1 \multimap T_2$.

To obtain a *grammar* based on $\text{ILL}_{\multimap}$, we consider the logic in combination with a *lexicon*, assigning one or more type formulas to the words of the language. In this setting, the proof of a sequent $x_1 : T_1, \ldots, x_n : T_n \vdash M : C$ constitutes an algorithm to compute a meaning M of type C, given by substituting parameters x_i with lexical meanings w_i. In the type lexicon, atomic types are used to denote syntactically autonomous, stand-alone units (words and phrases); e.g. NP for noun-phrase, S for sentence, etc. Function types are assigned to incomplete expressions, e.g. NP $\multimap$ S for an intransitive verb consuming a noun-phrase to produce a sentence, NP $\multimap$ NP $\multimap$ S for a transitive verb, etc.[2] Higher-order types, i.e. types of order greater than 1, denote functions that apply to functions; these give the grammar access to hypothetical reasoning, in virtue of the implication introduction rule.[3] Combined with parametric polymorphism,

---

[2] Read $\multimap$ as right-associative.

[3] $\mathcal{O}(A)$, the order of an atomic type, equals zero; for function types $\mathcal{O}(T_1 \multimap T_2) = \max(\mathcal{O}(T_1) + 1, \mathcal{O}(T_2))$.

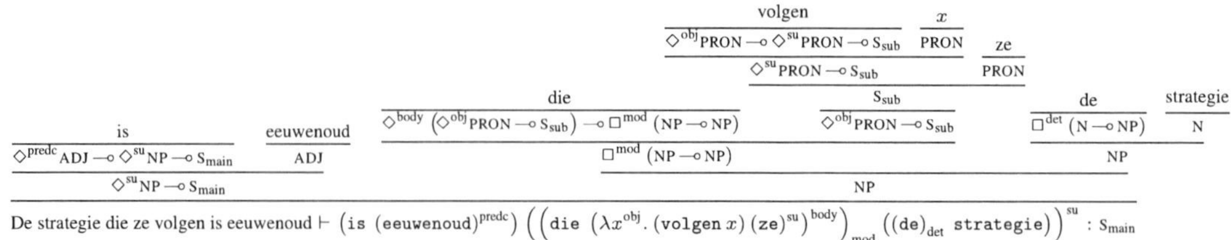

$$\text{De strategie die ze volgen is eeuwenoud} \vdash (\texttt{is } (\texttt{eeuwenoud})^{\mathrm{predc}}) \left(\left(\texttt{die } \left(\lambda x^{\mathrm{obj}}. (\texttt{volgen } x) (\texttt{ze})^{\mathrm{su}}\right)^{\mathrm{body}}\right)_{\mathrm{mod}} ((\texttt{de})_{\mathrm{det}} \texttt{ strategie})\right)^{\mathrm{su}} : \mathsf{S}_{\mathrm{main}}$$

Figure 1: Example derivation and Curry-Howard λ-term for the phrase *De strategie die ze volgen is eeuwenoud* ("The strategy that they follow is ancient") from Æthel sample `dpc-ind-001645-nl-sen.p.12.s.1_1`, showcasing how hypothetical reasoning enables the derivation of an object-relative clause (note how the instantiation of variable x of type PRON followed by its subsequent abstraction creates an argument for the higher-order function assigned to "die"). Judgement premises and rule names have been omitted for brevity's sake.

higher-order types eschew the need for phantom syntactic nodes, enabling straightforward derivations for apparent non-linear phenomena involving long-range dependencies, elliptical conjunctions, wh-movement and the like.

2.2 ILL$_{-\circ,\diamond,\square}$

For our experimental setup, we will be utilizing the Æthel dataset, a Dutch corpus of typelogical derivations (Kogkalidis et al., 2020). Noncommutative categorial grammars in the tradition of Lambek (1958) attempt to directly capture syntactic fine-structure by making a distinction between left- and right-directed variants of the implication. In order to deal with the relatively free word order of Dutch and contrary to the former, Æthel's type system sticks to the directionally non-committed $-\circ$ for function types, but compensates with two strategies for introducing syntactic discrimination. First, the *atomic* type inventory distinguishes between major clausal types $\mathsf{S}_{\mathrm{sub}}, \mathsf{S}_{\mathrm{v1}}, \mathsf{S}_{\mathrm{main}}$, based on the positioning of their verbal head (clause final, clause initial, verb second, respectively). Secondly, *function* types are enhanced with dependency information, expressed via a family of unary modalities $\diamond^d, \square^m$, with dependency labels d, m drawn from disjoint sets of complement vs adjunct markers. The new constructors produce types $\diamond^d \mathrm{A} -\circ \mathrm{B}$, used to denote the *head* of a phrase B that selects for a *complement* A and assigns it the dependency role d, and types $\square^m (\mathrm{A} -\circ \mathrm{B})$, used to denote *adjuncts*, i.e. non-head functions that project the dependency role m upon application. Following dependency grammar tradition, determiners and modifiers are treated as non-head functions.

The type enhancement induces a dependency marking on the derived λ-term, reflecting the introduction/elimination of the $\diamond, \square$ constructors; each dependency domain has a unique head, together with its complements and possible adjuncts, denoted by superscripts and subscripts, respectively. Figure 1 provides an example derivation and the corresponding λ-term.

A shallow dependency graph can be trivially reconstructed by traversal of the decorated λ-term, recursively establishing labeled edges along the path from a phrasal head to the head of each of its dependants while skipping abstractions; see Figure 4 for an example.

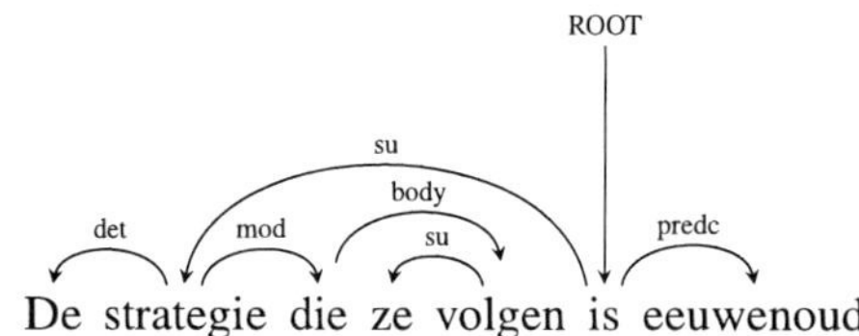

Figure 4: Shallow graph for the term of Figure 1.

2.3 Proof Nets

Despite their clear computational interpretation (Girard et al., 1988; Troelstra and Schwichtenberg, 2000; Sørensen and Urzyczyn, 2006), proofs in natural deduction format are arduous to obtain; reasoning with hypotheticals necessitates a mixture of forward and backward chaining search strategies. The sequent calculus presentation, on the other hand, permits exhaustive proof search via pure backward chaining, but does so at the cost of spurious ambiguity. Moreover, both the above assume a tree-like proof structure, which hinders their parallel processing and impairs compatibility with neural methods. As an alternative, we turn

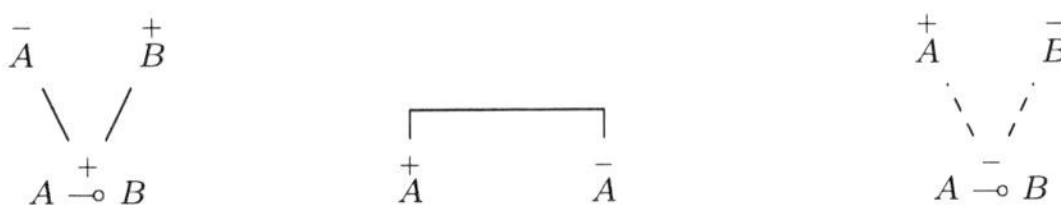

Figure 2: Links for linear logic proof nets. Left/right: positive/negative implication. Center: axiom link.

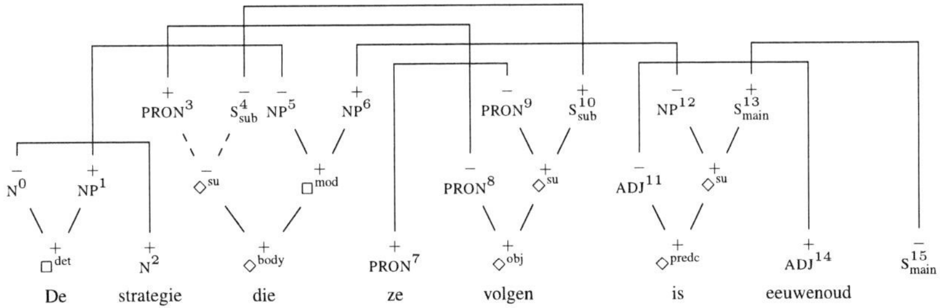

Figure 3: Proof net corresponding to the natural deduction derivation of Figure 1, with modal markings in place of implication arrows. Atomic types at the fringe of the formula decomposition trees are marked with superscript indices denoting their position for ease of identification. During decoding, the proof frame is flattened as the linear sequence: $[\,[\mathtt{SOS}],\Box^{det},N,NP,[\mathtt{SEP}],N,[\mathtt{SEP}],\Diamond^{body},\Diamond^{su},PRON,S_{sub},\Box^{mod},NP,NP,[\mathtt{SEP}],PRON,[\mathtt{SEP}],\Diamond^{obj},\dots]$

our attention towards *proof nets* (Girard, 1987), a graphical representation of linear logic proofs that captures hypothetical reasoning in a purely geometric manner. Proof nets may be seen as a parallelized version of the sequent calculus or a multi-conclusion version of natural deduction and combine the best of both words, allowing for flexible and easily parallelized proof search while maintaining the 1-to-1 correspondence with the terms of the linear λ-calculus.

To define ILL proof nets, we first need the auxiliary notion of *polarity*. We assign *positive* polarity to resources we have, *negative* polarity to resources we seek. Logically, a formula with negative polarity appears in *conclusion* position (right of the turnstile), whereas formulas with positive polarity appear in *premise* position (left of the turnstile). Given a formula and its polarity, the polarity of its subformulas is computed as follows: for a positive formula $T_1 \multimap T_2$, T_1 is negative and T_2 is positive, whereas for a negative formula $T_1 \multimap T_2$, T_1 is positive and T_2 is negative.

With respect to proof search, proof nets present a simple but general setup as follows. (1) Begin by writing down the formula decomposition tree for all formulas in a sequent $P_1, \ldots P_n \vdash C$, keeping track of polarity information; the result is called a *proof frame*. (2) Find a perfect matching between the positive and negative atomic formulas; the result is called a *proof structure*. (3) Finally, verify that the proof structure satisfies the correctness condition;

if so, the result is a *proof net*.

Formula decomposition is fully deterministic, with the decomposition rules shown in Figure 2. There are two logical links, denoting positive and negative occurrences of an implication (corresponding to the elimination and introduction rules of natural deduction, respectively). A third rule, called the axiom link, connects two equal formulas of opposite polarity.

To transform a proof frame into a proof structure, we first need to check the *count invariance* property, which requires an equal count of positive and negative occurrences for every atomic type, and then connect atoms of opposite polarity. In principle, we can connect any positive atom to any negative atom when both are of the same type; the combinatorics of proof search lies, therefore, in the axiom connections (the number of possible proof structures scales factorial to the number of atoms). Not all proof structures are, however, proof nets. Validating the correctness of a proof net can be done in linear time (Guerrini, 1999; Murawski and Ong, 2000); a common approach is to attempt a traversal of the proof net, ensuring that all nodes are visited (connectedness) and no loops exist (acyclicity) (Danos and Regnier, 1989). There is an apparent tension here between finding just *a* matching of atomic formulas (which is trivial once we satisfy the count invariance) and finding *the* correct matching, which produces not only a proof net, but also the preferred semantic reading of the sentence.

29

Deciding the provability of a linear logic sequent is an NP-complete problem (Lincoln, 1995), even in the simplest case where formulas are restricted to order 1 (Kanovich, 1994). Figure 3 shows the proof net equivalent to the derivation of Figure 1.

3 Neural Proof Nets

To sidestep the complexity inherent in the combinatorics of linear logic proof search, we investigate proof net construction from a neural perspective. First, we will need to convert a sentence into a proof frame, i.e. the decomposition of a logical judgement of the form $P_1, \ldots P_n \vdash C$, with P_i the type of word i and C the goal type to be derived. Having obtained a correct proof frame, the problem boils down to establishing axiom links between the set of positive and negative atoms and verifying their validity according to the correctness criteria. We address each of these steps via a functionally independent neural module, and define *Neural Proof Nets* as their composition.

3.1 Proof Frames

Obtaining proof frames is a special case of supertagging, a common problem in NLP literature (Bangalore and Joshi, 1999). Conventional practice treats supertagging as a discriminative sequence labeling problem, with a neural model contextualizing the tokens of an input sentence before passing them through a linear projection in order to convert them to class weights (Xu et al., 2015; Vaswani et al., 2016). Here, instead, we adopt the generative paradigm (Kogkalidis et al., 2019; Bhargava and Penn, 2020), whereby each type is itself perceived as a sequence of primitive symbols.

Concretely, we perform a depth-first-left-first traversal of formula trees to convert types to prefix (Polish) notation. This converts a type to a linear sequence of symbols $s \in \mathcal{V}$, where $\mathcal{V} = \mathcal{A} \cup \mathcal{D}$, the union of atomic types and dependency-decorated modal markings.[4] Proof frames can then be represented by joining individual type representations, separated with an extra-logical token [SEP] denoting type breaks and prefixed with a special token [SOS] to denote the sequence start (see the caption of Figure 3 for an example). The resulting sequence becomes the goal of a decoding process conditional on the input sentence, as implemented by a sequence-to-sequence model.

---

[4]Dependency decorations occur only within the scope of an implication, so the two are merged into a single symbol for reasons of length economy.

Treating supertagging as auto-regressive decoding enables the prediction of any valid type in the grammar, improving generalization and eliminating the need for a strictly defined type lexicon. Further, the decoder's comprehension of the type construction process can yield drastic improvements for beam search, allowing distinct branching paths within individual types. Most importantly, it grants access to the atomic sub-formulas of a sequent, i.e. the primitive entities to be paired within a proof net – a quality that will come into play when considering the axiom linking process later on.

3.2 Proof Structures

The conversion of a proof frame into a proof structure requires establishing a correct bijection between positive and negative atoms, i.e. linking each positive occurrence of an atom with a single unique negative occurrence of the same atom.

We begin by first noting that each atomic formula occurrence within a proof frame can be assigned an identifying index according to its position in the sequence (refer to the example of Figure 3). For each distinct atomic type, we can then create a table with rows enumerating negative and columns enumerating positive occurrences of that type, ordered by their indexes. We mark cells indexing linked occurrences and leave the rest empty; tables for our running example can be seen in Figure 5. The resulting tables correspond to a *permutation matrix* Π_A for each atomic type A, i.e. a set of matrices that are square, binary and doubly-stochastic, encoding the permutation over the *chain* (i.e. ordered set) of negative elements that aligns them with the chain of matching positive elements. This key insight allows us to reframe automated proof search as learning the latent space that dictates the permutations between disjoint and non-contiguous sub-sequences of the primitive symbols constituting a decoded proof frame.

Permutation matrices are discrete mathematical objects that are not directly attainable by neural models. Their continuous relaxations are, however, valid outputs, approximated by means of the Sinkhorn operator (Sinkhorn, 1964). In essence, the operator and its underlying theorem state that the iterative normalization (alternating between rows and columns) of a square matrix with positive entries yields, in the limit, a doubly-stochastic matrix, the entries of which are *almost* binary. Put differently, the Sinkhorn operator gives rise to a

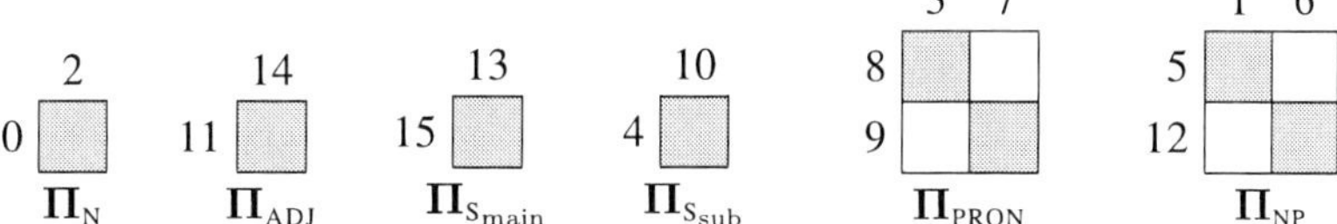

Figure 5: An alternative view of the axiom links of Figure 3, with tables $\mathbf{\Pi}_{\mathrm{N}}$, $\mathbf{\Pi}_{\mathrm{ADJ}}$, $\mathbf{\Pi}_{S_{\mathrm{main}}}$, $\mathbf{\Pi}_{S_{\mathrm{sub}}}$, $\mathbf{\Pi}_{\mathrm{PRON}}$, $\mathbf{\Pi}_{\mathrm{NP}}$ depicting the linked indices and corresponding permutations for each atomic type in the sentence.

non-linear activation function that applies on matrices, pushing them towards binarity and bistochasticity, analogous to a 2-dimensional softmax that preserves assignment (Mena et al., 2018). Moving to the logarithmic space eliminates the positive entry constraint and facilitates numeric stability through the log-sum-exp trick. In that setting, the Sinkhorn-normalization of a real-valued square matrix $\boldsymbol{X}$ is defined as:

$$\mathrm{Sinkhorn}(\boldsymbol{X}) = \lim_{\tau \to \infty} \exp\left(\mathrm{Sinkhorn}^{\tau}(\boldsymbol{X})\right)$$

where the induction is given by:

$$\mathrm{Sinkhorn}^{0}(\boldsymbol{X}) = \boldsymbol{X}$$

$$\mathrm{Sinkhorn}^{\tau}(\boldsymbol{X}) = \mathcal{T}_r\left(\mathcal{T}_r\left(\mathrm{Sinkhorn}^{(\tau-1)}(\boldsymbol{X})\right)^{\top}\right)$$

with $\mathcal{T}_r$ the row normalization in the log-space:

$$\mathcal{T}_r(\boldsymbol{X})_{i,j} = \boldsymbol{X}_{i,j} - log \sum_{r=0}^{N-1} e^{(\boldsymbol{X}_{r,j} - \max(\boldsymbol{X}_{r,:}))}$$

Bearing the above in mind, our goal reduces to assembling a matrix for each atomic type in a proof frame, with entries containing the unnormalized agreement scores of pairs in the cartesian product of positive and negative occurrences of that type. Given contextualized representations for each primitive symbol within a proof frame, scores can be simply computed as the inter-representation *dot-product attention*. Assuming, for instance, $\boldsymbol{I}_{\mathrm{A}}^{+}$ and $\boldsymbol{I}_{\mathrm{A}}^{-}$ the vectors indexing the positions of all a positive and negative occurrences of type A in a proof frame sequence, we can arrange the matrices $\boldsymbol{P}_{\mathrm{A}}, \boldsymbol{N}_{\mathrm{A}} \in \mathbb{R}^{a \times d}$ containing their respective contextualized d-dimensional representations (recall that the count invariance property asserts equal shapes). The dot-product attention matrix containing their element-wise agreements will then be given as $\tilde{\boldsymbol{S}}_{\mathrm{A}} = \boldsymbol{P}_{\mathrm{A}} \boldsymbol{N}_{\mathrm{A}}^{\top} \in \mathbb{R}^{a \times a}$. Applying the Sinkhorn operator, we obtain $\boldsymbol{S}_{\mathrm{A}} = \mathrm{Sinkhorn}(\tilde{\boldsymbol{S}}_{\mathrm{A}})$, which, in our setup, will be modeled as a continuous approximation of the underlying permutation matrix $\mathbf{\Pi}_{\mathrm{A}}$.

3.3 Implementation

Encoder-Decoder We first encode sentences using BERTje (de Vries et al., 2019), a pretrained BERT-Base model (Devlin et al., 2019) localized for Dutch. We then decode into proof frame sequences using a Transformer-like decoder (Vaswani et al., 2017).

Symbol Embeddings In order to best utilize the small, structure-rich vocabulary of the decoder, we opt for lower-dimensional, position-dependent symbol embeddings. We follow insights from Wang et al. (2020) and embed decoder symbols as continuous functions in the complex space, associating each output symbol $s \in \mathcal{V}$ with a magnitude embedding $\boldsymbol{r_s} \in \mathbb{R}^{128}$ and a frequency embedding $\boldsymbol{\omega_s} \in \mathbb{R}^{128}$. A symbol s occurring in position p in the proof frame is then assigned a vector $\tilde{\boldsymbol{v}}_{\boldsymbol{s,p}} = \boldsymbol{r_s} e^{j\boldsymbol{\omega_s}p} \in \mathbb{C}^{128}$. We project to the decoder's vector space by concatenating the real and imaginary parts, obtaining the final representation as $\boldsymbol{v}_{\boldsymbol{s,p}} = \mathrm{conc}(\Re(\tilde{\boldsymbol{v}}_{\boldsymbol{s,p}}), \Im(\tilde{\boldsymbol{v}}_{\boldsymbol{s,p}})) \in \mathbb{R}^{256}$.

Tying the embedding parameters with those of the pre-softmax transformation reduces the network's memory footprint and improves representation quality (Press and Wolf, 2017). In duality to the input embeddings, we treat output embeddings as functionals parametric to positions. To classify a token occurring in position p, we first compute a matrix $\boldsymbol{V_p}$ consisting of the local embeddings of all vocabulary symbols, $\boldsymbol{V_p} = \boldsymbol{v}_{:,\boldsymbol{p}} \in \mathbb{R}^{||\mathcal{V}|| \times 256}$. The transpose of that matrix acts then as a linear map from the decoder's representation to class weights, from which a probability distribution is obtained by application of the softmax function.

Proof Frame Contextualization Proof frames may generally give rise to more than one distinct proof, with only a portion of those being linguistically plausible. Frames eligible to more than one potential semantic reading can be disambiguated by accounting for statistical preferences, as exhibited by lexical cues. Consequently, we need our contextualization scheme to incorporate the sentential representation in its processing flow. To that end, we employ another Transformer decoder, now modified to operate with no causal mask, thus allowing all decoded symbols to freely attend over one another regardless of their relative position. This effectively converts it into a *bi-modal encoder* which operates on two input sequences of different length and dimensionality, namely the BERT output and the sequence of proof frame symbols, and constructs contextualized representations of the latter as informed by the former.

Axiom Linking We index the contextualized proof frame to obtain a pair of matrices for each distinct atomic type in a sentence, easing the complexity of the problem by preemptively dismissing the possibility of linking unequal types; this also alleviates performance issues noted when permuting sets of high cardinality (Mena et al., 2018). Post contextualization, positive and negative items are projected to a lower dimensionality via a pair of feed-forward neural functions, applied token-wise. Normalizing the dot-product attention weights between the above with Sinkhorn yields our final output.

4 Experiments

We train, validate and test our architecture on the corresponding subsets of the Æthel dataset, filtering out samples the proof frames of which exceed 100 primitive symbols. Implementation details and hyper-parameter tables, an illustration of the full architecture, dataset statistics and example parses are provided in Appendix A.[5]

4.1 Training

We train our architecture end-to-end, including all BERT parameters apart from the embedding layer, using AdamW (Loshchilov and Hutter, 2018).

In order to jointly learn representations that accommodate both the proof-frame and the proof-structure outputs, we back-propagate a loss signal derived as the addition of two loss functions. The first is the Kullback-Leibler divergence between the predicted proof frame symbols and the label-smoothed ground-truth distribution (Müller et al., 2019). The second is the negative log-likelihood between the Sinkhorn-activated dot-product weights

and the corresponding binary-valued permutation matrices.

Throughout training, we validate by measuring the per-symbol and per-sentence typing accuracy of the greedily decoded proof frame, as well as the linking accuracy under the assumption of an error-free decoding. We perform model selection on the basis of the above metrics and reach convergence after approximately 300 epochs.

4.2 Testing

We test model performance using beam search. For each input sentence, we consider the β best decode paths, with a path's score being the sum of its symbols' log probabilities, counting all symbols up to the last expected [SEP] token. Neural decoding is followed by a series of filtering steps. We first parse the decoded symbol sequences, discarding beams containing subsequences that do not meet the inductive constructors of the type grammar. The atomic formulas of the passing proof frames are polarized according to the process of §2.3. Frames failing to satisfy the count invariance property are also discarded. The remaining ones constitute potential candidates for a proof structure; their primitive symbols are contextualized by the bimodal encoder, and are then used to compute soft axiom link strengths between atomic formulas of matching types. Discretization of the output yields a graph encoding a proof structure; we follow the net traversal algorithm of Lamarche (2008) to check whether it is a valid proof net, and, if so, produce the λ-term in the process (de Groote and Retoré, 1996). Terms generated this way contain no redundant abstractions, being in β-normal η-long form.

4.3 Analysis

Table 1 presents a breakdown of model performance at different beam widths. To evaluate model performance, we use the first valid beam of each sample, defaulting to the highest scoring beam if none is available. On the token level, we report *supertagging accuracy*, i.e. the percentage of types correctly assigned. We further measure the percentage of samples satisfying each of the following sentential metrics: 1) *invariance property*, a condition necessary for being eligible to a proof structure, 2) *frame correctness*, i.e. whether the decoded frame is identical to the target frame, meaning all types assigned are the correct ones, 3) *untyped term accuracy*, i.e. whether, regardless of the proof frame,

---

[5]The implementing code can be found at `github.com/konstantinosKokos/neural-proof-nets`.

Metric (%)	Beam Size β					Baseline
	$\beta = 1$	$\beta = 2$	$\beta = 3$	$\beta = 5$	$\beta = 7$	*alpino*
Token Level						
Types Correct	85.5	91.4	92.4	93.2	93.4	56.2
Sentence Level						
Invariance Correct	87.6	93.4	94.9	96.1	96.6	*n/a*
Frame Correct	57.6	65.3	68.0	69.6	70.2	*n/a*
Term Correct (w/o types)	60.0	65.6	67.7	69.1	69.6	45.7
Term Correct (/w types & deps)	56.9	63.7	65.9	67.1	67.6	30.4

Table 1: Test set model performance broken down by beam size, and baseline comparison.

the untyped λ-term coincides with the true one, and 4) *typed term accuracy*, meaning that both the proof frame and the untyped term are correct.

Numeric comparisons against other works in the literature is neither our prime goal nor an easy task; the dataset utilized is fairly recent, the novelty of our methods renders them non-trivial to adapt to other settings, and ILL-friendly categorial grammars are not particularly common in experimental setups. As a sanity check, however, and in order to obtain some meaningful baselines, we employ the Alpino parser (Bouma et al., 2001). Alpino is a hybrid parser based on a sophisticated hand-written grammar and a maximum entropy disambiguation model; despite its age and the domain difference, Alpino is competitive to the state-of-the-art in UD parsing, remaining within a 2% margin to the last reported benchmark (Bouma and van Noord, 2017; Che et al., 2018). We pair Alpino with the extraction algorithm used to convert its output into ILL$_{-\circ,\diamond,\square}$ derivations (Kogkalidis et al., 2020); together, the two faithfully replicate the data generating process our system has been trained on, modulo the manual correction phase of van Noord et al. (2013). We query Alpino for the globally optimal parse of each sample in the test set (enforcing no time constraints), perform the conversion and log the results in Table 1.

Our model achieves remarkable performance even in the greedy setting, especially considering the rigidity of our metrics. Untyped term accuracy conveys the percentage of sentences for which the function-argument structure has been perfectly captured. Typed term accuracy is even stricter; the added requirement of a correct proof frame practically translates to no erroneous assignments of part-of-speech and syntactic phrase tags or dependency labels. Keeping in mind that dependency information are already incorporated in the proof frame, obtaining the correct proof structure fully subsumes dependency parsing.

The filtering criteria of the previous paragraph yield significant benefits when combined with beam search, allowing us to circumvent logically unsound analyses regardless of their sequence scores. It is worth noting that our metrics place the model's bottleneck at the supertagging rather than the permutation component. Term accuracy closely follows along (and actually surpasses, in the untyped case) frame accuracy. This is further evidenced when providing the ground truth types as input to the parser, in which case term accuracy reaches as high as 85.4%, indicative of the high expressive power of Sinkhorn on top of the the bi-modal encoder's contextualization. On the negative side, the strong reliance on correct type assignments means that a single mislabeled word can heavily skew the parse outcome, but also hints at increasing returns from improvements in the decoding architecture.

5   Related Work

Our work bears semblances to other neural methodologies related to syntactic/semantic parsing. Sequence-to-sequence models have been successfully employed in the past to decode directly into flattened representations of parse trees (Wiseman and Rush, 2016; Buys and Blunsom, 2017; Li et al., 2018). In dependency parsing literature, head selection involves building word representations that act as classifying functions over other words (Zhang et al., 2017), similar to our dot-product weighting between atoms.

Akin to graph-based parsers (Ji et al., 2019; Zhang et al., 2019), our model generates parse structures in the form of graphs. In our case, however, graph nodes correspond to syntactic primitives (atomic types & dependencies) rather than words, while the discovery of the graph structure is subject to hard constraints imposed by the decoder's output.

Transcription to formal expressions (logical forms, λ-terms, database queries and executable program instructions) has also been a prominent theme in NLP literature, using statistical methods (Zettlemoyer and Collins, 2012) or structurally-constrained decoders (Dong and Lapata, 2016; Xiao et al., 2016; Liu et al., 2018; Cheng et al., 2019). Unlike prior approaches, the decoding we employ here is unhindered by explicit structure; instead, parsing is handled in parallel across the entire sequence by the Sinkhorn operator, which biases the output towards structural correctness while requiring neither backtracking nor iterative processing. More importantly, the λ-terms we generate are not in themselves the product of a neural decoding process, but rather a corollary of the isomorphic relation between $ILL_{-\circ}$ proofs and linear λ-calculus programs.

In machine learning literature, Sinkhorn-based networks have been gaining popularity as a means of learning latent permutations of visual or synthetic data (Mena et al., 2018) or imposing permutation invariance for set-theoretic learning (Grover et al., 2019), with so far limited adoption in the linguistic setting (Tay et al., 2020; Swanson et al., 2020). In contrast to prior applications of Sinkhorn as a final classification layer, we use it over chain element representations that have been mutually contextualized, rather than set elements vectorized in isolation. Our benchmarks, combined with the assignment-preserving property of the operator, hint towards potential benefits from adopting it in a similar fashion across other parsing tasks.

6 Conclusion

We have introduced neural proof nets, a data-driven perspective on the proof nets of $ILL_{-\circ}$, and successfully employed them on the demanding task of transcribing raw text to proofs and computational terms of the linear λ-calculus. The terms construed constitute type-safe abstract program skeletons that are free to interpret within arbitrary domains, fulfilling the role of a practical intermediary between text and meaning. Used as-is, they can find direct application in logic-driven models of natural language inference (Abzianidze, 2016).

Our architecture marks a departure from other parsing approaches, owing to the novel use of the Sinkhorn operator, which renders it both fully parallel and backtrack-free, but also logically grounded. It is general enough to apply to a variety of grammar formalisms inheriting from linear logic; if augmented with Gumbel sampling (Mena et al., 2018), it can further a provide a probabilistic means to account for derivational ambiguity. Viewed as a means of exposing deep tecto-grammatic structure, it paves the way for graph-theoretic approaches at syntax-aware sentential meaning representations.

Acknowledgements

We would like to thank the anonymous reviewers for their detailed feedback, which helped improve the presentation of the paper. Konstantinos and Michael are supported by the Dutch Research Council (NWO) under the scope of the project "A composition calculus for vector-based semantic modelling with a localization for Dutch" (360-89-070).

References

Lasha Abzianidze. 2016. Natural solution to FraCaS entailment problems. In *Proceedings of the Fifth Joint Conference on Lexical and Computational Semantics*, pages 64–74, Berlin, Germany. Association for Computational Linguistics.

Jimmy Lei Ba, Jamie Ryan Kiros, and Geoffrey E Hinton. 2016. Layer normalization. *arXiv preprint arXiv:1607.06450v1*.

Srinivas Bangalore and Aravind K Joshi. 1999. Supertagging: An approach to almost parsing. *Computational linguistics*, 25(2):237–265.

Aditya Bhargava and Gerald Penn. 2020. Supertagging with CCG primitives. In *Proceedings of the 5th Workshop on Representation Learning for NLP*, pages 194–204, Online. Association for Computational Linguistics.

Gosse Bouma and Gertjan van Noord. 2017. Increasing return on annotation investment: The automatic construction of a Universal Dependency treebank for Dutch. In *Proceedings of the NoDaLiDa 2017 Workshop on Universal Dependencies (UDW 2017)*, pages 19–26, Gothenburg, Sweden. Association for Computational Linguistics.

Gosse Bouma, Gertjan van Noord, and Robert Malouf. 2001. Alpino: Wide-coverage computational analysis of dutch. In *Computational linguistics in the Netherlands 2000*, pages 45–59. Brill Rodopi.

Nicolaas Govert de Bruijn. 1979. Wiskundigen, let op uw Nederlands. *Euclides*, 55(juni/juli):429–435.

Jan Buys and Phil Blunsom. 2017. Robust incremental neural semantic graph parsing. In *Proceedings of the 55th Annual Meeting of the Association for Computational Linguistics (Volume 1: Long Papers)*, pages 1215–1226.

Wanxiang Che, Yijia Liu, Yuxuan Wang, Bo Zheng, and Ting Liu. 2018. Towards better UD parsing: Deep contextualized word embeddings, ensemble, and treebank concatenation. In *Proceedings of the CoNLL 2018 Shared Task: Multilingual Parsing from Raw Text to Universal Dependencies*, pages 55–64, Brussels, Belgium. Association for Computational Linguistics.

Jianpeng Cheng, Siva Reddy, Vijay Saraswat, and Mirella Lapata. 2019. Learning an executable neural semantic parser. *Computational Linguistics*, 45(1):59–94.

Vincent Danos and Laurent Regnier. 1989. The structure of multiplicatives. *Archive for Mathematical Logic*, 28:181–203.

Jacob Devlin, Ming-Wei Chang, Kenton Lee, and Kristina Toutanova. 2019. Bert: Pre-training of deep bidirectional transformers for language understanding. In *Proceedings of the 2019 Conference of the North American Chapter of the Association for Computational Linguistics: Human Language Technologies, Volume 1 (Long and Short Papers)*, pages 4171–4186.

Li Dong and Mirella Lapata. 2016. Language to logical form with neural attention. In *Proceedings of the 54th Annual Meeting of the Association for Computational Linguistics (Volume 1: Long Papers)*, pages 33–43.

Jean-Yves Girard. 1987. Linear logic. *Theoretical computer science*, 50(1):1–101.

Jean-Yves Girard, Yves Lafont, and P. Taylor. 1988. *Proofs and Types*. Cambridge Tracts in Theoretical Computer Science 7. Cambridge University Press.

Philippe de Groote. 2001. Towards abstract categorial grammars. In *Proceedings of the 39th Annual Meeting of the Association for Computational Linguistics*, pages 252–259.

Philippe de Groote and Christian Retoré. 1996. On the semantic readings of proof-nets. In *Proceedings Formal grammar*, pages 57–70, Prague, Czech Republic. FoLLI.

Aditya Grover, Eric Wang, Aaron Zweig, and Stefano Ermon. 2019. Stochastic optimization of sorting networks via continuous relaxations. In *International Conference on Learning Representations*.

Stefano Guerrini. 1999. Correctness of multiplicative proof nets is linear. In *Fourteenth Annual IEEE Symposium on Logic in Computer Science*, pages 454–263. IEEE Computer Science Society.

Dan Hendrycks and Kevin Gimpel. 2016. Bridging nonlinearities and stochastic regularizers with gaussian error linear units.

Tao Ji, Yuanbin Wu, and Man Lan. 2019. Graph-based dependency parsing with graph neural networks. In *Proceedings of the 57th Annual Meeting of the Association for Computational Linguistics*, pages 2475–2485.

Max I. Kanovich. 1994. The complexity of horn fragments of linear logic. *Annals of Pure and Applied Logic*, 69(2-3):195–241.

Konstantinos Kogkalidis, Michael Moortgat, and Tejaswini Deoskar. 2019. Constructive type-logical supertagging with self-attention networks. In *Proceedings of the 4th Workshop on Representation Learning for NLP (RepL4NLP-2019)*, pages 113–123.

Konstantinos Kogkalidis, Michael Moortgat, and Richard Moot. 2020. Æthel: Automatically extracted typological derivations for dutch. In *Proceedings of The 12th Language Resources and Evaluation Conference*, pages 5259–5268, Marseille, France. European Language Resources Association.

Ysuke Kubota and Robert Levine. 2020. *Type-Logical Syntax*. MIT Press.

François Lamarche. 2008. Proof nets for intuitionistic linear logic: Essential nets. Research report, INRIA Nancy.

Joachim Lambek. 1958. The mathematics of sentence structure. *The American Mathematical Monthly*, 65(3):154–170.

Zuchao Li, Jiaxun Cai, Shexia He, and Hai Zhao. 2018. Seq2seq dependency parsing. In *Proceedings of the 27th International Conference on Computational Linguistics*, pages 3203–3214.

Patrick Lincoln. 1995. Deciding provability of linear logic formulas. In Jean-Yves Girard, Yves Lafont, and Laurent Regnier, editors, *Advances in Linear Logic*, pages 109–122. Cambridge University Press.

Jiangming Liu, Shay B Cohen, and Mirella Lapata. 2018. Discourse representation structure parsing. In *Proceedings of the 56th Annual Meeting of the Association for Computational Linguistics (Volume 1: Long Papers)*, pages 429–439.

Ilya Loshchilov and Frank Hutter. 2018. Fixing weight decay regularization in adam.

Gonzalo Mena, David Belanger, Scott Linderman, and Jasper Snoek. 2018. Learning latent permutations with Gumbel-Sinkhorn networks. In *International Conference on Learning Representations*.

Michael Moortgat. 1996. Multimodal linguistic inference. *Journal of Logic, Language and Information*, 5(3/4):349–385.

Glyn Morrill. 2014. A categorial type logic. In *Categories and Types in Logic, Language, and Physics - Essays Dedicated to Jim Lambek on the Occasion of His 90th Birthday*, volume 8222 of *Lecture Notes in Computer Science*, pages 331–352. Springer.

Rafael Müller, Simon Kornblith, and Geoffrey E Hinton. 2019. When does label smoothing help? In *Advances in Neural Information Processing Systems*, pages 4696–4705.

Andrzej S. Murawski and C.-H. Luke Ong. 2000. Dominator trees and fast verification of proof nets. In *Logic in Computer Science*, pages 181–191.

Reinhard Muskens. 2001. Lambda grammars and the syntax-semantics interface. In *Proceedings of the 13th Amsterdam Colloquium*, pages 150–155.

Reinhard Muskens and Mehrnoosh Sadrzadeh. 2018. Static and dynamic vector semantics for lambda calculus models of natural language. *Journal of Language Modelling*, 6(2):319–351.

Gertjan van Noord, Gosse Bouma, Frank van Eynde, Daniel de Kok, Jelmer van der Linde, Ineke Schuurman, Erik Tjong Kim Sang, and Vincent Vandeghinste. 2013. Large scale syntactic annotation of written dutch: Lassy. In *Essential speech and language technology for Dutch*, pages 147–164. Springer, Berlin, Heidelberg.

Ofir Press and Lior Wolf. 2017. Using the output embedding to improve language models. In *Proceedings of the 15th Conference of the European Chapter of the Association for Computational Linguistics: Volume 2, Short Papers*, pages 157–163.

Dirk Roorda. 1991. *Resource Logics: Proof-theoretical Investigations*. Ph.D. thesis, Universiteit van Amsterdam.

Richard Sinkhorn. 1964. A relationship between arbitrary positive matrices and doubly stochastic matrices. *The annals of mathematical statistics*, 35(2):876–879.

Morten Heine Sørensen and Pawel Urzyczyn. 2006. *Lectures on the Curry-Howard isomorphism*. Elsevier.

Kyle Swanson, Lili Yu, and Tao Lei. 2020. Rationalizing text matching: Learning sparse alignments via optimal transport. *arXiv preprint arXiv:2005.13111*.

Yi Tay, Dara Bahri, Liu Yang, Donald Metzler, and Da-Cheng Juan. 2020. Sparse sinkhorn attention. *arXiv preprint arXiv:2002.11296v1*.

Anne Sjerp Troelstra and Helmut Schwichtenberg. 2000. *Basic Proof Theory*, 2 edition, volume 43 of *Cambridge Tracts in Theoretical Computer Science*. Cambridge University Press.

Ashish Vaswani, Yonatan Bisk, Kenji Sagae, and Ryan Musa. 2016. Supertagging with lstms. In *Proceedings of the 2016 Conference of the North American Chapter of the Association for Computational Linguistics: Human Language Technologies*, pages 232–237.

Ashish Vaswani, Noam Shazeer, Niki Parmar, Jakob Uszkoreit, Llion Jones, Aidan N Gomez, Łukasz Kaiser, and Illia Polosukhin. 2017. Attention is all you need. In *Advances in neural information processing systems*, pages 5998–6008.

Wietse de Vries, Andreas van Cranenburgh, Arianna Bisazza, Tommaso Caselli, Gertjan van Noord, and Malvina Nissim. 2019. BERTje: A Dutch BERT model. *arXiv preprint arXiv:1912.09582v1*.

Philip Wadler. 1993. A taste of linear logic. In *International Symposium on Mathematical Foundations of Computer Science*, pages 185–210. Springer.

Benyou Wang, Donghao Zhao, Christina Lioma, Qiuchi Li, Peng Zhang, and Jakob Grue Simonsen. 2020. Encoding word order in complex embeddings. In *International Conference on Learning Representations*.

Sam Wiseman and Alexander M Rush. 2016. Sequence-to-sequence learning as beam-search optimization. In *Proceedings of the 2016 Conference on Empirical Methods in Natural Language Processing*, pages 1296–1306.

Chunyang Xiao, Marc Dymetman, and Claire Gardent. 2016. Sequence-based structured prediction for semantic parsing. In *Proceedings of the 54th Annual Meeting of the Association for Computational Linguistics (Volume 1: Long Papers)*, pages 1341–1350.

Wenduan Xu, Michael Auli, and Stephen Clark. 2015. Ccg supertagging with a recurrent neural network. In *Proceedings of the 53rd Annual Meeting of the Association for Computational Linguistics and the 7th International Joint Conference on Natural Language Processing (Volume 2: Short Papers)*, pages 250–255.

Luke S Zettlemoyer and Michael Collins. 2012. Learning to map sentences to logical form: Structured classification with probabilistic categorial grammars. *arXiv preprint arXiv:1207.1420v1*.

Sheng Zhang, Xutai Ma, Kevin Duh, and Benjamin Van Durme. 2019. AMR parsing as sequence-to-graph transduction. In *Proceedings of the 57th Annual Meeting of the Association for Computational Linguistics*, pages 80–94, Florence, Italy. Association for Computational Linguistics.

Xingxing Zhang, Jianpeng Cheng, and Mirella Lapata. 2017. Dependency parsing as head selection. In *Proceedings of the 15th Conference of the European Chapter of the Association for Computational Linguistics: Volume 1, Long Papers*, pages 665–676.

A Appendix

A.1 Model

Table 2 presents model hyper-parameters, as selected by greedy grid search. An illustration of the model can be seen in Figure 6.

Parameter	Value
BERTje (*BERT-Base*)	
# Layers	12
# Self-attention heads	12
Feed-forward dimensionality	3 072
Feed-forward activation	GELU
Input/output dimensionality	768
Vocabulary size	30 000
Decoder	
# Layers	3
# Self-attention heads	8
# Encoder-attention heads	8
Feed-forward dimensionality	512
Input/output dimensionality	256
Vocabulary size	58
Bi-modal Encoder	
# Layers	1
# Self-attention heads	8
# Encoder-attention heads	8
Feed-forward dimensionality	512
Feed-forward activation	GELU
Input/output dimensionality	256
Pre-Sinkhorn Transformations	
Input/Feed-forward dimensionality	256
Feed-forward activation	GELU
Output dimensionality	32
Output activation	LayerNorm

Table 2: Model hyper-parameters

A.2 Optimization

We train with an adaptive learning rate following Vaswani et al. (2017), such that the learning rate at optimization step i is given as:

$$768^{-0.5} \cdot \min\left(i^{-0.5},\ i \cdot \text{warmup\_steps}^{-1.5}\right)$$

For BERT parameters, learning rate is scaled by 0.1. We freeze the oversized word embedding layer to reduce training costs and avoid overfitting. Optimization hyper-parameters are presented in Table 3.

We provide strict teacher guidance when learning axiom links, whereby the network is provided with the original proof frame symbol sequence instead of the predicted one. To speed up computation, positive and negative indexes are arranged per-length rather than type for each batch; this allows us to process symbol transformations, dot-product attentions and Sinkhorn activations in parallel for many types across many sentences. During training, we set the number of Sinkhorn iterations to 5; lower values are more difficult to reach convergence with, hurting performance, whereas higher values can easily lead to vanishing gradients, impeding learning (Grover et al., 2019).

Parameter	Value
Batch size	32
Warmup epochs	5
Weight decay	10^{-5}
Weight decay (BERT)	0
LR scale (BERT)	0.1
LR scale (BERT embedding)	0
Dropout rate	0.1
Label smoothing	0.1

Table 3: Optimizer hyper-parameters

A.3 Data

Figure 7 presents cumulative distributions of dataset statistics. The kept portion of the dataset corresponds to roughly 97% of the original, enumerating 55 683 training, 6 971 validation and 6 957 test samples.

A.4 Performance

Table 4 summarizes the model's performance in terms of untyped term accuracy over the test set in the greedy setting, binned according to input sentence lengths. Table 5 presents input-output pairs from sample sentences not included in the dataset.

Sentence Length	Total	Correct	(%)
1 – 5	808	743	92
5 – 10	1 491	1 104	74
10 – 15	1 576	919	58
15 – 20	1 206	501	42
20 –	592	154	26

Table 4: Test set model performance broken down by sentence length.

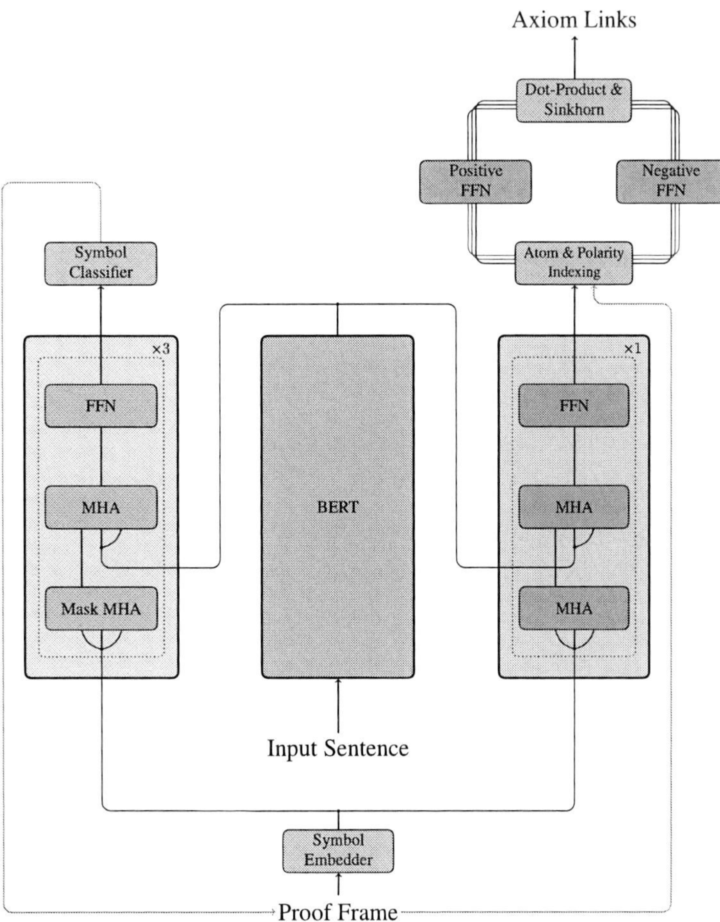

Figure 6: Schematic diagram of the full network architecture. The supertagger (orange, left) iteratively generates a proof frame by attending over the currently available part of it plus the full input sentence. The axiom linker (green, right) contextualizes the complete proof frame by attending over it as well as the sentence. Representations of atomic formulas are gathered and transformed according to their polarity, and their Sinkhorn-activated dot-product attention is computed. Discretization of the result yields a permutation matrix denoting axiom links for each unique atomic type in the proof frame. The final output is a proof structure, i.e. the pair of a proof frame and its axiom links.

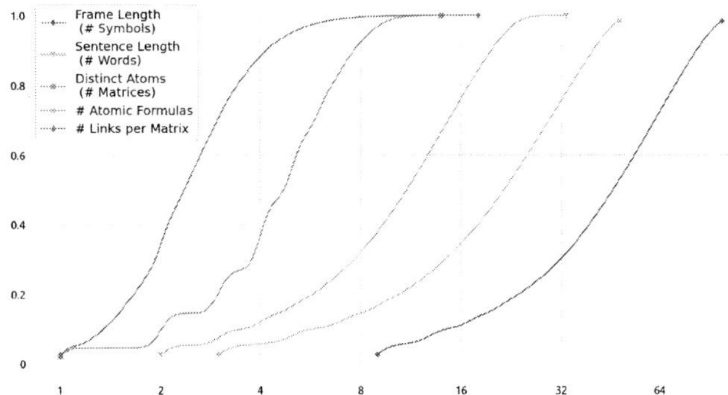

Figure 7: log2-transformed cumulative distributions of symbol and word lengths, counts of atomic formulas, matrices and matrix sizes from the portion of the dataset trained on.

De voorafgaande stukjes over Wiskundige Omgangstaal hadden het vooral over het samenspel tussen woorden en formules.
"The preceding articles on the Mathematical Vernacular mainly focused on the interplay between words and formules."
$((\texttt{hadden} :: \text{PP} \multimap \text{PRON} \multimap \text{S}_\text{main}\ ((\texttt{vooral} :: \text{PP} \multimap \text{PP})_\text{mod}\ (\texttt{over} :: \text{NP} \multimap \text{PP}\ ((\texttt{tussen} :: \text{WW} \multimap \text{NP} \multimap \text{NP}\ ((\texttt{en} :: \text{NP} \multimap \text{NP} \multimap \text{NP}\ (\texttt{woprden} :: \text{NP})^\text{cnj})\ (\texttt{formules} :: \text{NP})^\text{cnj})^\text{obj})_\text{mod}\ ((\texttt{het} :: \text{N} \multimap \text{NP})_\text{det}\ \texttt{samenspel} :: \text{N}))^\text{obj}))^\text{pc}\ (\texttt{het} :: \text{PRON})^\text{obj})\ ((\texttt{over} :: \text{NP} \multimap \text{NP} \multimap \text{NP}\ (\texttt{Wiskundige\_Omgangstaal} :: \text{NP})^\text{obj})_\text{mod}\ ((\texttt{voorafgaande} :: \text{NP} \multimap \text{NP})_\text{mod}\ ((\texttt{De} :: \text{N} \multimap \text{NP})_\text{det}\ \texttt{stukjes} :: \text{N})))^\text{su}$

In het wiskundig Nederlands worden vaak dezelfde fouten gemaakt als in het gewone Nederlands.
"The same mistakes are often made in mathematical Dutch as in common Dutch." $(\texttt{worden} :: \text{PPART} \multimap \text{NP} \multimap \text{S}_\text{main}\ ((\texttt{vaak} :: \text{PPART} \multimap \text{PPART})_\text{mod}\ ((\texttt{In} :: \text{NP} \multimap \text{PPART} \multimap \text{PPART}\ ((\texttt{wiskundig} :: \text{NP} \multimap \text{NP})_\text{mod}\ ((\texttt{het} :: \text{N} \multimap \text{NP})_\text{det}\ \texttt{Nederlands} :: \text{N}))^\text{obj})_\text{mod}\ \texttt{gemaakt} :: \text{PPART}))^\text{vc})\ ((\texttt{dezelfde} :: \text{CP} \multimap \text{N} \multimap \text{NP}\ (\texttt{als} :: \text{PP} \multimap \text{CP}\ (\texttt{in} :: \text{NP} \multimap \text{PP}\ ((\texttt{gewone} :: \text{NP} \multimap \text{NP})_\text{mod}\ ((\texttt{het} :: \text{N} \multimap \text{NP})_\text{det}\ \texttt{Nederlands} :: \text{N}))^\text{obj})^\text{cmp\_body})^\text{obcomp})_\text{det}\ (\texttt{fouten} :: \text{N})^\text{su}$

In het wiskundige taalgebruik is er meestal een scheiding aan te brengen tussen de echte wiskundige taal en de taal waarmee we over die wiskundige taal of over het wiskundige bedrijf spreken.
"In mathematical discourse, there is usually a distinction to be made between the real mathematical language and the language with which we speak about the mathematical language or about the mathematical practice."
–

Probeer zinnen steeds zo te stellen dat ze alleen op de door de schrijver bedoelde wijze zijn terug te lezen.
"Try to always formulate sentences in such a way that they can only be read in the manner intended by the author."
–

In het Nederlands kunnen vele zinnen wat volgorde betreft omgegooid worden.
"In Dutch, many sentences can be restructured as far as order is concerned."
$(\texttt{kunnen} :: \text{INF} \multimap \text{NP} \multimap \text{S}_\text{main}\ (\texttt{worden} :: \text{PPART} \multimap \text{INF}\ ((\texttt{wat} :: (\text{PRON} \multimap \text{S}_\text{sub}) \multimap \text{PPART} \multimap \text{PPART}\ \lambda x_0^\text{su}.((\texttt{betreft} :: \text{N} \multimap \text{PRON} \multimap \text{S}_\text{sub}\ (\texttt{volgorde} :: \text{N})^\text{obj})\ x_0)^\text{rel\_body})_\text{mod}\ ((\texttt{In} :: \text{NP} \multimap \text{PPART} \multimap \text{PPART}\ ((\texttt{het} :: \text{N} \multimap \text{NP})_\text{det}\ \texttt{Nederlands} :: \text{N})^\text{obj})_\text{mod}\ \texttt{omgegooid} :: \text{PPART}))^\text{vc})^\text{vc})\ ((\texttt{vele} :: \text{NP} \multimap \text{NP})_\text{mod}\ \texttt{zinnen} :: \text{NP})^\text{su}$

In het Nederlands kunnen vaak twee zinnen tot èèn kortere worden samengetrokken.
"In Dutch, two sentences can often be merged into a shorter one."
$(\texttt{kunnen} :: \text{INF} \multimap \text{NP} \multimap \text{S}_\text{main}\ (\texttt{worden} :: \text{PPART} \multimap \text{INF}\ ((\texttt{vaak} :: \text{PPART} \multimap \text{PPART})_\text{mod}\ ((\texttt{In} :: \text{NP} \multimap \text{PPART} \multimap \text{PPART}\ ((\texttt{het} :: \text{N} \multimap \text{NP})_\text{det}\ \texttt{Nederlands} :: \text{N})^\text{obj})_\text{mod}\ (\texttt{samengetrokken} :: \text{PP} \multimap \text{PPART}\ (\texttt{tot} :: \text{NP} \multimap \text{PP}\ ((\texttt{èèn} :: \text{ADJ} \multimap \text{NP})_\text{det}\ \texttt{kortere} :: \text{ADJ})^\text{obj})^\text{ld}))^\text{vc})^\text{vc})\ ((\texttt{twee} :: \text{N} \multimap \text{NP})_\text{det}\ \texttt{zinnen} :: \text{N})^\text{su}$

Populaire taal is vaak minder beveiligd tegen dubbelzinnigheid dan nette taal, en het mengsel van beide talen is nòg gevaarlijker.
"Informal language is often less protected against ambiguity than formal language, and the mixture of both languages is even more dangerous."
$(\texttt{en} :: \text{S}_\text{main} \multimap \text{S}_\text{main} \multimap ((\texttt{is} :: \text{PPART} \multimap \text{NP} \multimap \text{S}_\text{main}\ ((\texttt{minder} :: \text{CP} \multimap \text{PPART} \multimap \text{PPART}\ (\texttt{dan} :: \text{NP} \multimap \text{CP}\ ((\texttt{nette} :: \text{NP} \multimap \text{NP})_\text{mod}\ \texttt{taal} :: \text{NP})^\text{cmp\_body})^\text{obcomp})_\text{mod}\ ((\texttt{vaak} :: \text{PPART} \multimap \text{PPART})_\text{mod}\ (\texttt{beveiligd} :: \text{PP} \multimap \text{PPART}\ ((\texttt{tegen} :: \text{NP} \multimap \text{PP}\ (\texttt{dubbelzinnighead} : \text{NP})^\text{obj})^\text{pc})))^\text{vc}\ ((\texttt{Populaire} :: \text{NP} \multimap \text{NP})_\text{mod}\ \texttt{taal} :: \text{NP})^\text{su})^\text{cnj})\ ((\texttt{is} :: \text{AP} \multimap \text{NP} \multimap \text{S}_\text{main}\ ((\texttt{nòg} :: \text{AP} \multimap \text{AP})_\text{mod}\ \texttt{gevaarlijker} :: \text{AP})^\text{predc}\ ((\texttt{van} :: \text{NP} \multimap \text{NP} \multimap \text{NP}\ ((\texttt{beide} :: \text{N} \multimap \text{NP})_\text{det}\ \texttt{talen} :: \text{N})^\text{obj})_\text{mod}\ (\texttt{het} :: \text{N} \multimap \text{NP})_\text{det}\ \texttt{mengsel} :: \text{N}))^\text{su})^\text{cnj}$

Table 5: Greedy parses of the opening sentences of the first seven paragraphs of de Bruijn (1979), in the form of type- and dependency-annotated λ expressions. Two of them (3 & 4) yield no valid proof net; the remaining five are both valid and correct.

TaxiNLI: Taking a Ride up the NLU Hill

Pratik Joshi[2†*], **Somak Aditya**[1†], **Aalok Sathe**[3†*], and **Monojit Choudhury**[1]
[1]Microsoft Research India, 9 Lavelle Road, Vigyan, Bengaluru, India
[2]Google Research, Carina East Tower Bagmane Constellation Business Park, Bengaluru, India
[3]University of Richmond, 410 Westhampton Way, Richmond, VA, USA
pratikmjoshi123@gmail.com, aalok.sathe@richmond.edu, {t-soadit,monojitc}@microsoft.com

Abstract

Pre-trained Transformer-based neural architectures have consistently achieved state-of-the-art performance in the Natural Language Inference (NLI) task. Since NLI examples encompass a variety of linguistic, logical, and reasoning phenomena, it remains unclear as to which specific concepts are learnt by the trained systems and where they can achieve strong generalization. To investigate this question, we propose a taxonomic hierarchy of categories that are relevant for the NLI task. We introduce TAXINLI, a new dataset, that has 10k examples from the MNLI dataset (Williams et al., 2018) with these taxonomic labels. Through various experiments on TAXINLI, we observe that whereas for certain taxonomic categories SOTA neural models have achieved near perfect accuracies—a large jump over the previous models—some categories still remain difficult. Our work adds to the growing body of literature that shows the gaps in the current NLI systems and datasets through a systematic presentation and analysis of reasoning categories.

1 Introduction

The Natural Language Inference (NLI) task tests whether a hypothesis (H) in text contradicts with, is entailed by, or is neutral with respect to a given premise (P) text. This 3-way classification task, popularized by Bowman et al. (2015), which was in turn inspired by Dagan et al. (2005), now serves as a benchmark for *evaluation* of natural language *understanding* (NLU) capability of models; for example, NLI datasets (Bowman et al., 2015; Williams et al., 2018) are included in all NLU benchmarks such as GLUE and SuperGLUE (Wang et al., 2018). These corpora, in turn, have been successfully used to train models such as BERT (Devlin et al.,

2019) to achieve state-of-the-art (SOTA) performance in these tasks. Despite the wide adoption of NLI datasets, a growing concern in the community has been the lack of clarity as to *which linguistic or reasoning concepts these trained NLI systems are truly able to learn and generalize* (see, for example (Linzen, 2020) and (Bender and Koller, 2020), for a discussion). Over the years, as models have shown steady performance increases in NLI tasks, many authors (Nie et al., 2019; Kaushik et al., 2019) demonstrate steep drops in performance when these models are tested against adversarially (or counterfactually) created examples by non-experts. Richardson et al. (2019) use templated examples to show trained NLI systems fail to capture essential logical (negation, boolean, quantifier) and semantic (monotonicity) phenomena.

Herein lie the central questions of our work: 1) what is the distribution of various categories of *reasoning tasks* in the NLI datasets? 2) which categories of tasks are rarely captured by current NLI datasets (owing to the nature of the task and the non-expert annotators)? 3) which categories are well-understood by the SOTA models? and 4) are there categories where Transformer-based architectures are consistently deficient?

In order to answer these questions, we first discuss why performance-specific error analysis categories (Wang et al., 2018; Nie et al., 2019), and stress testing categories (Naik et al., 2018) are inadequate. We then propose a taxonomy of the various reasoning tasks that are commonly covered by the current NLI datasets (Sec 2). Next, we annotate 10,071 P-H pairs from the MNLI dataset (Williams et al., 2018) with the lowest level taxonomic categories, 18 in total (Sec 3). Then we conduct various experiments and careful error analysis of the SOTA models—BERT and RoBERTa, as well as other baselines, such as Bag-of-words Naïve Bayes and ESIM, on their performance across these categories

---

† denotes equal contribution. *Work was done while Authors were at Microsoft Research India.

41

Proceedings of the 24th Conference on Computational Natural Language Learning, pages 41–55
Online, November 19-20, 2020. ©2020 Association for Computational Linguistics
https://doi.org/10.18653/v1/P17

(Sec 4). Our analyses indicate that while these models perform well on some categories such as linguistic reasoning, the performance on many other categories, such as those that require world knowledge or temporal reasoning, are quite poor. We also look into the embeddings of the P-H pairs to understand which of these categorical distinctions are captured well in the learnt representations, and which get conflated (Sec 5). Inline with our previous finding, we observe strong correlation between the level of clustering within the representation of the examples from a category, and the performance of the models for that particular category.

2   A New Taxonomy for NLI

2.1   Necessity for a New Taxonomy

According to Wittgenstein (1922), "Language disguises the thought", and human beings try to gauge such thought from colloquial language using "complex silent adjustments". The journey from lexicon and syntax of "language" to the aspects of semantics and pragmatics can be thought of as a journey that portrays important milestones that an ideal NLU system should achieve. Irrespective of the order of such milestones[1], we believe that NLU (and NLI) systems should be tested and analyzed with respect to fundamental linguistic and logical phenomena. Recently, different types of phenomena have been tested through 1) creating new datasets, 2) probing tasks, and 3) error-analysis categorizations. Researchers have created new datasets by recasting various NLU tasks to a large NLI dataset (Poliak et al., 2018), eliciting counter-factual examples from non-experts by considering different lexical and reasoning factors (Kaushik et al., 2019), and adversarial example (Nie et al., 2019) elicitation by letting non-experts come up with examples through interacting with SOTA systems. However, these datasets do not expose the linguistic aspects where the current systems have difficulty. Using the probing task methodology, researchers (Jawahar et al., 2019; Goldberg, 2019) observed that BERT captures syntactic structure, along with some semantics such as NER, and semantic role labels (Tenney et al., 2019b). However, BERT's ability to reason is questioned by the observed performance degradation in MNLI (McCoy et al., 2019). Linzen (2020) also called for a pretraining-agnostic evaluation setup, where the setup is not limited to pre-trained

---

[1]"For an infant, a foreigner, or an instant-message addict, context is more important than syntax" (Sowa, 2010).

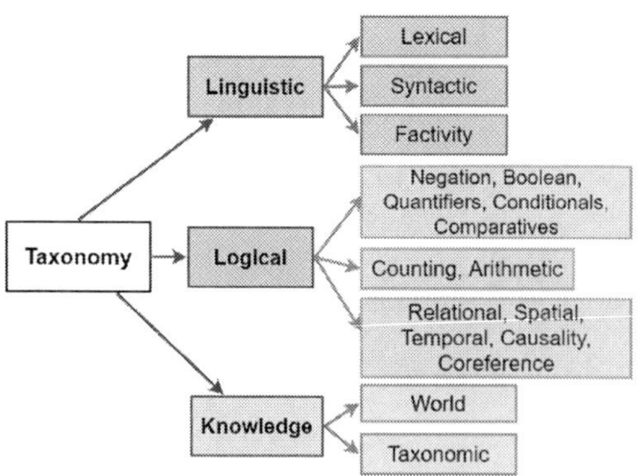

Figure 1: Taxonomic Categorization of the NLI task.

language models. Our taxonomic categorization is meant to serve as a set of necessary inferencing capabilities that one would expect a competing NLI system to possess; thereby promoting more probing tasks along unexplored categories.

Existing categorization efforts have centred around informing feature creation in the pre-Transformer era, and model-specific error analysis in more recent times. Previously, (LoBue and Yates, 2011) enumerated the type of commonsense knowledge required for NLI. Among recent error analysis efforts, the GLUE diagnostic dataset (Wang et al., 2018), inference types for Adversarial NLI (Nie et al., 2019), the new CheckList (Ribeiro et al., 2020) system and the Stress Tests (Naik et al., 2018) are mentionworthy. As we attempted to group the categorizations in Nie et al. (2019) and Wang et al. (2018) into four high-level categories (lexical, syntactic, semantic, and pragmatic)[2], we observe that there is a lack of consensus, non-uniformity and repetitiveness of these categories. For example, the *Tricky* label in Nie et al. (2019) groups examples that involve "wordplay, linguistic strategies such as syntactic transformations, or inferring writer intentions from contexts"; thereby spanning aspects of syntax and pragmatics. Similarly, *Reference and Names* requires both reasoning and knowledge. The GLUE diagnostic categories (Wang et al., 2018) does not include interesting reasoning categories such as *temporal*, and *spatial*. The stress types proposed by Naik et al. (2018) are specific to mostly lexical and some semantic corner cases. This is expected, as these categorizations are analysis-oriented and often dependent on the performance of a set of models in question. Here, we propose a taxonomic categorization that delineates

---

[2]Table provided in Appendix

a set of necessary uniform inferencing capabilities for the NLI task.

2.2 Taxonomic Categories: Definitions and Examples

In Figure 1, we present our taxonomic categorization. Our categorization is based on the following principles. First, we take a model-agnostic approach, where we work from the first principles to arrive at a set of basic inferencing processes that are required in NLI task. These include an unrestricted variety of linguistic and logical phenomena, and may require knowledge beyond text, thus providing us with the higher-level categories: *linguistic*, *logical* and *knowledge*-based. Second, we retain categories that are non-overlapping and sufficiently represented in NLI datasets. For example, for sub-categories under *linguistic*, we prune *semantics* because necessary aspects are covered by `logical` and `knowledge`-based categories. We omit specific aspects of *pragmatics* such as implicatures and pre-suppositions, as they are rarely observed in NLI datasets (Jeretic et al., 2020). Thirdly, we aim to list a set of necessary sub-categories. For example, for logical deduction sub-categories, we take inspiration from Davis and Marcus (2015), who list the commonsense reasoning categories where systems have seen success. Lastly, since we aim to employ non-experts for collecting annotations, we decide to restrict further sub-division wherever the definitions get complicated, or pre-suppose certain expertise; for example the `lexical` category is not sub-divided further (as followed in Wang et al. (2018)). Thus, we take a pragmatic approach that is theory neutral and does not warrant coverage of all reasoning tasks, though we do believe that the taxonomy is sufficiently deep and generic that allows systematic and meaningful analysis of NLI models with respect to their reasoning capabilities.

Next we define the categories. For a full set of examples, please see Table 1.

High-Level Categories: The **Linguistic** category represents NLI examples where the inference process to determine the entailment are internal to the provided text. We classify examples as **Logical** when the inference process may involve processes external to text, such as mapping words to percepts and reason with them (Sowa, 2010). **Knowledge**-based category represents examples where some form of external, domain or commonly assumed knowledge is required for inferencing.

Linguistic category is further sub-divided into `lexical`, `syntactic`, and `factivity`.

1. **Lexical**: This category captures P-H pairs where the text is almost the same apart from removal, addition or substitution of some lexical items. **Example**: P: Anakin was kind. H: Anakin was cruel.

2. **Syntactic**: `Syntactic` deals with examples where syntactic variations or paraphrases are essential to detecting entailment. **Example**: P: Anakin was an excellent pilot. H: The piloting skills of Anakin were excellent.

3. **Factivity**: Here the hypothesis contains an assumed fact from the premise, mostly an assumption about the existence of an entity or the occurrence of an action (inspired from Wang et al. (2018)). **Example**: P: Padme recognized that Anakin was intelligent. H: Anakin was intelligent.

Based on commonalities, **Logical** categories are grouped under "Connectives", "Mathematical" and "Deduction".

1. **Connectives (Negation, Boolean, Quantifiers, Conditionals, Comparatives)**: We group the logical categories `negation`, `boolean`, `quantifier`, `conditional` and `comparative` (Salvatore et al., 2019) under the "Connectives" label. `Negation` applies when P negates one (or more) of the facts in H. We apply the category `boolean` when P is a set of statements connected by *or, and* and H talks about one of the statements. `Quantifier` is applied when P or H requires understanding of words denoting existential or universal quantifiers. Similarly, `conditional` is applicable where P or H has conditional statements. If P (or H) compares entities via comparative phrases, then we label it as `comparative`. **Examples**: (`boolean` and `negation`) P: Jar Jar, R2D2 and Padme only visited Anakin's house. H: Jar Jar Binks didn't visit Anakin's shop.

2. **Mathematical (Counting, Arithmetic)**: This group of categories is concerned with examples that require mathematical reasoning. For brevity, we concentrate on examples that require counting and simple arithmetic operations. However, we observed exceedingly low number of examples in this category group from our pilot study on SNLI and MNLI, and hence we remove these from our final annotations.

3. **Deductions (Relational, Spatial, Temporal, Causal, Coreference)**: Motivated by predicate logic, success of qualitative representation and

Taxonomic Category	MNLI Examples	Taxonomic Category	MNLI Examples
Lexical	P: so it's stayed cold for the <u>entire</u> week H: It has been cold for the <u>whole</u> week.	Relational	P: Actually, <u>my sister</u> wrote a story on it. H: <u>My sibling</u> created a story about it.
Syntactic	P: Those in Egypt, Libya, Iraq, and Yemen were eventually overthrown by secular nationalist revolutionaries. H: Secular nationalist revolutionaries eventually overthrew them in Egypt and Libya.	Spatial	P: At the eastern end of Back Lane and turning right, Nicholas Street becomes Patrick Street, and in St. Patrick's Close is St. Patrick's Cathedral . H: Nicholas Street becomes Patrick Street after turning left at the eastern end of Back Lane.
Factivity	P: The best place to view the spring azaleas is at the Azalea Festival in the last week of April at Tokyo's Nezu shrine. H:There is an Azalea Festival at the Nezu Shrine.	Temporal	P: See you <u>Aug. 12, or soon thereafter</u>, we hope. H: The person told not to come <u>until December</u>.
Negation	P: They <u>post</u> loads of newspaper articles–Yahoo! H: Yahoo does <u>not post</u> any articles from newspapers.	Causal	P: Acroseon the mountainside is another terrace on which imperial courtiers and dignitaries would sit while enjoying dance performances and music recitals on the <u>hondo's broad terrace</u>. H: There is a <u>terrace</u> where musicians play.
Boolean	P:According to contemporaneous notes, at 9:55 the Vice President was still on the phone with the President advising that three planes were missing <u>and</u> one had hit the Pentagon. H: The President called the Vice President to tell him the plane hit the Pentagon.	Coreference	P: A dozen minor wounds crossed his forearms and body. H: The grenade explosion left him with a lot of wounds.
Quantifier	P: <u>Some</u> travelers add Molokai and Lanai to their itineraries. H: <u>No one</u> decides to go to Molokai and Lanai.	World	P: In this respect, bringing Steve Jobs back to save Apple is like bringing Gen. H: Steve Jobs unretired in 2002.
Conditional	P: If the revenue is transferred to the General Fund, it is recognized as nonexchange revenue in the Government-wide consolidated financial statements. H: Revenue from the General Fund is not considered in financial statements	Taxonomic	P: Benson's action picture in Lucia in London (Chapter 8)- Georgie stepped on a beautiful <u>pansy</u>. H: Georgie crushed a beautiful <u>flower</u> in Chapter 8 of Lucia in London.
Comparative	P: Load time is divided into elemental and coverage related load time. H: The coverage related load time <u>is longer than</u> elemental.		

Table 1: For each category, we provide an example from the MNLI dataset. For a full set of synthetic examples and definitions, please look at appendix.

reasoning in dealing with temporal and spatial reasoning (Gabelaia et al., 2005), and causality (Pearl, 2009), we list `relational, temporal, spatial` and `causal` under "Deductions". The `relational` reasoning stands for the requirement to perform deductive reasoning using relations present in text. `Spatial` (and `temporal`) denotes reasoning using spatial (and temporal) properties of objects represented in text. We also consider language-inspired reasoning categories such as co-reference resolution, which is known to often require event-understanding (Ng, 2017) beyond superficial cues. **Example**: (`relational`) P: The lamp was working properly. H: The lightbulb from the lamp was not functioning.

Lastly, we define two sub-categories under **Knowledge**, namely `world` and `taxonomic`.
1. **World**: Examples that require knowledge about named entities, knowledge about historical, current events; and domain-specific knowledge. **Example**: (`world`) P: Michelle Obama stayed in the White House during 2009-17. H: Michelle was living in the White House legally during 2009.
2. **Taxonomic**: Examples that require taxonomies and hierarchies. For example, *IsA, hasA, hasProperty* relations. **Example**: (`taxonomic`) P: Norman hated all musical instruments. H: Norman loves the piano.

Note that presence of a certain lexical trigger for a category (such as negation) does not warrant the labeling with the category, unless understanding of that concept is invoked in the deduction process.

3 TaxiNLI: Dataset Details

We present TaxiNLI, a dataset collected based on the principles and categorizations of the aforementioned taxonomy. We curate a subset of examples from MultiNLI (Williams et al., 2018) by sampling uniformly based on the entailment label and the domain. We then annotate this dataset with fine-grained category labels.

3.1 Annotation Process

Task Design For large-scale data collection, our aim was to propose an annotation methodology that is relatively flexible in terms of annotator qualifications, and yet results in high quality annotations. To employ non-expert annotators, we designed a simplified guideline (questionnaire/interface) for the task, that does not pre-suppose expertise in language or logic. As an overhead, the guideline requires a few rounds of one-on-one training of the annotators. Because it is expensive to perform such rounds of training in most crowdsourcing platforms, we hire and individually train a few chosen annotators. Upon conducting the previously-discussed pilot study and using the given feedback, we created a hierarchical questionnaire which first asked the annotator to do the NLI inference on the P-H pair, and then asked targeted questions to get the desired category annotations for the datapoints. The questionnaire is shared in the Appendix.

For the MNLI datapoints with 'neutral' gold labels, we realized, through observation and annotator feedback, that annotating the categories were difficult, as sometimes the hypotheses could not be connected well back to their premise. Hence, we created 2 questionnaires, one for the 'entailment/contradiction' examples, and one for 'neutral' examples. For the entailment/contradiction examples, We collected binary annotations for each of the 15 categories in our NLI taxonomy, for datapoints in MNLI which had 'entailment' or 'contradiction' as gold labels. To resolve this, for the 'neutral' examples we specifically asked them whether the premise and hypothesis were discussing 1) the same general topic (politics, geology, etc.), and if so, 2) had the same subject and/or object of discussion (Obama, Taj Mahal, etc.). If the response to 2) was 'yes', then they were asked to provide the category annotations as previously defined.

Annotator Training/Testing We first tested our two annotators by asking them to do inference on a set of randomly selected premise-hypothesis pairs from MultiNLI. This was to familiarize them with the inference task. After giving the category annotation task, we also continuously tested and trained the two annotators. After a set of datapoints were annotated, we reviewed and went through clarification and feedback sessions with the annotators to ensure they understood the task, and the categories, and what improvements were required. More details are provided in the Appendix.

3.1.1 Annotation Metrics

Here, we assess the individual annotator performance and inter-annotator agreement. Since, automated metrics for individual complex category annotations are hard to define, we use an indicative metric that matches the annotated inference label with the gold label, i.e., their **inference accuracy**. We also calculated inter-annotator agreement between the two annotators for an overlapping subset of 600 examples. For agreement, we use the Fleiss' Kappa (κ) (Fleiss, 1971). We also compute another simple statistic, namely the 'IOU' (Intersection-Over-Union) of categories per datapoint, defined as: $IOU = \frac{1}{N} \sum_{i=1}^{N} \frac{|C_{A1}^i \cap C_{A2}^i|}{|C_{A1}^i \cup C_{A2}^i|}$, where C_{Ai}^j are the

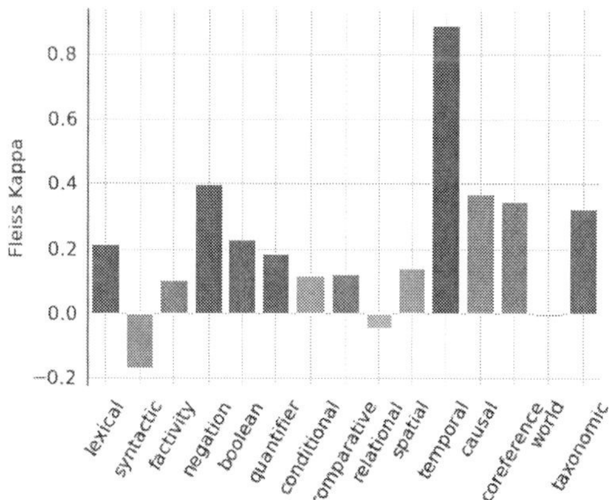

Figure 2: Inter-annotator Agreement (IAA) values between the two annotators, plotted category-wise.

category annotations for Annotator i for datapoint j, averaged over total datapoints N. Looking at the category-wise Fleiss' κ values in Fig. 2, we observe that there are promising levels of agreement in most of the categories except `syntactic`, `relational`, and `world`. We observe the average inference accuracy (86.7%) is high despite known issues in MNLI example ambiguity. Similarly, both the average Fleiss' κ (**0.226**) and the IOU metric (**0.241**) suggest an overall reasonable inter-annotator agreement.

3.2 Dataset Statistics

Each datapoint in TaxiNLI[3] consists of a premise-hypothesis pair, the entailment label, and binary annotations for 18 features. 15 features correspond to the 15 categories discussed in the taxonomy, and 3 additional features for the 'neutral' gold label datapoints based on same general topic, same subject, and same object. The statistics are listed in Tab. 2.

Total datapoints	10,071
Datapoints overlapping with MNLI	2343 (train) 7728 (dev)
Avg. datapoints per domain	1007.1
Datapoints per NLI label	3375 (C), 3201 (N), 3495 (E)
Avg. categories per datapoint	1.6
Neutral example characteristics	3087 (Same general topic), 2843 (Same object), 877 (Same subject)

Table 2: TaxiNLI Statistics

Categorical Observations From our annotations, we observe that inferencing each MNLI ex-

---

[3]The dataset is available for download from `https://github.com/microsoft/TaxiNLI`.

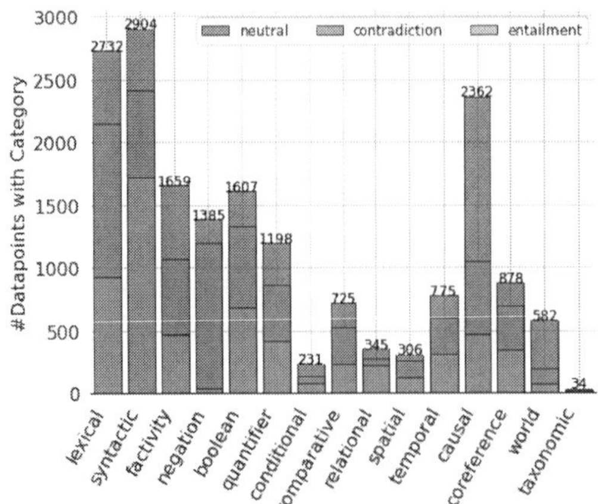

Figure 3: The number of datapoints annotated with each category, split by the gold label of the datapoints. For `taxonomic`, the gold label split is 13(E)/13(C)/8(N).

ample requires about 2 categories. Fig. 3 shows the distribution of categories in the TaxiNLI dataset. We see that a large number of P-H pairs in MNLI require `lexical` and `syntactic` knowledge to make an inference; whereas the challenges of `relational`, `spatial`, and `taxonomic` for inference are not adequately represented. There is a large proportion of examples in the `syntactic` category which have the 'entailment' label, and a large proportion of `negation` examples have the 'contradiction' label. Additionally, many 'neutral' examples were classified as requiring `causal` knowledge. The feedback session with annotators revealed that there were many 'neutral' examples where the hypothesis was essentially an unverifiable intent or detail of a certain action mentioned in the premise. An example is "**P:** *Another influence was that patrician politician Franklin Roosevelt, who was, like John D. Rockefeller, the focus of Nelson's relentless sycophancy and black-belt bureaucratic infighting.* **H:** *Nelson targeted Roosevelt in order to gain political favor.*".

Categorical Correlations Fig. 4 shows correlations among categories in our dataset. We observe that most categories show weak correlation in the MNLI dataset, hinting at a possible independence of categories with respect to each other. Relatively stronger positive correlations are seen between `boolean-quantifier`, and `boolean-comparative` categories. We specifically looked at the genre-wise split of datapoints containing `boolean-quantifier` and saw that

nearly 25% of them came from the 'telephone' genre of MNLI. An example is "**P:** *have that well and it doesn't seem like very many people uh are really i mean there's a lot of people that are on death row but there's not very many people that actually um do get killed* **H:** *Most people on death row end up living out their lives awaiting execution.*". `Factivity`, on the other hand, is negatively correlated with almost all the other categories, except `world`, which means P-H pairs labeled with `factivity` typically have no other categories marked.

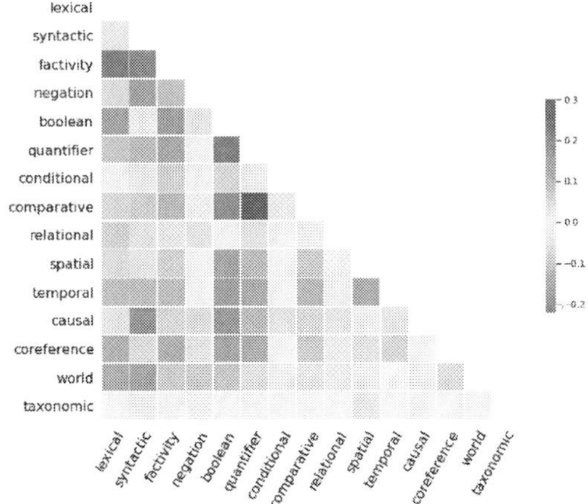

Figure 4: The correlation matrix between the taxonomic categories.

4 (Re)Evaluation of SOTA Models

We re-evaluate two Transformer-based and two standard baseline machine learning models on TAXINLI, under the lens of the taxonomic categories. As baselines, we choose BERT-base (Devlin et al., 2019), and RoBERTa-large (Liu et al., 2019b) as two state-of-the-art NLI systems. For our experiments, we use the pre-trained BERT-base and RoBERTa models from HuggingFace's Transformers implementation (Wolf et al., 2019). As pre-Transformer baselines, we use the bidirectional LSTM-based Enhanced Sequential Inference model (ESIM) (Chen et al., 2017). We also train a Naive Bayes (NB) model using bag-of-words features for the P-H pairs after removing stop words[4].

4.1 TAXINLI Error Analysis

We report the NLI task accuracy of the baseline systems on the MNLI validations sets in Table 3.

---

[4]Using NLTK's `RTEFeatureExtractor`

The systems are fine-tuned on the MNLI training set using the procedures followed in Devlin et al. (2019); Liu et al. (2019b); Chen et al. (2017).

MNLI-dev	NB	ESIM	BERT$_{BASE}$	RoBERTa$_{LARGE}$
Matched	51.46	72.3	84.7	92.3
Mismatched	52.31	72.1	84.8	90.0

Table 3: MNLI-validation set accuracy.

We evaluate the systems on a total of 7.7k examples, which are in the intersection of TAXINLI and the validation sets of MNLI.

Figure 5 shows for each category c_i, the normalized frequency for a model predicting an NLI example of that category accurately, i.e., $\frac{\#c_i=1,correct=1}{\#c_i=1}$. We observe that compared to NB, the improvements in BERT have been higher in `lexical`, `syntactic` categories compared to others. Improvements in ESIM compared to NB show a very similar trend, and show for knowledge categories the improvements are negligible. ESIM shows largest improvement on `negation`.

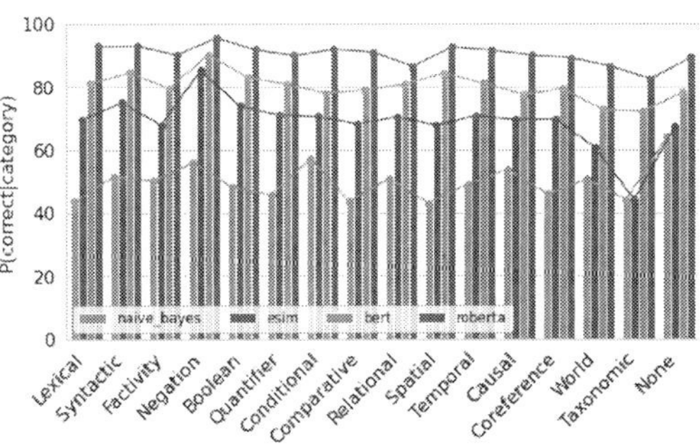

Figure 5: The normalized frequency of the systems predicting an example correctly, provided a category.

4.2 Factor Analysis

In order to quantify the precise influence of the category labels on the prediction of the NLI models, we probe into indicators and confounding factors using two methods: linear discriminant analysis (LDA) and logistic regression (LR). We use indicators for each category (0 or 1) and for two potential confounding variables (lengths of P,H), to model the correctness of prediction of the NLI system. The coefficients of these analyses on BERT are shown in Fig 6. The values for RoBERTa follow a similar trend, and are presented in the appendix. We see that presence of certain taxonomic categories strongly influence the correctness

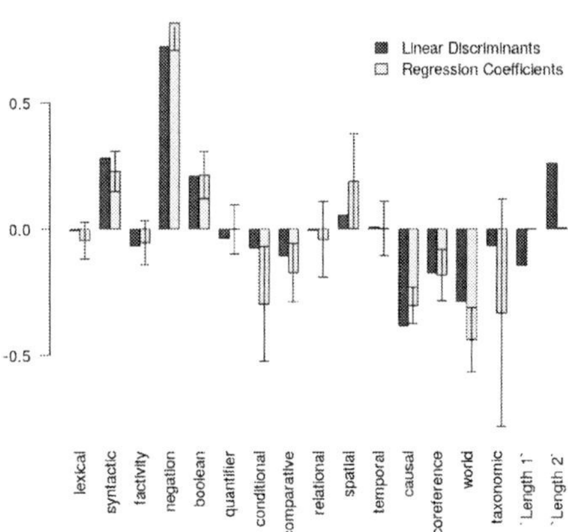

Figure 6: Coefficients obtained through Linear Discriminant Analysis (LDA) and Logistic Regression (LR) to model the correctness of NLI prediction by BERT, given taxonomy categories and possible confound variables. Significant LR coefficients: `syntactic**`, `negation***`, `boolean*`, `causal***`, `world***`, `Length2**`; where p value is smaller than: 0.001***, 0.01**, 0.05*.

of prediction. As we found in the analysis presented in Sec. 4, we observe that `syntactic`, `negation`, and `spatial` categories are strong indicators of correctness of prediction. On the other hand, `conditional`, `relational`, `causal`, `coreference` are harder to predict accurately. Sentence length does not play a significant role.

We also make an observation for categories such as `lexical`, `syntactic`, where the proportion of a single NLI label is high, also correlated with a high prediction accuracy (Fig. 6).

5 Discussion

Visual Analysis Section 4 paints a thorough picture by analysing the fine-grained capabilities of SOTA NLI systems at a *behavioral*[5] level. Whereas we can say the systems are lacking in certain aspects despite their high overall performance, it naturally also raises questions at the *understanding* level: 1) Is there any implicit knowledge acquired by the NLI-finetuned systems about the *kinds* of reasoning required in the inference task? 2) If not, do the systems simply lack the understanding of what kind of reasoning is required per example, or despite understanding that, are unable to do the

---

[5]Similar to social sciences, as a black-box system

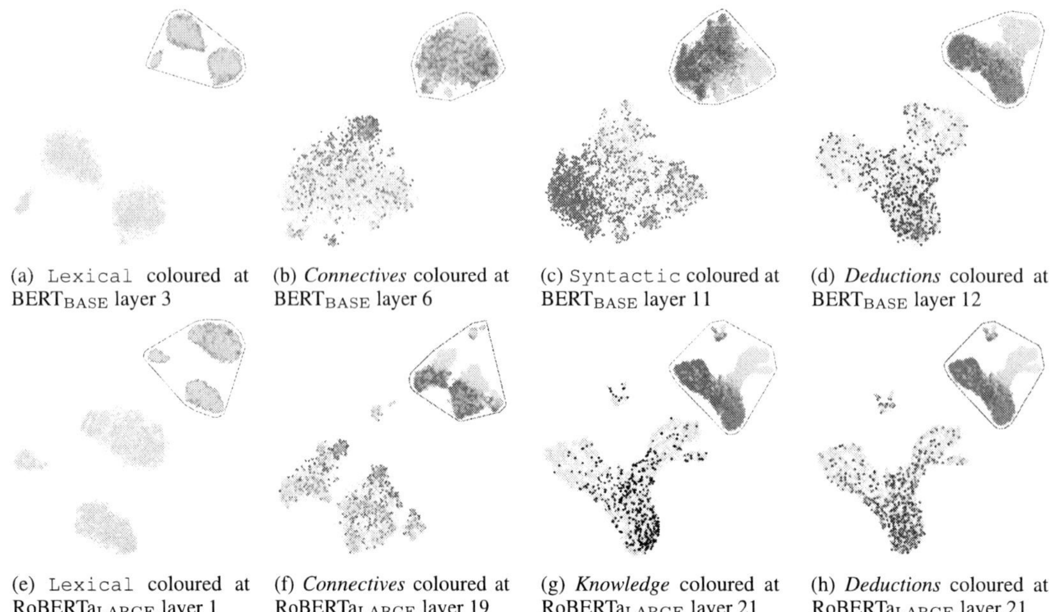

(a) Lexical coloured at BERT$_{\text{BASE}}$ layer 3

(b) *Connectives* coloured at BERT$_{\text{BASE}}$ layer 6

(c) Syntactic coloured at BERT$_{\text{BASE}}$ layer 11

(d) *Deductions* coloured at BERT$_{\text{BASE}}$ layer 12

(e) Lexical coloured at RoBERTa$_{\text{LARGE}}$ layer 1

(f) *Connectives* coloured at RoBERTa$_{\text{LARGE}}$ layer 19

(g) *Knowledge* coloured at RoBERTa$_{\text{LARGE}}$ layer 21

(h) *Deductions* coloured at RoBERTa$_{\text{LARGE}}$ layer 21

Figure 7: Layer-wise 2D t-SNE plots of pooled contextualized embeddings of the TaxiNLI examples extracted from BERT and RoBERTA finetuned on MNLI with no retraining on the taxonomic labels. Color codes represent taxonomic categories (inset shows NLI categories: **entailment** (■), **neutral** (■), **contradiction** (■)) and their combinations. Only combinations of up to two categories are included for brevity.

reasoning? 3) Can we make an argument for future work and model architecture that can more consciously use this information?

In light of recent probing task literature (Tenney et al., 2019a; Jawahar et al., 2019; Liu et al., 2019a), we specifically investigate whether representations of examples cluster meaningfully into taxonomic categories relevant to the reasoning required for NLI. We use the t-SNE (Maaten and Hinton, 2008) algorithm to visualize pooled contextualized representations of NLI examples, under the lens of our taxonomy. For an NLI example, we construct the embeddings at a Transformer layer by max-pooling hidden states over all input token positions concatenated with the [CLS] token (typically used for classification tasks) representation. The resulting visualizations (Fig. 7) reveal definitive patterns of clustering by taxonomic categories. The earliest separation is observed for the lexical category, at layer 3 in BERT (and layer 1 in RoBERTa), much before any other categories are realized. At layers 6 in BERT, and 19 in RoBERTa, about the same time as clustering by NLI label is seen, the *connectives* cluster is revealed. The *deductions* (see Sec. 2), and syntactic categories are revealed in later layers (layer 11 and 12 in BERT and layer 21 in RoBERTa). The *knowledge* cate-

gory is revealed more prominently in RoBERTa at layer 21, while BERT does not seem to show such a cluster. By the last few layers, separation into most categories becomes apparent. This means, along various layers of a NLI finetuned language model, taxonomic information is implicitly captured. Despite this, as discussed in the previous sections, SOTA models seem to be deficient in some of the categories—certain categories remain harder to perform inference on. In the latter layers, the separation along taxonomic categories also corresponds strongly with separation along NLI labels. For instance, in Fig. 7 (c), the examples categorized as syntactic almost entirely lie in the entailment cloud, which matches our intuition based on the statstics in Fig. 3.

The layer-wise separation of examples by taxonomy raises an interesting possibility to motivate model architectures that may attempt to use its discriminative power to identify such taxonomic categories, for specialized treatment to examples requiring certain reasoning capabilities.

Recasting: The under-representation of certain categories in the MNLI dataset raises a need for more balanced data collection. A possible alternative is to build recast diagnostic datasets for each category, and create probing tasks. Some datasets

(Zhang et al., 2019; Richardson et al., 2020) can be recast to the `syntactic` and **Logical** categories respectively, as their data creation aligns with our category definitions. However, most categories lack such aligned synthetic data, and crowd-sourced data would require manual annotation as above. This poses an avenue for future work.

6 Conclusion

To bridge the gap between accuracy-led performance measurement and linguistic analysis of state-of-the-art NLI systems, we propose a taxonomic categorization of necessary inferencing capabilities for the NLI task, and a re-evaluation framework of systems on a re-annotated NLI dataset using this categorization; which underscores the reasoning categories that current systems struggle with.

We would like to emphasize that unlike the case with challenge and adversarial datasets, TAXINLI re-annotates samples from existing NLI datasets which the SOTA models have been exposed to. Therefore, a lower accuracy in certain taxonomic categories in this case cannot be simply explained away by the "lack of data" and "unnatural distribution" arguments.

Acknowledgements

We gratefully acknowledge Sandipan Dandapat and Rohit Nargunde for their help regarding annotations. We would like to thank the anonymous reviewers for their insightful comments.

References

Emily M. Bender and Alexander Koller. 2020. Climbing towards NLU: On meaning, form, and understanding in the age of data. In *Proceedings of the 58th Annual Meeting of the Association for Computational Linguistics*, pages 5185–5198, Online. Association for Computational Linguistics.

Samuel Bowman, Gabor Angeli, Christopher Potts, and Christopher D Manning. 2015. A large annotated corpus for learning natural language inference. In *Proceedings of the 2015 Conference on Empirical Methods in Natural Language Processing*, pages 632–642.

Qian Chen, Xiaodan Zhu, Zhen-Hua Ling, Si Wei, Hui Jiang, and Diana Inkpen. 2017. Enhanced LSTM for natural language inference. In *Proceedings of the 55th Annual Meeting of the Association for Computational Linguistics (Volume 1: Long Papers)*, pages 1657–1668, Vancouver, Canada. Association for Computational Linguistics.

Ido Dagan, Oren Glickman, and Bernardo Magnini. 2005. The pascal recognising textual entailment challenge. In *Machine Learning Challenges Workshop*, pages 177–190. Springer.

Ernest Davis and Gary Marcus. 2015. Commonsense reasoning and commonsense knowledge in artificial intelligence. *Communications of the ACM*, 58(9):92–103.

Jacob Devlin, Ming-Wei Chang, Kenton Lee, and Kristina Toutanova. 2019. Bert: Pre-training of deep bidirectional transformers for language understanding. In *Proceedings of the 2019 Conference of the North American Chapter of the Association for Computational Linguistics: Human Language Technologies, Volume 1 (Long and Short Papers)*, pages 4171–4186.

JL Fleiss. 1971. Measuring nominal scale agreement among many raters. *Psychological bulletin*, 76(5):378—382.

David Gabelaia, Roman Kontchakov, Agi Kurucz, Frank Wolter, and Michael Zakharyaschev. 2005. Combining spatial and temporal logics: expressiveness vs. complexity. *Journal of Artificial Intelligence Research*, 23:167–243.

Yoav Goldberg. 2019. Assessing bert's syntactic abilities. *arXiv preprint arXiv:1901.05287*.

Ganesh Jawahar, Benoît Sagot, and Djamé Seddah. 2019. What does BERT learn about the structure of language? In *Proceedings of the 57th Annual Meeting of the Association for Computational Linguistics*, pages 3651–3657, Florence, Italy. Association for Computational Linguistics.

Paloma Jeretic, Alex Warstadt, Suvrat Bhooshan, and Adina Williams. 2020. Are natural language inference models IMPPRESsive? Learning IMPlicature and PRESupposition. In *Proceedings of the 58th Annual Meeting of the Association for Computational Linguistics*, pages 8690–8705, Online. Association for Computational Linguistics.

Divyansh Kaushik, Eduard Hovy, and Zachary C. Lipton. 2019. Learning the difference that makes a difference with counterfactually-augmented data.

Tal Linzen. 2020. How can we accclerate progress towards human-like linguistic generalization? In *Proceedings of the 58th Annual Meeting of the Association for Computational Linguistics*, pages 5210–5217, Online. Association for Computational Linguistics.

Nelson F Liu, Matt Gardner, Yonatan Belinkov, Matthew E Peters, and Noah A Smith. 2019a. Linguistic knowledge and transferability of contextual representations. *arXiv preprint arXiv:1903.08855*.

Yinhan Liu, Myle Ott, Naman Goyal, Jingfei Du, Mandar Joshi, Danqi Chen, Omer Levy, Mike Lewis, Luke Zettlemoyer, and Veselin Stoyanov. 2019b.

Roberta: A robustly optimized bert pretraining approach. *arXiv preprint arXiv:1907.11692.*

Peter LoBue and Alexander Yates. 2011. Types of common-sense knowledge needed for recognizing textual entailment. In *Proceedings of the 49th annual meeting of the association for computational linguistics: human language technologies*, pages 329–334.

Laurens van der Maaten and Geoffrey Hinton. 2008. Visualizing data using t-sne. *Journal of machine learning research*, 9(Nov):2579–2605.

Tom McCoy, Ellie Pavlick, and Tal Linzen. 2019. Right for the wrong reasons: Diagnosing syntactic heuristics in natural language inference. In *Proceedings of the 57th Annual Meeting of the Association for Computational Linguistics*, pages 3428–3448, Florence, Italy. Association for Computational Linguistics.

Aakanksha Naik, Abhilasha Ravichander, Norman Sadeh, Carolyn Rose, and Graham Neubig. 2018. Stress test evaluation for natural language inference. In *Proceedings of the 27th International Conference on Computational Linguistics*, pages 2340–2353, Santa Fe, New Mexico, USA. Association for Computational Linguistics.

Vincent Ng. 2017. Machine learning for entity coreference resolution: A retrospective look at two decades of research. In *Thirty-First AAAI Conference on Artificial Intelligence.*

Yixin Nie, Adina Williams, Emily Dinan, Mohit Bansal, Jason Weston, and Douwe Kiela. 2019. Adversarial nli: A new benchmark for natural language understanding. *arXiv preprint arXiv:1910.14599.*

Judea Pearl. 2009. *Causality.* Cambridge university press.

Adam Poliak, Aparajita Haldar, Rachel Rudinger, J. Edward Hu, Ellie Pavlick, Aaron Steven White, and Benjamin Van Durme. 2018. Collecting diverse natural language inference problems for sentence representation evaluation. In *Proceedings of the 2018 Conference on Empirical Methods in Natural Language Processing*, pages 67–81, Brussels, Belgium. Association for Computational Linguistics.

Marco Tulio Ribeiro, Tongshuang Wu, Carlos Guestrin, and Sameer Singh. 2020. Beyond accuracy: Behavioral testing of NLP models with CheckList. In *Proceedings of the 58th Annual Meeting of the Association for Computational Linguistics*, pages 4902–4912, Online. Association for Computational Linguistics.

Kyle Richardson, Hai Hu, Lawrence Moss, and Ashish Sabharwal. 2020. Probing natural language inference models through semantic fragments. *Proceedings of the AAAI Conference on Artificial Intelligence*, 34:8713–8721.

Kyle Richardson, Hai Na Hu, Lawrence S. Moss, and Ashish Sabharwal. 2019. Probing natural language inference models through semantic fragments. *ArXiv*, abs/1909.07521.

Felipe Salvatore, Marcelo Finger, and Roberto Hirata Jr. 2019. A logical-based corpus for cross-lingual evaluation. In *Proceedings of the 2nd Workshop on Deep Learning Approaches for Low-Resource NLP (DeepLo 2019)*, pages 22–30.

John F Sowa. 2010. The role of logic and ontology in language and reasoning. In *Theory and applications of ontology: philosophical perspectives*, pages 231–263. Springer.

Ian Tenney, Dipanjan Das, and Ellie Pavlick. 2019a. Bert rediscovers the classical nlp pipeline. *arXiv preprint arXiv:1905.05950.*

Ian Tenney, Patrick Xia, Berlin Chen, Alex Wang, Adam Poliak, R Thomas McCoy, Najoung Kim, Benjamin Van Durme, Samuel Bowman, Dipanjan Das, et al. 2019b. What do you learn from context? probing for sentence structure in contextualized word representations. In *7th International Conference on Learning Representations, ICLR 2019.*

Alex Wang, Amanpreet Singh, Julian Michael, Felix Hill, Omer Levy, and Samuel R Bowman. 2018. Glue: A multi-task benchmark and analysis platform for natural language understanding. *EMNLP 2018*, page 353.

Adina Williams, Nikita Nangia, and Samuel Bowman. 2018. A broad-coverage challenge corpus for sentence understanding through inference. In *Proceedings of the 2018 Conference of the North American Chapter of the Association for Computational Linguistics: Human Language Technologies, Volume 1 (Long Papers)*, pages 1112–1122. Association for Computational Linguistics.

L. Wittgenstein. 1922. Tractatus logico-philosophicus. *London: Routledge, 1981.*

Thomas Wolf, Lysandre Debut, Victor Sanh, Julien Chaumond, Clement Delangue, Anthony Moi, Pierric Cistac, Tim Rault, R'emi Louf, Morgan Funtowicz, and Jamie Brew. 2019. Huggingface's transformers: State-of-the-art natural language processing. *ArXiv*, abs/1910.03771.

Yuan Zhang, Jason Baldridge, and Luheng He. 2019. PAWS: Paraphrase adversaries from word scrambling. In *Proceedings of the 2019 Conference of the North American Chapter of the Association for Computational Linguistics: Human Language Technologies, Volume 1 (Long and Short Papers)*, pages 1298–1308, Minneapolis, Minnesota. Association for Computational Linguistics.

	ANLI Inference Types	GLUE Diagnostic
Lexical	Standard Inference Lexical Inference	Lexical Entailment Morphological Negation Factivity, Redundancy
Syntactic	Tricky	Syntactic Ambiguity, Prepositional Phrase Alternations: Active/Passive, Genitives/Partitives, Nominalization, Datives
Semantic	Standard Inference	Propositional Structure, Intersectivity Quantifiers, Restrictivity, Quantification
	Numerical, Quantitative	Counting
	Reference and Names	Symmetry/Collectivity, Coreference, Richer Logical Structures
	Reference and Names Reasoning about Facts	Named Entities Knowledge and Commonsense
Pragmatics	Tricky	Ellipsis/Implicits

Table 4: We show existing NLI error-analysis categorizations proposed by the recent papers, and group them in higher-level categories.

A Other Categorizations

B Bayesian Estimate of Correctness Correlation with Categories

Since, examples are annotated with multiple categories, we capture the dependencies by defining a Bayesian Network (BN) where, each category (a boolean random variable) has a directed edge to the *correct* node (representing correctness of prediction)[6]. We learn the parameters by fitting this BN to the observed data. In Figure 9, we see from the Bayesian estimate again that, the improvements by BERT in categories such as `relational` reasoning has been low. It also shows, that there is a sharp decrease in accuracy for examples requiring the use of `taxonomic` knowledge. However, RoBERTa improves over NB and ESIM by large margins, albeit non-uniformly.

C Factor Analysis of Correctness of Prediction by RoBERTa

In Fig. 9, we show the results of Linear Discriminant Analysis (LDA) and Linear Regression (LR) results for RoBERTa predictions. A very similar trend as BERT can be seen here as well.

---

[6]Additionally, we attempted to learn a Bayes Net from the data using `bnlearn` package. But the limited number of observations yield non-intuitive results.

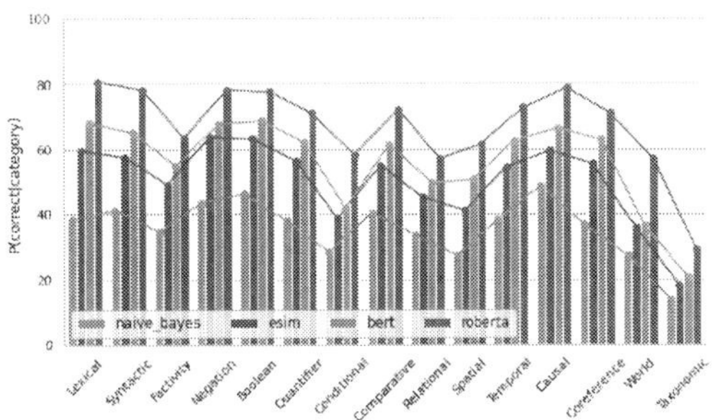

Figure 8: We show a Bayesian Estimate of $P(\texttt{correct} = 1 | \texttt{category} = 1)$ for different systems.

D Annotation Questionnaire

Our annotation process went through several steps of refinement and improvement. We started with the most basic annotation flow, which was to have a manual which defines each taxonomic category in detail, and then have the annotator mark for each category. For the pilot study, we took roughly 300 examples from MNLI and asked an initial annotator to annotate. The feedback was the following:

- The manual describing each taxonomic category had a lot of information and took time to understand and digest.

- It was difficult to keep referring to the guide, although after sufficient examples, it became easier.

- There was confusion and ambiguity about the definitions, and the annotator interpreted the definitions differently than what we intended.

- Figuring out the categorical annotations for neutral examples was a challenge, as sometimes the topic or subject of what the hypothesis was discussing was separate from what the premise was discussing.

Through the analysis of these annotations, we also observed that some of the initial categories we had were either exceedingly underrepresented in the MNLI dataset, or were consistently confused with others. Thus, we revised the set of categories, setting more distinct boundaries, and ensuring independence of categories. We revised the questionnaire into a hierarchical 'if-else' multi-choice design. The questionnaire is structured as follows:

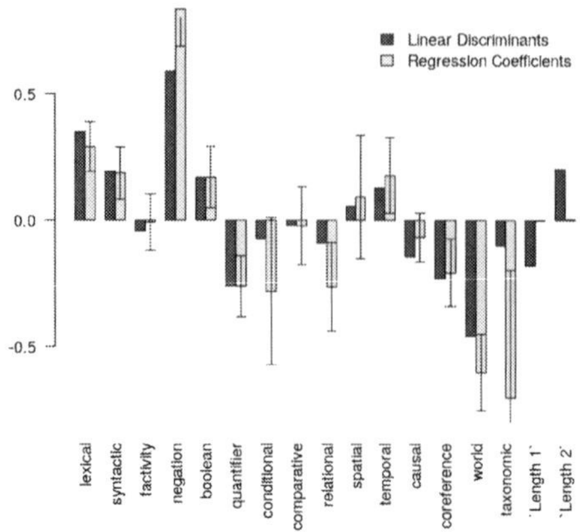

Figure 9: Coefficients obtained through Linear Discriminant Analysis (LDA) and Logistic Regression (LR) to model the correctness of NLI prediction by RoBERTa, given taxonomy categories and possible confound variables. Significant LR coefficients: `lexical**, negation***, world***, quantifier*, boolean*, Length1*`; where p value is smaller than: $0.001***, 0.01**, 0.05*$.

D.0.1 Questionnaire 1

"We present you with a set of statements. Statement 1 (S1) is the truth and context. Statement 2 (S2) is a claim/hypothesis. The task is to evaluate statement 2 as true, false, can't say.

S1: ... S2: ...

1. Can you evaluate S2 by just using the information/context given in S1? Or do you require knowledge from external documents, say history books, news articles, science books, etc.?

   (a) Need more information

   (b) Do not need more information

2. If yes, what kind of information did you require? (More than one answer can be ticked)

   (a) Knowledge about certain facts from say history books, news articles, tech magazines, etc.? This is also knowledge about named entities (e.g. Obama, Taj Mahal, New York etc.). E.g:
   - S1: Barack Obama lived in the White House during 2009-17.
   - S2: Barack Obama was the President in 2009.

This is TRUE and requires external knowledge that US presidents live in the White House.

   (b) Knowledge about taxonomies and hierarchies. A few examples are animal groups (snakes are reptiles), currencies (dollar is a currency), types of activities (football is a sport, sport is an activity). Basically, how a common noun (snake) belongs to a class (say reptiles), which can belong to yet another class (animals). Do not select this if the name of one object belongs (or is a substring) of the other class of objects (e.g. green snake is a snake isn't part of this category), or if the names of the objects are pronouns (e.g. Barack Obama - president and related examples are part of category 2a, not this one). E.g:
   - S1: Norman hated all musical instruments.
   - S2: Norman loves the piano.

This is FALSE and requires external knowledge that a piano belongs to the class of instruments, hence Norman cannot love the piano.

   (c) No extra knowledge required

3. Using just the information from S1, and given that you have the required knowledge from the above question, did you have to use some reasoning to figure out the answer, or did you just need the knowledge of words and paraphrasing, or both? (More than one can be ticked)

   (a) Some reasoning was required, which wasn't explicitly written down in S1, but was implicitly understood.

   (b) Knowledge of words (e.g. synonyms, antonyms), and recognizing paraphrases. The information I needed was explicitly written down in S1.

4. What kind of reasoning was required (if applicable) (More than one can be ticked)?

   (a) You needed reasoning about relations in S1. You observed that there were objects/entities in S1 and there were explicit mentions of how they were related (e.g. Jack and his son went to the circus), and you used your reasoning about the nature of those relations to arrive to the answer (e.g. Jack and a stranger went to the circus is FALSE) E.g:

- S1: Jack and his son went to the circus.
- S2: Jack and a stranger went to the circus.

This is FALSE, but you need to reason that S1 contains the relation "father of" between Jack and some person X (who is his son). S2 is false because if X is a stranger, it cannot be Jack's son.

(b) You needed reasoning about spatial setup. S1 contained information about relative locations of objects/entities (e.g. Jack was on the right of Jim, and Jim was on the right of John) and you needed to reason about how objects/entities were located, when it wasn't explicitly stated (e.g. John was on the left of Jack is TRUE).

(c) You needed reasoning about time intervals, duration, or temporal reasoning. S1 contained information about events and time information (e.g. Jack went to the shop from 8:00am to 10:00am), and you needed to reason about the timing to arrive at the answer (e.g. Jack was at the shop at 9:30am is TRUE).

(d) You needed reasoning about cause, effect, and intent behind it. S1 contained information about an event or an action (e.g. Jack was hurt). S2 contains either a cause or an intent, and you needed to reason whether S1 and S2 were possible cause/effect or intent/effect pairs (e.g. Jack was hit by a car is CAN'T SAY)
- S1: X shot Y
- S2: Y is hurt

This is TRUE, but you needed to reason that upon getting shot, Y should get hurt.

(e) You needed to be able to reason about who is being referred to in the text. Better demonstrated via example:
- S1: Jane didn't visit Janette because <u>she</u> didn't want to speak with her.
- S2: Jane didn't want to speak with Janette.

This is TRUE. 'She' refers to Jane, and you needed to reason about that to get the answer.

5. Did you need logical reasoning? This applies if S1 and/or S2 consist of statements connected by logical connective words (and, or, not, every, some, only, either, neither, etc. or any synonyms of these words). These connectives were important for arriving at the answer. If so, which connectives? (Can tick multiple choices)

(a) Negation (not, no, <u>in</u>capable etc.), where S2 negates one of the facts in S1. E.g:
- S1: Laurie has visited Nephi, Marion has only visited Calistoga.
- S2: Laurie didn't visit Nephi.

This is FALSE, and S2 is a negation of the first statement in S1.

(b) Boolean (or, and), where S1 is a set of statements connected by Or and AND, and S2 talks about one or more of these statements. E.g:
- S1: Jar Jar Binks, R2D2 and Padme only visited Anakin's house.
- S2: Jar Jar Binks didn't visit Anakin's shop.

This is TRUE, and S1 is connected by 'and' statements for three entities who visited Anakin's house. S2 talks about the sub-statement "Jar Jar Binks only visited Anakin's house" in the 'and' connective, and it is true because Jar Jar Binks didn't visit anywhere else.

(c) Quantifier (every, some, at least, at most, etc.), where S1 and S2 contain the use of these terms.
- S1: Everyone visited Anakin's home.
- S2: Padme didn't visit Anakin's home.

This is FALSE, with S1 containing the quantifier 'everyone', and S2 stating that someone, Padme, didn't visit.

(d) Conditionals (if-else, if-then, etc.), where S1 has if-then, if-else statements or similar.
- S1: Francisco has visited Potsdam and if Francisco has visited Potsdam then Tyrone has visited Pampa.
- S2: Tyrone has visited Pampa

This is TRUE, since there is a if-then condition in S1, and it is satisfied to make S2 true.

(e) Comparatives (e.g. as tall as, taller than, faster than, etc.) where S1 compares entities via these comparative phrases, and S2 needs knowledge about the comparisons.

- S1: John is taller than Gordon and Erik, and Mitchell is as tall as John
- S2: Gordon is taller than Mitchell.

This is FALSE. This are comparative statements "Is taller than" in S1, and S2 needs logical reasoning on who is taller than whom to get S2. In addition to this, this also needs knowledge of Boolean due to the presence of the 'and' in S1.

6. Finally, can you describe some word/phrase (explicitly written) properties of S1 and S2 which helped to arrive to the answer? (more than one can be ticked)

(a) S1 and S2 were almost the same, apart from the removal, addition, or substitution of a few words. If substituted, the words were synonyms or antonyms. E.g:
- S1: Anakin Skywalker was compassionate.
- S2: Anakin Skywalker was cruel.

This is FALSE, with S1 and S2 being very similarly framed statements, with the substitution of a word for it's antonym. Thus it belongs to this category.

(b) S1 and S2 were paraphrases of each other. S2 is a paraphrase of S1 or a certain part of information mentioned in S1
- S1: Anakin was an excellent pilot.
- S2: The piloting skills of Anakin were excellent.

This is TRUE, and S1 and S2 being paraphrases of one another. Also, to note, if 'excellent' in S2 were replaced by 'terrible', it would still fit this category, but would also fit category 6a, since it would be a paraphrase with a swapped word.

(c) S2 contains an assumed fact from S1, mostly an assumption about the existence or the occurrence of an action.
- S1: Anakin found the Death Star.
- S2: The Death Star exists.

This is TRUE. The Death Star exists if Anakin has found it, thus S1 makes the assumption that it exists.

- S1: James was happy that his plane could fly.
- S2: His plane couldn't fly.

This is FALSE. Since James was happy that the plane flew (S1 makes the assumption that it happened), it is FALSE that his plane couldn't fly since it happened."

The above questionnaire was given along with premise-hypothesis pairs having the gold label of 'entailment' or 'contradiction' . However, to prevent biasing the annotator, we allowed them to choose 'neutral' (CAN'T SAY) as well.

D.0.2 Questionnaire 2

This questionnaire was given to the annotators after they had done a sufficient number of 'entailment/contradiction' samples using Questionnaire 1. For Questionnaire 2, annotators were told that the datapoints were 'neutral', and asked them to first answer these 3 questions:

"Given S1, there isn't enough information to decide whether S2 is TRUE or FALSE. Please answer the following questions for each datapoint which has been annotated as CAN'T SAY.

1. Are S1 and S2 talking about the same general topic (e.g. sports, politics, religion)? [Yes/No]

2. If yes, are S1 and S2 talking about the same subject? (e.g. S1: Obama was the president of USA, S2: Obama was a nice guy, subject of sentence is Obama) [Yes/No]

3. If yes, are S1 and S2 talking about the same objects of discussion? (e.g. S1: Obama lived in the White House often, S2: Obama said the White House was huge. Here both subject (Obama) and object (White House) of discussion are the same)

4. If yes, what kinds of information are required which you used, and what kinds of information are missing? If no, what kinds of information are required which you used, and what kinds of information are missing? "

Upon answering the above, if the answer to the second question was yes, then they proceeded with the category annotation, else they moved on to the next question. This helped eliminate the random hypotheses.

D.0.3 Annotator Feedback

We received a lot of important feedback from our annotators during the clarification and training sessions. They are listed below:

- Many premise sentences seems out of place, and the context is still insufficient many times. As a result, the hypothesis also introduces ambiguity, making the process a bit tricky.

- There were cases where a certain name of an entity in the premise is switched for something else in the hypothesis. This created some confusion because it fell somewhere between lexical and coreference (according to the annotator).

- Another confusion arose from the quantifier category, where initially the name of the category led the annotators to believe that it referred to not just what we described (e.g. some, all), but quantities (say 5000 in the premise was swapped with 2000 in the hypothesis). This was again a middle ground between lexical and quantifier.

- Many of the premises contained incoherent, difficult to understand sentences. A lot of premises (which we later found to be from the telephone category), contained many filler words (uh, uhm, etc.) which made comprehension difficult.

- Another issue lies with an implicit rigidity of the annotation process using just the questionnaire. The targeted questions were written so as to allow annotators to generalize and apply intuitive principles along those thought lines that we try to demarcate via the questions. We wanted to prevent them completely However, as annotators have not been exposed to the exact intentions behind the annotation (so as to prevent bias), they followed the questionnaire strictly, and did not always generalize until subsequent training/clarification sessions where we encouraged them to generalize. However, the implicit rigidity still impacts the annotations to some extent, although mitigated to a large level by the training. This remains a challenge due to the tradeoff between open interpretation of the task, as well as a rigidity of desired annotations which stem from an analysis perspective (from our side).

- Idiomatic references, metaphors, and common phrases were also a source of confusion, and although to some extent were marked as world knowledge, did leave annotators unsure about where to place them.

The above feedback only strengthened our belief in an iterative training system for a complicated task such as this. It also sheds light on how difficult a task like this is to crowdsource.

Modeling Subjective Assessments of Guilt in Newspaper Crime Narratives

Elisa Kreiss[1,*]   Zijian Wang[2,*]   Christopher Potts[1,2]

[1]Department of Linguistics   [2]Symbolic Systems Program
Stanford University
{ekreiss, zijwang, cgpotts}@stanford.edu

Abstract

Crime reporting is a prevalent form of journalism with the power to shape public perceptions and social policies. How does the language of these reports act on readers? We seek to address this question with the **SuspectGuilt Corpus** of annotated crime stories from English-language newspapers in the U.S. For Suspect-Guilt, annotators read short crime articles and provided text-level ratings concerning the guilt of the main suspect as well as span-level annotations indicating which parts of the story they felt most influenced their ratings. SuspectGuilt thus provides a rich picture of how linguistic choices affect subjective guilt judgments. We use SuspectGuilt to train and assess predictive models which validate the usefulness of the corpus, and show that these models benefit from genre pretraining and joint supervision from the text-level ratings and span-level annotations. Such models might be used as tools for understanding the societal effects of crime reporting.

1 Introduction

News outlets around the world routinely report on crimes and alleged crimes, ranging from petty misdemeanors to large-scale international criminal conspiracies. Each of these reports will frame events in ways that shape reader perceptions, and these perceptions will in turn shape public perception of how much crime there is, who is responsible for crime, and what policy decisions should be made to address crime. It is therefore important to understand how the language in these reports acts on readers, and there is clear value in developing NLP models that approximate these reader perceptions at a large scale, as a tool for estimating the aggregate effects of crime reporting on society.

To begin to address these needs, we present the **SuspectGuilt Corpus** of annotated crime stories

A Canton man accused of brandishing a handgun when his estranged wife showed up with another man to pick up their children is facing criminal charges, police said. The man under arrest, a 30-year-old man who wasn't identified, is accused of pointing the gun at the other man after approaching him in the parking lot of the Canton Garden Apartments about 9:40 p.m. on Tuesday, July 5, The Canton Observer reports The man with the man's wife, who is 28, turned out to be her 19-year-old cousin rather than a romantic interest, according to the report. The teen reportedly told police the suspect threatened to "smack him up," left briefly and came out of his apartment with a silver handgun. The teen took cover. The suspect's brother defused the situation, according to the report. Police confiscated the handgun and five rounds of ammunition and took the suspect into custody. » For more Canton police news, go to hometownlife.com.

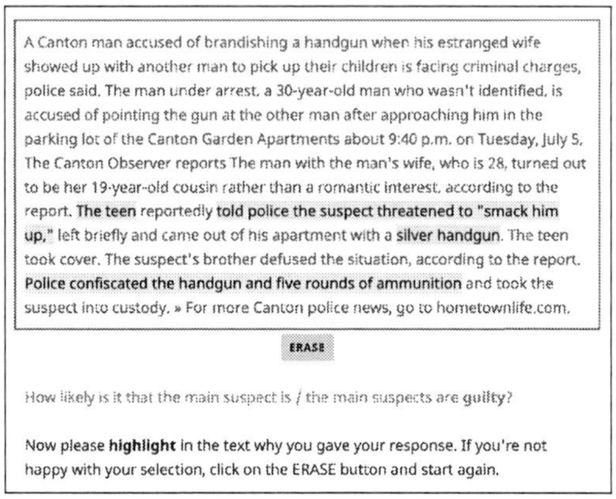

Figure 1: The SuspectGuilt corpus highlighting interface. After participants responded to a question about the guilt of the main suspect in the report, they completed this highlighting phase intended to provide insights into how they took themselves to be reasoning about the text. SuspectGuilt contains 1.8K stories with at least 5 participants responding to each.

from English-language newspapers in the U.S.[1] Each story in the corpus is multiply-annotated with participants' assessments (on a continuous scale) of the guilt of the main suspect(s) and of the author's belief in the guilt of the suspect(s). In addition, for each of these guilt-rating questions, the participants highlighted the spans of text in the story that they felt contributed to their decision (Figure 1). These additional annotations provide a window into the language that participants took themselves to be attending to as part of their personal verdicts, and thus they are especially useful for understanding how authors' low-level linguistic choices feed into readers' overall judgments.

We also explore a range of methods for developing predictive models on the basis of SuspectGuilt annotations which exemplify the usefulness of the

---

*Equal contribution.

[1]https://github.com/zijwang/modeling_guilt

Proceedings of the 24th Conference on Computational Natural Language Learning, pages 56–68
Online, November 19-20, 2020. ©2020 Association for Computational Linguistics
https://doi.org/10.18653/v1/P17

resource. Our models are built on top of pretrained BERT parameters. In the simplest case, we learn to predict the author or subject guilt ratings without any other supervision. This basic model is improved if it is jointly trained on the guilt ratings and the span-level annotations that SuspectGuilt provides, which helps to quantify the value of these low-level linguistic annotations. In addition, we explore unsupervised pretraining on a modestly-sized unlabeled corpus of crime stories, finding that it too increases the effectiveness of SuspectGuilt models.

The span-level annotations offer new opportunities for analysis as well. Using the Integrated Gradients method of Sundararajan et al. (2017), we identify the token-level features that our models rely on when trained without span-level supervision, and we compare this to the span-level annotations provided by SuspectGuilt. Overall, the correspondence between the two is not high, which explains why the span-level objective helps our models and suggests that the document-level ratings alone might not suffice to yield models that attend to texts in the same ways that humans do.

2 Related Work

Our work draws on prior research into the relationship between language and assessments of guilt, as well as work seeking to jointly model text-level and token-level annotations using neural networks.

2.1 Predicting Guilt

The challenge of predicting guilt judgments from text sources has not yet received much attention. However, Fausey and Boroditsky (2010) show that using agentive language increases blame and financial liability judgments people make. Their results suggest that even subtle linguistic changes in crime reports will shape people's judgments of the events. More recent work has focused on predicting guilt verdicts from the Supreme Courts in the Philippines (Virtucio et al., 2018) and Thailand (Kowsrihawat et al., 2018) on the basis of presented facts and legal texts. Kowsrihawat et al. employ a recurrent neural network with attention to make these predictions. These findings are for courtroom verdicts based on legal texts, and thus they are a useful complement to SuspectGuilt, which provides subjective guilt judgments based on crime reporting.

2.2 Veridicality Markers

We use the label 'veridicality markers' to informally identify a large class of lexical items that includes hedges, evidentials, and other markers of (un)certainty. Analysis of the span-level annotations in SuspectGuilt shows that veridicality markers play an out-sized role in shaping people's judgments of guilt. The annotations are dominated not only by conventionalized devices like *allegedly*, *suspect*, and *according to*, but also by more context-specific locutions like *police say* and *arrest*.

There is extensive prior literature on how veridicality markers affect the perceptions of the speaker and proposition (Erickson et al., 1978; Durik et al., 2008; Bonnefon and Villejoubert, 2006; Rubin, 2007; Jensen, 2008; Ferson et al., 2015). These studies suggest such markers affect people's judgments of credibility in differing ways. For example, an increase in the number of hedges decreases the credibility of witness reports (Erickson et al., 1978) but increases the trustworthiness of journalists and scientists (Jensen, 2008). Additionally, the interpretation of hedges is context dependent (Bonnefon and Villejoubert, 2006; Durik et al., 2008; Ferson et al., 2015) and show high individual variation (Rubin, 2007; Ferson et al., 2015).

Similarly, attitude predications like *X reported S* can be used to reduce commitment, but they can also be used to provide evidence in favor of *S* (Simons 2007; de Marneffe et al. 2012; White and Rawlins 2018; White et al. 2018). Stone (1994) and von Fintel and Gillies (2010) address similar uses of epistemic modal verbs. These findings show how complex these markers are pragmatically and highlight the value of usage-based studies of them.

2.3 Span-Level Supervision

BERT models (Devlin et al., 2019) define an output representation for every token-level input (see also Vaswani et al. 2017). The parameters of these models can be fine-tuned in many ways (Lee et al., 2020; Mosbach et al., 2020). Our models combine text-level prediction with sequence modeling; the supervision signals come from the guilt judgments and span highlighting in the SuspectGuilt corpus. This basic model structure has been used in a wide variety of settings before. What is perhaps special about our use of it is that the two levels of annotation each provide evidence about the other; the highlighting can be seen as guiding the regression model to pay attention to certain words, and the regression label is likely to create helpful biases for particular token-level classifications. Rei and Søgaard (2019) define models that similarly make use complementary tasks. This is also conceptually very similar to the token-level supervision in the debiasing model of Pryzant et al. (2020). However, while their token-level labels come from a fixed lexicon, ours were created in their linguistic context with a particular set of guilt-related issues in mind.

3 Data

The SuspectGuilt corpus is a resource to investigate how the language of crime reports affects readers. This section describes the data collection and annotation process. We provide qualitative and quantitative analyses of SuspectGuilt that exemplify its usefulness for psycholinguistic investigations and NLP applications.

3.1 Data Collection

The SuspectGuilt corpus is derived from a dataset of crime-related newspaper stories from regional, English-language newspapers in the U.S. We chose to focus on such stories because they are generally brief and self-contained. By contrast, crime-related stories from major news outlets tend to involve public figures, political issues, and important global events, and readers' prior exposure to the issues might affect their judgments in unpredictable ways.

Inspired by Davani et al. (2019), we collected our corpus from Patch.com. The Patch dataset contains independent, hyper-local news articles compiled from local news sites. We crawled all stories in the "Crime & Safety" section for all news up through December 2019, yielding 474k news stories from 1,226 communities in the U.S. We then filtered this collection to just stories with (1) at most 300 words and (2) at least 4 of the following word-stems: `suspect*`, `alleg*`, `arrest*`, `crim*`, `accus*`[2]. In addition, we filtered out stories that either have the same title, for which we only keep one copy, or are collections of multiple reports, e.g., records of incidents. As a post-processing step, we removed phone numbers and Patch.com advertisements. The final collection has 4.2K stories, of which we selected 1,957 for annotation.

---

[2]The word-stems were chosen to maximize the retrieval of news stories that report on criminal acts where a suspect has been identified but that still communicate uncertainty about the case.

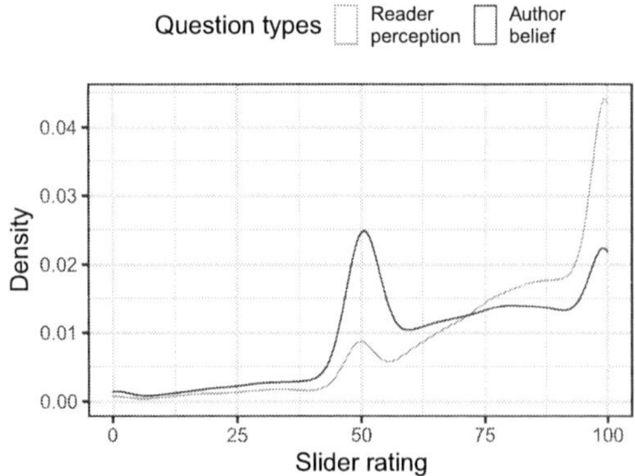

Figure 2: Slider rating density distribution for the *Reader perception* and *Author belief* questions.

3.2 Annotation Effort

For the annotation phase of SuspectGuilt, participants were recruited on Amazon's Mechanical Turk and asked to read five stories and respond to three questions about them:

1. *Reader perception*: "How likely is it that the main suspect is / the main suspects are guilty?"

2. *Author belief*: "How much does the author believe that the main suspect is / the main suspects are guilty?"

3. An attention check question, such as "How likely is it that this story contains more than five words?"

Responses were collected on a continuous slider, coded as ranging from 0 (very unlikely) to 1 (very likely). After submitting the slider response for each question, participants were asked to "highlight in the text why [they] gave [their] response". They additionally had the option to opt out of the slider response by indicating that the question didn't apply to the story. Stories with more than 30% of "Doesn't apply" responses were excluded from the corpus, yielding 1,821 unique news reports.

Guilt judgments are subjective and known to be highly variable (Section 2.2), and we expect the span-level highlighting to be even more variable. To accommodate this natural variation, we had multiple participants rate each story. Every story was annotated at least 5 times, and after excluding "Doesn't apply" responses, 99.2% of the stories still have 5 annotations or more for the *Reader perception* question and 86.7% for the *Author belief*

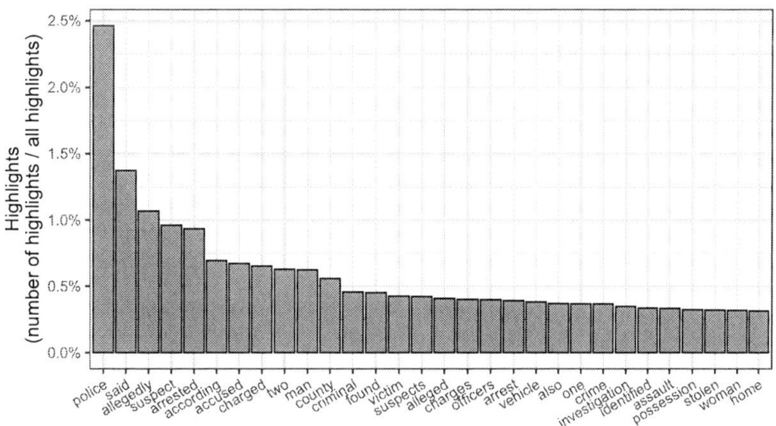

Figure 3: The 30 most highlighted words across questions.

question. For our analyses and modeling in this paper, we generally average these annotations, but the corpus supports work at finer-grained levels. Our appendices include additional details, including screenshots of the annotation interface, exclusion criteria for participants, and aggregated participant demographics.

3.3 Text-Level Annotations

Figure 2 shows the distribution of responses for the *Reader perception* and *Author belief* questions. Both distributions are skewed towards the middle and maximum portions of the slider scale. Relatively few participants chose ratings in the "very unlikely" range, which potentially reflects underlying biases about news reporting: readers expect suspects mentioned in these stories to be guilty. We also begin to see differences between the two questions. While *Reader perception* ratings are rather skewed to the maximum portion of the scale, *Author belief* responses are concentrated around the center. This already suggests a disconnect between what readers believe about the suspect's guilt more generally and what readers believe about the author's beliefs. The cluster around the center also suggests that participants feel uncertainty, especially in the *Author belief* case. The clustering might also reflect a presumption that journalists will seek to appear unbiased.

We find high levels of interannotator agreement for both the *Reader perception* and *Author belief* questions. The mean squared error (MSE) for each story is lower for the *Reader perception* question (mean MSE = 0.0313) than *Author belief* (mean MSE = 0.0410). To provide some context for these numbers, we also calculated them after first shuffling all ratings. The MSE for this setting is 0.0443 for *Author belief* and 0.0353 for *Reader perception*. Both are significantly higher than their non-shuffled counterparts according to a Welch Two Sample t-test ($p < 0.0001$).

3.4 Span-Level Annotations

When highlighting text spans, participants primarily marked passages shorter than 200 characters (approximately 33 words). *Author belief* highlights tended to be shorter than those for *Reader perception*. Overall, highlights had a length between 1 and 1,717 characters (about 286 words). (A highlight here is defined as a consecutive mark without a non-highlighted character in between. If a participant highlighted two passages that are directly connected, they count as one highlighting.)

We would like to estimate agreement levels for span highlighting as well. Because our stories have varying numbers of annotations, we cannot calculate a Fleiss kappa value for this problem. Krippendorff's alpha is a standard test that can accommodate this kind of variation, but its symmetric treatment of highlighting and non-highlighting is problematic since only 15% of the tokens are highlighted.[3] Nonetheless, to provide some insight into how alike our participants were in their highlighting behavior, we compared the percentage of anno-

---

[3]Due to this inequality, the random baseline in Krippendorff's alpha (which is computed by shuffling each story's highlights) is disproportionately strong. The highlighting data still achieves a positive Krippendorff's alpha of 0.16 for *Reader perception* and 0.08 for *Author belief*.

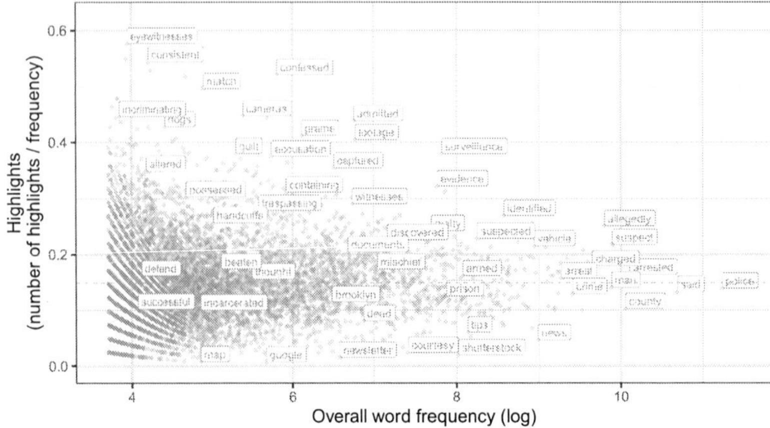

Figure 4: Proportion of token selections by frequency. Words that received the most highlights overall (see Figure 3) are presented in red, other words in grey. By chance, words would be highlighted 14.88% of the time, indicated by the dashed grey line. Words that are highlighted more often than predicted by chance are above this line, suggesting that they take on an important role in annotators' judgments.

tators who highlighted each character with a random baseline. The random baseline highlights were created by randomly shuffling the underlying highlight distribution for each annotation. We find that it was more likely that at least half of the annotators considered a token as important in the actual data as opposed to the random baseline (Welch Two Sample t-test: $p < 0.0001$).

Token-level analysis of the highlighted spans reveals many connections with the markers of veridicality discussed in Section 2.2. Figure 3 shows the most highlighted words across the two guilt questions.[4] The list is dominated by conventionalized devices for signaling lack of commitment in newspaper reporting (e.g., forms of *allege*), devices for shifting attribution to others (e.g., *said, accused*), and genre-specific words that play into how we assess evidence in criminal contexts (e.g., *accused, charged, investigation*).

However, as we might expect, the number of times a word is highlighted highly correlates with its frequency ($r = 0.97$). Figure 4 brings out this relationship. The x-axis is token frequency, and the y-axis gives the proportion of tokens for a word that were highlighted. (For example, if a word appeared 100 times and was highlighted 10 of those times, it would appear at 0.1 on the y-axis.) We excluded words with a frequency below 25, since these tend to get exaggerated proportions. The words from Figure 3 are displayed in red and are

highly frequent, and they are also the words with the highest highlighting proportion for their frequency, suggesting that these patterns are robust. Many of the other proportionally frequently highlighted words fall into the same categories as those in Figure 3: forms of *confess, eyewitnesses*, words picking out devices that provide evidence, and so forth. Words which were highlighted less than expected by chance (i.e., below the dashed grey line) rather reference meta-information of the news stories, such as *google, newsletter, shutterstock*, and *map*. In sum, the highlighting patterns seem aligned with the linguistic picture outlined in Section 2.2.

Figure 5 seeks to add a further dimension to this analysis. Thus far, we have ignored the distinction between the two guilt-rating questions, *Reader perception* and *Author belief*. The two questions are semantically quite different and might even come apart in some cases. For example, a reader might attend only to the evidence presented in a text and arrive at a high guilt-rating of their own, while ignoring clear indicators that the author wishes to remain non-committal about the origin or strength of that evidence. Kreiss et al. (2019) found that hedges affect responses of *Author belief* but not *Reader perception*, suggesting that the use of words like *allegedly* affects reader's perception about the author's beliefs but not their general guilt perception. This seems to be reflected in the selection data as well. In Figure 5, we give the words with the largest differences between the two guilt questions.

---

[4]Punctuation and stopwords taken from the *tm: Text mining package* in R were excluded for this analysis.

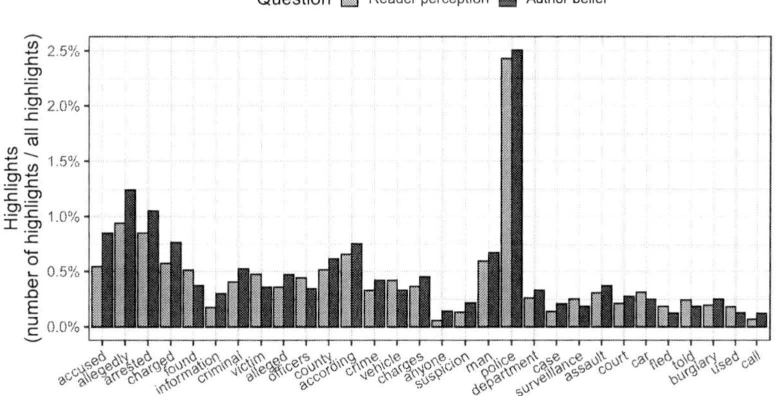

Figure 5: Words with the largest highlighting difference between the two guilt questions.

Conventionalized devices like these hedges, which signal lack of commitment in reporting, become even more prominent in the *Author belief* condition. This supports Kreiss et al.'s earlier findings of the relevance of these words for *Author belief* and not *Reader perception*, and further suggests that readers appear to have some metalinguistic awareness for this difference.

4 Models

This section summarizes the family of models we consider in this work. All of them begin with BERT. We explore models with and without additional unsupervised pretraining on crime stories. We build regression models on top of these parameters using just the CLS token, which is the initial token in all BERT input sequences and is often taken to provide an aggregate sequence representation, as well as mean-pooling over all the final output states, and we additionally define extensions for predicting token-level highlighting.

4.1 Guilt Ratings

BERT (Devlin et al., 2019) is a Transformer-based architecture (Vaswani et al., 2017) that is usually trained jointly to do masked language modeling and next sentence prediction. The inputs are sequences of tokens $[x_0, \ldots, x_n]$, with x_0 designated as CLS and x_n designated as SEP. BERT maps these inputs to a sequence of output representations $[h_0, \ldots, h_n]$.

Our two rating categories, *Reader perception* and *Author belief*, define two separate tasks. We model them separately. For each, the core regres-

sion model is given by $hW_r + b_r$, where W_r is a vector of weights, b_r is a bias term, and h is derived from the states $[h_0, \ldots, h_n]$. In the CLS-based approach, $h = h_0$. In the mean-pooling approach, $h = \mathbf{mean}([h_0, \ldots, h_n])$.

The individual regression models are trained using a mean squared error (MSE) loss:

$$J_r(\theta_r) = \frac{1}{m} \sum_{i=1}^{m} \frac{1}{2} \| H_{\theta_r}(x_i) - y_i^r \|^2 \quad (1)$$

Here, m is the number of examples, θ_r represents all the parameters of BERT plus our new task-specific parameters W_r and b_r, y_i^r is the true label for example x_i, and $H_{\theta_r}(x_i)$ is the prediction of the model for example x_i.

4.2 Genre Pretraining

BERT was trained on the BookCorpus (Zhu et al., 2015) and Wikipedia. It often performs well on tasks involving very different data, but any domain shift has the potential to lower performance, and crime stories are a specialized genre. Previous work has shown that in-domain continued pretraining is often beneficial for end-task performance in such situations (e.g. Han and Eisenstein, 2019; Gururangan et al., 2020). We thus evaluate models with and without pretraining on unlabeled crime stories. For this, we use the unlabeled portion of the dataset described in Section 3.1.

4.3 Span Highlighting

We want to understand how authors' low-level linguistic choices affect readers' judgments of suspect

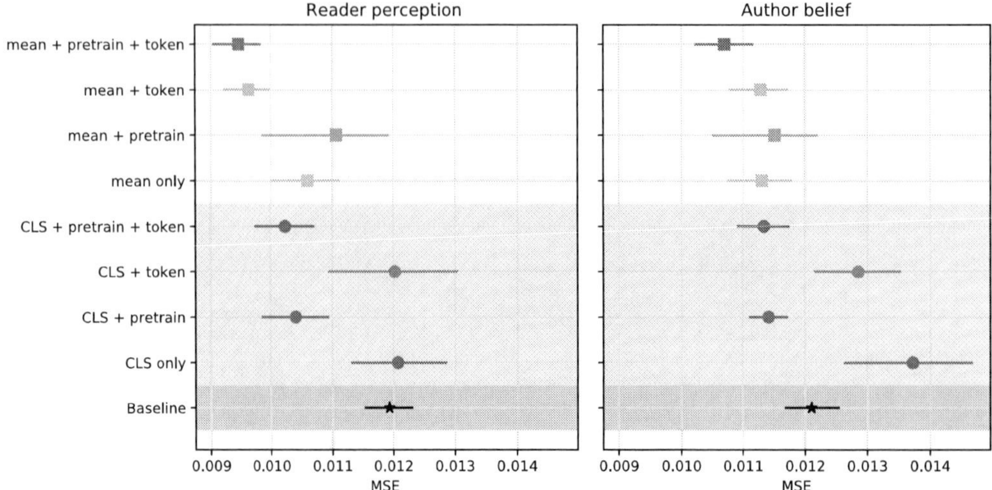

Figure 6: MSE (lower is better) for predicting guilt ratings for the *Reader perception* and *Author belief* questions, with bootstrapped 95% confidence intervals from 20 runs per model. 'CLS' models use just the CLS token for the regression, whereas 'mean' models average all the output heads (Section 4.1). 'pretrain' refers to genre pretraining (Section 4.2), and 'token' refers to token-level supervision from highlighting (Section 4.3).

guilt. To do this, we utilize the span-level annotation in SuspectGuilt. Annotations are coded as 1 if the token was highlighted, and 0 otherwise. We merge the annotations of each news story to form a supplemental regression task, where the target value is the mean of the annotations. We use the output representation of each token from BERT and apply a linear regression similar to (1):

$$J_t(\theta_t) = \frac{1}{n}\frac{1}{m}\sum_{i=1}^{n}\frac{1}{2}\|H_{\theta_t}(x_{ij}) - y_{ij}^t\|^2 \quad (2)$$

Here, m is the number of examples, n is the number of tokens, and x_{ij} and y_{ij} stand for the jth token in example i, with corresponding token label y_{ij}^t. θ_t denotes all the BERT parameters plus token-level regression parameters W_t and b_t, and $H_{\theta_t}(x_{ij})$ is the prediction of the model for x_{ij}.

Our problem formulation might be taken to more naturally suggest a logistic regression. However, we opted for a linear regression objective instead, in the hopes that this would better capture not just the probability that a token is important, but also *how important these tokens are*. The linear regression performed better in our evaluations, though the improvements over the logistic were modest.

	dev	test
BERT-based	2.224	2.223
Genre Pretrained	0.884	0.887

Table 1: Losses with and without genre pretraining.

4.4 Joint Objective

The joint loss is a combination of the guilt-rating and span-highlighting objectives (1) and (2):

$$J = J_r(\theta_r) + \lambda J_t(\theta_t) \quad (3)$$

where λ is a ratio of the losses that can be tuned.

5 Experiments

In this section, we report the evaluation procedure for the models described in Section 4. The results underline the usefulness of genre-pretraining and the rich annotations in the SuspectGuilt corpus.

5.1 Methods

We use the BERT-base uncased parameters for all of our experiments.

As discussed in Section 4.2, we performed pretraining with the ≈470K unlabeled articles from the dataset described in Section 3.1. We split the dataset into 80% training, 10% dev, and 10% test sets. Additional details are in Appendix B.1. Table 1 summarizes the quality of pretraining. The

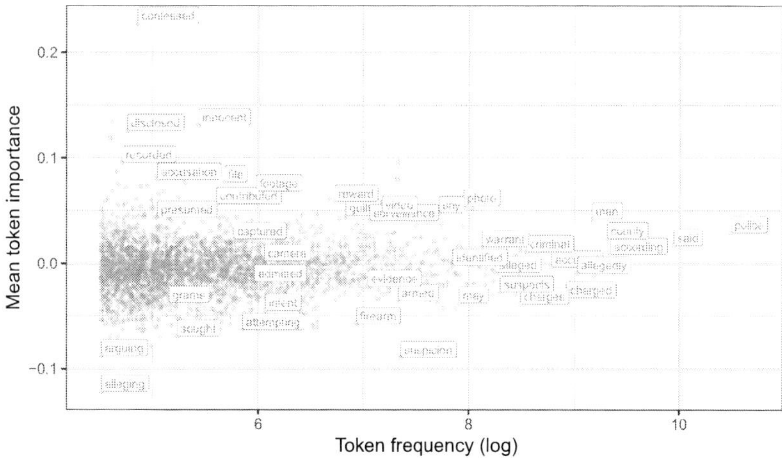

Figure 7: Mean model token importance by frequency. Words that received the most highlights overall (see Figure 3) are presented in red, other words in grey. In contrast to the highlighting data in Section 3.1, the token importance measure differentiates between tokens that increase (above 0 mean token importance) and decrease the predicted rating (below 0 mean token importance).

loss reduces up to 74%, suggesting that genre pretraining could significantly improve in-domain performance. We evaluate the end-to-end performance of the genre pretraining next.

For the core guilt-rating prediction tasks, we split the SuspectGuilt dataset into 85% training and 15% held-out test sets. We perform 5-fold cross validation and grid search on the training set. We then pick the best hyperparameters based on the best averaged loss of the 5-fold models, train our final model using the full training set for that fold, and report the final performance on the test set using the final model. We repeat the whole experiment with 20 different training-test splits to test the stability and significance of the performance. Additional details are given in Appendix B.2. We obtain a mean baseline by predicting everything as the mean values of the training set. We test the significance of *whether A is better than B* using the Wilcoxon signed-rank test (Wilcoxon, 1992).

5.2 Results and Discussion

Our results are summarized in Figure 6, which gives means and bootstrapped 95% confidence intervals. (Table 2 in our appendix gives the precise numerical values with standard deviations, and expands on the statistical analyses.)

The results suggest that *Author belief* is a harder task than *Reader perception*. This is aligned with the human results in Section 3.3.

In general, the mean-pooling models are sub-

stantially better than the CLS-based ones. Indeed, we fail to find evidence that BERT with the CLS token improves performance over the baseline ($p = 0.440$ for *Reader perception*; $p = 0.996$ for *Author belief*). Furthermore, when using both genre pretraining and token supervision, mean pooling is also significantly better than using the CLS token ($p = 0.001$ for *Reader perception*; $p = 0.022$ for *Author belief*).

Overall, a mean pooling model that makes use of genre pretraining as well as span-level supervision achieves the best performance. Span-level annotations are especially beneficial for the task of *Author belief* prediction, where this model significantly outperforms its closest competitors (e.g., when comparing against token supervision alone, $p = 0.022$). We thus conclude that both token-level supervision and genre pretraining provide important information for SuspectGuilt tasks.

6   Gradient-Based Token Importance

Although our models predict human guilt judgments well, the performance metrics don't tell us *how* they make predictions. Do they use information similarly to what we see in the human highlighting? Recent gradient-based methods for assessing feature importance in models like BERT (Sundararajan et al., 2017; Shrikumar et al., 2017) can help us answer this question.

Figure 7 presents one analysis of this form. We ran the Integrated Gradients method of Sundararajan et al., as implemented in the PyTorch Captum library, on models which received genre pretraining but no highlighting supervision. The figure includes test-set runs averaged across 20 models with different random train–test splits. A positive score means that the token increases the predicted rating; a negative score corresponds to a decrease.

Like our highlighting data, the neural network's importance scores show the highest variance for words with low frequency. Words that received higher highlighting proportions for their frequency primarily affect the model predictions positively. In addition, we find that words that are more likely than random to be highlighted (as described in Section 3) are also significantly more likely to receive a higher token importance score in the model (Welch Two Sample t-test: $p < 0.01$). Beyond this, however, there is little correlation between the absolute attribution score for each word and its highlighting proportion ($r = 0.07$). While we can't rule out the possibility that this traces to the approximations introduced by Integrated Gradients, it seems likely that it helps explain why the span highlighting objective has a large impact on model predictions, as it is bringing in very different information than the model would otherwise attend to.

7 Conclusion

We introduced the SuspectGuilt corpus, which provides a basis for a quantitative study of how readers arrive at judgments of *Reader perception* and *Author belief*. We also showed that SuspectGuilt can be used to train predictive models on top of BERT parameters, and that these models are improved by genre-specific pretraining and supervision derived from token-level highlighting.

Understanding how news reporting affects reader judgments is a difficult task. The span-level highlighting in SuspectGuilt provides some insight into the factors at work here. We sought to match this with an introspective analysis of our predictive models using the gradient-based token importance method of Sundararajan et al. (2017). This yielded a very different picture from what we see in SuspectGuilt. Ultimately, this combination of annotations and model introspection might lead to new insights concerning how our models make decisions in this and other domains.

We also hope that this work paves the way to large-scale studies of how readers formulate judgments of guilt in crime reporting and encourages the development of systems that provide guidance on the presentation of these reports.

8 Acknowledgments

We thank the anonymous reviewers, Judith Degen, Daniel Lassiter, Michael Franke, and Sebastian Schuster for their generous comments and valuable suggestions on earlier versions of this work. Special thanks also to our Mechanical Turk workers for their essential contributions. This work is supported in part by a Google Faculty Research Award. Any remaining errors are our own.

References

Jean-François Bonnefon and Gaëlle Villejoubert. 2006. Tactful or doubtful? expectations of politeness explain the severity bias in the interpretation of probability phrases. *Psychological Science*, 17(9):747–751.

Aida Mostafazadeh Davani, Leigh Yeh, Mohammad Atari, Brendan Kennedy, Gwenyth Portillo Wightman, Elaine Gonzalez, Natalie Delong, Rhea Bhatia, Arineh Mirinjian, Xiang Ren, et al. 2019. Reporting the unreported: Event extraction for analyzing the local representation of hate crimes. In *Proceedings of the 2019 Conference on Empirical Methods in Natural Language Processing and the 9th International Joint Conference on Natural Language Processing (EMNLP-IJCNLP)*, pages 5757–5761.

Jacob Devlin, Ming-Wei Chang, Kenton Lee, and Kristina Toutanova. 2019. BERT: Pre-training of deep bidirectional transformers for language understanding. In *Proceedings of the 2019 Conference of the North American Chapter of the Association for Computational Linguistics: Human Language Technologies, Volume 1 (Long and Short Papers)*, pages 4171–4186, Minneapolis, Minnesota. Association for Computational Linguistics.

Amanda M Durik, M Anne Britt, Rebecca Reynolds, and Jennifer Storey. 2008. The effects of hedges in persuasive arguments: A nuanced analysis of language. *Journal of Language and Social Psychology*, 27(3):217–234.

Bonnie Erickson, E Allan Lind, Bruce C Johnson, and William M O'Barr. 1978. Speech style and impression formation in a court setting: The effects of "powerful" and "powerless" speech. *Journal of Experimental Social Psychology*, 14(3):266–279.

Caitlin M Fausey and Lera Boroditsky. 2010. Subtle linguistic cues influence perceived blame and financial liability. *Psychonomic Bulletin & Review*, 17(5):644–650.

Scott Ferson, Jason O'Rawe, Andrei Antonenko, Jack Siegrist, James Mickley, Christian C Luhmann, Kari

Sentz, and Adam M Finkel. 2015. Natural language of uncertainty: numeric hedge words. *International Journal of Approximate Reasoning*, 57:19–39.

Kai von Fintel and Anthony S. Gillies. 2010. Must ... stay ... strong. *Natural Language Semantics*, 18(4):351–383.

Suchin Gururangan, Ana Marasović, Swabha Swayamdipta, Kyle Lo, Iz Beltagy, Doug Downey, and Noah A Smith. 2020. Don't stop pretraining: Adapt language models to domains and tasks. *Proceedings of ACL*.

Xiaochuang Han and Jacob Eisenstein. 2019. Unsupervised domain adaptation of contextualized embeddings: A case study in early modern english. *Proceedings of EMNLP-IJCNLP*.

Jakob D Jensen. 2008. Scientific uncertainty in news coverage of cancer research: Effects of hedging on scientists' and journalists' credibility. *Human communication research*, 34(3):347–369.

Kankawin Kowsrihawat, Peerapon Vateekul, and Prachya Boonkwan. 2018. Predicting judicial decisions of criminal cases from Thai Supreme Court using bi-directional GRU with attention mechanism. In *2018 5th Asian Conference on Defense Technology (ACDT)*, pages 50–55. IEEE.

Elisa Kreiss, Michael Franke, and Judith Degen. 2019. Uncertain evidence statements and guilt perception in iterative reproductions of crime stories. In *Proceedings of the Annual Meeting of the Cognitive Science Society*, volume 41.

Cheolhyoung Lee, Kyunghyun Cho, and Wanmo Kang. 2020. Mixout: Effective regularization to finetune large-scale pretrained language models. In *International Conference on Learning Representations*.

Marie-Catherine de Marneffe, Christopher D. Manning, and Christopher Potts. 2012. Did it happen? The pragmatic complexity of veridicality assessment. *Computational Linguistics*, 38(2):301–333.

Marius Mosbach, Maksym Andriushchenko, and Dietrich Klakow. 2020. On the stability of fine-tuning bert: Misconceptions, explanations, and strong baselines. *arXiv preprint arXiv:2006.04884*.

Adam Paszke, Sam Gross, Francisco Massa, Adam Lerer, James Bradbury, Gregory Chanan, Trevor Killeen, Zeming Lin, Natalia Gimelshein, Luca Antiga, Alban Desmaison, Andreas Kopf, Edward Yang, Zachary DeVito, Martin Raison, Alykhan Tejani, Sasank Chilamkurthy, Benoit Steiner, Lu Fang, Junjie Bai, and Soumith Chintala. 2019. Pytorch: An imperative style, high-performance deep learning library. In *Advances in Neural Information Processing Systems 32*, pages 8024–8035. Curran Associates, Inc.

Reid Pryzant, Richard Diehl Martinez, Nathan Dass, Sadao Kurohashi, Dan Jurafsky, and Diyi Yang. 2020. Automatically neutralizing subjective bias in text. In *Proceedings of the AAAI Conference on Artificial Intelligence*, volume 34, pages 480–489.

Marek Rei and Anders Søgaard. 2019. Jointly learning to label sentences and tokens. In *Proceedings of the AAAI Conference on Artificial Intelligence*, volume 33, pages 6916–6923.

Victoria L. Rubin. 2007. Stating with certainty or stating with doubt: Intercoder reliability results for manual annotation of epistemically modalized statements. In *Human Language Technologies 2007: The Conference of the North American Chapter of the Association for Computational Linguistics; Companion Volume, Short Papers*, pages 141–144, Rochester, New York. Association for Computational Linguistics.

Avanti Shrikumar, Peyton Greenside, and Anshul Kundaje. 2017. Learning important features through propagating activation differences. In *Proceedings of the 34th International Conference on Machine Learning-Volume 70*, pages 3145–3153. JMLR. org.

Mandy Simons. 2007. Observations on embedding verbs, evidentiality, and presupposition. *Lingua*, 117(6):1034–1056.

Matthew Stone. 1994. The reference argument of epistemic 'must'. Technical Report IRCS TR 97-06, Institute for Research in Cognitive Science, University of Pennsylvania.

Mukund Sundararajan, Ankur Taly, and Qiqi Yan. 2017. Axiomatic attribution for deep networks. In *Proceedings of the 34th International Conference on Machine Learning-Volume 70*, pages 3319–3328. JMLR. org.

Ashish Vaswani, Noam Shazeer, Niki Parmar, Jakob Uszkoreit, Llion Jones, Aidan N Gomez, Ł ukasz Kaiser, and Illia Polosukhin. 2017. Attention is all you need. In I. Guyon, U. V. Luxburg, S. Bengio, H. Wallach, R. Fergus, S. Vishwanathan, and R. Garnett, editors, *Advances in Neural Information Processing Systems 30*, pages 5998–6008. Curran Associates, Inc.

Michael Benedict L Virtucio, Jeffrey A Aborot, John Kevin C Abonita, Roxanne S Aviñante, Rother Jay B Copino, Michelle P Neverida, Vanesa O Osiana, Elmer C Peramo, Joanna G Syjuco, and Glenn Brian A Tan. 2018. Predicting decisions of the philippine supreme court using natural language processing and machine learning. In *2018 IEEE 42nd Annual Computer Software and Applications Conference (COMPSAC)*, volume 2, pages 130–135. IEEE.

Aaron Steven White and Kyle Rawlins. 2018. The role of veridicality and factivity in clause selection. In *Proceedings of the 48th Annual Meeting of the North East Linguistic Society*, Amherst, MA. GLSA Publications.

Aaron Steven White, Rachel Rudinger, Kyle Rawlins, and Benjamin Van Durme. 2018. Lexicosyntactic inference in neural models. In *Proceedings of the 2018 Conference on Empirical Methods in Natural Language Processing*, pages 4717–4724, Brussels, Belgium. Association for Computational Linguistics.

Frank Wilcoxon. 1992. Individual comparisons by ranking methods. In *Breakthroughs in statistics*, pages 196–202. Springer.

Thomas Wolf, Lysandre Debut, Victor Sanh, Julien Chaumond, Clement Delangue, Anthony Moi, Pierric Cistac, Tim Rault, R'emi Louf, Morgan Funtowicz, and Jamie Brew. 2019. Huggingface's transformers: State-of-the-art natural language processing. *ArXiv*, abs/1910.03771.

Yukun Zhu, Ryan Kiros, Rich Zemel, Ruslan Salakhutdinov, Raquel Urtasun, Antonio Torralba, and Sanja Fidler. 2015. Aligning books and movies: Towards story-like visual explanations by watching movies and reading books. In *Proceedings of the IEEE international conference on computer vision*, pages 19–27.

Appendices

A Data

2,818 annotators contributed to 3,463 submissions on Amazon's Mechanical Turk. The approximate time for completion was 15 minutes, and each participant was paid $2.50. We restricted participation to IP addresses within the US and an approval rate higher than 97%. Participants were asked to read 5 stories and respond to three questions about them (as described in Section 3.2). The full design of the trials is shown in Figure 8.

We excluded participants who indicated that they did the study incorrectly or were confused (544), whose self-reported native language was not English (71), who spent less than 3.5 minutes on the task (53), and who gave more then 2 out of 5 erroneous responses in the control questions (359). A response is considered erroneous when a clearly true or false question incorrectly received a slider value below or above 50 (the center of the scale) respectively. Additionally, we excluded 120 annotations because annotators had seen this story in a previous submission. Overall, we excluded 1,035 submissions and 120 annotations (15,405 annotations out of 51,945, resulting in 36,420 annotations).

A majority of annotators (89%) only participated once, which makes up 74% of all annotations. Only 14 annotators participated more than three times (0.7%).

The average age of annotators was 36 with a slightly higher proportion of male over female participants. The median time annotators spent on the study was 15.2 minutes, which is in-line with our original time estimates. Overall, annotators indicated that they enjoyed the study.

Annotators also had the option to indicate that the question cannot be applied to the news report. Overall, participants rarely used that option, but more so for the question about the *Author belief* (1.6%) than the *Reader perception* (10.5%) question. If several annotators agree that a question cannot be answered in the context of one particular story, it might be an indication that this story is not suitable for the corpus. We therefore decided to exclude stories where this box was selected more than 30% of the time with that particular question. Further inspection showed that this mainly affected summary news articles which addressed multiple stories and suspects and therefore the questions could not be uniquely attributed to one specific case.

B Experiments

B.1 Genre Pretraining

In this section, we describe the details of genre pretraining of BERT on our corpus. We set the maximum length to 400 tokens, with the tokens determined by the BERT tokenizer. This covers most of the instances in our corpus. We trained the model for 100K steps (roughly 30 epochs) using masked language modeling as described in (Devlin et al., 2019), with a mask probability of 0.15, a batch size of 128, and a learning rate of $5 \cdot 10^{-5}$. All experiments throughout this paper are based on PyTorch (Paszke et al., 2019) and Huggingface's Transformers (Wolf et al., 2019).

B.2 Predicting Guilt

In this section, we describe the hyperparameters used in our experiment.

For the basic models where there is no token supervision, we use the following hyperparameters

- Number of epochs: 5
- Warmup ratio: 10%
- Learning rate: 3E−5, 5E−5
- Random Seed: 0, 1
- Batch size: 16
- Checkpoints: 100 steps per checkpoint

1) Slider Rating

A Canton man accused of brandishing a handgun when his estranged wife showed up with another man to pick up their children is facing criminal charges, police said. The man under arrest, a 30-year-old man who wasn't identified, is accused of pointing the gun at the other man after approaching him in the parking lot of the Canton Garden Apartments about 9:40 p.m. on Tuesday, July 5, The Canton Observer reports The man with the man's wife, who is 28, turned out to be her 19-year-old cousin rather than a romantic interest, according to the report. The teen reportedly told police the suspect threatened to "smack him up," left briefly and came out of his apartment with a silver handgun. The teen took cover. The suspect's brother defused the situation, according to the report. Police confiscated the handgun and five rounds of ammunition and took the suspect into custody. » For more Canton police news, go to hometownlife.com.

How likely is it that the main suspect is / the main suspects are **guilty**?

very unlikely ———————————————————— very likely

☐ Doesn't apply.

SUBMIT RESPONSE

Optional: Is there something else you would like to add?

2) Highlights

A Canton man accused of brandishing a handgun when his estranged wife showed up with another man to pick up their children is facing criminal charges, police said. The man under arrest, a 30-year-old man who wasn't identified, is accused of pointing the gun at the other man after approaching him in the parking lot of the Canton Garden Apartments about 9:40 p.m. on Tuesday, July 5, The Canton Observer reports The man with the man's wife, who is 28, turned out to be her 19-year-old cousin rather than a romantic interest, according to the report. **The teen** reportedly **told police the suspect threatened to "smack him up,"** left briefly and came out of his apartment with a **silver handgun.** The teen took cover. The suspect's brother defused the situation, according to the report. **Police confiscated the handgun and five rounds of ammunition** and took the suspect into custody. » For more Canton police news, go to hometownlife.com.

ERASE

How likely is it that the main suspect is / the main suspects are **guilty**?

Now please **highlight** in the text why you gave your response. If you're not happy with your selection, click on the ERASE button and start again.

NEXT

Optional: Is there something else you would like to add?

Figure 8: Participants rated a story on a continuous slider. After submitting, they highlighted the passages in the story that they considered to be most relevant for their assessment. At this point, they could not return to the previous screen to change the rating they gave.

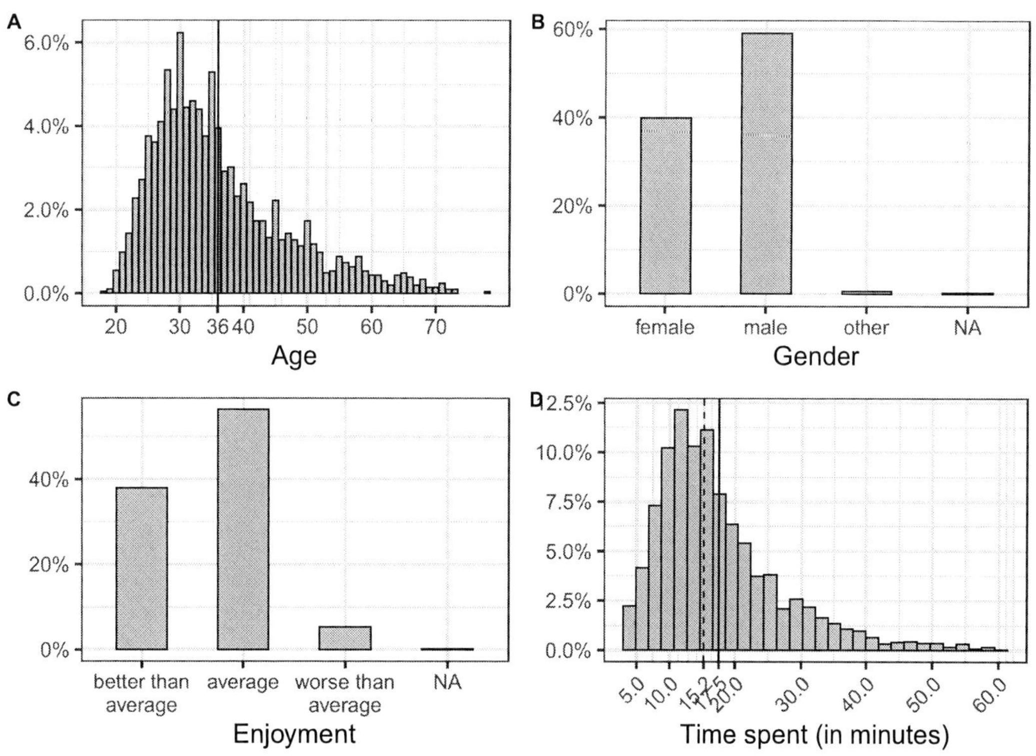

Figure 9: Participant demographics after exclusions.

	Reader perception Mean $_{\pm\text{std}}$	Author belief Mean $_{\pm\text{std}}$
Mean Baseline	0.0119 $_{\pm0.0009}$	0.0121 $_{\pm0.0010}$
BERT (CLS)	0.0121 $_{\pm0.0018}$	0.0137 $_{\pm0.0025}$
+ pretraining	0.0104 $_{\pm0.0013}$	0.0114 $_{\pm0.0007}$
+ token supervision	0.0120 $_{\pm0.0024}$	0.0129 $_{\pm0.0015}$
+ pretraining + token supervision	0.0102 $_{\pm0.0011}$	0.0113 $_{\pm0.0009}$
BERT (Mean)	0.0106 $_{\pm0.0013}$	0.0113 $_{\pm0.0012}$
+ pretraining	0.0111 $_{\pm0.0024}$	0.0115 $_{\pm0.0019}$
+ token supervision	0.0096 $_{\pm0.0009}$	0.0113 $_{\pm0.0011}$
+ pretraining + token supervision	**0.0095** $_{\pm0.0009}$	**0.0107** $_{\pm0.0011}$

Table 2: MSE for predicting guilt ratings for the *Reader perception* and *Author belief* questions. The models themselves are defined in Section 4. We report the mean and standard derivation values from 20 different runs. Bold denotes the best performance.

We also experimented with different number of epochs, batch sizes, and oversampling tail cases with different ratios in an initial small-scale study. We found that the current set of hyperparameters performs well in general. As adding more hyperparameter options is computationally intensive, we decided to use this set for our full-scale experiments.

When training the final model, we use the checkpoint whose corresponding steps are closet to 1.25 times the average number of steps of best performing checkpoints in the 5-fold cross validation.

For the models with token supervision, we use the same set of hyperparameters of no token supervision models except we only use one seed and add a hyperparameter of the loss ratio λ, with options of $[1, 2]$.

B.3 Numerical Results

Table 2 gives the corresponding numerical values for Figure 6. Whereas Figure 6 gives bootstrapped confidence intervals, here we given standard deviations to quantify the amount of variation seen across runs. Below are some additional details on these comparisons ('AB' = *Author belief*; 'RP' = *Reader perception*. Our statistical test here is the Wilcoxon signed-rank test.)

1. BERT with the CLS token does not improve performance compared to a simple mean baseline ($p = 0.449$ for RP and $p = 0.998$ for AB), while BERT with mean-pooling achieves better performance compared to the mean baseline ($p < 0.001$ for RP and $p = 0.004$ for AB).

2. The differences between using mean pooling and the CLS token are significant ($p = 0.003$ for RP and $p < 0.001$ for AB).

3. When using both the genre pretraining and the token supervision, mean pooling is significantly better than using the CLS token ($p = 0.001$ for RP and $p = 0.022$ for AB).

4. Overall, a mean pooling model that makes use of genre pretraining as well as span-level supervision achieves the best performance, significantly outperforming other models ($p < 0.001$ for RP and $p = 0.027$ for AB when comparing with the mean baseline; $p = 0.001$ for RP and $p = 0.020$ for AB with genre pretraining; and $p = 0.131$ for RP and $p = 0.022$ for AB with joint supervision).

5. Neither mean pooling models with genre pretraining ($p = 0.649$ for RP and $p = 0.464$ for AB) nor span-level supervision ($p = 0.001$ for RP and $p = 0.215$ for AB) alone can improve performance substantially in comparison to the mean baseline (only joint supervision for RP is significant).

On the Frailty of Universal POS Tags for Neural UD Parsers

Mark Anderson   **Carlos Gómez-Rodríguez**
Universidade da Coruña, CITIC
FASTPARSE Lab, LyS Research Group,
Departamento de Ciencias de la Computación y Tecnologías de la Información
Campus Elviña, s/n, 15071 A Coruña, Spain
{m.anderson, carlos.gomez}@udc.es

Abstract

We present an analysis on the effect UPOS accuracy has on parsing performance. Results suggest that leveraging UPOS tags as features for neural parsers requires a prohibitively high tagging accuracy and that the use of gold tags offers a non-linear increase in performance, suggesting some sort of exceptionality. We also investigate what aspects of predicted UPOS tags impact parsing accuracy the most, highlighting some potentially meaningful linguistic facets of the problem.

1 Introduction

Part-of-speech (POS) tags and dependency parsing have formed a long-standing union in NLP. But equally long-standing has been the question of its efficacy. Prior to the prevalence of deep learning in NLP, they were shown to be useful for syntactic disambiguation in certain contexts (Voutilainen, 1998; Dalrymple, 2006; Alfared and Béchet, 2012). However, for neural network implementations, especially those which utilise character embeddings, POS tags have been shown to be much less useful (Ballesteros et al., 2015; de Lhoneux et al., 2017).

Others have found that POS tags can still have a positive impact when using character representations given that the accuracy of the predicted POS tags used is sufficiently high (Dozat et al., 2017). Smith et al. (2018) undertook a systematic study of the impact of features for Universal Dependency (UD) parsing and found that using universal POS (UPOS) tags does still offer a marginal improvement for their transition-based neural parser. The use of fine-grained POS tags still seems to garner noticeable improvements (Ammar et al., 2016).

Latterly, POS tags have been commonly utilised implicitly for neural network parsers in multi-learning frameworks where they can be leveraged without the cost of error-propagation (Zhang and Weiss, 2016; Yang et al., 2017; Li et al., 2018; Nguyen and Verspoor, 2018; Zhang et al., 2020). Beyond multi-learning systems, Strzyz et al. (2019) introduced dependency parsing as sequence labelling by encoding dependencies using relative positions of UPOS tags, thus explicitly requiring them at runtime.

We follow the work of Smith et al. (2018) and evaluate the interplay of word embeddings, character embeddings, and POS tags as features for two modern parsers, one a graph-based parser, Biaffine, and the other a transition-based parser, UUParser (Dozat and Manning, 2017; Smith et al., 2018). Similar to Zhang et al. (2020), we focus on the contribution of POS tags but evaluate UPOS tags.

Contribution We analyse the effect UPOS accuracy has on two dependency parser systems for a number of UD treebanks. Our results suggest that in order to leverage UPOS tags as explicit features for these neural parsers, a prohibitively high tagging accuracy is needed, and that gold tag annotation seems to possess some exceptionality. We also investigate what aspects of predicted UPOS tags have the most impact on parsing accuracy.

2 Experimental details

We ran three experiments to measure the impact POS[1] tagging accuracy has on parsing performance when using POS tags as features. Experiment 1 considered the POS tagging accuracy as a controlled variable, set by training taggers as described below and then using the output of these taggers as features for parsers. Experiment 2 was similar, except the size of character embeddings were also changed. Experiment 3 was an extension to test the impact of taggers in an optimal setting where they achieve very high accuracies.

---

[1] From this point on we refer to universal POS tags as POS tags rather than UPOS tags for sake of efficiency.

Proceedings of the 24th Conference on Computational Natural Language Learning, pages 69–96
Online, November 19-20, 2020. ©2020 Association for Computational Linguistics
https://doi.org/10.18653/v1/P17

Data We use the same subset of UD v2.4 tree-banks (Nivre et al., 2019) as Anderson and Gómez-Rodríguez (2020): Ancient Greek Perseus, Chinese GSD, English EWT, Finnish TDT, Hebrew HTB, Russian GSD, Tamil TTB, Uyghur UDT, and Wolof WTB. We used fastText word embeddings for each language except for Ancient Greek and Wolof (Grave et al., 2018). For Ancient Greek we use embeddings from Ginter et al. (2017) and for Wolof those from Heinzerling and Strube (2018). When necessary, we reduced the dimensions to 100 using the algorithm of Raunak (2017).

2.1 Methodology

POS taggers We train POS taggers for each tree-bank separately using the sequence-labelling framework NCRF++ (Yang and Zhang, 2018). We train taggers so as to have POS taggers with varying accuracies ranging from 60 to the maximum score the network can achieve (that fits our binning procedure). The accuracy bins we used were increments of 2.5 ± 0.3 from 60 to 80 and increments of 1 ± 0.3 from 80 onwards. We allowed a small window around the desired accuracy for each bin to account for the fact we might never see a model with that exact accuracy. To obtain taggers with varying accuracies, we train each tagger as normal and save models when they reach a certain accuracy. We chose to vary the accuracy of the taggers in this more *natural* way so as to better represent how the taggers would likely behave if they were trained normally but never exceeded the accuracy of a given bin, so it is more likely that easier patterns are learnt first and systematic failures are more likely than if we randomly added noise.

Network details We use the default parameters for both parsers, i.e. those reported in each subsequent paper. We use v2.3 of UUParser[2] and use a PyTorch implementation of Biaffine.[3] The features to the networks are the word embeddings as mentioned above, character embeddings, and POS tag embeddings, with the latter two embeddings being randomly initialised. For Experiment 1, the character embedding size was 32 and varied as specified below for Experiment 2. The BiLSTM output dimension of the character embedding layer was 100 and the embedding dimension of the word and POS embeddings were also 100. These dimensions were chosen to control the contribution from each feature, but it is obviously feasible that optimising these contributions could result in different absolute results. However, keeping these static unless purposefully changing them for controlled input means we can make relative comparisons.

Experiment 1 We trained parsers for each tree-bank with gold tags and with predicted tags using a subset of the POS taggers with accuracy bins 60, 70, 80, 86, 91, and 93. The values were chosen such that we could cover a reasonable range and include as many treebanks as possible (e.g. only English, Hebrew, and Russian have taggers which achieve 93% accuracy). The parsers trained with predicted tags are run on inputs tagged by the same model, and those trained with gold tags are tested both on gold and a range of predicted tags. The goal of this experiment was to test the sensitivity of parsers to POS tagging accuracy for different treebanks. We also trained parsers without POS tags as a baseline for comparison.

Experiment 2 We trained parsers for each tree-bank with gold tags and with predicted tags using a subset of the POS taggers with accuracy bins 80, 86, and the max accuracy for each treebank which was on average 91(3). Each parser is run on inputs tagged by the same model. We used varying character embedding sizes of 32, 100, 180, 325, and 500. We also train parsers with these varying character embedding sizes with no POS tags as a baseline.

Experiment 3 We trained parsers with and without predicted POS tags for treebanks for which we obtained high-scoring POS taggers with a mean accuracy of 96(2) to evaluate the trend observed in Experiment 1. We use the settings from Experiment 1. The treebanks used were Catalan AnCora, Japanese GSD, Latin ITTB, and Polish PDB.

3 Results and analysis

Experiment 1 The results of Experiment 1 are shown in Figure 1, where the average difference in attachment scores between the baseline parsers (without POS tags) and those with differing POS tag accuracies are shown. We show the differences in attachment scores rather than the absolute values, as averaging over treebanks obscures differences.

There is an unsurprising relation between parsing score and tagging performance when training with gold POS tags. What is less expected is how

---

[2]UUParser GitHub from Smith et al. (2018).

[3]Biaffine PyTorch GitHub based on Dozat et al. (2017).

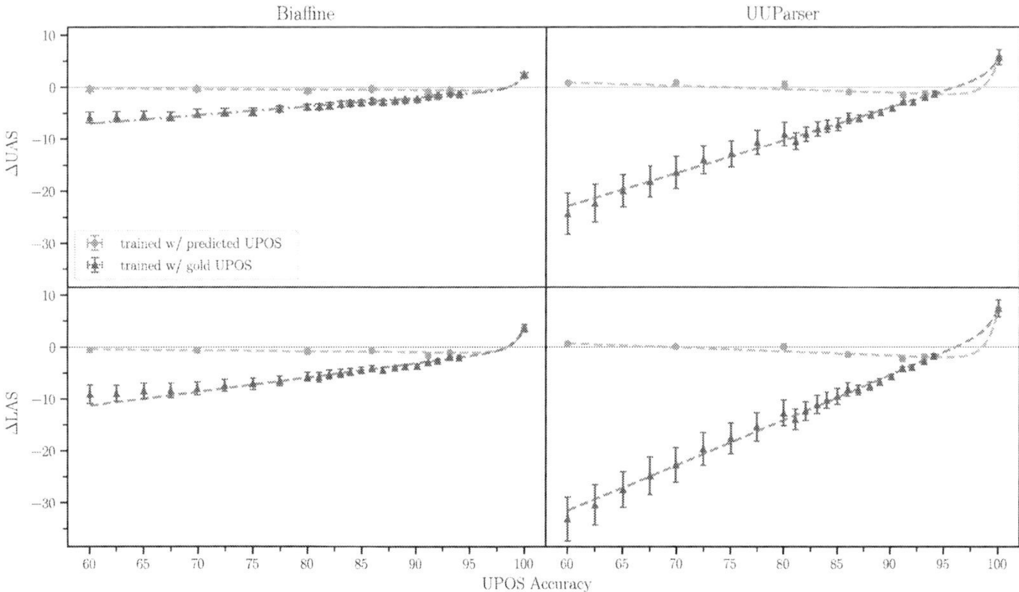

Figure 1: Average Δ attachment scores across all treebanks over the relative baseline parsers trained without POS tags, plotted with respect to POS tag accuracy for parsers trained with predicted (blue, circles) and gold (red, triangles) tags.

little of an impact is observed when using predicted tags during training, with an almost consistent performance with respect to POS tag accuracy.

The gold training trend for the graph-based parser suggests that it is less sensitive to POS tag accuracy than the transition-based parser. This is likely due to the transition-based parser being able to leverage POS tags more, so that it will see more of an impact when tagging accuracy is low. This is somewhat corroborated by the larger positive difference over the baseline when using gold tags at prediction time for UUParser compared to the increase seen for Biaffine.

Another notable phenomenon is that the results for parsing texts annotated with gold POS (rightmost point in each plot) outperform what could be expected from extrapolating the general trends. This raises the question as to whether this is due to smooth nonlinear accuracy increases in the rightmost part of the curves (where we couldn't obtain taggers) or to a sudden jump at the very end in a hockey-stick shape, indicating an exceptionality of gold POS tags and inadequacy of even very accurate but imperfect POS tags (which is relevant under the assumption that tagging accuracy can be pushed further with future model and/or training data improvements). Answering this question was the motivation for Experiment 3.

Almost exclusively, using predicted POS tags

does not outperform the parser trained without any POS tags. Curiously, the only parsers that are marginally better are those trained with predicted POS tags from the least accurate POS taggers.

Figures 6–9 in the Appendix show these results for each treebank separately, and almost all treebanks follow the general trend seen for both parsers. The only exception is Tamil TTB for UUParser, which benefits from POS tags both when training with gold and predicted tags. Tamil TTB is the smallest treebank, and it has the additional difficulty for parsing and tagging of being an agglutinative language, so possibly this combination of factors lends itself well to leveraging POS tags even in less than optimal circumstances. Tamil is also the lowest performing language with respect to POS tagging and parsing accuracy, but compared to Uyghur and Ancient Greek (the next two lowest performing languages) it outperforms both when using gold tags. In fact, Tamil has the biggest difference when using gold tags over the baseline than any other language, suggesting that they might be particularly useful when there is a heightened probability of ambiguity coupled with a dearth of data.

Experiment 2 The average attachment score differences for Experiment 2 are shown in Figure 2. This experiment was initially devised as we anticipated POS tags would have more of a positive

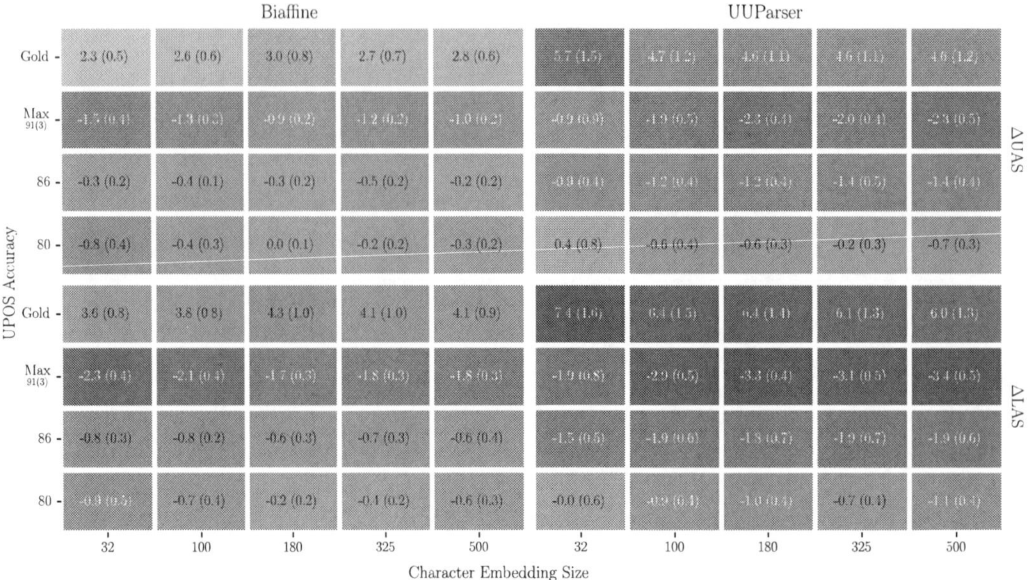

Figure 2: Average Δ attachment scores across all treebanks over the relative baseline parsers trained without POS tags for different character embedding sizes and different POS tag accuracies (80%, 86%, max (average of 91%) tagger accuracy for each treebank, and gold).

effect, especially for higher accuracy taggers, and we wanted to evaluate if having larger character embeddings would offset this. However, as the results of Experiment 1 showed no improvement over not using POS tags at all, this experiment became a verification of the inutility of predicted POS tags instead. And it is clear that in all contexts where predicted tags are used, no matter what the character embedding size is or what parser is used, predicted POS tags perform worse than not using POS tags at all. The unexpected dip in performance as tagging accuracy increases is even clearer here, as this trend is consistent across different character embedding sizes and is the case for both parsers. This decrease in performance is even more marked as the performance actually increases when increasing the character embedding size and not using POS tags at all for UUParser, as shown in

Table 1. This result corroborates one of the many observations from Smith et al. (2018). For the graph-based parser there is a negligible negative impact at higher character embedding sizes. Both parser implementations use a BiLSTM to create the character vector input to the network, so this seems more likely to be a result of the transition-based decoder leveraging features more than the graph-based one. The transition-based parser's ability to leverage POS tags in optimal settings is even clearer in Figure 2, as UUParser has twice the improvement using gold tags than that of Biaffine. Also, the impact of predicted POS tags is more pronounced as character embedding sizes increase for UUParser, but for Biaffine there is only a slight tendency to decrease as the character embedding size increases. We show the breakdown for each treebank in Figures 10–13 where again Tamil is clearly an outlier for UUParser, as it is the only language where any settings with predicted POS tags result in a positive increase (80 POS tag accuracy, character embedding size of 32) and has by far and away the largest increase when using gold tags (a factor of 2 greater than the next best improving language, Wolof, for both UAS and LAS).

Experiment 3   In Figure 1, there is a point around 96-98 POS tag accuracy where the parsers outperform the baselines without POS tags. Due to a lack

	Biaffine		UUParser	
Char	UAS	LAS	UAS	LAS
32	84.0 (5.9)	78.6 (8.7)	77.9 (8.3)	71.9 (10.0)
100	83.9 (6.3)	78.6 (8.9)	79.0 (7.3)	73.0 (9.3)
180	83.4 (6.8)	78.1 (9.4)	79.1 (7.2)	73.1 (9.2)
325	83.6 (6.7)	78.1 (9.5)	79.2 (7.1)	73.3 (8.9)
500	83.6 (6.4)	78.1 (9.1)	79.3 (7.0)	73.4 (8.8)

Table 1: Average attachment scores for different character embedding sizes (Char) without POS tags.

of models in that range, this is just an extrapolation. So we trained parsers with treebanks, listed above in the description of Experiment 3, for which we could obtain high POS tagging accuracy. The results of these parsers are shown in Table 2. Only the top two treebanks with the highest tagging accuracy (Catalan AnCora and Japanese GSD) perform better than using no POS tags, and only for UUParser. However, when the performance is below the baseline the difference is marginal. These results are consistent with the extrapolations in Figure 1 and suggest a sharp increase in the Δ attachment score slopes when POS tagging accuracy is in the 98-100 range, i.e., that predicted POS tags suddenly start being useful when they are very close to gold POS tags. This suggests that there may be certain tag patterns or contexts that are particularly relevant for parsing, but especially difficult for taggers to learn.

3.1 Parsing difficulty of POS tags

We then delved deeper by looking at the difficulty of predicting arcs and labels for each POS tag type. The full results are shown in Figures 14 and 15 in the Appendix, where the average differences in score with respect to the baseline model (no POS tags) are given. X (the UPOS tag for "other") is consistently difficult across parsers and parser types, except that the loss in UAS for UUParser is much smaller than for Biaffine for both training

	Biaffine		UUParser		
	UAS	LAS	UAS	LAS	POS$_{ACC}$
Catalan-AnCora					
Predicted	92.59	89.57	**90.88**	**88.03**	98.26
None	**92.89**	**90.33**	90.82	87.92	n/a
Japanese-GSD					
Predicted	95.02	93.66	**94.56**	**92.94**	97.69
None	**95.12**	**93.54**	94.47	92.74	n/a
Polish-PDB					
Predicted	92.78	89.97	89.25	85.57	97.52
None	**93.64**	**90.94**	**89.32**	**85.60**	n/a
Latin-ITTB					
Predicted	90.92	88.47	86.99	83.99	97.46
None	**91.09**	**88.74**	**87.25**	**84.25**	n/a

Table 2: Performance for treebanks with high scoring POS taggers trained with predicted POS tags, compared to the performance on the same treebanks without using POS tags.

with predicted and gold tags. However, the only time X is consistently better than the baseline model for LAS is when using gold tags at runtime and only with UUParser.

Another noticeable feature in these results is that for the max POS predicted accuracy and gold tag parsers for UUParser, INTJ (interjection) performs significantly better, both using predicted POS tags and gold tags for training, compared to the lower POS tag accuracy parsers. Beyond this, the performances echo the global scores with respect to the tagging accuracy.

Next, we evaluated the correlations (Pearson co-

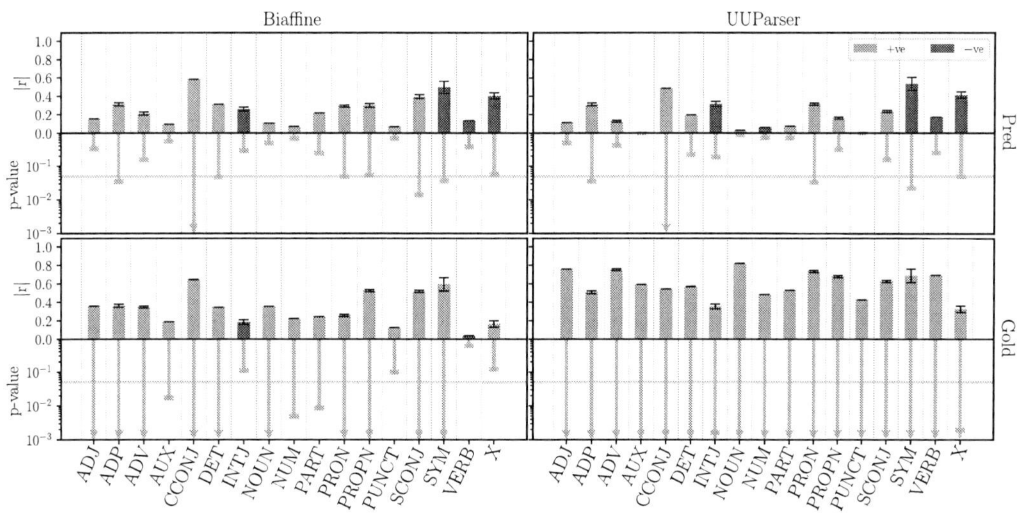

Figure 3: Pearson coefficients for the F1-score for separate POS tags and global LAS where positive (+ve) coefficients are shown in blue and negative (-ve) are shown in red. The corresponding p-values are shown below (orange) where an arrow head means the value was below 0.001. Left subplots are for Biaffine parsers, right for UUParsers, top row is for parsers trained with predicted tags, and bottom for parsers trained with gold tags.

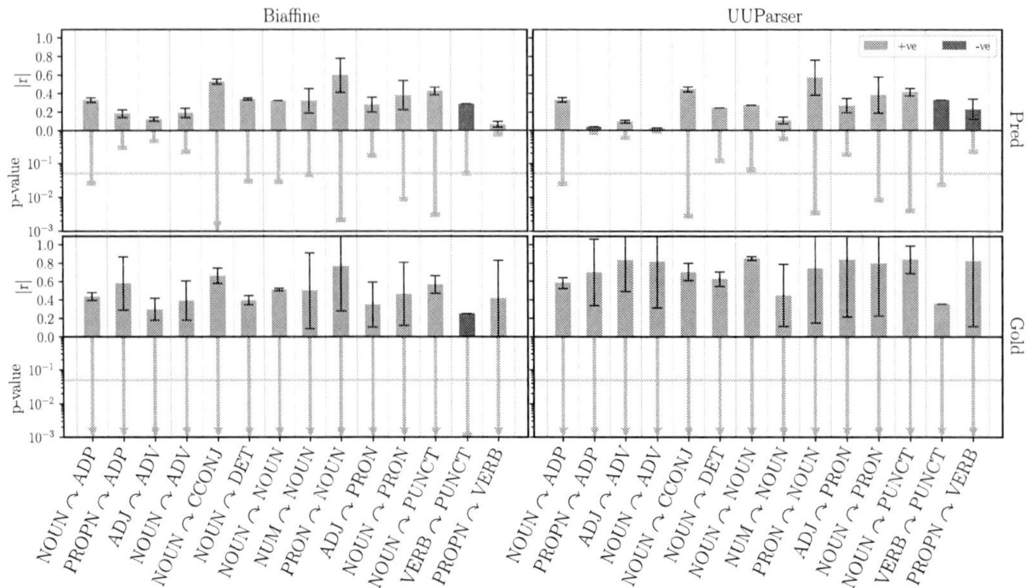

Figure 4: Pearson coefficients for the tagging F1-score for child⌢head pairs and global LAS where positive (+ve) coefficients are shown in blue and negative (-ve) are shown in red. The corresponding p-values are shown below (orange) where an arrow head means the value was below 0.001. Left subplots are for Biaffine parsers, right for UUParsers, top row is for parsers trained with predicted tags, and bottom for parsers trained with gold tags.

efficient) between tagging accuracy for each POS tag and global parsing performance. For these correlation results and all those that follow, we use the same taggers and parsers from Experiment 1. We only report results for LAS for the sake of space.

Figure 3 shows the Pearson coefficient with the corresponding p-value for the correlations between the F1-score for each POS tag and the global LAS score for both Biaffine and UUParser, for both predicted and gold POS tags used in training. Training with gold tags, the accuracy for every tag is positively correlated with parsing performance for UUParser and the correlations are all statistically meaningful. The correlations range from about 0.4 (INTJ and X) to about 0.8 (ADJ, ADV, NOUN, and PRON). For Biaffine, the correlations are much weaker ranging from 0.2 (AUX) to 0.6 (CCONJ, coordinating conjunction, and SYM, symbol) for those which are statistically significant.

For the systems trained with predicted POS tags, the correlations are much weaker for UUParser and only 5 are statistically significant. UUParser and Biaffine have much more similar correlations under these settings, where Biaffine has 2 other tags significantly correlated but its set contains those of UPParser. Of those that are significantly correlated for both, SYM and X are actually negatively correlated, suggesting that the taggers either fail

to generalise or fail to capture certain tagging patterns. A noticeable exception is the CCONJ tag which is both strongly correlated (about 0.6 for both) and statistically significant for both parsers. This is likely due to the nature of conj relations, where dependents are connected to the conjunct rather than the head of the conjunct (e.g. the second conjoined object of a verb is connected to the first) and so should be parsed differently than if they occurred without a CCONJ.

Figure 24 in the Appendix shows the correlation for the tagging accuracy of the head for each tag type. Across all systems, there is a correlation for the head of INTJ nodes (0.7 for predicted training, 0.5 for gold). This is perhaps due to INTJ nodes typically being attached to VERB or NOUN nodes, and that this narrow context means that the parsers will always look for a node like these and if the correct node is incorrectly tagged, this could disrupt the arc predictions and would be better off without the tagging information.

ADP (adposition) nodes are similar but with a lower correlation (about 0.4 for all systems). And again this might be due to these nodes occuring in less diverse contexts. X nodes are strongly negatively correlated for Biaffine for both gold and predicted training systems (0.6 and and 0.8 respectively) and similarly SCONJ (subordinating con-

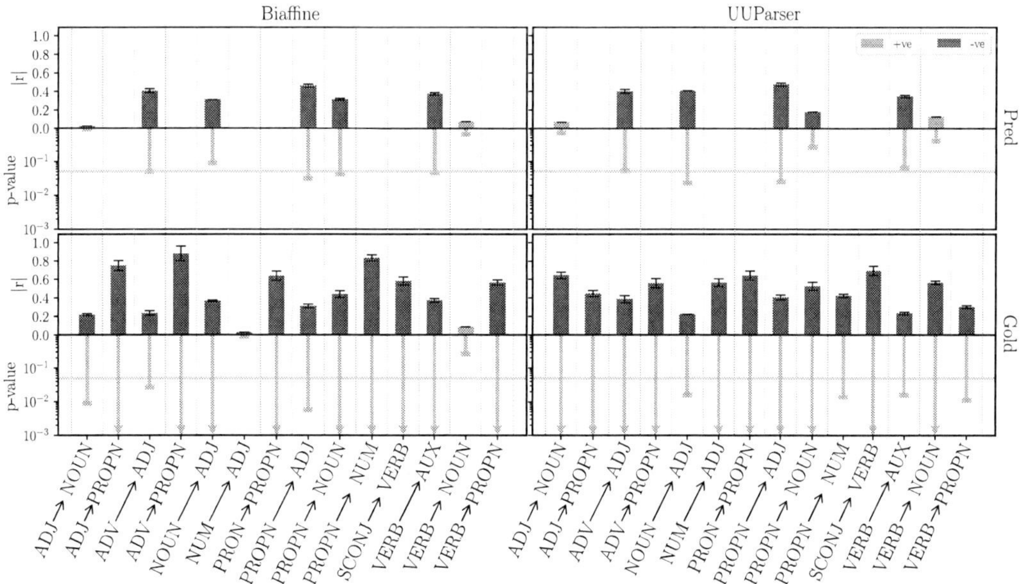

Figure 5: Pearson coefficients for the error rate of individual error types $POS_X \rightarrow POS_Y$ and global LAS where positive (+ve) coefficients are shown in blue and negative (-ve) are shown in red. The corresponding p-values are shown below (orange) where an arrow head means the value was below 0.001. Left subplots are for Biaffine parsers, right for UUParsers, top row is for parsers trained with predicted tags, and bottom for parsers trained with gold tags.

junction) nodes (0.7 and 0.5). Perhaps the diversity of the contexts in which these tags occur makes it difficult for the parser to leverage POS information. ADV nodes follow a similar trend, being negatively correlated for 3 of the 4 systems (gold UUParser being the exception), which could also be related to diversity of contexts: adverbs such as *very* never attach to verbs, but to other adverbs, and often the use of ADV covers situations where a word doesn't satisfy the definition of another POS tag.

Figure 4 shows the correlation of combining the accuracy of POS tags and the tags that govern them with global LAS scores. Only pairs that occur 10 times in 4 treebanks are included. The union of pairs with the highest correlations across all systems are shown (the 10 most highly correlated and statistically significant for each parser). The correlations are positive with one exception of PUNCT nodes headed by VERB nodes, which are weakly negative for all systems except gold UUParser. Conversely, PUNCT nodes headed by NOUN nodes have positive correlations for all systems (0.4 for all except gold UUParser which is about 0.8). Other than this, CCONJ nodes headed by NOUN nodes are positively correlated (0.6-0.7) for all systems, which adds to the discussion above regarding CCONJ tags and suggests that it helps

more specifically when conjuncts are NOUN nodes.

3.2 Dependency distance

Figures 16–19 in the Appendix show the attachment scores and occurence rates for each POS tag in dependency distance bins. Most tags decrease in performance as the distance increases. Other than NOUN, PUNCT, and VERB, the occurrence of longer-distanced edges are significantly lower than short-distanced ones. Of these, NOUN has a much more significant drop in performance as distance increases across all systems.

Figure 25 in the Appendix shows the combinations of POS tag and dependency distance with highest correlation with LAS. CCONJ appears in 8 pairs (out of 24) and appears 3 out of 6 times for the distances of 3 or less. This further supports the findings from above that awareness of CCONJ nodes is especially beneficial. Beyond this, most pairs (19) have distances of 4 or greater which is larger than the mean dependency distance typically observed in natural languages, e.g. it is 3.6 (0.4) averaged over all treebanks in UD v.2.4 using the equation from Liu (2008).

3.3 Error types

Finally, we evaluated which type of tagging errors are the most likely to impact parsing performance.

In Figures 20–23 in the Appendix, we show the corresponding attachment scores and counts of each error of tagging a gold tag of POS$_X$ as POS$_Y$ in confusion matrices for both parser types, for training with gold tags and with predicted tags with taggers of accuracy 80, 86, 91(3). We include these to supplement the following analysis and allow for comparisons to other error types that aren't shown. However, we can see that a lower occurrence rate of errors is associated with lower attachment scores and errors have a larger impact on LAS than UAS.

Figure 5 shows the highest correlated and statistically significant tagging errors. Correlations are between the error rate and the global LAS scores. Only error types that occur 10 times in the output of at least two taggers for at least 4 treebanks are included (the 5 most correlated for each parser). This is due to the fact that looking at the correlation between error rates and LAS when an error type rarely occurs will still give *statistically meaningful* correlations, as the absence of stats is one step removed from the correlation calculation. Error types are negatively correlated with parsing performance (the exceptions are those which aren't statistically significant for some systems). Correlations are strongest when training with gold POS tags. For Biaffine they are either much stronger or much weaker than UUParser, e.g. ADJ→PROPN is over 0.8 whereas it is only about 0.5 for UUParser, PROPN→NUM is about 0.8 for Biaffine and about 0.4 for UPParser. In contrast, ADJ→NOUN and ADV→ADJ are only about 0.2 for Biaffine but are about 0.6 and 0.4, respectively, for UUParser.

Two POS tag pairs appear in error types where both directions are observed, PROPN↔ADJ and NOUN↔ADJ for both parsers trained with gold tags. For the former, it appears that qualifiers that refer to nations or groups are often problematic as a similar form or the same one appear as PROPN and ADJ, e.g. *Sunni, African, Mexican*. For the error type ADJ→PROPN, another issue seems to be the capitalisation of certain words which either appear on their own or with limited punctuation, e.g *Wonderful!*, *Marvelous!*, or refer to something fixed but not quite a named entity, e.g. *Parliamentary elections, Perfect Score*. This is the case in English, and we apologise for the Anglo-bias, but the author isn't proficient in the other languages used. However, these errors do occur at a general level. It appears to be similar in Russian (Бургундского - *Burgundy*, Гомельская - *Gomel Region*); Finnish (*Suomalaisen - Finnish, eurooppalaisen - Euro-*

pean); and in Hebrew (איטלקית - *Italian*, גרמנית - *German*). The only language where neither of these error types occur is Wolof as it doesn't have an adjective category (Dione, 2019).

For the other bidirectional error type (NOUN↔ADJ), there appears a similar issue for ADJ→NOUN as ADJ↔PROPN for nations or groups, but NOUN is used instead of PROPN. Beyond this, when a NOUN is incorrectly tagged as an ADJ this occurs 44.7 (14.4)% when it is governed by another NOUN. This is especially prominent for English and Hebrew (65.8% and 64.4% respectively) with the lowest rate occurring for Ancient Greek and Tamil (25.8% and 28.9% respectively). The issue of tagging NOUN tokens governed by another NOUN token is also apparent in Figure 4 where this pair has a correlation coefficient of about 0.4 for both Biaffine systems and 0.8 for the gold trained UUParser system (for the predicted POS tag UUParser system, it isn't statistically significant). Again Wolof is an outlier as the error NOUN→ADJ never occurs, presumably because it never has any ADJ tokens to learn.

Only two error types are statistically significant for all systems: ADV→ADJ and PROPN→ADJ, the latter having been discussed above. The former isn't particularly prevalent, occurring with an error rate of 5.8 (5.7)% on average across all languages (except Wolof) with Russian and Tamil having the highest rates (15.5% and 15.0%, respectively) and Chinese and Hebrew having the lowest (0.6% and 1.7%). For English at least, two issues are clear. Words that have the same form when used as an adverb or adjective are commonly mis-tagged as ADJ when they should be ADV, e.g. *more, worst, better*, and so on. And also when an adverb is used in hyphenated adjectival phrases such as *fully* in *fully-fledged* and *ill* in *ill-advised*.

As Wolof was such an outlier with respect to common tagging errors (with those that impacted parsing performance) we looked at those most common in Wolof. DET→TAG occur more often than average, especially DET→VERB (error rate of 10.0% compared to 2.4(4.1)% for other languages) and DET→PRON (error rate of 13.5% compared to 7.6(6.3)% for other languages). DET→NOUN is also common but similar to the other languages (error rate of 8.0% compared to 7.0(7.0)% for other languages). DET→VERB and DET→NOUN are negatively correlated for Wolof with an average coefficient of $-0.85(0.11)$ across all systems and all with p< 0.05. Clearly, further language-specific analyses are needed.

4 Conclusion

We have evaluated the impact POS tag accuracy has on parsing performance for leading graph- and transition-based parsers across a diverse range of UD treebanks, highlighting the stark difference between using predicted POS tags and gold POS tags at runtime. We observed a non-linear increase in performance when using gold tags, suggesting they are somehow exceptional, i.e., precisely the tag patterns that not even the most accurate taggers can correctly predict (the last 2-3 percentage points towards 100% accuracy) seem to be the most important for parsing. This could be due to the parsers implicitly learning POS tag information, in such a way that the taggers learn nothing new to contribute or not enough to avoid a loss in performance due to the errors disrupting what the parsers have learnt. Our analysis also shows that practitioners should evaluate the efficacy of using predicted tags for a given system or language. We have also analysed what aspects of erroneous tagging predictions have the greatest impact and correlation to parsing performance. We observed some global trends, like the importance of CCONJ, but also language-specific issues which highlight the need to evaluate the usefulness of POS tags per language. The results also suggest that using a subset of POS tags might be effective.

Acknowledgments

This work has received funding from the European Research Council (ERC), under the European Union's Horizon 2020 research and innovation programme (FASTPARSE, grant agreement No 714150), from MINECO (ANSWER-ASAP, TIN2017-85160-C2-1-R), from Xunta de Galicia (ED431C 2020/11), and from Centro de Investigación de Galicia "CITIC", funded by Xunta de Galicia and the European Union (ERDF - Galicia 2014-2020 Program), by grant ED431G 2019/01. The authors would also like to the thank *all* the reviewers for their detailed and constructive comments and criticisms.

References

Ramadan Alfared and Denis Béchet. 2012. POS taggers and dependency parsing. *International Journal of Computational Linguistics and Applications*, 3(2):107–122.

Waleed Ammar, George Mulcaire, Miguel Ballesteros, Chris Dyer, and Noah A Smith. 2016. Many languages, one parser. *Transactions of the Association for Computational Linguistics*, 4:431–444.

Mark Anderson and Carlos Gómez-Rodríguez. 2020. Distilling neural networks for greener and faster dependency parsing. In *Proceedings of the 16th International Conference on Parsing Technologies*, pages 2–13.

Miguel Ballesteros, Chris Dyer, and Noah A. Smith. 2015. Improved transition-based parsing by modeling characters instead of words with LSTMs. In *Proceedings of the 2015 Conference on Empirical Methods in Natural Language Processing*, pages 349–359.

Mary Dalrymple. 2006. How much can part-of-speech tagging help parsing? *Natural Language Engineering*, 12(4):373–389.

Cheikh M Bamba Dione. 2019. Developing universal dependencies for Wolof. In *Proceedings of the Third Workshop on Universal Dependencies (UDW, SyntaxFest 2019)*, pages 12–23.

Timothy Dozat and Christopher D Manning. 2017. Deep biaffine attention for neural dependency parsing. *Proceedings of the 5th International Conference on Learning Representations*.

Timothy Dozat, Peng Qi, and Christopher D Manning. 2017. Stanford's graph-based neural dependency parser at the CoNLL 2017 shared task. In *Proceedings of the CoNLL 2017 Shared Task: Multilingual Parsing from Raw Text to Universal Dependencies*, pages 20–30.

Filip Ginter, Jan Hajic, Juhani Luotolahti, Milan Straka, and Daniel Zeman. 2017. CoNLL 2017 shared task-automatically annotated raw texts and word embeddings. LINDAT/CLARIN digital library at the Institute of Formal and Applied Linguistics, Charles University.

Edouard Grave, Piotr Bojanowski, Prakhar Gupta, Armand Joulin, and Tomas Mikolov. 2018. Learning word vectors for 157 languages. In *Proceedings of the International Conference on Language Resources and Evaluation (LREC 2018)*.

Benjamin Heinzerling and Michael Strube. 2018. BPEmb: Tokenization-free pre-trained subword embeddings in 275 languages. In *Proceedings of the Eleventh International Conference on Language Resources and Evaluation (LREC 2018)*.

Miryam de Lhoneux, Yan Shao, Ali Basirat, Eliyahu Kiperwasser, Sara Stymne, Yoav Goldberg, and Joakim Nivre. 2017. From raw text to universal dependencies - Look, no tags! In *Proceedings of the CoNLL 2017 Shared Task: Multilingual Parsing from Raw Text to Universal Dependencies*, pages 207–217.

Zuchao Li, Shexia He, Zhuosheng Zhang, and Hai Zhao. 2018. Joint learning of POS and dependencies for multilingual universal dependency parsing. In *Proceedings of the CoNLL 2018 Shared Task: Multilingual Parsing from Raw Text to Universal Dependencies*, pages 65–73.

Haitao Liu. 2008. Dependency distance as a metric of language comprehension difficulty. *Journal of Cognitive Science*, 9(2):159–191.

Dat Quoc Nguyen and Karin Verspoor. 2018. An improved neural network model for joint POS tagging and dependency parsing. *CoNLL 2018*, page 81.

Joakim Nivre, Mitchell Abrams, Željko Agić, et al. 2019. Universal Dependencies 2.4. LINDAT/CLARIN digital library at the Institute of Formal and Applied Linguistics (ÚFAL), Faculty of Mathematics and Physics, Charles University.

Vikas Raunak. 2017. Simple and effective dimensionality reduction for word embeddings. *Proceedings of NIPS LLD Workshop*.

Aaron Smith, Bernd Bohnet, Miryam de Lhoneux, Joakim Nivre, Yan Shao, and Sara Stymne. 2018. 82 treebanks, 34 models: Universal dependency parsing with multi-treebank models. In *Proceedings of the CoNLL 2018 Shared Task: Multilingual Parsing from Raw Text to Universal Dependencies*, pages 113–123.

Aaron Smith, Miryam de Lhoneux, Sara Stymne, and Joakim Nivre. 2018. An investigation of the interactions between pre-trained word embeddings, character models and POS tags in dependency parsing. In *EMNLP 2018: 2018 Conference on Empirical Methods in Natural Language Processing*, pages 2711–2720.

Michalina Strzyz, David Vilares, and Carlos Gómez-Rodríguez. 2019. Viable dependency parsing as sequence labeling. In *NAACL-HLT 2019: Annual Conference of the North American Chapter of the Association for Computational Linguistics*, pages 717–723.

Atro Voutilainen. 1998. Does tagging help parsing? A case study on finite state parsing. In *Proceedings of the International Workshop on Finite State Methods in Natural Language Processing*, pages 25–36. Association for Computational Linguistics.

Jie Yang and Yue Zhang. 2018. NCRF++: An opensource neural sequence labeling toolkit. In *Proceedings of the 56th Annual Meeting of the Association for Computational Linguistics*.

Liner Yang, Meishan Zhang, Yang Liu, Maosong Sun, Nan Yu, and Guohong Fu. 2017. Joint POS tagging and dependence parsing with transition-based neural networks. *IEEE/ACM Transactions on Audio, Speech, and Language Processing*, 26(8):1352–1358.

Yu Zhang, Zhenghua Li, Houquan Zhou, and Min Zhang. 2020. Is POS tagging necessary or even helpful for neural dependency parsing? *arXiv preprint arXiv:2003.03204*.

Yuan Zhang and David Weiss. 2016. Stack-propagation: Improved representation learning for syntax. *arXiv preprint arXiv:1603.06598*.

Appendix A Treebank performances

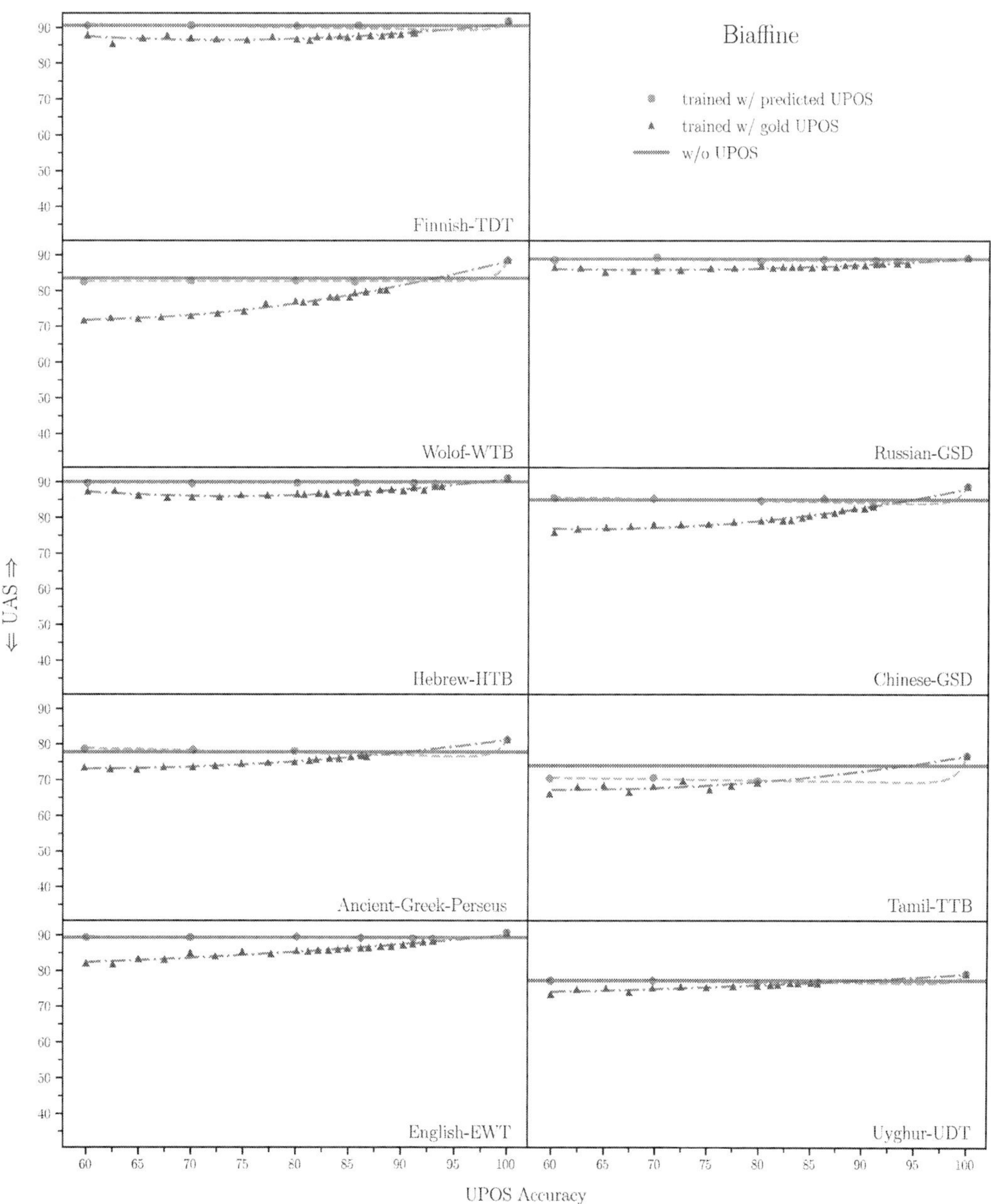

Figure 6: UAS for each treebank for Biaffine training with gold (red, triangles) and predicted (blue, circles) POS tags. Baseline parser trained without POS tags is shown in grey.

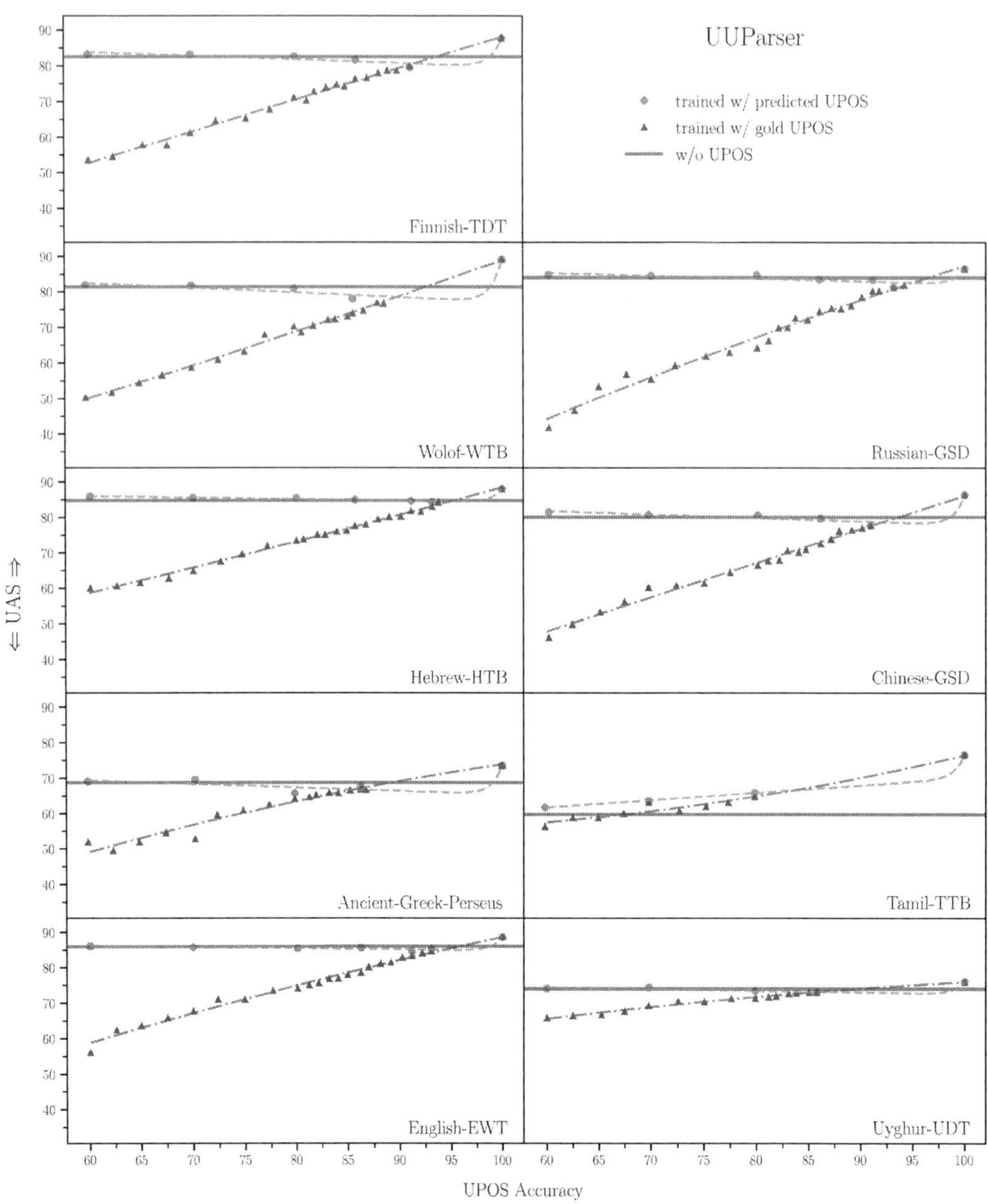

Figure 7: UAS for each treebank for UUParser training with gold (red, triangles) and predicted (blue, circles) POS tags. Baseline parser trained without POS tags is shown in grey.

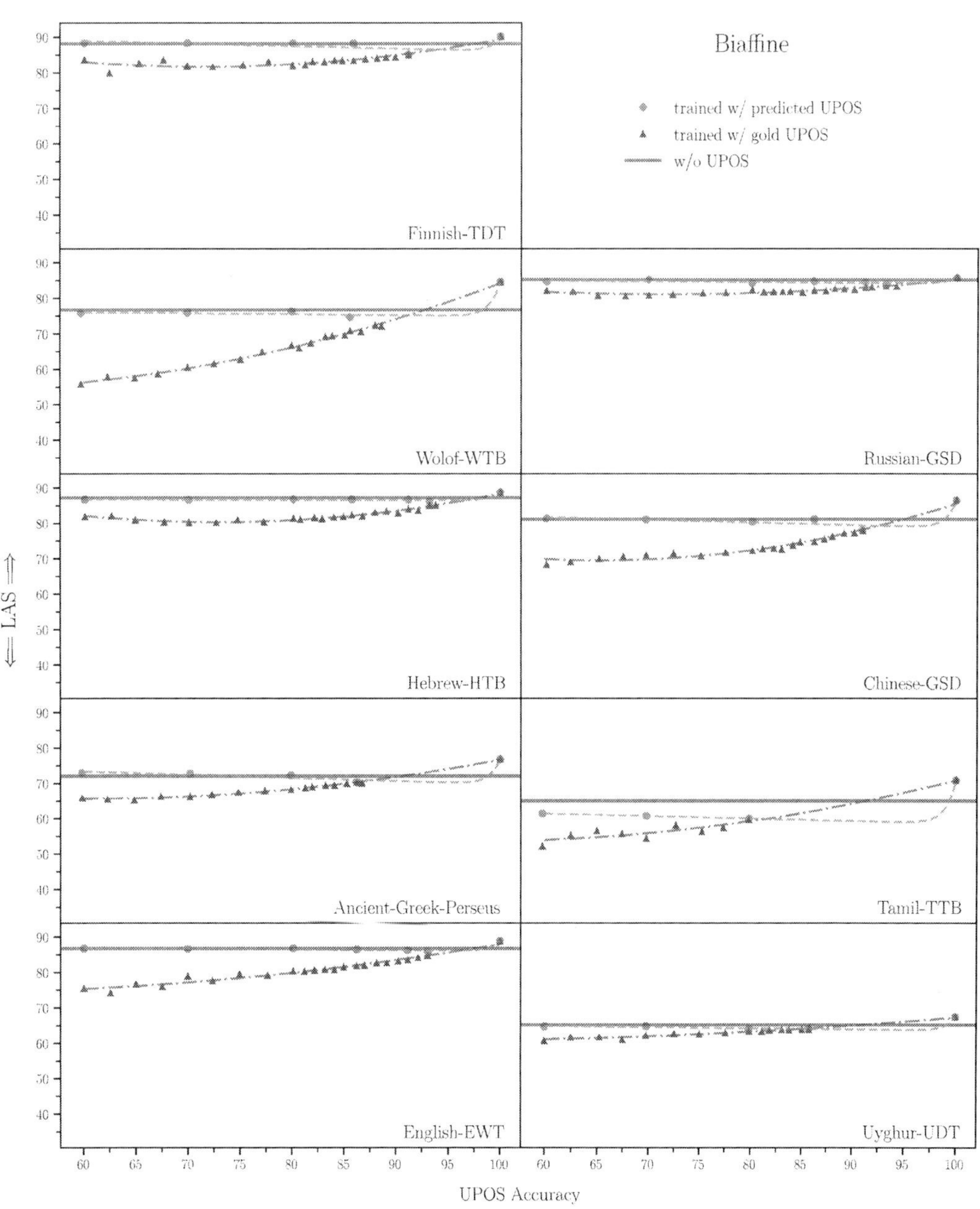

Figure 8: LAS for each treebank for Biaffine training with gold (red, triangles) and predicted (blue, circles) POS tags. Baseline parser trained without POS tags is shown in grey.

81

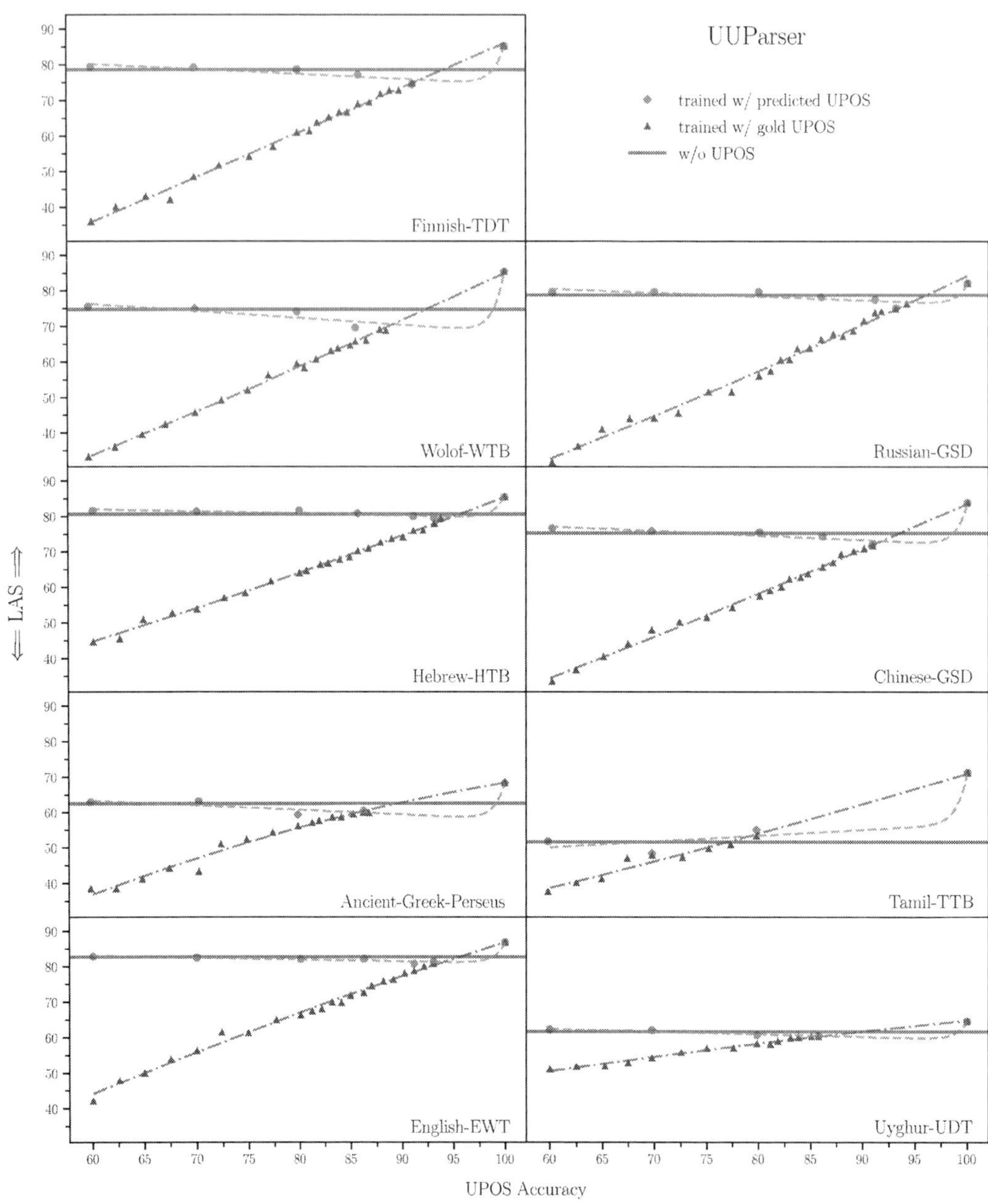

Figure 9: LAS for each treebank for UUParser training with gold (red, triangles) and predicted (blue, circles) POS tags. Baseline parser trained without POS tags is shown in grey.

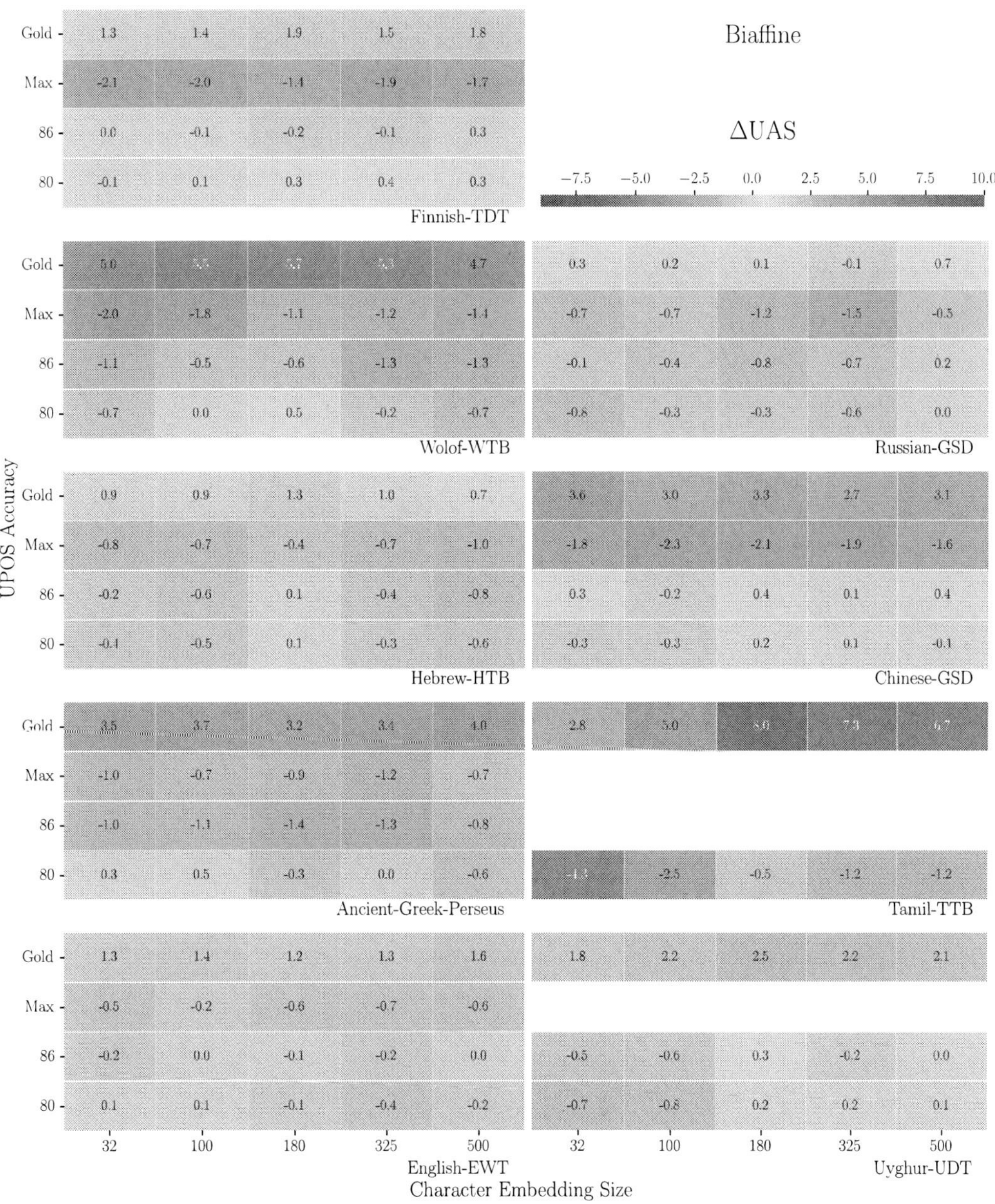

Figure 10: Δ UAS for each treebank for Biaffine compared to the baseline parsers trained without POS tags for different character embedding sizes and different POS tag accuracies.

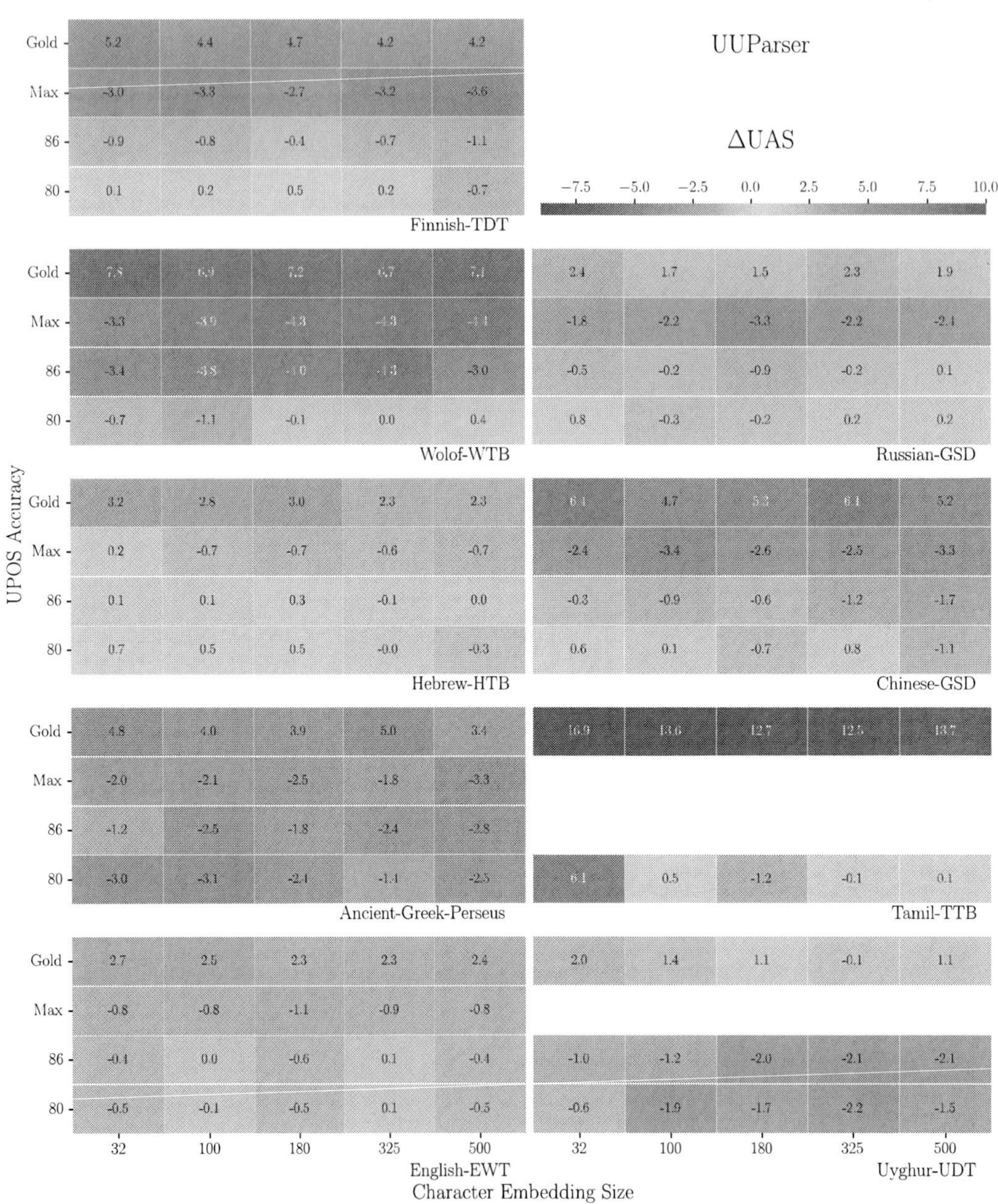

Figure 11: Δ UAS for each treebank for UUParser compared to the baseline parsers trained without POS tags for different character embedding sizes and different POS tag accuracies.

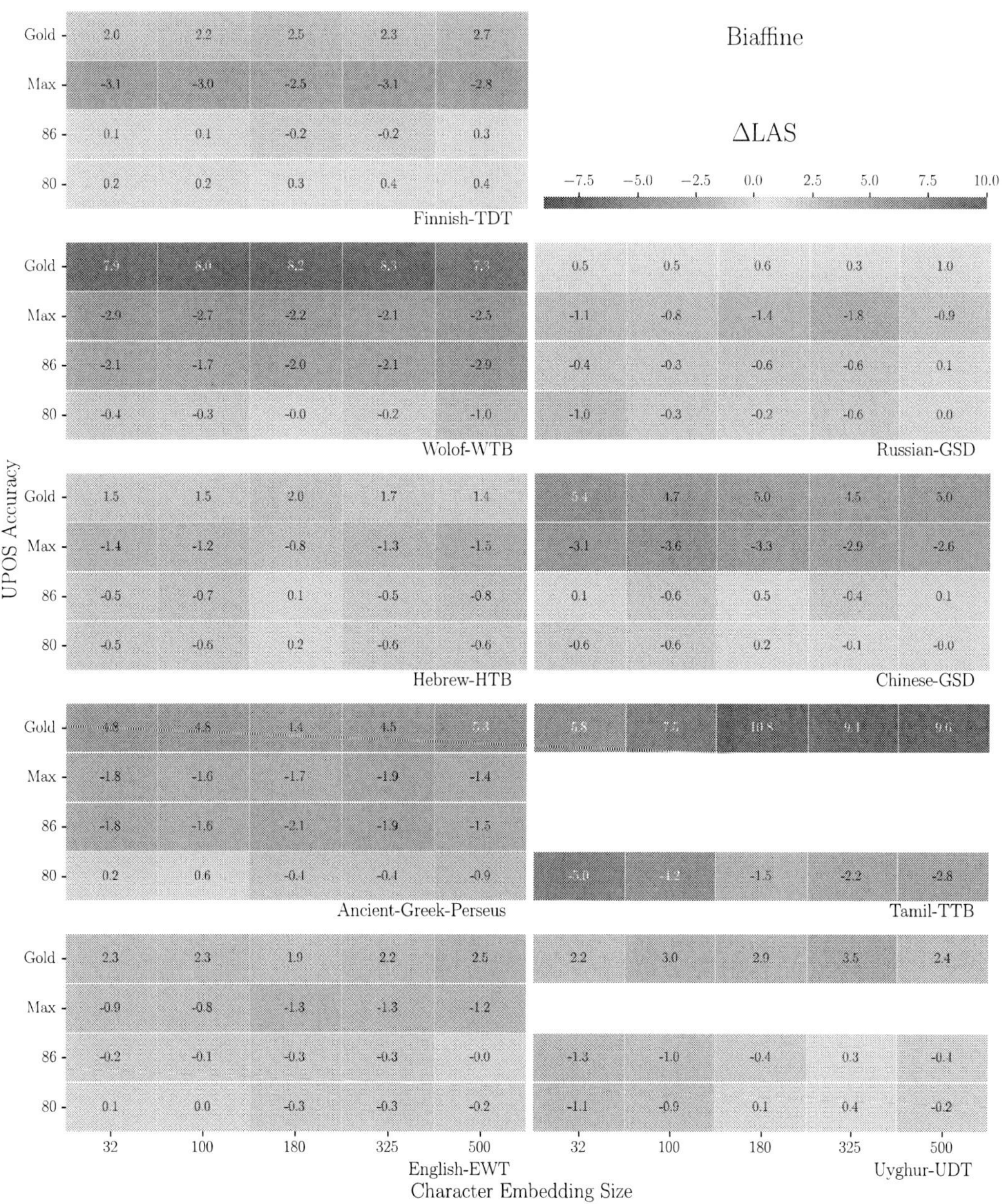

Figure 12: Δ LAS for each treebank for Biaffine compared to the baseline parsers trained without POS tags for different character embedding sizes and different POS tag accuracies.

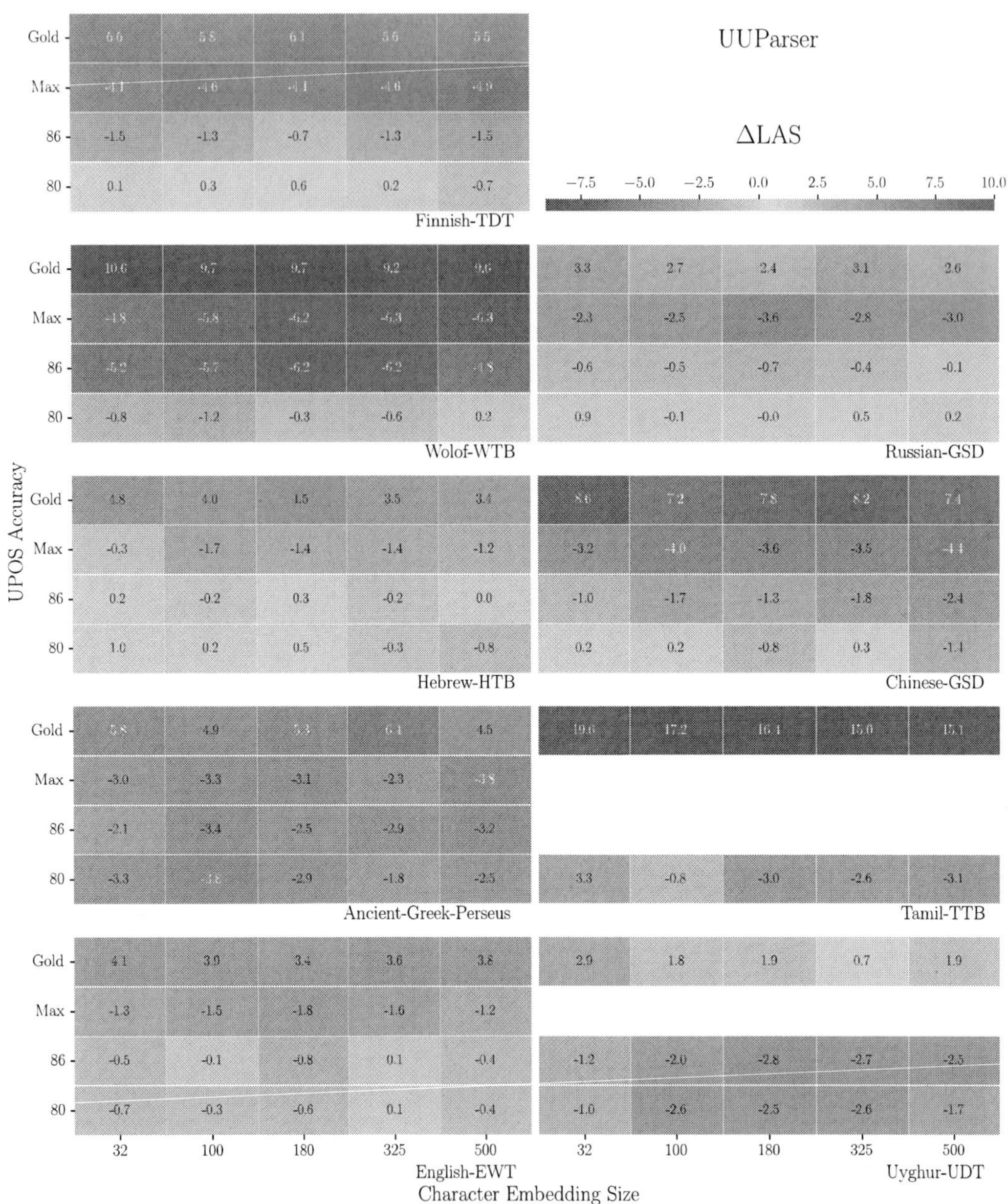

Figure 13: Δ LAS for each treebank for UUParser compared to the baseline parsers trained without POS tags for different character embedding sizes and different POS tag accuracies.

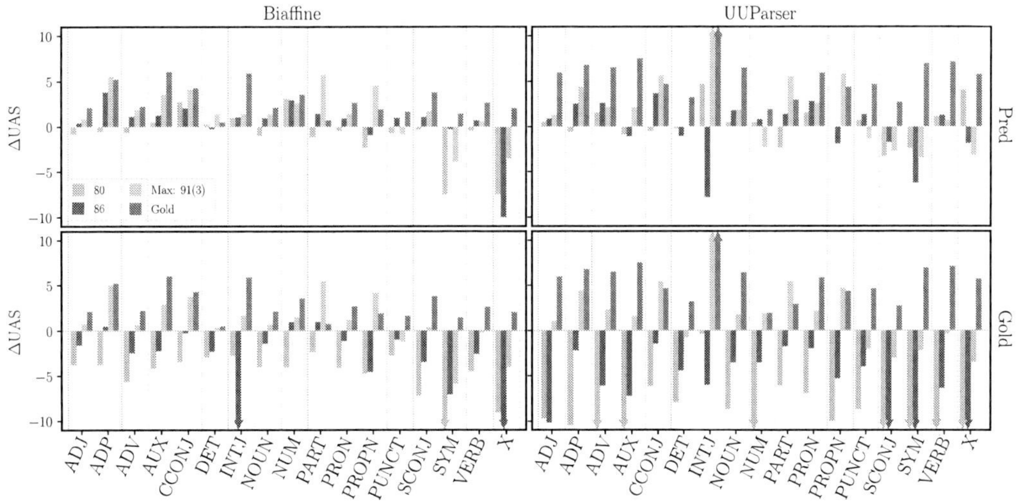

Figure 14: Average ΔUAS across all treebanks for models trained with POS tags from taggers of 80, 86, max POS accuracy of 91(3), and with gold tags for each POS tag.

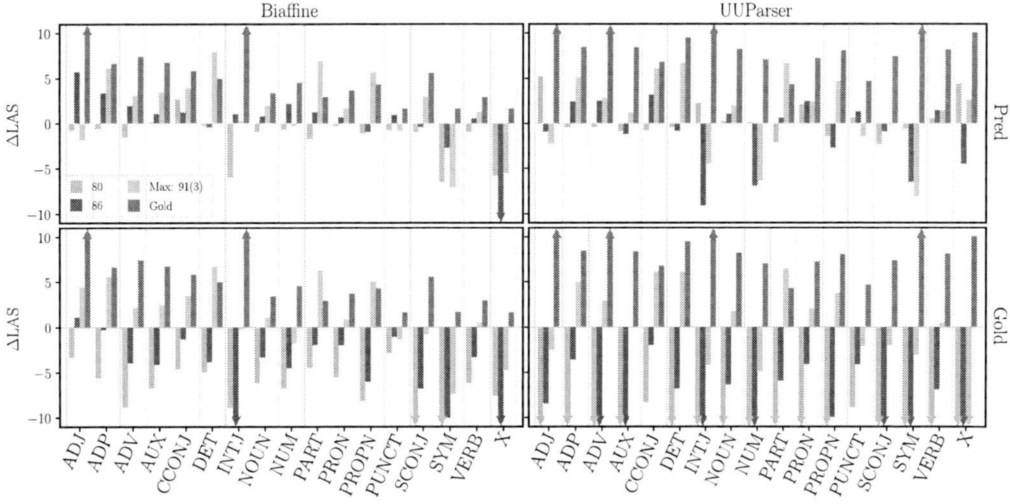

Figure 15: Average ΔLAS across all treebanks for models trained with POS tags from taggers of 80, 86, max POS accuracy of 91(3), and with gold tags for each POS tag.

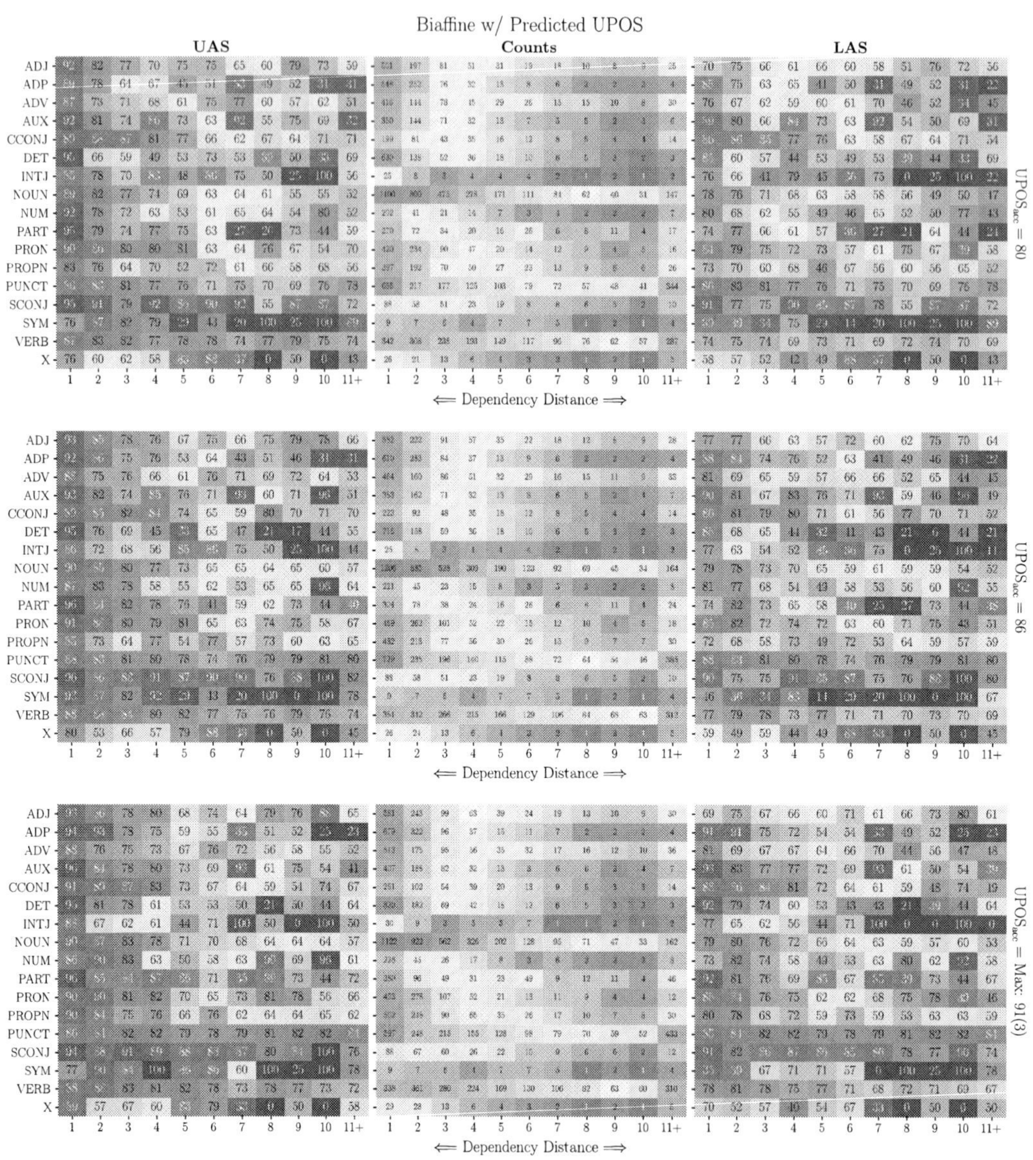

Figure 16: Average UAS (left column) and LAS (right column) across treebanks with Biaffine for models trained with predicted tags from taggers with 80, 86, and max POS accuracy of 91(3). UAS and LAS metrics are shown for each gold tag (y-axis) with a given dependency distance (x-axis). The counts of each pair of POS tag and dependency distance are shown in the middle column.

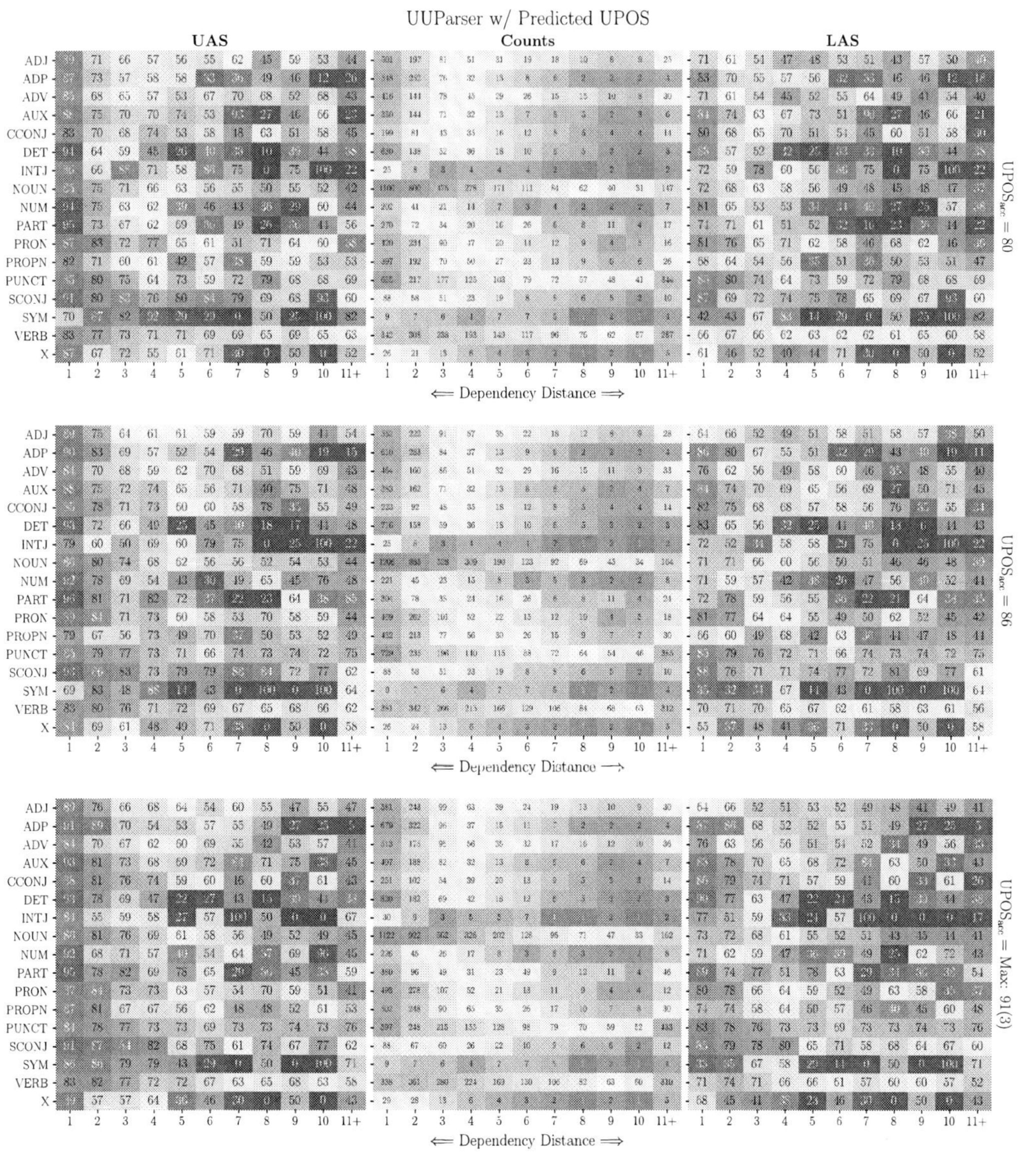

Figure 17: Average UAS (left column) and LAS (right column) across treebanks with UUParser for models trained with predicted tags from taggers with 80, 86, and max POS accuracy of 91(3). UAS and LAS metrics are shown for each gold tag (y-axis) with a given dependency distance (x-axis). The counts of each pair of POS tag and dependency distance are shown in the middle column.

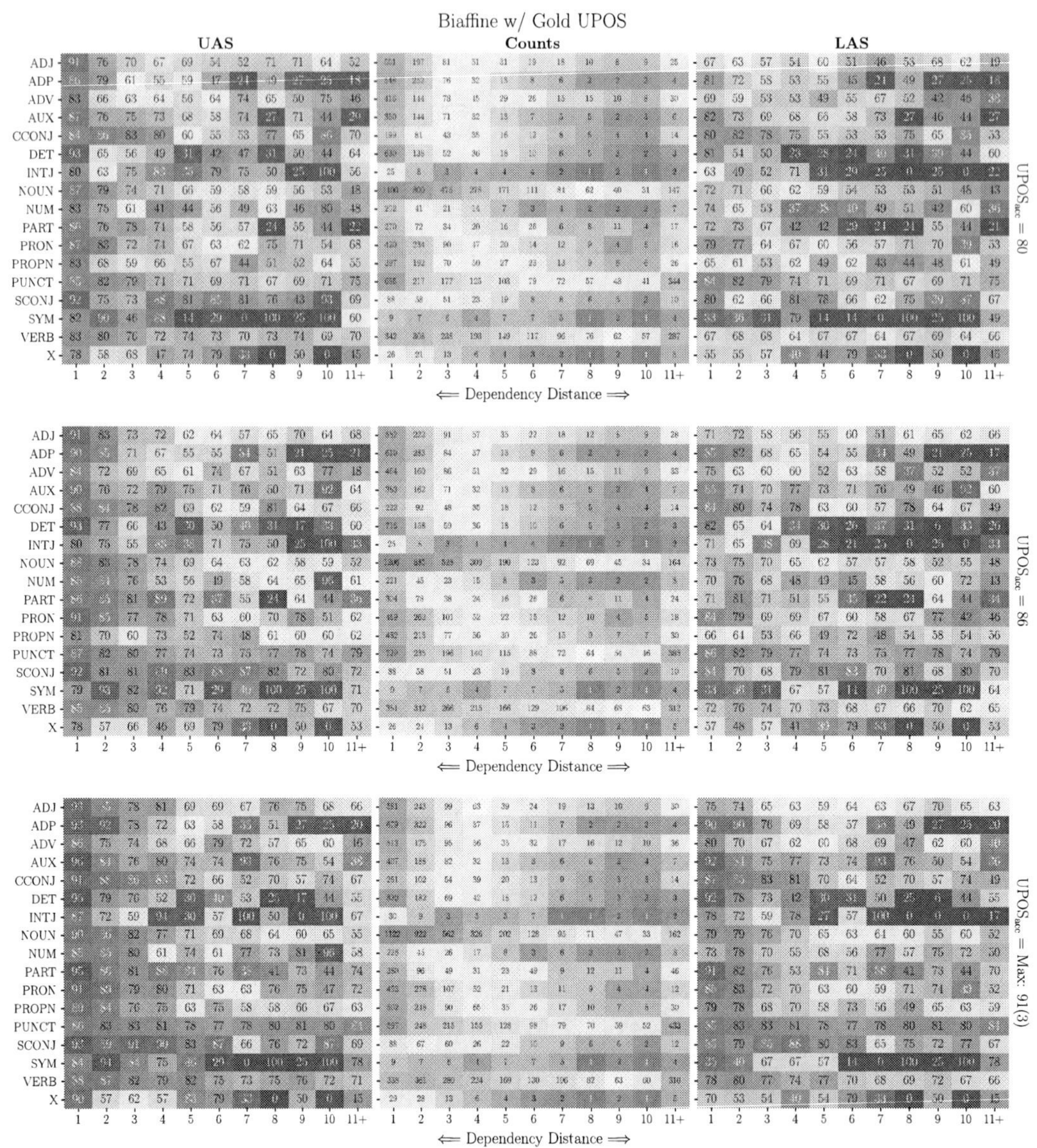

Figure 18: Average UAS (left column) and LAS (right column) across treebanks with Biaffine for models trained with gold tags but using predicted tags from taggers with 80, 86, and max POS accuracy of 91(3). UAS and LAS metrics are shown for each gold tag (y-axis) with a given dependency distance (x-axis). The counts of each pair of POS tag and dependency distance are shown in the middle column.

90

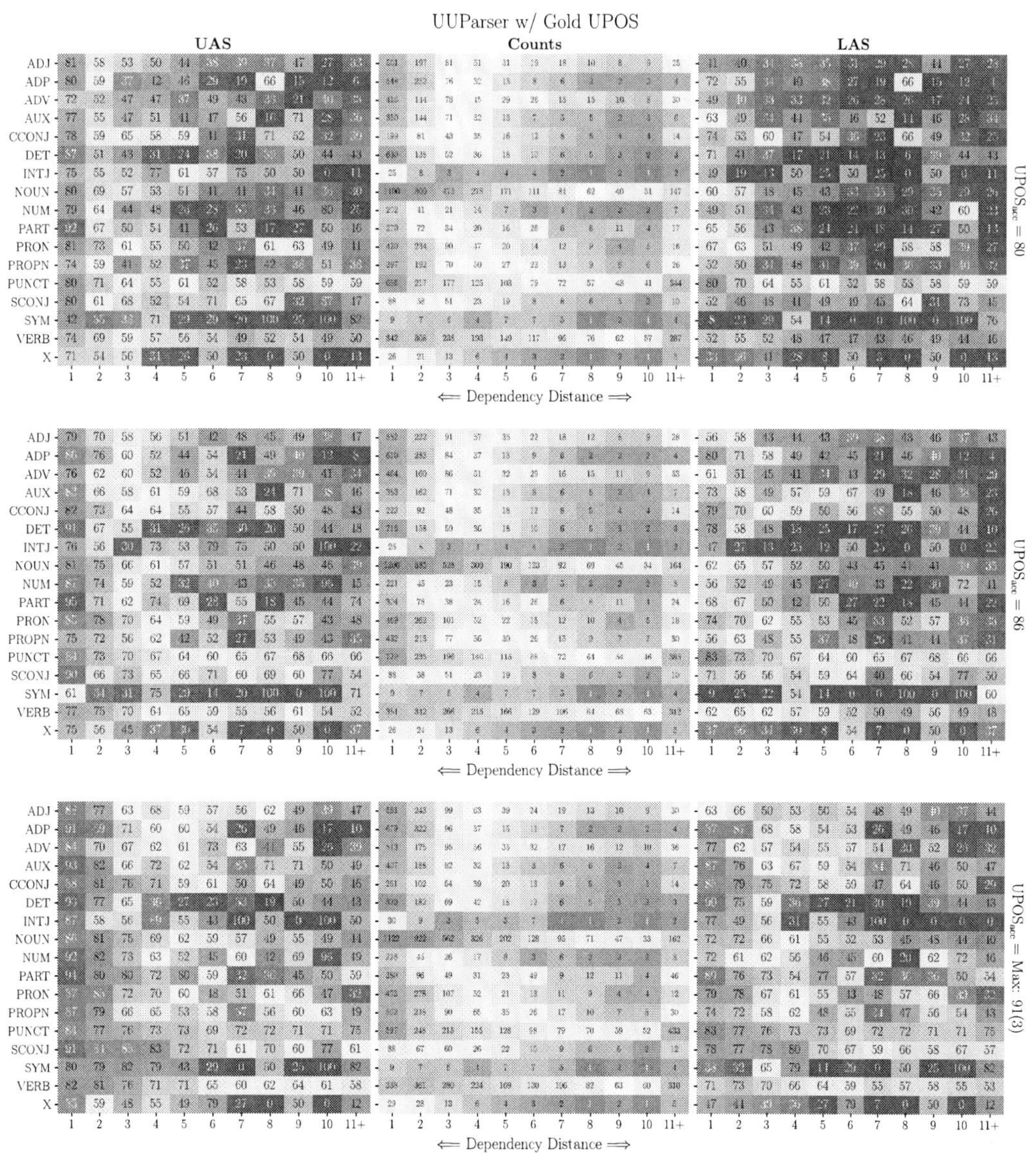

Figure 19: Average UAS (left column) and LAS (right column) across treebanks with UUParser for models trained with gold tags but using predicted tags from taggers with 80, 86, and max POS accuracy of 91(3). UAS and LAS metrics are shown for each gold tag (y-axis) with a given dependency distance (x-axis). The counts of each pair of POS tag and dependency distance are shown in the middle column.

Figure 20: Average UAS (left column) and LAS (right column) across treebanks with Biaffine for models trained with POS tags from taggers of 80, 86, and max POS accuracy of 91(3). UAS and LAS metrics are shown for each gold tag (y-axis) predicted as any other tag (x-axis). The numbers are annotated when the average count (shown in the centre column) of a particular error is greater than 20.

Figure 21: Average UAS (left column) and LAS (right column) across treebanks with UUParser for models trained with POS tags from taggers of 80, 86, and max POS accuracy of 91(3). UAS and LAS metrics are shown for each gold tag (y-axis) predicted as any other tag (x-axis). The numbers are annotated when the average count (shown in the centre column) of a particular error is greater than 20.

Figure 22: Average UAS (left column) and LAS (right column) across treebanks with Biaffine for models trained with gold tags but using predicted tags from taggers with 80, 86, and max POS accuracy of 91(3). UAS and LAS metrics are shown for each gold tag (y-axis) predicted as any other tag (x-axis). The numbers are annotated when the average count (shown in the centre column) of a particular error is greater than 20.

Figure 23: Average UAS (left column) and LAS (right column) across treebanks with UUParser for models trained with gold tags but using predicted tags from taggers with 80, 86, and max POS accuracy of 91(3). UAS and LAS metrics are shown for each gold tag (y-axis) predicted as any other tag (x-axis). The numbers are annotated when the average count (shown in the centre column) of a particular error is greater than 20.

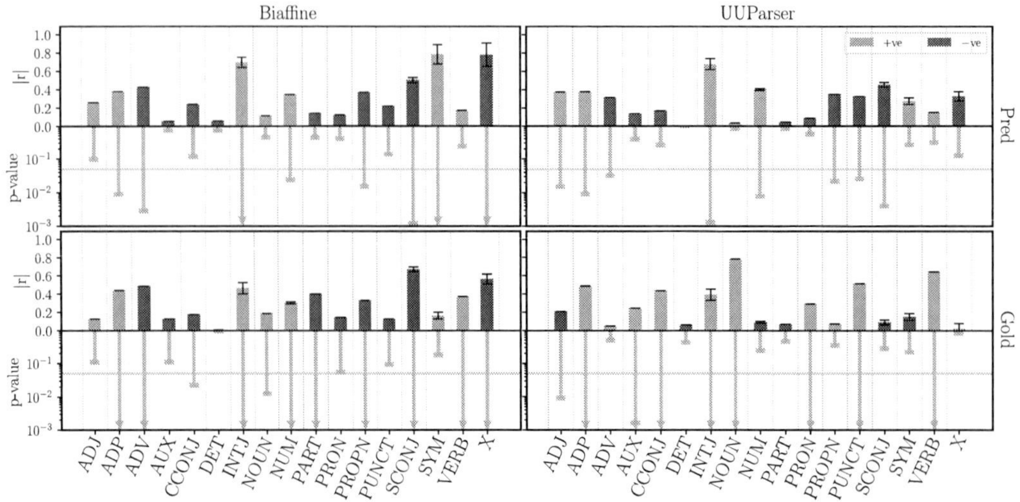

Figure 24: Pearson coefficients for the F1-score of the *head* of separate POS tags and global LAS where positive (+ve) coefficients are shown in blue and negative (-ve) are shown in red. The corresponding p-values are shown below (orange) where an arrow head means the value was below 0.001. Left subplots are for Biaffine parsers, right for UUParsers, top row is for parsers trained with predicted tags, and bottom for parsers trained with gold tags.

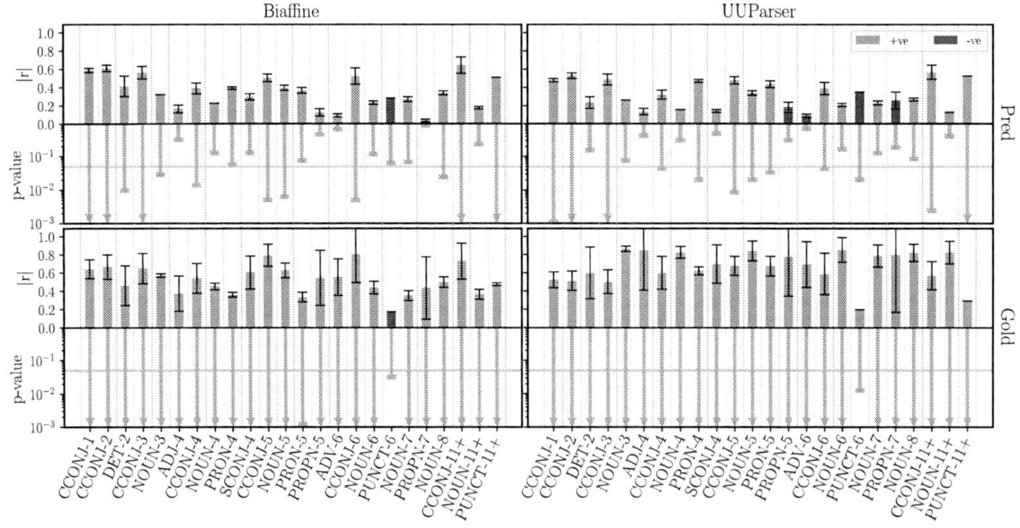

Figure 25: Pearson coefficients for the F1-score for individual POS tags with different dependency distances (POS-distance) and global LAS where positive (+ve) coefficients are shown in blue and negative (-ve) are shown in red. The corresponding p-values are shown below (orange) where an arrow head means the value was below 0.001. Left subplots are for Biaffine parsers, right for UUParsers, top row is for parsers trained with predicted tags, and bottom for parsers trained with gold tags.

Classifying Syntactic Errors in Learner Language

Leshem Choshen[*]
Department of Computer Science
Hebrew University of Jerusalem
leshem.choshen@mail.huji.ac.il

Dmitry Nikolaev[*]
Department of Linguistics
Stockholm University
dnikolaev@fastmail.com

Yevgeni Berzak
BCS
MIT
berzak@mit.edu

Omri Abend
Department of Computer Science
Hebrew University of Jerusalem
omri.abend@mail.huji.ac.il

Abstract

We present a method for classifying syntactic errors in learner language, namely errors whose correction alters the morphosyntactic structure of a sentence. The methodology builds on the established Universal Dependencies syntactic representation scheme, and provides complementary information to other error-classification systems. Unlike existing error classification methods, our method is applicable across languages, which we showcase by producing a detailed picture of syntactic errors in learner English and learner Russian. We further demonstrate the utility of the methodology for analyzing the outputs of leading Grammatical Error Correction (GEC) systems.

1 Introduction

Taxonomies of grammatical errors are important for linguistic and computational analysis of learner language, as well as for Grammatical Error Correction (GEC) systems.[1] Such taxonomies divide the complex space of errors into meaningful categories and enable characterizing their distribution in learner productions. This information can be beneficial for GEC: it can support the development of systems that focus on specific error types, serve as a form of inductive bias (for example, by regularizing the system's output to have a desired distribution over correction types), and guide data augmentation and data filtering by controlling the distribution of error types. Error taxonomies can also improve the interpretability of system outputs for error analysis and learner feedback.

A number of annotation efforts for learner language developed error taxonomies (Nicholls, 2003; Dahlmeier et al., 2013), and statistical classifiers

---

[*]First two authors contributed equally.
[1]Code can be found in github repo GEC_UD_divergences. Matrices directly mentioned are included in the appendix.

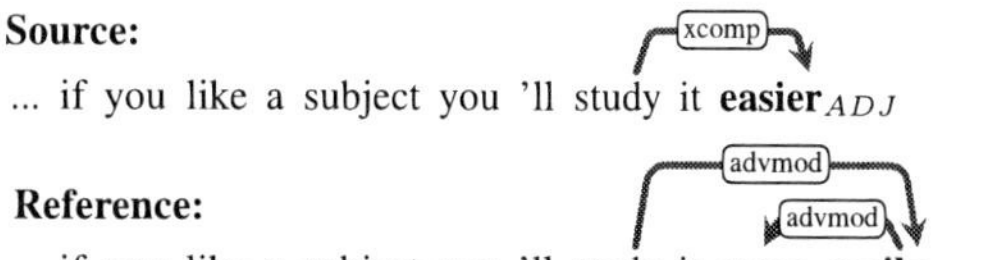

Figure 1: Example of an edit of type ADJ → ADV in POS terms and xcomp → advmod in edge-label terms. Corresponding spans are boldfaced.

into such taxonomies, notably ERRANT (Bryant et al., 2017). Taking error types into consideration in learning has also been shown to improve GEC performance (Kantor et al., 2019, cf. §6). However, most existing taxonomies are fairly coarse-grained and language specific, and do not produce meaningful types for a large proportion of the errors. For example, 25% of the errors in the standard NUCLE corpus (Dahlmeier et al., 2013) are mapped to the residual category OTHER (see §3.3).

We propose SERCL, a taxonomy of *Syntactic Errors* (SEs) and an automatic **C**lassification. Inspired by a longstanding tradition in Machine Translation (MT) which analyses divergences between source and translated texts based on syntactic structure (Dorr, 1994; Nikolaev et al., 2020), SERCL is based on divergences between ungrammatical sentences and their corrections. We define SEs as errors whose correction involves changing morphological features, POS labels or the syntactic structure labels. SERCL takes as input edits, i.e., grammatically incorrect text spans and their corrections, and compares their labels. For example, the error in Fig. 1 is an adjective replaced with an adverb (ADJ→ADV) in POS terms, and an xcomp→advmod in edge-label terms. Thus, SEs are defined by changes in form, rather than by the principles governing the choice of a correct form.

SERCL is the first taxonomy derived from a syntactic representation framework, and it uses the Universal Dependencies formalism (UD; Nivre et al., 2016). This approach provides three ma-

Proceedings of the 24th Conference on Computational Natural Language Learning, pages 97–107
Online, November 19-20, 2020. ©2020 Association for Computational Linguistics
https://doi.org/10.18653/v1/P17

jor advantages over prior learner error taxonomies. First, the SERCL taxonomy is derived automatically from UD annotations, circumventing the need for constructing ad-hoc manually defined error categories. Second, using the UD formalism makes the method applicable across languages, allowing for consistent analyses and comparisons of learner errors across different languages within one unified framework. Third, SERCL is compatible with standard representations and tools in NLP.

Further, the UD based approach to error classification can yield finer distinctions compared to existing schemes. For example, it divides the commonly used class of adposition errors into errors in the use of prepositions as nominal modifiers (e.g., "a mention ~~to~~ **of** previous work"), and the use of prepositions in prepositional objects or adjuncts (e.g., "referring ~~for~~ **to** previous work"). POS tags alone cannot distinguish them, but the UD trees expose this distinction straightforwardly. UD can also help classify agreement and case-assignment errors thanks to its morphological-feature layer containing information about case, number, gender, and other features relevant for inflection.

We validate SERCL's reliability by showing (1) SEs based on automatic parses are similar to ones based on manual parses. (§3.1); (2) SERCL types map well to NUCLE's manually curated taxonomy (§3.2); (3) SERCL is complementary to the standard type classifier ERRANT: 60% of the errors not classified by ERRANT are classified by SERCL.

We demonstrate SERCL's unique features, notably cross-linguistic applicability, by analyzing SE distributions in available corpora for learner English (§4.1) and learner Russian (§4.2).

Finally, we find in GEC systems (1) certain SEs are harder to correct (2) SEs are harder than non-SEs (c.f. 5) (3) the granular types can help devising rules to improve products (e.g. Grammarly, §5.2).

2 Methodology

This section defines our taxonomy of SEs and how SERCL classifies into it. Given a parsed learner sentence and its correction, and given an edit $e = (e_s, e_c)$, i.e., a sub-string of the source sentence e_s that contains a grammatical error and its reference correction e_c, we define its class in the following way. We select a representative token in e_s and in e_c. Specifically, each sub-string defines a sub-forest of the dependency parse, and the representative is taken to be the node closest

Acronym + Ref.	Notes
TLE (Berzak et al., 2016)	Manual parses
NUCLE (Dahlmeier et al., 2013)	Standard GEC benchmark
Lang8 (Mizumoto et al., 2012)	No error classes
W&I (Bryant et al., 2019)	Varied proficiency levels ERRANT classes
RULEC (Rozovskaya and Roth, 2019)	Learner Russian

Table 1: Datasets used in this work.

to the root.[2] The rationale for this decision is that UD treats grammatical markers as dependents of content words. Therefore, in most cases the semantic and syntactic heads correspond to one another, even if lexical items are changed. For example, in **went→was walking**, the semantic and syntactic head of the target has the lemma *walk* and not *be*.[3]

We define an SE as an edit where the two representative's labels do not match. The SE type is defined as the ordered pair of labels with the source label going first. Special cases of SEs are additions and deletions, i.e., edits in which the source or target span is empty.

This definition of SEs is straightforward to implement and requires no further annotation on top of the edits and parses, but it leaves out cases where the representative tokens retain their labels (e.g., agreement errors or inappropriate determiners), although these distinctions can be made in some cases based on UD's morphological features. For practical use, one can annotate all these non-SE errors by the feature that is retained (e.g. Plural Noun errors, if POS tag and morphological features are used). Given a corpus, a confusion matrix could be extracted, where the diagonal counts the non-SEs.

We focus in this work on universal POS-tag pairs, which are sufficient to classify and explain the majority of SEs in English. Dependency labels are analyzed as well, although we find that edge-label-based types and POS-based types are strongly correlated (§4.1). We also explore the use of morphological features, and apply it to Russian that has a rich morphology (§4.2).

---

[2]We select the leftmost token to break ties (3.5% of TLE SEs).

[3]In order to investigate the type correspondences of other tokens in the sub-strings, we may extract dependents of the representative nodes and compare their labels. This is an avenue for future work.

3 Reliability

3.1 Reliance on Automatic Parses

SERCL relies on syntactic trees. Manual annotation is currently only available for the TLE corpus (Berzak et al., 2016, all datasets addressed in the paper are summarized in Table 1), which includes POS and dependency relations, but no morphological features. Hence, we assess the outcomes of using a UD parser instead. We use UDPiPE (Straka et al., 2016) as our parser of choice. It is among the top-scoring parsers in CoNLL 2018 shared task (Zeman et al., 2018) for both English and Russian, the languages we consider in this paper.[4]

We begin by comparing the distribution of SEs in automatically parsed TLE and manual TLE. We focus the discussion on POS-based SEs for conciseness; the full distributions of SE types, both edge-label-based and POS-based are found in Appendix §3.1. When normalising by the number of tokens per POS, class frequencies are quite close to those obtained by manual edits (0.4% absolute change on average and Pearson correlation of $r = 0.998$). This is also the case when normalising by the amount of SEs per POS (0.05% change). The results suggest that the use of a parser does not qualitatively change the distribution of SEs, and that current UD parsing technologies are mature enough to be used for extracting SEs.

While trends are similar with manual and automatic parses, perhaps unsurprisingly, more SEs are found when using automatic parses. This is particularly clear for the "other" tag "X" and for interjections. Symbols are the only category where we find less SEs. We ignore these non-lexical tags in our analysis, suspecting that this is a weakness of the parser. Finding the parsing reliable, we move to compare SERCL to existing approaches.

3.2 Comparing to Manually Typed Edits

Unlike many NLP tasks, this work does not aim to mimic human behavior. Still, there is sense in comparing SERCL to a manually annotated taxonomy. We compare NUCLE annotated train errors and SERCL's (confusion matrix in appendix Table 17). We ignore relocation errors as edits lack the necessary information to discern relocation from deletion.

---

[4]A number of works designed parsers with learner language specifically in mind. However, as such parsers exist only for learner English, we use UDPipe for uniformity.

Source POS	Target POS	#	Source label	Target label	#
NOUN	VERB	51	compound	amod	32
NOUN	ADJ	50	cop	aux	32
ADJ	NOUN	49	xcomp	ccomp	32
VERB	NOUN	46	obl	obj	26
VERB	ADJ	37	obl	advmod	25
DET	PRON	34	det	nmod:poss	25
PRON	DET	32	advmod	obl	24

Table 2: Most prevalent types of SEs involving replacement in the TLE in terms of POS tags (left) and edge labels (right). Numbers are absolute counts. See §2 in the supplementary material for example sentences.

SE types are generally contained within a single NUCLE error type. Indeed, on average 62% of the instances of a given SE type are contained in the maximally overlapping NUCLE category, i.e., when assigning each SE a NUCLE category most of the SE's instances are NUCLE's category instances as well. 82% of the instances on average belong to one of the three maximally overlapping NUCLE categories. CCONJ→ADV, for example, is almost solely (95%) mapped to "transition" error type, addressing linking and phrase errors. This shows that SE types contain much of the information conveyed by NUCLE types. Qualitatively, SERCL has more categories and splits NUCLE types to meaningful sub-types. It is thus usually more informative. For example, the "article or determiner" NUCLE type is split to insertions and deletions of determiners in addition to other SEs (mostly from or to determiner).

3.3 Comparing to the Automatic ERRANT

This section studies the relation between SERCL's predictions and those of ERRANT. For comparability, we apply SERCL to the edit spans produced by ERRANT. For brevity, we focus on POS-based SEs.

ERRANT (Bryant et al., 2017) is essentially the only classifier in use today, and is therefore a natural point of comparison. ERRANT taxonomy is coarse-grained. It assumes for the most part that POS tags are not altered in corrections, classifying many errors by their POS tag (e.g. adverb error). Consequently, ERRANT covers mostly spelling and word-form errors.

We note three important differences between SERCL and ERRANT. First, being based on UD, SERCL is applicable across languages (see §4.2), while ERRANT requires new rules or other modifications per language (Boyd, 2018). Second, relying on an established framework with broad usability accords validity to SERCL's taxonomy, which is otherwise hard to validate (Bryant et al., 2017). Last, ERRANT classifies most SEs as OTHER. SERCL therefore complements ERRANT and is able to classify what ERRANT leaves unclassified.

Empirically, we find that ERRANT does not meaningfully classify a large portion of the errors: about 25% of ERRANT's predictions fall into the residual category Other in NUCLE and Lang8, and about 15% of them in W&I and TLE. We analyze which of those Other edits are SEs, finding most of them are. In W&I, of the 842 errors classified as OTHER, only 338 errors (40.1%) are cases where the POS remains unaltered, while the remaining 504 errors (59.9%) are POS-based SEs. The effective number of SE types that OTHER classifies into is 80.6, i.e., an entropy of 4.4 nets of the POS-based type distribution in edits classified as OTHER.

As for SEs not classified as OTHER, our manual analysis reveals that there too SERCL provides complementary information to ERRANT. Of the remaining errors, 620 are POS-based SEs, while 3211 are not (19.3%). Leaving out errors that involve punctuation leaves us with 522 SEs in W&I. Of those, the most common class is "morphological inflection" (indicating that the correction and the source share a lemma). On it, SERCL provides additional information, e.g., that the most frequent morphological inflection SE is NOUN→ADJ (31% of the cases), while the reverse direction is much rarer (7%). The second most common type, spelling, proved to be challenging for the parser and ERRANT is hence more informative for those. This is also the case for word-order errors. While verb errors are only the third most common, together with its subcategories, such as VERB:FORM, they account for 131 SEs. These might benefit from the SE categorization of common cases (e.g., VERB↔AUX errors suggest an error in the syntactic structure, unlike non-SE errors that usually involve lexical selection). Similarly, the 56 orthography errors could benefit from subcategorization of the common errors. For example, NOUN→PROPN is a common orthography error by ERRANT; ERRANT's type thus does not specify that it is a proper noun lacking capitalization. The other cases are either similar in spirit and can benefit from categorization of frequently appearing SEs, or cases where the POS tagging of the source and target disagree, either due to the UD guidelines

or to parser inconsistency (e.g., the source parse may consider a word a particle, while the target parse considers it an adposition).

To conclude, about 60% of the errors classified as OTHER by ERRANT receive a POS-based SE class. SE classification further provides non-trivial information in many instances of other ERRANT categories. Together, these demonstrate that SERCL provides value beyond ERRANT's classification, even where only English is considered.

4 Cross-linguistic Corpus Studies

In this section, we apply SERCL to available datasets, comparing between different English datasets, originally annotated in different taxonomies, and between English and Russian datasets.

4.1 English

We analyze the English datasets and learner language characteristics through SEs. We start with TLE, which provides manual UD and edit annotation. Our analysis is based upon the available tokenization and edit annotations. To avoid double-counting, we merge overlapping edits to form a set of non-overlapping ones. After removing some noise in the XML markup, we extract 4584 SEs. Of those, 2042 are additions, 1048 are deletions, and 1495 are replacements. In 657 cases of replacement, both the POS and edge label are changed; in 306 cases, only the POS is changed; in 532 cases, only the edge-label is changed.

Figure 2 presents the most frequent addition and deletion types. Frequent POS tags are often frequently deleted or added POS tags, but not necessarily (e.g., nouns are almost twice as frequent as determiners). Additions are drastically more frequent than deletions for determiners, punctuation and pronouns and only slightly more for adpositions. Thus, we replicate the results that learners omit more than they add (Bryant et al., 2019), and give a detailed view on where they do not.

It is often straightforward to connect major types of POS and edge-label additions and deletions: the relationship between DET and `det` is trivial, and missing/redundant adpositions mostly correspond to `mark` and `case`. Deletions and additions of lexical categories with more variegated syntactic functions (such as nouns and verbs) correspond to more varied edge labels. Generally, however, changes in edge labels and POS tags are found to

	A	B	C	Native
SCONJ	0.804	0.864	0.923	0.942
DET	0.857	0.907	0.960	0.971
ADV	0.844	0.893	0.945	0.950
ADJ	0.875	0.923	0.962	0.972
ADP	0.891	0.935	0.969	0.976
PART	0.887	0.924	0.963	0.985
AUX	0.901	0.943	0.973	0.987
PROPN	0.902	0.930	0.966	0.968
NUM	0.897	0.929	0.960	0.950
PRON	0.908	0.930	0.963	0.953
NOUN	0.934	0.963	0.983	0.983
CCONJ	0.922	0.944	0.968	0.971
VERB	0.945	0.964	0.983	0.980
PUNCT	0.978	0.980	0.990	0.981

Table 3: Percentage of unchanged POS tags per type (rows) and proficiency level (columns) in the W&I dataset. Proficiency levels are A-C where C is the most proficient, the last column is for native speakers. Sorted by the average of columns A-C.

be highly correlated both for additions and deletions (Cramer's V = 0.78 for both categories) and replacements (Cramer's V = 0.76).

Most prevalent types of replacements are presented in Table 2. These may suggest a direction to focus GEC efforts towards, a direction we explore in §5.2. Full matrices are in appendix §3.1; incidentally, 44.4% of the errors are POS SEs.

Investigating SEs across levels (see Table 3), we find the most error-prone SEs are among the least difficult to natives. However, on the easiest SEs advanced learners outperform natives. Being out of scope, we leave the details, as well as comparison between levels across datasets to Appendix 1.

4.2 Russian

To demonstrate the generality of the proposed approach, we apply SERCL to RULEC, a corpus of learner Russian (Rozovskaya and Roth, 2019). Russian syntax is characterised by pervasive agreement and complex rules of case selection for nouns. UD morphological features, parsed by UDPipe, make it possible to analyze learners' errors arising due to these phenomena; they are taken up in §4.2.2.

4.2.1 POS mismatches in learners' Russian

An overview of POS additions and deletions is presented in Figure 3. Compared to English (cf. §4.1), learners of Russian tend to more actively underuse nouns (177 additions vs. 64 deletions) and pronouns (111 additions vs. 34 deletions). The latter may stem from Russian being a pro-drop language where subject pronouns can be omitted in certain contexts. The precise rules, however, are rather

	Acc	Dat	Gen	Ins	Loc	Nom
Acc	0	46	132	43	96	40
Dat	17	0	25	21	7	11
Gen	78	45	0	71	73	83
Ins	19	19	53	0	16	15
Loc	66	14	62	12	0	7
Nom	88	19	163	75	22	0

Table 4: Case corrections in nouns in Russian learners' sentences. Source(rows) against reference (columns).

complicated, and it takes a lot of practice knowing when the result sounds felicitous (Zdorenko, 2010).

Most dominant types of POS replacements are similar (ADJ→NOUN, 80 cases; NOUN→ADJ, 75; VERB→NOUN, 65, PRON→DET, 50; NOUN→VERB, 45); however, ADV→ADJ (66) and ADJ→ADV (51) are also prominent, which may be since adjectives and adverbs are more strictly distinct in Russian.

4.2.2 Morphological Features

Russian possess a mildly complex conjugation and inflection system, which leaves a lot of room for errors even in cases when a correct POS is selected. The feature layer of UD makes it possible to identify these errors, which are dominated by three large classes: agreement errors (wrong person/number/gender features on verbs and wrong number/gender/case features on adjectives), case-assignment errors on nouns and pronouns, and verbal errors regarding aspect and voice.

A breakdown of case-assignment errors for nouns is presented in Table 4. It shows, among other things, that learners tend to use accusative and nominative cases in contexts where Russian demands the genitive case (which, in addition to the cross-linguistically frequent possessive meaning, also has numerous more subtle uses, e.g. in some types of negative sentences). Case-agreement errors on adjectives, on the other hand, tend to be more symmetric: 27 cases of an accusative case ending instead of a genitive vs. 19 cases of the converse error (see confusion matrices for case, gender, and number on adjectives in Appendix §3.5).

The Russian verbal system also presents learners with several difficulties that our analysis echoes. Verbs fall into two aspectual classes (with *perfective* verbs denoting completed actions and *imperfective* verbs actions-in-progress and habitual actions), and it is difficult for learners with native languages lacking this distinction to use them correctly (e.g., the English phrase *I went to work* will be translated differently depending on whether it is modified by *yesterday* or *every day*). The feature analysis shows

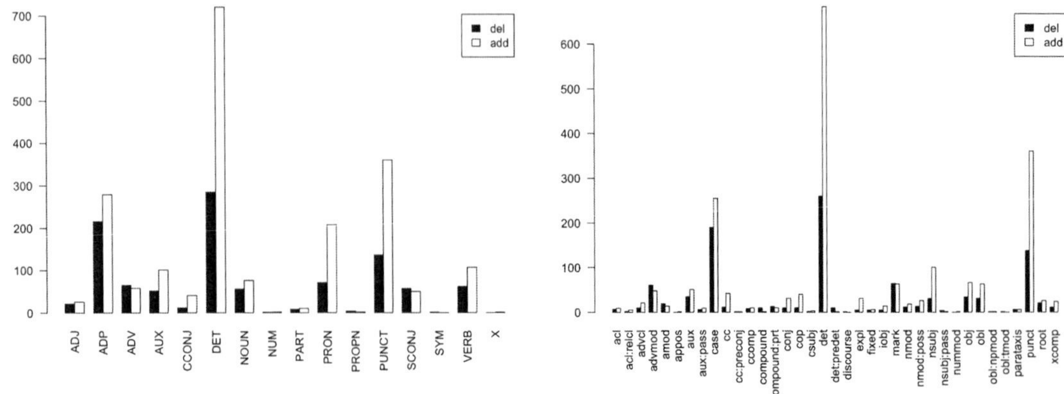

Figure 2: Left: POS tags of words deleted or added in corrected sentences in absolute counts; Right: edge labels of words deleted or added in corrected sentences in absolute counts (y).

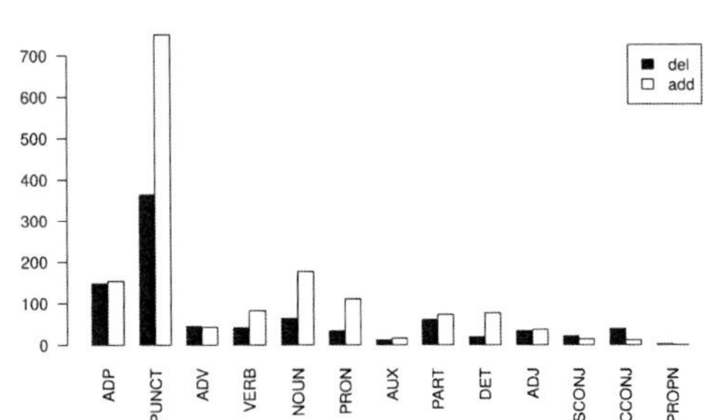

Figure 3: POS tags of words deleted or added in corrected Russian sentences.

that incorrect perfective verbs were changed into imperfective ones 210 times, and imperfective was changed into perfective 223 times.

Another complication stems from the use of middle voice in Russian. English is dominated by *labile* verbs denoting both spontaneous and caused actions (*The cup broke* vs. *I broke the cup*). In Russian, verbs for spontaneous actions are usually derived from transitive verbs (*razbil*[broke.smth]→*razbilsja*[got.broken]). Derived intransitive verbs are analyzed as "middle voice", and the inspection of verbal voice mismatches shows that the dominant type of error is the use of active voice instead of middle voice (108 cases vs. 45 cases of the converse error). These findings can inform future efforts of GEC evaluation and development, in addressing these recurring error patterns.

5 Analyzing GEC System Outputs

To further showcase the utility of SERCL, we demonstrate GEC system analysis with it.

	AIP-TOHOKU	UEDIN-MS	GOLD
ADJ→ADV	18	21	55
ADJ→NOUN	37	46	105
ADJ→VERB	21	33	59
NOUN →VERB	76	87	142
VERB→ADJ	17	21	38
NUM→DET	3	2	5
PART→DET	0	3	1

Table 5: AIP-TOHOKU, UEDIN-MS and Gold annotation changes (correct or not) on selected replacement types of SEs in absolute counts. The non-uniform behaviour of the systems over types indicates that SERCL produces meaningful results.

5.1 Experiments with Leading GEC Systems

We use the outputs of several systems that participated in the BEA2019 shared task (Bryant et al., 2019), namely: the winning system UEDIN-MS (Grundkiewicz et al., 2019), as well as KAKAO&BRAIN (Choe et al., 2019), SHUYAO (Xu et al., 2019), CAMB-CUED (Stahlberg and Byrne, 2019), and AIP-TOHOKU (Asano et al., 2019), that were ranked second, fifth, eighth and ninth respectively.[5] We extract matrices for the system outputs using the same method as in §3.1. Recall is bounded by the amount of predicted SEs, divided by their number in the gold standard. The full matrices are given in Appendix §3.2.

Our results in Table 5 show that the top-ranking UEDIN-MS makes consistently more changes in general and per source SE than AIP-TOHOKU ranked 9th, but less than CAMB-CUED, ranked 8th (found in appendix §3.2). However, there is no correlation between the number of SE changes in general or per source tag and the rank of the system

---

[5]The outputs will be published with the rest of our code, as they were deleted from the contests' page. We thank Yoav Kantor for providing us with the data.

(both yield a partial-order Kendall $\tau = 0$). This is in line with Choshen and Abend's (2018b), who found no relation between a system's performance and its conservatism.

Some SE types are harder for the examined systems than others. There is a slight negative correlation ($r = -0.16$) between the average recall bound of the systems and frequency in the gold standard. For example, pronouns are well addressed across systems, with 65% average recall bound, while numerals are less so, with 43%. This implies that less frequent corrections are handled less well, but also opens room for improvement. An example is numerals and coordinating conjunctions, which are handled less well.

	UEDIN-MS	GOLD	Ratio (%)
CCONJ	71	158	44.9
NUM	22	48	45.8
SCONJ	114	233	48.9
AUX	153	310	49.4
VERB	202	405	49.9
ADP	232	461	50.3
PROPN	62	114	54.4
NOUN	346	618	56.0
ADV	273	472	57.8
PART	97	166	58.4
PUNCT	116	191	60.7
ADJ	283	462	61.3
DET	348	568	61.3
PRON	367	584	62.8
Overall	2686	4790	56.1

Table 6: Amount of syntactic changes per source POS tags for UEDIN-MS and the gold standard in absolute counts. The ratio is an upper bound on the recall.

We further revisit the replacement types discussed in §4.1 and compute the recall upper bound for the top system UEDIN-MS (Table 5 and aggregation per source POS in 6). Putting aside the rare types NUM→DET and PART→DET, we find that UEDIN-MS tackles considerably more SEs than Grammarly (see §5.2 below and Table 7). However, the recall bound is not uniform across types, where two types receive very low recall (ADJ→ADV with 38% and ADJ→NOUN with 44%), indicating these as potential directions for future work.

The bound over all SEs for UEDIN-MS is 56% (50% on the subset of errors discussed above). If we assume the precision on SE is similar to the overall reported precision (72%), we may conclude that recall for SEs is around 40%. For comparison, the overall reported recall is 60%, which suggests that SEs are harder on average than non-SEs, underscoring the value in classifying them.

5.2 Prospects for Improving GEC using Fine-grained SE Classification

To demonstrate the benefits of fine-grained SE categories, we analyze several SE types involving word replacements that are not as prevalent in TLE as additions and deletions of determiners and prepositions, but are still recurrent and form a closed-class that is likely to be addressable through designated GEC modules. We also consider the open-class VERB→ADJ for comparison. We examine the performance of a leading GEC tool, Grammarly in handling these types and analyze the capabilities of end-to-end systems in §5.

NUM→DET. Almost all examples include *One* instead of *any* or *another*. Example: *Technology is also important in ~~one~~ another area for me.*

PART→DET. All examples show *not* used instead of *no*. Example: *There was ~~not~~ no discount.*

ADJ→NOUN. Such replacements mostly involve quantifiers (*many →a lot of, small →a few*) which constitute a closed class. Example: *But some schools in my country don't allow ~~many~~ a lot of things.* Another subtype of this SE is more openended in that it involves using adjectives instead of morphologically related nouns (e.g., *joyful→joy, late →lateness*). Example: *Second, there should be friends and family members in the home to provide ~~joyful~~ joy and fun.* These SEs should be easy to detect because derivational relations are mostly transparent. However, there are a handful of harder cases (e.g., *I felt like a ~~dumb~~ fool*) whose correction demands more nuanced lexical knowledge.

NOUN→VERB. This SE type usually involves a morphologically-related form (*entrance→enter, product→produce*). However, some of the examples of this type are ambiguous due to English zero-derivation of deverbal nouns. Cf. *I love sleep in tents*, where *to sleep* and *sleeping* are both valid corrections found in the corpus. Example: *When we ~~entrance~~ entered the place our problems began.*

VERB→ADJ. Those replacements are diverse and often include large changes, mostly when the original sentence uses a completely wrong form of expression. Errors involving a verb rather a passive participle, which acts as an adjective, are also frequent (*trust was broken→betrayed trust, have conscience→are aware, problems involve with →problems involved with*).

		Amount	Detected	Valid	Precision	Recall
Add	None→ADV	58	0	0	0%	0%
	None→DET	44	13	10	77%	23%
	None→PRON	120	4	1	25%	1%
	None→VERB	107	0	0	0%	0%
Delete	ADV→None	64	3	0	0%	0%
	DET→None	49	20	20	100%	41%
	Pron→None	71	4	4	100%	6%
	VERB→None	41	4	0	0%	0%
Replace	ADJ→ADV	101	19	12	63%	12%
	ADJ→NOUN	45	4	2	50%	4%
	ADJ→VERB	18	0	0	0%	0%
	NOUN→VERB	44	10	8	80%	18%
	VERB→ADJ	26	3	0	0%	0%
	NUM→DET	7	0	0	0%	0%
	PART→DET	6	4	4	100%	67%

Table 7: Grammarly's performance on selected SE types in absolute counts. The varying behaviour per type indicates the separation to types is meaningful.

We turn to analyzing Grammarly's performance on the types discussed, as well as the four most frequent SE types of deletions, additions, and replacements (two of which are not among the above types). Grammarly's performance is of particular interest due to its reliance on designated modules (classifiers and rules) for addressing specific error types. Our results thus demonstrate how such a system may benefit from uncovering error types that can be addressed by integrating additional modules.

We manually annotate whether the edit in question is at all detected and whether it is validly corrected by Grammarly. As Grammarly may offer more than a single correction, we deem correct any case where at least one of the corrections is valid.

Results (Table 7) indicate that Grammarly fares poorly in addressing SEs, with the possible exception of superfluous determiners. Indeed, in many of the cases, only a small portion of the SEs was detected. While it is possible that Grammarly tends to overlook such cases because of the dominance of punctuation, spelling, and determiner errors in learner language, some of the types here involve only a handful of lexemes, suggesting that targeted treatment or data augmentation may be effective.

6   Related Work

Error types are often used to improve performance and evaluation in GEC. Taxonomies have been used to construct classifiers and rule-based engines to correct specific error types (e.g., Rozovskaya et al., 2014; Farra et al., 2014; Zheng et al., 2018). When using end-to-end systems, balancing the distribution of errors in the train and test sets has been shown to improve results (Junczys-Dowmunt et al., 2018). Ensembling black-box systems relying on per-type performance has been shown superior to each system's performance and over average ensembling (Kantor et al., 2019). Augmenting the training data with synthetic errors of a particular type is effective for improving performance on that type (Belinkov and Bisk, 2018). The classification of grammatical error types is also used to analyze system performance (e.g., Lichtarge et al., 2019). Choshen and Abend (2018a,b) showed that current systems and evaluation measures essentially ignore some error types, suggesting that targeted evaluation of these types may be needed.

To date, several error taxonomies have been proposed and applied for annotating errors in major English learner-language corpora (Bryant et al., 2019; Dahlmeier et al., 2013; Nicholls, 2003, *inter alia)*. There has been interest lately in other languages, for which different datasets and taxonomies were created (Rozovskaya and Roth, 2019; Rao et al., 2018; Zaghouani et al., 2014). However, different taxonomies are used by different corpora, based on commonly observed error types in the target domain and language, which impedes direct comparison across corpora. Moreover, these taxonomies are not formulated based on a specific theory or annotation scheme for morphosyntactic representation, which may promote accessibility to non-experts but often leads to non-uniform terminology and difficulty in leveraging available NLP tools.

Another automatic type classification was suggested apart from ERRANT. Swanson and Yamangil (2012) trained a log-linear model to predict types defined by Nicholls (2003). This taxonomy resembles ours in that it uses grammatical categories (POS tags), but differs in that it only distinguishes types based on the POS tag of the

correction and not of the source sentence. Moreover, relying solely on POS tags yields difficulties
in classifying constructions that involve more than
a single word. For such cases, it defines specialized
error types, such as *Incorrect Argument Structure*,
which serves as a residual category for argument
structure errors that cannot be accounted for by
adposition or agreement errors. However, unlike
SERCL, it does not provide any information as to
what particular incorrect argument structure was
used or how it should be corrected.

Choshen and Abend (2018c) used a semantic
annotation(Abend and Rappoport, 2013) to show
semantics, unlike syntax is kept upon changes. UD
was previously used in GEC in the TLE corpus and
in a learner language parser (e.g., Sakaguchi et al.,
2017) (we do not apply their parser, as it is made
specifically for English, and might alter the origin
parse).

7 Conclusion

We presented SERCL, a novel method for classifying SEs based on UD parses of learner text and
its correction. We show that SERCL provides a
detailed picture of the prevalence of different SEs
in two languages, and can be straightforwardly automated. We further show that the method manages
to classify about 60% of the unclassified edits by
ERRANT, the standard tool for error classification,
and provides useful complementary information
for many of the classified edits.

Future work will combine SERCL and ERRANT
into a single tool for English error classification
(work in this direction has already begun). The
experiments we presented show that several leading GEC systems of different types make errors of
types that are not well-addressed by current systems. These results can inform the future development of tailored solutions for these cases.

Acknowledgments

We thank Yarden Gavish for her help with coding
and data preparation assignments. This work was
supported by the Israel Science Foundation (grant
no. 929/17). Leshem Choshen is supported

References

Omri Abend and A. Rappoport. 2013. Universal conceptual cognitive annotation (UCCA). In *ACL*.

Hiroki Asano, Masato Mita, Tomoya Mizumoto, and
Jun Suzuki. 2019. The AIP-tohoku system at the
BEA-2019 shared task. In *Proceedings of the Fourteenth Workshop on Innovative Use of NLP for Building Educational Applications*, pages 176–182, Florence, Italy. Association for Computational Linguistics.

Yonatan Belinkov and Yonatan Bisk. 2018. Synthetic
and natural noise both break neural machine translation. *ICLR*.

Yevgeni Berzak, Jessica Kenney, Carolyn Spadine,
Jing Xian Wang, Lucia Lam, Keiko Sophie Mori,
Sebastian Garza, and Boris Katz. 2016. Universal
Dependencies for learner english. In *Proceedings of
the 54th Annual Meeting of the Association for Computational Linguistics (Volume 1: Long Papers)*, volume 1, pages 737–746.

Adriane Boyd. 2018. Using Wikipedia edits in low
resource grammatical error correction. In *Proceedings of the 2018 EMNLP Workshop W-NUT: The
4th Workshop on Noisy User-generated Text*, pages
79–84, Brussels, Belgium. Association for Computational Linguistics.

Christopher Bryant, Mariano Felice, Øistein E. An-
dersen, and Ted Briscoe. 2019. The BEA-2019
shared task on grammatical error correction. In *Proceedings of the Fourteenth Workshop on Innovative
Use of NLP for Building Educational Applications*,
pages 52–75, Florence, Italy. Association for Computational Linguistics.

Christopher Bryant, Mariano Felice, and Ted Briscoe.
2017. Automatic annotation and evaluation of error
types for grammatical error correction. In *ACL*.

Yo Joong Choe, Jiyeon Ham, Kyubyong Park, and
Yeoil Yoon. 2019. A neural grammatical error cor-
rection system built on better pre-training and se-
quential transfer learning. In *Proceedings of the
Fourteenth Workshop on Innovative Use of NLP for
Building Educational Applications*, pages 213–227,
Florence, Italy. Association for Computational Lin-
guistics.

Leshem Choshen and Omri Abend. 2018a. Automatic
metric validation for grammatical error correction.
In *Proceedings of the 56th Annual Meeting of the
Association for Computational Linguistics (Volume
1: Long Papers)*.

Leshem Choshen and Omri Abend. 2018b. Inherent biases in reference-based evaluation for grammatical
error correction and text simplification. In *Proceedings of the 56th Annual Meeting of the Association
for Computational Linguistics (Volume 1: Long Papers)*.

Leshem Choshen and Omri Abend. 2018c. Reference-
less measure of faithfulness for grammatical error
correction. In *Proceedings of the 2018 Conference
of the North American Chapter of the Association
for Computational Linguistics: Human Language
Technologies*.

Daniel Dahlmeier, Hwee Tou Ng, and Siew Mei Wu. 2013. Building a large annotated corpus of learner english: The nus corpus of learner english. In *Proceedings of the eighth workshop on innovative use of NLP for building educational applications*, pages 22–31.

Bonnie J. Dorr. 1994. Machine translation divergences: a formal description and proposed solution. *Computational linguistics*, 20(4):597–635.

Noura Farra, Nadi Tomeh, Alla Rozovskaya, and Nizar Habash. 2014. Generalized character-level spelling error correction. In *Proceedings of the 52nd Annual Meeting of the Association for Computational Linguistics (Volume 2: Short Papers)*, volume 2, pages 161–167.

Roman Grundkiewicz, Marcin Junczys-Dowmunt, and Kenneth Heafield. 2019. Neural grammatical error correction systems with unsupervised pre-training on synthetic data. In *Proceedings of the Fourteenth Workshop on Innovative Use of NLP for Building Educational Applications*, pages 252–263, Florence, Italy. Association for Computational Linguistics.

Marcin Junczys-Dowmunt, Roman Grundkiewicz, Shubha Guha, and Kenneth Heafield. 2018. Approaching neural grammatical error correction as a low-resource machine translation task. In *NAACL-HLT*.

Yoav Kantor, Yoav Katz, Leshem Choshen, Naftali Naftali, and Noam Slonim. 2019. Learning to combine grammatical error corrections. In *BEA 2019 Shared Task: Grammatical Error Correction*.

Jared Lichtarge, Christopher Alberti, Shankar Kumar, Noam Shazeer, Niki Parmar, and Simon Tong. 2019. Corpora generation for grammatical error correction. In *NAACL-HLT*.

Tomoya Mizumoto, Yuta Hayashibe, Mamoru Komachi, Masaaki Nagata, and Yuji Matsumoto. 2012. The effect of learner corpus size in grammatical error correction of esl writings. In *COLING*.

Diane Nicholls. 2003. The cambridge learner corpus: Error coding and analysis for lexicography and elt. In *Proceedings of the Corpus Linguistics 2003 conference*, volume 16, pages 572–581.

Dmitry Nikolaev, Ofir Arviv, Taelin Karidi, Neta Kenneth, Veronika Mitnik, Lilja Maria Saeboe, and Omri Abend. 2020. Fine-grained analysis of cross-linguistic syntactic divergences. In *Proceedings of the 58th Annual Meeting of the Association for Computational Linguistics*, pages 1159–1176, Online. Association for Computational Linguistics.

Joakim Nivre, Marie-Catherine de Marneffe, Filip Ginter, Yoav Goldberg, Jan Hajic, Christopher D. Manning, Ryan McDonald, Slav Petrov, Sampo Pyysalo, Natalia Silveira, Reut Tsarfaty, and Daniel Zeman. 2016. Universal Dependencies v1: A multilingual treebank collection. In *Proc. of LREC*.

Gaoqi Rao, Qi Gong, Baolin Zhang, and Endong Xun. 2018. Overview of nlptea-2018 share task chinese grammatical error diagnosis. In *Proceedings of the 5th Workshop on Natural Language Processing Techniques for Educational Applications*, pages 42–51.

Alla Rozovskaya and Dan Roth. 2019. Grammar error correction in morphologically rich languages: The case of russian. *Transactions of the Association for Computational Linguistics*, 7:1–17.

Alla Rozovskaya, Dan Roth, and Vivek Srikumar. 2014. Correcting grammatical verb errors. In *Proceedings of the 14th Conference of the European Chapter of the Association for Computational Linguistics*, pages 358–367.

Keisuke Sakaguchi, Matt Post, and Benjamin Van Durme. 2017. Error-repair dependency parsing for ungrammatical texts. In *Proceedings of the 55th Annual Meeting of the Association for Computational Linguistics (Volume 2: Short Papers)*, pages 189–195.

Felix Stahlberg and Bill Byrne. 2019. The CUED's grammatical error correction systems for BEA-2019. In *Proceedings of the Fourteenth Workshop on Innovative Use of NLP for Building Educational Applications*, pages 168–175, Florence, Italy. Association for Computational Linguistics.

Milan Straka, Jan Hajic, and Jana Straková. 2016. Udpipe: Trainable pipeline for processing conll-u files performing tokenization, morphological analysis, pos tagging and parsing. In *LREC*.

Ben Swanson and Elif Yamangil. 2012. Correction detection and error type selection as an ESL educational aid. In *Proceedings of the 2012 Conference of the North American Chapter of the Association for Computational Linguistics: Human Language Technologies*, pages 357–361, Montréal, Canada. Association for Computational Linguistics.

Shuyao Xu, Jiehao Zhang, Jin Chen, and Long Qin. 2019. Erroneous data generation for grammatical error correction. In *Proceedings of the Fourteenth Workshop on Innovative Use of NLP for Building Educational Applications*, pages 149–158, Florence, Italy. Association for Computational Linguistics.

Wajdi Zaghouani, Behrang Mohit, Nizar Habash, Ossama Obeid, Nadi Tomeh, Alla Rozovskaya, Noura Farra, Sarah Alkuhlani, and Kemal Oflazer. 2014. Large scale Arabic error annotation: Guidelines and framework. In *Proceedings of the Ninth International Conference on Language Resources and Evaluation (LREC'14)*, Reykjavik, Iceland. European Language Resources Association (ELRA).

Tatiana Zdorenko. 2010. Subject omission in russian: a study of the russian national corpus. In Stefan Th. Gries, Stefanie Wulff, and Mark Davies, editors, *Corpus-linguistic applications. Current studies, new directions*, pages 119–133. Brill Rodopi.

Daniel Zeman, Jan Hajič, Martin Popel, Martin Potthast, Milan Straka, Filip Ginter, Joakim Nivre, and Slav Petrov. 2018. Conll 2018 shared task: multilingual parsing from raw text to universal dependencies. In *Proceedings of the CoNLL 2018 Shared Task: Multilingual Parsing from Raw Text to Universal Dependencies*, pages 1–21.

Junchao Zheng, Courtney Napoles, Joel Tetreault, and Kostiantyn Omelianchuk. 2018. How do you correct run-on sentences it's not as easy as it seems. In *Proceedings of the 2018 EMNLP Workshop W-NUT: The 4th Workshop on Noisy User-generated Text*, pages 33–38.

How to Probe Sentence Embeddings in Low-Resource Languages:
On Structural Design Choices for Probing Task Evaluation

Steffen Eger, Johannes Daxenberger, Iryna Gurevych
Computer Science Department, Technische Universität Darmstadt, Germany
`eger@aiphes.tu-darmstadt.de,`
`{daxenberger,gurevych}@ukp.informatik.tu-darmstadt.de`

Abstract

Sentence encoders map sentences to real valued vectors for use in downstream applications. To peek into these representations—e.g., to increase interpretability of their results— probing tasks have been designed which query them for linguistic knowledge. However, designing probing tasks for lesser-resourced languages is tricky, because these often lack large-scale annotated data or (high-quality) dependency parsers as a prerequisite of probing task design in English. To investigate how to probe sentence embeddings in such cases, we investigate sensitivity of probing task results to structural design choices, conducting the first such large scale study. We show that design choices like size of the annotated probing dataset and type of classifier used for evaluation do (sometimes substantially) influence probing outcomes. We then probe embeddings in a multilingual setup with design choices that lie in a 'stable region', as we identify for English, and find that results on English do not transfer to other languages. Fairer and more comprehensive sentence-level probing evaluation should thus be carried out on multiple languages in the future.

1 Introduction

Sentence embeddings (a.k.a. sentence encoders) have become ubiquitous in NLP (Kiros et al., 2015; Conneau et al., 2017), extending the concept of word embeddings to the sentence level. In the context of recent efforts to open the black box of deep learning models and representations (Linzen et al., 2019), it has also become fashionable to *probe* sentence embeddings for the linguistic information signals they contain (Perone et al., 2018), as this may not be clear from their performances in downstream tasks. Such probes are linguistic micro tasks—like detecting the length of a sentence or its dependency tree depth—that have to be solved by

		classifier			
		LR	MLP	NB	RF
size	High	(A,B,C)	(A,B,C)	(C,A,B)	(C,B,A)
	Mid	(A,C,B)	(C,B,A)	(A,B,C)	(C,B,A)
	Low	(A,B,C)	(B,A,C)	(B,C,A)	(A,B,C)

Table 1: Schematic illustration of our concept of stability across two dimensions (classifier and training size). Here, three encoders, dubbed A,B,C, are ranked. The region of stability is given by those settings that support the majority ranking of encoders, which is A≻B≻C.

a classifier using given representations.

The majority of approaches for probing sentence embeddings target English, but recently some works have also addressed other languages such as Polish, Russian, or Spanish in a multi- and cross-lingual setup (Krasnowska-Kieraś and Wróblewska, 2019; Ravishankar et al., 2019). Motivations for considering a multi-lingual analysis include knowing whether findings from English transfer to other languages and determining a universal set of probing tasks that suits multiple languages, e.g., with richer morphology and freer word order.

Our work is also inspired by probing sentence encoders in multiple (particularly low-resource) languages. We are especially interested in the formal structure of probing task design in this context. Namely, when designing probing tasks for low-resource languages, some questions arise naturally that are less critical in English. One of them is the size of training data for probing tasks, as this training data typically needs to be (automatically or manually) annotated, an inherent obstacle in low-resource settings.[1]

Thus, at first, we ask for the training data size

---

[1] The main issue is that high-quality dependency parsers, as required for standard probing tasks, exist only for a handful of languages. E.g., UDPipe (Straka, 2018) is available for only about 100 languages, and performance scores for some of these are considerably below those of English (Straka, 2018).

Proceedings of the 24th Conference on Computational Natural Language Learning, pages 108–118
Online, November 19-20, 2020. ©2020 Association for Computational Linguistics
https://doi.org/10.18653/v1/P17

required for obtaining reliable probing task results. This question is also relevant for English: on the one hand, Conneau et al. (2018) claim that training data for a probing task should be plentiful, as otherwise (highly parametrized) classifiers on top of representations may be unable to extract the relevant information signals; on the other hand, Hewitt and Liang (2019) note that a sufficiently powerful classifier with enough training data can in principle learn any task, without this necessarily allowing to conclude that the representations adequately store the linguistic signal under scrutiny. Second, we ask how stable probing task results are across different classifiers (e.g., MLP vs. Naive Bayes). This question is closely related to the question about size, since different classifiers have different sensitivities to data size; especially deep models are claimed to require more training data.

We evaluate the sensitivity of probing task results to the two outlined parameters—which are *mere* machine learning design choices that do not affect the linguistic content stored in the sentence representations under scrutiny—and then determine a 'region of stability' for English (en), where outcomes are predicted to be similar for the majority of parameter choices. Table 1 illustrates this. Using parameter choices within our region of stability, we turn to three lower-resource languages, *viz.*: Turkish (tr), Russian (ru), and Georgian (ka). tr is a Turkic language written in Latin script which makes exhaustive use of agglutination. ru is a Slavic language written in Cyrillic script characterized by strong inflection and rich morphology. ka is a South-Caucasian language using its own script called Mkhedruli. It makes use of both agglutination as well as inflection. For these, our main research questions are whether probing task results transfer from English to the other languages.

Overall, our research questions are:

- **(i)** How reliable are probing task results across machine learning design choices?

- **(ii)** Will encoder performances correlate across languages, even though the languages and their linguistic properties may differ?

- **(iii)** Will probing task performances correlate across languages?

- **(iv)** Will the correlation between probing and downstream tasks be the same across languages?

These questions are important because they indicate whether or not probing tasks (and their relation to downstream tasks) have to be re-evaluated in languages other than en.[2]

2 Related work

Our goal is to probe for sentence-level linguistic knowledge encoded in sentence embeddings (Perone et al., 2018) in a multilingual setup which marginalizes out the effects of probing task design choices when comparing sentence representations.

Sentence embeddings have become central for representing texts beyond the word level, e.g., in small data scenarios, where it is difficult to induce good higher-level text representations from word embeddings (Subramanian et al., 2018) or for clustering or text retrieval applications (Reimers and Gurevych, 2019). To standardize the comparison of sentence embeddings, Conneau and Kiela (2018) proposed the SentEval framework for evaluating the quality of sentence embeddings on a range of downstream and 10 probing tasks.

Probing tasks are used to introspect embeddings for linguistic knowledge, by taking "probes" as dedicated syntactic or semantic micro tasks (Köhn, 2016). As opposed to an evaluation in downstream applications or benchmarks like GLUE (Wang et al., 2018), probing tasks target very specific linguistic knowledge which may otherwise be confounded in downstream applications. Since they are artificial tasks, they can also be better controlled for to avoid dataset biases and artifacts. Probing is typically either executed on type/token (word) (Tenney et al., 2019) or sentence level (Adi et al., 2017). For sentence level evaluation, SentEval thus far only includes en data. Each probing task in SentEval is balanced and has 100k train, 10k dev, and 10k test instances. The effects of these design choices are unclear, which is why our work addresses their influence systematically.

In the **multilingual** setting, Sahin et al. (2019) propose 15 token and type level probing tasks. Their probing task data is sourced from UniMorph 2.0 (Kirov et al., 2018), Universal Dependency treebanks (McCarthy et al., 2018) and Wikipedia word frequency lists. To deal with lower-resourced languages, they only use 10K samples per probing task/language pair (7K/2K/1K for train/dev/test) and exclude task/language pairs for which this amount cannot be generated. Their final experi-

---

[2]Code and data are available from `https://github.com/UKPLab/conll2020-multilingual-sentence-probing`.

ments are carried out on five languages (Finnish, German, Spanish, `ru`, `tr`), for which enough training data is available. They find that for morphologically rich (agglutinative) languages, several probing tasks positively correlate with downstream applications. Our work also investigates correlation between probing and downstream performance, but we do so on sentence level.

On sentence level, Ravishankar et al. (2019) train an InferSent-like encoder (Conneau et al., 2017) on `en` and map this encoder to four languages (`ru`, French, German, Spanish) using parallel data. Subsequently, they probe the encoders on the probing tasks proposed by Conneau et al. (2018) using Wikipedia data for each language, with the same size of probing task data as in SentEval, i.e., 100k/10k/10k for train/dev/test. Their interest is in whether probing tasks results are higher/lower compared to `en` scores. They find particularly the `ru` probing scores to be low, which they speculate to be an artifact of cross-lingual word embedding induction and the language distance of `ru` to `en`. In contrast to us, their focus is particularly on the effect of transferring sentence representations from `en` to other languages. The problem of such an analysis is that results may be affected by the nature of the cross-lingual mapping techniques.

Krasnowska-Kieraś and Wróblewska (2019) probe sentence encoders in `en` and Polish (`pl`). They use tasks defined in Conneau et al. (2018) but slightly modify them (e.g., replacing dependency with constituency trees), reject some tasks (Bigram-Shift, as word order may play a minor role in `pl`), and add two new tasks (Voice and Sentence Type). Since `pl` data is less abundant, they shrink the size of the `pl` datasets to 75k/7.5k/7.5k for train/dev/test and, for consistency, do the same for `en`. They extract probing datasets from an `en`-`pl` parallel corpus using COMBO for dependency parsing (Rybak and Wróblewska, 2018). They find that `en` and `pl` probing results mostly agree, i.e., encoders store the same linguistic information across the two languages.

3 Approach

In the absence of ground truth, our main interest is in a 'stable' structural setup for probing task design—with the end goal of applying this design to multilingual probing analyses (keeping their restrictions, e.g., small data sizes, in mind). To this end, we consider a 2d space $\mathcal{X}$ comprising probing data size and classifier choice for probing tasks.[3] For a selected set of points $p_0, p_1, \ldots$ in $\mathcal{X}$, we evaluate all our encoders on p_i, and determine the 'outcomes' O_i (e.g., ranking) of the encoders at p_i. We consider a setup p_i as stable if outcome O_i is shared by a majority of other settings p_j. This can be considered a region of agreement, similarly to inter-annotator agreement (Artstein and Poesio, 2008). In other words, we identify 'ideal' test conditions by minimizing the influence of parameters p_i on the outcome O_i. Below, we will approximate these intuitions using correlation.

3.1 Embeddings

We consider two types of sentence encoders, **non-parametric methods** which combine word embeddings in elementary ways, without training; and **parametric methods**, which tune parameters on top of word embeddings. As non-parametric methods, we consider: (i) average word embeddings as a popular baseline, (ii) the concatenation of average, min and max pooling (*pmeans*) (Rücklé et al., 2018); and Random LSTMs (Conneau et al., 2017; Wieting and Kiela, 2019), which feed word embeddings to randomly initialized LSTMs, then apply a pooling operation across time-steps. As parametric methods, we consider: InferSent (Conneau et al., 2017), which induces a sentence representation by learning a semantic entailment relationship between two sentences; QuickThought (Logeswaran and Lee, 2018) which reframes the popular SkipThought model (Kiros et al., 2015) in a classification context; LASER (Artetxe and Schwenk, 2019) derived from massively multilingual machine translation models, and BERT base (Devlin et al., 2019), where we average token embeddings of the last layer for a sentence representation. Dimensionalities of encoders are listed in the appendix.

3.2 Probing Tasks

Following Conneau et al. (2018), we consider the following probing tasks: **BigramShift** (en, `tr`, `ru`, `ka`), **TreeDepth** (en), **Length** (en, `tr`, `ru`, `ka`), **Subject Number** (en, `tr`, `ru`), **WordContent** (en, `tr`, `ru`, `ka`), and **TopConstituents** (en).

---

[3]We also looked at further parameters, in particular, the class (im)balances of training datasets. Details and results can be found in the appendix. Since, however, their influence seemed to be less critical and an increased search space would blow up computational costs, we decided to limit our investigation to the described dimensions.

Task	Description	Example
Bigram Shift	Whether two words in a sentence are inverted	This is my Eve Christmas. $\longrightarrow$ True
Tree Depth	Longest path from root to leaf in constituent tree	"One hand here , one hand there , that 's it" $\longrightarrow$ 5
Length	Number of tokens	I like cats $\longrightarrow$ 1-4 words
Subject Number	Whether the subject is in singular or plural	They work together $\longrightarrow$ Plural
Word Content	Which mid-frequency word a sentence contains	Everybody should step back $\longrightarrow$ everybody
Top Constituents	Classific. task where classes are given by 19 most common top constituent sequences in corpus	Did he buy anything from Troy $\longrightarrow$ VDP_NP_VP
Voice	Whether sent. contains a passive construct	He likes cats $\longrightarrow$ False
SV-Agree	Whether subject and verb agree	They works together $\longrightarrow$ Disagree
SV-Dist	Distance between subject and verb	The delivery was very late $\longrightarrow$ 1

Table 2: Probing tasks, their description and illustration. Upper tasks are defined as in SentEval.

We choose Length, BigramShift and WordContent because they are unsupervised tasks that require no labeled data and can thus be easily implemented across different languages—they also represent three different types of elementary probing tasks: surface, syntactic and semantic/lexical. We further include Subject Number across all our languages because number marking is extremely common across languages and it is comparatively easy to identify. We adopt **Voice** (en, tr, ru, ka) from Krasnowska-Kieraś and Wróblewska (2019). For en, we additionally evaluate on TreeDepth and TopConstituents as hard syntactic tasks. We add two tasks not present in the canon of probing tasks given in SentEval: **Subject-Verb-Agreement (SV-Agree)** (en, tr, ru, ka) and **Subject-Verb-Distance (SV-Dist)** (en, tr, ru). We probe representations for these properties because we suspect that agreement between subject and verb is a difficult task which requires inferring a relationship between pairs of words which may stand in a long-distance relationship (Gulordava et al., 2018). Moverover, we assume this task to be particularly hard in morphologically rich and word-order free languages, thus it could be a good predictor for performance in downstream tasks.

To implement the probing tasks, for en, we use the probing tasks datasets defined in Conneau and Kiela (2018) and we apply spaCy[4] to sentences extracted from Wikipedia for the newly added probing tasks Voice and SV-Agree. For tr, ru, and ka, we do not rely on dependency parsers because of quality issues and unavailability for ka. Instead, for tr and ru, we use information from Universal Dependencies (UD) (Nivre et al., 2016). E.g., for SV-Dist, we determine the dependency distance between the main verb and the subject from UD.

Instead of the exact distances, we predict binned classes: [1], [2,4], [5,7], [8,12], [13,∞). For ka, we use data and grammatical information from the Georgian National Corpus (GNC)[5]. We could not implement SV-Dist for ka, due to missing dependency information in the GNC. For the same reason, we omit Subject Number for ka.

For SV-Agree, we create a list of frequently occurring verbs together with their corresponding *present tense conjugations* for all involved languages including English. We check each individual candidate sentence from Wikipedia for the presence of a verb form in the list. If no word is present, we exclude the sentence from consideration. Otherwise, we randomly replace the verb form by a different conjugation in 50% of the cases.

An overview of the probing tasks, along with descriptions and examples, is given in Table 2.

3.3 Downstream Tasks

In addition to probing tasks, we test the embeddings in downstream applications. Our focus is on a diverse set of high-level sentence classification tasks. We choose **Argument Mining**, **Sentiment Analysis** and **TREC question answering**. Required training data for languages other than en has been machine translated using Google Translate[6] for Argument Mining and TREC.[7] Statistics for all datasets are reported in Table 6.

Argument Mining (AM) AM is an emergent NLP task requiring sophisticated reasoning capabilities. We reuse the sentence-level argument (stance)

---

[4]https://spacy.io

[5]https://clarino.uib.no/gnc

[6]http://translate.google.com

[7]To estimate the quality of the machine translation, we measured its performance on parallel data. Details can be found in the appendix. While the machine translation is generally of acceptable quality, we cannot exclude the possibility that it may effect some of our downstream tasks results reported below.

detection dataset by Stab et al. (2018), which labels sentences extracted from web pages as pro-, con-, or non-arguments for eight different topics. A sentence only qualifies as pro or con argument when it both expresses a stance towards the topic and gives a reason for that stance. The classifier input is a concatenation of the sentence embedding and the topic encoding. In total, there are about 25,000 sentences.

Sentiment Analysis As opposed to AM, sentiment analysis only determines the opinion flavor of a statement. Since sentiment analysis is a very established NLP task, we did not machine translate en training data, but used original data for en, ru and tr and created a novel dataset for ka. For en, we use the US Airline Twitter Sentiment dataset, consisting of 14,148 tweets labeled in three sentiment classes[8]. For tr, we took the Turkish Twitter Sentiment Dataset with 6,172 examples and three classes[9]. For ru, we used the Russian Twitter Corpus (RuTweetCorp), which we reduced to 30,000 examples in two classes.[10] For ka, we followed the approach by Choudhary et al. (2018) and crawled sentiment flavored tweets in a distant supervision manner. Emojis were used as distant signals to indicate sentiment on preselected tweets from the Twitter API. After post-processing, we were able to collect 11,513 Georgian tweets in three sentiment classes. The dataset will made available publicly, including more details on the creation process.

TREC Question Type Detection Question type detection is an important part of Question-Answering systems. The Text Retrieval Conference (TREC) dataset consists of a set of questions labeled with their respective question types (six labels including e.g. "description" or "location") and is part of the SentEval benchmark (Conneau and Kiela, 2018). We used the data as provided in SentEval, yielding 5,952 instances.

4 Experiments

Experimental Setup To the SentEval toolkit (Conneau and Kiela, 2018), which addresses both probing and downstream tasks and offers Logistic Regression (LR) and MLP classifiers on top of representations, we added implementations of Random Forest (RF) and Naive Bayes (NB) from scikit-learn as other popular but 'simple' classifiers. SentEval defines specific model validation techniques for each task. Following SentEval, we tune the size of the hidden layer in $\{50, 100, 200\}$, dropout in $\{0.0, 0.1, 0.2\}$ and L^2 regularization in $\{10^{-5}, 10^{-1}\}$ when training an MLP. For RF, we tune the maximum tree depth in $\{10, 50, 100, \infty\}$. For LR, we tune the L^2 regularization in $\{10^{-5}, 10^{-1}\}$. We do not tune any hyperparameters for NB. For all probing tasks and TREC, we use predefined splits. For AM and sentiment analysis, we use 10-fold inner cross validation.

4.1 Probing task design in en

In our design, we consider (a) four well-known and popular classifiers—LR, MLP, NB, RF—on top of sentence representations, and (b) six different training data sizes (between 2k and 100k). We perform an exhaustive grid-search for size and classifier design, considering all combinations.

Size For each classifier, we obtain results (on 10k test instances) when varying the training data size over 2k, 5k, 10k, 20k, 30k, 100k. Downsampling was implemented by selecting the same percentage of samples that appears in the full dataset for each class. We then report average Spearman/Pearson correlations ρ/p between any two training set sizes s and t over all 9 probing tasks:[11]

$$\text{sim}_c(s, t) = \frac{1}{n} \sum_{i=1}^{n} \rho^*(\mathbf{c}_i(s), \mathbf{c}_i(t)) \qquad (1)$$

where n is the number of probing tasks ($n = 9$ for en), and $\mathbf{c}_i(s)$ is the vector that holds scores for each of the 7 sentence encoders in our experiments, given training size s, for probing task i and classifier c. We set correlations to zero if the p-value > 0.2.[12] In Table 3, we then report the minimum and average scores $\min_{(s,t)} \text{sim}_c(s, t)$ and $\frac{1}{M} \sum_{(s,t)} \text{sim}_c(s, t)$, respectively, per classifier c. We observe that the minimum values are small to moderate correlations between 0.2 (for NB) and 0.6 (for RF). The average correlations are moderate to high correlations ranging from 0.6 (for NB) to above 0.8 (for the others).

---

[11] We report both Spearman and Pearson for some of the results but give only Pearson for the remainder, reporting Spearman in the appendix.

[12] We choose a high p-value, because we correlate small vectors of size 7.

In Figure 1 (left), we show all the values $\text{sim}_c(s, t)$ for $c = \text{LR, NB}$. We observe that, indeed, LR has high correlations between training sizes especially starting from 10k training data points. The corresponding correlations of NB are much lower comparatively.

In Figure 2, we plot the stability of each training data size s

$$\text{sim}_c(s) = \frac{1}{N} \sum_t \text{sim}_c(s, t) \qquad (2)$$

for all of our classifiers c and where N is a normalizer equal to the number of different training set sizes, $N = 6$ in our case. The higher this score for a training size s, the more similar are the probing results for another training size t, on average. Across all classifiers, 2k and 100k are least stable— 100k is the default setting of SentEval. Most stable are 10k and 20k.

Classifier	Min		Avg	
	ρ	p	ρ	p
MLP	.480	.420	.810	.843
LR	.524	.502	.808	.805
RF	.529	.623	.800	.853
NB	.174	.292	.626	.671

Table 3: Stability over training sizes, in terms of minimum and average Spearman (ρ) / Pearson (p) correlation between any two sizes.

Classifier Next, we add the classifier choice as a second dimension: we examine whether correlations (Spearman/Pearson) between vectors $\mathbf{c}$ (holding scores for each of 7 sentence encoders for a classifier c) and $\mathbf{d}$ (holding the same scores for a classifier d) are similar in the same sense as in Eq. (1):

$$\text{sim}_{c,d}(s, t) = \frac{1}{n} \sum_{i=1}^{n} \rho^*(\mathbf{c}_i(s), \mathbf{d}_i(t)) \qquad (3)$$

Again, we average across all probing tasks, and set correlation values to zero if the p-value exceeds 0.2. In Table 4, we give min/avg values across data set sizes in this setup. We observe that LR and MLP most strongly agree. They have acceptable average agreement with RF, but low agreement with NB, on average, and, in the worst cases, even negative correlations with NB.

In Figure 1 (right), we illustrate correlations between LR and NB, on the one side, and LR and RF, on the other side, across all possible training set

	LR	RF	NB
MLP	.481/.790	.492/.632	-.043/.236
LR		.406/.640	-.057/.197
RF			.029/.320

Table 4: Min/Avg values $\text{sim}_{c,d}(s, t)$ across (s, t) (using Pearson) between classifiers c and d.

sizes. We observe that as the training data set sizes for RF and LR become larger, these two classifiers agree more strongly with LR. RF starts to have acceptable agreement with LR from 10k training instances onwards, while NB has acceptable agreement with LR only in the case of 100k training instances.

We now operationalize our intuition of 'region of stability' outlined in Table 1. For each of nine probing tasks, we compute the following. Let $r_j = E_{\zeta(1)} \succ E_{\zeta(2)} \succ E_{\zeta(3)} \succ \cdots$ be a specific ranking of encoders, where ζ is a fixed permutation. Let $r_{(c,s)}$ be the ranking of encoders according to the classifier, size combination (c, s). We compute the Spearman correlation $\tau_{(c,s,j)}$ between $r_{(c,s)}$ and r_j. For each possible ranking r_j of our 7 encoders, we then determine its support as the average over all values $\tau_{(c,s,j)}$ and then find the ranking $r_{\max}$ with most support according to this definition. Finally, we assign a score to the combination (c, s) not only when $r_{(c,s)}$ equals $r_{\max}$, but also when $r_{(c,s)}$ is close to $r_{\max}$: we again use the Spearman correlation between $r_{(c,s)}$ and $r_{\max}$ as a measure of closeness (we require a closeness of at least 0.75). The final score for (c, s) is given by (ignoring the threshold of 0.75 in the equation):

$$\mu_{(c,s)} = \sum_{i=1}^{n} \rho^*\left(r_{(c,s)}^{(i)}, r_{\max}^{(i)}\right) \qquad (4)$$

Table 5 shows classifier, size combinations with highest μ scores. LR and MLP are at the top, along with RF in the setting of 100k training data size. LR with size 10k is most stable overall, but the distance to the other top settings is small. Least stable (not shown) is NB.

classifier	LR	LR	RF	MLP	MLP	MLP
size	10k	20k	100k	20k	30k	10k
$\mu_{(c,s)}$	7.6	7.3	7.2	7.0	7.0	6.9

Table 5: Most stable classifier, size combinations according to Eq. (4).

Overall, we answer our first research question—

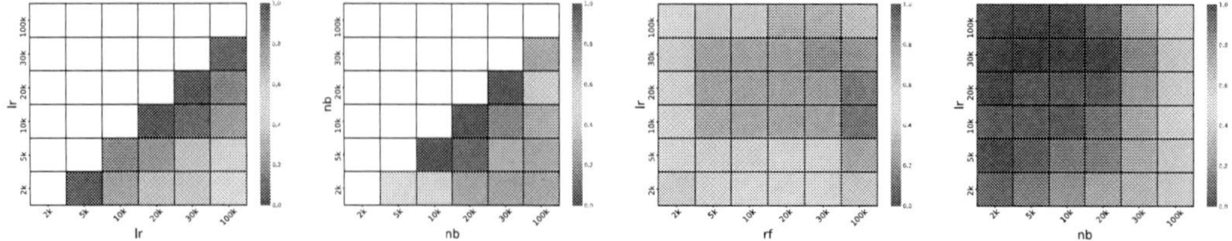

Figure 1: Left two: Average correlations $\text{sim}_c(s,t)$ for LR (first) and NB (second), using Pearson, for any two sizes $s,t \in \{2k, 5k, 10k, 20k, 30k, 100k\}$. Right two: Average correlations $\text{sim}_{c,d}(s,t)$ for $c = \text{LR}$ and $d = \text{RF}$ (third) and $c = \text{LR}$ and $d = \text{NB}$ (fourth). Best viewed in color.

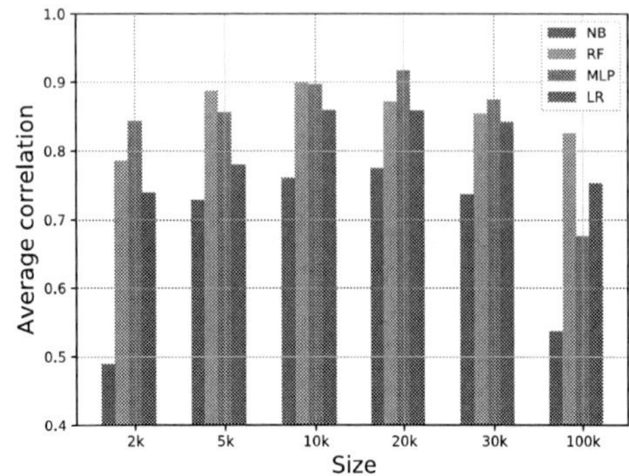

Figure 2: Stability of each training size computed using Eq. (2) for different classifiers c.

(i) How reliable are probing task results across machine learning design choices?—as follows (for en): probing tasks results can be little reliable and may vary greatly among machine learning parameter choices. The standard training set size of SentEval, 100k, appears to be less stable. As region of stability, we postulate especially the setting with 10k training instances for the LR classifier.

4.2 Multi-lingual results

Experimental Setup Given our results for en, we choose the LR classifier with a size of roughly 10k instances overall. Table 6 provides more details about the datasets. In line with SentEval (and partly supported by our results on dataset balance given in the appendix), we aim for as balanced label distributions as possible. Because of the small test sizes, we use inner 5-fold cross validation for all tasks except for SubjNumber, where we use pre-defined train/dev/test splits as in Conneau et al. (2018) to avoid leaking lexical information from train to test splits.

We obtain average and pmeans embeddings through pooling over pre-trained FastText embeddings (Grave et al., 2018). The same embeddings

are used for the random LSTM. For average BERT, we use the base-multilingual-cased model. We machine translate the AllNLI corpus into tr, ru and ka, to obtain training data for Infersent.[13] The models are then trained using default hyperparameters and with pre-trained FastText embeddings. Compared to en, we modify the WC probing task in the multilingual setting to only predict 30 mid-frequency words instead of 1000. This is more appropriate for our much smaller data sizes.

4.2.1 Probing tasks

Results are shown in Figures 3 and 4.

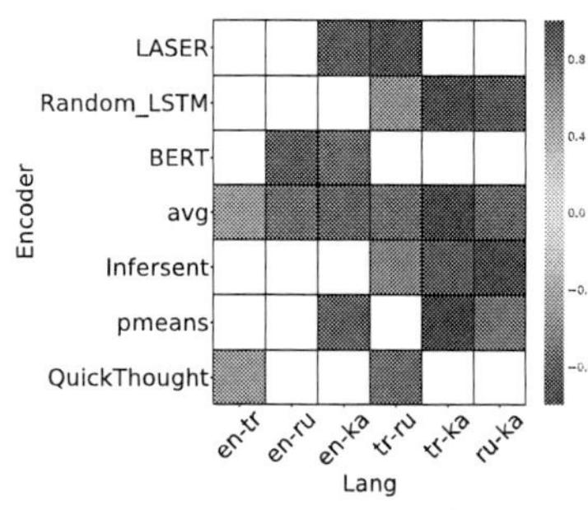

Figure 3: Pearson correlations across languages for different encoders.

(ii) Will encoder performances correlate across languages? For each encoder e, we correlate performances of e between en and the other languages on 5 (for ka) and 7 (for tr, ru) probing tasks (using 10k dataset size and LR for all involved languages, including en). In Figure 3, we observe that correlations between en and other languages are generally either zero or weakly positive. Only average embeddings have more than 1 positive correlation scores across the 3 language combinations with en. Among low-resource languages, there

---

[13]Using Google Translate, see appendix for details.

Task	EN		TR		RU		KA	
	Size	Balance	Size	Balance	Size	Balance	Size	Balance
Bigram Shift	100k	1:1	10k	1:1	10k	1.1:1	10k	1.1:1
Length	100k	1:1	10k	1:1	12k	1:1	10k	1:1
Subject Number	100k	1:1	4,093	5:1	11,877	1:1	-	-
Word Content	100k	1:1	10k	1.5:1	10k	1.2:1	10k	4:1
Top Constituents	100k	1:1	-	-	-	-	-	-
Tree Depth	100k	2.2:1	-	-	-	-	-	-
Voice	100k	1:1	8,417	6:1	10k	2:1	10k	1.9:1
SV-Agree	100k	1:1	10k	1:1	10k	1:1	10k	1:1
SV-Dist	100k	1:1	1,642	1.9:1	8,231	1.1:1	-	-
Arg. Mining (macro-F1)	25,303	3:1	25,303	3:1	25,303	3:1	25,303	3:1
TREC (Accuracy)	5,952	14:1	5,952	14:1	5,952	14:1	5,952	14:1
Sentiment Analysis (macro-F1)	14,148	4.2:1	6,172	1.7:1	30k	1:1	11,513	5.5:1

Table 6: Probing and downstream tasks. We report the balance between the class with the most and the least samples. For downstream tasks, the evaluation measure is given in brackets.

are no negative correlations and fewer zero correlations. All of the low-resource languages correlate more among themselves than with en. This makes sense from a linguistic point of view, since en is clearly the outlier in our sample given its minimal inflection and fixed word order. Thus, the answer to this research question is that our results support the view that transfer is better for typologically similar languages.

(iii) Will probing task performances correlate across languages? For each probing task π, we report Pearson correlations, between all language pairs, of vectors holding scores of 7 encoders on π. Figure 4 shows the results. The pattern is overall

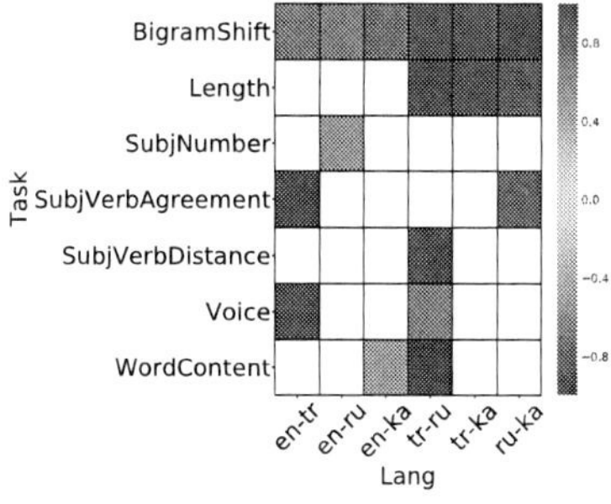

Figure 4: Pearson correlations across languages for different probing tasks.

similar as for (ii) in that there are many zero correlations between en and the other languages. tr also negatively correlates with en for SV-Agree. Only BigramShift has positive correlations throughout. Low-resource languages correlate better among themselves as with en. Our conclusions are the same as for question **(ii)**.

Note that our findings contrast with Krasnowska-

Kieraś and Wróblewska (2019), who report that probing results for en and pl are mostly the same. Our results are more intuitively plausible: e.g., a good encoder should store linguistic information relevant for a particular language.

4.2.2 Downstream Tasks

Results are shown in Figure 5.

(iv) Will the correlation between probing and downstream tasks be the same across languages? For each of our languages, we correlate probing and downstream task performances. The results show that the answer to research question (iv) is clearly negative. In particular, en behaves differently to the other languages—while ru and tr behave more similarly. ka is the only language with negative correlations for Length, en the only one with positive scores. For the sentiment task, Word Content correlates positively for all languages except ka. The AM task correlates only in en and ka, but with different probing tasks. SV-Agree correlates positively with TREC and sentiment in all languages but en. This might be because determining the agreement of subject and verb is more grammatically complex in the other languages compared to English, and storing an adequate amount of grammatical information may be beneficial for certain downstream tasks. Predicting the performances of embeddings in downstream tasks via probing tasks thus appears idiosyncratic for individual languages. Opposed to Sahin et al. (2019), who suggest a direct relation between word level probing and downstream performance on agglutinative languages, we see little to no systematic correlation on the sentence level. Overall, SV-Agree is the best predictor across languages, with

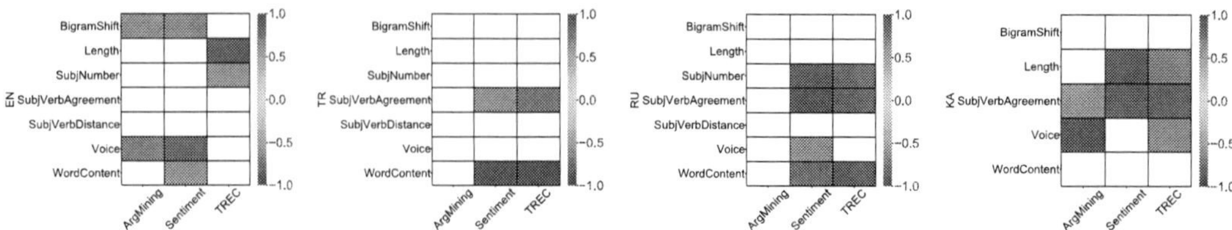

Figure 5: Pearson correlation among probing task and downstream performance for all languages.

7 positive correlations out of 12 possible. Interestingly, this task is missing from the current canon of SentEval.

5 Concluding Remarks

We investigated formal aspects of probing task design, including probing data size and classifier choice, in order to determine structural conditions for multilingual (low-resource) probing. We showed that probing tasks results are at best partly stable even for en and that the rankings of encoders varies with design choices. However, we identified a partial region of stability where results are supported by a majority of settings—even though this may not be mistaken for a 'region of truth'. This region was identified in en, which has most resources available. Our further findings then showed that probing and downstream results do not transfer well from English to our other languages, which in turn challenges our identified region of stability.

Overall, our results have partly negative implications for current practices of probing task design as they indicate that probing tasks are to some degree unreliable tools for introspecting linguistic information contained in sentence encoders. The relation of probing to downstream tasks is also unclear, as our multilingual results show. This is supported by recent findings giving contradictory claims regarding, e.g., the importance of the Word Content probing task for downstream performances (Eger et al., 2019; Wang and Kuo, 2020; Perone et al., 2018). Our findings further add to contemporaneous work by Ravichander et al. (2020) and Elazar et al. (2020), who showed that probes do not necessarily identify linguistic properties required for solving an actual task, thus questioning a common interpretation of probing itself.

An important aspect to keep in mind for correlation analyses as we conducted is that results may heavily depend on the selection of encoders involved—in our case, we selected a number of recently proposed state-of-the-art models in conjunction with weaker baseline models, for a diverse collection of encoders. While the small number of encoders we examined is a clear limitation of our approach, many of our results are significant (at relatively large p-values).

To the degree that the supervised probing tasks examined here will remain important tools for interpretation of sentence encoders in the future, our results indicate that multilingual probing is important for a fairer and more comprehensive comparison of encoders.

Acknowledgments

We thank the anonymous reviewers for their useful comments and suggestions. Wei Zhao and Benjamin Schiller gave useful feedback on earlier versions of this paper. Daniel Wehner and Martin Kerscher greatly helped to extend the SentEval code and collect the probing data for the low-resource languages. We finally thank Paul Meurer from the University of Bergen for making the Georgian National Corpus (GNC) available for our experiments in ka. The first author has been funded by the HMWK (Hessisches Ministerium für Wissenschaft und Kunst) as part of structural location promotion for TU Darmstadt in the context of the Hessian excellence cluster initiative "Content Analytics for the Social Good" (CA-SG). The second author has been supported by the German Federal Ministry of Education and Research (BMBF) under the promotional reference 03VP02540 (ArgumenText).

References

Yossi Adi, Einat Kermany, Yonatan Belinkov, Ofer Lavi, and Yoav Goldberg. 2017. Fine-grained analysis of sentence embeddings using auxiliary prediction tasks. *CoRR*, abs/1608.04207.

Mikel Artetxe and Holger Schwenk. 2019. Massively multilingual sentence embeddings for zero-shot cross-lingual transfer and beyond. *TACL*, 7:597–610.

Ron Artstein and Massimo Poesio. 2008. Inter-coder agreement for computational linguistics. *Comput. Linguist.*, 34(4):555–596.

Nurendra Choudhary, Rajat Singh, Vijjini Anvesh Rao, and Manish Shrivastava. 2018. Twitter corpus of resource-scarce languages for sentiment analysis and multilingual emoji prediction. In *Proceedings of the 27th International Conference on Computational Linguistics*, pages 1570–1577, Santa Fe, New Mexico, USA. Association for Computational Linguistics.

Alexis Conneau and Douwe Kiela. 2018. SentEval: An evaluation toolkit for universal sentence representations. In *Proceedings of the Eleventh International Conference on Language Resources and Evaluation (LREC 2018)*, Miyazaki, Japan. European Language Resources Association (ELRA).

Alexis Conneau, Douwe Kiela, Holger Schwenk, Loïc Barrault, and Antoine Bordes. 2017. Supervised learning of universal sentence representations from natural language inference data. In *Proceedings of the 2017 Conference on Empirical Methods in Natural Language Processing*, pages 670–680, Copenhagen, Denmark. Association for Computational Linguistics.

Alexis Conneau, Germán Kruszewski, Guillaume Lample, Loïc Barrault, and Marco Baroni. 2018. What you can cram into a single vector: Probing sentence embeddings for linguistic properties. *CoRR*, abs/1805.01070.

Jacob Devlin, Ming-Wei Chang, Kenton Lee, and Kristina Toutanova. 2019. BERT: Pre-training of deep bidirectional transformers for language understanding. In *Proceedings of the 2019 Conference of the North American Chapter of the Association for Computational Linguistics: Human Language Technologies, Volume 1 (Long and Short Papers)*, pages 4171–4186, Minneapolis, Minnesota. Association for Computational Linguistics.

Steffen Eger, Andreas Rücklé, and Iryna Gurevych. 2019. Pitfalls in the evaluation of sentence embeddings. In *Proceedings of the 4th Workshop on Representation Learning for NLP (RepL4NLP-2019)*, pages 55–60, Florence, Italy. Association for Computational Linguistics.

Yanai Elazar, Shauli Ravfogel, Alon Jacovi, and Yoav Goldberg. 2020. When bert forgets how to pos: Amnesic probing of linguistic properties and mlm predictions. *ArXiv*, abs/2006.00995.

Edouard Grave, Piotr Bojanowski, Prakhar Gupta, Armand Joulin, and Tomas Mikolov. 2018. Learning word vectors for 157 languages. In *Proceedings of the International Conference on Language Resources and Evaluation (LREC 2018)*.

Kristina Gulordava, Piotr Bojanowski, Edouard Grave, Tal Linzen, and Marco Baroni. 2018. Colorless green recurrent networks dream hierarchically. *CoRR*, abs/1803.11138.

John Hewitt and Percy Liang. 2019. Designing and interpreting probes with control tasks. In *Proceedings of the 2019 Conference on Empirical Methods in Natural Language Processing and the 9th International Joint Conference on Natural Language Processing (EMNLP-IJCNLP)*, pages 2733–2743, Hong Kong, China. Association for Computational Linguistics.

Ryan Kiros, Yukun Zhu, Ruslan Salakhutdinov, Richard Zemel, Antonio Torralba, Raquel Urtasun, and Sanja Fidler. 2015. Skip-thought vectors. *CoRR*, abs/1506.06726.

Christo Kirov, Ryan Cotterell, John Sylak-Glassman, Géraldine Walther, Ekaterina Vylomova, Patrick Xia, Manaal Faruqui, Sabrina J. Mielke, Arya McCarthy, Sandra Kübler, David Yarowsky, Jason Eisner, and Mans Hulden. 2018. UniMorph 2.0: Universal morphology. In *Proceedings of the Eleventh International Conference on Language Resources and Evaluation (LREC 2018)*, Miyazaki, Japan. European Language Resources Association (ELRA).

Arne Köhn. 2016. Evaluating embeddings using syntax-based classification tasks as a proxy for parser performance. In *Proceedings of the 1st Workshop on Evaluating Vector-Space Representations for NLP*, pages 67–71, Berlin, Germany. Association for Computational Linguistics.

Katarzyna Krasnowska-Kieraś and Alina Wróblewska. 2019. Empirical linguistic study of sentence embeddings. In *Proceedings of the 57th Annual Meeting of the Association for Computational Linguistics*, pages 5729–5739, Florence, Italy. Association for Computational Linguistics.

Tal Linzen, Grzegorz Chrupała, Yonatan Belinkov, and Dieuwke Hupkes, editors. 2019. *Proceedings of the 2019 ACL Workshop BlackboxNLP: Analyzing and Interpreting Neural Networks for NLP*. Association for Computational Linguistics, Florence, Italy.

Lajanugen Logeswaran and Honglak Lee. 2018. An efficient framework for learning sentence representations. *CoRR*, abs/1803.02893.

Arya D. McCarthy, Miikka Silfverberg, Ryan Cotterell, Mans Hulden, and David Yarowsky. 2018. Marrying universal dependencies and universal morphology. In *Proceedings of the Second Workshop on Universal Dependencies (UDW 2018)*, pages 91–101, Brussels, Belgium. Association for Computational Linguistics.

Joakim Nivre, Marie-Catherine de Marneffe, Filip Ginter, Yoav Goldberg, Jan Hajič, Christopher D. Manning, Ryan McDonald, Slav Petrov, Sampo Pyysalo, Natalia Silveira, Reut Tsarfaty, and Daniel Zeman. 2016. Universal dependencies v1: A multilingual treebank collection. In *Proceedings of the Tenth International Conference on Language Resources and Evaluation (LREC'16)*, pages 1659–1666, Portorož, Slovenia. European Language Resources Association (ELRA).

Christian Perone, Roberto Silveira, and Thomas Paula. 2018. Evaluation of sentence embeddings in downstream and linguistic probing tasks. *CoRR*, abs/1806.06259.

Abhilasha Ravichander, Yonatan Belinkov, and Eduard H. Hovy. 2020. Probing the probing paradigm: Does probing accuracy entail task relevance? *ArXiv*, abs/2005.00719.

Vinit Ravishankar, Lilja Øvrelid, and Erik Velldal. 2019. Probing multilingual sentence representations with x-probe. In *Proceedings of the 4th Workshop on Representation Learning for NLP (RepL4NLP-2019)*, pages 156–168, Florence, Italy. Association for Computational Linguistics.

Nils Reimers and Iryna Gurevych. 2019. Sentence-BERT: Sentence embeddings using siamese BERT-networks. In *Proceedings of the 2019 Conference on Empirical Methods in Natural Language Processing*. Association for Computational Linguistics.

Andreas Rücklé, Steffen Eger, Maxime Peyrard, and Iryna Gurevych. 2018. Concatenated power mean word embeddings as universal cross-lingual sentence representations. *CoRR*, abs/1803.01400.

Piotr Rybak and Alina Wróblewska. 2018. Semi-supervised neural system for tagging, parsing and lematization. In *Proceedings of the CoNLL 2018 Shared Task: Multilingual Parsing from Raw Text to Universal Dependencies*, pages 45–54, Brussels, Belgium. Association for Computational Linguistics.

Gözde Gül Sahin, Clara Vania, Ilia Kuznetsov, and Iryna Gurevych. 2019. LINSPECTOR: multilingual probing tasks for word representations. *CoRR*, abs/1903.09442.

Christian Stab, Tristan Miller, Benjamin Schiller, Pranav Rai, and Iryna Gurevych. 2018. Cross-topic argument mining from heterogeneous sources. In *Proceedings of the 2018 Conference on Empirical Methods in Natural Language Processing*, pages 3664–3674, Brussels, Belgium. Association for Computational Linguistics.

Milan Straka. 2018. UDPipe 2.0 prototype at CoNLL 2018 UD shared task. In *Proceedings of the CoNLL 2018 Shared Task: Multilingual Parsing from Raw Text to Universal Dependencies*, pages 197–207, Brussels, Belgium. Association for Computational Linguistics.

Sandeep Subramanian, Adam Trischler, Yoshua Bengio, and Christopher J Pal. 2018. Learning general purpose distributed sentence representations via large scale multi-task learning. In *International Conference on Learning Representations*.

Ian Tenney, Patrick Xia, Berlin Chen, Alex Wang, Adam Poliak, R Thomas McCoy, Najoung Kim, Benjamin Van Durme, Sam Bowman, Dipanjan Das, and Ellie Pavlick. 2019. What do you learn from context? probing for sentence structure in contextualized word representations. In *International Conference on Learning Representations*.

Alex Wang, Amanpreet Singh, Julian Michael, Felix Hill, Omer Levy, and Samuel Bowman. 2018. GLUE: A multi-task benchmark and analysis platform for natural language understanding. In *Proceedings of the 2018 EMNLP Workshop BlackboxNLP: Analyzing and Interpreting Neural Networks for NLP*, pages 353–355, Brussels, Belgium. Association for Computational Linguistics.

Bin Wang and C. C. Jay Kuo. 2020. Sbert-wk: A sentence embedding method by dissecting bert-based word models.

John Wieting and Douwe Kiela. 2019. No training required: Exploring random encoders for sentence classification. *CoRR*, abs/1901.10444.

Understanding the Source of Semantic Regularities in Word Embeddings

Hsiao-Yu Chiang
School of Information
University of California, Berkeley, USA
hsiaoyuchiang@berkeley.edu

Jose Camacho-Collados
School of Computer Science and Informatics
Cardiff University, United Kingdom
camachocolladosj@cardiff.ac.uk

Zachary A. Pardos
Graduate School of Education
University of California, Berkeley, USA
pardos@berkeley.edu

Abstract

Semantic relations are core to how humans understand and express concepts in the real world using language. Recently, there has been a thread of research aimed at modeling these relations by learning vector representations from text corpora. Most of these approaches focus strictly on leveraging the co-occurrences of relationship word pairs within sentences. In this paper, we investigate the hypothesis that examples of a lexical relation in a corpus are fundamental to a neural word embedding's ability to complete analogies involving the relation. Our experiments, in which we remove all known examples of a relation from training corpora, show only marginal degradation in analogy completion performance involving the removed relation. This finding enhances our understanding of neural word embeddings, showing that co-occurrence information of a particular semantic relation is the not the main source of their structural regularity.

1 Introduction

The representation of words has been a long-standing task in natural language processing (NLP). The main underlying principle is known for decades, as explained by Firth (1957). This principle was based on the idea that the meaning of a word can be understood by its surrounding company (i.e., the words in its context). Most modern representation learning theory in NLP is based on this assumption, with vector representation being the most successful area to date (Turney and Pantel, 2010). More recently, low-dimensional word representations learned from text corpora using neural networks (i.e., *word embeddings*) have emerged (Mikolov et al., 2013a; Pennington et al., 2014; Bojanowski et al., 2017) stemming from cognitive frameworks based on distributed representation (Hinton et al., 1986; Feldman and Ballard,

1982). Neural word embeddings have been proven to contain useful information about concepts and entities, and provide a generalization boost to many NLP applications (Goldberg, 2017). Surprisingly, these representations have also been shown to exhibit linear relationships between words in the vector space, demonstrated by *analogy*. For example, Mikolov et al. (2013b) showed that a simple operation such as *king-man+woman* will result in a point near queen in the vector space[1]. These word analogies have been extensively investigated in the literature, aiming to shed light on this surprising property. However, while there has been a body of research seeking to understand how these analogies work (Arora et al., 2016; Gittens et al., 2017; Ethayarajh et al., 2019; Allen and Hospedales, 2019), and noting issues about their methodology (Linzen, 2016; Gladkova et al., 2016; Nissim et al., 2020), there has not been a specific analysis on the source of statistical cues that leads to their high performance on this task.

Concurrently, a thread of research has focused on explicitly modeling lexical relationships of word pairs in text corpora (Jameel et al., 2018; Espinosa-Anke and Schockaert, 2018; Washio and Kato, 2018; Joshi et al., 2019; Camacho-Collados et al., 2019). While these methods employ different means for learning relation vectors, they share a common initial premise: only co-occurring words in the corpus are considered[2]. While this simplified assumption works well enough in practice, providing a useful signal even in downstream NLP applications, in this paper we find that valuable information is likely lost in the process. In fact, we

---

[1]More information of how word analogies work can be found in Section 2.1.

[2]Some of these methods also provide tools to learn representations for out-of-vocabulary pairs (Joshi et al., 2019; Camacho-Collados et al., 2019). However, their initial vector spaces are based on co-occurring word pairs only.

119

Proceedings of the 24th Conference on Computational Natural Language Learning, pages 119–131
Online, November 19-20, 2020. ©2020 Association for Computational Linguistics
https://doi.org/10.18653/v1/P17

find that a text corpus provides enough information to infer pairwise relations without training on any specific examples of a given relation.

In our experiments, we focus on semantic relations in particular, which are the most suited for both word and relation embedding models. Neural word embeddings are used to learn representations from text corpora, with word analogies as the evaluation mechanism to test our hypothesis. We run an extensive set of control experiments where the co-occurrence information is completely removed from the reference corpora. The results show that, with relationship instance removal, analogy performance degrades to only a limited extent, overall.[3] This finding suggests that neural embeddings do not learn lexical relation regularities from examples of the relation, but that they are still able to be inferred through the semantic featurization of individual words.

2 Related Work

2.1 Understanding analogies in word embeddings

The surprising result of Mikolov et al. (2013b), showing that word embedding can solve linear analogy problems, led to a careful investigation by researchers from different fields. A line of research proposed mathematical formalisms to try to understand the intrinsic properties of word embeddings. Arora et al. (2016) was one of the first to provide a rigorous theoretical explanation on the linear algebraic structure of word embeddings. Their formalism is based on a latent variable model that makes assumptions on the nature of the vector space. Later works rely on the notion of paraphrasing (Gittens et al., 2017; Allen and Hospedales, 2019), based on the observation that different words can be used in similar contexts interchangeably, dropping some of the previous assumptions made by Arora et al. (2016). Concurrently, other works have attempted to provide explanations of the compositional properties of distributional models through additions (Levy and Goldberg, 2014a; Paperno and Baroni, 2016; Ethayarajh et al., 2019), which lie at the core of word analogy completion.

While these works formalize word analogies and attempt to explain how they work mathematically,

our empirical analysis is focused on understanding the source of signal in corpora that affect the performance of word analogy completion, without asserting any predefined assumption. In particular, we are mostly interested in determining whether relationship pair co-occurrence in sentences is necessary in order for a word embedding to succeed at analogy completion.

2.2 Issues in word analogies

A number of publications have encountered methodological issues in the word analogy task through word embeddings. Levy and Goldberg (2014a) found that the addition operations may not be optimal, as they are reduced to three separate similarity problems that can be solved through more appropriate operations. Linzen (2016) showed that simple baselines based on nearest neighbour searches are competitive in the analogy categories proposed by Mikolov et al. (2013b). Because of this, Gladkova et al. (2016) proposed a new dataset, partially addressing some of the previous shortcomings. Other works have shown that linear relationships, while being implicit, are not directly apparent in the word embedding space, and therefore word analogies may not be the best method to retrieve this information (Drozd et al., 2016; Schluter, 2018; Bouraoui et al., 2018). Finally, Gonen and Goldberg (2019) and Nissim et al. (2020) cautioned against over-reliance on analogies as a means to uncover and correct for biases in word embeddings.

These methodological observations challenge the supremacy of analogy evaluations as the optimal proxy for downstream task performance of a word embedding. Nevertheless, they represent a valuable mechanism with which to compare the semantic regularities of two different neural embeddings. In particular, word analogies represent an ideal benchmark for our research questions, as the impact of co-occurrence statistics within word relations can be evaluated directly through analogy validation. This would not be the case for other more complicated tasks such as relation classification or extraction, which may add additional confounds.

3 Methodology

In this section we explain the experimental methodology we follow to answer our main research question. First, we briefly describe how to solve word

---

[3]In a few specific relations the degradation is more marked. Nonetheless, this degradation does not surpass 50% even in the most unfavorable case for accuracy, and for other metrics this degradation does not surpass 20%.

analogies using word embeddings (Section 3.1). We then explain our methodology to compile corpora to train word embeddings (Section 3.2).

3.1 Solving word analogies with neural word embeddings

The first step to solve word analogies using neural word embeddings is to first learn word vectors from an unlabeled text corpora. To do so, standard word embedding models such as Word2Vec (Mikolov et al., 2013a), GloVe (Pennington et al., 2014) or FastText (Bojanowski et al., 2017) are often used. The output of these models is a vector space where each word is represented as a single point. With these vectors, mathematical operations can then be made to solve a given analogy.

Formally, given three words (a, b and c), the task of word analogy completion consists of predicting the most appropriate word d that satisfies a is to b as c is to d. In this case, both a-b and c-d are part of the same relationship. For instance, in the case of *Paris*, *France* and *Berlin*, the word to retrieve would be *Germany*. In this case both *Paris-France* and *Berlin-Germany* belong to the *capital-of* relation. With word embeddings this can be solved with the simple vector operation[4] $\vec{b} - \vec{a} + \vec{c}$, retrieving the word whose vector is closest to that point in the space.

Word analogy completion is used as the main evaluation for our experiments.

3.2 Corpus preparation

Our main research question is whether an explicit observation of a relationship in a corpus is necessary to complete an example of that relationship via analogy. To this end, given a reference unlabeled corpus, we devise the following methodology per lexical relation type.

3.2.1 Sentence removal

First, for each relation type (e.g. *capital-of*) in a dataset, we remove all sentences from the corpus that contain word pairs belonging to the relation. This results in a modified corpus for each relation type and a respective word embedding for each relation type trained on the modified corpus. For example, for the pair *Lisbon-Portugal*, we would remove all sentences from our reference corpus

where *Lisbon* and *Portugal* co-occur, and this process would be repeated for all pairs of the *capital-of* relation.

3.2.2 Sentence replacement

This setting is similar to the sentence removal strategies with the added inclusion of new sentences to replace the removed ones. In particular, for each removed sentence containing a word pair of a relation type, two sentences from a similar corpus replace it, where each sentence contains one of the words in the pair. This is arguably the most fairly comparable setting to no removal, as the number of occurrences for each word in the relation would be approximately the same with respect to the default setting. The overall number of sentences would be slightly higher, though this is negligible in comparison to the full corpus (see Section 4.1 for the specific details on the corpora used for the evaluation).

For both the sentence replacement and sentence removal strategies, we also experiment with a more aggressive setting. In this setting (referred to as *removal+* or *replacement+* in our experiments), all sentences containing any two words from the vocabulary of the relation[5] are removed, in the case of removal+, or replaced, in the case of replacement+. This is the most aggressive setting where no co-occurrence information of a given relation is preserved.

4 Evaluation

In this section we provide the details of our experimental setup (Section 4.1) and then, the main results of our evaluation (Section 4.2).

4.1 Experimental Setting

In the following we describe the experimental setting for all our experiments. More details and code to reproduce our experiments can be found online[6].

Text corpora. As our reference corpus we selected UMBC (Han et al., 2013), which is a diverse 3-billion-token corpus of paragraphs extracted from the web, amounting to a total of 132M sentences. In particular, we randomly select 80% of all sentences which would be the base corpus for the experiments. Then, we used the remaining

---

[4]Levy and Goldberg (2014a) showed that a multiplication operation can also be used to solve analogies. However, for this analysis we focused on the traditional solution of the problem proposed by Mikolov et al. (2013b).

[5]Recall from the previous subsection (Section 3.1) that each analogy instance is formed by four words.

[6]https://github.com/h-yuc/Lexical-Relations-Analogies

20% to add replacement sentences when necessary (see Section 3.2.2 for more details on the replacement setting). To complement the main results and test the generalization of our findings, we also use Wikipedia[7] (2 billion tokens and 104M sentences) for the base removal experiments.

Word embedding models. For word embedding models, we use both the CBOW and Skip-Gram variants of Word2Vec (Mikolov et al., 2013a). These neural representation learning approaches have shown to be amenable to analogy completion since their introduction (Mikolov et al., 2013b). Unlike FastText (Bojanowski et al., 2017), they do not include character information and are therefore more suitable for our experiments as pure word-based models. We use standard hyperparameters for both CBOW and Skip-Gram, with 300-dimensions and a window size of 10 in both cases. Given the difference in speed (CBOW being around five times faster to train) and the small performance difference, we considered CBOW for all our main experiments, but included Skip-Gram results in the appendix.

Validation datasets. Google (Mikolov et al., 2013b) and BATS (Gladkova et al., 2016) relation example datasets are used for analogy completion. BATS was introduced after the Google dataset to address some of its shortcomings in the number and type of relations, so the inclusion of both datasets in our experiments help give a more general overview. In particular, we focus on the semantic relations of each dataset. Table 1 shows the statistics of the relations considered in each of the datasets.

Evaluation protocol. For solving word analogies, we follow the original methodology of Mikolov et al. (2013b)[8], as explained in Section 3.1. For simplicity, we unify the evaluation setting for both datasets where we only consider a single solution. In the case of BATS, we consider the first answer as provided in the dataset, which is generally the most specific. With the expectation that performance after co-occurrence removal may degrade substantially, we report analogy completion results using recall at 1 (accuracy), 10, and 50. Recall@50, for example, reports the percentage of analogy completions in which the expected word was among the 50 nearest neighbors to the three

Relation type	#inst	#word	Example
cap-comm-country	506	46	Cairo, Egypt, Paris, France
capital-world	4,524	232	Muscat, Oman, Tokyo, Japan
currency	866	60	Europe, euro, Korea, won
city-in-state	2,467	94	Toledo, Ohio, Dallas, Texas
family	506	46	king, queen, man, woman
nationality-adj.	1,599	82	Greece, Greek, Spain, Spanish
country-capital	2450	100	Hanoi, Vietnam, Rome, Italy
country-language	2,450	100	Jordan, Arabic, USA, English
UK_city-county	2,450	100	Exeter, Devon, Wells, Somerset
name-nationality	2,450	100	Caesar, Roman, Plato, Greek
name-occupation	2,450	100	Plato, philosopher, Dante, poet
animal-young	2,450	100	bee, larva, ox, calf
animal-sound	2,450	100	bee buzz frog ribbit
animal-shelter	2,450	100	horse, stable, ant, anthill
things-color	2,450	100	coffee, black, cream, white
male-female	2,450	100	son, daughter, father, mother
hypernym-animal	2,450	100	human, primate, cat, feline
hypernym-misc	2,450	100	pastry, food, plum, fruit
hyponym-misc	2,450	100	bag, pouch, dessert, cake
meronym-subst.	2,450	100	bag, leather, penny, metal
meronym-member	2,450	100	bird, flock, page, book
meronym-part	2,450	100	day, hour, dollar, cent
synonym-intensity	2,450	100	angry, furious, ask, beg
synonym-exact	2,450	100	help, aid, child, kid
antonym-gradable	2,450	100	aware, unaware, slow, fast
antonym-binary	2,450	100	after, before, below, above

The first six relations (cap-comm-country through nationality-adj.) belong to *Google*; the remaining relations belong to *BATS*.

Table 1: Statistics of the word analogy datasets used in our experiments: Number of instances (#inst) and unique words (#word).

word subtraction and addition. The inclusion of recall at different thresholds allows for a more complete overview of the performance, as the standard accuracy measure alone may not reflect the full picture (Gladkova et al., 2016; Schluter, 2018).

Training. For each relation type, we utilized three different variants of each corpora that are used to train word embeddings (i.e., the original corpus and two resulting from our removal and replacement strategies, as explained in Section 3.2). To reduce the amount of training, we only considered the default and removal strategy for Wikipedia[9], while all experiments are performed on the main UMBC reference corpus. In total, we compiled 156 different corpora, occupying 2.2TB of disk space, and learned 184 different word embedding models, totalling around 1,980 hours (around 83 full days) of model training on a high performance single node (48-core) system.

4.2 Results

As explained in the previous section, our experiments are aimed at understanding the role of co-occurring words in a given relation type (e.g.

---

[7]We use the Wikipedia dump of November 2016.

[8]As in the original protocol, words that are included in the instance are excluded from the nearest neighbours search.

[9]Likewise, for Skip-Gram we only considered the Google analogy dataset and a single strategy per corpus (results in appendix).

	Sentences removed		Recall@1 (accuracy)					Recall@10					Recall@50				
	Rm/Rp	Rm+/Rp+	Def	Rm	Rp	Rm+	Rp+	Def	Rm	Rp	Rm+	Rp+	Def	Rm	Rp	Rm+	Rp+
cap.-country	49,248	245,677	61.7	53.0	52.4	51.4	51.6	89.7	81.6	82.6	83.4	83.4	98.2	90.3	90.5	91.3	92.3
cap.-world	79,060	452,915	49.4	31.3	32.7	30.1	33.6	82.0	65.8	67.9	65.0	67.2	91.2	79.2	80.5	78.6	80.8
currency	4,260	145,179	8.7	5.1	6.9	5.8	6.2	37.3	32.6	34.2	33.1	34.5	63.5	58.7	59.6	58.4	60.4
city-state	96,666	247,238	14.1	7.7	7.7	8.6	9.1	40.4	28.0	28.0	28.9	31.5	62.1	50.1	50.0	49.9	53.8
family	450,875	2,830,852	91.1	85.0	82.0	69.8	72.9	100.0	95.3	94.7	88.1	89.7	100.0	98.4	96.8	90.5	91.1
nation-adj	145,064	492,671	86.4	80.2	81.7	81.3	83.1	96.0	96.1	95.6	96.4	95.9	97.9	97.8	97.9	97.7	97.4
AVERAGE	**137,529**	**735,755**	**51.9**	**43.7**	**43.9**	**41.2**	**42.7**	**74.2**	**66.5**	**67.1**	**65.8**	**67.0**	**85.5**	**79.1**	**79.2**	**77.7**	**79.3**
country-cap	66,988	369,463	71.6	54.7	55.8	56.7	59.6	90.9	86.9	87.3	86.1	86.5	95.1	93.0	93.1	91.6	91.2
country-lang	21,066	649,071	26.7	24.0	24.9	16.9	19.6	60.8	56.9	57.4	47.5	52.5	74.8	73.3	73.1	62.6	69.1
city-county	2,599	56,719	1.8	1.2	1.2	0.2	0.7	10.4	7.8	8.3	2.5	5.7	27.7	25.3	25.0	6.3	17.8
name-nation.	12,069	1,808,784	20.6	17.5	18.1	18.9	16.1	54.7	50.7	51.6	50.6	46.9	72.5	68.9	69.6	65.1	65.9
name-occup.	10,934	1,030,106	45.1	41.8	42.1	12.0	34.9	72.2	70.6	69.8	30.4	65.1	80.6	79.4	79.0	44.9	76.0
animal-young	3,238	221,647	3.6	2.7	3.0	1.2	3.4	15.5	13.6	12.4	5.8	10.2	28.4	26.4	25.6	10.7	21.4
animal-sound	1,307	75,529	3.8	2.7	3.5	0.8	2.0	12.2	9.0	11.0	2.8	6.4	20.0	15.9	17.2	4.5	11.1
animal-shelter	11,892	569,567	3.3	1.7	1.7	0.6	1.0	16.6	12.4	12.5	3.4	9.3	32.0	26.0	25.7	8.0	18.8
things-color	52,219	1,179,341	11.2	11.5	11.8	12.5	10.9	41.6	39.1	41.0	41.1	33.7	59.4	55.2	56.7	54.7	49.5
male-female	108,898	445,429	48.0	42.8	43.5	38.6	40.0	70.4	69.3	68.3	63.6	64.7	79.0	77.4	77.0	73.6	72.7
hyper-animal	3,410	93,258	9.6	8.4	7.8	1.6	4.4	41.1	37.5	38.4	9.8	29.3	67.1	63.8	64.8	24.1	52.5
hyper-misc	15,157	456,525	4.7	4.4	4.2	1.6	3.1	23.8	22.9	22.3	14.8	20.9	43.0	41.5	40.8	28.2	37.6
hypo-misc	32,118	274,377	9.8	10.3	9.3	8.8	10.9	55.9	54.2	55.4	49.1	55.1	81.3	79.3	79.1	73.4	79.0
mero-subst.	68,128	1,548,273	6.5	5.4	5.3	2.9	3.7	30.7	26.0	25.8	15.6	20.8	52.5	45.2	45.4	30.5	40.7
mero-member	257,447	4,897,322	3.1	2.9	2.8	2.3	3.0	26.9	24.7	25.3	17.9	25.9	44.7	41.8	42.1	30.4	43.4
mero-part	30,016	364,053	2.9	2.7	2.4	2.7	2.7	29.0	27.4	27.2	23.9	26.9	49.8	48.1	48.1	42.0	46.7
syn-intens.	40,241	1,329,093	17.9	17.7	17.4	14.8	19.0	49.6	47.1	49.0	42.3	47.2	70.2	68.4	68.9	59.8	68.3
syn-exact	49,292	882,075	27.8	26.0	25.8	26.6	27.5	69.0	66.2	65.4	66.9	68.6	85.8	84.2	83.8	84.4	84.9
auto-grad.	237,221	2,397,131	21.3	20.0	19.8	17.1	22.1	46.2	43.3	43.6	40.4	46.9	65.1	61.5	61.6	59.1	65.4
auto-binary	1,648,965	42,023,189	27.6	26.2	27.6	28.6	35.1	59.2	56.1	56.7	57.4	67.2	71.1	69.9	70.0	71.8	80.6
AVERAGE	**133,660**	**3,033,547**	**18.3**	**16.2**	**16.4**	**13.3**	**16.0**	**43.8**	**41.1**	**41.4**	**33.6**	**39.5**	**60.0**	**57.2**	**57.3**	**46.3**	**54.6**

Table 2: UMBC corpus word analogy results using CBOW with five different configurations: Default (Def), Remove (Rm), Replace (Rp) and their more aggressive counterparts removing all pairwise co-occurrences (Rm+ and Rp+).

capital-of) as they pertain to analogy completion. Table 2 shows the main set of results of the CBOW model on the UMBC corpus. As can be observed, and as expected, the default model (i.e., no co-occurrence removal) trained on the original corpus provides the highest analogy completion results, overall. However, less expected is the low magnitude decrease in performance of the experiments involving co-occurrence removal. The default experiments performed analogies with 51.9% accuracy (R@1), on average, compared to 42.7% with the most aggressive replace plus (Rp+) strategy on the Google dataset, and 18.1% vs. 16.0%, respectively, on the BATS dataset. Figure 1 shows the average decrease in performance of the replace strategy (Rp) per relation type as a percentage of the default performance. For R@1, the decrease in performance is lower than 10% for the majority of relations. When considering R@10 and R@50, this decrease in performance is even less pronounced, which suggests that the main geometrical features of the space were largely preserved (a more visu-

alization of the space is presented in Section 5.2). The *animal-shelter* significant decrease in performance is a special case as the performance of the default model was very low to start with (3.3%), which highlights the difficulty to model that particular relationship via word analogies. The same could be attributed to the *city-state* (Default accuracy of 14.1%), which is the relation with the second highest decrease in performance for R@1.

Finally, Table 3 shows experimental results for the default, remove (Rm) and remove plus (Rm+) strategies for models trained on the Wikipedia corpus. The results are slightly higher overall, given the clean, consistent, and topically comprehensive nature of the corpus. The overall difference between default and removal strategies was similar to that of UMBC (reminder that the remove plus strategy consisted of removing all sentences where any two words from a given relation co-occur). No co-occurrence removal (Def) vs. removal plus (Rm+) had analogy completion accuracies of 59% vs. 52.5%, respectively, on the Google dataset, and

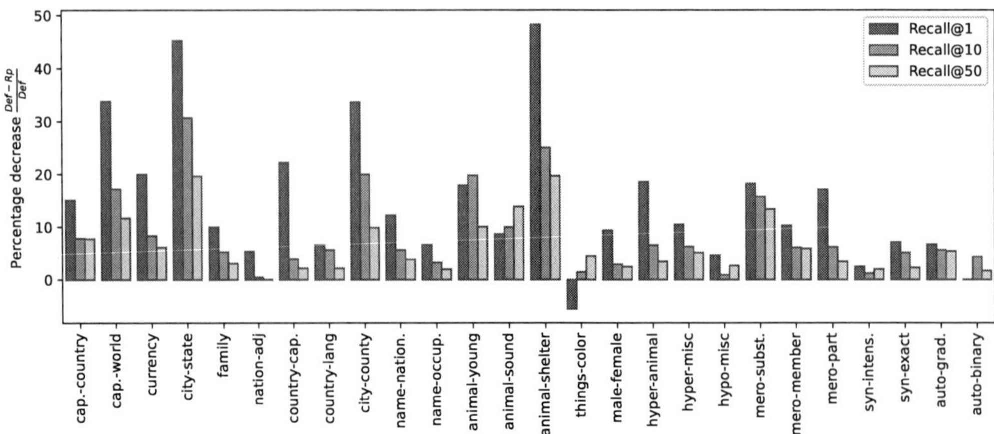

Figure 1: Average decrease in performance (%) of the CBOW model trained on the original UMBC corpus with respect to the replace strategy (Rp) per relation type (Google and BATS datasets).

21.7% vs. 20.3% on the BATS dataset.

5   Analysis

In this section we aim to better understand the results presented in the previous section. In particular, we analyze to what extent the performance drops that exist are correlated with frequencies of words in the relationship (Section 5.1). We also compare, through principal component analysis (PCA) visualization, the structure of the relation with the highest point decrease, before and after co-occurrence removal (Section 5.2).

5.1   Correlation with word frequency

A natural question that may arise when looking at the results is whether word frequency has any influence on the performance drop of co-occurring word pairs. For instance, one may wonder if getting a high-quality word embedding, which is generally achieved when word frequency is sufficiently high in the corpus, is enough to compensate for the lack of sentences with words forming a certain relation. Or, alternatively, if the relative frequency of co-occurring words in a relation has an effect on the final embedding, as this would mean that frequency is a necessary condition for learning robust semantic regularities. To answer these questions, we computed the correlation between word and pair frequencies in a word analogy instance and the performance drop. For the frequency indicator, we computed two numbers, H_{ind} and H_{pair}:

1. Harmonic mean[10] between all individual

words in the analogy instance (H_{ind}) was computed as follows:

$$H_{ind} = \frac{n}{\sum_{i=1}^{n} \frac{1}{x_i}} \qquad (1)$$

where x_i is the frequency of a word in the given word analogy instance and n is the number of words, i.e., four in the case of individual words in word analogies. For example, the harmonic mean of the four words, *king* (220,958 occurrences in UMBC), *queen* (52,262), *man* (751,262), and *woman* (296,915) would be 141,048.

2. The relative pairwise frequency (H_{pair}) was computed as the previous number divided by the harmonic mean of the number of sentences where two words of a pair co-occur (i.e., H_{co}):

$$H_{pair} = \frac{H_{co}}{H_{ind}} = \frac{2 \cdot p_1 \cdot p_2}{(p_1 + p_2)} \cdot \frac{1}{H_{ind}} \qquad (2)$$

where p_i corresponds to the frequency of a relation pair in a word analogy instance. This number can give a better indication of how relevant the co-occurrence information of a given word pair is. Following the previous example, the relative pairwise frequency H_{pair} of the instance composed of *king-queen* (5,498 joint co-occurrences in UMBC) and *man-woman* (36,189) is 0.068.

---

[10]We decided to use the harmonic mean because it is generally more robust to outliers (e.g., a highly frequent word) than the usual arithmetic mean.

		Sentences removed		Recall@1 (accuracy)			Recall@10			Recall@50		
		Rm	Rm+	Def	Rm	Rm+	Def	Rm	Rm+	Def	Rm	Rm+
Google	capital-country	162,671	521,038	61.9	54.6	55.5	93.3	89.5	90.3	97.6	94.9	96.1
	capital-world	320,106	1,102,291	66.8	48.1	51.4	92.9	80.6	82.1	97.2	90.3	91.1
	currency	4,327	223,588	31.4	28.5	25.3	60.9	58.2	51.3	77.9	78.4	71.0
	city-in-state	344,196	659,539	19.7	12.6	15.2	54.0	34.8	39.4	72.3	55.7	58.5
	family	375,904	1,012,935	78.1	73.3	72.3	94.3	92.9	89.7	95.7	94.5	93.9
	nationality-adjective	437,316	1,381,200	95.9	94.9	95.5	98.5	98.6	97.6	99.8	99.7	98.9
	AVERAGE	**274,087**	**816,765**	**59.0**	**52.0**	**52.5**	**82.3**	**75.8**	**75.1**	**90.1**	**85.6**	**84.9**
BATS	country-capital	267,095	885,924	83.8	79.5	78.7	91.1	90.0	88.9	93.6	91.8	91.3
	country-language	82,842	527,339	28.6	25.3	23.9	62.0	58.5	58.9	72.7	70.9	71.2
	UK_city-county	39,780	198,005	17.0	9.1	9.7	43.5	34.0	34.3	59.0	52.3	51.8
	name-nationality	31,980	390,864	31.4	29.5	30.7	56.0	53.9	56.5	67.8	65.2	69.1
	name-occupation	24,798	136,447	39.9	35.9	34.7	63.0	59.5	58.3	72.1	68.8	67.8
	animal-young	7,021	135,815	5.4	2.4	2.4	20.0	12.5	10.5	33.1	24.4	22.3
	animal-sound	2,921	121,416	5.3	2.8	1.7	15.2	10.5	7.6	24.2	18.6	14.5
	animal-shelter	23,832	262,708	2.0	1.3	0.9	8.7	5.4	4.6	17.5	12.1	10.7
	things-color	47,298	445,312	14.5	15.0	15.2	39.9	38.6	42.8	55.6	52.7	56.2
	male-female	400,035	1,387,664	51.8	47.4	46.5	77.6	73.7	71.6	84.5	82.4	80.7
	hypernyms-animals	11,723	77,632	20.1	16.8	14.4	57.6	52.7	47.4	75.4	71.0	66.6
	hypernyms-misc	16,825	164,097	7.4	6.7	6.2	33.1	29.9	30.3	55.8	53.0	51.9
	hyponyms-misc	90,811	594,541	12.4	12.4	10.9	52.2	51.2	49.4	72.7	70.6	69.8
	meronyms-substance	70,896	510,291	7.8	6.7	6.9	28.9	24.2	24.9	48.7	43.4	41.4
	meronyms-member	774,473	4,259,786	10.4	9.1	12.0	33.3	28.2	35.6	49.9	44.7	53.0
	meronyms-part	91,041	539,371	6.7	6.1	5.5	34.0	31.5	31.7	56.5	52.0	51.4
	synonyms-intensity	44,149	624,662	15.6	14.9	14.4	42.9	40.4	40.7	61.3	60.7	58.7
	synonyms-exact	83,651	1,308,183	23.2	20.7	25.4	52.6	50.0	54.4	69.1	67.1	70.2
	antonyms-gradable	282,330	1,233,454	21.6	18.5	22.3	49.0	46.3	49.6	67.1	64.6	66.5
	antonyms-binary	1,726,724	21,329,952	29.4	26.1	44.6	57.7	55.4	77.2	72.2	70.7	85.6
	AVERAGE	**206,011**	**1,756,673**	**21.7**	**19.3**	**20.3**	**45.9**	**42.3**	**43.8**	**60.4**	**56.8**	**57.5**

Table 3: Wikipedia corpus word analogy results using CBOW with three different configurations: Default (Def), Remove (Rm), and its more aggressive setting removing all pairwise co-occurrences (Rm+)

With respect to performance drops, for each analogy completion instance we considered the ranks[11] of the correct completion words in both the default and replace settings and computed the difference. Table 4 shows the results of the correlation results in the Google analogy dataset. Not surprisingly, the correlation between the individual frequency of the words in an instance and the rank difference is negative in all relation types except for one (*nationality-adjective*). However, the correlation is rather weak, as the addition of new sentences compensate for the initial removal, even if the sentences are of a different kind. As for the relative frequency of pairs in the instance, the correlation is positive as expected. In this case, the signal is higher than with the individual frequency case, especially in the *family* relationship. Overall, this experiment shows a level of support for our initial premises on the effect of relative pair frequencies, but further research would be necessary to understand other reasons behind the performance drop.

	Frequency		Drop	Correlation	
	Ind	Pair		H_{ind}	H_{pair}
cap.-country	26,111	2,002	15.1	-0.239	-0.114
cap.-world	4,328	434	33.8	-0.128	+0.188
currency	3,815	52	20.0	-0.092	+0.041
city-state	14,226	1,121	45.3	-0.012	+0.192
family	58,197	5,617	10.0	-0.065	+0.315
nation-adj	30,076	2,238	5.4	+0.063	+0.021
AVERAGE	**22,792**	**1,911**	**22.9**	**-0.079**	**+0.107**

Table 4: Pearson correlations between frequency (average among all instances in the dataset) and performance drop between the default and replace (Rp) corpora.

5.2 Visualization

In this section, we present visualizations of the word pairs from one lexical relation, before and after co-occurrence removal, in order to gain insight into the effect of removal on the learned structure of the space. In particular, we selected the relation from the Google datasets with the largest raw

---

[11]We only considered the position of the fifty first nearest neighbours. If the correct word was not among the fifty nearest neighbours, 51 was used as the position, which would be equivalent to a wrong answer.

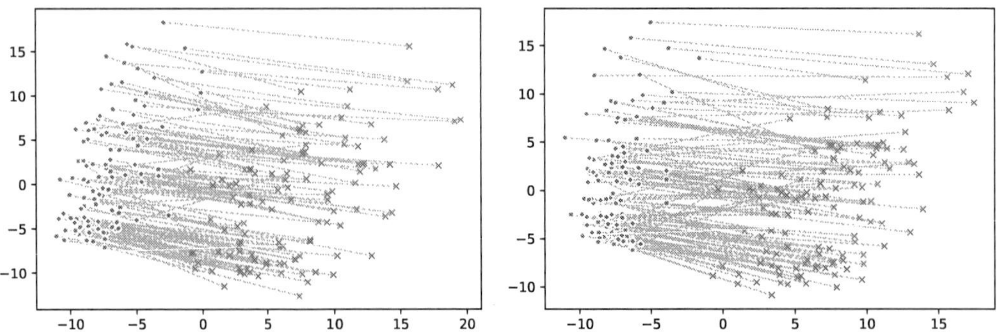

Figure 2: *Capital-world* vectors projected by PCA. All models trained on different subsets of UMBC: default (left) and remove (right). Red marks (x) correspond to *countries* and blue dots, *capitals*.

performance point drop[12]. Figure 2 shows the two principal components of word pairs in the *capital-world* relation for both the default (Def) and remove (Rm) settings. A reminder from Section 3.2.1, the remove setting involves removing all sentences where both words from a relation co-occur, without any replacement. As can be seen, even in the case of a relation with a R@1 performance gap as high as 36.6%, the linear relations are largely preserved in the word embedding space. This can also be supported by the fact that the performance drop is much smaller for R@10 and R@50 (see Figure 1), suggesting that the correct completion word is still somewhere near in the space. For example, for the instance *Australia, Canberra, Spain*, the correct word *Madrid* is found as the fifth nearest neighbours in the Rm vector space, with the top two words being *Barcelona* and *Valencia* (other large Spanish cities). Intuitively, this error does not affect the overall representation of the relation in the vector space, as those words were already in a similar linear relationship in the default model.

6   Discussion

6.1   The source of semantic regularities

In this paper, we find that neural word embeddings (i.e., Word2Vec models) do not require observation of instances of the relation (e.g., Madrid is the *capital of* Spain) in order to maintain nominal accuracy in relation completion tasks. We believe this is the first time such an observation has been made, empirically, using natural language, though it has been observed in neural embeddings trained

on non-linguistic data (Pardos and Nam, 2020).

In Mikolov et al. (2013b), where Word2Vec models were first introduced, the phrase "Linguistic Regularities" was used. While it was not made explicit what the word regularities referred to, analogy completion was exclusively used for validation, leaving open the possibility that regularities referred to some pattern of structure allowing for lexical relationships to be expressed. If the regularities relevant to analogy completion are not formed from examples of the lexical relationship contained in the analogy, then how are they formed and how was the accuracy of the completion mostly retained in our experiments in the absence of examples? Instead, it may leverage the robustness of regularities, or features, learned about individual words to lay the structural foundation for inferences to then be made about a lexical relation. Removing co-occurrences of capitals and countries, for example, would not completely remove the concept of capitals and countries from the corpus. The embedding of "Madrid" would likely still encode features associated with a busy city, government buildings, culture, and European regionality. This is also related to work that showed relations and relevant information from relations can be captured from word embeddings (Jadhav et al., 2020), even if the relation cannot be retrieved explicitly from linear transformations (Drozd et al., 2016; Bouraoui et al., 2018). Interestingly, however, our results indicate that the frequency of an individual word in a corpus is only weakly related to the robustness of features leveraged for successful analogy completion.

Finally, even though co-occurrences of pairs from a specific relation are not necessary to learn the necessary features, word pairs still may play a critical role in regularity development. Most

---

[12]In the appendix we also include the same visualizations for the relations with the second largest performance drop (*city-in-state*) and the smallest performance drop (*nationality-adjective*), which largely share the same conclusions.

word embedding models (including the Skip-Gram model of Word2Vec) are trained in pairwise fashion after-all, making predictions and calculating loss based on each pair of input and context words.

6.2 Cognitive perspective

Neural embeddings come from a cognitive perspective on semantic representation. They stem from a hypothesized architecture of the mind called Connectionism (Feldman and Ballard, 1982) in which emergent concepts (Hopfield, 1982; Hinton, 1986) are learned as distributed representations across the embedding space (Hinton et al., 1986). If neural word embeddings are a candidate model of a component of human cognition, then our results suggest that the faculties of the mind that understand relational concepts (e.g., male and female) may establish these concepts primarily through induction and observations of behavior. For example, this would mean that we learn features of male and female separately, rather than through explicit declaration of representative pairs (i.e., explicit co-occurrences). It is perhaps a separate faculty of the mind that queries this conceptual representation framework for inferences to be made about relationships between new elements. These inferences, conducted by way of analogy, may indeed be key to innovation (Hope et al., 2017) and a possible component of human creativity (Holyoak et al., 1996).

7 Conclusion and Future Work

In this paper we have presented a large-scale analysis on the role of co-occurring relational word pairs in completing analogies. In the analyses we have measured to what extent the loss of co-occurrence information within relation types affects analogy completion using neural word embeddings. Perhaps surprisingly, this effect is quite small, to the point that word embeddings can complete analogies of a relationship in the vector space even if the co-occurrence information from the reference corpus is totally removed.

In order to complement this analysis, for future work it would be interesting to analyze to what extent the conclusions of this analysis apply to purely distributional models, e.g., PMI-based, as they have shown to share similarity properties with word embeddings (Levy et al., 2015), to the point of Skip-Gram being viewed as an implicit co-occurrence matrix factorization (Levy and Goldberg, 2014b).

Moreover, the analysis could be extended to other types of relations, not only semantic. Further investigation could then focus on how the main sources of concepts and linguistic regularities in word embeddings are learned, and how they can be leveraged to improve unsupervised relation models, e.g., (Jameel et al., 2018; Joshi et al., 2019). Finally, as a follow-up to recent work aiming at understanding how language models and contextualized embeddings capture relations (Petroni et al., 2019; Bouraoui et al., 2020; Jiang et al., 2020), further research could be devoted to analyze the performance of such models with and without pairwise co-occurrence information.

References

Carl Allen and Timothy Hospedales. 2019. Analogies explained: Towards understanding word embeddings. In *International Conference on Machine Learning*, pages 223–231.

Sanjeev Arora, Yuanzhi Li, Yingyu Liang, Tengyu Ma, and Andrej Risteski. 2016. A latent variable model approach to pmi-based word embeddings. *Transactions of the Association for Computational Linguistics*, 4:385–399.

Piotr Bojanowski, Edouard Grave, Armand Joulin, and Tomas Mikolov. 2017. Enriching word vectors with subword information. *Transactions of the Association of Computational Linguistics*, 5(1):135–146.

Zied Bouraoui, Jose Camacho-Collados, and Steven Schockaert. 2020. Inducing relational knowledge from BERT. In *Proceedings of AAAI*.

Zied Bouraoui, Shoaib Jameel, and Steven Schockaert. 2018. Relation induction in word embeddings revisited. In *Proceedings of the 27th International Conference on Computational Linguistics*, pages 1627–1637, Santa Fe, New Mexico, USA. Association for Computational Linguistics.

Jose Camacho-Collados, Luis Espinosa-Anke, Shoaib Jameel, and Steven Schockaert. 2019. A latent variable model for learning distributional relation vectors. In *Proceedings of IJCAI*.

Aleksandr Drozd, Anna Gladkova, and Satoshi Matsuoka. 2016. Word embeddings, analogies, and machine learning: Beyond king-man+ woman= queen. In *Proceedings of coling 2016, the 26th international conference on computational linguistics: Technical papers*, pages 3519–3530.

Luis Espinosa-Anke and Steven Schockaert. 2018. SeVeN: Augmenting word embeddings with unsupervised relation vectors. In *Proceedings of the 27th International Conference on Computational Linguistics*, pages 2653–2665, Santa Fe, New Mexico, USA. Association for Computational Linguistics.

Kawin Ethayarajh, David Duvenaud, and Graeme Hirst. 2019. Towards understanding linear word analogies. In *Proceedings of the 57th Annual Meeting of the Association for Computational Linguistics*, pages 3253–3262.

Jerome A. Feldman and Dana H. Ballard. 1982. Connectionist models and their properties. *Cognitive Science*, 6(3):205–254.

John R. Firth. 1957. A synopsis of linguistic theory. *Studies in Linguistic Analysis (special volume of the Philological Society)*, 1952-59:1–32.

Alex Gittens, Dimitris Achlioptas, and Michael W Mahoney. 2017. Skip-gram- zipf+ uniform= vector additivity. In *Proceedings of the 55th Annual Meeting of the Association for Computational Linguistics (Volume 1: Long Papers)*, pages 69–76.

Anna Gladkova, Aleksandr Drozd, and Satoshi Matsuoka. 2016. Analogy-based detection of morphological and semantic relations with word embeddings: what works and what doesn't. In *Proceedings of the Student Research Workshop at NAACL*, pages 8–15.

Yoav Goldberg. 2017. Neural network methods for natural language processing. *Synthesis Lectures on Human Language Technologies*, 10(1):1–309.

Hila Gonen and Yoav Goldberg. 2019. Lipstick on a pig: Debiasing methods cover up systematic gender biases in word embeddings but do not remove them. In *Proceedings of the 2019 Conference of the North American Chapter of the Association for Computational Linguistics: Human Language Technologies, Volume 1 (Long and Short Papers)*, pages 609–614.

Lushan Han, Abhay Kashyap, Tim Finin, James Mayfield, and Jonathan Weese. 2013. UMBC EBIQUITY-CORE: Semantic textual similarity systems. In *Proceedings of the Second Joint Conference on Lexical and Computational Semantics*, volume 1, pages 44–52.

Geoffrey E. Hinton. 1986. Learning distributed representations of concepts. In *Proceedings of the eighth annual conference of the cognitive science society*, volume 1, page 12. Amherst, MA.

Geoffrey E. Hinton, James L. McClelland, and David E. Rumelhart. 1986. Distributed representations. *Parallel distributed processing: explorations in the microstructure of cognition, vol. 1*, pages 77–109.

Keith J Holyoak, Keith James Holyoak, and Paul Thagard. 1996. *Mental leaps: Analogy in creative thought*. MIT press.

Tom Hope, Joel Chan, Aniket Kittur, and Dafna Shahaf. 2017. Accelerating innovation through analogy mining. In *Proceedings of the 23rd ACM SIGKDD International Conference on Knowledge Discovery and Data Mining*, pages 235–243.

John J. Hopfield. 1982. Neural networks and physical systems with emergent collective computational abilities. *Proceedings of the National Academy of Sciences*, 79(8):2554–2558.

Aishwarya Jadhav, Yifat Amir, and Zachary A. Pardos. 2020. Lexical relation mining in neural word embeddings. In *Proceedings of the 29th International Conference on Computational Linguistics*.

Shoaib Jameel, Zied Bouraoui, and Steven Schockaert. 2018. Unsupervised learning of distributional relation vectors. In *Proceedings of the 56th Annual Meeting of the Association for Computational Linguistics (Volume 1: Long Papers)*, pages 23–33, Melbourne, Australia. Association for Computational Linguistics.

Zhengbao Jiang, Frank F. Xu, Jun Araki, and Graham Neubig. 2020. How can we know what language models know? *Transactions of the Association for Computational Linguistics*, 8:423–438.

Mandar Joshi, Eunsol Choi, Omer Levy, Daniel Weld, and Luke Zettlemoyer. 2019. pair2vec: Compositional word-pair embeddings for cross-sentence inference. In *Proceedings of the 2019 Conference of the North American Chapter of the Association for Computational Linguistics: Human Language Technologies, Volume 1 (Long and Short Papers)*, pages 3597–3608, Minneapolis, Minnesota. Association for Computational Linguistics.

Omer Levy and Yoav Goldberg. 2014a. Linguistic regularities in sparse and explicit word representations. In *Proceedings of the Eighteenth Conference on Computational Natural Language Learning*, pages 171–180, Ann Arbor, Michigan. Association for Computational Linguistics.

Omer Levy and Yoav Goldberg. 2014b. Neural word embedding as implicit matrix factorization. In *Advances in neural information processing systems*, pages 2177–2185.

Omer Levy, Yoav Goldberg, and Ido Dagan. 2015. Improving distributional similarity with lessons learned from word embeddings. *Transactions of the Association for Computational Linguistics*, 3:211–225.

Tal Linzen. 2016. Issues in evaluating semantic spaces using word analogies. In *Proceedings of the 1st Workshop on Evaluating Vector-Space Representations for NLP*, pages 13–18.

Tomas Mikolov, Kai Chen, Greg Corrado, and Jeffrey Dean. 2013a. Efficient estimation of word representations in vector space. *CoRR*, abs/1301.3781.

Tomas Mikolov, Wen-tau Yih, and Geoffrey Zweig. 2013b. Linguistic regularities in continuous space word representations. In *Proceedings of HLT-NAACL*, pages 746–751.

Malvina Nissim, Rik van Noord, and Rob van der Goot. 2020. Fair is better than sensational: Man is to doctor as woman is to doctor. *Computational Linguistics*, 46(2):487–497.

Denis Paperno and Marco Baroni. 2016. When the whole is less than the sum of its parts: How composition affects pmi values in distributional semantic vectors. *Computational Linguistics*, 42(2):345–350.

Zachary A. Pardos and Andrew J. H. Nam. 2020. A university map of course knowledge. *PLoS ONE*, 15(9).

Jeffrey Pennington, Richard Socher, and Christopher D Manning. 2014. GloVe: Global vectors for word representation. In *Proceedings of EMNLP*, pages 1532–1543.

Fabio Petroni, Tim Rocktäschel, Sebastian Riedel, Patrick Lewis, Anton Bakhtin, Yuxiang Wu, and Alexander Miller. 2019. Language models as knowledge bases? In *Proceedings of the 2019 Conference on Empirical Methods in Natural Language Processing and the 9th International Joint Conference on Natural Language Processing (EMNLP-IJCNLP)*, pages 2463–2473.

Natalie Schluter. 2018. The word analogy testing caveat. In *Proceedings of the 2018 Conference of the North American Chapter of the Association for Computational Linguistics: Human Language Technologies, Volume 2 (Short Papers)*, pages 242–246.

Peter D. Turney and Patrick Pantel. 2010. From frequency to meaning: Vector space models of semantics. *Journal of Artificial Intelligence Research*, 37:141–188.

Koki Washio and Tsuneaki Kato. 2018. Filling missing paths: Modeling co-occurrences of word pairs and dependency paths for recognizing lexical semantic relations. In *Proceedings of the 2018 Conference of the North American Chapter of the Association for Computational Linguistics: Human Language Technologies, Volume 1 (Long Papers)*, pages 1123–1133, New Orleans, Louisiana. Association for Computational Linguistics.

Appendix

A Additional Experiments

In this appendix we include some additional results that complement our main experiments.

Skip-gram results. Table 5 and 6 present the results of the Skip-gram model of Word2Vec trained in UMBC and Wikipedia, respectively.

Performance drop. Figure 3 presents the performance drop percentage of the remove setting (Rm) with respect to the default setting in UMBC.

B Visualizations

Figures 4 and 5 present visualizations of the word embedding space for the relations *nationality-adjective* and *city-in-state*, respectively, in both default (Def) and remove (Rm) settings. These figures complement Figure 2 of the main paper.

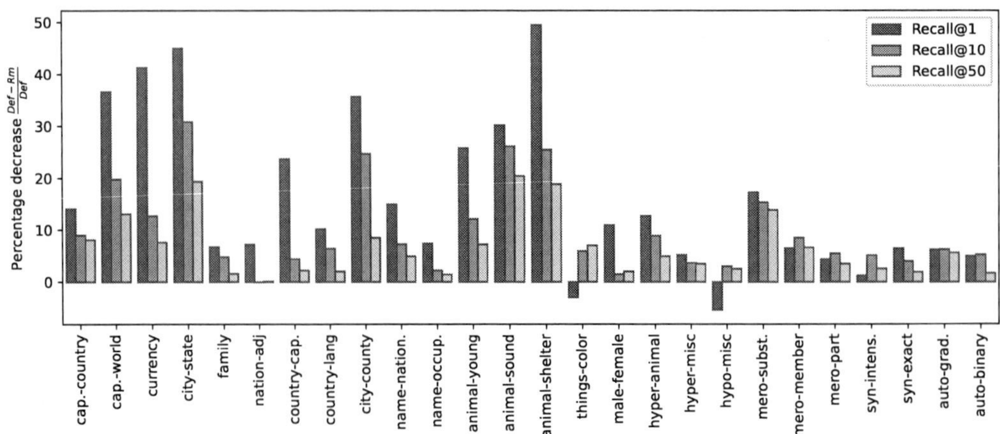

Figure 3: Average decrease in performance (%) of the CBOW model trained on the original UMBC corpus with respect to the removal strategy (Rm) per relation type (Google and BATS datasets).

		Recall@1			Recall@10			Recall@50		
		Def	Rp	Rp+	Def	Rp	Rp+	Def	Rp	Rp+
Google	**cap.-country**	61.7	51.0	48.2	91.7	85.2	86.2	98.4	95.1	93.1
	cap.-world	49.8	34.0	33.5	79.1	66.5	65.3	92.2	81.0	80.4
	currency	12.1	9.5	5.8	35.7	30.6	28.1	61.8	57.7	53.0
	city-state	16.6	10.2	10.7	54.6	37.5	38.4	76.3	62.5	62.8
	family	82.0	67.2	63.2	100.0	90.9	82.0	100.0	94.9	87.6
	nation-adj	92.4	89.2	87.9	98.0	96.6	95.9	99.8	99.3	97.2
	AVERAGE	**52.4**	**43.5**	**41.5**	**76.5**	**67.9**	**66.0**	**88.1**	**81.7**	**79.0**

Table 5: UMBC corpus word analogy results using Skip-gram with three different configurations: Default (Def), Replace (Rp), its more aggressive setting replacing all pairwise co-occurrences, i.e., Rp+.

		Recall@1			Recall@10			Recall@50		
		Def	Rm	Rm+	Def	Rm	Rm+	Def	Rm	Rm+
Google	**cap.-country**	68.0	52.0	45.9	96.1	86.8	84.6	99.2	97.0	95.9
	cap.-world	70.0	44.6	42.2	93.7	78.6	78.1	97.9	89.1	89.9
	currency	31.2	23.6	19.2	59.9	53.1	44.8	73.2	67.7	59.5
	city-state	19.9	8.9	10.5	56.8	29.9	32.4	75.4	50.4	51.2
	family	71.2	61.5	59.1	94.9	83.8	82.6	95.5	90.7	89.5
	nation-adj	99.7	98.7	96.7	100.0	99.9	99.3	100.0	100.0	99.8
	AVERAGE	**60.0**	**48.2**	**45.6**	**83.6**	**72.0**	**70.3**	**90.2**	**82.5**	**80.9**

Table 6: Wikipedia corpus word analogy results using Skip-gram with three different configurations: Default (Def), Remove (Rm), its more aggressive setting removing all pairwise co-occurrences, i.e., Rm+.

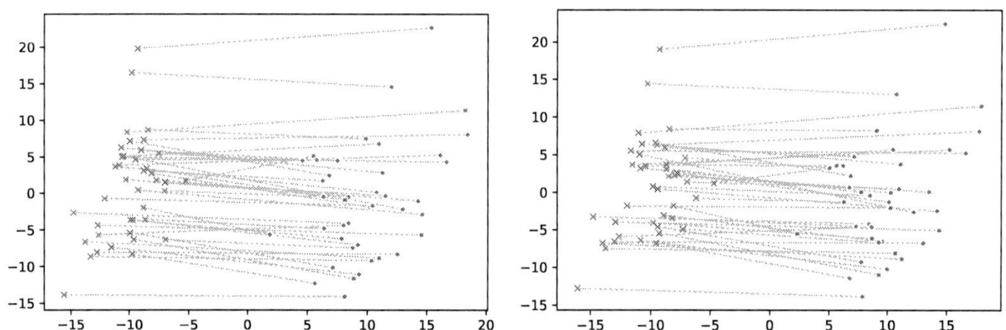

Figure 4: *Nationality-adjective* vectors projected by PCA. All models trained on different subsets of UMBC: default (left) and remove (right). Red marks (x) correspond to *country-adjectives* and blue dots, *countries*.

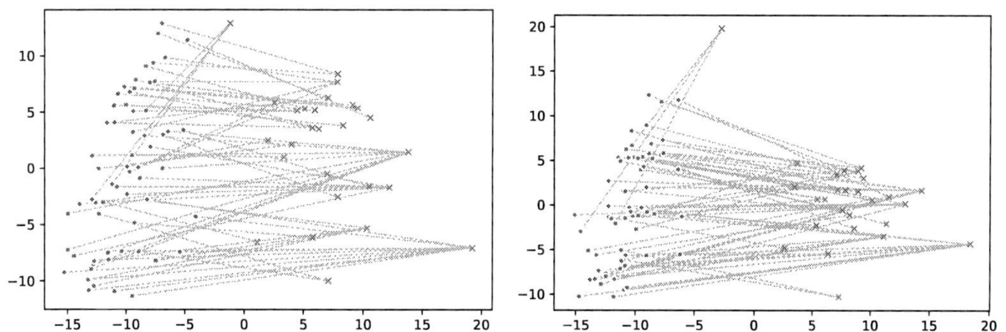

Figure 5: *City-in-state* vectors projected by PCA. All models trained on different subsets of UMBC: default (left) and remove (right). Red marks (x) correspond to *states* and blue dots, *cities*.

Finding the Right *One* and Resolving it

Payal Khullar   **Arghya Bhattacharya**   **Manish Shrivastava**

Language Technologies Research Centre
International Institute of Information Technology Hyderabad
Gachibowli, Hyderabad, Telangana-500032
{payal.khullar@research., arghya.b@research.,
m.shrivastava@}iiit.ac.in

Abstract

One-anaphora has figured prominently in theoretical linguistic literature, but computational linguistics research on the phenomenon is sparse. Not only that, the long standing linguistic controversy between the determinative and the nominal anaphoric element *one* has propagated in the limited body of computational work on one-anaphora resolution, making this task harder than it is. In the present paper, we resolve this by drawing from an adequate linguistic analysis of the word *one* in different syntactic environments - once again highlighting the significance of linguistic theory in Natural Language Processing (NLP) tasks. We prepare an annotated corpus marking *actual* instances of one-anaphora with their textual antecedents, and use the annotations to experiment with state-of-the art neural models for one-anaphora resolution. Apart from presenting a strong neural baseline for this task, we contribute a gold-standard corpus, which is, to the best of our knowledge, the biggest resource on one-anaphora till date.

1 Introduction

One-anaphora is an anaphoric relation between a non-lexical proform (i.e. *one* or *ones*) and the head noun or the nominal group inside a noun phrase (NP). Consider the example sentence in (1) from The British National Corpus (2001), where the word *one* can be easily understood as *room*, from the preceding context.

> 1. The furniture in the lower **room**, which in every respect corresponds to the upper *one*, consists of one chair, of most antique and unsafe appearance.[1]

The context from where the anaphor gets its sense and/or reference from is called the antecedent. For

---

[1] Following the typographical conventions for one-anaphora and their antecedents by Gardiner (2003), we denote an antecedent noun phrase **like this** and one-anaphora *like this*.

one-anaphora, the antecedent can be a single word (head noun of the antecedent NP), as in (1), or group of nominal words – a compound noun or a head noun with its dependent, as in (2). However, the antecedent of one anaphora is never the whole NP.

> 2. There was much competition during the war as to who could come up with the best **bomb story** , and my mother had a great time telling this *one* to all the aunties...

One-anaphora can represent a particular case of identity-of-sense anaphora where the anaphor shares only the sense of the antecedent and not the complete reference. This category of one-anaphora is named as sense sharing one-anaphors as opposed to "contrastive anaphors" presented in (1) (Luperfoy, 1991), where the "lower" room that the anaphor refers to is in contrast with the the "upper" room as antecedent. Such an interpretation can also be vague in some cases, as in (2), where the bomb story that the mother is telling might in fact be the best bomb story in the competition, but not necessarily. In other cases, it is possible that the entity that the anaphor one refers to is a subset of the entities the antecedent denotes, such as in (3), where the black car that Jack liked is actually one amongst the many cars that he saw.

> 3. Of all the **cars** Jack saw, he liked the black *one* the most.

This category of one-anaphora is discussed by some linguists as "member anaphora" for representative sampling (Luperfoy, 1991), or "nominal substitutes" that stand in for a meaningful head (Halliday and Hasan, 1976). The antecedent can also be the head noun with its propositional argument, such as in (4), where the anaphor resolves as *point of agreement*.

> 4. Even so, there are possible **points of agreement** — if not in principle, then at least in

Proceedings of the 24th Conference on Computational Natural Language Learning, pages 132–141
Online, November 19-20, 2020. ©2020 Association for Computational Linguistics
https://doi.org/10.18653/v1/P17

practice. The most obvious *one* is commercial animal agriculture in its dominant form.

Sometimes, the antecedent boundary selection decision is vague, even for human evaluators. For instance, the antecedent in (5) can be *presentation on global warming* or just *presentation*, depending on the context.

5. My **presentation** on global warming was the longest *one* in the conference.

However, for a sentence like (6), there is little ambiguity that the antecedent is only the head noun *book* without its prepositional argument.

6. This **book** with yellow cover is the best *one* in the library.

It will be absurd for the anaphor to be interpreted as *book with yellow cover*, although a sloppy reading such as this is also possible.

2   Previous Work

The nominal anaphoric element one is extensively discussed in theoretical linguistics as one-anaphora, noun anaphora, one-insertion, one-substitution and pronominalization (Menzel, 2017, 2014; Kayne, 2015; Hankamer and Sag, 2015; Payne et al., 2013; Corver and van Koppen, 2011; Gunther, 2011; Culicover and Jackendoff, 2005; Akhtar et al., 2004; Cowper, 1992; Luperfoy, 1991; Dalrymple et al., 1991; Dahl, 1985; Radford, 1981; Baker, 1978; Halliday and Hasan, 1976; Bresnan, 1971). In computational linguistics literature, however, it has largely been ignored, despite the evident impact of one-anaphora resolution in improving the accuracy of downstream Natural Language Processing (NLP) tasks such as Machine Translation (MT) and Question Answering (QA).

To the best of our knowledge, the earliest computational approach to one-anaphora detection and resolution comes from Gardiner (2003), who presented several linguistically-motivated heuristics to distinguish one-anaphora from other non-anaphoric uses of one in English. For the resolution task, she used web search to select potential antecedent candidates. The second seminal work comes from Ng et al. (2005) that uses Gardiner's heuristics as features to train a Machine Learning (ML) model. The most recent work on one-anaphora comes from Recasens et al. (2016) where it has been treated as

one of the several sense anaphoric relations in English. The authors create sAnaNotes corpus where they annotate one third of the OntoNotes corpus for sense Anaphora. They use a Support Vector Machine (SVM) classifier - LIBLINEAR implementation (Fan et al., 2008) along with 31 lexical and syntactic features, to distinguish between the anaphoric and the non-anaphoric class. Trained and tested on one-third of the OntoNotes dataset annotated as the SAnaNotes corpus, their system achieves 61.80% F1 score on the detection of all anaphoric relations, including one-anaphora. Their baseline statistical model outeperforms the existing ML model for one-anaphora detection. This work, however, only limits itself to the detection part, deeming resolution of sense anaphora as a hard NLP task.

3   Getting to Know Every *One*

English has three distinct lexemes spelled as one– the regular third person indefinite pronoun, the indefinite cardinal numeral (determinative) and regular common count noun. There is no visible difference in their orthographic base form. However, they are totally different with respect to their morphological, syntactic, and semantic properties. On the surface, this difference can be observed in the way these forms inflect (morphology), behave in a sentence (syntax) and impart meaning (semantics) (Payne et al., 2013).

Previous efforts to classify the word *one* in English involve classification based on different functions of the word in discourse– numeric, partitive, anaphoric, generic, idiomatic, and unclassifiable; and in terms of the type of antecedent the anaphoric one takes– a kind, a set, an individual instance (Payne et al., 2013; Gardiner, 2003; Luperfoy, 1991; Dahl, 1985). This scheme has been extended for classification of other sense anaphoric relations as well (Recasens et al., 2013). This distinction clubs closely related types like numeric and partitive (both are determinative, roughly mean "1") to different classes. It also treats the regular count noun anaphora and determinative anaphora together as the anaphoric class. This makes the previous research miss important underlying linguistic generalisations in these forms. In syntactic literature, one-anaphora refers to an anaphoric instance of the word *one*, where its syntactic properties resemble that of a count noun (Payne et al., 2013; HuddlestonRodnry and Pullum, 2005). Like an En-

	One in English	**Identifying Features**	**Examples**
Pronoun	Regular, third-person, indefinite pronoun.	Refers to an arbitrary person. As with pronouns, no plural form.	<u>One</u> must respect his elders.
Determiner	Indefinite cardinal numeral (Most common usage). Means '1'.	1. When used with a head noun, it is oligatory and non-anaphoric.	I will have <u>one</u> glass of water.
		2. Partitive function. It means, one entity in a set of many. Often, followed by the preposition "of".	<u>One</u> of the keys is missing.
		3. When used as a noun modifier, it means 'sole', and is ommissible.	You are the <u>one</u> reason I am here.
		4. When used without a noun, it acts as a noun ellipsis licensor. Anaphoric to whole NP.	I have two pens and my friend has <u>one</u>.
Noun	Regular, common count noun.	1. Means roughly 'instance thereof'- refers back to some class or type in discourse or salient in context. Anaphoric to the head noun, with or without a dependent, but never to the whole NP. Has both singular and plural forms **(One Anaphora).**	The fictitious **example** being used here isn't the easiest *one* to give to an informant, but many much more difficult *ones* have been explained.
		2. Derivative, non-anaphoric. Has both singular and plural forms.	Always take care of your loved <u>ones</u>.

Table 1: The three uses of the word <u>one</u> in English.

glish noun, it has four inflected forms – singular (one), plural (ones), genetive singular (one's) and genetive plural (ones'). In its singular form, it can occur after a singular demonstrative determiner, a determiner followed by an adjective. It can not occur solely with an indefinitive article, but a construction where an indefinitive article is followed by an adjective is acceptable. With the definitve article, it occurs when followed by a relative clause (Kayne, 2015).

Interestingly, this count noun instance of *one* looks very similar to the anaphoric subtype of the determinative instance of *one* on the surface. However, a close linguistic investigation clarifies that they have completely different morphological, syntactic and semantic properties (Payne et al., 2013). More importantly, they are different with respect to the kind of antecedent they take. While anaphoric noun takes noun heads as antecedents, the determinative one takes the whole NP. Consider the following example that Gardiner (2003) takes from

Luperfoy (1991) as an instance of one-anaphora.

7. All the officers wore hats so Joe wore one too.

The problem here is that the occurrence such as in (7) is not an anaphoric noun; it is the determinative anaphor. Note that the plural form of this element is *some*, and not *ones*. Further, the constituent whose repetition this *one* word avoids is not *hats*, but the entire NP *a hat*. In ellipsis theory, this determinative *one* word here is not one-anaphora, but the licensor or trigger of an elided noun. Detection and resolution of this determinative one anaphor has actually been carried out in a part of our previous computational research on ellipsis (Khullar et al., 2020, 2019)

Right from Baker (1978), the traditional linguistic literature on one-anaphora and noun ellipsis too has confused between the noun and determiner uses of the word *one*, using them interchangeably in discussions and analysis. The faulty understanding on this phenomenon in earlier syntactic discourse,

No.	POS String Template	Example Sentences from BNC
1.	Determiner – Adjective – "one"	Her idea of the value of art criticism was <u>a simple one</u>.
2.	Determiner – (Adverb)+ – Adjective – "one"	The need for volunteers from churches, particularly in London and Scotland in the day-time, is <u>an ever constant one</u>.
3.	Determiner – "one" – Preposition	The only room available is <u>this one on</u> Friday the ninth.
4.	Determiner – "one" – Gerund/Participle	The songs contain upto eight themes, <u>each one consisting</u> of repeated phrases.
5.	Determiner – "one" –(Punct) Complementizer	Freeman wrote another clause, wrote <u>another one which</u> meant that you had to go.

Table 2: Template for fetching one-anaphora from POS tagged data.

unfortunately, propagated into the limited body of computational work on one-anaphora, and made this task harder than it really is. In the current paper, we aim to bridge this gap by drawing from a thorough linguistic investigation of anaphoric instances of the word *one* in recent linguistic studies, where clear differences between these two forms of the word have been discussed (Payne et al., 2013). Note that although Kayne (2015) prefers to give all instances of the word *one* a homogeneous internal structure, comprising a classifier merged with an indefintive article through a variety of examples, he too identifies subtypes within this class and points out how they behave differently than one another.

The crux of the discussion on different types of *ones* in English in this section is summarised in Table 1, listing details of the classification scheme–in terms of how the word *one* behaves morphologically, syntactically and semantically in a sentence, along with identifying features and sentence examples for each type[2]. Using this wisdom, we extend the computational research on the phenomenon.

4   Corpus Creation

In this section, we explain our efforts to build a one-anaphora corpus that contains actual instances of one-anaphora and is sizeable enough for training supervised machine learning models. We make this process easier by using linguistic theory on syntactic environment of one-anaphora. To begin with, since one-anaphora is a count noun, we select all plural *ones* as plurality is a feature of count nouns. For the singular form, we identify five POS

string sequences that capture the syntactic distribution of one-anaphora in English. The basic idea is that one-anaphora, being a regular count noun, will always occur inside of an NP. In other words, it will be proceeded by a determiner or noun modifier like category and could be followed by a relative clause. All the syntactically possible combinations for one-anaphora to exist are presented in Table 1.

For our annotation purpose, we use The British National Corpus that contains over one hundred million words of British English, drawn from written and spoken sources. The text comes from a variety of sources like books, periodicals, media, letters, conversations and monologues. The text also has part of speech tags assigned by the CLAWS part-of-speech tagger (The British National Corpus, 2001). To fetch potential one-anaphora, we perform a semi-automatic search using the POS string templates discussed above. To calculate accuracy of our POS string templates, we check their output on 5000 randomly selected sentences containing the word *ones* or *ones* . Our templates retrieve 153 positive sentences. We manually check all the 5000 sentences and do not find any one-anaphora instance missed by the templates. However, of the 153 results, 18 are incorrect (false positives). Hence, we get a full recall, a precision of 88.24 and F1 score of 93.75. Although the precision is slightly low and the high F1 score is mainly contributed from the prediction of 4,847 negative instances correctly, these results show that the templates are good enough to fetch a variety of one-anaphora candidates that can be followed by manual confirmation. This is also much less expensive than previous entirely manual annotation efforts.

A simple search for the word *ones* and *ones*

---

[2]The table is an extended version of the one presented in Payne et al. (2013).

in the BNC yields 2,72,469 results. We run the templates on these sentences, which yields 15,647 unique matches. Of these, we manually check the first 1058 sentences only.[3] We keep the true positive cases for the final corpus. From these 1058 sentences, we get 912 positive sentences containing 921 one-anaphora. For these 921 anaphors, we look for antecedents. Since the distance between the one-anaphor and antecedent is generally not that large (Gardiner, 2003), for finding and marking the antecedents, we only consider a context of up to three sentences, including the current sentence. If an antecedent is not present within this context or is not present at all endophorically, we leave the anaphor without its resolution marked. This decision speeds up the annotation effort.

4.1 Annotation Format

We use a stand off annotation scheme that does not modify the original text. The format of the annotation is as follows:

ANA   sentence ID   start index   end index

ANT   sentence ID   start index   end index

Here, ANA is short for anaphor and ANT for antecedent. Sentence ID is the unique ID given to a sentence in the BNC. We mark the boundaries with word offsets of the anaphor and antcedent in a given sentence. The simplicity of the format and stand-off annotation scheme make these annotations easy to understand and reuse.

4.2 Inter-annotator agreement

Annotation is carried out manually. Three annotators who are linguists by training and proficient in the language perform the task independently on all the sentences. For each sentence, the first annotation decision involves checking if the marked one-anaphora is correct or not. In the second step, the annotators mark antecedents for sentences they they mark as correct in the first step. We calculate the inter-annotator agreement for both these steps separately. We use the Fleiss's Kappa coefficient to calculate the inter-annotator agreement between multiple annotators. For the first task, we get Fleiss's Kappa coefficient of 0.89 and for the second task, we get 0.81. These numbers confirm reliability of our annotations. Most of the disagreements occur in distinguishing between derivative

---

[3] We do not manually check all of these as it would be very arduous and expensive.

non-anaphoric and exophoric one-anaphora for the first task and boundary selection decision for the second task. All the disagreements are finally resolved at the end of the task by discussion among the three annotators and the agreed-upon cases are included in the final corpus.

4.3 Corpus Summary

In this section, we present a summary of major statistical observations of our annotated corpus along with a brief discussion.

- In the 100-million-word BNC, the word *one* occurs 2,61,093 and the word *ones* occurs 11,376. This makes their respective frequencies 0.26% and 0.01% in the corpus. Sentence wise, these frequencies are 3.97% and 0.18% respectively. From our templates, we fetch 15,647 matching sentences that contain 18,669 one-anaphora words (some sentences contain more than one one-anaphora words), both singular and plural (subject to precision error described previously). Roughly, this makes the sentence-wise frequency of one-anaphora 6.25% and word wise frequency 6.85%. We get a significantly lower frequency value as compared to that in the previous annotation efforts, which came out to be 15.2% (Ng et al., 2005) and 12.3% (Recasens et al., 2016). This is expected as most of the one-anaphora cases marked in these papers are not one-anaphoric nouns, but determinative anaphora.

- We note an interesting observation about the location of the anaphor and antecedent in the text. About 92% of the fetched one-anaphora instances come from the first and second templates alone, see Figure 1 for reference. Both these template require the anaphor to be preceded by one or more adjectives. This means that one-anaphora is most frequently followed by adjectives. This observation in line with the analysis of one-anaphora as NP-ellipsis with adjectival remnants (Corver and van Koppen, 2011).

- In the annotated part of our corpus, we get a total of 921 one-anaphora in 912 sentences. Of these, the antecedents of 895 anaphors is present endophorically (i.e. in the text) within a context window of 3 sentences. For the remaining 26 anaphors, either the antecedent is

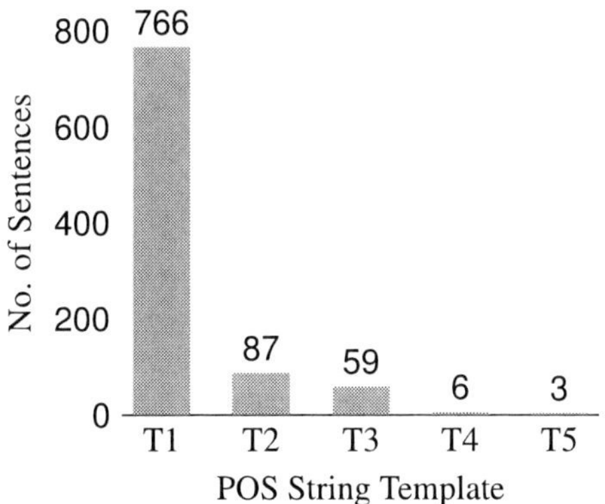

Figure 1: Number of sentences containing one-anaphora, fetched using five different templates, labelled T1 to T5.

not present in the text at all (exophoric cases), is present but not in the considered context window (and ignored for practical reasons), or the annotators are not able to agree on a single decision with certainty. This means that in our corpus, a majority one-anaphora are endophoric and, thus, can be resolved.

- We also note that a majority of the antecedents in our corpus comprise a single word only. Only 31 antecedents of out 895 are more than one word long. This implies that one-anaphora most often resolves to just the head noun of the antecedent NP. This is an important observation as antecedent boundary selection is presumably as a hard NLP task. As discussed previously, even human annotators find it difficult to make this decision in some cases. Hence, as far as one-anaphora is considered, resolving it to just the head noun of the antecedent NP is a simple and practical choice for NLP tasks.

- Finally, over 90% of the antecedents are present in the same sentence as one-anaphora, about 7% in the first previous sentence and less than 2% in the second previous sentence. The antecedent can go beyond the second previous sentence too but we do not annotate it as discussed in the annotation scheme. Although antecedents can follow one-anaphora, we do not find any such cases in our annotated corpus. Since we consider only a small part of the actual number of occurrences in the BNC, it can be safely concluded that cataphoric in-

stances are rare or very less frequent. This is in line with the observation made by Gardiner (2003) that the antecedent is generally located closer to one-anaphora and lies frequently in the previous context. For computational work, both these observations can be employed as manual features to improve the search for the antecedents of one-anaphora.

5 One-anaphora Resolution

In this section, we describe a framework to resolve one-anaphora in free text. We break the complete task in two subtasks – the first being the detection of the anaphor and the second the selection of the antecedent candidate from its context. See Figure 2 for an overview of the framework.

5.1 Detecting One-Anaphors

Detecting instances of *one* that are one-anaphora is not a trivial task as the word *one* occurs very frequently in text and most of the times, it is not one-anaphora.[4] To begin with, we can test the efficacy of our POS string templates on real world data, which does not come with gold tags. To do this, we use the state-of-the-art spaCy parser (Honnibal and Johnson, 2015) to automatically tag sentences from our annotated dataset and then apply the template rules to filter out matching candidates. Apart from fetching wrong candidates or missing correct ones, this template system is now also subject to parser errors. Using gold annotations, we automatically check for recall and precision value. After application of the templates on the tagged sentences from spaCy, we get a precision of 78.34%, a recall of 85.92% and F1 score of 81.96%. We now turn to supervised machine learning models to see if they offer a more accurate and robust solution.

5.1.1 Task Description

The one-anaphora detection task can be modelled as a classification problem, where, given an instance of the words *one* or *ones*, the classifier has to predict whether it is one-anaphora or not. Formally, for a given anaphor candidate ana_i in the context c, the task of one-anaphora detection is represented as follows:

$$f(ana_i, c) \rightarrow \{0, 1\}$$

where 1 denotes that ana_i is a one-anaphor in c, and and 0 otherise.

---

[4]The most frequent tag assigned to the word *one* in BNC is cardinal numeral (Gardiner, 2003).

5.1.2 Training/Dev/Test Data

We take the 912 sentences containing 921 one-anaphora marked in our annotated dataset as our positive set. For the negative set, we take an equal number of sentences from BNC that contain instances of *one* other than one-anaphora. Hence, our data size becomes 1824 sentences. We perform a standard 70-10-20 split to obtain the train, development and test set respectively, and follow the 5-fold cross validation procedure to capture both classes properly in each case.

5.2 Selecting Antecedents

There is evidence that parallelism in discourse can be applied to resolve possible readings for anaphoric entities and reference phenomenon (Hobbs and Kehler, 1997). Linguistic research also shows structural similarities between antecedent and anaphoric clauses (Luperfoy, 1991; Halliday and Hasan, 1976). An antecedent selection procedure can possibly benefit from capturing this similarity.

5.2.1 Task Description

This subtask involves selecting the right antecedent for one-anaphora, if it can be resolved. Formally, in a given context c, for an instance of one-anaphora ana_i, and the antecedent candidate ant_j; the task of antecedent selection can be defined as follows:

$$f(ant_j, ana_i, c) \rightarrow \{0, 1\}$$

where 1 denotes that the antecedent candidate ant_j is the actual resolution of the one-anaphora ana_i, and 0 otherise. Thus, for a given input sentence, the model can potentially select one or more antecedent candidates.

5.2.2 Training/Dev/Test Data

For antecedents, we have 895 positive samples in the annotated corpus. For the negative samples, we take all noun words other than the antecedent from the positive sentences and undersample to deal with the resulting skewed class distribution. We only take noun words since the antecedent of one-anaphora can only be a noun (optionally with dependents). As in the previous step, we perform a standard 70-10-20 split to obtain the train, development and test set respectively, and follow the 5-fold cross validation procedure to capture both classes properly in each case.

5.2.3 Experiments

To get representations of the word and its context, we experiment with both static and contextual types of word embeddings. For the former, we choose state-of-the-art fastText (FT) embeddings (Bojanowski et al., 2016) as they are able to provide representations of rare words and non words that might be frequent in movie dialogues. For the latter, we use BERT (Bidirectional Encoder Representations from Transformers) base uncased word-piece model for English (Devlin et al., 2019) as it currently provides the most powerful word embeddings taking into account a large left and right context. For the first subtask, we take word embeddings for the one-anaphora candidate and its context; and for the second subtask, we take word embeddings for the antecedent candidate, the gold one-anaphora vector from the annotations and their context. This way, we are able to evaluate the performance of both the subtasks separately. For fastText, we use pretrained embeddings and sumpool the embeddings of the given word and its context to obtain a single vector that we employ for training our classifiers. For both the subtasks, we experiment with a simple Multilayer Perceprton (MLP) and bidirectional Long Short Term Memory (bi-LSTM) networks. In MLP, we have a simple, two-layer feedforward network (FFNN) or two layers of multiple computational units interconnected in a feed-forward way without loops. We have a single hidden layer with 768 neurons and a sigmoid function. A unidirectional weight connection exists between the two successive layers. The classification decision is made by turning the input vector representations of a word with its context into a score. The network has a softmax output layer. For the bi-LSTM, we have embedding layer, time-distributed translate layer, Bi-LSTM (RNN) layer, batch normalization layer, dropout layer and prediction layer. The activation used is Softmax. In case of BERT, we fine tune the pretrained BERT model. We seperate the sentence and the candidate words with a [SEP] token and keep the sequence length to 300 as this is the maximum sentence length in the training data. After creating the concatenated set of tokens, if the number of tokens are greater than 300, we clip it to 300, otherwise we add [PAD] tokens which correspond to the embedding of 768 dimensional zero-vector. Attention mask tells the model to not focus on [PAD] tokens. The [CLS] output of the BERT model is used for classification.

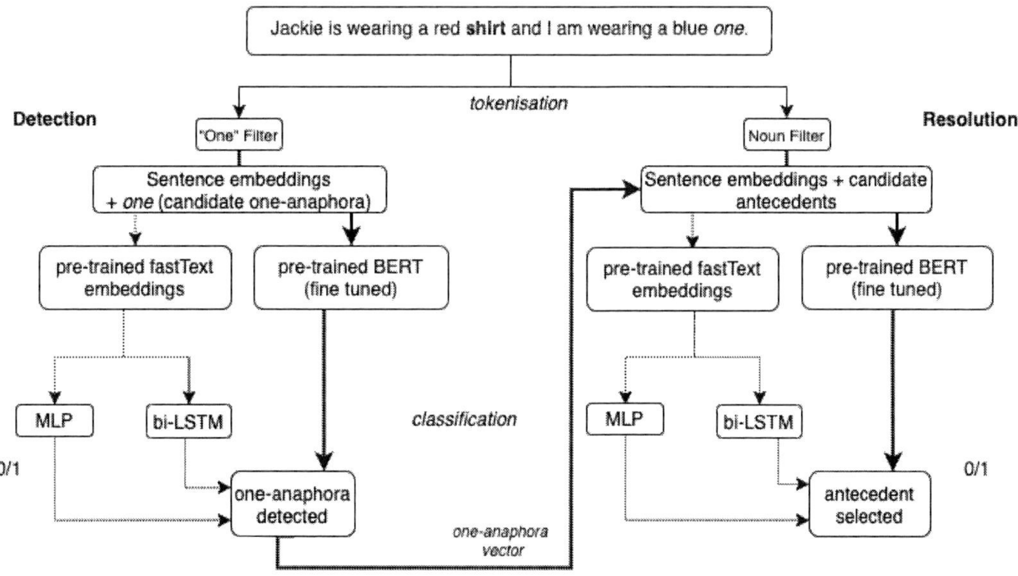

Figure 2: One anaphora detection and resolution pipeline. Classification decision is first taken on a given word one as anaphoric or non-anaphoric. The detected anaphoric one vector is passed on to the second model where the resolution decision is taken. Dotted lines represent model choices that were not included in the final pipeline.

Mathematically;

$$P(y|x) = softmax(W \cdot x + b)$$

where x denotes the input vector and y denotes the one-anaphora or antecedent for the first and second subtasks respectively. The loss function is calculated with cross entropy. We train in batch sizes of 16 and early stopping with max epochs of 100. In early stopping the patience is kept to be 10 and the optimizer used is Adam. We use default values for the learning rate. We use Keras (Chollet, 2015) for coding these models.

5.2.4 Results and Discussion

We evaluate the performance of all our detection models in terms of F1-score, computed by taking an average F1-scores obtained from the 5-folds results. The precision, recall and F1-score values of all the experiments for one-anaphora detection and antecedent selection are presented in Table 3. The majority of errors come from failing to detect actual anaphors, wrongly identifying non-anaphoric words and correct anaphor detection but failed antecedent selection. We also treat the result as incorrect when the system gives multiple antecedents for the same one-anaphora (as currently there is no way the system can make a decision in such a case).

Our experiments show that, the pre-trained fine tuned BERT model renders robust and high scores for both the subtasks. This is expected as BERT has been previously shown to give promising scores on a number of classification tasks. In our task, the model is robust and efficiently makes generalisations on the syntactic and semantic dependency between the one-anaphora with the determiners and adjectival modifiers in its context, as well as between antecedents and the anaphor. The results with the pre-trained fastText embeddings with a simple MLP are also promising. The sufficient neurons in the hidden layer with sigmoidal function ensures network approximate the nonlinear relationships between the input and output. Even though FFNNs are not designed to capture long range dependencies in a sentence that are inevitably required for handling a discourse device like one-anaphora, they can perform exceedingly well when they are infused with the contexual knowledge that they lack (Dumpala et al., 2018). This makes them suitable to resolve one-anaphora efficiently from low resource datasets like the one we use to train. This knowledge comes from the pre-trained embeddings.

We finally integrate the neural network models for each subtask into an end-to-end pipeline, see Figure 2 for an overview. Now, instead of the gold vectors, the resolution model is fed the one-

Task	P	R	F
One-Anaphora			
Detection			
FT, MLP	65.49	79.35	71.76
FT, Bi-LSTM	64.22	71.74	67.77
BERT (fine-tuned)	**78.87**	**89.35**	**83.78**
Antecedent			
Selection			
FT, MLP	55.24	61.29	58.11
FT, Bi-LSTM	58.97	65.74	62.17
BERT (fine-tuned)	**63.07**	**72.33**	**67.38**
Final Model			
See Figure 2.	59.99	70.01	64.61

Table 3: Precision (**P**), Recall **R** and F1-Score (**F**) values of different models for one-anaphora detection and antecedent selection tasks. Values in bold depict best performance. The two subtasks are finally integrated into a final model.

anaphora vectors from the detection model. This obviously results into error propagation into the second model, and lowers the precision value to 59.99, recall to 70.01 and consequently, the F1-score to 64.61 of the final system. Although, we achieve promising results on both the subtasks separately as well as in the pipeline process, the results can be further improved with hyperparameter tuning, additional regularization and manual feature addition.

6 Conclusion

In this paper, we used the most recent linguistic understanding of the word *one* in English to define and classify the one-anaphora phenomenon for computational linguistics research. We built a big corpus containing actual instances of one-anaphora by hand annotating sentences from BNC and used the annotations to experiment with state-of-the-art neural models for one-anaphora detection and resolution. For word and context representation, we experimented with pre-trained fastText and BERT word embeddings. We achieve promising results on a task that was deemed hard in previous NLP work, highlighting the importance of linguistic theory in NLP research. The gold standard corpus prepared for this task, containing 921 instances of one-anaphora marked in an easy-to-reuse standoff annotation scheme, will be released with this paper for future work.

References

Nameera Akhtar, Maureen Callanan, Geoffrey K Pullum, and Barbara C Scholz. 2004. Learning antecedents for anaphoric one. *Cognition*, 4:141–145.

Carl Lee Baker. 1978. Introduction to generative transformational syntax. *Englewood Cliffs, NJ:: Prentice-Hal*.

Piotr Bojanowski, Edouard Grave, Armand Joulin, and Tomas Mikolov. 2016. Enriching word vectors with subword information. *arXiv preprint arXiv:1607.04606*.

Joan Bresnan. 1971. A note on the notion "identity of sense anaphora". *Linguistic Inquiry*, 2:589–597.

Francois Chollet. 2015. Keras. `https://keras.io`.

Norbert Corver and Marjo van Koppen. 2011. Np-ellipsis with adjectival remnants: a microcomparative perspective. *Natural Language & Linguistic Theory*, 29(2):371–421.

Elizabeth A. Cowper. 1992. A concise introduction to syntactic theory. *Chicago, IL: University of Chicago Press*.

Peter W Culicover and Ray Jackendoff. 2005. Simpler syntax. *Oxford, England: Oxford University Press*.

Deborah Anna Dahl. 1985. The structure and function of one-anaphora in english. *Ph.D. thesis, University of Minnesota*.

Mary Dalrymple, Stuart M. Shieber, and Fernando C.N. 1991. Ellipsis and higher order unification. *Linguistics and Philosophy*, 14:399–452.

Jacob Devlin, Ming-Wei Chang, Kenton Lee, and Kristina Toutanova. 2019. Bert: Pre-training of deep bidirectional transformers for language understanding. In *NAACL-HLT*.

Sri Harsha Dumpala, Rupayan Chakraborty, and Sunil Kumar Kopparapu. 2018. Knowledge-driven feed-forward neural network for audio affective content analysis. Workshops at the Thirty-Second AAAI Conference on Artificial Intelligence.

Rong-En Fan, Kai-Wei Chang, Cho-Jui Hsieh, Xiang-Rui Wang, and Chih-Jen Lin. 2008. Liblinear: A library for large linear classification. volume 9, page 1871–1874. Journal of Machine Learning Research.

Mary Gardiner. 2003. Identifying and resolving one-anaphora. Department of Computing, Division of ICS, Macquarie University.

Christine Gunther. 2011. Noun ellipsis in english: adjectival modifiers and the role of context. *The structure of the noun phrase in English: synchronic and diachronic explorations*, 15(2):279–301.

Michael Alexander Kirkwood Halliday and Ruqaiya Hasan. 1976. Cohesion in english. *Longman London*, page 76.

Jorge Hankamer and Ivan Sag. 2015. Deep and surface anaphora. *Linguistic Inquiry*, 7:391–428.

Jerry R. Hobbs and Andrew Kehler. 1997. A theory of parallelism and the case of vp ellipsis. In *Proceedings of the 35th Annual Meeting of the Association for Computational Linguistics and Eighth Conference of the European Chapter of the Association for Computational Linguistics*, ACL '98/EACL '98, pages 394–401, Stroudsburg, PA, USA. Association for Computational Linguistics.

Matthew Honnibal and Mark Johnson. 2015. An improved non-monotonic transition system for dependency parsing. In *Proceedings of the 2015 Conference on Empirical Methods in Natural Language Processing*, pages 1373–1378, Lisbon, Portugal. Association for Computational Linguistics.

Rodnry HuddlestonRodnry and Geqffrry Pullum. 2005. The cambridge grammar of the english language. *Zeitschrift für Anglistik und Amerikanistik*, 53.

Richard S Kayne. 2015. English one and ones as complex determiners. *New York University*.

Payal Khullar, Allen Anthony, and Manish Shrivastava. 2019. Using syntax to resolve npe in english. In *Proceedings of Recent Advances in Natural Language Processing*, pages 535–541.

Payal Khullar, Kushal Majmundar, and Manish Shrivastava. 2020. Noel: An annotated corpus for noun ellipsis in english. In *Language Resources Evaluation Conference*.

Susann Luperfoy. 1991. Discourse pegs: A computational analysis of context-dependent referring expressions. *Ph.D. thesis, University of Texas at Austin*.

Katrin Menzel. 2014. A corpus linguistic study of ellipsis as a cohesive device1. *Proceedings of Corpus Linguistics*.

Katrin Menzel. 2017. *Understanding English-German contrasts: a corpus-based comparative analysis of ellipses as cohesive devices*. Ph.D. thesis, Universitat des Saar- ¨ landes, Saarbrucken.

Hwee Tou Ng, Yu Zhou, Rober Dale, and Mary Gardiner. 2005. A machine learning approach to identification and resolution of one-anaphora. pages 1105–1110.

John Payne, Geoffrey K. Pullum, Barbara C. Scholz, and Eva Berlage. 2013. Anaphoric one and its implications. *Language*, 4:794–829.

Andrew Radford. 1981. Transformational syntax: A student's guide to chomsky's extended standard theory. *Cambridge, UK: Cambridge University Press*.

Marta Recasens, Cristian Danescu-Niculescu-Mizil, and Dan Jurafsky. 2013. Linguistic models for analyzing and detecting biased language. In *Proceedings of the 51st Annual Meeting of the Association for Computational Linguistics (Volume 1: Long Papers)*, pages 1650–1659, Sofia, Bulgaria. Association for Computational Linguistics.

Marta Recasens, Zhichao Hu, and Olivia Rhinehart. 2016. Sense anaphoric pronouns: Am i one? page 1–6. Proceedings of the Workshop on Coreference Resolution Beyond OntoNotes (CORBON 2016).

The British National Corpus. 2001. *Oxford University Computing Services on behalf of the BNC Consortium*, (2).

Bridging Information-Seeking Human Gaze and Machine Reading Comprehension

Jonathan Malmaud
MIT BCS
malmaud@mit.edu

Roger Levy
MIT BCS
rplevy@mit.edu

Yevgeni Berzak
MIT BCS
berzak@mit.edu

Abstract

In this work, we analyze how human gaze during reading comprehension is conditioned on the given reading comprehension question, and whether this signal can be beneficial for machine reading comprehension. To this end, we collect a new eye-tracking dataset with a large number of participants engaging in a multiple choice reading comprehension task. Our analysis of this data reveals increased fixation times over parts of the text that are most relevant for answering the question. Motivated by this finding, we propose making automated reading comprehension more human-like by mimicking human information-seeking reading behavior during reading comprehension. We demonstrate that this approach leads to performance gains on multiple choice question answering in English for a state-of-the-art reading comprehension model.

1 Introduction

Much of the work in NLP strives to develop systems that are able to perform linguistic tasks similarly to humans. To achieve this goal, one typically provides NLP systems with *human knowledge* about the task at hand. This knowledge can come in the form of linguistic annotations, hand-crafted rules and access to linguistic databases, as well as various model design choices.

In this work, we study the possibility of providing the model with an inductive bias by using *human behavioral signals* based on eye movements in reading as an additional source of information which can guide NLP models to adequately process linguistic input and solve linguistic tasks. As a case study, we examine reading comprehension, a task of central importance for probing both human and machine understanding of text. To enable this study, we collect eye movement data from 269 participants who engage in a reading comprehension

task using the materials of OneStopQA (Berzak et al., 2020).

We argue that reading comprehension is a particularly well-suited task for linking human eye movement information to NLP modelling due to the substantial correspondence between reading times and the relevance of the text segment for answering the question. Hahn and Keller (2018) have shown this correspondence by establishing increased reading times on the correct answer in a question answering task where answers are named entities. Our study generalizes this result to an arbitrary QA setting, and demonstrates longer reading times for portions of the text which are most pertinent for answering the question correctly.

Building on this observation, we develop a new approach to machine reading comprehension in which the model is directed to *mimic human fixation times* over the text, given the question. The idea behind this approach is to encourage the model to focus on question-relevant information. Specifically, we introduce a multi-task reading comprehension architecture in which a state-of-the-art transformer model jointly performs question-answering and prediction of the human reading time distribution over the text.

Our modelling framework is *behavioral*, treating the reading comprehension model itself as a blackbox. This leads to both theoretical and practical advantages. From a theoretical perspective, this approach is appealing as it creates a direct parallel to human reading, in which eye movements are an external behavior. Practically, our approach has the advantage of being modular, allowing swapping our model with other reading comprehension models, and the task with other NLP tasks.

Our experiments demonstrate that our approach leads to consistent gains in question-answering performance across different training regimes, model variants, and on both in- and out-of-domain evalu-

142

Proceedings of the 24th Conference on Computational Natural Language Learning, pages 142–152
Online, November 19-20, 2020. ©2020 Association for Computational Linguistics
https://doi.org/10.18653/v1/P17

ations. In particular, our model outperforms baseline models with gaze from human reading without exposure to the question. It also performs better than using manual annotations of the textual span critical for answering the question.

To summarize, we present three contributions:

1. We collect an eye-tracking dataset with a large number of participants engaging in free-form multiple choice question answering.

2. We show that human gaze behavior during question answering is strongly task-conditioned.

3. We demonstrate that human gaze can improve the performance of a state-of-the-art reading comprehension model.

While this work is a proof of concept and uses a relatively costly data collection procedure, as eye-tracking technology continues to become more ubiquitous and affordable, it will be feasible to perform large scale data collection and deployment of similar approaches for QA and other NLP tasks.

2 Related Work

Our work contributes to two areas of research. The first is how human gaze is conditioned on the reading task. This question was previously investigated in the domain of question answering by Hahn and Keller (2018), who collected eye-tracking data in an experimental setup similar to ours for materials from the CNN and Daily Mail corpus (Hermann et al., 2015). They demonstrate that reading times on the named entity which is the correct answer to the question are longer if participants are shown the question before reading the passage as compared to ordinary reading. Our work builds on this result, introducing a more general QA setup which is not restricted to questions whose answer is a named entity. Crucially, we further leverage this information for improving machine question answering.

The second research area to which or work contributes is augmenting NLP models with gaze data. In this area, gaze during reading has been used for tasks such as syntactic annotation (Barrett and Søgaard, 2015a,b; Barrett et al., 2016; Strzyz et al., 2019), text compression (Klerke et al., 2016), text readability (González-Garduño and Søgaard, 2017), Named Entity Recognition (Hollenstein and Zhang, 2019), and sentiment classification (Mishra et al., 2016, 2017, 2018). Work on the first four tasks

used task-independent eye-tracking corpora, primarily the Dundee corpus (Kennedy et al., 2003) and GECO (Cop et al., 2017). For the task of sentiment classification, the authors used task specific eye-tracking corpora in which the participants were asked to perform sentiment classification.

Our study differs from this literature in several aspects. First, we address the previously unexplored task of reading comprehension, which has established theoretical and empirical connections to eye movements in reading (Just and Carpenter, 1980; Reichle et al., 2010; Rayner et al., 2016; Hahn and Keller, 2018, *among others*). Also differently from these studies, we cover and directly compare both a task specific reading condition (Hunting) and a task-independent condition (Gathering), as well as both external (Dundee) and corpus specific (OneStopQA) eye-tracking data.

Our QA task can be viewed as a generalization of the work in Mirsha et al. (2016; 2017; 2018), where instead of being asked about the sentiment of a paragraph, subjects are presented with arbitrary questions. Our multitask approach for jointly performing the QA task and predicting gaze is similar to Klerke et al. (2016), Berrett et al. (2018) and Mishra et al. (2018). In particular, in Equation 4 we use the same loss term as Barrett et al. (2018) which consists of a linear combination of an NLP task loss and gaze prediction loss. Our approach differs from Barrett et al. (2018) in that their model uses the gaze predictions as input attention weights for the NLP task, while our model treats gaze only as an output. Our approach provides a parallel to human reading, in which eye movements are an external behavior rather than an input to language processing tasks. Our work differs from Mishra et al. (2018) in the model and the use of a single auxiliary objective based on gaze. Finally, we note that in Vajjala et al. (2016) eye-tracking data from ESL learners was collected for 4 articles from the same source of OneStopEnglish articles (Vajjala and Lučić, 2018) used here, and utilized to study the influence of text difficulty level on fixation measures and reading comprehension. Our work focuses on a different task and a different population of readers.

A large body of work exists on QA, including span prediction (e.g. BiDAF (Seo et al., 2017)), cloze (e.g. (Hermann et al., 2015)), and multiple choice QA (e.g. Stanford Attentive Reader (Chen et al., 2016)). Here, we focus on multiple choice

QA due to its prevalence in human evaluations of reading comprehension, and use RoBERTa due to its state-of-the-art performance on this task. Further, neural models for QA deploy various notions of *internal attention*. The study of NLP model internal attention has drawn much interest in recent years (Adi et al., 2017; Clark et al., 2019; Serrano and Smith, 2019; Kovaleva et al., 2019; Hoover et al., 2019, *among others*). In this work we abstract away from model internal dynamics due to their complexity, and the theoretical justification for treating gaze as an external behavior rather than an internal model property. Examination of internal model attention and its relation to human gaze is however an intriguing research direction that we intend to pursue in future work.

3   Data

3.1   Reading Comprehension Data

We use two reading comprehension resources, OneStopQA (Berzak et al., 2020) and RACE (Lai et al., 2017).

OneStopQA is a reading comprehension dataset containing paragraph-level multiple choice reading comprehension questions for 30 Guardian articles (162 paragraphs) taken from the OneStopEnglish dataset (Vajjala and Lučić, 2018). Each article is available in three parallel text difficulty levels: the original Advanced text and two simplified versions, Intermediate and Elementary. Each paragraph has three multiple choice reading comprehension questions. All the questions are answerable based on any of the text level versions of the paragraph. We use the Advanced and Elementary text versions, corresponding to 972 question–paragraph pairs.

The answers for each OneStopQA question are structured as follows.

A is the correct answer. Answering a question correctly requires information from a textual span in the paragraph called the *critical span*. Importantly, the critical span does not contain the answer in verbatim form.

B is a distractor which represents a plausible miscomprehension of the critical span.

C is a distractor which is anchored in an additional span in the paragraph, called the distractor span.

D is a distractor which has no support in the text. Both the critical span and the distractor span are annotated manually in the text.

RACE is the standard dataset in NLP for training and evaluation of multiple choice reading com-

prehension. It comprises reading comprehension examination materials for middle school and high school students in China. Similarly to OneStopQA, RACE questions are multiple choice, with four possible answers for each question. As opposed to OneStopQA, the questions are based on an entire article rather than a specific paragraph and the answers have no systematic structure with respect to the text. Although RACE has been widely used in NLP, it was recently shown that it has substantial quality assurance drawbacks; 47% of its questions are guessable by RoBERTa without the passage, and 18% do not have a unique correct answer (Berzak et al., 2020). We therefore treat RACE as a secondary evaluation benchmark. Statistics on the reading comprehension materials are presented in Table 1.

	OneStopQA		RACE	
	Ele	Adv	Mid	High
Words per text	112.3	138.6	232.1	354.1
# Passages	162	162	6,409	18,728
# Questions	486	486	25,421	62,445

Table 1: Statistics for OneStopQA and the RACE training set. The term *passage* refers to a single paragraph in OneStopQA and an article in RACE.

3.2   OneStopQA Eye-Tracking Data

We collected a dataset of eye movements for the 30 OneStopQA articles. The articles are divided into three 10-article batches with 54 paragraphs in each batch. Each participant read a single 10-article batch. Following the experimental setup of (Hahn and Keller, 2018), a given batch is presented in one of two possible between subject conditions: *Hunting* and *Gathering*. In the Hunting condition participants are presented with the question prior to reading the text, while in the Gathering condition the question is provided only after the participant has completed reading the text.

A single experiment trial consists of reading a paragraph and answering one reading comprehension question about it. In the Hunting condition, a trial has 5 pages in which the screen shows one page at a time. In the first page, the participant reads the question (henceforth *question preview* page). In the second page, they read the paragraph. In the third page they read the question again. The fourth page retains the question, and also displays the four answers. After choosing one of the answers, the fifth page informs the participant on whether they answered the question correctly. The Gathering condition is identical to the Hunting condition, except that participants are not presented with the question preview page. Consequently, subjects in this condition have to be prepared for any question.

Each trial was randomly assigned to one of six conditions in a Latin square design, where each condition is a combination of one of the three questions and one of the two paragraph levels. The presentation order of the articles and the assignment of answers to A – D letters was randomized. Eye movements were recorded using an EyeLink 1000 Plus eye tracker (SR Research) at a sampling rate of 1000Hz. The experiment duration was typically 1 - 1.5 hours. Further details on the eye-tracking experiment are provided in Appendix A.

We collected data from 269 participants, with an average of 7.5 participants per trial (question - paragraph level pair). We excluded trials in which participants did not answer the question correctly, remaining with 6.3 participants per trial. The overall question answering accuracy rate was 86.9% in the Hunting condition and 81.9% in the Gathering condition, which is lower ($p < 10^{-4}$).[1]

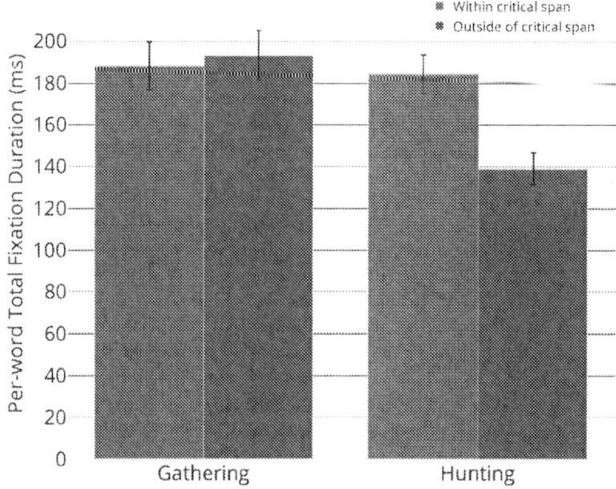

Figure 1: Mean Total Fixation Duration inside and outside the critical span in the Hunting (with question preview) and Gathering (without question preview) conditions. Error bars correspond to a 95% confidence interval from a mixed-effects model that accounts for variation of fixation durations across subjects and questions.

4 Question Conditioned Gaze in Human Reading Comprehension

We motivate our approach by demonstrating that human gaze distributions are strongly conditioned on the reading comprehension task. This conditioning has been previously established for the case of named entities (Hahn and Keller, 2018), and we examine it here in a more general QA setting. Specifically, we consider speed-normalized Total Fixation Duration; for each subject, we take the Total Fixation Duration (i.e. sum of all the fixation times) on a word and normalize it by the subject's total reading time for the passage. Consider the example in Figure 2, where we visualize the speed-normalized gaze on each word averaged across subjects for the same question – paragraph pair in the Hunting (with question preview) and Gathering (without question preview) conditions. As can be seen from the heatmaps, the gaze distributions are fundamentally different between these conditions. In particular, in the Hunting condition we observe a noticeable correspondence between gaze and the annotated critical span. Although the degree of correspondence between gaze and the critical span in the Hunting condition depends on the specifics of the question and the text, the presented example is representative of a large portion of our items.

To further substantiate this observation, in Figure 1 we compare the average Total Fixation Duration within versus outside the critical span in both the Hunting and Gathering conditions. We observe that in the Hunting condition, reading times are significantly longer within the critical span compared to outside of the critical span ($p < 10^{-15}$),[2] while in the Gathering condition they are slightly shorter within the critical span ($p < 10^{-4}$). The difference between within-span vs outside-of-span reading times between Hunting and Gathering conditions is also significant ($p < 10^{-15}$). We further note that the total reading time for the passage is shorter in the Hunting condition ($p < 10^{-4}$), consistent with more targeted reading as compared to the Gathering condition.

While our analysis provides evidence for an increased concentration of gaze time around text that is critical for answering the question, the potential

---

[1] Satterhwaite's method on a mixed-effects model: correct $\sim$ preview + (preview||subject) + (preview||example).

[2] This and subsequent tests are calculated using Satterthwaite's method applied to a mixed-effects model that treats subjects and questions as crossed random effects. Using R formula notation, the model is gaze $\sim$ span $*$ condition + (span||subject) + (condition*span||example)). Tests were performed with the lme4 and lmerTest R packages.

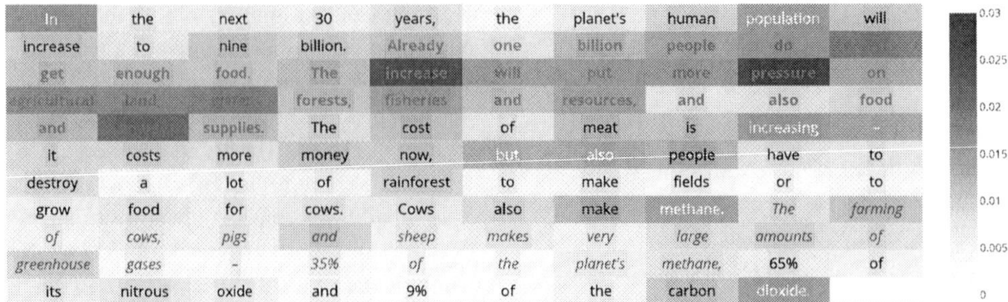

(a) Hunting condition (with question preview)

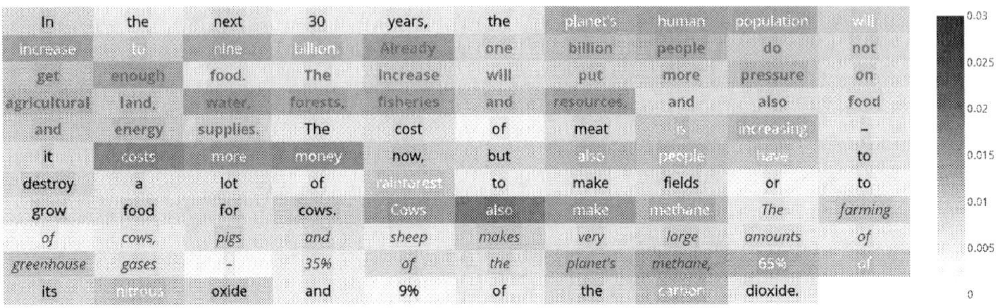

(b) Gathering condition (without question preview)

Figure 2: Example of gaze distributions in the Hunting and Gathering conditions for an Elementary level paragraph. The color of each word corresponds to its Total Fixation Duration divided by the overall passage reading time, averaged across participants. The critical span appears in bold red. The distractor span appears in purple italics.

utility of human gaze is not limited to this aspect alone. Human gaze can be viewed as a soft form of text annotation that relates the entire text to cognitive load during processing. In particular, it can in principle provide valuable fine-grained information within the critical span.

5 Method: Joint Question Answering and Human Gaze Prediction

To test the effectiveness of utilizing human gaze data for enhancing the performance of a reading comprehension system, we trained a reading comprehension model to perform the same multiple choice task as the human subjects. We then conducted a series of controlled experiments to assess how the accuracy of the model is affected by providing it with human eye movements information.

5.1 Model

We utilize the RoBERTa transformer architecture, which has shown state-of-the-art performance on the multiple choice reading comprehension task

(Liu et al., 2019). We experiment with both the Base and the Large variants of this model. To allow RoBERTa to benefit from the gaze data, we use multi-task learning with hard parameter sharing (Caruana, 1993), and modify RoBERTa to jointly predict the answer to each question and the human gaze times allocated to each passage word.

Each multiple-choice example is composed of the passage d, the question Q, and the four possible answers $\{y_1, y_2, y_3, y_4\}$. We follow the standard procedure for using transformer architectures for multiple-choice tasks, concatenating the passage, question, and answer $[CLS, d, SEP, Q, y]$ for each possible answer y. The resulting string is encoded through RoBERTa. We then take the final embedding of the CLS token for each answer and run it through a logistic layer to return the probability of each answer being correct. This probability is used to calculate a cross-entropy QA loss term L_{QA} for each example.

$$L_{QA} = -\log p(y_c) \qquad (1)$$

Where y_c is the correct answer for the question.

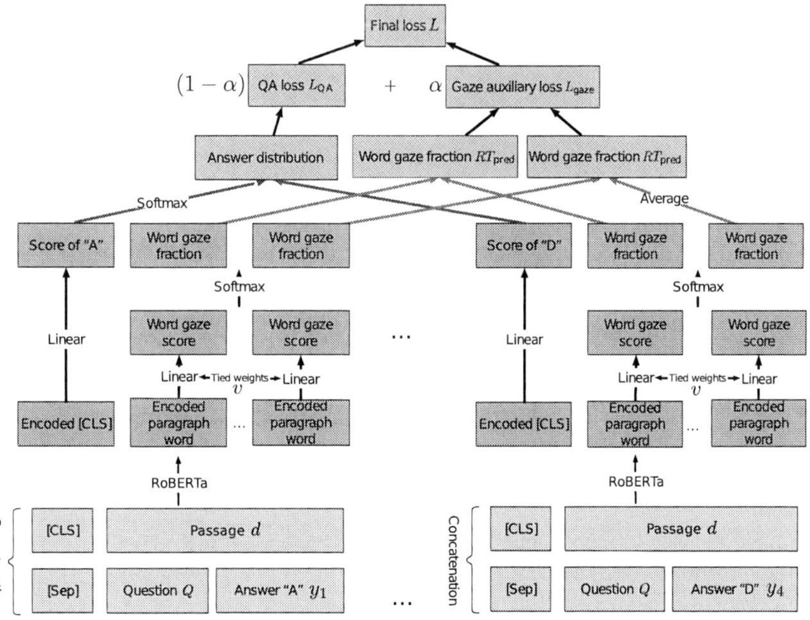

Figure 3: Model diagram. The model uses the standard transformer architecture for multiple choice QA, augmented to simultaneously predict human reading times over the passage.

We additionally calculate an auxiliary loss based on gaze information. As in Figure 2, our reference metric $RT(w)$ is speed-normalized Total Fixation Duration (TF). Specifically, for each passage word w and subject s, we consider the subject's Total Fixation Duration on the word $TF_s(w)$ normalized by the sum of all their fixation durations over the passage, and then average this quantity across all subjects who read the passage.

$$RT(w) = \frac{1}{S} \sum_s \frac{TF_s(w)}{\sum_{w'} TF_s(w')} \quad (2)$$

In cases where RoBERTa's byte pair tokenizer (Sennrich et al., 2016) splits a single word into multiple tokens, we evenly split the gaze time associated with the word among the resulting tokens.

We take the encoding of each passage word at the last layer of RoBERTa for each candidate answer y and add a linear layer parameterized by a weight vector $v \in R^d$ shared across all passage word positions, where d is the RoBERTa embedding dimension. For each passage word w, this layer maps from the d-dimensional word embedding to a scalar gaze value. These values are put through a softmax layer, obtaining predictions $RT_{pred_y}(w)$ which are guaranteed to be between 0 and 1 for each word and sum to 1 for each passage, making them comparable to our normalized human gaze measurements

RT. These predictions are then averaged across the four possible answers to obtain reading time predictions for each passage word $RT_{pred}(w)$. Finally, we compute the cross-entropy loss between the gaze predictions and observed human gaze.

$$L_{gaze} = -\sum_w RT(w) \log RT_{pred}(w) \quad (3)$$

The final loss term is a convex combination of the gaze loss term and the answer prediction loss, where a hyperparameter α is the relative weight assigned to the gaze loss term:

$$L = (1 - \alpha)L_{QA} + \alpha L_{gaze} \quad (4)$$

Figure 3 presents a diagram of our model.

Our modelling approach is fundamentally behavioral, as it attempts to mimic human eye movements as an external behavior. It treats the model itself largely as a black-box, relying only on the model's final query-conditioned representations of the passage words. It is therefore also modular – the RoBERTa model can be substituted with any QA model which provides passage word representations. Furthermore, our framework is compatible not only with the multiple choice variant of the QA task, but also with other answer output formats.

We also note that the standard multiple choice QA transformer architecture requires a copy of the passage and the question for each answer, and thus the reading time predictions are generated for each copy and averaged. In QA models were the query and passage are encoded only once, such averaging would not be required. Further, other architectures are conceivable for joint multiple choice QA and gaze prediction. In particular, one may consider architectures which do not include the answers for gaze prediction; for example, through soft parameter-sharing multi-task approaches. We chose hard parameter sharing as it enables predicting gaze with only a minimal architecture change and a small number of additional parameters to the standard multiple choice QA transformer model.

5.2 Training Procedure

Each experiment consists of a training set of QA examples from OneStopQA accompanied by gaze data, a development set, and a test set. For each experiment, we fine-tune an initial model for 15 epochs for each $\alpha \in [0, .2, .4, .6, .8, 1.0]$. We pick the epoch and α that have the highest question-answering accuracy on the development set and report accuracy on the test set. For experiments on OneStopQA, we perform five-fold cross validation where each fold has 18 training articles, 6 development articles and 6 test articles. Each article appears three times in train, once in dev and once in test across the 5 folds.

5.3 Conditions

We test two initial models:

1. **No RACE fine-tuning** using RoBERTa that has not been fine-tuned for QA on RACE. This experiment shows the value of incorporating eye-tracking data in data-scarce scenarios where only a small amount of data is available for fine-tuning on the given task.

2. **With RACE fine-tuning** using RoBERTa that has been fine-tuned on RACE to perform multiple choice question answering, following the procedure in (Liu et al., 2019).

For each fine-tuning regime, we test the model for two levels of generalization:

1. **Within-domain** where we use our five-fold cross validation setup to train and test on OneStopQA.

2. **Out-of-domain** where we train on all 30 OneStopQA articles and use the RACE dev and test sets for development and testing.

We note that in addition to the quality assurance issues with RACE mentioned in Section 3.1, the out-of-domain RACE evaluations are particularly challenging due to substantial differences in the genres and questions types between OneStopQA and RACE, and the small size of OneStopQA as compared to RACE.

5.4 Baselines

We compare our model with two baselines which do not use auxiliary loss. We further introduce four auxiliary loss models, which replace Hunting condition gaze with alternative information sources for measuring the importance of each passage word.

No Auxiliary Loss

These two baselines do not utilize the auxiliary loss during model fine-tuning.

1. **No OneStopQA Fine-tuning** The model is not fine-tuned for QA on OneStopQA.

2. **With OneStopQA Fine-tuning** The model is fine-tuned for QA on OneStopQA.

With Auxiliary Loss

These four models are fine-tuned for QA on OneStopQA, and use an auxiliary loss where gaze in the Hunting condition is replaced with other ways for weighting each word in the passage.

1. **Question–Passage Similarity** In this baseline, the auxiliary information is based on the similarity between the question and each passage word. We encode the question and the passage separately with an off-the-shelf encoder (here, RoBERTa that has not been fine-tuned for question-answering) and compute the dot-product between each encoded passage word and the final encoding of the question's CLS token. These values are then normalized by applying a softmax function.

2. **Gaze Gathering Dundee** Here, we utilize gaze data from the Dundee corpus (Kennedy et al., 2003), allowing us to examine the benefit of predicting gaze on the same texts used for QA, versus unrelated texts. We split each Dundee article into passages of size equal to the average OneStopQA passage (125 words), yielding 453 passages. We then normalize the average Total Fixation Duration across Dundee's 10 subjects as for OneStopQA. In each training step, we predict answers on one

		OneStopQA				RACE			
		No RACE Fine-tuning		With RACE Fine-tuning		No RACE Fine-tuning		With RACE Fine-tuning	
		Base	Large	Base	Large	Base	Large	Base	Large
	No OneStopQA Fine-tuning	23.5	23.1	68.5	85.8	24.2	24.3	68.4	82.9
	With OneStopQA Fine-tuning	48.9	62.9	68.3	85.9	36.8	42.9	68.4	82.9
+ Aux. Loss	Question–Passage Similarity	54.7	78.9	72.3	87.3	**41.2**	52.6	68.2	82.9
	Gaze Gathering Dundee	55.9	78.2	72.5	86.6	39.3	52.5	68.4	82.9
	Gaze Gathering OneStopQA	54.7	80.2	71.5	87.0	39.6	48.4	68.4	**83.0**
	Critical Spans OneStopQA	54.7	**80.7**	70.1	86.5	40.4	51.6	68.4	82.9
	Gaze Hunting OneStopQA	**57.1**	80.5	**73.1**	**88.0**	41.1	**53.0**	**68.5**	**83.0**

Table 2: Question Answering accuracy for RoBERTa Base and Large on OneStopQA and RACE. RACE Fine-tuning denotes whether the model has been first fine-tuned for QA on RACE. The first two rows are baselines without an auxiliary loss, without and with QA fine-tuning on OneStopQA. The following four rows are baselines fine-tuned for QA on OneStopQA with auxiliary loss, using four different alternatives for measuring the importance of each passage word. The last row is our primary model variant, which uses gaze in the Hunting condition. All the results with OneStopQA fine-tunings are averaged over three runs of the model.

batch of OneStopQA questions and gaze distributions on one batch of Dundee paragraphs chosen at random, and perform a step of gradient descent. This interleaved procedure is similar to that used by Barrett et al. (2018), and is analogous to the other baselines, where we predict answers on one batch of OneStopQA examples and gaze distribution on those same examples for each gradient descent step.

3. **Gaze Gathering OneStopQA** In this method, we use gaze data from the Gathering variant of the OneStopQA reading experiment where subjects do not see the question before seeing the paragraph they will later be questioned about, and hence their gaze is necessarily not question-dependent.

4. **Critical Span Annotations OneStopQA** In OneStopQA, each question includes a manual annotation which indicates the span in the passage which is critical for answering the question. We assign a gaze value of 1 to the tokens within the span and 0 to those outside it, and normalize with softmax as before. This corresponds to a theoretical subject who looks equally at each word within the critical span and not anywhere else in the passage.

We note that the last two baselines are new methods for improving machine QA using human-generated behavioral data (gaze and span annotations) that have not been previously proposed in the literature, and constitute very strong alternatives to our model.

6 Experimental Results

Our results are summarized in Table 2. All the results involving OneStopQA fine-tunings are averaged across three runs. In the following, p values are indicated when the difference in the performance of the compared models is statistically significant at the $p < 0.05$ level.

Fine-tuning the model for QA on OneStopQA is most beneficial in the two resource-lean regimes when the model has not been previously fine-tuned on RACE ($p < 10^{-10}$, Wald test). Similarly, adding auxiliary loss to the QA model in these two regimes has a substantially larger impact on model performance compared to performing prior fine-tuning on RACE ($p < 10^{-8}$ for all baselines).

In our within-domain evaluations on OneStopQA, we observe improvements of our model over all the baselines in all evaluations, except for the case of the Large model without RACE fine-tuning where our model comes second. We also observe improvements in the out-of-domain evaluations on RACE. When the Large model is fine-tuned for QA only on OneStopQA, it obtains an accuracy of 53.0, reflecting a 0.4 improvement over the strongest baseline. The Base model comes second in this evaluation. When first fine-tuning the model for QA on RACE, then performing additional fine-tuning on OneStopQA, the Base model obtains an improvement of 0.1 over the strongest auxiliary loss baseline. For the Large model we observe a similar improvement when using gaze, with the same performance in the Hunting and Gathering conditions.

Interestingly, we do not observe a consistent ordering in the performance of the baselines. In particular, we do not observe a clear advantage of using gaze in the Gathering condition over Question–Passage Similarity. We also obtain comparable performance when gaze data in the Gathering condition comes from OneStopQA and Dundee. Notably, in nearly all the evaluations our model performs better compared to the manual Critical Span Annotation baseline. We hypothesize that this may be because the annotated spans do not capture potential inter-annotator variation in span annotations, as well as within-span information which is informative for our task.

We note that while the gains over the strongest baselines are not statistically significant at the .05 level, the overall consistent pattern across evaluation regimes suggests the promise of using Hunting gaze data as the target of the auxiliary loss objective over any other single baseline. Finally, we note that an α of $0.2 - 0.4$ was most often chosen.

7 Conclusion

We present a framework for performing automated reading comprehension in a human-like fashion, yielding performance gains for a state-of-the art reading comprehension model. Our work also contributes to the study of human reading, providing evidence for a systematic conditioning of human reading on the reading comprehension task. In the future we intend to study the relation between gaze and internal model attention, and further explore the relation between gaze, task and task performance in QA and well as other tasks.

Acknowledgments

We gratefully acknowledge support from Elemental Cognition and from NSF grant IIS1815529, a Google Faculty Research Award, and a Newton Brain Science Award to RPL.

References

Yossi Adi, Einat Kermany, Yonatan Belinkov, Ofer Lavi, and Yoav Goldberg. 2017. Fine-grained analysis of sentence embeddings using auxiliary prediction tasks. In *ICLR*.

Maria Barrett, Joachim Bingel, Nora Hollenstein, Marek Rei, and Anders Søgaard. 2018. Sequence classification with human attention. In *CoNLL*, pages 302–312.

Maria Barrett, Joachim Bingel, Frank Keller, and Anders Søgaard. 2016. Weakly supervised part-of-speech tagging using eye-tracking data. In *ACL*, volume 2, pages 579–584.

Maria Barrett and Anders Søgaard. 2015a. Reading behavior predicts syntactic categories. In *CoNLL*, pages 345–349.

Maria Barrett and Anders Søgaard. 2015b. Using reading behavior to predict grammatical functions. In *Workshop on Cognitive Aspects of Computational Language Learning*, pages 1–5.

Yevgeni Berzak, Jonathan Malmaud, and Roger Levy. 2020. STARC: Structured annotations for reading comprehension. *ACL*.

Rich Caruana. 1993. Multitask learning: A knowledge-based source of inductive bias. In *ICML*.

Danqi Chen, Jason Bolton, and Christopher D Manning. 2016. A thorough examination of the cnn/daily mail reading comprehension task. pages 2358–2367.

Kevin Clark, Urvashi Khandelwal, Omer Levy, and Christopher D Manning. 2019. What does BERT look at? an analysis of BERT's attention. In *BlackboxNLP Workshop*, pages 276–286.

Uschi Cop, Nicolas Dirix, Denis Drieghe, and Wouter Duyck. 2017. Presenting geco: An eyetracking corpus of monolingual and bilingual sentence reading. *Behavior research methods*, 49(2):602–615.

Ana Valeria González-Garduño and Anders Søgaard. 2017. Using gaze to predict text readability. In *Proceedings of the 12th Workshop on Innovative Use of NLP for Building Educational Applications*, pages 438–443.

Michael Hahn and Frank Keller. 2018. Modeling task effects in human reading with neural attention. *arXiv preprint arXiv:1808.00054*.

Karl Moritz Hermann, Tomas Kocisky, Edward Grefenstette, Lasse Espeholt, Will Kay, Mustafa Suleyman, and Phil Blunsom. 2015. Teaching machines to read and comprehend. In *NeurIPS*, pages 1693–1701.

Nora Hollenstein and Ce Zhang. 2019. Entity recognition at first sight: Improving NER with eye movement information. In *NAACL-HLT*.

Benjamin Hoover, Hendrik Strobelt, and Sebastian Gehrmann. 2019. exBERT: A visual analysis tool to explore learned representations in transformers models. *arXiv preprint arXiv:1910.05276*.

Marcel A Just and Patricia A Carpenter. 1980. A theory of reading: From eye fixations to comprehension. *Psychological review*, 87(4):329.

Alan Kennedy, Robin Hill, and Joël Pynte. 2003. The dundee corpus. In *European conference on eye movement*.

Sigrid Klerke, Yoav Goldberg, and Anders Søgaard. 2016. Improving sentence compression by learning to predict gaze. In *NAACL-HLT*.

Olga Kovaleva, Alexey Romanov, Anna Rogers, and Anna Rumshisky. 2019. Revealing the dark secrets of BERT. In *EMNLP*, pages 4365–4374.

Guokun Lai, Qizhe Xie, Hanxiao Liu, Yiming Yang, and Eduard Hovy. 2017. Race: Large-scale reading comprehension dataset from examinations. In *EMNLP*, pages 785–794.

Yinhan Liu, Myle Ott, Naman Goyal, Jingfei Du, Mandar Joshi, Danqi Chen, Omer Levy, Mike Lewis, Luke Zettlemoyer, and Veselin Stoyanov. 2019. RoBERTa: A robustly optimized BERT pretraining approach. *arXiv preprint arXiv:1907.11692*.

Abhijit Mishra, Kuntal Dey, and Pushpak Bhattacharyya. 2017. Learning cognitive features from gaze data for sentiment and sarcasm classification using convolutional neural network. In *ACL*, pages 377–387.

Abhijit Mishra, Diptesh Kanojia, Seema Nagar, Kuntal Dey, and Pushpak Bhattacharyya. 2016. Leveraging cognitive features for sentiment analysis. In *CoNLL*.

Abhijit Mishra, Srikanth Tamilselvam, Riddhiman Dasgupta, Seema Nagar, and Kuntal Dey. 2018. Cognition-cognizant sentiment analysis with multitask subjectivity summarization based on annotators' gaze behavior. In *AAAI*.

Keith Rayner, Elizabeth R Schotter, Michael EJ Masson, Mary C Potter, and Rebecca Treiman. 2016. So much to read, so little time: How do we read, and can speed reading help? *Psychological Science in the Public Interest*, 17(1):4–34.

Erik D Reichle, Andrew E Reineberg, and Jonathan W Schooler. 2010. Eye movements during mindless reading. *Psychological Science*, 21(9):1300–1310.

Rico Sennrich, Barry Haddow, and Alexandra Birch. 2016. Neural machine translation of rare words with subword units. In *ACL*.

Minjoon Seo, Aniruddha Kembhavi, Ali Farhadi, and Hannaneh Hajishirzi. 2017. Bidirectional attention flow for machine comprehension. *ICLR*.

Sofia Serrano and Noah A Smith. 2019. Is attention interpretable? pages 2931–2951.

Michalina Strzyz, David Vilares, and Carlos Gómez-Rodríguez. 2019. Towards making a dependency parser see. In *EMNLP-IJCNLP*.

Sowmya Vajjala and Ivana Lučić. 2018. Onestopenglish corpus: A new corpus for automatic readability assessment and text simplification. In *Workshop on Innovative Use of NLP for Building Educational Applications*.

Sowmya Vajjala, Detmar Meurers, Alexander Eitel, and Katharina Scheiter. 2016. Towards grounding computational linguistic approaches to readability: Modeling reader-text interaction for easy and difficult texts. In *Proceedings of the Workshop on Computational Linguistics for Linguistic Complexity (CL4LC)*, pages 38–48, Osaka, Japan. The COLING 2016 Organizing Committee.

A Supplemental Material: OneStopQA Eye-Tracking Experiment

Eye Tracker

We used a Tower Mount Eyelink 1000 Plus eye tracker (SR Research) at a sampling rate of 1000Hz. Eye movements were recorded for participants' dominant eye.

Monitor

The experiment was presented on a 27inch monitor (Dell U2715H) with a display area of 597mm×336mm, resolution of 2560px×1440px and refresh rate of 60Hz. Participants' eye level was 750mm away from the top of the monitor's display area and 795 away from its bottom. In this setup participants eyes were about 45mm below top of the monitor's display, approximately at the same height as the top most position of the text.

Controller

Participants used a controller (Logitech Gamepad F310) during the experiment. The button A was used for proceeding to the next page after finishing reading as well as for confirming the answer selection. The four buttons of the directional pad were used for choosing answers.

Text

We used the Lucida Sans Typewriter monospace font, with font size of 25pt (each letter occupying 19px×38px). We used triple spacing (76px) between lines. The top left position of the questions and the paragraphs was (300, 186) with a text area width of 1824px (96 characters). Questions were 1-2 lines and paragraphs were 3-10 lines. Answers were presented in a cross arrangement, with text width of 700px, and were 1-3 lines.

Calibration

We used 9 point calibration with bulls-eye targets (18px outer circle 6px inner circle). Calibration was performed at least 3 times during the experiment: once at the beginning of the experiment and once after each of two breaks. Calibration was also performed upon failure to trigger the text at the beginning of a trial as described below. The experimenters were instructed repeat calibration until an average validation error below $0.3°$ was reached.

Text Triggering and Recalibration

Prior to the presentation of the question preview, paragraph and question, participants were presented with a page presenting a fixation target located at (300, 186), the same position as the first letter of text on the following page. The targets were **q** for the question preview, **p** for the paragraph and **Q** for the question. The presentation of the following text page was triggered by a fixation of at least 250ms within a 39px×48px rectangular area centered around the 19px×38px area of the target letter. This corresponds to a horizontal margin of about half a letter width, and vertical margin of about quarter of a line space around the target letter.

Failure to produce a 250ms fixation within 4 seconds on the first target of the trial (**q** target in the Hunting condition and **p** target in the Gathering condition), automatically triggered recalibration. For subsequent trial targets (**p** and **Q** in the Hunting condition and **Q** in the Gathering condition) the next page was presented even if the participant was not able to produce a 250ms fixation on the target letter within 4 seconds.

A Corpus of Very Short Scientific Summaries

Yifan Chen
University of Cambridge, UK
yc462@cam.ac.uk

Tamara Polajnar
Royal Society of Chemistry
and University of Cambridge, UK
polajnart@rsc.org

Colin Batchelor
Royal Society of Chemistry, UK
batchelorc@rsc.org

Simone Teufel
University of Cambridge, UK
sht25@cam.ac.uk

Abstract

We present a new summarisation task, taking scientific articles and producing journal table-of-contents entries in the chemistry domain. These are one- or two-sentence author-written summaries that present the key findings of a paper. This is a first look at this summarisation task with an open access publication corpus consisting of titles and abstracts, as input texts, and short author-written advertising blurbs, as the ground truth. We introduce the dataset and evaluate it with state-of-the-art summarisation methods.

1 Introduction

Table-of-contents (TOC) entries are short summaries written by authors that are placed in the table of contents of journals, often with an eye-catching accompanying image, to advertise their paper to readers. They are meant to be a clear and concise summary of a paper's main contribution, but different from the title and abstract, which have a different communicative function. We take the titles and abstracts from chemistry papers published by the Royal Society of Chemistry as input in this initial study, as they are freely available and more numerous, but will also release full text for the smaller subset of open access publications. As such, this particular corpus is different from other scientific corpora, which normally take the abstract as the summary.

We include an analysis of the corpus properties, and experimental results with strong baselines and three different state-of-the-art deep learning models: an attention-based RNN, a reinforcement learning approach, and a BERT-based transformer method. We also perform a human evaluation study to compare the models and to validate the usefulness of the summarisation task.

The main aim of releasing this particular corpus is to see how useful deep learning models are in producing a latent semantic representation of chemical texts. Within this paper we constrain ourselves to the question: Can we decode this representation into a useful summary and perhaps aid in the journal editing process? But the real goal would be to transfer this representation into useful editing tasks like plagiarism detection or semantic search and discovery.

In addition, chemistry has a complex domain lexicon involving a potentially infinite set of molecules that can be described both by formulae and (often multi-word) terms, as well as a set of other techniques. While everything from tokenisation onward in an NLP pipeline would benefit from customisation, there is a lack of domain-specific resources. In this paper we start addressing this problem by introducing a summarisation corpus, but we hope this is the first of many resources that will aid researchers in this field. Ultimately, underlying all these tasks is an ability to produce representations that can accurately substitute multi-word terms for chemical formulae or an accurate hyponym like *ketone*, without ontological knowledge. This corpus is one in a set of tools that will help us compare models' abilities to do this.

2 Related Work

Supervised summarisation tasks are primarily evaluated on large news text corpora: CNN/Daily Mail (See et al., 2017), XSum (Narayan et al., 2018), and Newsroom (Grusky et al., 2018). Most of these use professionally written summaries consisting of one or more sentences provided by the publisher. There are also domain-specific datasets like arXiv/PubMed (Cohan et al., 2018) for mixed science summarisation and BIGPATENT (Sharma et al., 2019), both of which use abstracts as the ground truth. The number of documents in these datasets varies between 200,000 and 1.3 million.

Proceedings of the 24th Conference on Computational Natural Language Learning, pages 153–164
Online, November 19-20, 2020. ©2020 Association for Computational Linguistics
https://doi.org/10.18653/v1/P17

While initial efforts in the field concentrated on unsupervised extractive summarisation methods (Mihalcea and Tarau, 2004; Vanderwende et al., 2007; Moratanch and Chitrakala, 2017), recent work has seen an explosion of deep learning-based models that leverage these large datasets to produce more abstractive and natural-sounding summaries. Out of these we choose three methods that each take a different approach. First is the pointer-generator method by See et al. (2017), which balances extractive and abstractive summarisation by substituting phrases according to a learned parameter. The second method from Chen and Bansal (2018) uses a reinforcement learning (RL) algorithm to extract informative sentences and then rewrites them using a sequence-2-sequence model with an additional re-ranking algorithm to avoid repetitive phrasings. The final method we test is a BERT-based model introduced by Liu and Lapata (2019) which uses BERT embeddings as the pre-trained encoder, stacked Transformer layers as a decoder and a fine-tuning process to produce more natural abstractive summaries. Although Cohan et al. (2018) designed a method for use with scientific text, it was specifically created for full text documents and our input text is much shorter.

There are a few historic examples of extractive summarisation in the chemistry domain (Boudin et al., 2008; Pollock and Zamora, 1975), but the research in this subfield was not as active as in other NLP applications. In their summarisation approach, Boudin et al. (2008) highlight the need for keeping the case in chemical names and for using character-based similarity measures for relevance ranking. We, likewise, employ customised tokenisation and named entity recognition while pre-processing the corpus (Corbett and Boyle, 2018) to enable future researchers to forgo the NER step. Further related applications of NLP include information retrieval (Sun et al., 2011; Hawizy et al., 2011) and literature mining (Zaslavsky et al., 2017; Öztürk et al., 2020), while lessons learned from deep learning in NLP have been applied to strings representing chemical structures to successfully discover new potential antibiotics (Stokes et al., 2020).

3 Corpus Description

The RSCSUM corpus contains 307,847 papers published in the chemistry domain between 2000 and

Split	Training set examples	246268
	Test set examples	30776
	Validation set examples	30803
Training set stats	Total vocabulary size	487610
	Appearing over 10 times	52230
	Average summary length	29.07
	Average title length	18.37
	Average abstract length	169.08
	Compression ratio	21.01
	Named entities in title	11.11%
	Named entities in summary	10.40%
	Named entities in abstract	8.28%

Table 1: RSCSUM statistics.

2019.[1] It is split into around 80% training set, 10% test set, and 10% validation set. The titles and abstracts comprise input documents, while the reference is the short table-of-contents summary.

Tab. 1 shows some vital statistics of the corpus. The compression ratio ($R_i = L_{D_i}/L_{S_i}$) indicates the ratio between the length of the input document and the gold standard summary. Our compression ratio is 21, substantially higher than that of CNN and DM (14). On the other hand, titles and abstracts are very information-dense and provide a large part of the relevant information useful for the summary. Our vocabulary size is similar to that of the CNN/DM and XSum corpora (Narayan et al., 2018), although many of the tokens occur very rarely. Of course, this is a count of lower case tokens, which in chemistry can lead to the undesired effect of collapsing significantly different chemical names into the same string. About 10% of the text is also taken up by chemical named entities, including chemical formulae. These are difficult to abstract, and this process may require knowledge from the full text documents or external sources. In fact about 1% of summaries have 3 or more chemical names that do not appear in the input text, while 26% of them have at least one. Tab. 2 shows an example document where automatically extracted chemical named entities (Corbett and Boyle, 2018) are highlighted.

Tab. 3 shows how our corpus compares to frequently used standard summarisation corpora. Although we have a relatively high number of training instances, both the summary and document lengths are at the short end of the spectrum. This will obviously make abstractive summarisation a more difficult task.

The concepts of *extractive fragment coverage*

[1]You can download the corpus at `http://rsc.li/RSCsum`

doc id: C2JM16014E
Summary: Highly luminescent Cd1-xZnxSe1-ySy quantum dot (QD)-encoded poly(styrene-co-ethylene glycol dimethacrylate-co-methacrylic acid) beads (PSEMBs) were prepared by a novel in situ synthesis method.
Title: Facile single step preparation of high-performance quantum dot barcodes.
Abstract: We demonstrate the facile preparation of highly luminescent Cd1-xZnxSe1-ySy quantum dot (QD)-encoded poly(styrene-co-ethylene glycol dimethacrylate-co-methacrylic acid) beads (PSEMBs) in a straightforward and reproducible manner. The monodisperse mesoporous PSEMBs are first swelled in chloroform. Afterwards , the reaction precursors, composed of Cd, Zn, Se and S, are impregnated into the microspheres. Subsequently, the Cd1-xZnxSe1-ySy QDs are synthesised directly within the polymer beads by thermal decomposition......

Table 2: Example document "C2JM16014E" from RSCsum: summary, title and abstract.

dataset	documents	Avg. length (char)	
		article	summary
CNN	92K	656	43
DM	219K	693	53
XSum	227K	431	23
arXiv	215K	4938	220
PubMed	133K	3016	203
RSCsum	308K	187	29

Table 3: Comparison of corpora statistics.

and *extractive fragment density* were introduced by Grusky et al. (2018). The extractive fragment coverage is the percentage of unigrams in the summary that were directly copied from the input text, regardless of their order. The extractive fragment density is the average of the sum of squares of lengths of the extracted n-grams. The higher the coverage score is, the more individual words the summary extracts from the input text, but this may indicate re-wording using the same tokens and not necessarily direct copying of phrases. On the other hand, high density suggests a higher number of copied n-grams and therefore a more extractive dataset. Fig. 1 visualises the distribution of fragment density and coverage of the five compared corpora[2]. As we can see, RSCSUM has lower coverage and lower density. The graphs also indicate that the ground truth summaries in RSCSUM and XSum are more distinct from the reference content, compared to the bullet point summaries in CNN/DM or the abstracts in arXiv and PubMed.

If we take as reasonable that chemical names should be copied we can adapt the idea of fragment coverage to this dataset. We use the following formula to detect the percentage overlap between the tokens in each sentence n in the abstract A_i and the tokens in the summary S_i^t, disregarding the tokens that belong to chemical named entities t_c. We take the maximum value of all sentence overlaps.

$$\theta(A_i, S_i) = \max(\frac{|S_i^t \cap A_{i1}^{t-t_c}|}{|A_{i1}^{t-t_c}|}, ... \frac{|S_i^t \cap A_{in}^{t-t_c}|}{|A_{in}^{t-t_c}|}) \tag{1}$$

This allows us to examine the abstractiveness of the corpus in finer detail, as show in Tab. 2. In about 54k cases, authors appear to have taken the easy route of directly copying at least one sentence from the abstract.

4 Methods

We implement three extractive baselines and three abstractive deep models.

4.1 Baselines

The most basic extractive baseline is **Lead-2**, where we take the first two sentences of an abstract as the summary. We also use SumBasic[3] and a GloVe vector[4] enhanced TextRank algorithm.

4.2 Deep models

4.2.1 Pointer–Generator

We adapt the PyTorch re-implementation[5] of the original pointer–generator network (PGN) (See et al., 2017) by inserting ELMo embeddings (Peters et al., 2018) trained on PubMed texts,[6] hereafter refered to as PGN-E. The added ELMo embeddings were computed by a pre-trained two-layered bidirectional language model (biLM) resulting in 512-dimensional word vectors, which is more than twice of the original pointer generator embedding size. We also experimented with the original PGN, and while we found the difference in performance as evaluated by ROUGE metrics negligible, PGN-E produced a higher rate of novel n-grams indicating better abstractiveness.

---

[2]The data for CNN/DM and XSum is gathered from Hugging Face (https://huggingface.co/datasets), and PubMed and arXiv from Cohan et al. (2018). For all datasets, we consider the training set only.

[3]https://pypi.org/project/sumy/
[4]https://github.com/stanfordnlp/GloVe
[5]https://github.com/atulkum/pointer_summarizer
[6]https://allennlp.org/elmo/

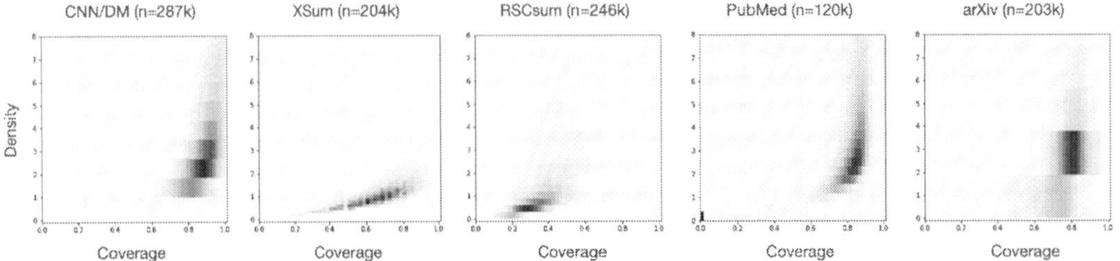

Figure 1: Extractive fragment coverage and density distributions across the compared datasets, where n indicates the number of documents.

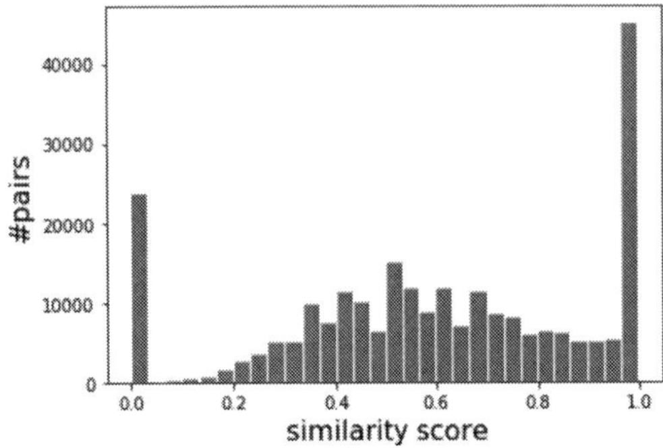

Figure 2: Distribution of the similarity scores between summary and abstract according to Eq. 1.

Likewise, we adjusted some of the hyperparameters: the vocabulary size is 100K for both the source and target text, and the Adagrad (Duchi et al., 2011) learning rate 0.05 was chosen from 0.15,[7] 0.1 and 0.05 with the initial accumulator value set to 0.1. We used gradient clipping with a maximum gradient norm of 2 and early stopping triggered by the loss on the validation set. The generated summaries were constrained to the range from 25 to 100 tokens. During training, the batch size was 8, and at test time the beam size of the beam search algorithm was 4. We trained the enhanced model for a maximum of 35K iterations due to computational restrictions. Finally, to speed up the training process, input content sentences were truncated to a maximum length of 100 tokens and summary sentences to 30 tokens.

4.2.2 Reinforcement Learning

We use the model introduced by Chen and Bansal (2018) (RL-EA) which has two separate learning mechanisms, maximum likelihood (ML) and reinforcement learning (RL). When training with Adam (Kingma and Ba, 2014), their respective learning

rates were 10^{-3} and 10^{-4} respectively, and the discount factor was 0.95. The abstractor and extractor were trained separately until convergence with ML objectives, then RL was applied to the trained sub-modules. Each single-layered LSTM network includes 256 hidden units in all models. The final encoder states linearly map to the initial decoder states in the abstractor module. We also applied early stopping and the 2-norm of 2.0 gradient clipping (Pascanu et al., 2012) here.

To prime the embedding matrix of the ML model, we trained 128-dimensional word2vec (Mikolov et al., 2013) vectors with a constrained vocabulary size of 30K tokens. These embeddings were then updated in downstream training. A sentence ending token (v_{EOE}) was added as a trainable parameter for RL to learn when to stop extracting sentences from the input source, so the total summary length has no strict limitation compared with the other two abstractive models. At test time, input content was not limited, but the output summary was constrained to a maximum of 30 tokens per sentence for the abstractor.

We also tested the re-ranking mechanism of this algorithm, but decided not to include results as they produced similar ROUGE scores and lower percentages of novel n-grams.

4.2.3 Transformer

We adapt the open-source code provided by Liu and Lapata and replace the "BERT-base-uncased" pre-trained model with SciBERT (Beltagy et al., 2019). SciBERT follows the BERT model architecture, which is a multi-bidirectional transformer, by training an objective which predicts masked tokens and the next sentence, but is trained on scientific texts including PubMed. The input source content and target summaries were tokenised with BERT's subword tokeniser. We refer to this model as SciBERT Abstractive, SciBERTA for short.

---

[7]0.15 is the best learning rate for the CNN/DM dataset.

The specific hyperparameter values of the abstractive component are shown in Appendix A.1. The maximum encoding text size is set to 512, because only 210 input texts in our corpus are longer than 512, and 512 is the maximum length in the original BERT model position embeddings. The model was trained for 100K steps with gradient accumulation for every five steps. Its intermediate models were saved every 2000 iterations and evaluated on the validation set every 2500 steps. The top-3 intermediate results which have the highest validation accuracy are chosen, and results on the test set are averaged to provide the final score.

The transformer decoder contains 768 hidden units and a hidden size of 2048 for all feed-forward layers. During decoding the beam search size is 5 and the output summary is limited the the range of 20 to 100 tokens. The decoding ends when an end-of-sequence token is generated. Trigram blocking (Paulus et al., 2017) is used to avoid repetition. Because of the sub-word tokeniser, OOV tokens are rarely observed.

5 Quantitative Evaluation

We perform a set of classic quantitative experiments by training and tuning on the train and validation portions of the data and testing once on the test portion. We evaluate the performance of the models using four standard variations of ROUGE (Lin, 2004) and report the F1 values and the confidence interval (CI) in Tab. 4. ROUGE-1 and ROUGE-2 measure the unigram and bigram overlap between the automatic and reference summaries, whereas ROUGE-L measures the longest extended matching sequence of words using the longest common subsequence (LCS). An advantage of using LCS is that it uses all in-sequence matches that reflect sentence-level word order, rather than requiring consecutive matches. Since it automatically includes the longest in-sequence common n-grams, a predefined n-gram length is not necessary. Finally, the skip-bigram/unigram variation ROUGE-SU measures overlap of word pairs that have a maximum of two gaps between words combined with unigram overlap.

5.1 Results

Results are presented in Tab. 4. We can observe from the CI overlap that SciBERTA is significantly better than the other two deep learning methods, whereas Lead-2 provides the most competitive

baseline. In fact PGN-E barely outperforms the Lead-2 baseline. An examination of the summaries produced on the validation set confirms that this method most often adopts the Lead-2 strategy by copying first and/or second sentence, an issue that was also observed in prior work (Qiu et al., 2020; Gehrmann et al., 2018). This result pattern is also confirmed by prior work (Tab. 5) where we see that the original PGN does not even beat the Lead-3 baseline, while the BERT-based model outperforms the other two. The introduction of ELMo vectors slightly alleviates this issue over the original PGN-coverage model. The original PGN has 71.28% unigram overlap with Lead-2, while PGN-E is at 68.22%. RL-EA has unigram overlap of 61.35% and SciBERTA again shows highest diversity with only about 53.86% overlap with the Lead-2 baseline.

As an indication of abstractiveness, Fig. 4 shows the average percentage of novel n-grams for each of the deep learning methods. We can see that SciBERTA also outperforms the other methods with this measure, and although PGN-E and RL-EA were indistinguishable based on ROUGE, PGN-E is actually producing more novel n-grams.

5.2 Filtering Training Data

As we saw in Sec.3 we filter out the training examples which have at least one sentence with 80% overlap and higher and we are left with 174180 training examples. We call this training set RSCSUM-T80, and leave the test and validation sets untouched, with 30776 and 30803 examples respectively. The exclusion of the strong extractive signal changes the training data profile and also reduces the training data size, resulting in a decrease in ROUGE results by between 1 and 4 F1 points. On the other hand, this strategy does lead to a larger proportion of novel n-grams for PGN-E and RL-EA (Fig. 5). PGN-E's performance increases slightly over the original SciBERTA scores, which unfortunately drop slightly on the pruned training data. This indicates that SciBERTA is more resilient to biased signals in the training data, but benefits from more training data. The unigram overlap between the generated summaries and the Lead-2 baseline is also reduced across the board (PGN: 59.61%, PGN-E: 59.49%, RL-EA:49.44%, SciBERTA: 52.46%).

Models	ROUGE-1		ROUGE-2		ROUGE-L		ROUGE-SU	
	F1	CI	F1	CI	F1	CI	F1	CI
Lead-2	**45.4**	(-0.2, +0.2)	**30.5**	(-0.3, +0.3)	**38.1**	(-0.2, +0.2)	**21.8**	(-0.2, +0.2)
SumBasic	38.5	(-0.2, +0.2)	20.4	(-0.2, +0.2)	29.8	(-0.2, +0.2)	15.0	(-0.2, +0.2)
Textrank	38.2	(-0.2, +0.2)	21.8	(-0.3, +0.3)	30.7	(-0.3, +0.3)	16.6	(-0.2, +0.2)
PGN-E	46.2	(-0.2, +0.3)	31.0	(-0.4, +0.3)	41.2	(-0.3, +0.3)	26.5	(-0.3, +0.3)
RL-EA	47.4	(-0.3, +0.3)	31.7	(-0.3, +0.3)	40.8	(-0.3, +0.3)	25.8	(-0.3, +0.3)
SciBERTA	**48.3**	(-0.3, +0.3)	**32.4**	(-0.4, +0.3)	**42.4**	(-0.3, +0.4)	**28.1**	(-0.3, +0.3)

Table 4: Results of extractive and abstractive models on RSCSUM (best in each section bold-faced). Fig. 3 gives the bar chart for a better view.

Models	ROUGE-1	ROUGE-2	ROUGE-L
Baseline			
Lead-3 (See et al., 2017)	40.3	17.7	36.6
Abstractive models			
PGN (See et al., 2017)	36.4	15.7	33.4
PGN+coverage (See et al., 2017)	39.5	17.3	36.3
RL-EA+rerank (Chen and Bansal, 2018)	40.9	17.8	38.5
BERTSumAbs (Liu and Lapata, 2019)	**41.7**	**19.4**	**38.8**

Table 5: Performance of related algorithms from prior work on the non-anonymised CNN/Daily Mail dataset.

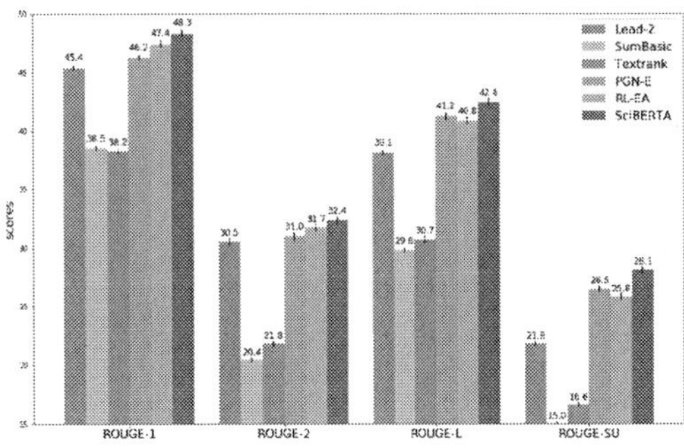

Figure 3: Bar chart for Tab. 4.

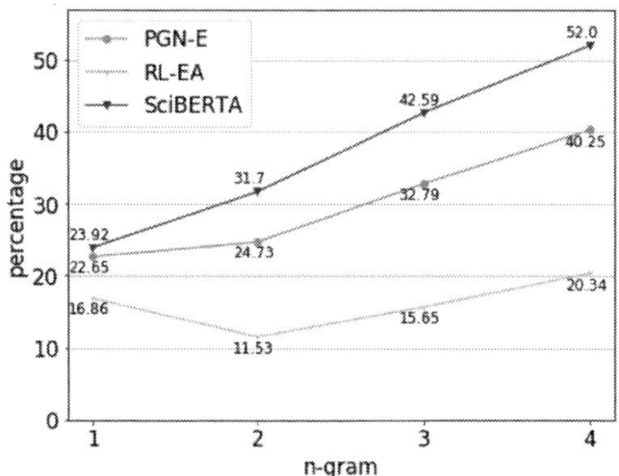

Figure 4: Average percentage of novel n-grams in the generated summaries.

6 Qualitative Evaluation

Reference-based automatic evaluation has accepted limitations such as the fact that any given reference is not the only possible summary or even necessarily the best one. We, therefore, perform a small-scale human evaluation using three participants with a background in the chemical sciences. They volunteered to help. We choose to compare SciB-ERTA as the best-performing system, in addition to RL-EA, which is less similar to the Lead-2 baseline than PGN-E and also has a different learning objective. In order to test the quality of the gold standard reference summaries objectively, we also evaluate them in our setup.

We perform a 3×3 Latin Square design with 42 items (documents) and three conditions (systems). The advantage of the Latin Square design (cf. Tab. 6) is that each participant sees each item in only one condition, thus avoiding repetition bias.

The systems (α, β, γ) are run on different batches of 14 items (1, 2, 3) and then shown to judges (A_1, A_2, A_3), so that A_1 is seeing summaries from batch 1 generated by system α, batch 2 generated by system β, and batch 3 summaries by system γ. We then randomise the order of items shown. So that the conditions are not readily distinguishable, we aim to provide a distribution of summary lengths which is as even as possible. Fig. 6 shows the natural distribution of the summary lengths produced on the test set.

The participants were presented with the document title and abstract (concatenated together) and a summary, which they rated on scale of 0-5 according to the criteria in Tab. 7. Dimensions considered are grammaticality, informativeness, relevance and overall quality. We report the systems' mean scores

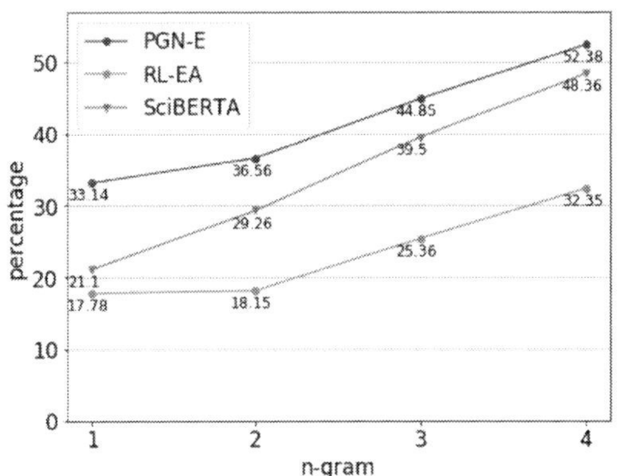

Figure 5: Average percentage of novel n-grams in the generated summaries with the filtered training dataset RSCsum-80.

	batch 1	batch 2	batch 3
A_1	$\alpha 1$	$\beta 2$	$\gamma 3$
A_2	$\gamma 1$	$\alpha 2$	$\beta 3$
A_3	$\beta 1$	$\gamma 2$	$\alpha 3$

Table 6: 3×3 Latin square design with conditions (systems) α, β, and γ, participants A_1, A_2, A_3 and item batches 1, 2, 3.

for each dimension separately as well as the average across dimensions.

6.1 Results

Tab. 8 shows the results, with SciBERTA outperforming both RL-EA and the ground truth (GT) on all counts. SciBERTA achieves the highest mean score on all four criteria at 4.52, 4.81, 3.55 and 3.48 respectively, whereas the ground truth has only 3.33 overall quality and 3.86 on average, which is quite unexpected. One possible reason is that a few of the ground truth examples are sentences directly extracted from the abstracts and are thus less in-

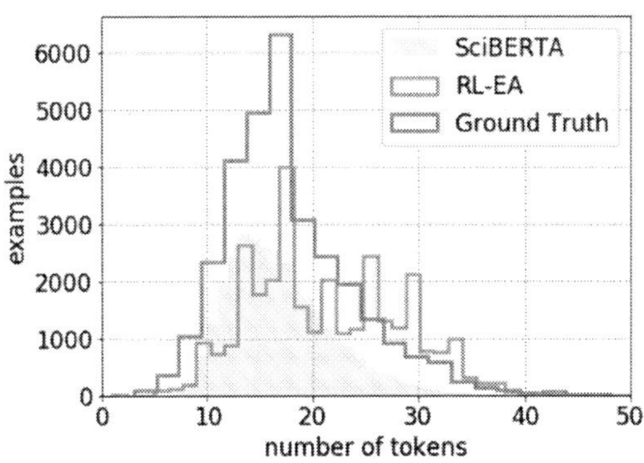

Figure 6: Distribution of model summary length (test set).

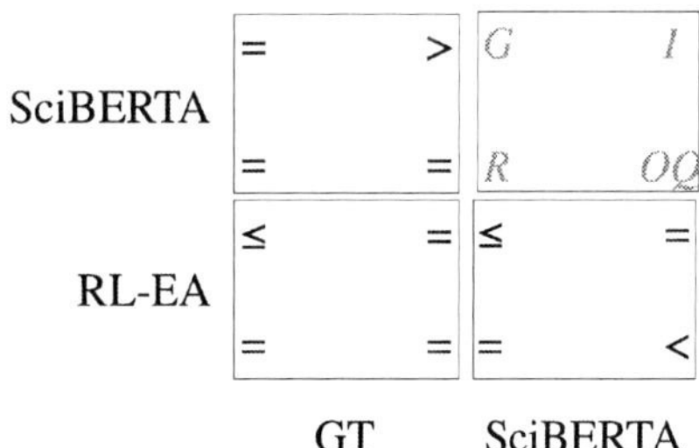

Figure 7: Statistical significance test on the values in Tab. 8. The four positions correspond to **G**rammaticality, **I**nformativeness, **R**elevance and **O**verall **Q**uality respectively, as shown in upper left box. "=" means no statistical difference, ">" means the row performs significantly better than the column at the significance level $\alpha = 0.05$, whereas "$\leqslant$" indicates the same at $\alpha = 0.01$.

teresting for this task. Although we took care to distribute the summary lengths as evenly as possible, in general RL-EA favours longer summaries, yet the more succinct summaries of SciBERTA are preferred even in the informativeness dimension. RL-EA also sometimes produces unfinished sentence fragments and this could be one of the reasons for its relatively low grammaticality and quality values.

We use the two-tailed Wilcoxon signed-rank test to compute the statistical significance between the systems (Fig. 7). Though SciBERTA performs the best in all the evaluation dimensions as well as the overall average, it is significantly better than the ground truth only in terms of the informativeness and outperforms RL-EA regarding grammaticality and overall quality. Except for grammaticality, there is no statistically-significant difference detected between RL-EA and the ground truth.

As an indication of the degree to which participants agreed in their judgements, Fig. 8 shows the mean scores given by each judge to each of the three conditions.[8] We can see that the judgements by A_2 pattern in a different way to those of participants A_1 and A_3, which are more similar to each other. This might be due to the different backgrounds of the participants, as the former is a materials scientist by training, whereas the latter two are chemists.

Anecdotally, the participants independently re-

---

[8] In a Latin Square design, agreement can only be measured within experimental groups, not across them. However, as the experimental group size is 1 in our 3×3 setting, this is of no use to us here.

Dimension	Prompt	Rating range $0 < - - - - - - > 5$	
Grammaticality	Are the individual sentences of the summary well-written and grammatical?	Disagree	Agree
Informativeness	To which degree does the summary contain false or misleading information?	A lot	Zero
Relevance	Does the summary capture the main points of the abstract?	Disagree	Agree
Overall quality	If I were a journal editor, I would accept this summary for enticing readers to the website.	Disagree	Agree

Table 7: Human evaluation of the question-answering rating system.

dimension	SciBERTA	RL-EA	GT
Grammaticality	**4.52**	3.29	4.24
Informativeness	**4.81**	4.62	4.38
Relevance	**3.55**	3.52	3.50
Overall quality	**3.48**	2.71	3.33
Average	**4.09**	3.53	3.86

Table 8: Mean scores of human evaluation on RSC-SUM.

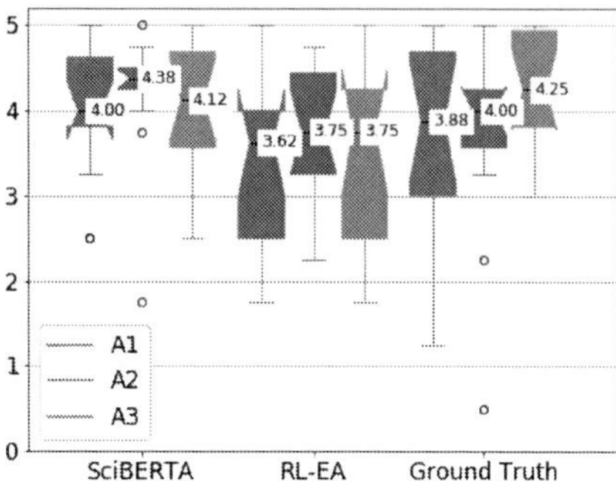

Figure 8: Participants' individual mean scores, by conditions.

ported that the fact that the summaries were uncased would be a barrier to use of automatic summarisation in chemistry, but that it didn't cause them trouble in the small number of examples they were looking at. For example, "no" (stop word), "No" (nobelium), and "NO" (nitrogen oxide), all have vastly different meanings.

One explicitly stated reason for the lower scores of human summaries is that they often contain grammatical errors. In their feedback, the participants noted that they were generous when grading the grammaticality as the summaries are mostly right regardless of the case. Nevertheless, when looking closely at a few ground truth summaries, we noticed that they seem to have been marked down for grammatical mistakes. The overarching reason is probably that writing the summaries was an after-acceptance task for the authors, which may not have had their full attention. For example in the Appendix A.2 Tab. 10 we can see that the ground truth summary consists of the motivation sentence, while every method accurately picked out the contribution sentence. Of these, the one by SciBERTA is the most grammatically pleasing. As the input source document is the abstract of a paper, authors have a tendency to start with motivational statements, e.g. "we synthesised something and then studied its properties, applications etc". One participant remarked that they tended to mark down the summaries that only focused on this aspect of the abstract. Conversely, some ground truth summaries draw on the full paper and the domain knowledge of the authors, and so could contain information beyond the abstract. While we do not have specific feedback on this point, this could also lead to an undesirable score.

7 Discussion

In this paper we introduced a corpus that consists of titles and abstracts of papers in the scientific domain as input text, and author-written table-of-contents summaries. The summaries are meant to be distinct from the titles and abstracts, but at least one fifth of the training data contains significant extractive elements. Overall the corpus compares favourably to others in its abstractive qualities. It contains scientific terminology in the chemistry domain, and some of the terminology in the summaries does not occur in the available input text. Consequently, as part of a larger effort of enriching chemical NLP, in the future we will also release about 40K full text open access articles that have corresponding TOC summaries.

We tested three state-of-the-art deep summarisation methods and found that a transformer-based method that uses pretrained scientific BERT embeddings produces the best overall results in both quantitative evaluation and a qualitative study with three domain expert participants. It is surprisingly resistant to the strong extractive component in the training data, and produces novel content despite the short input text. A qualitative study showed that automatic summaries yield acceptable results and are in some aspects significantly better than author-written summaries. However, in order to be truly useful, the summarisation methods and associated embeddings need to be adapted to deal with the cased text, which may lead to difficulties with an expanded vocabulary. In conclusion, this study paves the way for future exploration of summarisation and semantics in the chemistry domain.

8   Acknowledgements

The authors would like to thank Aileen Day and Peter Corbett who participated in our evaluation and the reviewers for their thoughtful comments.

References

Iz Beltagy, Kyle Lo, and Arman Cohan. 2019. Scibert: Pretrained language model for scientific text. In *EMNLP*.

Florian Boudin, Juan-Manuel Torres-Moreno, and Patricia Velázquez-Morales. 2008. An efficient statistical approach for automatic organic chemistry summarization. In *International Conference on Natural Language Processing*, pages 89–99. Springer.

Yen-Chun Chen and Mohit Bansal. 2018. Fast abstractive summarization with reinforce-selected sentence rewriting. In *Proceedings of the 56th Annual Meeting of the Association for Computational Linguistics (Volume 1: Long Papers)*, pages 675–686, Melbourne, Australia. Association for Computational Linguistics.

Arman Cohan, Franck Dernoncourt, Doo Soon Kim, Trung Bui, Seokhwan Kim, Walter Chang, and Nazli Goharian. 2018. A discourse-aware attention model for abstractive summarization of long documents. *Proceedings of the 2018 Conference of the North American Chapter of the Association for Computational Linguistics: Human Language Technologies, Volume 2 (Short Papers)*.

Peter Corbett and John Boyle. 2018. Chemlistem: chemical named entity recognition using recurrent neural networks. *Journal of cheminformatics*, 10(1):59.

John Duchi, Elad Hazan, and Yoram Singer. 2011. Adaptive subgradient methods for online learning and stochastic optimization. *Journal of machine learning research*, 12(Jul):2121–2159.

Sebastian Gehrmann, Yuntian Deng, and Alexander M Rush. 2018. Bottom-up abstractive summarization. *arXiv preprint arXiv:1808.10792*.

Max Grusky, Mor Naaman, and Yoav Artzi. 2018. Newsroom: A dataset of 1.3 million summaries with diverse extractive strategies. In *Proceedings of the 2018 Conference of the North American Chapter of the Association for Computational Linguistics: Human Language Technologies, Volume 1 (Long Papers)*, pages 708–719, New Orleans, Louisiana. Association for Computational Linguistics.

Lezan Hawizy, David M Jessop, Nico Adams, and Peter Murray-Rust. 2011. Chemicaltagger: A tool for semantic text-mining in chemistry. *Journal of cheminformatics*, 3(1):17.

Diederik P. Kingma and Jimmy Ba. 2014. Adam: A method for stochastic optimization.

Chin-Yew Lin. 2004. ROUGE: A package for automatic evaluation of summaries. In *Text Summarization Branches Out*, pages 74–81, Barcelona, Spain. Association for Computational Linguistics.

Yang Liu and Mirella Lapata. 2019. Text summarization with pretrained encoders.

Rada Mihalcea and Paul Tarau. 2004. Textrank: Bringing order into text. In *Proceedings of the 2004 conference on empirical methods in natural language processing*, pages 404–411.

Tomas Mikolov, Ilya Sutskever, Kai Chen, Greg S Corrado, and Jeff Dean. 2013. Distributed representations of words and phrases and their compositionality. In *Advances in neural information processing systems*, pages 3111–3119.

N Moratanch and S Chitrakala. 2017. A survey on extractive text summarization. In *2017 international conference on computer, communication and signal processing (ICCCSP)*, pages 1–6. IEEE.

Shashi Narayan, Shay B. Cohen, and Mirella Lapata. 2018. Don't give me the details, just the summary! topic-aware convolutional neural networks for extreme summarization.

Razvan Pascanu, Tomas Mikolov, and Yoshua Bengio. 2012. On the difficulty of training recurrent neural networks.

Romain Paulus, Caiming Xiong, and Richard Socher. 2017. A deep reinforced model for abstractive summarization.

Matthew E. Peters, Mark Neumann, Mohit Iyyer, Matt Gardner, Christopher Clark, Kenton Lee, and Luke Zettlemoyer. 2018. Deep contextualized word representations. In *Proc. of NAACL*.

Joseph J Pollock and Antonio Zamora. 1975. Automatic abstracting research at chemical abstracts service. *Journal of Chemical Information and Computer Sciences*, 15(4):226–232.

Xipeng Qiu, Tianxiang Sun, Yige Xu, Yunfan Shao, Ning Dai, and Xuanjing Huang. 2020. Pre-trained models for natural language processing: A survey. *arXiv preprint arXiv:2003.08271*.

Abigail See, Peter J. Liu, and Christopher D. Manning. 2017. Get to the point: Summarization with pointer-generator networks.

Eva Sharma, Chen Li, and Lu Wang. 2019. Bigpatent: A large-scale dataset for abstractive and coherent summarization.

Jonathan M. Stokes, Kevin Yang, Kyle Swanson, Wengong Jin, Andres Cubillos-Ruiz, Nina M. Donghia, Craig R. MacNair, Shawn French, Lindsey A. Carfrae, Zohar Bloom-Ackermann, Victoria M. Tran, Anush Chiappino-Pepe, Ahmed H. Badran, Ian W. Andrews, Emma J. Chory, George M. Church, Eric D. Brown, Tommi S. Jaakkola, Regina Barzilay, and James J. Collins. 2020. A deep learning approach to antibiotic discovery. *Cell*, 180(4):688 – 702.e13.

Bingjun Sun, Prasenjit Mitra, C Lee Giles, and Karl T Mueller. 2011. Identifying, indexing, and ranking chemical formulae and chemical names in digital documents. *ACM Transactions on Information Systems (TOIS)*, 29(2):1–38.

Lucy Vanderwende, Hisami Suzuki, Chris Brockett, and Ani Nenkova. 2007. Beyond sumbasic: Task-focused summarization with sentence simplification and lexical expansion. *Information Processing & Management*, 43(6):1606–1618.

Leonid Zaslavsky, Daniel Lowe, Chih-Hsuan Wei, Zhiyong Lu, and Evan Bolton. 2017. Improving chemical names matching for verification, rating, and validation of pubchem compound records. In *ABSTRACTS OF PAPERS OF THE AMERICAN CHEMICAL SOCIETY*, volume 253. AMER CHEMICAL SOC 1155 16TH ST, NW, WASHINGTON, DC 20036 USA.

Hakime Öztürk, Arzucan Özgür, Philippe Schwaller, Teodoro Laino, and Elif Ozkirimli. 2020. Exploring chemical space using natural language processing methodologies for drug discovery. *Drug Discovery Today*, 25(4):689–705.

A Appendices

A.1 SciBERTA hyperparameter setting

Table 9 provides the specific hyperparameter setting for the SciBERTA system.

hyperparameter	SciBERTA
training_steps	100,000
warmup steps	10,000
max_pos	512
batch size	8
grad_accum_cnt	5
dropout	0.2
learning rate	0.002
learning rate$_{dec}$	0.01

Table 9: Hyperparameter settings in SciBERTA.

A.2 Summary examples

The real examples generated by the three systems are shown in Tables 11–14. Compared to training on full RSCSUM, training on RSCSUM-T80 could lead to mistakes using PGN-E and RL-EA models.

Candidate$_{PGN-E}$: hydrogen peroxide (h2o2) plays a significant role in regulating the redox balance in the living body . this work illustrated a high sensitivity hydrophilic photoacoustic probe for ratiometric imaging of h2o2 in living mice .
Candidate$_{RL-EA}$: a high sensitivity hydrophilic photoacoustic probe for ratiometric imaging of hydrogen peroxide in vitro and vivo .
Candidate$_{SciBERTA}$: a hydrophilic photoacoustic probe was developed for ratiometric imaging of h2o2 in vitro and vivo .
Ground truth: Hydrogen peroxide (H2O2) plays a significant role in regulating the redox balance in the living body .
Abstract: Enhancing hydrophilicity of photoacoustic probes for effective ratiometric imaging of hydrogen peroxide . Hydrogen peroxide (H2O2) plays a significant role in regulating the redox balance in the living body . Compared with traditional imaging techniques , ratiometric photoacoustic imaging is no doubt a superior choice for H2O2 visualization . However , the difficult design of ratiometric probes with only one activatable agent that exhibits two changeable absorption peaks under H2O2 activation remains a big challenge . In this work , we developed a near - infrared absorbing probe , which responded to H2O2 selectively and permitted the ratiometric photoacoustic imaging of H2O2 in living mice . The probe was constructed from an Aza-BODIPY backbone attached with a benzeneboronic acid pinacol ester moiety though a quaternization reaction . Oligo(ethylene glycol) (OEG) was introduced into hydrophobic Aza-BODIPY to enhance the water - solubility of the probe . The OEG-Aza-BODIPY-BAPE probe exhibited sensitive and specific ratiometric PA signals towards H2O2 . In vivo experiments also showed that the OEG-Aza-BODIPY-BAPE probe can be used for ratiometric PA imaging . Overall , our work illustrated a high sensitivity hydrophilic photoacoustic probe for ratiometric imaging of hydrogen peroxide in vitro and vivo .

Table 10: An example "C8AY01644E" produced by PGN-E, RL-EA and SciBERTA on full RSCSUM. Overlaps are highlighted by different colours.

Candidate$_{full}$: β-amyloid (aβ) plays a central role in alzheimer's disease (ad), but the specific molecular mechanism and associated structures remain unknown.
Candidate$_{T80}$: β-amyloid (aβ) plays a central role in alzheimer's disease (ad), but the specific molecular mechanism and associated structures remain unknown in contrast to structured conformations and associated structures.
Ground truth: Direct correlation of Alzheimer patient data to a spectrum of NMR structures and chemical properties of beta amyloid (Aβ) variants allows identification of conformation - dependent disease properties .
Abstract: Pathogenic properties of Alzheimer's β-amyloid identified from structure – property patient-phenotype correlations . β-Amyloid (Aβ) plays a central role in Alzheimer's disease (AD), but the specific molecular mechanism and associated structures remain unknown. We compiled patient data for carriers......We conclude that disordered monomers are likely to be pathogenically important in contrast to structured conformations......

Table 11: An example "C4DT03122A" produced by PGN-E training on full RSCSUM and RSCSUM-T80 respectively. The underlined phrase is a repetitive expression.

Candidate$_{full}$: the addition of inbr3 to the oxidative sonogashira cross - coupling reaction of 2 - ethynylaniline with (e) - trimethyl (3,3,3 - trifluoroprop -1-enyl) silane led ~~the subsequent cyclization of these 1,3 - enynes under palladium catalysis provides access to the corresponding indoles bearing a 3,3,3 - trifluoroprop -1-enyl group at their 2 - position~~ .
Candidate$_{T80}$: the addition of inbr3 to the oxidative sonogashira cross - coupling reaction of 2 - ethynylaniline with (e) - trimethyl (3,3,3 - trifluoroprop -1-enyl) silane led ~~the oxidative sonogashira coupling of 2 - ethynylanilineselectronic with a affords~~ a dramatic enhancing effect of inbr3 .
Ground truth: A dramatic enhancing effect of InBr3 was observed towards the oxidative Sonogashira cross - coupling reaction of 2-ethynylaniline with (E)-trimethyl(3,3,3-trifluoroprop-1-enyl)silane .
Abstract: The addition of InBr3 to the oxidative Sonogashira cross - coupling reaction of 2-ethynylaniline with (E)-trimethyl(3,3,3-trifluoroprop-1-enyl)silane led to a dramatic increase in the reactivity to afford the corresponding 1,3-enynes bearing a trifluoromethyl group on their terminal sp2 carbon . The subsequent cyclization of these 1,3-enynes under palladium catalysis provides access to the corresponding indoles bearing a 3,3,3-trifluoroprop-1-enyl group at their 2- position .

Table 12: An example "C5OB02558C" produced by RL-EA on full RSCSUM and RSCSUM-T80 respectively. The strikethrough denotes a wrong expression.

Candidate$_{full}$: a novel visible light promoted carbodifluoroalkylation of allylic alcohols is disclosed. a series of difluoro 1,5 - dicarbonyl compounds were obtained through a tandem radical addition and 1,2-aryl migration process.
Candidate$_{T80}$: a novel visible light promoted carbodifluoroalkylation of allylic alcohols was developed via a tandem radical addition and 1,2-aryl migration process , which proceeds via a radical intermediate.
Ground truth: A novel visible light promoted carbodifluoroalkylation of allylic alcohols is disclosed.
Abstract: Visible light promoted carbodifluoroalkylation of allylic alcohols via concomitant 1,2-aryl migration. A novel visible light promoted carbodifluoroalkylation of allylic alcohols is disclosed. A series of difluoro 1,5-dicarbonyl compounds were obtained through a tandem radical addition and 1,2-aryl migration process. Mechanistic analysis indicated that the 1,2-aryl rearrangement proceeded via a radical intermediate.

Table 13: An example "C5CC01189B" produced by SciBERTA on full RSCSUM and RSCSUM-T80 respectively.

Recurrent babbling:
evaluating the acquisition of grammar from limited input data

Ludovica Pannitto
CIMeC
University of Trento
`ludovica.pannitto@unitn.it`

Aurélie Herbelot
CIMeC/DISI
University of Trento
`aurelie.herbelot@unitn.it`

Abstract

Recurrent Neural Networks (RNNs) have been shown to capture various aspects of syntax from raw linguistic input. In most previous experiments, however, learning happens over unrealistic corpora, which do not reflect the type and amount of data a child would be exposed to. This paper remedies this state of affairs by training a Long Short-Term Memory network (LSTM) over a realistically sized subset of child-directed input. The behaviour of the network is analysed over time using a novel methodology which consists in quantifying the level of grammatical abstraction in the model's generated output (its 'babbling'), compared to the language it has been exposed to. We show that the LSTM indeed abstracts new structures as learning proceeds.

1 Do RNNs learn grammar?

Artificial Neural Networks, and Long Short-Term Memory Networks more specifically, have consistently demonstrated great capabilities in the area of language modeling. In addition to generating credible surface patterns, they show excellent performances when tested on very specific grammatical abilities (Gulordava et al., 2018; Lakretz et al., 2019), without requiring any prior bias towards the syntactic structure of natural languages.

From a theoretical point of view, these results seem to contradict the well-known argument of the *poverty of the stimulus* (Chomksy, 1959; Chomsky, 1968) and raise questions about the *continuity hypothesis* in language acquisition (Lust, 1999; Crain and Pietroski, 2001). At the same time, a number of results give a much more mitigated view of RNNs' abstraction capabilities (Marvin and Linzen, 2018; Chowdhury and Zamparelli, 2018). It thus remains unclear how and to what extent grammatical abilities emerge in artificial language models, and how this knowledge is encoded in their representations – especially when considering notions such as *productivity* and *compositionality* (Baroni, 2020), which are recognised as defining traits of natural languages.

This paper proposes that the evaluation of RNN grammars should be widened to include the effect of the type of input data fed to the network, as well as the theoretical paradigm used to analyse its output. We specifically remark that much of the discussion concerning language modeling remains influenced by the mainstream *generativist* approach, which posits a sharp distinction between syntax and the lexicon. Our own approach will be to depart from this account by testing the grammatical abilities of an RNN in a *usage-based* perspective. Specifically, we ask what kind of structures are abstracted and used productively by the network, and how the abstraction process takes place over time.

In contrast with previous models: (i) we train a vanilla char-LSTM on a more realistic variety and amount of data, focusing on a limited amount of child-directed language; (ii) we do not rely on extrinsic evaluations or downstream tasks, instead we introduce a methodology to evaluate how the distribution of grammatical items, over time, comes to approximate the one in the input, through a continuous process and (iii) we tentatively explore the interaction between meaning representations and the abstraction abilities of the network, blurring the distinction between lexicon and syntax, in a way more akin to Construction Grammar (CxG, Fillmore, 1988; Goldberg, 1995; Kay and Fillmore, 1999). Our evaluation focuses on the network's generated output (its 'babbling'), asking to what extent the system simulates the type of grammatical abstraction observed in human children. The study is conducted on English.

In what follows, we review related work (§ 2), we then formulate the question of grammar modelling in a broader theoretical framework (§ 3) in-

165

Proceedings of the 24th Conference on Computational Natural Language Learning, pages 165–176
Online, November 19-20, 2020. ©2020 Association for Computational Linguistics
https://doi.org/10.18653/v1/P17

volving three parameters: the type of acquisition mechanism under study, the nature of the input data, and the representational paradigm adopted for the analysis. We configure this broad framework with particular choices of parameters and implement it in § 4, 5 and 6. We provide two analyses of the distributional properties of the network's 'babbling', discussed in § 7.

2 Related Work

A considerable amount of literature has investigated the ability of ANNs to acquire grammar, and the list we present here is by no means exhaustive. The analysis of the syntactic abilities of LSTMs (Hochreiter and Schmidhuber, 1997) and ANN-based language models dates back quite a few years (McClelland, 1992; Lewis and Elman, 2001). Recent contributions have followed a general tendency to analyze the inner-workings of networks, and the specific type of knowledge they acquire (Alishahi et al., 2019; Linzen and Baroni, 2020). For instance, Linzen et al. (2016) show how a network acquires *abstract* information about number agreement, albeit in a supervised setting. The same study is expanded in Gulordava et al. (2018), which shows how a language modeling task is enough for a network to predict long-distance number agreement, both on semantically sound and nonsensical sentences. The authors conclude that "LM-trained RNNs can construct abstract grammatical representations", but their model is trained on a rather consequent amount of data (90M tokens) from a rather peculiar distribution (a Wikipedia snapshot). Similarly, it has been shown that LSTMs (McCoy et al., 2018; Wilcox et al., 2018) can learn tricky syntactic rules like the English auxiliary inversion and filler-gap dependencies, although, in later work, McCoy et al. (2020) find that only models with an explicit inductive bias (Shen et al., 2018) learn to generalize the MOVE-MAIN rule with respect to auxiliary inversion. Marvin and Linzen (2018) show instead poor performance of RNNs in grammaticality evaluation, due to their sensitivity to the specific lexical items encountered during training, a limitation that, they say, "would not be expected if its syntactic representations were fully abstract". Similarly Chowdhury and Zamparelli (2018) state that their model "is sensitive to linguistic processing factors and probably ultimately unable to induce a more abstract notion of grammaticality". Moreover, despite the fact that the model of Gulordava et al. (2018) is tested on four languages, the most promising results may not be generalizable to languages showing different surface patterns from English. Ravfogel et al. (2018) fail to replicate Gulordava et al. (2018)'s results on Basque, and Davis and van Schijndel (2020), after testing the network on relative clause attachment cases in English and Spanish, conjecture that the associative (non-linguistic) bias of RNNs overlaps with English syntactic structure but represents an obstacle to learn attachment rules for Spanish.

Other puzzling results concern the relation of perplexity to syntactic performance (Warstadt et al., 2019; Hu et al., 2020): having evaluated their models on 34 benchmarks, Hu et al. (2020) conclude with a call for a wider variety of syntactic phenomena to test on. Further studies have shown that networks carrying explicit inductive bias perform better than vanilla LSTMs. In a recent paper, Lepori et al. (2020) show that a constituency-based network generalizes more robustly than a dependency-based one, and that both outperform a more basic BiLSTM. Lastly, we mention the study carried out by Kuncoro et al. (2018) who perform their study using a character-based LSTM – a choice we will follow in this work.

A very similar scientific discussion, which we won't report in depth here, is blooming around Transformer-based language models (Tran et al., 2018; Goldberg, 2019; Bacon and Regier, 2019; Jawahar et al., 2019; Lin et al., 2019), leading to similar contrasting results.

Finally, a separate line of work focuses on a more indirect test of the information encoded in the internal representation, assessing which aspects of the original syntactic structure can be reconstructed through diagnostic classifiers (Adi et al., 2017; Giulianelli et al., 2018; Hewitt and Manning, 2019; Tenney et al., 2019).

In summary, a clear trend has not yet emerged (Linzen and Baroni, 2020). All the models we cited, however, seem to idealize syntactic structure as a separate and more abstract ability from the knowledge of statistical regularities or lexical co-occurrences. This perspective may reflect a belief in a sharp distinction between the *lexicon* and *compositional rules*. That is, ANNs are expected to gain *abstract grammatical abilities* through compositional generalization, where compositionality is understood as the ability to produce an unbounded number of sentences by means of a set of algebraic rules (Baroni, 2020). In contrast with this approach, usage-based models encourage us to adopt a different perspective, and to analyze LSTMs' grammatical abilities with respect to the kind of representations (more in §3.3) posited by theories such as Construction Grammar (CxG, Fillmore, 1988; Goldberg, 1995; Kay and Fillmore, 1999).

3 Framework

In essence, the question of language acquisition asks how much language (Λ) can be learned with a certain level of computational complexity (C) by being exposed to a certain type of data (I). The corresponding formalization, $a : C \times I \mapsto \Lambda$, describes both human and artificial acquisition processes, and its components have been central in the linguistic debate. Below, we will discuss each term (C, I and Λ) in further detail.

3.1 Computational complexity of the acquisition mechanism (C)

Our aim is to test how much grammatical structure can be induced from linguistic input through a pattern-finding mechanism such as that provided by ANNs. Therefore, we fix the level of computational complexity to a vanilla, character-based LSTM, which we train exploring different sources of input in a specific range $\{I_i\}$, selected based on their complexity level. We then use the trained model to generate some amount of text (to *babble*), to explore the structure of the produced output $\ell \in \Lambda$, mainly with respect to productivity.

$$(LSTM, I_i) \xrightarrow{a} \ell_i \qquad (1)$$

Our choice of model has consequences from a theoretical point of view. Different stances have been taken about how much has to be *hard-coded* or *innate* in order for language acquisition to happen: while formal innatist theories have always posited the need for a specialized and innate ability, a dedicated *device* for language learning (Chomsky, 1981, 1995; Hauser et al., 2002), cognitive theories have argued for a more systemic vision, showing how general purpose memory and cognitive mechanisms can account for the emergence of linguistic abilities (Tomasello, 2003; Goldberg, 2006; Christiansen and Chater, 2016; Cornish et al., 2017; Lewkowicz et al., 2018).

LSTMs, under this perspective, can be seen as a domain-general attention and memory mechanism, without any explicitly hard-coded grammatical knowledge. They have been applied, without substantial modifications, to a variety of tasks, ranging from time series prediction to object co-segmentation, and encompassing grammar learning as well. On the continuum between specialized devices and general purpose associative mechanisms, LSTMs place themselves on the latter side, with their recurrent structure seeming to be crucial in the linguistic abstraction process (Tran et al., 2018).

3.2 Structure and role of the input (I)

Because of the traditional sharp distinction between *competence* and *performance*, the role of the input and the linguistic environment has been minimized by theories in the realm of Universal Grammar (UG). Usage-based theories, on the other hand, have granted the input a central role to the end of explaining why language is structured as it is (Fillmore, 1988; Kay and Fillmore, 1999; Hoffmann et al., 2013; Christiansen and Chater, 2016; Goldberg, 2019): one of the striking points to make here is that in the usage-based framework the acquisition problem is framed as an incremental process. Acquiring language essentially entails learning how to process the linguistic input in an error-driven procedure, where full linguistic creativity and productivity are acquired gradually by speakers (Bannard et al., 2009), building up on knowledge about specific items and restricted abstractions.

In this sense, the specific features of the language on which ANNs are trained cannot be overlooked when it comes to describing their acquired grammatical abilities. Compared to what a child is exposed to during the most crucial months of language acquisition, ANNs are trained on an input that is often unrealistic in size: the LSTM introduced in Gulordava et al. (2018) is for example exposed to 90M tokens, and sees them multiple times over training. It is hard to come up with a precise estimate of the amount of language children are exposed to during the years of acquisition, as the variation depends on a huge number of factors including the socio-economic environment (Bee et al., 1969) or the societal organization (Cristia et al., 2019). Hart and Risley (1995), in a seminal work, estimate that, by the age of 3, welfare children have heard about 10 millions words while the average working-class child has heard around 30 millions. Finally, the domain of the data also matters: child-directed language is characterized by specific features (Matthews and Bannard, 2010) that are not present in the most widely used corpora.[1]

3.3 Shape and features of the generated language (Λ)

Any analysis of the language Λ generated by a learner implies the availability of a *representation*. Much has been written on the respective benefits of various representations of linguistic structures: the exact nature of their shape and content is the ultimate conundrum of linguistic theory. Of course, this paper is not the place to review the wide variations that exists among theories, so we will just limit ourselves to motivate our choice with respect to the broader theoretical framework.

Constituency-based representations have been prevalent in the description of natural language syntax, becoming primarily associated with derivational theories. Due to the Fregean view of compositionality, they have also become the natural building blocks for meaning composition. Dependency representations have, on the other hand, re-gained popularity over constituency representations in the last decades, showing desirable properties from a computational perspective (they adapt to a wider array of languages, representing ill-formed sentences results easier and the output is more easily incorporated in semantic graphs) while taking a more functional approach to language description, more in line with cognition oriented-approaches.

In order to represent the features of $\ell \in \Lambda$, we choose a representation which makes the least possible assumptions on the acquisition process and on the content of the generated language, and is at the same time flexible and computationally tractable. We therefore rely on dependency representations, more specifically the universal dependencies framework (Nivre et al., 2020), from which we extract subtrees called *catenae* (Osborne et al., 2012). As we will see below, the notion of catena is more flexible than that of constituent, and allows us to describe a larger set of generalizations.

Generally speaking, CxG approaches seem to lack a shared representational framework[2], relying on box diagrams or Attribute-Value Matrices to describe the traits of the fragments they study. The

Strings	A, AB, ABC, ... B, BC, ...E
Catenae	A, B, C, D, E, AB, ABCE, ABDE, ABCDE, ABE, BCE,BDE, BE, CE, DE, CDE
Constituents	A, ABCDE, C, D, CDE

Table 1: Possible structures that can be extracted from the dependency tree in Figure 2

structures introduced by Osborne (2006) are characterized instead as fundamental meaning-bearing units (Osborne and Groß, 2012), in line with the theoretical tenets of CxGs, thus being ideal candidates for the lexicon (or *'Constructicon'*) postulated in such theories: catenae have in fact been applied in the description of construction-like structures (Osborne and Groß, 2012; Dunn, 2017) and allow for the representation of non-adjacent structures while encompassing the notion of constituent as well (Osborne, 2006, 2018).

A catena is defined as "a word, or a combination of words which is continuous with respect to dominance" (Osborne et al., 2012): given a dependency tree, this definition selects a broader set of elements than the definition of constituent[3]. Unlike constituents, catenae can include both contiguous and non contiguous words. They however capture something more refined than generic subsets of sentence items, as the elements are grouped depending on the syntactic links holding in the sentence.

From a graph-theory perspective, catenae form subtrees (i.e., subsets of nodes and edges that constitute a tree themselves) of the original tree.

Let's consider for example the structures represented in Figures 1a, 1b and 1c: the same elements (nodes A to G) are arranged differently in the structure of dependency tree, and this leads to a different number and composition of catenae.

As a concrete example, Figure 2 represents a dependency tree, and Table 1 the structures that can be extracted from it: considering the lexical level, we can extract *Mary had lamb*, *had a lamb*, *a little lamb* as catenae. As the morpho-syntactic and syntactic levels are available, however, we can also extract partially filled structures as *Mary had NOUN*, *nsubj VERB dobj* and so on.

Of interest for our analysis, CxG argues that grammar items above the lexical level bear meaning themselves, and that this emerges from patterns of usage. According to Goldberg (2006), for example, the meaning of the ditransitive pattern *Sbj V*

---

[1]Specifically, those that contain data harvested from the web such as Wikipedia or UKWaC.

[2]an exception should be made for the formalisms derived from the FrameNet project (`https://framenet.icsi.berkeley.edu/`)

[3]which can be seen as a subtype of catena as "A catena that consists of a word plus all the words that that word dominates"

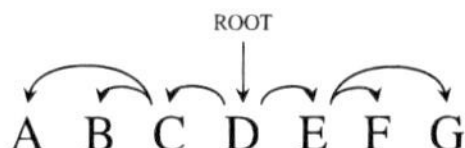

(a) The case of a flat structure, where all nodes are linked to the *root*: from a tree like this we can extract $2^6 - 1$ catenae, each one containing A plus a subset of its children nodes.

(b) The case where nodes are arranged in a full dependency chain: here the number of catenae corresponds to the number of substrings that could be extracted from the linear signal, that is 20.

(c) The case of a hierarchical structure, typically what we would find in linguistic trees, where the counts are less trivial to make. In particular, for each node we find that the number of catenae *rooted* in that node can be estimated depending on the number of catenae *rooted* in his children nodes, and depends therefore on the specific structure of the tree.

Figure 1

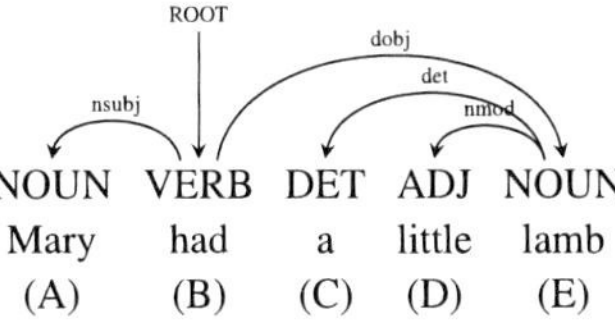

Figure 2: The dependency representation of the sentence *Mary had a little lamb*, annotated with morpho-syntactic and syntactic information.

Obj Obj2, and thus its productivity, emerges from its strong association with *give* in child-directed speech: part of the meaning of *give* remains attached to the construction. A natural, and promising (Rambelli et al., 2019), solution to represent the semantics of catenae is given by Distributional Semantics (Harris, 1954), where each element of the *'Constructicon'* is implicitly described in terms of its context of use (Erk, 2012; Lenci, 2018). We will see in §6 how we can use such distributional representations to investigate the level of abstraction of our network's babbling.

4 Data and language modelling

4.1 Corpus

Our corpus is composed of three parts, each presenting different features with respect to linguistic complexity: (1) Child-directed utterances of the publicly available North American and United Kingdom portions of the CHILDES database (MacWhinney, 2000); (2) movie and TV series subtitles from the OpenSubtitle corpus (Lison and Tiedemann, 2016), filtered by content-rating label (G for movies and TV-Y, TV-Y7, TV-G for TV series), available from *The Movie Database*[4]; (3) a 2019 snapshot of Simple English Wikipedia[5], an English-language edition of Wikipedia written in basic English.

These different corpora vary in size: for our experiments we randomly (with uniform probability) extract sentences from each source so that the total number of tokens approximates 3 millions (10% are kept for validation and 10% for testing).

4.2 Language models

For each of the considered corpora, we train a character-based LSTM on the tokenized, raw text. To do so, we slightly modify the PyTorch implementation of a vanilla LSTM.[6], adapting it to a character-based setting. We run a Bayesian optimization process (Nogueira, 2014–) to select the best hyperparameters for the corpus (values can be found in the supplementary material). We then produce a model every 5 epochs of training (for a total of 7 models for CHILDES, 9 models for Open Subtitles and 7 models for simple Wikipedia), as to be able to produce *snapshots* of the network's abilities at different stages during training. For each of the saved models, we sample[7] utterances until we reach the size of the input (the 'babbling' stage). An example of babbling is reported in Table 2.

4.3 Extracting catenae

As introduced in § 3, the outcome of the acquisition process is a language sample ℓ_i, that we want to compare to the input language I_i or to other language samples ℓ_j produced at different stages of acquisition. For the next steps, both the input text

---

[4]https://www.themoviedb.org/

[5]https://simple.wikipedia.org/

[6]https://github.com/pytorch/examples/tree/master/word_language_model

[7]The sampling happens as follows: a random initial letter is picked, with a probability depending on the distribution of letters at the beginning of sentences in the input data, then letters are sampled with a greedy algorithm until an *end of sentence* marker is reached or the length surpasses the average sentence length of the input plus 2 standard deviations.

	CHILDES	opensubtitles	simplewiki
input	you tinker tot let 's see if I can make this turn here that 's Jim 's business	this is no way to treat a lion ! re-entry into earth 's atmosphere in 37 minutes . are you worried i 'm going to try and stop you ?	She is the rector of the National Autonomous University of Honduras (UNAH) since 2009 .
best model	she 's a fire if I put it down for a snack oh I love you	some of horases are here down . just lost it all . i said we 've ... lucky .	She is a former municipality in the center of an arrondissement in the southwest of France .

Table 2: Examples from input text and babbling produced by the best model, for each corpus. Sentences have been sampled according to the distribution of sentence lengths in the data.

(the corpus) and the network's babbling are linguistically processed and annotated up to the syntactic level with the UDPipe toolkit (Straka and Straková, 2017) (a schema of the full processing pipeline is presented in Figure 3). Since our aim is to monitor the syntactic behaviour of the network throughout learning, we extract catenae from the input corpus and from each babbling stage. To do so, we perform a recursive depth-first visit of dependency trees (pseudocode is provided in the supplementary material). That is, if the node A is a leaf, then the only possible catena is the one containing A itself; otherwise, all catenae rooted in A are formed by A plus a (eventually empty) combination of catenae rooted in its children nodes.

With this procedure, we extract catenae from sentences (with length between 1 and 25). For efficiency reasons, we exclude catenae longer than 5 elements. Many structures are generated, not all of which are relevant: since we see catenae as pieces of the lexicon, frequency is not the only relevant parameter and elements should be positively associated in order to be recorded as objects. We therefore weigh the produced structures with a multivariate version of Mutual Information (MI), based on Van de Cruys (2011):

$$MI(x_1, ..., x_n) = f(x_1, ..., x_n) \log_2 \frac{p(x_1, ..., x_n)}{\prod_{i=1}^{n} p(x_i)} \quad (2)$$

where $p(x_1, ..., x_m) = \frac{f(x_1,...,x_m)}{\sum_{(y_1,...,y_m)} f(y_1,...,y_m)}$.

Table 3 shows some of the structures with highest and lowest MI: from a qualitative perspective, it is evident that the measure is able to isolate linguistically relevant patterns, such as the basic intransitive and transitive structures ($@nsubj\ @root$ and $@nsubj\ \_VERB\ @obj$).

It is important to remark that the linguistic annotation process (except for the tokenization step) and the catenae extraction processes are completely independent from the language modeling performed

catena	frequency	mi
largest mi		
@nsubj @root	294.59K	633.93K
_DET _NOUN	189.97K	552.32K
_VERB @obj	190.72K	520.82K
_PRON _VERB	271.44K	503.17K
@nsubj _AUX @root	129.60K	478.86K
smallest mi		
_PRON @nsubj	17.50K	-35.54K
@root @nsubj	27.61K	-34.89K
@nsubj _PRON	11.63K	-30.47K
_VERB @nsubj	12.79K	-26.82K
_AUX _PRON	15.75K	-26.67K

Table 3: Examples of catenae extracted from CHILDES. Largest and smallest mutual information are reported, in top and bottom tier of the table respectively. Part of Speech are prefixed by "_" and syntactic relations are prefixed by "@"

by the LSTM, which is only fed with raw text and is therefore completely agnostic about the linguistic categories superimposed by the parser.

5 What do ANNs approximate?

Our first analysis demonstrates that the language generated by the LSTM reproduces the distribution of the input, and that this happens well beyond the lexical level: in other words, the network has acquired statistical regularities at the level of grammatical patterns, and is able to use them productively to generate novel language fragments that adhere to the same distribution as the input.

Fig. 4 shows the extent of this approximation for various pairs: (i) $(\ell_i^c, \ell_j^c) \in \ell_{1...k}^c$ (language fragments output by a particular stage of babbling, for each corpus c), (ii) $(\ell_i^c, I^c), \ell_i^c \in \ell_{1...k}^c$ (fragments output by a particular stage of babbling, compared to those extracted from the respective input c), (iii) $(I^{c_i}, I^{c_j}), (BM^{c_i}, BM^{c_j}), (I^{c_i}, BM^{c_j})$ (fragments extracted from the input or the best babbling stage, compared among different corpora c_i, c_j). It emerges from the plot that correlations are very high within each corpus (on average, 0.935 for

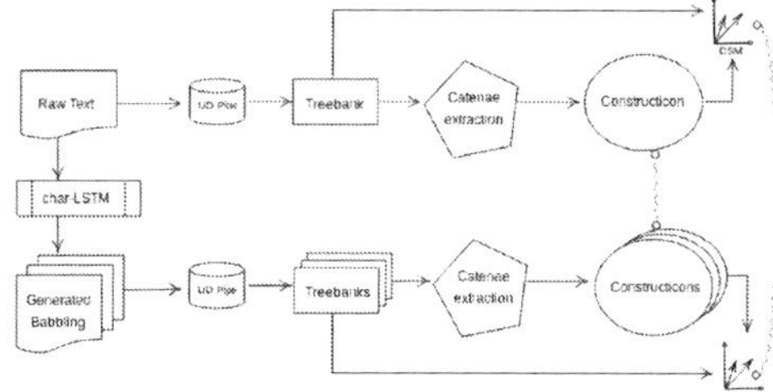

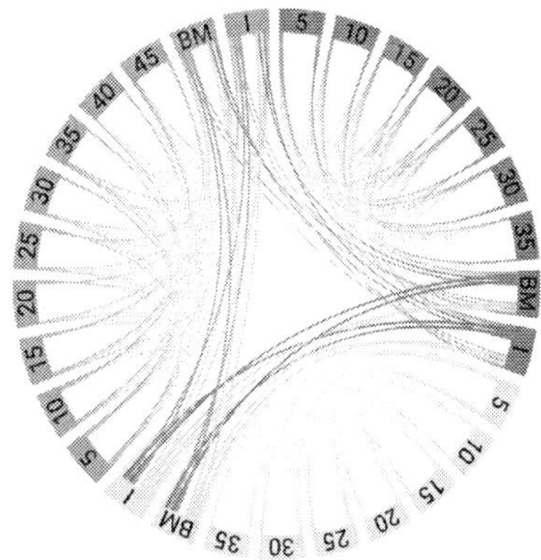

Figure 3: The figure depicts the processing pipeline used for the experiments: raw text from corpora serves as input to the LSTM, that in turn produces raw text at different training stages (i.e., the babbling). Both the corpus and the babbling texts are then processed with a NLP pipeline in order to build treebanks, from which catenae are then extracted. These extracted structures form the constructicons, which are compared in the experiments described in Section 5 (dashed line). The structures in each constructicon are then represented in a Distributional Semantic Model, through co-occurrences extracted from the respective treebanks. The distributional semantic models are then used for the experiments in § 6 (dashed line).

Figure 4: Correlation values (Spearman ρ) over top 10K catenae for each corpus (OpenSubtitles in green on the left of the plot, CHILDES in red in the top right and Simple Wikipedia in yellow at the bottom) compared to the respective babbling (at intermediate stages of learning) and the best models (BM). The thickness of the connections is inversely proportional to correlation.

CHILDES, 0.929 for OpenSubtitles and 0.917 for Simple Wikipedia). In particular, the correlations between the best models (BM) and the respective input series (I) show values that are among the highest, demonstrating that the network acquires structures and reproduces them with a distribution that almost perfectly matches the input. On the other hand, it is clear that different corpora show different distributions, as correlations between pairs of input series I and best models show much lower values[8]. Overall, CHILDES scores the best correlation values, probably due to the specific features of child-directed speech, specifically its repetitiousness Clark (2009). OpenSubtitles interestingly shows intermediate properties, sharing quite a lot of catenae with CHILDES,[9] while Simple Wikipedia shows a completely different distribution.

6 Meaning and abstraction

Our second analysis relies on the idea that we can state that the network *has learned some grammar* once it is able to use an acquired pattern in a pro-

ductive and creative way. Following the basic hypothesis of CxG, stated in § 3.3, we expect this generalization ability to evolve during training and the distributional properties of patterns to be in relation with the grammatical abilities of the network at various stages of learning.

Let's consider the structures cat_1 : *the dog* and cat_2 : *DET NOUN*. For the purpose of our analysis, we will consider (cat_1, cat_2) to be a minimal pair, as *the dog* can be considered a lexicalized instance of the more abstract construction *DET NOUN*. Using a distributional analysis, we can capture how the contexts of cat_1 and cat_2 vary, and how this variation is associated with generalization. If their cosine similarity decreases during training, it means that their contexts become more and more dissimilar: the network produces *DET NOUN* in new contexts which do not perfectly overlap with those of *the dog*, indicating that the network's babbling is becoming more productive (a graphical representation is given in Figure 5). In this case, we theorize that cat_2 has been recognised as a partially independent pattern from cat_1. If, on the contrary, their cosine similarity increases, we might deduce that the network has recognized cat_2 as partly unnecessary: it is correcting an overgeneralization.

We restrict this analysis to the CHILDES corpus. We build distributional vector spaces for the input and each stage of babbling using the DISSECT toolkit (Dinu et al., 2013). We consider catenae

---

[8]The complete set of correlation values is reported in supplementary material

[9]The Jaccard index between CHILDES and OpenSubtitles remains above 0.5, even when considering the top 1M catenae, while the same index computed between CHILDES and Simple Wikipedia drops to around 0.13.

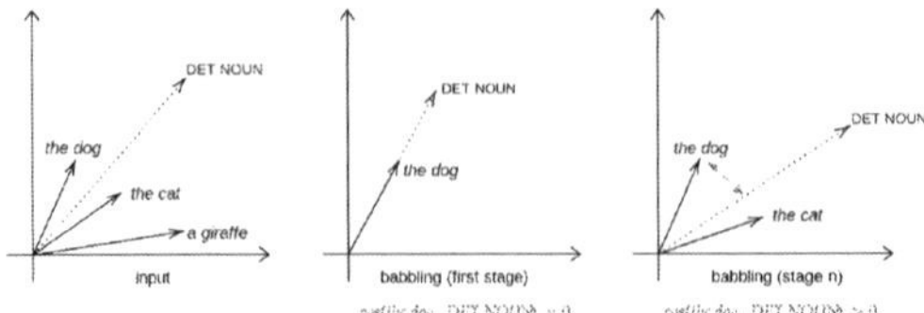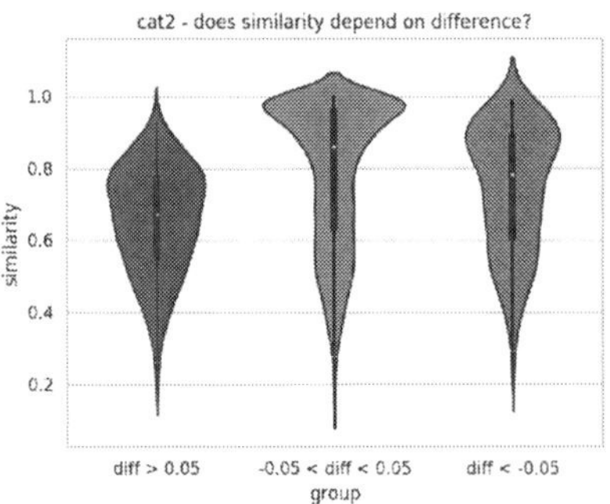

Figure 5: Let us assume that the input presents various lexicalized instances of the pattern *DET NOUN* (e.g. *the dog, the cat, a giraffe*). Our hypothesis is that the network will only be able to capture its more stereotypical instances (i.e., *the dog*), and the distributions of *the dog* and *DET NOUN* will thus almost perfectly overlap in the first stages of babbling (the length of vectors in the figure is just for exemplification). At later stages, the language produced by the network will show greater traits of productivity: the distribution of *DET NOUN* might show that its cosine distance to *the dog* has increased as it is now instantiated by two different lexicalized patterns (*the dog* and *the cat*) that are produced in dissimilar contexts.

Figure 6: Distribution of average cosine similarities for the three groups of cat_2, showing low, intermediate and high average shifts respectively.

composed by 2 or 3 elements as targets/contexts, and define co-occurrence as the presence of two catenae in the same sentence. Co-occurrences are weighted with PPMI and the space reduced to 300 dimensions with SVD. We then extract minimal pairs (cat_1, cat_2) of catenae from the input text, where cat_1 is an instance of cat_2. For each pair, we compute their cosine similarity in all distributional spaces, and the difference in cosine between the last and first babbling (see Table 4).

We then compute average distributional shifts and cosine similarities, grouping all pairs by cat_1 and cat_2 values (for instance, we average all pairs that show abstractions of cat_1 : *a minute*, as well as pairs that show instantiations of cat_2 : *DET NOUN*). Some averages are shown in Table 5.

We finally split catenae in three bins based on average distributional shift and investigate the influence of input similarity over the abstraction behaviour of a construction. Our hypothesis is that catenae that underwent the highest shifts during training were those showing intermediate levels of similarities in the input distributional space. Indeed, pairs with very high input similarities are unlikely to exhibit abstraction: according to constructionist intuition, their distributional similarity means that the catena that is part of the *Constructicon* is the least abstract one, and there is no need for the more abstract category. Low similarity pairs, on the other hand, may simply contain unrelated catenae.

To test our hypothesis, we perform a Kruskall-

Wallis one-way analysis of variance test, that turn out to be significant for groupings made on both cat_1 and cat_2 lists.[10] The result is confirmed by Dunn's posthoc test. We show results for the test performed on the cat_2 list in Table 6 and Figure 6.

7 Discussion and future work

Usage-based computational accounts have already shown to be able to explain puzzling phenomena in acquisition (Freudenthal et al., 2015; McCauley and Christiansen, 2019) or to induce syntactic rules in an unsupervised manner (Solan et al., 2005), making use of surface properties of the language signal like transitional probabilities or basic distributional analysis. However, despite being rooted in the psychological literature and yielding fundamental psycholinguistic results, the models presented in such investigations are often not comparable to studies involving neural language models, as the former are usually less flexible and less scalable to large amounts of data than the latter.

In this paper, we have reviewed relevant work concerning the assessment of grammatical abilities in neural language models and noted the lack of variety in both the input data fed to ANNs (I) and the theoretical framework used in analysing the output language (Λ). In line with the existing usage-based computational accounts, we have introduced a methodology to evaluate the level of productivity of an LSTM trained on limited, child-directed data, using inspirations from constructionist approaches.

We have been able to show that neural networks approximate the distribution of constructions at a quite refined level when trained over a bare 3M

---

[10]p = 6.988142426844016e-28 for cat_1 and p = 7.420868598608134e-32 for cat_2

cat_1	cat_2	input	BM	5	10	15	20	25	30	35	distributional shift
a minute	a _NOUN	0.28	0.32	0.71	0.51	0.44	0.39	0.38	0.37	0.34	0.37
a minute	a @root	0.13	0.19	0.49	0.37	0.26	0.20	0.21	0.22	0.20	0.30
you _VERB it	_PRON @root @expl	0.10	0.19	0.46	0.28	0.25	0.25	0.19	0.17	0.21	0.25
you _VERB you	you _VERB @iobj	0.28	0.40	0.68	0.56	0.47	0.49	0.39	0.42	0.43	0.25
we can _VERB	_PRON can @root	0.51	0.54	0.79	0.74	0.59	0.54	0.55	0.61	0.57	0.22
go _VERB @obj	_VERB @conj @obj	0.64	0.72	0.56	0.74	0.70	0.74	0.72	0.72	0.72	-0.16
_AUX hungry	@cop @conj	0.68	0.52	0.36	0.39	0.44	0.45	0.47	0.42	0.59	-0.24
can get	can @advcl	0.55	0.54	0.24	0.36	0.45	0.48	0.43	0.39	0.52	-0.28

Table 4: Pairs of catenae (cat_1, cat_2), their cosine similarity in the space obtained from CHILDES, in the space obtained from the best model (BM) and in all the intermediate models. The last column shows the difference between cosine similarity at epoch 5 and cosine similarity at epoch 35.

cat_1	shift	cosine	cat_2	shift	cosine
@nsubj @root so	0.18	0.43	more @root	0.2	0.21
@nsubj only @root	0.18	0.41	_AUX know @obj	0.19	0.66
what @root @obj	0.18	0.39	@advmod tell	0.17	0.64
what @advmod _VERB	0.16	0.19	@aux know @obj	0.16	0.71
only @root	0.16	0.38	@advmod can _VERB	0.15	0.76
more @root	0.16	0.23	know @obj	0.15	0.62
@root it @xcomp	0.15	0.61	a _NOUN	0.13	0.52
@det minute	0.15	0.25	might @root	0.13	0.70
_PRON only @root	0.15	0.53	_PRON @root n't	0.12	0.53
_VERB _DET minute	0.15	0.33	@root that _VERB	0.12	0.65
_PRON @root so	0.14	0.54	_VERB 'll @ccomp	0.12	0.71
_DET minute	0.134	0.33	_VERB me @obl	0.12	0.76

Table 5: Catenae with highest average shifts.

	negative	none	positive
negative	-	6.83e-06	4.57e-05
none	0.000	-	4.15e-29
positive	0.000	4.15e-29	-

Table 6: Dunn posthoc test on the three groups of c_2, showing low (< -0.05), intermediate ($-0.05 < x < 0.05$) and high (< 0.05) average shifts respectively.

words from the CHILDES corpus, reproducing the distribution of grammatical patterns even when they are not fully lexicalized. The analysis in § 5 indicates that the linguistic variety of OpenSubtitles is a potentially relevant benchmark to further investigate language acquisition, due to its similarity to the CHILDES data. In contrast, Simple Wikipedia has proved to be dissimilar to child-directed speech. This large difference should be taken into consideration when it comes to evaluating the grammatical abilities on the network: many of the studies cited in § 2 use models trained on Wikipedia or similar varieties, which may complicate the acquisition of generic grammatical phenomena heavily present in child-directed language. The analysis in § 6 further illustrated how we can follow paths of abstraction by putting our grammar formalism in a vector space. Additional investigations are of course needed to confirm our results. In particular, we would like to target the behavior of some

specific sets of structures.

Most importantly, the introduced methodology, despite being preliminary, presents a number of features that make our study fit in the usage-based theoretical framework while also using neural networks as language modeling tools, more specifically: (i) it posits no sharp distinction between lexicon and grammar: fully lexicalized, partially filled and purely syntactic patterns are all part of our constructicon and can play a similar role in production. Different items can therefore be represented compared, irrespective of their *lexical* nature; (ii) it makes no assumption about the stability of the constructicon: what is relevant for productivity at the earliest stages of learning might become superfluous later on; (iii) all items are seen as form-meaning pairs (i.e., constructions by definition, as in Goldberg, 2006): a novel way of modeling constructional meaning is therefore introduced and represents a promising path for future studies; (iv) distributional semantics is used both as a powerful quantitative tool and as a usage-based cognitive hypothesis, which leads us to specific assumptions about the cognitive format and origin of semantic representations (Lenci, 2008), and seems in line with the view of constructions as "invitations to form categories" (Goldberg, 2019).

Finally, we must account for potential biases introduced by applying dependency parsing to both input data and neural babbling: while this step is necessary to extract catenae, it introduces a non-negligible amount of noise, as the available pipelines are typically trained on different varieties than the ones considered in this study. In particular, the parser is somehow projecting its own categories, which have been acquired in a different setting and probably on a different variety, on our data. This currently limits the transferability of our results. Besides looking for ways to circumvent this issue, further work includes a comparison of our results with a wider choice of models.

Acknowledgements

We thank Dr. Lucia Busso for useful discussions on an earlier version of this work and Lucio Messina for helping us in condensing results into figures and tables. We gratefully acknowledge the support of NVIDIA Corporation with the donation of the Titan V GPU used for this research. We would also like to thank the anonymous reviewers for their helpful suggestions and comments.

References

Yossi Adi, Einat Kermany, Yonatan Belinkov, Ofer Lavi, and Yoav Goldberg. 2017. Fine-grained analysis of sentence embeddings using auxiliary prediction tasks. In *International Conference on LearningRepresentations*.

Afra Alishahi, Grzegorz Chrupała, and Tal Linzen. 2019. Analyzing and interpreting neural networks for nlp: A report on the first blackboxnlp workshop. *Natural Language Engineering*, 25(4):543–557.

Geoff Bacon and Terry Regier. 2019. Does bert agree? evaluating knowledge of structure dependence through agreement relations. *arXiv preprint arXiv:1908.09892*.

Colin Bannard, Elena Lieven, and Michael Tomasello. 2009. Modeling children's early grammatical knowledge. *Proceedings of the National Academy of Sciences*, 106(41):17284–17289.

Marco Baroni. 2020. Linguistic generalization and compositionality in modern artificial neural networks. *Philosophical Transactions of the Royal Society B*, 375(1791):20190307.

Helen L Bee, Lawrence F Van Egeren, Ann Pytkowicz Streissguth, Barry A Nyman, and Maxine S Leckie. 1969. Social class differences in maternal teaching strategies and speech patterns. *Developmental Psychology*, 1(6p1):726.

Noam Chomksy. 1959. Review of skinner's verbal behaviour. *Language*, 35:26–58.

Noam Chomsky. 1968. *Language and Mind*. New York: Harcourt Brace Jovanovich.

Noam Chomsky. 1981. Lectures on government and binding. *Dordrecht: Foris*.

Noam Chomsky. 1995. *The minimalist program*. MIT Press.

Shammur Absar Chowdhury and Roberto Zamparelli. 2018. Rnn simulations of grammaticality judgments on long-distance dependencies. In *Proceedings of the 27th international conference on computational linguistics*, pages 133–144.

Morten H Christiansen and Nick Chater. 2016. *Creating language: Integrating evolution, acquisition, and processing*. MIT Press.

Eve V Clark. 2009. *First language acquisition*. Cambridge University Press.

Hannah Cornish, Rick Dale, Simon Kirby, and Morten H Christiansen. 2017. Sequence memory constraints give rise to language-like structure through iterated learning. *PloS one*, 12(1).

Stephen Crain and Paul Pietroski. 2001. Nature, nurture and universal grammar. *Linguistics and philosophy*, 24(2):139–186.

Alejandrina Cristia, Emmanuel Dupoux, Michael Gurven, and Jonathan Stieglitz. 2019. Child-directed speech is infrequent in a forager-farmer population: a time allocation study. *Child development*, 90(3):759–773.

Tim Van de Cruys. 2011. Two multivariate generalizations of pointwise mutual information. In *Proceedings of the Workshop on Distributional Semantics and Compositionality*, pages 16–20. Association for Computational Linguistics.

Forrest Davis and Marten van Schijndel. 2020. Recurrent neural network language models always learn English-like relative clause attachment. In *Proceedings of the 58th Annual Meeting of the Association for Computational Linguistics*, pages 1979–1990, Online. Association for Computational Linguistics.

Georgiana Dinu, Nghia The Pham, and Marco Baroni. 2013. DISSECT - DIStributional SEmantics composition toolkit. In *Proceedings of the 51st Annual Meeting of the Association for Computational Linguistics: System Demonstrations*, pages 31–36, Sofia, Bulgaria. Association for Computational Linguistics.

Jonathan Dunn. 2017. Learnability and falsifiability of construction grammars. *Proceedings of the Linguistic Society of America*, 2:1–1.

Katrin Erk. 2012. Vector space models of word meaning and phrase meaning: A survey. *Language and Linguistics Compass*, 6(10):635–653.

Charles J Fillmore. 1988. The mechanisms of "construction grammar". In *Annual Meeting of the Berkeley Linguistics Society*, volume 14, pages 35–55.

Daniel Freudenthal, Julian M Pine, Gary Jones, and Fernand Gobet. 2015. Simulating the cross-linguistic pattern of optional infinitive errors in children's declaratives and wh-questions. *Cognition*, 143:61–76.

Mario Giulianelli, Jack Harding, Florian Mohnert, Dieuwke Hupkes, and Willem Zuidema. 2018. Under the hood: Using diagnostic classifiers to investigate and improve how language models track agreement information. In *Proceedings of the 2018*

EMNLP Workshop BlackboxNLP: Analyzing and Interpreting Neural Networks for NLP, pages 240–248.

Adele E Goldberg. 1995. *Constructions: A construction grammar approach to argument structure*. University of Chicago Press.

Adele E Goldberg. 2006. *Constructions at work: The nature of generalization in language*. Oxford University Press on Demand.

Adele E Goldberg. 2019. *Explain me this: Creativity, competition, and the partial productivity of constructions*. Princeton University Press.

Kristina Gulordava, Piotr Bojanowski, Édouard Grave, Tal Linzen, and Marco Baroni. 2018. Colorless green recurrent networks dream hierarchically. In *Proceedings of the 2018 Conference of the North American Chapter of the Association for Computational Linguistics: Human Language Technologies, Volume 1 (Long Papers)*, pages 1195–1205.

Zellig S Harris. 1954. Distributional structure. *Word*, 10(2-3):146–162.

Betty Hart and Todd R Risley. 1995. *Meaningful differences in the everyday experience of young American children*. Paul H Brookes Publishing.

Marc D Hauser, Noam Chomsky, and W Tecumseh Fitch. 2002. The faculty of language: what is it, who has it, and how did it evolve? *science*, 298(5598):1569–1579.

John Hewitt and Christopher D Manning. 2019. A structural probe for finding syntax in word representations. In *Proceedings of the 2019 Conference of the North American Chapter of the Association for Computational Linguistics: Human Language Technologies, Volume 1 (Long and Short Papers)*, pages 4129–4138.

Sepp Hochreiter and Jürgen Schmidhuber. 1997. Long short-term memory. *Neural computation*, 9(8):1735–1780.

Thomas Hoffmann, Graeme Trousdale, and Ray Jackendoff. 2013. Constructions in the parallel architecture.

Jennifer Hu, Jon Gauthier, Peng Qian, Ethan Wilcox, and Roger P Levy. 2020. A systematic assessment of syntactic generalization in neural language models. *arXiv preprint arXiv:2005.03692*.

Ganesh Jawahar, Benoît Sagot, and Djamé Seddah. 2019. What does bert learn about the structure of language? In *Proceedings of the 57th Annual Meeting of the Association for Computational Linguistics*, pages 3651–3657.

Paul Kay and Charles J Fillmore. 1999. Grammatical constructions and linguistic generalizations: the what's x doing y? construction. *Language*, pages 1–33.

Adhiguna Kuncoro, Chris Dyer, John Hale, Dani Yogatama, Stephen Clark, and Phil Blunsom. 2018. LSTMs can learn syntax-sensitive dependencies well, but modeling structure makes them better. In *Proceedings of the 56th Annual Meeting of the Association for Computational Linguistics (Volume 1: Long Papers)*, pages 1426–1436, Melbourne, Australia. Association for Computational Linguistics.

Yair Lakretz, Cognitive Neuroimaging Unit, German Kruszewski, Theo Desbordes, Dieuwke Hupkes, Stanislas Dehaene, and Marco Baroni. 2019. The emergence of number and syntax units in lstm language models. In *Proceedings of NAACL-HLT*, pages 11–20.

Alessandro Lenci. 2008. Distributional semantics in linguistic and cognitive research. *Italian journal of linguistics*, 20(1):1–31.

Alessandro Lenci. 2018. Distributional models of word meaning. *Annual review of Linguistics*, 4:151–171.

Michael A Lepori, Tal Linzen, and R Thomas McCoy. 2020. Representations of syntax [mask] useful: Effects of constituency and dependency structure in recursive lstms. *arXiv preprint arXiv:2005.00019*.

John D Lewis and Jeffrey L Elman. 2001. Learnability and the statistical structure of language: Poverty of stimulus arguments revisited. In *Proceedings of the 26th annual Boston University conference on language development*, volume 1, pages 359–370. Citeseer.

David J Lewkowicz, Mark A Schmuckler, and Diane MJ Mangalindan. 2018. Learning of hierarchical serial patterns emerges in infancy. *Developmental psychobiology*, 60(3):243–255.

Yongjie Lin, Yi Chern Tan, and Robert Frank. 2019. Open sesame: Getting inside bert's linguistic knowledge. In *Proceedings of the 2019 ACL Workshop BlackboxNLP: Analyzing and Interpreting Neural Networks for NLP*, pages 241–253.

Tal Linzen and Marco Baroni. 2020. Syntactic structure from deep learning. *arXiv preprint arXiv:2004.10827*.

Tal Linzen, Emmanuel Dupoux, and Yoav Goldberg. 2016. Assessing the ability of lstms to learn syntax-sensitive dependencies. *Transactions of the Association for Computational Linguistics*, 4:521–535.

Pierre Lison and Jörg Tiedemann. 2016. Opensubtitles2016: Extracting large parallel corpora from movie and tv subtitles.

Barbara Lust. 1999. Universal grammar: The strong continuity hypothesis in first language acquisition. *Handbook of Child Language Acquisition*.

Brian MacWhinney. 2000. *The CHILDES Project: Tools for analyzing talk. Third Edition*. Lawrence Erlbaum Associates.

Rebecca Marvin and Tal Linzen. 2018. Targeted syntactic evaluation of language models. In *Proceedings of the 2018 Conference on Empirical Methods in Natural Language Processing*, pages 1192–1202.

Danielle Matthews and Colin Bannard. 2010. Children's production of unfamiliar word sequences is predicted by positional variability and latent classes in a large sample of child-directed speech. *Cognitive science*, 34(3):465–488.

Stewart M McCauley and Morten H Christiansen. 2019. Language learning as language use: A cross-linguistic model of child language development. *Psychological review*, 126(1):1.

James L McClelland. 1992. Can connectionist models discover the structure of natural language. *Minds, Brains and Computers*, pages 168–189.

R Thomas McCoy, Robert Frank, and Tal Linzen. 2018. Revisiting the poverty of the stimulus: hierarchical generalization without a hierarchical bias in recurrent neural networks. In *Proceedings of the 40th Annual Conference of the Cognitive Science Society*.

R Thomas McCoy, Robert Frank, and Tal Linzen. 2020. Does syntax need to grow on trees? sources of hierarchical inductive bias in sequence-to-sequence networks. *arXiv preprint arXiv:2001.03632*.

Joakim Nivre, Marie-Catherine de Marneffe, Filip Ginter, Jan Hajic, Christopher D Manning, Sampo Pyysalo, Sebastian Schuster, Francis Tyers, and Daniel Zeman. 2020. Universal dependencies v2: An evergrowing multilingual treebank collection. In *Proceedings of The 12th Language Resources and Evaluation Conference*, pages 4034–4043.

Fernando Nogueira. 2014–. Bayesian Optimization: Open source constrained global optimization tool for Python.

Timothy Osborne. 2006. Beyond the constituent-a dependency grammar analysis of chains. *Folia Linguistica*, 39(3-4):251–297.

Timothy Osborne and Thomas Groß. 2012. Constructions are catenae: Construction grammar meets dependency grammar.

Timothy Osborne, Michael Putnam, and Thomas Groß. 2012. Catenae: Introducing a novel unit of syntactic analysis. *Syntax*, 15(4):354–396.

Timothy J Osborne. 2018. Tests for constituents: What they really reveal about the nature of syntactic structure. *Language Under Discussion*, 5(1):1–41.

Giulia Rambelli, Emmanuele Chersoni, Philippe Blache, Chu-Ren Huang, and Alessandro Lenci. 2019. Distributional semantics meets construction grammar. towards a unified usage-based model of grammar and meaning. In *Proceedings of the First International Workshop on Designing Meaning Representations*, pages 110–120.

Shauli Ravfogel, Yoav Goldberg, and Francis Tyers. 2018. Can lstm learn to capture agreement? the case of basque. In *Proceedings of the 2018 EMNLP Workshop BlackboxNLP: Analyzing and Interpreting Neural Networks for NLP*, pages 98–107.

Yikang Shen, Shawn Tan, Alessandro Sordoni, and Aaron Courville. 2018. Ordered neurons: Integrating tree structures into recurrent neural networks. In *International Conference on Learning Representations*.

Zach Solan, David Horn, Eytan Ruppin, and Shimon Edelman. 2005. Unsupervised learning of natural languages. *Proceedings of the National Academy of Sciences*, 102(33):11629–11634.

Milan Straka and Jana Straková. 2017. Tokenizing, pos tagging, lemmatizing and parsing ud 2.0 with udpipe. In *Proceedings of the CoNLL 2017 Shared Task: Multilingual Parsing from Raw Text to Universal Dependencies*, pages 88–99, Vancouver, Canada. Association for Computational Linguistics.

Ian Tenney, Patrick Xia, Berlin Chen, Alex Wang, Adam Poliak, R Thomas McCoy, Najoung Kim, Benjamin Van Durme, Samuel Bowman, Dipanjan Das, et al. 2019. What do you learn from context? probing for sentence structure in contextualized word representations. In *7th International Conference on Learning Representations, ICLR 2019*.

Michael Tomasello. 2003. *Constructing a language: A usage-based theory of language acquisition*. Harvard University Press.

Ke M Tran, Arianna Bisazza, and Christof Monz. 2018. The importance of being recurrent for modeling hierarchical structure. In *Proceedings of the 2018 Conference on Empirical Methods in Natural Language Processing*, pages 4731–4736.

Alex Warstadt, Alicia Parrish, Haokun Liu, Anhad Mohananey, Wei Peng, Sheng-Fu Wang, and Samuel R Bowman. 2019. Blimp: A benchmark of linguistic minimal pairs for english. *arXiv preprint arXiv:1912.00582*.

Ethan Wilcox, Roger Levy, Takashi Morita, and Richard Futrell. 2018. What do rnn language models learn about filler–gap dependencies? In *Proceedings of the 2018 EMNLP Workshop BlackboxNLP: Analyzing and Interpreting Neural Networks for NLP*, pages 211–221.

A simple repair mechanism can alleviate computational demands of pragmatic reasoning: simulations and complexity analysis

Jacqueline van Arkel[1] Marieke Woensdregt[2] Mark Dingemanse[2] Mark Blokpoel[3]

[1]Faculty of Science and Engineering, University of Groningen, Groningen, the Netherlands
[2]Centre for Language Studies, Radboud University, Nijmegen, the Netherlands
[3]Donders Centre for Cognition, Radboud University, Nijmegen, the Netherlands
jacquelinevanarkel@gmail.com, m.woensdregt@let.ru.nl
m.dingemanse@let.ru.nl, m.blokpoel@donders.ru.nl

Abstract

How can people communicate successfully while keeping resource costs low in the face of ambiguity? We present a principled theoretical analysis comparing two strategies for disambiguation in communication: (i) pragmatic reasoning, where communicators reason about each other, and (ii) other-initiated repair, where communicators signal and resolve trouble interactively. Using agent-based simulations and computational complexity analyses, we compare the efficiency of these strategies in terms of communicative success, computation cost and interaction cost. We show that agents with a simple repair mechanism can increase efficiency, compared to pragmatic agents, by reducing their computational burden at the cost of longer interactions. We also find that efficiency is highly contingent on the mechanism, highlighting the importance of explicit formalisation and computational rigour.

1 Introduction

Natural languages are rife with ambiguity (Wasow et al., 2005), yet people seem to communicate efficiently regardless. How can people communicate successfully in the face of ambiguity while keeping resource costs low? There seem to be at least three strategies communicators have at their disposal. First, contextual information can be used to disambiguate the speaker's intended meaning (Piantadosi et al., 2012; Sperber and Wilson, 1986; MacDonald et al., 1994), though context-sensitive computations are notorious in computational cognitive science for the astronomical demands they make on computation time (Fodor, 2000; Haselager, 1997; van Rooij et al., 2011). Second, pragmatic reasoning allows taking into account the speaker's goal (e.g. 'being informative') (Grice, 1975; Sperber and Wilson, 1986; Goodman and Frank, 2016), but this alone is not always enough to fully disambiguate

meaning (Schegloff, 1992). Finally, communicators can leverage the interaction itself by explicitly requesting clarification (e.g. by asking 'Huh?' or 'Who?') in a process known as other-initiated repair (Schegloff et al., 1977; Purver et al., 2018). This provides a possible way for communicators to reduce their computational burden through interaction, potentially increasing communicative efficiency (Dingemanse, 2020).

To investigate the computational plausibility of this potential gain in communicative efficiency we present a theoretical analysis of other-initiated repair and pragmatic reasoning. Following Gibson et al. (2019), we define efficient communication as communication in which participants reach mutual understanding while requiring minimal effort in terms of resource costs (deconstructed here as the sum of computational and interactional cost). We compare a novel agent-based model of other-initiated repair with one of pragmatic reasoning (Goodman and Frank, 2016) for both their communicative success and use of computational and interactional resources. Simulations are used to evaluate the models' success and interactional resource costs while a computational complexity analysis is used to determine the computational resource demands (van Rooij, 2008; van Rooij et al., 2019).

The results show that, on roughly equal terms of communicative success, agents with a simple repair mechanism can reduce their computational burden compared to pragmatic agents, at the cost of longer interactions. While this shows that an efficiency-increasing trade-off is in principle possible, the question remains whether the computational advantage scales to more complex forms of other-initiated repair. The work we present here makes two contributions: 1) a proof of concept that a simple form of repair can help communicators outsource computational demands in interaction, and 2) a framework for the careful theoretical anal-

177

Proceedings of the 24th Conference on Computational Natural Language Learning, pages 177–194
Online, November 19-20, 2020. ©2020 Association for Computational Linguistics
https://doi.org/10.18653/v1/P17

ysis of the interplay of cognitive and interactional resources in human communication.

2 Background

A computational model of pragmatic reasoning in communication that is widely used and has been shown to fit empirical data of human communicative behaviour well, is the rational speech act (RSA) model (Frank and Goodman, 2012; Goodman and Frank, 2016). This model formalises communication as rational behaviour in which a speaker chooses an utterance by maximising its utility, where utility is defined as the probability that the listener will correctly infer the speaker's communicative intention[1]. This means that the speaker reasons about a listener when choosing an utterance. Likewise, the listener in the RSA model reasons about a speaker by inverting this model of rational utterance production: inferring what the speaker's most likely communicative intention is given the utterance produced (using Bayesian inference). Thus, both RSA production and RSA interpretation consist of a chain of recursive social reasoning, eventually bottoming out in a literal (i.e. zero-order) speaker or listener, which is where the interaction is grounded in semantic meaning. We take this model as our basis to implement pragmatic reasoning for disambiguation in communication.

As mentioned above, another mechanism that human communicators use to reach mutual understanding is repair (Schegloff et al., 1977; Clark and Schaefer, 1987). Cross-linguistic work on informal face-to-face conversation has shown that repair is frequent (on average once every 1.4 minutes) and that it is highly similar in form and function across unrelated languages (Dingemanse et al., 2015). Attested repair initiations fall into three basic types, which differ in the grasp they display of the trouble source: (i) *open request* (e.g. 'Huh?'), (ii) *restricted request* (e.g. 'Who?') and (iii) *restricted offer* (e.g. 'At the market?'). These types are used according to similar principles across languages, with participants requesting clarification when necessary and reusing material when possible, resulting in repair sequences that appear to minimise the joint effort of speaker and listener (Dingemanse et al., 2015; Clark and Wilkes-Gibbs, 1986).

Interactive repair is a universal and frequently used mechanism for resolving trouble in communication. Here we hypothesise that it provides an affordance that inference based on context or pragmatic reasoning does not: it allows at least part of the computational burden of making inferences to be offloaded onto interaction, in effect distributing the process of reaching mutual understanding over multiple interactional turns (Dingemanse, 2020). This can be seen as a form of cognitive offloading (Risko and Gilbert, 2016), with turns at talk constituting material symbols that can augment cognitive processes (Clark, 2006). In this paper we combine agent-based simulations with a computational complexity analysis to investigate the relative resource demands of pragmatic reasoning and interactive repair. We aim to find out whether other-initiated repair can increase communicative efficiency by relieving communicators of the computational demands of pragmatic reasoning, without that causing a decrease in communicative success.

3 Methods

3.1 Computational models[2]

We use agent-based simulations to compare the communicative efficiency (in terms of both success and resource costs) of other-initiated repair (OIR) and pragmatic reasoning. As reviewed above, people use both strategies for disambiguation in natural conversation. Here, however, we separate them in order to create a baseline comparison between the two. We design two separate models: (i) an interactional model, in which agents have the ability to use repair, but do not use pragmatic reasoning, and (ii) a pragmatic model, in which agents use pragmatic reasoning, but do not have the ability to use repair.

Both models of communication start from a lexicon consisting of binary signal-referent mappings (see Table 1 for an example). Depending on the model of communication (interactional or pragmatic), speakers and listeners use this lexicon in different ways in order to arrive at signal productions and interpretations.

3.1.1 Interactional model

In the interactional model, agents are literal communicators who do not use pragmatic reasoning but can initiate repair. The main innovation we present here is a model of other-initiated repair

---

[1] We use the conventional 'speaker' and 'listener', though we are aware that natural languages are produced and perceived in diverse modalities.

[2] The implementation code and simulation data are available at: `https://osf.io/fxphv/`.

	r_1	r_2	r_3	r_4
s_1	0	1	1	0
s_2	1	0	1	0
s_3	1	1	0	0
s_4	1	0	0	1

Table 1: Example of a simple lexicon. s denotes a signal, and r a referent. This lexicon has an ambiguity level of 0.5: every signal is associated with half of the referents.

governed by the listener's level of certainty about the speaker's intended referent. Our model consists of three parts. First, after each signal production by the speaker, we measure the listener's uncertainty as the conditional entropy of the probability distribution over referents given the signal (MacKay, 2003). Second, we define an entropy threshold parameter which simulates the amount of uncertainty that the listener is willing to tolerate: when a listener's uncertainty falls above this threshold (i.e. uncertainty is too high), they initiate repair using an open request (which one can think of as saying 'Huh?' or 'What did you say?') (for a related use of entropy as a trigger for repair, see de Ruiter and Cummins, 2012). Finally, we provide a simple mechanism for solving the ambiguity problem indicated by the listener: the speaker can send another signal associated with the intended referent, and the listener then performs a conjunction operation to determine what referents are in the intersection of the current signal and the previous signal(s), thereby (potentially) reducing referential uncertainty. When the conditional entropy of the listener's probability distribution over referents given the signal(s) received falls below the entropy threshold (i.e. when uncertainty is low enough), an interpretation is reached by choosing the referent that has maximum posterior probability.

For example, imagine a speaker with an intention to communicate referent 2 who has just uttered signal 3 based on the lexicon in Table 1. After the listener has initiated repair, the speaker utters signal 1, which leads to the association vector of $[0, 1, 0, 0]$ after conjunction, and now the listener can be certain referent 2 is the speaker's intended referent. Below we give a computational-level description of production and interpretation in this interactional model.

PRODUCTION

Input: A set of signals S, a set of referents R, a lexicon $\mathcal{L} : S \times R \to \mathbb{B}$ mapping signal-referent pairs to a Boolean value. We write $\mathcal{L}(s)$ to denote the list of values for all referents given signal s. A dialogue history D_r which is a set of signals produced earlier in a conversation $\{s, \dots\}$. The dialogue history D_r is relative to the intended referent r by the speaker. An order of pragmatic inference $n = 0$. And finally an intended referent $r \in R$.

Output: The signal s that maximizes the probability $\Pr_{S_0}^S(s \mid r, \mathcal{L}_{D_r})$, where

$$\mathcal{L}_{D_r}(s, r) = \mathcal{L}(s, r) \bigwedge_{s' \in D_r} \mathcal{L}(s', r)$$

For interactional production, the following equations are relevant:

$$\Pr_{S_0}^S(s \mid r, \mathcal{L}_{D_r}) = \delta_S(s|r, \mathcal{L}_{D_r}) \tag{1}$$

$$\delta_S(s|r, \mathcal{L}_{D_r}) = \frac{\mathcal{L}_{D_r}(s, r)}{\sum_{s' \in S} \mathcal{L}_{D_r}(s', r)} \tag{2}$$

Equation 1 shows the probability of a signal s given the intended referent r and the lexicon updated according to the dialogue history $\mathcal{L}_{D_r}$. For an interactional speaker (who uses literal production), this probability is given by Equation 2, which normalises the lexicon over signals, given the intended referent.

INTERPRETATION

Input: $\mathcal{L}$, $\mathcal{L}(s)$, and D_r as defined for the production model above. An order of pragmatic inference $n = 0$. An entropy threshold H_t determining whether the entropy H is too high or sufficiently low. And finally an observed signal $s \in S$.

Output: $\mathcal{L}_{D_r}(s, r)$ as defined for the production model above. Let $\Pr_{L_0}^L(r \mid s, \mathcal{L}_{D_r})$ provide the posterior distribution over referents given s and $\mathcal{L}_{D_r}$, and let $H(R|s, \mathcal{L}_{D_r})$ be the conditional entropy (i.e. uncertainty) of that distribution. The output is of one of two types: a repair signal, or an inferred referent given the signal and dialogue history:

$$\begin{cases} \text{repair signal} & \text{if } H(R|s, \mathcal{L}_{D_r}) \\ & \quad > H_t \\ \arg\max_{r \in R} \Pr_{L_0}^L(r \mid s, \mathcal{L}_{D_r}) & \text{if } H(R|s, \mathcal{L}_{D_r}) \\ & \quad \leq H_t \end{cases}$$

For interactional interpretation, the following equations are relevant:

$$\Pr_{L_0}^L(r \mid s, \mathcal{L}_{D_r}) = \delta_L(r|s, \mathcal{L}_{D_r}) \tag{3}$$

$$\delta_L(r|s, \mathcal{L}_{D_r}) = \frac{\mathcal{L}_{D_r}(s, r)}{\sum_{r' \in R} \mathcal{L}_{D_r}(s, r')} \quad (4)$$

$$H(R|s, \mathcal{L}_{D_r}) = \sum_{r \in R} \Pr(r \mid s, \mathcal{L}_{D_r}) \times$$

$$\log_2 \frac{1}{\Pr(r \mid s, \mathcal{L}_{D_r})} \quad (5)$$

Equation 3 shows the probability of a referent r given the received signal s and the lexicon updated according to the dialogue history $\mathcal{L}_{D_r}$. For an interactional listener (who uses literal interpretation), this probability is given by Equation 4, which normalises the lexicon over referents given the received signal. Finally, the conditional entropy of the probability distribution over referents given the signal and the lexicon updated according to the dialogue history is shown in Equation 5.

3.1.2 Pragmatic model

The pragmatic model is based on the RSA framework (Frank and Goodman, 2012; Goodman and Frank, 2016). This framework models pragmatic reasoning as a chain of social recursion, in which the speaker reasons about the listener when choosing a signal, and the listener reasons about the speaker when interpreting a signal. Figure 1 shows the chain of reasoning used in the current model.

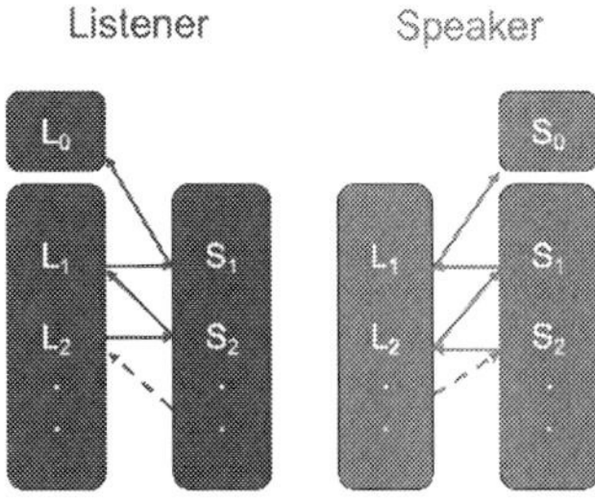

Figure 1: Pragmatic reasoning model for listener and speaker. Arrow direction represents a 'reasons about' relationship, illustrating the recursive reasoning being done by the agents. Agents reason about increasingly lower levels, eventually bottoming out in a literal listener or speaker respectively.

In order to not stack the deck against the pragmatic agents in terms of computational burden, we further distinguish between two subtypes of pragmatic agents: 'frugally pragmatic' and 'fully pragmatic'. A frugally pragmatic listener starts out at a low level of social recursion (order $n = 1$), and only 'levels up' to a higher order of pragmatic reasoning $(n + 1)$ when too uncertain about the speaker's intended referent. Thus, they decide how to proceed based on their own uncertainty, somewhat analogously to how the interactional listener decides whether to initiate repair. In contrast, a fully pragmatic listener starts at the maximum order of pragmatic reasoning straight away (here we cap pragmatic reasoning at order 2, as previous simulation work has shown that orders higher than 2 yield diminishing returns in terms of communicative success; Blokpoel et al., 2020). As this paper focuses on disambiguation by the listener, we keep the speaker model that these two subtypes of pragmatic listener interact with constant: a 'fully pragmatic' speaker who starts at the maximum order of pragmatic reasoning straight away. Below we give a computational-level description of production and interpretation in this pragmatic model.

PRODUCTION
Input: $\mathcal{L}$ and $\mathcal{L}(s)$ as defined above (see Production in Interactional Model; Section 3.1.1). An order of pragmatic inference $n = 2$, and an intended referent $r \in R$.
Output: The signal s that maximizes the probability $\Pr^S_{S_n}(s \mid r, \mathcal{L})$.

$$\Pr^S_{S_n}(s \mid r, \mathcal{L}) = \frac{\Pr^S_{L_n}(r \mid s, \mathcal{L})}{\sum_{s' \in S} \Pr^S_{L_n}(r \mid s', \mathcal{L})} \quad (6)$$

$$\Pr^S_{L_n}(r \mid s, \mathcal{L}) = \frac{\Pr^S_{S_{n-1}}(s \mid r, \mathcal{L})}{\sum_{r' \in R} \Pr^S_{S_{n-1}}(s \mid r', \mathcal{L})} \quad (7)$$

$$\Pr^S_{S_0}(s \mid r, \mathcal{L}) = \delta_S(s|r, \mathcal{L}) \quad (8)$$

$$\delta_S(s|r, \mathcal{L}) = \frac{\mathcal{L}(s, r)}{\sum_{s' \in S} \mathcal{L}(s', r)} \quad (9)$$

For pragmatic production, the speaker reasons about the listener (Equation 6), who in turn reasons about the speaker being one order of pragmatic reasoning below (Equation 7). Finally, this bottoms out to reasoning about a literal (zero-order) speaker (Equation 8), where the normalised lexicon comes into play (Equation 9).

INTERPRETATION
Input: $\mathcal{L}$ and $\mathcal{L}(s)$ as defined above (see Production in Interactional Model; Section 3.1.1). An order of pragmatic inference n with a maximum at $n_{max} = 2$. An entropy threshold H_t determining whether the entropy H is too high or sufficiently

low. And finally an observed signal $s \in S$.

Output: Let $\mathrm{Pr}^L_{L_n}(r \mid s, \mathcal{L})$ be the posterior distribution over referents given s and $\mathcal{L}$, and let $H(R|s, \mathcal{L})$ be the conditional entropy (i.e. uncertainty) of that distribution. The output is an inferred referent r given the signal, if needed by moving a level up on the order of pragmatic reasoning:

$$
\begin{cases}
\text{RSA INTERPRETATION}(n+1) & \text{if } H(R|s, \mathcal{L}) \\
& > H_t, \text{ and} \\
& n < n_{max} \\
\arg\max_{r \in R} \mathrm{Pr}^L_{L_n}(r \mid s, \mathcal{L}) & \text{if } H(R|s, \mathcal{L}) \\
& \leq H_t, \text{ or} \\
& n = n_{max}
\end{cases}
$$

$$
\mathrm{Pr}^L_{L_n}(r \mid s, \mathcal{L}) = \frac{\mathrm{Pr}^L_{S_n}(s \mid r, \mathcal{L})}{\sum_{r' \in R} \mathrm{Pr}^L_{S_n}(s \mid r', \mathcal{L})} \quad (10)
$$

$$
\mathrm{Pr}^L_{S_n}(s \mid r, \mathcal{L}) = \frac{\mathrm{Pr}^L_{L_{n-1}}(r \mid s, \mathcal{L})}{\sum_{s' \in S} \mathrm{Pr}^L_{L_{n-1}}(r \mid s', \mathcal{L})} \quad (11)
$$

$$
\mathrm{Pr}^L_{L_0}(r \mid s, \mathcal{L}) = \delta_L(r|s, \mathcal{L}) \quad (12)
$$

$$
\delta_L(r|s, \mathcal{L}) = \frac{\mathcal{L}(s, r)}{\sum_{r' \in R} \mathcal{L}(s, r')} \quad (13)
$$

$$
H(R|s, \mathcal{L}) = \sum_{r \in R} \mathrm{Pr}(r \mid s, \mathcal{L}) \times
$$

$$
\log_2 \frac{1}{\mathrm{Pr}(r \mid s, \mathcal{L})} \quad (14)
$$

For pragmatic interpretation, the listener reasons about the speaker (Equation 10), who in turn reasons about the listener being one order of pragmatic reasoning below (Equation 11). This bottoms out to reasoning about a literal (zero-order) listener (Equation 12), where the normalised lexicon comes into play (Equation 13). Finally, the conditional entropy of the probability distribution over referents given the signal is shown in Equation 14.

3.2 Complexity theory

Computational-level models such as those above have very specific computational resource demands. These demands can be analysed using mathematical proof techniques from computational complexity theory (Garey and Johnson, 1979). A model's resource demands (also referred to as computational complexity) are defined by the worst-case running time of the fastest possible algorithm that computes the specified input-output mapping. Worst-case complexity is most appropriate assuming that all instances from the model's input domain may possibly occur.[3] The computational complexity of a model can be proven by reduction or by proposing an algorithm, and is given in terms of the input size of the model (e.g., the size of the lexicon).

In the first method (reduction), one constructs a mathematical relationship, i.e., a polynomial-time reduction, between the model of interest (say M_I) and a model who's complexity is known (say M_K). A reduction proves that either M_I is a special case of M_K or the other way around.[4] Depending on the complexity of M_K, the reduction may inform us about the complexity of M_I. If M_I reduces to M_K and M_K is easy, then M_I must be easy too, because we can use the 'fast' algorithm that exists for M_K to compute M_I. If M_K reduces to M_I and M_K is hard, then M_I must be hard too, otherwise if M_I would be easy, we could compute M_K easily too. A reduction is denoted as $A \leq B$, where A reduces to B.

$$
M_I \text{ is easy} \iff M_I \leq M_K \text{ and } M_K \text{ is easy}
$$
$$
M_I \text{ is hard} \iff M_I \geq M_K \text{ and } M_K \text{ is hard}
$$

Polynomial time reductions can be used to prove that models are easy or hard. Easy models belong to the complexity class P and for these models there exist polynomial-time (or faster) algorithms. Hard models belong to class NP-hard; these models are as hard as all other models in NP and require exponential time or worse, assuming that $P \neq NP$. See Table 2 for example resource requirements.

In the second method (proposing an algorithm), one creates an algorithm that computes the model *exactly* and then analyses the algorithm's complexity profile. Unless one can prove the algorithm is the fastest, this method gives an upperbound on the model's computational complexity. This method affords comparison between models of similar complexity class. This is the method we use to deter-

---

[3] If one finds this assumption to generic, one can propose a restricted special case model. Such a model may have a different computational complexity. Parameterized complexity analysis (Downey and Fellows, 1999; van Rooij et al., 2019) is a sophisticated approach for investigating various special case models.

[4] A polynomial-time reduction from A to B does not strictly prove a special case relationship. Formally it proves that at polynomial cost any input of A can be transformed into an equivalent input for B such that the output of B is consistent with the output of A.

mine the complexity of the interactional and pragmatic models, because they are both polynomial-time computable. We illustrate this method using matrix row normalization. Given a definition of basic computation step (e.g., multiplication), input size (e.g., $\max(|\text{rows}|, |\text{columns}|)$) and an algorithm (see Algorithm 1), one expresses the number of required computation steps. Here, n^2 computations steps are required.

Algorithm 1: Matrix row normalization taking $2kl = n^2$ steps, where $n = \max(k, l)$.

Data: M is a $k \times l$ matrix

```
1  for i ← 1 to k do
2  │   for j ← 1 to l do
3  │   │   S_i ← S_i + M_ij ;      // k x l steps
4  │   end
5  end
6  for i ← 1 to k do
7  │   for j ← 1 to l do
8  │   │   M_ij ← M_ij/S_i ;       // k x l steps
9  │   end
10 end
```

		Easy		**Hard**
n	$\log n$	n	n^3	2^n
5	.0069ms	.5ms	12.5ms	3.2ms
20	.013ms	2ms	.8s	105s
50	.017ms	5mss	1.3s	31,274,997h
100	.020ms	10ms	100s	9.6×10^{19}y
250	.026ms	25mss	26min	1.4×10^{65}y
500	.027ms	50mss	3.5h	9.6×10^{140}y

Table 2: Illustration of time required to compute models of varying complexity with input size n.

Using the second method, we derived upper bounds on the computational complexity of each model (see Appendix B for the full proofs). Table 3 shows the computational complexity for the different agent types.

Interactional	Frugally pragmatic	Fully pragmatic
$2m(t - 1) +$ $2mt + 2m$	**1:** $16m^2 + 4m$ **2:** $20m^2 + 4m$	$20m^2 + 2m$

Table 3: Computational complexity comparison across agent types. m denotes the maximum of $|S|$ and $|R|$ (number of signals and referents, respectively), and t denotes the number of turns. Frugally pragmatic agents may end up in one of two scenarios: either (1) they are sufficiently certain about their 1st-order inference or (2) they will make an additional 2nd-order inference.

3.3 Simulation details

For the purposes of this paper, we assume that there is no disparity between the agent types within a given speaker-listener pair, meaning that interactional speakers always converse with an interactional listener, and pragmatic speakers always converse with a pragmatic listener. This provides a clear-cut contrast to compare the effect of OIR versus pragmatic reasoning on efficiency in communication.

We ran simulations to see which agent type performs best at communicating efficiently (which we break down into communicative success and resource costs). These simulations consist of a set of interactions between two agents. An interaction starts with the speaker being assigned a randomly chosen intended referent, and ends when the listener reaches an interpretation based on the signal(s) sent by the speaker. If the agents are of the interactional type, they can use multiple turns; if the agents are pragmatic, the speaker can only send one signal. We cap the number of turns at $2 \times |S| - 1$, to make sure agents do not get stuck in an infinite loop of other-initiated repair. In addition to interacting agents being of the same type, we also assume that there is no asymmetry between interacting agents: they always share the same lexicon.

In the simulations described below, we looked at three different lexicon sizes ($|S| \times |R|$=6x4, 15x10, and 30x20) in order to investigate how the efficiency of the different strategies scales with lexicon size. We kept the ambiguity of the lexicons constant at a moderate level of 0.5 (given that we are interested in disambiguation), and the entropy threshold constant at $H_t = 1.0$ bits (which corresponds approximately to a probability distribution where most of the probability mass is distributed equally over two referents).Following Blokpoel et al. (2020), we define lexicon ambiguity as mean signal ambiguity, and signal ambiguity as the relative number of referents a signal is associated with. Appendix A shows additional simulation results that explore the effects of varying the ambiguity level and entropy threshold parameters.

For each combination of parameter settings, we randomly generate 1,000 lexicons of the corresponding size and ambiguity level, and have the corresponding pair of agents interact for $2 \times |R|$ times (about randomly selected referential intentions). We constrain the set of possible lexicons such that (i) each referent has at least one signal associated with it, and (ii) each signal has an equal level of ambiguity. The latter constraint is to avoid potential effects of skewed ambiguity (e.g. when half of the signals refer to all referents and the other signals to none, in the case of a mean ambiguity of 0.5) (Blokpoel et al., 2020).

3.4 Measures: Communicative success and resource costs

For each simulation, we measured (i) the communicative success, (ii) the interactional cost, and (iii) the computational cost. We define communicative success as 1.0 if the listener's interpretation matches the speaker's intended referent, and 0.0 otherwise. We define interactional cost as the number of turns (i.e. the total number of signals and repair initiators that are sent back and forth between speaker and listener). Computational resource requirements are based on the complexity upper bound derived for each model (see Table 3 and Appendix B).

4 Results

Figure 2a shows the mean communicative success for the different agent types and lexicon sizes. The frugally pragmatic listeners were always sufficiently certain about the intended referent of the speaker when using a lexicon of size 6x4, resulting in the agents staying with their first order inference for that lexicon size. For the lexicon sizes of 15x10 and 30x20, the frugally pragmatic listeners were always too *un*certain about the speaker's intended referent, and therefore always went up to order $n = 2$.[5]

As Figure 2a shows, the pragmatic agents have an advantage in terms of communicative success for the smallest lexicon size (6x4), while for bigger lexicon sizes (15x10 and 30x20) the interactional agents have an advantage. This can be accounted for by the fact that the interactional agents do not use OIR for a lexicon with only 4 referents and an ambiguity level of 0.5 (see Figure 2b), as they are already certain enough[6], and therefore choose ran-

---

[5]This model behaviour depends on the entropy threshold (lower values mean agents tolerate less uncertainty), ambiguity level (more ambiguous lexicons lead to more uncertainty), and lexicon size (larger lexicons result in more dispersed probability distributions, which causes higher uncertainty). See Appendix A for results with different parameter settings.

[6]Recall that the entropy threshold of 1.0 bits corresponds approximately to an equal distribution of probability mass over two referents.

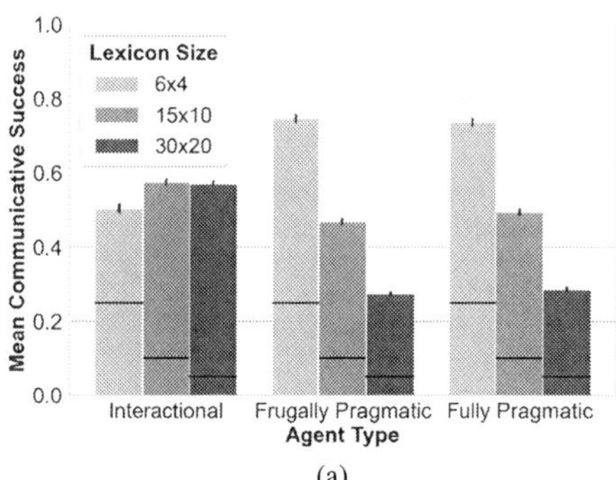

(a)

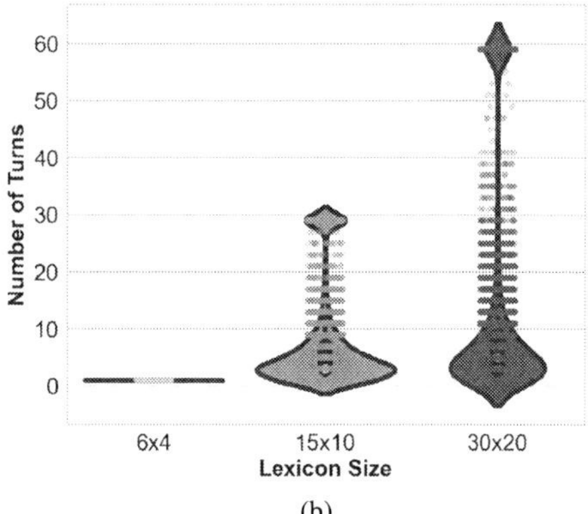

(b)

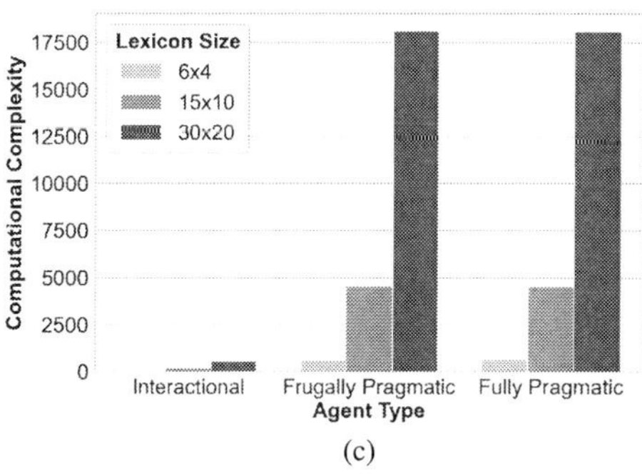

(c)

Figure 2: (a) Communicative success by agent type and lexicon size (horizontal lines indicate chance level, error bars 95% CIs). (b) Number of turns by lexicon size (interactional agents only); turns >1 increment by 2 since repair sequences are paired turns. (c) Computational complexity (in basic computation steps) by agent type and lexicon size. For interactional agents with a 6×4 lexicon no data is visible as the computation cost is very small (48) relative to the range of the y-axis.

domly between two referents straight away (resulting in ~50% communicative success). For bigger lexicons, however, they do use OIR, which explains the increased communicative success: through multiple turns they can reduce referential uncertainty.

183

Interactional agents perform approximately equally well with the bigger lexicons of 15x10 and 30x20, while the pragmatic agents show a steady decline in communicative success for bigger lexicon sizes. This decline can be explained by bigger lexicons resulting in more dispersed probability distributions, which causes less certainty for both speakers and listeners when choosing their productions and interpretations. This is more of a problem for pragmatic agents as they cannot do anything other than go one level up in pragmatic reasoning, while interactional agents can take as many turns as needed to reduce referential uncertainty (for as far as their lexicon allows). For pragmatic agents, we see no difference in communicative success between the Frugally Pragmatic and Fully Pragmatic strategies. This is as expected since they have access to the same pragmatic reasoning mechanisms and differ only in the successive deployment of orders of reasoning.

Figure 2b shows the distribution of the number of turns for the interactional agents. Here, a clear effect of lexicon size is visible: the bigger the lexicon, the more turns are used. This is unsurprising given that larger lexicons (given a constant ambiguity level) contain more referent associations per signal. Therefore, a larger lexicon causes more uncertainty, which results in more turns. (Note that we allowed agents to take more turns for bigger lexicons: we set a cap at $2 \times |S| - 1$ turns.) For the smallest lexicon size of 6x4, only one turn (i.e. one speaker production) is needed for the listener to be certain enough to end the interaction, meaning that listeners do not make use of OIR for this lexicon size. Most interactional sequences take less than 10 turns in total regardless of lexicon size. This means that interactional listeners need on average less than 5 repair attempts to reach a sufficiently certain interpretation.

Figure 2c shows the computation cost (as means of the computational complexity) by agent type and lexicon size. For the interactional agents, the average number of turns per lexicon size (6x4: 1.0, 15x10: 3.0, and 30x20: 4.7 turns) is entered into the computation cost, since the worst case is defined by an artificial limit on interaction length. As mentioned above, the frugally pragmatic agents always went up to order $n = 2$ for lexicon sizes 15x10 and 30x20, resulting in almost the same computation cost as for the fully pragmatic agents (see also Table 3). Only for a lexicon of size 6x4 the frugally

pragmatic agents were certain enough to stay with their first-order inference, ending up with a slightly lower computation cost than the fully pragmatic agents.

There is a substantial difference in computation cost between the interactional and pragmatic agent types. Especially for larger lexicons the computation cost is considerably lower for interactional than for pragmatic agents. Compared to this difference, the degree to which computation cost is reduced for Frugally Pragmatic compared to Fully Pragmatic agents is a lot smaller. The effect of lexicon size is smaller for the interactional compared to the pragmatic agents, as the computation cost increases linearly with lexicon size for interactional agents, while it increases quadratically with lexicon size for pragmatic agents (see Table 3).

5 Discussion

Can communicators reduce their computational burden through interaction? We showed using a theoretical analysis that the use of other-initiated repair can be more efficient than pragmatic reasoning in communication, by reducing the computational demands of pragmatic reasoning through interaction. The chief computational advantage of repair in our model derives from the fact that it trades recursive pragmatic inferences (which scale quadratically with lexicon size) for computationally simpler conjunctions (which scale linearly). This advantage seems to scale to bigger lexicon sizes as well, with the communicative success of the interactional agents not being affected by lexicon size, whereas pragmatic agents' communicative success decreases. This supports the hypothesis that communicating agents can leverage interactive repair to reduce their computational burden, essentially outsourcing individual computation to interaction.

A number of design choices may affect the generalisability of these results. First, we have modelled only a simple form of interactive repair, albeit one corresponding to a widely used repair format (the open request). Other forms of repair may have different computational complexity profiles. For instance, restricted offers hold up a candidate understanding for confirmation, and their formulation likely requires some degree of pragmatic reasoning, adding to the computational complexity (Schlöder and Fernández, 2015). Also, dealing with some forms of repair may involve belief revision (Wilkes-Gibbs and Clark, 1992), which requires context-sensitive abductive inferences known to be computationally intractable (Abdelbar and Hedetniemi, 1998; Bylander et al., 1991; Thagard and Verbeurgt, 1998). In sum, other-initiated repair is not a monolithic phenomenon, and the analytical tools we supply here can be used to systematically investigate the computational tractability of a range of possible interactional strategies (see e.g. Ginzburg and Fernández, 2010; van Rooij et al., 2011).

Another limitation is that the conditions under which the agents communicate are unrealistic in that all agent pairs share the exact same lexicon. Any potential misunderstanding thus stems solely from ambiguity, and not from one agent associating a given signal with a slightly different set of referents than their interlocutor. Relaxing this assumption is likely to cause problems for the simple repair strategy presented here, because it is based on conjunction. If interactional agents would base their (literal) productions and interpretations on conjunctions of more asymmetrical lexicons, divergences between intended referent and interpretation would soon arise, in which case we predict a decrease in communicative success, and therefore in efficiency. Pragmatic agents, on the other hand, have been shown to be able to leverage a moderate level of ambiguity in their lexicons to overcome asymmetry (Blokpoel et al., 2020).

We now consider two possible extensions to the current modelling work. Note, however, that these both come with additional computational demands and require careful theoretical re-analysis to investigate where efficiency trade-offs may play a role.

First, a hybrid model of pragmatic inference and other-initiated repair might combine the best of both worlds. The question then is if agents can achieve communicative success while keeping resource demands low by having their choice of strategy depend on an assessment of the situation. For example, in a speaker role, such a hybrid agent could 'level up' to a higher order of pragmatic reasoning in response to a repair initiator. Such hybrid agents will of course need a meta-cognitive capacity to decide which strategy to use (for instance by reasoning about the level of asymmetry between themselves and their interlocutor). This meta-level reasoning would bring additional computational resource demands that would affect the agents' efficiency. While a hybrid strategy may be able to preserve some of the efficiency trade-offs we have documented here, it is an open question whether they would not be dwarfed by the added computational cost of meta-cognition (see e.g. Otworowska et al., 2018).

Second, agents may revise their beliefs about the way their interlocutors use signals on the basis of conversation history, in order to overcome asymmetry (Hawkins et al., 2017). This form of updating might be able to explain why people are successful communicators while spending minimal interactional resources, but it comes at a computational cost too. Consider that agents would have to entertain the possibility that their interlocutor has any in principally possible lexicon, and from those infer the ones that are most likely given their conversation history. There exist, however, exponentially many possible lexicons (viz. 2^n for a lexicon of binary mappings, where n is the lexicon size, Blokpoel et al., 2020)[7].

Which of these (or other) models best explains the relation between interactive repair and pragmatic reasoning is an empirical question. Here we have shown that formal models informed by research on human interaction (Albert and Ruiter, 2018) can bring us closer to an understanding of the cognitive and communicative capacities of interacting people. The question of communicative efficiency is inherently one of computational plausibility. This question is best addressed through careful theoretical analysis as we have shown here. Further modelling can be used to refine our computational understanding of the phenomenon prior to empirical testing (cf. van Rooij and Baggio, 2020).

6 Conclusion

Using theoretical analysis, we showed that a simple form of other-initiated repair can ease the computational burden of pragmatic reasoning and thereby contribute to communicative efficiency. Our models make several simplifying assumptions, so scaling them to other interactional strategies will increase computational demands and perhaps alter the division of labour. Besides offering a proof of concept of how repair can ease the computational demands of communication, our methods pave the way for principled theory-driven analyses of how people balance cognitive and interactional resources in human interaction.

---

[7]For 30 signals and 20 referents there exist $2^{30 \times 20} = 1152921504606846976$ possible alternatives lexicons to consider. Even when agents can consider a million alternatives per second, it would take them about 3.6 years to update each time they hear their interlocutor speak.

Acknowledgments

This work is funded by the Netherlands Organisation for Scientific Research (NWO): MB is funded by Gravitation grant 024.001.006 of the Language in Interaction consortium, and MD and MW are supported by Vidi grant *Elementary particles of conversation* (016.Vidi.185.205). We would like to thank the reviewers for their valuable comments.

References

Aashraf M. Abdelbar and Sandra M. Hedetniemi. 1998. Approximating MAPS for belief networks is NP-hard and other theorems. *Artificial Intelligence*, 102(1):21–38.

Saul Albert and Jan-Peter de Ruiter. 2018. Improving Human Interaction Research through Ecological Grounding. *Collabra: Psychology*, 4(1).

Mark Blokpoel, Mark Dingemanse, Marieke Woensdregt, George Kachergis, Sara Bögels, Ivan Toni, and Iris van Rooij. 2020. Pragmatic communicators can overcome asymmetry by exploiting ambiguity. Preprint, Open Science Framework.

Tom Bylander, Dean Allemang, Michael C Tanner, and John R Josephson. 1991. The computational complexity of abduction. *Artificial Intelligence*, 49(1–3):25–60.

Andy Clark. 2006. Material Symbols. *Philosophical Psychology*, 19(3):291–307.

Herbert H. Clark and Edward Schaefer. 1987. Collaborating on contributions to conversations. *Language and Cognitive Processes*, 2(1):19–41.

Herbert H. Clark and Deanna Wilkes-Gibbs. 1986. Referring as a collaborative process. *Cognition*, 22(1):1–39.

Mark Dingemanse. 2020. Resource-rationality beyond individual minds: the case of interactive language use. *Behavioral and Brain Sciences*, 43:e9.

Mark Dingemanse, Seán G. Roberts, Julija Baranova, Joe Blythe, Paul Drew, Simeon Floyd, Rosa S. Gisladottir, Kobin H. Kendrick, Stephen C. Levinson, Elizabeth Manrique, Giovanni Rossi, and Nick Enfield, J. 2015. Universal principles in the repair of communication problems. *PLoS ONE*, 10(9):1–15.

Robert Downey and Mike Fellows. 1999. *Parameterized complexity*. Springer, Berlin.

Jerry A. Fodor. 2000. *The Mind Doesn't Work That Way: The Scope and Limits of Computational Psychology*. MIT press, Cambridge, MA.

Michael C. Frank and Noah D. Goodman. 2012. Predicting pragmatic reasoning in language games. *Science*, 336(6084):998.

Micheal R Garey and David S. Johnson. 1979. *Computers and intractability: A guide to the theory of NP-completeness*. W. H. Freeman, San Francisco, CA.

Edward Gibson, Richard Futrell, Steven T. Piandadosi, Isabelle Dautriche, Kyle Mahowald, Leon Bergen, and Roger Levy. 2019. How Efficiency Shapes Human Language. *Trends in Cognitive Sciences*, 23(5):389–407.

Jonathan Ginzburg and Raquel Fernández. 2010. Computational models of dialogue. In Alexander Clark, Chris Fox, and Shalom Lappin, editors, *The handbook of computational linguistics and natural language processing*, Blackwell handbooks in linguistics. Wiley-Blackwell, Chichester, West Sussex ; Malden, MA.

Noah D. Goodman and Michael C. Frank. 2016. Pragmatic language interpretation as probabilistic inference. *Trends in Cognitive Sciences*, 20(11):818–829.

Herbert P. Grice. 1975. Logic and Conversation. In Herbert P. Grice, editor, *Studies in the Way of Words*, pages 305–315. Harvard University Press.

Pim F. Haselager. 1997. *Cognitive Science and Folk Psychology: The Right Frame of Mind*. Sage, London.

Robert X. D. Hawkins, Michael C. Frank, and Noah D. Goodman. 2017. Convention-formation in iterated reference games. *Proceedings of the 39th Annual Meeting of the Cognitive Science Society*.

Maryellen C. MacDonald, Neal J. Pearlmutter, and Mark S. Seidenberg. 1994. Lexical nature of syntactic ambiguity resolution. *Psychological Review*, 101(4):676–703.

David J. C. MacKay. 2003. *Information Theory, Inference and Learning Algorithms*. Cambridge University Press.

Maria Otworowska, Mark Blokpoel, Marieke Sweers, Todd Wareham, and Iris van Rooij. 2018. Demons of ecological rationality. *Cognitive Science*, 42(3):1057–1066.

Steven T. Piantadosi, Harry Tily, and Edward Gibson. 2012. The communicative function of ambiguity in language. *Cognition*, 122(3):280–291.

Matthew Purver, Julian Hough, and Christine Howes. 2018. Computational Models of Miscommunication Phenomena. *Topics in Cognitive Science*.

Evan F. Risko and Sam J. Gilbert. 2016. Cognitive Offloading. *Trends in Cognitive Sciences*, 20(9):676–688.

Jan-Peter de Ruiter and Chris Cummins. 2012. A model of intentional communication: AIRBUS (Asymmetric Intention Recognition with Bayesian Updating of Signals). *Proceedings of SemDial 2012*, pages 149–50.

Emanuel A. Schegloff. 1992. Repair After Next Turn: The Last Structurally Provided Defense of Intersubjectivity in Conversation. *American Journal of Sociology*, 97(5):1295–1345.

Emanuel A. Schegloff, Gail Jefferson, and Harvey Sacks. 1977. The Preference for Self-Correction in the Organization of Repair in Conversation. *Language*, 53(2):361–382. ArticleType: primary_article / Full publication date: Jun., 1977 / Copyright © 1977 Linguistic Society of America.

Julian J. Schlöder and Raquel Fernández. 2015. Clarifying Intentions in Dialogue: A Corpus Study. In *Proceedings of the 11th International Conference on Computational Semantics (IWCS-2015)*, London.

Dan Sperber and Deirdre Wilson. 1986. *Relevance: Communication and Cognition*, first edition. Blackwell Publishing.

Paul Thagard and Karsten Verbeurgt. 1998. Coherence as constraint satisfaction. *Cognitive Science*, 22(1):1–24.

Iris van Rooij. 2008. The Tractable Cognition Thesis. *Cognitive Science*, 32(6):939–984.

Iris van Rooij and Giosuè Baggio. 2020. Theory before the test: How to build high-verisimilitude explanatory theories in psychological science. Preprint, PsyArXiv.

Iris van Rooij, Mark Blokpoel, Johan Kwisthout, and Todd Wareham. 2019. *Cognition and Intractability: A Guide to Classical and Parameterized Complexity Analysis*. Cambridge University Press.

Iris van Rooij, Johan Kwisthout, Mark Blokpoel, Jakub Szymanik, Todd Wareham, and Ivan Toni. 2011. Intentional Communication: Computationally Easy or Difficult? *Frontiers in Human Neuroscience*, 5.

Thomas Wasow, Andrew Perfors, and David Beaver. 2005. The puzzle of ambiguity. In O Orgun and P Sells, editors, *Morphology and The Web of Grammar: Essays in Memory of Steven G. Lapointe*, pages 265–282. CSLI Publications.

Deanna Wilkes-Gibbs and Herbert H Clark. 1992. Coordinating beliefs in conversation. *Journal of Memory and Language*, 31(2):183–194.

A Additional Results

This appendix shows the simulation results for all different parameter settings that were run, by way of a robustness check. The parameters that were manipulated are (i) the ambiguity level, (ii) the entropy threshold (i.e. the level of uncertainty that the listener is willing to tolerate) and (iii) the lexicon size.

Figure 3 shows the mean communicative success for the different parameter settings for which simulations were run. For lexicon size 6x4, no data is shown for the agents of type Frugally Pragmatic 1 for the entropy thresholds of 0.8 and 1.0 bits combined with an ambiguity level of 0.8, as in these conditions all frugally pragmatic listeners levelled up to a higher order of pragmatic reasoning (for which the data can be found under Frugally Pragmatic Agents 2). For agents of type Frugally Pragmatic 2 with lexicon size 6x4, no data is available for any of the entropy thresholds combined with an ambiguity level of 0.2, and for the entropy thresholds of 1.0 and 1.5 bits combined with an ambiguity level of 0.5, because the frugally pragmatic listeners never levelled up to second-order reasoning in these conditions. For the Frugally Pragmatic Agents 1 the same happened for the larger lexicons of 15x10 and 30x20 with an ambiguity level of either 0.5 or 0.8 (and for the combination of an ambiguity level of 0.2 with an entropy threshold of either 0.8 or 1.0 bits for the lexicon size of 30x20), as all agents went an order up here as well (i.e., data for these parameter settings is shown under Frugally Pragmatic Agents 2). For the Frugally Pragmatic Agents 2, there is no data for the lexicon size of 15x10, an ambiguity level of 0.2 and entropy thresholds of 1.0 and 1.5 bits, as no agents went up from order 1 to order 2 in these conditions. Finally, the fully pragmatic agents did not have the possibility to move an order up, therefore no entropy threshold was set.

First of all, the expected effect of ambiguity level is visible: the higher the ambiguity level, the lower the communicative success. This holds for almost all conditions, except for the Frugally Pragmatic Agents 1 with a lexicon size of 6x4 and an entropy threshold of 1.5 bits. Here we can see a slight improvement in communicative success when the ambiguity goes up from 0.5 to 0.8, which can be explained by the fact that for a high ambiguity level, these agents decide to go up to order 2 of pragmatic reasoning most of the time, and only stay with order 1 when they are sufficiently certain about the speaker's intended referent. Another exception when it comes to the effect of ambiguity level on the communicative success can be detected for the interactional agents with a lexicon size of 15x10, for the entropy thresholds of 1.0 and 1.5 bits and an ambiguity level of 0.2 and 0.5: here, the interactional agents perform better with an ambiguity level of 0.5 than 0.2. This is due to the fact that an ambiguity level of 0.2 for a lexicon size of 15x10

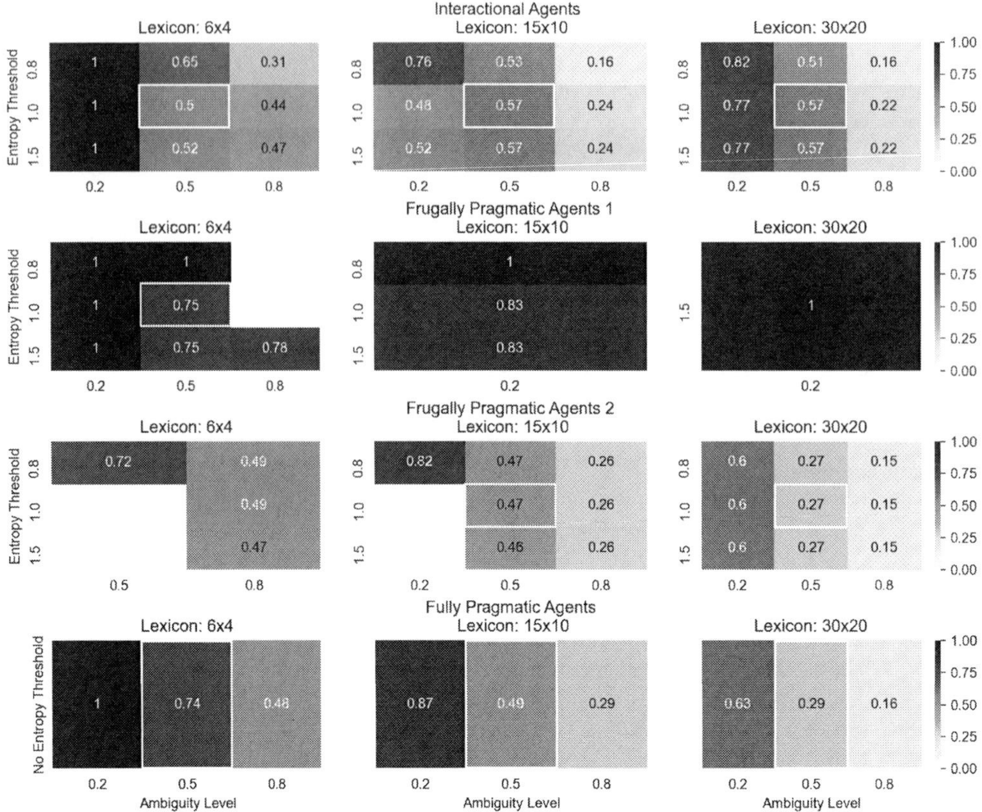

Figure 3: The mean communicative success for the different parameter settings: different agent types, entropy thresholds, ambiguity levels and lexicon sizes. For the frugally pragmatic agents 1, a lexicon size of 6x4, entropy thresholds of 1.0 and 0.8 bits, and an ambiguity level of 0.8 there is no data available as all agents went up on the order of pragmatic reasoning, for which the data is represented below at the frugally pragmatic agents 2 for a lexicon size of 6x4 (because the agents went up from an order of 1 to 2). Notice though that for a lexicon size of 6x4 no data is shown for an ambiguity level of 0.2 or an ambiguity level of 0.5 combined with an entropy threshold of either 1.0 or 1.5 bits, as no agents decided to go up from an order of 1 to 2. Again, for the frugally pragmatic agents 1 for the larger lexicons of 15x10 and 30x20 with an ambiguity level of either 0.5 or 0.8 (and for the combination of an ambiguity level of 0.2 and an entropy threshold of either 0.8 or 1.0 bits for the lexicon size of 30x20), all agents went an order up as well, explaining why no data is shown here. For the frugally pragmatic agents 2, there is no data for the lexicon size of 15x10, an ambiguity level of 0.2 and entropy thresholds of 1.0 and 1.5 bits, as no agents went up from an order of 1 to 2. Finally, the fully pragmatic agents did not have the possibility to move an order up, therefore no entropy threshold was set. The white outlines indicate the simulation results reported in the main body of the paper.

means that every signal refers to 2 referents. Therefore, agents do not use OIR for this ambiguity level as they have already reached the entropy threshold from the start; when the entropy threshold is set to 1.0 bits (or higher), agents are satisfied with having their set of possible interpretations narrowed down to two approximately equiprobable candidates. With a higher ambiguity level the agents

do need to use OIR for these entropy thresholds, therefore they can reach an entropy level under the entropy threshold and only have one referent left to choose from in some cases.

Secondly, the entropy threshold is used to manipulate how much uncertainty a listener allows for in a conversation; we ran simulations with three different entropy thresholds: 0.8, 1.0 and 1.5. With an

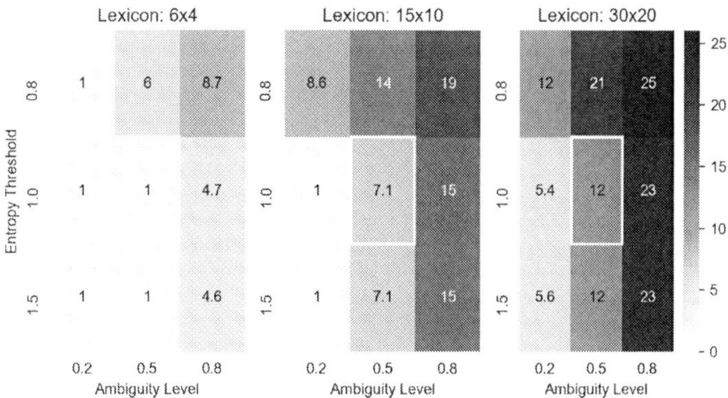

Figure 4: The mean number of turns for the interactional agents for the different parameter settings: different entropy thresholds, ambiguity levels and lexicon sizes. The white outlines indicate the simulation results reported in the main body of the paper.

entropy threshold of 0.8 bits, listeners are quite certain about which referent to choose, as one referent has a higher probability than the others. An entropy threshold of 1.0 bits means that the listener still has to choose between two more or less equally probable referents given a signal. Finally, with an entropy threshold of 1.5 bits, listeners have to choose between three more or less equally probable referents given a signal.[8] For the fully pragmatic agents the entropy threshold does not play a role, as these agents start at the maximum order of pragmatic reasoning ($n = 2$) from the beginning, regardless of their level of (un)certainty. When looking at the results in Figure 3, a clear effect of entropy threshold is not detectable. Overall, we can spot a small effect of the lowest entropy threshold of 0.8 bits leading to a higher communicative success, but this effect is not consistent across conditions and not very visible between the entropy thresholds of 1.0 and 1.5 bits.

Finally, an effect of lexicon size can be seen as well: for bigger lexicons the communicative success tends to be lower than for smaller ones. As discussed in the main body of the paper, this is due to bigger lexicons resulting in more dispersed probability distributions over signals and referents (for speakers and listeners respectively). Furthermore, we can observe that frugally pragmatic listeners go an order up in pragmatic reasoning (thereby entering the Frugally Pragmatic 2 scenario) when the ambiguity level is higher and when the lexicon size

is larger, which happens more often for the agents who tolerate less uncertainty (i.e. have a lower entropy threshold). This is in line with our expectations, as bigger lexicons with higher ambiguity levels cause more dispersed probabilities over the referents given a signal. A listener who is uncertain about the speaker's intended referent is more likely to go up on the order of reasoning, and this effect will be stronger if the listener has a lower entropy threshold.

Figure 4 shows the mean number of turns for the interactional agents for the different ambiguity levels and entropy thresholds. These parameters have a clear effect on the number of turns. The higher the ambiguity level, the more turns are used to be certain enough about the speaker's intended referent. Next, the lower the entropy threshold, the more turns are needed to be certain enough (as a lower entropy threshold means that the agent tolerates *less* uncertainty). And finally, regarding the lexicon size: the bigger the lexicon, the more turns are needed to be certain enough, as bigger lexicons lead to more dispersed probability distributions over the referents given the signal(s).

As mentioned above, for lower entropy thresholds, agents want to eliminate more uncertainty (i.e. gain a lower conditional entropy), which they try to achieve by taking more turns. However, we can observe in Figure 4 that there is not a (big) difference in the number of turns that the agents take between an entropy threshold of 1.0 and 1.5 bits, which means that after some turns agents are equally certain for both entropy thresholds (probably both fall under 1.0, regardless of the threshold).

---

[8]We can make these generalisations based on the definition of conditional entropy, but note that a given conditional entropy value can in principle correspond to a number of different probability distributions.

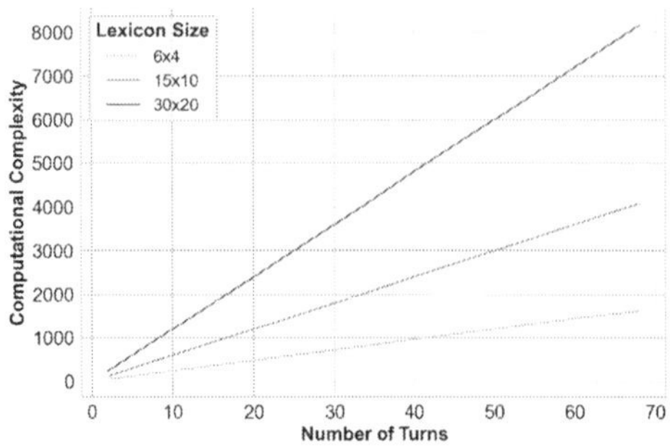

Figure 5: The computational complexity for different numbers of turns for different lexicon sizes, for the interactional agents.

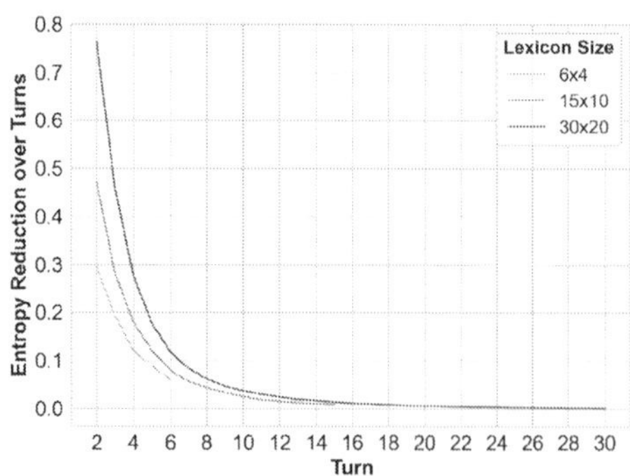

Figure 6: The difference in entropy between the number of turns for different lexicon sizes for the interactional agents.

Next, Figure 5 shows the computational complexity for the interactional agents for the different lexicon sizes and numbers of turns. Here, we can see that the computational complexity goes up for bigger lexicons and more turns, as expected.

Finally, Figure 6 shows the difference in conditional entropy over turns for different lexicon sizes for the interactional agents (as the pragmatic agents only perform one turn), meaning that the entropy difference of turn 2 for instance is given by:

$$\Delta_H = H(t_2) - H(t_1)$$

Here we can see that for the smaller lexicon sizes, the entropy difference between turns is smaller. Moreover, we can observe that around 10 turns the entropy does not differ much anymore when taking more turns, meaning that taking more than 10 turns in total (i.e. 5 per agent; including 5 counts of OIR) is not very effective when it comes to the listener's certainty about their interpretation. This is in line with the result discussed in the body of the paper that the interactional agents, regardless of lexicon size, take less than 5 turns most of the time.

B Computational Complexity Analysis of Interactional, Frugally Pragmatic and Fully Pragmatic Communication Strategies

B.1 Agent types and computational operations

We distinguish three agent types:

1. **Interactional agents:** Use other-initiated repair and conjunction to get to mutual understanding

2. **Frugally pragmatic agents:** Speaker is always order 2, but listener starts at order 1, and only levels up to order 2 when uncertainty is too high

3. **Fully pragmatic agents:** Both speaker and listener are order 2. Listener's strategy doesn't depend on their uncertainty

Together, these three agent types make use of three different operations of which we can analyse the computational complexity:

1. **Conjunction** (only used by interactional agents)

2. **Entropy** (only used by listeners of the interactional and frugally pragmatic agent types)

3. **Inference** (used by all agent types)

Below, we will analyse the computational complexity of the relevant operations for the three different agent types listed above in turn.

B.2 Computational complexity analysis

Let's start with distinguishing between $|S|$ (number of signals) and $|R|$ (number of referents) in our computational complexity analysis. We can later simplify by subsuming these two variables under a single variable m, which simply takes on whichever value is the maximum out of $|S|$ and $|R|$.

B.2.1 Interactional agents

Interactional speaker The interactional speaker has to do one conjunction step and one inference step per turn.

The conjunction step updates the lexicon L' (which exists only within a particular interaction and is 'reset' to the speaker's original lexicon at the start of each new interaction) by multiplying each value in the column corresponding to $r_{intended}$ in L' with the corresponding value in the signal row corresponding to the signal that was last sent s_{t-1}. This operation is specified below in algorithm 2.

Algorithm 2: Conjunction operation for interactional speaker

Data: L' is a lexicon matrix with $|S|$ rows and $|R|$ columns. $r_{intended}$ is the speaker's intended referent. s_{t-1} is the latest signal in the dialogue history D_r. Note that we assume that at each turn t, L' contains the outcome of the conjunction operation that was performed at the previous turn $t - 1$ (if such a previous turn exists). If $t = 1$, L' is identical to the speaker's lexicon L.

Result: An updated lexicon L' on which the conjunction operation has been performed given $r_{intended}$ and s_{t-1}. Note that the only values that are updated in L' are the cells in the column corresponding to $r_{intended}$.

1 **for** $i \leftarrow 1$ **to** $|S|$ **do**
2 $\quad\big|\quad L'_{i,r_{intended}} = L'_{i,r_{intended}} * L_{s_{t-1},r_{intended}}$;
3 **end**

The computational complexity of step 2 in algorithm 2 is $|S|$ (i.e. the multiplication operation has to be done exactly once for each cell in the column corresponding to $r_{intended}$).

Algorithm 2 has to be performed exactly once for each turn $t > 1$ after the first turn. Therefore, this conjunction operation has to be performed exactly $t - 1$ times in a given interaction. Thus, the overall computational complexity of conjunction for the interactional speaker is $|S|(t - 1)$.

To determine which signal to send next, the speaker has to go along the column of their intended referent, and select the signal that has the highest value. Given that every agent type has to do this inference step, let's assume that lookup is free. In that case the speaker has to make $|S|$ comparisons to check which signal has the highest value.

Taken together, this means that the computational complexity for the interactional speaker strategy as a whole (per interaction) is $|S|(t - 1) + |S|$.

Interactional listener In addition to the conjunction and inference steps, the interactional *listener* has to do an entropy step in between, to decide whether to move on to the inference step (if entropy is low), or whether to respond with a repair initiator (if entropy is high).

Let's again go through the steps in order:

The conjunction step updates the lexicon L' (which exists only within a particular interaction and is 'reset' to the listener's original lexicon at the start of each new interaction) by multiplying the signal row corresponding to the first signal that was received in the interaction $s_{t=1}$ with the signal row corresponding to the signal that was last received s_{t-1}. This operation is specified below in algorithm 3.

The computational complexity of step 2 in algorithm 3 is $|R|$ (i.e. the multiplication operation has to be done exactly once for each cell in the row corresponding to signal $s_{t=1}$).

Just like for the interactional speaker, algorithm 3 has to be performed exactly once for each turn $t > 1$ after the first turn. Therefore, this conjunction operation has to be performed exactly $t - 1$ times in a given interaction. Thus, the overall computational complexity of conjunction for the interactional listener is $|R|(t - 1)$.

At each turn of the interaction (including the very first turn), the listener does an entropy step to check how certain they are about their inference over possible intended referents. The entropy of the probability distribution over referents given the received signal s and the lexicon updated according to the dialogue history L_{D_r} (what is called L'

Algorithm 3: Conjunction operation for interactional listener

Data: L' is a lexicon matrix with $|S|$ rows and $|R|$ columns. s_{t-1} is the latest signal in the dialogue history D_r. Note that we assume that at each turn t, L' contains the outcome of the conjunction operation that was performed at the previous turn $t-1$ (if such a previous turn exists). If $t=1$, L' is identical to the listener's lexicon L.

Result: An updated lexicon L' on which the conjunction operation has been performed given $s_{t=1}$ (the first signal in the interaction) and s_{t-1} (the latest signal in the interaction). Note that the only values that are updated in L' are the cells in the row corresponding to $s_{t=1}$ (i.e. the signal that was received in the very first turn of the interaction).

1 **for** $i \leftarrow 1$ **to** $|R|$ **do**
2 $\quad L'_{s_{t=1},i} = L'_{s_{t=1},i} * L'_{s_{t-1},i}$;
3 **end**

above) is given by equation 15.

$$H(R|s, L_{D_r}) = \sum_{r \in R} Pr(r|s, L_{D_r}) log_2 \frac{1}{Pr(r|s, L_{D_r})}$$

(15)

Thus, the listener has to first do a multiplication operation for each $r \in |R|$, and then sum each of the $|R|$ resulting values together. This means that the computational complexity of the entropy calculation is $2|R|$. Because the entropy calculation happens at every single turn, the overall computational complexity of the entropy operation for a given interaction is $2|R|t$.

Once the entropy falls below the entropy threshold, or once the cap on the number of turns has been reached, the listener will decide to move to the inference step to actually interpret the signal(s). In order to do that, the listener has to go along the row corresponding to the first signal that was sent $s_{t=1}$ and select the referent that has the highest value. To do this, the listener has to make $|R|$ comparisons.

Taken together, this means that the computational complexity for the interactional listener strategy as a whole (per interaction) is $|R|(t-1) + 2|R|t + |R|$.

B.2.2 Pragmatic agents

We can consider the RSA operation of updating the matrix of production/reception probabilities separately from the inference step of choosing an actual utterance or interpretation. The computational complexity of that RSA step by itself (for speakers and listeners alike) is $(2 + 4n)|S||R|$, where n is the order of pragmatic reasoning.

The idea behind this is that a pragmatic agent has to normalise $2n$ times (first along the rows and then along the columns for production, or first along the columns and then along the rows for interpretation; and that n times). Each normalisation step itself takes $2|S||R|$ (taking the sum over rows or columns takes $|S||R|$ steps, then dividing each cell by the relevant sum also takes $|S||R|$ steps). Taken together, this makes $2n \cdot 2|S||R| = (4n)|S||R|$ steps. However, we haven't yet incorporated the first normalisation step which turns the lexicon of binary mappings into a level-0 speaker (in the case of pragmatic production) or a level-0 listener (in the case of pragmatic interpretation). As explained above, this initial normalisation operation consists of $2|S||R|$ steps, so if we add it in, we get: $(2 + 4n)|S||R|$.

If we combine this with the inference step (which, as we saw above, is $|S|$ for speakers, and $|R|$ for listeners), we get $(2 + 4n)|S||R| + max(|S|, |R|)$. Which is a generic computational complexity analysis for pragmatic agents in general. But we can make this more specific by considering speakers and listeners separately, as we do below.

Frugally pragmatic speaker The frugally pragmatic speaker strategy is exactly the same as the fully pragmatic speaker strategy; see the corresponding complexity analysis below under 'Fully pragmatic speaker'.

Frugally pragmatic listener For the frugally pragmatic listener, the computational complexity of this strategy depends on whether the listener decides to level up to order 2 or not.

- **Scenario 1:** In this scenario, the listener *doesn't* level up, which means that $n = 1$. This yields: $(2 + 4n)|S||R| = (2 + (4 * 1))|S||R| = 6|S||R|$ for the RSA operation. This is then combined with the entropy calculation, which, as shown above, takes $2|R|$

	Interactional	**Frugally pragmatic**	**Fully pragmatic**
Speaker	$\|S\|(t-1)+\|S\|$	$10\|S\|\|R\|+\|S\|$	$10\|S\|\|R\|+\|S\|$
Listener	$\|R\|(t-1)+2\|R\|t+\|R\|$	**1:**$6\|S\|\|R\|+2\|R\|+\|R\|$ **2:**$10\|S\|\|R\|+2\|R\|+\|R\|$	$10\|S\|\|R\|+\|R\|$

Table 4: Computational complexity comparison across agent types (with speaker and listener strategy summed together).

	Interactional	**Frugally pragmatic**	**Fully pragmatic**
Speaker	$m(t-1)+m$	$10m^2+m$	$10m^2+m$
Listener	$m(t-1)+2mt+m$	**1:**$6m^2+2m+m$ **2:**$10m^2+2m+m$	$10m^2+m$

Table 5: Computational complexity comparison across agent types (with speaker and listener strategy summed together).

steps.

And finally, the listener has to do an inference step to come to an actual interpretation. As shown above, this takes $|R|$ steps.

Taken together, this means that the computational complexity for the frugally pragmatic listener who *doesn't* level up is $6|S||R| + 2|R| + |R|$.

- **Scenario 2:** In this scenario, the listener *does* level up, which means that $n = 2$. This yields: $(2 + 4n)|S||R| = (2 + (4*2))|S||R| = 10|S||R|$ for the RSA operation. (Note that this subsumes the initial RSA operation at order $n = 1$; we assume that the listener can hold on to the outcome of that first $n = 1$ operation to use it as the basis for their subsequent $n = 2$ inference.)

  This is then combined with the entropy calculation, which, as shown above, takes $2|R|$ steps.

  And finally, the listener has to do an inference step to come to an actual interpretation. As shown above, this takes $|R|$ steps.

  Taken together, this means that the computational complexity for the frugally pragmatic listener who *does* level up is $10|S||R| + 2|R| + |R|$.

Fully pragmatic speaker The frugally pragmatic speaker and fully pragmatic speaker strategies are exactly the same: they both start at order $n = 2$, and don't do anything other than regular RSA production. The RSA operation part for order $n = 2$ is $(2 + 4n)|S||R| = (2 + (4*2))|S||R| = 10|S||R|$.

As shown above, the inference step for production takes $|S|$ steps.

Taken together, this means that the computational complexity for the frugally *or* fully pragmatic speaker is $10|S||R| + |S|$.

Fully pragmatic listener The fully pragmatic listener starts at order $n = 2$ straight away, and doesn't do any entropy calculation.

Taken together, this means that the computational complexity for the fully pragmatic listener is $10|S||R| + |R|$.

B.2.3 Comparison across agent types

Table 4 shows a comparison of the computational complexity of each strategy.

We can make the computational complexity of the speaker and listener roles more comparable by subsuming $|S|$ and $|R|$ under one combined variable $m = max(|S|, |R|)$, which simply takes on whichever is the highest value out of $|S|$ and $|R|$. (Given the parameter settings used in the simulations, this will always be $|S|$, given that $|S|$ was fixed at $1.5 \times |R|$.)

Division of labour between speaker and listener From Table 5 we can read off how the division of labour between speaker and listener differs between the different strategies. Only in the fully pragmatic agent types do speaker and listener do an exactly equal amount of work. In the interactional strategy,

Interactional	Frugally pragmatic		Fully pragmatic
$2m(t-1) + 2mt + 2$	**1:**$16m^2$ **2:**$20m^2 + 4m$	$+\quad 4m$	$20m^2 + 2m$

Table 6: Computational complexity comparison across agent types (with speaker and listener strategy summed together).

the listener always does a bit more work than the speaker (because the listener thinks about how uncertain they are about their inference; the speaker in contrast only has to react when they get a repair request). In the frugally pragmatic strategy, the listener does *less* work than the speaker when they can stay at order $n = 1$ (scenario 1), but *more* work than the speaker when they have to level up to order $n = 2$ because their initial inference was too uncertain (scenario 2).

Comparison across agent types (collapsing across speaker and listener role) Ultimately however, we are interested in comparing across agent types. In order to do this, we can sum the complexity of the speaker and listener within each agent type together, as shown in Table 6.

As described in Section 4, we used the formulas in Table 6 in combination with the mean number of turns derived from the simulations for each separate strategy to yield the computational cost results shown in Figure 2c.

Acquiring language from speech by learning to remember and predict

Cory Shain
Ohio State University
`shain.3@osu.edu`

Micha Elsner
Ohio State University
`elsner.14@osu.edu`

Abstract

Classical accounts of child language learning invoke *memory* limits as a pressure to discover sparse, language-like representations of speech, while more recent proposals stress the importance of *prediction* for language learning. In this study, we propose a broad-coverage unsupervised neural network model to test memory and prediction as sources of signal by which children might acquire language directly from the perceptual stream. Our model embodies several likely properties of real-time human cognition: it is strictly incremental, it encodes speech into hierarchically organized labeled segments, it allows interactive top-down and bottom-up information flow, it attempts to model its own sequence of latent representations, and its objective function only recruits local signals that are plausibly supported by human working memory capacity. We show that much phonemic structure is learnable from unlabeled speech on the basis of these local signals. We further show that remembering the past and predicting the future both contribute to the linguistic content of acquired representations, and that these contributions are at least partially complementary.

1 Introduction

How children acquire language from the environment is one of the fundamental mysteries of cognitive science. Much theoretical, experimental, and computational research into this question has focused on acquiring abstractions over lower-order symbols, such acquiring morphemes from phoneme sequences or syntactic structures from word sequences (Chomsky, 1965; Gold, 1967; Elman, 1991; Saffran et al., 1996; Albright, 2002; Klein and Manning, 2004; Goldwater et al., 2009; Christodoulopoulos et al., 2012, *inter alia*). Children, however, do not get symbolic input; symbolic representations at any level of granularity

constitute abstractions inferred from highly variable, noisy, and information-rich perceptual signals like audition and vision. This work joins a growing computational literature exploring the kinds of architectures and learning objectives that best support acquisition of linguistic representations directly from the speech signal without supervision (Versteegh et al., 2015; Dunbar et al., 2017). Such models can be used to test questions about language acquisition under more realistic assumptions about the input signal, especially to the extent that they reflect known constraints on human cognition (Shain and Elsner, 2019; Beguš, 2020).

This study uses computational modeling to examine two influential and possibly complementary ideas about how people learn abstract representations, including language, from data: learning to remember, and learning to predict. Both hypotheses have been advocated by prior work in language acquisition, cognitive neuroscience, and computational modeling, yet their relative contributions to language learning are not yet clear. Our model permits precise manipulation of memory and prediction pressures during acquisition, allowing direct comparison of these hypotheses.

In so doing, we implement several constraints on real-time language processing that have not been simultaneously present in prior modeling of this domain: (1) we jointly segment and label the speech signal without supervision; (2) the learning objective is applied incrementally during real-time processing using only locally available feedback; (3) the encoded signal is segmental, sparse, and hierarchically organized; (4) segments are represented featurally as patterns of activation, rather than discrete category symbols; and (5) the system is optimized by modeling its own state at multiple timescales, rather than by modeling the data alone.

Results show a systematic improvement along multiple measures of phoneme induction quality

Proceedings of the 24th Conference on Computational Natural Language Learning, pages 195–214
Online, November 19-20, 2020. ©2020 Association for Computational Linguistics
https://doi.org/10.18653/v1/P17

from both learning to remember and learning to predict, suggesting that these two kinds of signals may play complementary roles during child language acquisition. The contributions of this work are as follows:

- We propose a novel deep neural encoder-decoder for unsupervised speech processing that is incremental, segmental, and useful for testing hypothesized cognitive constraints.

- We show empirically that memory-based and prediction-based signals contribute separately to the acquisition of linguistic regularities, simultaneously supporting two existing classes of theories about the learning pressures that underlie human language acquisition.

2 Background

2.1 Memory, Prediction, and Learning

Many proposals from the language acquisition literature appeal to memory pressures as a learning signal (Newport, 1990; Pinker, 1991; Carstairs-McCarthy, 1994; Rissanen and Ristad, 1994; Baddeley et al., 1998; Goldsmith, 2003; Yang, 2005, *inter alia*). For example, Baddeley et al. (1998) invoke constraints on working memory, arguing that because the speech signal is too rich to support full retention during real-time language processing (Baddeley and Hitch, 1974), infants are guided toward phonemic representations, which constitute an efficient encoding of that signal. Meanwhile, classical theories of language acquisition such as Newport (1990) and Pinker (1991) invoke constraints on long-term memory, arguing that linguistic regularities constitute compressed descriptions of the learner's input and that their discovery reduces the amount of information that must by idiosyncratically stored. Artificial language learning patterns in humans (Kersten and Earles, 2001) and recent computational modeling of the speech domain (e.g. Lee and Glass, 2012; Lee et al., 2015; Kamper et al., 2015; Elsner and Shain, 2017; Kamper et al., 2017a; Shain and Elsner, 2019) have supported a contribution from memory constraints to language learning. This position also aligns with an extensive computational neuroscience literature on *sparse coding*, which holds that biological neurons are tuned for memory-efficient representations of recent stimuli (Attneave, 1954; Olshausen and Field, 1996, 2004; Sheridan et al., 2017).

Nonetheless, debate exists about the role of memory in language learning. For example, Rohde and Plaut (1999) fail to replicate findings from Elman (1993) in favor of Newport (1990). In addition, Perfors (2012) fails to find evidence that memory bottlenecks encourage discovery of underlying linguistic regularities in adults and argues that such limitations only support language learning in concert with strong inductive priors. Furthermore, evidence suggests that mental representations during language processing preserve acoustic details over and above symbolic codes (Andruski et al., 1994; McMurray et al., 2002). Related work has called into question both the memory efficiency of human mental representations and the severity of long-term memory limits. For example, experimental evidence indicates that human mental representations contain redundant information, both of language (Baayen et al., 1997) and of other constructs such as logical relations (Piantadosi et al., 2016). In addition, recent estimates of mental storage requirements indicate that lexical information, especially semantics, already requires vastly more storage than e.g. phonemes and syntax, suggesting little added memory benefit from optimizing the efficiency with which regularities are stored (Mollica and Piantadosi, 2019). Finally, recent computational evidence linking memory bottlenecks to success in unsupervised speech processing has relied on storage of arbitrarily long acoustic sequences in their full detail in order to compute reconstruction losses (Kamper et al., 2015; Elsner and Shain, 2017). This design is inconsistent with known constraints on the storage duration (< 1s) of unanalyzed acoustic traces in human working memory (Baddeley and Hitch, 1974; Cowan, 1984). It is thus not yet clear (1) how strongly memory pressures constrain mental representations of speech or (2) how much they encourage language learning.

Memory efficiency is not the only objective that can be constructed to learn abstractions over data without supervision. It has also been proposed that language learning may be driven by optimizing prediction of future input (Rohde and Plaut, 1999; Johnson et al., 2013; Phillips and Ehrenhofer, 2015; Apfelbaum and McMurray, 2017). This proposal aligns with an extensive neuroscience literature arguing that *predictive coding* for future inputs is a "canonical computation" of the human brain (Keller and Mrsic-Flogel, 2018) and may better characterize the tuning of biological neurons than sparse coding (Singer et al., 2018), possibly because prediction affords advantages in critical tasks (Nijhawan, 1994) and may help organisms filter noise from the perceptual signal by focusing attention on features relevant to prediction (Bialek et al., 2001). Additional support for a role of prediction in language learning comes from the success of incremental *language models* in natural language processing, which optimize prediction of future words (Ney et al., 1994; Heafield et al., 2013; Jozefowicz et al., 2016; Radford et al., 2019). Language models support dramatic performance improvements in language processing tasks (Radford et al., 2019) and have been shown to both (1) acquire linguistic abstractions without direct supervision (Linzen et al., 2016) and (2) covary with human language comprehension measures (Frank and Bod, 2011; Goodkind and Bicknell, 2018; van Schijndel and Linzen, 2018). Finally, experimental evidence indicates that infants chunk the speech stream at points of low transition probability, suggesting that predictive signals are exploited to learn word-like units (Saffran et al., 1996).

We address these questions computationally by manipulating the presence or absence of memory and prediction pressures in the joint objective of an unsupervised incremental speech processing model, allowing us to quantify the contributions of these two hypothesized learning signals under realistic constraints on real-time processing.

2.2 Recurrent, Hierarchical, and Segmental Speech Processing in Humans

Artificial recurrent neural networks such as those employed here were initially proposed as algorithmic-level (Marr, 1982) models of activity in biological neural networks (Little, 1974; Hopfield, 1982), and subsequent studies support ubiquitous recurrence in the cortex (Harris and Mrsic-Flogel, 2013). In addition, influential theories of biological neural information processing argue that biological neural circuits integrate information at multiple hierarchically-organized timescales (Kiebel et al., 2008; Hasson et al., 2015; Norman-Haignere et al., 2020). Further neuroscientific evidence indicates that segmentation of the time dimension plays a critical role in human cognition, both in domain-general event processing (Zacks et al., 2001; Jensen, 2006, *inter alia*) and in speech processing specifically (Sanders and Neville, 2003; Cunillera et al., 2006, 2009; Kooijman et al., 2013;

Lee and Cho, 2016, *inter alia*). Segmentation or "chunking" also plays a central role in several theories of language comprehension (Sanford and Sturt, 2002; Hale, 2006; Frank and Christiansen, 2018) and learning (Monaghan and Christiansen, 2010; McCauley and Christiansen, 2019). Our model incorporates these notions architecturally, with segment boundaries implemented by "detector neurons" that govern information flow between neural populations at larger and smaller timescales (Masquelier, 2018).

2.3 Modeling the Mental State

Many theories of linguistic structure posit multiple, hierarchically organized levels of representation (Chomsky, 1957; Goldsmith, 1976). Such theories predict the existence of abstractions over abstractions, latent structures that describe the distribution of other latent structures. This idea accords with recent theories of generalized Bayesian learning in biological agents, in which neural populations are thought to model the activity of other neural populations within their Markov blanket (Friston, 2010). The notion of learning through modeling other elements of the agent's own mental state has been exploited in symbolic computational models of language acquisition (Lee and Glass, 2012; Lee et al., 2015), but not in the context of artificial neural zero-resource speech models, which have so far derived their objective exclusively from the data (Kamper et al., 2017a; Elsner and Shain, 2017). Our approach incorporates this idea by optimizing higher layers to predict the sequence of activations at lower layers.

2.4 Related Computational Approaches

This work is part of a growing interest in unsupervised representation learning from raw speech, especially the Zerospeech 2015 (Versteegh et al., 2015) and 2017 (Dunbar et al., 2017) shared tasks and participating systems (Badino et al., 2015; Renshaw et al., 2015; Agenbag and Niesler, 2015; Chen et al., 2015; Baljekar et al., 2015; Räsänen et al., 2015; Lyzinski et al., 2015; Zeghidour et al., 2016; Heck et al., 2016; Srivastava and Shrivastava, 2016; Kamper et al., 2017b; Chen et al., 2017; Yuan et al., 2017; Heck et al., 2017; Shibata et al., 2017; Ansari et al., 2017a,b), as well as subsequent deep neural autoencoders (Van Den Oord et al., 2017; Chorowski et al., 2019) inspired by the WaveNet architecture (van den Oord et al., 2016). Much of this work concerns the discovery of word-like units, while our analyses focus on learning at the phoneme level (see section 4.3).

A symbolic Bayesian framework for joint unsupervised phoneme segmentation and clustering is proposed by Lee and Glass (2012) and extended by Lee et al. (2015). Their system infers a Dirichlet process hidden Markov model to learn a symbolic sequential encoding of the speech stream. A disadvantage of this approach for the present research question is that the categorically distributed phone labels lack any notion of featural relatedness, contrary to widely held assumptions about natural language phonology (Clements, 1985). In addition, the learning signal derives from a next-frame prediction objective, making it difficult to use the model to factorially manipulate memory and prediction pressures. Another recent framework for unsupervised phone segmentation identifies boundaries at points of high surprisal in a frame-level language model (Michel et al., 2017). This approach does not generate segment encodings and cannot straightforwardly be used to test claims about the role of memory in language learning.

3 Model

Like many prior ANN zero-resource speech processing models (e.g. Kamper et al., 2015, 2017a; Elsner and Shain, 2017; Shain and Elsner, 2019), we employ an encoder-decoder framework. However, unlike previous approaches, our model decodes incrementally and hierarchically, with each layer decoding its inputs at their own timescale over a short window backward into the past and/or forward into the future. The model is thus required not only to describe the input signal (speech), but also its own sequence of latent representations (e.g. phones, words, etc.), much as people are implicitly thought to do in prior symbolic work on unsupervised language learning (Goldwater et al., 2009; Lee et al., 2015). Our encoder model closely follows Chung et al. (2017), and thus the primary technical contribution of this work lies in the cascaded incremental decoder and the layerwise incremental objective described below, both of which are designed to encourage repurposable segment representations based on locally available information. Although encodings are ultimately the quantity of interest in unsupervised encoder-decoder models, prior work has shown that decoder design can be a major determinant of acquired representations (McCoy et al., 2018, 2020). The overall design

is schematized in Figure 1. Code is available at `https://github.com/coryshain/dnnseg`.

3.1 Encoder

Our encoder closely follows a hierarchical multiscale extension (HM-LSTM, Chung et al., 2017) of long short-term memory (LSTM) networks (Hochreiter and Schmidhuber, 1997). The encoder consists of multiple LSTM layers linked by discrete boundary neurons that govern memory retention and information flow between layers. When a boundary neuron fires in layer l, it terminates a *segment*. Layer l then ejects its hidden state representation to layer $l + 1$, receives top-down input from the hidden state of layer $l + 1$, and resets its cell state (incremental memory) in order to process the next segment. The hidden state at a boundary thus constitutes a *label* for the segment terminating at that boundary, which is used to summarize the content of the segment when communicating with other layers. When the boundary neuron at layer l does not fire, layer $l + 1$ is inert and simply copies its representation forward. As a result, higher layers track information at longer timescales than lower layers, and the segmentation behavior at l determines the input timescale at $l + 1$. Each layer proceeds by segmenting and labeling its input signal at a timescale learned from data, resulting in a hierarchical sequence of labeled segments. As argued in Chung et al. (2017), this design enforces a trade-off between recurrent information (which is erased by segmentation) and top-down information (which is made available by segmentation).[1] Although the linguistic quality of discovered HM-LSTM segments is not systematically examined in the original proposal (Chung et al., 2017) and recent analysis has called it into question (Kádár et al., 2018), our results indicate that HM-LSTMs can discover segmental structure from speech, at least at the phonemic level.

3.2 Decoder

The decoder consists of two multi-layer attentional sequence-to-sequence (seq2seq) LSTMs with L layers each, one backward-directional (memory) and one forward directional (prediction). The LSTMs respectively decode the B previous input segment labels and the F following input segment labels given an encoder representation at layer l and

---

[1]See Appendix A for definition of the encoder and B for comparison to Chung et al. (2017).

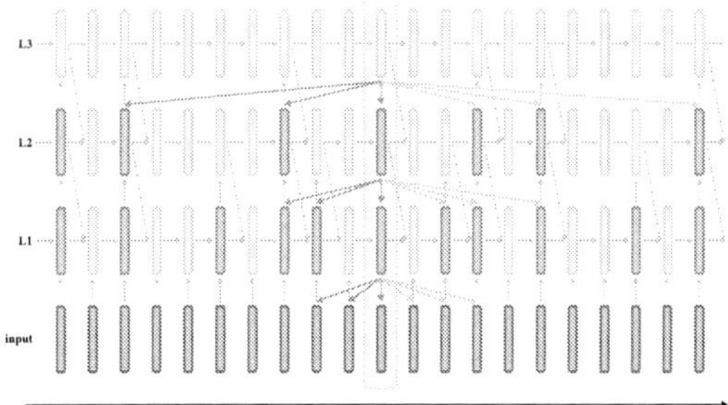

Figure 1: *Incremental layerwise encoder-decoder framework.* Shown here with 3 layers and a forward/backward window size of 3. Segment boundaries are shown in cyan. Gray arrows indicate information flow through the encoder, as governed by the boundary decisions. Colored arrows indicate information flow from encodings to decoder targets in the backward (orange) and forward (green) directions, starting from the encoded timestep at the center of the figure.

time t. In addition, the predicted sequence from the layer above serves as attention values to inform decoding at the current layer, at a timescale determined by the segmentation patterns of the current layer and the layer below. The internal behavior of the decoder is thus tightly coupled with the segmental behavior of the encoder, providing direct feedback into the encoder decisions. In addition, the label sequence of the decoder at all layers must support both (1) decoding of the perceptual signal (the data), since top-down connections allow higher-level representations to inform lower-level ones, and (2) decoding of lower-level state sequences.[2]

3.3 Objective

We employ an incremental layerwise objective that both *reconstructs* backward and *predicts* forward from time t at layer l over the segment labels from layer $l - 1$ at a timescale defined by the segmentation behavior of layer $l-1$. Thus only the first layer decodes at the timescale of the data; higher layers l decode at the timescale of $l-1$, and representations associated with non-boundaries in $l-1$ are ignored by the objective. The objective scans incrementally over the time dimension and imposes a forward and backward cost at every segment boundary identified by layer $l - 1$. As a result, the first layer ("phonemes") is responsible for incrementally decoding the local past and future realization of the acoustic stream, the second layer is responsible for decoding the local past and future realization of the

"phoneme" sequence, etc.[3]

Although it is possible to backpropagate into the decoding targets (i.e. encoder representations) at higher layers, thereby encouraging the encoder to discover more predictable segment sequences, we found in practice that doing so resulted in a form of mode collapse where labels became insensitive to the data and converged to a single value for all timesteps. For this reason, we stop the gradients into decoding targets and backpropagate only into the decoder predictions. Thus, the objective encourages encodings at higher layers to change to better predict structures at lower layers— but does not alter the representations at those lower layers to make them more uniform and therefore easier to predict.

4 Experimental Design

We assess the contribution of memory and prediction pressures to phoneme acquisition by (1) manipulating these pressures on models exposed to speech data from two unrelated languages (Xitsonga and English) and (2) evaluating the effect of these manipulations on multiple measures of phoneme induction quality.

4.1 Data

We use the Zerospeech 2015 (Versteegh et al., 2015) challenge data in English and Xitsonga, a Bantu language spoken in South Africa. The Xitsonga data come from the NCHLT corpus (De Vries et al., 2014) and contain 2h29m07s of read speech from 24 speakers. The English data come from the Buckeye Corpus (Pitt et al., 2005) and contain 4h59m05s of spontaneous speech from 12 speakers. For English, we additionally include the official development set in training, which contains 1h39m45s of spontaneous speech from 2 speakers, also from the Buckeye Corpus. English development set performance was used for model development and tuning, but the development set is not included in the evaluations presented here. Xitsonga lacks a development set, so designs selected on the English development set are applied directly to Xitsonga for evaluation. Before fitting, we convert the source audio files into a cochleagram-based spectral representation that approximates the signal generated by the human auditory system (McDermott and Simoncelli, 2011).[4]

---

[2]See Appendix C for definition of the decoder.

[3]See Appendix D for definition of the objective.
[4]See Appendix F for full preprocessing details.

4.2 Experimental Manipulations

We seek to assess the contribution of both memory and prediction pressures to the content of model representations. To this end, our principal manipulations are the backward ($B \in \{0, 5, 25, 50\}$) and forward ($F \in \{0, 1, 5, 10\}$) window lengths used by the decoder, which respectively impose a pressure to efficiently remember and accurately predict. Note that the condition $B = 0$, $F = 0$ (no reconstruction or prediction) is not well defined because the objective is 0 at any parameterization and thus has no gradient, and we therefore exclude it from consideration in these results. In addition, we manipulate the number of encoder layers ($L \in \{2, 3, 4\}$). This is because it is unclear *a priori* which layers of the encoder are expected to correspond to quantities of interest like phonemes or words, since the representations are unsupervised and the model could additionally or instead discover e.g. subphonemic, morphemic, phrasal, intonational, and other kinds of structures. Although detection of these and other levels of linguistic representation is of interest and is the target of future work, the annotations provided by the Zerospeech 2015 data support phoneme-level and word-level analyses only, and we concentrate our evaluation there. Varying the number of layers allows us to investigate which layers emergently discover more phoneme-like units, and under what conditions.

4.3 Evaluation

Because our model generates a segmental encoding of the speech signal, we apply two classes of evaluation in this study: phoneme segmentation and phoneme-level probing classification. The segmentation evaluation measures the degree of correspondence between the model-generated segment boundaries and expert-annotated phoneme boundaries, using a boundary F-measure which assigns a true positive for up to one predicted boundary that falls within some tolerance of each gold boundary, false positives for all other predicted boundaries, and false negatives for all gold boundaries that lack a predicted boundary within the tolerance. Following Lee and Glass (2012), we use a tolerance of 20ms. The classification evaluation measures the amount of signal in model-generated encodings as to (1) the true identity of the phoneme being encoded and (2) the cluster of phonological features associated with that phoneme (Hayes, 2011). Following e.g. Shain and Elsner (2019) and

Chrupała et al. (2020), we do so using probing classifiers. In particular, for each layer of each model's encoder, we fit linear classifiers to (1) the phoneme labels and (2) the phonological feature labels associated with the gold phoneme segment corresponding to each phone boundary. We extract the gold and predicted phoneme encodings at the human-annotated phoneme boundaries, regardless of whether the model segmented at that location. This supports direct comparison of metrics across models, since the set of evaluated segments is held constant. Phonological features are extracted at the same timepoints, following the procedure described in Shain and Elsner (2019).[5]

Although our model is designed to support joint discovery of multiple layers of representation, we find empirically that no model appreciably improves at any layer in word boundary F-score over a baseline that segments only at the ends of voice activity regions, and qualitative inspection does not indicate systematic correspondence to an unannotated level of representation such as syllables, morphemes, or intonational units. Despite differences in segmentation rate, and thereby in word boundary precision-recall trade-off, models generally converge on similar (low) word boundary F-scores, and thus our manipulations are not informative about word learning. Probe-based classification metrics are not well suited to word-level evaluation due to the size of the vocabulary. Though human speech processing involves units between the phoneme and word level, detailed analysis of such units is difficult due to the lack of annotation in the corpus. We believe poor word discovery at higher layers may be due in part to the fact that non-initial layers have both a non-stationary objective (the evolving representations of the layer below) and slower learning dynamics, perhaps making it difficult for these layers to "catch up" with moving targets (Ioffe and Szegedy, 2015). We leave exploration of possible remedies to future research and focus here only on the phoneme level.

While it is *a priori* unclear which layer of the encoder is expected to encode phonemes (for example, the initial layers may encode sub-phonemic units), we find systematically better phoneme segmentation and classification performance in the first layer of the network. For simplicity, we therefore only present metrics from this layer.

In addition to reporting raw model performance,

---

[5]See Appendix E for probe implementation details.

Model	English			Xitsonga		
	Bd	Pc	Fc	Bd	Pc	Fc
Full	**65.3**	**22.9**	**49.3**	39.3	**28.6**	**53.8**
Baseline U	30.4	12.3	42.2	22.1	15.4	46.2
Baseline X	52.4	20.5	47.1	**44.8**	27.8	53.2

Table 1: F-measures for boundary discovery (Bd), phoneme classification (Pc), and phonological feature classification (Fc), using $B = 25$, $F = 1$, $L = 3$.

we report performance improvements from each model relative to (1) baseline U (*untrained*), an architecturally matched model left at random initialization (Chrupała et al., 2020), and (2) baseline X (*cross-language*), the architecturally matched model trained on the opposite language.[6] These two baselines quantify different contributions of the acquisition process. Baseline U quantifies architectural inductive bias: how well does the architecture alone guide linguistic representations, without learning? Baseline X quantifies modality inductive bias: how well does general knowledge of human speech guide linguistic representations, without exposure to the target language? Improvement against either of these baselines supports language learning from experience, over and above any prior knowledge that might more efficiently be innately encoded.[7]

5 Results and Discussion

Boundary and macro-averaged phoneme and feature classification F-measures from the best-performing configuration on the English development set ($B = 25$, $F = 1$, $L = 3$) are given in Table 1. English boundary performance ($F = 65.3$) approaches previously reported unsupervised phoneme segmentation scores on different and therefore not directly comparable datasets (Lee and Glass, 2012; Michel et al., 2017, both around

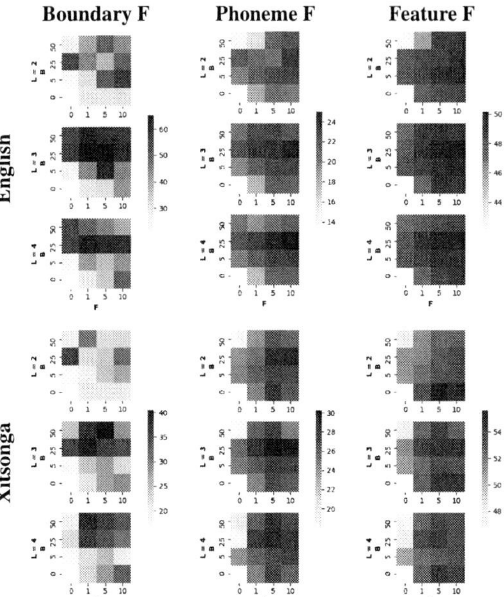

Figure 2: **Phoneme acquisition scores.** F-measures for boundary detection (left), phoneme classification (center), and phonological feature classification (right).

$F = 75$). The overall segmentation performance in Xitsonga is considerably worse than that of English, consistent with prior evidence that word segmentation in the Zerospeech 2015 Xitsonga partition is harder than English (e.g. Kamper et al., 2017a). By contrast, classification metrics in Xitsonga are better than in English, which is again consistent with prior findings of stronger unsupervised classification performance in Xitsonga (Shain and Elsner, 2019).

The difference in relative performance between segmentation and classification in the two languages could be due in part to differences in register: the English data is spontaneously produced, while the Xitsonga data is read speech. Longer average phoneme duration (100ms vs 70ms) and cleaner articulations in Xitsonga could plausibly give rise to this asymmetry, and further investigation is left to future work. The model substantially outperforms the untrained baseline (U) on all metrics and outperforms the cross-language baseline (X) on all metrics but boundary F in Xitsonga, which could be due in part to the larger size of the English-language training set. Results therefore indicate that the reconstruction and prediction objectives have contributed to unsupervised discovery of phonemic patterns in both languages.

Segmentation and macro-averaged classification

---

[6]For Xitsonga, baseline X is the architecturally matched English-trained model. For English, baseline X is the architecturally matched Xitsonga-trained model.

[7]We do not evaluate directly against a previous state of the art because no state of the art exists for unsupervised phoneme segmentation and classification in the Zerospeech 2015 data. A previous model that performed the same task (Lee and Glass, 2012) achieved an average boundary F-score of 76.1 on a different dataset that used a different boundary annotation standard (automatic forced alignment instead of human annotation). To our knowledge, the dataset is no longer publicly available. A recent segmentation-only model (Michel et al., 2017) achieved a boundary F of 75 on the TIMIT dataset (Fisher et al., 1986). However, because TIMIT is restricted to 10 unique utterances of English, we believe Zerospeech 2015, which contains more linguistically diverse speech from two unrelated languages, is a better dataset for investigating language acquisition patterns.

F-measures by language and experimental condition are given in Figure 2. Results show a contribution of both memory ($B > 0$) and prediction ($F > 0$), with a similar distribution of relative performance between the two languages, supporting the existence of language-general influences of prediction and memory on phoneme learning.

As shown in Figure 2, models without memory pressures ($B = 0$) find substantially worse boundaries than models with memory pressures. There also appears to be a ceiling effect of backward reconstruction size, with a jump in performance at $B = 25$ but no systematic improvement at $B = 50$. Importantly, at layer 1, $B = 25$ covers a 250ms interval, which falls within even conservative estimates of the storage duration of unanalyzed auditory traces in humans (Cowan, 1984). The $B = 25$ objective could therefore plausibly be used during online speech processing. Prediction pressures also support discovery of phoneme boundaries, as shown by the generally worse boundary performance of $F = 0$ vs. $F > 0$ in both languages.

In addition, Figure 2 shows that memory and prediction both modulate phoneme classification performance, with a roughly convex performance surface around a peak at $B = 25$, $F = 10$ for English and $B = 25$, $F = 5$ for Xitsonga. A similar peak emerges in the feature classification results for English, along with a local feature classification peak in Xitsonga for $L > 2$. A 250ms auditory memory window thus supports both phoneme segmentation and classification in our models, with additional benefits from predicting over short intervals (Singer et al., 2018). For feature classification, the primary determinant of performance across languages is the prediction objective, with performance generally increasing up to $F = 5$. There is also an effect of encoder depth in these results, such that encoders with more layers ($L > 2$) tend to perform better across metrics, despite the fact that all metrics reflect performance at the first layer. This result supports a contribution of multiscale modeling, even if the segmentation behavior at higher layers does not clearly correspond to a theory-driven level of representation (see section 4.3).

Figure 3 reports performance differences by metric against baseline U (untrained). Training yields consistent and often substantial improvements across metrics in multiscale ($L > 0$) encoders with both memory ($B > 0$) and prediction ($F > 0$) pressures, but can fail to improve in the

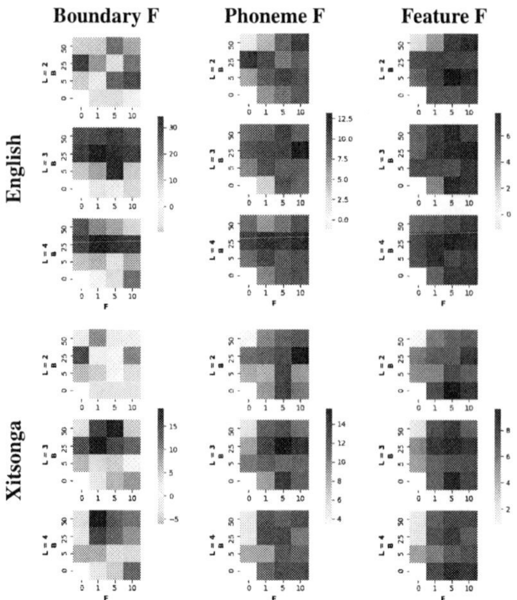

Figure 3: **Effect of learning.** Change in F-measure by metric over baseline U.

absence of these characteristics. Memory and prediction therefore modulate not only absolute performance, but also the utility of language experience.

Figure 4 reports performance differences by metric against baseline X (cross-language). English segmentation is substantially helped by experience with (i.e. training on) English, especially under strong memory pressures. However, Xitsonga segmentation is generally worse for the Xitsonga-trained model than the English-trained one. This might be due to the fact that the English training set is larger, and/or to low overall levels of segmentation performance in Xitsonga. While we leave further investigation of this exception to future work, the classification metrics still show a clear benefit of in-domain training in both languages, but only in the presence of prediction pressures.

The baseline X results bear on the degree to which speech processing patterns can plausibly be innately specified. Although the set of phonological categories and features are classically regarded as universal (Chomsky and Halle, 1968; Clements, 1985), it is well known that the "same" phonological abstraction (e.g. voicing) can be phonetically cached out in different ways depending on the language (e.g. Gordon and Ladefoged, 2001; Gordon et al., 2002). Our results suggest that, at least between Xitsonga and English, this variation is both (1) constrained enough to permit recognition of

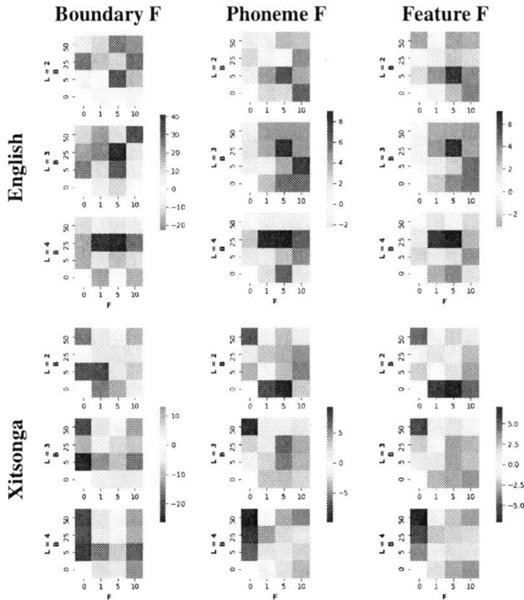

Figure 4: **Effect of language.** Change in F-measure by metric over baseline X.

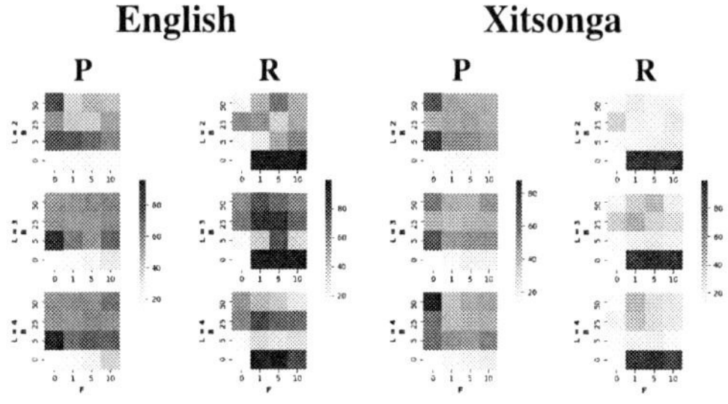

Figure 5: **Boundary P/R trade-off.** Boundary precision (left) and recall (right) by experimental configuration in Xitsonga and English.

non-trivial patterns from speech in other languages on the basis of general, possibly innate processing biases, and (2) substantial enough to give rise to a benefit of direct experience with the target language, even for language-general constructs like phoneme categories and phonological features.

We use linear regression on the combined metrics to quantitatively evaluate the contribution of both memory and prediction pressures to phoneme acquisition. Results show significant positive contributions to acquisition from memory pressures ($p = 0.006$), prediction pressures ($p < 0.001$), and multiscale encoding ($p < 0.001$).[8]

The boundary precision/recall trade-off illuminates the mechanisms by which memory and prediction pressures affect learning (Figure 5). Without memory pressures ($B = 0$), segmentation rates are high, resulting in high recall and low precision. Introducing memory pressures ($B > 0$) slows the segmentation rate, resulting in a more balanced P/R trade-off. Without prediction pressures ($F = 0$), segmentation rates are generally low, resulting in higher precision and lower recall. Introducing prediction pressures ($F > 0$) increases the segmentation rate, again resulting in a more balanced trade-off. To understand this pattern, recall that a boundary in our model represents both a cost

(flushing the memory cell) and a benefit (injecting top-down feedback). The cost of forgetting is plausibly greater for reconstruction than prediction, since only the current layer has had direct access to the sequence of reconstruction targets. By contrast, the benefit of top-down feedback is plausibly greater for prediction than reconstruction, since the prediction can condition on contextual representations at multiple timescales. In our segmental model of speech processing, the objectives therefore induce countervailing biases that boost signal for phonological constructs, supporting their joint influence on phoneme acquisition from speech.

6 Conclusion

We proposed an unsupervised deep neural model of speech processing that is incremental, segmental, and optimized by local feedback. We manipulated the model's objective function in order to investigate prior hypotheses about the role in human language acquisition of memory constraints on the one hand and predictive processing on the other. Results support a role for both memory and prediction pressures for acquiring phonemes from speech. Both objectives inform the model's segmentation behavior and the content of its segment encodings. In addition, results suggest that these two mechanisms coordinate to support phoneme discovery by introducing countervailing pressures toward retention of previously encountered signals (memory) and consultation of top-down signals (prediction).

Acknowledgements

We thank Aren Jansen and the Clippers discussion group at Ohio State for providing valuable feedback on this research. This work was funded in part by a Google Faculty Research Award to Micha Elsner.

---

[8]See Appendix G for details.

References

Wiehan Agenbag and Thomas Niesler. 2015. Automatic segmentation and clustering of speech using sparse coding and metaheuristic search. In *Sixteenth Annual Conference of the International Speech Communication Association*.

Adam Albright. 2002. Islands of reliability for regular morphology: Evidence from Italian. *Language*, pages 684–709.

Jean E Andruski, Sheila E Blumstein, and Martha Burton. 1994. The effect of subphonetic differences on lexical access. *Cognition*, 52(3):163–187.

T K Ansari, Rajath Kumar, Sonali Singh, and Sriram Ganapathy. 2017a. Deep learning methods for unsupervised acoustic modeling—Leap submission to ZeroSpeech challenge 2017. In *Automatic Speech Recognition and Understanding Workshop (ASRU), 2017 IEEE*, pages 754–761. IEEE.

T K Ansari, Rajath Kumar, Sonali Singh, Sriram Ganapathy, and Susheela Devi. 2017b. Unsupervised HMM posteriograms for language independent acoustic modeling in zero resource conditions. In *Automatic Speech Recognition and Understanding Workshop (ASRU), 2017 IEEE*, pages 762–768. IEEE.

Keith S Apfelbaum and Bob McMurray. 2017. Learning during processing: Word learning doesn't wait for word recognition to finish. *Cognitive science*, 41:706–747.

Fred Attneave. 1954. Some informational aspects of visual perception. *Psychological review*, 61(3):183.

R Harald Baayen, Ton Dijkstra, and Robert Schreuder. 1997. Singulars and plurals in Dutch: Evidence for a parallel dual-route model. *Journal of Memory and Language*, 37(1):94–117.

Alan Baddeley, Susan Gathercole, and Costanza Papagno. 1998. The Phonological Loop as a Language Learning Device. *Psychological Review*, 105(1):158–173.

Alan D Baddeley and Graham Hitch. 1974. *Working Memory*. University of Stirling, Stirling, Scotland.

Leonardo Badino, Alessio Mereta, and Lorenzo Rosasco. 2015. Discovering discrete subword units with binarized autoencoders and hidden-markov-model encoders. In *Sixteenth Annual Conference of the International Speech Communication Association*.

Pallavi Baljekar, Sunayana Sitaram, Prasanna Kumar Muthukumar, and Alan W Black. 2015. Using articulatory features and inferred phonological segments in zero resource speech processing. In *Sixteenth Annual Conference of the International Speech Communication Association*.

Gašper Beguš. 2020. Modeling unsupervised phonetic and phonological learning in Generative Adversarial Phonology. *Proceedings of the Society for Computation in Linguistics*, 3(1):138–148.

Pascal Belin, Robert J Zatorre, Philippe Lafaille, Pierre Ahad, and Bruce Pike. 2000. Voice-selective areas in human auditory cortex. *Nature*, 403(6767):309–312.

Yoshua Bengio, Nicholas Léonard, and Aaron Courville. 2013. Estimating or propagating gradients through stochastic neurons for conditional computation. *arXiv preprint arXiv:1308.3432*.

William Bialek, Ilya Nemenman, and Naftali Tishby. 2001. Predictability, complexity, and learning. *Neural computation*, 13(11):2409–2463.

Anna Blasi, Evelyne Mercure, Sarah Lloyd-Fox, Alex Thomson, Michael Brammer, Disa Sauter, Quinton Deeley, Gareth J Barker, Ville Renvall, Sean Deoni, and others. 2011. Early specialization for voice and emotion processing in the infant brain. *Current biology*, 21(14):1220–1224.

Guy J Brown and Martin Cooke. 1994. Computational auditory scene analysis. *Computer speech and language*, 8(4):297–336.

Andrew Carstairs-McCarthy. 1994. Inflection classes, gender, and the principle of contrast. *Language*, pages 737–788.

Hongjie Chen, Cheung-Chi Leung, Lei Xie, Bin Ma, and Haizhou Li. 2015. Parallel inference of Dirichlet process Gaussian mixture models for unsupervised acoustic modeling: A feasibility study. In *Sixteenth Annual Conference of the International Speech Communication Association*.

Hongjie Chen, Cheung-Chi Leung, Lei Xie, Bin Ma, and Haizhou Li. 2017. Multilingual bottle-neck feature learning from untranscribed speech. In *Automatic Speech Recognition and Understanding Workshop (ASRU), 2017 IEEE*, pages 727–733. IEEE.

Noam Chomsky. 1957. *Syntactic Structures*. Mouton, The Hague.

Noam Chomsky. 1965. *Aspects of the Theory of Syntax*. MIT Press, Cambridge, MA.

Noam Chomsky and Morris Halle. 1968. *The Sound Pattern of English*. Harper \& Row.

Jan Chorowski, Ron J Weiss, Samy Bengio, and Aäron van den Oord. 2019. Unsupervised speech representation learning using wavenet autoencoders. *IEEE/ACM transactions on audio, speech, and language processing*, 27(12):2041–2053.

Christos Christodoulopoulos, Sharon Goldwater, and Mark Steedman. 2012. Turning the pipeline into a loop: Iterated unsupervised dependency parsing and PoS induction. In *Proceedings of the NAACL-HLT Workshop on the Induction of Linguistic Structure*, pages 96–99.

Grzegorz Chrupała, Bertrand Higy, and Afra Alishahi. 2020. Analyzing analytical methods: The case of phonology in neural models of spoken language. *arXiv preprint arXiv:2004.07070*.

Junyoung Chung, Sungjin Ahn, and Yoshua Bengio. 2017. Hierarchical Multiscale Recurrent Neural Networks. In *International Conference on Learning Representations 2017*.

George N Clements. 1985. The geometry of phonological features. *Phonology*, 2(1):225–252.

Djork-Arné Clevert, Thomas Unterthiner, and Sepp Hochreiter. 2015. Fast and accurate deep network learning by exponential linear units (elus). *arXiv preprint arXiv:1511.07289*.

Matthieu Courbariaux, Itay Hubara, Daniel Soudry, Ran El-Yaniv, and Yoshua Bengio. 2016. Binarized neural networks: Training deep neural networks with weights and activations constrained to+1 or-1. *arXiv preprint arXiv:1602.02830*.

Nelson Cowan. 1984. On short and long auditory stores. *Psychological bulletin*, 96(2):341.

Toni Cunillera, Estela Càmara, Juan M Toro, Josep Marco-Pallares, Nuria Sebastián-Galles, Hector Ortiz, Jesús Pujol, and Antoni Rodr\'\iguez-Fornells. 2009. Time course and functional neuroanatomy of speech segmentation in adults. *Neuroimage*, 48(3):541–553.

Toni Cunillera, Juan M Toro, Nuria Sebastián-Gallés, and Antoni Rodr\'\iguez-Fornells. 2006. The effects of stress and statistical cues on continuous speech segmentation: an event-related brain potential study. *Brain Research*, 1123(1):168–178.

Nic J De Vries, Marelie H Davel, Jaco Badenhorst, Willem D Basson, Febe De Wet, Etienne Barnard, and Alta De Waal. 2014. A smartphone-based ASR data collection tool for under-resourced languages. *Speech communication*, 56:119–131.

Ewan Dunbar, Xuan Nga Cao, Juan Benjumea, Julien Karadayi, Mathieu Bernard, Laurent Besacier, Xavier Anguera, and Emmanuel Dupoux. 2017. The zero resource speech challenge 2017. In *Automatic Speech Recognition and Understanding Workshop (ASRU), 2017 IEEE*, pages 323–330. IEEE.

Jeffrey L Elman. 1991. Distributed representations, simple recurrent networks, and grammatical structure. *Machine Learning*, 7:195–225.

Jeffrey L Elman. 1993. Learning and development in neural networks: The importance of starting small. *Cognition*, 48:71–99.

Ryan Eloff, André Nortje, Benjamin van Niekerk, Avashna Govender, Leanne Nortje, Arnu Pretorius, Elan van Biljon, Ewald van der Westhuizen, Lisa van Staden, and Herman Kamper. 2019. Unsupervised Acoustic Unit Discovery for Speech Synthesis Using Discrete Latent-Variable Neural Networks. *Proc. Interspeech 2019*, pages 1103–1107.

Micha Elsner and Cory Shain. 2017. Speech segmentation with a neural encoder model of working memory. In *Proceedings of the 2017 Conference on Empirical Methods in Natural Language Processing*, pages 1070–1080.

Shirley Fecteau, Jorge L Armony, Yves Joanette, and Pascal Belin. 2005. Sensitivity to voice in human prefrontal cortex. *Journal of Neurophysiology*, 94(3):2251–2254.

William M Fisher, George R Doddington, and Kathleen M Goudie-Marshall. 1986. The DARPA Speech Recognition Research Database: Specifications and Status. In *Proceedings of DARPA Workshop on Speech Recognition*, pages 93–99.

Stefan L Frank and Rens Bod. 2011. Insensitivity of the Human Sentence-Processing System to Hierarchical Structure. *Psychological Science*, 22(6):829–834.

Stefan L Frank and Morten H Christiansen. 2018. Hierarchical and sequential processing of language. *Language, Cognition and Neuroscience*, 33(9):1213–1218.

Karl Friston. 2010. The free-energy principle: a unified brain theory? *Nature reviews neuroscience*, 11(2):127.

Xavier Glorot and Yoshua Bengio. 2010. Understanding the difficulty of training deep feedforward neural networks. In *Proceedings of the thirteenth international conference on artificial intelligence and statistics*, pages 249–256.

Mark E. Gold. 1967. Language Identification in the Limit. *Information and Control*, (10):447–474.

John Goldsmith. 1976. *Autosegmental phonology*. Ph.D. thesis, MIT Press London.

John Goldsmith. 2003. Unsupervised learning of the morphology of a natural language. *Computational Linguistics*, 27(2):153–189.

Sharon Goldwater, Thomas Griffiths, and Mark Johnson. 2009. A {Bayesian} framework for word segmentation: {Exploring} the effects of context. *Cognition*, 112:21–54.

Adam Goodkind and Klinton Bicknell. 2018. Predictive power of word surprisal for reading times is a linear function of language model quality. In *Proceedings of the 8th Workshop on Cognitive Modeling and Computational Linguistics (CMCL 2018)*, pages 10–18.

Matthew Gordon, Paul Barthmaier, and Kathy Sands. 2002. A cross-linguistic acoustic study of voiceless fricatives. *Journal of the International Phonetic Association*, pages 141–174.

Matthew Gordon and Peter Ladefoged. 2001. Phonation types: a cross-linguistic overview. *Journal of phonetics*, 29(4):383–406.

John Hale. 2006. Uncertainty about the rest of the sentence. *Cognitive Science*, 30(4):643–672.

Kenneth D Harris and Thomas D Mrsic-Flogel. 2013. Cortical connectivity and sensory coding. *Nature*, 503(7474):51–58.

Uri Hasson, Janice Chen, and Christopher J Honey. 2015. Hierarchical process memory: memory as an integral component of information processing. *Trends in cognitive sciences*, 19(6):304–313.

Bruce Hayes. 2011. *Introductory phonology*, volume 32. John Wiley \& Sons, Hoboken.

Kenneth Heafield, Ivan Pouzyrevsky, Jonathan H Clark, and Philipp Koehn. 2013. Scalable modified Kneser-Ney language model estimation. In *Proceedings of the 51st Annual Meeting of the Association for Computational Linguistics*, pages 690–696, Sofia, Bulgaria.

Michael Heck, Sakriani Sakti, and Satoshi Nakamura. 2016. Unsupervised linear discriminant analysis for supporting DPGMM clustering in the zero resource scenario. *Procedia Computer Science*, 81:73–79.

Michael Heck, Sakriani Sakti, and Satoshi Nakamura. 2017. Feature optimized dpgmm clustering for unsupervised subword modeling: A contribution to zerospeech 2017. In *Automatic Speech Recognition and Understanding Workshop (ASRU), 2017 IEEE*, pages 740–746. IEEE.

Geoffrey Hinton. 2012. Neural Networks for Machine Learning. *Coursera, video lectures*.

Sepp Hochreiter and Jürgen Schmidhuber. 1997. Long Short-Term Memory. *Neural Comput.*, 9(8):1735–1780.

John J Hopfield. 1982. Neural networks and physical systems with emergent collective computational abilities. *Proceedings of the national academy of sciences*, 79(8):2554–2558.

Sergey Ioffe and Christian Szegedy. 2015. Batch Normalization: Accelerating Deep Network Training by Reducing Internal Covariate Shift. In *International Conference on Machine Learning*, pages 448–456.

Ole Jensen. 2006. Maintenance of multiple working memory items by temporal segmentation. *Neuroscience*, 139(1):237–249.

Matt A Johnson, Nicholas B Turk-Browne, and Adele E Goldberg. 2013. Prediction plays a key role in language development as well as processing. *Behavioral and Brain Sciences*, 36(4):360.

Rafal Jozefowicz, Oriol Vinyals, Mike Schuster, Noam Shazeer, and Yonghui Wu. 2016. Exploring the limits of language modeling. *arXiv preprint arXiv:1602.02410*.

Ákos Kádár, Marc-Alexandre Côté, Grzegorz Chrupała, and Afra Alishahi. 2018. Revisiting the Hierarchical Multiscale LSTM. In *Proceedings of the 27th International Conference on Computational Linguistics*, pages 3215–3227.

Herman Kamper, Micha Elsner, Aren Jansen, and Sharon Goldwater. 2015. Unsupervised neural network based feature extraction using weak top-down constraints. In *Acoustics, Speech and Signal Processing (ICASSP), 2015 IEEE International Conference on*, pages 5818–5822. IEEE.

Herman Kamper, Aren Jansen, and Sharon Goldwater. 2017a. A segmental framework for fully-unsupervised large-vocabulary speech recognition. *Computer Speech & Language*, 46:154–174.

Herman Kamper, Karen Livescu, and Sharon Goldwater. 2017b. An embedded segmental k-means model for unsupervised segmentation and clustering of speech. In *Automatic Speech Recognition and Understanding Workshop (ASRU), 2017 IEEE*, pages 719–726. IEEE.

Georg B Keller and Thomas D Mrsic-Flogel. 2018. Predictive Processing: A Canonical Cortical Computation. *Neuron*, 100(2):424–435.

Alan W Kersten and Julie L Earles. 2001. Less really is more for adults learning a miniature artificial language. *Journal of Memory and Language*, 44(2):250–273.

Stefan J Kiebel, Jean Daunizeau, and Karl J Friston. 2008. A hierarchy of time-scales and the brain. *PLoS Comput Biol*, 4(11):e1000209.

Diederik P Kingma and Jimmy Ba. 2014. Adam: A method for stochastic optimization. *CoRR*, abs/1412.6.

Dan Klein and Christopher D. Manning. 2004. Corpus-based induction of syntactic structure: Models of dependency and constituency. In *Proceedings of the Annual Meeting on Association for Computational Linguistics*, volume 1, pages 478–485.

Valesca Kooijman, Caroline Junge, Elizabeth K Johnson, Peter Hagoort, and Anne Cutler. 2013. Predictive brain signals of linguistic development. *Frontiers in psychology*, 4:25.

Byeongwook Lee and Kwang-Hyun Cho. 2016. Brain-inspired speech segmentation for automatic speech recognition using the speech envelope as a temporal reference. *Scientific reports*, 6:37647.

Chia-ying Lee and James Glass. 2012. A Nonparametric {Bayesian} Approach to Acoustic Model Discovery. In *Proceedings of the 50th Annual Meeting of the Association for Computational Linguistics*, pages 40–49.

Chia-ying Lee, Timothy J O'Donnell, and James Glass. 2015. Unsupervised Lexicon Discovery from Acoustic Input. In *Transactions of the Association for Computational Linguistics*, volume 3, pages 389–403.

Tal Linzen, Emmanuel Dupoux, and Yoav Goldberg. 2016. Assessing the ability of LSTMs to learn syntax-sensitive dependencies. *Transactions of the Association for Computational Linguistics*, 4:521–535.

William A Little. 1974. The existence of persistent states in the brain. *Mathematical biosciences*, 19(1-2):101–120.

Vince Lyzinski, Gregory Sell, and Aren Jansen. 2015. An evaluation of graph clustering methods for unsupervised term discovery. In *Sixteenth Annual Conference of the International Speech Communication Association*.

David Marr. 1982. *Vision: A Computational Investigation into the Human Representation and Processing of Visual Information*. W.H. Freeman and Company.

Timothée Masquelier. 2018. STDP allows close-to-optimal spatiotemporal spike pattern detection by single coincidence detector neurons. *Neuroscience*, 389:133–140.

Stewart M McCauley and Morten H Christiansen. 2019. Language learning as language use: A cross-linguistic model of child language development. *Psychological review*, 126(1):1.

R Thomas McCoy, Robert Frank, and Tal Linzen. 2018. Revisiting the poverty of the stimulus: Hierarchical generalization without a hierarchical bias in recurrent neural networks. In *Proceedings of the 40th Annual Conference of the Cognitive Science Society*, pages 2093–2098.

R Thomas McCoy, Robert Frank, and Tal Linzen. 2020. Does syntax need to grow on trees? Sources of hierarchical inductive bias in sequence-to-sequence networks. *Transactions of the Association for Computational Linguistics*, 8:125–140.

Josh H McDermott and Eero P Simoncelli. 2011. Sound texture perception via statistics of the auditory periphery: evidence from sound synthesis. *Neuron*, 71(5):926–940.

Bob McMurray, Michael K Tanenhaus, and Richard N Aslin. 2002. Gradient effects of within-category phonetic variation on lexical access. *Cognition*, 86(2):B33–B42.

Paul Mermelstein. 1976. Distance measures for speech recognition, psychological and instrumental. *Pattern recognition and artificial intelligence*, 116:374–388.

Paul Michel, Okko Rasanen, Roland Thiollière, and Emmanuel Dupoux. 2017. Blind Phoneme Segmentation With Temporal Prediction Errors. In *Proceedings of ACL 2017, Student Research Workshop*, pages 62–68.

Francis Mollica and Steven T Piantadosi. 2019. Humans store about 1.5 megabytes of information during language acquisition. *Royal Society open science*, 6(3):181393.

Padraic Monaghan and Morten H Christiansen. 2010. Words in puddles of sound: Modelling psycholinguistic effects in speech segmentation. *Journal of child language*, 37(3):545–564.

Elissa Newport. 1990. Maturational constraints on language learning. *Cognitive Science*, 14:11–28.

Hermann Ney, Ute Essen, and Reinhard Kneser. 1994. On structuring probabilistic dependences in stochastic language modelling. *Computer Speech and Language*, 8(1):1–38.

R Nijhawan. 1994. Motion extrapolation in catching. *Nature*, 370(6487):256.

Sam V Norman-Haignere, Laura K Long, Orrin Devinsky, Werner Doyle, Ifeoma Irobunda, Edward Merricks, Neil A Feldstein, Guy M V McKhann, Catherine Schevon, Adeen Flinker, and Nima Mesgarani. 2020. Hierarchical integration across multiple timescales in human auditory cortex. *bioRxiv*.

Bruno A Olshausen and David J Field. 1996. Emergence of simple-cell receptive field properties by learning a sparse code for natural images. *Nature*, 381(6583):607.

Bruno A Olshausen and David J Field. 2004. Sparse coding of sensory inputs. *Current opinion in neurobiology*, 14(4):481–487.

Aäron van den Oord, Sander Dieleman, Heiga Zen, Karen Simonyan, Oriol Vinyals, Alex Graves, Nal Kalchbrenner, Andrew Senior, and Koray Kavukcuoglu. 2016. WaveNet: A Generative Model for Raw Audio. In *9th ISCA Speech Synthesis Workshop*, page 125.

Fabian Pedregosa, Gaël Varoquaux, Alexandre Gramfort, Vincent Michel, Bertrand Thirion, Olivier Grisel, Mathieu Blondel, Peter Prettenhofer, Ron Weiss, Vincent Dubourg, and others. 2011. Scikit-learn: Machine learning in Python. *Journal of machine learning research*, 12(Oct):2825–2830.

Amy Perfors. 2012. When do memory limitations lead to regularization? An experimental and computational investigation. *Journal of Memory and Language*, 67(4):486–506.

Cyril R Pernet, Phil McAleer, Marianne Latinus, Krzysztof J Gorgolewski, Ian Charest, Patricia E G Bestelmeyer, Rebecca H Watson, David Fleming, Frances Crabbe, Mitchell Valdes-Sosa, and others.

2015. The human voice areas: Spatial organization and inter-individual variability in temporal and extra-temporal cortices. *Neuroimage*, 119:164–174.

Colin Phillips and Lara Ehrenhofer. 2015. The role of language processing in language acquisition. *Linguistic approaches to bilingualism*, 5(4):409–453.

Steven T Piantadosi, Joshua B Tenenbaum, and Noah D Goodman. 2016. The logical primitives of thought: Empirical foundations for compositional cognitive models. *Psychological review*, 123(4):392.

Steven Pinker. 1991. Rules of language. *Science*, 253(5019):530–535.

Mark A Pitt, Keith Johnson, Elizabeth Hume, Scott Kiesling, and William Raymond. 2005. The Buckeye corpus of conversational speech: labeling conventions and a test of transcriber reliability. *Speech Communication*, 45(1):89–95.

Alec Radford, Jeffrey Wu, Rewon Child, David Luan, Dario Amodei, and Ilya Sutskever. 2019. Language models are unsupervised multitask learners. *OpenAI Blog*, 1(8):9.

Okko Räsänen, Gabriel Doyle, and Michael C Frank. 2015. Unsupervised word discovery from speech using automatic segmentation into syllable-like units. In *Sixteenth Annual Conference of the International Speech Communication Association*.

Daniel Renshaw, Herman Kamper, Aren Jansen, and Sharon Goldwater. 2015. A comparison of neural network methods for unsupervised representation learning on the zero resource speech challenge. In *Sixteenth Annual Conference of the International Speech Communication Association*.

Jorma Rissanen and Eric Sven Ristad. 1994. Language acquisition in the MDL framework. *Language computations*, pages 149–166.

Douglas L T Rohde and David C Plaut. 1999. Language acquisition in the absence of explicit negative evidence: How important is starting small? *Cognition*, 72(1):67–109.

Jenny R Saffran, Richard N Aslin, and Elissa L Newport. 1996. Statistical learning by 8-month-old infants. *Science*, 274(5294):1926–1928.

Lisa D Sanders and Helen J Neville. 2003. An ERP study of continuous speech processing: I. Segmentation, semantics, and syntax in native speakers. *Cognitive Brain Research*, 15(3):228–240.

Anthony J Sanford and Patrick Sturt. 2002. Depth of processing in language comprehension: Not noticing the evidence. *Trends in cognitive sciences*, 6(9):382–386.

Andrew M Saxe, James L McClelland, and Surya Ganguli. 2013. Exact solutions to the nonlinear dynamics of learning in deep linear neural networks. *arXiv preprint arXiv:1312.6120*.

Marten van Schijndel and Tal Linzen. 2018. A Neural Model of Adaptation in Reading. In *EMNLP 2018*, pages 4704–4710.

Cory Shain and Micha Elsner. 2019. Measuring the perceptual availability of phonological features during language acquisition using unsupervised binary stochastic autoencoders. In *Proceedings of the 2019 Conference of the North American Chapter of the Association for Computational Linguistics: Human Language Technologies, Volume 1 (Long and Short Papers)*, pages 69–85.

Patrick M Sheridan, Fuxi Cai, Chao Du, Wen Ma, Zhengya Zhang, and Wei D Lu. 2017. Sparse coding with memristor networks. *Nature nanotechnology*, 12(8):784.

Hayato Shibata, Taku Kato, Takahiro Shinozaki, and Shinji Watanabet. 2017. Composite embedding systems for ZeroSpeech2017 Track1. In *Automatic Speech Recognition and Understanding Workshop (ASRU), 2017 IEEE*, pages 747–753. IEEE.

Yosef Singer, Yayoi Teramoto, Ben D B Willmore, Jan W H Schnupp, Andrew J King, and Nicol S Harper. 2018. Sensory cortex is optimized for prediction of future input. *eLife*, 7:e31557.

Brij Mohan Lal Srivastava and Manish Shrivastava. 2016. Articulatory gesture rich representation learning of phonological units in low resource settings. In *International Conference on Statistical Language and Speech Processing*, pages 80–95. Springer.

Aaron Van Den Oord, Oriol Vinyals, and others. 2017. Neural discrete representation learning. In *Advances in Neural Information Processing Systems*, pages 6306–6315.

Ashish Vaswani, Noam Shazeer, Niki Parmar, Jakob Uszkoreit, Llion Jones, Aidan N Gomez, Łukasz Kaiser, and Illia Polosukhin. 2017. Attention is all you need. In *Advances in neural information processing systems*, pages 5998–6008.

Maarten Versteegh, Roland Thiollière, Thomas Schatz, Xuan Nga Cao, Xavier Anguera, Aren Jansen, and Emmanuel Dupoux. 2015. The zero resource speech challenge 2015. In *Sixteenth Annual Conference of the International Speech Communication Association*.

Charles Yang. 2005. On productivity. *Linguistic variation yearbook*, 5(1):265–302.

Yougen Yuan, Cheung-Chi Leung, Lei Xie, Hongjie Chen, Bin Ma, and Haizhou Li. 2017. Extracting bottleneck features and word-like pairs from untranscribed speech for feature representation. In *Automatic Speech Recognition and Understanding Workshop (ASRU), 2017 IEEE*, pages 734–739. IEEE.

Jeffrey M Zacks, Todd S Braver, Margaret A Sheridan, David I Donaldson, Abraham Z Snyder, John M Ollinger, Randy L Buckner, and Marcus E Raichle.

2001. Human brain activity time-locked to perceptual event boundaries. *Nature neuroscience*, 4(6):651–655.

Pavel Zahorik and Frederic L Wightman. 2001. Loudness constancy with varying sound source distance. *Nature neuroscience*, 4(1):78–83.

Neil Zeghidour, Gabriel Synnaeve, Maarten Versteegh, and Emmanuel Dupoux. 2016. A deep scattering spectrum—deep siamese network pipeline for unsupervised acoustic modeling. In *Acoustics, Speech and Signal Processing (ICASSP), 2016 IEEE International Conference on*, pages 4965–4969. IEEE.

Ciyou Zhu, Richard H Byrd, Peihuang Lu, and Jorge Nocedal. 1997. Algorithm 778: L-BFGS-B: Fortran subroutines for large-scale bound-constrained optimization. *ACM Transactions on Mathematical Software (TOMS)*, 23(4):550–560.

A   Encoder Definition

Given encoder inputs $\mathbf{x}_t^{\mathrm{e}} \in \mathbb{R}^{D_0}$ for $0 < t \leq T$, an encoder with L layers is a recurrent neural network that computes its D_l-dimensional hidden state $\mathbf{h}_t^{\mathrm{e}(l)} \in \mathbb{R}^{D_l}$ at timestep t and layer l from the hidden state below $\mathbf{h}_t^{\mathrm{e}(l-1)}$ (bottom-up connection), the previous hidden state $\mathbf{h}_{t-1}^{\mathrm{e}(l)}$ (recurrent connection), and the previous hidden state above $\mathbf{h}_{t-1}^{\mathrm{e}(l+1)}$, where the layer zeroth state $\mathbf{h}_t^{\mathrm{e}(0)} \in \mathbb{R}^{D_0}$ is the data $\mathbf{x}_t^{\mathrm{e}}$. The hidden state $\mathbf{h}_t^{\mathrm{e}(l)}$ serves as a *label* at layer l and timestep t. Information flow between these layers is governed by a discrete boundary neuron $z_t^{(l)} \in \{0, 1\}$ at each layer. Let $t^{(l)'}$ be the location of the most recent segment boundary preceding time t in layer l:

$$t^{(l)'} \stackrel{\text{def}}{=} \tau \mid \left[(z_\tau^{(l)} = 1) \wedge \right.$$
$$\left. \left(z_{\tau'}^{(l)} = 0,\ \forall \tau' \in \{\tau+1, \ldots, t-1\} \right) \right] \tag{A1}$$
$$\forall \tau \in \{1, \ldots, t-1\}$$

Let $f^{\mathrm{f}(l)}(a, b)$ be a filter function dropping labels of l at non-boundaries between timepoints a and b:

$$f^{\mathrm{f}(l)}(a, b) \stackrel{\text{def}}{=} \mathbf{h}_\tau^{\mathrm{e}(l)} \mid \left(z_\tau^{(l)} = 1 \right),$$
$$\forall \tau \in \{a, \ldots, b\} \tag{A2}$$

A *segment* $\mathbf{S}_t^{(l)}$ at layer l and timestep t is defined as:

$$\mathbf{S}_t^{(l)} \stackrel{\text{def}}{=} f^{\mathrm{f}(l-1)}(t^{(l)'} + 1, t) \tag{A3}$$

In other words, the segment $\mathbf{S}_t^{(l)}$ consists of the sequence of segment labels from layer $l - 1$ at boundaries from $l - 1$ that intervene since the last segment boundary at l.

The bottom-up, recurrent, and top-down inputs are respectively linearly transformed into vectors in $\mathbf{s}^{\mathrm{b}(l)}, \mathbf{s}^{\mathrm{r}(l)}, \mathbf{s}^{\mathrm{t}(l)} \in \mathbb{R}^{4D_l+1}$ using weight matrices $\mathbf{W}_i^j$ mapping from layer i to layer j, and masked using the boundary decisions z:

$$\mathbf{s}_t^{\mathrm{b}(l)} \stackrel{\text{def}}{=} z_t^{(l-1)} \mathbf{W}_{l-1}^l \mathbf{h}_t^{\mathrm{e}(l-1)} \tag{A4}$$

$$\mathbf{s}_t^{\mathrm{r}(l)} \stackrel{\text{def}}{=} \mathbf{W}_l^l \begin{pmatrix} \mathbf{h}_t^{\mathrm{e}(l)} \\ \mathbf{h}_t^{\mathrm{e}(l)'} \\ n_t^{(l)} \end{pmatrix} \tag{A5}$$

$$\mathbf{s}_t^{\mathrm{t}(l)} \stackrel{\text{def}}{=} z_{t-1}^{(l)} \mathbf{W}_{l+1}^l \mathbf{h}_t^{\mathrm{e}(l+1)} \tag{A6}$$

where $\mathbf{h}_t^{\mathrm{e}(l)'}$ records the label at the preceding segment boundary $\mathbf{h}_{t^{(l)'}}^{\mathrm{e}(l)}$ and $n_t^{(l)}$ is the number of timesteps since the preceding segment boundary at l. We pass this additional information into the recurrent connection to relieve pressure on the cell state to encode it. These vectors are summed together with a bias $\mathbf{b}^{(l)}$ to create a vector of preactivations $\mathbf{s}^{(l)}$, normalized by the boundary decisions so that the weights on active connections sum to 1:

$$\mathbf{s}_t^{(l)} \stackrel{\text{def}}{=} \frac{\mathbf{s}^{\mathrm{b}(l)} + \mathbf{s}^{\mathrm{r}(l)} + \mathbf{s}^{\mathrm{t}(l)} + \mathbf{b}^{(l)}}{1 + z_t^{(l-1)} + z_{t-1}^{(l)}} \tag{A7}$$

In this way, information is only passed upward and downward at boundaries, and the boundaries thus govern information flow between adjacent layers.

The vector $\mathbf{s}_t^{(l)}$ is split into state preactivations $\mathbf{u}_t^{(l)} \in \mathbb{R}^{4D_l}$ and scalar boundary preactivation $v_t^{(l)} \in \mathbb{R}$. Discrete boundary $z_t^{(l)}$ is computed from $v_t^{(l)}$ stochastically during training:

$$z_t^{\mathrm{train}(l)} \sim \mathrm{Bernoulli}\left(\mathrm{sigmoid}(v_t^{(l)}) \right) \tag{A8}$$

and deterministically during evaluation:

$$z_t^{\mathrm{eval}(l)} = \begin{cases} 1 & v_t^{(l)} > 0 \\ 0 & \text{otherwise} \end{cases} \tag{A9}$$

We additionally require that $z_t^{(0)} = 1$ (the input always "segments") and $z_t^{(L)} = 0$ (the top layer never segments). To enforce hierarchical segmentation behavior, we mask the boundaries by the boundaries at the layer below:

$$z_t^{(l)} \leftarrow z_t^{(l)} z_t^{(l-1)} \tag{A10}$$

Gradients through these discrete decisions are approximated using straight-through estimation (Hinton, 2012; Bengio et al., 2013; Courbariaux et al., 2016; Chung et al., 2017; Shain and Elsner, 2019; Eloff et al., 2019).

The forget gates $\mathbf{f}_t^{\mathrm{e}(l)}$, input gates $\mathbf{i}_t^{\mathrm{e}(l)}$, output gates $\mathbf{o}_t^{\mathrm{e}(l)}$, and cell proposal $\mathbf{g}_t^{\mathrm{e}(l)}$ are computed as follows:

$$\mathbf{f}_t^{\mathrm{e}(l)} \stackrel{\text{def}}{=} \mathrm{sigmoid}\left(\mathbf{u}_t^{(l)}{}_{[1:D_l]} \right) \tag{A11}$$

$$\mathbf{i}_t^{\mathrm{e}(l)} \stackrel{\text{def}}{=} \mathrm{sigmoid}\left(\mathbf{u}_t^{(l)}{}_{[D_l+1:2D_l]} \right) \tag{A12}$$

$$\mathbf{o}_t^{\mathrm{e}(l)} \stackrel{\text{def}}{=} \mathrm{sigmoid}\left(\mathbf{u}_t^{(l)}{}_{[2D_l+1:3D_l]} \right) \tag{A13}$$

$$\mathbf{g}_t^{\mathrm{e}(l)} \stackrel{\text{def}}{=} \tanh\left(\mathbf{u}_t^{(l)}{}_{[3D_l+1:4D_l]} \right) \tag{A14}$$

The cell state $\mathbf{c}_t^{\mathrm{e}(l)}$ is a weighted sum of three terms: a *flush* operation $\mathbf{c}_t^{\mathrm{f}(l)}$ that erases the cell memory, a standard LSTM *update* $\mathbf{c}^{\mathrm{u}(l)}$, and a *copy* operation $\mathbf{c}^{\mathrm{c}(l)}$ that copies the preceding cell state forward:

$$\mathbf{c}_t^{\mathrm{f}(l)} \stackrel{\mathrm{def}}{=} \mathbf{i}_t^{\mathrm{e}(l)} \odot \mathbf{g}_t^{(\mathrm{e}l)} \tag{A15}$$

$$\mathbf{c}_t^{\mathrm{u}(l)} \stackrel{\mathrm{def}}{=} \mathbf{f}_t^{\mathrm{e}(l)} \odot \mathbf{c}_{t-1}^{\mathrm{e}(l)} + \mathbf{i}_t^{\mathrm{e}(l)} \odot \mathbf{g}_t^{\mathrm{e}(l)} \tag{A16}$$

$$\mathbf{c}_t^{\mathrm{c}(l)} \stackrel{\mathrm{def}}{=} \mathbf{c}_{t-1}^{\mathrm{e}(l)} \tag{A17}$$

These terms are weighted by the boundary decision such that a flush occurs when the preceding timestep finds a boundary, an update otherwise occurs when the layer below finds a boundary, and a copy occurs when neither layer finds a boundary:

$$\begin{aligned} \mathbf{c}_t^{\mathrm{e}(l)} \stackrel{\mathrm{def}}{=}\ & z_{t-1}^{(l)} \mathbf{c}_t^{\mathrm{f}(l)} + \\ & \left(1 - z_{t-1}^{(l)}\right) z_t^{(l-1)} \mathbf{c}_t^{\mathrm{u}(l)} + \\ & \left(1 - z_{t-1}^{(l)}\right) \left(1 - z_t^{(l-1)}\right) \mathbf{c}_t^{\mathrm{c}(l)} \end{aligned} \tag{A18}$$

The hidden state $\mathbf{h}_t^{\mathrm{e}(l)}$ is computed as:

$$\mathbf{h}_t^{\mathrm{e}(l)} \stackrel{\mathrm{def}}{=} \tanh\left(\mathbf{c}_t^{\mathrm{e}(l)}\right) \tag{A19}$$

The previous segment encoding $\mathbf{h}_t^{e(l)'}$ is updated following a boundary and copied forward otherwise:

$$\mathbf{h}_t^{\mathrm{e}(l)'} \stackrel{\mathrm{def}}{=} z_{t-1}^{(l)} \mathbf{h}_{t-1}^{\mathrm{e}(l)} + \left(1 - z_{t-1}^{(l)}\right) \mathbf{h}_{t-1}^{\mathrm{e}(l)'} \tag{A20}$$

The current segment length $n_t^{(l)}$ is reset to 0 if $z_{t-1}^{(l)} = 1$, incremented if $z_t^{(l-1)} = 1$, and copied forward otherwise:

$$n_t^{(l)} \stackrel{\mathrm{def}}{=} \left(1 - z_{t-1}^{(l)}\right) n_{t-1}^{(l)} + z_t^{(l-1)} \tag{A21}$$

B Comparison of Encoder Model to Chung et al. (2017)

Although our encoder model closely follows the definition in Chung et al. (2017), it differs in the following ways:

- The recurrent connection includes both the previous segment label and the current segment length in addition to the previous hidden state. We found this to be helpful during model development, and we hypothesize that this is because doing so removes the need for this information to be encoded by the model.

- We implement the case-wise reasoning of the segmentation decisions using multiplicative masking rather than logical selection. This is intended to boost signal into the boundary decisions.

- We enforce hierarchical segmentation behavior by multiplicatively masking the segmentation decision at layer l with the segmentation decision at layer $l - 1$, thus preventing higher layers from segmenting where lower layers do not.

- We compute boundaries during training via Bernoulli sampling rather than rounding. We found this to substantially improve performance on the development set, and we hypothesize that sampling may improve the straight-through gradient estimates by ensuring that the segmentation decision is unbiased with respect to the underlying segmentation probability.

- We renormalize the preactivations $\mathbf{s}_t^{(l)}$ by the incoming boundary decisions (eq. A7). We found this to be helpful during model development, and we hypothesize that this is because it avoids fluctuation in the scale of preactivations as a function of the boundaries.

- We do not apply the Chung ct al. (2017) technique of *slope annealing*, i.e. gradually increasing the steepness of the sigmoid activation function to reduce bias in the straight-through estimator. We did not find an appreciable benefit from slope annealing during development, and it had a tendency to produce training instability. Eliminating it also reduces experimenter degrees of freedom by removing design decisions about the annealing function.

C Decoder Definition

The decoder consists of two attentional seq2seq LSTMs with L layers each, one backward-directional (memory) and one forward directional (prediction). Given a backward window size B and a forward window size F, each backward decoder layer generates reconstructions $\mathbf{Y}_t^{\mathrm{B}(l)} \in \mathbb{R}^{B \times D_{l-1}}$ and each forward decoder layer generates predictions $\mathbf{Y}_t^{\mathrm{F}(l)} \in \mathbb{R}^{F \times D_{l-1}}$, corresponding respectively to the B preceding and F following segment labels of layer $l - 1$ at time t. The initial decoder hidden and cell states — $\mathbf{h}_{t,0}^{\mathrm{dB}(l)}$ and $\mathbf{c}_{t,0}^{\mathrm{dB}(l)}$ for the backward decoder and $\mathbf{h}_{t,0}^{\mathrm{dF}(l)}$ and $\mathbf{c}_{t,0}^{\mathrm{dF}(l)}$ for the forward decoder — are generated using multilayer feedforward transforms $f^{\mathrm{hB}(l)}$, $f^{\mathrm{cB}(l)}$, $f^{\mathrm{hF}(l)}$, and $f^{\mathrm{cF}(l)}$:

$$\mathbf{h}_{t,0}^{\mathrm{dB}(l)} \stackrel{\text{def}}{=} f^{\mathrm{hB}(l)}\left(\mathbf{h}_t^{\mathrm{e}(l)}\right) \tag{A22}$$

$$\mathbf{c}_{t,0}^{\mathrm{dB}(l)} \stackrel{\text{def}}{=} f^{\mathrm{cB}(l)}\left(\mathbf{h}_t^{\mathrm{e}(l)}\right) \tag{A23}$$

$$\mathbf{h}_{t,0}^{\mathrm{dF}(l)} \stackrel{\text{def}}{=} f^{\mathrm{hF}(l)}\left(\mathbf{h}_t^{\mathrm{e}(l)}\right) \tag{A24}$$

$$\mathbf{c}_{t,0}^{\mathrm{dF}(l)} \stackrel{\text{def}}{=} f^{\mathrm{cF}(l)}\left(\mathbf{h}_t^{\mathrm{e}(l)}\right) \tag{A25}$$

Decoder states are doubly time indexed by t, i, where t indexes the encoder timestamp (i.e. the input timestep at which decoding begins) and i indexes the decoder timestamp (i.e. progress through the B or F decoder frames). Given decoder states $\mathbf{h}_{t,i}^{\mathrm{dB}(l)}$, $\mathbf{h}_{t,i}^{\mathrm{dF}(l)}$, predictions $\mathbf{Y}_t^{\mathrm{B}(l)}{}_{[i]}$, $\mathbf{Y}_t^{\mathrm{F}(l)}{}_{[i]} \in \mathbb{R}^{D_{l-1}}$ are generated using multilayer feedforward transforms $f^{\mathrm{yB}(l)}$, $f^{\mathrm{yF}(l)}$:

$$\mathbf{Y}_t^{\mathrm{B}(l)}{}_{[i]} \stackrel{\text{def}}{=} f^{\mathrm{yB}(l)}\left(\mathbf{h}_{t,i}^{\mathrm{dB}(l)}\right) \tag{A26}$$

$$\mathbf{Y}_t^{\mathrm{F}(l)}{}_{[i]} \stackrel{\text{def}}{=} f^{\mathrm{yF}(l)}\left(\mathbf{h}_{t,i}^{\mathrm{dF}(l)}\right) \tag{A27}$$

The decoder takes as input a periodic positional encoding $\mathbf{e}_i$, generated following Vaswani et al. (2017). Non-final layers additionally take as an attention values the predictions from the layer above, i.e. $\mathbf{Y}_t^{\mathrm{B}(l+1)}$ (for backward reconstruction) and $\mathbf{Y}_t^{\mathrm{F}(l+1)}$ (for forward prediction) and compute a weighted sum of these values over time with attention weight vectors $\mathbf{a}_{t,i}^{\mathrm{B}(l)} \in (0,1)^B$ and $\mathbf{a}_{t,i}^{\mathrm{F}(l)} \in (0,1)^F$ to generate context vectors $\mathbf{w}_{t,i}^{\mathrm{B}(l)}$ and $\mathbf{w}_{t,i}^{\mathrm{F}(l)}$:

$$\mathbf{w}_{t,i}^{\mathrm{B}(l)} \stackrel{\text{def}}{=} \mathbf{Y}_t^{\mathrm{B}(l+1)\top} \mathbf{a}_{t,i}^{\mathrm{B}(l)} \tag{A28}$$

$$\mathbf{w}_{t,i}^{\mathrm{F}(l)} \stackrel{\text{def}}{=} \mathbf{Y}_t^{\mathrm{F}(l+1)\top} \mathbf{a}_{t,i}^{\mathrm{F}(l)} \tag{A29}$$

Attention weights $\mathbf{a}^{\mathrm{B}(l)}$ and $\mathbf{a}^{\mathrm{F}(l)}$ are computed using Gaussian kernel $k(i; \mu, \sigma^2)$:

$$k(i; \mu, \sigma^2) \stackrel{\text{def}}{=} \exp\left(\frac{(i-\mu)^2}{\sigma^2}\right) \tag{A30}$$

Kernel k is applied to decoder time, with concentration $\sigma^{\mathrm{B}(l)}, \sigma^{\mathrm{F}(l)} = 0.25$ and with location $\mu_{t,i}^{\mathrm{B}(l)}, \mu_{t,i}^{\mathrm{F}(l)} \in \mathbb{R}_+$ computed by transforming the previous decoder state using a feedforward transform $f^{\mathrm{qB}(l)}$, $f^{\mathrm{qF}(l)}$ and adding the result to the previous attention location:

$$\mu_{t,i}^{\mathrm{B}(l)} \stackrel{\text{def}}{=} \mathrm{abs}\left(f^{\mathrm{qB}(l)}\left(\mathbf{h}_{t,i-1}^{\mathrm{dB}(l)}\right)\right) + \mu_{t,i-1}^{\mathrm{B}(l)} \tag{A31}$$

$$\mu_{t,i}^{\mathrm{F}(l)} \stackrel{\text{def}}{=} \mathrm{abs}\left(f^{\mathrm{qF}(l)}\left(\mathbf{h}_{t,i-1}^{\mathrm{dF}(l)}\right)\right) + \mu_{t,i-1}^{\mathrm{F}(l)} \tag{A32}$$

where $\mu_{t,0}^{\mathrm{B}(l)} = 1$. Unit-normalized attention vectors are computed from timestamp vectors $\mathbf{t}^{\mathrm{B}} \stackrel{\text{def}}{=} (1, \dots, B)^\top$ and $\mathbf{t}^{\mathrm{F}} \stackrel{\text{def}}{=} (1, \dots, F)^\top$ as:

$$\mathbf{a}_{t,i}^{\mathrm{B}(l)} \stackrel{\text{def}}{=} \frac{k\left(\mathbf{t}^{\mathrm{B}}; \sigma^{\mathrm{B}(l)}, \mu_{t,i}^{\mathrm{B}(l)}\right)}{\sum_{j=1}^{B} k\left(\mathbf{t}_{[j]}^{\mathrm{B}}; \sigma^{\mathrm{B}(l)}, \mu_{t,j}^{\mathrm{B}(l)}\right)} \tag{A33}$$

$$\mathbf{a}_{t,i}^{\mathrm{F}(l)} \stackrel{\text{def}}{=} \frac{k\left(\mathbf{t}^{\mathrm{F}}; \sigma^{\mathrm{F}(l)}, \mu_{t,i}^{\mathrm{F}(l)}\right)}{\sum_{j=1}^{B} k\left(\mathbf{t}_{[j]}^{\mathrm{F}}; \sigma^{\mathrm{F}(l)}, \mu_{t,j}^{\mathrm{F}(l)}\right)} \tag{A34}$$

The attention weights are thus constrained to march monotonically in time from t into the decoded past or future predicted segment labels from the layer above. Using fixed concentration 0.25 yields an effective kernel width $[-2\sigma, 2\sigma]$ of one timestep, ensuring that the bulk of the attention kernel either falls on a single segment label or straddles two consecutive segment labels and preventing the decoder from spreading its attention over many higher-level segments. This design encourages one-to-many temporal alignment between decoded segment labels and decoded inputs, while allowing the decoder to determine how long to attend to a predicted segment label before moving on to the next one. At the final (top) layer, no top-down predictions are available, so the context vectors are omitted (or, equivalently, set to $\mathbf{0}$).

The inputs to the decoder $\mathbf{x}_{t,i}^{\mathrm{dB}(l)}$, $\mathbf{x}_{t,i}^{\mathrm{dF}(l)}$ are constructed as the vertical concatenation of $\mathbf{e}$, $\mathbf{w}$, and the previously generated decoder output, and a standard LSTM state update is applied:

$$\mathbf{x}_{t,i}^{\mathrm{dB}(l)} \stackrel{\text{def}}{=} \begin{pmatrix} \mathbf{e}_i \\ \mathbf{w}_{t,i}^{\mathrm{B}(l)} \\ \mathbf{Y}_t^{\mathrm{B}(l)}{}_{[i-1]} \end{pmatrix} \tag{A35}$$

$$\mathbf{x}_{t,i}^{\mathrm{dF}(l)} \stackrel{\text{def}}{=} \begin{pmatrix} \mathbf{e}_i \\ \mathbf{w}_{t,i}^{\mathrm{F}(l)} \\ \mathbf{Y}_t^{\mathrm{F}(l)}{}_{[i-1]} \end{pmatrix} \tag{A36}$$

$$\mathbf{h}_{t,i}^{\mathrm{dB}(l)}, \mathbf{c}_{t,i}^{\mathrm{dB}(l)} \stackrel{\text{def}}{=} \mathrm{LSTM}\left(\mathbf{x}_{t,i}^{\mathrm{dB}(l)}, \mathbf{h}_{t,i-1}^{\mathrm{dB}(l)}\right), i > 0 \tag{A37}$$

$$\mathbf{h}_{t,i}^{\mathrm{dF}(l)}, \mathbf{c}_{t,i}^{\mathrm{dF}(l)} \stackrel{\text{def}}{=} \mathrm{LSTM}\left(\mathbf{x}_{t,i}^{\mathrm{dF}(l)}, \mathbf{h}_{t,i-1}^{\mathrm{dF}(l)}\right), i > 0 \tag{A38}$$

The decoder is only applied to elements of $f^{\mathrm{f}(l)}(1, T)$ (i.e. only to frames where layer l segments) and only decodes the last B elements of $f^{\mathrm{f}(l-1)}(1, t)$ and the first F elements of $f^{\mathrm{f}(l-1)}(t + 1, T)$; that is, it decodes only the B preceding segment labels and F following segment labels from layer $l - 1$, ignoring labels at non-boundaries. Therefore, like encoding, decoding is also multiscale, taking place at the timescale of the encoder representations.

D Objective

Each decoder layer contributes two terms to the objective, a forward objective and a backward objective. Layer 1 decodes the data and uses a squared error loss:

$$f^{\mathcal{L}(1)}(x, y) \stackrel{\text{def}}{=} ||x - y||_2^2 \qquad \text{(A39)}$$

Layers $2, \ldots, L$ decode the representations from the layer below, which are tanh-activated and thus constrained to the interval $(-1, 1)$. Encoder features $\mathbf{h}_t^{\mathrm{e}(l)}$ are deterministically cast into bitwise feature probabilities $\mathbf{p}_t^{\mathrm{e}(l)}$ and decoded using sigmoid cross-entropy loss:

$$\mathbf{p}_t^{\mathrm{e}(l)} \stackrel{\text{def}}{=} (\mathbf{h}_t^{\mathrm{e}(l)} + 1)/2 \qquad \text{(A40)}$$

$$f^{\mathcal{L}(l)}(x, y) \stackrel{\text{def}}{=} \text{sigmoid-xent}(x, y), 1 < l \leq L \qquad \text{(A41)}$$

Let $T^{(l)'}$ denote the number of segment boundaries in layer l. Let $\mathbf{Z}_{t,i,d}^{\mathrm{B}(l)}$, $\mathbf{Z}_{t,i,d}^{\mathrm{F}(l)}$, $\hat{\mathbf{Z}}_{t,i,d}^{\mathrm{B}(l)}$, and $\hat{\mathbf{Z}}_{t,i,d}^{\mathrm{F}(l)}$ respectively denote the backward and forward targets and model predictions at encoder time t, decoder time i, and dimension d, defined as follows:

$$\mathbf{Z}_{t,i,d}^{\mathrm{B}(l)} \stackrel{\text{def}}{=} \text{rev}\left(f^{\mathrm{f}(l-1)}(1, t)\right)_{[i,d]} \qquad \text{(A42)}$$

$$\mathbf{Z}_{t,i,d}^{\mathrm{F}(l)} \stackrel{\text{def}}{=} f^{\mathrm{f}(l-1)}(t + 1, T)_{[i,d]} \qquad \text{(A43)}$$

$$\hat{\mathbf{Z}}_{t,i,d}^{\mathrm{B}(l)} \stackrel{\text{def}}{=} \mathbf{Y}_t^{\mathrm{B}(l)}{}_{[i,d]} \qquad \text{(A44)}$$

$$\hat{\mathbf{Z}}_{t,i,d}^{\mathrm{F}(l)} \stackrel{\text{def}}{=} \mathbf{Y}_t^{\mathrm{F}(l)}{}_{[i,d]} \qquad \text{(A45)}$$

The backward and forward loss components $\mathcal{L}^{\mathrm{B}(l)}$ and $\mathcal{L}^{\mathrm{F}(l)}$ are computed as:

$$\mathcal{L}^{\mathrm{B}(l)} \stackrel{\text{def}}{=} \frac{\sum_{t=1}^{T^{(l)'}} \sum_{i=1}^{B} \sum_{d=1}^{D_{l-1}} f^{\mathcal{L}(l)}\left(\mathbf{Z}_{t,i,d}^{\mathrm{B}(l)}, \hat{\mathbf{Z}}_{t,i,d}^{\mathrm{B}(l)}\right)}{T^{(l)'} B D_{l-1}} \qquad \text{(A46)}$$

$$\mathcal{L}^{\mathrm{F}(l)} \stackrel{\text{def}}{=} \frac{\sum_{t=1}^{T^{(l)'}} \sum_{i=1}^{F} \sum_{d=1}^{D_{l-1}} f^{\mathcal{L}(l)}\left(\mathbf{Z}_{t,i,d}^{\mathrm{F}(l)}, \hat{\mathbf{Z}}_{t,i,d}^{\mathrm{F}(l)}\right)}{T^{(l)'} F D_{l-1}} \qquad \text{(A47)}$$

The overall loss $\mathcal{L}$ is:

$$\mathcal{L} \stackrel{\text{def}}{=} \sum_{l=1}^{L} \mathcal{L}^{\mathrm{B}(l)} + \mathcal{L}^{\mathrm{F}(l)} \qquad \text{(A48)}$$

E Implementation Details

We apply the following implementation decisions in this study:

- $D_l = 128$ for $1 \leq l \leq L$

- One hidden layer of 128 units for all feedforward transforms

- Positional encoding dimensionality of 128

- Exponential linear unit (elu) activations for all internal feedforward layers (Clevert et al., 2015)

- Glorot uniform initialization for bottom-up, top-down, and feedforward encoder and decoder weight matrices (Glorot and Bengio, 2010)

- Orthogonal initialization for recurrent weight matrices (Saxe et al., 2013)

- Adam optimizer (Kingma and Ba, 2014) with learning rate 0.001, a minibatch size of 8, and default TensorFlow parameters.

- **Probing classifier implementation**

  - Logistic regression using `scikit-learn` (Pedregosa et al., 2011)

  - Phoneme prediction is multinomial, feature prediction is binary

  - Minority feature class is always coded as positive

  - 2-fold cross-validation

  - L2 $\lambda = 1$

  - 100 LBFGS iterations (Zhu et al., 1997) per fold

F Data Preprocessing

We convert the audio recordings into sequences of 50-dimensional cochleagrams (Brown and Cooke, 1994; McDermott and Simoncelli, 2011), each representing 10ms of audio data. Although this differs from the standard automatic speech recognition pipeline based on Mel frequency cepstral coefficients (Mermelstein, 1976), it is motivated for our study because the model is unsupervised. Since we wish to test theories about cognition by extracting features from the acoustic stream without supervision, it is critical not only that the speech representation contain features that support identification of linguistic units, but that the representation emphasize those features in a plausibly similar manner to that of the human auditory system. Cochleagrams support this goal by incorporating more recent insights about human auditory perception (McDermott and Simoncelli, 2011). Our implementation uses the `pycochleagram` library `https://github.com/mcdermottLab/pycochleagram`.

We L2 normalize the cochleagrams in order to encourage the decoder to focus on the spectral power envelope rather than absolute variation in loudness, since the former plausibly contains more linguistic signal. This procedure is supported by evidence of loudness constancy in human auditory perception, suggesting that similar kinds of normalization may take place in the brain (Zahorik and Wightman, 2001). We additionally z-transform the normalized cochleagrams over time within each audio file, since this proved beneficial during model development.

The source audio files contain many non-speech regions that are not of direct relevance for this study. We use the voice activity detection (VAD) intervals provided with the Zerospeech 2015 challenge data to remove these regions as a preprocess, and we force boundaries at the ends of VAD intervals. This greatly speeds training by removing irrelevant data, and it aligns with neuroscientific evidence of a prelinguistic capacity to detect human voices (Belin et al., 2000; Fecteau et al., 2005; Blasi et al., 2011; Pernet et al., 2015).

G   Regression Model Design and Results

We use linear regression to test the relationship between performance and memory pressures, prediction pressures, and multiscale encoding. To do so, we combine raw boundary, phoneme classification, and feature classification metrics, along with deltas in these metrics over baselines U and X, into a single vector of performance statistics, each of which measures one aspect of the contribution of these dimensions to phoneme learning in our unsupervised models. To improve normality of performance metrics which are bounded on the interval $[0, 1]$, as well as comparability of performance across metrics, we first (1) cast the metrics onto the interval

Predictor	β	t	p
Intercept	-1.22	-7.73	**3.89e-14*****
Memory	0.247	2.75	**0.006****
Prediction	0.959	9.86	**2.0e-16*****
Multiscale	0.305	4.10	**4.58e-5*****
Comparison=Full	0.037	0.453	0.651
Comparison=BaselineX	-0.064	-0.709	0.479
Metric=Phoneme	0.021	0.240	0.810
Metric=Feature	0.022	0.250	0.803

Table A1: Linear regression results

$[-1, 1]$, (2) apply Fisher's Z transformation (i.e. arctanh), and (3) Z-score the transformed vectors within each metric type.

We use binary coding for our predictors of interest: presence/absence of memory pressures ($B > 0$), presence/absence of prediction pressures ($F > 0$), and presence/absence of multiscale segmental encoding ($L > 2$). We also include categorical controls for comparison type (full, full - baseline U, full - baseline X) and metric type (boundary, phoneme, feature). Results, shown in Table A1, support a contribution of all three critical variables to phoneme acquisition.

Identifying Incorrect Labels in the CoNLL-2003 Corpus

Frederick Reiss[1,2], Hong Xu[2]*, Bryan Cutler[2]*,
Karthik Muthuraman[2]* and Zachary Eichenberger[1,3]*
[1]IBM Research – Almaden, San Jose, CA 95120, USA
[2]IBM Center for Open Source Data and AI Technologies (CODAIT),
San Francisco, CA 94105, USA
[3]University of Michigan, Ann Arbor, MI 48109, USA
frreiss@us.ibm.com, hongx@ibm.com, bjcutler@us.ibm.com
karthik.muthuraman@ibm.com, zachary.eichen@gmail.com

Abstract

The CoNLL-2003 corpus for English-language named entity recognition (NER) is one of the most influential corpora for NER model research. A large number of publications, including many landmark works, have used this corpus as a source of ground truth for NER tasks. In this paper, we examine this corpus and identify over 1300 incorrect labels (out of 35089 in the corpus). In particular, the number of incorrect labels in the test fold is comparable to the number of errors that state-of-the-art models make when running inference over this corpus.

We describe the process by which we identified these incorrect labels, using novel variants of techniques from semi-supervised learning. We also summarize the types of errors that we found, and we revisit several recent results in NER in light of the corrected data. Finally, we show experimentally that our corrections to the corpus have a positive impact on three state-of-the-art models.

1 Introduction

The English-language portion of the CoNLL-2003 shared task (Tjong Kim Sang and De Meulder, 2003) (henceforth CoNLL-2003) is one of the most widely-used benchmarks for named entity recognition (NER) models. It consists of news articles from the Reuters RCV1 corpus (Lewis et al., 2004).

Since its debut, CoNLL-2003 has played a central role in NLP research. Over 2300 research papers have cited the original CoNLL-2003 paper[1]. Among these works, many are landmark results that have revolutionized the field of natural language processing, including Glove embeddings (Pennington et al., 2014), BERT embeddings (Devlin et al., 2019), conditional random fields (Sutton and McCallum, 2012), and bidirectional LSTM models (Lample et al., 2016).

The CoNLL-2003 corpus continues to be used in NER research. The Papers with Code website (Paper with Code, 2020), which tracks state-of-the-art F1 scores[2] for this corpus, currently (as of July 2020) shows 43 results from 2016 through 2019 that improved this metric.

While researchers have relied heavily on the CoNLL-2003 corpus as a source of ground truth, few have paid attention to the corpus itself. Errors in the corpus could potentially mislead and even divert the course of future research. Recent work has pointed out that improper benchmarking can have significant impact on evaluating machine learning algorithms (Smith-Miles et al., 2014). The fact that Stanislawek et al. (2019) and Wang et al. (2019) found many errors while examining parts of the corpus is even more alarming. A detailed examination of the corpus has become imperative.

In this paper, we present our work on correcting labeling errors in the CoNLL-2003 corpus. Section 2 gives an overview of the corpus itself, the high-level process we followed, and related work. Section 3 describes how we used a novel form of semi-supervised labeling to identify potentially-incorrect labels. Sections 4 and 5 describe how we examined and categorized the flagged labels. And Sections 6 and 7 describe how we created a corrected version of the corpus and reevaluated past results.

2 Overview

The CoNLL-2003 corpus contains news articles from a subset of the Reuters RCV1 corpus (Lewis et al., 2004). Entities are tagged using an extended version of the tagging policy from the Message Understanding Conference (Tjong Kim Sang and

---

*The last four authors have contributed equally.

[1]https://scholar.google.com/scholar?cites=1710381009831973011 5

[2]"F1 score" here means "harmonic mean of precision and recall over the test fold for models trained on the train fold".

Proceedings of the 24th Conference on Computational Natural Language Learning, pages 215–226
Online, November 19-20, 2020. ©2020 Association for Computational Linguistics
https://doi.org/10.18653/v1/P17

De Meulder, 2003) (MUC), with the addition of a new tag `MISC` to cover entities not mentioned in MUC's labeling rules. The data consists of text files in which each line holds information about one token. Associated with each token are tags in inside-outside-begin (IOB) format (Ramshaw and Marcus, 1995). The files, `eng.train`, `eng.testa`, and `eng.testb`, contain the `train`, `dev`, and `test` folds of the corpus, respectively.

2.1 Our Work

In this paper, we identify and correct labeling errors in the CoNLL-2003 corpus. We used a semi-supervised approach to flag potentially-incorrect labels in the corpus, then manually reviewed the labels thus flagged.

Our approach builds on previous work in semi-supervised labeling, with some key differences. Because we were looking for incorrect labels in a corpus that already had many high-quality labels, we needed a sieve with especially high sensitivity. We used ensembles of NER models trained on the corpus, and we focused on cases where the models agreed strongly on a particular label, but that label does not appear in the corpus. One of these ensembles was the outputs of the original 16 entries in the 2003 competition. We also trained two other 17-model ensembles ourselves by applying Gaussian random projections to the BERT embeddings space.

We deliberately used models with F1 scores significantly below the state of the art. To find incorrect labels, we needed models that disagree with the original CoNLL-2003 corpus. Our initial experiments with the CoNLL-2003 competition entries showed that this ensemble, with F1 scores between 0.6 and 0.88, was particularly effective for finding incorrect labels. We tuned the models that we trained ourselves to have F1 scores in this range.

Our technique flagged 3182 out of a total of 35089 entity labels. Manual inspection determined that 850 of these labels — 27% — were incorrect. We also found 470 additional incorrect labels in close proximity to the labels that our techniques flagged, for a total of 1320 incorrect labels across the corpus.

Of a particular note, our analysis found 421 incorrect labels in the `test` fold. The `test` fold for this corpus contains 5648 labels. An F1 score of 0.93, as current state-of-the-art models produce, corresponds to approximately 400 errors on this

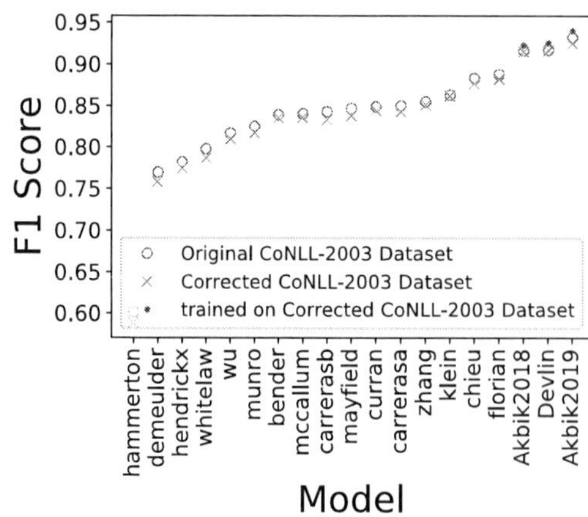

Figure 1: F1 scores on the `test` fold for 18 different NER models before and after correcting labeling errors in the `test` fold. Correcting these errors widened the spread in F1 scores between the more sophisticated models at the right and the less sophisticated models at the left.

fold. The change in F1 score over the past 17 years (0.934 - 0.888 = 0.046) corresponds to eliminating approximately 300 errors. The error rate of state-of-the-art models is comparable to the error rate of the corpus itself.

We used the results of our hand labeling to build a corrected version of the corpus. Then we re-evaluated the original entries in the competition, plus selected NER models from recent work, over the corrected corpus.

Figure 1 shows how the reported accuracy of these models changed. Surprisingly, we did not observe any change in the relative ranking of the models. Even though we corrected almost 8% of the labels in the `test` fold, no model's F1 score changed by more than 0.01. Without retraining, the changes in F1 score were all in the downward direction, but the F1 scores of the more sophisticated models dropped by less. The highest F1 score dropped from 0.932 to 0.927, while the lowest dropped from 0.601 to 0.589. When we retrained the three state-of-the-art models on the corrected data, their F1 scores became higher than their original scores.

2.1.1 Reproducibility

We have shared the full data set for this paper at `https://github.com/CODAIT/Identifying-Incorrect-Labels-In-CoNLL-2003`. This data set includes a complete list of the errors that we found in the corpus, with notes from the labelers about the nature of each error. We also include scripts for generating a corrected version of the full CoNLL-2003 corpus in its original format. We have also released the code for our experiments as part of our open source *Text Extensions for Pandas* project[3].

2.2 Related Work

Most of the previous work we have mentioned so far has treated the CoNLL-2003 corpus as ground truth. Two recent exceptions to this trend are Stanislawek et al. (2019) and Wang et al. (2019).

Stanislawek et al. (2019) identified some of the same incorrect labels that we found. This paper categorized the errors that modern NER models make on the `test` fold of the corpus. As a side-effect of the error analysis, the authors of this paper flagged cases where the output of a model had been considered "wrong" because a label in the corpus was incorrect. The authors identified 99 such errors in the `test` fold of this corpus.

There are several important differences between this paper and our work. Stanislawek et al. (2019) flagged errors as a side-effect of another task, while our primary focus was on identifying as many errors as possible. Due to our broader focus, we identified 421 errors in the `test` fold, compared to the 99 errors they found. We also examined the other two folds of the corpus, while the previous paper focused only on the `test` fold. The previous paper used models with high precision and recall; and they examined all the incorrect outputs of these models. We deliberately used less accurate models so as to widen the scope of potential errors flagged, and we focused on cases where there was strong agreement between these models plus disagreement with the ground truth data.

Wang et al. (2019) hired human labelers to label all sentences in the `test` fold of the corpus and found that 5.38% of sentences in this fold contained errors. This number is a lower error rate than we report, mostly due to the fact that the labelers did not look for errors in tokenization or sentence identification. Excluding those types of errors, our work flagged 348 out of 5648 entities in the `test` fold, for an error rate of 6.16%. We attribute the remaining 0.78 percent increase in error rate to the fact that our labelers examined entire documents and looked for consistency across doc-

uments, while Wang et al. (2019)'s labelers only viewed individual sentences in isolation.

Beyond the larger number of types of errors we searched for, there are two other important differences between our work and that of Wang et al. (2019). We developed a novel semi-supervised approach to identifying incorrect labels, and we used this approach to examine the entire corpus instead of just the `test` fold.

Our general approach of training an ensemble of models, then focusing attention on areas where most of the models disagree with the existing labels, has parallels to other work on human-in-the-loop methods for creating ground truth. Liang et al. (2017) used confidence estimates from a model trained on a data set to flag potential errors in the same data set for further review. The specific NLP task studied in that work was that of extracting a list of patient problems from an electronic medical record.

Fusing together the output of multiple models and/or rules is a also common approach when using weak supervision to train models over unlabeled NLP corpora. Lison et al. (2020) used hidden Markov models to generate labeled NER data from the outputs of multiple labeling functions. The Snorkel system (Ratner et al., 2020) provides a general framework for using the outputs of labeling functions to estimate both labels and the confidence of those labels.

The data management and data mining communities have a long history of building systems and algorithms to identify errors in ground truth data. Abedjan et al. (2016) provide a through survey. Although the primary focus of this previous work was on structured data, subtasks like address normalization have an NLP component.

3 Automated Labeling

We did not set out to relabel the CoNLL-2003 corpus. When we started looking at this corpus, our intent was to identify entity mentions that older models are not able to extract, but that state-of-the-art models are able to extract. We had hoped to use this information to drive continued improvements to these models.

3.1 Initial Results

The downloadable archive[4] for the corpus includes the outputs from the original entrants in the 2003

[3]`https://github.com/CODAIT/
text-extensions-for-pandas`

[4]https://www.clips.uantwerpen.be/conll2003/ner/

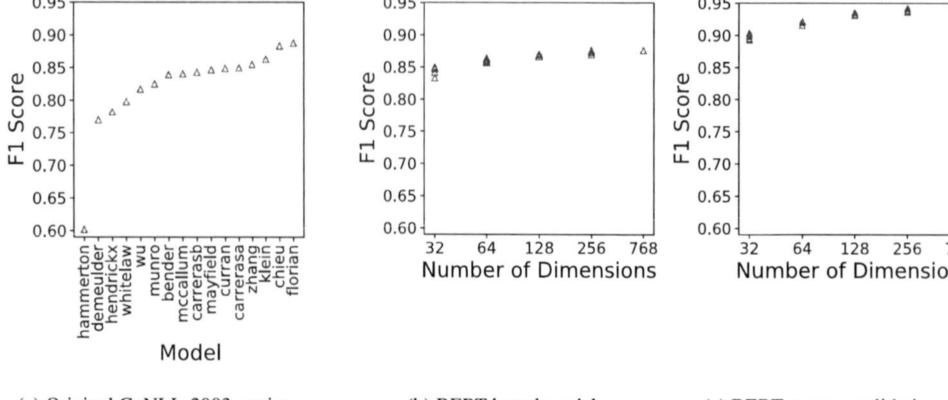

(a) Original CoNLL-2003 entries. (b) BERT-based models. (c) BERT + cross-validation.

Figure 2: F1 scores of the models in our three ensembles. Each scatter point in these plots represents a trained model. The x-axes of Figures 2b and 2c represent the number of dimensions of embeddings.

competition. These entrants used a variety of different models, drawing on the technology available at the time.

We believed that these model outputs would provide an objective picture of what kinds of entities were difficult to extract for state-of-the-art models circa 2003. We hypothesized that there would be entity mentions that none of the models could extract correctly, due to limitations of 2003-era technology. We further believed that modern models would be able to tag some of these previously impossible mentions. To test this hypothesis, we aggregated together the outputs of the original entrants to find these "difficult" entities.

The corpus ships as a collection of tokens with tags in IOB format. Using *Text Extensions for Pandas*[5], a library of extension types for `pandas` DataFrames (Reback et al., 2020; McKinney et al., 2010), we translated the labeled tokens of the corpus into *entity mentions* — that is, *spans* of tokens within the corpus's document, plus the corresponding entity type *tag* for each span.

We performed the same translation on each of the entrants' outputs. This process produced seventeen sets of entity mentions: One for the original corpus and one for each of the sixteen entrants. Next, we merged these sets together to find the mentions that were present in the original corpus but were *not* present in the competition entries.

Then we looked at some of these entity mentions in the context of the original news articles, and our original hypothesis fell apart. About one third the examples we looked at turned out to be incorrect la-

bels. It would be hard to argue that these "incorrect" answers were due to inadequacies of early-2000's technology, when it was in fact the *corpus* that was incorrect.

Next, we took a slightly different view of the aggregate data we had. Instead of looking for entity mentions that were in the corpus but not in the entrants' outputs, we looked for entity mentions that were in all the entrants' outputs but were *not* in the corpus. As before, a third of the examples that we looked at involved incorrect or missing labels. We decided at this point to focus on identifying and correcting these incorrect labels.

3.2 Training Custom Models

The model outputs from the original CoNLL-2003 competition had proven useful for zeroing in on incorrect labels, but this data had a significant shortcoming. The model outputs only cover the `dev` and `test` folds of the corpus. No model outputs on the `train` fold are available. To apply the technique we had used so far to the `train` fold, we would need to train our own collection of models.

We used a BERT embeddings layer from the `transformers` open source library (Wolf et al., 2019), tuned on the CoNLL-2003 corpus, to produce BERT embeddings over sliding windows of text from the `train` fold. Then we applied 16 different Gaussian random projections to these 768-dimensional embeddings to reduce them to between 32 and 256 dimensions. We trained multinomial logistic regression classifiers over these random projections. We also trained an additional classifier over the full embeddings, for a total of 17 different models.

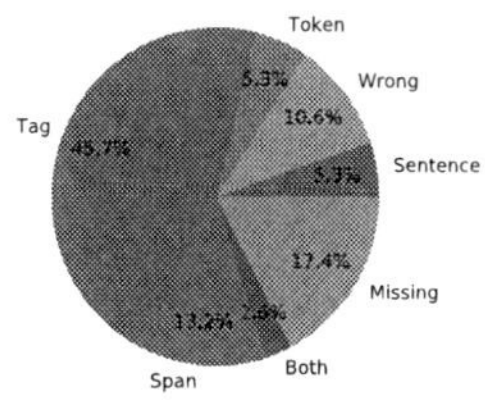
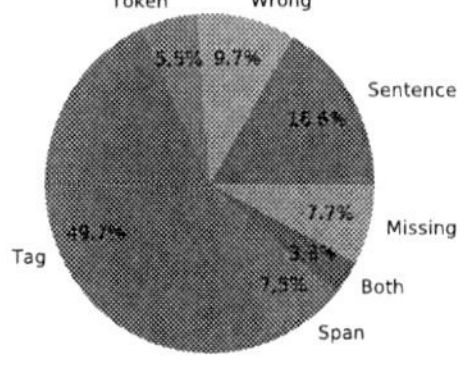
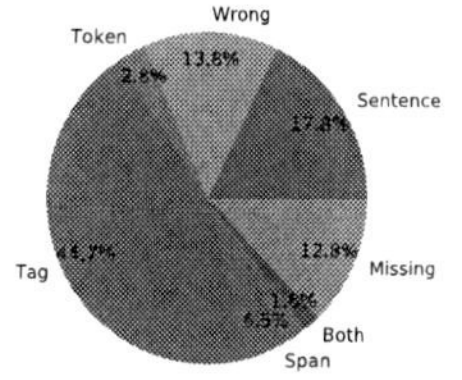
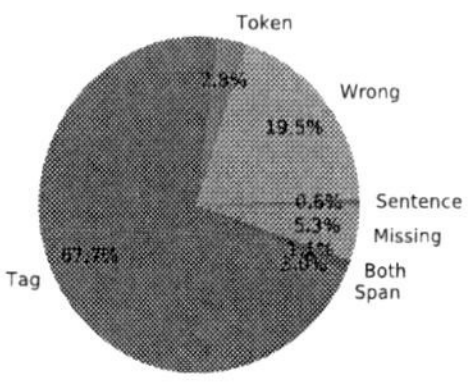

(a) Percentage of each error type correctly flagged by using original entrants.

(b) Percentage of each error type correctly flagged by the method using custom models.

(c) Percentage of each error type correctly flagged by the method using cross-validation.

(d) Percentage of Each Error Type Correctly Flagged By hand labeling.

Figure 3: Distribution of error types found by each of the four methods.

Our goal in building these models was not to attain the highest possible precision and recall. In fact, high levels of accuracy could be detrimental to our task, as high levels of accuracy imply a high congruence with the ground-truth labels we were trying to correct. Instead, we wanted a collection of models that would produce diverse results and F1 scores in line with the accuracy of the original CoNLL-2003 entrants.

With one exception, the CoNLL-2003 competition produced F1 scores between 77% and 89% on the `test` fold. We tuned our models' training and inference until they produced results approximately within this range. Figure 2 shows the resulting F1 scores on the `test` fold. Figure 2a shows the original CoNLL-2003 competition entries' F1 scores, while Figure 2b shows the F1 scores of the models we trained, plotted against the dimensionality of their Gaussian random projection stages.

Based on published results on BERT embeddings for NER, we expect that additional tuning would have raised the F1 scores of our models by about 0.02. We judged that the lower F1 scores in Figure 2 are better for this application.

As with our previous analysis of the original competition results, we aggregated together the outputs of these 17 models on the `test` fold of the corpus, then aligned these results with the corpus labels. A manual spot-check of these aligned results verified that these aggregated results also functioned as an effective sieve for identifying incorrect labels. Roughly half of the entity mentions that were found by all 17 models but were not in the corpus were due to incorrect or missing labels in the corpus. We found similar results on the `dev` fold.

3.3 Cross-Validation

Next, we applied our ensemble of models to the `train` fold of the corpus and compared the aggregated results against the corpus's labels. As with the `test` fold, we were able to use the aggregate model outputs to identify a list of entity mentions with a high fraction of incorrect corpus labels. However, this list was significantly shorter than the lists we were able to produce on the `test` and `dev` folds. Because the models were themselves trained on the `train` fold, there were fewer discrepancies between the model outputs and the corpus labels.

To produce a larger list of potentially incorrect labels, we divided the entire corpus randomly into ten folds and performed a ten-fold cross-validation. For each of the ten folds, we retrained our ensemble of models on the other 9 folds and ran model inference on the current fold. This process involved training 170 different models, but because we only needed to generate the BERT embeddings once, we were able to perform all training in a few hours on a 4-year-old MacBook.

Interestingly, this cross-validation approach produced models with significantly higher F1 scores on the random holdout sets, compared with our earlier approach of training on the `train` fold and testing on the `test` fold. As Figure 2c shows, F1 scores for the holdout sets for each of the models — which together encompass the entire corpus — ranged from 0.89 to 0.94, an increase of roughly 5%.

We attribute this improvement to the non-random split of the original corpus. The contest judges used article publication date to split the corpus into folds. The `train` and `dev` folds used articles from August of 1996, while the `test` fold was from December of that year (Tjong Kim Sang and De Meulder, 2003).

This non-random split matches common industry practices[6]. However, dividing the the corpus by time means that any systematic changes in the target domain over time are not visible to the optimizer during training. Models trained on a random sample of the corpus are able to achieve a higher F1 score because they have better information about the types of articles that were published in December 1996.

In both ensembles that we trained, our model outputs aligned well with the labels on the `train` fold. Consequently, our sieve identified fewer potentially incorrect labels in the `train` fold of the corpus, which in turn would lead to our identifying fewer incorrect labels during manual relabeling. Better accuracy led to worse results.

4   Hand Labeling

Each of our three ensembles produced two lists of labels: one list of labels that were in the corpus but not in the model outputs; and a second list of labels that were in the model outputs but not in the corpus. Overall, we produced six lists of potentially-incorrect labels. Four of these lists spanned the entire corpus, while the remaining two (from the original contest entries) only spanned the `test` and `dev` folds.

We proceeded to examine these lists by hand, looking at each flagged label in the context of the target document. We focused on the labels where there was a strong agreement between the models in each ensemble. We started out by examining the labels where all models agreed, then moved onto the labels where all models but one agreed, and so on. As we progressed to labels with less agreement among models, the fraction of flagged labels that was actually incorrect decreased. When this fraction dropped below 20 percent, we stopped going through the ordered list of flagged labels.

For each list of potentially-incorrect labels, one member of our team examined the labels, and a second member of our team audited the decisions that the first member had made. In total, we made 12 passes (3 ensembles × 2 sets of labels × 2 human reviewers) of manual review over the `train` and `test` folds of the corpus and 8 passes over the `test` fold.

---

[6]In our experience, most organizations that use machine learning do not have the ability to travel backwards in time. Hence, they train models on data from the past and apply those models to data from the future.

When we found that a label was incorrect, we coded the type of error and the required correction so that the error could be corrected automatically later on. We divided errors into several categories:

- `Tag`: The corpus correctly identifies the span of an entity mention, but the span is associated with the wrong entity type.

- `Span`: The corpus correctly identifies the type of an entity mention, but the boundaries of the span of tokens containing the mention are incorrect.

- `Both`: The corpus correctly identifies an entity mention, but both the tag and the span boundaries are incorrect.

- `Wrong`: The corpus incorrectly identifies an entity mention.

- `Sentence`: The corpus contains an incorrect sentence boundary, and as a result the span and/or tag of one or more entity mentions are incorrect. This type of error especially problematic because incorrect labels on both sides of the sentence boundary count as two mistakes when computing precision and recall.

- `Token`: The corpus contains an incorrect token boundary, and as a result the span and/or tag of one or more entity mentions are incorrect.

Appendix 9.1 shows examples of each error type. The data set that we have published as a companion to this paper (See Section 2.1.1) includes complete lists of the errors that we found, both before and after manual review.

4.1   Inter-Annotator Agreement

Each manual pass over the corpus involved validating a set of suggested changes, not reannotating the corpus in its entirety. As a result, conventional metrics of inter-annotator agreement between our human evaluators do not apply. Instead, we report the similarity between the outputs of the three *ensembles*.

Table 1 summarizes the Jaccard similarity between the three ensembles' outputs before and after manual review. Figure 4 shows a Venn diagram view of the relationship between the sets of flagged labels after manual review. The raw outputs of the two BERT-based ensembles showed a high degree

Ensemble 1	Ensemble 2	Fold(s)	Before Review	After First Review	After Second Review
Original models	Custom models	`dev`/`test`	0.5153	0.2500	0.2533
Original models	Custom + Cross-val.	`dev`/`test`	0.5179	0.2072	0.2052
Custom models	Custom + Cross-val.	`dev`/`test`	0.8220	0.5167	0.5532
Custom models	Custom + Cross-val.	`train`	0.8707	0.6677	0.6592

Table 1: Jaccard similarity between the flagged labels from different pairs of ensembles before and after human review. The original models flagged a substantially different set of labels from our BERT-based custom models, and this divergence increased after manual review.

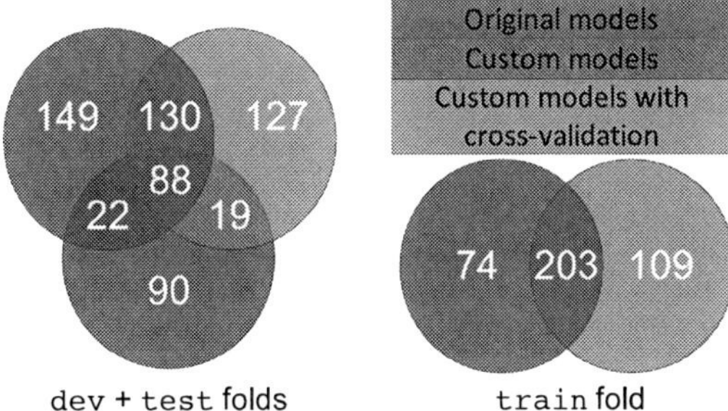

Figure 4: Number of errors flagged by different combinations of ensembles after filtering by human labelers.

of overlap, but this overlap reduced substantially after manual review. The original models flagged a very different set of labels from the BERT based models, especially after manual review.

5 Incorrect Labels Identified

In total, we examined 3182 labels our ensembles had flagged in the three folds of the corpus. We considered any label where fewer than 7 models agreed with the corpus label to be "flagged". Of these labels, 1274 came from the `test` fold, 854 came from the `dev` fold, and 1054 came from the `train` fold; accounting for 22.6%, 14.3%, and 4.5% of their folds, respectively.

As we noted in Section 3.3, our models had significantly higher F1 scores on the `train` fold, both with and without cross-validation. Because model outputs were closer to the corpus labels, the ensembles flagged fewer labels on this fold. However, the fraction of these labels that were actually incorrect was higher than that on the other folds: 34% versus 23%.

Of the errors correctly flagged, 184 were found by the ensemble composed of the original entrants' results; 641 were flagged by our custom models; and 275 errors were found by custom models with cross-validation. 372 of these errors were correctly flagged by two or more approaches. While ex-

amining the affected documents, we found 470 additional errors in the vicinity of flagged errors.

Figure 3 shows the distribution of errors broken down by error type and source. The most frequent error type we found in the corpus was a `Tag` type error, accounting for 48% of errors in total. `Both` type errors were least frequent.

Our BERT-based models found a higher fraction of `Sentence` type errors, largely because these models were able to express spans that cross sentence boundaries. The entrants' outputs in our first ensemble, being constrained by the IOB file format, were physically incapable of expressing a span that crosses a sentence boundary. We also suspect that many of these older models operated on one sentence at a time, while the document context feeding our BERT embeddings could span multiple sentences.

Had we been aiming to maximize the F1 scores of our BERT-based models, we would have postprocessed the outputs of these models to split spans along sentence boundaries. This lack of postprocessing led to a decrease in F1 score, but it enabled us to find more errors.

The distribution of error types remained relatively constant across folds, with one exception: `Sentence` errors accounted for a much larger fraction in the `train` fold — 26% of errors, as opposed to the 8% and 10% rates in the `dev` and `test` folds, respectively.

6 Corrected CoNLL-2003 Corpus

After identifying incorrect tags, spans and sentence boundaries, we created a corrected version of the original CoNLL-2003 corpus, which we refer to as the corrected CoNLL-2003 corpus.

We used the *Text Extensions for Pandas* library to parse the original corpus and extract tokens and spans for each entity. We created data files containing all of the vetted corrections from our hand labeling of ensemble outputs. We wrote a script that applies all of these corrections to the CoNLL-2003 corpus, producing a corrected version of the

Entrant	**Original** test Fold			**Corrected** test Fold		
	Precision	Recall	F1 Score	Precision	Recall	F1 Score
bender	0.8468	0.8318	0.8392	0.8412	0.8279	0.8347
carrerasa	0.8405	0.8596	0.8500	0.8325	0.8517	0.8420
carrerasb	0.8581	0.8284	0.8430	0.8466	0.8192	0.8327
chieu	0.8812	0.8851	0.8831	0.8733	0.8791	0.8762
curran	0.8429	0.8550	0.8489	0.8376	0.8501	0.8438
demeulder	0.7584	0.7813	0.7697	0.7468	0.7693	0.7579
florian	0.8899	0.8854	0.8876	0.8837	0.8800	0.8818
hammerton	0.6909	0.5326	0.6015	0.6749	0.5210	0.5881
hendrickx	0.7633	0.8017	0.7820	0.7548	0.7936	0.7737
klein	0.8612	0.8649	0.8631	0.8593	0.8634	0.8614
mayfield	0.8445	0.8490	0.8467	0.8354	0.8411	0.8382
mccallum	0.8452	0.8355	0.8404	0.8398	0.8315	0.8356
munro	0.8087	0.8421	0.8251	0.8003	0.8327	0.8162
whitelaw	0.8160	0.7805	0.7978	0.8045	0.7702	0.7870
wu	0.8202	0.8139	0.8170	0.8112	0.8075	0.8094
zhang	0.8613	0.8488	0.8550	0.8574	0.8459	0.8516

Table 2: Experimental results on the original CoNLL 2003 (English) competition.

corpus.

For information on how to obtain the code and data necessary to recreate our corrected corpus, as well as all the experiment code for this paper, see Section 2.1.1.

7 Experimental Evaluation

In this section, we first re-evaluate the entries from the original competition against the corrected test fold of the corpus. We then re-evaluate the metrics of three state-of-the-art NER models from recent literature on the corrected corpus.

7.1 Re-evaluation of the Original Competition Entries

We evaluated the original 16 CoNLL-2003 competition entries on the original and corrected CoNLL-2003 test folds.

Before evaluating on the corrected data, we needed to adjust sentence boundaries and tokenization in the entrants' output files to match that of the corrected corpus. The evaluation metric for this corpus relies on perfect alignment between tokens and sentences of the files being compared. When we split a token, we copied the token's label to the new, smaller tokens.

We recomputed precision, recall, and F1 scores. Our results are shown in Table 2 and Figure 1. All of the entries have lower precision, recall, and F1 scores on the corrected CoNLL-2003 test fold than on the original test fold. Although we changed nearly 8% of the labels in the test fold, all the models' metrics decreased by 1% or less.

The more accurate entries saw their F1 scores decline by less than the entries with lower F1 scores. For example, the top-scoring entry's F1 score dropped by 0.0054, while the bottom-scoring entry dropped by 0.0122 — more than twice as much. As a result, the ranking of entries did not change. It appears that the errors in the original corpus penalize models that produce answers closer to the actual ground truth.

Since we did not have access to the original models, we only performed inference and scoring on the corrected CoNLL-2003 corpus. We expect that the metrics would improve if the models are entirely re-trained on the corrected corpus' train fold. This would constitute relevant future work and point towards new reliable benchmarks.

7.2 Experimental Results on Recent Models

We evaluated three state-of-the-art NER models. We selected three models (Akbik et al., 2018, 2019; Devlin et al., 2019) according to the ranking of models on the CoNLL-2003 NER task compiled on Papers with Code (Paper with Code, 2020)[7]. Table 3 summarizes our experimental results. We have the following observations.

---

[7]We initially planned to select all of the models that rank top 10 from (Paper with Code, 2020). However, we were able to reproduce only three of them. We were unable to apply the rest of the models for the following technical reasons: two of which we requested code from the authors never received any responses; one of which we could find code but there is no instruction on how to use the code; three of which we could find code with instructions but we could not reproduce by following the instructions; one of which uses a nonstandard tagging scheme. We have contacted the authors of all of these papers for help with their code.

Model		**Original** `test` Fold			**Corrected** `test` Fold		
		Precision	Recall	F1 Score	Precision	Recall	F1 Score
Trained on	(Akbik et al., 2018)	0.9133	0.9207	0.9165	0.9108	0.9177	0.9142
Original	(Akbik et al., 2019)	0.9290	0.9354	0.9322	0.9226	0.9286	0.9256
Corpus	(Devlin et al., 2019)	0.9119	0.9229	0.9173	0.9110	0.9217	0.9163
Trained on	(Akbik et al., 2018)	0.9073	0.9120	0.9096	0.9206	0.9248	0.9227
Corrected	(Akbik et al., 2019)	0.9252	0.9260	0.9256	0.9400	0.9407	0.9404
Corpus	(Devlin et al., 2019)	0.9228	0.9309	0.9268	0.9218	0.9295	0.9256

Table 3: Experimental results for recent models. We trained each of the three models (Akbik et al., 2018), (Akbik et al., 2019), and (Devlin et al., 2019) on the original and corrected `train` folds, respectively. For each trained model, we evaluated on the original and corrected `test` folds, respectively. For (Akbik et al., 2018) and (Akbik et al., 2019), we trained on both `train` and `dev` folds. For (Devlin et al., 2019), we trained on the `train` fold. For all models, we used the hyperparameter settings specified in their respective papers.

On the corrected `test` fold, all the listed metrics (the F1 scores, precision, and recall) are higher for the models trained on the corrected corpus than those on the original corpus. This indicates that our correction on the corpus has a positive impact on the quality of training of the three models.

Comparing the metrics of models trained and evaluated on the original corpus (the top-left section of the table) and the metrics of models trained and evaluated on the corrected corpus (the bottom-right section of the table), we see that all metrics have been improved on the corrected corpus. This might indicate that these three models are actually more effective (according to the evaluation on the corrected corpus) than they were thought to be (according to the evaluation on the original corpus).

However, on the original `test` fold, all the listed metrics (the F1 scores, precision, and recall) are not higher for the models trained on the original corpus than those on the corrected corpus. This might be explained by the fact that the errors in the original `test` fold are not consistent with the original `train` and `dev` folds, hence models trained on the original corpus are not necessarily more advantageous than those trained on the corrected corpus when evaluated on the original `test` fold.

For models trained on the original corpus, all the listed metrics (the F1 scores, precision, and recall) on the corrected `test` fold are very close to those on the original `test` fold (differences are mostly within 0.002 and no larger than 0.01). Once again, this might be explicable by the fact that the errors the errors in the original `test` fold are not consistent with the original `train` and `dev` folds. Hence, models trained on the original corpus are not necessarily more advantageous when evaluated on the original `test` fold than on the corrected `test` fold.

8 Conclusion and Future Work

The CoNLL-2003 corpus is highly influential in named entity recognition (NER) research. It has been used for benchmarking many landmark NER models and has been continuing to play a critical role in recent research. In this paper, we took a closer look at the CoNLL-2003 corpus and identified a number of errors. We used a semi-supervised method to identify these errors and then systematically corrected them.

The primary contribution of this paper is the creation of a more error-free version of the CoNLL-2003 corpus, which can potentially be used to evaluate past NER models more accurately and make future benchmarking more reliable. Indeed, as our experiments on three recent state-of-the-art NER models have shown, our corrections to the corpus have a positive impact on these models: When evaluated on our corrected `test` fold, all three models trained on our corrected corpus outperformed their counterparts trained on the original corpus by a non-negligible margin.

We firmly believe that benchmarking corpora are the lighthouses for research, and improving the quality of benchmarking corpora is of utmost importance in guiding the research community. We hope that others can replicate the process we applied to this corpus on other key corpora, and in doing so, improve the utility of these vital resources.

References

Ziawasch Abedjan, Xu Chu, Dong Deng, Raul Castro Fernandez, Ihab F. Ilyas, Mourad Ouzzani, Paolo Papotti, Michael Stonebraker, and Nan Tang. 2016. Detecting data errors: Where are we and what needs to be done? *Proceedings of the VLDB Endowment*, 9(12):993–1004.

Alan Akbik, Tanja Bergmann, and Roland Vollgraf. 2019. Pooled contextualized embeddings for named entity recognition. In *Proceedings of the Annual Conference of the North American Chapter of the Association for Computational Linguistics: Human Language Technologies*, pages 724–728.

Alan Akbik, Duncan Blythe, and Roland Vollgraf. 2018. Contextual string embeddings for sequence labeling. In *Proceedings of the International Conference on Computational Linguistics*, pages 1638–1649.

Walter Daelemans, Jakub Zavrel, A. van den Bosch, and Ko van der Sloot. 2002. MBT: Memory based tagger, version 1.0, reference guide. Technical report, University of Antwerp.

Jacob Devlin, Ming-Wei Chang, Kenton Lee, and Kristina Toutanova. 2019. BERT: Pre-training of deep bidirectional transformers for language understanding. In *Proceedings of the Annual Conference of the North American Chapter of the Association for Computational Linguistics*, pages 4171–4186.

Guillaume Lample, Miguel Ballesteros, Sandeep Subramanian, Kazuya Kawakami, and Chris Dyer. 2016. Neural architectures for named entity recognition. In *Proceedings of the Annual Conference of the North American Chapter of the Association for Computational Linguistics: Human Language Technologies*.

David D. Lewis, Yiming Yang, Tony G. Rose, and Fan Li. 2004. Rcv1: A new benchmark collection for text categorization research. *Journal of Machine Learning Research*, 5:361–397.

Jennifer J. Liang, Ching-Huei Tsou, and Murthy V. Devarakonda. 2017. Ground truth creation for complex clinical nlp tasks – an iterative vetting approach and lessons learned. *AMIA Summits on Translational Science Proceedings*, 2017:203 – 212.

Pierre Lison, Jeremy Barnes, Aliaksandr Hubin, and Samia Touileb. 2020. Named entity recognition without labelled data: A weak supervision approach. In *Proceedings of the Annual Meeting of the Association for Computational Linguistics*, pages 1518–1533.

Wes McKinney et al. 2010. Data structures for statistical computing in Python. In *Proceedings of the 9th Python in Science Conference*, volume 445, pages 51–56.

Paper with Code. 2020. Named Entity Recognition on CoNLL 2003 (English). `https://paperswithcode.com/sota/ named-entity-recognition-ner-on-conll-2003`.

Jeffrey Pennington, Richard Socher, and Christopher Manning. 2014. GloVe: Global vectors for word representation. In *Proceedings of the 2014 Conference on Empirical Methods in Natural Language Processing (EMNLP)*, pages 1532–1543, Doha, Qatar. Association for Computational Linguistics.

Lance Ramshaw and Mitch Marcus. 1995. Text chunking using transformation-based learning. In *Proceedings of the third Workshop on Very Large Corpora*.

Alexander Ratner, Stephen H. Bach, Henry R. Ehrenberg, Jason Alan Fries, Sen Wu, and Christopher Ré. 2020. Snorkel: Rapid training data creation with weak supervision. *The VLDB Journal*, 29:709–730.

Jeff Reback, Wes McKinney, jbrockmendel, Joris Van den Bossche, Tom Augspurger, Phillip Cloud, gfyoung, Sinhrks, Adam Klein, Simon Hawkins, and et al. 2020. pandas-dev/pandas: Pandas 1.0.5.

Kate Smith-Miles, Davaatseren Baatar, Brendan Wreford, and Rhyd Lewis. 2014. Towards objective measures of algorithm performance across instance space. *Computers & Operations Research*, 45:12–24.

Tomasz Stanislawek, Anna Wróblewska, Alicja Wójcicka, Daniel Ziembicki, and Przemyslaw Biecek. 2019. Named entity recognition - is there a glass ceiling? In *Proceedings of the 23rd Conference on Computational Natural Language Learning (CoNLL)*, pages 624–633, Hong Kong, China. Association for Computational Linguistics.

Charles Sutton and Andrew McCallum. 2012. An introduction to conditional random fields. *Foundations and Trends in Machine Learning*, 4(4):267–373.

Erik F. Tjong Kim Sang and Fien De Meulder. 2003. Introduction to the CoNLL-2003 shared task: Language-independent named entity recognition. In *Proceedings of the SIGNLL Conference on Computational Natural Language Learning*, pages 142–147, USA. Association for Computational Linguistics.

Zihan Wang, Jingbo Shang, Liyuan Liu, Lihao Lu, Jiacheng Liu, and Jiawei Han. 2019. Crossweigh: Training named entity tagger from imperfect annotations. In *Proceedings of the 2019 Conference on Empirical Methods in Natural Language Processing and the 9th International Joint Conference on Natural Language Processing*, pages 5153–5162. Association for Computational Linguistics.

Thomas Wolf, Lysandre Debut, Victor Sanh, Julien Chaumond, Clement Delangue, Anthony Moi, Pierric Cistac, Tim Rault, Rémi Louf, Morgan Funtowicz, Joe Davison, Sam Shleifer, Patrick von Platen, Clara Ma, Yacine Jernite, Julien Plu, Canwen Xu, Teven Le Scao, Sylvain Gugger, Mariama Drame, Quentin Lhoest, and Alexander M. Rush. 2019. HuggingFace's transformers: State-of-the-art natural language processing. *ArXiv*, abs/1910.03771.

9 Appendix

9.1 Types of Errors

We classified the errors that we found into several categories. In this section, we give concrete examples of each type.

9.1.1 Tag Errors

In some cases, the corpus had correctly identified the span of the entity mention, but the tokens of that span were labeled with an incorrect entity type. For example, the 156th document in the `test` fold contains the token/label sequence:

```
smuggled O
heroin O
from O
Turkey I-LOC
to O
Antwerp I-ORG
```

This sequence incorrectly tags a mention of the city `Antwerp` as an `ORG` entity when it should be tagged `LOC`.

We call errors of this type `Tag` errors.

9.1.2 Span Errors

In other cases, the corpus correctly identified the entity type of an entity mention, but there was an error in labeling the precise range of tokens containing that entity. For example, the 113th document of the `test` fold contains the token/label sequence:

```
Ingeborg I-PER
Helen I-PER
Markein O
```

This sequence incorrectly marks the span 'Ingeborg Helen' as a 'PER' entity, when the correct span is 'Ingeborg Helen Markein', the full name of a Norwegian skier.

We call errors of this type `Span` errors.

9.1.3 Both Errors

At some locations in the corpus, an entity was subject to both a `Span` error and a `Tag` error at the same time. For example, the headline for the 23rd document of the `test` fold contains the token/label sequence:

```
ARAB I-MISC
CONTRACTORS O
WIN O
AFRICAN I-MISC
CUP I-MISC
```

These labels miss an instance of the `ORG` entity `ARAB CONTRACTORS`, a reference to The Arab Contractors Sporting Club, an Egyptian soccer team. In lieu of labeling `ARAB CONTRACTORS`, the sequence labels `ARAB` as a single-token `MISC` entity, which is not correct because that token is part of the longer `ORG` entity.

We call errors of this type `Both` errors.

9.1.4 Wrong Errors

In some cases, the corpus marks tokens that do not match any entity type at all. For example, the 153rd document in the `test` fold contains the token/label sequence:

```
next O
Wednesday I-ORG
```

This sequence of labels incorrectly marks `Wednesday` as an `ORG` entity when that token is in fact a reference to a day of the week.

We call errors of this type `Wrong` errors.

9.1.5 Sentence Errors

The creators of the corpus used automatic tools to break each document into sentences. Some of these sentence boundaries were incorrect, and some of these incorrect sentence boundaries occurred in the middle of an entity mention. For example, the 20th document of the `dev` fold contains the token/label sequence:

```
the O
Berlin I-MISC

Grand I-MISC
Prix I-MISC
```

(where the blank line encodes a sentence boundary).

Because the labeling and scoring scheme for this corpus does not permit entity mentions to span sentence boundaries, this sequence marks `Berlin` and `Grand Prix` as two separate 'MISC' entities.

This type of error is especially problematic because incorrect labels on these tokens will count as two mistakes when computing precision and recall. In addition, many models process one sentence at a time. When processing the above document, such models will see a sentence that ends with the token `Berlin`, followed by a sentence that starts with `Grand Prix`.

In other cases, an incorrect sentence boundary led the human labeler to conclude incorrectly that the period after an abbreviation is not part of the abbreviation. For example, the 208th document of the `train` fold contains the token/label sequence:

```
The I-ORG
Walt I-ORG
Disney I-ORG
Co I-ORG
. O

said O
Thursday O
```

(where the blank line encodes a sentence boundary).

In this example, `Co.` should be labeled as an `ORG` entity, but only `Co` (without the period) is marked.

We call errors of both these types `Sentence` errors.

9.1.6 "Token"-Type Errors

The authors of the original corpus used the MBT tagger (Daelemans et al., 2002) to tokenize the original news articles. Occasionally, the tokenizer made a mistake; and occasionally, a tokenization mistake happened to coincide with an entity mention. For example, the 169th document of the `train` fold contains the token/label sequence:

```
Nigerian I-MISC
terms O
jeopardize O
Commonwealth I-ORG
trip-Canada I-MISC
. O
```

Here, the tokenizer has incorrectly tokenized "trip — Canada" as a single token, and the human labeler has labeled this token as `MISC`, even though `Canada` is a `LOC` entity. Correcting this kind of problem involves splitting the incorrect token into its corrected parts, then relabeling those parts as needed. The above example turns into:

```
Nigerian I-MISC
terms O
jeopardize O
Commonwealth I-ORG
trip O
- O
Canada I-LOC
. O
```

We call errors of this type `Token` errors.

When is a bishop not like a rook? When it's like a rabbi!
Multi-prototype BERT embeddings for estimating semantic relationships

Gabriella Chronis
Department of Linguistics
The University of Texas at Austin
Austin, TX 78705 USA
gabriellachronis@utexas.edu

Katrin Erk
Department of Linguistics
The University of Texas at Austin
Austin, TX 78705 USA
katrin.erk@utexas.edu

Abstract

This paper investigates contextual language models, which produce *token* representations, as a resource for lexical semantics at the word or *type* level. We construct multi-prototype word embeddings from `bert-base-uncased` (Devlin et al., 2018). These embeddings retain contextual knowledge that is critical for some type-level tasks, while being less cumbersome and less subject to outlier effects than exemplar models. Similarity and relatedness estimation, both type-level tasks, benefit from this contextual knowledge, indicating the context-sensitivity of these processes. BERT's token level knowledge also allows the testing of a type-level hypothesis about lexical abstractness, demonstrating the relationship between token-level behavior and type-level concreteness ratings. Our findings provide important insight into the interpretability of BERT: layer 7 approximates semantic similarity, while the final layer (11) approximates relatedness.

1   Introduction

The rampant success enjoyed by contextualized language models (CLMs) like CoVe (McCann et al., 2017), ElMo (Peters et al., 2018), BERT (Devlin et al., 2018), and RoBERTa (Liu et al., 2019b) has precipitated a deluge of research into analyzing and interpreting their functionality. But to date, there has been little work analyzing their lexical semantic knowledge. This paper seeks to answer two questions: 1) Is it possible to generate useful static word-type embeddings from BERT activations for word tokens? 2) What sort of semantic relations are represented in embeddings generated from BERT?

'Useful' word embeddings are those which successfully represent target semantic relations and enable the testing of linguistic and cognitive hypotheses. Many linguistic tasks and questions concern word meanings at the type level—that is, what

a word means in general, abstracted away from any particular context. Similarity, relatedness, and abstractness are often construed as properties at the type-level: most similarity and relatedness datasets contain judgments on isolated word pairs, and abstractness datasets contain judgments on isolated words.

CLMs produce representations at the token level: the vector representation of a word varies depending on its context of occurrence. How can contextual representations be helpful for type-level tasks? Similarity and relatedness are context-sensitive processes. For example, the relevant features of *water* used for calculating its similarity to *land* are different from those for calculating its similarity to *coffee*. BERT's contextual knowledge is useful for dealing with the effects of this variation on similarity and relatedness judgments. Relative abstractness/concreteness is another property often treated as a type-level phenomenon. However, this property may be detectable through token-level interactions. We hypothesize that a high degree of contextual variation may be an indicator of type-level abstractness. In other words, abstract words are more 'heterogeneous' than concrete words. Traditional static representations, which represent words as infinitesimal points, are not suitable to test this hypothesis. In contrast, BERT enables the representation of a single word as a constellation of points, with each point corresponding to a different usage or usage type. In BERT, heterogeneity translates to the dispersion of tokens or prototypes in space.

The most obvious extension of contextualized word embeddings to the type level is to build exemplar models from token representations. Such models represent a word as the sum total of observed occurrences, i.e. the set of all token vectors. Full exemplar representations are computationally expensive, and subject to noise from outliers. At the other end of the spectrum, some have tried av-

227

Proceedings of the 24th Conference on Computational Natural Language Learning, pages 227–244
Online, November 19-20, 2020. ©2020 Association for Computational Linguistics
https://doi.org/10.18653/v1/P17

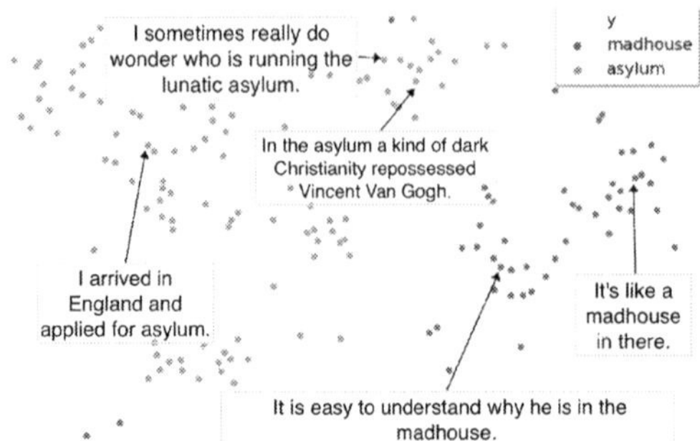

Figure 1: 2D t-SNE visualization of layer 8 vectors for tokens of *asylum* and *madhouse* sampled from the BNC.

eraging over exemplar models to generate a single vector for each word (Bommasani et al., 2020). However, these models do not leverage the contextual knowledge resident in BERTs later layers.

Our approach aims to capture the regularities in contextual variation while reducing the noise it introduces. A set of BERT token vectors for a single word naturally tends to separate spatially into groups of similar usages, or 'usage types' (Giulianelli et al., 2020). Usage types often correspond to polysemous or homonymous senses, idiomatic constructions, and affordances.[1] Figure 1 shows a t-SNE visualization of tokens for *madhouse* and *asylum*. The dominant usage of asylum is as political refuge, but there is a cluster corresponding to *asylum* as an institution of confinement for people with psychiatric diagnoses, which shares similar negative connotations to *madhouse*, a derogatory colloquialism for such institutions.

To test whether these usage types retain enough contextual information to aid in context-sensitive lexical tasks, we use K-means clustering of BERT token representations to derive multi-prototype lexical embeddings. The embeddings are evaluated on the standard lexical tasks of similarity and relatedness estimation. Clustered BERT-based representations provide high-quality predictions of human judgments for both tasks. They are also employed to test a cognitive hypothesis which holds that one of the factors contributing to relative abstractness/concreteness a word is how much its meaning varies in context. We find that the average

dispersion of tokens in a cluster bears a significant relationship to abstractness.

The contributions of this paper are as follows:

1. Application of BERT for type-level lexical modeling, and the testing of type-level lexical-semantic hypotheses.

2. Clustering of contextualized representations into multi-prototype embeddings, which maintain the advantages of contextualization without the complexity burden of exemplar models, leading to improved performance on similarity and relatedness estimation.

3. Insight into the semantic interpretability of BERT, most notably that middle layers best approximate similarity while the final layer approximates relatedness.

2   Related work

The pre-trained BERT language model is a bidirectional Transformer (Vaswani et al., 2017) encoder. It has either 12 fully-connected layers (`bert-base`) or 24 (`bert-large`). The model is trained on two tasks: masked token prediction and next sentence prediction. For `bert-base`, the representation of an input sequence consists in a 12-layer activation network with 768-dimensional vectors for each input token (where tokens correspond to sub-word WordPieces [Schuster and Nakajima, 2012]) at each of 12 layers. The preponderance of research surrounding analysis and interpretability of BERT has been dubbed BERTology, after the poster-child of the contextual revolution (cf. Rogers et al., 2020 for an excellent survey).

Probing Tasks   Most studies of word meaning in BERT follow an agenda of extrinsic evaluation (Artetxe et al., 2018). Tenney et al. (2019a) found that CLMs improve over non-contextual counterparts largely on syntactic tasks, with smaller gains on semantic tasks. Tenney et al. (2019b) introduced *edge*-probing tasks to analyze the layer-wise structure of BERT, and found that early layers perform syntactic tasks like part-of-speech and dependency tagging, while later layers encode information pertinent to semantic tasks like coreference resolution, relation labeling, and semantic proto-role labeling. We aim to advance this kind of structural analysis of BERT through the *intrinsic* evaluation of representations at different layers.

---

[1] Affordances are the different ways a thing can present itself to an individual (Gibson, 2015 [1979]). For instance, water can manifest as a drink, a chemical substance to be studied, a span to be travelled across, a medium for recreational sports, or a municipal resource, just to name a few.

Contextual Word Embeddings Existing applications of CLMs to lexical tasks use exemplar models or single-prototype models. Wiedemann et al. (2019) successfully employed a K-nearest-neighbor approach to BERT exemplar models for word sense disambiguation (WSD). Coenen et al. (2019) created a visualization tool that generates a 'word cloud' from BERT tokens, browsable by layer.[2] They also achieved a state-of-the-art F1 score on a WSD task with the simple scheme involving sense-annotated training data from Peters et al. (2018).

Ethayarajh (2019) generated static embeddings from CLM models, using the first PCA component sets of token representations. Bommasani et al. (2020) experimented with averaging tokens for context-agnostic word vectors. This approach performs well on similarity and relatedness tasks compared to traditional static embeddings. However, averaging evaporates much of BERT's contextual variation, cutting off its potential to aid in similarity estimation. It's no surprise that averages derived from earlier layers of BERT performed best at similarity estimation. Later layers demonstrate more contextual variation (Ethayarajh, 2019), making the mean less meaningful.

Similarity The most common method for intrinsic evaluation of word embeddings is similarity estimation. However, major critiques have been leveled at the standard similarity datasets, and even at the construct of similarity itself. Depending on which comparison a word enters into, there is variation in which senses (and/or features) of the word are considered for the calculation. Nelson Goodman's (1972) dismissal of similarity argues that the *selection* of properties to consider varies so widely as to be essentially arbitrary. Thus, similarity datasets which ask raters to assess the similarity between two words out of context are argued to be premised on the flawed notion that similarity is fixed (Faruqui et al., 2016).

Two words are never absolutely similar or dissimilar. Rather, in assessing the likeness between two words, one implicitly selects some grounds for assessing their likeness. In Tversky's classic (1977) feature-matching model, the similarity of two items is computed from the number of shared properties they have as compared to the number of properties they hold distinct. Tversky notes that property se-

lection is subject to variation. To give an extreme example involving polysemy, the relevant features for comparing *bishop* with *rabbi* are different from those for relevant for comparing *bishop* and *rook*.

Given the complaints lodged against similarity, and the existence of contextual similarity datasets (Erk et al., 2013; Pilehvar and Camacho-Collados, 2019; Stanovsky and Hopkins, 2018), why bother applying BERT to non-contextual datasets at all? And for that matter, what is the value of modeling word-pair similarity judgments? The pared down format of word-pair judgments foregrounds the cognitive regularities of the underlying process by which humans select a grounds for comparison. Despite potential variability in similarity judgments, inter-annotator agreement for word-pair similarity ratings is fairly high (Medin et al., 1993). In one sense, an apple is like candy: both are sweet snack foods. However, they are consistently judged to be dissimilar (2.08 in Simlex999 on a scale of 1-10; SD=0.75). Together, *apple* and *candy* co-determine a grounds for likeness, narrowing the context or the features under consideration (one is healthy, the other rots your teeth).

Medin et al. (1993) argue that similarity is a *process*, and this process is governed by constraints which give rise to regularities. For example, antonyms such as *black-white* are judged to be maximally dissimilar in isolation, but are judged more similar when presented alongside a comparison such as *black-red* containing a related word. As the authors so vividly put it, "Nelson Goodman (1972) called similarity a chameleon, but we believe that similarity is more like two yoked chameleons: The entities entering into a comparison jointly constrain one another and jointly determine the outcome of a similarity comparison" (272).

Viewed as a context-sensitive, constraint-based process, it seems natural that similarity judgments should benefit from context-sensitive lexical representations. In single-prototype embeddings, the properties or features which are considered are necessarily constant. The same vector is considered in every similarity calculation for a single word. By representing a word as a set of vectors, each corresponding to a prototypical usage, we can access the usage types relevant to different comparisons separately.

Relatedness Similarity is paradigmatic: highly similar words are more likely to occupy the same 'slot' in a sentence (i.e., *The bug is on the*

---

rug/carpet). Semantic relatedness, on the other hand is syntagmatic: two highly related words are likely to appear in succession, as in *She filled the car with gasoline*. As a comparison between two isolated words, the argument for context-sensitivity of similarity also applies to relatedness judgments. The next section describes a BERT-based approach to inject a degree of context-sensitivity into similarity and relatedness estimation.

3 Multi-prototype BERT embeddings

As stated, BERT token representations demonstrate greater contextual variation at each progressive layer (Ethayarajh, 2019). To capture the contextual knowledge of later layers, we construct multi-prototype embeddings from many token representations of a single word.

The usage types captured by clusters do not always correspond directly to dictionary word senses, but they often discriminate between senses of polysemous and homonymous words, metaphorical senses, as well as syntactic roles and constructions. (Giulianelli et al., 2020). For this reason, count-based multi-prototype models have long been recognized for their usefulness to WSD tasks (Schütze, 1998; Reisinger and Mooney, 2010; Pilehvar and Camacho-Collados, 2019). We observed that natural clusters often capture cognitive affordances. Whether or not they are linguistically significant, these loose categories likely play a role in cognitive processes like similarity. To recast our earlier observation: the affordance(s) of *water* that comes to mind in the comparison of *water-land* are different from the idea that surfaces when comparing *water-coffee*. We use clustering to approximate BERT's usage-types and the affordances they capture, and demonstrate their usefulness for lexical tasks.

3.1 Materials & Methods

The transformation of token-vectors into multi-prototype vectors requires several steps, described here for a single word w.

Data Collection First, a set S of up to 100 sentences containing a token t of w was sampled at random from the British National Corpus (BNC, Burnard, 2000).[3] As the human judgments in our evaluation datasets were collected agnostic to part of speech, and are particular to word forms, no

lemmatization or tagging was used. Any sentences too large to input to BERT were discarded.

Then, each sentence $s \in S$ was passed to the pre-trained `bert-base-uncased` model, and the layer-wise network activations obtained. If BERT split the token t into subword WordPieces[4], we followed the now-standard practice of averaging t's subword vectors to obtain a single token vector for t at each layer. This process yielded a vector for each token at each of 12 layers.

Clustering At each layer, w's token vectors at that layer were clustered using K-means. Separate embeddings were calculated for each layer $l \in L = \{0..11\}$, and for each number of K-means clusters $K \in \{1, ..., 10, 50\}$.[5] For a given choice of K and l, the set of cluster centroids $\pi(w)_1^l \ldots \pi(w)_K^l$ constitute the multi-prototype representation for w. These centroids correspond to K prototypical usages of w. In the rare case that $|S| < K$ for w, it was not possible to construct a K-prototype representation for w. Consequently, scores could not be calculated for a handful of words for some parameter combinations. However, scores for at least 99% of the comparisons for all datasets were collected for K=1-10 (See A.2). This detail renders comparison between models less than ideal, but the differences are so minimal as to make the issue negligible.

Evaluation Cosine distance, the typical method of relation estimation, will not work for multi-prototype models, as it is a function of two vectors. Reisinger and Mooney (2010) compute distance using the centroids of clusters. MAXSIM of words w, w' is the maximum cosine similarity of any cluster centroid of w to any centroid of w'. In our case, the layer l introduces an additional parameter, such that $MaxSim(w, w', l, K) =$

$$\max_{1 \leq j \leq K, 1 \leq k \leq K} cos(\pi_j^l(w), \pi_k^l(w'))$$

where $\pi_{j,l}(w)$ corresponds to the centroid of the jth cluster for word w at layer l. Effectively, the similarity of two words is equal to the similarity

---

[3]Indices of the sampled sentences are available at `https://github.com/gchronis/MProBERT`

[4]Note that this process is referred to as 'tokenization', and the resulting WordPieces are typically referred to as tokens. To avoid confusion, this paper reserves the word 'token' to refer to an occurrence of an entire word in sentential context.

[5]Results for k=50 were evaluated for the sake of curiosity about the extreme case but are not discussed—such embeddings are more like exemplar models than multi-prototype models.

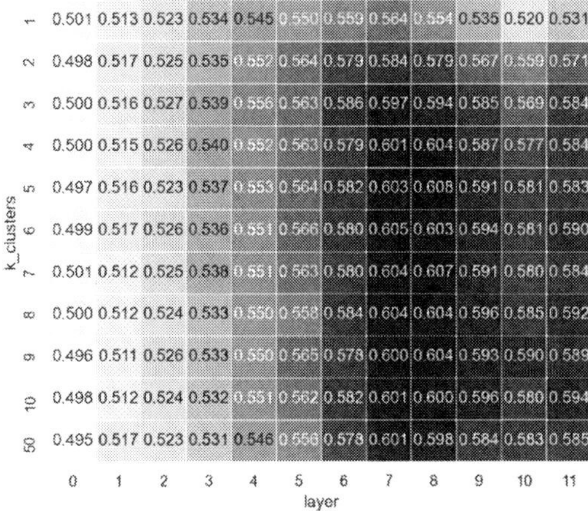

Figure 2: Spearman's ρ for BERT multi-prototype embeddings correlated against SimLex-999 **similarity** for each combination of layer and number of K-means clusters ($p < 1e^{-60}$).

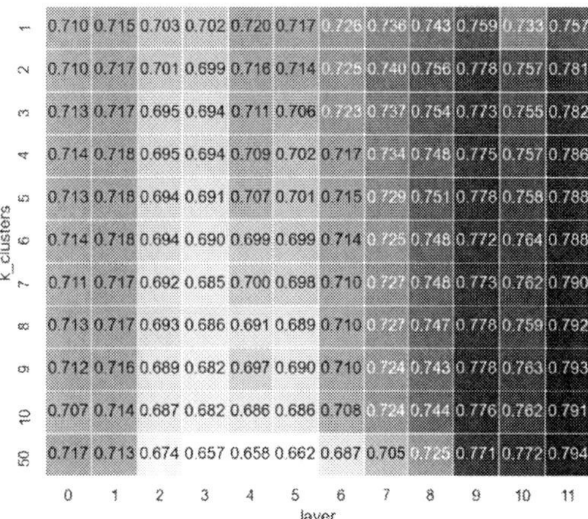

Figure 3: Spearman's ρ for BERT multi-prototype embeddings correlated against MEN **relatedness** ratings for each combination of layer and number of K-means clusters ($p < 1x10^{-100}$).

of their two closest prototypes. We also experimented with their AVGSIM, defined as the mean of all pairwise similarities between w's centroids against those of w'. For AVGSIM, two words are close if many of their prototypes are close. In stark contrast to Reisinger and Mooney (2010), we found MAXSIM to universally outperform AVGSIM, and so report results on the former only.

4 Similarity and Relatedness

4.1 Datasets

The embeddings were evaluated against three similarity datasets and four relatedness datasets. For similarity, we used SimLex999 (Hill et al., 2015), SimVerb3500 (Gerz et al., 2016), and WordSim353$_{sim}$ (Agirre et al., 2009). The latter is a partition of WordSim353 (Finkelstein et al., 2001) devised to approximate similarity. SimLex999 contains 999 word pairs balanced for concreteness and annotated specifically for similarity. SimVerb3500, containing 3500 verb pairs, was also designed specifically to target similarity. For relatedness datasets we used WordSim353$_{rel}$ (Agirre et al. (2009)'s complementary relatedness subset); MEN, containing 3000 word pairs (Bruni et al., 2014), and YP-130, consisting of 130 verb pairs (Yang and Powers, 2006). Though it was not collected with specific instructions to the raters, for the sake of comparison to other approaches, we also evaluate on the original WordSim353 dataset, and report results with the relatedness datasets.

4.2 Results

Overall, clustering yielded great improvement, especially at later layers.

Similarity Performance on all similarity datasets peaked between layers 7-9, somewhere between 5-8 clusters. This pattern is exemplified by the heatmap in Figure 1, which displays Spearman's ρ correlations against SimLex999 for embeddings at each layer and each choice of K. Performance on SimLex999 reaches a peak score at layer 8 with 5 clusters ($\rho = 0.608$). SimVerb3500 follows a strikingly similar pattern, with the highest performance at layer 7 with 7 clusters ($\rho = 0.531$). For WordSim353$_{sim}$, performance peaks at layer 9 with 8 clusters ($\rho = 0.826$), but the performance is nearly matched by layer 11 with 4/5 clusters ($\rho = 0.825$).

Relatedness Across the board, layer 11 achieves the best performance on relatedness tasks. The pattern is illustrated in Figure 3, which shows Spearman's ρ correlations between MAXSIM predictions and MEN ratings for each layer and choice of K. Clustering induces significant performance improvements at layers 8 and up. Layers 0-1 show little variation due to clustering, and layer 2-7 performance actually degrades. MEN performance peaks at layer 11 with 9 clusters ($\rho = 0.793$). The other datasets show a similar pattern, with peak performance at layer 11 between 7 and 9 clusters: K=7 for WordSim353$_{rel}$ ($\rho = 0.665$), K=9 for YP-130 ($\rho = 0.715$), and K=7 for WordSim353 ($\rho = 0.747$).

	Similarity			Relatedness			
	SL-999	*SV-3500*	*WS-353$_{sim}$*	*WS-353*	*WS-353$_{rel}$*	*MEN*	*YP-130*
Distributional	0.563 SP-15	0.364 CBOW	0.795 GloVe	0.738 FastText	**0.681** FastText	**0.801** GloVe	0.535 GloVe
CLM-based	0.550 XLNet-24 (4)	0.455 XLNet-24 (3)	- -	0.730 BERT-24 (6)	- -	0.200 BERT-pca-1 (1)	- -
MProBERT	**0.605**	**0.528** (layer=7, K$\leq$9)	**0.807**	**0.741**	0.653	0.781 (layer=11, K$\leq$9)	**0.711**

Table 1: Performance of best unioned multi-prototype BERT embeddings (M-ProBert) for both similarity and relatedness estimation tasks (Spearman's ρ) compared to other CLM-based word embeddings and to state-of-the-art corpus-based distributional models. Best results in bold. Parentheses for CLM models indicate layer number.

Model Selection It is possible to sidestep the issue of model selection by following Reisinger and Mooney (2010) in taking the union of all of the prototypes of different cluster sizes. This method works as well or nearly as well as selecting the best value for K, with the union of all clusters for $K \leq 9$ giving the best results overall.

As a general model for similarity estimation, we suggest layer 7 with the union of all clusters for $K \leq 9$. For relatedness, we suggest embeddings built from layer 11 using the union of all clusters $K \leq 9$. For both similarity and relatedness, $K = 7$ does provide marginally better results, but the success of the unioned model demonstrates that *post hoc* selection of K is not necessary to achieve good performance.

Table 1 compares the best unioned models for similarity and relatedness to state-of-the-art distributional approaches trained on running monolingual text (without the injection of structured knowledge), as well as to other CLM-based static embeddings. For distributional models we compared to Symmetric Pattern embeddings (SP-15, [Schwartz et al., 2015]), GloVe (Pennington et al., 2014), CBOW (Mikolov et al., 2013), and Fast-Text (Bojanowski et al., 2017). For other CLM-based embeddings, we compared to Bommasani et al. (2020), who tested layer-wise token aggregations for numerous architectures: BERT, RoBERTa, GPT2, XLNet, and DistilBert. We also compared to Ethayarajh (2019), who examined the first PCA component of individual layers of several CLMs. Performance drastically improves over other CLM-based embeddings, and our generalized similarity estimation model surpasses the distributional state-of-the-art on all three datasets.[6]

4.3 Discussion

In contrast with Bommasani et al. (2020), who find performance to peak at early layers, our model's performance peaks at later layers, which we know to possess more fine-grained contextual information (Ethayarajh, 2019). Multi-prototype embeddings harness the power of this contextual information for the type-level tasks of similarity and relatedness estimation. The fact that contextual information aids in similarity estimation supports the hypothesis that similarity, even between isolated words, is a dynamic, context-sensitive process. Indeed, word-pair or 'context-free' similarity estimation is not truly a type-level task. Each word in a pair constitutes the linguistic context for the interpretation of the other word. By capturing the most typical contexts for a word, multi-prototype embeddings enable the selection of a grounds for likeness, approximated here with MAXSIM.

Multi-prototype vs Exemplar The optimal number of prototypes is relatively small. Performance increases with K up to a point, after which it begins to degrade minimally but steadily (Figure 4.2). This behavior can be explained in terms of the model taking into account more outliers with a very high K. The higher K is, the more likely we are to find small clusters very far from the rest of the tokens, representing a rare but highly specific usage type, or even totally unique usages in clusters all by themselves. As K is maximized towards an exemplar model, the likelihood increases that any pair of words will have exemplars that are near to each other, thus increasing the predicted similarity. We hypothesize that this kind of overestimation of similarity is the reason performance degrades.

More generally, we found multi-prototype models with relatively few (K$\leq$10) prototypes better

---

[6]Benchmark scores are self-reported by the authors or obtained from Lastra-Díaz et al. (2019)'s reproducible survey. Future work should reimplement these models to test the statistical significance of the performance gains.

purposed than more exemplar-like models (K=50) for estimating semantic relationships. In addition to being more lightweight, multi-prototype vectors appear to be a beneficial abstraction over exemplar models, at least for the present task. Whether or not exemplars are stored in memory, knowledge of individual outliers is not relevant to these tasks, which deal with stereotypical or prototypical class relationships rather than relationships between individuals.

Similarity vs Relatedness The analysis also uncovered differences in the semantic relations approximated by different layers. The final layer of BERT approximate relatedness, while layer 7 is optimal for estimating similarity. This finding bears an interesting connection to recent insights in BERTology. The middle layers of `bert-base` (6-9) are consistently noted to be the most transferable, i.e., to perform the best across tasks (Hewitt and Manning, 2019; Goldberg, 2019; Jawahar et al., 2019; Liu et al., 2019a). The final layers, on the other hand, are the most specific to the next sentence prediction task. The connection suggests that successful representation of semantic similarity may be critical to many NLP tasks, moreso than relatedness. Our results support the thesis that static vectors cannot surfaces all aspects of lexical semantic meaning at once (Artetxe et al., 2018). But, perhaps when forced to compromise on one general purpose embedding for downstream applications, one which approximates similarity may be preferable over those which approximate relatedness—these embeddings appear to work best on a wide variety of downstream tasks.

The difference in preferred layer for different tasks confirms that similarity and relatedness, so important a distinction to distributional models, ought to be treated separately in CLMs as well.

Clusters While we do not undertake a systematic analysis into the types of usage-clusters captured by K-means, qualitative examination indicates that the gains from clustering come from expected behavior. For example, at layer 8 with $K=3$, the clusters for *river* correspond to the natural feature and associated sensory imagery, the name construction *river X*, and adjectival uses (e.g. *river warden, river dolphin*). The clusters for *stream* correspond to to a a fluid *medium* through which other entities pass (e.g. *blood stream, gas stream*), the natural feature, and a *substance in motion* constituting the

stream (many but not all of which examples take the form *stream of X*, where X is not a typical fluid).[7] Among these clusters, MAXSIM selects the two corresponding to the concrete natural feature.

The clusters selected by MAXSIM do not always correspond to a clear cohesive usage-type. Sometimes it selects a catchall prototype, or one one that encompasses multiple distinct usage types. However, even in these cases, K-means separates out distractor usages such as proper names and specific constructions that would otherwise shift the mean of a single prototype into less relevant realms. The SimLex999 rating between *cat* and *lion* is 6.75 (SD=0.84). The single prototype model (l=8) predicts 5.79. The multi-prototype model (l=8, k=7) is more accurate at 6.33. MAXSIM selects a *cat* cluster that lacks an obvious interpretation (though it does frequently contrast cats to other animal species). Importantly, MAXSIM *excludes* a cluster containing cats as pets, a cluster in which a cat is a grammatical subject, and one for a colloquialism meaning 'obtain'. The selected *lion* cluster contains lions which interact directly with humans. They have surprising docile characteristics like being 'tamed' or 'lying down like a lamb'. The discarded clusters correspond to lion as wild animal, as a name, the idiom *lion's share*, and metaphorical human lions.

The *cat-lion* example shows that the model implements the principle of context-sensitivity for similarity estimation. The chosen prototypes are not the most stereotypical, but actually those which *downplay* the distinctive features of domesticity in cats and wildness in lions. The relatively high human rating may be attributed to the recognition that the two species have many shared biological traits compared to other animals, and MAXSIM is able to find this common ground. Refer to Appendix B for example sentences from different clusters.

5   Abstractness and contextual variation

To demonstrate the potential of multi-prototype embeddings, we next leverage our model to test a cognitive hypothesis about concreteness. Specifically, we examine the difference between abstract and

---

[7]The blend between syntactico-grammatical and semantic prototypes underscores the relationship between form and meaning. The construction *stream of X* invites a focus on the movement of the substance and tends towards more metaphorical uses, allowing count nouns, whereas *X stream* invites a focus on the channel created by the substance and is limited to more 'fluidlike' fluids.

concrete words with respect to spatial dispersion among prototypes.

Roughly speaking, abstract concepts are classically characterized as those that are "neither purely physical nor spatially constrained" (Barsalou and Wiemer-Hastings, 2005, 129). Concrete words are recognized and comprehended faster (West and Holcomb, 2000), remembered longer (Paivio, 1971, 2013; Fliessbach, Weis, Klaver, Elger, and Weber, 2006), and more resilient to brain damage (Katz and Goodglass, 1990) than abstract words.

The dominant explanation for concreteness effects is called the Dual-Coding Hypothesis (Paivio, 1971, 2013; Crutch and Warrington, 2005). It holds that concrete and abstract concepts are organized differently in the brain: the former are grounded in experience, while the latter are based solely on other concepts. The sensory richness of concrete concepts explains their memory advantage. Significant distributional-semantic research has tested the Dual-Coding Hypothesis, with mixed results (cf. Hill et al., 2013, 2014a,b).

Dual-Coding Theory demands discrete types of conceptual representations, and raises an uncomfortable metaphysical issue of whether a concept can be about anything other than the purely physical. Embodied views of abstract representation (Kousta et al., 2011) hold that both linguistic and experiential information contribute to rich representations for *all* concepts, and that the apparent distinction arises from statistical patterns in the proportion of sensorimotor to affective experiential information undergirding the concepts. The question then arises of how to account for concreteness effects without positing distinct representations.

A recent psychological theory contends that concreteness effects are a consequence of 'situational systematicity' (Davis et al., 2020): abstract concepts are constituted by a larger and more complex set of relationships, dispersed through space and time, and are therefore more subject to contextual variation. If the hypothesis is valid, it might contribute to an explanation of concreteness effects without reliance on the claim that abstract concepts lack experiential grounding: simple, systematic, contextually invariant concepts would naturally be easier to remember.

Testing the situational systematicity hypothesis demands a way to measure the complexity and contextual variability in concepts. Multi-prototype BERT meets this demand, at least for modeling

variability, which can be viewed a proxy for complexity. Single-prototype models cannot be used to test this hypothesis—they lack such fine-grained information about contexts of occurrence.

5.1 Setup

We analyze the 1028 unique words in the SimLex999 dataset, each of which is annotated with its USF concreteness norm (Nelson et al., 2004). As a measure of heterogeneity we use average pairwise token distance among clusters. For a given K and l, we calculate the average pairwise cosine distance between all tokens in a cluster, and then average that value across clusters. This value measures how heterogeneous a word's usage-types tend to be.

5.2 Results

Results indicate a relationship between abstractness and dispersion. However, the nature of this relationship changes throughout the layers of the network. Figure 4 shows the correlation between concreteness and average pairwise token distance throughout the layers of `bert-base` with K set to 9. The strongest correlations are observed for this choice of K, reaching a maximum of $\rho = -0.264$ at layer 9. The same pattern of correlations, from significantly positive to significantly negative, was observed for all choices of K.

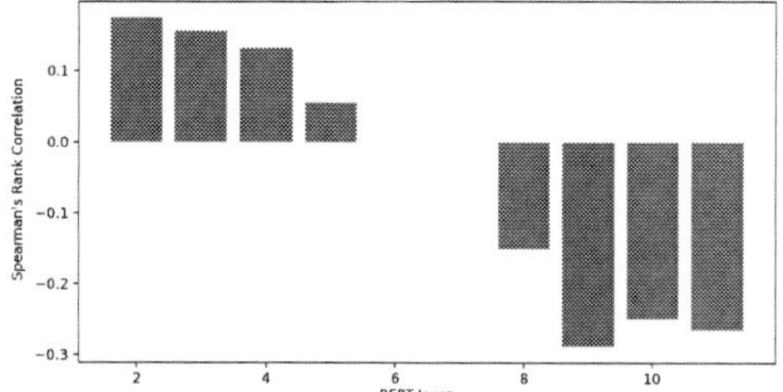

Figure 4: Spearman's correlation between USF concreteness norms and average inter-token distance for K=9 multi-prototype vectors ($p < 0.1, N = 1028$). Correlations for layers 0, 5, and 6 were not significant.

The correlation changes direction depending on the layer: there is a significant positive correlation at layers 1-5, and a significant negative correlation at 7-11. A strong negative correlation means that abstract words tend to demonstrate greater variance at these layers than do concrete words.

5.3 Discussion

The heterogeneity hypothesis predicts a negative correlation between concreteness and variance.

This pattern is upheld at layers 7-11. At these layers, tokens in the clusters of an abstract word tend to be somewhat farther apart from one another than those in a concrete word. Ethayarajh (2019) noted that inter-token variance increases throughout the layers of BERT. While true in general, variance increases more for abstract words than concrete words. However, the hypothesis is not upheld at early layers. Early layers tend to separate concrete tokens while later layers tend to separate abstract tokens.

Where the model demonstrates more variance between tokens, it encodes more detailed knowledge of that word. Where it displays less variance, these internal differences are collapsed. That is, where variance is low, the model is 'focused', or zoomed in, on representing differences between words, and where variance is high, the model is 'focused' on representing variation in how one word is used. The reason for this shift in correlation from positive to negative, or in other words the shift in 'focus' from concrete to abstract words, remains opaque. The immediate conclusion to be drawn from this analysis is that abstractness, a type-level property, bears a significant connection to behavior at the token level. This supports the idea that properties at the word level are dependent on interactions at the token level, and demonstrates the utility of token-level representations for lexical semantics at the type level.

Implications for the situational systematicity hypothesis are inconclusive. Contextual variation represents just one dimension along which concrete and abstract concepts vary. On its own, the correlation between dispersion and concreteness does not capture the data explained by Dual-Coding Theory. The results of the present analysis, while preliminary, constitute a proof-of-concept for how at least some differences between abstract and concrete words might be accounted for without positing richer representations for one type over the other. Incorporating more properties and using of more sophisticated measures of contextual variation may prove to distinguish representations of concrete and abstract words even further.

6   Conclusion

We have presented evidence that the spatially complex lexical representations afforded by CLMs are useful in type-level lexical modeling, and in investigating type-level semantic questions. We first addressed the common tasks of predicting word similarity and relatedness, and demonstrated that BERT produces high-quality multi-prototype word embeddings. We then used these representations test a hypothesis about word-level abstractness, and uncovered a significant connection between this type-level property and the relationships between tokens.

Multi-prototype embeddings represent word meaning as a *constellation* of points, as opposed to a single point. The strength of multi-prototype embeddings (and other alternatives such as probabilistic, Gaussian, and exemplar-based models) lies in this word-internal complexity. A vector lacks internal complexity—it is infinitesimal. As such, it can only be compared to other vectors on the basis of their location in space. Internally complex representations, on the other hand, can be compared on the basis of their internal geometry. When words have a shape, we can ask how the shape of words, or of lexical categories, compare to one another. Computational lexical semantics ought to seek out and apply mathematical methods for comparing the higher-order structure or topology of word meaning in such models.

Future Work   In this experiment we limit the sample size for each word to 100, and use a fixed K for each word. While increasing the number of data points would perhaps lead to more natural fine-grained clusters, and therefore more sensible K-means clusters for a higher K, we predict that outliers would still lead to the over-prediction of similarities. In order to maximize the contribution to the longstanding debate between exemplar and prototype models for semantic memory, the effects of increased sample size should be evaluated. In addition, the optimal number of prototypes is not the same for every word. We hypothesize that the application of non-parametric and hierarchical clustering methods will demonstrate a tendency towards a relatively low number of prototypes, further validating multi-prototype models of semantic memory as well as improving performance.

Future work will apply CLMs to to other lexical tasks and questions, such as metaphor. Metaphor interpretation is a context-sensitive process akin to similarity judgment. The Rational Speech Act formalization of metaphor interpretation (Kao et al., 2014) utilizes hand-crafted feature vectors; it might be extended by inducing metaphorical sense representations from BERT-based prototypes.

References

Eneko Agirre, Enrique Alfonseca, Keith Hall, Jana Kravalova, Marius Paşca, and Aitor Soroa. 2009. A study on similarity and relatedness using distributional and WordNet-based approaches. In *Proceedings of Human Language Technologies: The 2009 Annual Conference of the North American Chapter of the Association for Computational Linguistics*, pages 19–27. Association for Computational Linguistics.

Mikel Artetxe, Gorka Labaka, Iñigo Lopez-Gazpio, and Eneko Agirre. 2018. Uncovering divergent linguistic information in word embeddings with lessons for intrinsic and extrinsic evaluation. In *Proceedings of the 22nd Conference on Computational Natural Language Learning*, pages 282–291. Association for Computational Linguistics.

L Barsalou and K Wiemer-Hastings. 2005. Situating abstract concepts. In *Grounding Cognition: The Role of Perception and Action in Memory, Language, and Thought*, pages 129–163.

Piotr Bojanowski, Edouard Grave, Armand Joulin, and Tomas Mikolov. 2017. Enriching word vectors with subword information. *arXiv:1607.04606 [cs]*.

Rishi Bommasani, Kelly Davis, and Claire Cardie. 2020. Interpreting pretrained contextualized representations via reductions to static embeddings. In *Proceedings of the 58th Annual Meeting of the Association for Computational Linguistics*, pages 4758–4781. Association for Computational Linguistics.

Elia Bruni, Nam Khanh Tran, and Marco Baroni. 2014. Multimodal distributional semantics. *Journal of Artificial Intelligence Research*, 49(1):1–47.

Lou Burnard. 2000. *User Reference Guide for the British National Corpus*. Technical report, Oxford University Computing Services.

Andy Coenen, Emily Reif, Ann Yuan, Been Kim, Adam Pearce, Fernanda Viégas, and Martin Wattenberg. 2019. Visualizing and measuring the geometry of BERT. *arXiv:1906.02715 [cs, stat]*. Version: 1.

Sebastian J. Crutch and Elizabeth K. Warrington. 2005. Abstract and concrete concepts have structurally different representational frameworks. *Brain*, 128(3):615–627.

Charles P. Davis, Gerry T. M. Altmann, and Eiling Yee. 2020. Situational systematicity: A role for schema in understanding the differences between abstract and concrete concepts. *Cognitive Neuropsychology*, 37(1):142–153.

Jacob Devlin, Ming-Wei Chang, Kenton Lee, and Kristina Toutanova. 2018. BERT: Pre-training of deep bidirectional transformers for language understanding. *arXiv:1810.04805 [cs]*.

Katrin Erk, Diana McCarthy, and Nicholas Gaylord. 2013. Measuring word meaning in context. *Computational Linguistics*, 39(3):511–554.

Kawin Ethayarajh. 2019. How contextual are contextualized word representations? comparing the geometry of BERT, ELMo, and GPT-2 embeddings. In *Proceedings of the 2019 Conference on Empirical Methods in Natural Language Processing and the 9th International Joint Conference on Natural Language Processing*, pages 55–65. Association for Computational Linguistics.

Manaal Faruqui, Yulia Tsvetkov, Pushpendre Rastogi, and Chris Dyer. 2016. Problems with evaluation of word embeddings using word similarity tasks. *arXiv:1605.02276 [cs]*.

Lev Finkelstein, Evgeniy Gabrilovich, Yossi Matias, Ehud Rivlin, Zach Solan, Gadi Wolfman, and Eytan Ruppin. 2001. Placing search in context: the concept revisited. In *Proceedings of the 10th international conference on World Wide Web*, pages 406–414. Association for Computing Machinery.

K. Fliessbach, S. Weis, P. Klaver, C. E. Elger, and B. Weber. 2006. The effect of word concreteness on recognition memory. *NeuroImage*, 32(3):1413–1421.

Daniela Gerz, Ivan Vulić, Felix Hill, Roi Reichart, and Anna Korhonen. 2016. SimVerb-3500: A large-scale evaluation set of verb similarity. In *Proceedings of the 2016 Conference on Empirical Methods in Natural Language Processing*, pages 2173–2182. Association for Computational Linguistics.

James J. Gibson. 2015 [1979]. *The Ecological Approach to Visual Perception: Classic Edition*. Psychology Press, New York ; Hove, England.

Mario Giulianelli, Marco Del Tredici, and Raquel Fernández. 2020. Analysing lexical semantic change with contextualised word representations. In *Proceedings of the 58th Annual Meeting of the Association for Computational Linguistics*, pages 3960–3973. Association for Computational Linguistics.

Yoav Goldberg. 2019. Assessing BERT's syntactic abilities. *arXiv:1901.05287 [cs]*.

Nelson Goodman. 1972. Seven strictures on similarity. In *Problems and Projects*. Bobs-Merril, Indianapolis.

John Hewitt and Christopher D. Manning. 2019. A structural probe for finding syntax in word representations. In *Proceedings of the 2019 Conference of the North American Chapter of the Association for Computational Linguistics: Human Language Technologies, Volume 1 (Long and Short Papers)*, pages 4129–4138. Association for Computational Linguistics.

Felix Hill, Douwe Kiela, and Anna Korhonen. 2013. Concreteness and corpora: A theoretical and practical study. In *Proceedings of the Fourth Annual Workshop on Cognitive Modeling and Computational Linguistics (CMCL)*, pages 75–83, Sofia, Bulgaria. Association for Computational Linguistics.

Felix Hill, Anna Korhonen, and Christian Bentz. 2014a. A quantitative empirical analysis of the abstract/concrete distinction. *Cognitive Science*, 38(1):162–177.

Felix Hill, Roi Reichart, and Anna Korhonen. 2014b. Multi-modal models for concrete and abstract concept meaning. *Transactions of the Association for Computational Linguistics*, 2:285–296.

Felix Hill, Roi Reichart, and Anna Korhonen. 2015. SimLex-999: Evaluating semantic models with (genuine) similarity estimation. *Computational Linguistics*, 41(4):665–695.

Ganesh Jawahar, Benoît Sagot, and Djamé Seddah. 2019. What does BERT learn about the structure of language? In *Proceedings of the 57th Annual Meeting of the Association for Computational Linguistics*, pages 3651–3657. Association for Computational Linguistics.

Justine Kao, Leon Bergen, and Noah Goodman. 2014. Formalizing the pragmatics of metaphor understanding. *Proceedings of the Annual Meeting of the Cognitive Science Society*, 36(36).

R. B. Katz and H. Goodglass. 1990. Deep dysphasia: analysis of a rare form of repetition disorder. *Brain and Language*, 39(1):153–185.

Stavroula-Thaleia Kousta, Gabriella Vigliocco, David P. Vinson, Mark Andrews, and Elena Del Campo. 2011. The representation of abstract words: Why emotion matters. *Journal of Experimental Psychology: General*, 140(1):14–34.

Juan J. Lastra-Díaz, Josu Goikoetxea, Mohamed Ali Hadj Taieb, Ana García-Serrano, Mohamed Ben Aouicha, and Eneko Agirre. 2019. A reproducible survey on word embeddings and ontology-based methods for word similarity: Linear combinations outperform the state of the art. *Engineering Applications of Artificial Intelligence*, 85:645–665.

Nelson F. Liu, Matt Gardner, Yonatan Belinkov, Matthew E. Peters, and Noah A. Smith. 2019a. Linguistic knowledge and transferability of contextual representations. In *Proceedings of the 2019 Conference of the North American Chapter of the Association for Computational Linguistics: Human Language Technologies, Volume 1 (Long and Short Papers)*, pages 1073–1094. Association for Computational Linguistics.

Yinhan Liu, Myle Ott, Naman Goyal, Jingfei Du, Mandar Joshi, Danqi Chen, Omer Levy, Mike Lewis, Luke Zettlemoyer, and Veselin Stoyanov. 2019b. RoBERTa: A robustly optimized BERT pretraining approach. *arXiv:1907.11692 [cs]*.

Bryan McCann, James Bradbury, Caiming Xiong, and Richard Socher. 2017. Learned in translation: Contextualized word vectors. In I. Guyon, U. V. Luxburg, S. Bengio, H. Wallach, R. Fergus, S. Vishwanathan, and R. Garnett, editors, *Advances in Neural Information Processing Systems 30*, pages 6294–6305. Curran Associates, Inc.

Douglas L. Medin, Robert L. Goldstone, and Dedre Gentner. 1993. Respects for similarity. *Psychological Review*, 100(2):254–278.

Tomas Mikolov, Kai Chen, Greg Corrado, and Jeffrey Dean. 2013. Efficient estimation of word representations in vector space. *arXiv:1301.3781 [cs]*.

Douglas Nelson, Cathy McEvoy, and Thomas Schreiber. 2004. The university of south florida free association, rhyme, and word fragment norms. *Behavior research methods, instruments, & computers : a journal of the Psychonomic Society, Inc*, 36:402–7.

Allan Paivio. 1971. *Imagery and verbal processes*. Holt, Rinehart & Winston, New York.

Allan Paivio. 2013. Dual coding theory, word abstractness, and emotion: A critical review of Kousta et al. (2011). *Journal of Experimental Psychology: General*, 142(1):282–287.

Jeffrey Pennington, Richard Socher, and Christopher Manning. 2014. Glove: Global vectors for word representation. In *Proceedings of the 2014 Conference on Empirical Methods in Natural Language Processing (EMNLP)*, pages 1532–1543. Association for Computational Linguistics.

Matthew Peters, Mark Neumann, Mohit Iyyer, Matt Gardner, Christopher Clark, Kenton Lee, and Luke Zettlemoyer. 2018. Deep contextualized word representations. In *Proceedings of the 2018 Conference of the North American Chapter of the Association for Computational Linguistics: Human Language Technologies, Volume 1 (Long Papers)*, pages 2227–2237, New Orleans, Louisiana. Association for Computational Linguistics.

Mohammad Taher Pilehvar and Jose Camacho-Collados. 2019. WiC: the word-in-context dataset for evaluating context-sensitive meaning representations. In *Proceedings of the 2019 Conference of the North American Chapter of the Association for Computational Linguistics: Human Language Technologies, Volume 1 (Long and Short Papers)*, pages 1267–1273. Association for Computational Linguistics.

Joseph Reisinger and Raymond J. Mooney. 2010. Multi-prototype vector-space models of word meaning. In *Human Language Technologies: The 2010 Annual Conference of the North American Chapter of the Association for Computational Linguistics,* pages 109–117. Association for Computational Linguistics.

Anna Rogers, Olga Kovaleva, and Anna Rumshisky. 2020. A primer in BERTology: What we know about how BERT works. *arXiv:2002.12327 [cs]*.

Mike Schuster and Kaisuke Nakajima. 2012. Japanese and Korean voice search. In *International Conference on Acoustics, Speech and Signal Processing*, pages 5149–5152.

Roy Schwartz, Roi Reichart, and Ari Rappoport. 2015. Symmetric pattern based word embeddings for improved word similarity prediction. In *Proceedings of the Nineteenth Conference on Computational Natural Language Learning*, pages 258–267, Beijing, China. Association for Computational Linguistics.

Hinrich Schütze. 1998. Automatic word sense discrimination. *Computational Linguistics*, 24(1):97–123.

Gabriel Stanovsky and Mark Hopkins. 2018. Spot the odd man out: Exploring the associative power of lexical resources. In *EMNLP*.

Ian Tenney, Dipanjan Das, and Ellie Pavlick. 2019a. BERT rediscovers the classical NLP pipeline. In *Proceedings of the 57th Annual Meeting of the Association for Computational Linguistics*, pages 4593–4601, Florence, Italy. Association for Computational Linguistics.

Ian Tenney, Patrick Xia, Berlin Chen, Alex Wang, Adam Poliak, R. Thomas McCoy, Najoung Kim, Benjamin Van Durme, Samuel Bowman, Dipanjan Das, and Ellie Pavlick. 2019b. What do you learn from context? probing for sentence structure in contextualized word representations. *arXiv:1905.06316 [cs.CL]*.

Amos Tversky. 1977. Features of Similarity. *Psychological Review*, 84(4):327–352.

Ashish Vaswani, Noam Shazeer, Niki Parmar, Jakob Uszkoreit, Llion Jones, Aidan N. Gomez, Lukasz Kaiser, and Illia Polosukhin. 2017. Attention is all you need. *arXiv:1706.03762 [cs]*.

W. Caroline West and Phillip J. Holcomb. 2000. Imaginal, semantic, and surface-level processing of concrete and abstract words: An electrophysiological investigation. *Journal of Cognitive Neuroscience*, 12(6):1024–1037.

Gregor Wiedemann, Steffen Remus, Avi Chawla, and Chris Biemann. 2019. Does BERT make any sense? interpretable word sense disambiguation with contextualized embeddings. *arXiv:1909.10430 [cs.CL]*.

Dongqiang Yang and David Powers. 2006. Word similarity on the taxonomy of WordNet. In *Proceedings of GWC 2006*, pages 121–128.

A Reproducibility Details

A.1 Data Collection

Tokens from the British National Corpus (Burnard, 2000) were collected using NLTK v3.4.5. The sentences in the corpus were shuffled to ensure a random sample of tokens for each word. Lists of token sentences for each word, along with their original BNC indices, are available in the `word_data` directory in the supplemental material. To generate token vector representations, we used the HuggingFace `pytorch_pretrained_bert` implementation of the pre-trained `bert-base-uncased`.

A.2 Evaluation Datasets

For a few words, the BNC did not contain enough tokens to generate multi-prototype embeddings for some choices of K. These words are not included in the analyses for that choice of K. For instance, if only 7 tokens of a word were collected, and $K=8$, predictions were not calculated for pairs containing that word. Fortunately, this was very rare, and most words in the evaluations datasets have at least 50 tokens in the BNC, if not more. Tables 2 and 3 give detailed information about which word-pairs from each dataset, if any, were not evaluated at each cluster. As a consequence of the pruning, the Spearman's ρ correlation was sometimes calculated on minimally different data from one cluster to the next. However, the differences are so minimal as to make the issue negligible. Importantly, for the unioned models which we compare to other approaches, over 99% of all word-pairs were evaluated for each dataset.

A.3 Supplemental Material

The codebase for this project, including scripts for collecting data, generating BERT representations, calculating clusters, evaluating models, and visualizing results, is available at `https://github.com/gchronis/MProBERT`. Here one can also find lists of the tokens included in this analysis along with their BNC indices.

B Clusters

K-means clustering of token BERT representations captures polysemy as well as different usage types. Tables 4 and 5 shows a selection of sentences in clusters for *stream* and *river* at layer 8 for $k=3$ clusters. Tables 7 and 6 show a representative selection of tokens from each of the clusters at layer 8 for $k=7$. While the prototypes are often aligned

Dataset	K	Percentage Evaluated	Omitted Words	Omitted pairs
WordSim353_sim	8	99.51	{aluminum}	{aluminum-metal}
	9	99.01	{aluminum, kilometer}	{mile-kilometer, aluminum-metal}
	10	99.01	{aluminum, kilometer}	{mile-kilometer, aluminum-metal}
WordSim353_rel	9	99.6	{kilometer}	{territory-kilometer}
	10	99.6	{kilometer}	{territory-kilometer}
WordSim353	8	99.72	{aluminum}	{aluminum-metal}
	9	99.15	{kilometer, aluminum}	{mile-kilometer, territory-kilometer, aluminum-metal}
	10	99.15	{kilometer, aluminum}	{mile-kilometer, territory-kilometer, aluminum-metal}
SimLex999	4	99.8	{orthodontist}	{orthodontist-dentist, doctor-orthodontist}
	5	99.7	{disorganize, orthodontist}	{orthodontist-dentist, doctor-orthodontist, disorganize-organize}
	6	99.7	{disorganize, orthodontist}	{orthodontist-dentist, doctor-orthodontist, disorganize-organize}
	7	99.7	{disorganize, orthodontist}	{orthodontist-dentist, doctor-orthodontist, disorganize-organize}
	8	99.5	{aluminum, disorganize, orthodontist}	{metal-aluminum, tin-aluminum, orthodontist-dentist, doctor-orthodontist, disorganize-organize}
	9	99.5	{aluminum, disorganize, orthodontist}	{metal-aluminum, tin-aluminum, orthodontist-dentist, doctor-orthodontist, disorganize-organize}
	10	99.5	{aluminum, disorganize, orthodontist}	{metal-aluminum, tin-aluminum, orthodontist-dentist, doctor-orthodontist, disorganize-organize}

Table 2: Words from each dataset for which fewer than K tokens were collected, along with word pairs that were consequently omitted from evaluation. Where K is not listed, the number of tokens collected for each word was sufficient to construct K-prototype vectors. Each entry reports the percentage of word-pairs in the dataset evaluated for that K.

Dataset	K	Percentage Evaluated	Omitted Words	Omitted pairs
YP-130	3	99.23	{commercialize}	{distribute-commercialize}
	4	99.23	{commercialize}	{distribute-commercialize}
	5	99.23	{commercialize}	{distribute-commercialize}
	6	99.23	{commercialize}	{distribute-commercialize}
	7	99.23	{commercialize}	{distribute-commercialize}
	8	99.23	{commercialize}	{distribute-commercialize}
	9	99.23	{commercialize}	{distribute-commercialize}
	10	99.23	{commercialize}	{distribute-commercialize}
MEN	1	99.93	{ipod}	{chair-ipod, ipod-rope}
	2	99.93	{ipod}	{chair-ipod, ipod-rope}
	3	99.93	{ipod}	{chair-ipod, ipod-rope}
	4	99.87	{donut, ipod}	{cafe-donut, chair-ipod, ipod-rope, donut-panda}
	5	99.87	{donut, ipod}	{cafe-donut, chair-ipod, ipod-rope, donut-panda}
	6	99.87	{donut, ipod}	{cafe-donut, chair-ipod, ipod-rope, donut-panda}
	7	99.67	{donut, colorful, ipod}	{colorful-outfit, cafe-donut, colorful-toy, colorful-frame, colorful-duck, colorful-wood, colorful-lab, chair-ipod, ipod-rope, donut-panda}
	8	99.67	{donut, colorful, ipod}	{colorful-outfit, cafe-donut, colorful-toy, colorful-frame, colorful-duck, colorful-wood, colorful-lab, chair-ipod, ipod-rope, donut-panda}
	9	99.67	{donut, colorful, ipod}	{colorful-outfit, cafe-donut, colorful-toy, colorful-frame, colorful-duck, colorful-wood, colorful-lab, chair-ipod, ipod-rope, donut-panda}
	10	99.67	{donut, colorful, ipod}	{colorful-outfit, cafe-donut, colorful-toy, colorful-frame, colorful-duck, colorful-wood, colorful-lab, chair-ipod, ipod-rope, donut-panda}
SimVerb3500	1	99.94	{misspend}	{misspend-pass, pass-misspend}
	2	99.94	{misspend}	{misspend-pass, pass-misspend}
	3	99.8	{broil, misspend}	{bake-broil, broil-cook, broil-burn, broil-fry, broil-boil, misspend-pass, pass-misspend}
	4	99.8	{broil, misspend}	{bake-broil, broil-cook, broil-burn, broil-fry, broil-boil, misspend-pass, pass-misspend}
	5	99.69	{broil, plow, misspend}	{plow-dig, bake-broil, sow-plow, mow-plow, broil-cook, broil-burn, broil-fry, broil-boil, plow-hit, misspend-pass, pass-misspend}
	6	99.6	{intoxicate, broil, plow, misspend}	{plow-dig, bake-broil, sow-plow, drink-intoxicate, mow-plow, broil-cook, broil-burn, broil-fry, broil-boil, plow-hit, dislike-intoxicate, belong-intoxicate, misspend-pass, pass-misspend}
	7	99.6	{intoxicate, broil, plow, misspend}	{plow-dig, bake-broil, sow-plow, drink-intoxicate, mow-plow, broil-cook, broil-burn, broil-fry, broil-boil, plow-hit, dislike-intoxicate, belong-intoxicate, misspend-pass, pass-misspend}
	8	99.6	{intoxicate, broil, plow, misspend}	{plow-dig, bake-broil, sow-plow, drink-intoxicate, mow-plow, broil-cook, broil-burn, broil-fry, broil-boil, plow-hit, dislike-intoxicate, belong-intoxicate, misspend-pass, pass-misspend}
	9	99.6	{intoxicate, broil, plow, misspend}	{plow-dig, bake-broil, sow-plow, drink-intoxicate, mow-plow, broil-cook, broil-burn, broil-fry, broil-boil, plow-hit, dislike-intoxicate, belong-intoxicate, misspend-pass, pass-misspend}
	10	99.51	{intoxicate, hypnotize, broil, plow, misspend}	{plow-dig, bake-broil, sow-plow, drink-intoxicate, mow-plow, spell-hypnotize, hypnotize-control, broil-cook, broil-burn, broil-fry, broil-boil, plow-hit, hypnotize-remember, dislike-intoxicate, belong-intoxicate, misspend-pass, pass-misspend}

Table 3: Continued from last page. Words from each dataset for which fewer than K tokens were collected, along with word pairs that were consequently omitted from evaluation. Where K is not listed, the number of tokens collected for each word was sufficient to generate K clusters. Each entry reports the percentage of word-pairs in the dataset evaluated for that K.

in part by grammatical constructions, there is an interesting concordance between form and semantic subsense or conceptual affordance. Cluster 2 for *stream* mostly contains examples of the phrase *stream of X*. This construction has the effect of focusing attention on the substance constituting the stream and emphasizing its movement. Interestingly, the examples in this cluster which do not contain this construction also emphasize the movement of a substance. Compare with *X stream*, where the stream is construed as a medium or channel through which other entities pass.

Cluster ID	Sentences
0	Care must be taken to select the correct neutralizing agent for the specific odorous gas to be treated and there are obvious difficulties when both acidic and alkaline compounds are present in the gas **stream**. Alcohol is absorbed into the blood **stream** via the stomach and takes effect within 5-10 minutes. Every infected **stream** has a 'parent' **stream**, and it may have more than one 'daughter' **stream**. That is to say, the infant must convert stimulation from light rays, sound waves, from the speech **stream** into the appropriate representational grist if it is to get the kind of information that it requires from the world; but this gleaning of information does not constitute thought.
1	Without waiting for the others he plunged down the bank into the **stream**, slipping and slithering heedlessly over the protruding roots and rocks. The horses were quietly cropping the rich grass by the **stream**. Using cement of their own manufacture, they skilfully build tubular houses for themselves out of materials that they pick up from the bed of the **stream**. A small lagoon is formed by the **stream** between a sandbank and the rock wall.
2	Thus a **stream** of pulses lasting 1 second each and given at 10 second intervals could be the 'background' (they could be sound pulses or pulses on a screen, for example); the 'signal' being sought could be the absence of a pulse, one that was shorter or longer than the standard value or one that appeared too soon or too late. Without stopping, the combine disgorged a **stream** of grain into the trailer. Burning straw was the best fun — it was poked through the grill at the front of the grate and, when it caught fire, smoke would **stream** out of the other end. As he ate and drank she found herself chattering away to him out of nervousness, a **stream** of things that went through her head, the small happenings of a day.

Table 4: Example sentences from each *stream* cluster with $k=3$ and $l=8$. Cluster 0 is a bit of a catchall cluster, encompassing idioms like 'came on stream', but it contains all mentions of a stream as a medium through which other media pass. Cluster 1 represents the natural feature. Cluster 2 captures, but is not limited to, the usage 'stream of X'. Other usages in this cluster share with the construction a focus on the movement of the substance constituting the stream rather than the substance as a medium to move through. Consequently, cluster 2 contains more abstract streams, in that many of its arguments (often count nouns) are not typically thought of as fluids. Note the relationship between grammatical form and semantic subsense / conceptual affordance.

Cluster ID	Sentences
0	In this tale, two weeds grew on a **river** bank; one of them conserved its energy, and grew low and small and brown, with its sights set on a long life, while the other put forth all its strength into growing tall and into colouring itself a beautiful green. The lights dazzled, but on the broad face of the water there were innumerable V shaped eddies, showing the exact position of whatever the **river** had not been able to hide. Across the **river** and through the streets of Cliffe men fought in close combat before the royalists scattered. How can he get all three safely over the **river**?
1	The **River** Doon flows north-west from Dalmellington, past Patna and Dalrymple, under the Auld Brig o' Doon at Alloway, where Tam o' Shanter escaped from pursuing witches in Burns's magnificent poem : The Malá Strana or Lesser Town spreads beneath the castle to the banks of the **River** Vltava. Turkey's Prime Minister Suleyman Demirel arrived in Nakhichevan on May 28 to attend the opening of a bridge between Azerbaijan and Turkey over the **river** Arax. The **river** Sol is the southernmost of the Empire's rivers.
2	A few low hovels that had once been homes to **river** people were now derelict, and an empty building which was once a sailmaker's and then a barge-builder's premises now stood empty after its last owner, a steam-traction engineer, foundered in the changing times. In 1972 the Government of Sind Province declared the **river** dolphin protected by law and prohibited its killing and trapping. As in India, a **river**, a hill, mountain or lake, in Celtic legend, is personified by a god-like person. The same accountants apparently proposed getting rid of **river** wardens and people in pollution control.

Table 5: Four occurrences of *river* in the BNC belonging to each cluster with $k=3$ and $l=8$. Cluster 0 corresponds to a river as a natural feature, cluster 1 is captures the construction *river X* where X is the name of the river, and cluster 2 contains river used as an adjective to describe things associated with rivers.

Cluster ID	Sentences
0	Homer described it as a monster with the body of a goat, tail of a DRAGON and head of a **lion**, belching flames.
	With one sister slightly older and another two years younger there were real female " spats' at times with the sisters fighting like young **lion** cubs.
	A creature appeared, a **lion**, red and huge, bounding up the narrow winding streets of Edinburgh, splashing through rivers of blood which poured from the castle.
	The vertebrates found from that period include mammoth and other extinct elephants, extinct rhino, hippopotamus, giant deer, **lion**, spotted hyaena, tortoise and macaque (from the 'monkey gravel' of West Runton, Norfolk — where else?).
1	Finally, let us rekindle that vision in Isaiah 11 where the **lion** does not eat the lamb but lies down in a symbiotic relationship with it.
	Looking down from a height of ten or twelve feet, she saw an old friend, the MGM **lion**.
	He was like a man fearing his moment had come, he said, covering his eyes in silent prayer — yet astonished to find the **lion** in the same pose.
	The peace-keepers successfully tame the roaring **lion**.
2	The Blue Lagoon was the old Red **Lion** renamed, no one knew why, on the corner of Bankside and Trinity Street.
	Mrs Johnston, 35, was found dead at The **Lion** public house on Moorfields in Liverpool city centre last Thursday lunchtime.
	It was further established that Bacon had purchased some arsenic from a shop in Red **Lion** Square only days before, allegedly to kill rats.
	Glaxo sold its factory, as did Gresham **Lion**, and its successor, Dowty, which could not make the business succeed, sold to the Taiwanese.
3	The company, which claims the **lion**'s share of the object database market, has yet to record a profit.
	If this is done, care must be taken to ensure that each slice receives its proper priority in order of payment, otherwise one party may take the **lion**'s share of the income at the expense of the other.
	But he gave the **lion**'s share of the credit for the victory to Snodin, playing his first full 90 minutes for two and a half years after a series of hamstring and knee injuries put his career in doubt.
	Yet last week he had married Magda Tannenbaum, daughter of Sigmund Tannenbaum of Bradford and Hamburg, a wool merchant of legendary wealth, enormous possessions, and no son to inherit the **lion**'s share of them.
4	Three days after Fraser's departure a large new flag bearing the arms of Dunbar and March, a white **lion** on red, flew from the castle's topmost tower, indicative that the Earl had arrived.
	The arms granted to his chosen foundation were the fleur-de-lis of France and the royal **lion** of England, above the three lilies of the Virgin Mary.
	The sun shone through an elaborate crest of arms in coloured glass, with the **lion** of Venice rampant above a flurry of plumes and a Latin motto, the glass throwing dark Harlequin patterns on to his expressionless face.
	The green left sleeve brassard carries a red-on-yellow rampant **Lion** of Scotland patch, which we are told is special to the CO and his crew.
5	Henry the **Lion**
	At Acre, the ramparts of Richard Coeur de **Lion**'s massive fortress stretch down to a tideless Mediterranean while tiny Arab figures promenade in the dusk past the serail.
	The play was the true story of bachelor Mr Lewis, author of The **Lion**, The Witch And The Wardrobe, and his meeting at the age of 50 with writer Joy Davidman.
	They sent ambassadors to England to encourage marriage arrangements between two of Henry's daughters and Henry the **Lion** and one of Barbarossa's sons.
6	He was one of the first eminent European scientists to make a career in the USA, and rapidly became a **lion** : his lectures and books were popular, and he built up a school and museum at Harvard.
	She was one fine **lion** and I do n't blame Raja, only it wasn't me.
	He was only too well aware of the Talmudic dictum that a handful does not satisfy a **lion**, but he was neither apologetic nor guilty over it.
	He looked frightening and she had a momentary sensation of having caged herself in with an angry **lion**.

Table 6: Four tokens from the BNC from each cluster for *lion* with k=7 and l=8. Cluster 0 corresponds to a lion as a wild animal, with respect to other animals and the features which distinguish lions from them. Cluster 1 corresponds to lions interacting with humans and especially acting in ways that are unstereotypically docile. Cluster 2 corresponds to place names containing *Lion*. Cluster 3 corresponds to the idiom *lion's share*. Cluster 4 corresponds to lions on heraldic coats of arms. Cluster 5 corresponds to human or character names containing *Lion*. Cluster 6 corresponds to metaphorical senses of *lion* to describe a human.

Cluster ID	Sentences
0	Did you believe that, Thomas is part of an eight **cat** routine at Circus International at, it's been at Sutton Coldfield, it's at Northfield over the weekend, but these are just domestic cats, ordinary domestic cats.
1	'Cat got yer' tongue?' Paul says he saw a little **cat** swallowing a big dog. The list consisted of an assortment of well known mammals, birds, reptiles, fish and invertebrates, and also included three domestic species : dog, horse and **cat**. I, I know that one hey diddle diddle the **cat** and the fiddle the cow jumped over the moon, the little dog laughed to see such fun and the dish ran away with the spoon
2	He sat looking at the fire with lowered eyelids, a contented expression on his face, looking like a big overfed **cat**. Ecstatic, the boy tried on one mask after another, roaring like a lion or mewing like a **cat**. He took off his clothes, and Isobel curled up on the bed watching him, like a little **cat**. Lacuna was looking like a **cat** that had seen its prey.
3	Obviously, if you are eating more fibre-rich food you are likely to **cat** more grams of fibre.
4	A FAMILY gave up their holiday to pay £700 for a life-saving operation on their **cat** Tilly. She lives in a terraced house in Lancashire with her mum and dad and her **cat**, Arthur. He sat up and stroked the **cat** gently, scratching between the backs of its ears, making Bonaventure purr with pleasure. She took out her pen and paper and wrote a very angry letter to the doctor about the death of her valuable **cat**.
5	A **cat** does not want to die with the smell of humanity in his nostrils and the noise of humanity in his delicate peaked ears. 'All right,' said the **Cat**. After this, he became a nicer **cat**, + was n't so proud of himself all the time. 'There you are !' she said, and the **cat** lifted its tail up with pleasure and rubbed its head against the branch.
6	**Cat.** **Cat.** **Cat.**

Table 7: Four tokens from the BNC from each cluster for *cat* with k=7 and l=8. Cluster 0 corresponds to a unique circus context. Cluster 1 corresponds (loosely) to a cat in relation to other animals. Cluster 2 corresponds to similes likening people to cats by way of stereotypical catlike behavior. Cluster 3 contains a colloquial use of the word to mean 'obtain'. Cluster 4 corresponds to domestic pets. Cluster 5 is not very cohesive, but includes many examples of cats as grammatical subjects or in more agentive roles. Cluster 6 is the word *Cat* in isolation.

Uniform processing difficulty is a poor predictor of cross-linguistic word order frequency

Brennan Gonering
Linguistics Department
University of California, Davis
`btgonering@ucdavis.edu`

Emily Morgan
Linguistics Department
University of California, Davis
`eimorgan@ucdavis.edu`

Abstract

Some have argued that word orders which are more difficult to process should be rarer cross-linguistically. Our current study fails to replicate the results of Maurits, Navarro, and Perfors (2010), who used an entropy-based Uniform Information Density (UID) measure to moderately predict the Greenbergian typology of transitive word orders. We additionally report an inability of three measures of processing difficulty - entropy-based UID, surprisal-based UID, and pointwise mutual information - to correctly predict the correct typological distribution, using transitive constructions from 20 languages in the Universal Dependencies project (version 2.5). However, our conclusions are limited by data sparsity.

1 Introduction

Cross-linguistic typologies of word order preferences have shown a robust pattern for oderings of subjects, objects, and verbs (see the World Atlas of Language Structures (WALS) data in Table 3 and Figure 4) (Greenberg, 1963; Hawkins, 2014). Several hypotheses have been proposed to explain this pattern, including the Animate First Principle, Verb-Object Bonding, and the Theme First Principle (Tomlin, 1986). However, these are somewhat circular in their reasoning: they are motivated based on the prevalence of subject-first languages and languages where the verb and object are adjacent. These principles are then used to explain the very same word order patterns that motivated them in the first place. With the goal of achieving a more robust explanation, some have argued in more recent work that processing difficulty (broadly construed) is inversely proportional to typological frequency (Hawkins, 2004, 2014; Fedzechkina et al., 2018). Languages are claimed to evolve from word orders that are more difficulty to process to orders that are easier to process. Therefore, a word order that is more difficult to process should be rarer

cross-linguistically. Within this context, Maurits et al. (2010) attempted to use the Uniform Information Density (UID) hypothesis to explain the distributional patterns of subject-verb-object constructions. Maurits et al. (2010) (henceforth MNP) constructed simplified sets of events, ranking each possible ordering of subject, verb, and object by deviation from UID ideal.

MNP's results showed a consistent high ranking for VSO and VOS, and a consistent low ranking for SOV, contrary to the observed cross-linguistic frequency. While MNP used an entropy-based UID measure, there are other measures of processing difficulty that could be applied to the underlying question of whether languages evolve from difficult-to-process word orders to easy-to-process word orders. This paper therefore seeks to test the claim that languages evolve in this way, by comparing the predicted processing difficulty of the six possible subject-verb-object word orders. To do this, we use the following three metrics of processing difficulty, defined in the following sections: deviation from a UID ideal based on changes in entropy, deviation from a UID ideal based on surprisal, and total pointwise mutual information.

To that end, this paper is divided into two major components. In the first, we attempted to replicate the entropy-based UID results MNP obtained on their toyworld and on child-directed corpus data. In the second, we evaluate the ranking of word orders produced by each of the three processing difficulty measures using event datasets derived from corpora in 20 different languages. [1]

2 Processing difficulty measures

2.1 Entropy

The UID hypothesis models human language as a noisy communication channel. A speaker/signer

---

[1] All code and data for this project are available at `https://github.com/ucdavis/gonering_morgan-conll2020`

Proceedings of the 24th Conference on Computational Natural Language Learning, pages 245–255
Online, November 19-20, 2020. ©2020 Association for Computational Linguistics
https://doi.org/10.18653/v1/P17

should attempt to convey as much information as possible for a comprehender to reasonably reconstruct their message, given the possibility for misunderstanding, interference, cognitive misrepresentation, or literal noise in the surrounding environment (Levy and Jaeger, 2007; Frank and Jaeger, 2008). Under the UID hypothesis, the optimal solution is for a speaker/signer to spread the information as evenly as possible across the component parts of a message. Theoretically, this increases the likelihood of successful reconstruction by the comprehender (Levy and Jaeger, 2007; Frank and Jaeger, 2008). Additionally, because language is modelled as a noisy channel, there exists some maximum speed at which a language user can communicate successfully – termed the channel capacity. The UID hypothesis therefore further claims that as a language user approaches this capacity, they will make linguistic choices that distribute the information density of their utterance more uniformly. This should enable a language user to communicate both quickly and without errors (Levy and Jaeger, 2007).

"Information" can be conceptualized as the amount of uncertainty that is reduced by a message, calculated using entropy. If we model words in an incoming language stream as random variables which identify a random event, we can calculate how much each word reduces the uncertainty (entropy) about what event is being described. We can thereby quantify how much information each word contains. For the purposes of investigating transitive word order preferences, we adopt here the same simplified model as MNP. Each event is composed of an agent[2], a, drawn randomly from a set of possible agents, A; a verb, v, drawn randomly from a set of possible verbs, V; and a patient, p, drawn randomly from a set of possible patients, P. We then define an event, (a, v, p), as a variable drawn randomly from a set of possible events, (A, V, P). We can then assume a particular event is discussed with probability $P(a, v, p)$. Because we represent an event using just these three components, the words of an utterance based on such an event can be artificially permuted to derive all six possible word orders.

In this model, we assume that the comprehender always begins with the maximum uncertainty about

what will be discussed:

$$H_0 = - \sum_{a,v,p \,\epsilon\, A,V,P} P(a, v, p) \log_2(P(a, v, p))$$

After all words are communicated (and sometimes before), the entropy will always be zero. This signifies that the comprehender has uniquely identified the event discussed out of all the other potential events. In between, each word provides an amount of information to decrease the comprehender's uncertainty about the event being discussed. The information provided by a word, then, is the change in uncertainty, calculated as the difference in entropy before and after the word was communicated: for word i, $I_i = H_{i-1} - H_i$.

Given the simplified three word utterance modelled here, an utterance that achieves the UID ideal would have exactly $\frac{1}{3}$ of the total entropy, H_0, provided by each word. How far a particular utterance deviates from this ideal is therefore dependent on how much information each word provides above or below this $\frac{1}{3}$ mark. Figure 1 illustrates the deviation from this entropy-based UID ideal for two events taken from MNP's toyworld, (Eve,ate,rice) and (Eve,ate,bread) (see Table 1), in SOV and VOS order. By summing the individual deviations of each word, we can arrive at an overall deviation score for a particular utterance. Multiplying the current deviation sum by $\frac{3}{4}$ rescales the maximum deviation value to 1, deriving a final equation:

$$D(I) = \frac{3}{4} \sum_{i=1}^{3} \left| \frac{I_i}{H_0} - \frac{1}{3} \right|$$

A weighted average of the deviation scores for each utterance in a word order, using the probability of the event as the weight, creates an overall score for that word order. This metric allows us to systematically compare how close each of the six possible orderings of subjects, verbs, and objects approach the ideal of uniform information density. This is the deviation metric that MNP used, and which we adopt here as well.

2.2 Surprisal

Surprisal is defined as the negative log of a probability (i.e. $S(x) = -\log(P(x))$) and has been posited as a good model of incremental language processing, particularly in capturing difficulty of processing a sentence (Hale, 2001; Levy, 2011). Surprisal is closely related to entropy and is compatible with the UID hypothesis as well. In this case the UID hypothesis would state that the total surprisal of an event should be distributed equally

---

246

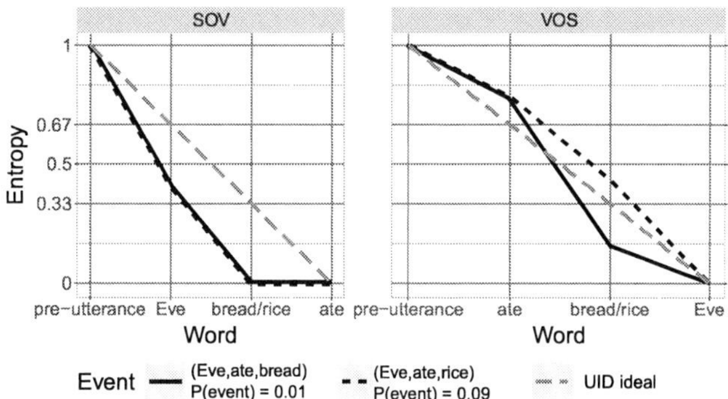

Figure 1. The deviation of the higher-probability event (Eve,ate,rice) (dotted black lines) and the lower-probability event (Eve,ate,bread) (solid black lines) from the UID ideal (dashed purple lines), using entropy to quantify the amount of information per word. Example utterances and probabilities were taken from the MNP toyworld.

across the words of an utterance. As such, surprisal provides a measure that is sensitive to the probabilities of each word of an utterance, and the probability of the utterance as a whole, whereas the MNP entropy-based measure was not. More specifically, the surprisal of an event is given by $S(event) = -\log_2 P(event)$, and the surprisal of the individual words that make up an utterance is the negative log probability of that word, given the history of words previously encountered (i.e. $S(word) = -\log_2 P(word|history)$).

We define here a surprisal-based deviation from UID ideal, analogous to the entropy-based deviation proposed by MNP:

$$D(S_{utt}) = \frac{3}{4} \sum_{i=1}^{3} \left| \frac{S_{word_i}}{S_{event}} - \frac{1}{3} \right|$$

Again, a weighted average of the deviation scores for each utterance in a word order, using the probability of the event as the weight, creates an overall score for that word order. Figure 2 illustrates the deviation from this surprisal-based UID ideal for two events (see Table 1) in SOV and VOS order. Fig. 2 also underscores that despite passing similarities in the underlying equations, these two processing difficulty measures may indeed lead to ultimately different results.

2.3 The information locality hypothesis

So far we have discussed the information structure of utterances within the framework of a single theory, UID. The UID hypothesis is not without critique though. Specifically, UID ignores findings from traditional linguistics about how the information structure of utterances is specifically nonuniform, e.g. new information and contrastive focus (Rizzi, 1997; Choudhury, 2015). Information local-

ity on the other hand, offered as an explanation for a range of syntactic phenomena, claims that words with high mutual information are placed as close as possible to each other in order to ease processing for a comprehender (Futrell, 2019; Futrell et al., 2019; Gibson et al., 2019).

In the context of the current paper, information locality would predict that the components of a transitive utterance should be placed such that the pointwise mutual information of adjacent words is maximized:

$$pmi_{utt} = pmi(word_1, word_2) + pmi(word_2, word_3)$$
$$= \log_2 \frac{P(word_1, word_2)}{P(word_1)P(word_2)} + \log_2 \frac{P(word_2, word_3)}{P(word_2)P(word_3)}$$

Note that because of this formulation, this measure does not distinguish between mirror word orders (i.e. SOV has the same overall PMI value as VOS). One method, which we adopt here, of converting these PMI values into a metric that can be compared across event sets is to z-score the pointwise mutual information values. We can use this standardized PMI score to rank word orders from greatest total PMI score to lowest. Figure 3 illustrates the total pointwise mutual information for two events (see Table 1) in SOV/VOS, SVO/OVS, and VSO/OSV orders.

3 Attempted replication of MNP

3.1 Background

MNP used three different methods to construct sets of events and event probabilities: they constructed an artificial set of events as a "toyworld," they extracted transitive utterances from corpora, and finally they asked participants to rank the likelihood of certain events occurring. We focus here on the first two methods they used. Their corpora-derived

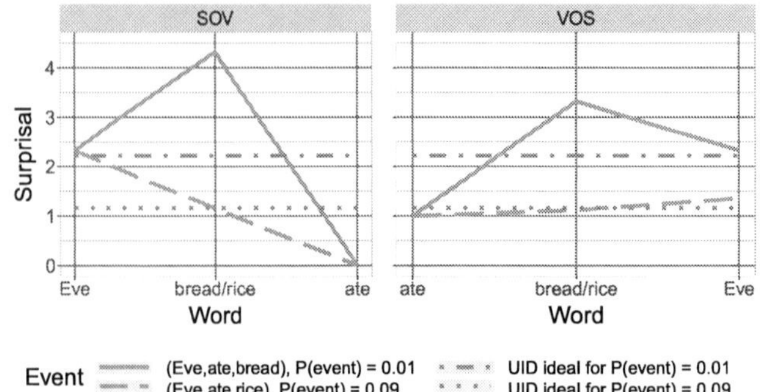

Figure 2. The deviation of the higher-probability event (Eve,ate,rice) (dashed blue lines) and the lower-probability event (Eve,ate,bread) (solid blue lines) from the UID ideal (dotted and dot-dashed purple lines), using surprisal to quantify the amount of information per word.

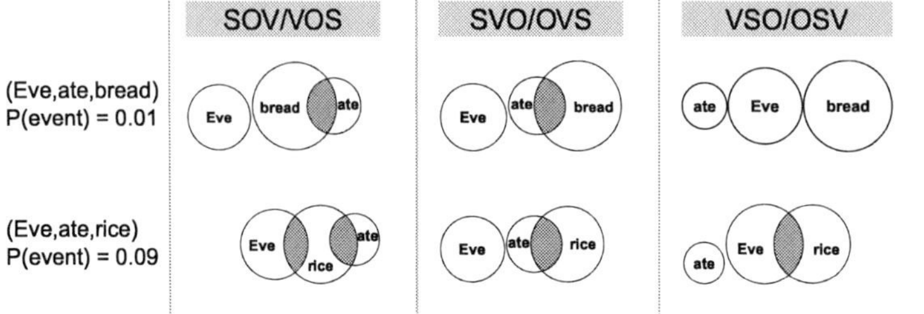

Figure 3. The pointwise mutual information of the events (Eve,ate,bread) and (Eve,ate,rice). Each circle represents the information content of the labeled word, measured as $-log_2(P(word))$, and the orange-shaded intersections represent the pointwise mutual information between two adjacent labeled words.

event sets were constructed by extracting transitive utterances from the Brown corpus of English child-directed speech from the CHILDES database. From the Brown corpus, MNP extracted transitive events from adult utterances in the transcripts related to just one child (of the three in the Brown corpus), "Adam." They discarded events involving pronouns that could refer to a broad range of agents or patients (e.g. "it" and "this"), resulting in a total of 544 transitive utterances. Each unique utterance was defined as an event, and these events were assigned a probability based on the frequency that an utterance involving the event was observed in the corpus. MNP's results showed a consistent low ranking for SOV and consistent high rankings for both VSO and VOS, in contrast to their actual distributions (see Table 2).

3.2 Methods

We tested the entropy-based measure on the original toyworld events from MNP and a dataset of event probabilities generated by extracting transitive utterances from the Brown corpus of child-directed speech (Brown, 1973; MacWhinney, 2000). We created two separate, exact implementations of the entropy-based UID algorithm described by MNP, one in the Java programming language and the other in R. In recreating the MNP toyworld, we used the exact probability distributions specified in their supplementary materials, except for two events with clear typographical errors. We then input these event probabilities into both the Java and R algorithm implementations, to derive weighted mean entropy-based UID deviation scores for each of the six possible word orders. The word orders were finally ranked from least deviation to greatest.

In attempting to replicate MNP's results on child-directed speech data, we decided to use all utterances from all transcripts in the Brown corpus (Brown, 1973; MacWhinney, 2000). This was motivated by a desire to lessen the potential impact of data sparsity. We also did not exclude utterances with broad-referent pronouns (such as "it" or "what"), as MNP did, so as not to exclude highly probable, naturalistic speech. In total, 30,166 transitive utterances were automatically extracted using an algorithm we created for that purpose, with 14,381 unique utterance types. In comparison, MNP used just 544 utterance tokens. We then assigned each transitive utterance a probability based

	Eat				Drink			
	Apple	**Bread**	**Cake**	**Rice**	**Coffee**	**Cola**	**Juice**	**Water**
Alice	0.05	0.00	0.03	0.02	0.07	0.03	0.00	0.00
Bob	0.02	0.00	0.04	0.04	0.02	0.04	0.02	0.02
Eve	0.00	0.01	0.00	0.09	0.03	0.01	0.00	0.06
Mallory	0.04	0.04	0.01	0.01	0.00	0.01	0.09	0.00
Trent	0.02	0.00	0.01	0.07	0.02	0.03	0.03	0.02

Table 1. MNP's toyworld. Each cell represents the joint probability P(a,v,p) of an event.

on the proportion of times it occurred in the corpus, similarly to MNP. Then, we input these event probabilities into the Java algorithm implementation to derive weighted mean entropy-based UID deviation scores for each of the six of the possible word orders. The word orders were finally ranked from least deviation to greatest.

3.3 Results

Both the Java and R implementations of the MNP entropy-based UID model failed to replicate their toyworld results. However, both of these implementations did produce the exact same ranking and the exact same numerical results (Table 2). Having used their exact event probabilities and an exact recreation of their algorithm (as best we understand it), we expected to get the exact same rankings as they did. We note though that they did not release their numerical results for us to compare to. We further failed to replicate MNP's ranking from the "Adam" transcripts-derived data using our full Brown-derived data (Table 2). The difference between our Brown corpus based rankings and MNP's "Adam" transcripts based rankings seems larger than the differences between the two toyworld rankings. Although the Brown-derived dataset we used was larger than MNP's, we still expected substantial overlap in the word order rankings.

3.4 Discussion

Despite failing to replicate MNP's results exactly, as expected, we are inclined to trust our results. Both of our separate implementations of their model – in two different programming languages – produced exactly identical numerical and rank order results. This is also backed by our further failure to replicate MNP's results using child-derived speech. Although we did not expect perfect alignment of results, our ranking appears, qualitatively, to be quite different from that reported by MNP (Table 2). Taken together, these results call into question all of the rankings reported by MNP. Ad-

ditionally, our results cast doubt on MNP's main conclusion that processing difficulty, as conceptualized by the Uniform Information Density hypothesis, is likely to have played a role in the evolution of subject-verb-obejct word order preferences across the world's languages.

4 Universal Dependencies languages

4.1 Methods

Having evaluated just one processing difficulty measure on data from a single language, we next sought to test all three measures on event probabilities derived from corpus data from a wide variety of languages. For this task, the Universal Dependencies (UD) project (version 2.5) was chosen (Zeman et al., 2019). The claim that languages evolve from orders that are difficult to process to orders that are easier to process assumes that certain word orders are inherently easier or more difficult to process. The dominant word order of a language from which we derive event data should therefore not matter. Nevertheless, to try to reduce this potential confound, we chose 20 languages from the UD project, from as many different dominant word orders as possible, based on two primary criteria: (1) genetic diversity, and (2) a large dataset in the UD treebanks. The languages we chose consisted of six SVO-dominant languages (English, Mandarin, Mbya Guarani, Indonesian, Vietnamese, and Wolof), five SOV-dominant languages (Basque, Hindi, Japanese, Korean, and Turkish), five VSO-dominant languages (Breton, Irish, Scottish Gaelic, Tagalog, and Welsh), and four languages considered to have no single dominant subject-verb-object word order (Dutch, German, Hungarian, and Warlpiri) according to WALS (Dryer, Matthew S., 2013). Transitive constructions were thus extracted from all treebanks that included the underlying text and the CoNLL-U parse annotation. Lemma-level information from the CoNLL-U annotation, instead of word-level information, was extracted whenever possible. In

MNP's toyworld rankings	Our toyworld replication rankings	MNP's rankings from the "Adam" transcripts	Our Brown corpus rankings
VSO	VOS, 0.206	VSO, 0.38	SVO, 0.427
VOS	VSO, 0.288	SVO, 0.41	SOV, 0.439
SVO	SVO, 0.291	VOS, 0.48	VSO, 0.585
OVS	SOV, 0.500	SOV. 0.64	VOS, 0.588
SOV	OVS = OSV, 0.530	OSV, 0.78	OVS = OSV, 0.684
OSV		OVS, 0.79	

Table 2. Side-by-side comparison of MNP's results and our attempted replication.

addition to the words of each utterance, we also automatically determined the word order of each construction extracted.

Each extracted event was assigned a probability based on the frequency it was observed in the UD treebanks for a given language. Despite the large size of many of the underlying treebanks, this method proved to create a very sparse model. This led to underestimating the probabilities of events that occurred rarely in the corpora while overestimating the probabilities of events that occurred more frequently. This also influences the amount of information each word provides: if an event occurs rarely, the words that make up an utterance corresponding to it will better disambiguate the event than those words otherwise would. Across our subset of languages, more than 46% of utterances tested in each language were deterministically predicted by the first two words alone. Due to this, we eliminated events where any one of the words only occurred once in a language's corpus. This improved the problem of sparsity somewhat, dropping the proportion of deterministically predictable utterances from a minimum of 46% to 8%. However, some languages still had 100% of utterances being deterministically predicted by the first two words, with a mean across the subset of 72%. The consequences of this will be discussed in more detail in section 4.4.

The weighted mean entropy-based and surprisal-based UID scores for each word order in each language of our subset were aggregated, then averaged over languages to derive an overall deviation score for each word order. In doing so, we made the assumption that a subject is as predictive of a verb in one language as in every other; that a verb is as predictive of an object in one language as in every other; etc. In order to compare pointwise mutual information scores across languages, raw PMI scores for every utterance were z-scored within each language. This is necessary because different sized event sets in each language would lead to different magnitudes of raw PMI scores. A weighted mean for each word order within each language was then taken. The means for each word order were finally averaged across languages.

4.2 Results

As shown in Table 3, the entropy-based and surprisal-based UID measures both generated the same ordinal rankings for word orders, though their deviation scores differed. These results differ partially from the observed distribution of transitive word orders. To test whether means for each word order were significantly different from each other or not, a one-way ANOVA with unequal variance was performed for each processing difficulty measure. Word orders did not show significant differences in means for either the entropy-based or the surprisal-based UID measures, ($F(5,53) = 1.40$, $p = 0.239$ and $F(5,53) = 1.91$, $p = 0.108$, respectively).

Our mutual information measure likewise failed to produce a ranking of word orders that resembles the actual cross-linguistic distribution (Table 3). A one-way ANOVA with unequal variance indicated a significant effect of word order for this measure ($F(5,53) = 3.65$, $p = 0.00649$). Post hoc two-tailed Welch's t-tests indicated that SOV/VOS orders had a significantly greater mean PMI value than either VSO/OSV ($t(34) = 2.54$, $p = 0.0157$) or SVO/OVS ($t(37) = 2.98$, $p = 0.00508$) at the 95% confidence level. However, there was no significant difference in mean PMI values between VSO/OSV and SVO/OVS ($t(37) = 0.700$, $p = 0.488$).

Under the hypothesis we test, our three measures of processing difficulty should produce a distribution of highest-ranked word orders that, when aggregated, roughly matches the observed typological distribution. Figure 4 shows the proportion of word orders that were ranked highest by each processing difficulty measure across our subset of 20 languages from the UD project.

WALS	Entropy-based UID	Surprisal-based UID	Pointwise mutual information
SOV (47.6%)	**VSO**, 0.583 (0.163)	**VSO**, 0.604 (0.141)	**SOV = VOS**, -0.00677 (0.229)
SVO (41.1%)	**VOS**, 0.590 (0.172)	**VOS**, 0.612 (0.146)	**VSO = OSV**, -0.166 (0.160)
VSO (8.0%)	**SVO**, 0.628 (0.183)	**SVO**, 0.652 (0.153)	**SVO = OVS**, -0.204 (0.187)
VOS (2.1%)	**SOV**, 0.648 (0.179)	**SOV**, 0.674 (0.147)	
OVS (0.9%)	**OVS**, 0.694 (0.205)	**OVS**, 0.716 (0.175)	
OSV (0.3%)	**OSV**, 0.699 (0.197)	**OSV**, 0.720 (0.169)	

Table 3. Rankings of word orders generated by our three processing difficulty measures, compared to the observed distribution of word orders as catalogued by WALS. Mean values are indicated after the word order with standard deviations in parentheses.

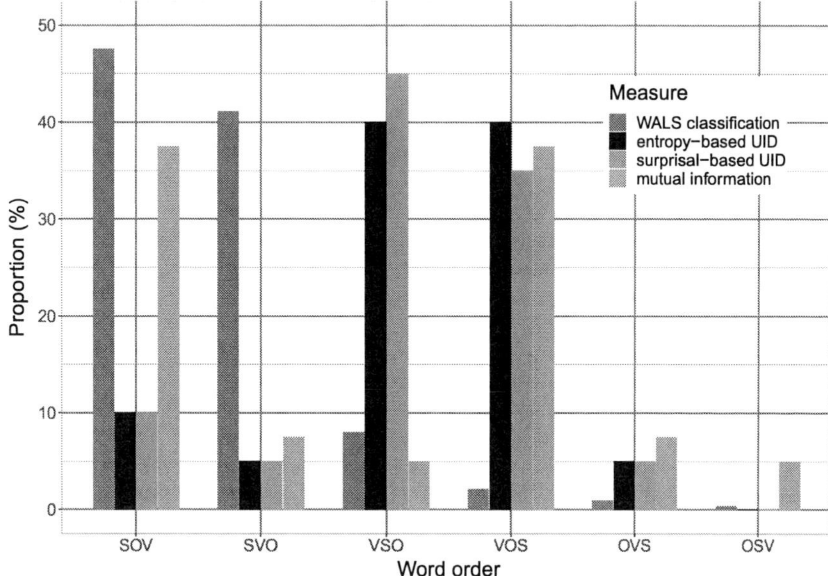

Figure 4. The proportion of word orders predicted across the 20 languages of our UD subset, by the entropy-based UID measure (black), the surprisal-based UID measure (blue), and the pointwise mutual information measure (orange), compared to the observed proportion of word orders catalogued by WALS (cyan).

4.3 Discussion

The rankings from our UID-based measures, and their overprediction of VSO and VOS orders, would suggest that verb-initial languages should be most frequent, contrary to the actual typological distribution. The rankings of our mutual information measure, and its overprediction of VOS word order, would suggest an abundance of languages with dominant SOV and VOS word orders and a dearth of languages with any other order. Although the prediction about SOV does accord with its typological frequency, these results do not accord with the observed frequencies of the other word orders. This is most notable in regards to SVO and VOS orders, which are greatly underpredicted and overpredicted, respectively. A limitation of the mutual information measure we used though, is that mirror word orders are indistinguishable. There may be other ways to define such a measure that would distinguish between mirror orders in future work. That said, the underprediction of SVO orders presents a serious challenge to the hypotheses we tested.

Overall, our raw data would suggest tendency for languages to evolve to be verb-initial. Evidence in favor of this is rather weak or nonexistent though (Givn, 1979; Li, 2014). Only one measure ranked SOV highly, which is both the most typologically frequent order and has been argued to be a target order for language evolution. Strong evidence that languages evolve towards SVO order contradict the results from all of our three measures (Givn, 1979; Li, 2014; Maurits and Griffiths, 2014). However, our results do agree with Maurits and Griffiths (2014)'s suggestion that processing difficulty is not the primary motivator of language change.

Given that ANOVA tests indicated no significant difference between the means of the six word orders in the entropy-based and surprisal-based UID measures, our data further suggest that UID either plays no role in language evolution of transitive constructions, or that it exerts equal pressure toward every possible ordering. This conclusion is weakly supported by the ANOVA and t-tests conducted on the PMI results. These PMI results would suggest a strong pressure for languages to evolve towards SOV or VOS order. While we can't rule out the possibility that other, stronger, forces act to push language evolution in specific directions, there does not appear to be evidence for languages evolving in such ways.

4.4 Limitations

As mentioned previously, these event data were very sparse, even after removing utterances where any word occurred just once in the corpus. Because of the semantic of some verbs, we would expect a non-zero percentage of utterances where the first two words deterministically predict the third. Nevertheless, the levels obtained in some languages though were unacceptably high. This disproportionately affected SOV and OSV utterances more (80.5% of utterances) compared to VOS and OVS (70.1% of utterances), and compared to VSO and SVO (67.4% of utterances). Both the entropy-based and surprisal-based UID deviation scores are likely to be higher for these utterances, potentially depressing the rankings of SOV, OSV, VOS, and OVS compared to VSO and SVO. Conversely, the PMI values for these utterances may be inflated. This is a considerable limitation, and as such, our conclusions should be considered tentative. This problem even affected the largest corpora we used, but could be addressed in future work using a smoothing algorithm.

Another criticism of this work could be that the use of events and event probabilities is an inadequate model of human language. Although we concede that this model fails to capture the infinitely productive nature of language, it is still a suitable, if imperfect approximate model of speech. The benefit of using a corpus to generate model events is the potential to capture naturalistic speech. There is also evidence that people draw on their knowledge of events when comprehending sentences, suggesting that information about events is an important aspect of language use (Nieuwland, 2015; Tieu et al., 2019).

5　General discussion

With regard to the original MNP paper, we identify three main claims: (1) that object-initial languages have the least uniform information structure; (2) that SVO and VSO have the most uniform information structures; and (3) that UID influenced the distribution of word orders beyond what would be expected by chance. The raw orders from our MNP replication attempts and the entropy-based and surprisal-based UID rankings from our subset of UD languages supports the first point, in that OVS and OSV were consistently placed as the last orders in all rankings. However, the statistical tests we conducted on our UD-derived entropy-based and surprisal-based UID scores suggest there was no difference between the deviation scores of all six word orders. Our pointwise mutual information results are similarly murky on this question, with both our rankings and statistical tests indicating object-initial word orders performing worse than object-medial orders, but with no distinction possible between SVO and OVS or between VSO and OSV.

On the second claim of MNP, our raw UD derived entropy-based and surprisal-based UID orderings support the claim that VSO order results in the most uniform distribution of information, while again our statistical tests fail to support this. SVO, on the other hand, consistently performed worse in our raw rankings than in MNP's, suggesting that SVO does not have one of the most uniform information structures – and again, our statistical tests suggesting that SVO is no more or less uniform in its information structure than any other order. Meanwhile, our PMI results contradict MNP's claim with regard to both VSO and SVO. For both of these first claims, the discrepancies between what the raw rankings suggest and what the statistical tests indicate could be due to not testing enough languages, or due to the other limitations outlined in section 4.4.

On claim three of MNP, the data presented here suggest that uniform processing difficulty may not have played a large role in the evolution of transitive constructions. This follows other lines of evidence that suggest word order evolution is lineage specific (Dunn et al., 2011; Maurits and Griffiths, 2014). Evidence also points to language evolution being subject to a number of complex, interacting factors, including the number of speakers (Lupyan and Dale, 2010; Raviv et al., 2019) and geography

(Norris, 1998; Lupyan and Dale, 2010). Noisy-channel surprisal models further strongly predict SVO word order, as it reliably encodes which noun is the subject and which is the object (Gibson et al., 2019). This suggests that the pressure for a language to transition to SVO order is based in faithful transmission of an utterance rather than in easing processing costs. This pressure for faithful communication may itself be influenced by the factors mentioned earlier.

The contribution of language contact cannot be ignored either, and researchers have long been aware of areal distributions in typological patterns. A growing idea is that bilinguals are the cause of these areal effects, by inducing language change in one or both of their language communities (see e.g. Fernndez et al., 2017; Kootstra and ahin, 2018). Examining the language processing and mental representations of bilinguals will be a fruitful area of research to shed more light on this issue. Indeed, some studies are already showing that an L2 can exert influence on a bilingual's L1 (Carando, 2015; Higby, 2016; de Oliveira et al., 2017).

Finally, it is pertinent we point out that many languages with typologically infrequent word orders are spoken by minoritized peoples, oftentimes ethnically or racially. Arguments that these languages are difficult to process can reinforce assimilationist narratives that such languages are inferior and their speakers should speak supposedly superior dominant languages instead. Given that many settler-colonial powers have instituted programs to this effect, and continue to, with justifications based on the supposed deficiencies or inferiorities of minoritized languages, this warning is not hyperbole (DeGraff, 2005; Baloy, 2011; Zentella, 2014; Campbell, 2016; Rosa and Flores, 2017; Flores, 2020). Additionally, such explanations can whitewash the potential role of imperialism and colonialism in causing a dearth of non-SVO/SOV languages. There is value in examining the communicative and cognitive pressures that shape human language, but we must be diligent in how we frame our research questions and findings so as not to uphold oppressive language ideologies.

References

Natalie J. K. Baloy. 2011. We Can't Feel Our Language: Making Places in the City for Aboriginal Language Revitalization. *American Indian Quarterly*, 35(4):515.

Roger Brown. 1973. *A first language: The early stages.* Harvard U. Press, Cambridge, MA.

Rebecca Ann Campbell. 2016. *Reification, Resistance, and Transformation? The Impact of Migration and Demographics on Linguistic, Racial, and Ethnic Identity and Equity in Educational Systems: An Applied Approach.* Ph.D. thesis, University of South Florida.

Agustina Carando. 2015. The emergence of L1 innovations in Spanish-English bilinguals: Evidence from cross-linguistic structural priming. *CUNY Academic Works*.

Arunima Choudhury. 2015. *Interaction between prosody and information structure: experimental evidence from Hindi and Bangla.* Ph.D. thesis, University of Southern California.

Michel DeGraff. 2005. Linguists' most dangerous myth: The fallacy of Creole Exceptionalism. *Language in Society*, 34(04).

Dryer, Matthew S. 2013. Order of subject, object and verb. In Matthew S. Dryer and Martin Haspelmath, editors, *The world atlas of language structures online.* Max-Planck-Institut fr evolutionre Anthropologie., Leipzig.

Michael Dunn, Simon J. Greenhill, Stephen C. Levinson, and Russell D. Gray. 2011. Evolved structure of language shows lineage-specific trends in word-order universals. *Nature*, 473(7345):79–82.

Maryia Fedzechkina, Becky Chu, and T. Florian Jaeger. 2018. Human Information Processing Shapes Language Change. *Psychological Science*, 29(1):72–82.

Eva M. Fernndez, Ricardo A. De Souza, and Agustina Carando. 2017. Bilingual innovations: Experimental evidence offers clues regarding the psycholinguistics of language change. *Bilingualism: Language and Cognition*, 20(2):251–268. Publisher: Cambridge University Press.

Nelson Flores. 2020. From academic language to language architecture: Challenging raciolinguistic ideologies in research and practice. *Theory Into Practice*, 59(1):22–31.

Austin F Frank and T Florian Jaeger. 2008. Speaking Rationally: Uniform Information Density as an Optimal Strategy for Language Production. In *Proceedings of the annual meeting of the cognitive science society*, volume 30, page 7.

Richard Futrell. 2019. Information-theoretic locality properties of natural language. In *Proceedings of the First Workshop on Quantitative Syntax (Quasy, SyntaxFest 2019)*, pages 2–15, Paris, France. Association for Computational Linguistics.

Richard Futrell, Peng Qian, Edward Gibson, Evelina Fedorenko, and Idan Blank. 2019. Syntactic dependencies correspond to word pairs with high mutual information. In *Proceedings of the Fifth International Conference on Dependency Linguistics (Depling, SyntaxFest 2019)*, pages 3–13, Paris, France. Association for Computational Linguistics.

Edward Gibson, Richard Futrell, Steven P. Piantadosi, Isabelle Dautriche, Kyle Mahowald, Leon Bergen, and Roger Levy. 2019. How Efficiency Shapes Human Language. *Trends in Cognitive Sciences*, 23(5):389–407.

Talmy Givn. 1979. *On understanding grammar*. Academic Press, London.

Joseph H Greenberg. 1963. Some Universals of Grammar with Particular Reference to the Order of Meaningful Elements. In *Universals of Language*, pages 73–113. MIT Press.

John Hale. 2001. A probabilistic Earley parser as a psycholinguistic model. In *Proceedings of the second meeting of the North American Chapter of the Association for Computational Linguistics on Language technologies*, pages 1–8. Association for Computational Linguistics.

John A. Hawkins. 2004. *Efficiency and complexity in grammars*. Oxford University Press on Demand.

John A. Hawkins. 2014. *Cross-linguistic variation and efficiency*. OUP Oxford.

Eve Higby. 2016. Native Language Adaptation to Novel Verb Argument Structures by Spanish-English Bilinguals: An Electrophysiological Investigation. *CUNY Academic Works*.

Gerrit Jan Kootstra and Hlya ahin. 2018. Crosslinguistic structural priming as a mechanism of contact-induced language change: Evidence from Papiamento-Dutch bilinguals in Aruba and the Netherlands. *Language*, 94(4):902–930.

Roger Levy. 2011. Integrating surprisal and uncertain-input models in online sentence comprehension: formal techniques and empirical results. In *Proceedings of the 49th Annual Meeting of the Association for Computational Linguistics: Human Language Technologies*, volume 1, pages 1055–1065. Association for Computational Linguistics.

Roger Levy and T Florian Jaeger. 2007. Speakers optimize information density through syntactic reduction. In *Advances in Neural Information Processing Systems*.

Charles N Li. 2014. *Mechanisms of syntactic change*, 3rd edition. University of Texas Press.

Gary Lupyan and Rick Dale. 2010. Language Structure Is Partly Determined by Social Structure. *PLoS ONE*, 5(1):e8559.

Brian MacWhinney. 2000. The CHILDES Project: Tools for Analyzing Talk (third edition): Volume I: Transcription format and programs, Volume II: The database. *Computational Linguistics*, 26(4):657–657.

Luke Maurits and Thomas L. Griffiths. 2014. Tracing the roots of syntax with Bayesian phylogenetics. *Proceedings of the National Academy of Sciences*, 111(37):13576–13581.

Luke Maurits, Amy Perfors, and Danielle Navarro. 2010. Why are some word orders more common than others? A uniform information density account. In *Advances in Neural Information Processing Systems*, pages 1585–1593.

Mante S. Nieuwland. 2015. The Truth Before and After: Brain Potentials Reveal Automatic Activation of Event Knowledge during Sentence Comprehension. *Journal of Cognitive Neuroscience*, 27(11):2215–2228.

Mary Jane Norris. 1998. Canada's aboriginal languages. *Canadian social trends*, 51(36):19–27.

Cndido Samuel Fonseca de Oliveira, Ricardo Augusto de Souza, and Fernando Luiz Pereira de Oliveira. 2017. Bilingualism effects on L1 representation and processing of argument structure. *Journal of the European Second Language Association*, 1(1):23–37.

Limor Raviv, Antje Meyer, and Shiri Lev-Ari. 2019. Larger communities create more systematic languages. *Proceedings of the Royal Society B: Biological Sciences*, 286(1907):20191262.

Luigi Rizzi. 1997. The fine structure of the left periphery. In *Elements of Grammar*, pages 281–337. Springer.

Jonathan Rosa and Nelson Flores. 2017. Unsettling race and language: Toward a raciolinguistic perspective. *Language in Society*, 46(5):621–647.

Lyn Tieu, Philippe Schlenker, and Emmanuel Chemla. 2019. Linguistic inferences without words. *Proceedings of the National Academy of Sciences*, 116(20):9796–9801.

Russell S. Tomlin. 1986. Basic word order – functional principles. *London: Croom Helm*.

Daniel Zeman, Joakim Nivre, Mitchell Abrams, Noëmi Aepli, Željko Agić, Lars Ahrenberg, Gabrielė Aleksandravičiūtė, Lene Antonsen, Katya Aplonova, Maria Jesus Aranzabe, Gashaw Arutie, Masayuki Asahara, Luma Ateyah, Mohammed Attia, Aitziber Atutxa, Liesbeth Augustinus, Elena Badmaeva, Miguel Ballesteros, Esha Banerjee, Sebastian Bank, Verginica Barbu Mititelu, Victoria Basmov, Colin Batchelor, John Bauer, Sandra Bellato, Kepa Bengoetxea, Yevgeni Berzak, Irshad Ahmad Bhat, Riyaz Ahmad Bhat, Erica Biagetti, Eckhard Bick, Agnė Bielinskienė, Rogier Blokland, Victoria Bobicev, Loïc Boizou, Emanuel Borges Völker, Carl Börstell, Cristina Bosco, Gosse Bouma, Sam Bowman, Adriane Boyd, Kristina Brokaitė, Aljoscha Burchardt, Marie Candito, Bernard Caron, Gauthier Caron, Tatiana Cavalcanti, Gülşen Cebiroğlu Eryiğit, Flavio Massimiliano Cecchini, Giuseppe G. A.

Celano, Slavomír Čéplö, Savas Cetin, Fabricio Chalub, Jinho Choi, Yongseok Cho, Jayeol Chun, Alessandra T. Cignarella, Silvie Cinková, Aurélie Collomb, Çağrı Çöltekin, Miriam Connor, Marine Courtin, Elizabeth Davidson, Marie-Catherine de Marneffe, Valeria de Paiva, Elvis de Souza, Arantza Diaz de Ilarraza, Carly Dickerson, Bamba Dione, Peter Dirix, Kaja Dobrovoljc, Timothy Dozat, Kira Droganova, Puneet Dwivedi, Hanne Eckhoff, Marhaba Eli, Ali Elkahky, Binyam Ephrem, Olga Erina, Tomaž Erjavec, Aline Etienne, Wograine Evelyn, Richárd Farkas, Hector Fernandez Alcalde, Jennifer Foster, Cláudia Freitas, Kazunori Fujita, Katarína Gajdošová, Daniel Galbraith, Marcos Garcia, Moa Gärdenfors, Sebastian Garza, Kim Gerdes, Filip Ginter, Iakes Goenaga, Koldo Gojenola, Memduh Gökırmak, Yoav Goldberg, Xavier Gómez Guinovart, Berta González Saavedra, Bernadeta Griciūtė, Matias Grioni, Normunds Grūzītis, Bruno Guillaume, Céline Guillot-Barbance, Nizar Habash, Jan Hajič, Jan Hajič jr., Mika Hämäläinen, Linh Hà Mỹ, Na-Rae Han, Kim Harris, Dag Haug, Johannes Heinecke, Felix Hennig, Barbora Hladká, Jaroslava Hlaváčová, Florinel Hociung, Petter Hohle, Jena Hwang, Takumi Ikeda, Radu Ion, Elena Irimia, Ọlájídé Ishola, Tomáš Jelínek, Anders Johannsen, Fredrik Jørgensen, Markus Juutinen, Hüner Kaşıkara, Andre Kaasen, Nadezhda Kabaeva, Sylvain Kahane, Hiroshi Kanayama, Jenna Kanerva, Boris Katz, Tolga Kayadelen, Jessica Kenney, Václava Kettnerová, Jesse Kirchner, Elena Klementieva, Arne Köhn, Kamil Kopacewicz, Natalia Kotsyba, Jolanta Kovalevskaitė, Simon Krek, Sookyoung Kwak, Veronika Laippala, Lorenzo Lambertino, Lucia Lam, Tatiana Lando, Septina Dian Larasati, Alexei Lavrentiev, John Lee, Phng Lê H`ông, Alessandro Lenci, Saran Lertpradit, Herman Leung, Cheuk Ying Li, Josie Li, Keying Li, KyungTae Lim, Maria Liovina, Yuan Li, Nikola Ljubešić, Olga Loginova, Olga Lyashevskaya, Teresa Lynn, Vivien Macketanz, Aibek Makazhanov, Michael Mandl, Christopher Manning, Ruli Manurung, Cătălina Mărănduc, David Mareček, Katrin Marheinecke, Héctor Martínez Alonso, André Martins, Jan Mašek, Yuji Matsumoto, Ryan McDonald, Sarah McGuinness, Gustavo Mendonça, Niko Miekka, Margarita Misirpashayeva, Anna Missilä, Cătălin Mititelu, Maria Mitrofan, Yusuke Miyao, Simonetta Montemagni, Amir More, Laura Moreno Romero, Keiko Sophie Mori, Tomohiko Morioka, Shinsuke Mori, Shigeki Moro, Bjartur Mortensen, Bohdan Moskalevskyi, Kadri Muischnek, Robert Munro, Yugo Murawaki, Kaili Müürisep, Pinkey Nainwani, Juan Ignacio Navarro Horñiacek, Anna Nedoluzhko, Gunta Nešpore-Bērzkalne, Lng Nguy˜ên Thị, Huy`ên Nguy˜ên Thị Minh, Yoshihiro Nikaido, Vitaly Nikolaev, Rattima Nitisaroj, Hanna Nurmi, Stina Ojala, Atul Kr. Ojha, Adédayọ Olúòkun, Mai Omura, Petya Osenova, Robert Östling, Lilja Øvrelid, Niko Partanen, Elena Pascual, Marco Passarotti, Agnieszka Patejuk, Guilherme Paulino-Passos, Angelika Peljak-Łapińska, Siyao Peng, Cenel-Augusto Perez, Guy Perrier, Daria Petrova, Slav Petrov, Jason Phelan, Jussi Piitulainen, Tommi A Pirinen, Emily Pitler, Barbara Plank, Thierry Poibeau, Larisa Ponomareva, Martin Popel, Lauma Pretkalniņa, Sophie Prévost, Prokopis Prokopidis, Adam Przepiórkowski, Tiina Puolakainen, Sampo Pyysalo, Peng Qi, Andriela Rääbis, Alexandre Rademaker, Loganathan Ramasamy, Taraka Rama, Carlos Ramisch, Vinit Ravishankar, Livy Real, Siva Reddy, Georg Rehm, Ivan Riabov, Michael Rießler, Erika Rimkutė, Larissa Rinaldi, Laura Rituma, Luisa Rocha, Mykhailo Romanenko, Rudolf Rosa, Davide Rovati, Valentin Roca, Olga Rudina, Jack Rueter, Shoval Sadde, Benoît Sagot, Shadi Saleh, Alessio Salomoni, Tanja Samardžić, Stephanie Samson, Manuela Sanguinetti, Dage Särg, Baiba Saulīte, Yanin Sawanakunanon, Nathan Schneider, Sebastian Schuster, Djamé Seddah, Wolfgang Seeker, Mojgan Seraji, Mo Shen, Atsuko Shimada, Hiroyuki Shirasu, Muh Shohibussirri, Dmitry Sichinava, Aline Silveira, Natalia Silveira, Maria Simi, Radu Simionescu, Katalin Simkó, Mária Šimková, Kiril Simov, Aaron Smith, Isabela Soares-Bastos, Carolyn Spadine, Antonio Stella, Milan Straka, Jana Strnadová, Alane Suhr, Umut Sulubacak, Shingo Suzuki, Zsolt Szántó, Dima Taji, Yuta Takahashi, Fabio Tamburini, Takaaki Tanaka, Isabelle Tellier, Guillaume Thomas, Liisi Torga, Trond Trosterud, Anna Trukhina, Reut Tsarfaty, Francis Tyers, Sumire Uematsu, Zdeňka Urešová, Larraitz Uria, Hans Uszkoreit, Andrius Utka, Sowmya Vajjala, Daniel van Niekerk, Gertjan van Noord, Viktor Varga, Eric Villemonte de la Clergerie, Veronika Vincze, Lars Wallin, Abigail Walsh, Jing Xian Wang, Jonathan North Washington, Maximilan Wendt, Seyi Williams, Mats Wirén, Christian Wittern, Tsegay Woldemariam, Tak-sum Wong, Alina Wróblewska, Mary Yako, Naoki Yamazaki, Chunxiao Yan, Koichi Yasuoka, Marat M. Yavrumyan, Zhuoran Yu, Zdeněk Žabokrtský, Amir Zeldes, Manying Zhang, and Hanzhi Zhu. 2019. Universal dependencies 2.5. LINDAT/CLARIAH-CZ digital library at the Institute of Formal and Applied Linguistics (ÚFAL), Faculty of Mathematics and Physics, Charles University.

Ana Celia Zentella. 2014. TWB (Talking while Bilingual): Linguistic profiling of Latina/os, and other linguistic torquemadas. *Latino Studies*, 12(4):620–635.

Relations between comprehensibility and adequacy errors
in machine translation output

Maja Popović
ADAPT Centre, School of Computing
Dublin City University, Ireland
maja.popovic@adaptcentre.ie

Abstract

This work presents a detailed analysis of translation errors perceived by readers as comprehensibility and/or adequacy issues. The main finding is that good comprehensibility, similarly to good fluency, can mask a number of adequacy errors. Of all major adequacy errors, 30% were fully comprehensible, thus fully misleading the reader to accept the incorrect information. Another 25% of major adequacy errors were perceived as almost comprehensible, thus being potentially misleading. Also, a vast majority of omissions (about 70%) is hidden by comprehensibility. Further analysis of misleading translations revealed that the most frequent error types are ambiguity, mistranslation, noun phrase error, word-by-word translation, untranslated word, subject-verb agreement, and spelling error in the source text. However, none of these error types appears exclusively in misleading translations, but are also frequent in fully incorrect (incomprehensible inadequate) and discarded correct (incomprehensible adequate) translations. Deeper analysis is needed to potentially detect underlying phenomena specifically related to misleading translations.

1 Introduction

While automatic evaluation metrics are very important and invaluable tools for rapid development of machine translation (MT) systems, they are only a substitution for human assessment of translation quality. Various methods have been proposed and used for the human evaluation of MT quality by assigning overall scores to MT outputs, such as (ALPAC, 1966; White et al., 1994; Koehn and Monz, 2006; Callison-Burch et al., 2007; Roturier and Bensadoun, 2011; Graham et al., 2013; Barrault et al., 2019), and all of them rely on at least one of the three translation quality criteria: comprehensibility (comprehension, intelligibility), adequacy

(fidelity, semantic accuracy), and fluency (grammaticality). Comprehensibility reflects the degree to which a translated text can be understood, adequacy reflects the degree to which the translation conveys the meaning of the original text in the source language, and fluency reflect the grammar of the translated text. The raters are usually asked to assign an overall score for the given translation criterion. In order to get more details about translation performance, error classification and analysis emerged in the field of MT (Vilar et al., 2006; Lommel et al., 2014; Klubička et al., 2018; Van Brussel et al., 2018).

However, there is less work dealing with human perception of MT quality and errors. For statistical phrase-based MT systems (SMT), Kirchhoff et al. (2014) and Federico et al. (2014) were identifying error types which are mostly disliked by readers. In the last five years, systems based on artificial neural networks (NMT) have become the new state of the art. Several evaluation studies, such as (Castilho et al., 2017; Klubička et al., 2018; Van Brussel et al., 2018) reported that these systems are able to produce more fluent and readable translations, but that they are still suffering from adequacy issues. In addition, many participants mentioned that good fluency of NMT outputs makes it more difficult to spot adequacy errors such as omissions or mistranslations. Such "fluently inadequate" errors may mislead readers into trusting the content based on fluency alone, especially when surrounded by fluent and adequate parts of a text (Martindale and Carpuat, 2018). Automatic identification of such errors for both SMT and NMT systems has been investigated in (Martindale et al., 2019) and it is confirmed that these errors appear much more often in NMT system.

To the best of our knowlegde, comprehensibility, while being a very important translation quality factor, has not been investigated in depth yet. It

256

Proceedings of the 24th Conference on Computational Natural Language Learning, pages 256–264
Online, November 19-20, 2020. ©2020 Association for Computational Linguistics
https://doi.org/10.18653/v1/P17

should be stressed that comprehensibility is very different from fluency – a fluent text can be incomprehensible (for example "Colorless green ideas sleep furiously."), and vice versa (for example "All these experiment was carry out this year.").

Our main research questions are:

RQ1 Are there "comprehensible inadequate" translations which are misleading human readers so that they fully trust the MT output despide adequacy errors?

In other words: how many adequacy errots are perceived as comprehensible?

RQ2 If the answer to the RQ1 is "yes", which types of translation errors are mainly related to these translations?

As a first step, a group of evaluators annotated problematic parts of the given machine translated text. They were not asked to assign any error labels, only to mark the parts of the text which they perceived as problematic for the given translation criterion. They first annotated all comprehensibility issues, and after about two weeks, all adequacy issues. For each criterion, they were asked to distinguish major and minor issues. We then analysed all major issues in order to examine relations between comprehensibility and adequacy and identify error types.

The analysis was carried out on English user reviews (as a case of "mid-way" genre between formal and informal written language) translated into Croatian and Serbian (as a case of mid-size less-resourced morphologically rich European languages).

It is worth noting that the aim of this work is not to compare MT systems, nor to estimate their overall performance for the given language pairs and domain in order to potentially improve them. The aim of this work is to explore relations between two aspects of human perception of translation quality.

2 Related work

Lot of research on MT evaluation deals with classification and analysis of MT errors, for example (Vilar et al., 2006; Farrús et al., 2010; Stymne and Ahrenberg, 2012; Lommel et al., 2014; Klubička et al., 2018). Few papers deal with human perception of these errors, but neither of them defines precisely which criterion is the translation quality based on.

Kirchhoff et al. (2014) uses conjoint analysis to investigate user preferences for error types of SMT systems. First, the errors in MT outputs were annotated, and then MT outputs with different error types were given to the crowd evaluators. They were asked to choose the MT output which they like best and to give the reason for their preference. One of the findings is that the frequencies of error types are not related to the user preferences. The most dispreferred error type was word order error, although it was the least frequent one. It was followed by word sense errors (ambiguity), then morphological errors (most frequent ones), whereas errors in function words were the most tolerable.

A similar study on SMT outputs based on linear mixed-effects models is described in (Federico et al., 2014), aiming to estimate the impact of different translation errors to the overall translation quality. For each MT output, experts were asked to assign a score on a 5-point scale while other experts annotated the errors. The results confirmed that the frequency of errors of a given type does not correlate with human preferences. Another finding is that omissions and mistranslations have the highest impact on the overall translation quality. In addition, it is observed that certain combinations of errors have less impact than each of those error types ocurring in isolation.

In the last few years, with the emergence of NMT systems which generate much more fluent and readable outputs but still are prone to adequacy errors, some studies have concentrated on investigating adequacy and fluency errors. Martindale and Carpuat (2018) carried out a survey to determine how users respond to good translations compared to translations that are either adequate but not fluent, or fluent but not adequate. This study showed that users strongly disliked disfluent translations, but were much less bothered with adequacy errors. Therefore, it was concluded that fluent translations with adequacy errors can mislead the reader to trust an incorrect meaning. Automatic identification of these misleading "fluently inadequate" translations using source text, reference human translation and MT output was proposed in (Martindale et al., 2019), and the main finding was that NMT systems generate more misleading translations than SMT systems. However, the question about how many adequacy errors are actually hidden by fluency remained open.

To the best of our knowledge, the relation be-

tween adequacy and comprehensibility has not
been investigated yet. Comprehensibility, similarly
to fluency, has an immediate effect on the reader,
while adequacy problems can be perceived only
if the reader has access to the source text or to a
correct translation to find out that the meaning is
wrong. This means that comprehensibility may
have the same misleading effect making the reader
accept an incorrect information. On the other hand,
because comprehensibility is different than fluency
(fluent sentences can be incomprehensible and vice
versa), the effects might be different.

3 Data set

Our analysis has been carried out on written user-
generated content, namely user reviews. Two
types of publicly available user reviews written
in English have been analysed: IMDb movie reviews[1] (Maas et al., 2011) and Amazon product
reviews[2] (McAuley et al., 2015). A set of those
user reviews was translated into Croatian and Serbian, two closely related mid-size less-resourced
morphologically rich European languages. The reviews were translated[3] by three on-line systems:
Google Translate[4], Bing[5] and Amazon translate[6].
The analysed text consists of a mixture of MT outputs from the three systems including 222 translated reviews consisting of about 1500 sentences
(segments) and 19837 untokenised words in total.

This text was then given to the annotators to
mark comprehensibility and adequacy issues, and
the process is described in details in the next section.

The annotated text is publicly available under
the Creative Commons CC-BY licence.[7]

3.1 Annotating comprehensibility and adequacy issues

As mentioned in Introduction, comprehensibility
reflects the degree to which a translated text can
be understood, and adequacy reflects the degree
to which the translation conveys the meaning of

the original text in the source language. Comprehension should be assessed without access to the
original text in the source language (or a correct
translation), while the original text (or a correct
translation) is mandatory for adequacy. Therefore,
each annotator first completed the annotation
of comprehension issues while reading only the
translation. After completing (usually after about
two weeks), they annotated adequacy issues by
comparing the translation with the original source
text. For each criterion, the annotators were asked
to distinguish two levels of issues: major issues
and minor issues. While for this particular study
we are interested only in major issues, we did
not want any errors to remain unannotated. The
following guidelines were given to the annotators:

Comprehensibility:

- mark all parts of the text (single words, small
  or long phrases, or entire sentences) which are
  not understandable (it does not make sense,
  it is not clear what it is about, etc.) as major
  issues;

- mark all parts of the text (again: words,
  phrases or sentences) which seem understandable but contain grammatical or stylistic errors
  as minor issues;

- if it seems that something is missing, add
  "XXX" to the corresponding position.

Adequacy:

- mark all parts of the translation (single words,
  small or long phrases, or entire sentences)
  which have different meaning than the original
  English text as major issues;

- mark all parts of the translation (again: words,
  phrases or sentences) which do not actually
  change the meaning of the source text, but contain sub-optimal lexical choices or grammar
  errors as minor issues;

- if some parts of the original English text are
  missing in the translation, add "XXX" to the
  corresponding position in the translation;

- if there are any errors in the source language[8]
  (spelling or grammar errors, etc.), mark its

---

[1]https://ai.stanford.edu/~amaas/data/
sentiment/
[2]http://jmcauley.ucsd.edu/data/amazon/
[3]at the end of January 2020
[4]https://translate.google.com/
[5]https://www.bing.com/translator
[6]https://aws.amazon.com/translate/
[7]https://github.com/m-popovic/
QRev-annotations/tree/master/
initial-analysis

[8]Detailed instructions for errors in the source text are particularly relevant for evaluating user generated content.

translation as major or minor issue if it does not correspond to the *intented* English word even though it is a correct translation of the erroneous English word.

The annotators were seeing the entire reviews during the process, not only isolated segments or blocks of 2-3 segments. In this way, it was ensured that the annotators were able to spot any context-dependent issues.

We wanted the texts to be annotated by a reliable group of readers which is neither too homogeneous as a group of professional translators nor too heterogeneous as crowd evaluators. Therefore, the annotation was performed by computational linguistics researchers and students, fluent in the source language and native speakers of the target language. They had different backgrounds, coming from technical studies, translation studies as well as from humanities.

Because the annotators were not asked to perform any fine-grained categorisation, the inter-annotator agreement was high – annotators assigned identical issue tags to more than 70% of words. More details about the annotation process can be found in (Popović, 2020).

4 Analysis of comprehensibility and adequacy issues

Table 1 presents overall percentages[9] of words perceived as issues, separately for each of the two translation criteria. In total (including both target languages and all three MT systems), 9.5% words in the text were perceived as incomprehensible, and the meaning of 9.9% words was changed in the translation process. As for minor issues, 13.5% words were perceived as slightly difficult to understand, and 12.8% were not translated in the optimal way.

It can be noted that the overall amounts of comprehensibility and adequacy issues are similar. However, it does not necessarily mean that the majority of words is perceived both as incomprehensible and inadequate. Therefore, we examined major comprehensibility and adequacy issues in depth.

---

[9]raw counts divided by the total number of words in the text including those without issues and the omission marks "XXX"

quality aspect	grade	raw count	%words
comprehension	major	1887	9.5
	minor	2673	13.5
adequacy	major	1963	9.9
	minor	2539	12.8

Table 1: Raw counts and percentages of words (normalised by the total number of words, including those without issues and the omission marks "XXX") perceived as problematic for comprehensibility and adequacy.

4.1 Relations between different types of issues

In order to determine presence or absence of misleading translations, we explored the following cases of different relations between comprehensibility and adequacy errors:

- only major adequacy issue A_{maj}
  (comprehensible inadequate translation)
  – incorrect information is accepted –

  The meaning of the original text is changed but the translation is readable and comprehensible. The reader feels comfortable with the text and does not notice any problem, thus accepting the incorrect meaning.

- $A_{maj}+C_{min}$ – major adequacy and minor comprehension issues
  (almost comprehensible inadequate translation)
  – incorrect information can be accepted –

  The meaning of the original text is changed, and the reader finds this incorrect meanining slightly difficult to understand. The reader is therefore susceptible to accept this incorrect meaning.

- $A_{maj}+C_{maj}$ – both major issues
  (incomprehensible inadequate translation)
  – incorrect information is discarded –

  The meaning of the original text is changed, and the reader is not able to understand this changed meaning. The reader clearly notices that there is something wrong with the text.

- $C_{maj}+A_{min}$ – major comprehension and minor adequacy issues
  (incomprehensible almost adequate translation)
  – almost correct information is discarded –

  The meaning of the original text is basically conveyed to the translation, only not in an

issue types	affected words		
	raw count	%words	%A$_{maj}$
only A$_{maj}$	588	2.96	30.0
A$_{maj}$+C$_{min}$	490	2.47	24.9
A$_{maj}$+C$_{maj}$	885	4.46	45.1
C$_{maj}$+A$_{min}$	342	1.72	
only C$_{maj}$	660	3.33	
C$_{min}$+A$_{min}$	1254	6.32	
only C$_{min}$	929	4.68	
only A$_{min}$	943	4.75	

Table 2: Raw counts and percentages of words (normalised by the total number of words, including those without issues and the omission marks "XXX") of all combinations of perceived issue types. For cases involving major adequacy issues, the percentages normalised by the total number of major adequacy issues are shown, too, in order to estimate the portion of hidden adequacy issues. For the sake of completenes, the numbers are presented for minor issues, too, although they were not further analysed in this work.

optimal way, but the reader cannot understand it. The reader is thus missing some correct information.

- only major comprehension issue C$_{maj}$ (incomprehensible adequate translation) – correct information is discarded –

  The meaning of the original text is correctly conveyed to the translation, but the reader cannot understand it. The reader is therefore not able to get the fully correct information.

Table 2 presents raw counts and percentages of words perceived in the described ways. For the sake of completeness, the numbers for minor issue types are shown as well. The numbers are generally in line with the findings of the previous work (Kirchhoff et al., 2014; Federico et al., 2014) regarding lack of correlation between the error frequency and perception of severity – in our texts, the frequencies of words perceived only as minor issues are higher than the frequencies of words perceived as major issues.

As already mentioned, minor issues were not further analysed in this work, because by definition they were not perceived as essential: either the meaning was preserved although not conveyed in the best way, or the translation was slightly difficult to understand, or both.

Misleading translations Table 2 shows that about 3% of words in the translated text are mis-

leading, and 2.5% are potentially misleading. This means that of every 100 words in the translation, 3 are fully accepted by the reader although their meaning is not correct, and 2 can be potentially accepted. Furthermore, from all major adequacy errors in the text, only 45.5% are incomprehensible. About 30% of adequacy errors are fully hidden so that the reader does not notice any problem, and about 25% are partially hidden because the reader is not fully sure that s/he understands the text, but s/he is very susceptible to accept the meaning.

All in all, the portion of misleading translations is not negligible, so we continued our analysis by trying to identify error types associated with such translations. Also, we wanted to explore whether there are error types related (almost) exclusively to them.

4.2 Error types

For each (group of) word(s) perceived as compreensibility or adequacy major issue, we assigned an error type. The error types were not predefined by any particular error typology, but identified while looking into the text. It is worth noting that many error types were identified, but most of them are ocurring rarely in the text. Also, for some of the annotated words no particular error type could be defined, which is probably an effect of annotators' personal preferences. The most frequent error types perceived as misleading translations can be defined as follows:

- **ambiguity**

  The obtained translation for the given word is in principle correct, but not in the given context (word sense error).

- **mistranslation**

  The obtained translation for the given word is incorrect.

- **noun phrase**

  An English sequence consisting of a head noun and additional nouns and adjectives is incorrectly translated. Formation rules for Serbian and Croatian are rather different than for English and there is often no unique solution. The examples in the table below represent two English noun collocations and their reference translations into Serbian and Croatian together with the corresponding English glosses. This type of issue is relevant for many Slavic languages.

language	NP1	NP2
en	grill cover	chocolate cake
sr/hr	poklopac za roštilj	čokoladni kolač
gloss	cover for grill	'chocolaty' cake

- **spelling error in source**

  A word in the original text in the source language has spelling errors which result in incorrect translation. This type of issue is especially relevant for user-generated content.

- **subject-verb agreement**

  A verb inflection in the translation denoting person does not correspond to the subject.

- **untranslated**

  A word in the source language is simply copied to the translated text.

- **word-by-word translation**

  A sequence of source words is translated as single words – the translation choice of each word looks random, both lexically and morphologically, without taking into account any context.

Table 3 shows these error types and their percentages for misleading translations. These error types are the certainly "dangerous" because they can easily mislead the reader to accept incorrect information. However, the very same error types are often perceived as fully incorrect (incomprehensible inadequate), too. Furthermore, they (except of untranslated words) even often lead to discarding correct information (incomprehensible adequate). Further in-depth analysis is needed to determine whether there are some underlying phenomena related exclusively to the misleading translations.

Five examples of different perceptions of ambiguity errors, noun phrase errors and word-by-word translations are presented in Table 4. All sentences except 3) have misleading parts (fully misleading marked as red and potentially misleading as green). In the sentences 1) and 2) there is only one misleading ambiguous word. The incorrectly chosen variants of these words are fully comprehensible so that without the source text, the reader was not able to figure out that the information is not correct. On the other hand, the ambiguous word in the sentence 3), together with the noun phrase, is perceived as both incomprehensible and inadequate (marked as violet). Sentences 4) and 5) illustrate how different parts of a phrase translated word-by-word are perceived in different ways: violet denotes fully incorrect, red denotes misleading, and cyan denotes discarding almost correct translation. It might be worth noting that all sentences are perfectly fluent except the sentence 3) which is very disfluent.

Propagation effect   Table 3 also shows that there is a strong effect of *propagation* for comprehensibility – many correct words are perceived as incomprehensible because of errors in surrounding words. In many cases, the reader finds the whole sentence incomprehensible. An example of propagation can be seen in Table 5. All words in bold are correct, but all were perceived as major comprehensibility issues due to different types of errors in surrounding words: a red misleading omission, a fully incorrect violet word, and an incomprehensible group of almost correct cyan words. It should be mentioned that for some adequacy errors, annotators also marked one or two neighbouring words which were not really incorrect, but that happened very rarely.

Omissions   Since several studies reported that the omissions are generally problematic to spot without access to the source text, we compared the frequencies of omissions percieved only as comprehensibility issue, only as adequacy issue, and as both (regardless of the severity grade).

Table 6 confirms the previous findings: a vast majority of omissions (71.5%) was perceived only as adequacy error. Only 9% of actual omissions were also perceived as comprehensibility issues. Apart from this, 19% of omissions were perceived as exclusively comprehensibility issues and are not related to anything actually omitted from the source text. The most probable reason is the influence of other surrounding errors, but further analysis is needed to better understand this effect.

5   Conclusions

This work presents the results of a detailed analysis of translation errors perceived by readers as major comprehensibility and/or major adequacy issues. The main finding is that good comprehensibility, similarly to good fluency, can mask a number of adequacy errors. Of all major adequacy errors, 30% were fully comprehensible, thus fully misleading the reader to accept the incorrect information. An-

incorrect information is:			discarded information is:	
accepted only A_{maj}	potentially accepted $A_{maj}+C_{min}$	discarded $A_{maj}+C_{maj}$	almost correct $C_{maj}+A_{min}$	correct only C_{maj}
ambiguity 24.0	ambiguity 24.8	ambiguity 26.7	ambiguity 16.4	*propagation 33.3*
mistranslation 6.0	mistranslation 8.9	mistranslation 8.2	noun phrase 8.4	ambiguity 14.4
word-by-word 5.0	noun phrase 8.4	noun phrase 6.9	mistranslation 5.8	noun phrase 7.0
noun phrase 4.4	untranslated 8.2	untranslated 6.7	{noun case 5.8}	word-by-word 4.1
source spelling 3.8	word-by-word 5.4	word-by-word 5.5	word-by-word 5.8	mistranslation 3.7
subject-verb 3.8	(subject-verb 3.2)	(subject-verb 4.5)	subject-verb 4.9	(subject-verb 2.0)
untranslated 3.8	(source spelling 2.4)	(source spelling 3.5)	{POS ambiguity 3.5}	(source spelling 1.2)

Table 3: The most frequent error types perceived as a particular issue combination. The numbers represent percentages of the error type perceived as the issue combination – 24.0% of all comprehensible inadequate translations (accepted incorrect information) are ambiguity errors, 6.0% are mistranslations, etc. Parentheses indicate that the error type was not in the top list for the given issue combination, but it is presented for comparison because it is in the top list for misleading traslations.

other 25% of major adequacy errors were perceived as almost comprehensible, thus being potentially misleading. In addition, a vast majority of omissions (about 70%) is hidden by comprehensibility.

Further analysis of those misleading translations was carried out in order to find out which types of translation errors are perceived in this way. Ambiguous words, mistranslations, noun phrases, untranslated words, word-by-word translations, subject-verb agreement and spelling errors in the original text were identified as the most frequent error types in misleading translations. Although noun phrase problems are typical for Slavic languages and errors in the source text are typical for user generated content, the rest of the error types is rather general. However, none of these error types is exclusively related to misleading translations, but are also frequent in fully incorrect (incomprehensible inadequate) and discarded correct (incomprehensible adequate) translations. Deeper analysis is needed to potentially detect underlying phenomena specifically related to misleading translations.

Apart from the obvious directions for future work such as analysing more texts and including more language pairs and domains, the presented analysis can be expanded in the following directions: including fluency in the analysis, including all minor issues in the analysis, further analysis of omissions, and investigating co-ocurrences of different error types. Another experiment could include monolingual annotators for comprehensibility in order to completely eliminate potential influence of knowlegde of the source language.

Acknowledgments

This research is being conducted with the financial support of the European Association for Machine Translation (EAMT) under its programme "2019 Sponsorship of Activities" at the ADAPT Research Centre at Dublin City University. The ADAPT SFI Centre for Digital Media Technology is funded by Science Foundation Ireland through the SFI Research Centres Programme and is co-funded under the European Regional Development Fund (ERDF) through Grant 13/RC/2106.

We would like to thank all the evaluators for providing us with annotations and feedback.

References

ALPAC. 1966. Language and machines. Computers in translation and linguistics.

Loïc Barrault, Ondřej Bojar, Marta R. Costa-jussà, Christian Federmann, Mark Fishel, Yvette Graham, Barry Haddow, Matthias Huck, Philipp Koehn, Shervin Malmasi, Christof Monz, Mathias Müller, Santanu Pal, Matt Post, and Marcos Zampieri. 2019. Findings of the 2019 conference on machine translation (WMT19). In *Proceedings of the Fourth Conference on Machine Translation (Volume 2: Shared Task Papers, Day 1)*, pages 1–61, Florence, Italy. Association for Computational Linguistics.

Chris Callison-Burch, Cameron Fordyce, Philipp Koehn, Christof Monz, and Josh Schroeder. 2007. (meta-) evaluation of machine translation. In *Proceedings of the Second Workshop on Statistical Machine Translation*, pages 136–158, Prague, Czech Republic.

Sheila Castilho, Joss Moorkens, Federico Gaspari, Iacer Calixto, John Tinsley, and Andy Way. 2017. Is neural machine translation the new state of the art? *The Prague Bulletin of Mathematical Linguistics*, 108(1):109 – 120.

1)	A_{maj} (misleading)	
	source	Extremely uncomfortable
	MT	Izuzetno neprijatno AMB
	gloss	Extremely awkward
2)	A_{maj} (misleading)	
	source	The special effects with the mummy's ghost
	MT	Specijalni efekti s duhom mame AMB
	gloss	The special effects with the mother's ghost
3)	A_{maj}+C_{maj} (fully incorrect)	
	source	Best readily available food coloring
	MT	Najbolje lako AMB obojenje hrane NP
	gloss	Best easy coloring of_food
4)	A_{maj} (misleading), A_{maj}+C_{min} (potentially misleading)	
	source	they fit easily under my snow pants and they don't show through
	MT	lako se uklapaju AMB ispod mojih snežnih pantalona i ne prolaze WBW kroz njih WBW
	gloss	they concord easily under my snow pants and not they_go through them
5)	A_{maj} (misleading), A_{maj}+C_{maj} (fully incorrect), A_{min}+C_{maj} (almost correct discarded)	
	source	No matter how much care I used in throwing it
	MT	Bez obzira koliko briga WBW sam koristio WBW u bacanju WBW
	gloss	No matter how_many cares I used in the throwing

Table 4: Examples of ambiguity errors (AMB), noun phrase errors (NP) and word-by-word translations (WBW) perceived as comprehensible inadequate (red), almost comprehensible inadequate (green), incomprehensible almost adequate (cyan) and incomprehensible inadequate translations (violet).

source	For the kind of shipping they want it would be reasonable to expect a better presentation.
MT	**Za vrstu dostave** XXX žele da bi bilo **razumno očekivati bolju prezentaciju.**
gloss	**For the kind of shipping** {which} they_want that would be **reasonable to expect better presentation.**

Table 5: Example of propagation effect for major comprehensibility issues. All words in bold are correct, but perceived as incomprehensible due to different types of errors in surrounding words (presented in colour).

percentage of omissions perceived:	
only as comprehensibility issues	19.2
only as adequacy issues	71.5
as both	9.3

Table 6: Percentage of omissions perceived only as comprehensibility issues, only as adequacy issues, and as both types of issues.

Mireia Farrús, Marta Ruiz Costa-Jussà, José B. Mario, and José Adrián R. Fonollosa. 2010. Linguistic-based evaluation criteria to identify statistical machine translation errors. In *Proceedings of the 14th Annual Conference of the European Association for Machine Translation (EAMT 2010)*, St. Raphaël, France.

Marcello Federico, Matteo Negri, Luisa Bentivogli, and Marco Turchi. 2014. Assessing the impact of translation errors on machine translation quality with mixed-effects models. In *Proceedings of the 2014 Conference on Empirical Methods in Natural Language Processing (EMNLP 2014)*, Doha, Qatar.

Yvette Graham, Timothy Baldwin, Alistair Moffat, and Justin Zobel. 2013. Continuous measurement scales in human evaluation of machine translation. In *Proceedings of the 7th Linguistic Annotation Workshop and Interoperability with Discourse*, pages 33–41, Sofia, Bulgaria. Association for Computational Linguistics.

Katrin Kirchhoff, Daniel Capurro, and Anne M. Turner. 2014. A conjoint analysis framework for evaluating user preferences in machine translation. *Machine Translation*, 28(1):117.

Filip Klubička, Antonio Toral, and Víctor M. Sánchez-Cartagena. 2018. Quantitative Fine-grained Human Evaluation of Machine Translation Systems: A Case Study on English to Croatian. *Machine Translation*, 32(3):195–215.

Philipp Koehn and Christof Monz. 2006. Manual and automatic evaluation of machine translation between European languages. In *Proceedings on the Workshop on Statistical Machine Translation*, pages 102–121, New York City.

Arle Lommel, Aljoscha Burchardt, Maja Popović, Kim Harris, Eleftherios Avramidis, and Hans Uszkoreit. 2014. Using a new analytic measure for the annotation and analysis of MT errors on real data. In *Proceedings of the 17th Annual Conference of the European Association for Machine Translation (EAMT 2014)*, pages 165–172.

Andrew L. Maas, Raymond E. Daly, Peter T. Pham, Dan Huang, Andrew Y. Ng, and Christopher Potts. 2011. Learning Word Vectors for Sentiment Analysis. In *Proceedings of the 49th Annual Meeting of the Association for Computational Linguistics and Human Language Technologies (ACL-HLT 2011)*, pages 142–150, Portland, Oregon, USA.

Marianna Martindale and Marine Carpuat. 2018. Fluency over adequacy: A pilot study in measuring user trust in imperfect MT. In *Proceedings of the 13th Conference of the Association for Machine Translation in the Americas (AMTA 2018)*, pages 13–25, Boston, MA.

Marianna Martindale, Marine Carpuat, Kevin Duh, and Paul McNamee. 2019. Identifying fluently inadequate output in neural and statistical machine translation. In *Proceedings of Machine Translation Summit XVII*, pages 233–243, Dublin, Ireland.

Julian McAuley, Christopher Targett, Qinfeng Shi, and Anton van den Hengel. 2015. Image-Based Recommendations on Styles and Substitutes. In *Proceedings of the 38th International ACM SIGIR Conference on Research and Development in Information Retrieval (SIGIR 2015)*, pages 43–52, Santiago, Chile.

Maja Popović. 2020. Informative manual evaluation of machine translation output. In *Proceedings of the 28th International Conference on Computational Linguistics (COLING 2020)*, Online.

Johann Roturier and Anthony Bensadoun. 2011. Evaluation of MT Systems to Translate User Generated Content. In *Proceedings of the MT Summit XIII*, Xiamen, China.

Sara Stymne and Lars Ahrenberg. 2012. On the practice of error analysis for machine translation evaluation. In *Proceedings of the Eighth International Conference on Language Resources and Evaluation (LREC 2012)*, pages 1785–1790, Istanbul, Turkey.

Laura Van Brussel, Arda Tezcan, and Lieve Macken. 2018. A fine-grained error analysis of NMT, SMT and RBMT output for English-to-Dutch. In *Proceedings of the Eleventh International Conference on Language Resources and Evaluation (LREC 2018)*, Miyazaki, Japan.

David Vilar, Jia Xu, Luis Fernando D'Haro, and Hermann Ney. 2006. Error analysis of statistical machine translation output. In *Proceedings of the Fifth International Conference on Language Resources and Evaluation (LREC'06)*, Genoa, Italy. European Language Resources Association (ELRA).

John White, Theresa O'Connell, and Francis O'Mara. 1994. The ARPA MT evaluation methodologies: evolution, lessons, and future approaches. In *Proceedings of the 1994 Conference, Association for Machine Translation in the Americas*, pages 193–205.

Cross-lingual Embeddings Reveal Universal and Lineage-Specific Patterns in Grammatical Gender Assignment

Hartger Veeman
Uppsala University
Department of linguistics and philology
Box 635, 75126 Uppsala
hartger.veeman.7544@student.uu.se

Marc Allassonnière-Tang
University Lyon 2
Lab Dynamics of Language
14 avenue Berthelot 69363 Lyon
marc.tang@univ-lyon2.fr

Aleksandrs Berdicevskis
University of Gothenburg
Språkbanken
Box 200, 40530 Gothenburg
aleksandrs.berdicevskis@gu.se

Ali Basirat
Uppsala University
Department of linguistics and philology
Box 635, 75126 Uppsala
ali.basirat@lingfil.uu.se

Abstract

Grammatical gender is assigned to nouns differently in different languages. Are all factors that influence gender assignment idiosyncratic to languages or are there any that are universal? Using cross-lingual aligned word embeddings, we perform two experiments to address these questions about language typology and human cognition. In both experiments, we predict the gender of nouns in language X using a classifier trained on the nouns of language Y, and take the classifier's accuracy as a measure of transferability of gender systems. First, we show that for 22 Indo-European languages the transferability decreases as the phylogenetic distance increases. This correlation supports the claim that some gender assignment factors are idiosyncratic, and as the languages diverge, the proportion of shared inherited idiosyncrasies diminishes. Second, we show that when the classifier is trained on two Afro-Asiatic languages and tested on the same 22 Indo-European languages (or vice versa), its performance is still significantly above the chance baseline, thus showing that universal factors exist and, moreover, can be captured by word embeddings. When the classifier is tested across families and on inanimate nouns only, the performance is still above baseline, indicating that the universal factors are not limited to biological sex.

1   Grammatical gender assignment

Grammatical gender is one of the nominal classification systems found in natural languages (Seifart, 2010). In languages with grammatical gender, certain words agree in a specific form with the noun they modify depending on the gender of the modified noun (Corbett, 1991, 2001). For instance,

Swedish has a binary gender system with the common/neuter values, in which the articles and adjectives must have grammatical gender agreement with the noun they are modifying, c.f., *ett stor-t äpple* (SG.NEUT big-SG.NEUT apple.SG.NEUT) 'a big apple' and *en stor-∅ häst* (a.SG.UTER big-SG.UTER horse.SG.UTER) 'a big horse'.

The most common gender distinctions are masculine/feminine (e.g., in French and Italian), masculine/feminine/neuter (e.g., in Russian and German), and common/neuter (e.g., in Swedish and Danish) (Corbett, 2013a).[1] Within these distinctions, grammatical gender does not necessarily fully agree with the biological sex. By way of illustration, the German word for 'girl', *Mädchen*, is a neuter noun. Moreover, nouns with the same meaning may belong to different grammatical gender in different languages. For example, the German noun for 'sun', *Sonne*, is feminine, but its French equivalent, *soleil*, is masculine.

Based on these observations, several questions have been developed in the literature. First of all, what are the main factors that influence gender assignment in individual languages? Second, are there any principles that are shared cross-linguistically or are they all language- and/or culture-specific? With regard to the first question, two main factors have been identified in the literature: formal features of the noun and its meaning (Corbett and Fraser, 2000; Rice, 2006; Corbett, 2013b; Fedden and Corbett, 2019). With regard to the second question, it is generally believed that

---

[1]More complex distinctions are also found. As an example, Swahili has a more complex system with 18 classes. These systems are generally referred to as 'noun classes' in the literature and are not covered by the term 'grammatical gender' in the current paper.

Proceedings of the 24th Conference on Computational Natural Language Learning, pages 265–275
Online, November 19-20, 2020. ©2020 Association for Computational Linguistics
https://doi.org/10.18653/v1/P17

gender assignment is based on a mix of shared cognitive principles (Kemmerer, 2017) and linguistic/cultural idiosyncrasies (Takamura et al., 2016; Di Garbo et al., 2019).

One of the most common way to answer the second question is to measure the transferability of gender across languages. If the gender assignment rules of a language can be easily used to predict the gender of nouns in another language, it shows that the principles of gender assignment are partly shared and transferable between the two languages. If such a transfer is possible within most languages, one can then assume that gender assignment is to a large extent based on universal patterns. Most empirical studies that adopted this approach followed the perspective of language acquisition and analyzed how native speakers of language X could predict the gender of a selected amount of nouns from language Y (Sabourin et al., 2006; Jarvis and Pavlenko, 2010, p.132-136). No studies known to the authors investigated the transferability of grammatical gender for a large amount of nouns from a large sample of languages by using natural language processing methods, which is the gap we aim at filling.

We use a transfer learning setting to measure the transferability of grammatical gender across languages. In this setting, a neural classification model is trained to predict the grammatical gender of nouns in a source language. This model is then applied to a set of test nouns in a target language to predict their grammatical gender. The classifier's ability to classify the test nouns is interpreted as an indication of the transferability of grammatical gender system from the source language to the target language (i.e., the higher the accuracy is, the more transferable the gender systems are). The entire setting is founded on the cross-lingual representation of words, providing for knowledge transfer between the gender classification models across languages. The embeddings are used to represent nouns in both source and target languages. The use of word embeddings for the study of grammatical gender is based on the premise that they can capture linguistically-motivated information about words (Nastase and Popescu, 2009; Andreas and Klein, 2014; Artetxe et al., 2018; Basirat and Tang, 2019; Williams et al., 2019), including information about the gender of nouns within a language (Basirat and Tang, 2019; Williams et al., 2019; Nastase and Popescu, 2009; Basirat et al., in press).

We ask the following research questions. Is successful gender transfer possible between non-related languages (if yes, it means that there exist universal factors in gender assignment)? When the classifier is applied to related languages, does its success depend on how related they are (if yes, this in an indication that some factors are not universal)? Does gender transfer work in the same way for all nouns or are there differences between certain noun classes?

2 Experimental materials and settings

In this section, we present the languages involved in this study along with the source of our data. Then, we provide an overview of the cross-lingual word embedding method and the settings of the classifier used for gender transfer.

2.1 Materials

Two sources of data are selected for each language. First, a noun-gender dictionary is constructed from the morphological annotations of the Universal Dependencies 2.6 (Zeman et al., 2020). For each language, a dictionary is created by iterating through all available UD treebanks for the given language. For every unique downcased noun form in these treebanks, the grammatical gender is extracted from the treebank and labeled to the noun as one of four classes: neuter, feminine, masculine and common (underspecified values such as "Fem,Masc" were ignored). The same four-class label structure was used for all languages, to ensure compatibility of the models. Second, word embeddings are selected from pre-trained cross-lingual embeddings published on the fastText website (Joulin et al., 2018).[2] Further details about the embeddings are provided in the following subsection.

We selected all languages that have grammatical gender and are present in both data sources, with the exception of Albanian due to its small treebank size and Norwegian because in pilot experiments, our classifier showed unexpectedly poor performance for reasons we were not able to establish. This results in the selection of 24 languages that are shown in Table 1. Three types of gender systems are found: masculine/feminine (42%, 10/24), masculine/feminine/neuter (46%, 11/24), and common/neuter (12%, 3/24). Only a few languages belong to the third type, which is actually the result of a merge between the masculine and the feminine

---

[2] https://fasttext.cc/docs/en/aligned-vectors.html

categories existing originally in those languages (Enger, 2017, p.1439). The Indo-European language family is over-represented, which is due to practical limitations from the available resources. Nevertheless, our sample has its advantages. First, the Indo-European language family is considered to be one of the 'typical' grammatical gender language families (Audring, 2016, p.2), which represents an ideal starting point for a quantitative analysis. Second, comparing languages mostly from the same family allows us to address our second research question about the correlation between relatedness of the languages and the transferability of gender.

Language		m	f	n	c	Size
Arabic*	ar	33	67	-	-	3
Bulgarian	bg	24	33	43	-	9
Catalan	ca	49	51	-	-	9
Czech	cs	17	41	43	-	44
Danish	da	-	-	72	28	7
German	de	24	40	36	-	56
Greek	el	25	52	23	-	4
Spanish	es	44	56	-	-	1
French	fr	43	57	-	-	13
Hebrew*	he	44	57	-	-	6
Hindi	hi	33	67	-	-	8
Croatian	hr	17	39	45	-	12
Italian	it	45	55	-	-	13
Lithuanian	lt	38	62	-	-	7
Latvian	lv	49	51	-	-	13
Dutch	nl	-	-	72	28	9
Polish	pl	21	35	45	-	26
Portuguese	pt	45	55	-	-	8
Romanian[3]	ro	64	37	-	-	17
Russian	ru	17	34	49	-	44
Slovak	sk	18	39	43	-	9
Slovenian	sl	16	41	43	-	12
Swedish	sv	-	-	75	25	11
Ukrainian	uk	14	38	48	-	11

Table 1: Languages included in the data. Asterisk (*) denotes Afro-Asiatic languages, the rest are Indo-European. The gender distribution (in %) is shown in columns m = masculine, f = feminine, c = common (uter), n = neuter. The "Size" column indicates the number of nouns in thousand tokens (K).

---

[3]Traditionally, Romanian is considered to have three genders: masculine, feminine, and neuter, but an alternative two-gender analysis has also been proposed (Bateman and Polinsky, 2010). UD follows the two-gender annotation.

2.2 Cross-lingual Word Embeddings

Cross-lingual word embeddings aim at representing words of multiple languages in a joint embedding space such that similar words (in each language and across all languages) are clustered together. These resources provide a foundation for the cross-lingual study of words and the development of transfer learning models between languages.

The cross-lingual word embeddings can be trained in different ways (Ruder et al., 2019). One of the main approaches is to find a mapping between monolingual word embedding spaces using a seed dictionary that contains words and their translations in different languages. This approach is based on the observation made by Mikolov et al. (2013) that word embeddings exhibit similar structures across languages. Mikolov et al. (2013) formulate the mapping as a least-square linear regression between the monolingual embeddings of the seed lexicon to minimize the mean square error of the word translations. The mapping model is then generalized to all words in the languages. This approach is improved by Xing et al. (2015); Smith et al. (2017), imposing an orthogonal constraint on the transformation weights. Later attempts were made to reduce the need for the seed dictionary (Smith et al., 2017; Artetxe et al., 2017). Conneau et al. (2018); Zhang et al. (2017) leverage adversarial training to automatically produce the dictionary during training and completely eliminate its necessity as a supervision source. Joulin et al. (2018) further enhance the loss function of the regression model using the retrieval model of Conneau et al. (2018), providing for the representation of unseen words.

In this study, we use fastText cross-lingual word embeddings trained on the monolingual word embeddings of Bojanowski et al. (2017) using the mapping approach of Joulin et al. (2018). The monolingual embeddings are trained on Wikipedia data for words that appear at least five times. The embeddings encode information about the form and semantics of words from sub-word units and word co-occurrences, respectively. The information about the form and semantics plays a critical role in the assignment of grammatical gender to nouns (Corbett, 1991; Rice, 2006). This motivates us to use fastText embeddings for the study of cross-lingual grammatical gender transfer. The original embeddings are distributed in a 300-dimensional space and cover 44 languages belonging to different language families. In the current study, we retrieved the embeddings for the 24 languages that have gender systems and a sufficiently large data size.

2.3 Settings

A multi-layer perceptron is used to predict the grammatical gender of nouns from their cross-lingual embeddings. The choice of a multi-layer perceptron instead of a recurrent model is motivated by 1) the fact that the grammatical gender is an inherent static property of a noun that does not change in different contexts, and 2) the proven ability of a multi-layer perceptron for the task (Basirat and Tang, 2019). The network has three layers, an input layer that reads the 300-dimensional word embeddings, a single hidden layer twice the size of the input layer with ReLu activation, and an output layer with softmax activation consisting of four neurons related to the four genders masculine, feminine, neuter, and common. This provides for modeling the three gender systems masculine/feminine, masculine/feminine/neuter, and common/neuter and analysing the extent to which these systems are transferable.

The classifier is trained on pairs of the noun embeddings and genders collected from the dictionary. The data is split into 80%, 10% and 10% for training, validation and testing. The data is randomly split in folds, of which the designations of training, test and validation are rotated between runs. The final results are the average of multiple runs covering a full rotation of the folds. We label the language the classifier is trained on *source* and the language to which it attempts predicting gender *target*. The train and the validation data is used for training a classification model on the source language and the test data is used for testing the model on the target language. We go through all possible source-target combinations, 576 (24×24) language pairs.

PyTorch (Paszke et al., 2019) is used to implement the classifier using the stochastic gradient descent optimizer with a learning rate of 0.1 and the cross-entropy loss function. Early stopping was employed if the model stopped improving over 20 epochs, with a minimum of 2200 epochs and a maximum of 25000 epochs. We ran the classifier ten times with different random seeds to measure the variability between training runs. For every language pair, we calculate Fleiss' kappa across the ten runs. The kappas vary from 0.73 (substan-

tial agreement) to 0.99, the average value is 0.91 (almost perfect agreement), and the standard deviation is 0.04. We conclude that the results are robust with respect to random seed.

3 Gender transfer at the language level

In this section, we analyse the results of the experiment from two different perspectives. First, we consider the broad transferability of gender across languages by measuring the accuracy across all possible pairs of languages in the dataset (section 3.1, figures 1 and 3). While this step provides an overview of the accuracy of gender transfer, it is also extremely influenced by the different gender systems across languages. For instance, asking a language that has the masculine/feminine system to predict the categories on a language that has a masculine/feminine/neuter system is by definition going to result in a low accuracy since the source language does not have information about neuter nouns. To overcome this issue, we perform an additional analysis with narrower scope, where we compare pairs of only those languages that have isomorphic systems (section 3.2). As an example, we use languages that have masculine/feminine to predict the gender in languages that also have masculine/feminine. The rationale behind narrowing the scope is that it enables us to focus on the question of how similar the distributions of nouns across gender classes are, abstracting away from possible differences between the number of classes and their types.

We define a random guessing baseline for the transfer between each pair of languages. The baseline is the accuracy that would have been achieved by a classifier that makes a random guess based solely on gender probabilities in the source language. The accuracy it would achieve is

$$\sum_{g \in \{m,f,c,n\}} p(g_s)p(g_t)$$

where $p(g_s)$ is the probability of the given gender in the source language and $p(g_t)$ is the probability of the given gender in the target language. In all our experiments, we report the absolute improvement (or degradation) of the transfer learning accuracy from the random baseline accuracy. In this way, a negative value indicates that the transfer accuracy is below the baseline, a positive value indicates that the transfer accuracy is higher than the baseline, and a zero value indicates that the transfer accuracy is only as good as the random baseline.[4]

3.1 Gender transfer between all systems

The mean accuracy from the ten different-seed runs of each transfer is compared with the random baseline and plotted in Figure 1. Each entry is the difference between the result and the baseline, i.e. an improvement (or degradation) from the baseline results.

We run three two-sided paired t-tests to check whether the accuracy is significantly different from the baseline: one for language pairs within the Indo-European family ($t(483) = 27.013$, *p-value* < 0.001), one for language pairs where the source language is from an Afro-Asiatic family and the target language is Indo-European ($t(43) = 10.454$, *p-value* < 0.001), one for language pairs where the source is Indo-European and the target is Afro-Asiatic ($t(43) = 9.5251$, *p-value* < 0.001), in all cases the average classifier accuracy is higher than the baseline.

Three main observations are worth noting. First, word embeddings do provide sufficient information to generate an accuracy significantly above the baseline for the majority of languages, as shown by the diagonal line in the plot and the output of the t-tests. Second, Danish, Dutch, and Swedish do not transfer well to other languages. These three languages are the only languages that have a common/neuter system, which explains the low accuracy of gender transfer. Third, even though Arabic and Hebrew are not related to the Indo-European language family, both as source and target languages they yield accuracy that is comparable to that yielded by Indo-European languages and is significantly higher than the baseline (see Section 4). These points imply that while the relatedness of languages affect the transferability of gender, we are also likely to find some shared principles of gender assignment across non-related languages.

Then, we compare the accuracy of the transfer with phylogenetic distance within the Indo-European language family. To do so, we extract the phylogenetic distance from the broad Indo-European tree published by Chang et al. (2015, tree

A3), as shown in Figure 2. The branch lengths are annotated in terms of years, which allows a direct comparison of phylogenetic distance defined as the time depth of the first common ancestor shared by a pair of compared languages. The larger the distance, the less related is a pair of languages. The output of the comparison is shown in Figure 3.

A linear regression shows a significant relationship between accuracy and phylogenetic distance ($t(4838) = -60.12$, $p < 0.001$). The slope coefficient for phylogenetic distance is -0.00005, which means that the accuracy decreases by 5% for each 1000 years of phylogenetic distance. The R^2 value shows that 43% of the variation in accuracy can be explained by phylogenetic distance. A closer analysis indicates that the transfer accuracy of a pair of languages sharing the same system is generally higher than the transfer accuracy of pair of languages having different systems. For instance, the lower values between 1000 and 2000 years of phylogenetic distance are gender transfers between common/neuter and masculine/feminine/neuter languages. Further details are explained in subsection 3.2.

Finally, we performed a correlation test to see whether gender transferability in a language pair is affected by how different gender distributions in the two languages are. By gender distribution we mean a distribution of the marginal probabilities of seeing each gender over all nouns in the vocabulary set, and we measure the difference between two distributions as the KL-divergence. We find that the transferability correlates negatively with the KL-divergence both globally over all languages (Spearman $\rho = -0.7$, $p < 0.001$) and locally within each branch (Slavic: $\rho = -0.4$, $p = 0.002$, Germanic: $\rho = -0.9$, $p < 0.001$, and Romance: $\rho = -0.8$, $p < 0.001$), indicating that gender transfer becomes weaker as the marginal distributions of gender become more different.

3.2 Gender transfer between isomorphic systems

Three types of comparisons are made. First, the accuracy of transfer between languages with masculine/feminine systems is measured. Then, the same process is conducted for languages with masculine/feminine/neuter systems and common/neuter systems.

To estimate the combined effect of phylogenetic distance and system type (masculine/feminine,

---

[4]Note that our measure is not of course a perfect quantification of gender-system similarity, since it does not yield the accuracy of 1 for all the cases when source and target languages are the same (the diagonal in Figure 1). It can, however, be viewed as an approximation (in principle, the accuracy of transfer X → Y can be normalized by dividing it by the accuracy of X → X).

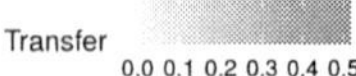

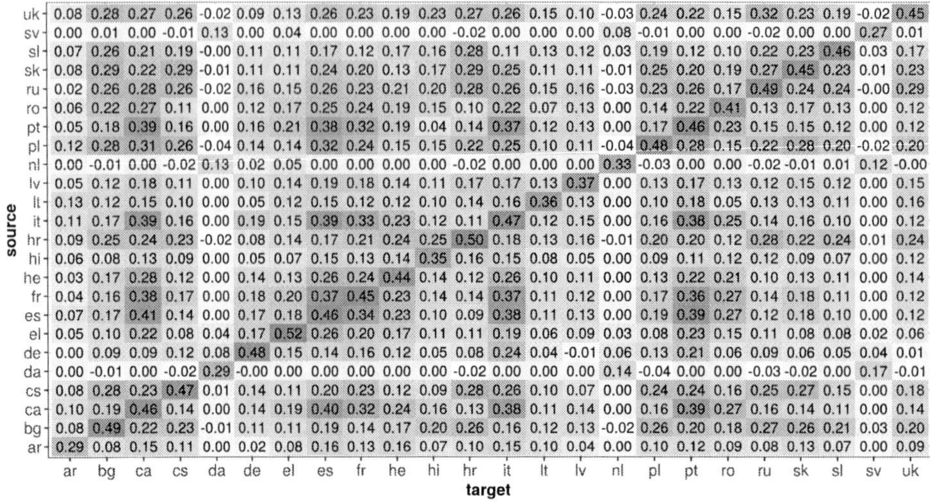

Figure 1: Average difference between accuracy and the random baseline. A positive value represents an accuracy above the baseline while a negative value indicates an accuracy below the baseline.

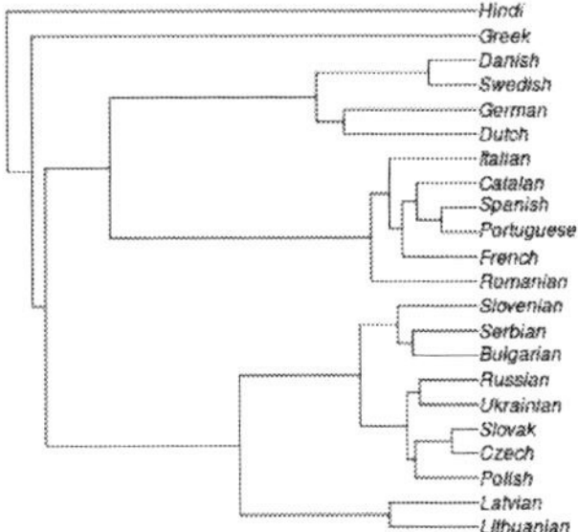

Figure 2: The phylogenetic tree of the Indo-European languages included in the analysis.

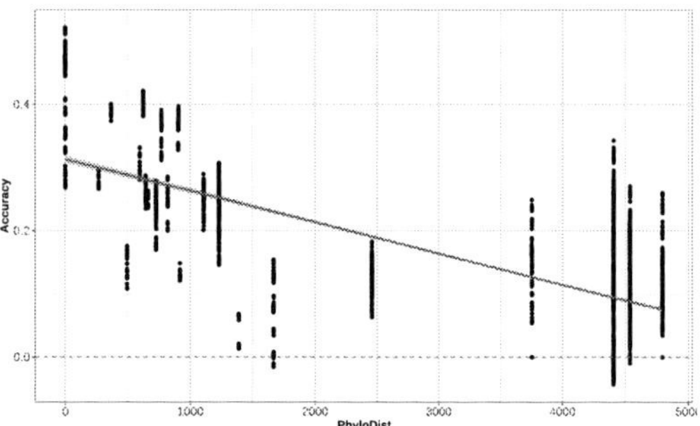

Figure 3: A comparison of the accuracy improvement (or degradation) of gender transfer (Y-axis) and the phylogenetic distance between each language pair (X-axis). The dashed line refers to the random baseline. The phylogenetic distance refers to the years separating each pair of languages in the Indo-European tree. Each point represents the average of the transfer accuracy over 10 runs.

masculine/feminine/neuter, common/neuter), we fit a linear regression model with the values of the accuracy improvement (or degradation) from the baseline as the dependent variable, phylogenetic distance a continuous predictor, and system type a categorical predictor (common/neuter is the reference level). The two-way interaction between the predictors is also included. The summary of the model is presented in Table 2. The R^2 value shows that 74% of the variation of accuracy in the sample can be explained by phylogenetic distance and gender system types.

The results again show a negative relationship between accuracy and phylogenetic distance. With regard to gender systems, having masculine/feminine or masculine/feminine/neuter has a positive effect on the accuracy, when considering common/neuter systems as the reference level. Within all three systems, masculine/feminine has the highest coefficient (0.12), which implies that transfers between languages having masculine/feminine gender systems generally result in higher accuracy than masculine/feminine/neuter and common/neuter. The interactions show that the negative effect of phylogenetic distance on accuracy is attenuated if both languages in the pair have masculine/feminine or

270

Predictor	Estimate	t(1894)	P value
PhyDis	-0.00009	-10.926	< 0.001
m/f	0.12251	12.053	< 0.001
m/f/n	0.06577	6.589	< 0.001
PhyDis:m/f	0.00003	4.104	< 0.001
PhyDis:m/f/n	0.00004	4.679	< 0.001

Table 2: Summary of the regression model: Accuracy as predicted by phylogenetic distance and gender system type (m = masculine, f = feminine, n = neuter).

masculine/feminine/neuter gender systems.

4 Gender transfer at the word level

In this section, we perform a finer-grained analysis: focus not on languages, but on individual nouns. Our main question is if there are any patterns in the distribution of errors. Is it random or are certain classes of nouns systematically more difficult to predict than others?

To obtain a single prediction for every noun from the 10 random-seed runs, we pick the gender which has the largest sum of confidence scores (softmax activation values). This is virtually equivalent to taking the gender that gets most votes across the runs, but has an advantage of avoiding ties.

We test whether the following factors play a role: how frequent a noun is, whether it is animate or not and whether its form is equivalent to lemma (citation form, baseform) or not.

It is reasonable to expect that embeddings of frequent nouns will capture more useful information and thus yield better accuracy. Note, however, that very infrequent nouns (frequency <5) have already been excluded from consideration, since for them the embeddings are not available. We calculate frequency of every noun form using the UD corpora.

Nouns denoting living beings, especially human beings, can be expected to yield higher accuracy, since for them the semantic motivation behind gender assignment is often more transparent (based on biological sex). That is not always the case (cf. the already-mentioned German *Mädchen* 'girl', which is neuter), and the proportion of nouns where grammatical gender is predicted by biological sex is likely to vary across languages. Furthermore, it is unknown to what extent the embeddings can actually capture the relevant semantics. Nonetheless, at least in some cases sex can predict gender (cf. French *garçon* 'boy' and *fille* 'girl', or Russian *kot* 'tomcat' and *koška* 'female cat' that are resp.

masculine and feminine). For nouns that do not denote living things no such predictor is known.

As a proxy for "denoting a living thing" we use the animacy category available in some UD treebanks for Slavic languages (Czech, Slovak, Polish, Russian, Ukrainian, Slovenian and Croatian). In Slavic, animacy is manifested on the grammatical level, primarily through differential object marking (Janda, forthcoming). Animacy annotation is also available in the Hindi-PUD treebank, but that treebank lacks lemmas, which makes it unsuitable for our analysis; see below.

We extract animacy information in the following way: we go through all treebanks available for every language and calculate how often a form is annotated as "animate" or "inanimate". Polish has more detailed annotation: animate human and animate non-human, we collapse these two categories into "animate". Note that Slavic animacy is a formal feature that is not exactly isomorphic to living vs. non-living distinction.

Finally, at least in some languages it is easier to infer gender from the citation form (that is, the form which is equivalent to lemma) than from inflected forms (see (Berdicevskis, forthcoming) for an overview of Slavic languages). This presumably happens because cues are more transparent in the citation form. It can also be easier to learn the cues for the citation form, which is often the most frequent one. We test whether this tendency is observed in our data. Alternatively, we could have tested whether certain morphological features (number: singular vs plural, case: nominative vs oblique etc.) play a role, but the analysis we choose is more universal: it can be applied to any language without adjustments.

Other formal, semantic and historical properties can potentially affect how easy it is to infer the gender of a noun (e.g. whether a noun is a recent borrowing or not), but there is no straightforward way to reliably extract this information for all the nouns in our datasets.

We run two logistic regression models. Both include data only from those language pairs where the target language is one of the seven Slavic languages with detailed animacy information: Czech, Slovak, Polish, Russian, Ukrainian, Slovenian, Croatian. In both models, the dependent variable is whether a noun has its gender correctly predicted by the classifier. In Model 1, the independent variables are frequency, animacy, citation form and phylogenetic distance between source and target languages. It is applied to all language pairs except those where source language is Arabic or Hebrew (since for them the distance cannot be estimated). To the remaining pairs we apply Model 2, which has only three independent variables: frequency, animacy, citation form. The results are reported in Table 3 and Table 4.

Predictor	Estimate	z	P value
Freq	-0.004	-0.95	0.340
Inan	-0.999	-13.4	< 0.001
Non-cit	-0.789	-10.4	< 0.001
PhyDis	-0.0004	-24.4	< 0.001
Freq:Inan	0.006	1.4	0.168
Freq:Non-cit	0.009	2.0	0.042
Inan:Non-cit	-0.311	-3.9	< 0.001
Freq:PhyDis	1e-06	1.0	< 0.302
Inan:PhyDis	5.7e-05	3.0	< 0.003
Non-cit:PhyDis	6.9e-05	3.6	< 0.001
Freq:Inan:Non-cit	-0.009	-2.1	0.034
Freq:Inan:PhyDis	-1.7e-06	-1.6	0.106
Freq:Non-cit:PhyDis	-2.1e-06	-1.9	0.059
Inan:Non-cit:PhyDis	6.5e-05	3.1	0.002
Freq:Inan:Non-cit:PhyDis	2.4e-06	2.2	0.030

Table 3: Summary of Model 1: Correctness of the guess as predicted by noun frequency, animacy (Anim vs Inan), citation form (Cit vs Non-Cit) and phylogenetic distance (PhyDis).

Coefficient	Estimate	z	P value
Freq	-0.003	-0.4	0.707
Inan	-1.871	-14.0	< 0.001
Non-cit	-1.455	-10.7	< 0.001
Freq:Inan	0.002	0.3	0.800
Freq:Non-cit	0.002	0.3	0.7744
Inan:Non-cit	0.852	6.0	< 0.001
Freq:Inan:Non-cit	-0.001	-0.1	0.897

Table 4: Summary of Model 2 (Arabic and Hebrew as source languages): Correctness of the guess as predicted by noun frequency, animacy (Anim vs Inan) and citation form (Cit vs Non-Cit).

Model 1 (Indo-European languages only) shows that the prediction accuracy is significantly lower for inanimate nouns than for animate nouns and for inflected forms than for citation forms. The following predictors also have significant negative effects: the interaction of inanimacy and non-citation form; the interaction of frequency, inanimacy and non-citation form; phylogenetic distance between source and target languages (the coefficient is small, but it shows change per year, and the distance in

our dataset vary from approx. 300 to 5000 years). Interestingly, all other significant predictors (most of which all are interactions of distance with other predictors) are positive. It means that the negative effects (for instance, those of inanimacy and non-citation form) described above are smaller for less related languages. The negative effect of inflected forms is also smaller for more frequent nouns.

Model 2 (Afro-Asiatic languages as source) shows similar results: inanimacy and non-citation forms have significant and strong negative effect. This similarity with Model 1 provides further evidence in favor of the universal factors in gender assignment. What is different, however, is that the interaction of these two factors has a strong positive effect (that is, inflected forms of inanimate nouns have higher accuracy than can be expected).

Finally, we perform one more test. Our results indicate that gender systems are partly transferable across non-related languages (see Section 3.1), which suggests there are certain universalities in gender assignment. We want to test whether these universalities are limited to the aforementioned fact that grammatical gender for living creatures closely (even though not perfectly) matches biological sex. To investigate that, we focus on those language pairs where source language is Afro-Asiatic and target language is one of those for which the animacy information is available. From these pairs, we exclude those treebanks where animacy is annotated only for a small proportion of nouns (Slovenian and Croatian), and that leaves us with 10 pairs (Arabic and Hebrew as source, Russian, Czech, Polish, Slovak and Ukrainian as target). We focus on inanimate nouns only (thus eliminating any possible contribution of biological sex) and test whether the classifier still performs above the chance baseline. With only 10 datapoints, we cannot run a reliable t-test. Instead, we perform 10 simulation tests, running a naive classifier that guesses the gender relying solely on the source-language probabilities 10000 times for every language pair and taking the proportion of cases when it achieves the same accuracy as our classifier (or higher) as the p-value. The p-value is 0 in all pairs apart from four: Arabic $\rightarrow$ Czech: 0.009, Arabic $\rightarrow$ Polish: 0.718, Arabic $\rightarrow$ Slovak: 0.923, Hebrew $\rightarrow$ Polish: 0.003. In other words, in eight cases out of 10, the classifier, applied only to inanimate nouns, still performs significantly better than chance.

5   Conclusion

This study investigates how grammatical gender is transferable across languages from a transfer learning point of view. The cross-lingual word embeddings are considered as the source of knowledge shared between languages from which the grammatical gender of nouns are predicted using a multi-layer perceptron. The empirical results reveals that there exist some universal and lineage-specific patterns in the grammatical gender assignment.

First, our analysis of gender transfer between Afro-Asiatic and Indo-European languages indicated that partly successful gender transfer is possible between non-related languages. This observation supports the existence of universal factors in gender assignment. The accuracy of the classifier is higher than the random baseline even when it is tested on inanimate nouns only, which means that the universal factors are not limited to biological sex.

Second, our analysis of gender transfer between Indo-European languages demonstrates that the phylogenetic distance between languages has a negative effect on the success of the transfer, which suggests that some factors of gender assignment are not universal. These results match with the literature by showing that gender assignment is a mixture of universal and idiosyncratic factors.

Third, we also found that gender transfer does not work in the same way for all nouns. The prediction accuracy is significantly lower for inanimate nouns than for animate nouns and for inflected forms than for citation forms. This effect is found when considering both family-internal and family-external transfers, which provides further evidence in favor of the universal factors in gender assignment.

We would like to make a few caveats and suggestions about the future development of the current study. While we address the universality of gender assignment cross-linguistically, our data is restricted to languages from two families and our word embeddings are trained on data from specific domains. Additional data from a more diverse sample is needed to further confirm our observations. Furthermore, we cannot fully exclude that the observed similarities are an areal effect caused by contact.

It should also be noted that we cannot identify which universal factors enable the classifier to perform above the baseline. A more fine-grained word-level analysis would be required to find the possible contributors to this. Linguistically, grammatical gender is strongly tied to the semantic and formal properties of nouns. Since the cross-lingual word embeddings used in this study encode both the formal and semantic information, we cannot disentangle the relative contributions of form and semantics to gender transfer.

Finally, it should be mentioned that an important line of research in modern NLP focuses on gender bias present in naturally occurring texts (Caliskan et al., 2017; Gonen et al., 2019). The combination of these questions and approaches with our perspective might become an interesting research direction.

Supplementary materials, including raw data and scripts for analysis are openly available.[5]

Acknowledgments

The authors are thankful for the constructive comments from the anonymous referees and editors, which helped to significantly improve the quality of the paper. The second author is thankful for the support of the IDEXLYON (16-IDEX-0005) Fellowship grant.

References

Jacob Andreas and Dan Klein. 2014. How much do word embeddings encode about syntax? In *Proceedings of the 52nd Annual Meeting of the Association for Computational Linguistics (Volume 2: Short Papers)*, pages 822–827, Baltimore, Maryland. Association for Computational Linguistics.

Mikel Artetxe, Gorka Labaka, and Eneko Agirre. 2017. Learning bilingual word embeddings with (almost) no bilingual data. In *Proceedings of the 55th Annual Meeting of the Association for Computational Linguistics (Volume 1: Long Papers)*, pages 451–462, Vancouver, Canada. Association for Computational Linguistics.

Mikel Artetxe, Gorka Labaka, Iñigo Lopez-Gazpio, and Eneko Agirre. 2018. Uncovering divergent linguistic information in word embeddings with lessons for intrinsic and extrinsic evaluation. In *Proceedings of the 22nd Conference on Computational Natural Language Learning*, pages 282–291, Brussels, Belgium. Association for Computational Linguistics.

Jenny Audring. 2016. Gender. In Mark Aronoff, editor, *Oxford research encyclopedia of linguistics*. Oxford University Press, Oxford.

---

[5]https://github.com/marctang/Cross-lingual-embeddings-Grammatical-gender

Ali Basirat, Marc Allassonnière-Tang, and Aleksandrs Berdicevskis. in press. An empirical study on the contribution of formal and semantic features to the grammatical gender of nouns. *Linguistics Vanguard*.

Ali Basirat and Marc Tang. 2019. Linguistic information in word embeddings. In *Agents and Artificial Intelligence*, pages 492–513, Cham. Springer International Publishing.

Nicoleta Bateman and Maria Polinsky. 2010. Romanian as a two-gender language. In *Hypothesis A/Hypothesis B*, pages 41–77. MIT Press.

Aleksandrs Berdicevskis. forthcoming. Gender and declension. In Neil Bermel and Jan Fellerer, editors, *Oxford Guides to the World's Languages: The Slavonic Languages*. Oxford University Press.

Piotr Bojanowski, Edouard Grave, Armand Joulin, and Tomas Mikolov. 2017. Enriching word vectors with subword information. *Transactions of the Association for Computational Linguistics*, 5:135–146.

Aylin Caliskan, Joanna J Bryson, and Arvind Narayanan. 2017. Semantics derived automatically from language corpora contain human-like biases. *Science*, 356(6334):183–186.

Will Chang, Chundra Cathcart, David Hall, and Andrew Garrett. 2015. Ancestry-constrained phylogenetic analysis supports the Indo-European steppe hypothesis. *Language*, 91(1):194–244.

Alexis Conneau, Guillaume Lample, Marc'Aurelio Ranzato, Ludovic Denoyer, and Hervé Jégou. 2018. Word translation without parallel data.

G. G. Corbett. 2001. Grammatical gender. In *International Encyclopedia of the Social Sciences*, pages 6335–6340.

Greville G Corbett. 1991. *Gender*. Cambridge University Press, Cambridge.

Greville G Corbett. 2013a. Number of Genders. In Matthew S Dryer and Martin Haspelmath, editors, *The World Atlas of Language Structures Online*. Max Planck Institute for Evolutionary Anthropology, Leipzig.

Greville G Corbett. 2013b. Sex-based and non-sex-based gender systems. In Matthew S Dryer and Martin Haspelmath, editors, *The world atlas of language structures online*. Max Planck Institute for Evolutionary Anthropology, Leipzig.

Greville G Corbett and Norman Fraser. 2000. Gender assignment: A typology and a model. In Gunter Senft, editor, *Systems of nominal classification*, pages 293–325. Cambridge University Press, Cambridge.

Francesca Di Garbo, Bruno Olsson, and Bernhard Wälchli. 2019. Grammatical gender and linguistic complexity : Volume ii: World-wide comparative studies.

Hans-Olav Enger. 2017. The Nordic languages in the 19th century II: Morphology. In Oskar Bandle, Kurt Braunmüller, Ernst Hakon Jahr, Allan Karker, Hans-Peter Naumann, Ulf Teleman, Lennart Elmevik, and Gun Widmark, editors, *The Nordic Languages, Part 2*, pages 1437–1442. De Gruyter, Berlin.

Sebastian Fedden and Greville G Corbett. 2019. The continuing challenge of the German gender system. *Paper presented at the International Symposium of Morphology*.

Hila Gonen, Yova Kementchedjhieva, and Yoav Goldberg. 2019. How does grammatical gender affect noun representations in gender-marking languages? In *Proceedings of the 23rd Conference on Computational Natural Language Learning (CoNLL)*, pages 463–471, Hong Kong, China. Association for Computational Linguistics.

Laura Janda. forthcoming. Gender and animacy. In Neil Bermel and Jan Fellerer, editors, *Oxford Guides to the World's Languages: The Slavonic Languages*. Oxford University Press.

Scott Jarvis and Aneta Pavlenko. 2010. *Crosslinguistic influence in language and cognition*, paperback ed edition. Routledge, New York, NY. OCLC: 845735473.

Armand Joulin, Piotr Bojanowski, Tomas Mikolov, Hervé Jégou, and Edouard Grave. 2018. Loss in translation: Learning bilingual word mapping with a retrieval criterion. In *Proceedings of the 2018 Conference on Empirical Methods in Natural Language Processing*.

David Kemmerer. 2017. Categories of object concepts across languages and brains: the relevance of nominal classification systems to cognitive neuroscience. *Language, Cognition and Neuroscience*, 32(4):401–424.

Tomas Mikolov, Quoc V Le, and Ilya Sutskever. 2013. Exploiting similarities among languages for machine translation. *arXiv preprint arXiv:1309.4168*.

Vivi Nastase and Marius Popescu. 2009. What's in a name? In some languages, grammatical gender. In *Proceedings of the 2009 Conference on Empirical Methods in Natural Language Processing*, pages 1368–1377, Singapore. Association for Computational Linguistics.

Adam Paszke, Sam Gross, Francisco Massa, Adam Lerer, James Bradbury, Gregory Chanan, Trevor Killeen, Zeming Lin, Natalia Gimelshein, Luca Antiga, Alban Desmaison, Andreas Kopf, Edward Yang, Zachary DeVito, Martin Raison, Alykhan Tejani, Sasank Chilamkurthy, Benoit Steiner, Lu Fang,

Junjie Bai, and Soumith Chintala. 2019. Pytorch: An imperative style, high-performance deep learning library. In H. Wallach, H. Larochelle, A. Beygelzimer, F. dAlché-Buc, E. Fox, and R. Garnett, editors, *Advances in Neural Information Processing Systems 32*, pages 8024–8035. Curran Associates, Inc.

Curt Rice. 2006. Optimizing gender. *Lingua*, 116(9):1394–1417.

Sebastian Ruder, Ivan Vulić, and Anders Søgaard. 2019. A survey of cross-lingual word embedding models. *J. Artif. Int. Res.*, 65(1):569–630.

Laura Sabourin, Laurie A Stowe, and Ger J De Haan. 2006. Transfer effects in learning a second language grammatical gender system. *Second Language Research*, 22(1):1–29.

Frank Seifart. 2010. Nominal classification. *Language and Linguistics Compass*, 4(8):719–736.

Samuel L Smith, David HP Turban, Steven Hamblin, and Nils Y Hammerla. 2017. Offline bilingual word vectors, orthogonal transformations and the inverted softmax.

Hiroya Takamura, Ryo Nagata, and Yoshifumi Kawasaki. 2016. Discriminative analysis of linguistic features for typological study. In *Proceedings of the Tenth International Conference on Language Resources and Evaluation (LREC'16)*, pages 69–76, Portorož, Slovenia. European Language Resources Association (ELRA).

Adina Williams, Damian Blasi, Lawrence Wolf-Sonkin, Hanna Wallach, and Ryan Cotterell. 2019. Quantifying the semantic core of gender systems. In *Proceedings of the 2019 Conference on Empirical Methods in Natural Language Processing and the 9th International Joint Conference on Natural Language Processing (EMNLP-IJCNLP)*, pages 5734–5739, Hong Kong, China. Association for Computational Linguistics.

Chao Xing, Dong Wang, Chao Liu, and Yiye Lin. 2015. Normalized word embedding and orthogonal transform for bilingual word translation. In *Proceedings of the 2015 Conference of the North American Chapter of the Association for Computational Linguistics: Human Language Technologies*, pages 1006–1011, Denver, Colorado. Association for Computational Linguistics.

Daniel Zeman, Joakim Nivre, et al. 2020. Universal dependencies 2.6. LINDAT/CLARIAH-CZ digital library at the Institute of Formal and Applied Linguistics (ÚFAL), Faculty of Mathematics and Physics, Charles University.

Meng Zhang, Yang Liu, Huanbo Luan, and Maosong Sun. 2017. Adversarial training for unsupervised bilingual lexicon induction. In *Proceedings of the 55th Annual Meeting of the Association for Computational Linguistics (Volume 1: Long Papers)*, pages 1959–1970, Vancouver, Canada. Association for Computational Linguistics.

Modelling Lexical Ambiguity with Density Matrices

Francois Meyer
University of Amsterdam
`francoisrmeyer@gmail.com`

Martha Lewis
University of Bristol,
ILLC, University of Amsterdam
`martha.lewis@bristol.ac.uk`

Abstract

Words can have multiple senses. Compositional distributional models of meaning have been argued to deal well with finer shades of meaning variation known as polysemy, but are not so well equipped to handle word senses that are etymologically unrelated, or homonymy. Moving from vectors to density matrices allows us to encode a probability distribution over different senses of a word, and can also be accommodated within a compositional distributional model of meaning. In this paper we present three new neural models for learning density matrices from a corpus, and test their ability to discriminate between word senses on a range of compositional datasets. When paired with a particular composition method, our best model outperforms existing vector-based compositional models as well as strong sentence encoders.

1 Introduction

An integral part of natural language understanding is the ability to handle lexical ambiguity. Words can have multiple meanings, and the precise meaning of a word only becomes clear when we see it in use - the surrounding context disambiguates it. Word sense disambiguation (WSD) is said to be an 'AI complete' problem (Navigli, 2009), that is, a problem that is at least as hard as any other problem in AI, and as such has been the subject of extensive research. Standard approaches treat WSD as a classification problem: given a word in context, the task is to classify it into one of a range of possible senses (Lesk, 1986; Schütze, 1998; Navigli, 2009). A more difficult task is to disambiguate every word in a sentence (Chaplot and Salakhutdinov, 2018). A summary of the state of the art is given in (Raganato et al., 2017). More recently, neural approaches (Hadiwinoto et al., 2019; Huang et al., 2019) use contextualised embeddings

as input to WSD systems, together with knowledge from WordNet. Other neural approaches generate multiple sense vectors per word (Neelakantan et al., 2014; Cheng and Kartsaklis, 2015) or vectors representing a context (Melamud et al., 2016).

Disambiguation can be costly. Each word should be disambiguated with respect to the correct senses of the other words in the sentence, meaning that the computational complexity of the task can become problematic (Chaplot and Salakhutdinov, 2018). Within a compositional framework, the idea is for words to disambiguate automatically in the process of composition (Kintsch, 2001; Mitchell and Lapata, 2008; Baroni et al., 2014; Boleda, 2020).

Within purely vector-based models, the amount of ambiguity that a word vector can represent is limited. Baroni et al. (2014) argue that distributional vectors work well for polysemy, but less so for homonymy. Piedeleu et al. (2015) extend the vector based model of meaning to encompass homonymy by using the notion of a *density matrix*. These can be used to encode a probability distribution over possible meanings of a word in a single representation. Density matrices can also be accommodated within a compositional framework, allowing the ambiguity encoded in the matrix to be resolved via composition.

We use density matrices within a compositional distributional framework to model word and sentence meaning. We propose three new models for building density matrices, based on neural word embedding models. We survey several composition methods for density matrices and evaluate how well our density matrices encode ambiguity and to what extent the composition methods achieve disambiguation, on four disambiguation datasets that test disambiguation in a compositional setting. One of our models (multi-sense Word2DM) emerges as the best model overall. When paired with a particular composition method (Phaser), multi-sense

276

Proceedings of the 24th Conference on Computational Natural Language Learning, pages 276–290
Online, November 19-20, 2020. ©2020 Association for Computational Linguistics
https://doi.org/10.18653/v1/P17

Word2DM outperforms all other models (including existing baselines and high-performing sentence encoders) on most of the disambiguation tasks.

2 Background

Compositional distributional models come in a range of flavours. Mitchell and Lapata (2008) use simple element-wise operations on vectors. More recently, neural models of composition (Socher et al., 2012; Bowman et al., 2015) and large networks such as BERT (Devlin et al., 2019) have been extremely successful. A third flavour is the type-logical tensor-based models of composition (Baroni and Zamparelli, 2010; Coecke et al., 2010; Paperno et al., 2014; Sadrzadeh and Muskens, 2018). The tensor-based model of composition works as follows. We choose a vector space N for nouns, and another S for sentences, and represent relational words as multilinear maps over these spaces. Intransitive verbs are represented as linear maps $N \to S$, i.e. matrices in $N \otimes S$. Transitive verbs are represented as maps from two copies of N to S, i.e. order 3 tensors or 'cubes' of parameters in $N \otimes S \otimes N$. Composition is performed via *tensor contraction* - an extension of matrix multiplication. Matrices and tensors require many parameters. To alleviate this problem, Grefenstette and Sadrzadeh (2011a,b); Kartsaklis et al. (2012) develop ways of building matrices and tensors from word vectors, some of which are described in section 4.1.1.

We use an extension of the tensor-based approach, based on methods given in Piedeleu et al. (2015); Bankova et al. (2018). Nouns and sentences are represented as *density matrices* and relational words (adjectives, verbs, etc.) are represented as *completely positive maps*, which take density matrices to density matrices.

Representing words with density matrices A density matrix over $\mathbb{R}^n$ is a matrix of the form

$$\rho = \sum_i p_i \vec{v_i}\vec{v_i}^\top \tag{1}$$

where $\{p_i\}_i$ are the probabilities assigned to the vectors $\{\vec{v_i}\}_i$. Density matrices over $\mathbb{R}^n$ are:

1. Symmetric: $\rho^\top = \rho$.
2. Positive semidefinite: $\forall \vec{x} \in \mathbb{R}^n,\ \vec{x}^\top \rho \vec{x} \geq 0$
3. Unit trace: $\mathrm{tr}(\rho) = 1$

To represent words, we view each word as a probability distribution over senses, and we view the vectors $\vec{v_i}$ in equation (1) as representing its different senses. For example, the word *bright* could mean *shiny* or *clever*. Suppose that when *bright* is used, it is twice as likely to mean *shiny* as it is to mean *clever*. The density matrix for *bright*, denoted ⟦bright⟧, is computed as follows:

$$⟦\text{bright}⟧ = \frac{2}{3}\overrightarrow{\text{shiny}}\,\overrightarrow{\text{shiny}}^\top + \frac{1}{3}\overrightarrow{\text{clever}}\,\overrightarrow{\text{clever}}^\top$$

Composition with density matrices Since we are working with density matrices, nouns are now maps $N \to N$, i.e. matrices in $N \otimes N$. Sentences are matrices in $S \otimes S$. This means that intransitive verbs are order-4 tensors that take a noun density matrix as input and give back a sentence density matrix. They live in a space $N \otimes N \otimes S \otimes S$. Transitive verbs are order-6 tensors. Clearly, these spaces get very big very quickly.

To deal with this increase in dimensionality, tricks to create completely positive maps out of density matrices have been proposed (Lewis, 2019b; Coecke and Meichanetzidis, 2020). This allows composition mechanisms to be specified at the level of density matrices, rather than having to work in the high-order spaces described above. We describe these composition mechanisms in section 3.2.

Other applications of density matrices in NLP include modelling entailment in a compositional setting (Balkir et al., 2015; Bankova et al., 2018; Sadrzadeh et al., 2018; Lewis, 2019a; Bradley and Vlassopoulos, 2020). Blacoe et al. (2013) also use density matrices to model ambiguity, but in a different setting.

WSD in compositional distributional semantics Baroni et al. (2014) argue that compositional distributional semantic models are particularly able to pick out the more subtle shades of meaning termed *polysemy*. This idea is used in (Mitchell and Lapata, 2008; Grefenstette and Sadrzadeh, 2011a,b; Kartsaklis et al., 2013), where a range of semantic composition models are tested on datasets built to distinguish different senses of words in context. Neural and distributional models for disambiguation are compared in Milajevs et al. (2014), and the role of ellipsis in disambiguation is investigated in Wijnholds and Sadrzadeh (2019).

3 Methods

3.1 Density Matrix Models

We now introduce the three novel methods that we propose for building density matrices.

3.1.1 BERT2DM

Algorithm 1: BERT2DM training

---

for *each sentence s in a corpus* **do**
| Process s with BERT.
| Extract and store the contextualised embeddings produced by BERT for the words in s.
end
Discard all contextualised embeddings corresponding to stop words.
Apply PCA/SVD to the remaining contextualised embeddings.
for *each word v in the vocabulary* **do**
| Compute the density matrix of v as

$$[\![v]\!] = \sum_{i \in \mathrm{ind}(v)} \vec{v_i}\, \vec{v_i}^{\top},$$

| where $\mathrm{ind}(v)$ are the indices at which the word v occurs in the corpus and $\vec{v_i}$ is the reduced embedding for v.
end

BERT (Devlin et al., 2019) produces *contextualised embeddings* for words and sentences. Given a sentence, it produces vectors for each word that are specific to that particular context (BERT actually models subword units, but we average the subword embeddings of a word to obtain a contextualised word embedding). BERT2DM uses the contextualised embeddings of BERT to build density matrices that encode multiple senses of a word. BERT is applied to a corpus and the contextualised embeddings for a word w are combined to compute w's density matrix according to equation (1). The procedure is outlined in algorithm 1.

Since the vectors produced by BERT are fairly large, we apply a dimensionality reduction step (either PCA or SVD) over all content word embeddings before combining to form a density matrix.

We also experiment with clustering the contextual embeddings of a word and applying dimensionality reduction to the cluster centroids instead of the contextualised embeddings. The motivation for this is that clustering contextualised embeddings can produce clusters that correspond to distinct senses (as shown by Wiedemann et al. (2019)).

3.1.2 Word2DM

Word2DM is an extension of Word2Vec (Mikolov et al., 2013a,b) skip-gram with negative sampling

---

Algorithm 2: Word2DM training

---

for *each word v in the vocabulary* **do**
| Randomly initialise a $n \times m$ matrix B_v.
end
for *each target word w_t in the corpus* **do**
| **for** *each context word w_c* **do**
| | Sample K negative samples from some noise distribution.
| | Maximise equation 2 with respect to B_t, B_c, and B_{w_k} for $k = 1, ...K$.
| **end**
end
for *each word v in the vocabulary* **do**
| Compute its density matrix as $A_v = B_v B_v^{\top}$.
end

(SGNS). SGNS modifies word vectors to become closer to words they do occur with, and further away from words they don't occur with (the negative samples). When extending the SGNS algorithm to produce density matrices, we must ensure that the matrices satisfy the conditions resulting from their definition: symmetry, positive semidefiniteness, and unit trace. The first and last are easy to enforce, but preserving positivity is more challenging. To preserve positivity, we utilise the following property of positive semi-definiteness:

Property 3.1. *For any matrix B, the product $BB^{\top}$ is positive semi-definite.*

We enforce positive semi-definiteness by training the weights of an intermediary matrix B and computing our density matrix as $A = BB^{\top}$. By updating the weights of B and computing A we indirectly train positive semi-definite matrices. We modify the training objective of SGNS to maximise the similarity of the density matrices of co-occurring words. The objective function at each target-context prediction is then:

$$J(\theta) = \log \sigma(\mathrm{tr}(A_t A_c)) + \sum_{k=1}^{K} \log \sigma(-\mathrm{tr}(A_t A_{w_k}))$$

$$(2)$$

where A_t and A_c are the the density matrices of the target and context words respectively, $A_1, A_2, ..., A_K$ are the density matrices of K negative samples, and θ is the set of weights of the intermediary matrices B_t, B_c and $B_1, B_2, ..., B_K$.

Word2DM is a straightforward extension of Word2Vec for learning density matrices. However, it turns out that enforcing positive semi-definiteness by introducing intermediary matrices leads to sub-optimal training updates. This can be shown by examining the gradients of equation (2) with respect to the intermediary matrices (derivation in supplementary material).

3.1.3 Multi-sense Word2DM

Multi-sense Word2DM is a modification of Word2DM designed to overcome the gradient issues of Word2DM and to explicitly model ambiguity. Multi-sense Word2DM achieves this through the following changes to Word2DM:

- The columns of the intermediary $n \times m$ matrix B now represent the m different senses of the word. Each sense of a word has its own n-dimensional embedding. The density matrix of a word is still computed as before, and can be expressed in terms of the sense embeddings as

$$A = BB^{\top} = \sum_{i=1}^{m} \vec{b_i}\,\vec{b_i}^{\top} \quad (3)$$

where $\vec{b_1}, ..., \vec{b_m}$ are the columns of B corresponding to different senses.
- Each word is also associated with a single vector v_w, which represents it as a context word.
- The following objective function is maximised:

$$J(\theta) = \log \sigma(b_t^{\top} c_t) + \sum_{k=1}^{K} \log \sigma(-b_t^{\top} v_{w_k}) \quad (4)$$

where c_t is the sum of context vectors for all words surrounding the target word and b_t is the the embedding for the relevant sense of the target word. We select b_t by finding the column of B_t most similar to c_t (measured by either cosine similarity or dot product). The full training procedure is outlined in algorithm 3.

Multi-sense Word2DM explicitly models ambiguity by letting the columns of the intermediary matrix represent the different senses of a word. During training the column closest to the context embedding is selected as the relevant sense embedding and only this column is updated. This enables the model to avoid the gradient issues of Word2DM. The objective function being maximised (equation 4) has the same gradient as Word2Vec and therefore does not lead to suboptimal training updates.

3.2 Composition methods

The composition methods we use are based on methods in (Lewis, 2019a; Coecke and Meichanet-zidis, 2020). These reduce the high-dimensional representations needed for relation words to com-position of density matrices. The relational word is seen as a map that takes nouns as arguments. The composition methods are as follows, using the example of an adjective modifying a noun:

Add : $[\![\text{adj}]\!] + [\![\text{noun}]\!]$
Mult : $[\![\text{adj}]\!] \odot [\![\text{noun}]\!]$
Tensor : $[\![\text{adj}]\!] \otimes [\![\text{adj}]\!] \times [\![\text{noun}]\!]$, where $\otimes$ denotes the Kronecker product and $\times$ denotes tensor contraction.
Phaser : $[\![\text{adj}]\!]^{1/2}[\![\text{noun}]\!][\![\text{adj}]\!]^{1/2}$

More complex phrases are combined according to their parse. So, a transitive sentence modified with an adjective is composed as $(\text{subj}(\text{verb}(\text{adj obj})))$. For example, composing the sentence *Bob likes old cars* would consist of the following steps:

$$[\![\text{old cars}]\!] = f([\![\text{old}]\!], [\![\text{cars}]\!])$$
$$[\![\text{likes old cars}]\!] = f([\![\text{likes}]\!], [\![\text{old cars}]\!])$$
$$[\![\text{Bob likes old cars}]\!] = f([\![\text{Bob}]\!], [\![\text{likes old cars}]\!])$$

where the composer f can be substituted by any of the composition methods listed above.

4 Experimental Setup

We evaluate our models on three tasks - word similarity, disambiguation, and a word level ambiguity analysis. The code for training and evaluating our models has been made available at `https://github.com/francois-meyer/lexical-ambiguity-dms`. In this section we introduce the experimental setup used in all of these tasks.

4.1 Baselines

Throughout the experiments we compare our models to existing word and sentence embedding models. For our word embedding baselines we use embeddings produced by three existing models - Word2Vec, GloVe, and FastText. We use the publicly available[1] embeddings trained by Wijn-holds and Sadrzadeh (2019). The embeddings are 300-dimensional and were trained on the combined and lemmatised ukWaC and Wackypedia corpora[2]. In the tasks that involve sentence-level semantics (the disambiguation tasks) we compare our models

---

[1] https://github.com/gijswijnholds/compdisteval-ellipsis
[2] wacky.sslmit.unibo.it

Algorithm 3: MS-Word2DM training

---

for *each word w in the vocabulary* **do**
    Randomly initialise a $n \times m$ matrix B_w and a n-dimensional vector v_w.
end

for *each target word w_t in the corpus* **do**
    Sum the context vectors of the words surrounding w_t within a window of size $2l$ to get a context embedding c_t:

$$c_t = \sum_{i=t-l, i \neq t}^{t+l} v_i$$

    Compute the similarity (with either cosine similarity or dot product) of the columns $b_1, ..., b_m$ of B_t and c_t and extract the most similar column as b_t (the embedding of the relevant sense).
    Sample K negative samples from some noise distribution. Maximise equation 4 with regards to b_t, c_t, and v_{w_k} for $k = 1, ...K$.
end

for *each word v in the vocabulary* **do**
    Compute its density matrix as $A_v = B_v B_v^\top$.
end

---

to existing compositional distributional semantic (CDS) models and neural sentence encoders.

4.1.1 CDS models

CDS models compute a sentence vector as a function of the distributional vectors of the words in the sentence. We use the pre-trained word embeddings of Wijnholds and Sadrzadeh (2019) and compute sentence embeddings by either summing, element-wise multiplying, or applying tensor-based composition. For the phrase *big house* with vectors $\overrightarrow{big}$ and $\overrightarrow{house}$ the different compositional distributional methods will be computed as follows:

Add : $\overrightarrow{big} + \overrightarrow{house}$
Mult : $\overrightarrow{big} \odot \overrightarrow{house}$
Tensor : $\overrightarrow{big} \times \overrightarrow{big}^\top \times \overrightarrow{house}$

4.1.2 Sentence encoders

We compare our models to two well-known neural sentence encoders - InferSent (Conneau et al., 2017) and BERT (Devlin et al., 2019). InferSent embeddings are 4096-dimensional, which is much larger than the word embeddings used in our CDS baselines. We use two pre-trained InferSent models that are publicly available[3], referred to as InferSent1 and InferSent2 in our results. We also compare our models to BERT as a sentence encoder. BERT produces an embedding for the entire sentence by adding a special classification token (`[CLS]`) to the start of every sequence. When BERT is used in a sentence-level task, the `[CLS]` embedding can be used as a semantic representation for the entire sentence.

Some of our evaluation data contains phrases that are not fully formed sentences. To ensure a fair comparison, we convert all phrases to fully formed sentences for evaluation of the sentence encoders. We added "the" before noun phrases and converted verbs to their present tense form.

4.1.3 Context2DM

We also compare our models to a baseline density matrix model, which we call Context2DM. It is based on the procedure of Schütze (1998) for building multi-sense embeddings. Context2DM builds the density matrix of a word w as follows:

1. Context embeddings are obtained for all the contexts in which w occurs (computed by summing the pre-trained embeddings of all the words that occur around w in a particular context).
2. These context embeddings are clustered (using hierarchical agglomerative clustering for $k = 2, ..., 10$ and the variance reduction criterion to select the number of clusters) and the resulting cluster centroids subsequently represent the different senses of w.
3. The density matrix of w is computed as the mixture of its sense embeddings i.e. the sum of the outer products of the cluster centroids, normalised to have unit trace.

For the pre-trained word embeddings required for step 1 of the above procedure, we use 17-dimensional word embeddings, trained with the gensim implementation[4] of Word2Vec on the combined ukWaC+Wackypedia corpus.

4.2 Training

All our density matrices are 17×17 (so 289 parameters). This is closest in size to the 300-dimensional baseline embeddings. We train our

---

[3]https://github.com/facebookresearch/InferSent
[4]https://radimrehurek.com/gensim/models/word2vec

Data set	Format	High similarity example	Low similarity example	# Pairs	# Annotators
ML2008	S$\underline{V}$	value slump value decline	value slump value slouch	120	53
GS2011	S$\underline{V}$O	people buy house people purchase house	people buy house people bribe house	200	25
GS2012	AS$\underline{V}$AO	local family run small hotel local family operate small hotel	local family run small hotel local family move small hotel	194	50
KS2013 -CoNLL	AS$\underline{V}$AO	young woman file long nail young woman smooth long nail	young woman file long nail young woman register long nail	194	43

Table 1: Details of the disambiguation data sets (A: adjective, S: subject, V: verb, O: object).

Word2DM and multi-sense Word2DM models on the ukWaC+Wackypedia corpus, consisting of 2.8 billion words. Hyperparameters are provided in the supplementary material. Training these models on a single GPU (Nvidia GeForce GTX 1080 Ti) with 60GB of memory takes around 20 hours per iteration of the training corpus. We present results for four different multi-sense Word2DM models. Two use cosine similarity to compare sense vectors to context vectors, while the other two use the dot product. We also vary the number of senses modelled (the number of columns in the intermediary matrix) between 5 and 10.

We present results for four different BERT2DM models. Two of these cluster the BERT representations into senses before dimensionality reduction, while the other two do not. One of the advantages of clustering the representations is that it reduces the size of the matrix on which dimensionality reduction is applied, so it becomes computationally feasible to train on a larger corpus. We train the unclustered variants on a 10-million word subcorpus of Wackypedia, and the clustered variants on a 20-million word subcorpus. We also vary the dimensionality reduction algorithm between PCA and SVD, to test whether or not centering the contextual embeddings before dimensionality reduction makes any difference. Training BERT2DM takes only a few hours on a 16-core CPU (Intel Xeon Gold 6130) but requires around 4.5GB of memory per 1 million words that it is trained on.

4.3 Data Sets

We test our models on data sets designed to test disambiguation in a compositional setting. Data sets for this task contain sentence pairs with:

- An ambiguous *target* word used in a disambiguating phrase.
- A *landmark* word that has the same meaning as one of the target word's senses.

- Human judgements of how similar the meaning of the phrase is when the ambiguous word is replaced by the landmark word.

We use four disambiguation data sets to evaluate our models. Three of the four data sets - GS2011 (Grefenstette and Sadrzadeh, 2011a), GS2012, and KS2013-CoNLL (Kartsaklis et al., 2013) - are publicly available[5], while ML2008 (Mitchell and Lapata, 2008) was obtained privately from the authors of Wijnholds and Sadrzadeh (2019). We show examples and statistics of the data sets in table 1.

5 Results

We introduce each of the evaluation tasks and present our results. For multi-sense Word2DM and BERT2DM we trained four models each, with different hyperparameter settings (as described in section 4.2 and listed in table 2).

	RG	WS	MC	SL	MEN
Word2Vec	.818	**.662**	**.765**	.404	**.781**
GloVe	**.826**	.571	.732	.399	.773
FastText	.767	.517	.682	**.404**	.768
Context2DM	.228	.234	.331	.094	.267
Word2DM	.541	.473	.452	.157	.540
MS-Word2DM					
- cos, 5 senses	**.768**	.556	**.670**	**.290**	.680
- cos, 10 senses	.727	.580	.659	.256	**.682**
- dot, 5 senses	.662	.578	.568	.247	.663
- dot, 10 senses	.679	**.596**	.612	.281	.663
BERT2DM					
- PCA	.452	.275	.388	.226	.351
- SVD	.428	.317	.392	.234	.327
- PCA + cluster	.383	.219	.381	.153	.251
- SVD + cluster	.315	.205	.294	.091	.207

Table 2: Spearman ρ obtained on word similarity tasks.

	Verb	Mult	Add	Tensor	Phaser
Word2Vec	.215	.256	.299	.231	
GloVe	.332	.098	.304	**.397**	
FastText	.181	.281	.198	.137	
BERT			.140		
InferSent1			.207		
InferSent2			.174		
Context2DM	-.069	-.025	-.058	-.025	-.064
Word2DM	-.022	.057	.010	.057	-.007
MS-Word2DM					
- cos, 5 senses	.235	.195	.254	.195	**.328**
- cos, 10 senses	.248	.204	.210	.204	.217
- dot, 5 senses	.216	.145	.280	.145	.311
- dot, 10 senses	.157	.195	.170	.195	.325
BERT2DM					
- PCA	-.055	-.016	-.101	-.016	-.114
- SVD	.072	.170	.075	.170	.067
- PCA + cluster	.105	.170	.062	.170	.130
- SVD + cluster	.090	-.002	.057	-.002	.049

Table 3: Spearman ρ obtained on ML2008.

	Verb	Mult	Add	Tensor	Phaser
Word2Vec	.209	.203	.268	.204	
GloVe	**.304**	.211	.252	.256	
FastText	.210	.187	.154	.185	
BERT			.266		
InferSent1			.241		
InferSent2			.194		
Context2DM	.037	-.027	.012	-.021	.036
Word2DM	-.059	.001	.019	-.064	-.039
MS-Word2DM					
- cos, 5 senses	.187	.286	.206	.289	**.365**
- cos, 10 senses	.091	.237	.161	.200	<u>.323</u>
- dot, 5 senses	-.016	.091	-.002	.010	.077
- dot, 10 senses	-.021	.116	.025	.131	.118
BERT2DM					
PCA	-.024	-.107	-.001	-.097	-.046
SVD	-.105	-.304	-.078	-.057	-.074
PCA + cluster	-.056	.030	.008	.007	-.028
SVD + cluster	.045	.013	.031	.037	-.029

Table 4: Spearman ρ obtained on GS2011.

5.1 Word Similarity

To validate the quality of our density matrices as general semantic representations we evaluate them on the following standard word similarity data sets: RG (Rubenstein and Goodenough, 1965), WS (Finkelstein et al., 2001), MC (Miller and Charles, 1991), SL (Hill et al., 2015), and MEN (Bruni et al., 2012). We use the evaluation scripts and data sets made publicly available[6] by Faruqui and Dyer (2014). The results are shown in table 2.

Multi-sense Word2DM performs best out of all the density matrix models, achieving scores comparable to the word embeddings. It substantially improves upon Word2DM, supporting our theoretical findings about Word2DM's learning issues. Using cosine similarity to select the relevant sense results in slightly better scores. The BERT2DM models perform worst of all our models, but still demonstrate some ability to judge word similarity. There is no clear performance difference between using PCA or SVD for dimensionality reduction. Clustering the BERT representations before dimensionality reduction leads to worse correlation scores.

5.2 Disambiguation

The results we obtain on the disambiguation data sets are presented in tables 3 to 6. In each of these tables our density matrix models are compared to our baselines. Column headings specify the composition methods used to compute the phrase representation. These do not apply to the sentence encoders (BERT and InferSent). The rightmost composition method (Phaser) does not apply to the CDS models. The leftmost column (Verb) compares the semantic representations of the verbs without composition. The best performing models, among the baselines and the density matrices, are indicated in bold. We compare the best-performing density matrix models to the best-performing baseline using a one-sided paired t-test (applying the Bonferroni correction to account for multiple comparisons). We indicate statistically significant improvements over the baseline models, or statistically equivalent scores, by underlining the corresponding scores.

Multi-sense Word2DM is by far the best performing density matrix model. It outperforms all the baseline models on 3 out of the 4 data sets. Among all the composition methods, Phaser most consistently achieves high correlation scores (especially on the more complex data sets). In some cases BERT2DM achieves correlation scores that are comparable to multi-sense Word2DM and the baselines. But in general the BERT2DM density matrices cannot reliably be used to achieve disambiguation.

5.3 Ambiguity Analysis

To investigate to what extent our models encode ambiguity at a word level, we turn to von Neumann entropy (VNE). For a density matrix $\rho = \sum_i p_i \overrightarrow{v_i} \overrightarrow{v_i}^\top$ the VNE is defined as

$$S(\rho) = -\mathrm{tr}(\rho \ln \rho). \tag{5}$$

<hr>

[6]https://github.com/mfaruqui/eval-word-vectors

	Verb	Mult	Add	Tensor	Phaser
Word2Vec	.270	.155	.334	.260	
GloVe	.413	.219	.297	.231	
FastText	.302	.176	.175	.264	
BERT			**.471**		
InferSent1			.370		
InferSent2			.372		
Context2DM	-.025	.015	-.063	-.033	.005
Word2DM	-.047	.019	-.092	.043	.074
MS-Word2DM					
- cos, 5 senses	.266	.203	.270	.329	**.500**
- cos, 10 senses	.214	.208	.263	.304	.397
- dot, 5 senses	-.067	.068	-.103	.022	.126
- dot, 10 senses	-.059	.082	-.040	.068	.126
BERT2DM					
- PCA	.025	.031	.122	.056	.056
- SVD	-.071	.001	-.042	-.037	-.056
- PCA + cluster	-.232	-.073	-.141	-.155	-.232
- SVD + cluster	-.132	-.117	-.154	-.089	-.172

Table 5: Spearman ρ obtained on GS2012.

	Verb	Mult	Add	Tensor	Phaser
Word2Vec	.201	.222	.194	.190	
GloVe	.152	.154	.127	.083	
FastText	.081	.285	.073	.196	
BERT			**.314**		
InferSent1			.187		
InferSent2			.190		
Context2DM	-.017	-.074	-.037	-.064	-.006
Word2DM	.149	-.118	.114	-.014	.081
MS-Word2DM					
- cos, 5 senses	.135	.075	.190	.147	.309
- cos, 10 senses	.171	.008	.207	.118	.288
- dot, 5 senses	-.026	.034	.039	.117	.275
- dot, 10 senses	.094	.016	.070	.053	**.345**
BERT2DM					
- PCA	.084	.082	.089	.081	.187
- SVD	.037	.160	.054	.128	.037
- PCA + cluster	.075	.075	.073	.067	-.011
- SVD + cluster	.036	-.058	.020	.052	.017

Table 6: Spearman ρ obtained on KS2013-CoNLL.

This can be seen as an extension of Shannon entropy to matrices, and quantifies the amount of information encoded in a density matrix.

We perform two analyses of ambiguity with VNE. First we test whether our density matrices model lexical ambiguity. We do this by investigating whether or not the measured ambiguity of a word's density matrix correlates with the number of meanings associated with the word. Secondly, we perform a systematic analysis of how ambiguity changes when words are composed into phrases. Using the four disambiguation data sets, we measure the VNE before and after composition, expecting ambiguity to decrease after composition. Something similar was done by Piedeleu et al. (2015), at a smaller scale.

For these experiments, we only report results for one variant of multi-sense Word2DM (cosine similarity, 5 senses) and two variants of BERT2DM (SVD and PCA).

Ambiguity and polysemy To determine the number of senses that a word has, we use WordNet synsets (senses) (Miller, 1995). We compute the correlation between the VNE of density matrices and the number of synsets associated with words. The correlation coefficients are shown in table 7 and the relationships are plotted in figure 1.

The results show that both BERT2DM and multi-sense Word2DM successfully encode how ambiguous words are. Word2DM exhibits a very low correlation and Context2DM (not plotted) shows none.

Model	Pearson r	Spearman ρ
Context2DM	-.081	-.043
Word2DM	.053	.112
MS-Word2DM	.296	.295
BERT2DM SVD	.367	.418
BERT2DM PCA	**.405**	**.463**

Table 7: Correlation coefficient between the VNE of a word's density matrix and the number of WordNet synsets to which the word belongs.

Ambiguity and composition VNE allows us to measure how ambiguity evolves through composition. We can compare the ambiguity of a word to the ambiguity of a phrase containing the word. Seeing the context in which a word occurs can reveal which sense of the word is being employed, and should therefore reduce the amount of ambiguity present. The multi-sense Word2DM density matrix for the ambiguous word *run* has a VNE of 1.491. After composition in the sentence *The family run the hotel*, the sentence has a VNE of 0.144, so ambiguity has decreased.

We test whether this phenomenon holds true for our models on the disambiguation data sets, which consist of ambiguous verbs and disambiguating phrases. For each of the data sets we compute the average VNE of the verb density matrices. We compare this to the average VNE of the disambiguating phrases, where the density matrices are composed using different composition methods. The results are presented in tables 8 to 11.

In each of the tables, the leftmost column (Verb) contains the average von Neumann entropy of the

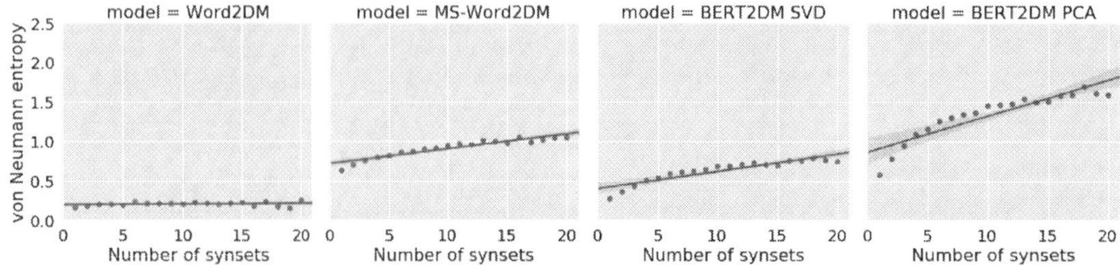

Figure 1: The average VNE of density matrices plotted against the number of WordNet synsets of words.

	Verb	Mult	Add	Tensor	Phaser
Context2DM	0.344	0.354	0.429	0.354	**0.007**
Word2DM	0.103	0.257	0.707	0.257	**0.019**
MS-Word2DM	0.953	1.751	1.537	1.751	**0.468**
BERT2DM*	0.667	**0.132**	0.938	**0.132**	**0.060**

Table 8: Average VNE before and after composition on ML2008. *SVD variant

	Verb	Mult	Add	Tensor	Phaser
Context2DM	0.174	0.187	0.359	0.402	**0.000**
Word2DM	0.245	0.522	1.096	0.797	**0.038**
MS-Word2DM	1.444	1.821	1.906	4.012	**0.224**
BERT2DM*	0.763	**0.008**	0.961	**0.174**	**0.003**

Table 9: Average VNE before and after composition on GS2011. *SVD variant

	Verb	Mult	Add	Tensor	Phaser
Context2DM	0.167	**0.137**	0.417	0.387	**0.000**
Word2DM	0.140	0.623	1.445	0.908	**0.005**
MS-Word2DM	1.340	**1.181**	2.043	3.534	**0.029**
BERT2DM*	0.659	**0.000**	1.080	**0.014**	**0.000**

Table 10: Average VNE before and after composition on GS2012. *SVD variant

	Verb	Mult	Add	Tensor	Phaser
Context2DM	0.233	**0.183**	0.524	0.537	**0.000**
Word2DM	0.161	0.604	1.405	0.889	**0.010**
MS-Word2DM	1.224	1.453	2.032	3.704	**0.033**
BERT2DM*	0.689	**0.000**	1.124	**0.026**	**0.000**

Table 11: Average VNE before and after composition on KS2013-CoNLL. *SVD variant

ambiguous verbs alone, while the other columns contain the average von Neumann entropy after composing the disambiguating phrases with the different composition methods. Cases where the average von Neumann entropy decreases after composition (as expected) are highlighted in bold.

The results are quite similar across the data sets. Phaser emerges as the best method for decreasing ambiguity through composition. This nicely supports the results of the disambiguation experiments, in which Phaser also emerged as the best composition method for disambiguating the meaning of ambiguous words through composition. Besides Phaser, none of the other composition methods reliably decrease the measured ambiguity.

6 Conclusion and Future Work

In this paper we addressed the problem of modelling ambiguity in NLP, and how ambiguous words can be disambiguated in context. We investigated density matrices as semantic representations for modelling ambiguity. Our results confirmed the value of density matrices over vector-based approaches. Equipped with a compositional frame-work, one of our density matrix models (multi-sense Word2DM) outperformed all other models (including existing compositional models and strong neural baselines) on most of the disambiguation tasks. We also performed a mathematical analysis of the ambiguity encoded by our models. This revealed that the density matrices built by two of our models (multi-sense Word2DM and BERT2DM) reflect true word level ambiguity. We have shown the value in designing neural models that learn density matrices from scratch.

Possible directions for future work includes extending our models to larger datasets and longer sentences, and modifying techniques for differing sentences as in the Word in Context dataset (Pilehvar and Camacho-Collados, 2019) and other WSD tasks. We focused on ambiguity here, but it would be possible to do similar experiments focused on other aspects of meaning such as metaphor or entailment, and examining how these interact with composition.

Acknowledgments

Martha Lewis is supported by NWO Veni grant 'Metaphorical Meanings for Artificial Agents'.

References

Esma Balkir, Mehrnoosh Sadrzadeh, and Bob Coecke. 2015. Distributional sentence entailment using density matrices. In *Proceedings of the First International Conference on Theoretical Topics in Computer Science*, volume 9541, pages 1–22.

Dea Bankova, Bob Coecke, Martha Lewis, and Dan Marsden. 2018. Graded hyponymy for compositional distributional semantics. *Journal of Language Modelling*, 6:225–260.

Marco Baroni, Raffaella Bernardi, Roberto Zamparelli, et al. 2014. Frege in space: A program for compositional distributional semantics. *Linguistic Issues in language technology*, 9(6):5–110.

Marco Baroni and Roberto Zamparelli. 2010. Nouns are vectors, adjectives are matrices: Representing adjective-noun constructions in semantic space. In *Proceedings of the 2010 Conference on Empirical Methods in Natural Language Processing*, pages 1183–1193.

William Blacoe, Elham Kashefi, and Mirella Lapata. 2013. A quantum-theoretic approach to distributional semantics. In *Proceedings of the 2013 Conference of the North American Chapter of the Association for Computational Linguistics: Human Language Technologies*, pages 847–857. Association for Computational Linguistics.

Gemma Boleda. 2020. Distributional semantics and linguistic theory. *Annual Review of Linguistics*.

Samuel Bowman, Christopher Potts, and Christopher D Manning. 2015. Recursive neural networks can learn logical semantics. In *Proceedings of the 3rd workshop on continuous vector space models and their compositionality*, pages 12–21.

Tai-Danae Bradley and Yiannis Vlassopoulos. 2020. Language modeling with reduced densities.

Elia Bruni, Gemma Boleda, Marco Baroni, and Nam-Khanh Tran. 2012. Distributional semantics in technicolor. In *Proceedings of the 50th Annual Meeting of the Association for Computational Linguistics (Volume 1: Long Papers)*, pages 136–145, Jeju Island, Korea. Association for Computational Linguistics.

Devendra Singh Chaplot and Ruslan Salakhutdinov. 2018. Knowledge-based word sense disambiguation using topic models. In *Thirty-Second AAAI Conference on Artificial Intelligence*.

Jianpeng Cheng and Dimitri Kartsaklis. 2015. Syntax-aware multi-sense word embeddings for deep compositional models of meaning. In *Proceedings of the 2015 Conference on Empirical Methods in Natural Language Processing*, pages 1531–1542, Lisbon, Portugal. Association for Computational Linguistics.

Bob Coecke and Konstantinos Meichanetzidis. 2020. Meaning updating of density matrices. *ArXiv*, 2001.00862.

Bob Coecke, Mehrnoosh Sadrzadeh, and Stephen Clark. 2010. Mathematical foundations for a compositional distributed model of meaning. *Lambek Festschrift, Linguistic Analysis*, 36.

Alexis Conneau, Douwe Kiela, Holger Schwenk, Loïc Barrault, and Antoine Bordes. 2017. Supervised learning of universal sentence representations from natural language inference data. In *Proceedings of the 2017 Conference on Empirical Methods in Natural Language Processing*, pages 670–680, Copenhagen, Denmark. Association for Computational Linguistics.

Jacob Devlin, Ming Wei Chang, Kenton Lee, and Kristina Toutanova. 2019. BERT: Pre-training of deep bidirectional transformers for language understanding. In *Proceedings of the 2019 Conference of the North American Chapter of the Association for Computational Linguistics: Human Language Technologies, Volume 1 (Long and Short Papers)*, pages 4171–4186.

Manaal Faruqui and Chris Dyer. 2014. Community evaluation and exchange of word vectors at wordvectors.org. In *Proceedings of ACL: System Demonstrations*.

Lev Finkelstein, Evgeniy Gabrilovich, Yossi Matias, Ehud Rivlin, Zach Solan, Gadi Wolfman, and Eytan Ruppin. 2001. Placing search in context: The concept revisited. volume 20, pages 406–414.

Edward Grefenstette and Mehrnoosh Sadrzadeh. 2011a. Experimental support for a categorical compositional distributional model of meaning. In *Proceedings of the Conference on Empirical Methods in Natural Language Processing*, pages 1394–1404. Association for Computational Linguistics.

Edward Grefenstette and Mehrnoosh Sadrzadeh. 2011b. Experimenting with transitive verbs in a DisCoCat. In *Proceedings of the GEMS 2011 Workshop on GEometrical Models of Natural Language Semantics*, pages 62–66, Edinburgh, UK. Association for Computational Linguistics.

Christian Hadiwinoto, Hwee Tou Ng, and Wee Chung Gan. 2019. Improved word sense disambiguation using pre-trained contextualized word representations. In *Proceedings of the 2019 Conference on Empirical Methods in Natural Language Processing and the 9th International Joint Conference on Natural Language Processing (EMNLP-IJCNLP)*, pages 5297–5306, Hong Kong, China. Association for Computational Linguistics.

Felix Hill, Roi Reichart, and Anna Korhonen. 2015. SimLex-999: Evaluating semantic models with (genuine) similarity estimation. *Computational Linguistics*, 41(4):665–695.

Luyao Huang, Chi Sun, Xipeng Qiu, and Xuanjing Huang. 2019. Glossbert: Bert for word sense disambiguation with gloss knowledge. *Proceedings of the 2019 Conference on Empirical Methods in Natural Language Processing and the 9th International Joint Conference on Natural Language Processing (EMNLP-IJCNLP)*.

Dimitri Kartsaklis, Mehrnoosh Sadrzadeh, and Stephen Pulman. 2012. A unified sentence space for categorical distributional-compositional semantics: Theory and experiments. In *Proceedings of COLING 2012: Posters*, pages 549–558, Mumbai, India. The COLING 2012 Organizing Committee.

Dimitri Kartsaklis, Mehrnoosh Sadrzadeh, and Stephen Pulman. 2013. Separating disambiguation from composition in distributional semantics. In *Proceedings of the Seventeenth Conference on Computational Natural Language Learning*, pages 114–123, Sofia, Bulgaria. Association for Computational Linguistics.

Walter Kintsch. 2001. Predication. *Cognitive science*, 25(2):173–202.

Michael Lesk. 1986. Automatic sense disambiguation using machine readable dictionaries: how to tell a pine cone from an ice cream cone. In *Proceedings of the 5th annual international conference on Systems documentation*, pages 24–26.

Martha Lewis. 2019a. Compositional hyponymy with positive operators. In *Proceedings of Recent Advances in Natural Language Processing*, pages 638–647.

Martha Lewis. 2019b. Modelling hyponymy for discocat. Presented at Applied Category Theory Conference 2019.

Oren Melamud, Jacob Goldberger, and Ido Dagan. 2016. context2vec: Learning generic context embedding with bidirectional LSTM. In *Proceedings of The 20th SIGNLL Conference on Computational Natural Language Learning*, pages 51–61, Berlin, Germany. Association for Computational Linguistics.

Tomas Mikolov, Kai Chen, Greg Corrado, and Jeffrey Dean. 2013a. Efficient estimation of word representations in vector space. *CoRR*, abs/1301.3781.

Tomas Mikolov, Ilya Sutskever, Kai Chen, Gregory S. Corrado, and Jeffrey Dean. 2013b. Distributed representations of words and phrases and their compositionality. In *Advances in Neural Information Processing Systems 26: 27th Annual Conference on Neural Information Processing Systems 2013.*, pages 3111–3119.

Dmitrijs Milajevs, Dimitri Kartsaklis, Mehrnoosh Sadrzadeh, and Matthew Purver. 2014. Evaluating neural word representations in tensor-based compositional settings. In *Proceedings of the 2014 Conference on Empirical Methods in Natural Language Processing (EMNLP)*, pages 708–719.

George A. Miller. 1995. Wordnet: A lexical database for english. *Commun. ACM*, 38(11):39–41.

George A. Miller and Walter G. Charles. 1991. Contextual correlates of semantic similarity. *Language and Cognitive Processes*, 6(1):1–28.

Jeff Mitchell and Mirella Lapata. 2008. Vector-based models of semantic composition. In *Proceedings of ACL-08: HLT*, pages 236–244.

Roberto Navigli. 2009. Word sense disambiguation: A survey. *ACM Comput. Surv.*, 41(2).

Arvind Neelakantan, Jeevan Shankar, Alexandre Passos, and Andrew McCallum. 2014. Efficient nonparametric estimation of multiple embeddings per word in vector space. In *Proceedings of the 2014 Conference on Empirical Methods in Natural Language Processing (EMNLP)*, pages 1059–1069, Doha, Qatar. Association for Computational Linguistics.

Denis Paperno, Nghia The Pham, and Marco Baroni. 2014. A practical and linguistically-motivated approach to compositional distributional semantics. In *Proceedings of the 52nd Annual Meeting of the Association for Computational Linguistics (Volume 1: Long Papers)*, pages 90–99, Baltimore, Maryland. Association for Computational Linguistics.

Robin Piedeleu, Dimitri Kartsaklis, Bob Coecke, and Mehrnoosh Sadrzadeh. 2015. Open system categorical quantum semantics in natural language processing. In *Proceedings of the 6th Conference on Algebra and Coalgebra in Computer Science*, volume 35, pages 270–289. Schloss Dagstuhl-Leibniz-Zentrum fuer Informatik.

Mohammad Taher Pilehvar and José Camacho-Collados. 2019. WiC: the word-in-context dataset for evaluating context-sensitive meaning representations. In *Proceedings of the 2019 Conference of the North American Chapter of the Association for Computational Linguistics: Human Language Technologies*, pages 1267–1273.

Alessandro Raganato, Jose Camacho-Collados, and Roberto Navigli. 2017. Word sense disambiguation: A unified evaluation framework and empirical comparison. In *Proceedings of the 15th Conference of the European Chapter of the Association for Computational Linguistics: Volume 1, Long Papers*, pages 99–110, Valencia, Spain. Association for Computational Linguistics.

Herbert Rubenstein and John B. Goodenough. 1965. Contextual correlates of synonymy. *Commun. ACM*, 8(10):627–633.

Mehrnoosh Sadrzadeh, Dimitri Kartsaklis, and Esma Balkir. 2018. Sentence entailment in compositional distributional semantics. *Annals of Mathematics and Artificial Intelligence*, 82(4):189–218.

Mehrnoosh Sadrzadeh and Reinhard Muskens. 2018. Static and dynamic vector semantics for lambda calculus models of natural language. *Journal of Language Modelling Vol*, 6(2):319–351.

Hinrich Schütze. 1998. Automatic word sense discrimination. *Computational Linguistics*, 24(1):97–123.

Richard Socher, Brody Huval, Christopher D Manning, and Andrew Y Ng. 2012. Semantic compositionality through recursive matrix-vector spaces. In *Proceedings of the 2012 joint conference on empirical methods in natural language processing and computational natural language learning*, pages 1201–1211.

Gregor Wiedemann, Steffen Remus, Avi Chawla, and Chris Biemann. 2019. Does BERT make any sense? Interpretable word sense disambiguation with contextualized embeddings. In *Proceedings of KONVENS 2019*.

Gijs Wijnholds and Mehrnoosh Sadrzadeh. 2019. Evaluating composition models for verb phrase elliptical sentence embeddings. In *Proceedings of the 2019 Conference of the North American Chapter of the Association for Computational Linguistics: Human Language Technologies, Volume 1 (Long and Short Papers)*, pages 261–271, Minneapolis, Minnesota. Association for Computational Linguistics.

A Word2DM Gradients

The objective function that SGNS optimises at each prediction with regard to model parameters θ is

$$J(\theta) = \log \sigma(v_t{}^\top v_c) + \sum_{k=1}^{K} \log \sigma(-v_t{}^\top v_{w_k}) \quad (6)$$

where v_t is the embedding of target word, v_c is the embedding of the context word, and $v_1, v_2, ..., v_K$ are the embeddings of K negative samples. By optimising equation 6 over a large corpus, skip-gram learns word embeddings that encode distributional information.

Maximising equation 6 adjusts the embeddings of words occurring in the same context to be more similar and adjusts the embeddings of words that don't occur together to be less similar. This becomes clear when we consider the gradients used to update embeddings during training. We briefly recall the details of the gradient calculation so as to refer back to it later in this section. The derivative of equation 6 with respect to the target vector v_t is

$$\frac{\partial J}{\partial v_t} = (1-\sigma(v_t{}^\top v_c))v_c - \sum_{k=1}^{K}(1-\sigma(v_t{}^\top v_{w_k}))v_{w_k} \quad (7)$$

which is used to update the target vector as follows:

$$v_t \leftarrow v_t + \alpha \frac{\partial J}{\partial v_t} \quad (8)$$

The target vector is updated by adding the scaled context vector to it and subtracting the scaled negatively sampled vectors from it. The vectors are scaled proportionally to how dissimilar they are to the target vector. This ensures that the target vector is "pulled closer" to the true context vector and "pushed away" from the negative context vectors. It is this computationally simple training procedure which makes SGNS effective.

Word2DM extends SGNS to learn density matrices, replacing equation 6 with the following objective function:

$$J(\theta) = \log \sigma(\mathrm{tr}(A_t A_c)) + \sum_{k=1}^{K} \log \sigma(-\mathrm{tr}(A_t A_{w_k})) \quad (9)$$

where A_t and A_c are the density matrices of the target and context words respectively, $A_1, A_2, ..., A_K$ are the density matrices of K negative samples, and θ is the set of weights of the intermediary matrices B_t, B_c and $B_1, B_2, ..., B_K$.

Computing this objective function requires multiple matrix multiplications. For each $\mathrm{tr}(A_t A_c)$ term (including the terms of the K negative samples), the matrices A_t and A_c have to be computed respectively as $A_t = B_t B_t^\top$ and $A_c = B_c B_c^\top$ and then the matrix product $A_t A_c$ has to be computed. This means that, for each target-context prediction, we require $3(K+1)$ matrix multiplications. One of the most attractive features of SGNS is its computational efficiency, which enabled training on very large corpora in reasonable time. The introduction of multiple matrix multiplications into the objective function means that much of this efficiency is lost. In order to reduce the complexity of our model, we make use of the following property and lemma to find a new objective function that is computationally simpler, but equivalent to equation 9.

Property A.1. *The trace of the product of two matrices can be expressed as the sum of the element-wise products of their elements. If A is an $n \times m$ matrix and B is an $m \times n$ matrix, then the trace of the $n \times n$ matrix AB can be computed as*

$$\mathrm{tr}(AB) = \sum_{i=1}^{n} \sum_{j=1}^{m} a_{ij} b_{ji}$$

Lemma A.2. *If B_t and B_c are $n \times m$ intermediary matrices, then trace of the matrix product $A_t A_c$ can be written as the sum of the squared elements of an $m \times m$ matrix $C = B_c^\top B_t$:*

$$\mathrm{tr}(A_t A_c) = \sum_{i=1}^{m} \sum_{j=1}^{m} c_{ij}^2$$

Proof. We can express $\mathrm{tr}(A_t A_c)$ as a trace computation involving intermediary matrices B_t and B_c:

$$\mathrm{tr}(A_t A_c) = \mathrm{tr}(B_t B_t^\top B_c B_c^\top)$$

Then we can use the cyclic property of the trace function to rewrite this as the product of a matrix C and its transpose:

$$\begin{aligned}
\mathrm{tr}(A_t A_c) &= \mathrm{tr}(B_c^\top B_t B_t^\top B_c) \\
&= \mathrm{tr}(B_c^\top B_t (B_c^\top B_t)^\top) \\
&= \mathrm{tr}(C C^\top), \quad \text{where } C = B_c^\top B_t
\end{aligned}$$

Now we can use property A.1 to express this as the element-wise products of the elements of C and its transpose:

$$\operatorname{tr}(A_t A_c) = \sum_{i=1}^{m}\sum_{j=1}^{m}[C]_{ij}[C^{\top}]_{ji}$$

$$= \sum_{i=1}^{m}\sum_{j=1}^{m} c_{ij}c_{ij}$$

$$= \sum_{i=1}^{m}\sum_{j=1}^{m} c_{ij}^{2}$$

$\square$

This allows us to rewrite equation 9 to find an equivalent objective function that requires fewer computations than straightforward matrix multiplication would. The objective function at each target-context prediction becomes

$$J(\theta) = \log\sigma\left(\sum_{i=1}^{m}\sum_{j=1}^{m}[B_c^{\top}B_t]_{ij}^2\right) \quad (10)$$

$$+ \sum_{k=1}^{K}\log\sigma\left(-\sum_{i=1}^{m}\sum_{j=1}^{m}[B_{w_k}^{\top}B_t]_{ij}^2\right).$$

By using the result of lemma A.2 we have reduced the number of matrix multiplications required for each target-context prediction from $3(K+1)$ to $(K+1)$. Density matrices are trained by maximising equation 10 with respect to the intermediary matrices $B_t, B_c, B_{w_1}, ..., B_{w_K}$ over a large corpus.

The model is trained using stochastic gradient descent. We now derive the gradients used to update B_t during training, and subsequently show that these gradients lead to suboptimal updates to the density matrices during training. Deriving the gradient with respect to B_c and B_{w_k} would proceed similarly. To compute the gradients of equation 10 we first rewrite it in terms of the elements of the $n \times m$ matrices B_t, B_c, and B_{w_k}:

$$J(\theta) = \log\sigma\left(\sum_{i=1}^{m}\sum_{j=1}^{m}(\sum_{l=1}^{n} b_{li}^c b_{lj}^t)^2\right) \quad (11)$$

$$+ \sum_{k=1}^{K}\log\sigma\left(-\sum_{i=1}^{m}\sum_{j=1}^{m}(\sum_{l=1}^{n} b_{li}^{w_k} b_{lj}^t)^2\right),$$

where b_{pq}^x denotes the pqth element of B_x. We derive the gradient of this objective function with respect to b_{pq}^t, an element of the intermediary target word matrix B_t. In order to use the chain rule in

gradient calculations we rewrite $J(\theta)$ as a composite function:

$$J(\theta) = \log\sigma(y(\theta)) + \sum_{k=1}^{K}\log\sigma(z_k(\theta)), \quad (12)$$

where

$$y(\theta) = \sum_{i=1}^{m}\sum_{j=1}^{m}(\sum_{l=1}^{n} b_{li}^c b_{lj}^t)^2 \quad \text{and}$$

$$z_k(\theta) = -\sum_{i=1}^{m}\sum_{j=1}^{m}(\sum_{l=1}^{n} b_{li}^{w_k} b_{lj}^t)^2.$$

The derivative of J with respect to b_{pq}^t can now be computed as follows:

$$\frac{\partial J}{\partial b_{pq}^t} = \frac{\partial \log}{\partial \sigma}\frac{\partial \sigma}{\partial y}\frac{\partial y}{\partial b_{pq}^t} + \sum_{k=1}^{K}\frac{\partial \log}{\partial \sigma}\frac{\partial \sigma}{\partial z_k}\frac{\partial z_k}{\partial b_{pq}^t}$$

$$= \frac{1}{\sigma(y)}(1 - \sigma(y))\sigma(y)\frac{\partial y}{\partial b_{pq}^t}$$

$$+ \sum_{k=1}^{K}\frac{1}{\sigma(z_k)}(1 - \sigma(z_k))\sigma(z_k)\frac{\partial z_k}{\partial b_{pq}^t}$$

$$= (1 - \sigma(y))\frac{\partial y}{\partial b_{pq}^t} + \sum_{k=1}^{K}(1 - \sigma(z_k))\frac{\partial z_k}{\partial b_{pq}^t}$$

$$= (1 - \sigma(y))\sum_{i=1}^{m} 2b_{pi}^c \sum_{l=1}^{n} b_{li}^c b_{lq}^t$$

$$- \sum_{k=1}^{K}(1 - \sigma(z_k))\sum_{i=1}^{m} 2b_{pi}^{w_k}\sum_{l=1}^{n} b_{li}^{w_k} b_{lq}^t$$

$$= (1 - \sigma(y))2[B_c B_c^{\top} B_t]_{pq}$$

$$- \sum_{k=1}^{K}(1 - \sigma(z_k))2[B_{w_k} B_{w_k}^{\top} B_t]_{pq}$$

The last line in the above derivation is obtained by rewriting the summation expressions as equivalent matrix multiplications. We can now write the derivative of J with respect to the full intermediary matrix B_t:

$$\frac{\partial J}{\partial B_t} = (1 - \sigma(y(\theta)))2B_c B_c^{\top} B_t \quad (13)$$

$$+ \sum_{k=1}^{K}(1 - \sigma(z_k(\theta)))2B_{w_k} B_{w_k}^{\top} B_t$$

As opposed to the gradients of Word2Vec (equation 7), the gradients of Word2DM do not lead to simple and easily interpretable training updates. As discussed in the paragraph following equation 8, in Word2Vec the target vector is made more similar to the context vector and less similar to the negative context vectors. Ideally we would like something

289

similar to occur in Word2DM with density matrices, but equation 13 shows that we lose the intuitive training updates of Word2Vec through the introduction of intermediary matrices. Furthermore, we can show that the gradients of Word2DM sometimes lead to unwanted consequences in training.

Consider the case where the density matrices of a target and context word are highly dissimilar. Recall from equation 9 that the y is in equation 13 is the trace inner product of the density matrices A_t and A_c (the measure we use to quantify semantic similarity). The minimum value of the trace inner product of two density matrices is zero (this follows from the fact that density matrices are positive semi-definite), so two density matrices are highly dissimilar when their trace inner product is close to zero i.e. $y \approx 0$. From equation 10 we can recall how y can be written in terms of the intermediary matrices:

$$y = \sum_{i=1}^{m} \sum_{j=1}^{m} [B_c^{\top} B_t]_{ij}^2$$

Consider that $y \approx 0$ if and only if the elements of $B_c^{\top} B_t$ are close to zero in value, since squaring the elements in the summation makes them all positive. We have established the following equivalence:

$$\mathrm{tr}(A_t A_c) \approx 0 \iff B_c^{\top} B_t \approx O,$$

where O is the $m \times m$ matrix with all zero entries. Consider how this will affect the target-context update during training. The first term of the gradient in equation 13 becomes

$$(1 - \sigma(y(\theta)))2B_c B_c^{\top} B_t = (1 - \sigma(0))2B_c O \approx O$$

so the target-context update becomes ineffective for true contexts. The update should make the density matrix of the target word more similar to that of the context word, but the gradient is so small that it makes this impossible. Moreover, the more dissimilar the target and context density matrices are before the update, the less effective the update will be. This is the opposite of the intended effect (achieved by Word2Vec) in which the magnitude of the target-context update should increase if the target and context representations are less similar. This is an example of how the introduction of intermediary matrices in Word2DM leads to suboptimal training updates. We ensure that our density matrices are positive semi-definite, but lose the guarantee that the algorithm will learn high-quality semantic representations.

B Hyperparameters for Word2DM and Multi-Sense Word2DM

Word2DM additional details We use a dynamic window size i.e. the size of each context window is sampled uniformly between 1 and the maximum window size. We also discard words that occur less than some minimum threshold and subsample frequently occurring words. Negative samples are drawn from a unigram distribution raised to the power of $\frac{3}{4}$. Furthermore, we train two density matrices for each word - one that represents it as a target word and another that represents it as a context word. After training we use the target density matrices as our final density matrices.

Hyperparameters We train our Word2DM and multi-sense Word2DM models on the ukWaC+Wackypedia corpus, consisting of 2.8 billion words. We use a window size of 5, a minimum word count of 50, 5 negative samples per positive context, and a subsampling rate of 1e-5. We train the model for 4 iterations of the ukWaC+Wackypedia corpus, using the Adam optimisation algorithm, a learning rate of 0.001, and 16 sentences per batch.

Catplayinginthesnow: Impact of Prior Segmentation on a Model of Visually Grounded Speech

William N. Havard[1,2]**, Laurent Besacier**[1]**, Jean-Pierre Chevrot**[2]

[1] LIG, Univ. Grenoble Alpes, CNRS, Grenoble INP, 38000 Grenoble, France
[2] LIDILEM, Univ. Grenoble Alpes, 38000 Grenoble, France
`first-name.lastname@univ-grenoble-alpes.fr`

Abstract

The language acquisition literature shows that children do not build their lexicon by segmenting the spoken input into phonemes and then building up words from them, but rather adopt a top-down approach and start by segmenting word-like units and then break them down into smaller units. This suggests that the ideal way of learning a language is by starting from full semantic units. In this paper, we investigate if this is also the case for a neural model of Visually Grounded Speech trained on a speech-image retrieval task. We evaluated how well such a network is able to learn a reliable speech-to-image mapping when provided with phone, syllable, or word boundary information. We present a simple way to introduce such information into an RNN-based model and investigate which type of boundary is the most efficient. We also explore at which level of the network's architecture such information should be introduced so as to maximise its performances. Finally, we show that using multiple boundary types at once in a hierarchical structure, by which low-level segments are used to recompose high-level segments, is beneficial and yields better results than using low-level or high-level segments in isolation.

1 Introduction and Prior Work

Visually Grounded Speech (VGS) models whether CNN-based (Harwath and Glass, 2015; Harwath et al., 2016; Kamper et al., 2017) or RNN-based (Chrupała et al., 2017; Merkx et al., 2019) became recently popular as they enable to model complex interaction between two modalities, namely speech and vision, and can thus be used to model child language acquisition, and more specifically lexical acquisition. Indeed, these models are trained to solve a speech-image retrieval task. That is, given a spoken input description, they are trained to retrieve the image that matches the description the

best. This task requires the model to identify lexical units that might be relevant in the spoken input, detect which objects are present in the image, and finally see if those objects match the detected spoken lexical units. Their task is thus very close to that of a child learning its mother tongue, who is surrounded by a visually perceptible context and tries to match parts of the acoustic input to surrounding visible situations. Research in language acquisition have put forward that children do not build their lexicon by segmenting the spoken input into phonemes and then building up words, but rather adopt a top-down approach (Bortfeld et al., 2005) and start by identifying and memorising whole words (Jusczyk and Aslin, 1995) or chunks of words (Bannard and Matthews, 2008) and then segment the spoken input into smaller units, such as phonemes. This suggests that the most efficient way of segmenting the spoken input to map a visual context to its description is at word level. From a more technological point of view, speech-based models lag behind their textual counterparts. For example, speech-image retrieval performs worse than text-image retrieval, despite being trained on the same data, the only changing factor being the modality where text or speech is used as a query. This begs the question: what makes text inherently better than speech for such applications? Is it because text is made up of already-segmented (discrete) units which lack internal variation, or because these discrete units (usually tokens) stand for full semantic units, or a combination of both?

Since the pioneering computational modelling work of lexical acquisition by Roy and Pentland (2002), neural network enabled an even tighter interaction between the visual and the audio modalities. Recent works suggest that networks trained on a speech-image retrieval task perform an implicit segmentation of their input. Whether CNN-based approaches or RNN-based approaches are

291

Proceedings of the 24th Conference on Computational Natural Language Learning, pages 291–301
Online, November 19-20, 2020. ©2020 Association for Computational Linguistics
https://doi.org/10.18653/v1/P17

employed, all seem to segment individual words from the inputted spoken utterance (Harwath et al., 2016; Chrupała et al., 2017; Havard et al., 2019; Havard et al., 2019; Merkx et al., 2019). This result stands also for languages other than English, such as Hindi or Japanese (Harwath et al., 2018; Havard et al., 2019; Azuh et al., 2019; Ohishi et al., 2020). Chrupała et al. (2017) and Merkx et al. (2019), however, observed that not all layers encode word-like units, suggesting that some layers specialise in lexical processing whereas some other do not encode such information.

Contributions Our research question can be framed as follows: what is the segmentation that maximises the performance of an audio-visual network if speech were to be segmented? To answer this question we investigate *how* it is possible to give speech boundary information to a neural network and explore *which* type of boundary (phone, syllable, or word) is the most efficient. We also explore *where* such information should be provided, that is, at which layer of the architecture is the addition of this information the most beneficial?

2   Model & Data

Data We use two different data sets in our experiments: MS COCO (Lin et al., 2014) and Flickr8k (Hodosh et al., 2013). Both corpora were initially conceived for computer vision purposes and both feature a set of images along with five written descriptions of the images. The captions were not computer generated but written by humans. We use the audio extensions of both data sets: for Flickr8k, we use the captions provided by Harwath and Glass (2015), and for COCO we use Synthetic COCO data set introduced by (Chrupała et al., 2017; Chrupała et al., 2017). The captions of Harwath and Glass (2015) were gathered using Amazon Mechanical Turk and were thus uttered by humans. This data set is particularly challenging as it features multiple speakers and the quality of the recording is uneven from one caption to another. The spoken captions of Chrupała et al. (2017) feature synthetic speech generated with Google's Text-to-Speech system. For both corpora, we extracted speech-to-text alignments through the *Maus* forced aligner (Kisler et al., 2017) online platform, resulting in alignments at word and phone levels.

Architecture The models we train in our experiments all have the same architecture and are based on that of Chrupała et al. (2017).[1] As all models of VGS, be they CNN-based or RNN-based, this architecture has two main components: an image encoder and a speech encoder. Such models are trained to solve a speech-image retrieval task, that is, given a query in the form of a spoken description, they should retrieve the closest matching image fitting the description.

The image encoder is a simple linear layer that reduces pre-computed VGG image vectors to the desired dimension. The speech encoder, which receives MFCC vectors as input, consists of a 1D convolutional layer, followed by five stacked recurrent layers with residual connections, followed by an attention mechanism. We use uni-directional recurrent layers and not bi-directional recurrent layers even though it has been shown they lead to better results (Merkx et al., 2019). Indeed, we aim at having a cognitively plausible model: humans process speech in a left-to-right fashion, as speech is being gradually uttered, and not from both ends simultaneously. We use the same loss function as initially used by Chrupała et al. (2017):

$$\mathcal{L}(u, i, \alpha) = \sum_{u,i} \left(\sum_{u'} \max[0, \alpha + d(u, i) - d(u', i)] \right. $$
$$\left. + \sum_{i'} \max[0, \alpha + d(u, i) - d(u, i')] \right) \tag{1}$$

This contrastive loss function encourages the network to minimise the cosine distance d by a margin α between an image i and its corresponding utterance u, while maximising the distance between mismatching image/utterance pairs i'/u and i/u'. In our experiments we set $\alpha = 0.2$.

Hyperparameters For both COCO and Flickr8k we use 1D convolutions with 64 filters of length 6 and a stride of 1 to preserve the original time resolution (and hence, boundary position). We use 512 units per recurrent layer for COCO and 1024 for Flickr8k. All models were trained using Adam optimiser and an initial learning rate of 0.0002. For our experiments we use the pre-computed MFCC vectors and pre-computed VGG vectors provided by Chrupała et al. (2017).[2] We also use the same training, validation and testing splits.[3]

---

[1]The code we use is based on `https://github.com/gchrupala/vgs`

[2]12 MFCC coef. plus energy for COCO; 12 MFCC coef. plus energy as well as deltas and delta deltas for Flickr8k.

[3]Training/Validation/Test   split   contain

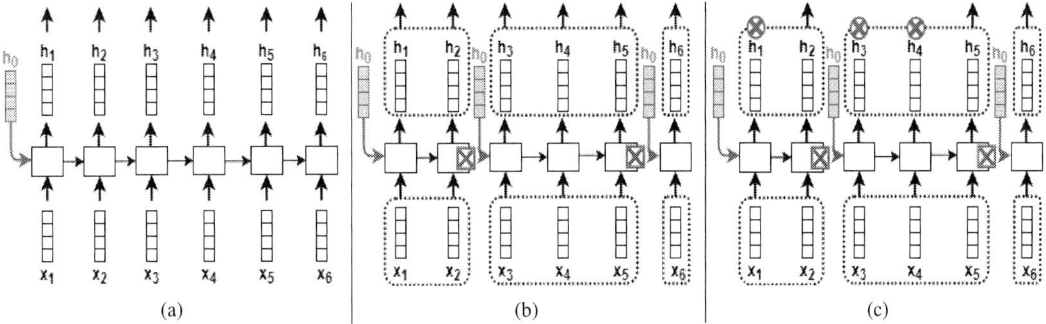

(a)   (b)   (c)

Figure 1: Graphical representation of the different GRUs used in our experiments. Figure 1a shows a Vanilla GRU. Figure 1b shows GRU$_{\text{PACK.}}$ in the ALL condition where all the vectors produced at each time step are passed on to the next layer. 1c shows GRU$_{\text{PACK.}}$ in the KEEP condition where only the last vector of a segment is passed on to the next layer, thus resulting in a output sequence shorter than the input sequence. The red crosses inscribed in a square (⊠) signal that the output vector computed at a given timestep is not passed on to the next timestep and that the initial state h_0 is passed on instead. The red crosses inscribed in a circle (⊗) signal that the output vector computed at a given timestep is not passed on to the next layer. Dotted line group vectors belonging to a same segment (either phone, syllable-connected, syllable-word, or word). Note that h_0 is only passed on to the next state at the end of a segment, thus effectively materialising a boundary by manually resetting the history. Also note that the $x_1, x_2, ..., x_t$ figured in this representation could either be the original input sequence (in our case, acoustic vectors) or could also be the output of the previous recurrent layer.

3 Integrating Segmentation Information

3.1 Boundary Types

As previously stated, we are interested in supplying our network with linguistic information such as segment boundaries. We define a segment as either being a phoneme, a syllable, or a word. We consider two different types of syllables. Indeed, when we speak, words are not uttered one after the other in a disconnected fashion, but are rather blended together through a process called "resyllabification". In English, this phenomenon is visible when a word ending with a consonant is followed by a word starting with a vowel. In this case, the final consonant of the first word tends to be detached from it and attached to the next word, thus crossing the word boundary. This phenomenon is illustrated in Example (1) where phonemes in red indicate a resyllabification phenomenon.

(1)   This is an article.
       Transcription[4]   /ðɪs#ɪz#ən#ɑɹtɪkəl/
       a. *No resyllabification*   /ðɪs.ɪz.ən.ɑɹ.tɪ.kəl/
       b. *With resyllabification*   /ðɪ.sɪ.zə.nɑɹ.tɪ.kəl/

For the rest of this article "syllables-word" will refer to syllables that result of a segmentation that does not take into account resyllabification (1-a), whereas "syllables-connected" will refer to syllables that result of a segmentation that takes into account resyllabification (1-b). It should be noted that in the syllables-connected condition, most word boundaries are lost.[5] In the syllables-word condition, however, all word boundaries are preserved and the segmentation inside a word may result in a morphemic segmentation (as for example in "runway" /ɹʌn.weɪ/ or "air.plane" /ɛɹ.pleɪn/). Nevertheless, this is not always the case, especially for longer words that are of non-germanic origin (such as "elephant" /ɛ.lɛ.fant/ or "computer" /kəm.pju.tɚ/). We expect models trained in the syllables-connected condition to perform worse than those trained in the syllables-word condition as resyllabification hinders word recognition (Vroomen and Gelder, 1999).

Segment boundaries were derived from the forced alignment metadata so as to indicate which MFCC vector constitutes a boundary or not.[6] Therefore, for each caption we have a sequence X of length T of d-dimensional acoustic vectors $X = \left[x_1^d, x_2^d, ..., x_T^d\right]$ and a corresponding

---

113,287/5,000/5,000 images (COCO) and 6,000/1,000/1,000 images (Flickr8k).

[4]We use "#" to signal word boundaries and "." to signal syllable boundaries.

[5]Word boundaries are not lost in the following cases: V#V and C#C when CC is not an allowed complex onset. C and V respectively refer to "consonant" and "vowel".

[6]As the force aligner used does not provide alignment at the syllable level, we wrote a custom script to recreate syllables from the phonemic transcription.

sequence of scalars B representing boundaries $B = [b_1, b_2, ..., b_T]$, $b_t \in \{0, 1\}$, where $b_t \triangleq 1$ if x_t is a segment boundary, 0 otherwise.

3.2 Integrating Boundary Information

In order to integrate boundary information into the model, we take advantage of how recurrent neural networks compute their output. They can be formalised as follows:

$$h_t = f\left(h_{t-1}, x_t; \theta\right) \tag{2}$$

where the hidden state at timestep t noted h_t is a function f of the previous hidden state h_{t-1} and the current input at x_t, with θ being learnable parameters of the function f. A special case arises at the very first time step $t = 1$ as h_{t-1} does not exist. In this case, the initial state h_{t-1} noted h_0 is set to be a vector of 0. The output of such a network at timestep T is thus dependent on all the previous timesteps. An illustration of such a network is depicted in Figure 1a. In this work, we use GRUs (Cho et al., 2014), but our methodology is applicable to any other type of recurrent cell such as vanilla RNNs or LSTMs.

Our approach to integrate boundary information into the network can be formalised as follows:

$$h_t = \begin{cases} f\left(h_0, x_t; \theta\right), \text{ if } b_{t-1} = 1 \\ f\left(h_{t-1}, x_t; \theta\right), \text{ otherwise} \end{cases} \tag{3}$$

In our approach, h_t is only dependent on the previous timestep h_{t-1} if the previous timestep was not an acoustic vector corresponding to segment boundary ($b_{t-1} \neq 0$). If the previous timestep corresponds to a segment boundary ($b_{t-1} = 1$), we reset the hidden state so that it is equal to h_0. Hence, vectors in the same segment are temporally dependent, but vectors belonging to two different segments are not. The GRUs that use this computing scheme will from now on be referred to as GRU$_\text{PACK.}$, as vectors belonging to the same segment are "packed" together.

We derived two different conditions from this initial setting: ALL and KEEP. In the ALL condition (see Figure 1b), all the vectors belonging to a segment are forwarded to the next layer (which can either be a recurrent layer, or an attention mechanism depending on the position of the GRU$_\text{PACK.}$ layer.) In the KEEP condition, only the last vector of each segment is forwarded to the next layer (see Figure 1c). The length of the output and input sequence stays the same in the ALL condition.

However, it should be noted that in the KEEP condition, the length of the output sequence is shorter than the input sequence. Potentially, the length of the sequences can be different for different items inside a batch as the captions have a different number of segments (be they phones, syllables or words). For this reason, and as the subsequent layers expect a 3D rectangular matrix,[7] we add padding vectors on the sequence dimension until all the elements of the batch have the same sequence length. The difference between ALL and KEEP is motivated by the fact that we believe that keeping the last vector of a segment could constrain the network to build more consistent representations for different occurrences of the same segment, as the subsequent layers will have less information to rely on. A similar approach to ours was proposed by Chen et al. (2019) in an Audio-Word2Vec experiment, where instead of being given gold segment boundaries, a classifier outputs a probability that a given frame constitutes a segment boundary.

4 Experiments and Results

4.1 GRU$_\text{PACK.}$ Position and Random Boundaries

In order to understand where boundary information should be introduced (that is, at which level of the architecture), we train as many models as the number of recurrent layers, where each time one layer of GRUs is replaced with one GRU$_\text{PACK.}$ layer. For example, "GRU$_\text{PACK.}$-3" refers to a model where the third layer of GRUs is a GRU$_\text{PACK.}$ layer and other layers (1st, 2nd, 4th, and 5th layer) are vanilla GRU layers. This setting will allow to explore *where* introducing boundary information is the most efficient.

To understand if introducing boundary information helps the network in its task, we compare the performance of the models using boundary information with a baseline model which does not use any (thus, all the recurrent layers of the baseline architecture are Vanilla GRU layers). This model will from now on be referred to as BASELINE. We also introduce another condition, where, instead of training models with real segment boundaries (which from now on will be referred to as TRUE), we train models with random boundaries (which from now on will be referred to as RANDOM). Indeed, it could be that randomly slicing speech into sub-units leads to better results, even though the resulting units do

---

[7]Of shape batch size $\times$ sequence $\times$ embedding dimension.

Data set	R@1	R@5	R@10
COCO	9.0	27.0	39.5
Flickr8k	4.3	13.4	21.4

Table 1: Mean recalls at 1, 5, and 10 (in %) on a speech-image retrieval task COCO and Flickr8k in the BASE-LINE condition. Chance scores are 0.0002/0.001/0.002 for COCO and 0.001/0.005/0.01 for Flickr8k.

not constitute linguistically meaningful units. Consequently, training models with random boundaries will enable us to verify this claim. Random boundaries were generated by simply shuffling the position of the real boundaries (vector B introduced in §3.1), resulting in as many randomly positioned boundaries as there are real ones. Note that we do still expect the models to have reasonable results even when using random boundaries, as acoustic vectors are kept untouched. Nonetheless, we expect that placing random boundaries will hinder network's learning process and thus yield results significantly lower than when using true boundaries. We expect results to be significantly lower in the RANDOM-KEEP condition as this condition is equivalent to randomly subsampling the input, and thus removing a lot of information.

4.2 Evaluation

Models are evaluated in term of Recall@k (R@k). Given a spoken query, R@k evaluates the models ability to rank the target paired image in the top k images. In order to evaluate if the results observed in our different experimental conditions (TRUE-ALL, TRUE-KEEP, RANDOM-ALL, RANDOM-KEEP) are different from one another and from the BASE-LINE condition, we used a two-sided proportion Z-Test. This test is used to check if there is a statistical difference between two independent proportions. As for each spoken query there is only one target image, R@k becomes a binary value which equals 1 if the target image is ranked in the top k images and 0 otherwise. In our case, the proportion that we test is the number of successes over the number of trials (which corresponds to the number of different caption/image pairs in the test set).

4.3 Results

Overall, our experimental settings led to the training of 81 different models per data set.[8] BASE-

LINE results are shown in Table 1, results for the TRUE/RANDOM conditions obtained on the Flickr8k are shown in Table 2 and results on COCO in Table 5 (Appendix A). We obtain lower results on Flickr8k than on COCO which shows how difficult the task is on natural speech. The results obtained on synthetic speech are also very low compared to their textual counterpart.[9] For space reasons, and as the results on both Flickr8k and COCO show the same trend, we will focus in the following pages on analysing the results obtained on the Flickr8k data set. The results obtained on the COCO data set are reported in Appendix A.

TRUE/RANDOM and ALL/KEEP Boundaries One of the questions our experiments aim at answering is whether introducing boundary information helps the network in solving its task or not. To do so, we first compare the difference between TRUE and RANDOM boundaries. We notice different patterns depending on the position of the GRU$_{PACK.}$ layer and also depending on the ALL and KEEP conditions.

We observe that in the ALL condition the results between TRUE and RANDOM boundaries are overall not statistically different from one another, and are not significantly better or worse from the baseline results. There is only one case where such differences are statistically significant: for the 1st layer when using word segments. However, in the KEEP condition, we observe a strong difference between TRUE and RANDOM boundaries across all boundary types and across most of the layers. Overall, in the KEEP condition, models trained with TRUE boundaries have statistically different results from models trained with RANDOM boundaries. Also, in such settings, the results obtained are generally statistically better than the baseline, while in the RANDOM-KEEP condition the results are statistically worse than the baseline.

These results show that there is overall no difference between using TRUE or RANDOM boundaries in the ALL condition (except for one layer), hence showing that boundary information is not used effectively by the network. In contrast, the difference between TRUE and RANDOM in the KEEP condition shows that boundary information is effectively used by the network. Using random boundaries which do not delimit meaningful linguistic units really hurts the performance of the network, espe-

---

[8](Seg. type $\in$ {phone,syl.-connected,syl.-word,word} $\times$ GRU$_{PACK.}${1,2,3,4,5} $\times$ {TRUE,RANDOM} $\times$ {ALL,KEEP}) + BASELINE

[9]Merkx and Frank (2019) report R@1 $= 27.5$ on a GRU-based model using characters as input.

	Flickr8k — KEEP condition								Flickr8k — ALL condition							
GRU	Phones		Syl.-Co.		Syl.-Word		Word		Phones		Syl.-Co.		Syl.-Word		Word	
Pack.	T	R	T	R	T	R	T	R	T	R	T	R	T	R	T	R
5	3.6	**3.7**	*3.6*	*2.5⁻*	**3.3**	3.0	**3.2**	**3.2**	**4.0**	3.9	**4.1**	**4.1**	**4.3**	3.9	3.4	**4.2**
4	**3.8**	**3.8**	**4.4**	3.5	**3.9**	*2.6⁻*	*5.2⁺*	*2.5⁻*	4.0	**4.4**	3.9	**4.1**	**4.3**	3.8	**4.5**	**4.5**
3	*4.9⁺*	*3.8*	**4.5**	*3.1*	*5.3⁺*	*3.1*	*4.9⁺*	3.3	**4.5**	4.4	**4.3**	4.2	**4.4**	4.2	**4.5**	3.8
2	*4.8⁺*	3.9	*5.1⁺*	*3.6*	**4.8**	3.4	*5.4⁺*	*3.4*	**4.5**	3.8	*4.8*	*3.6*	**4.4**	4.2	**4.7**	4.1
1	**4.8**	*2.4⁻*	**3.4**	*1.9⁻*	**4.4**	*2.0⁻*	**3.9**	*1.9⁻*	**4.3**	3.4	**4.0**	**4.0**	**4.4**	4.3	*5.3⁺*	*4.1*

Table 2: Maximum R@1 (in %) for each model trained on test set of the Flickr8k data set (models were selected based on the maximum R@1 on the validation set). "T" stands for TRUE (boundaries) and "R" stands for RANDOM (boundaries). "Syl-Co." and "Syl-Word" stand for "Syllables-Connected" and "Syllables-Word" respectively. Each line shows the results for when a specific recurrent layer is a GRU$_{PACK.}$ layer (see §4.1). The 1st layer is the lowest layer and the 5th the highest. The highest R@1 in the table is shown in red. Best results between each TRUE and RANDOM pair (columnwise) are shown in **bold**. ○⁺ and ○⁻ indicate that the results are statistically better (respectively worse) than the baseline. Results in *italics* show statistical significance (two-sided Z-Test, p-value $< 1e^{-2}$, see §4.2) between each TRUE and RANDOM pair (columnwise).

cially in the KEEP condition as most of the vectors are removed. In the ALL condition, using TRUE or RANDOM boundaries yields results close to that of the BASELINE, suggesting boundary information might act as noise and help the network regularise. Thus, as expected, the network was effectively constrained to learn better representations in the KEEP condition. We believe it is the case because in the ALL condition, boundary information is diluted among the neighbouring vectors while this is not the case in the KEEP condition, as each segment is represented by a single vector.

Phones, Syllables, or Words From now on, we will focus on the results obtained in the KEEP condition, as the ALL condition brings only slight improvement over the BASELINE condition. In our experiments we used four different type of segments corresponding to different type of linguistic units: phones, syllables-connected, syllables-word, and words. These different type of segments vary in *length* (words and syllables are longer than phones), *quantity* (there are more phones and syllables than words), and *intrinsic linguistic information*: phones only show which are the basic acoustic units of the language, while word segments represent meaningful units, and syllables-word and syllables-connected are a higher form of acoustic unit that may contain morphemic information. Given the task the network is trained for (speech-image retrieval), we do not expect these different units to perform equally well. Indeed, as this task implies mapping an image vector describing which objects are present in a picture and a spoken description of an image, we expect word-like segments (or segments that preserve word bound-

aries and that bear a substantial amount of semantic information) to perform better.

This is in fact what we observe in practice: word units obtain statistically better results ($R@1 = 5.4$) than the baseline ($+1.1$pp). Syllables-word also bring significant improvement ($R@1 = 5.3$), however, slightly less than when using word units. It should be noted that syllables-connected segments also obtain statistically significant improvement over the baseline (GRU$_{PACK.}$$-2$) despite not preserving all the word boundaries. However, these results are slightly worse than the syllables-word and word segments, suggesting that preserving word boundaries is a property that helps the network. It appears that the size of a segment is also an important parameter. Indeed, phone segments (naturally) preserve word boundaries, but of course naturally lack the internal cohesion of a morpheme or a word as nothing links two adjacent phonemes together. Thus, it seems that segments that preserve meaning (such as words) or from which meaning can be more easily recomposed (syllable) may facilitate the network's task. The fact that syllable-like segments perform as well as word segments might only be an artefact of using English where a high proportion of word is monosyllabic.[10] Working on a language such as Japanese where the syllable-to-morpheme ratio is higher would be a future line of work that would enable to test this hypothesis.

GRU$_{PACK.}$ Layer Position We introduced boundary information at different levels of our architecture in order to better understand at which layer it is the most useful to add such information.

---

[10] Jespersen (1929) estimates that at least 8,000 commonly frequent words are monosyllabic in English.

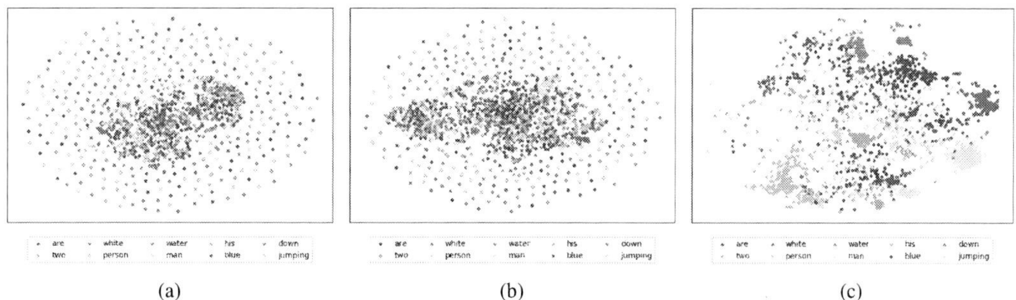

(a)   (b)   (c)

Figure 2: t-SNE projections of the final vector of different occurrences of eigth randomly selected words (Flick8k) in the BASELINE condition (2a), in the ALL condition (2b), and in the KEEP condition (2c). Plot 2a shows that the representation learnt in the BASELINE and ALL conditions are not word-based as the final vectors of different occurrences of the same word do not cluster together. In the KEEP condition, the model succeeded in learning similar representations for different occurrences of the same word as words cluster together.

Our results clearly show that introducing boundary information at different layers has a clear impact on the results: using such information at the first or the fifth layer is useless, as we notice it either yields similar results to the baseline or worsens the results regardless of the type of boundary used ($GRU_{PACK}.-5$). When using syllable-word segments the best results are obtained when introducing the information at $GRU_{PACK}.-3$, and at $GRU_{PACK}.-2$ when using word segments. Word-like segments seem to be the most robust representation to be used as they yield significantly better results at three different layers ($GRU_{PACK}.-2,3,4$). We also notice that phone segments bring no improvement over the baseline at $GRU_{PACK}.-4,5$ showing that these layers do not handle phone like information. All in all, these results are in line with that of Chrupała et al. (2017) who found that the intermediate representations of the fifth layer is the less informative in predicting word presence, while lower layers encode this information better. This confirms that the middle layers of our architecture deal with lexical units whereas the fifth layer encodes information that disregards that type of information.

4.4 Segmentation as a Means for Compression

Recall that in the KEEP condition, only the last vector comprising a segment is kept while the other vectors are discarded. This can be interpreted as a form of "guided" subsampling, as usually subsampling does not take into consideration linguistic factors. To understand how much information is kept between the input and the output of a GRU_{PACK}.

layer in the KEEP condition, we compute an average compression rate (in %) for each of the segment types for Flickr8k. The results are the following: phones = 90.57%, syllables-connected = 93.41%, syllables-word = 94.36%, and words = 94.90%.[11] When we re-analyse our results in light of this information, it appears we can remove a large part of the original input (up to 94.90% if using word segments) while conserving or increasing the original R@1. It is not simply the effect of subsampling that helps, but subsampling with *meaningful* linguistic units. The effect of informed subsampling is striking when we compare R@1 for RANDOM-KEEP, which are always below the BASELINE, while TRUE-KEEP are on a par with the BASELINE or better. A counter-intuitive finding of our experiments is that it is better to subsample early on (in the first layers) and thus remove most of the information early on than later on. Subsampling with word segments in $GRU_{PACK}.-2$ (and thus only keeping 5.1% of the original amount of information for the subsequent layers) yields better results than subsampling with the same resolution at $GRU_{PACK}.-5$.

5 Towards Hierarchical Segmentation

In our current approach, only one out of the five recurrent layers is a GRU_{PACK}. layer, which handles only one type of segment. However, we can stack as many GRU_{PACK}. as desired, provided they are supplied with boundary information. Stacking such layers enables us to not only integrate bound-

---

[11] Note that the compression rate for syllables-word and words is very close, suggesting there is a significant overlap between syllables-word units and word units.

Architecture		5 layers					4 layers				3 layers			2 layers	
1st GRU$_{\text{PACK.}}$ \\ 2nd GRU$_{\text{PACK.}}$		1	2	3	4	5	1	2	3	4	1	2	3	1	2
1			7.7	7.7	7.3	3.9		7.6	7.9	5.7		**8.1**	5.3		**6.4**
2				8.2	7.6	5.8			**8.1**	6.3			7.3		
3					7.1	6.5				6.7					
4						6.1									
5															
Baseline (No GRU$_{\text{PACK.}}$)		4.3					4.4				3.4			3.5	

Table 3: R@1 obtained on the test set of the Flickr8k data set with a hierarchical architecture consisting of two GRU$_{\text{PACK.}}$ layers using phone and word segments (models were selected based on the maximum R@1 on the validation set). Best score overall is shown in red. Best score (layer-wise) is shown in **bold**. Greyed out cell signal impossible configurations. We also indicate R@1 obtained on a baseline architecture without any GRU$_{\text{PACK.}}$.

ary information, but also introduce structure, where one layer handles one type of segment (e.g. phone) and the following GRU$_{\text{PACK.}}$ layer handles another type of segment, that is hierarchically above the preceding (e.g. syllable, or word).[12] Harwath et al. (2020) explored such hierarchical architecture using a CNN-based model that incorporated vector quantisation layers and found that it improves R@k. Our work thus attempts to verify if it is also the case for an RNN-based model.

Phones and Words: We first explore hierarchical segmentation with phones and words on the Flickr8k data set.[13] We only consider the KEEP condition as it yields better results than the ALL condition. We vary the position of the GRU$_{\text{PACK.}}$ layers as well as the number of layers (from 2 to 5) and test all possible positions with two GRU$_{\text{PACK.}}$ layers. For each configuration, the lowest GRU$_{\text{PACK.}}$ will receive phone boundary information, and the next GRU$_{\text{PACK.}}$ layer will receive word boundary information. Note that such configuration results in a double sequence reduction. Indeed, after the first GRU$_{\text{PACK.}}$ layer, they are only as many output vectors as there are phones, and in the second, the resulting phone vectors are recomposed together to form words, resulting in as many output vectors as there are words. Results are shown in Table 3. Training an architecture with two GRU$_{\text{PACK.}}$ layers, each handling two different types of segments results in much better R@1 than the baseline (+3.9pp) and than a single-GRU$_{\text{PACK.}}$-layered architecture (+2.8pp), thus showing that introducing hierarchy is beneficial. Results also confirm that

the layer 2 and 3 of our architecture are those that benefit the most from adding linguistic information, and confirm the fact that the upper layers (such as the fifth) do not take as much advantage of this information as the lower layers. Introducing structure allowed us to remove two recurrent layers without a big loss of performance ($R@1 = 8.1$ for a three-layered architecture with two GRU$_{\text{PACK.}}$ layers) while the baseline architecture with only three layers performs poorly.

Phones, Syllables, and Words: We also explore an architecture with 3 GRU$_{\text{PACK.}}$ layers, to which we provide phone, syllable-word and word boundaries. As in our previous experiments, we vary the number of layers (from 3 to 5), and test all possible configurations. The results of this experiment are presented in Table 4. We notice that the best result obtained with this architecture is far superior to the best result of a single-layered architecture ($R@1 = 9.6$, +4.2pp), but also superior to the best result of a double-layered architecture (+1.4pp over the phone-word architecture). Our best results are obtained by a five-layered architecture with GRU$_{\text{PACK.}}$ in position 1, 3 and 4. However, we notice that the four-layered architecture obtains more consistent results across all layers, the maximum result being only -0.3pp away from best five-layered architecture. We also notice that the 3 layered architecture obtains a very high R@1 of 8.0 which is about two times over the baseline results.

Our results show that the more structure we introduce into the network, the better it performs. Additionally, introducing structure enables us to reduce the number of layers (and hence the number of computations) while increasing the performances compared to the baseline. Overall, it is better to

---

[12]Note that it could also be possible to use larger units, such as chunks.

[13]We also explored two other hierarchical architectures that use phones and syllables-word, and syllables-word and words. The results are reported in Appendix B in Table 6 and Table 7.

use boundary information in coordination in a hierarchical structure than using them in isolation.

Architecture $GRU_{PACK.}$	5 layers	4 layers	3 layers
1 + 2 + 3	8.5	**9.3**	8.0
1 + 2 + 4	8.1	8.6	
1 + 2 + 5	7.8		
1 + 3 + 4	9.6	8.4	
1 + 3 + 5	7.9		
1 + 4 + 5	7.8		
2 + 3 + 4	8.8	8.3	
2 + 3 + 5	8.5		
2 + 4 + 5	8.3		
3 + 4 + 5	7.8		

Table 4: R@1 obtained on the test set of the Flickr8k data set with a hierarchical architecture consisting of three $GRU_{PACK.}$ layers using phone, syllable-word and word segments (models were selected based on the maximum R@1 on the validation set).

6 Discussion and Future Work

The goal of our experiments is to see if segmenting speech in sub-units is beneficial, and if so, which units maximise the performance. It is indeed the case that segmenting speech into sub-units helps. As to which segment obtains the best performance we observe mixed results. Indeed, word segmentation yields better results than phone segmentation, but we do also observe that syllable-like segmentation also gives results that are in the same ballpark as word segmentation. Nevertheless, word segmentation seems to be a *more robust* representation compared to syllable as such word segments consistently yield better results at various levels of our architecture.

Another finding of our experiments which we believe is important is that one cannot subsample speech without taking into account its linguistic nature. Indeed, random subsampling might yield results on a par with the baseline, but this might only be a regularisation effect. *Linguistically informed subsampling* (KEEP condition) yields however much better results and should be favoured.

Regarding the question of why textual approaches perform better than spoken approaches, we conclude that the fact that tokens stand for full semantic units plays little in their performance. The fact that text-based models use segmented input (either tokens or characters) also seems to play little in the final performance, otherwise we should have observed better results as our input was also segmented. What seems most crucial is that the representation of a token never changes whereas speech exhibits lots of variation, as no word is pronounced exactly in the same fashion when uttered. Our approach helped the network in building more consistent representations for the same word (especially in the KEEP condition, see Figure 2), even though it did not succeed for every word. Consistent representation across various occurrences seems to be the most important factor.

Finally, our experiments allowed us to observe that, such as for humans, the use of large units, such as words, is indeed the most efficient solution to learn a reliable speech-to-image mapping. Indeed, even if phone and syllable-like units yield non trivial results, they are less robust than word segments. Our $GRU_{PACK.}$ setting also allowed us to simply introduce hierarchy in a neural network by simply stacking $GRU_{PACK.}$ layers and providing different boundary information to each of them. Our experiments allowed us to confirm the results obtained by Harwath et al. (2020) on a CNN-based VGS model, stating that introducing hierarchical structures proves beneficial overall even for shallower architectures. Interestingly, our hierarchical experiments allowed us to notice that using segment boundaries in isolation only brings slight improvements. It is only when different levels are combined (phones and words, or phones, syllables and words) that the performance of the network reaches its peak.

The future lines of work we imagine consist in *learning* where the boundaries are located instead of supplying boundary information to the network at training and testing time. We could indeed use ACT recurrent cells (Kreutzer and Sokolov, 2018) or an architecture such as (Chen et al., 2019) that would dynamically and unsupervisedly learn how to segment the input signal into sub-units. The additional advantage of such methods is that they make no presupposition on the form/size of the segments, and consequently on what a good segment should or should not be, but lets the network find the optimal solution. Finally, we plan to also introduce syntactic information and integrate chunk boundaries and measure the impact of syntactical grouping of spoken units.

Acknowledgments

This work was supported by grants from NeuroCoG IDEX UGA as part of the "Investissements d'avenir" program (ANR-15-IDEX-02).

References

Emmanuel Azuh, David Harwath, and James Glass. 2019. Towards Bilingual Lexicon Discovery From Visually Grounded Speech Audio. In *Proc. Interspeech 2019*, pages 276–280.

Colin Bannard and Danielle Matthews. 2008. Stored word sequences in language learning: The effect of familiarity on children's repetition of four-word combinations. *Psychological Science*, 19(3):241–248. PMID: 18315796.

Heather Bortfeld, James L. Morgan, Roberta Michnick Golinkoff, and Karen Rathbun. 2005. Mommy and me: Familiar names help launch babies into speech-stream segmentation. *Psychological Science*, 16(4):298–304. PMID: 15828977.

Y. Chen, S. Huang, H. Lee, Y. Wang, and C. Shen. 2019. Audio word2vec: Sequence-to-sequence autoencoding for unsupervised learning of audio segmentation and representation. *IEEE/ACM Transactions on Audio, Speech, and Language Processing*, 27(9):1481–1493.

Kyunghyun Cho, Bart van Merrienboer, Caglar Gulcehre, Dzmitry Bahdanau, Fethi Bougares, Holger Schwenk, and Yoshua Bengio. 2014. Learning phrase representations using rnn encoder–decoder for statistical machine translation. In *Proceedings of the 2014 Conference on Empirical Methods in Natural Language Processing (EMNLP)*, pages 1724–1734. Association for Computational Linguistics.

Grzegorz Chrupała, Lieke Gelderloos, and Afra Alishahi. 2017. Representations of language in a model of visually grounded speech signal. In *Proceedings of the 55th Annual Meeting of the Association for Computational Linguistics (Volume 1: Long Papers)*, pages 613–622. Association for Computational Linguistics.

Grzegorz Chrupała, Lieke Gelderloos, and Afra Alishahi. 2017. Synthetically spoken coco. [Data set] http://doi.org/10.5281/zenodo.400926.

D. Harwath, G. Chuang, and J. Glass. 2018. Vision as an interlingua: Learning multilingual semantic embeddings of untranscribed speech. In *2018 IEEE International Conference on Acoustics, Speech and Signal Processing (ICASSP)*, pages 4969–4973.

David Harwath and James Glass. 2015. Deep multimodal semantic embeddings for speech and images. In *2015 IEEE Workshop on Automatic Speech Recognition and Understanding (ASRU)*, pages 237–244.

David Harwath, Wei-Ning Hsu, and James R. Glass. 2020. Learning hierarchical discrete linguistic units from visually-grounded speech. In *8th International Conference on Learning Representations, ICLR 2020, Addis Ababa, Ethiopia, April 26-30, 2020*. OpenReview.net.

David Harwath, Antonio Torralba, and James R. Glass. 2016. Unsupervised learning of spoken language with visual context. In *Proceedings of the 30th International Conference on Neural Information Processing Systems*, NIPS'16, page 1866–1874, Red Hook, NY, USA. Curran Associates Inc.

William N. Havard, Jean-Pierre Chevrot, and Laurent Besacier. 2019. Models of Visually Grounded Speech Signal Pay Attention to Nouns: A Bilingual Experiment on English and Japanese. In *ICASSP 2019 - 2019 IEEE International Conference on Acoustics, Speech and Signal Processing (ICASSP)*, pages 8618–8622.

William N. Havard, Jean-Pierre Chevrot, and Laurent Besacier. 2019. Word Recognition, Competition, and Activation in a Model of Visually Grounded Speech. In *Proceedings of the 23rd Conference on Computational Natural Language Learning (CoNLL)*, pages 339–348, Hong Kong, China. Association for Computational Linguistics.

Micah Hodosh, Peter Young, and Julia Hockenmaier. 2013. Framing image description as a ranking task: Data, models and evaluation metrics. *Journal of Artificial Intelligence Research*, 47:853–899.

Otto Jespersen. 1929. *Monosyllabism in English*.

P.W. Jusczyk and R.N. Aslin. 1995. Infants′ detection of the sound patterns of words in fluent speech. *Cognitive Psychology*, 29(1):1–23.

Herman Kamper, Shane Settle, Gregory Shakhnarovich, and Karen Livescu. 2017. Visually grounded learning of keyword prediction from untranscribed speech. pages 3677–3681.

Thomas Kisler, Uwe Reichel, and Florian Schiel. 2017. Multilingual processing of speech via web services. *Computer Speech & Language*, 45:326 – 347.

Julia Kreutzer and Artem Sokolov. 2018. Learning to segment inputs for NMT favors character-level processing. *Proceedings of the International Workshop on Spoken Language Translation October 29-30, 2018 Bruges, Belgium*, 1:166–172.

Tsung-Yi Lin, Michael Maire, Serge Belongie, James Hays, Pietro Perona, Deva Ramanan, Piotr Dollár, C. Lawrence Zitnick, Tomas Pajdla, Bernt Schiele, and Tinne Tuytelaars. 2014. Microsoft coco: Common objects in context. In *Computer Vision – ECCV 2014*, pages 740–755, Cham. Springer International Publishing.

Danny Merkx and Stefan L. Frank. 2019. Learning semantic sentence representations from visually grounded language without lexical knowledge. *Natural Language Engineering*, 25(4):451–466.

Danny Merkx, Stefan L. Frank, and Mirjam Ernestus. 2019. Language Learning Using Speech to Image Retrieval. In *Proc. Interspeech 2019*, pages 1841–1845.

Y. Ohishi, A. Kimura, T. Kawanishi, K. Kashino, D. Harwath, and J. Glass. 2020. Trilingual semantic embeddings of visually grounded speech with self-attention mechanisms. In *ICASSP 2020 - 2020 IEEE International Conference on Acoustics, Speech and Signal Processing (ICASSP)*, pages 4352–4356.

Deb K. Roy and Alex P. Pentland. 2002. Learning words from sights and sounds: a computational model. *Cognitive Science*, 26(1):113–146.

Jean Vroomen and Beatrice De Gelder. 1999. Lexical access of resyllabified words: Evidence from phoneme monitoring. *Memory & Cognition*, 27(3):413–421.

Learning to Ground Medical Text in a 3D Human Atlas

Dusan Grujicic*, Gorjan Radevski*, Tinne Tuytelaars, Matthew B. Blaschko
Department of Electrical Engineering (ESAT-PSI)
KU Leuven
`firstname.lastname@esat.kuleuven.be`

Abstract

In this paper, we develop a method for grounding medical text into a physically meaningful and interpretable space corresponding to a human atlas. We build on text embedding architectures such as BERT and introduce a loss function that allows us to reason about the semantic and spatial relatedness of medical texts by learning a projection of the embedding into a 3D space representing the human body. We quantitatively and qualitatively demonstrate that our proposed method learns a context sensitive and spatially aware mapping, in both the inter-organ and intra-organ sense, using a large scale medical text dataset from the "Large-scale online biomedical semantic indexing" track of the 2020 BioASQ challenge. We extend our approach to a self-supervised setting, and find it to be competitive with a classification based method, and a fully supervised variant of approach.

1 Introduction

The quantity of available medical literature increases daily (Wang et al.; Tsatsaronis et al., 2015), however, it is often provided in a non-systematized, free form. The development of BERT (Devlin et al., 2018), and the increased popularity of transfer learning in natural language processing (NLP), prompted notable works that aim to leverage publicly available medical and scientific articles to develop domain specific pre-trained language models (Lee et al., 2019; Alsentzer et al., 2019; Beltagy et al., 2019; Jin et al., 2019). High quality sentence representations that capture the semantics and structure of the text can be obtained by training models to solve the Natural Language Inference (NLI) task on open-domain datasets (Bowman et al., 2015; Williams et al., 2017) and predict whether two pieces of text entail, contradict or are neutral to

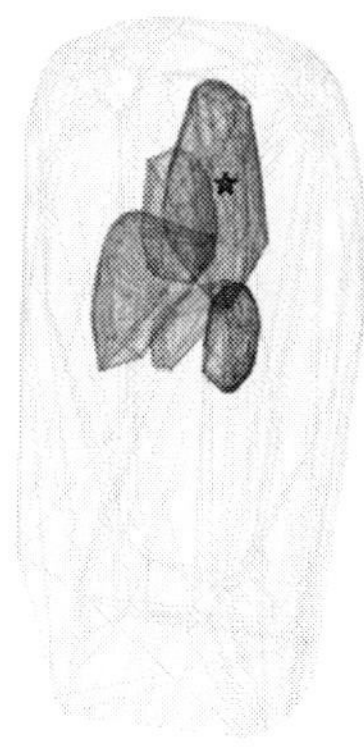

Figure 1: Given the text with implicit reference to lungs: "Divided into two lobes, an upper and a lower lobe, by the oblique fissure, which extends from the costal to the mediastinal surface" (Drake et al., 2009), our model learns the grounding indicated by the star.

each other (Conneau et al., 2017). The aforementioned BERT-based models can serve as the encoder backbone for such approaches (Reimers and Gurevych, 2019), and the setup can be trivially extended to enable searching through and retrieving relevant documents from large datasets. Despite proving useful in a variety of settings, these works suffer from the following limitations:

(i) The documents are embedded in a non-interpretable space. (ii) There is no clear visually intuitive indication of how similar two retrieved documents are, i.e., black box retrieval. (iii) Visualizing the embeddings requires dimensionality reduction techniques (Hotelling, 1933; Maaten and Hinton, 2008).

By contrast, we propose a method that embeds medical text into a universal, small dimensional space corresponding to the human body that is easy to navigate and interpret (Figure 1). The propensity of functionally similar organs towards being physically close represents an inductive bias that can be leveraged for computing compact, 3D text representations that are competitive with standard higher dimensional text embeddings. Additionally, our approach allows to search through and retrieve documents grounded within the physical space of the human body. To that end, our contributions are:

---

*Equal Contribution

302

Proceedings of the 24th Conference on Computational Natural Language Learning, pages 302–312
Online, November 19-20, 2020. ©2020 Association for Computational Linguistics
https://doi.org/10.18653/v1/P17

(i) We propose the task of the grounding medical text in the physical space of the human body, where anatomically related substructures tend to be close to one another. (ii) We develop a loss function that allows us to reason about the semantic relatedness of medical texts. (iii) We develop a concrete use-case for medical text retrieval where we outperform several competitive baselines.

We perform extensive evaluation to measure the performance of our method in two scenarios, namely, grounding in the human atlas (relevant for visualization and navigation), and medical text-to-text retrieval (directly assessing the performance of our model in an information retrieval setting). Furthermore, we set up an experimental setting explicitly tailored to measure the spatial reasoning ability of our model within an organ, a setting never directly imposed during training. We empirically demonstrate that our method is highly successful in all aforementioned experimental settings, effectively addressing the previously stated limitations. The codebase and the trained models are released at: `www.github.com/gorjanradevski/text2atlas`

2   Related work

(Medical) text embeddings. Before the development of BERT, a common approach to embedding text was leveraging a pre-trained recurrent neural network (RNN) language model (LM) (Peters et al., 2018; Kiros et al., 2015). An extension of such LM for the biomedical domain is BioELMO (Jin et al., 2019). Despite being successful in a transfer learning setting, the usefulness of the generated embeddings for medical text navigation and retrieval is arguably limited. Furthermore, BERT-based medical language representation models such as BIOBERT (Lee et al., 2019) and CLINICALBERT (Alsentzer et al., 2019), despite outperforming RNN based LMs on a variety of downstream tasks, also make embedded text navigation impractical. We, on the other hand, directly focus on learning embeddings that are rich with visual information, i.e., are by default represented in a physically meaningful space of the human body.

(Medical) text grounding. There has been a variety of approaches (Krishnamurthy and Kollar, 2013; Kong et al., 2014; Rohrbach et al., 2016; Hu et al., 2016; Wang et al., 2018) and datasets, such as ReferIt (Kazemzadeh et al., 2014) and RefCOCO (Yu et al., 2016), focusing on the visual grounding of natural language in the general domain. However, the application of text grounding in the medical domain has been limited, and to the best of our knowledge, there are no works that ground medical text in the human body. The main differences between these works and ours are: (i) we perform a grounding which is universal, and not specific to a single environment (e.g. the image), (ii) their models are trained with expensive bounding box annotations for the desired grounding location, (iii) the methods rely on explicit annotations of every concept referred in the text, i.e., these models can not reason about the particular referred region unless explicitly trained to do so. Furthermore, our method is designed to reduce the labeling costs, as it relies on high level annotations of the referred organs in a paragraph, which, in a self-supervised setting, can be inferred from the text itself.

(Medical) Document retrieval. Retrieving a set of relevant documents given a query requires that both the query and the documents are embedded in a joint latent space. A straight-forward approach to obtaining a single text representation is to use the `[CLS]` token representation concatenated with the mean-pooled and max-pooled representations of the remaining tokens from a pre-trained BERT model. However, it is shown that this often leads to a worse representation than averaging GloVe embeddings (Pennington et al., 2014; Reimers and Gurevych, 2019). Recently, such embeddings are obtained using a pre-trained BERT subsequently fine-tuned as a Siamese model (Reimers and Gurevych, 2019) on the NLI task using general domain datasets (Bowman et al., 2015; Williams et al., 2017). The proxy-task is proven to be effective as models trained this way generate embeddings in which documents that share similar semantics map nearby. Despite this useful feature, without inspecting the documents' content, it is not immediately obvious why a set of documents is clustered together in the latent space, and why they are considered to be semantically similar. We address this issue by embedding documents in the physical space of the human body, where the document similarity is expressed in terms of physical proximities in 3D. This leads to an intuitive interpretation of why a set of documents are considered to be similar.

3 Data collection

3.1 Human body atlas

We leverage the Segmented Inner Organs (SIO)
(Pommert et al., 2001) (see Appendix, Figure A.1),
though the approach is readily extended to other
models of the human anatomy. We refer to this
3D model as the *atlas*. We base the 3D atlas on
the segmentation labels of the tissues in the human
body provided in SIO, which come in the form
of image slices that form a 3D voxel model of the
male torso when stacked on top of one another. The
stacked images from the torso represent a volume
of $573 \times 330 \times 774$ voxels, with 1-millimeter resolution along each axis. The value of each voxel
represents the segmentation label of its corresponding organ or tissue. An organ can be represented as
the set of indices of voxels in the aforementioned
volume which contain the value corresponding to
the organ's segmentation label.[1]

3.2 Dataset

The dataset used in this work is built upon the training set of the Task 8a: "Large-scale online biomedical semantic indexing" of the 2020 BioASQ challenge (Tsatsaronis et al., 2015). Originally, it consists of 14,913,939 samples, where each sample
pertains to one medical article, and contains the
abstract text and the Medical Subject Headings
(MeSH) (Lipscomb, 2000) vocabulary terms of the
organs. We consider the grounding of article abstracts to the locations in the atlas that correspond
to the article MeSH terms. Therefore, we use the
articles that contain one or more MeSH terms that
match the names or the alias terms of the organs in
the atlas glossary. To accommodate the maximal
sequence length of BERT$_{\text{BASE}}$, we keep the articles
whose abstracts have fewer than 512 WordPiece
(Wu et al., 2016) tokens. For each organ in the
atlas glossary, we take 500 articles that mention
it individually, and another 500 articles that mention it in addition to another organ(s). Subsequent
removal of duplicates resulted in the final dataset
of 25,552 abstracts annotated with organ MeSH
terms, of which 70% are used for training, 15% for
validation and 15% for testing.[2]

4 Proposed task and methods

4.1 Text-to-atlas grounding objective

Our goal is to ground medical texts into the 3D
space of the human body. To achieve this, we
project the representations of text referring to one
or more atlas organs into the 3D volume in the atlas that corresponds to the mentioned organs. The
volume of each organ is characterized by a set of
voxels in the atlas, which capture its position, size
and shape. The voxels of one organ can, in turn, be
represented by a point cloud in 3D space, where
each point represents the coordinate indices of one
voxel[3]. The most straightforward way to associate
texts with predefined regions of a physical space,
is to have a model trained to simply minimize the
cross-entropy between the predicted probability
distribution over the set of all organs (e.g., each
indexing their predefined location), and the target
vector with 1's at the indices corresponding to the
target organs and 0's elsewhere. This approach is
expected to yield a high accuracy of selecting the
right organ, however, has a critical downside of not
providing any meaningful within organ reasoning,
i.e., during inference, it grounds all articles pertaining to a single organ to either a random location
within the organ, or a single predefined one. On
the other hand, framing the task as minimization of
the mean squared error between the predicted 3D
location and an average of the ground truth organ
positions would result in a grounding to some mid-
way location, potentially belonging to some other,
unrelated organ. To overcome both of these issues,
and retain as much of the predictive power as possible, we frame the task as predicting a set of 3D
coordinates within the human body, while forcing
the prediction to snap to the most nearby ground
truth organ. Namely, we design a loss function –
Soft Organ Distance loss, henceforth abbreviated as
SOD (Section 4.3), which gives the model freedom
to choose the most relevant organ in case there are
multiple organ annotations for a particular sample.

4.2 Model

We use BERT (Devlin et al., 2018) as our model
backbone due to its applicability in a wide range of
domains. As per Devlin et al. (2018), we tokenize
the input text using WordPiece (Wu et al., 2016),
and take the representation of the `[CLS]` token as
the sequence representation. Finally, to obtain the

---

[1]Details about the creation of the 3D human atlas can be
found in the Appendix Section A.

[2]Additional details about the dataset found in the Appendix
Section B.

[3]For brevity, we will also use the term voxel or organ point
for a vector of indices of the actual voxel in the 3D volume.

3D atlas grounding for a piece of medical text, we project BERT's output with a linear layer, mapping from BERT's hidden space to the 3D space:

$$\hat{y} = \text{Linear}(\text{BERT}(x)), \quad (1)$$

where x is a vector of tokens representing the medical text and $\hat{y}$ is the 3D grounding in the human body. During training, we normalize $\hat{y}$ by applying tanh, which is subsequently rescaled to the dimensions of the atlas during inference.

4.3 Soft Organ Distance loss

The proposed loss function – SOD, allows us to sacrifice the least amount of predictive power and in turn, achieve within organ contextual reasoning, i.e., not only grounding the medical article to the right organ but also to the appropriate location within the organ without any explicit annotations at that level of granularity. Furthermore, a medical text may simultaneously refer to a single or multiple organs in the human body. In the former setting, we would like to have an approach based on mean squared error minimization, while in the latter, we would like to relax the target and pull the model's prediction to the location of the closest ground truth organ. Finally, the organs themselves are distributed in nature, and their volumes are characterized by a set of points in 3D space, rather than just one.

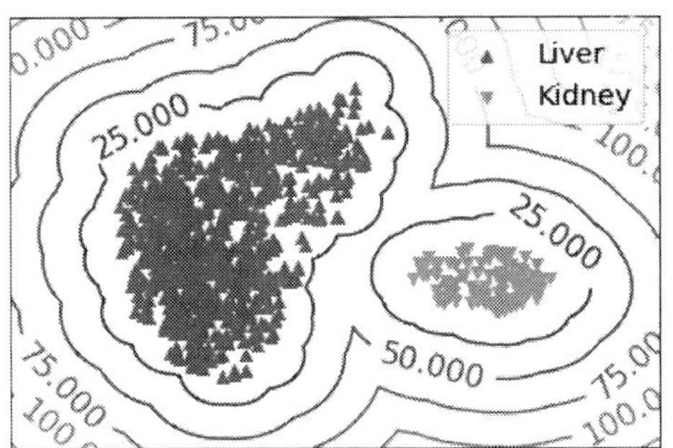

Figure 2: Loss isocurves around "liver" and "kidney" point clouds projected into 2D with PCA (Hotelling, 1933).

In Figure 2, we observe our desired scenario when there are two ground truth organs – "liver" and "kidney". As the grounding approaches the "liver", we observe that the loss contribution from the "kidney" organ voxels diminishes, and vice versa. This effect extends to the loss contributions of individual voxel points. Namely, as the grounding approaches a particular region in the organ, the loss contribution from the other voxel points diminishes – thus allowing the model to ground the input text within the most appropriate organ substructure.

In order to account for the distributed nature of the organs and take a step towards the desired within organ semantic reasoning, for each sample during training, we randomly sample a set of N points from the point cloud of each of its organs. Then, we calculate (1) the Euclidean distances between the prediction and each sampled organ point, and (2) the soft-min[4] across these distances as weights for the contributions of individual points. The loss contribution $\mathcal{L}_p$ of an organ point y is the product of its distance from the predicted point $\hat{y}$ and its corresponding weight produced by the soft-min:

$$\mathcal{L}_p = \|\hat{y} - y\|_2 \frac{\exp(-\|\hat{y} - y\|_2/\gamma_p)}{\sum_{i=1}^{N} \exp(-\|\hat{y} - y_i\|_2/\gamma_p)}, \quad (2)$$

where N is the number of points sampled from the organ point cloud and γ_p is a temperature term. We calculate the loss for one organ $\mathcal{L}_o$ as the sum of contributions of its points: $\mathcal{L}_o = \sum_{i=1}^{N} \mathcal{L}_p^i$.

We calculate the loss for each individual target organ in the way described above. Then, we compute the soft-min over the set of such loss terms as contribution weights for each organ. The total loss is the sum of soft-min-weighted losses over each organ:

$$\mathcal{L}_t = \sum_{i=1}^{M} \mathcal{L}_o^i \frac{\exp(-\mathcal{L}_o^i/\gamma_o)}{\sum_{j=1}^{M} \exp(-\mathcal{L}_o^j/\gamma_o)}, \quad (3)$$

where M is the total number of target organs, $\mathcal{L}_o^i$ is the organ loss for the i-th organ, and γ_o is a temperature term.

5 Experimental setup

We use BERT$_{\text{BASE}}$ (Devlin et al., 2018) as the backbone of the trained models. We use AdamW (Loshchilov and Hutter, 2017) with a learning rate of 10^{-5} as per Devlin et al. (2018), weight decay of 10^{-2} and clip the gradients when the global norm exceeds 2.0. We perform early stopping by saving the model with the best performance on the validation set. We only tune the hyperparameters related to the SOD loss function, and we keep everything else fixed as per the standard practice

---

[4]Soft-max on the inputs reversed in sign, used to emphasize smaller quantities - in this case, shortest distances.

(Devlin et al., 2018). Our implementation utilizes PyTorch (Paszke et al., 2019) and the HuggingFace Transformers library (Wolf et al., 2019).

6 Evaluation

We quantitatively evaluate our trained models in two scenarios: (1) Grounding to the human atlas – measuring to what extent our trained model can ground medical articles to the correct location. (2) Medical information retrieval – to directly assess the quality of the document embeddings, i.e., evaluate to what extent medical articles characterized by a certain set of MeSH terms are grouped together in the physical space of the human body.

6.1 Grounding to the human atlas

To evaluate the quality of the grounding, we measure each of the models performance on three evaluation metrics (more details in Appendix C):

(1) Rate at which the texts are grounded within, or sufficiently close[5], to the volume of the correct organ, or the hit rate, which we denote as Inside Organ Ratio – **IOR**, expressed as percentage. (2) Distance to the nearest voxel of the nearest correct organ, denoted as Nearest Voxel Distance – **NVD**, expressed in centimeters. (3) Distance to the nearest voxel of the nearest correct organ, calculated only on samples for which the projection is outside the organ volume, denoted as Nearest Voxel Distance Outside – **NVD-O**, expressed in centimeters.

We compute the aforementioned metrics in four distinct inference scenarios specifically tailored to measure the grounding ability of our models. In the following experiments we show that our approach has an advantage over multiple baselines and demonstrate its ability to reason within the substructures of the organ and generalize to out-of-atlas organs, in addition to its other desirable properties that we demonstrate qualitatively.

6.1.1 General setting

We generate a 3D grounding for each of the articles in the test set and measure our model's performance against the following baselines:

(i) **Random** – We predict a randomly sampled point within a randomly chosen organ for each sample. (ii) **Center** – We use the center of the 3D atlas as the prediction. (iii) **Frequency (Freq.)** – We measure the frequency of the organ terms in the

training set, and always predict the point within the most frequent organ. (iv) **MSE** – We frame the task as regression, and minimize the mean squared error (MSE) between the prediction and the average of a set of randomly sampled points from all the target organs. (v) **CLS** – We frame the task as classification and train a model to predict an organ index. The model is trained to minimize the cross-entropy between the output probability distribution and the target vector with 1's at the positions corresponding to the indices of organs present in the text and 0's elsewhere. During evaluation, the prediction is considered to be correct when it corresponds to any one of the target MeSH terms. When measuring NVD and NVD-O, we randomly sample a voxel point from the predicted organ as a 3D grounding.[6]

Method	IOR	NVD	NVD-O
Random	8.9 ± 0.5	17.9 ± 0.3	19.0 ± 0.3
Center	6.7 ± 0.4	13.3 ± 0.2	13.3 ± 0.2
Freq.	10.9 ± 0.5	13.9 ± 0.2	15.4 ± 0.2
MSE	$9,9 \pm 0.5$	6.8 ± 0.1	7.0 ± 0.1
CLS	$\mathbf{90.8 \pm 0.5}$	0.9 ± 0.1	8.2 ± 0.5
SOD	89.4 ± 0.5	$\mathbf{0.8 \pm 0.1}$	$\mathbf{2.5 \pm 0.1}$

Table 1: Mean IOR, NVD and NVD-O measured on the test set. The error bars represent the standard error.

In Table 1 we observe that SOD outperforms all baselines, and achieves nearly the same IOR as CLS. Furthermore, SOD significantly outperforms CLS according to the NVD and NVD-O metrics, which give a strong indication of the overall grounding performance, as per the one-sided Wilcoxon signed-rank test (Wilcoxon, 1945) ($p \approx 0$). We conclude that despite framing the task as soft regression, we sacrificed the least amount of predictive power (as per IOR), and exploited the atlas's inductive bias to achieve successful grounding (as per NVD and NVD-O).

6.1.2 Within organ reasoning

We perform a simulation to demonstrate that the grounding can infer anatomical substructures not present at the granularity of labeling in a specific atlas. Therefore, we perform experiments in which we merge the voxels of two different organs – effectively treating them as a single organ, and keep only instances from the training set that contain

---

[5]As some organs are hollow (small intestine, colon, etc.), we record a "hit", when the grounding is less than 1cm away from the most nearby voxel.

[6]We do not use the organ voxels centroids as prediction, as they can be outside of the organ volume for non-convex organs and yield a non-zero distance even when the correct organ is predicted, unfairly penalizing the classification baseline.

these "super-organs".[7] Then, we train a new model on each of these subsets and subsequently generate 3D groundings for each of the test set samples that only contain the individual occurrences of the two merged organs. The merged organ pairs are: (i) the "lung" and the "stomach", functionally different organs that belong to different groups, respiratory and digestive, respectively; and (ii) the "duodenum"[8] and the "small intestine", organs which are functionally related and frequently jointly referred to as "small intestine" in the literature.

Then, we train three different models for each merger: (1) **SMP** – We train a classification baseline on each of the subsets. During inference, we substitute the organ index with a randomly sampled voxel point within the predicted organ (2) **SOD w/** – We train a model using SOD with (w/) individual organs from the filtered training set. (3) **SOD w/o** – We train a model with the two organs merged into one "super-organ", effectively training without (w/o) the per-organ annotations.

With the functionally different "lung" and "stomach" merged together, in Table 2 we observe that SOD w/o significantly outperforms SMP, which can predict the coarse label corresponding to the super-organ, but is unable to reason about the organ's subregions. We also observe that SOD w/o performance is relatively close to SOD w/, which is trained with the separated organs. In Figure 3 we observe the grounding of 136 articles related to the "lung" and the "stomach" generated with SOD w/o. A notably harder problem is the "small intestine"-"duodenum" merger, which involves functionally related organs. We again observe that SOD w/o significantly outperforms SMP in both the micro-averaged performance and the grounding within the "duodenum". SMP achieves higher IOR on the articles that belong to the "small intestine," which is a result of the roughly 3 times larger number of "small intestine" voxels compared to the "duodenum" making the SMP performance skewed. We further examine the approximate locations of anatomical structures that co-occur most frequently with a given organ. For the organs co-occurring with the "lung", the frequency-weighed arithmetic mean of their centroids lies roughly 13.8 centimeters above that of the organs that co-occur with the "stomach". Similarly, such mean location of organs co-occurring with the "duodenum" lies 6.5 cen-

timeters to the upper-left of the one of the "small intestine".

We conclude that despite the lack of explicit within organ annotations, SOD w/o learns to spatially reason about substructures within the organ based on the target organs' co-occurrences. In particular, the model learns to disambiguate between the organ regions because terms associated with different sub-regions tend to co-occur with different organs, typically the ones to which they are closer to (See Appendix Section F). This is an important observation from the following aspects: (i) Medical articles would get mapped to the appropriate organ regions they refer to, even though never explicitly annotated as such during training. (ii) Given an atlas with increased granularity, our method would, to a degree, accommodate for the newly added sub-regions without the need for re-training.

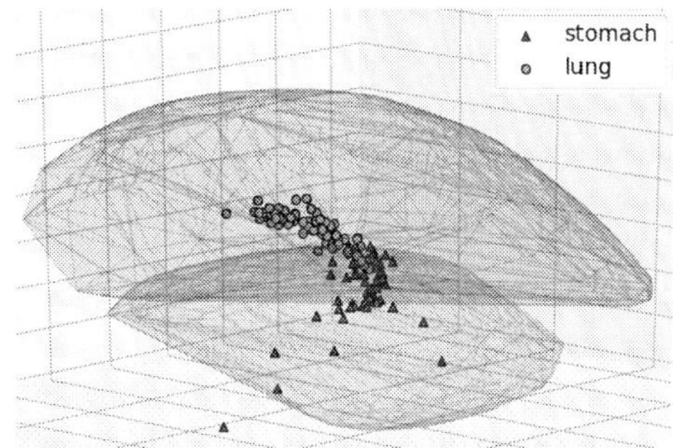

Figure 3: Groundings of articles referring exclusively to either the "lung" or the "stomach", obtained from a model trained with the two organs fused into one.

6.1.3 Generalization to unseen organs

To verify that our approach captures the locations of organs which are absent in the atlas segmentation labels, we evaluate the generalization ability of our method to organs unseen during training. For every organ, we remove its annotation from the training set, train a separate model, perform inference on the test set samples referring to it, and finally report the metrics averaged over all held-out organs.[9] In addition to NVD, we measure the rate at which the prediction is within the convex hull enveloping the organs of the same functional group as the held out organ, denoted as Inside Group Ratio – **IGR**. We compare SOD's performance against Random, Center and CLS, defined in Section 1.

---

[7] It may occur individually or co-occur with other organs.

[8] The duodenum is the first section of the small intestine in most higher vertebrates, including mammals.

[9] Samples referring solely to the held-out organ are removed, and the ones referring to it in addition to some other organs retain only the annotations of the other organs.

Method	IOR	NVD	IOR	NVD	IOR	NVD
	Lung		Stomach		Total	
SOD w/	100.0 ± 0.0	0.0 ± 0.0	95.4 ± 2.6	0.2 ± 0.1	97.8 ± 1.3	0.1 ± 0.0
SMP	46.5 ± 6.0	2.5 ± 0.3	44.6 ± 6.2	4.2 ± 0.6	45.6 ± 4.3	3.3 ± 0.3
SOD w/o	$\mathbf{94.4 \pm 2.8}$	$\mathbf{0.2 \pm 0.1}$	$\mathbf{81.5 \pm 4.8}$	$\mathbf{0.5 \pm 0.1}$	$\mathbf{88.2 \pm 2.8}$	$\mathbf{0.3 \pm 0.1}$
	Small intestine		Duodenum		Total	
SOD w/	97.4 ± 1.8	0.1 ± 0.0	90.9 ± 3.6	0.2 ± 0.1	94.4 ± 1.9	0.2 ± 0.0
SMP	$\mathbf{71.1 \pm 5.2}$	$\mathbf{1.0 \pm 0.2}$	33.3 ± 5.8	5.1 ± 0.6	53.5 ± 4.2	2.9 ± 0.3
SOD w/o	50.0 ± 5.8	1.1 ± 0.1	$\mathbf{93.9 \pm 3.0}$	$\mathbf{0.2 \pm 0.0}$	$\mathbf{70.4 \pm 3.8}$	$\mathbf{0.7 \pm 0.1}$

Table 2: Within organ reasoning evaluated on test set subsets obtained according choice of organs merged.

Method	IGR	NVD
Random	34.5 ± 4.0	21.1 ± 1.5
Center	37.0 ± 9.5	15.8 ± 2.0
CLS	$72.1 \pm 5.8 \ (84.21)$	$8.3 \pm 1.0 \ (6.9)$
SOD	$\mathbf{76.5 \pm 5.3 \ (86.15)}$	$\mathbf{7.5 \pm 1.0 \ (5.9)}$

Table 3: Results on test set samples referring to organs held out during training. Median values are in parentheses.

Method	IOR	NVD	NVD-O
Occ	68.7 ± 0.7	3.2 ± 0.1	9.7 ± 0.3
CLS	74.1 ± 0.7	2.5 ± 0.1	8.4 ± 0.3
CLS + M	80.4 ± 0.6	1.7 ± 0.1	7.3 ± 0.3
SOD	79.7 ± 0.7	1.6 ± 0.1	5.1 ± 0.2
SOD + M	$\mathbf{83.2 \pm 0.6}$	$\mathbf{1.2 \pm 0.1}$	$\mathbf{3.9 \pm 0.2}$

Table 4: Results on the full test set when the models are trained in a self-supervised fashion.

In Table 3, we observe that SOD significantly outperforms Random and Center. We also confirm a significant advantage of SOD over CLS by performing a Wilcoxon signed-rank test (IGR: $p = 0.0063$; NVD: $p = 0.0014$). Therefore, we conclude that besides grounding texts regarding organs present in the atlas, SOD reasons about unannotated structures, i.e., it learns to leverage the shared context between the held out organ and the functionally similar organs nearby. Consequently, we conclude that SOD learns to relate the articles' context with the spatial domain of the human body, and exploits this knowledge to improve generalization in a *zero-shot* setting. This suggests that our approach is robust to the granularity of the atlas used in training.

6.1.4 Self-supervised extension

We additionally evaluate our method in a self-supervised setting. Specifically, we ground medical abstracts in the atlas using only self-supervision in the form of occurrences of organ related terms. For that, we aggregate a list of all organ names corresponding to the MeSH terms, together with their UMLS synonyms (Bodenreider, 2004). During training, instead of providing the ground truth MeSH term annotation as target organs, we provide the target organs that correspond to the elements of the aggregated list of organ terms that appear in the abstract. We then train two different variants of our method: (1) **SOD** – A model trained with our regular SOD loss function. (2) **SOD + M** – During training, we stochastically substitute the occurrences of organ names or their synonyms in the text with a [MASK] [10] token with 50% probability.

We evaluate the performance of our method against the following baselines: (i) **Occ** – A naive model that predicts one of the organ names that appear in the text at random. When there is no explicit organ occurrence, it predicts the center of the atlas. (ii) **CLS** – A classification baseline, trained to predict one of the organ name occurrences from the text. (iii) **CLS + M** – A classification baseline boosted with the "masking" extension. Finally, we perform inference on the annotated test set and measure the IOR, NVD and NVD-O.

In Table 4 we observe that our method outperforms all baselines when trained both without (SOD), and with the masking extension (SOD + M). Since masking the organ names and their synonyms puts additional emphasis on their surrounding context, it allows the model to generalize better to the semantically annotated test set, yielding a considerable improvement for all metrics. It is noteworthy that in spite of training the model using organ names + synonym occurrences that appear

---

[10]The [MASK] token is included in BERT's vocabulary.

within the medical articles as ground truth targets, we obtain performance competitive to the fully-supervised training, included in Table 1. This data efficiency feature of our method is especially important since obtaining annotated data for medically relevant NLP tasks requires the time and effort of medical experts.

6.2 Medical information retrieval

We formulate a text-to-text retrieval setting where each test set article serves as a query and the remaining articles as the database from which we retrieve the relevant ones. We measure the retrieval quality using the standard Recall@K metric, i.e., the fraction of queries for which the correct article is retrieved among the top K articles. A retrieved article is considered correct when it has an identical set of MeSH term annotations as the query article. We fix K to 1, 5 or 10. We evaluate the performance of our method against the following supervised (w/) and pre-trained (w/o) baselines:

(i) **3D-Sms** (w/) – We train a Siamese BERT to group articles by optimizing the triplet loss, enforcing the embedding of articles with matching sets of MeSH annotations to nearby locations, and the non-matching ones to distant locations in the embedding space. We set the embedding space dimension to 3, and use the Euclidean distance measure and online triplet mining to obtain the positives and negatives for each sample during training (Hermans et al., 2017). (ii) **Large-Sms** (w/) – We follow the same procedure as 3D-Sms, however, we extend the embedding space dimension to 768[11]. (iii) **BaseBert** (w/o) – We use a general domain pre-trained BERT and concatenate the mean-pooled, max-pooled and [CLS] representations into a 2304 dimensional vector for each of the test articles. (iv) **BioBert** (w/o) – We use BERT pre-trained on PubMed abstracts and follow the same procedure as with BASEBERT. (v) **SciBert-NLI** – We use the mean-pooled embeddings from SCIBERT, fine-tuned for the NLI task on the datasets of Bowman et al. (2015); Williams et al. (2017).

In all baselines, we perform retrieval by taking the top K elements from the list of articles ranked by the Euclidean distance between their representation vectors and that of the query. The distance is computed in the representation space for the models trained on the retrieval task and the pre-trained sentence representation models, while for the SOD

models we consider the physical distance in the 3D atlas.

Method	Dims.	R@1	R@5	R@10
Large-Sms (w/)	768	**42.9 ± 0.8**	**68.7 ± 0.7**	**75.4 ± 0.7**
3D-Sms (w/)	3	34.6 ± 0.8	61.4 ± 0.8	69.7 ± 0.7
SOD (w/)	3	37.4 ± 0.8	64.3 ± 0.8	71.3 ± 0.7
BaseBert (w/o)	2304	9.8 ± 0.5	26.1 ± 0.7	37.5 ± 0.8
BioBert (w/o)	2304	13.6 ± 0.6	35.2 ± 0.8	48.5 ± 0.8
SciBert-NLI (w/o)	768	16.9 ± 0.6	41.8 ± 0.8	55.4 ± 0.8
SOD+M (w/o)	3	**26.7 ± 0.7**	**56.8 ± 0.8**	**65.9 ± 0.8**

Table 5: Medical text retrieval. **Top:** Methods that use MeSH term supervision (w/), and **Bottom:** Methods that do not use MeSH annotation (w/o).

In Table 5 (upper), we compare our method with supervised (w/) Siamese models trained to group documents based on their MeSH term annotations. An interesting observation is that despite being trained to choose between the target organs when there are multiple, SOD outperforms 3D-Sms, which is explicitly trained to group articles in 3D based on the whole set of MeSH annotations, without being limited to organizing the article embeddings in the rather constrained 3D human atlas. It is worth noting that SOD falls slightly short compared to Large-Sms, most likely because Large-Sms is trained to embed text in 768 dimensions, thus having a higher representational power.

In Table 5 (lower), we evaluate the retrieval performance of our self-supervised method SOD+M (trained on occurrences of atlas glossary terms and their synonyms, see Section 6.1.4) against the pre-trained BERT baselines, in a setting that does not rely on ground truth MeSH term annotations. We observe that SOD+M significantly outperforms all of them, including SciBert-NLI[12].

We observe a performance gap between SOD+M (w/o) and SOD (w/), as well as the methods that are explicitly trained to optimize the retrieval performance (3D-Sms, Large-Sms). However, in a (realistic) scenario of having large quantities of unannotated medical texts that require systematization, such fully-supervised approaches would not be feasible.

6.3 Qualitative evaluations and use-cases

We further demonstrate several desirable properties of our approach in a qualitative fashion. Although training was performed using a single male atlas, in Figure 4a, we observe the grounding of a paragraph

---

[11]The dimensionality of the BERT embedding.

[12]We report SciBert-NLI as it outperformed BioBert-NLI.

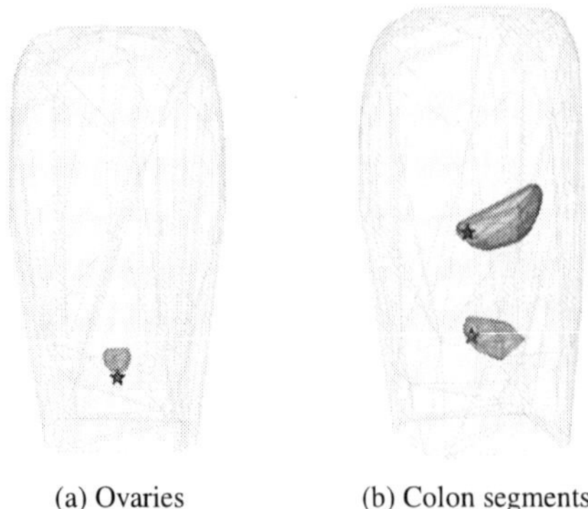

(a) Ovaries   (b) Colon segments

Figure 4: **Left**: Grounding of the paragraph about the "ovaries" (Appendix Section D). The red structure is the "urinary bladder", which serves as a location reference. **Right:** Grounding of Wikipedia articles describing the "transverse colon" (upper) and "sigmoid colon" (lower), which were contained within the common label "colon" during training.

describing the "ovaries" (See Appendix Section D) to a reasonably close vicinity of their actual location. We additionally qualitatively evaluate the results of Section 6.1.2 by mapping Wikipedia articles referring to the "transverse colon" and the "sigmoid colon" to the 3D atlas. In Figure 4b, we observe that the articles are mapped to the actual locations of the colon segments, despite that the terms shared a common label ("colon") during training.

The low dimensional text embeddings in the 3D atlas space can be put to use in multiple real-world applications. Integrated with a speech recognition system, they could be used to provide real time localization of the steps taken during medical procedures based on the narrative operative reports. Additionally, the grounding to a 3D atlas can be used as a way to systematize large corpora of unannotated text while being able to observe the relationship between embedded texts in an intuitively meaningful setting. Another advantage of text retrieval in the physical 3D space is the ability to retrieve information by directly specifying an observable locations in the human atlas space, as opposed to using textual queries. To demonstrate this, we built a tool which accepts a query in the form of 3D coordinates and matches articles related to Covid-19 based on the proximity of their embeddings in 3D space (Grujicic et al., 2020). The tool for visual-based retrieval of Covid-19 related articles can be accessed at: `www.github.com/dusangrujicic/cord19-visualizer`

7 Discussion and conclusions

One limitation of our method is that it does not explicitly take into account spatial descriptions and other modifier expressions. Rather, it uses abstract level annotation to ground whole abstracts to the most semantically relevant regions, and uses the co-occurrences between terms (which also reflect their spatial relationships to a significant degree) to organize and distribute the grounding to within the same organ or to out-of-atlas organs. A natural extension of this work would be to move up from the entity level, and explicitly address the spatial language and descriptions of relationships between anatomical structures.

In this paper, we formulated a novel task of medical text grounding within an atlas of the human body. We proposed a loss function, Soft Organ Distance, which enables us to reason about inter-organ and intra-organ relatedness of medical text, without explicit annotations for the latter. In particular, we addressed the following limitations of prior work: (i) The text is embedded within a non-interpretable space – we embed, and systematically organize all articles in the 3D model of the human body, thus interpretability is intrinsic to our approach. (ii) There is no immediate, visually intuitive indication of the similarity between the retrieved articles – we perform retrieval directly in the 3D atlas, where the text embeddings and the relationships between them are visually comprehensible. Namely, while standard embedding and visualization techniques uncover hidden data clusters, the underlying similarity grouping the articles is not clear. On the other hand, our approach provides semantically and spatially meaningful grounding together with off-the-shelf successful retrieval, which we believe to be essential for many NLP applications involving medical information retrieval and visualization.

Acknowledgements

This work was supported by KU Leuven Internal Funds (MACCHINA) and the Flemish Government under the Onderzoeksprogramma Artificiële Intelligentie (AI) Vlaanderen programme.

References

Emily Alsentzer, John R Murphy, Willie Boag, Wei-Hung Weng, Di Jin, Tristan Naumann, and Matthew McDermott. 2019. Publicly available clinical bert embeddings. *arXiv preprint arXiv:1904.03323*.

Iz Beltagy, Arman Cohan, and Kyle Lo. 2019. Scibert: Pretrained contextualized embeddings for scientific text. *arXiv preprint arXiv:1903.10676*.

Olivier Bodenreider. 2004. The unified medical language system (umls): integrating biomedical terminology. *Nucleic acids research*, 32(suppl_1):D267–D270.

Samuel R Bowman, Gabor Angeli, Christopher Potts, and Christopher D Manning. 2015. A large annotated corpus for learning natural language inference. *arXiv preprint arXiv:1508.05326*.

Andreas Christ, Wolfgang Kainz, Eckhart G Hahn, Katharina Honegger, Marcel Zefferer, Esra Neufeld, Wolfgang Rascher, Rolf Janka, Werner Bautz, Ji Chen, et al. 2009. The virtual family—development of surface-based anatomical models of two adults and two children for dosimetric simulations. *Physics in Medicine & Biology*, 55(2):N23.

Alexis Conneau, Douwe Kiela, Holger Schwenk, Loic Barrault, and Antoine Bordes. 2017. Supervised learning of universal sentence representations from natural language inference data. *arXiv preprint arXiv:1705.02364*.

Jacob Devlin, Ming-Wei Chang, Kenton Lee, and Kristina Toutanova. 2018. Bert: Pre-training of deep bidirectional transformers for language understanding. *arXiv preprint arXiv:1810.04805*.

Richard Drake, A Wayne Vogl, and Adam WM Mitchell. 2009. *Gray's Anatomy for Students E-Book*. Elsevier Health Sciences.

Marie-Christine Gosselin, Esra Neufeld, Heidi Moser, Eveline Huber, Silvia Farcito, Livia Gerber, Maria Jedensjö, Isabel Hilber, Fabienne Di Gennaro, Bryn Lloyd, et al. 2014. Development of a new generation of high-resolution anatomical models for medical device evaluation: the virtual population 3.0. *Physics in Medicine & Biology*, 59(18):5287.

Dusan Grujicic, Gorjan Radevski, Tinne Tuytelaars, and Matthew B Blaschko. 2020. Self-supervised context-aware covid-19 document exploration through atlas grounding. In *ACL Workshop on Natural Language Processing for COVID-19*.

Alexander Hermans, Lucas Beyer, and Bastian Leibe. 2017. In defense of the triplet loss for person re-identification. *arXiv preprint arXiv:1703.07737*.

Karl Heinz Höhne, Bernhard Pflesser, Andreas Pommert, Martin Riemer, Rainer Schubert, Thomas Schiemann, Ulf Tiede, and Udo Schumacher. 2001. A realistic model of human structure from the visible human data. *Methods of information in medicine*, 40(02):83–89.

Harold Hotelling. 1933. Analysis of a complex of statistical variables into principal components. *Journal of educational psychology*, 24(6):417.

Ronghang Hu, Huazhe Xu, Marcus Rohrbach, Jiashi Feng, Kate Saenko, and Trevor Darrell. 2016. Natural language object retrieval. In *Proceedings of the IEEE Conference on Computer Vision and Pattern Recognition*, pages 4555–4564.

Qiao Jin, Bhuwan Dhingra, William W Cohen, and Xinghua Lu. 2019. Probing biomedical embeddings from language models. *arXiv preprint arXiv:1904.02181*.

Sahar Kazemzadeh, Vicente Ordonez, Mark Matten, and Tamara Berg. 2014. Referitgame: Referring to objects in photographs of natural scenes. In *Proceedings of the 2014 conference on empirical methods in natural language processing (EMNLP)*, pages 787–798.

Ryan Kiros, Yukun Zhu, Russ R Salakhutdinov, Richard Zemel, Raquel Urtasun, Antonio Torralba, and Sanja Fidler. 2015. Skip-thought vectors. In *Advances in neural information processing systems*, pages 3294–3302.

Chen Kong, Dahua Lin, Mohit Bansal, Raquel Urtasun, and Sanja Fidler. 2014. What are you talking about? text-to-image coreference. In *Proceedings of the IEEE conference on computer vision and pattern recognition*, pages 3558–3565.

Jayant Krishnamurthy and Thomas Kollar. 2013. Jointly learning to parse and perceive: Connecting natural language to the physical world. *Transactions of the Association for Computational Linguistics*, 1:193–206.

Jinhyuk Lee, Wonjin Yoon, Sungdong Kim, Donghyeon Kim, Sunkyu Kim, Chan Ho So, and Jaewoo Kang. 2019. Biobert: pre-trained biomedical language representation model for biomedical text mining. *arXiv preprint arXiv:1901.08746*.

Carolyn E Lipscomb. 2000. Medical subject headings (mesh). *Bulletin of the Medical Library Association*, 88(3):265.

Ilya Loshchilov and Frank Hutter. 2017. Decoupled weight decay regularization. *arXiv preprint arXiv:1711.05101*.

Laurens van der Maaten and Geoffrey Hinton. 2008. Visualizing data using t-sne. *Journal of machine learning research*, 9(Nov):2579–2605.

Mark Neumann, Daniel King, Iz Beltagy, and Waleed Ammar. 2019. Scispacy: Fast and robust models for biomedical natural language processing.

Adam Paszke, Sam Gross, Francisco Massa, Adam Lerer, James Bradbury, Gregory Chanan, Trevor Killeen, Zeming Lin, Natalia Gimelshein, Luca Antiga, et al. 2019. Pytorch: An imperative style, high-performance deep learning library. In *Advances in neural information processing systems*, pages 8026–8037.

Jeffrey Pennington, Richard Socher, and Christopher D Manning. 2014. Glove: Global vectors for word representation. In *Proceedings of the 2014 conference on empirical methods in natural language processing (EMNLP)*, pages 1532–1543.

Matthew E Peters, Mark Neumann, Mohit Iyyer, Matt Gardner, Christopher Clark, Kenton Lee, and Luke Zettlemoyer. 2018. Deep contextualized word representations. *arXiv preprint arXiv:1802.05365*.

Andreas Pommert, Karl Heinz Höhne, Bernhard Pflesser, Ernst Richter, Martin Riemer, Thomas Schiemann, Rainer Schubert, Udo Schumacher, and Ulf Tiede. 2001. Creating a high-resolution spatial/symbolic model of the inner organs based on the visible human. *Medical Image Analysis*, 5(3):221–228.

Nils Reimers and Iryna Gurevych. 2019. Sentence-bert: Sentence embeddings using siamese bert-networks. *arXiv preprint arXiv:1908.10084*.

Anna Rohrbach, Marcus Rohrbach, Ronghang Hu, Trevor Darrell, and Bernt Schiele. 2016. Grounding of textual phrases in images by reconstruction. In *European Conference on Computer Vision*, pages 817–834. Springer.

Thomas Schiemann, Ulf Tiede, and Karl Heinz Höhne. 1997. Segmentation of the visible human for high-quality volume-based visualization. *Medical image analysis*, 1(4):263–270.

George Tsatsaronis, Georgios Balikas, Prodromos Malakasiotis, Ioannis Partalas, Matthias Zschunke, Michael R Alvers, Dirk Weissenborn, Anastasia Krithara, Sergios Petridis, Dimitris Polychronopoulos, et al. 2015. An overview of the bioasq large-scale biomedical semantic indexing and question answering competition. *BMC bioinformatics*, 16(1):138.

Liwei Wang, Yin Li, Jing Huang, and Svetlana Lazebnik. 2018. Learning two-branch neural networks for image-text matching tasks. *IEEE Transactions on Pattern Analysis and Machine Intelligence*, 41(2):394–407.

Lucy Lu Wang, Kyle Lo, Yoganand Chandrasekhar, Russell Reas, Jiangjiang Yang, Darrin Eide, Kathryn Funk, Rodney Kinney, Ziyang Liu, William Merrill, et al. Cord-19: The covid-19 open research dataset. *ArXiv*.

Frank Wilcoxon. 1945. Individual comparisons by ranking methods. *Biometrics*, 1(6):80–83.

Adina Williams, Nikita Nangia, and Samuel R Bowman. 2017. A broad-coverage challenge corpus for sentence understanding through inference. *arXiv preprint arXiv:1704.05426*.

Thomas Wolf, Lysandre Debut, Victor Sanh, Julien Chaumond, Clement Delangue, Anthony Moi, Pierric Cistac, Tim Rault, Rémi Louf, Morgan Funtowicz, et al. 2019. Transformers: State-of-the-art natural language processing. *arXiv preprint arXiv:1910.03771*.

Yonghui Wu, Mike Schuster, Zhifeng Chen, Quoc V Le, Mohammad Norouzi, Wolfgang Macherey, Maxim Krikun, Yuan Cao, Qin Gao, Klaus Macherey, et al. 2016. Google's neural machine translation system: Bridging the gap between human and machine translation. *arXiv preprint arXiv:1609.08144*.

Licheng Yu, Patrick Poirson, Shan Yang, Alexander C Berg, and Tamara L Berg. 2016. Modeling context in referring expressions. In *European Conference on Computer Vision*, pages 69–85. Springer.

Representation Learning for Type-Driven Composition

Gijs Wijnholds
Utrecht Institute of Linguistics OTS
Utrecht University
g.j.wijnholds@uu.nl

Mehrnoosh Sadrzadeh
Department of Computer Science
University College London
m.sadrzadeh@ucl.ac.uk

Stephen Clark
School of Electronic Engineering and Computer Science
Queen Mary University of London
stephen.clark609@gmail.com

Abstract

This paper is about learning word representations using grammatical type information. We use the syntactic types of Combinatory Categorial Grammar to develop multilinear representations, i.e. maps with n arguments, for words with different functional types. The multilinear maps of words compose with each other to form sentence representations. We extend the skipgram algorithm from vectors to multilinear maps to learn these representations and instantiate it on unary and binary maps for transitive verbs. These are evaluated on verb and sentence similarity and disambiguation tasks and a subset of the SICK relatedness dataset. Our model performs better than previous type-driven models and is competitive with state of the art representation learning methods such as BERT and neural sentence encoders.

1 Introduction

We develop a novel technique for learning word representations by using syntactic type information of the words to learn representations for them and the constituency-based structure of the sentence to compose the representations. The word representations are multilinear maps, i.e. maps with variable number of arguments, where the number of arguments and the type of each map come from the syntactic type of each word. The word representation are composed via the application and further composition of the results of these maps, based on constituency structure.

For instance, a noun such as $\overrightarrow{children}$ or $\overrightarrow{ball}$ is represented by a vector, i.e. $\overrightarrow{children}$ or $\overrightarrow{ball}$, which can be thought of as 0-linear maps as they have no input or output. An adjective such as *young* is represented by a unilinear map $young$, i.e. a linear map of one argument, which at input takes an argument of type noun, e.g. *children* and at output returns an argument of type noun, i.e. *young children*. A transitive verb such as *play*, is represented

by a bilinear map *play*, i.e. a linear map with two arguments, which at input takes two arguments of type noun, e.g. *children* and *ball*, and at output returns an argument of type sentence, i.e. *young children play ball*. An adjective-noun phrase representation is obtained by applying the representation of the adjective to the representation of its noun, i.e. by applying the unilinear map of the adjective to the vector of the noun. A sentence representation is obtained by the composition of two applications, i.e. by first applying the representation of the verb, e.g. *play* to the representation of the object, e.g. $\overrightarrow{ball}$, resulting in a unilinear map for the representation of the verb phrase *play ball*, and subsequently applying this verb phrase to the representation of the subject, e.g. $\overrightarrow{children}$.

The representations are learnt by generalising the skipgram model with negative sampling of Mikolov et al. (2013) from vectors to higher order tensors, which are the intended multilinear maps. The types and composition operations come from the syntactic types and combinators of Combinatory Categorial Grammar (CCG) (Steedman, 2000). CCG is a phrase structure grammar formalism based on the combinatory logic of Curry and Feys (Curry and Feys, 1958). It assigns types defined in the notation of the combinatory logic to words of language and uses the operations of the combinatory logic to compose these types to obtain types for the phrases and sentences containing them. For instance, a word can have a CCG functional type of n arguments; this word will be represented in our setting by an n-ary map that uses the representations of its arguments, in a skipgram-style model, to predict the representations of the contexts of their composed phrases. As an example, consider a transitive verb; it has a CCG functional type of two arguments. Its representation is thus a binary map that predicts the contexts of its subject-verb-

313

Proceedings of the 24th Conference on Computational Natural Language Learning, pages 313–324
Online, November 19-20, 2020. ©2020 Association for Computational Linguistics
https://doi.org/10.18653/v1/P17

object phrases. Since the specific subject-verb-object phrases obtained may be sparse, we approximate the higher order maps with a set of lower order ones. As a result, a word with a CCG type of n arguments, gets represented by n maps of $n - 1$ arguments; these transform the representations of a certain number of the arguments to predict the contexts of the remaining arguments. A transitive verb is now represented by two unary maps of one argument each; one of them transforms the object representation to predict its subject contexts, and the other transforms its subject representations to predict its object contexts. These lower order approximations are combined with each other to produce one single representation for the word with functional type.

Our generalised skipgram algorithm is modular, i.e. the skipgram model of Mikolov et al. (2013) and its extension to adjective matrices (Maillard and Clark, 2015) are special cases of it. We instantiate our model on binary and unary maps for transitive verbs. After learning these representations, we evaluate them on verb similarity, compositional sentence similarity and disambiguation tasks, and a subset of the SICK relatedness dataset (Marelli et al., 2014).

In the verb and sentence similarity and verb disambiguation datasets, our model outperforms all previous type-driven models, and in most cases it also outperforms InferSent and Universal Sentence encoders, as well as pre-trained ELMo and BERT embeddings. However, it does not outperform BERT embeddings fine-tuned on NLI data. In the subset of SICK, our model only outperforms all previous type-driven models. Despite that, our model is motivated by linguistic theory, is simple and quick to train, and has the potential for improvement (which we expand on in the conclusion).

Code and data to train representations and reproduce our work is available online.[1]

Background There is a plethora of methods for word embeddings, with few of them distinguishing the grammatical types of the words. For adjectives, we have the regression model of Baroni and Zamparelli (2010) that approximates the holistic adjective-noun vectors to learn adjective matrices; we also have the skipgram model of Maillard and Clark (2015) that learns a transformation between fixed vectors for nouns and adjective-noun combi-nations. The model of Grefenstette and Sadrzadeh (2011) takes the sum of the outer products of the vectors of subjects and objects, and the Kronecker product of the verb vector with itself, to learn verb matrices. Later work uses multi-step regression to learn a verb cube, i.e. a multidimensional array of depth 1, by iteratively approximating a holistic subject-verb and verb-object vector (Grefenstette et al., 2013). The model of Paperno et al. (2014) overcomes the sparsity issues of this technique and approximates the cubes by two matrices. The plausibility model of Polajnar et al. (2014), learns a verb matrix/cube by optimising a model that distinguishes between observed subject-verb-object triples and randomly generated ones. Our work is different from these, since we use a skipgram-style model rather than combining the subject and object vectors or the verb vectors, as done by Grefenstette and Sadrzadeh (2011), or performing regression, as done by Paperno et al. (2014) and Polajnar et al. (2014).

Sentence embeddings are either learnt by mixing word embeddings e.g. the additive models of (Mitchell and Lapata, 2010; Mikolov et al., 2013), or as a whole, e.g. the supervised InferSent (Conneau et al., 2017) and Universal Sentence Encoder (Cer et al., 2018), and the unsupervised ELMo (Peters et al., 2018) and BERT (Devlin et al., 2019) models. None, however, explicitly take into account grammatical information. Tree-RNNs (Socher et al., 2013), Tree-LSTMs (Tai et al., 2015), and Lifted Matrix Space model (Chung et al., 2018), do use the constituency tree of a sentence as a guide, but to learn a semantic function composition rather than different types of representations for words. Our work is different from these, since we start our learning procedure by taking the grammatical types of words into account and then compose these initially learnt representations with each other based on the structure of phrases they are part of, rather then by adding or learning different composition operators, or learning the entire phrase/sentence at once.

On the other hand, formal distributional models, e.g. the categorial framework of Coecke et al. (2010, 2013), the linear regression approach of Baroni et al. (2014), and the Combinatory Categorial Grammar (CCG) tensor contraction model of Maillard et al. (2014), directly take the grammatical types of words into account, but fail to scale up to sentences of any length and complexity, and do not

---

[1] `github.com/gijswijnholds/`
`tensorskipgram-torch`

perform as well as their neural embedding counterparts. To remedy these issues, our model makes use of a simple neural network to learn the type-driven word representations in such a way that their composition leads to improved results.

2 Multilinear Skipgram Embeddings

The skipgram model with negative sampling generates word embeddings by optimising a logistic regression objective in which target vectors have high inner product with context vectors for positive contexts, and low inner product with negative ones. Given a target word n and a set of positive contexts C, a set of negative contexts $\overline{C}$ is sampled from a unigram distribution raised to some power (here: 3/4, after Levy et al. (2015)).

Initially, both target vectors $\mathbf{n}$ and context vectors $\mathbf{c}$ are randomly intialised, and during training the model updates both target and context vectors to maximise the following objective function:

$$\sum_{c \in C} \log \sigma(\mathbf{n} \cdot \mathbf{c}) + \sum_{\overline{c} \in \overline{C}} \log \sigma(-\mathbf{n} \cdot \overline{\mathbf{c}}) \quad (1)$$

We generalise the skipgram model following the typing of Combinatorial Categorial Grammar (CCG, Steedman (2000)). CCG has a transparent interface between syntax and semantics and robust wide-coverage parsers (Clark and Curran, 2007; Hockenmaier and Steedman, 2007). Syntactic types of CCG are either atomic, e.g. nouns/noun phrases: NP and sentences: S, or functional. Functional types are either of the form Y/X or $Y \backslash X$; they take an argument of type X and return an argument of type Y, where for $\backslash$ the argument occurs to the left and for $/$ it occurs to the right. Examples of functional types are adjectives: NP/NP, intransitive verbs: $S \backslash NP$ and transitive verbs: $(S \backslash NP)/NP$.

Types are composed with each other through the combinatorial rules of CCG, which include forward and backward application and composition, type-raising, and backward-cross and forward-cross composition. An example of forward application is when an adjective composes with a noun, producing a noun. An example of backward application is when a verb phrase composes with a noun phrase producing a sentence.

$$\frac{NP/NP \quad NP}{NP} > \qquad \frac{NP \quad S \backslash NP}{S} <$$

Forward and backward composition are used in composing auxiliary phrases; cross composition

and the type-raising combinators are used in cases of coordination and gapping.

Following the tensor semantics of CCG, developed in Maillard et al. (2014), in our model, we represent a word W with a functional type of n arguments by a n-ary map $\mathbb{W}$ from the argument spaces to the result space:

$$\mathbb{W}_{(n)} \colon V_1 \times \ldots \times V_n \to V_{n+1}$$

where V_i's are (finite dimensional) vector spaces over the field of reals and the subscript n denotes the arity of the map $\mathbb{W}$. Equivalently, $\mathbb{W}_{(n)}$ is an $(n+1)$th-order tensor $\mathbb{W}_{i_1 \ldots i_{n+1}}$ in the space $V_1 \otimes \ldots \otimes V_n \otimes V_{n+1}$. Given a functional word W of n arguments and representations $\mathbf{d}_1, \ldots, \mathbf{d}_n$ of its arguments, we denote by $\mathbb{W}_{(n)}\mathbf{d}_1 \ldots \mathbf{d}_n$ the application of the representation of W to its arguments' representations. The model that learns the maps has the following objective function:

$$\sum_{c \in C} \log \sigma(\mathbb{W}_{(n)}\mathbf{d}_1 \ldots \mathbf{d}_n \cdot \mathbf{c})$$
$$+ \sum_{\overline{c} \in \overline{C}} \log \sigma(-\mathbb{W}_{(n)}\mathbf{d}_1 \ldots \mathbf{d}_n \cdot \overline{\mathbf{c}})$$

When W is a noun, $\mathbb{W}_{(0)}$ is a 0-ary map, equivalent to $\mathbb{W}_{i_1}$: a 1st-order tensor, i.e., a vector. In this case, the objective function reduces to the original skipgram model of Equation 1. For W an adjective, $\mathbb{W}_{(1)}$ is a unary map, equivalent to $\mathbb{W}_{i_1 i_2}$: a 2-nd order tensor, i.e., a matrix. The objective function that learns it was developed in Maillard and Clark (2015), and is as follows:

$$\sum_{c \in C} \log \sigma(\mathbb{W}_{(1)}\mathbf{d}_1 \cdot \mathbf{c}) + \sum_{\overline{c} \in \overline{C}} \log \sigma(-\mathbb{W}_{(1)}\mathbf{d}_1 \cdot \overline{\mathbf{c}})$$

Since adjective-noun combinations are themselves nouns, taking the original skipgram linear context window will produce sensible adjective representations. This is however not the case for all words with functional types: for verbs, for example, subjects and objects may not be directly adjacent to the verb in a sentence and so one needs to commit to a full sentential context, leading to uninformative training data. Aside to that, training of a cube leads to over parameterisation. To overcome these issues simultaneously, we define lower order approximations of higher order tensors, where one argument of the functional type is left out of the composition and used as context.

More formally, a word W with a functional type of n arguments, is approximated by n maps of

$n-1$ arguments. Equivalently, in tensor form, we are approximating a *full* $n+1$th-order tensor, by decomposing it into n separate *partial* tensors of one lower order each. We denote the map equivalent of these partial tensors by $\widetilde{\mathbb{W}}^{i}_{(n-1)}$. The objective function of the model thus become as follows:

$$\sum_{d_i \in D_i} \log \sigma(\widetilde{\mathbb{W}}^{i}_{(n-1)} \mathbf{d}_1 ... \mathbf{d}_{i-1}\mathbf{d}_{i+1}...\mathbf{d}_n \cdot \mathbf{d}_i) +$$

$$\sum_{\overline{d}_i \in \overline{D}_i} \log \sigma(-\widetilde{\mathbb{W}}^{i}_{(n-1)} \mathbf{d}_1 ... \mathbf{d}_{i-1}\mathbf{d}_{i+1}...\mathbf{d}_n \cdot \overline{\mathbf{d}}_i)$$

Here, d_i is a word with representation $\mathbf{d}_i$: an *observed* argument of W, and D_i is the set of all such arguments. Whereas, $\overline{d}_i$ is a word with representation $\overline{\mathbf{d}}_i$, which can in principle serve as an argument of W, but it is randomly sampled, so it is an *unobserved* argument of W. Similarly, $\overline{D}_i$ is the set of all such arguments.

We can decrease the order of the tensors even more by parameterising over subsets of contexts. For a word W of n arguments, when including 1 to $i \leq n$ of its n arguments in the context, we obtain an $(n-i)$th-order tensor, with the equivalent map $\widetilde{\mathbb{W}}^{1...i|i+1...n}_{(n-i+1)}$. The application of this map to the remaining $i+1$ to n arguments is $\widetilde{\mathbb{W}}^{1...i|i+1...n}_{(n-i+1)} \mathbf{d}_{i+1}...\mathbf{d}_n$. So we predict as context the $1...i$th arguments by composing with the vectors for the $i+1...n$th arguments. We write $\widetilde{\mathbb{W}}^{1...i}_{(n-i+1)}$ when $i = n$, i.e. we use all arguments as context.

2.1 Instantiation to Verb Skipgram

We instantiate our model on transitive verbs. A transitive verb V has CCG type $(S \backslash NP)/NP$. Our *full* model learns a binary map $\mathbb{V}_{(2)}: V_1 \times V_2 \to V_3$, equivalent to a 3rd-order tensor, i.e. a cube, $\mathbb{V}_{i_1 i_2 i_3}$ to represent V. We denote d_1, i.e. the object of the verb, by o, its vector by $\mathbf{o}$, and d_2, i.e. its subject, by s, its vector by $\mathbf{s}$. The objective function of our *full* model for V is thus

$$\sum_{c \in C} \log \sigma(\mathbb{V}_{(2)}\mathbf{o}\mathbf{s}\cdot \mathbf{c}) + \sum_{\overline{c} \in \overline{C}} \log \sigma(-\mathbb{V}_{(2)}\mathbf{o}\mathbf{s}\cdot \overline{\mathbf{c}}) \quad (2)$$

We approximate $\mathbb{V}_{(2)}$ by training two unary maps, an object one $\widetilde{\mathbb{V}}^{1|2}_{(1)}$, which we denote by $\widetilde{\mathbb{V}}^{o|s}_{(1)}$, and a subject one $\widetilde{\mathbb{V}}^{2|1}_{(1)}$, which we denote by $\widetilde{\mathbb{V}}^{s|o}_{(1)}$. The map $\widetilde{\mathbb{V}}^{o|s}_{(1)}$ predicts the object of the verb, given a

Representation	Order	Context
$\mathbb{V}^{sent\|o,s}_{(2)}$	binary	sentence
$\widetilde{\mathbb{V}}^{o\|s}_{(1)} / \widetilde{\mathbb{V}}^{s\|o}_{(1)}$	unary	obj/sbj
$\widetilde{\mathbb{V}}^{o}_{(0)} / \widetilde{\mathbb{V}}^{s}_{(0)} / \widetilde{\mathbb{V}}^{o,s}_{(0)}$	0-ary	obj/sbj/both
$\mathbb{V}^{sent\|s}_{(1)}, \mathbb{V}^{sent\|o}_{(1)}$	unary	sentence
$\mathbf{v}_{skip}$	0-ary	linear window

Table 1: Verb representations, ranging from 0-ary (vectors) to binary maps (cubes).

fixed subject; it is learnt as follows:

$$\sum_{o \in O} \log \sigma(\widetilde{\mathbb{V}}^{o|s}_{(1)}\mathbf{s} \cdot \mathbf{o}) + \sum_{\overline{o} \in \overline{O}} \log \sigma(-\widetilde{\mathbb{V}}^{o|s}_{(1)}\mathbf{s} \cdot \overline{\mathbf{o}}) \quad (3)$$

The map $\widetilde{\mathbb{V}}^{s|o}_{(1)}$ predicts the subject of the verb, given a fixed object, and is learnt as follows:

$$\sum_{s \in S} \log \sigma(\widetilde{\mathbb{V}}^{s|o}_{(1)}\mathbf{o} \cdot \mathbf{s}) + \sum_{\overline{s} \in \overline{S}} \log \sigma(-\widetilde{\mathbb{V}}^{s|o}_{(1)}\mathbf{o} \cdot \overline{\mathbf{s}}) \quad (4)$$

Here, S and O are the sets of observed subjects and objects of V, and $\overline{S}$ and $\overline{O}$ are the sets of V's unobserved subjects and objects.

We push the approximation one level further to also produce three 0-ary maps, i.e. vectors, for the verb. We denote these by $\widetilde{\mathbb{V}}^{o}_{(0)}$, $\widetilde{\mathbb{V}}^{s}_{(0)}$, $\widetilde{\mathbb{V}}^{o,s}_{(0)}$; they respectively represent a verb vector by only considering its objects, subjects, or both as context. These vectors are similar to the dependency based embeddings of Levy and Goldberg (2014).

We summarise all trained models by the arity of their maps and the choice of their contexts in Table 1. As baselines, we additionally train unary maps $\mathbb{V}^{sent|s}_{(1)}$ and $\mathbb{V}^{sent|o}_{(1)}$, which predict a full sentence context given the subject or object of the verb, and $\mathbf{v}_{skip}$ for the original skipgram vector of the verb.

2.2 Fusion

We consider two ways of combining our unary map skipgram verb representations into a single representation: the *middle* and *late* fusion methods of Bruni et al. (2014). Middle fusion takes a weighted average of the two verb representations, using the result to compute similarity scores. Late fusion uses each representation to compute separate similarity scores and then averages the results. Given a weighted average $M_\alpha(A, B) = \alpha A + (1-\alpha)B$ for $\alpha \in [0..1]$, and V, W two verbs, with approximated

Metric	Formula
vecsim	$\cos(\mathbf{a}, \mathbf{b}) = \dfrac{\mathbf{a} \cdot \mathbf{b}}{|\mathbf{a}||\mathbf{b}|}$
matsim^S	$\underset{\mathbf{s} \in \mathcal{S}}{\text{med}}\, \cos(\widetilde{\mathbb{V}}_{(1)}\mathbf{s}, \widetilde{\mathbb{W}}_{(1)}\mathbf{s})$
matsim^O	$\underset{\mathbf{o} \in \mathcal{O}}{\text{med}}\, \cos(\widetilde{\mathbb{V}}_{(1)}\mathbf{o}, \widetilde{\mathbb{W}}_{(1)}\mathbf{o})$
cubesim	$\underset{\langle \mathbf{s}, \mathbf{o} \rangle \in \mathcal{A}}{\text{med}}\, \cos(\mathbb{V}_{(2)}\mathbf{os}, \mathbb{W}_{(2)}\mathbf{os})$

Table 2: Similarity metrics on vectors, matrices and cubes, based on clustering centroids.

subject and object matrices $\widetilde{\mathbb{V}}, \widetilde{\mathbb{V}}'$ and $\widetilde{\mathbb{W}}, \widetilde{\mathbb{W}}'$ the middle and late fusion operations are:

$$\text{mid} \qquad \text{sim}(M_\alpha(\widetilde{\mathbb{V}}, \widetilde{\mathbb{V}}'), M_\alpha(\widetilde{\mathbb{W}}, \widetilde{\mathbb{W}}')) \qquad (5)$$

$$\text{late} \qquad M_\alpha(\text{sim}(\widetilde{\mathbb{V}}, \widetilde{\mathbb{W}}), \text{sim}(\widetilde{\mathbb{V}}', \widetilde{\mathbb{W}}')) \qquad (6)$$

The same fusion methods are used in the compositional tasks, where either verb matrices are averaged before composition, or cosine scores are averaged after.

2.3 Clustering

In their adjective skipgram model, Maillard and Clark (2015) argued that cosine similarity, while suitable for vectors, does not capture any information about the function of matrices as unary maps and that instead one should measure how similarly the maps transform their arguments. The same holds for generalisations of unary maps to n-ary ones, equivalently, for matrices to higher order tensors. Following Maillard and Clark, we apply clustering to achieve this. The degree of similarity between two words W and W', each with a functional type of n arguments, is obtained by taking the median of the degrees of similarities of the applications of their maps $\mathbb{W}_{(n)}$ and $\mathbb{W}'_{(n)}$ on the clusters of their arguments. Since going through all the instantiations of the arguments is expensive, we cluster the most frequent argument vectors and work with the similarity between the two transformations applied to the centroids of each cluster. The resulting similarity function is defined as follows, for $\mathcal{D}$ the set of tuples of cluster centroids:

$$\text{tensorsim} :$$

$$\underset{\langle \mathbf{d}_1, ..., \mathbf{d}_n \rangle \in \mathcal{D}}{\text{med}}\, \cos(\mathbb{W}_{(n)}\mathbf{d}_1...\mathbf{d}_n, \mathbb{W}'_{(n)}\mathbf{d}_1...\mathbf{d}_n)$$

Model type	Formula
Middle	$T(\mathbf{s}, M_\alpha(\widetilde{\mathbb{V}}_{(1)}, \widetilde{\mathbb{V}}'_{(1)}), \mathbf{o})$
Late	$M_\alpha(T(\mathbf{s}, \widetilde{\mathbb{V}}_{(1)}, \mathbf{o}), T(\mathbf{s}, \widetilde{\mathbb{V}}'_{(1)}, \mathbf{o}))$
Two	$M_\alpha(T_s(\mathbf{s}, \widetilde{\mathbb{V}}_{(1)}, \mathbf{o}), T_o(\mathbf{s}, \widetilde{\mathbb{V}}'_{(1)}, \mathbf{o}))$
Cube	$\mathbb{V}_{(2)}\mathbf{os}$

Table 3: Building Representations for Transitive Sentences. T represents a n-ary map composition model for transitive sentences, T_s is subject-directed composition, T_o is object-directed composition. When $\alpha = 0$ or $\alpha = 1$, the models reduce to the case of using one of the two verb matrix embeddings.

For the case of transitive verbs, we are dealing with binary map transformations and the above definition simplifies to considering the most frequent subjects and objects of the verb, clustering them separately, then applying the map to the centroid vectors and taking the median. The details of the different map transformation similarities that we obtain for transitive verbs using our model are given in Table 2.

3 Implementation and Evaluation

3.1 Implementation

We implemented all models in Python, using the `tensorflow` package (Abadi et al., 2016)[2]. Vectors were 100-dimensional; unary and binary maps, i.e. matrices and cubes, were shaped accordingly. The functional type-driven information was extracted from a dependency parsed corpus[3] containing ca.130M sentences and ca. 3.2B words, on which the initial regular noun vectors were also trained.

In the case of matrices and cubes with full sentential contexts, a pair of networks was trained separately for each verb, sharing the context matrix from the noun skipgram model. For the matrices with subject (resp. object) contexts, we trained a pair of networks (a subject network and an object network), each with a single embedding layer encoding all the verbs. In these networks, the context matrix consists of all possible object (resp. subject) context vectors. Here we considered both a fixed context matrix (from the noun skipgram model) and a trainable context matrix and found that the

---

[2]Our code was later changed to Pytorch.
[3]UKWaCkypedia, `wacky.sslmit.unibo.it`

trainable context matrix gave the best results[4], so we work with the latter. Negative samples were drawn from the distribution over objects/subjects of all verbs in the case of the partial tensor models. We considered $k = 10$ negative samples per subject/object.

3.2 Evaluation and Datasets

We evaluate our verb representations on four types of tasks: verb similarity, verb disambiguation, sentence similarity, including SVO sentences and SVO sentences with elliptical phrases, and a subset of the SICK sentence relatedness task.

3.3 Verb Similarity

We considered five verb similarity datasets of varying size: pairs of words from the MEN (Bruni et al., 2012) and SimLex-999 (Hill et al., 2015) datasets that were labelled as verbs, obtaining 22 and 222 verb similarity pairs, respectively. Next to these partial datasets, we considered VerbSim (Yang and Powers, 2006), a dataset of 130 verb pairs, and the more recent SimVerb-3500 dataset (Gerz et al., 2016), containing 3500 verb pairs.

3.4 Verb Disambiguation and Sentence Similarity

We considered seven tasks. (1,2) The two datasets introduced by Mitchell and Lapata (2008, 2010), dubbed ML08 and ML10. These datasets contain pairs of intransitive sentences; the 2008 dataset aims to disambiguate the verb of each sentence, the 2010 dataset is for computing sentence similarity. (3,4) The transitive verb disambiguation datasets of Grefenstette and Sadrzadeh (2011) (GS11) and Kartsaklis and Sadrzadeh (2013) (KS13a), and (5) the transitive sentence similarity dataset of Kartsaklis et al. (2013) (KS13b). (6,7) We additionally test on two recent datasets (Wijnholds and Sadrzadeh, 2019) (ELLDIS and ELLSIM), which extend the KS13a and KS13b datasets to sentences with verb phrase ellipsis in them.

The datasets ML08 and ML10, respectively, contain pairs of subject-verb, and verb-object phrases. Next to the additive baseline, we apply the unary map representations of verbs to the subject (or

---

[4]We argue that this is because contexts in the noun skip-gram model are more general as they serve as contexts to many different target words.

Model	Formula
CA	$M_\alpha\big(\mathbf{s}^T\widetilde{\mathbb{V}}_{(1)} \odot \mathbf{o},\ \widetilde{\mathbb{V}}'_{(1)}\mathbf{o} \odot \mathbf{s}\big)$
CAS	$M_\alpha\big(\mathbf{s}^T\widetilde{\mathbb{V}}_{(1)} + \mathbf{o},\ \widetilde{\mathbb{V}}'_{(1)}\mathbf{o} + \mathbf{s}\big)$
CATA	$M_\alpha\big(\mathbf{s}^T\widetilde{\mathbb{V}}_{(1)},\ \widetilde{\mathbb{V}}'_{(1)}\mathbf{o}\big)$

Table 4: Two-map models. We compose partial sentence embeddings using the subject- and object-directed verb matrix, and merge the two embeddings into one. M_α is the mixing operator defined before.

object) to get sentence representations: $\widetilde{\mathbb{V}}_{(1)}\mathbf{s}$ for subject-verb phrases, $\widetilde{\mathbb{V}}_{(1)}\mathbf{o}$ for verb-object phrases. For the separate subject-verb and verb-object maps, we apply middle and late fusion. To model a transitive sentence of the form *subj verb obj*, we compare verb-only and additive baselines with n-ary map models as described in Table 3. In the Two model in this table, we first apply $\widetilde{\mathbb{V}}^o_{(1)}$ to the subject vector, then mix it with the application of $\widetilde{\mathbb{V}}^s_{(1)}$ to the object vector. We then mix in the object/subject vectors and obtain three different models: **CA** for Copy Argument, **CAS** for Copy Argument Sum and **CATA** for Categorical Argument; see Table 4.

The ELLDIS and ELLSIM datasets of Wijnholds and Sadrzadeh (2019) contain sentences of the form *subj verb obj and subj* does too*. We first resolve the ellipsis by replacing the marker *does too* with its antecedent *verb object*, then apply a transitive model to the resulting *subj verb obj* and *subj* verb object* conjunct and finally combine the representations by addition; formally

$$E(\mathbf{s}, \widetilde{\mathbb{V}}_{(1)}, \mathbf{o}, \mathbf{s}^*) = T(\mathbf{s}, \widetilde{\mathbb{V}}_{(1)}, \mathbf{o}) + T(\mathbf{s}^*, \widetilde{\mathbb{V}}_{(1)}, \mathbf{o})$$

where $\mathbf{s}^*$ is the representation of *subj**.

3.5 SICK-R

The SICK relatedness task of Marelli et al. (2014) contains sentence pairs that are scored between 1 and 5 on semantic relatedness to evaluate compositional distributional models for relatedness. To evaluate our verb representations, we extract the verbs with their arguments (subjects and/or objects) from dependency parsed sentences, use one of the previously described composition models to generate a single verb representation for the verb-argument tuple, and compose this with the vectors for the remaining words in the

	$\mathbf{MEN}_v$	$\mathbf{SL}_v$	**VS**	$\mathbf{SV}_d$	$\mathbf{SV}_t$
$\mathbf{v_{skip}}$	0.28	0.05	0.34	0.22	0.18
$\mathbf{V}_{Kron}$	0.38	0.1	0.37	0.22	0.18
$\mathbf{V}_{Rel}$	0.33	0.05	0.34	0.22	0.18
$\widetilde{\mathbb{V}}^{o/s/s,o}_{(0)}$	0.25	0.27	**0.56**	0.25	0.20
$\mathbb{V}^{sent\|s/o}_{(1)}$	0.50	0.16	0.09	-0.02	0.02
$\widetilde{\mathbb{V}}^{o\|s/s\|o}_{(1)}$	**0.59**	**0.34**	0.55	**0.29**	**0.24**
$\mathbb{V}^{sent\|s,o}_{(2)}$	0.04	0.02	-0.08	-0.01	-0.03
SoTA	n/a	0.39	0.65	0.40	0.30

Table 5: Spearman ρ correlation on verb similarity datasets. The subscript v indicates that we are looking at the partial verb-only dataset. For SimVerb we distinguish between the development and test set. State of the art scores are taken from (Chersoni et al. (2016), VS) and (Gerz et al. (2016), SL_v, SV_d, SV_t). For MEN, we did not find any results on the verb subset.

	ML08	**ML10**	**GS11**	**KS13a**	**KS13b**
$\mathbf{v_{skip}}$	0.07	0.40	0.23	0.18	0.45
$\mathbf{V}_{Kron}$	**0.25**	0.40	0.27	**0.26**	0.45
$\mathbf{V}_{Rel}$	0.11	0.43	0.31	0.18	0.47
$\widetilde{\mathbb{V}}^{o/s/s,o}_{(0)}$	0.06	0.53	0.33	0.10	0.64
$\mathbb{V}^{sent\|s/o}_{(1)}$	0.16	-0.00	0.37	0.06	-0.06
$\widetilde{\mathbb{V}}^{o\|s/s\|o}_{(1)}$	0.12	**0.64**	**0.40**	0.22	**0.69**
$\mathbb{V}^{sent\|s,o}_{(2)}$	0.18	0.00	-0.03	0.00	-0.03
SoTA	0.19	0.45	0.46	0.22	0.73
Human	0.66	0.71	0.74	0.58	0.75

Table 6: Spearman ρ correlation of verbs of SVO sentence level tasks. Each score is a maximum score out of possible clusters and fusion weights. State of the art scores are taken from (Mitchell and Lapata (2008),ML08), (Milajevs et al. (2014),GS11,KS13b) and (Kartsaklis and Sadrzadeh (2013),ML10,KS13a).

sentence. We used the Spacy[5] parser combined with a postprocessing script to correct cases of coordination of verbs and arguments, as we expected this to be vital information in the dataset. To keep this process manageable, we used the SemEval subset of the SICK dataset. We evaluate our best performing verb unary map representations ($\widetilde{\mathbb{V}}^{o\|s/s\|o}_{(1)}$), as well as the two analytical verb representations $\mathbf{V}_{Kron}$ and $\mathbf{V}_{Rel}$.

3.6 Comparison with Other Methods

At the verb level, we compare our skipgram verb representations (Table 1) with two verb representation methods from the type-driven literature (Grefenstette and Sadrzadeh, 2011). The first representation, referred to by *Kronecker*, lifts a verb vector to a matrix representation using outer product. The second representation is the *Relational* model, where a verb matrix is taken to be the sum of the outer products of its subject and object vectors; formally:

$$\mathbf{V}_{Kron} = \mathbf{v}_a \otimes \mathbf{v}_a \qquad \mathbf{V}_{Rel} = \sum_i \mathbf{s}_i \otimes \mathbf{o}_i$$

At the sentence level, we compare our model with that of Mitchell and Lapata (2010), which given a sentence adds the vectors of the words therein, and also with supervised sentence encoders, InferSent (Conneau et al., 2017), as well

as, Universal Sentence Encoder (Cer et al., 2018). For these latter, we take off-the-shelf encoders to map the sentence pairs in our evaluation datasets to a pair of embeddings, and compute the cosine similarity between these. We moreover compare to state-of-the-art contextualised encoders ELMo (Peters et al., 2018) and BERT (Devlin et al., 2019). For ELMo, we use a pre-trained model and apply mean pooling[6]. For BERT, we take the implementation of Reimers and Gurevych (2019)[7], as it implements both the original pre-trained BERT models and fine-tuned sentence embedding models. To this, we apply max, mean, and CLS token pooling, and report the best scores out of all models and pooling types, for the pre-trained models and the fine-tuned models.

4 Results

4.1 Verb Level Tasks

The correlation results on verb similarity tasks are displayed in Table 5. Here, for the case of verb vectors, the general skipgram model is outperformed by the vectors trained using our partial model on the verb arguments as context, and in fact these show the highest performance on the VerbSim dataset. That the unary and binary maps representations with the full sentence as context perform rather

[5] https://spacy.io/

[6] https://tfhub.dev/google/elmo/2
[7] https://github.com/UKPLab/
sentence-transformers

	ML08	ML10	GS11	KS13a	KS13b
$C(+)$	0.17	0.54	0.19	0.18	0.67
$C(\mathbf{V}_{Kron})$	0.08	0.40	0.20	0.28	0.53
$C(\mathbf{V}_{Rel})$	0.19	0.51	0.32	0.19	0.51
$C(\mathbb{V}^{sent|s/o}_{(1)})$	-0.04	0.00	0.25	0.20	0.54
$C(\widetilde{\mathbb{V}}^{o|s/s|o}_{(1)})$	**0.19**	**0.55**	**0.54**	**0.37**	**0.75**
$C(\mathbb{V}^{sent|s,o}_{(2)})$	—	—	-0.02	-0.04	0.06
Human	0.66	0.71	0.74	0.58	0.75

Table 7: Spearman ρ scores on compositional tasks. $C(+)$ denotes the additive model, whereas the other rows represent the best score for compositional models with different verb representations.

	ML08	ML10	GS11	KS13a	KS13b
$\widetilde{\mathbb{V}}^{o|s/s|o}_{(1)}$	0.19	0.55	0.54	**0.37**	0.75
IS	0.18	0.63	0.30	0.17	0.78
USE	0.04	0.33	0.09	0.21	0.54
ELMo	0.17	0.54	0.11	0.24	0.73
BERT$_p$	0.19	0.34	0.24	0.32	0.61
BERT$_f$	**0.32**	**0.74**	**0.61**	0.32	**0.82**
Human	0.66	0.71	0.74	0.58	0.75

Table 8: Spearman ρ scores on compositional tasks, for our proposed unary map verb representation versus state of the art sentence embedding methods.

poorly, and in many cases worse than the vector representations, illustrates that the choice of context is too general for these higher-order representations. On four out of the five tasks, our approximated models that train unary maps with a restricted notion of context, outperform all other models: the most significant of these increases are for the 3000 entry test subset of the SimVerb dataset: here we observe an increase from 0.18 to 0.24.

Table 6 shows the correlation scores on the verbs of the SVO sentence level tasks. In this experiment, we perform the sentence disambiguation and similarity tasks by only using the verbs of the sentences. We observe the same pattern in the results: training verb vectors on dependency label contexts slightly improves the performance. This is against the erratic performance of the binary map representations (on all but the ML2008 dataset). Again, our approximated unary map representations with a restricted context significantly outperforms the other methods.

In the majority of the verb similarity datasets we do not improve the state of the art, but in the majority of the verb parts of the SVO sentence datasets, we do.

4.2 Sentence Level Tasks

4.2.1 Verb Disambiguation and SVO Sentence Similarity Datasets

The most interesting results, however, come from the SVO sentence tasks. These compute a representation for each sentence of the dataset by composing the representations of the words of that sentence, rather than by only working with individual word representations, as was done in the previous two tasks. Table 7 contrasts the additive models (top row), type-driven methods that use the Kronecker (second row) and Relational (third row) verb representations, against the type-driven model that uses skipgram representations (resp. full context binary maps, full context unary maps, restricted context unary maps).

While the skipgram binary map verb representations with full sentences as context perform slightly better in a sentence context, they generally underperform the additive baseline and the non-skipgram tensors. We argue that this is mainly due to the choice of context: the full sentence doesn't tell us enough about the subjects and objects of the verb, whereas the Relational model directly encodes this information. Similarly to the verb similarity results, the binary map representations show a very poor performance, which we argue is due to data sparsity. Even though the binary map implicitly model properties of arguments of the verbs, their representation is too sparse to effectively model anything. Our proposed unary map model remedies both the sparsity problem and the choice of context, and outperforms all the other representations, save on the ML2008 dataset. This model also improves the state of the art in all the datasets.

4.2.2 Elliptical Phrase and SICK Datasets

The results in Tables 9 show that our proposed verb unary map representations achieve competitive results compared to the additive baseline, and pre-trained BERT embeddings, on the ELLDIS and ELLSIM tasks and on (a subset of) the SICK relatedness task. What is more, they clearly outperform the analytic tensors and in ellipsis datasets; they also improve the state of the art of ELLDIS, which

Add	Kron	Rel	$\widetilde{V}^{o|s/s|o}_{(1)}$	IS	USE	BERT$_p$	BERT$_f$
0.31	0.30	0.37	0.56	0.34	0.27	0.36	**0.65**
0.67	0.52	0.65	0.76	**0.80**	0.68	0.67	0.79
0.71	0.58	0.44	0.70	0.74	**0.76**	0.70	**0.76**

Table 9: Spearman ρ scores on the ELLDIS (top), ELL-SIM (middle), and SICK relatedness (bottom) tasks.

was 0.53, and provide equal results to the state of the art of ELLSIM, which was 0.76 , both reported in Wijnholds and Sadrzadeh (2019). However, they are surpassed by fine-tuned BERT sentence embeddings and sentence encoders, that achieve the highest. For SICK, to verify that the high performance of our verb maps is not caused simply by adding in the vectors for the remaining word of a sentence, we did an ablation in which the rest of the sentence was not considered. Using addition of vectors, this gave a ρ of 0.61, and for the compositional verb matrices this gave 0.62 (cf. 0.71 and 0.70 in Table 9).

4.3 Comparison with Sentence Embeddings

We compare our model with the InferSent encoder and the Universal Sentence Encoder, and with ELMo and BERT encodings in Table 8. Although our embeddings outperform Universal Sentence Encoder on all tasks, on the ML2010 and KS2014 dataset InferSent performs higher, possibly due to its high embedding dimensionality (4096). For the BERT embeddings we observe an interesting pattern: our proposed method outperforms any pre-trained BERT model, but after fine-tuning on NLI datasets, the BERT models score the highest on all datasets but KS2013. Although fully analysing the syntactic awareness of BERT is beyond the scope of this paper, it seems that both explicitly modelling syntax in the embeddings as our method does, and fine-tuning BERT embeddings are viable strategies.

5 Conclusion

We generalised the skipgram model (Mikolov et al., 2013) to learn multilinear map representations for words with functional types using the setting of Combinatory Categorial Grammar. Our model reduces to the original skipgram for atomic types such as nouns, and to the adjective skipgram model of Maillard and Clark (2015), for functional types

of one argument. To overcome potential sparsity issues we approximated higher arity maps with a set of lower arity ones and showed that such approximations provide better results.

The model was implemented on transitive verbs, learning binary and a set of approximated unary representations. These were evaluated on verb similarity and disambiguation and sentence similarity tasks. The unary map approximations significantly outperformed previous type-driven verb representations. They also outperformed sentence encoders and pre-trained BERT embeddings. When moving to datasets of longer sentences, e.g. sentences with elliptical phrases and the SICK relatedness, some sentence encoders and fine-tuned BERT representations were superior.

Our multilinear skipgram model paves the way for a new generation of type-driven representations, in line with recent research highlighting benefits of syntactic biases injected into representation learning (Kuncoro et al., 2020). Furthermore, our model is fast to train, guided by a linguistic calculus (CCG), and produces syntax-aware sentence embeddings. Performance could potentially be improved by adding non-linearities to the model, as in Socher et al. (2013) and by modelling complex syntactic phenomena such as auxiliaries and negation.

Acknowledgments

The authors gratefully acknowledge a multitude of reviewers for their careful efforts in reviewing this work. Wijnholds is grateful for receiving PGR student funding from the School of Electronic Engineering and Computer Science at Queen Mary University of London, and is currently supported by the Dutch Research Council (NWO) under the scope of the project "A composition calculus for vector-based semantic modelling with a localization for Dutch" (360-89-070). Sadrzadeh acknowledges the Royal Academy of Engineering Industrial Fellowship IF192058.

References

Martín Abadi, Paul Barham, Jianmin Chen, Zhifeng Chen, Andy Davis, Jeffrey Dean, Matthieu Devin, Sanjay Ghemawat, Geoffrey Irving, Michael Isard, et al. 2016. Tensorflow: A system for large-scale machine learning. In *12th USENIX Symposium on Operating Systems Design and Implementation (OSDI 16)*, pages 265–283.

Marco Baroni, Raffaela Bernardi, and Roberto Zamparelli. 2014. Frege in space: A program of compositional distributional semantics. *LiLT (Linguistic Issues in Language Technology)*, 9.

Marco Baroni and Roberto Zamparelli. 2010. Nouns are vectors, adjectives are matrices: Representing adjective-noun constructions in semantic space. In *Proceedings of the 2010 Conference on Empirical Methods in Natural Language Processing*, pages 1183–1193. Association for Computational Linguistics.

Elia Bruni, Gemma Boleda, Marco Baroni, and Nam-Khanh Tran. 2012. Distributional semantics in technicolor. In *Proceedings of the 50th Annual Meeting of the Association for Computational Linguistics: Long Papers-Volume 1*, pages 136–145. Association for Computational Linguistics.

Elia Bruni, Nam-Khanh Tran, and Marco Baroni. 2014. Multimodal distributional semantics. *Journal of Artificial Intelligence Research*, 49:1–47.

Daniel Cer, Yinfei Yang, Sheng-yi Kong, Nan Hua, Nicole Limtiaco, Rhomni St John, Noah Constant, Mario Guajardo-Cespedes, Steve Yuan, Chris Tar, et al. 2018. Universal sentence encoder. *arXiv preprint arXiv:1803.11175*.

Emmanuele Chersoni, Enrico Santus, Alessandro Lenci, Philippe Blache, and Chu-Ren Huang. 2016. Representing verbs with rich contexts: an evaluation on verb similarity. In *Proceedings of the 2016 Conference on Empirical Methods in Natural Language Processing*, pages 1967–1972, Austin, Texas. Association for Computational Linguistics.

WooJin Chung, Sheng-Fu Wang, and Samuel Bowman. 2018. The lifted matrix-space model for semantic composition. In *Proceedings of the 22nd Conference on Computational Natural Language Learning*, pages 508–518, Brussels, Belgium. Association for Computational Linguistics.

Stephen Clark and James R. Curran. 2007. Wide-coverage efficient statistical parsing with CCG and log-linear models. *Computational Linguistics*, 33(4):493–552.

Bob Coecke, Edward Grefenstette, and Mehrnoosh Sadrzadeh. 2013. Lambek vs. Lambek: Functorial vector space semantics and string diagrams for Lambek calculus. *Annals of Pure and Applied Logic*, 164(11):1079 – 1100. Special issue on Seventh Workshop on Games for Logic and Programming Languages (GaLoP VII).

Bob Coecke, Mehrnoosh Sadrzadeh, and Stephen Clark. 2010. Mathematical foundations for a compositional distributional model of meaning. *Linguistic Analysis*, 36(1):345–384.

Alexis Conneau, Douwe Kiela, Holger Schwenk, Loïc Barrault, and Antoine Bordes. 2017. Supervised learning of universal sentence representations from natural language inference data. In *Proceedings of the 2017 Conference on Empirical Methods in Natural Language Processing*, pages 670–680, Copenhagen, Denmark. Association for Computational Linguistics.

Haskell B. Curry and Richard Feys. 1958. *Combinatory Logic*. North-Holland, Amsterdam.

Jacob Devlin, Ming-Wei Chang, Kenton Lee, and Kristina Toutanova. 2019. BERT: Pre-training of deep bidirectional transformers for language understanding. In *Proceedings of the 2019 Conference of the North American Chapter of the Association for Computational Linguistics: Human Language Technologies, Volume 1 (Long and Short Papers)*, pages 4171–4186, Minneapolis, Minnesota. Association for Computational Linguistics.

Daniela Gerz, Ivan Vulić, Felix Hill, Roi Reichart, and Anna Korhonen. 2016. SimVerb-3500: A large-scale evaluation set of verb similarity. In *Proceedings of the 2016 Conference on Empirical Methods in Natural Language Processing*, pages 2173–2182, Austin, Texas. Association for Computational Linguistics.

E. Grefenstette, G. Dinu, Y. Zhang, M. Sadrzadeh, and M. Baroni. 2013. Multi-step regression learning for compositional distributional semantics. In *Proceedings of the 10th International Conference on Computational Semantics (IWCS 2013) – Long Papers*, pages 131–142, Potsdam, Germany. Association for Computational Linguistics.

Edward Grefenstette and Mehrnoosh Sadrzadeh. 2011. Experimental support for a categorical compositional distributional model of meaning. In *Proceedings of the 2011 Conference on Empirical Methods in Natural Language Processing*, pages 1394–1404, Edinburgh, Scotland, UK. Association for Computational Linguistics.

Felix Hill, Roi Reichart, and Anna Korhonen. 2015. SimLex-999: Evaluating semantic models with (genuine) similarity estimation. *Computational Linguistics*, 41(4):665–695.

Julia Hockenmaier and Mark Steedman. 2007. CCGbank: A corpus of CCG derivations and dependency structures extracted from the Penn treebank. *Computational Linguistics*, 33(3):355–396.

Dimitri Kartsaklis and Mehrnoosh Sadrzadeh. 2013. Prior disambiguation of word tensors for constructing sentence vectors. In *Proceedings of the 2013 Conference on Empirical Methods in Natural Language Processing*, pages 1590–1601, Seattle, Washington, USA. Association for Computational Linguistics.

Dimitri Kartsaklis, Mehrnoosh Sadrzadeh, and Stephen Pulman. 2013. Separating disambiguation from composition in distributional semantics. In *Proceedings of the Seventeenth Conference on Computational Natural Language Learning*, pages 114–123,

Sofia, Bulgaria. Association for Computational Linguistics.

Adhiguna Kuncoro, Lingpeng Kong, Daniel Fried, Dani Yogatama, Laura Rimell, Chris Dyer, and Phil Blunsom. 2020. Syntactic structure distillation pretraining for bidirectional encoders. *arXiv preprint arXiv:2005.13482*.

Omer Levy and Yoav Goldberg. 2014. Dependency-based word embeddings. In *Proceedings of the 52nd Annual Meeting of the Association for Computational Linguistics (Volume 2: Short Papers)*, pages 302–308, Baltimore, Maryland. Association for Computational Linguistics.

Omer Levy, Yoav Goldberg, and Ido Dagan. 2015. Improving distributional similarity with lessons learned from word embeddings. *Transactions of the Association for Computational Linguistics*, 3:211–225.

Jean Maillard and Stephen Clark. 2015. Learning adjective meanings with a tensor-based skip-gram model. In *Proceedings of the Nineteenth Conference on Computational Natural Language Learning*, pages 327–331, Beijing, China. Association for Computational Linguistics.

Jean Maillard, Stephen Clark, and Edward Grefenstette. 2014. A type-driven tensor-based semantics for CCG. In *Proceedings of the EACL 2014 Workshop on Type Theory and Natural Language Semantics (TTNLS)*, pages 46–54, Gothenburg, Sweden. Association for Computational Linguistics.

Marco Marelli, Stefano Menini, Marco Baroni, Luisa Bentivogli, Raffaella Bernardi, and Roberto Zamparelli. 2014. A SICK cure for the evaluation of compositional distributional semantic models. In *Proceedings of the Ninth International Conference on Language Resources and Evaluation (LREC-2014)*, pages 216–223, Reykjavik, Iceland. European Languages Resources Association (ELRA).

Tomas Mikolov, Ilya Sutskever, Kai Chen, Greg S Corrado, and Jeff Dean. 2013. Distributed representations of words and phrases and their compositionality. In C. J. C. Burges, L. Bottou, M. Welling, Z. Ghahramani, and K. Q. Weinberger, editors, *Advances in Neural Information Processing Systems 26*, pages 3111–3119. Curran Associates, Inc.

Dmitrijs Milajevs, Dimitri Kartsaklis, Mehrnoosh Sadrzadeh, and Matthew Purver. 2014. Evaluating neural word representations in tensor-based compositional settings. In *Proceedings of the 2014 Conference on Empirical Methods in Natural Language Processing (EMNLP)*, pages 708–719.

Jeff Mitchell and Mirella Lapata. 2008. Vector-based models of semantic composition. In *Proceedings of ACL-08: HLT*, pages 236–244, Columbus, Ohio. Association for Computational Linguistics.

Jeff Mitchell and Mirella Lapata. 2010. Composition in distributional models of semantics. *Cognitive Science*, 34(8):1388–1429.

Denis Paperno, Nghia The Pham, and Marco Baroni. 2014. A practical and linguistically-motivated approach to compositional distributional semantics. In *Proceedings of the 52nd Annual Meeting of the Association for Computational Linguistics (Volume 1: Long Papers)*, pages 90–99, Baltimore, Maryland. Association for Computational Linguistics.

Matthew Peters, Mark Neumann, Mohit Iyyer, Matt Gardner, Christopher Clark, Kenton Lee, and Luke Zettlemoyer. 2018. Deep contextualized word representations. In *Proceedings of the 2018 Conference of the North American Chapter of the Association for Computational Linguistics: Human Language Technologies, Volume 1 (Long Papers)*, pages 2227–2237, New Orleans, Louisiana. Association for Computational Linguistics.

Tamara Polajnar, Laura Rimell, and Stephen Clark. 2014. Using sentence plausibility to learn the semantics of transitive verbs. *Learning Semantics Workshop, NIPS*.

Nils Reimers and Iryna Gurevych. 2019. Sentence-BERT: Sentence embeddings using Siamese BERT-networks. In *Proceedings of the 2019 Conference on Empirical Methods in Natural Language Processing and the 9th International Joint Conference on Natural Language Processing (EMNLP-IJCNLP)*, pages 3982–3992, Hong Kong, China. Association for Computational Linguistics.

Richard Socher, Alex Perelygin, Jean Wu, Jason Chuang, Christopher D. Manning, Andrew Ng, and Christopher Potts. 2013. Recursive deep models for semantic compositionality over a sentiment treebank. In *Proceedings of the 2013 Conference on Empirical Methods in Natural Language Processing*, pages 1631–1642, Seattle, Washington, USA. Association for Computational Linguistics.

Mark Steedman. 2000. *The syntactic process*, volume 24. MIT Press.

Kai Sheng Tai, Richard Socher, and Christopher D. Manning. 2015. Improved semantic representations from tree-structured long short-term memory networks. In *Proceedings of the 53rd Annual Meeting of the Association for Computational Linguistics and the 7th International Joint Conference on Natural Language Processing (Volume 1: Long Papers)*, pages 1556–1566, Beijing, China. Association for Computational Linguistics.

Gijs Wijnholds and Mehrnoosh Sadrzadeh. 2019. Evaluating composition models for verb phrase elliptical sentence embeddings. In *Proceedings of the 2019 Conference of the North American Chapter of the Association for Computational Linguistics: Human Language Technologies, Volume 1 (Long and Short Papers)*, pages 261–271, Minneapolis, Minnesota. Association for Computational Linguistics.

Dongqiang Yang and David Martin Powers. 2006. Verb similarity on the taxonomy of wordnet. In *Pro-

*ceedings of the Third International WordNet Confer-
ence GWC 2006, South Jeju Island, Korea*, pages
121–128. Masaryk University.

Word Representations Concentrate and This is Good News!

Romain Couillet[1]**, Yagmur Gizem Cinar**[2]**, Eric Gaussier**[2] and **Muhammad Imran**[2]
[1]LargeDATA chair, GIPSA-lab, University Grenoble-Alpes, Grenoble, France
[2]University Grenoble-Alpes, CNRS, LIG-Lab, Grenoble, France

Abstract

This article establishes that, unlike the legacy tf*idf representation, recent natural language representations (word embedding vectors) tend to exhibit a so-called *concentration of measure phenomenon*, in the sense that, as the representation size p and database size n are both large, their behavior is similar to that of large dimensional Gaussian random vectors. This phenomenon may have important consequences as machine learning algorithms for natural language data could be amenable to improvement, thereby providing new theoretical insights into the field of natural language processing.

1 Introduction

One of the reasons of the success of deep learning (DNN) representations (such as image features or word embeddings) lies in their very high performing and stable behavior, when used for instance as inputs to classification or regression algorithms. We hypothesize that the underlying explanation is that, *from the point of view of these learning algorithms*, these (usually large dimensional) efficient representations exhibit a behavior "akin" (although formally different) to large dimensional random Gaussian vectors. In a sense, one may think of these "compressed raw data" representations as being all the better than they have a large "entropy", i.e., that they are composed of independent and isotropic components (otherwise, according to information theory, one may compress them even more). However, large dimensional "Gaussian-like" representation vectors $\mathbf{x} \in \mathbb{R}^p$ display quite counter-intuitive behavior when compared to small dimensional data, thereby disrupting our standard approach to machine learning. In particular, they naturally suffer from various sources of the curse of dimensionality: for instance, from the law of large numbers, $\frac{1}{p}\|\mathbf{x}\|^2 = \frac{1}{p}\sum_{i=1}^{p} x_i^2$ tends

to converge as $p \to \infty$, so that the representations, rather than occupying all of $\mathbb{R}^p$, concentrate at the edges of a sphere. Worse, the normalized distance $\frac{1}{p}\|\mathbf{x}_1 - \mathbf{x}_2\|^2 = \frac{1}{p}\|\mathbf{x}_1\|^2 + \frac{1}{p}\|\mathbf{x}_2\|^2 - \frac{2}{p}\mathbf{x}_1^\mathsf{T}\mathbf{x}_2 \simeq \frac{1}{p}\|\mathbf{x}_1\|^2 + \frac{1}{p}\|\mathbf{x}_2\|^2$ (due to $\frac{1}{p}\mathbf{x}_1^\mathsf{T}\mathbf{x}_2 \to 0$ for vectors of independent entries) loses the information of correlation between $\mathbf{x}_1$ and $\mathbf{x}_2$.

Fortunately, these curses of dimensionality can be turned into blessings. Again by (advanced versions of) the law of large numbers, the behavior of machine learning algorithms running on Gaussian-like data becomes amenable to theoretical analysis, in particular using recent advances in the fields of large dimensional statistics and random matrix theory. Therefore, these analyses allow for the performance prediction, improvement, and optimization of machine learning methods on *real data*. Consequently, proving that data representations behave like Gaussian vectors implies the possibility to theoretically control the learning algorithms designed to handle these data.

In a recent line of works, Couillet and co-authors suggest and theoretically support that DNN representations are indeed *not Gaussian* per se, but closely resemble *concentrated random vectors*. By definition, a concentrated random vector $\mathbf{x} \in \mathbb{R}^p$ is a vector which satisfies a concentration of measure phenomenon in the sense of Ledoux (2001): in essence, concentration means that $\mathbf{x}$ does *not* converge (quite the opposite) but any *scalar Lipschitz observation* $g(\mathbf{x}) \in \mathbb{R}$ of $\mathbf{x}$ converges around its statistical mean when the size p of $\mathbf{x}$ increases; Figure 1 schematically illustrates the concentration of measure phenomenon. In particular, a key property to the present article is that the distance between any two concentrated random vectors $\mathbf{x}_1$ and $\mathbf{x}_2$ with "nice properties" converges to a constant value, which *only depends* on the data statistics, and is in particular independent of their random re-

Proceedings of the 24th Conference on Computational Natural Language Learning, pages 325–334
Online, November 19-20, 2020. ©2020 Association for Computational Linguistics
https://doi.org/10.18653/v1/P17

alization. This fundamental phenomenon, not true for small data, is at the core of our present study.

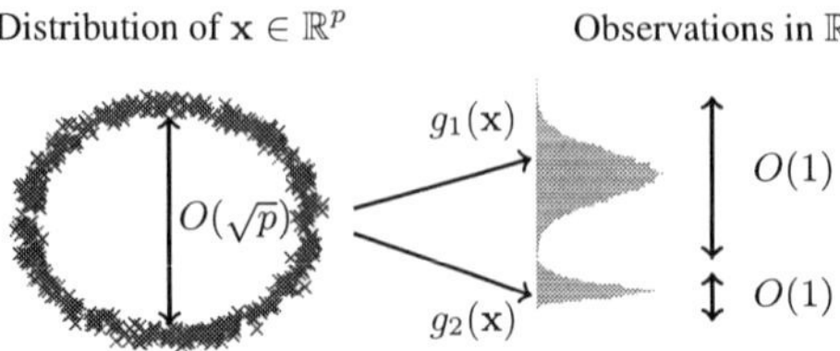

Figure 1: A visual interpretation of the concentration of measure phenomenon. **(Left)** Schematics of 500 realizations of p-dimensional Gaussian random vectors $\mathbf{x} \sim \mathcal{N}(0, \mathbf{I}_p)$ (concentrated by definition). **(Right)** Concentration of two Lipschitz functionals ($g_1(\mathbf{x}) = \mathbf{x}^\top \mathbf{1}_p/\sqrt{p}$ and $g_2(\mathbf{x}) = \|\mathbf{x}\|_\infty$). While $\mathbf{x}$ "spreads out" in its ambient space, $g_1(\mathbf{x})$ and $g_2(\mathbf{x})$ converge.

In detail, Seddik et al. (2020) shows that *natural images* and their modern representations (such as VGG, ResNet embeddings) can be appropriately modelled by concentrated random vectors: they precisely prove that the extremely realistic images produced by modern generative adversarial networks (GANs) are by definition concentrated random vectors. Besides, in Louart and Couillet (2018), the authors establish a *universality result* which proves that the performance of many machine learning algorithms – from support vector machines to (kernel) spectral clustering – applied to concentrated random data is asymptotically[1] the same as if the data had been Gaussian random vectors with the same first and second order statistics. These findings have important consequences to modern machine learning: they in particular ensure that even involved algorithms applied to real data are analytically tractable, and that their performances can be anticipated and improved offline (without the need for cross-validation).

As (possibly large dimensional) vector representations of words and documents have become a basic building block of many natural language processing methods (Turney and Pantel, 2010), in particular since the success of word embeddings such as *word2Vec* (Mikolov et al., 2013) and *Glove*[2] (Pennington et al., 2014), two natural questions arise: (i) do word (and document) representations exhibit concentration of measure phenomena?, and (ii) do some of the aforementioned findings on real images extend to words and textual documents?

The present article empirically investigates this question and claims to reach a positive answer[3]. Specifically, the main contributions of the article are as follows:

1. We empirically establish that recent word embedding representations can suffer a *distance concentration phenomenon*, typical of concentrated random vectors but usually considered as a manifestation of the curse of dimensionality;

2. We empirically confirm that these word embeddings, unlike tf*idf vectors, exhibit a *universality phenomenon* in the following sense: letting $\mathbf{x}_1, \ldots, \mathbf{x}_n \in \mathbb{R}^p$ be n words or document representations of dimension p, the kernel matrix $\mathbf{K} \in \mathbb{R}^{n \times n}$ with $\mathbf{K}_{ij} = f(\frac{1}{p}\|\mathbf{x}_i - \mathbf{x}_j\|^2)$ for some smooth function f has the same behavior (entry-wise and spectral) as a matrix $\mathbf{K}'$ built out of Gaussian random vectors $\mathbf{x}_i'$ having the same statistical mean and covariance as the original data.[4]

3. As a concrete application, the classification performances achieved by a kernel (least-square) support vector machine applied to classes of documents of popular databases are shown to be theoretically predictable and to match the theory established on mere Gaussian random vectors, thereby confirming the universality property of word embedding representations and the possibility to use a simple Gaussian vector theory to predict the performance of machine learning algorithms for natural language processing.

Related works. Several works similarly tried to reinterpret word embeddings, either in terms of matrix factorization (Levy and Goldberg, 2014b) or latent models Arora et al. (2016), and to account for the associations and analogies typical of the linear behavior of these embeddings (Levy and Goldberg, 2014a; Bolukbasi et al., 2016; Gittens et al., 2017; Ethayarajh et al., 2019a,b; Allen and

---

[1] In the limit of large number and dimension of the data.

[2] Recent *contextualized* word embeddings, such as BERT Devlin et al. (2019), cannot be reasonably used without fine tuning. These are not considered in the present study, even though we do believe our conclusions also apply to them, a point to be investigated in future extensions.

[3] The source code used for our experiments is available at https://github.com/ygcinar/nlp-concentration

[4] Those means and covariances being evaluated empirically from words and documents of a common class.

Hospedales, 2019). In a different line of research, many attempts were made to understand the syntactic and semantic generalization capabilities of different deep learning models based on word embeddings, as in Dessì and Baroni (2019); Hewitt and Manning (2019); Lakretz et al. (2019); Chi et al. (2020) to list a few. Our approach is however different in its trying to *statistically model* word embeddings so to grasp the behavior of related machine learning algorithms. To the best of the authors' knowledge, this the first time this approach is being investigated.

2 Preliminaries and first observations

2.1 Asymptotics of learning

From a crude viewpoint, machine learning algorithms may be seen as functionals $F_\theta : \mathbb{R}^{p \times n} \times \mathbb{R}^p \to \mathbb{R}$, $(\mathbf{X}, \mathbf{x}) \to F_\theta(\mathbf{X}, \mathbf{x})$ which, for an input training data matrix $\mathbf{X} = [\mathbf{x}_1, \ldots, \mathbf{x}_n]$ and a test datum $\mathbf{x}$ returns a soft scalar score or hard decision. Here θ accounts for the possible hyperparameter vector used to fine-tune the algorithm. Assuming the training dataset $\mathbf{X} \in \mathbb{R}^{p \times n}$ to be a random matrix with some prescribed distribution (and similarly for $\mathbf{x}$), evaluating the performances of F_θ boils down to establishing the statistics of the *random variable $F_\theta(\mathbf{X}, \mathbf{x})$*. This has long been a cumbersome, if not impossible, task which has mainly been studied so far using the asymptotic statistics $n \to \infty$ and p fixed. Yet, these results have long remained of little use, not very expressive, and of limited interest when n is not much larger than p; this being in particular due to the non-linear (and often even implicit) nature of F_θ. Random matrix theory and statistical physics have recently changed this paradigm and managed to break the non-linearity barrier by showing that, as $n, p \to \infty$ simultaneously (thereby mimicking the modern large and numerous data setting), the performances of many non-trivial learning algorithms become tractable since they *converge*, as $n, p \to \infty$, to some deterministic limits (Couillet et al., 2016).

These latest results are based on sufficiently "stable" random models for $\mathbf{X}$ (and $\mathbf{x}$): statistical physics uses isotropy and symmetries, which however often reduces to standard Gaussian data assumptions, while random matrix theory is richer and has lately exploited the *Lipschitz stability* offered by *concentrated random vector* models (Louart and Couillet, 2018). By definition, a random vector $\mathbf{z}$ in a vector space $\mathcal{S}$ is concentrated if, for all 1-Lipschitz functional $g : \mathcal{S} \to \mathbb{R}$, we have that for all $\varepsilon > 0$,

$$\mathbb{P}\left(|g(\mathbf{z}) - m_g| > \varepsilon\right) \leq C e^{-c\varepsilon^2}$$

for some constant $C, c > 0$ and m_g a median of $g(\mathbf{z})$. That is, $\mathbf{z}$ itself may not converge in any usual sense (in general it does not: for instance $z \sim \mathcal{N}(0, \mathbf{I}_p)$ is concentrated but does not converge) but its Lipschitz functionals, also called *observations of $\mathbf{z}$*, do converge (e.g., $\frac{1}{\sqrt{p}}\|\mathbf{z}\| \to 1$ almost surely). Recall Figure 1 for a visual intuition. Concentrated random vector modelling is particularly convenient as it ensures that, if $\mathbf{X}$ is, say, a concentrated random matrix, then for any Lipschitz function G (that outputs either small or large dimensional data), $G(\mathbf{X})$ is still concentrated and in particular functionals $G : \mathbb{R}^{p \times n} \to \mathbb{R}$ are such that $G(\mathbf{X})$ almost surely converges.

It is proved in Louart and Couillet (2018) that, for a rich family of functionals F_θ, if $\mathbf{X}$ and $\mathbf{x}$ are concentrated, not only does $F_\theta(\mathbf{X}, \mathbf{x})$ converge, but it converges *to the same limit* as $F_\theta(\mathbf{X}', \mathbf{x}')$ for $\mathbf{X}'$ and $\mathbf{x}'$ random Gaussian matrix and vector having the same statistics (mean and covariance) as $\mathbf{X}$ and $\mathbf{x}$, respectively. This is a classical but fundamental result in random matrix theory, referred to as *universality*.

Remark 1 (When are n, p large enough?). *If random matrix theory predicts the asymptotic convergence of algorithms as $n, p \to \infty$, these results are only useful if, in practice, n and p need not be extremely large. As a matter of fact, and quite surprisingly, the* large dimensional effects arise very rapidly *so that, in practice, n, p of the order of hundreds (sometimes even tens) is enough for an asymptotic behavior to emerge. This is explained by the numerous ($O(np)$) degrees of freedom inherent to the data which in particular induce rates of convergence, e.g., central limit theorems, at speed $1/\sqrt{np}$ instead of $1/\sqrt{n}$ when $n \to \infty$ alone. Word embedding vectors, of size $p \sim 100$ or more, naturally enter this regime.*

2.2 How to testify of a concentration of measure phenomenon?

With this introductory overview in mind naturally arises the question of the relevance of a concentrated random vector modelling for practical data. As pointed out in the introduction, the synthetic images produced by GANs (Goodfellow et al., 2014) are by definition concentrated random vectors: this is because they are bounded Lipschitz functions (the Lipschitz operator being the pre-trained neural network) of a Gaussian random vector which is itself concentrated. Genuine images being so well approximated by GAN synthetic images, this strongly suggests that real images can be modelled as concentrated random vectors, which is confirmed by simulation results in Seddik et al. (2020).

But words and documents are so far not reliably produced by GANs and it is unclear whether they might embrace the concentration of measure phenomenon. The objective of the article is to empirically assess whether the most pregnant phenomena occurring in concentration random vectors, namely the convergence of distances between distinct vectors and the (Gaussian-like) universality behavior, are observed on word and document representations.

2.3 Concentration of distances, and kernel spectrum

2.3.1 Concentration of distance

A first phenomenon arising in concentrated random vectors, which disrupts standard machine learning intuition, is the *convergence of distances phenomenon*. Specifically, if $x_1, \ldots, x_n \in \mathbb{R}^p$ are i.i.d. concentrated random vectors with $C \equiv \mathrm{Cov}(x_i)$ of bounded spectral norm, then, as $p, n \to \infty$ in such a way that n grows no more than polynomially with p (which is the case, for example, if p/n is constant),

$$\max_{1 \le i \ne j \le n} \left| \frac{1}{p} \|x_i - x_j\|^2 - \tau_p \right| \to 0 \quad (1)$$

almost surely, where $\tau_p \equiv \frac{2}{p}\mathrm{tr}C$. That is, the distances between any pair of data all converge to the same limit.

Besides, and most importantly, if the x_i's are drawn from a mixture of k distribution classes (with k fixed) such that $\|\mu_a - \mu_b\| = O_p(1)$, with $\mu_a = \mathbb{E}[x_i]$ for x_i in Class a, and $\mathrm{tr}(C_a - C_b) = O_p(\sqrt{p})$, with $C_a = \mathrm{Cov}(x_i)$, then (1) remains valid. This means that the *classes cannot asymptotically be distinguished* by the data distances. Here τ_p can be taken to be any $\frac{2}{p}\mathrm{tr}C_a$, for $a \in \{1, \ldots, k\}$. The setting $\|\mu_a - \mu_b\| = O_p(1)$ and $\mathrm{tr}(C_a - C_b) = O_p(\sqrt{p})$ is referred to as the *non-trivial classification regime*.

Remark 2 (On "non-trivial" classification). *The above two assumptions* $\|\mu_a - \mu_b\| = O_p(1)$ *and* $\mathrm{tr}(C_a - C_b) = O_p(\sqrt{p})$ *are quite natural to model a* non-trivial, *that is neither too easy nor too hard, classification scenario. In other words, if either* $\|\mu_a - \mu_b\|$ *or* $\frac{1}{\sqrt{p}}\mathrm{tr}(C_a - C_b)$ *were to increase with* p, *then a simple Bayesian analysis demonstrates that a trivial algorithm can achieve asymptotically perfect classification as p increases; conversely, if both* $\|\mu_a - \mu_b\|$ *and* $\frac{1}{\sqrt{p}}\mathrm{tr}(C_a - C_b)$ *were to vanish as p increases, it is theoretically impossible to retrieve the classes with any algorithm. In practice, of course, p remains fixed so that the conditions* $\|\mu_a - \mu_b\| = O_p(1)$ *and* $\mathrm{tr}(C_a - C_b) = O_p(\sqrt{p})$ *are mostly quantitative: in fact, "good" vector representations will tend to have rather large values of* $\|\mu_a - \mu_b\|$ *and sometimes fall in a rather trivial regime (the classification task is then easy in general and most standard algorithms perform well), while other representations may be less discriminative, in which case classification is non-trivial and a well-tailored classification algorithm must be devised.*

Our first result consists in empirically confirming that the concentration of distances phenomenon of Equation (1) occurs with popular word and document representations. Specifically, Figure 2 displays the histogram of distances of a set of n vector observations $x_1, \ldots, x_n \in \mathbb{R}^p$ under two main settings:

1. The x_i's are i.i.d. $\mathcal{N}(\mu, I_p)$ vs. $\mathcal{N}(-\mu, T)$ for $\mu = (4, 0, \ldots, 0)^\top$ (which satisfies the condition $\|\mu_1 - \mu_2\| = O_p(1)$), $[T]_{ij} = .4^{|i-j|}$ is a Toeplitz matrix, $n = 200$ and (i-a) $p = 4$ or (i-b) $p = 400$, which serves as a theoretical reference;

2. The x_i's correspond to $n = 1\,100$ balanced documents from two classes ("Christian" versus "Forsale") from the 20News-Group database[5]) obtained by selecting in each class the top $3\,500$ words according to their tf*idf scores, the idf being computed within the documents of the class, and encoded through (ii) tf*idf based weighted averages of the Glove embeddings of the words in the document, (iii) tf*idf based weighted averages of the word2vec embeddings of the words in the document, or merely through their (iv) tf*idf vectors.

---

[5]http://qwone.com/~jason/20Newsgroups/

For comparison purposes, all datasets have been centered.

A first observation is that the distances between two-class distributions of both Glove and word2vec representations seemingly "concentrate around $\sqrt{2}$" instead of displaying a bi-modal distribution. Besides, and possibly more importantly, the distribution closely matches the distribution of distances obtained for mere large dimensional Gaussian random vectors. This "resemblance to large (rather than small) Gaussian vector behavior" provides a first hint into a behavior typical of concentrated random vectors. This conclusion does however not hold for tf*idf representations, the distance histogram of which is far from being symmetrically centered around $\sqrt{2}$, which is naturally explained by the sparse nature of the the the tf*idf vectors. Together, these results are a first indicator of a peculiar concentration behavior of "modern" vector representations for documents, as opposed to tf*idf vectors.

The above results are further supported in Figure 3 based on all the classes of the 20NewsGroup dataset and detailed in the next section.

From a practical standpoint though, the mono-modal histograms of Figure 2 strongly suggest that "individual distance-based" document classification methods are likely to fail. The next section investigates this aspect by showing that more elaborate methods which treat data distances collectively rather than individually, such as spectral-based techniques, are more amenable to handle document vector classification than individual distance-based techniques.

2.3.2 Kernel spectral behavior

A broad range of machine learning algorithms $F_\theta(\mathbf{X}, \mathbf{x})$ are of the form $G_\theta(\mathbf{K}, \mathbf{x})$ where $\mathbf{K} \in \mathbb{R}^{n \times n}$ is a *kernel matrix* of the input data $\mathbf{X}$ (ker-

---

[6]Exact calculus reveals that, for $\mathbf{x}_i \sim \mathcal{N}(\boldsymbol{\mu}_a, \mathbf{C}_a)$ and $\mathbf{x}_j \sim \mathcal{N}(\boldsymbol{\mu}_b, \mathbf{C}_b)$, under the aforementioned non-trivial regime, for $\tau_p = \frac{1}{p}\mathrm{tr}(\mathbf{C}_a + \mathbf{C}_b)$ here,

$$\frac{1}{\sqrt{p}}\|\mathbf{x}_i - \mathbf{x}_j\| \sim \mathcal{N}\left(\sqrt{\tau_p}, \sigma_{a,b}^2\right) + o_p(1)$$

$$\sigma_{a,b}^2 \equiv \frac{1}{\tau_p}\frac{1}{p^2}\mathrm{tr}(\mathbf{C}_a\mathbf{C}_b) + \frac{1}{2\tau_p}\frac{1}{p^2}\mathrm{tr}(\mathbf{C}_a^2) + \frac{1}{2\tau_p}\frac{1}{p^2}\mathrm{tr}(\mathbf{C}_b^2)$$

the quantities appearing in the variance $\sigma_{a,b}^2$ being consistently estimated from: $\frac{1}{p}\mathrm{tr}(\hat{\mathbf{C}}_1\hat{\mathbf{C}}_2) = \frac{1}{p}\mathrm{tr}(\mathbf{C}_1\mathbf{C}_2) + o_p(1)$ and $\frac{1}{p}\mathrm{tr}(\hat{\mathbf{C}}^2) = \frac{1}{p}\mathrm{tr}(\mathbf{C}^2) + \frac{1}{np}(\mathrm{tr}(\hat{\mathbf{C}}))^2 + o_p(1)$ with n the number of independent samples used to evaluate the sample covariance matrix $\hat{\mathbf{C}}$ of $\mathbf{C}$.

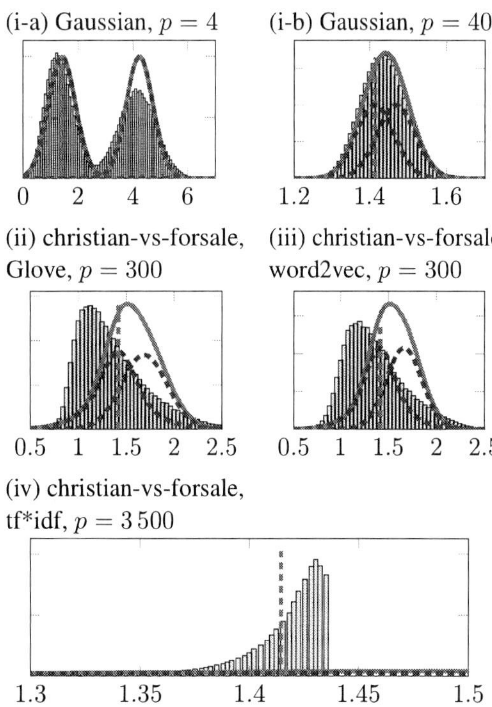

Figure 2: Distribution of (centered and normalized) input data distances $\{\frac{1}{\sqrt{p}}\|\mathbf{x}_i - \mathbf{x}_j\|\}_{1 \leq i \neq j \leq n}$ for (i) two-class Gaussian mixture with mean $\pm\boldsymbol{\mu}$ of size (i-a) $p = 4$ or (i-b) $p = 400$, and two-class documents (20NewsGroups, "Christian" vs. "Forsale") with (ii) Glove, (iii) word2vec, or (iv) tf*idf representations. In blue are displayed the intra- and inter-class distance distributions and in red the collective distance distribution, as if all data were Gaussian and all distances were independent (which they are not).[6] Dashed-red line pointing the $\sqrt{2}$ position (where distances theoretically concentrate).

nel spectral clustering, kernel SVM, graph kernel semi-supervised learning, etc.). Typically, following our distance-based development, $\mathbf{K}_{ij} = f(\frac{1}{p}\|\mathbf{x}_i - \mathbf{x}_j\|^2)$ for some smooth function f.

Studying the statistical behavior of such algorithms, even under a mere Gaussian mixture model setting, has long remained an open problem, due to the non-linearity of f and of the intricate dependence between the entries of $\mathbf{K}$. As a positive aftermath of the (a priori deleterious) concentration of distance phenomenon though, the authors in El Karoui et al. (2010); Couillet et al. (2016) prove that, when $p, n \to \infty$, the involved matrix $\mathbf{K}$ is asymptotically well approximated by a form

$$\mathbf{K} = \mathbf{W} + \mathbf{P} + o_{\|\cdot\|}(1) \tag{2}$$

where $\mathbf{W}$ is a non-informative full-rank noise matrix and $\mathbf{P}$ is a low-rank[7] informative matrix which carries in its few eigenvectors the information about (a) the k data classes *only through* the first and second order statistics $\{\boldsymbol{\mu}_a\}_{a=1}^k$ and $\{\mathbf{C}_a\}_{a=1}^k$ of the classes, and (b) the kernel function f *only through* its local behavior around the joint distance concentration point τ_p. For instance, the popular radial-basis (RBF) kernel $f(t) = \exp(-\frac{t}{2\sigma^2})$ behaves theoretically the same as any other function (for instance a mere polynomial of order 2) having the same first two derivatives as f in τ_p. This finding opens the perspective to improve kernel-based algorithms based on a careful choice of the behavior of f around τ_p.

One of the main consequences of the approximation (2) is the theoretical ability to anticipate the *spectral behavior*, so in particular to describe the statistics of the dominant eigenvectors[8] of $\mathbf{K}$, thereby allowing for a theoretical prediction of the performances of spectral learning (e.g., spectral clustering, manifold learning, etc.). These results are again universal in that they only depend on the statistical means and covariances of the data classes; see Couillet et al. (2016) for details.

We wish here to demonstrate that kernel matrices built on natural language data similarly conform to the behavior of large dimensional Gaussian vectors. To this end, we use both the same two-class data benchmark introduced in the previous section as well as the complete set of classes from 20News-Group. We design a matrix $\mathbf{K}$ for the popular RBF kernel $f(t) = \exp(-t/2)$ (that is with bandwidth $\sigma^2 = 1$) and extract its second dominant eigenvector $\mathbf{v}_2$.[9]

This is depicted in Figure 3 and Figure 4, which it is convenient to compare to Figure 2. It is first observed that, while, according to Figure 2 and subsequently supported by Figure 3, the *entries of* $\mathbf{K}$, i.e., $\exp(- \cdot /2)$ applied to the distances $\frac{1}{p}\|\mathbf{x}_i - \mathbf{x_j}\|^2$, are not discriminating – the distance distribution being unimodal in Figure 2 and the contrast between inner and outer class similarity being weak for Glove and word2vec in Figure 3 –, the *entries of* $\mathbf{v}_2$ are instead strongly informative and the eigenvector distribution is bi-modal: this is in essence explained by a "redundancy" effect

---

[7]Of rank usually equal or bounded by the number of classes in the dataset.

[8]Those associated to the largest (or smallest) isolated eigenvalues of $\mathbf{K}$.

[9]Which is known to be the best discriminating eigenvector in a two-class setting.

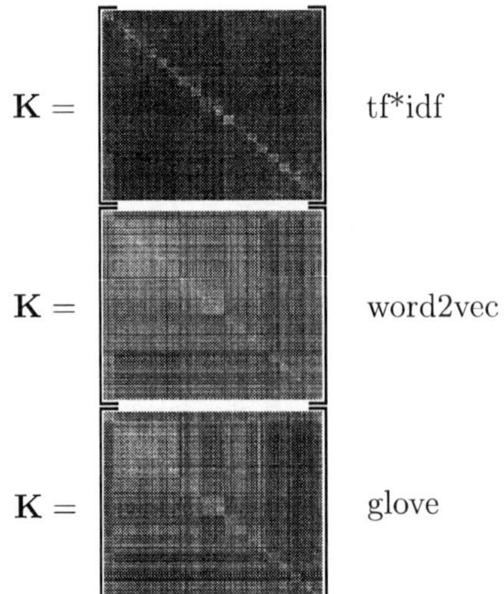

Figure 3: Display of the Gaussian kernel matrices for tf*idf, word2vec and Glove embeddings over the whole 20News-Groups database. Very low contrast is observed between inner and outer similarities, especially for glove and word2vec, as a consequence of the distance concentration effect.

in the numerous data belonging to the same class which "gather energy" into an isolated eigenvalue with eigenvector $\mathbf{v}_2$.[10] This cumulative effect is not exploited by algorithms which treat data distances *one-by-one* (such a KNN kernel with few neighbors) rather than collectively.

A second observation, more to the point for our present demonstration, is that the histogram of the entries of $\mathbf{v}_2$ for genuine natural language data is a close match to the histogram of the synthetic Gaussian vector counterparts: this is a second manifestation of the *universality of concentration of measure*.

Remark 3 ("Behaving like" is not "being" a Gaussian). *We wish to insist that this universality observation does* not *suggest that word and document vectors* look like *Gaussian vectors (this would be a mistake); it merely states that the observed* functional *of the learning data* $\mathbf{X}$ *(here the entries of an eigenvector of* $\mathbf{K}$*) has the same asymptotic behavior* as with Gaussian vector inputs.

These empirical results are strong indicators that natural language data representations may behave similar to concentrated random vectors and may adequately be modelled as such. This implies that

---

[10]In Couillet et al. (2016), a mathematical argument using random matrix theory is provided to fully justify this observation.

the *curse of dimensionality*, appearing here in the distance concentration phenomenon, is at play: as a main consequence, we expect many standard algorithms based on individual data distance evaluations to dramatically fail, where more elaborate techniques using spectral properties remain competitive and, in addition, are now prone to theoretical analysis. The next section investigates this claim in the specific case of SVMs.

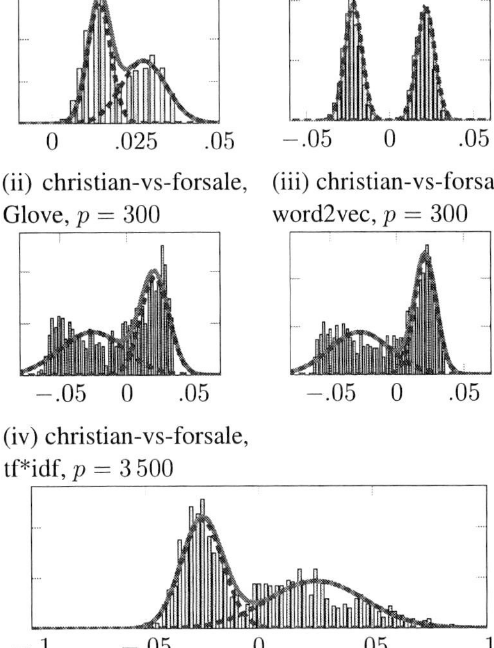

(i-a) Gaussian, $p = 4$

(i-b) Gaussian, $p = 400$

(ii) christian-vs-forsale, Glove, $p = 300$

(iii) christian-vs-forsale, word2vec, $p = 300$

(iv) christian-vs-forsale, tf*idf, $p = 3\,500$

Figure 4: Histogram of the entries of the second dominant eigenvector $\mathbf{v}_2$ of $\mathbf{K} = \{\exp(-\frac{1}{2p}\|\mathbf{x}_i - \mathbf{x}_j\|^2)\}_{1 \leq i,j \leq n}$. **(Left)** Real data (same setting as in Figure 2; **(Right)** Gaussian vectors with the same (empirically estimated) first and second order statistics as their left counterpart. In red are displayed the theoretical distributions under Gaussian data input (according to Couillet et al. (2016)).

3   Application to supervised learning

The concentration of measure phenomenon in real data (Equation (1)) has a fundamental advantage: the performance of many learning algorithms become predictable and, consequently, amenable to improvement. The results of the previous section therefore strongly suggest that, for the first time to the authors' knowledge, one can predict to some extent (so long that the non-trivial conditions are met

for the processed data) the performance of a host of machine learning algorithms for natural language processing.

Specifically, we consider here the standard least-square kernel support vector machine (LSSVM) classifier (used, *e.g.*, in Mitra et al. (2007) for text classification with some refinement), with kernel $\mathbf{K} = \{f(\frac{1}{p}\|\mathbf{x}_i - \mathbf{x}_j\|^2)\}_{1 \leq i,j \leq n}$, for some function f to be specified. The LSSVM classifier allocates the class of a new datum $\mathbf{x}$ based on its position with respect to a hyperplane in kernel space designed from the training set $\mathbf{X}$. Although not directly a spectral method (as in the unsupervised spectral clustering algorithm (Von Luxburg, 2007)), for large n, p, the LSSVM classifier inherently exploits the eigenspectrum of the kernel matrix $\mathbf{K}$ and its performance is proved in Liao and Couillet (2019) to be asymptotically predictable (for large enough p, n) and in closed form (which is thus simpler than the margin-based SVM, whose asymptotic performances do not admit a closed form).

Precisely, the class $\mathcal{C}_1$ or $\mathcal{C}_2$ allocated to $\mathbf{x}$ is the result of the binary test

$$g(\mathbf{x}) \underset{\mathcal{C}_1}{\overset{\mathcal{C}_2}{\gtrless}} \zeta_p$$

for some well-chosen threshold $\zeta_p \in \mathbb{R}$, where $g(\mathbf{x}) = \boldsymbol{\alpha}^\mathsf{T} \mathbf{k}(\mathbf{x}) + b$, with

$$\boldsymbol{\alpha} = \mathbf{S}^{-1}(\mathbf{y} - b\mathbf{1}_n), \quad b = \frac{\mathbf{1}_n^\mathsf{T}\mathbf{S}^{-1}\mathbf{y}}{\mathbf{1}_n^\mathsf{T}\mathbf{S}^{-1}\mathbf{1}_n}$$

and $\mathbf{S} = \mathbf{K} + \frac{n}{\gamma}\mathbf{I}_n$, for $\mathbf{y} \in \{\pm 1\}^n$ the vector of training data labels, $\mathbf{k}(\mathbf{x}) = \{f(\frac{1}{p}\|\mathbf{x}_i - \mathbf{x}\|^2)\}_{1 \leq i \leq n}$, and regularization $\gamma > 0$.

In Liao and Couillet (2019), the authors precisely show that, for a two-class mixture of concentrated random vectors with means $\boldsymbol{\mu}_1, \boldsymbol{\mu}_2$ and covariances $\mathbf{C}_1, \mathbf{C}_2$, as $n, p \to \infty$ in the non-trivial regime described above, for $\mathbf{x}$ genuinely in class $\mathcal{C}_i$,

$$g(\mathbf{x}) \to \mathcal{N}(m_i, \sigma_i^2)$$

where m_1, m_2, σ_1^2 and σ_2^2 only depend on (a) the ratio $f'(\tau_p)/f''(\tau_p)$ and (b) scalar functionals of the statistical means and covariances (specifically, only $\|\boldsymbol{\mu}_1 - \boldsymbol{\mu}_2\|^2$, $\mathrm{tr}(\mathbf{C}_1 - \mathbf{C}_2)/\sqrt{p}$ and $\mathrm{tr}((\mathbf{C}_1 - \mathbf{C}_2)^2)/p)$; see Liao and Couillet (2019) for details.[11] For instance, $f(t) = \exp(-t/2\sigma^2)$

---

[11] Of particular interest, Liao and Couillet (2019) proves that the optimal threshold ζ_p *must* be around $\frac{n_2}{n} - \frac{n_1}{n}$, with n_a the number of elements of class $\mathcal{C}_a$ in the training dataset, and not around 0 as conventionally assumed.

is the standard radial-basis function kernel (RBF) with bandwidth σ^2, the asymptotic performances of which only depend on $f'(\tau_p)/f''(\tau_p) = -2\sigma^2$.

Of utmost relevance here is that the asymptotic performances are *identical for concentrated random vectors as for Gaussian random vectors* having the same first and second order statistics.

Figure 5 reports the performances of LSSVM as a function of the ratio $f'(\hat{\tau}_p)/f''(\hat{\tau}_p)$, where $\hat{\tau}_p \equiv \frac{1}{n(n-1)}\sum_{1\leq i\neq j\leq n}\frac{1}{p}\|\mathbf{x}_i - \mathbf{x}_j\|^2$ is a consistent (and fast converging) estimate for τ_p, here for two kernels: (a) the second order polynomial kernel such that $f(\hat{\tau}_p) = 4$, $f''(\hat{\tau}_p) = 1$ and $f'(\tau_p)$ varying from -2 to 1, and (b) the RBF kernel with bandwidth σ^2 such that $-2\sigma^2$ varies from -2 to 0 (of course $-2\sigma^2$ cannot be positive).

The benchmark dataset are the Yahoo Answer classes "cult" versus "education", the feature vectors of which are either (ii) tf*idf based weighted averages of Glove embedding ($p = 300$), (iii) tf*idf based weighted averages of word2vec embeddings ($p = 300$) and (iv) tf*idf representation (with dictionary size $p = 3\,000$). A comparison to (i) Gaussian input data vectors is also provided for reference ($p = 300$). In each experiment, the number of training data is $n = 500$ or $n = 2\,000$.

Figure 5 first shows a trend for the performances to converge, as the results for both $n = 500$ and $n = 2\,000$ are similar: as such, these performances are not random and then possibly amenable to theoretical analysis.

More in detail, Figure 5 demonstrates that, for the tf*idf representation, the theoretical equivalent for concentrated vectors (red) and the empirical performance (blue) are quite different, clearly confirming that tf*idf representations are not appropriately modelled by concentrated vectors. This is again no surprise as these vectors are intrinsically sparse, which concentrated vectors cannot be.

The case of word2vec and Glove is more interesting as Figure 5 reports an extremely accurate fit between theory and practice for $f'(\hat{\tau}_p)/f''(\hat{\tau}_p)$ below -1 and above $.5$. More crucially, in these regions, the performances for both the RFB kernel and the polynomial kernel with $f'(\hat{\tau}_p)/f''(\hat{\tau}_p) = -2\sigma^2$ perfectly coincide, so that real data performance corroborates the theory. Only the region $[-1, .5]$ shows a severe discrepancy. This is explained by two factors: (a) for any kernel (here for the polynomial kernel), Liao and Couillet (2019) shows that the region where $f'(\tau_p) \simeq 0$ is particularly

unstable to "strongly mean-discriminative data", i.e., data mixtures strongly identifiable from their statistical means; this is what is observed here with a vanishing performance (dropping to 50%) when $f'(\hat{\tau}_p) = 0$, inducing instability; at this point of our analysis though, we cannot explain the performance increase near 0^- predicted by the theory while the empirical performance monotonously drops; (b) for the RBF kernel, in the vicinity of $\sigma^2 \sim 0$, the entries of $\mathbf{K}$ degenerate; $\mathbf{K}$ becomes sparse, which goes against concentration; this is already observed for Gaussian inputs (top display); this gap can only be covered with larger p, n values.

4   Concluding Remarks

The results of this article may scratch the surface of a new mathematical theory for harnessing modern natural language processing representations: recent word and document features (word2vec and Glove) were shown here to exhibit some key characteristics of concentrated random vectors, which tf*idf maps do not. This, as a consequence of recent works on the analysis of machine learning algorithms for concentration random vectors, opens the path to theoretical analyses, improved understanding, fine-tuned and new algorithms for natural language data processing.

Yet, the preliminary conclusions of the present article are less compelling than similar conclusions drawn for image representations (e.g., in Liao and Couillet (2019); Seddik et al. (2020), where the performance predictions on real images are extremely accurate for wide ranges of hyperparameters). This may be interpreted in two ways: either the document representation (Glove and word2vec) need be perfected to be as discriminative and "maximum entropic"[12] as VGG or ResNet are for images, or the *concentration power* of document embeddings is intrinsically weaker than image embeddings. If the latter hypothesis is correct, further mathematical efforts are needed to improve our understanding of these "weakly concentrated" data models. We plan to investigate these points in the future.

Acknowledgements

This work was partially funded by the MIAI@Grenoble Alpes project (ANR-19-P3IA-0003).

---

[12]We suggest here that good representations should extract all the information and leave residual noise as maximally uninformative; in the manner of isotropic Gaussian vectors.

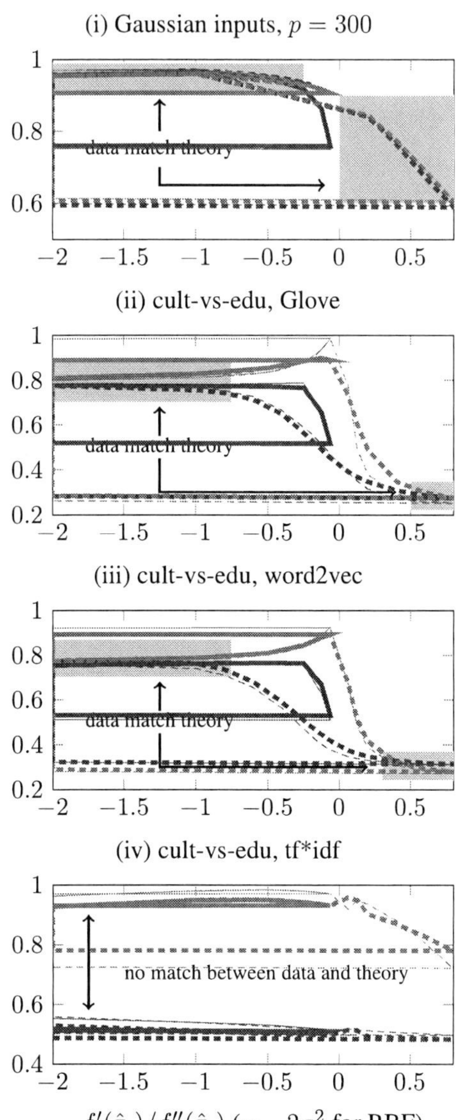

Figure 5: Comparative performance of LSSVM classification for various document vector representations: empirical results (**blue**) versus asymptotic theory (**red**), for $n = 500$ (**thick**) or $n = 2000$ (**light**), with either RBF (**plain**) or second-order polynomial (**dashed**) kernel. Good fit for word2vec and Glove embeddings away from unstability region of $f'(\hat{\tau}_p)/f''(\hat{\tau}_p)$, suggesting concentration (Gaussian-like) behavior; tf*idf data do not concentrate.

References

Carl Allen and Timothy M. Hospedales. 2019. Analogies explained: Towards understanding word embeddings. In *Proceedings of the 36th International Conference on Machine Learning, ICML 2019, 9-15 June 2019, Long Beach, California, USA*, pages 223–231. PMLR.

Sanjeev Arora, Yuanzhi Li, Yingyu Liang, Tengyu Ma, and Andrej Risteski. 2016. A latent variable model approach to pmi-based word embeddings. *Trans. Assoc. Comput. Linguistics*, 4:385–399.

Tolga Bolukbasi, Kai-Wei Chang, James Y. Zou, Venkatesh Saligrama, and Adam Tauman Kalai. 2016. Man is to computer programmer as woman is to homemaker? debiasing word embeddings. In *Advances in Neural Information Processing Systems 29: Annual Conference on Neural Information Processing Systems 2016, December 5-10, 2016, Barcelona, Spain*, pages 4349–4357.

Ethan A. Chi, John Hewitt, and Christopher D. Manning. 2020. Finding universal grammatical relations in multilingual BERT. In *Proceedings of the 58th Annual Meeting of the Association for Computational Linguistics, ACL 2020, Online, July 5-10, 2020*, pages 5564–5577.

Romain Couillet, Florent Benaych-Georges, et al. 2016. Kernel spectral clustering of large dimensional data. *Electronic Journal of Statistics*, 10(1):1393–1454.

Roberto Dessì and Marco Baroni. 2019. Cnns found to jump around more skillfully than rnns: Compositional generalization in seq2seq convolutional networks. In *Proceedings of the 57th Conference of the Association for Computational Linguistics, ACL 2019, Florence, Italy, July 28- August 2, 2019, Volume 1: Long Papers*, pages 3919–3923.

Jacob Devlin, Ming-Wei Chang, Kenton Lee, and Kristina Toutanova. 2019. BERT: pre-training of deep bidirectional transformers for language understanding. In *Proceedings of the 2019 Conference of the North American Chapter of the Association for Computational Linguistics: Human Language Technologies, NAACL-HLT 2019, Minneapolis, MN, USA, June 2-7, 2019, Volume 1 (Long and Short Papers)*, pages 4171–4186.

Noureddine El Karoui et al. 2010. The spectrum of kernel random matrices. *The Annals of Statistics*, 38(1):1–50.

Kawin Ethayarajh, David Duvenaud, and Graeme Hirst. 2019a. Towards understanding linear word analogies. In *Proceedings of the 57th Conference of the Association for Computational Linguistics, ACL 2019, Florence, Italy, July 28- August 2, 2019, Volume 1: Long Papers*, pages 3253–3262.

Kawin Ethayarajh, David Duvenaud, and Graeme Hirst. 2019b. Understanding undesirable word embedding associations. In *Proceedings of the 57th Conference of the Association for Computational Linguistics, ACL 2019, Florence, Italy, July 28- August 2, 2019, Volume 1: Long Papers*, pages 1696–1705.

Alex Gittens, Dimitris Achlioptas, and Michael W. Mahoney. 2017. Skip-gram - zipf + uniform = vector additivity. In *Proceedings of the 55th Annual Meeting of the Association for Computational Linguistics, ACL 2017, Vancouver, Canada, July 30 - August 4, Volume 1: Long Papers*, pages 69–76.

Ian Goodfellow, Jean Pouget-Abadie, Mehdi Mirza, Bing Xu, David Warde-Farley, Sherjil Ozair, Aaron Courville, and Yoshua Bengio. 2014. Generative adversarial nets. In *Advances in neural information processing systems*, pages 2672–2680.

John Hewitt and Christopher D. Manning. 2019. A structural probe for finding syntax in word representations. In *Proceedings of the 2019 Conference of the North American Chapter of the Association for Computational Linguistics: Human Language Technologies, NAACL-HLT 2019, Minneapolis, MN, USA, June 2-7, 2019, Volume 1 (Long and Short Papers)*, pages 4129–4138.

Yair Lakretz, Germán Kruszewski, Theo Desbordes, Dieuwke Hupkes, Stanislas Dehaene, and Marco Baroni. 2019. The emergence of number and syntax units in LSTM language models. In *Proceedings of the 2019 Conference of the North American Chapter of the Association for Computational Linguistics: Human Language Technologies, NAACL-HLT 2019, Minneapolis, MN, USA, June 2-7, 2019, Volume 1 (Long and Short Papers)*, pages 11–20.

Michel Ledoux. 2001. *The concentration of measure phenomenon*. 89. American Mathematical Soc.

Omer Levy and Yoav Goldberg. 2014a. Linguistic regularities in sparse and explicit word representations. In *Proceedings of the Eighteenth Conference on Computational Natural Language Learning, CoNLL 2014, Baltimore, Maryland, USA, June 26-27, 2014*, pages 171–180.

Omer Levy and Yoav Goldberg. 2014b. Neural word embedding as implicit matrix factorization. In *Advances in Neural Information Processing Systems 27: Annual Conference on Neural Information Processing Systems 2014, December 8-13 2014, Montreal, Quebec, Canada*, pages 2177–2185.

Zhenyu Liao and Romain Couillet. 2019. A large dimensional analysis of least squares support vector machines. *IEEE Transactions on Signal Processing*, 67(4):1065–1074.

Cosme Louart and Romain Couillet. 2018. Concentration of measure and large random matrices with an application to sample covariance matrices. *arXiv preprint arXiv:1805.08295*.

Tomas Mikolov, Ilya Sutskever, Kai Chen, Gregory S. Corrado, and Jeffrey Dean. 2013. Distributed representations of words and phrases and their compositionality. In *Advances in Neural Information Processing Systems 26: 27th Annual Conference on Neural Information Processing Systems 2013. Proceedings of a meeting held December 5-8, 2013, Lake Tahoe, Nevada, United States*, pages 3111–3119.

Vikramjit Mitra, Chia-Jiu Wang, and Satarupa Banerjee. 2007. Text classification: A least square support vector machine approach. *Applied Soft Computing*, 7(3):908–914.

Jeffrey Pennington, Richard Socher, and Christopher D. Manning. 2014. Glove: Global vectors for word representation. In *Proceedings of the 2014 Conference on Empirical Methods in Natural Language Processing, EMNLP 2014, October 25-29, 2014, Doha, Qatar, A meeting of SIGDAT, a Special Interest Group of the ACL*, pages 1532–1543.

Mohamed El Amine Seddik, Cosme Louart, Mohamed Tamaazousti, and Romain Couillet. 2020. Random matrix theory proves that deep learning representations of gan-data behave as gaussian mixtures. *arXiv preprint arXiv:2001.08370*.

Peter D. Turney and Patrick Pantel. 2010. From frequency to meaning: Vector space models of semantics. *J. Artif. Intell. Res.*, 37:141–188.

Ulrike Von Luxburg. 2007. A tutorial on spectral clustering. *Statistics and computing*, 17(4):395–416.

"LazImpa": *Laz*y and *Impa*tient neural agents learn to communicate efficiently

Mathieu Rita[1]   **Rahma Chaabouni[1,2]**   **Emmanuel Dupoux[1,2]**

[1]Cognitive Machine Learning (ENS/EHESS/PSL Research University/CNRS/INRIA)
[2]Facebook AI Research
mathieu.rita@polytechnique.edu, {rchaabouni, dpx}@fb.com

Abstract

Previous work has shown that artificial neural agents naturally develop surprisingly non-efficient codes. This is illustrated by the fact that in a referential game involving a speaker and a listener neural networks optimizing accurate transmission over a discrete channel, the emergent messages fail to achieve an optimal length. Furthermore, frequent messages tend to be longer than infrequent ones, a pattern contrary to the Zipf Law of Abbreviation (ZLA) observed in all natural languages. Here, we show that near-optimal and ZLA-compatible messages can emerge, but only if both the speaker and the listener are modified. We hence introduce a new communication system, "LazImpa", where the speaker is made increasingly *laz*y, i.e., avoids long messages, and the listener *impa*tient, i.e., seeks to guess the intended content as soon as possible.

1 Introduction

Recent emergent-communication studies, renewed by the astonishing success of neural networks, are often motivated by a desire to develop neural network agents eventually able to verbally interact with humans (Havrylov and Titov, 2017; Lazaridou et al., 2017). To facilitate such interaction, neural networks' emergent language should possess many natural-language-like properties. However, it has been shown that, even if these emergent languages lead to successful communication, they often do not bear core properties of natural language (Kottur et al., 2017; Bouchacourt and Baroni, 2018; Lazaridou et al., 2018; Chaabouni et al., 2020).

In this work, we focus on one basic property of natural language that resides on the tendency to use messages that are close to the informational optimum. This is illustrated in the Zipf's law of Abbreviation (ZLA), an empirical law that states that in natural language, the more frequent a word is, the shorter it tends to be (Zipf, 1949; Teahan et al., 2000; Sigurd et al., 2004; Strauss et al., 2007). Crucially, ZLA is considered to be an *efficient* property of our language (Gibson et al., 2019). Besides the obvious fact that an efficient code

would be easier to process for us, it is also argued to be a core property of natural language, likely to be correlated with other fundamental aspects of human communication, such as regularity and compositionality (Kirby, 2001). Encouraging it might hence lead to emergent languages that are also more likely to develop these other desirable properties.

Despite the importance of such property, Chaabouni et al. (2019) showed that standard neural network agents, when trained to play a simple signaling game (Lewis, 1969), develop an inefficient code, which even displays an *anti*-ZLA pattern. That is, counterintuitively, more frequent inputs are coded with longer messages than less frequent ones. This inefficiency was related to neural networks' "innate preference" for long messages. In this work, we aim at understanding which constraints need to be introduced on neural network agents in order to overcome their innate preferences and communicate efficiently, showing a proper ZLA pattern.

To this end, we use a reconstruction game where we have two neural network agents: speaker and listener. For each input, the speaker outputs a sequence of symbols (which constitutes the message) sent to the listener. The latter needs then to predict the speaker's input based on the given message. Also, similarly to the previous work, inputs are drawn from a power-law distribution.

We first describe the experimental and optimization framework (see Section 2). In particular, we introduce a new communication system called 'LazImpa', comprising two different constraints (a) *Laz*iness on the speaker side and (b) *Impa*tience on the listener side. The former constraint is inspired by the least-effort principle which is attested to be a ubiquitous pressure in human communication (Piantadosi et al., 2011; Zipf, 1949; Kanwal et al., 2017).

However, if such a constraint is applied too early, the system does not learn an efficient system. We show that incrementally penalizing long messages in the cost function enables an early exploration of the message space (a kind of 'babbling phase') and prevents converging to an inefficient local minimum.

The other constraint, on the listener side, relies on the prediction mechanism, argued to be important in language comprehension (e.g., Federmeier, 2007; Altmann and Mirković, 2009), and is achieved by allowing

335

Proceedings of the 24th Conference on Computational Natural Language Learning, pages 335–343
Online, November 19-20, 2020. ©2020 Association for Computational Linguistics
https://doi.org/10.18653/v1/P17

the listener to reconstruct the intended input as soon as possible. We also provide a two-level analytical method: first, metrics quantifying the efficiency of a code; second, a new protocol to measure its informativeness (see Section 3). Applying these metrics, we demonstrate that, contrary to the standard speaker/listener agents, our new communication system 'LazImpa' leads to the emergence of an efficient code. The latter follows a *ZLA-like* distribution, close to natural languages (see Sections 4.1 and 4.2). Besides the plausibility of the introduced constraints, our new communication system is, first, task- and architecture-agnostic (requires only communicating with sequences of symbols), and second allows stable optimization of the speaker/listener. We also show how both listener and speaker constraints are fundamental to the emergence of a ZLA-like distribution, as efficient as natural language (see Section 4.3).

2 Experimental framework

We explore the properties of emergent communication in the context of referential games where neural network agents, Speaker and Listener, have to cooperatively communicate in order to win the game.

Speaker network receives an input $i \in \mathcal{I}$ and generates a message m of maximum length `max_len`. The symbols of the message belong to a vocabulary $V = \{s_1, s_2, ..., s_{\texttt{voc\_size}-1}, \texttt{EOS}\}$ of size `voc_size` where `EOS` is the 'end of sentence' token indicating the end of Speaker's message. Listener network receives and consumes the message m. Based on this message, it outputs $\hat{i}$. The two agents are successful if Listener manages to guess the right input (i.e., $\hat{i} = i$).

We make two main assumptions. First inputs are drawn from $\mathcal{I}$ following a power-law distribution, where $\mathcal{I}$ is composed of 1000 one-hot vectors.

Consequently, the probability of sampling the kth most frequent input is: $\frac{1/k}{\sum_{j=1}^{1000} 1/j}$ modelling words' distribution in natural language (Zipf, 2013) (see details in Appendix A.1.1). Second, we experiment in the main paper with `max_len` $= 30$ and `voc_size` $= 40$.[1] We further discuss the influence of these assumptions in Appendix. A.4.2 and show the robustness of our results to assumptions change.

In our analysis, we only consider the successful runs, i.e., the runs with a uniform accuracy strictly higher than 97% over all possible 1000 inputs. An emergent language consists then of the input-message mapping. That is, for each input $i \in \mathcal{I}$ fed to Speaker after successful communication, we note its output m.

By $\mathcal{M}$, we define the set of messages m used by our agents after succeeding in the game.

2.1 Agent architectures

In our experiments, we compare two communication systems:

- Standard Agents: as a baseline, composed of Standard Speaker and Standard Listener;

- 'LazImpa': composed of *Lazy* Speaker and *Impa*tient Listener.

For both Speaker and Listener, we experiment with either standard or modified LSTM architectures (Hochreiter and Schmidhuber, 1997).

2.1.1 Standard Agents

Standard Speaker. Standard Speaker is a single-layer LSTM. First, Speaker's inputs i are mapped by a linear layer into an initial hidden state of Speaker's LSTM cell. Then, the message m is generated symbol by symbol: the current sequence is fed to the LSTM cell that outputs a new hidden state. Next, this hidden state is mapped by a linear layer followed by a softmax to a Categorical distribution over the vocabulary. During the training phase, the next symbol is sampled from this distribution. During the testing phase, the next symbol is deterministically selected by taking the argmax of the distribution.

Standard Listener. Standard Listener is also a single-layer LSTM. Once the message m is generated by Speaker, it is entirely passed to Standard Listener. Standard Listener consumes the symbols one by one, until the `EOS` token is seen (the latter is included and fed to Listener). At the end, the final hidden state is mapped to a Categorical distribution $L(m)$ over the input indices (linear layer + softmax). This distribution is then used during the training to compute the loss. During the testing phase, we take the argmax of the distribution as a reconstruction candidate.

Standard loss $\mathcal{L}_{std}$. For Standard Agents, we merely use the cross-entropy loss between the ground truth one-hot vector i and the output Categorical distribution of Listener $L(m)$.

2.1.2 LazImpa

Lazy Speaker. Lazy Speaker has the same architecture as Standard Speaker. The 'Laziness' comes from a cost on the length of the message m directly applied to the loss.

Impatient Listener. We introduce Impatient Listener, designed to guess the intended content as soon as possible. As shown in Figure 1, Impatient Listener consists of a modified Standard Listener that, instead of guessing i after consuming the entire message $m = (m_0, ..., m_t)$, makes a prediction $\hat{i}_k$ for each symbol m_k.[2] This modification takes advantage of the recurrent property of the LSTM, however, could be adapted to any causal sequential neural network model.

---

[1] This combination makes our setting comparable to natural languages; the latter has no upper bound on the maximum length, also a vocabulary size of 40 is close to the alphabet size of the natural languages we study of mean vocabulary size equal to 41.75. See Chaabouni et al. (2019) for more details.

[2] m_t=`EOS` by construction.

At training, a prediction of Impatient Listener, at a position k, is a Categorical distribution $L(m_{:k})$, constructed using a shared single linear layer followed by a softmax (with $m_{:k} = (m_0, ..., m_k)$). Eventually, we get a sequence of $t + 1$ distributions $L(m) = (L(m_{:0}), ..., L(m_{:t}))$, one for each reading position of the message.

At test time, we only take the argmax of the distribution generated by Listener when it reads the EOS token.

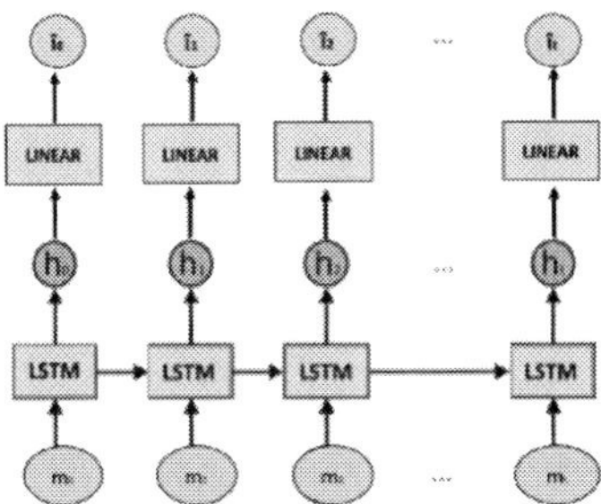

Figure 1: Impatient Listener architecture. The agent is composed of a single-layer LSTM cell and one shared linear layer followed by a softmax. It generates a prediction at each time step.

LazImpa Loss $\mathcal{L}_{laz}$. LazImpa loss is composed of two parts that model 'Impatience' ($\mathcal{L}_{laz/L}$) and 'Laziness' ($\mathcal{L}_{laz/S}$), such that,

$$\mathcal{L}_{laz}(i, m, L(m)) = \mathcal{L}_{laz/L}(i, L(m)) + \mathcal{L}_{laz/S}(m). \quad (1)$$

On one hand, $\mathcal{L}_{laz/L}$ forces Impatient Listener to guess the right candidate as soon as possible when reading the message m. For this purpose, with i the ground-truth input and $L(m) = (L(m_{:0}), ..., L(m_{:t}))$ the sequence of intermediate distributions, the Impatience Loss is defined as the mean cross-entropy loss between i and the intermediate distributions:

$$\mathcal{L}_{laz/L}(i, L(m)) = \frac{1}{t + 1} \sum_{k=0}^{t} \mathcal{L}_{std}(i, L(m_{:k})), \quad (2)$$

Hence, all the intermediate distributions contribute to the loss function according to the following principle: the earlier the Listener predicts the correct output, the larger the reward is.

On the other hand, $\mathcal{L}_{laz/S}$ consists of an adaptive penalty on message lengths. The idea is to first let the system explore long and discriminating messages (**exploration step**) and then, once it reaches good enough communication performances, we apply a length cost (**reduction step**). With $|m|$ the length of the message associated with the input i and 'acc' the estimation of the accuracy (proportion of inputs correctly communicated weighted by appearance frequency), the Laziness Loss is defined as:

$$\mathcal{L}_{laz/S}(m) = \alpha(\text{acc})|m| \quad (3)$$

To schedule this two-step training, we model α as shown in Figure 2. The regularization is mainly composed of two branches: (1) exploration step and (2) reduction step. The latter starts only when the two agents become successful.

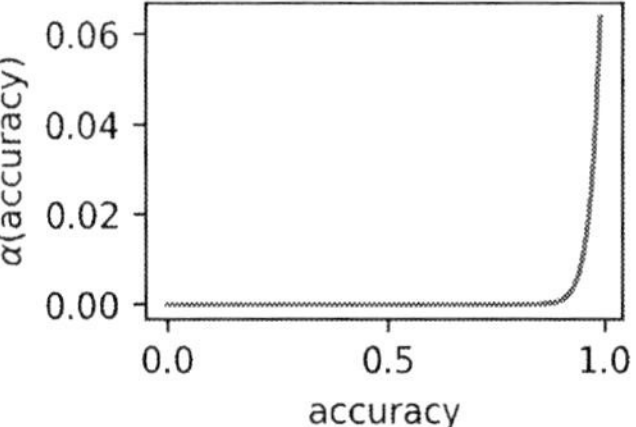

Figure 2: Scheduling of the regularization parameter α as a function of the accuracy. We distinguish two different regimes: the exploration and the reduction regimes. See the mathematical description in Appendix A.1.4

2.2 Optimization

The overall setting, which can be seen as a discrete auto-encoder, cannot be differentiated directly, as the latent space is discrete. We use a hybrid optimization between REINFORCE for Speaker (Williams, 1992) and classic back-propagation for Listener (Schulman et al., 2015).

With $\mathcal{L}$ the loss of the system, i the ground-truth input and $L(m)$ the output distribution of Listener that takes the message m as input, the training task consists in minimizing the expectation of the loss $\mathbb{E}[\mathcal{L}(i, L(m))]$. The expectation is computed w.r.t the joint distribution of the inputs and the message sequences. Let's denote θ_L and θ_S Listener and Speaker parameters respectively. The optimization task requires to compute the gradient $\nabla_{\theta_S \cup \theta_L} \mathbb{E}[\mathcal{L}(i, L(m))]$. An unbiased estimate of this gradient is the gradient of the following function:

$$\mathbb{E}[\underbrace{\mathcal{L}(i, L(m; \theta_L))}_{(A)} + \underbrace{(\{\mathcal{L}(i, L(m; \theta_L))\} - b) \log P_S(m|\theta_S)}_{(B)}],$$

$$(4)$$

where $\{.\}$ is the stop-gradient operation, $P_S(m|\theta_S)$ the probability that Speaker generates the message m, b the running-mean baseline used to reduce variance (Williams, 1992). We also promote exploration by encouraging Speaker's entropy (Williams and Peng, 1991).

The gradient of (4) w.r.t θ_L is found via conventional back-propagation (A) while gradient w.r.t θ_S is found with a REINFORCE-like procedure estimating the gradient via a Monte-Carlo integration calculated over samples of the messages (B). Once the gradient is estimated, it is eventually passed to the Adam optimizer (Kingma and Ba, 2014).

In Appendix A.3.1, we show that LazImpa leads to a stable convergence. We use the EGG toolkit (Kharitonov et al., 2019) as a starting framework. For reproducibility, the code can be found at `https://github.com/MathieuRita/Lazimpa` and the set of hyper-parameters used is presented in Appendix A.1.

3 Analytical method

As ZLA is defined informally, we first introduce reference distributions for comparison. Then, we propose some simple metrics to evaluate the overall efficiency of our emergent codes. Eventually, we provide a simple protocol to analyze the distribution of information within the messages.

3.1 Reference distributions

We compare the emergent languages to the reference distributions introduced in Chaabouni et al. (2019). We provide below a brief description of the different distributions, however, we invite readers to refer to the reference paper for more details.

Optimal Coding (Cover and Thomas, 2006) guarantees the shortest average message length with `max_len` = 30 and `voc_size` = 40. To do so, we deterministically associate the shortest messages to the most frequent inputs. See Ferrer i Cancho et al. (2013) for more details about the derivation of Optimal Coding.

Natural Language We also compare emergent languages with several human languages. In particular, we consider the same languages of the reference paper (English, Arabic, Russian, and Spanish). These references consist of the mapping from the frequency of the top 1000 most frequent words in each language to their length (approximated by the number of characters of each word).[3]

3.2 Efficiency metrics

In this work, we examine the constraints needed for neural agents to develop efficient languages. We use three metrics to evaluate how efficient the different codes are. For all metrics, N denotes the total number of messages (=1000) and $l(m)$ the length of a message m.

Mean message length L_{type}: measures the mean length of the messages assuming a *uniform* weight for each input/message:

$$L_{type} = \frac{1}{N} \sum_{m \in \mathcal{M}} l(m), \qquad (5)$$

Mean weighted message length L_{token} : measures the average length of the messages weighted by their generation frequency:

$$L_{token} = \sum_{m \in \mathcal{M}} p(m)l(m), \qquad (6)$$

where $p(m)$ is the probability of message m (equal to the probability of input i denoted by m) such that $\sum_{m \in \mathcal{M}} p(m) = 1$. Formally, the message m referring to the kth most frequent input would have a probability $\frac{1/k}{\sum_1^{1000} 1/j}$.
Note that, the Optimal Coding is the one that minimizes L_{token} (Cover and Thomas, 2006; Ferrer i Cancho et al., 2013).

ZLA significance score p_{ZLA}: Let's note $(l_i)_{i \in \mathcal{I}}$ a distribution of message lengths of a code. As a ZLA distribution is the one that minimizes L_{token}, we can check if $(l_i)_{i \in \mathcal{I}}$ follows ZLA by testing if its L_{token} is lower than any random permutation of its frequency-length mapping. This is the idea of the randomization test proposed by Ferrer i Cancho et al. (2013).

The test checks whether L_{token} coincides with $\sum_{i \in \mathcal{I}} l_i f_{\sigma(i)}$, with $\sigma(i)$ a random permutation of inputs. We can eventually compute a p-value p_{ZLA} (at threshold α) that measures to which extent L_{token} is likely to be smaller than any other weighted mean message length of a frequency-length mapping. $p_{ZLA} < \alpha$ indicates that any random permutation would have most likely longer weighted mean length. Thus $(l_i)_{i \in \mathcal{I}}$ follows *significantly* a ZLA distribution. Additional details are provided in Appendix A.3.2.

3.3 Information analysis

We also provide an analytical protocol to evaluate how information is distributed within the messages. We consider a symbol to be informative if replacing it randomly has an effect on Listener's prediction. Formally, let's take the message $m = (m_0, ..., m_t)$ associated to the ground truth input i after training. To evaluate the information contained in the symbol at position k, m_k, we substitute it randomly by drawing another symbol r_k uniformly from the vocabulary (except the `EOS` token). Then, we feed this new message $\tilde{m} = (m_1, ..., r_k, ..., m_t)$ into Listener that outputs $\tilde{o}_{m,k}$ (index m indicates that the original message was m, index k indicates that the kth symbol of the original message has been replaced). We define $\Lambda_{m,k}$ a boolean score that evaluates whether the symbol replaced at position k has an impact on the prediction, such that $\Lambda_{k,m} = \mathbf{1}(\tilde{o}_{m,k} \neq i)$. If $\Lambda_{m,k} = 1$, the kth symbol of message m is considered as informative. If $\Lambda_{m,k} = 0$, it is considered as non-informative. We do not consider misreconstructed inputs, neither the position t, as m_t=EOS.[4] This token is needed for Listener's prediction at test time.

This test allows us to introduce some variables that quantify to which extent information is effectively distributed within the messages. As previously, we note $l(m)$ the length of message m and N the total number of messages.

---

[3]We use the frequency lists from `http://corpus.leeds.ac.uk/serge/`.

[4]As we only consider successful runs, more than 97% of inputs are, by definition, well-reconstructed.

Positional encoding $(\Lambda_{.,k})_{1 \le k \le \texttt{max\_len}}$: analyzes the position of informative symbols within an emergent code. We assign a score $\Lambda_{.,k}$ for each position k that counts the proportion of informative symbols over all the messages of a language:

$$\Lambda_{.,k} = \frac{1}{N(k)} \sum_{m \in \mathcal{M}} \Lambda_{m,k}, \qquad (7)$$

where $N(k)$ is the number of messages that have a symbol (different from $\texttt{EOS}$) at position k.

Effective length L_{eff}: measures the mean number of informative symbols by message:

$$L_{eff} = \frac{1}{N} \sum_{m \in \mathcal{M}} \sum_{k=1}^{l(m)-1} \Lambda_{m,k}. \qquad (8)$$

L_{eff} counts the average number of symbols Listener relies on (removing all the uninformative symbols for which $\Lambda_{m,k} = 0$). A message with only informative symbols would have $L_{eff} = L_{type} - 1.$[5]

Information density ρ_{inf} : measures the fraction of informative symbols in a language:

$$\rho_{inf} = \frac{1}{N} \sum_{m \in \mathcal{M}} \frac{1}{l(m)-1} \sum_{k=1}^{l(m)-1} \Lambda_{m,k}. \qquad (9)$$

We integrate over the first $l(m) - 1$ positions as we disregard $\texttt{EOS}$ that occurs in all messages.[6] $0 \le \rho_{inf} \le 1$. If $\rho_{inf} = 1$, messages are limited to the informative symbols (all used by Listener to decode the message). The lower ρ_{inf} is, the more non-informative symbols are in the message.

As we do not have Listener when generating Optimal Coding, we compute these metrics for the latter reference by considering all symbols, but $\texttt{EOS}$, informative.

4 Results

In this section, we study the code of our new communicative system, LazImpa, and compare it to the Standard Agents baseline and the different reference distributions. We show that LazImpa leads to near-optimal and ZLA-compatible languages. Eventually, we demonstrate how both Impatience and Laziness are required to get human-level efficiency. All the quantitative results of the considered codes are gathered in Table 1.

4.1 LazImpa vs. Standard Agents

We compare here LazImpa to the baseline system Standard Agents both in terms of the length efficiency and the allocation of information.

---

[5]We subtract 1 as we disregard $\texttt{EOS}$ in all messages.
[6]By convention, for the case where m=($\texttt{EOS}$), $\frac{0}{0}$=1.

Length efficiency of the communication. Contrary to Standard Agents, LazImpa develops an efficient communication as presented in Figure 3. Indeed, its average length of the messages is significantly lower than the Standard Agents system (average L_{type}=29.6 for Standard Agents vs. L_{type}=5.49 for LazImpa). The latter demonstrates length distributions almost constant and close to the maximum length we set (=30). We demonstrate in Appendix A.2.1 how the exploration of long messages in Standard Agents is key for agents' success in the reconstruction game, even though, in theory, shorter messages are sufficient.

Interestingly, both systems do not only differ by their average length, but also by the distribution of messages length. Specifically, the Standard Agents system follows significantly an anti-ZLA distribution (see Appendix A.3.2 for quantitative support of this claim) while LazImpa has an average L_{token}=3.78 showing a ZLA pattern: the shortest messages are associated to the most frequent inputs. The randomization test gives quantitative support of this observation ($p_{ZLA} < 10^{-5}$).

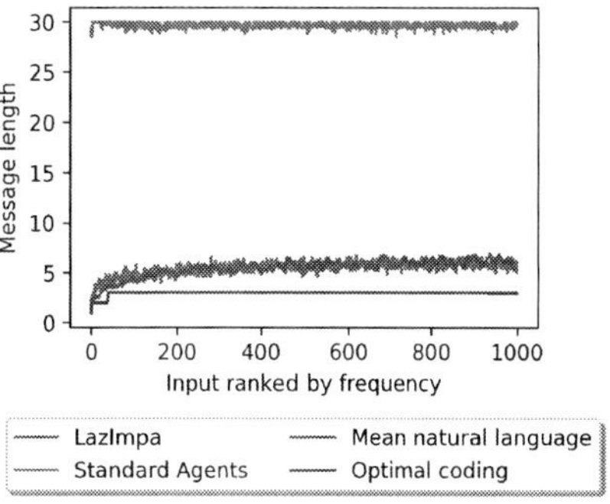

Figure 3: Average message length across successful runs as a function of input frequency rank.

Informativeness of the communication. When considering how Standard Agents system allocates information, shown in Figure 4a, we can make two striking observations. First, only a very small part of the messages are informative (on average $\rho_{inf} = 11\%$). Therefore, even if long messages seem necessary for the agents to succeed, most of the symbols are not used by Listener. In particular, if $L_{type} = 29.6$ on average, the average number of symbols used by Standard Listener (L_{eff}) is only equal to 3.33 (which is even smaller than natural languages' mean message length $L_{type} = 5.46$). Surprisingly, we also observe that, if we restrict the messages to their informative symbols (i.e. removing positions k with $\Lambda_{k,.} = 0$), the length statistics follow a ZLA-like distribution (see Figure 9 in Appendix A.2.2). Second, in all our experiments, the information is localized at the very end of the messages. That is, there is almost no actual information in the messages about Speaker's inputs before the last symbols.

Contrarily, Figure 4d shows a completely different

339

Class	Code	L_{type}	L_{token}	p_{ZLA}	L_{eff}	ρ_{inf}
Emergent	Standard Agents	29.6 ± 0.4	29.91 ± 0.07	$> 1 - 10^{-5}$	3.33 ± 0.46	0.11 ± 0.02
	LazImpa	5.49 ± 0.67	3.78 ± 0.34	$< 10^{-5}*$	2.67 ± 0.07	0.60 ± 0.07
References	Mean natural languages	5.46 ± 0.61	3.55 ± 0.14	$< 10^{-5}*$	/	/
	Optimal Coding	2.96	2.29	$< 10^{-5}*$	1.96	1.00

Table 1: Efficiency and information analysis of emergent codes and reference distribution. For each metric, we report the mean value and the standard deviation when relevant (across seeds when experimenting with emergent languages and across the natural languages presented in Section 3.1 for Mean natural languages). L_{type} is the mean message length, L_{token} is the mean weighted message length, p_{ZLA} the ZLA significance score, L_{eff} the effective length and ρ_{inf} the information density. '/' indicates that the metric cannot be computed. For p_{ZLA}, '*' indicates that the p-value is significant (< 0.001).

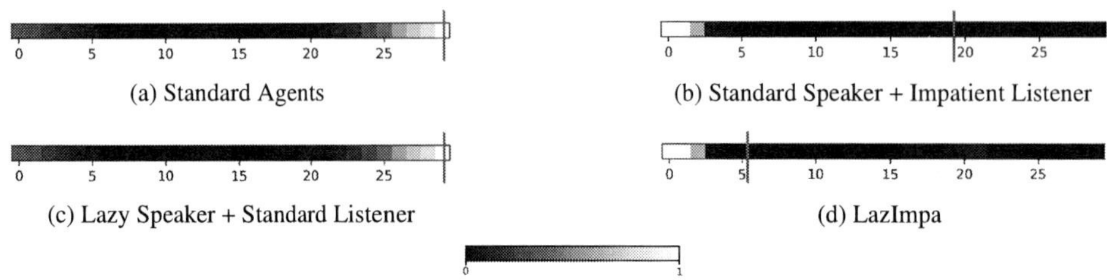

(a) Standard Agents

(b) Standard Speaker + Impatient Listener

(c) Lazy Speaker + Standard Listener

(d) LazImpa

Figure 4: Fraction of informative symbols at each position k averaged across all emergent messages of successful runs $((\Lambda_{k,.})_{0 \leq k \leq 29})$. Each box represents the proportion of informative symbols at a given position $\Lambda_{k,.}$ mapped to a color according to a gray gradient (black=0 ; white=1). The red vertical lines mark the mean message length L_{type} across successful runs.

spectrum for LazImpa. Indeed, Impatient Listener relies on $\rho_{inf} = 60\%$ of the symbols. This corresponds to a big increase compared to $\rho_{inf} = 19\%$ when using Standard Agents. Yet, we are still far from the 100% observed in Optimal Coding. That is, even with the introduction of a length cost (with Lazy Speaker), we still encounter non-informative symbols. Finally, these informative symbols are localized in the first positions, opposite to what we observed with Standard Agents. We will show in Section 4.3 how this immediate presence of information is crucial for the length reduction of the messages.

In sum, if we consider only *informative/effective* positions, Standard Agents use efficient and ZLA-like (effective) communicative protocol. However, they make it maximally long adding non-informative symbols at the beginning of each message. Introducing LazImpa reverses the length distribution. Indeed, we observe with LazImpa the emergence of efficient and ZLA-obeying languages, with significantly larger ρ_{inf}.

4.2 LazImpa vs. reference distributions

We demonstrated above how LazImpa leads to codes with length significantly shorter than the one obtained with Standard Agents.

We compare it here with stricter references, namely natural languages and Optimal Coding. We show that LazImpa results in languages as efficient as natural languages both in terms of length statistics and symbols distribution. However, agents do not manage to reach optimality.

Comparison with natural languages. We see in Figure 5a that the message lengths in the emergent communication are analogous to the words lengths in natural languages: close average L_{token} and L_{type} (see Table 1).

We further compare their unigram distributions. Chaabouni et al. (2019) showed that Standard Agents develop repetitive messages with a skewed unigram distribution. Our results, in Figure 5b, show that, on top of a ZLA-like code, LazImpa enables the emergence of natural-language-like unigram distribution, without any particular repetitive pattern. Intriguingly, this similarity with natural languages is an unexpected property as a uniform distribution of unigrams would lead to a more efficient protocol.

Comparison with Optimal Coding. If LazImpa leads to significantly more efficient languages compared to Standard Agents, these emergent languages are still not as efficient as Optimal Coding (see Figure 3). One obvious source of sub-optimality is the addition of uninformative symbols at the end of the messages (i.e. the difference between L_{eff}=2.67 and L_{type}-1=4.49). Interestingly, when analyzing the intermediate predictions of Impatient Listener, we see that this model is actually able to guess the right input only reading approximately the L_{eff} first positions (see Appendix A.4.1 for details). However, we still can note that the informative length L_{eff} is slightly sub-optimal ($L_{eff} = 2.67$ for LazImpa, $L_{eff} = 1.96$ for Optimal Coding). This difference

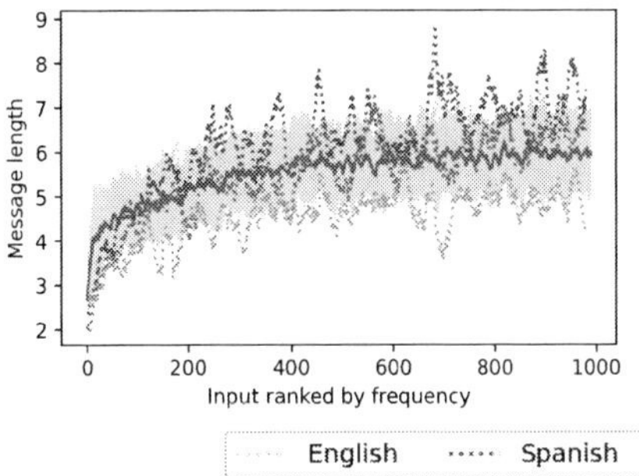
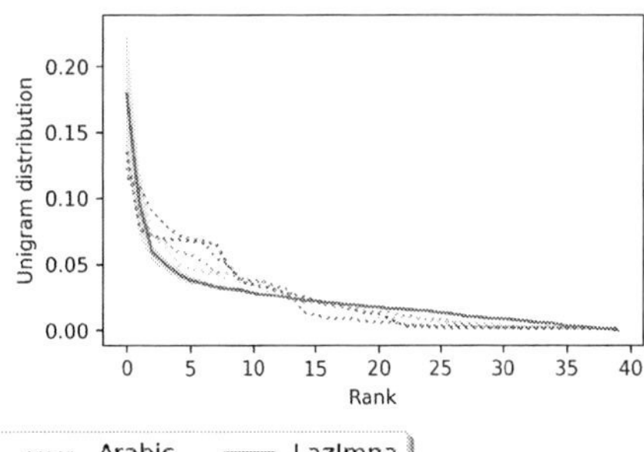

(a) Message length of natural languages and LazImpa (averaged across successful runs) as a function of input frequency rank. For readability, the curves have been smoothed using a sliding average of 20 consecutive lengths, see the real curves in Appendix A.4.3. The light blue interval shows 1 standard deviation for LazImpa's distribution.

(b) Unigrams distribution of natural languages and LazImpa (averaged across successful messages) ranked by unigram frequency. The light blue interval shows 1 standard deviation for LazImpa's unigrams distribution.

Figure 5: Comparison of LazImpa' statistics and natural languages.

can be explained by the non-uniform use of unigrams. Specifically, we show in Appendix A.4.1 that effective lengths of LazImpa messages approximate Optimal Coding when the latter uses the same skewed unigram distribution.

4.3 Ablation study

We have just seen that our new communication system LazImpa allows agents to develop an efficient and ZLA-obeying language whose statistical properties are close to those of natural languages. In this section, we analyze the effects of the modeling choices we have made.

We first look at the effect of Laziness. To do so, we compare LazImpa to the system "Standard Speaker + Impatient Listener" (i.e. removing the length regularization). Figure 6a shows the joint evolution of the mean length of messages (L_{type}) and game accuracy. We observe that our non-regularized system, similarly to LazImpa, initially explores long messages while being more successful (exploration step). Surprisingly, even in the absence of Laziness, the exploration step does not continue to maximally long messages, as it is the case for Standard Agents, but breaks at length ≈ 20. However, *contrary to LazImpa*, "Standard Speaker + Impatient Listener" does not present a reduction step (a reduction of mean length for a fixed good accuracy). Thus, as expected, the introduction of Laziness in LazImpa is responsible for the reduction step, and hence for a shorter and more efficient communication protocol. However, we note in Figure 6b, that Impatience alone is sufficient for the emergence of ZLA. Moreover, when looking at the information spectrum, comparing "Standard Speaker + Impatient Listener" (Figure 4b) to LazImpa (Figure 4d), we observe how alike both systems allocate information and differ only by their mean length.

Second, we investigate the role of Impatience. We see in Figure 6a that the system "Lazy Speaker + Standard Listener" admits a visually different dynamic compared to LazImpa. In particular, the exploration step leads to significantly longer messages, close to max_len. Interestingly, if we demonstrated above the necessity of Laziness for the reduction step, alone, it does not induce it: no reduction step in the "Lazy Speaker + Standard Listener" system is observed. This is due to the necessity of long messages when experimenting with Standard Listener. Specifically, as informative symbols are present only at the last positions (see Figure 4c), introducing a length regularization provokes a drop in accuracy, which in turn cancels the regularization. In other words, the length regularization scheduling stops at the exploration step, which makes the system almost equivalent to Standard Agents (this could be also seen experimentally in Figures 6a and 6b).

Taken together, our analysis emphasizes the importance of both Impatience *and* Laziness for the emergence of efficient communication.

5 Conclusion

We demonstrated that a standard communication system, where standard Speaker and Listener LSTMs are trained to solve a simple reconstruction game, leads to long messages, close to the maximal threshold. Surprisingly, if these messages are long, LSTM agents rely only on a small number of informative message symbols, located at the end. We then introduce LazImpa, a constrained system that consists of *Laz*y Speaker and *Impa*tient Listener. On the one hand, Lazy Speaker is obtained by introducing a cost on messages length once the communication is successful. We found that early exploration of potentially long messages is crucial for successful convergence (similar to the exploration in RL settings). On the other hand, Impatient Listener aims to succeed at the game as soon as possible, by predicting Speaker's input at each message's symbol.

We show that both constraints are *necessary* for the emergence of a ZLA-like protocol, as efficient as natural languages. Specifically, Lazy Speaker alone would

341

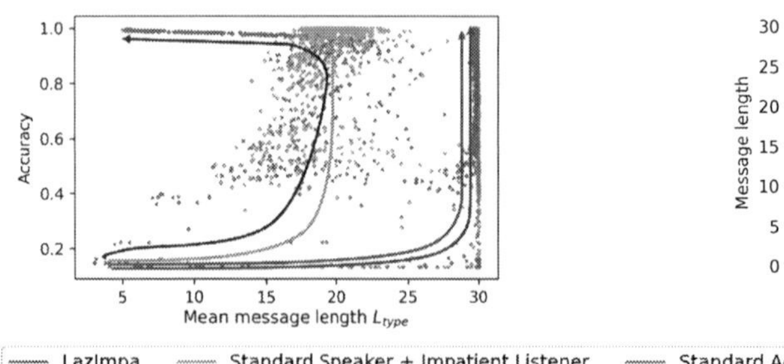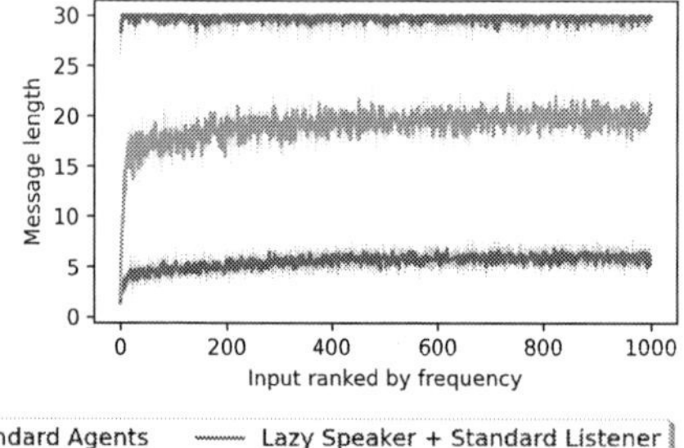

(a) Joint evolution of the accuracy and mean length for the different models. Each point shows the couple (L_{type},accuracy) of one training episode. Arrows represent the average joint evolution of the two variables.

(b) Average message length as a function of input frequency rank for the different systems. Light color intervals show 1 standard deviation.

Figure 6: Comparison of different communication systems.

fail to shorten the messages. We connect this to the importance of the Impatience mechanism to locate useful information at the beginning of the messages. If the function of this mechanism is subject to a standing debate (e.g., Jackendoff, 2007; Anderson and Chemero, 2013), many prior works had pointed to its necessity to human language understanding (e.g., Friston, 2010; Clark, 2013). We augment this line of works and suggest that impatience could be at play in the emergence of ZLA-obeying languages. However, if impatience leads to ZLA, it is not sufficient for human-level efficiency. In other words, efficiency needs constraints *both* on Speaker and Listener sides.

Our work highlights the importance of introducing the right pressures in the communication system. Indeed, to construct automated agents that would eventually interact with humans, we need to introduce task-agnostic constraints, allowing the emergence of more human-like communication. Moreover, while being general, LazImpa provides a more stable optimization compared to the unconstrained system. Finally, this study opens several lines of research. One would be to investigate further the gap from optimality. Indeed, while LazImpa emergent languages show human-level efficiency, they do not reach optimal coding. Specifically, emergent languages still have non-informative symbols at the end of the messages. If these additional non-useful symbols drift the protocol from optimality, we encounter similar trend in human (Marslen-Wilson, 1987) and animal communication (McLachlan and Magrath, 2020). We leave the understanding of the role of these non-informative symbols and how we can reach optimal coding for future works. A second line of research would be to apply this system to other games or NLP problems and study how it affects other properties of the language such as regularity or compositionality.

Acknowledgments

We would like to thank Emmanuel Chemla, Marco Baroni, Eugene Kharitonov, and the anonymous reviewers for helpful comments and suggestions.

This work was funded in part by the European Research Council (ERC-2011-AdG-295810 BOOT-PHON), the Agence Nationale pour la Recherche (ANR-17-EURE-0017 Frontcog, ANR-10-IDEX-0001-02 PSL*, ANR-19-P3IA-0001 PRAIRIE 3IA Institute) and grants from CIFAR (Learning in Machines and Brains), Facebook AI Research (Research Grant), Google (Faculty Research Award), Microsoft Research (Azure Credits and Grant), and Amazon Web Service (AWS Research Credits).

References

Gerry TM Altmann and Jelena Mirković. 2009. Incrementality and prediction in human sentence processing. *Cognitive science*, 33(4):583–609.

Michael L Anderson and Tony Chemero. 2013. The problem with brain guts: Conflation of different senses of" prediction" threatens metaphysical disaster. *Behavioral and Brain Sciences*, 36(3):204.

Diane Bouchacourt and Marco Baroni. 2018. How agents see things: On visual representations in an emergent language game. pages 981–985.

Rahma Chaabouni, Eugene Kharitonov, Diane Bouchacourt, Emmanuel Dupoux, and Marco Baroni. 2020. Compositionality and generalization in emergent languages. *arXiv preprint arXiv:2004.09124*.

Rahma Chaabouni, Eugene Kharitonov, Emmanuel Dupoux, and Marco Baroni. 2019. Anti-efficient encoding in emergent communication.

Andy Clark. 2013. Whatever next? predictive brains, situated agents, and the future of cognitive science. *Behavioral and brain sciences*, 36(3):181–204.

Thomas Cover and Joy Thomas. 2006. *Elements of Information Theory, 2nd ed.* Wiley, Hoboken, NJ.

Kara D Federmeier. 2007. Thinking ahead: The role and roots of prediction in language comprehension. *Psychophysiology*, 44(4):491–505.

Ramon Ferrer i Cancho, Antoni Hernández-Fernández, David Lusseau, Govindasamy Agoramoorthy, Minna Hsu, and Stuart Semple. 2013. Compression as a universal principle of animal behavior. *Cognitive Science*, 37(8):1565–1578.

Karl Friston. 2010. The free-energy principle: a unified brain theory? *Nature reviews neuroscience*, 11(2):127–138.

Edward Gibson, Richard Futrell, Steven P Piantadosi, Isabelle Dautriche, Kyle Mahowald, Leon Bergen, and Roger Levy. 2019. How efficiency shapes human language. *Trends in cognitive sciences*, 23(5):389–407.

Serhii Havrylov and Ivan Titov. 2017. Emergence of language with multi-agent games: Learning to communicate with sequences of symbols. pages 2149–2159.

Sepp Hochreiter and Jürgen Schmidhuber. 1997. Long short-term memory. *Neural computation*, 9(8):1735–1780.

Ray Jackendoff. 2007. A parallel architecture perspective on language processing. *Brain research*, 1146:2–22.

Jasmeen Kanwal, Kenny Smith, Jennifer Culbertson, and Simon Kirby. 2017. Zipf's law of abbreviation and the principle of least effort: Language users optimise a miniature lexicon for efficient communication. *Cognition*, 165:45–52. Copyright © 2017 Elsevier B.V. All rights reserved.

Eugene Kharitonov, Rahma Chaabouni, Diane Bouchacourt, and Marco Baroni. 2019. EGG: a toolkit for research on emergence of language in games. In *Proceedings of EMNLP (System Demonstrations)*.

Diederik P. Kingma and Jimmy Ba. 2014. Adam: A method for stochastic optimization.

Simon Kirby. 2001. Spontaneous evolution of linguistic structure-an iterated learning model of the emergence of regularity and irregularity. *IEEE Transactions on Evolutionary Computation*, 5(2):102–110.

Satwik Kottur, José Moura, Stefan Lee, and Dhruv Batra. 2017. Natural language does not emerge 'naturally' in multi-agent dialog.

Angeliki Lazaridou, Karl Moritz Hermann, Karl Tuyls, and Stephen Clark. 2018. Emergence of linguistic communication from referential games with symbolic and pixel input.

Angeliki Lazaridou, Alexander Peysakhovich, and Marco Baroni. 2017. Multi-agent cooperation and the emergence of (natural) language. Published online: `https://openreview.net/group?id=ICLR.cc/2017/conference`.

David Lewis. 1969. *Convention*. Harvard University Press, Cambridge, MA.

William D Marslen-Wilson. 1987. Functional parallelism in spoken word-recognition. *Cognition*, 25(1-2):71–102.

Jessica R McLachlan and Robert D Magrath. 2020. Speedy revelations: how alarm calls can convey rapid, reliable information about urgent danger. *Proceedings of the Royal Society B*, 287(1921):20192772.

Steven T Piantadosi, Harry Tily, and Edward Gibson. 2011. Word lengths are optimized for efficient communication. *Proceedings of the National Academy of Sciences*, 108(9):3526–3529.

John Schulman, Nicolas Heess, Theophane Weber, and Pieter Abbeel. 2015. Gradient estimation using stochastic computation graphs. In *Proceedings of the 28th International Conference on Neural Information Processing Systems - Volume 2*, page 3528–3536, Cambridge, MA, USA. MIT Press.

Bengt Sigurd, Mats Eeg-Olofsson, and Joost Van Weijer. 2004. Word length, sentence length and frequency–zipf revisited. *Studia Linguistica*, 58(1):37–52.

Udo Strauss, Peter Grzybek, and Gabriel Altmann. 2007. Word length and word frequency. In *Contributions to the science of text and language*, pages 277–294. Springer.

William J Teahan, Yingying Wen, Rodger McNab, and Ian H Witten. 2000. A compression-based algorithm for chinese word segmentation. *Computational Linguistics*, 26(3):375–393.

Ronald Williams and Jing Peng. 1991. Function optimization using connectionist reinforcement learning algorithms. *Connection Science*, 3:241–.

Ronald J. Williams. 1992. Simple statistical gradient-following algorithms for connectionist reinforcement learning. *Machine Learning*, 8(3):229–256.

George Zipf. 1949. *Human Behavior and the Principle of Least Effort*. Addison-Wesley, Boston, MA.

George Kingsley Zipf. 2013. *The psycho-biology of language: An introduction to dynamic philology*. Routledge.

Simulating the acquisition of core semantic competences from small data

Aurélie Herbelot
Center for Mind/Brain Sciences
Dept. of Information Engineering and Computer Science
University of Trento
`aurelie.herbelot@unitn.it`

Abstract

Many tasks are considered to be 'solved' in the computational linguistics literature, but the corresponding algorithms operate in ways which are radically different from human cognition. I illustrate this by coming back to the notion of semantic competence, which includes basic linguistic skills encompassing both referential phenomena and generic knowledge, in particular a) the ability to denote, b) the mastery of the lexicon, or c) the ability to model one's language use on others. Even though each of those faculties has been extensively tested individually, there is still no computational model that would account for their joint acquisition under the conditions experienced by a human. In this paper, I focus on one particular aspect of this problem: the amount of linguistic data available to the child or machine. I show that given the first competence mentioned above (a denotation function), the other two can in fact be learned from very limited data (2.8M token), reaching state-of-the-art performance. I argue that both the nature of the data and the way it is presented to the system matter to acquisition.

1 Introduction

Many tasks and datasets are considered solved problems in the computational linguistics literature. However, the data, training regimes and system architectures required to obtain top performance are unrealistic from the point of view of human cognition. Thus, state-of-the-art data-driven frameworks can be considered excellent engineering solutions to particular linguistic tasks, but they are not usable as 'models' of language acquisition, and thus of limited applicability to test hypotheses about human language.

This paper argues that core problems in computational linguistics should be 're-solved' – solved again – not as tasks, but as phenomena to *simulate*.

This would involve a more careful attention to i) the type of data fed to the system; ii) the knowledge already in-built in its architecture; iii) the mode of learning implied by the training regime; iv) the specific features exploited by the learning process; and of course, v) the theoretical proposals explaining the phenomenon. Some of these desiderata have started being explored in the literature: the BlackBox NLP events, for instance, are currently fostering important discussions on the interpretability of artificial neural systems (Linzen et al., 2018, 2019). Still, the field remains far from satisfying all of them.

The work described in the following pages is a step towards the simulation of a particular phenomenon: the acquisition of core semantic competences. Its specific focus is on data: more particularly, the type and size of the corpus a system is exposed to. As we will see, talking about input data (desideratum i. above) naturally brings in questions about learning mechanisms (ii. and iii.), and about representation (iv.) Let us first note that an NLP system is typically exposed to at least hundreds of millions of words, if not billions. In contrast, a 3-year-old US child has only observed 25M words; a Mayan child of the same age will hear as little as 5M words (Cristia et al., 2017). In spite of the limited data they are exposed to, a child will reliably learn their language – this is referred to as the 'poverty of stimulus' in Chomsky's work.

If the stimulus is poor, we have to posit the existence of extra cognitive mechanisms to compensate for the lack of explicit linguistic evidence. For human syntax, Chomsky famously advocated the existence of an innate Universal Grammar. I argue that there is an equivalent question to be asked in machine learning: indeed, the architecture (ii.) and hyperparameters (iii.) of a system, as well as the specific representation of the input data (iv.), are 'innate' features which are important to make

Proceedings of the 24th Conference on Computational Natural Language Learning, pages 344–354
Online, November 19-20, 2020. ©2020 Association for Computational Linguistics
https://doi.org/10.18653/v1/P17

explicit when describing a 'data-driven' system.

In what follows, I investigate a particular configuration of a semantic acquisition model. Specifically, I ask whether a particular type of input, based on individual grounded entities, can make up for data sparsity. Following this hypothesis, I propose a model nicknamed EVA (Entity Vector Aggregator)[1] and compare it to the behaviour of a character-based language model with no access to referential information. I perform a battery of tests including similarity, compatibility and acceptability judgements, as well as lexical relation categorisation, and demonstrate that when fed with the right data and the right representation, the model learns core semantic competences from as little as 2.8M words.

2 Semantic competence in the linguistic literature

The notion of linguistic *competence* was introduced by Chomsky *Aspects of the theory of syntax* (Chomsky, 1965): competence is 'knowing one's language', and it must be distinguished from performance, 'using one's language'. According to Chomsky, the study of linguistics is the study of competence. The linguist should try and elucidate the underlying structure of the *mental* phenomenon that leads to observable performance.

In syntax, competence is usually defined in terms of grammaticality. The semantic equivalent is more difficult to pinpoint, and various proposals have been made. We will focus on three major positions in this paper: semantic competence as mastery of a) the lexicon; b) reference; c) language use.

1. Mastery of the lexicon: following Chomskian grammar, Katz and Fodor (1963) propose that the goals of semantics can be obtained by *"subtracting grammar from the goals of a description of a language"* (p172). According to them, this subtraction results in elements of lexical semantics, including relations such as hyponymy or antonymy, as well as word senses. Semantic competence is then the ability to say that *The paint is silent* is not felicitous, that *The bill is large* is ambiguous, or again that *There are two chairs in the room* entails *There are at least two things in the room*.

2. Ability to refer: coming from formal semantics, Partee (1979) investigates the notion of a 'godly' speaker, who would have perfect ability to match words to extensions, and argues such a speaker might embody (intensional) semantic competence. She however also identifies logical issues with that notion, in particular with respect to propositional attitudes. In Partee (2014), she offers a compromise which recognises the important relation between linguistic constituents and external reality, but also admits that language users can be mistaken or simply ignorant when it comes to truth-theoretic judgements.

3. Distributional consistency: Kripke (1972) argues for a 'causal theory of reference', which posits that people use words in the way that they have seen other people use it. Competent usage follows from simple exposure to performance data, without assuming fully competent extensional knowledge: For instance, having heard *Frege came to dinner* from some speaker, a competent listener might ask **Who is Frege?**, having understood that Frege is a person, but being unable to identify that person in the world (see also Putnam, 1975 for a related argument). Seen from a statistical perspective, this position boils down to an idea of distributional consistency, that is, the belief that speakers model their language use on others. A notion of acceptability derives from the theory (i.e. it would be incorrect to ask **What is Frege?**), but in a way that is different from the felicity conditions posited by Katz and Fodor (1963): while Katz and Fodor assume that felicity comes from the rules of the lexicon, the Kripkian account implies that it emerges from the language use following an initial reference act.

This paper starts from the assumption that all three definitions should be satisfied to speak of semantic competence. That is, I will posit that we need meaning representations that allow us to denote (to satisfy 2), for which we have descriptions or referring expressions by actual language users (to satisfy 3), and over which we can learn lexical relations (to satisfy 1). To achieve this, I will hypothesise a semantics based on *instances* (which can be aggregated into sets in a formal semantics fashion), but represented in terms of the statistical properties of language use. I will propose a representation which satisfies both requirements in §4.

3 (Small) data

The input data we will work with is a set of grounded 'utterances' extracted from annotations in the Visual Genome (VG) dataset (Krishna et al.,

---

[1]The code for EVA is freely available at `https://github.com/minimalparts/EVA`.

2017). This annotated set displays several important properties. First, it is *small* (around 2.8M tokens), so compatible in scale with the limited data a learner is exposed to. Second, while it does not quite correspond to the type of sentences a child might be exposed to, it has some similarities with a realistic 'early' linguistic diet: the simple image annotations can be regarded as utterances of the type *Look! The dog is playing with the ball.* Third, it encodes the particular representational aspects we want to investigate: it is anchored in a clear notion of grounded instances (the individual objects in an image) and corresponding language use (the human-generated captions/annotations associated with each bounding box).

The VG itself consists of a set of 108,077 images annotated with 5.4M region descriptions as well as 3.8M object referents,[2] 2.8M attributes and 2.3M relationships. All objects are associated with a unique identifier, meaning that we can use such identifiers as a set of object variables for the particular universe defined by the VG.

I follow the methodology introduced by Kuzmenko and Herbelot (2019), who extract information about VG instances and use it to create a 'set-theoretic' vector space. The example below shows a subset of the annotation for image ID 1, after some initial pre-processing of the data. I assume that each image corresponds to some 'situation', in the spirit of Young et al. (2014). So situation 1 contains a tall brick building, identified by variable 1058508, on which we find a black sign, identified by variable 1058507. *Object types* are recognisable through their suffix (e.g. *building.n*, *sign.n*), *attributes* consist of all other one-place predicates (e.g. *tall*, *made|of|bricks*); and *relationships* consist of all two-place predicates (e.g. *on*).

```
<situation id=1>
    ...
    <entity id=1058508>
        building.n(1058508)
        tall(1058508)
        brick(1058508)
        made|of|bricks(1058508)
        on(1058507,1058508)
    </entity>
    <entity id=1058507>
        sign.n(1058507)
        black(1058507)
        on(1058507,1058508)
    </entity>
    ...
</situation>
```

---

[2] In the VG, object referents are associated with WordNet synsets. For simplicity, I collapse all WordNet senses together, but this has hardly any effect on the size of the object referents' set which, including sense annotations, would amount to 1203 unique types vs 1188 when ignoring sense.

We can straightforwardly obtain shallow logical forms associated with each situation, e.g.:

$$building.n'(1058508), tall'(1058508), brick'(1058508),$$
$$sign.n'(1058507), black'(1058507),$$
$$on(1058507, 1058508)$$

For simplicity (and because each entity only occurs once in VG), I transform two-place predicates into two one-place predicates: e.g. $on(1058507, 1058508)$ becomes $on(1058507, building.n')$, $on(sign.n', 1058508)$, respectively denoting the set of things that are on buildings, and the set of things that signs are on.

The provided annotations together with the associated objects, attributes and relations can be taken to be a *partial* description of some subset of the real world (i.e. the subset encapsulated by the images). This can be illustrated by considering the following two instances of bear (objects referents 158539 and 1617277), together will all their annotated relations:

```
158539    bear.n has(-,eye.n) has(-,claw.n) has(-,paw.n)
          has(-,mark.n) beside(grass.n,-)has(-,ear.n)
          on(-,land.n) has(-,leg.n) has(-,nose.n)
1617277   bear.n has(-,fur.n) has(-,nose.n)
```

We see that two instances can be annotated with different degrees of granularity in the VG. The first instance above includes many more details about the physical appearance of the bear, although the second includes the relation 'has fur', which is missed by the first one. That is, we have two different 'experiences' of bears, associated with utterances which, in a realistic situation, could have come from the learner's carer (*'Look at the bear next to the grass, look at its claws!'*) This is a typical example of the 'poverty of the stimulus' effect: the performance data associated with those instances of bear is both *incomplete* (the linguistic data only describes part of the bears) and *inconsistent* (the two descriptions are very dissimilar).

In order to fully exploit the information in the VG, the annotated *attributes* and *relationships* are supplemented with a third type of linguistic information: simple extensional co-occurrences are computed, thus modelling an implicit logical *and* (the comma in the shallow logical form). I.e., if a bear occurs in an image under a cloudy sky, the model registers the co-occurrence of a bear entity with a sky entity. In what follows, I refer to such implicit relations under the general term of *situational co-occurrences*, to express the fact that the extensional co-occurrence takes place within a single situation.

4 Models

In the field of computational linguistics, we often take models to be 'algorithms', independently of the data they are trained on, and often, independently from the assumptions that the algorithm is built upon. But as pointed out in the introduction to this paper, what is in the data, what is inbuilt in the algorithm, and how the data is presented to the learning process determines the extent to which one can speak of a scientific model of such or such phenomenon. Therefore, I will talk of a 'model' as a *combination* of a particular system / algorithm (with its specific assumptions) and a particular type of data.

In what follows, in the spirit of fixing the learning mechanism as much as possible, I present three models based on very similar algorithms (variants of skip-gram language models). I however vary the data input into the system, both in size and representation.

Pretrained FastText (FT): The first model under consideration is a pre-trained, state-of-the-art set of vectors, generated with FastText (Bojanowski et al., 2017). The system is a character-based language model and thus unsuitable for encoding extensions (that is, it will not satisfy the ability to refer in our set of semantic competences). However, it provides a helpful upper-bound for the tasks that language models excel at. The FastText vectors[3] were obtained from training over 16B tokens from a Wikipedia snapshot, the UMBC webbase corpus (Han et al., 2013) and statmt.org news dataset (Mikolov et al., 2018).

FastText trained on VG (FTVG): Being based on simple character ngrams, FastText is well suited to learning from smaller data (Mikolov et al., 2018). A FastText model is trained with default settings on a portion of the Visual Genome's 5.4M region descriptions. Such descriptions are short phrases or sentences of the type *man wearing red and black surf apparel* or *Red bus has advertisements that says 123 Current Account Santander*. From those descriptions, 2.8M tokens are used to match the size of the next system's background data (see 'EVA' below). FTVG differs from FT not only

with respect to the size but also the presentation of its data: while FTVG is exposed to raw utterances like FT, those utterances are broken down by instance (the data contains one description per line, so a target word is only ever found in contexts that pertain to the same instance).

EVA: Finally, a third model is proposed. Nicknamed EVA (Entity Vector Aggregator), it is generated straight from the extensional information contained in the VG annotations (the attributes, relationships and situational co-occurrences described in §3). Before being fed to the skip-gram, the data is converted into a form akin to a set-theoretic vector space, using the procedure below.

First, let P_L be the predicates in some logic and U the entities in some universe. Let us define a vector space model by using some interpretation function $||.||$ to return the denotations of P_L:

$$||.|| : (P_L \cup U)^* \to ((P_L \times U) \to \{0, 1\})$$

An example of such a vector space is shown on the left of Fig 1. I will refer to it as an *entity matrix*: each predicate is associated with a point expressed in terms of a vector basis U (so each dimension corresponds to an entity). The point is a straightforward representation of the extension of the predicate, and shows the entities that the predicate is true of. For instance, following the first row of the matrix, we find that the set of bears in our toy space is $\{x1, x2\}$.

We can then define an aggregation function A_D which groups context elements by predicate (e.g. all objects that are bears are aggregated into a single $bear'$ vector by pointwise addition):

$$A_D : ((P_L \times U) \to \{0, 1\}) \to ((P_L \times P_L) \to \mathbb{N}_0)$$

This operation results in a vector space such as the one shown on the right of Fig 1. I will refer to it as a *predicate matrix*, since the basis is now made of the predicates in P_L.

An entity and predicate matrix are built for the VG, using the following restrictions. We ignore objects which are not annotated with any attribute or relation and would result in $\vec{0}$ vectors, thus obtaining around 2M entities. Further, the entity matrix is constructed for predicates with frequency over 100. The result of this pre-processing is a 2M $\times 8284$ matrix, where the predicates include 1188 object types, 798 attributes and 6283 relationships.

	x1	x2	x3	x4	x5	x6
bear'	1	1	0	0	0	0
white'	1	0	0	0	0	0
black'	0	1	0	0	0	0
tree'	0	0	1	1	1	1
old'	0	0	1	1	0	0
young'	1	1	0	0	1	1

	bear'	white'	black'	tree'	old'	young'
bear'	2	1	1	0	0	2
white'	1	1	0	0	0	1
black'	1	0	1	0	0	1
tree'	0	0	0	4	2	2
old'	0	0	0	2	2	0
young'	2	1	1	2	0	2

Figure 1: **Left:** an entity matrix, showing the entities that a predicate is true of. **Right:** the corresponding predicate matrix, after aggregation with function A_D. The first row is simply the pointwise addition of the first two columns in the entity matrix (the two bear entities).

We can compare the figures above to the size of the large FT pretrained model by counting the number of unique tokens in the Visual Genome data, where 'unique' means that the token – whether object type, attribute or relationship – appears with a specific entity. Since two-place predicates are transformed into two one-place predicates, the token is incremented for each argument separately (e.g. *tree(3787077)* is one token but *parked-on(1058515,1058539)* gives two tokens). This comes to 1,590,861 tokens for one-place predicates (object type and attributes) and 1,224,582 tokens for two-place predicates (relationships), thus around 2.8M tokens in total.[4] So EVA is exposed to around 5700 *less* data than FT. It however has the advantage of being grounded in a clear notion of entity, thus matching the type of situated speech that forms most of a child's diet (Clark, 2009). Further, the corpus size is in line with the number of tokens that a child might get directed at them in around a year of early life.

The challenge for both FTVG and EVA is to deal with the poverty of the stimulus. It is worth recalling that Landauer and Dumais (1997) suggested a solution to the problem which involved the use of Principal Component Analysis (PCA) as a dimensionality reduction method over a distributional matrix. The use of PCA was meant to capture the main axes of variance over the limited data given to the model, allowing for fast generalisation. Later models of distributional semantics, in particular neural architectures (e.g. the skip-gram of Mikolov et al., 2013), do not explicitly mention dimensionality reduction as a way to successfully generalise over insufficient data, but the intuition remains implicit in the choice of dimensionality of the embedding layers. FTVG can rely on this mechanism, as well as its character-ngram model. EVA needs its own way to surmount the issue, and

because it encodes extensional information, it has to deal with the poverty of the stimulus not only at the level of the linguistic input, but also at the denotation level. (As we have seen before, the VG is in no way an exhaustive and accurate representation of the world.) In other words, we want EVA to learn word embeddings at reduced dimensionality like its competitors, but from co-occurring *extensions*.

The implementation of EVA's embedding function is extremely simple and does away with some of the hyperparameters used by the original skip-gram model. It takes a predicate matrix of size $m \times m$, as would be produced by the aggregation function A_D, subsamples the counts in that matrix (lowering very frequent counts), and performs a prediction task. That task consists in predicting whether a 'target' predicate (from the rows of the matrix) and a 'context' predicate (from the columns of the matrix) have been seen together in the description of a unique, grounded entity. A 'positive' example for the target bear$'$ might be the predicate brown$'$ (some bear entity has been seen to be brown). A 'negative' sample for the same target bear$'$ might be transparent$'$. Positive samples are taken in shuffled order from the subsampled matrix, while negative samples are randomly chosen amongst the zero values of the matrix. As in the original skip-gram with negative sampling, embeddings for each predicate are first randomly initialised and fine-tuned in the process of doing the prediction task. A dimensionality of 300 gives optimal results in preliminary experiments over our development set. Therefore, results shown in the next sections are for this dimensionality only.

We use two main approaches for testing representations: a) for the similarity task, as is standard in the literature, we directly compute the relative position of embeddings in the space using the cosine metric; b) for other tasks, we use the vectors as input to a very simple feedforward neural net architectures, learning dedicated weights for each task

---

[4]Note that in the original VG annotation, region descriptions are not fully aligned with object / attribute / relation annotations and typically contain more information. So the data given to FTVG and EVA may present slight variations.

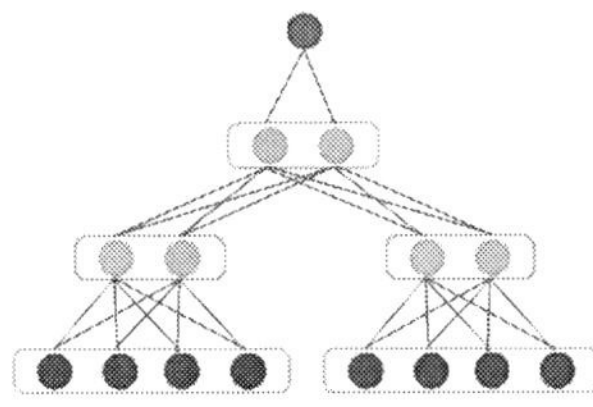

$$
\begin{aligned}
a_{11} &= RELu(x_{11}W_{11} + b_{11}) \\
a_{12} &= RELu(x_{12}W_{12} + b_{12}) \\
a_2 &= RELu([a_{11}, a_{12}]W_2 + b_2) \\
\hat{y} &= a_2 W_3
\end{aligned}
$$

Figure 2: A simple neural architecture.

over frozen background representations. The architecture used across tasks is shown in Fig. 2. It consists of an input taking two word vectors, mapped to a hidden layer with reduced dimensionality. All hidden layer representations are then concatenated and passed through a second hidden layer which is then fed to the output layer. The output layer may consist of a single node or several, depending on whether the task requires regression or classification. A RELu non-linearity is applied to the input layer and first (concatenated) hidden layer. A softmax is used on the last layer for classification tasks.

The training regime for all three models is as follows. A single grid search is performed over the hyperparameter space, using 200 iterations of Bayesian optimisation[5] with early stopping. For EVA, I follow results by Kuzmenko and Herbelot (2019) showing that linguistic phenomena are not all modelled by the same feature types in the VG. The validation data is used to select the best combination of feature types for a task (attributes, relations, situational co-occurrences), running the hyperparameter optimisation over all possible combinations. For all models, the five best hyperparameter sets are then selected according to validation results, and their stability is checked by performing 10 extra validation runs on each set, yielding 10 models per combination. The 10 models corre-

sponding to the best average score are then applied to the test set and an average score is reported over the test data, together with standard deviation.

5 Evaluation procedure

The entity matrix is evaluated in terms of the three aspects of competence we discussed in §2: knowledge of core lexical relations (Katz and Fodor, 1963), knowledge of 'acceptable' use of a term (again, Katz and Fodor, 1963, but also Putnam, 1975; Kripke, 1972), and of course, ability to retrieve the extension of a term (Partee, 1979).

Lexical relations: the models are evaluated on three different datasets encoding different aspects of lexical knowledge, namely the relation of *similarity*, the ability of the model to *classify specific relations* such as hyponymy or meronymy, and finally the relation of *incompatibility*. First, *Similarity* is evaluated against SimLex-999 (Hill et al., 2015), a set of 999 pairs meant to capture similar rather than merely related items. The second test is to evaluate the ability of the model to distinguish between particular *relations*, as encoded in the BLESS dataset (Baroni and Lenci, 2011). BLESS contains 26554 pairs annotated for hyponymy, meronymy, co-hyponymy, attribute and event relations (an additional class is included for the absence of relation and is marked as 'random'). Finally, the models are fed the *incompatibility* dataset of Kruszewski and Baroni (2015). This dataset contains 17973 word pairs associated with a compatibility judgement elicited from human annotators, on a scale from 1 to 7. So for instance, the pair *airplane-baby* has a mean score of 1 (fully incompatible), *dessert-vegetable* a score of 3 (somewhat compatible) and *airplane-jet* a score of 6.6 (close to full compatibility). All datasets are pre-processed to only keep the instances containing words present in the VG corpus, thus reducing the size of each available resource. The three models are evaluated on the same data.

The overall number of tested instances is shown for each dataset in Table 1, as well as the splits between training, validation and test sets. Note that SimLex-999 is evaluated in the standard fashion, by computing cosine distance between vectors in the space, with no further training involved. The data is nevertheless split into validation and test sets to allow for the selection of the best set of features for EVA at validation stage (out of the attributes, relationships and situational co-occurrences). To

---

[5]This step uses the package available at `https://github.com/fmfn/BayesianOptimization`. Hyperparameters are optimised in the following ranges: learning rate and regularisation, $[0.001 - 0.01]$; epochs, $[100 - 500]$; minibatch size, $[16 - 1024]$; size of hidden layer, from 100 to initial vector size for FastText, and EVA; and in the range $50 - 100$ for FTVG.

Dataset	# Instances post-filtering	Train	Val	Test
SimLex-999*	169	-	100	69
BLESS	1764	1200	300	264
Compatibility	2074	1500	300	274
Acceptability	1030	700	200	130

Table 1: Number of instances left in datasets after filtering against VG vocabulary. Splits into train, validation and test sets are shown. Due to the small number of instances in SimLex-999, systems are evaluated 10 times on that dataset, using 10 random splits.

confirm robustness of the reported results, systems are run over 10 random splits of the 169 instances in the dataset, and average correlations are reported.

Acceptability: there are various datasets for acceptability / plausibility judgements (e.g. Vecchi et al., 2017; Wang et al., 2018), but one is needed which contains a fair number of concrete nouns, to match the VG data. The compound dataset of Graves et al. (2013) fulfils this requirement: it consists of 2160 compound nouns annotated by humans on a scale of 0 to 4, made of 500 concrete nouns. Half of the compounds are attested collocations like *television chef*, while the others are unattested, like *bike barn* or *book puppy*. Again, the data is filtered to keep only the pairs containing words included in the VG dataset.

Let us note here that the acceptability task is interestingly different from learning the incompatibility relation, whilst sharing some aspects with it. The nouns tested for incompatibility in the previous section (e.g. *zebra - woman*) represent labels which may or may not denote the same sets: the task is extensional in nature. The acceptability task, on the other hand, tests to what extent a speaker might generate a plausible interpretation for a given compound noun. This involves inferring a tacit relation between the nouns. So for instance, *lawn guy* is judged fairly acceptable by humans (average score of 3.464 out of 4), presumably because a lawn guy might be the guy who is standing on the lawn, or the guy who normally mows the lawn, etc.

Extensions: reference is deterministically encoded in EVA. To make this clear, the next section provides illustrative examples of composition over VG categories. It also shows how referents are retrieved by the model and how dimensions can be aggregated to quantify over instances of subkinds.

6 Results

This section contains results obtained on the validation and test portions of our datasets (see Table 1 for data splits).

Table 2 shows how EVA's performance on the validation sets depends on the combination of VG feature types used in training. Various observations can be made with regard to the results, starting with the most striking effect: SimLex-999 is extremely sensitive to data type. The similarity dataset shows correlations between 0.14 (when using situational co-occurrence only) and 0.39 (when using attributes and relations). In general, it is clear that using situational co-occurrences is detrimental to the performance of the system. This is to be expected, since the similarity evaluation is geared towards identifying taxonomic siblings (e.g. *cat, dog*: kinds that are structurally similar) rather than related items (e.g. *cat, meow*: kinds or events that might co-occur in the same situations).

Other datasets are less affected by feature selection but still show a preference for certain inputs. Notably, BLESS performs at its best when using situation information. This is perhaps due to the distinctions that the model has to perform between classes such as taxonomic siblings, meronyms and 'other' relations. Meronymy, in particular, requires to distinguish between items that simply co-occur in a situation (*cat* and *garden*) and those that co-occur but are also part of a relation (*cat* has-a *paw*). Finally, relations seem crucial to get best performance on the incompatibility dataset.

Moving to the test set, we only retain the models with highest performance on the validation data (*Att+Rel* for SimLex-999, *Sit* for BLESS, *Att* for acceptability and *Att+Sit* for incompatibility). Overall results are provided in Table 3 for all three models (FT, FTVG and EVA), and discussed below.

Lexical relations: On the *similarity* task (SimLex-999), EVA outperforms FTVG by 10 points and lags behind the huge pre-trained FT by only one point. The *classification of lexical relations* (BLESS) is achieved by all systems with high accuracy, without significant differences. Finally, performance on *incompatibility* is slightly over state-of-the-art level for both systems trained on the VG. EVA gives the best overall score, outperforming pretrained FT by two points. In other words, the system built on denotations is the overall winner when considering lexical

	Att	Rel	Sit	Att+Rel	Att+Sit	Rel+Sit	Att+Rel+Sit
SimLex (ρ)	0.33 ± 0.04	0.38 ± 0.04	0.14 ± 0.05	$\mathbf{0.39} \pm 0.04$	0.16 ± 0.05	0.25 ± 0.05	0.24 ± 0.04
BLESS (acc.)	0.89 ± 0.00	0.89 ± 0.00	$\mathbf{0.92} \pm 0.01$	0.91 ± 0.00	0.91 ± 0.00	0.91 ± 0.00	0.91 ± 0.00
Accept. (ρ)	$\mathbf{0.50} \pm 0.01$	0.47 ± 0.01	0.47 ± 0.01	0.48 ± 0.02	0.48 ± 0.01	0.49 ± 0.02	0.46 ± 0.01
Incompat. (ρ)	0.42 ± 0.02	0.45 ± 0.03	0.43 ± 0.01	$\mathbf{0.47} \pm 0.04$	0.42 ± 0.02	0.45 ± 0.02	0.45 ± 0.03

Table 2: EVA performance on validation set, for different combinations of feature types. The figures shown are averaged over 10 runs.

	Corpus size	SimLex ρ	BLESS acc.	Incompatibility ρ	Acceptability ρ	Reference
FT	16B	$\mathbf{0.39} \pm 0.08$	$\mathbf{0.87} \pm 0.01$	0.43 ± 0.04	$\mathbf{0.59} \pm 0.02$	$\times$
FTVG	2.8M	0.28 ± 0.12	0.86 ± 0.01	0.44 ± 0.06	0.58 ± 0.01	$\times$
EVA	2.8M	0.38 ± 0.10	$\mathbf{0.87} \pm 0.01$	$\mathbf{0.45} \pm 0.04$	0.56 ± 0.02	$\checkmark$

Table 3: Test results on all datasets.

competence, despite being trained on very scarce data.

Semantic acceptability: This time, we see that FTVG slightly outperforms EVA ($\rho = 0.58$ vs $\rho = 0.56$), possibly by virtue of being a language model and thus more suited to encoding word usage, in the sense of 'distributional consistency' (see §2). It is nevertheless striking that minimal training over data which encodes no surface information achieves very reasonable performance, in the range of pretrained FT ($\rho = 0.59$). This can be taken as confirmation that acceptability *can* be learned successfully from an extensional representation.

Extensions: To complete the above results, let us recall that EVA encodes reference by default, since the raw entity matrix (before aggregation and dimensionality reduction) captures how predicates are associated with entities. Denotations are therefore returned fully deterministically. To illustrate this, I give here an example of basic intersective composition in the VG model. Given the entity matrix, set intersection is simply expressed as pointwise multiplication. For instance, the denotation of the phrase *brown bear* can be obtained by multiplication of the *bear* and *brown* entity vectors. The operation returns brown bear entities in the Visual Genome with their other properties, as exemplified below:

```
5460844    bear.n.01, brown, large, adult, big,
           with(-,bear.n.01)
5464728    bear.n.01, brown, furry, shaggy, fuzzy,
           splashing, posing, big, in(-,water.n.01)
4868617    bear.n.01, brown, wearing(-,jean.n.01),
           on(-,pillow.n.01), holding(baby.n.01,-)
...
```

Given the entity matrix, it is possible to multiply any number of vectors to obtain denotations for, say, 'playing brown bears', 'playing white bears',

or 'cute teddy bears', and inspect the corresponding subspaces (that is, the basis made of the individuals in the denotations). In those subspaces, only the vectors corresponding to annotated properties for the respective sets are non-zero. For instance, there are five playing white bears in the VG, forming a 5-dimensional subspace with 38 non-zero property vectors. Quantification can be defined for particular restrictors (subsets of playing white bears) and scopes (the property vectors) by aggregating individuals into a 1-dimensional basis representing a subkind and reading set overlap relations off the normalised version of that basis.

To illustrate this, let us consider the three subkinds 'playing white bears', 'playing brown bears' and 'cute teddy bears'. For each subkind, having applied intersective composition to the vectors in the entity matrix by pointwise multiplication, we obtain a denotation vector which can be aggregated using A_D. The result of such operation is shown in Fig 3, with some relevant property vectors. Following normalisation, the weight of a vector along a dimension can be read as the probability of an instance of the set represented by the dimension to have the property of the vector. So for instance, there is a 0.6 probability that a playing white bear is in water, versus a 0.36 probability for playing brown bears in the VG data. While being preliminary, such observations about the behaviour of the EVA representations indicate that it could encode a number of important set-theoretic properties, making it properly compatible with formal semantics approaches.

7 Conclusion

This paper made the case for solving existing tasks with models more in line with cognitive reality, ar-

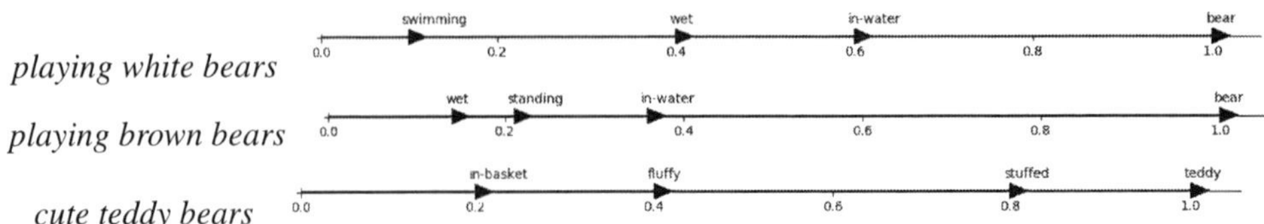

Figure 3: Result of intersective composition over EVA vectors.

guing in particular for the use of smaller corpora. Coming back to the points made in our introduction, I summarise the contributions of the model with respect to desirable aspects of a language acquisition 'simulation'.

First, we have seen that systems trained on 2.8M tokens of VG data are competitive with a large language model pretrained on 5700 times more data when tested on core lexical tasks. On the similarity task, the reference-based system EVA considerably outperforms a language model trained on the same amount of data, emerging as the best 'small data' model.

Notably, EVA exploits a very specific presentation of the data, capitalising on its access to individual instances and its ability to choose the semantic information relevant for solving a given task. Recent work has argued that language modeling is not enough for Natural Language Understanding, and in particular that the relation between language and world(s) matters to comprehension (Bender and Koller, 2020). The results presented here support this view: not only are instances the basic building blocks of reference, but they might also be crucial to support the acquisition of lexical competences.

With respect to the 'innate' mechanisms of the new model presented here, several shortcomings must be pointed out. First and foremost, EVA assumes the availability of a denotation function – some oracle able to map words to entities. This is of course something that children actually have to learn in the process of acquisition, and which probably proceeds in parallel with the training of other semantic competences. Ideally, this assumption should be relaxed in future versions of the model to understand how much the system learns when its reference module is imperfect (for instance, by linking EVA to an object recognition system from the Language and Vision literature).

Further, the learning mechanisms involved in EVA may be too generic. We have used simple co-occurrence prediction for the acquisition of word semantics and non-linear regression/classification

for task-specific competences, which goes well with claims that language can be acquired via generic cognitive functions. But the actual training regime used by those mechanisms may not be as plausible as it could be. In particular, it is unclear how much supervision is involved in the human acquisition of skills such as lexical relation recognition or acceptability judgements (see e.g. Saxton, 2000 on the amount of negative input received by children from their carer). It is for instance dubious to argue that meronymies should be learned in a supervised fashion, with the learner being explicitly told that an ear or a whisker is 'part of' a cat. This aspect will have to be investigated further before claiming plausibility of the model.

Finally, the data used for our experiments is currently anchored in a visual dataset, and is therefore focused on concrete entities. Linguistic competence involves mastery of abstract vocabulary, as well as reference to 'possible worlds', which can be different from the universe we perceive. It remains to be seen how the competences acquired over purely perceptual data can be usefully brought into skills that involve abstraction and modality.

Acknowledgments

I thank Ann Copestake and Katrin Erk for reading an early draft of this paper, as well as the participants to the GeCKo workshop in Barcelona for their helpful comments. I would also like to thank the anonymous reviewers for their helpful suggestions and comments. Finally, I gratefully acknowledge the support of NVIDIA Corporation with the donation of the Titan V GPU used for this research.

References

Marco Baroni and Alessandro Lenci. 2011. How we blessed distributional semantic evaluation. In *Proceedings of the GEMS 2011 Workshop on GEometrical Models of Natural Language Semantics*, pages 1–10. Association for Computational Linguistics.

Emily M Bender and Alexander Koller. 2020. Climbing towards NLU: On meaning, form, and understanding in the age of data. In *Proceedings of the 58th annual meeting of the Association for Computational Linguistics (ACL 2020)*, Seattle, United States.

Piotr Bojanowski, Edouard Grave, Armand Joulin, and Tomas Mikolov. 2017. Enriching word vectors with subword information. *Transactions of the Association for Computational Linguistics*, 5:135–146.

Noam Chomsky. 1965. *Aspects of the theory of syntax*. MIT Press.

Eve V Clark. 2009. *First language acquisition*. Cambridge University Press.

Alejandrina Cristia, Emmanuel Dupoux, Michael Gurven, and Jonathan Stieglitz. 2017. Child-directed speech is infrequent in a forager-farmer population: A time allocation study. *Child development*.

William W Graves, Jeffrey R Binder, and Mark S Seidenberg. 2013. Noun–noun combination: Meaningfulness ratings and lexical statistics for 2,160 word pairs. *Behavior research methods*, 45(2):463–469.

Lushan Han, Abhay L Kashyap, Tim Finin, James Mayfield, and Jonathan Weese. 2013. Umbc_ebiquity-core: Semantic textual similarity systems. In *Second Joint Conference on Lexical and Computational Semantics (*SEM), Volume 1: Proceedings of the Main Conference and the Shared Task: Semantic Textual Similarity*, volume 1, pages 44–52.

Aurélie Herbelot and Eva Maria Vecchi. 2015. Building a shared world: Mapping distributional to model-theoretic semantic spaces. In *Proceedings of EMNLP2015*, Lisbon, Portugal.

Felix Hill, Roi Reichart, and Anna Korhonen. 2015. Simlex-999: Evaluating semantic models with (genuine) similarity estimation. *Computational Linguistics*, 41(4):665–695.

Jerrold J Katz and Jerry A Fodor. 1963. The structure of a semantic theory. *Language*, 39(2):170–210.

Saul A Kripke. 1972. Naming and necessity. In *Semantics of natural language*, pages 253–355. Springer.

Ranjay Krishna, Yuke Zhu, Oliver Groth, Justin Johnson, Kenji Hata, Joshua Kravitz, Stephanie Chen, Yannis Kalantidis, Li-Jia Li, David A Shamma, et al. 2017. Visual genome: Connecting language and vision using crowdsourced dense image annotations. *International Journal of Computer Vision*, 123(1):32–73.

Germán Kruszewski and Marco Baroni. 2015. So similar and yet incompatible: Toward the automated identification of semantically compatible words. In *Proceedings of the 2015 Conference of the North American Chapter of the Association for Computational Linguistics: Human Language Technologies*, pages 964–969.

Elizaveta Kuzmenko and Aurélie Herbelot. 2019. Distributional semantics in the real world: building word vector representations from a truth-theoretic model. In *Proceedings of the 13th International Conference on Computational Semantics (IWCS 2019)*. Association for Computational Linguistics.

Thomas K Landauer and Susan T Dumais. 1997. A solution to Plato's problem: The latent semantic analysis theory of acquisition, induction, and representation of knowledge. *Psychological review*, pages 211–240.

Tal Linzen, Grzegorz Chrupała, and Afra Alishahi, editors. 2018. *Proceedings of the 2018 EMNLP Workshop BlackboxNLP: Analyzing and Interpreting Neural Networks for NLP*. Association for Computational Linguistics, Brussels, Belgium.

Tal Linzen, Grzegorz Chrupała, Yonatan Belinkov, and Dieuwke Hupkes, editors. 2019. *Proceedings of the 2019 ACL Workshop BlackboxNLP: Analyzing and Interpreting Neural Networks for NLP*. Association for Computational Linguistics, Florence, Italy.

Tomas Mikolov, Kai Chen, Greg Corrado, and Jeffrey Dean. 2013. Efficient estimation of word representations in vector space. *arXiv preprint arXiv:1301.3781*.

Tomas Mikolov, Edouard Grave, Piotr Bojanowski, Christian Puhrsch, and Armand Joulin. 2018. Advances in pre-training distributed word representations. In *Proceedings of the International Conference on Language Resources and Evaluation (LREC 2018)*.

Barbara H Partee. 1979. Semantics – mathematics or psychology? In *Semantics from different points of view*, pages 1–14. Springer.

Barbara H Partee. 2014. The history of formal semantics: Changing notions of linguistic competence. https://udrive.oit.umass.edu/ partee/Partee2014Harvard.pdf. 9th Annual Joshua and Verona Whatmough Lecture, Harvard.

Hilary Putnam. 1975. *Philosophical Papers: Mind, Language, and Reality*, volume 2. Cambridge University Press.

Matthew Saxton. 2000. Negative evidence and negative feedback: Immediate effects on the grammaticality of child speech. *First Language*, 20(60):221–252.

Eva M Vecchi, Marco Marelli, Roberto Zamparelli, and Marco Baroni. 2017. Spicy adjectives and nominal donkeys: Capturing semantic deviance using compositionality in distributional spaces. *Cognitive science*, 41(1):102–136.

Su Wang, Greg Durrett, and Katrin Erk. 2018. Modeling semantic plausibility by injecting world knowledge. In *Proceedings of the 2018 Conference of the*

North American Chapter of the Association for Computational Linguistics: Human Language Technologies, Volume 2 (Short Papers), pages 303–308.

Peter Young, Alice Lai, Micah Hodosh, and Julia Hockenmaier. 2014. From image descriptions to visual denotations: New similarity metrics for semantic inference over event descriptions. *Transactions of the Association for Computational Linguistics*, 2:67–78.

In Media Res: A Corpus for Evaluating Named Entity Linking with Creative Works

Adrian M.P. Brașoveanu
MODUL Technology GmbH
Vienna, Austria
`adrian.brasoveanu@`
`modul.ac.at`

Albert Weichselbraun
Fachhochschule Graubünden
Chur, Switzerland
`albert.weichselbraun@`
`fhgr.ch`

Lyndon J.B. Nixon
MODUL Technology GmbH
Vienna, Austria
`lyndon.nixon@`
`modul.ac.at`

Abstract

Annotation styles express guidelines that direct human annotators by explicitly stating the rules to follow when creating gold standard annotations of text corpora. These guidelines not only shape the gold standards they help create, but also influence the training and evaluation of Named Entity Linking (NEL) tools, since different annotation styles correspond to divergent views on the entities present in a document. Such divergence is particularly relevant for texts from the media domain containing references to creative works. This paper presents a corpus of 1000 annotated documents from sources such as Wikipedia, TVTropes and WikiNews that are organized in ten partitions. Each document contains multiple gold standard annotations representing various annotation styles. The corpus is used to evaluate a series of Named Entity Linking tools in order to understand the impact of the differences in annotation styles on the reported accuracy when processing highly ambiguous entities such as names of creative works. Relaxed annotation guidelines that include overlap styles, for instance, lead to better results across all tools.

1 Introduction

Identifying all entities from texts and linking them to modern Knowledge Graphs (KGs) like DBpedia and Wikidata is the core task of Named Entity Linking (NEL) (Rosales-Méndez et al., 2018b). A particular challenge in NEL is disambiguating the entity references in the surface form (original text). For example, mentions such as *NYT* or *NY Times* or even *Times* could all be surface forms referencing the entity *The New York Times* and they can then be linked to the associated entries from well-known public KGs like DBPedia and Wikidata (i.e., dbr:The_New_York_Times or wd:Q9684 [1]). In ad-

dition to entities, the relations between them, as defined in the texts themselves or extracted from a KG, can also help enlighten the narratives. All of the NEL related tasks are supported by large communities which have a vested interest in advancing their Knowledge Extraction (KE) capabilities. The various good results for general NEL benchmarks (e.g., F1 scores of 0.80 (Rosales-Méndez et al., 2018a)) are encouraging and suggest that the tasks tested for in these benchmarks may be solved soon. However, the main focus of most reported evaluations to date has been on the correct annotation of several specific types of entities like Persons (PER), Locations (LOC) or Organizations (ORG). Sometimes fine-grained typing was also allowed for locations, therefore allowing us to use types like natural locations (LOC) to depict naturally occurring locations like mountains or rivers, facility (FAC) to describe buildings or infrastructure like bridges or airports and Geo-Political Entities (GPE) to describe cities, region or countries (Ji et al., 2017). Only in the last half-decade the focus has slowly shifted towards expanding the typing to encompass a wider array of types, from dates and products to games, sports, books or movies. A large subset of the fine-grained types of entities found naturally in texts, especially in the media domain, are focused on what can generically be called *Works* or sometimes *Creative Works* and which would encompass all creative works (manifestations of creative effort by a creator or group of creators), from books or songs, to movies, television episodes and video games, for example. Collective works with unknown authors (e.g., religious works, folklore), festivals, concerts or sports events can also be considered creative works, even though they may be labelled differently (e.g., a concert might be labelled as an *Event*, whereas its audio or video recording could be labelled as a *Creative Work*).

---

[1] *dbr* represents the namespace abbreviation of DBpedia resources, *wd* for Wikidata resources

Proceedings of the 24th Conference on Computational Natural Language Learning, pages 355–364
Online, November 19-20, 2020. ©2020 Association for Computational Linguistics
https://doi.org/10.18653/v1/P17

The current generation of automated annotators provide a rather mixed set of results for media-related annotations due to inconsistent annotation guidelines related to this domain in the past. For example, a TV show like *Star Trek: Deep Space Nine* will either get no result or two different results, one marking the franchise (*Star Trek*) and the second the titular space station (*Deep Space Nine*), but will probably not be annotated with the full correct entity (*Star Trek: Deep Space Nine*) by many automated annotator tools. Such an annotation could alternatively be considered correct in our view, if instead of the space station, the second annotation would point to the TV show itself. Of course, if we examine the characters from the respective TV shows, we can run into similar problems, as some characters might be described by multiple resources, each of them highlighting a particular performance (e.g., *James Bond* is described both as literary character - dbr:James_Bond_(literary_character) - and Person dbr:James_Bond). In order to counteract such issues, we have developed a corpus focused around annotating such media-related entities. We share this corpus, together with the corresponding annotation guidelines, as well as a set of alternative annotations, especially for nested entities [2]. Since we plan to continuously update this corpus with new partitions every few months, one of its core concepts is the fact that for each ten partitions created there will be a summary partition, a partition that will combine annotations similar to those from the previous nine partitions. If users aim at performing a quick evaluation, they will be able to use this summary partition which we call 'core set' in order to have a first set of results and decide upon their preferred fine-tuning procedure.

The expression *media annotations* is typically used to refer to video or audio annotations, therefore in the context of this paper we have selected the expression *media entity annotations* to signify the annotation of texts created and/or published by various media conglomerates which contain entities of type Creative Work.

We consider our work as an important step in the road towards building culturally-aware AIs since a significant part of human culture is represented by the creative works humanity has produced, AIs are needed that can correctly annotate and interpret information about the referenced creative works.

The rest of the paper is organized as follows: Section 2 showcases somewhat similar work and articles that discuss some of the ideas that we followed during our design process; Section 3 describes the design of the corpora; Section 4 evaluates several tools on some of the partitions included in our corpora; whereas the final section provides a reflection upon the insights gained from designing a gold standard that focuses on creative works.

2   Related Work

Since this dataset uses several concepts that are not widely used in NEL evaluation datasets (e.g., lenses, core sets, multiple annotation styles), this section also includes explanations for those concepts.

After examining a rich set of media annotation papers we have discovered that very few papers actually discuss how to correctly annotate media assets with creative work entities. Early results were focused on the correct semantic annotation of text extracted from the multimedia content (e.g., transcription or subtitles), as presented in a set of papers that originated from the LinkedTV project like (Li et al., 2013; Nixon and Troncy, 2014), but using the classical entity types well supported by NEL tools (Person, Organization, Location). More recent media annotation work discussed cross-modal annotations (Zhang et al., 2017) and story identification (Nixon et al., 2019). None of these projects or papers focused on the correct identification of creative works or the various naming variants involved in creative works referencing. An episode name like *The Trouble with Tribbles* can be an episode of *Star Trek*, but also an instance of a chapter, comic book or book in the same franchise. Even though the existing research would help us annotate the respective episode's video, it will not really help us contextualize it, if mentioned in a press release, for example.

Due to the shortcomings of current approaches, we have also examined several other avenues, including corpora that contain creative works or historical entities that might otherwise be difficult to identify by the general public and were created for different purposes but in somewhat similar situations (e.g., no corpora available, specific domain, etc). The digital humanities domain, and in particular historical documents and literary criticism, are perhaps the closest scenarios to our use case

---

[2]The corpus is available online at: `https://github.com/modultechnology/in_media_res`.

that come to mind. Several works in this domain like the historical documents from the Impresso collection (Ehrmann et al., 2020), the multilingual news corpora MeanTime (Minard et al., 2016) and Dekker's work on extracting small snippets of literary criticism from social media (Dekker et al., 2018) have served as a starting point in our journey, helping us to define our annotation guidelines.

Some early ideas about naming variations (in particular (Ehrmann et al., 2017), (Rosales-Méndez et al., 2019) and (Weichselbraun et al., 2019b)), and nested annotations ((Ju et al., 2018) and (Ji et al., 2017)) have also shaped our understanding of the difficulties of correctly capturing names referencing entities, regardless of the domain, and have led us to multiple works on annotation styles and lenses. The idea of data lenses comes from multiple places, but it was generally inspired by photography where different lenses are used in order to get different views on an object. In NEL, and in NLP in general, the idea is to enable different views onto the same dataset. During the last few years, lenses have increasingly been used to transform data between different views (Rajkumar et al., 2013). In the NLP domain, lenses have traditionally been implemented as annotation sets that reflect the view of a human annotator upon the specific data, being an important feature of annotation packages like GATE (Maynard, 2009), as well as for implementation of large parallel corpora typically used for multilingual settings (e.g., (Iranzo-Sánchez et al., 2019). In the Semantic Web (SW), ontologies have traditionally been used to act as lenses over data eventually leading to an entire field of study: Ontology-Based Data Access (Calvanese et al., 2015). More recently, lenses have been used to create multiple views over chemistry data (Batchelor et al., 2014), help manage large data sets (Lenzerini, 2018), or understand big data and AI workloads (Gao et al., 2018).

With respect to entity linking, an early example of lenses was the concept of approximate matching implemented in tools like Neleval (Hachey et al., 2014) and Gerbil (Röder et al., 2018). The computation of partial matches was done based on the number of overlapping characters or entity types with respect to the measures that can be optimized (e.g., precision or recall). Many optimization strategies will fail to correctly identify either connections between entities (e.g., parent) or nested entities. What is missing and why, can generally be

discovered during the error analysis phase of the evaluations, as shown in (Braşoveanu et al., 2018b) and (Stanislawek et al., 2019). Understanding error classification schemes like the ones described in these publications can be the key towards moving the field forward.

More recently, lenses have been used to understand entity annotations (Braşoveanu et al., 2018a) and to study the effect of relaxed annotation schemas that include more types than usual (Rosales-Méndez et al., 2018a). A theoretical treatment of automatic procedures for building lenses is presented in (Weichselbraun et al., 2019a). The paper showcases how to automatically build lenses by following simple rules (e.g., expand the surface form to the maximum length - the longest mention - or reduce the surface form to the minimal possible length - the shortest mention). Using the longest mention leads to an annotation schema with less entities, whereas using the shortest mention will lead to more entities being annotated. Intermediary schemas are also possible, if we take into account the possibilities of combining the previous schemas or if we add additional rules. We test some of the lenses discussed in this paper, as it can be seen in Section 3.

Our In Media Res corpora contains partitions from multiple domains. Due to this aspect, it was decided to introduce core sets partitions at every nine partitions. By adding these core sets, evaluators can later build a summary dataset for the whole corpus, regardless of the number of partitions contained in it. The concept of core sets was borrowed from computational geometry and robotics. A core set is a small engineered subset of a very large dataset that retains its properties as accurately as possible (e.g., a set of points that approximate the shape of a figure). Its size typically depends on the desired accuracy, not necessarily on the size of the original data set. Core sets have been successfully applied to a variety of problems, from dimensionality reduction of massive data sets (Feldman et al., 2016), to vector summarization (Feldman et al., 2017) or compression of neural networks (Baykal et al., 2018).

3 The In Media Res Corpus

Since most corpora used in ground truth annotation are focused on news media or tweets that describe current events, there is no wide agreement on annotation styles for entities of type Creative Work.

We, therefore, started our corpus design by testing various annotation styles and creating an annotation guideline for Creative Work entities. After we identified a solution, we created multiple partitions from various domains.

The name of the corpus comes from the Latin expression *in media res* that refers to narratives (e.g., books or movies) that start in the middle of the story. Similarly, the created corpus has been designed with the aim of understanding different annotation styles, and rather than starting from zero builds upon prior research in this area. Also, the fact that most of the annotated documents are related to media (e.g., franchises, books, TV shows) has been one of the reasons why we have selected this name.

3.1 Annotation Styles

While classic corpora are quite good for identifying people, organizations or locations, there are less adequate corpora to help with evaluating works (e.g., books, TV shows, music, etc) or events. This has been the main reason why we have decided to create a corpus focused mostly on creative works to help us fine-tune media domain document annotations.

As opposed to the classic entity types in NEL evaluations (e.g., Person, Organization, Location), the annotation of documents from the media domain (TV, radio, film etc.) raises specific challenges. In addition to the core entity types like *Person*, *Organization* and *Location*, media domain document annotation also needs to support a fourth large class of entities: *Creative Work* or *Work* [3]. This class encompasses a large selection of entities that might be classified as creative works, from books and songs, through to games, movies, TV Shows and entire media franchises. It is important to note that, if we leave the temporal attributes aside (e.g., new positions for a person, key people for a company, new episodes for a TV show), there is a lot of variation when it comes to the main attributes of this entity type as opposed to the three core types (Person, Organization, Location). A TV show might have some executive producers, a production company, some actors starring in it, as well as a set of episodes, each with their own list of directors, writers or stars; a book will have some

author(s), publisher, and awards or links to a book series; and a song might have an interpret, author, music producer, and so on. As it can be seen, it is difficult to find common attributes between the various sub-classes, except for the fact that they are all types of creative works that were published in some format or medium in a certain period of time. It can even be argued that all these creative works should be modeled as their own entity types, but in order to perform such a fine-grained extraction, it is important to first identify the large class to which the entities belong. Adding works can also lead to a high number of false positives, as often fictional characters (e.g., *James Bond, Harry Potter*) might share names with real people, as well as with their own media franchises which can encompass different sets of series (e.g., books, tv shows, movies, comics, etc); fictional characters might be based on real people (e.g., see the recent trend of music biopics based on *N.W.A., Queen* or *Elton John* or TV shows like *Narcos* who often fictionalize real characters by changing their names or changing the events in which they participate) or the name of a work is later used for a different work (e.g., again the example of music biopics is relevant). Table 1 showcases some of the issues encountered by annotators such as AIDA (Hoffart et al., 2011), DBpedia Spotlight (Daiber et al., 2013) and Recognyze (Weichselbraun et al., 2019b) when performing named entity linking on works. As illustrated in the table, each annotator tends to return a different set of results based on its settings. Unfortunately, the best settings for annotators are not published, therefore, even when NEL annotators are integrated into benchmarking systems like Gerbil (Röder et al., 2018) or (Odoni et al., 2018) it is still difficult to understand if the obtained results really represent the best possible outcome. When examining these differences between tools, we decided to use lenses as a method for further investigating overlaps and partial matches.

For the current evaluation, we have considered the following annotation styles based on (Weichselbraun et al., 2019a) (here illustrated on the annotation of the text snippet *Star Trek: Picard* and its associated DBpedia resource $dbr : Star\_Trek : \_Picard$):

1. The annotation style $\emptyset MIN$ disregards overlapping entities and extracts the minimum number of entities: $m_{[\text{Star Trek: Picard}]}^{dbr:Star\_Trek:\_Picard}$, i.e. links the snippet to the *Star Trek: Picard* DB-

---

[3]represented by `http://dbpedia.org/ontology/Work` (abbreviated as dbo:Work) in DBpedia or `https://schema.org/CreativeWork` in the schema.org vocabulary

Example	AIDA	Spotlight	Recognyze
Sir Patrick Stewart OBE	1: Patrick Stewart	1: Patrick 2: Stewart 3: OBE	1: Patrick Stewart 2: OBE
Star Trek: Deep Space Nine	1: Star Trek	1: Star Trek 2: Deep Space Nine	1: Star Trek 2: Star Trek: Deep Space Nine
The British Broadcast Corporation (BBC)	1: British Broadcast Corporation 2: BBC	1: British 2: BBC	1: British Broadcast Corporation 2: BBC
Seinfeld	1: Seinfeld	1: Seinfeld	1: Seinfeld

Table 1: Understanding differences between annotator results. Numbers were added in order to clarify which entities were retrieved.

pedia entity.

2. The annotation style $\emptyset MAX$ also ignores overlapping entities but extracts the maximum number of entities from a given text snippet: $m_{\text{[Star Trek]}}^{dbr:Star\_Trek}, m_{\text{[Picard]}}^{dbr:Star\_Trek:\_Picard}$.

3. The annotation style $OMAX$ allows for overlaps and, again, will aim to extract the maximum number of entities whenever possible: $m_{\text{[Star Trek: Picard]}}^{Star\_Trek:\_Picard}, m_{\text{[Star Trek]}}^{dbr:Star\_Trek}$.

It has to be noted that two of the styles ($\emptyset MAX$ and $OMAX$) can also extract the person rather than the TV show *Picard* as a separate entity, but since this result would have a different type (*Person* instead of *Work*, as it points to the Jean-Luc Picard character from the same franchise) and different link (e.g., $dbr : Jean - Luc\_Picard$ instead of $dbr : Star\_Trek : \_Picard$), it would be an incorrect result that is automatically removed in our implementation. The presented rules only consider borderline cases, even though combinations of them can also be used within a corpus. A corpus which would not apply the OMAX rule, for example, might lose the extended reference to *Sir Patrick Stewart OBE* and only return *Patrick Stewart* or end up removing the references to the actor's titles (e.g., *Sir, OBE*). We consider OMAX annotation rule to be the best, as it essentially merges the other annotation styles. The advantage of using these rules comes from the fact that they can easily be automated. By using them we have generated alternative annotations (also known as lenses) for all of our dataset partitions. One such example is provided for the core set of our dataset in the evaluation from Section 4. The annotations in Table 2 illustrate the gold standard results for the different lenses described in this section. The $\emptyset MIN$ results are somewhat closer to the expected full annotation (e.g., the one presented in the example column) and only introduce minor variations. One of our assumptions was that lenses such as OMAX should even the playing field by reducing the penalty of overlaps in terms of false positives, while also offering some clues on what kind of surface forms are picked up more frequently by the various annotators.

3.2 Partitions and Statistics

The corpora currently has 10 sections each with 100 documents. We plan to add more partitions in time to cover different domains and therefore test different algorithms for domain adaptation in Named Entity Linking.

At every 900 documents, we include a numbered partition called *general* (e.g., general-1, general-2, etc) which will contain some documents from each of the domains covered in these 900 documents, therefore representing a summary or a core set of the previous set of partitions. This is done in order to create a large core set of the entire corpora. The General core sets can be used both as smaller standalone corpora, as well as small test beds in order to decide if certain partitions are useful.

We have started by collecting several sentences from the Wikipedia abstracts of 100 articles about creative works (as classified by their respective DB-Pedia resource). The initial set of entities contained books, TV shows, media companies, YouTube influencers and media franchises. Several entity types were annotated, include Person (PER), Orga-

Example	ØMIN	ØMAX	OMAX
Sir Patrick Stewart OBE	1: Sir Patrick Stewart OBE	1: Sir 2: Patrick Stewart 3: OBE	1: Sir Patrick Stewart OBE 2: Sir 3: OBE
MLB Advanced Media (MLBAM)	1: MLB Advanced Media (MLBAM)	1:MLB Advanced Media 2: MLBAM	1: MLB Advanced Media (MLBAM) 2: MLBAM
Burbank, California	1: Burbank, California	1: Burbank 2: California	1: Burbank, California 2: California
Seinfeld	1: Seinfeld	1: Seinfeld	1: Seinfeld

Table 2: Understanding differences between lenses. Numbers were added in order to clarify which entities were retrieved.

nization (ORG), Location (LOC), Work (WORK), Event (EVENT) or Other (OTHER). The corpus was annotated by two annotators following our annotation guideline. The human annotators were asked to use the ØMIN lens for creating the initial annotations, therefore disregarding overlapping entities and selecting the minimum possible number of matches. A judge was available for questions during the whole annotation process and helped solve disagreements after the annotation process has been completed. The rest of the lenses (e.g., ØMAX, OMAX) have later been automatically generated using a Python script. The judge has then verified the resulting annotations in order to eliminate mistakes. This process was iterative, therefore most of the errors reported being eliminated from the script until the end of the process. The resulting corpus was exported into multiple formats, including CSV and NIF.

The remaining texts were collected from the open source repositories TVTropes[4] and WikiNews[5]. Currently the following partitions are available (we indicate the sources in parentheses):

- *Franchises* (TV Tropes) set is focused on big multimedia franchises like *Marvel Cinematic Universe* or *Star Wars* and the creative works in various formats (movies, TV shows, books, video games) that support them. Due to the fact that many NEL tools are not trained to correctly recognize creative works and due to the popularity prior settings used by various

algorithms, this partition is generally considered difficult for current NEL tools.

- *RegionalTV* (TV Tropes) set contains texts about European TV Shows.

- *EuroFilm* (TV Tropes) is focused on classic and modern European films. We have typically included five to fifteen movies for the selected countries (France, Germany, Austria, Switzerland, U.K., Netherlands, Italy, Denmark, Sweden).

- The *WebMedia* (TV Tropes) set was built around YouTube influencers. Due to the dynamic nature of the YouTube platform, the channels of some of the annotated entities may not exist in the future. Therefore, the content from this partition should be considered time-sensitive and relatively difficult. For the current version of the corpus the various types of YouTube subcultures[6] were not annotated, but we consider including such types in future versions.

- *News* (Wiki News) collects general interest News on a variety of topics. As expected, the level of difficulty for this partition is medium, since most tools were trained for such content.

- *Politics* (Wiki News) encompasses general politics News related to elections, political events (e.g., Syrian Conflict, Arab Spring) and war-related News. In some cases there

---

[4] https://tvtropes.org/
[5] https://en.wikinews.org/

[6] https://tvtropes.org/pmwiki/pmwiki.php/
UsefulNotes/Subcultures

Category	Count
Partitions	10
Documents per partition	100
Documents	1000
Total entities	3422
Total entities (ØMIN)	3422
Total entities (ØMAX)	3655
Total entities (OMAX)	3809

Table 3: Basic statistics.

might be overlaps between this partition and the News partition, but this is simply due to the fact that they include the same types of entities.

- *Business* (Wikipedia) includes documents on corporations from the tech, medical and media domains. The difficulty level is medium.

- *Climate* (Wikipedia) contains coverage on Climate Change, sustainability and related entities (e.g., Greenpeace, Al Gore, Greta Thunberg).

- *Entertainment News* (Wikipedia) is a partition related to celebrity News during early 2020.

- *Core set (General)* (Wikipedia) partition contains the core set of the first 9 partitions, including short texts from domains like general news, politics, franchises, TV or movies. The level of difficulty is generally medium.

Some basic statistics about this corpus can be found in Table 3. Most of the documents have one to three sentences and can be considered equivalent to DBpedia abstracts, even though they were collected from various sources. Due to the nature of the collected information (e.g., franchises, TV shows, books) the early partitions often draw upon abstracts. Later partitions, in contrast, are randomly selected from the actual content of the articles. This assures that the collection is heterogeneous and that it can later be used for testing multiple use cases (e.g., media-related entities, news media, policies, etc).

4   Evaluation

This section describes the tools used during the evaluation, its design and a discussion around results.

4.1   Evaluation Design and Results

The following tools have been used during our general-purpose evaluation:

- **DBpedia Spotlight** (Daiber et al., 2013) is a statistical NEL engine that was originally built as a demo for showcasing DBpedia's capabilities and has been ported to multiple languages. The statistical models from Spotlight are really good for larger Knowledge Extraction or WSD challenges where all words need to be linked to their respective KG entities, but they are not necessarily fine-tuned for typed NEL tasks.

- **AIDA** (Hoffart et al., 2011) uses graph-based disambiguation algorithms and is considered one of the best NEL engines focused around Wikipedia linking.

- **Recognyze** (Weichselbraun et al., 2019b) is a multi-KG (e.g., DBpedia, Wikidata, Wikipedia) graph-based disambiguation engine focused on the issue of name variance.

We have created two different sets of evaluations. The first one (see Table 4) contains the results for the core set partition of the corpus. This evaluation also lists the results for different annotation styles (lenses) as they were presented in this paper. The second evaluation (see Table 5) compares the results of several tools on the entire corpora.

As it can be seen in Table 4, the multiple annotation styles had an impact on almost all of the evaluated tools. This suggests that most of the tools do seem to perform better when considering these annotation styles in succession, with Spotlight and Recognyze gaining up to 4%. It is interesting to note that the rules seem to improve the recall of DBpedia, Spotlight and Recognyze in all cases, whereas precision is not impacted by OMAX styles for Spotlight. There might be a need for multiple evaluations in a future publication to establish the full impact of these guidelines, but since such annotation styles can automatically be generated from any dataset following the outlined rules, they are definitely worth investigating.

As expected the results on the core set (Table 4) and the entire corpus (Table 5) are similar. They are between 2% and 3% lower for each tool, which due to the higher number of entities should be considered a good results. This also indicates that the content of the core set was indeed carefully chosen

Corpus	System	mP	mR	$mF1$	MP	MR	$MF1$
Core set	AIDA	0.47	0.48	0.47	0.43	0.48	0.43
ØMIN	Spotlight	0.53	0.43	0.48	0.35	0.42	0.37
(480 entities)	Recognyze	**0.61**	**0.52**	**0.56**	**0.52**	**0.50**	**0.51**
Core set	AIDA	0.49	0.48	0.49	0.45	0.48	0.44
ØMAX	Spotlight	0.55	0.43	0.48	0.35	0.40	0.36
(507 entities)	Recognyze	**0.62**	**0.54**	**0.58**	**0.55**	**0.52**	**0.53**
Core set	AIDA	0.49	0.48	0.49	0.45	0.48	0.44
OMAX	Spotlight	0.51	0.57	0.54	0.51	**0.58**	0.52
(527 entities)	Recognyze	**0.65**	**0.61**	**0.64**	**0.61**	0.57	**0.59**

Table 4: Core set experiments with multiple lenses (m - micro; M - macro; p - precision; r - recall; $F1$ - F1).

Corpus	System	mP	mR	$mF1$	MP	MR	$MF1$
	AIDA	0.50	**0.49**	0.50	0.46	0.47	0.46
All partitions	Spotlight	0.65	0.48	0.54	0.66	**0.50**	0.50
(3809 entities)	Recognyze	**0.69**	**0.49**	**0.57**	**0.70**	0.48	**0.56**

Table 5: Results on the entire corpora - with overlaps - OMAX lens (m - micro; M - macro; p - precision; r - recall; $F1$ - F1).

to reflect the content of the whole dataset up to this point in time.

4.2 Discussion

NEL performance on the *In Media Res* corpus is considerably lower than the results obtained on traditional data sets. This was expected due to the large amount of errors introduced by adding creative works to the corpora. Also as expected, the tools were not able to distinguish well between a character and the franchise that bears its name or offer good results on the YouTube influencer partition of the corpus. The influencer partition is especially difficult due to the fact that some of the works mentioned there (e.g., YouTube channels that were shut down or early gigs for famous influencers) are NIL (i.e. entities that have not been included in Wikipedia or related KGs such as DBpedia and Wikidata).

While some media franchises are well-covered by Wikipedia (e.g., *Harry Potter*) and related KGs, others are not. In such cases a good approach towards improving coverage and results might be leveraging Linked Data extracted from dedicated wikis such as *Memory Alpha* (covering the *Star Trek* franchise), *Wookieepedia* (covering *Star Wars*) or *Marvel Database* (covering both *Marvel Comics* and the *Marvel Cinematic Universe*). Most of the fandoms organize around such wikis and also many of them are published through *Fandom*[7] and similar wiki engines. Some of the information from these wikis is also collected in Linked Data form through DBkwik (Hertling and Paulheim, 2018).

---

[7] https://www.fandom.com/

5 Conclusion and Future Work

The road towards designing culturally-aware AIs has started with the expansion of fields like digital humanities during the last decade. While some steps towards this goal were made, the selected topics still depend on funding and on the researcher's own goals, as this is a relatively new field. Even so, we find it surprising that there was a lack of guidance in the NEL community related to name variation and nested entities for creative works. The corpus and concepts introduced in this paper are a first attempt to address this issue.

The results of the various annotators on the *In Media Res* corpus are understandably lower than on corpora from traditional domains such as news articles and social media. While applying different annotation lenses improves the results for some annotators, it is clear that there is a need for more progress in this area.

We plan to continue maintaining the corpus and provide updates, new partitions, or lenses. We hope that these efforts will contribute to increased accuracy in the annotation of creative work entities and, therefore, aid annotation systems in taking a further step towards culturally-aware AIs.

Acknowledgments

This research has been partially funded through the following projects: the ReTV project (www.retv-project.eu) funded by the European Union's Horizon 2020 Research and Innovation Programme (No. 780656), and MedMon (www.fhgr.ch/medmon) funded by the Swiss Innovation Agency Innosuisse.

References

Colin R. Batchelor, Christian Y. A. Brenninkmeijer, Christine Chichester, Mark Davies, Daniela Digles, Ian Dunlop, Chris T. A. Evelo, Anna Gaulton, Carole A. Goble, Alasdair J. G. Gray, Paul T. Groth, Lee Harland, Karen Karapetyan, Antonis Loizou, John P. Overington, Steve Pettifer, Jon Steele, Robert Stevens, Valery Tkachenko, Andra Waagmeester, Antony J. Williams, and Egon L. Willighagen. 2014. Scientific Lenses to Support Multiple Views over Linked Chemistry Data. In *The Semantic Web - ISWC 2014 - 13th International Semantic Web Conference, Riva del Garda, Italy, October 19-23, 2014. Proceedings, Part I*, volume 8796 of *Lecture Notes in Computer Science*, pages 98–113. Springer.

Cenk Baykal, Lucas Liebenwein, Igor Gilitschenski, Dan Feldman, and Daniela Rus. 2018. Data-Dependent Coresets for Compressing Neural Networks with Applications to Generalization Bounds. *CoRR*, abs/1804.05345.

Adrian M. P. Braşoveanu, Lyndon J.B. Nixon, and Albert Weichselbraun. 2018a. StoryLens: A Multiple Views Corpus for Location and Event Detection. In *Proceedings of the 8th International Conference on Web Intelligence, Mining and Semantics (WIMS 2018)*, Novi Sad, Serbia. ACM.

Adrian M. P. Braşoveanu, Giuseppe Rizzo, Philipp Kuntschick, Albert Weichselbraun, and Lyndon J.B. Nixon. 2018b. Framing Named Entity Linking Error Types. In *Proceedings of the Eleventh International Conference on Language Resources and Evaluation (LREC 2018)*, pages 266–271, Paris, France. European Language Resources Association (ELRA).

Diego Calvanese, Alessandro Mosca, José Remesal, Martín Rezk, and Guillem Rull. 2015. A 'historical case' of Ontology-Based Data Access. In *2015 Digital Heritage, Granada, Spain, September 28 - October 2, 2015*, pages 291–298. IEEE.

Joachim Daiber, Max Jakob, Chris Hokamp, and Pablo N. Mendes. 2013. Improving Efficiency and Accuracy in Multilingual Entity Extraction. In *I-SEMANTICS 2013 - 9th International Conference on Semantic Systems, ISEM '13, Graz, Austria, September 4-6, 2013*, pages 121–124. ACM.

Niels Dekker, Tobias Kuhn, and Marieke van Erp. 2018. Evaluating Social Network Extraction for Classic and Modern Fiction Literature. *PeerJ Prepr.*, 6:e27263.

Maud Ehrmann, Guillaume Jacquet, and Ralf Steinberger. 2017. Jrc-names: Multilingual entity name variants and titles as linked data. *Semantic Web*, 8(2):283–295.

Maud Ehrmann, Matteo Romanello, Simon Clematide, Phillip Ströbel, and Raphaël Barman. 2020. Language Resources for Historical Newspapers: The Impresso Collection. In *Proceedings of The 12th Language Resources and Evaluation Conference, LREC 2020, Marseille, France, May 11-16, 2020*, pages 958–968. European Language Resources Association.

Dan Feldman, Sedat Ozer, and Daniela Rus. 2017. Coresets for Vector Summarization with Applications to Network Graphs. *CoRR*, abs/1706.05554.

Dan Feldman, Mikhail Volkov, and Daniela Rus. 2016. Dimensionality Reduction of Massive Sparse Datasets Using Coresets. In *Advances in Neural Information Processing Systems 29: Annual Conference on Neural Information Processing Systems 2016, December 5-10, 2016, Barcelona, Spain*, pages 2766–2774.

Wanling Gao, Jianfeng Zhan, Lei Wang, Chunjie Luo, Daoyi Zheng, Fei Tang, Biwei Xie, Chen Zheng, Xu Wen, Xiwen He, Hainan Ye, and Rui Ren. 2018. Data Motifs: A Lens Towards Fully Understanding Big Data and AI Workloads. In *Proceedings of the 27th International Conference on Parallel Architectures and Compilation Techniques, PACT 2018, Limassol, Cyprus, November 01-04, 2018*, pages 2:1–2:14. ACM.

Ben Hachey, Joel Nothman, and Will Radford. 2014. Cheap and Easy Entity Evaluation. In *Proceedings of the 52nd Annual Meeting of the Association for Computational Linguistics, ACL 2014, June 22-27, 2014, Baltimore, MD, USA, Volume 2: Short Papers*, pages 464–469. The Association for Computer Linguistics.

Sven Hertling and Heiko Paulheim. 2018. DBkWik: A Consolidated Knowledge Graph from Thousands of Wikis. In *2018 IEEE International Conference on Big Knowledge, ICBK 2018, Singapore, November 17-18, 2018*, pages 17–24. IEEE Computer Society.

Johannes Hoffart, Mohamed Amir Yosef, Ilaria Bordino, Hagen Fürstenau, Manfred Pinkal, Marc Spaniol, Bilyana Taneva, Stefan Thater, and Gerhard Weikum. 2011. Robust Disambiguation of Named Entities in Text. In *Proceedings of the 2011 Conference on Empirical Methods in Natural Language Processing, EMNLP 2011, 27-31 July 2011, John McIntyre Conference Centre, Edinburgh, UK, A meeting of SIGDAT, a Special Interest Group of the ACL*, pages 782–792.

Javier Iranzo-Sánchez, Joan Albert Silvestre-Cerdà, Javier Jorge, Nahuel Roselló, Adrià Giménez, Albert Sanchís, Jorge Civera, and Alfons Juan. 2019. Europarl-ST: A Multilingual Corpus For Speech Translation Of Parliamentary Debates. *CoRR*, abs/1911.03167.

Heng Ji, Xiaoman Pan, Boliang Zhang, Joel Nothman, James Mayfield, Paul McNamee, and Cash Costello. 2017. Overview of TAC-KBP2017 13 Languages Entity Discovery and Linking. In *Proceedings of the 2017 Text Analysis Conference, TAC 2017, Gaithersburg, Maryland, USA, November 13-14, 2017*, page 4. NIST.

Meizhi Ju, Makoto Miwa, and Sophia Ananiadou. 2018. A Neural Layered Model for Nested Named Entity Recognition. In *Proceedings of the 2018 Conference of the North American Chapter of the Association for Computational Linguistics: Human Language Technologies, NAACL-HLT 2018, New Orleans, Louisiana, USA, June 1-6, 2018, Volume 1 (Long Papers)*, pages 1446–1459. Association for Computational Linguistics.

Maurizio Lenzerini. 2018. Managing Data through the Lens of an Ontology. *AI Magazine*, 39(2):65–74.

Yunjia Li, Giuseppe Rizzo, José Luis Redondo García, Raphaël Troncy, Mike Wald, and Gary Wills. 2013. Enriching Media Fragments with Named Entities for Video Classification. In *22nd International World Wide Web Conference, WWW '13, Rio de Janeiro, Brazil, May 13-17, 2013, Companion Volume*, pages 469–476. International World Wide Web Conferences Steering Committee / ACM.

Diana Maynard. 2009. GATE: Bridging the Gap between Terminology and Linguistics. In *Proceedings of the 8th International Conference on Terminology and Artificial Intelligence, Toulouse, France, November 18-20, 2009*, volume 578 of *CEUR Workshop Proceedings*. CEUR-WS.org.

Anne-Lyse Minard, Manuela Speranza, Ruben Urizar, Begoña Altuna, Marieke van Erp, Anneleen Schoen, and Chantal van Son. 2016. MEANTIME, the NewsReader Multilingual Event and Time Corpus. In *Proceedings of the Tenth International Conference on Language Resources and Evaluation LREC 2016, Portorož, Slovenia, May 23-28, 2016*. European Language Resources Association (ELRA).

Lyndon J. B. Nixon, Evlampios E. Apostolidis, Foteini Markatopoulou, Ioannis Patras, and Vasileios Mezaris. 2019. Multimodal Video Annotation for Retrieval and Discovery of Newsworthy Video in a News Verification Scenario. In *MultiMedia Modeling - 25th International Conference, MMM 2019, Thessaloniki, Greece, January 8-11, 2019, Proceedings, Part I*, volume 11295 of *Lecture Notes in Computer Science*, pages 143–155. Springer.

Lyndon J. B. Nixon and Raphaël Troncy. 2014. Survey of Semantic Media Annotation Tools for the Web: Towards New Media Applications with Linked Media. In *The Semantic Web: ESWC 2014 Satellite Events - ESWC 2014 Satellite Events, Anissaras, Crete, Greece, May 25-29, 2014, Revised Selected Papers*, volume 8798 of *Lecture Notes in Computer Science*, pages 100–114. Springer.

Fabian Odoni, Philipp Kuntschik, Adrian M. P. Braşoveanu, and Albert Weichselbraun. 2018. On the importance of drill-down analysis for assessing gold standards and named entity linking performance. In *Proceedings of the 14th International Conference on Semantic Systems, SEMANTICS 2018, Vienna, Austria, September 10-13, 2018,* volume 137 of *Procedia Computer Science*, pages 33–42. Elsevier.

Raghu Rajkumar, Nate Foster, Sam Lindley, and James Cheney. 2013. Lenses for Web Data. *ECEASST*, 57.

Michael Röder, Ricardo Usbeck, and Axel-Cyrille Ngonga Ngomo. 2018. GERBIL - Benchmarking Named Entity Recognition and Linking Consistently. *Semantic Web*, 9(5):605–625.

Henry Rosales-Méndez, Aidan Hogan, and Barbara Poblete. 2018a. VoxEL: A Benchmark Dataset for Multilingual Entity Linking. In *The Semantic Web - ISWC 2018 - 17th International Semantic Web Conference, Monterey, CA, USA, October 8-12, 2018, Proceedings, Part II*, volume 11137 of *Lecture Notes in Computer Science*, pages 170–186. Springer.

Henry Rosales-Méndez, Aidan Hogan, and Barbara Poblete. 2019. NIFify: Towards Better Quality Entity Linking Datasets. In *Companion of The 2019 World Wide Web Conference, WWW 2019, San Francisco, CA, USA, May 13-17, 2019.*, pages 815–818. ACM.

Henry Rosales-Méndez, Barbara Poblete, and Aidan Hogan. 2018b. What Should Entity Linking link? In *Proceedings of the 12th Alberto Mendelzon International Workshop on Foundations of Data Management, Cali, Colombia, May 21-25, 2018.*, volume 2100 of *CEUR Workshop Proceedings*, page 15. CEUR-WS.org.

Tomasz Stanislawek, Anna Wróblewska, Alicja Wójcicka, Daniel Ziembicki, and Przemyslaw Biecek. 2019. Named Entity Recognition - Is There a Glass Ceiling? In *Proceedings of the 23rd Conference on Computational Natural Language Learning, CoNLL 2019, Hong Kong, China, November 3-4, 2019*, pages 624–633. Association for Computational Linguistics.

Albert Weichselbraun, Adrian MP Brasoveanu, Philipp Kuntschik, and Lyndon JB Nixon. 2019a. Improving Named Entity Linking Corpora Quality. *RANLP 2019*, pages 1328–1337.

Albert Weichselbraun, Philipp Kuntschik, and Adrian M. P. Brasoveanu. 2019b. Name Variants for Improving Entity Discovery and Linking. In *2nd Conference on Language, Data and Knowledge, LDK 2019, May 20-23, 2019, Leipzig, Germany.*, volume 70 of *OASICS*, pages 14:1–14:15. Schloss Dagstuhl - Leibniz-Zentrum fuer Informatik.

Lei Zhang, Andreas Thalhammer, Achim Rettinger, Michael Färber, Aditya Mogadala, and Ronald Denaux. 2017. The xLiMe system: Cross-lingual and Cross-modal Semantic Annotation, Search and Recommendation over Live-TV, News and Social Media Streams. *J. Web Semant.*, 46-47:20–30.

Analogies minus analogy test: measuring regularities in word embeddings

Louis Fournier [1]   **Emmanuel Dupoux** [1 2]   **Ewan Dunbar** [1 3 4]

[1]Cognitive Machine Learning (ENS-CNRS-EHESS-INRIA-PSL Research University), France
[2]Facebook A.I. Research, Paris, France
[3]Laboratoire de Linguistique Formelle (CNRS-Paris Diderot-Sorbonne Paris Cite), France
[4]University of Toronto, Toronto, Canada
louis.fournier@polytechnique.edu   ewan.dunbar@utoronto.ca
emmanuel.dupoux@gmail.com

Abstract

Vector space models of words have long been claimed to capture linguistic regularities as simple vector translations, but problems have been raised with this claim. We decompose and empirically analyze the classic arithmetic word analogy test, to motivate two new metrics that address the issues with the standard test, and which distinguish between class-wise **offset concentration** (similar directions between pairs of words drawn from different broad classes, such as *France–London, China–Ottawa, …*) and **pairing consistency** (the existence of a regular transformation between *correctly*-matched pairs such as *France:Paris::China:Beijing*). We show that, while the standard analogy test is flawed, several popular word embeddings do nevertheless encode linguistic regularities.

1 Introduction

Vector semantic models saw a surge in interest after embeddings trained under the word2vec architecture (Mikolov et al., 2013a) were shown to encode linguistic regularities (Mikolov et al., 2013b). The demonstration relied on the arithmetic analogy test: relations such as $\text{king} + \text{woman} - \text{man} \approx \text{queen}$ were shown to hold for a variety of semantic and grammatical relations. Evaluation of word embeddings on analogy tests and training on related loss functions remains current. There is also continued interest in theoretically grounding the success of distributional embeddings on these tests (Allen and Hospedales, 2019; Ethayarajh et al., 2019).

There is, however, a substantial literature pointing to problems with word analogies (see Section 2), leading to the conclusion that word analogies are fragile in practice, and sometimes going so far as to imply that the positive results were erroneous. These critiques have been ambiguous as to whether the problem is that the embeddings in question do not really encode the relevant linguistic structure, or whether the issue is merely that the arithmetic analogy *test* as it is standardly defined, is flawed.

The current paper confirms that there are serious problems with the standard analogy test, as it confounds three different properties of word vectors while purporting to measure only one: class-wise **offset concentration** (similar directions between pairs of words drawn from different broad classes, such as *France–London, China–Ottawa*), **within-pair similarity** between test words (for example, the similarity between *Paris* and *France*), as well as the **pairing consistency** the test sets out to measure (the presence of a regular direction encoding relations such as *capital-of*: *France–Paris, China–Beijing*). We give an algebraic decomposition of the standard analogy test that explains previous negative results in terms of within-pair similarity. Using new measures, we show that, in practice, offset concentration, rather than true pairing consistency, may account for part of word embeddings' success. Nevertheless, we show that several standard word embeddings do show pairing consistency for the relations tested by the BATS analogy benchmark (Gladkova et al., 2016).[1]

2 Related work

The validity of the arithmetic analogy test has been questioned in several papers, starting with Levy and Goldberg (2014). We detail in Section 3 several major issues with the test as raised by Levy and Goldberg (2014), Linzen (2016), and Rogers et al. (2017). Finley et al. (2017), Newman-Griffis et al. (2017), Chen et al. (2017) and Schluter (2018) also raised concerns about the test and its assumptions. More recently, Nissim et al. (2020) argued against this test as an inadequate tool for studying bias in

---

[1]Code is available at www.github.com/bootphon/
measuring-regularities-in-word-embeddings.

365

Proceedings of the 24th Conference on Computational Natural Language Learning, pages 365–375
Online, November 19-20, 2020. ©2020 Association for Computational Linguistics
https://doi.org/10.18653/v1/P17

word embeddings. Rogers (2019) observes that many of the issues have been ignored.

Some works have proposed other measures of linguistic relations in word embeddings. Levy and Goldberg (2014), Vylomova et al. (2016), and Rogers et al. (2017) all examined the similarity of vector offsets in a more direct way than the standard analogy test (see Section 3 below). Drozd et al. (2016) proposed a method based on predicting the class of the unknown word, and Bouraoui et al. (2018) relaxed the assumptions by allowing probabilistic models to predict the relations.

We claim that these works still do not provide a satisfactory measure of how well word vector offsets encode linguistic relations. Without such a measure, it is impossible to assess whether the original conclusions are correct. We develop this argument, and then develop a new measure, below.

3 The arithmetic analogy test

Mikolov et al. (2013b) proposed to measure the presence of linguistic relations in the structure of word embeddings using vector arithmetic. For two pairs of words representing the same linguistic relation, (a, a^*) and (b, b^*), the test assesses whether:

$$b + (a^* - a) \approx b^* \qquad (1)$$

In practice, the test assesses whether b^* is the nearest neighbour to $b + a^* - a$, using the cosine similarity (cosine of the angle between x and y):

$$\text{sim}(x, y) = \frac{x \cdot y}{\|x\|\|y\|} \qquad (2)$$

The assumption is that, if the offset $o_a = a^* - a$ is parallel to the offset $o_b = b^* - b$, then this common offset direction encodes the same linguistic relation. For example, if *Paris* minus *France* goes in the same direction as *Beijing* minus *China*, and as other capital–country pairs, the common offset direction can be seen as encoding the relation *capital-of*.

Thus, the idea behind the arithmetic analogy test is that offsets corresponding to the same linguistic relation, if they are the same or roughly the same, should be interchangeable. Therefore, *France* + (*Beijing* − *China*) should be the same as *France* + (*Paris* − *France*) (modulo the vector magnitude, if we are hypothesizing that it is the direction, and not the precise normed vector, that encodes the relation *capital-of:* hence the use of the cosine similarity).

The criticisms of Mikolov et al. (2013b) and the research it inspired have often been characterized as problems with "word analogies." This is ambiguous: it does not distinguish between problems with the *method* of using the arithmetic test just described for testing the presence of linguistic regularities, and the veracity of the *conclusion* that there are linguistic regularities coded in word embeddings as vector offsets. In order to resolve this ambiguity, one would need to know for sure, using some better measure, whether linguistic regularities are coded. We propose such a measure beginning in Section 4. We first analyze the key problems that have been previously raised.

3.1 Within-pair similarity

The analogy will be scored correct if b^* is the $\arg\max_x \text{sim}(b + o_a, x)$. Levy and Goldberg (2014) call this objective 3COSADD. Let us call $\text{sim}(b + o_a, b^*)$ the "analogy score." Putting aside norms, the analogy score can be decomposed as:

$$\begin{aligned} \text{sim}(b + o_a, b^*) &\propto b \cdot b^* + o_a \cdot b^* \\ &\propto b \cdot b^* + o_a \cdot o_b + o_a \cdot b \end{aligned} \qquad (3)$$

The first term, the dot product of b and b^*, is proportional to the **within-pair similarity**, $\text{sim}(b, b^*)$. The second term is proportional to the similarity between the offsets, which would appear at first glance, to be the term of principal interest in assessing whether a linguistic relation is consistently coded by the offsets. The third term is proportional to the similarity between the start word b and the offset o_a, and does not depend on b^*.

We develop an analysis of the offset similarity in sections 4–5, deriving from it the offset concentration and pairing consistency properties we propose to measure. Previous work suggested that offset similarity is not very high in practice, compared to within-pair similarity. Levy and Goldberg (2014) showed that evaluating on the basis of similarity between offsets, using PAIRDIREC-TION to determine the nearest neighbours, leads to failure on analogy tests that would otherwise succeed using the 3COSADD objective. Rogers et al. (2017) showed that within-pair similarity is correlated with performance on the standard arithmetic analogy test. Clearly, measuring whether *Paris* is similar to *France* is not the same as measuring whether the relation *capital-of* is present in the word embedding. As Levy and Goldberg point out, within-pair similarity is not irrelevant to the question—if the idea is that there is a consistent dimension *capital-of* which should constitute the principal difference between *Paris* and *France*, then the two words should otherwise be similar. But a test dominated by within-pair similarity can lead to spurious results, since pairs of words may be similar without capturing the relation in question.

Using the Bigger Analogy Test Set (BATS) (Gladkova et al., 2016) and the pre-trained Google News skip-gram embeddings of Mikolov et al. (2013a), we examine the role of the three terms of (3). BATS consists of forty relations, each composed of fifty word pairs, grouped into four broad types: inflectional morphology, derivational morphology, encyclopedic semantics (like capitals and animal sounds), and lexicographic semantics (like synonyms and antonyms). When multiple pairs exist for the same input word, we only keep the first. For each of the forty relations, we take the mean for each term over all $a:a^{*}::b:b^{*}$ tuples.

Complementing previous analyses, we display means for these three terms in Figure 1, confirming that within-pair similarity is indeed positive and large compared to the other terms. Notably, offset similarities vary between relations, but are almost always smaller. However, they are always positive.

3.2 Honest analogies: predicting input words

Linzen (2016) observes that the arithmetic analogy test, as practised, excludes a, a^{*}, and b from the $\arg\max$—otherwise, one of these input words tends (incorrectly) to be the response—most of the time, b. Rogers et al. (2017) and Schluter (2018) imply that part of the issue may be that $\|o_a\|$ is small. This cannot be why: the offsets have similar magnitudes, so if $\|o_b\|$ is long enough to bring b to b^{*}, then $\|o_a\|$ should be too. Importantly, if we compute the decomposition in (3), but suppose that b^{*} is equal to $b + o_a$ ($o_a = o_b$: the analogy score is thus always 1), we observe empirically that the within-pair similarity- and offset similarity-driven terms have similar values (Figure 8 in the appendix). This means that $\|o_a\|$ is similar to $\|b\|$. The weakness of the offset-similarity term in the score is not driven by the offsets being small.

Define Δ_{sim} as the analogy score minus the similarity of $b + o_a$ to the start word b, which must be negative in order for the "honest" analogy test to return b. We observe that Δ_{sim} is equal to:

$$\Delta_{\text{sim}} = \frac{b+o_a}{\|b+o_a\|} \cdot \left(\frac{b^{*}}{\|b^{*}\|} - \frac{b}{\|b\|} \right) \qquad (4)$$

By replacing b^{*} by $b + o_a$, we can expand the score, which is then proportional to:

$$\frac{\|b\| - \|b^{*}\|}{\|b\|} \cdot (b + o_a) \cdot b + o_a \cdot o_b + b \cdot o_b \qquad (5)$$

This decomposes Δ_{sim} into three terms. The first term is proportional to the difference between the norms of b and b^{*}, which we have empirically observed to be small, and which will be null for normalized embeddings. The second term is proportional to the offset similarity, and the third term is proportional to the similarity between b and o_b. For normalized word vectors, the third term is equal to $\text{sim}(b, b^{*}) - 1$, which is the negative cosine distance between b and b^{*}. Since $\|b\|$ and $\|b^{*}\|$ tend to be similar, we find that this is a good approximation even for non-normalized vectors. Δ_{sim} is thus negative, roughly, whenever the offset similarity is less than the cosine distance between b and b^{*}. Intuitively, the similarity of the offsets must compensate for the difference between b^{*} and b.

In Figure 2, we plot means for the three terms from (5). We observe that the first term is indeed small and can be ignored. Importantly, we observe that the offset similarity term is smaller in magnitude than the negative b–b^{*} distance term).

Linzen's observation that an input word is typically predicted under the 3CosAdd objective—and not an unrelated vocabulary word—implies that not only is Δ_{sim} negative, but that the equivalent value is negative for all words in the vocabulary. This in turn would imply (for normalized embeddings) that the similarity between o_a and the offset of b with respect to any other word is smaller than the distance between b and that word. Far from staying in the neighbourhood of b, o_a moves b in a direction far from every word in the vocabulary.

Our analysis of these known problems with word analogies details the central problem: the pairs of offsets tested are not similar enough to support the kind of arithmetic demanded by the 3CosAdd objective. An illustration of the dominance of within-pair similarity is given in Figure 3. Note that we present this figure *only* to illustrate the dominance of within-pair similarity. Two-dimensional projections are misleading: the vectors in Figure 3 do not have the property, discussed above, that the offsets are of length similar to the word vectors themselves—this is difficult to reconcile with high within-pair similarity in two dimensions.

None of this, however, implies that word embed-

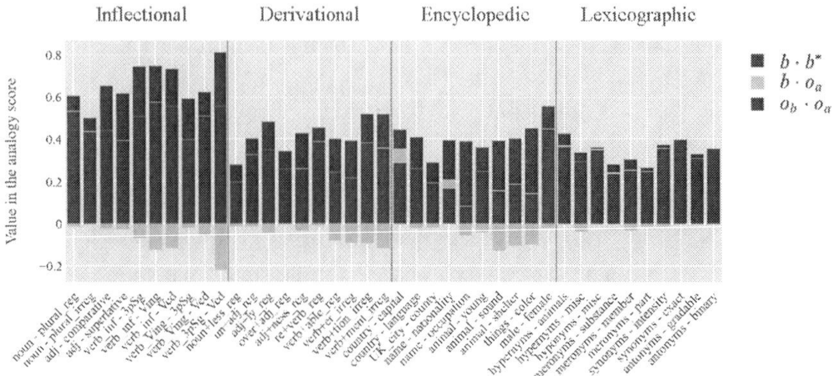

Figure 1: Decomposition of the analogy score in three terms, with only two depending on the word to predict. The largest component is $b \cdot b^*$, proportional to within-pair similarity. $b \cdot o_a$ is proportional to the similarity of the offset to the start word b. $o_b \cdot o_a$ is proportional to the similarity between offsets. All terms are divided by the same overall normalization term (not indicated in the legend).

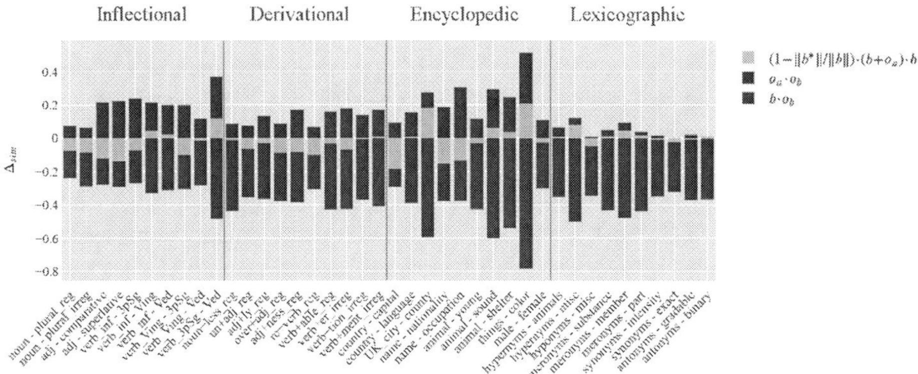

Figure 2: Decomposition of Δ_{sim}, the difference between the similarity of the analogy to b^* and to b. The term proportional to the dissimilarity of b to b^* is greater than the one proportional to the offset similarity, which means the common direction of the offset is not enough to bring the analogy closer to b^* than to b.

dings do not show linguistic regularities. It simply implies that the standard arithmetic analogy test does not measure these regularities correctly, and should not be used. While it may be true that the quantity of interest, the similarity between offsets, is generally insufficient to dominate the standard analogy test, that does not mean it is too small to be considered an encoding of a linguistic regularity. How similar is similar enough? In the following section, we propose an answer to this question.

4   Measuring Regularities

The similarity between offsets, $\text{sim}(o_a, o_b)$, is the quantity of primary interest to assess whether linguistic relations are represented as consistent directions. We seek a measure of whether they are. As noted, Levy and Goldberg (2014) showed that

$\arg\max_x \text{sim}(a^* - a, x - b)$ does not tend to find the right answer (b^*). However, the fact that b^* does not maximize offset similarity does not answer the question of what a meaningful level of offset similarity is. Rogers et al. (2017) analyzed examples of correct and false analogies and showed them to have comparable offset similarities. This makes sense: a baseline level of offset similarity can be found by looking at unrelated pairs. However, that paper examined only one isolated example.

We propose an **offset concentration score** (OCS) measuring the offset similarity among pairs belonging to the same relation and a **pairing consistency score** (PCS) measuring the distinctness of the similarities from a baseline. We propose PCS as the correct measure of linguistic regularity, with OCS a source of supplementary information.

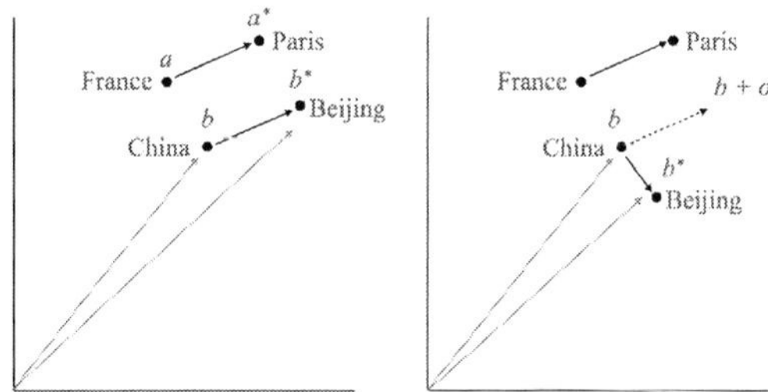

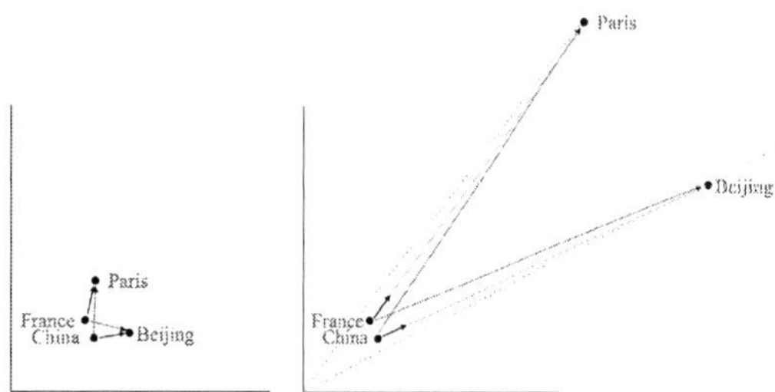

Figure 3: Schematic illustration of an analogy underlining the role of within-pair similarity in the arithmetic analogy test. At left, *China + (Paris − France)* predicts *Beijing* in part for the "right" reason (offsets are parallel). At right, the offsets are not parallel, but *Beijing* is likely to be predicted, since its cosine similarity to *China* is high. The problem is worse than the 2D schematic would suggests, since it can occur even when the word vectors are normalized, and when the offsets are quite long. *China* will be predicted if it is not excluded, since it is also in the neighbourhood.

Figure 4: Schematic illustration of an analogy underlining the pitfalls of offset concentration. At left, *Paris − France* appears nearly orthogonal to *Beijing − China*. At right, however, the offsets have much greater cosine similarity, simply because *Paris* and *Beijing* are far away. The similarity between *Paris − China* and *Beijing − France* (dotted lines) is almost as high. Unlike what might be suggested by the 2D schema, this can arise easily even for normalized word vectors.

Perfectly parallel offsets would imply that *France* and *Paris* differ on the same dimension as *China* and *Beijing*—*and on no other dimension*—and similarly for the other offsets of the same kind (*Canada−Ottawa*, ...). Perfect parallelism is not necessary for $\text{sim}(o_a, o_b)$ to contribute to success on the analogy test. By offset concentration, we mean the degree to which, for an entire set of word pairs, the offsets are parallel to one another (thus, concentrated in a single direction).

Once we take into account that offsets need not be perfectly parallel, we must bear in mind that positive cosine similarity between offsets does not imply that the embedding space captures linguistic relations. For example, recalling Schluter (2018), training embeddings to capture distributional regularities may group words into linguistic classes—with, for example, country names such as *France*, *China*..., occupying a region of the space distinct from that of *Paris*, *Beijing*..., due to distributional commonalities. This by itself could yield offset concentration: offsets would all come from a similar origin, and go to a similar destination. However, $\text{sim}(France\text{-}Paris, China\text{-}Beijing)$ would not necessarily be larger than $\text{sim}(France\text{-}Beijing, China\text{-}Paris)$. We illustrate this issue in Figure 4.

In such an example, we might be able to assert that the class of capital city names is distinct from the class of country names. But asserting that the relation *capital-__of__* is captured is a stronger property. It would require that moving from the *France*

vector in the direction of the common *capital-of* vector lead to *Paris* and not to *Beijing*, nor to any other capital city—or, at least, that it passes closer to *Paris*. We call this property pairing consistency.

4.1 Offset concentration

Figure 5 shows a histogram of the pairwise similarities between all pairs of BATS analogy offsets for the pre-trained word2vec embeddings used above, grouped by broad BATS relation type. As above, these similarities are small but generally positive. We propose an **offset concentration score**:

$$\text{OCS} = \frac{1}{N(N-1)} \sum_i \sum_{j \neq i} o_i \cdot o_j \quad (6)$$

which is the mean similarity between normalized offsets within a single relation, where the normalized offset vector o_i of a given word pair is $o_i = \frac{a_i^* - a_i}{\|a_i^* - a_i\|}$. We discuss in the appendix the link between the OCS and the mean direction of the offsets.

4.2 Pairing consistency

To measure the pairing consistency, we compare the direction of the offsets for a given set of word pairs against comparable shuffled offsets from the same BATS relation. Shuffled offsets are generated by holding the start words constant but permuting the end words (avoiding true pairs). We expect true offsets to be more parallel than shuffled offsets.

We sample sets of shuffled offsets for each relation. For each set, as for the true offsets, we

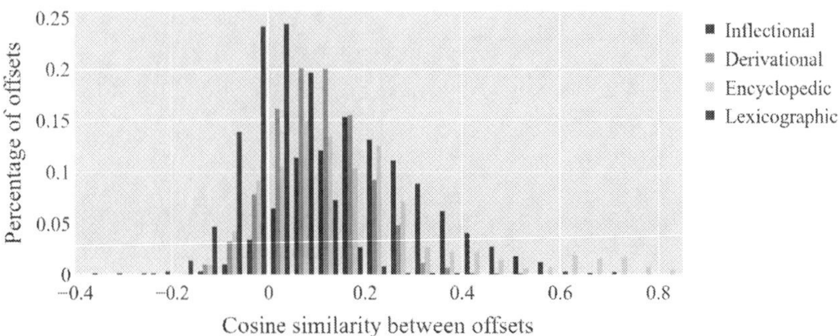

Figure 5: Distribution of the cosine similarities between vector offsets for word2vec embeddings, grouped by broad relation type. The Offset Concentration Score is the mean offset similarity for all pairs within a single relation (e.g., *country–capital*).

compute all pairwise similarities between offsets. Rather than averaging similarities as in the OCS, we calculate the separation between distributions— the true offset similarities versus each set of shuffled offset similarities. We empirically construct the receiver operating characteristic curve for linearly separating true versus shuffled similarities (i.e., setting a criterion on the similarity dimension above which offsets are true offsets and below which offsets are shuffled offsets). We calculate the area under the curve (AUC). The AUC will be 1 for perfectly separable distributions, 0.5 for indistinguishable distributions, and below 0.5 when true offsets are systematically less parallel than the baseline. We average AUC over all shuffled sets.

For any set of offsets O , we refer to the set of its offset similarities as $\mathrm{sim}(O) = \{o_i \cdot o_j, \forall (o_i, o_j) \in O^2, i < j\}$. For S_s a list of N_s sets of shuffled offsets O' (here $N_s = 50$), we define the following **pairing consistency score**, where O are the true offsets:

$$\mathrm{PCS} = \frac{1}{N_s} \sum_{O' \in S_s} \mathrm{AUC}\big(\mathrm{sim}(O), \mathrm{sim}(O')\big) \quad (7)$$

5 Exploration of word2vec

We perform a series of experiments to assess the presence of linguistic regularities in the pre-trained word2vec embeddings used above, and to show the behavior of our new measures.

5.1 Random baselines

In addition to the real BATS test, we apply our measures to artificial analogy sets, which we construct to show no pairing consistency. We seek to justify the use of pairing consistency, rather than directly using offset concentration, by demonstrating

that offset concentrations can remain non-zero even for arbitrarily associated pairs. For each BATS relation, we construct ten of each of the following types of permuted relations. We calculate the mean OCS and the mean PCS over the ten instances. We expect the mean PCS to be 0.5 in each case.

First, we construct sets of word pairs derived from the BATS by **permutation within-category**: for each category, the end words are randomly re-assigned to start words. In other words, we construct categories for which shuffling should have no effect (they are already shuffled). Comparing the OCS to that of the real BATS also allows us to measure the effect of shuffling on the OCS.

If permuted word pairs can show positive offset concentration simply because the start words and/or the end words are found in a coherent region of the embedding space, then positive OCS should be found in word pairs drawn from **mismatched categories**. For each pair of start/end word categories among the BATS relations (for example, the *noun–plural_reg* relation maps the start category *singular nouns* to the end category *regular plural nouns*), we randomly re-assign the end category (yielding, for example, *singular nouns–past tense verbs*). We then randomly construct fifty start/end pairs. We compare mismatched categories from **within** versus **across** broad BATS category types (inflectional morphology, derivational morphology, encyclopedic semantics, lexicographic semantics).

Finally, to assess the impact of the geometric coherence of words within categories on the OCS, we construct pairs without respect for category: we compare word pairs with **random start** words, **random end** words, and **random start and end** words, with ten different random word sets.

5.2 Offset concentration

Table 1 shows the OCS and PCS scores on real and randomized BATS relations using word2vec. The OCS scores for the real BATS sets are not close to one (as expected, given the results above).

The fully random set has an OCS of zero, confirming that offset concentration is unlikely to occur by chance, at least for these word vectors. The other random analogy sets all show non-zero OCS. Some random sets have even higher OCS scores than the real BATS sets. Thus, as predicted, offset concentration can exist even when linguistic relations are, by construction, not coded in any systematic way. Even the random-start and random-end pairs show non-zero OCS,[2] indicating that geometric coherence within one category is sufficient to give some degree of parallelism to the offsets. Surprisingly, the OCS is systematically lower for the permuted within-category baseline than for the mismatched-category baselines. Mismatched categories may be further apart than matched categories, reducing the angles between offsets overall.

These results have important consequences for how we measure meaningful regularities in vector embeddings. Not only is the arithmetic analogy test not fit to detect the presence of similar directions among related pairs, even if it were, similar directions alone are not sufficient to deduce that linguistic regularities are coded. The test can be dominated by spurious within-pair similarity *and* by spurious offset concentration—which can arise even when matching against random words.

5.3 Pairing consistency

The real BATS sets show PCS above chance, contrary to all random analogy sets, which show PCS of 0.5, as expected.[3] The PCS scores are low for the semantic (encyclopedic, lexicographic) relations.

In Section 3 above, we remarked that within-pair similarity is not completely irrelevant to analogies, as a higher within-pair similarity amplifies the component along the common direction. Here, the relations which show greater within-pair similarity (Figure 1) also show higher PCS.

---

[2] We observe a systematic difference between the random start and random end results, which seems to indicate a bias in the BATS analogy sets, with the end words being more susceptible to forming clusters.

[3] As noted, these scores are the mean over ten replications of the random sets. Even where the mean is not precisely 0.5, it is always within one half-interquartile-range of 0.5.

6 Comparing word embeddings

We evaluate the pairing consistency on the BATS test for popular word embeddings. We include Glove (Pennington et al., 2014), a purely distributional model similar to word2vec; two embeddings making use of external semantic knowledge: dict2vec (Tissier et al., 2017) and ConceptNet Numberbatch (Speer et al., 2017); and the static token embeddings of BERT (Devlin et al., 2019) and GPT-2 (Radford et al., 2019).

The left subfigure in Figure 6 presents the standard 3COSADD analogy test accuracy (input words excluded). Within broad relation types, we see similar results across embeddings, with a few exceptions (the static GPT-2 embeddings are poor throughout, but much better than the others on derivational morphology). Consistent with previous results using the arithmetic analogy test, derivational morphology and encyclopedic and lexical semantic relations obtain lower scores than inflectional morphology (Gladkova et al., 2016; Rogers et al., 2017).

The PCS scores are presented at right in Figure 6. The general picture is similar: there are systematic differences between relation types, and inflectional morphology tends to be well coded. However, contrary to the conclusions of the standard analogy test, the PCS reveals that Numberbatch codes linguistic relations better than the other embeddings, which is more consistent with the evaluations presented in Speer et al. (2017). The PCS also shows that derivational morphology occupies an intermediate position between inflectional morphology and semantics: word2vec, Glove, and Numberbatch in fact code derivational morphology better, in the PCS sense, than encyclopedic semantic relations. The elevated analogy test performance of some embeddings on encyclopedic relations is likely an artefact of the kind of category-level geometric coherence discussed in Section 5. As we show in the appendix in Table 2 , encyclopedic relations show higher OCS overall than derivational morphology relations, in spite of lower PCS.

7 Contributions

We have made new arguments against the use of the standard arithmetic analogy test in the evaluation of word embeddings. We show in detail how regularities in vector offsets, which are the object of primary interest for the analogy test, are, on the one hand, washed out by within-pair similarity, and,

Analogy set	Inflectional		Derivational		Encyclopedic		Lexicographic	
	OCS	PCS	OCS	PCS	OCS	PCS	OCS	PCS
Real BATS	**.295**	.851	**.156**	.679	.198	.559	.031	.539
Permuted within-category	.111	.500	.088	.500	.170	.500	.015	.500
Mismatched category (within type)	.147	.501	.120	.500	**.260**	.501	.093	.500
Mismatched category (across type)	.175	.500	.173	.500	.223	.500	**.134**	.500
Random start	.090	.500	.075	.500	.204	.499	.069	.500
Random end	.063	.500	.060	.500	.137	.501	.059	.499
Random start and end	.000	.500						

Table 1: Offset Concentration Scores and Pairing Consistency Scores for the real and random baseline analogy sets (higher is better; 0.5 is chance level for PCS). Random baseline scores are averaged across ten permutations. All scores are then averaged across BATS relations. Mismatched categories (across broad BATS relation type) are grouped along the start type. Random start and end is not assigned to a BATS type, as all the words are drawn randomly. Bold indicates the highest OCS score in a given column: we see that OCS is not always highest for real analogies. Random baseline PCS scores are always within a half-IQR of 0.5.

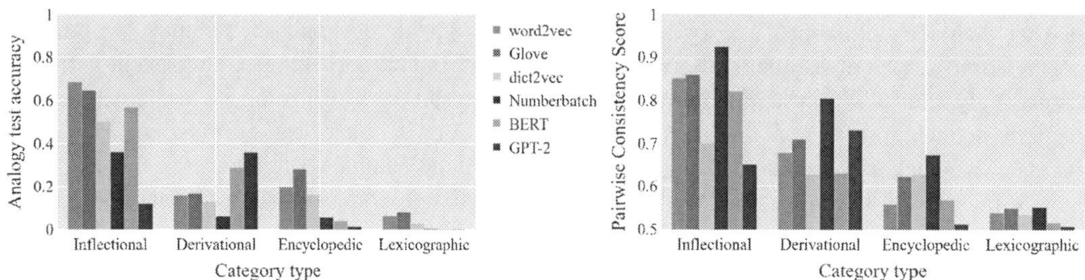

Figure 6: Left: accuracy on the standard arithmetic analogy test, across embeddings, averaged across BATS relations (within the four broad types). Right: the same figure for the Pairing Consistency Score, starting at .5 (chance-level).

on the other, insufficient to establish the existence of linguistic regularities. We explain the previously observed phenomenon that arithmetic analogy tests consistently predict the input words.

We propose a new measure of the presence of linguistic relations in word embeddings, the pairing consistency score, which measures the degree to which offsets between related pairs are parallel above chance, and the offset concentration score, a complementary measure of the absolute degree of parallelism. We show that a variety of word vectors really do capture linguistic regularities, in spite of distortions introduced by the arithmetic analogy test. We show that these distortions lead to spurious conclusions when comparing performance. Arithmetic analogy tests and loss functions based on them are deprecated and should be replaced by direct evaluation of pairing consistency.

Acknowledgments

This work was funded in part by the European Research Council (ERC-2011-AdG-295810 BOOTPHON), the Agence Nationale pour la Recherche (ANR-17-EURE-0017 Frontcog, ANR-17-CE28-0009 GEOMPHON, ANR-10-IDEX-0001-02 PSL*, ANR-19-P3IA-0001 PRAIRIE 3IA Institute, ANR-18-IDEX-0001 U de Paris, ANR-10-LABX-0083 EFL) and grants from CIFAR (Learning in Machines and Brains), Facebook AI Research (Research Grant), Google (Faculty Research Award), Microsoft Research (Azure Credits and Grant), and Amazon Web Service (AWS Research Credits).

References

Carl Allen and Timothy Hospedales. 2019. Analogies Explained: Towards Understanding Word Embeddings. In *Proceedings of the 36th International Conference on Machine Learning*, volume 97 of *Proceedings of Machine Learning Research*, pages 223–231, Long Beach, California, USA. PMLR.

Zied Bouraoui, Shoaib Jameel, and Steven Schockaert. 2018. Relation Induction in Word Embeddings Revisited. In *Proceedings of the 27th International Conference on Computational Linguistics*, pages 1627–1637, Santa Fe, New Mexico, USA. Association for Computational Linguistics.

Dawn Chen, Joshua C. Peterson, and Thomas L. Griffiths. 2017. Evaluating vector-space models of analogy. *CoRR*, abs/1705.04416.

Jacob Devlin, Ming-Wei Chang, Kenton Lee, and Kristina Toutanova. 2019. BERT: Pre-training of Deep Bidirectional Transformers for Language Understanding. In *Proceedings of the 2019 Conference of the North American Chapter of the Association for Computational Linguistics: Human Language Technologies, Volume 1 (Long and Short Papers)*, pages 4171–4186, Minneapolis, Minnesota. Association for Computational Linguistics.

Aleksandr Drozd, Anna Gladkova, and Satoshi Matsuoka. 2016. Word Embeddings, Analogies, and Machine Learning: Beyond King - Man + Woman = Queen. In *Proceedings of COLING 2016, the 26th International Conference on Computational Linguistics: Technical Papers*, pages 3519–3530, Osaka, Japan, December 11-17.

Kawin Ethayarajh, David Duvenaud, and Graeme Hirst. 2019. Towards Understanding Linear Word Analogies. In *Proceedings of the 57th Annual Meeting of the Association for Computational Linguistics*, pages 3253–3262, Florence, Italy. Association for Computational Linguistics.

Gregory Finley, Stephanie Farmer, and Serguei Pakhomov. 2017. What Analogies Reveal about Word Vectors and their Compositionality. In *Proceedings of the 6th Joint Conference on Lexical and Computational Semantics (*SEM 2017)*, pages 1–11, Vancouver, Canada. Association for Computational Linguistics.

Anna Gladkova, Aleksandr Drozd, and Satoshi Matsuoka. 2016. Analogy-Based Detection of Morphological and Semantic Relations with Word Embeddings: What Works and What Doesn't. In *Proceedings of the NAACL-HLT SRW*, pages 47–54, San Diego, California, June 12-17, 2016. ACL.

Omer Levy and Yoav Goldberg. 2014. Linguistic Regularities in Sparse and Explicit Word Representations. In *Proceedings of the Eighteenth Conference on Computational Natural Language Learning*, pages 171–180, Ann Arbor, Michigan. Association for Computational Linguistics.

Tal Linzen. 2016. Issues in Evaluating Semantic Spaces Using Word Analogies. In *Proceedings of the First Workshop on Evaluating Vector Space Representations for NLP*. Association for Computational Linguistics.

Tomas Mikolov, Kai Chen, Greg Corrado, and Jeffrey Dean. 2013a. Efficient Estimation of Word Representations in Vector Space. In *Proceedings of International Conference on Learning Representations (ICLR)*.

Tomas Mikolov, Wen-tau Yih, and Geoffrey Zweig. 2013b. Linguistic Regularities in Continuous Space Word Representations. In *Proceedings of NAACL-HLT 2013*, pages 746–751, Atlanta, Georgia, 9–14 June 2013.

Denis Newman-Griffis, Albert Lai, and Eric Fosler-Lussier. 2017. Insights into Analogy Completion from the Biomedical Domain. In *BioNLP 2017*, pages 19–28, Vancouver, Canada,. Association for Computational Linguistics.

Malvina Nissim, Rik van Noord, and Rob van der Goot. 2020. Fair Is Better than Sensational: Man Is to Doctor as Woman Is to Doctor. *Computational Linguistics*, 46(2):487–497.

Jeffrey Pennington, Richard Socher, and Christopher Manning. 2014. GloVe: Global Vectors for Word Representation. In *Proceedings of the 2014 Conference on Empirical Methods in Natural Language Processing (EMNLP)*, pages 1532–1543, Doha, Qatar. Association for Computational Linguistics.

Alec Radford, Jeffrey Wu, Rewon Child, David Luan, Dario Amodei, and Ilya Sutskever. 2019. Language Models are Unsupervised Multitask Learners. *OpenAI Blog*, 1(8):9.

Anna Rogers. 2019. On word analogies and negative results in NLP. *Hacking Semantics*.

Anna Rogers, Aleksandr Drozd, and Bofang Li. 2017. The (Too Many) Problems of Analogical Reasoning with Word Vectors. In *Proceedings of the 6th Joint Conference on Lexical and Computational Semantics (* SEM 2017)*, pages 135–148.

Natalie Schluter. 2018. The Word Analogy Testing Caveat. In *Proceedings of the 2018 Conference of the North American Chapter of the Association for Computational Linguistics: Human Language Technologies, Volume 2 (Short Papers)*, pages 242–246, New Orleans, Louisiana. Association for Computational Linguistics.

Robyn Speer, Joshua Chin, and Catherine Havasi. 2017. ConceptNet 5.5: An Open Multilingual Graph of General Knowledge. In *Proceedings of the Thirty-First AAAI Conference on Artificial Intelligence*, AAAI'17, page 4444–4451. AAAI Press.

Julien Tissier, Christophe Gravier, and Amaury Habrard. 2017. Dict2vec : Learning Word Embeddings using Lexical Dictionaries. In *Proceedings of the 2017 Conference on Empirical Methods in Natural Language Processing*, pages 254–263, Copenhagen, Denmark. Association for Computational Linguistics.

Ekaterina Vylomova, Laura Rimell, Trevor Cohn, and Timothy Baldwin. 2016. Take and Took, Gaggle and Goose, Book and Read: Evaluating the Utility of Vector Differences for Lexical Relation Learning. In *Proceedings of the 54th Annual Meeting of the Association for Computational Linguistics (Volume 1: Long Papers)*, pages 1671–1682, Berlin, Germany. Association for Computational Linguistics.

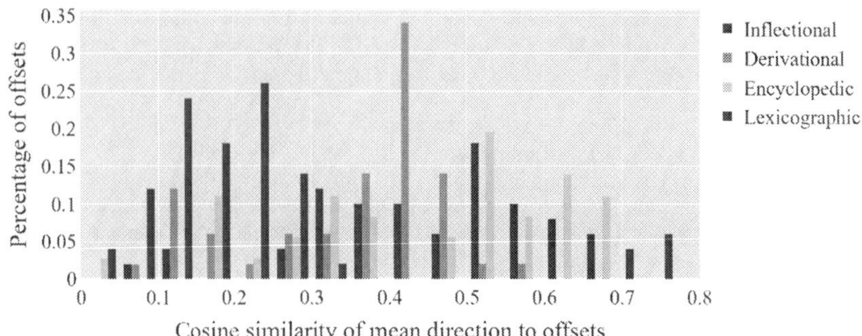

Figure 7: Distribution of the cosine similarity of vector offsets to the mean direction for the default word2vec embeddings for each category, then grouped by broad type. The mean similarity improves the similarity even for anisotropic offsets, as discussed. Variance changes seem category dependent.

Appendix A: The offsets' mean direction

For a set of offsets, the OCS measures how concentrated the hypercone of the offsets is. The center of this hypercone is the average normalized offset d, the unit vector defined by

$$d \propto \sum_i \frac{a_i^* - a_i}{\|a_i^* - a_i\|} \qquad (8)$$

This vector has different interesting properties. First, we can note that it is the unit vector maximizing the sum of the similarities of the offsets with it. With the normalized offsets $o_i = \frac{a_i^* - a_i}{\|a_i^* - a_i\|}$,

$$d = \arg\max_{u, \|u\|=1} \sum_i o_i \cdot u \qquad (9)$$

Furthermore, let's define MSM, the mean similarity of d to the offsets. We can first prove that the MSM is equal to the norm of d before normalization:

$$\mathrm{MSM} = \frac{1}{N} \sum_j \mathrm{sim}\Big(\frac{\frac{1}{N}\sum_i o_i}{\|\frac{1}{N}\sum_i o_i\|}, o_j\Big)$$

$$= \frac{1}{N} \cdot \frac{\sum_i o_i \sum_j o_j}{\|\sum_i o_i\|} = \Big\|\frac{1}{N} \cdot \sum_i o_i\Big\| \qquad (10)$$

Indeed, the average offset will have a norm close to 1 if the offsets are higly similar, but close to 0 if they are anisotropic. We can now go further and link the MSM to the OCS.

$$\frac{1}{N^2}\Big\|\sum_i o_i\Big\|^2 = \frac{1}{N^2}\Big(\sum_i o_i^2 + \sum_i \sum_{j \neq i} o_i \cdot o_j\Big)$$

$$= \frac{1}{N} + \frac{N(N-1)}{N^2} \cdot \mathrm{OCS}$$

$$\mathrm{MSM} = \sqrt{\frac{1}{N} + \frac{(N-1)}{N} \cdot \mathrm{OCS}} \qquad (11)$$

This result shows that the MSM is a strict (parabolic) improvement to the OCS, with a computable baseline decreasing with N. For BATS, $N = 50$ (if all words are in the vocabulary), and thus the minimal MSM is $\sqrt{1/50} \approx 0.14$ even for anisotropic offsets (with an OCS $= 0$). This score shows that offset concentration can be quickly amplified in unrealistic ways. Still, we can consider d as a close representation of the offsets' relation. We display in Figure 7 the distribution of the similarities of the offsets to d.

Appendix B: Additional figures

Embedding	Inflectional				Derivational				Encyclopedic				Lexicographic			
	Analogy		Metrics		Analogy		Metrics		Analogy		Metrics		Analogy		Metrics	
	N	H	OCS	PCS	N	H	OCS	PCS	N	H	OCS	PCS	N	H	OCS	PCS
word2vec	.686	.099	.295	.851	.158	.005	.156	.679	.198	.203	.198	.559	.063	.006	.031	.539
Glove	.645	.224	.345	.860	.167	.022	.237	.710	.281	.122	.255	.623	.080	.008	.004	.550
dict2vec	.503	.001	.099	.700	.127	.000	.079	.630	.162	.050	.213	.628	.030	.006	.024	.534
Numberbatch	.360	.226	.357	.924	.060	.029	.224	.805	.056	.066	.251	.674	.004	.006	.034	.552
BERT tokens	.568	.018	.217	.821	.288	.229	.178	.632	.041	.073	.151	.569	.002	.015	.016	.517
GPT-2 tokens	.119	.019	.097	.651	.359	.248	.270	.732	.014	.050	.071	.513	.003	.011	.011	.508

Table 2: Comparison of analogy test scores and our OCS and PCS metrics for different word embeddings, grouped by broad type. N designates the Normal analogy test scores, and H the Honest analogy test scores where the input words are allowed to be predicted. OCS and PCS designate the Offsets Concentration Scores and Pairwise Consistency Scores. Bold means highest score for this type.

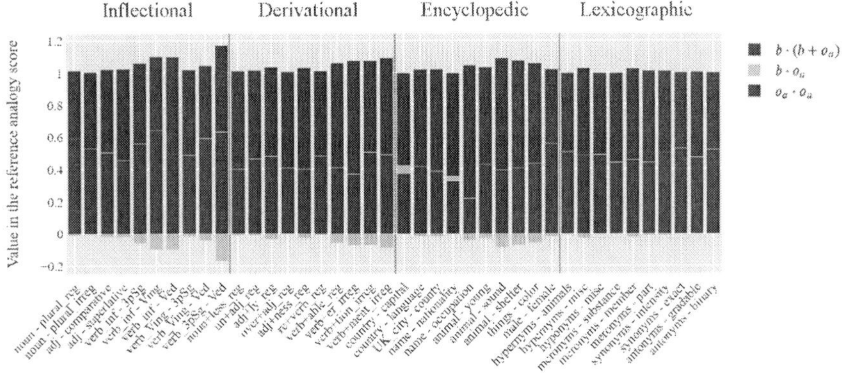

Figure 8: Decomposition of the analogy score if $o_a = o_b$ (the score being therefore equal to 1). The similar values of $b \cdot (b + o_a)$ and $o_a \cdot o_a$ indicates that the length of o_a and b is similar, and thus that the offset length does not explain the low value of $o_a \cdot o_b$ in the real decomposition.

Word associations and the distance properties of context-aware word embeddings

Maria A. Rodriguez
University of Geneva
Maria.AnduezaRodriguez@unige.ch

Paola Merlo
University of Geneva
Paola.Merlo@unige.ch

Abstract

What do people know when they know the meaning of words? Word associations have been widely used to tap into lexical representations and their structure, as a way of probing semantic knowledge in humans. We investigate whether current word embedding spaces (contextualized and uncontextualized) can be considered good models of human lexical knowledge by studying whether they have comparable characteristics to human association spaces. We study the three properties of association rank, asymmetry of similarity and triangle inequality.

We find that word embeddings are good models of some word associations properties. They replicate well human associations between words, and, like humans, their context-aware variants show violations of the triangle inequality. While they do show asymmetry of similarities, their asymmetries do not map those of human association norms.

1 Introduction

What do people know when they know the meaning of words? Lexical semantic knowledge is rich and structured and comprises the knowledge of the relation between a word and its related concept, the relationships between concepts among themselves and between words themselves. Word associations —spontaneous elicitation of words by similarity, contrast or contiguity— have been widely used to tap into lexical representations and their structure, as a way of probing semantic knowledge in humans (De Deyne and Storms, 2014).

To process language in a way that mirrors human expectations and to develop usable technology, we need computational representations of the meaning of words that correspond to speakers' knowledge of words (De Deyne et al., 2016). Current word embeddings methods, without context or context-aware, represent lexical semantic knowledge as

coordinates in a multi-dimensional space. Work in cognitive psychology, however, has argued that human lexical knowledge and in particular word associations are not well represented by geometrical models (Tversky, 1977; Gati and Tversky, 1982; Tversky and Hutchinson, 1986). More precisely, similarity judgments of associations in humans have been shown not to exhibit the properties of true distances. For example, associations are not symmetric: speakers will indicate that North Korea is more similar to China than China is to North Korea.

In an analysis inspired by Tversky (1977)'s critique of spatial measures of similarity in word associations, and by recent work on topic models and word embeddings (Griffiths et al., 2007; Nematzadeh et al., 2017), we compare current word embedding spaces to the large human norming study by Nelson et al. (2004) and investigate whether these word embedding spaces, especially those based on transformers, —the lexical representations used by almost all our current architectures— share some properties with human word associations, as human-like representations of lexical meaning.

2 Word Associations

The task of word free association consists in providing a *cue* word to a speaker and asking to produce, fast and without thinking, other words that come to mind, called the *target* words. These collections of free associations present interesting characteristics. First, they present a certain stability across speakers, so that it is possible to determine the most associated word on average, the second most associated and so forth. Second, they present interesting qualitative properties. They exhibit asymmetry of similarity judgments, as in the example on China and North Korea above. Finally, they also exhibit

376

Proceedings of the 24th Conference on Computational Natural Language Learning, pages 376–385
Online, November 19-20, 2020. ©2020 Association for Computational Linguistics
https://doi.org/10.18653/v1/P17

EXP.	DESCRIPTION	WORD EMBEDDING	HYPOTHESIS	METHOD
1	Find the top-k neighbors near the cue	BERT not in context, lemmatized and unlemmatized	Top-k near cue in BERT are associates in human associations.	kNN, median rank and P@K
2.1	Asymmetry of countries	BERT in context	Non-prominent countries are more similar to prominent countries than vice versa.	Cosine
2.2	Asymmetries as frequencies	Output of Exp.1	Frequent words are more often associates of less frequent words than vice versa.	Cues and targets from Nelson, cues and targets from Exp. 1; hits of Google's search engine.
2.3	Asymmetries of hypernyms and hyponyms	BERT in context	If salience = 'more general', hyponyms are more similar to hypernyms than the reverse. If salience = 'more specific', the effect is the opposite.	Nouns and verbs from Nelson; hypernyms/hyponyms from WordNet; cosine.
2.4	Asymmetry as neighbourhood density	BERT not in context unlemmatized; FastText (only for countries)	A semantically richer word elicits a greater number of close neighbours than a fainter word.	Extraction of asymmetric pairs from Nelson; kNN; cosine (threshold ≥ 0.2)
3	Violation of triangle inequality	BERT in context	BERT embedding space violates the triangle inequality.	Extraction of asymmetric triples; cosine, τ threshold.

Figure 1: Summary of experiments.

violation of transitivity (called in the literature, violation of the triangle inequality). For example, *asteroid* is highly associated with *belt*, and *belt* is highly associated with *buckle*, but *asteroid* and *buckle* show little association.

Feature-based explanations of these properties makes use of the richness of the representation, in terms of number of features and the proportion of shared features between two representations (Tversky, 1977). For example, the asymmetry of similarity is explained by the assumption that only a few of the large number of features in speakers' mental representation of China are shared with North Korea, while the representation of North Korea involves a small number of features, many of which are shared with China. More recent approaches have proposed probabilistic representations in terms of topic models (Griffiths et al., 2007). Violation of the triangle inequality is explained in these models as an effect of the fact that topic models represent different uses of a word as different topics, and different topics do not necessarily preserve similarity.

We investigate whether current word embedding spaces can be considered good models of human lexical knowledge by studying whether they have comparable characteristics to human association spaces. We study the three properties of associations mentioned above: rank, asymmetry of similarity and violation of triangle inequality (lack of transitivity). More specifically, first, we verify that the notion of word association makes sense in word embedding spaces and compare if the target words

that occur as preferentially associated with a cue word in a word embedding space correspond to the closest words in human association norms.

Then, we analyse asymmetry in similarity in several different ways: we look at its correlation with cue and target frequency, with neighbourhood densities and lexical entailment. Finally, we model violations of triangle inequality by looking at how similarity of words spreads across word embedding spaces. A summary of the experiments discussed in more detail in the following sections is given in Figure 1.

3 Data

To perform the studies indicated above, we use two sets of artificial word embedding data, and one set of human association norms.

3.1 Word embedding data

BERT Devlin et al. (2018) propose BERT, a transformer-based model that uses an attention mechanism to extract the context of words and subwords from text. The innovation of BERT is the application of a bi-directional training to the Transformer, achieving a better use of context from text than systems with unidirectional training. BERT is pretrained on the BookCorpus (800M words) and English Wikipedia (2500M words). The BookCorpus (Zhu et al., 2015) is a collection of 11,038 books available on the Web, from 16 different genres, taking into account only books with more than 20K words to avoid noise coming from shorter stories. In all experiments below, we use the Hugginface version of BERT[1], specifically the "bert-base-uncased" model that we expressly do not modify.

FastText The original FASTTEXT model is based on Wikipedia dumps[2] in nine differerent languages including English (Bojanowski et al., 2017). However, in this work, we used the pre-trained FASTTEXT embeddings provided by the official site of FASTTEXT, that we expressly do not modify.[3] The embeddings are trained on 600-billion tokens from CommonCrawl[4], resulting in two-million word vectors with subword information.

3.2 Human word association norms

Nelson et al. (2004) propose a large dataset of free association, rhyme and word fragment norms, elicited from more than 6000 participants. The participants were asked to write the first word that came to mind when presented a particular stimulus word. More than 750'000 free associations (called targets) from a total of 5019 stimulus words (called cues) were collected. The related quantitative information (such as number of participants and measures of association strength) were calculated.[5]

Other word association norms exist, such as the Small World of Words (De Deyne et al., 2019), but in this study, we wanted to be able to compare, at least indirectly, our work to previous work where the Nelson's norms were used (Griffiths et al., 2007; Nematzadeh et al., 2017).

4 Experiment 1: The notion of association

To simulate the process of production of associates of a free association task, we used the k-nearest neighbours algorithm (kNN) to find the top-k words that are near the cue. The intuition is that words near the cue word in the embedding space are probably associates. We use cosine similarity as the metric to find the nearest neighbours.

We compare if the target words that occur as preferentially associated with a cue word in a word embedding space correspond to the closest words in human association norms. For this comparison,

Rank	Unlemmatized		Lemmatized	
	Median Rank	P@K (%)	Median Rank	P@K (%)
1	4	13.02	3	24.18
2	12	28.09	10	43.26
3	35	43.64	27	55.86
4	94	53.59	69	64.53
5	230	61.62	157.5	69.94

Table 1: Results of Experiment 1 for the unlemmatized and lemmatized data. For each rank in human associations (Rank column), we computed the median ranking on the basis of the BERT vector space. Furthermore, we computed the precision at K (P@K with K = 1, 2, 3, 4, 5 corresponding to the ranks) where we check if the first associate in the human associations appears in the top K associates of BERT.

we use two measures: median ranking and P@k, following Griffiths et al. (2007).

Method As human associations in Nelson are lemmatized, we tested both the lemmatized and unlemmatized versions on the "raw" BERT word embeddings obtained from the vocabulary of the model. [6]

The median rank is a measure of central tendency of the median rank in BERT for the n-ranked associate target in Nelson. For example, in Figure 2 for the unlemmatized data, we would have to take the median across ranks of the ranks given in BERT (1, 1, 2, 32, 22) for the first ranked target in Nelson.

This measure is calculated as follows. For each cue in Nelson, we extract the top-k nearest neighbours in the BERT space and rank the results by their cosine similarity in descending order. Then, for each same cue and each one of its targets in Nelson, we calculate the target's rank in BERT (see Figure 2). The median of these ranks is calculated for each of the Nelson's rank (see Table 1).

Using the same ranked lists, we calculate Precision at K (P@K), where $K = 1, 2, 3, 4, 5$. P@K tells us if the first associate in the human associa-

---

[1]https://github.com/huggingface/transformers

[2]https://dumps.wikimedia.org

[3]https://fasttext.cc/docs/en/english-vectors.html

[4]https://commoncrawl.org

[5]The words we use in this work are found in appendix A and B in Nelson et al. (2004). Appendix A presents the list of targets produced by each cue and Appendix B presents the list of cues that elicit a particular target.

[6]These raw vectors come with the pre-trained model of BERT. They are extracted from the vocabulary of the model, thus not in context. They can be downloaded from `https://github.com/ajitrajasekharan/bert_mask`. Their unlemmatized version uses the words and the embeddings as they come with the model. Their lemmatized words are derived using the WordNet lemmatizer from NLTK `http://www.nltk.org/api/nltk.stem.html#module-nltk.stem.wordnet` and the word embeddings corresponding to a lemmatised word is the sum of all the word embeddings of the unlemmatised word forms.

	ABDOMEN	YELL	SAW	RISE	NECESSARY
	Unlemmatized				
Human Associations	**stomach (1)**	**shout (1)**	**see (2)**	lift (32)	important (22)
	belly (4)	scream (5)	hammer (207)	fall (37)	need (27)
	organ (3399)	whisper (27)	look (239)	stand (38)	must (263)
	body (4418)	loud (189)	cut (294)	wake (72)	money (11869)
	muscle (8368)	cheer (194)	tool (350)	shine (73)	object (13096)
BERT Predictions	**stomach**	**shout**	sees	rises	required
	abdominal	yells	**see**	risen	needed
	torso	yelled	seen	rising	essential
	belly	yelling	seeing	Rise	unnecessary
	groin	scream	Saw	rose	appropriate
	Lemmatized				
Human Associations	**stomach (1)**	**shout (1)**	**see (1)**	lift (23)	**need (3)**
	belly (4)	scream (3)	look (57)	lower (25)	important (20)
	organ (217)	whisper (15)	hammer (80)	fall (43)	must (221)
	body (250)	noise (39)	cut (221)	wake (52)	object (1867)
	sex (276)	anger (83)	tool (229)	stand (70)	money (9684)
BERT Predictions	**stomach**	**shout**	**see**	Rising	essential
	abdominal	yelled	Saw	arise	require
	torso	scream	noticed	raise	**need**
	belly	roar	felt	ascend	unnecessary
	groin	growl	heard	Rise	appropriate

Figure 2: Unlemmatized and lemmatized rankings in word associations from Nelson et al. (2004) and from BERT predictions, listed in descending order from the first to the fifth rank. Human associations are ranked by cosine similarity. In parentheses, the rankings of the human associations in the BERT space. See the text for how the examples were chosen.

tions appears in the top-k associates of BERT. For example, Figure 2 for the unlemmatized data shows a P@K=1 of 2 out of 5 and a P@K=3 of 3 out of 5. For the lemmatized data, we have a P@K=1 of 3 out of 5 and a P@K=3 of 4 out of 5.

Results The results are shown in Table 1 and examples are shown in Figure 2. The median BERT ranking for the first human associate in unlemmatized and lemmatized associations is respectively 4 and 3.

For the unlemmatized version, the first associate in the human word associations is the word with the highest ranking in BERT in 13.02% of cases and in the top 5 ranks of BERT in 61.62% of the cases. For the lemmatized version, these values improve to, respectively, 24.18% of cases and 69.62% of the cases.

As can be seen in Table 2, the results in BERT are convincing. For the unlemmatized data, the first three columns show examples where BERT ranks the right associate at or near the top of its list. The last two columns are examples of not very good association rankings in BERT. Notice the third column, which shows the limitations of an unlemmatized approach as BERT does not correctly distinguish between forms of the same word. For the lemmatized data, we see an improvement in

the prediction of BERT: the rankings of the human associations are in general lower than the rankings of the unlemmatized version. As a measure of indirect comparison, previous work (Griffiths et al., 2007) indicates that a topic model trained on the TASA corpus (Landauer and Dumais, 1997)[7], and compared to the same norms by Nelson's gives a median rank of 50.5 and predicts the first associate correctly in 10.24% of cases with an improvement of over 60% over a frequency baseline. They indicate that this improvement over the baseline results from having reduced dimensionality. Clearly, word embeddings benefit from similar properties, and to an even greater extent, being trained on much larger data sets and being based on non-linear dimensionality reductions.

5 Experiment 2: Asymmetries

Perhaps more interestingly than simple ranking measures, human word associations also exhibit peculiar qualitative properties that computational systems must also exhibit if they want to be considered human-like. These properties are especially interesting in a discussion of word embeddings as they seem to specifically defy a representation of

---

[7]This is a collection of reading materials spanning the school years from grade school to college.

the lexicon as a geometric space, in that they violate metric axioms, such as symmetry of distances and the triangle inequality.

Our intuition is, however, that context-aware word embeddings are no longer linear geometric representations in multi-dimensional space and that, as such, could mirror the geometrically-warped properties of human associations. For this reason, we use cosine, a symmetric similarity operator: any asymmetry found this way is to be ascribed to the context-aware vector and not to the similarity operator. Here we want to model the asymmetric association between cue and target words (Tversky, 1977). We want to model the intuition that these asymmetries stem from a richer and more specific representation for certain words (like China) and less specific or vaguer representation for less salient words (like North Korea).

5.1 Experiment 2.1: Asymmetry of countries

We start by testing the data discussed in Tversky (1977). It has been observed that in contexts that elicit similarity, the more prominent word is preferentially the second element in the similarity. So, for example, speakers prefer *North Korea is similar to China* to *China is similar to North Korea*.

Twenty-one pairs of country names served as stimuli. The pairs were constructed so that one element was more prominent (A) than the other (B) (e.g., China-North Korea, USA-Mexico, Belgium-Luxembourg). We used the pairs found in Tversky and Gati (1978), but also updated the list of countries. As Tversky's list was created in the 70s, some countries do not exist today or have changed their name (e.g., USSR is replaced by Russia, West Germany by Germany, Ceylon by Sri Lanka).[8]

Method Following Tversky's experimental procedure, we contextualised word embeddings of the country names by setting the names in three context sentences: "A is similar to B", "A is essentially B" and "A is roughly B". We indicate this context below as (A, B). As we wanted to test asymmetries, we also constructed these sentences in the opposite direction e.g. "B is similar to A". We indicate this context below as (B, A). In what follows, A refers to prominent countries and B to less prominent countries, so people prefer "B is similar to A".

On this basis, we used the sentences as input for BERT, we extracted the word vectors (in context)

Context	$cos(B, A) \geq cos(A, B)$
A is similar to B	76.19%
A is essentially B	57.14%
A is roughly B	66.67%

Table 2: Results of Experiment 2.1: percent of times the cosine similarity in BERT is higher when the more prominent country is in second position ($cos(B, A)$), matching people's preferences, compared to when it is in first position ($cos(A, B)$).

of each country name and we tested, for example, if $cos(A{=}China, B{=}NK){\geq}cos(B{=}NK, A{=}China)$ or if $cos(B{=}NK, A{=}China){\geq}cos(A{=}China, B{=}NK)$.

Since BERT spaces take context into account, they should be able to detect the differences between the order of the words in the context and if they replicate human associations, we should find that $cos(B{=}NK, A{=}China){\geq}cos(A{=}China, B{=}NK)$ more often than the reverse.

Results As showed by Table 2, the cosine similarity is higher when the less prominent country is in the first position. This results, then, confirms human judgements. But why is it so?

The explanation for the human result has been in terms of richness of representation and the relative proportion of common features and contrasting features, features unique to one of the two elements being compared (Tversky's contrast model). Griffiths et al. (2007) also show, however, that frequency is a strong predictor of salience, so that this effect could be simply due to frequency. We verify then how much frequency in general is related to salience.

5.2 Experiment 2.2: Asymmetries as frequencies

Frequency is a strong aspect of saliency and it could be that frequent words are more often evoked as associates of less frequent words than vice versa (Griffiths et al., 2007).

Method We use the hits of Google's search engine, because the British National Corpus[9], a properly balanced corpus of over 100 million tokens, did not contain all the countries we needed. We find that more prominent countries are more frequent than less prominent countries in 76.19% of the cases. The results are the same if we use the updated list of countries.

---

[8]The word lists are shown in the supplementary materials.

[9]http://www.natcorp.ox.ac.uk/

Rank	Avg Frequency Word Association	Avg Frequency BERT
1	1369	8716
2	1942	8432
3	2804	9691
4	2696	10619
5	2546	13136

Table 3: Results of Experiment 2.2 for unlemmatized associations. For each rank, we compute the average frequency of the targets in human associations and BERT predictions for a given cue.

Context	Mean cos(he,ho)	Mean cos(ho,he)	p-value
similar	0.452	0.443	< 0.0001
essentially	0.455	0.447	< 0.0001
roughly	0.450	0.443	< 0.0001

Table 4: Paired samples t-test on asymmetric verbs and nouns with He/Ho relation extracted from human word associations with BERT.

Given that we know that word embeddings encode information about the frequency of the underlying words (Schnabel et al., 2015), then the effect of country similarity could be an effect of frequency.

Could a frequency explanation, though, be extended to all words in BERT embeddings? We quantify the frequency of each cue ($freq_{cue}$) and target word ($freq_{target}$). As in Experiment 1, we conduct two tests for unlemmatized and lemmatized data. We used both unlemmatized and lemmatized lists of words in the British National Corpus to retrieve the frequency of words. Then, we extract from the corpus both the pairs of cues and targets from Nelson's human associations and the pairs from BERT, ordered by the rankings obtained in Experiment 1.

Results As shown in Table 3, the average frequency for unlemmatized (and lemmatized) associations in BERT is higher than in human word associations.

The human associations confirm what had already been found in Griffiths et al. (2007): cues tend to elicit targets with higher frequencies than themselves. Precisely, in the unlemmatized version, 62.95% of associations have a target with higher frequency. In contrast, if we compute the frequency of the targets found by BERT, we find that only 30% of associations have a target with higher frequency.

This indicates that, in general, if we were to find human-like asymmetric judgments of similarity in

BERT spaces it would not be a frequency effect. The question remains, however, of how to operationalise the notion of salience.

5.3 Experiment 2.3: Asymmetry of hypernyms and hyponyms

Similarly to the experiment in section 5.1, we also tested the asymmetric associations where cues and targets are common nouns and verbs, and not proper nouns. Unlike proper nouns, such as country names, whose salience is related to the external world and the prominence of the referred country in it, for common nouns and verbs, the notion of salience also needs to be defined in linguistic terms, possibly as richness of representation.

We test here two possible interpretations that make opposite predictions in the case of common nouns and verbs: a rich representation can be interpreted as meaning 'more prototypical, more general', but also 'more specified'. These two operationalisations can be teased apart by looking at lexical entailment: the hypernym is more general and the hyponym is more specified. We conducted a test where the cue-target pairs were in a hyponym-hypernym relation, for short Ho/He relation.

Pairs of nouns and pairs of verbs were extracted from the Appendix A of Nelson et al. (2004), using only asymmetric pairs for a total of 2735 pairs. We further extract the pairs that are in a hyponym-hypernym relation using WordNet (Miller, 1995). If the target possesses some hyponyms in Wordnet, then we check that there is a hyponym that has the same category as the target in the list of hyponyms, i.e. if the target is a verb then the hyponym, in addition to being an existing association of the target, has to be the first verb in the list of hyponyms. We extracted a total of 79 pairs of verbs and 573 pairs of nouns.[10] From these pairs, we constructed three types of sentences, as in section 5.1.

Depending on whether salience and richness of representation means 'more general' or 'more specific', we have two different expectations. If it means 'more general', then we should find the same effect as for proper nouns, where the preference is for the hyponym to be more similar to the hypernym than the reverse (e.g. *Dancing is similar to moving, A dog is essentially an animal*), an intuitive preference.

But an interpretation as 'more specified' yields a different prediction. In a He/Ho pair, the relation

---

[10]The word lists are shown in the supplementary materials.

is formalised by subsumption, so the features of the hypernym are all present in the representation of the hyponym. Hence, the number of matching features will be a greater proportion for the hypernym than for the hyponym and thus the expectation is reversed. We expect to prefer *Moving is similar to dancing, An animal is essentially a dog*, which does not seem natural.

The results in Table 4 show that, in general, the (He, Ho) pairs have a higher cosine similarity than (Ho, He) pairs. In all contexts, these results are confirmed by a paired samples t-test, where p-value< 0.05. This confirms that BERT spaces encode salience in terms of richness of specifying features. But this is contrary to human intuition, at least to our intuition, which appears to prefer to identify salience with prototypicality and generality.

5.4 Experiment 2.4: Asymmetry as neighbourhood density

The intuition of vectorial spaces is that the meaning of a word is determined by the neighbouring words. If that is the case, then, a semantically richer word will elicit a greater number of close neighbours than a fainter word. We model this asymmetry by looking at the density of neighbouring words.

Method We extract words from human associations where we can find an asymmetric association: the cue word produces a certain target, but this specific target does not produce back the initial cue. There are 18'571 of these pairs of words. We compute the density around these words in the embedding space using kNN with cosine as the metric. We quantify the number of associates around a word given a threshold for the cosine similarity ($cosine \geq 0.2$). The threshold 0.2 was chosen to have enough data to analyse, a higher threshold would not provide samples with adequate numbers of responses.

Results In human associations, there is an imbalance between cue and target suggesting that targets are more salient, so that we expect them to have a denser neighbourhood in vectorial space. But in BERT's vectors corresponding to human asymmetric associations (those where a cue elicits a target but not the reverse), the target is denser than the cue in only 26.58% of cases.[11]

We also tested the country data described in section 5.1 with the same procedure. The results show that the more prominent country has a higher density in 23.8% of cases. Recall that this result is not a frequency effect, as indicated by the country frequencies reported in experiment 2.2.[12]

In conclusion, context-aware vectorial spaces do not encode asymmetries in similarities analogously to human associations. In human associations, targets are more frequent, and more general, while in vectorial spaces only targets as proper nouns are more frequent, but both common nouns and verbs as targets are less frequent, more specific and have a sparser neighbourhood than their cues.

6 Experiment 3: Violations of triangle inequality

Human word associations violate the triangle inequality, also called transitivity here. It is easy to find sets of words that have this property. For example, *asteroid* is highly associated with *belt*, and *belt* is highly associated with *buckle*, but *asteroid* and *buckle* have little association.

The triangle inequality restricts the possible relationships between three words in embedding spaces: If w_1 and w_2 are highly associated and w_2 and w_3 are highly associated, then we expect w_1 and w_3 to be highly associated.

However, as already motivated in section 5, our intuition is that context-aware word embeddings are no longer following the rules of linear geometric representations. For this reason, we use the cosine that, in addition to being symmetric, does not violate the triangle inequality. If any violation of the triangle inequality is found, it is attributable to the context-aware vector and not to the similarity operator.

Method We extracted a subset of the triples (w_1, w_2, w_3) from Appendix A in Nelson et al. (2004)'s norms for a total of 12664 triples, where both (w_1, w_2) and (w_2, w_3) are pairs of asymmetric nouns that share the same word w_2. We call these "pivot triples". Of these 12664 pivot triples only 263 are transitive, that is, they do not violate the triangle inequality and (w_1, w_3) exists in the

---

[11] As a control, we also extract bi-directional associations: the cue word produce a certain target and this specific target produces back the initial cue. For example, given the cue *ball*, one of the produced associates is the target *baseball*. Conversely, *baseball* elicits *ball* as target. For these 6232 pairs, in 50.09% of cases, the target is denser than the cue.

[12] For this experiment, we used FASTTEXT, as countries cannot be used in context with this model and not all the countries were included in the BERT "raw" word embeddings.

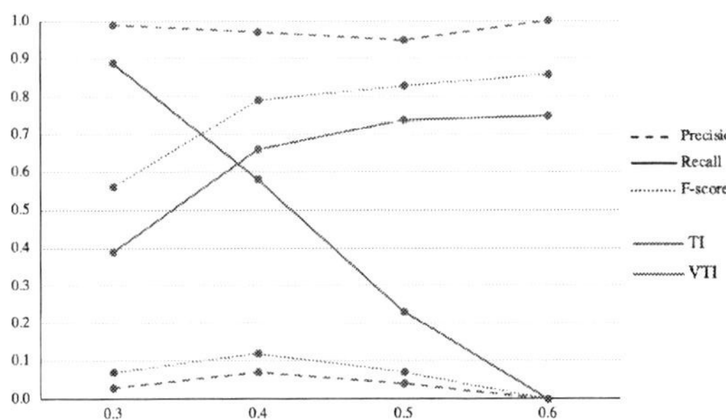

Figure 3: Precision, recall and F-score for transitive and intransitive triples. TI indicates tuples that respect the triangle inequality, and VTI refers to tuples that violate the triangle inequality. The x-axis indicates the different values of τ and the y-axis the score. Calculations are done considering Nelson's norms as the gold and BERT word embeddings as the system output.

human associations as a cue-target pair.[13] To calculate the BERT word embeddings, we contextualise each pair in the three different contexts already shown for previous experiments. To determine if the two pairs of words violate the triangle inequality in BERT space, we follow a procedure similar to Griffiths et al. (2007)'s. We set a threshold τ and extract those (w_1, w_2) and (w_2, w_3) whose cosine is greater than τ. Then, for each of these pivot triples, we quantify how many (w_1, w_3) pairs exist in the associations as a cue-target pair. If the pair exists and (w_1, w_3) is greater than τ, then BERT's embeddings also show transitivity; if the pair exists, but (w_1, w_3) is less than τ, then (w_1, w_3) in BERT does not reflect the transitivity found in humans; if the pair does not exist and (w_1, w_3) is lesser than τ, then there is a lack of transitivity both in human associations and in BERT embeddings.

Results Figure 3 shows some comparisons, in terms of precision and recall, of the BERT spaces against the gold human associations for different values of τ. The results show that the BERT space has many more triples for which there is triangle inequality (transitive triples), especially for low values of τ. This is expected, as BERT is trained on a much larger vocabulary space. The really interesting and relevant results are the measures of recall of the violations of triangle inequality (recall of VTI, blue solid line in the figure). As the results show, for increasing values of τ and more and more stringent definitions of similarity,

the agreement of BERT with the human norms on violations of triangle inequality is high, and this despite a clear tendency to overestimate triangle inequalities (transitivity), as the TI values show.

7 Discussion

We have found converging evidence for BERT being like human word associations in ranks of associations, quantitatively and qualitatively. In studying whether BERT similarity spaces are asymmetric, we find converging evidence to human experiments, using country names, both in the fact that the notion of salience influences the calculation of similarity and also in the fact that frequency correlates with the preferential direction of similarity. However, using a larger test set, we do not find convergence with frequency, or generality (hyperym/hyponym pairs of verbs and nouns) or neighbourhood density. Finally, human word associations violate the triangle inequality. So do BERT embedding spaces, for reasonably high values of the similarity measure.

In conclusion, we confirm the properties of rank association and triangle inequality and also the influence of frequency for certain kinds of associations. We find, instead, that the property of asymmetric similarity does not appear to conform to the operationalisations we tested.

8 Related work

Recent interest in vectorial representations of words derives from the realisation that the meaning of words is much better represented when the rich networks of similarities and dissimilarities among words are taken into account. But the realisation that such notions are central to our word representations, that they can be estimated from a corpus and that such representations can be very technologically apt is not new.

Church and Hanks (1990) brought to the attention of the computational linguistic community a notion of word association as the information-theoretic measure of mutual information estimated on large corpora. It was shown that if word order was taken into account the measure could be asymmetric. Mutual information and other word association measures have been intensely studied to describe multi-word expressions or collocations, a stumbling block for many NLP applications (for a recent survey, see Constant et al. (2017)). Levy and Goldberg (2014) show that word embeddings are closely related to information-theoretic notions

---

[13] Samples of the word lists are shown in the supplementary materials.

of mutual information, although denser and better performing in many tasks.

Our work builds on previous work in the non-associationist tradition: Word associations are a reflex of underlying properties and representations of words and their meaning (Clark, 1970; Tversky, 1977; Griffiths et al., 2007; De Deyne et al., 2016) and not the reverse. Tversky and colleagues's body of work is centred in a *contrast model*, a model of objects, concepts and words based on features and not on a position in a multi-dimensional space. In this model, the similarity between objects increases with shared common features and decreases with distinctive features (Tversky, 1977; Tversky and Gati, 1978). From this point of view, computation of similarity is based on set-theoretic operations, rather than the computation of metric distances (Tversky, 1977). In a probabilistic topic model, Griffiths et al. (2007), words are a set of probability distributions on topics so that words that have a high probability under the same topic will be highly predictive of one another. The representations induced by the topic model and their correspondence to human memory are compared to a spatial representation model (Latent Semantic Analysis, LSA) (Landauer and Dumais, 1997) and found to better reflect human association norms.

Current vector space semantic representations can be seen as inheriting from both the feature-based tradition and the similarity space tradition, exemplified by LSA. While initial similarity-space proposals like LSA represent words as atomic and occupying a single point in space, current geometric approaches represent words as vectors. The approaches proposed by Mikolov et al. (2013a,b); Bojanowski et al. (2017); Devlin et al. (2018) are based on a distributed representation of words, and aim to produce vectors that represent a word, or the substrings that compose a word, with information about its surroundings, so that word vectors that share the same meaning tend to be close. A recent comparison of word embeddings, Word2vec and Glove, to Nelson's norms indicates that vectorial representations that do not take context into account, unlike BERT, still are unable to capture the triangle inequality (Nematzadeh et al., 2017).

Investigations of word associations also belongs to the growing literature of evaluating vector spaces for natural language applications. Word associations are an interesting, intrinsic way to evaluate vector spaces (Vulić et al., 2017; Thawani et al., 2019), and have revealed important properties of these spaces, from gender stereotypes and demographic variation (Du et al., 2019; Garimella et al., 2017) to their usefulness in the detection of puns (Sevgili et al., 2017), among many others.

9 Conclusions

The work described in this paper starts from the assumption that word associations are the expression of underlying meaning properties of words. It confirms that context-aware word embeddings exhibit some properties of human association norms, despite being a vectorial representation of words in space. Future work needs to clarify the underlying mechanisms that give rise to these properties, extend the study to new languages, leveraging also newer association norms (De Deyne et al., 2019). It will also extend the investigation of word associations to other properties, such as the minimal contrast rule —associations tend to establish a minimal contrast— or the marking rule —marked cues elicit unmarked targets more often than the reverse (Clark, 1970), and model documented differences between adults and children.

Acknowledgments

We are very grateful to Suzanne Stevenson and the anonymous reviewers for useful suggestions.

References

Piotr Bojanowski, Edouard Grave, Armand Joulin, and Tomas Mikolov. 2017. Enriching word vectors with subword information. *Transactions of the Association for Computational Linguistics*, 5:135–146.

Kenneth Church and Patrick Hanks. 1990. Word association norms, mutual information, and lexicography. *Computational linguistics*, 16(1):22–29.

Herbert H Clark. 1970. Word associations and linguistic theory. *New horizons in linguistics*, 1:271–286.

Mathieu Constant, Gülşen Eryiğit, Johanna Monti, Lonneke Van Der Plas, Carlos Ramisch, Michael Rosner, and Amalia Todirascu. 2017. Multiword expression processing: A survey. *Computational Linguistics*, 43(4):837–892.

Simon De Deyne, Danielle J Navarro, Amy Perfors, Marc Brysbaert, and Gert Storms. 2019. The "Small World of Words" English word association norms for over 12,000 cue words. *Behavior research methods*, 51(3):987–1006.

Simon De Deyne, Amy Perfors, and Daniel J Navarro. 2016. Predicting human similarity judgments with distributional models: The value of word associations. In *Proceedings of COLING 2016, the 26th International Conference on Computational Linguistics: Technical Papers*, pages 1861–1870, Osaka, Japan. The COLING 2016 Organizing Committee.

Simon De Deyne and Gert Storms. 2014. Word associations. In John R. Taylor, editor, *The Oxford Handbook of the Word*. Oxford University Press.

Jacob Devlin, Ming-Wei Chang, Kenton Lee, and Kristina Toutanova. 2018. Bert: Pre-training of deep bidirectional transformers for language understanding. In *Proceedings of NAACL-HLT 2019*, pages 4171—4186, Minneapolis, Minnesota, USA.

Yupei Du, Yuanbin Wu, and Man Lan. 2019. Exploring Human Gender Stereotypes with Word Association Test. In *Proceedings of the 2019 Conference on Empirical Methods in Natural Language Processing and the 9th International Joint Conference on Natural Language Processing (EMNLP-IJCNLP)*, pages 6133–6143, Hong Kong, China. Association for Computational Linguistics.

Aparna Garimella, Carmen Banea, and Rada Mihalcea. 2017. Demographic-aware word associations. In *Proceedings of the 2017 Conference on Empirical Methods in Natural Language Processing*, pages 2285–2295, Copenhagen, Denmark. Association for Computational Linguistics.

Itamar Gati and Amos Tversky. 1982. Representations of qualitative and quantitative dimensions. *Journal of Experimental Psychology: Human Perception and Performance*, 8(2):325–340.

Thomas L Griffiths, Mark Steyvers, and Joshua B Tenenbaum. 2007. Topics in semantic representation. *Psychological review*, 114(2):211–244.

Thomas K Landauer and Susan T Dumais. 1997. A solution to Plato's problem: The latent semantic analysis theory of acquisition, induction, and representation of knowledge. *Psychological review*, 104(2):211–240.

Omer Levy and Yoav Goldberg. 2014. Neural word embedding as implicit matrix factorization. In *Advances in neural information processing systems*, pages 2177–2185.

Tomas Mikolov, Kai Chen, Greg Corrado, and Jeffrey Dean. 2013a. Efficient estimation of word representations in vector space. *arXiv preprint arXiv:1301.3781*.

Tomas Mikolov, Ilya Sutskever, Kai Chen, Greg S Corrado, and Jeff Dean. 2013b. Distributed representations of words and phrases and their compositionality. In *Advances in neural information processing systems*, pages 3111–3119.

George A Miller. 1995. Wordnet: a lexical database for English. *Communications of the ACM*, 38(11):39–41.

Douglas L Nelson, Cathy L McEvoy, and Thomas A Schreiber. 2004. The University of South Florida free association, rhyme, and word fragment norms. *Behavior Research Methods, Instruments, & Computers*, 36(3):402–407.

Aida Nematzadeh, Stephan C Meylan, and Thomas L Griffiths. 2017. Evaluating Vector-Space Models of Word Representation, or, The Unreasonable Effectiveness of Counting Words Near Other Words. In *Proceedings of the 39th Annual Meeting of the Cognitive Science Society*, pages 859–854, London, UK.

Tobias Schnabel, Igor Labutov, David Mimno, and Thorsten Joachims. 2015. Evaluation methods for unsupervised word embeddings. In *Proceedings of the 2015 Conference on Empirical Methods in Natural Language Processing*, pages 298–307, Lisbon, Portugal. Association for Computational Linguistics.

Özge Sevgili, Nima Ghotbi, and Selma Tekir. 2017. N-hance at SemEval-2017 task 7: A Computational Approach using Word Association for Puns. In *Proceedings of the 11th International Workshop on Semantic Evaluation (SemEval-2017)*, pages 436–439, Vancouver, Canada. Association for Computational Linguistics.

Avijit Thawani, Biplav Srivastava, and Anil Singh. 2019. SWOW-8500: Word Association task for Intrinsic Evaluation of Word Embeddings. In *Proceedings of the 3rd Workshop on Evaluating Vector Space Representations for NLP*, pages 43–51, Minneapolis, USA. Association for Computational Linguistics.

Amos Tversky. 1977. Features of similarity. *Psychological review*, 84(4):327–352.

Amos Tversky and Itamar Gati. 1978. Studies of similarity. *Cognition and categorization. Hillsdale, Erlbaum*, pages 79–98.

Amos Tversky and J Hutchinson. 1986. Nearest neighbor analysis of psychological spaces. *Psychological review*, 93(1):3–22.

Ivan Vulić, Douwe Kiela, and Anna Korhonen. 2017. Evaluation by Association: A Systematic Study of Quantitative Word Association Evaluation. In *Proceedings of the 15th Conference of the European Chapter of the Association for Computational Linguistics: Volume 1, Long Papers*, pages 163–175, Valencia, Spain. Association for Computational Linguistics.

Yukun Zhu, Ryan Kiros, Rich Zemel, Ruslan Salakhutdinov, Raquel Urtasun, Antonio Torralba, and Sanja Fidler. 2015. Aligning books and movies: Towards story-like visual explanations by watching movies and reading books. In *Proceedings of the IEEE international conference on computer vision*, pages 19–27.

TrClaim-19: The First Collection for Turkish Check-Worthy Claim Detection with Annotator Rationales

Yavuz Selim Kartal and **Mucahid Kutlu**
Department of Computer Engineering
TOBB University of Economics and Technology
Ankara, Turkey
{ykartal,m.kutlu}@etu.edu.tr

Abstract

Massive misinformation spread over Internet has many negative impacts on our lives. While spreading a claim is easy, investigating its veracity is hard and time consuming, Therefore, we urgently need systems to help human fact-checkers. However, available data resources to develop effective systems are limited and the vast majority of them is for English. In this work, we introduce TrClaim-19, which is the very first labeled dataset for Turkish check-worthy claims. TrClaim-19 consists of labeled 2287 Turkish tweets with annotator rationales, enabling us to better understand the characteristics of check-worthy claims. The rationales we collected suggest that claims' topics and their possible negative impacts are the main factors affecting their check-worthiness.

1 Introduction

In 2013, World Economic Forum (WEF) listed massive digital misinformation as one of the top global risks likely to occur in 10 years[1]. Unfortunately, we witnessed many unpleasant incidents due to misinformation spread over Internet such as massive stock price changes[2], gunfights[3], and others. Since the start of COVID-19 pandemic, we have also observed many incidents showing the value of true information and how misinformation about health issues can be deadly (e.g., misusing disinfectants to prevent coronavirus after Donald Trump suggested injecting disinfectants as treatment[4]).

In order to prevent the negative outcomes of misinformation, many fact-checking websites emerged all over the world in the last decade (Cherubini and Graves, 2016). The fact-checking websites manually investigate veracity of claims and share their findings with their readers. While they play an important role in the combat against misinformation, their precious journalistic effort is not enough to reduce spread of misinformation and its negative outcomes. While making a claim is so easy, investigating its veracity is highly time consuming, taking around one day (Hassan et al., 2017). Furthermore, Vosoughi et al. (2018) report that misinformation spread eight times faster than true information. Hence, we need effective solutions to help human fact-checkers and to reduce the negative impact of misinformation.

As Nakov et al. (2018) outline, the first task of a fact-checking system is to detect whether a statement contains a check-worthy claim or not. Considering the massive amount of messages shared on social media platforms, check-worthy claim detection models help human fact-checkers to filter out unimportant claims and use their valuable time to detect veracity of the most important claims. A number of researchers worked on this problem (e.g., (Lespagnol et al., 2019; Hassan et al., 2017; Jaradat et al., 2018)) and shared tasks for check-worthy claim detection have been organized (Nakov et al., 2018; Atanasova et al., 2019; Barrón-Cedeno et al., 2020).

While researchers showed great interest in fact-checking, the available resources are still limited and the vast majority of the studies focused on English. Regarding the task of detecting check-worthy claims, the only available labeled datasets are for English and Arabic (Nakov et al., 2018; Atanasova et al., 2019). However, as WEF notes in its aforementioned report, misinformation is a global problem affecting all countries. Misinformation can

---

[1] http://reports.weforum.org/global-risks-2013
[2] www.reuters.com/article/net-us-usa-whitehouse-ap/hackers-send-fake-market-moving-ap-tweet-on-white-house-explosions-idUSBRE93M12Y20130423
[3] www.nytimes.com/2016/12/05/business/media/comet-ping-pong-pizza-shooting-fake-news-consequences.html
[4] https://www.reuters.com/article/us-health-coronavirus-disinfectants-idUSKBN23C2P2

Proceedings of the 24th Conference on Computational Natural Language Learning, pages 386–395
Online, November 19-20, 2020. ©2020 Association for Computational Linguistics
https://doi.org/10.18653/v1/P17

also spread internationally. For instance, during 2019 European elections, same or similar stories have been shared in different languages across European countries (Fletcher et al., 2018). Hence, in order to have an effective combat against spread of misinformation, we need research studies for a wide range of languages.

In this work, we focus on Turkish and introduce TrClaim-19, which is the very *first* labeled Turkish tweets with the rationales of annotators for check-worthy claim detection task. Turkish is a particularly important language for fact-checking studies because Fletcher et al. (2018) report that 49% of Internet users in Turkey coincide with at least one fake news in a week, which is higher than all other countries investigated in their study. Furthermore, being a member of Altaic language family, Turkish language has different linguistic features than other languages studied for fact-checking, such as being an agglutinative language and having flexible word order structure in sentences. In addition to developing a useful resource for the research community, we also seek answers for the following research questions.

- RQ-1: What is the agreement level between non-expert fact-checkers on check-worthiness of claims?

- RQ-2: Do non-experts have different opinion about check-worthiness of claims than experts?

- RQ-3: What are the main rationales to label claims as check-worthy?

In particular, we have first crawled Turkish tweets for 344 days in 2019, tracking important events happened in Turkey such as local elections, earthquake in Istanbul, and military operation in Syria. Eventually, we gathered around 225 millions Turkish tweets. Subsequently, we crawled 765 claims fact-checked by two Turkish fact-checking websites. Next, for each claim, we retrieved three tweets from our tweet crawl using Lucene search engine library[5]. Each retrieved tweet has been labeled by three separate annotators. For each tweet, we asked annotators whether it is relevant to the respective claim, and whether it contains a check-worthy claim. Inspired by McDonnell et al. (2016)'s study, we also asked their rationale for the tweets labeled as check-worthy.

---

⁵ https://lucene.apache.org/core/

Table 1: General Statistics about TrClaim-19.

The number of tweets crawled	225M
The number of tweets annotated	2287
The number of check-worthy claims	875
The number of rationale categories	26

Table 1 summarizes general features of TrClaim-19. In total, we collected labels for 2287 tweets, and 875 of them are labeled as check-worthy when labels are aggregated by majority voting. We have observed that agreement on check-worthiness of tweets among non-experts are low (Fleiss' kappa = 0.23). In 36% of cases, non-experts disagreed with experts on check-worthiness of claims. Assessors provided rationales in 26 different categories. Rationales we collect suggest that topics and possible negative impacts of claims are the main factors in making a claim check-worthy.

The contributions of our work are as follows.

- We develope and share TrClaim-19, which is the very first labeled data resource for Turkish check-worthy claim detection [6].

- TrClaim-19 is also the first data resource with annotator rationales for check-worthy claim detection task, enabling better understanding of the research problem to develop effective solutions.

- We investigate the subjectivity of check-worthiness of claims. In particular, we explore how much non-expert and expert fact-checkers agree on check-worthiness of claims.

- We provide performance results of four models on TrClaim-19 to provide reference baselines for future studies.

2 Related Work

A number of researchers created annotated datasets for check-worthy claim detection. To our knowledge, Hassan et al. (2015) created the first check worthiness dataset using transcripts of the U.S. presidential debates. They invited journalists, professors and university students to label the data. Each sentence in debates is labeled by at least two annotators. They used a three-scale label which are "non factual", "unimportant factual" and "check-worthy factual". In total, they labeled 1571 sentences.

---

⁶ https://github.com/YSKartal/TrClaim19

Following Hassan et al. (2015), US political debates have been used in many other studies. Patwari et al. (2017) constructed a check-worthy detection dataset using US primary and presidential debates. They identified 9 reputable news portals and fact-checking websites (e.g., Polifact, CNN and factcheck.org), and considered statements which are fact-checked by at least one of these websites, as check-worthy. Gencheva et al. (2017) also applied the same method to build their dataset using again US debates. They report that the agreement between fact-checking websites is low: Only one sentence is fact-checked by all nine websites they listed while 880 statements are fact-checked by only one website. In a follow-up study, Jaradat et al. (2018) introduce ClaimRank for detecting check-worthy claims in English and Arabic. However, the Arabic data they use is just the translation of the US election debates.

CLEF Check That! Lab have been organizing shared tasks for detecting check-worthy claims since 2018. In 2018, similar to other datasets, they used US debates and political speeches, and considered statements fact-checked by FactCheck.org as check-worthy (Elsayed et al., 2018). For Arabic check-worthy detection task, they just used translations of the English dataset. In 2019, the organizers of the lab used the extension of the previous year's dataset (Atanasova et al., 2019). In 2020, CLEF Check That! Lab[7] organizers constructed datasets using tweets and again political debates (Barrón-Cedeno et al., 2020). The English tweet dataset consists of 962 tweets about COVID-19 pandemic. The Arabic dataset consists of 7500 tweets about 15 trending topics at the time of crawling among Arab social media users such as COVID-19 and Trump Peace Plan[8].

Overall, the vast majority of the existing datasets are English and use U.S. political speeches and debates. TrClaim-19 distinguishes from the existing data resources as follows. 1) Tr-Claim19 is the first collection for Turkish check-worthy claims. 2) TrClaim-19 is the first collection providing with the rationales of annotators. 3) We collect labels for each tweet from three annotators, enabling us to analyze subjectivity of the task and different rationales for the same check-worthy claims.

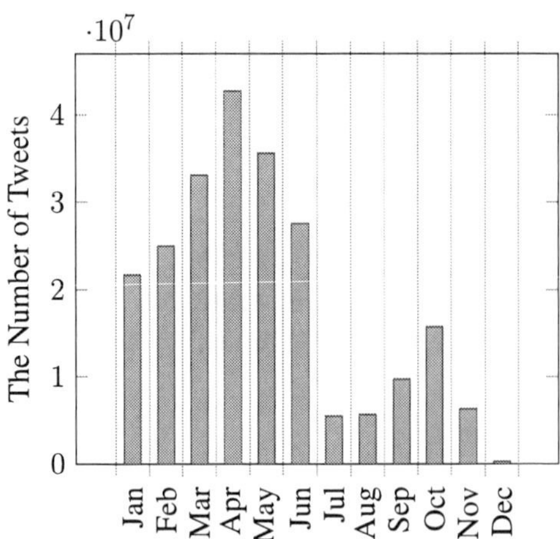

Figure 1: The number of tweets crawled in each month of 2019.

3 Tweet Collection

Social media platforms play an important role in spreading misinformation. Therefore, we focus on claims spread on Twitter. In order to gather tweets with check-worthy claims, we crawled Turkish tweets between January 1, 2019 and December 31, 2019[9] using Twitter API. We used keyword tracking approach enabling us to gather tweets about important topics. In 2019, there were many major events happened in Turkey, such as local elections[10], an earthquake in Istanbul [11], a military operation in Syria[12], and others. Therefore, we used keywords related to these major events such as "seçim" (election), "terrör" (terror), "ekonomi" (economics), "mülteci" (refugee), "Suriye" (Syria), politician names (e.g., "Erdoğan"), and others. We used a dynamic keyword list, instead of a static one, such that we updated the list whenever a new important event happened. For instance, after the earthquake in Istanbul in September 26, 2019, we added the word "deprem" (earthquake) in our keyword list.

At the end of our long crawling process, we have collected around 225 millions Turkish tweets. The distribution of tweets crawled for each month is shown in **Figure 1**. The number of tweets collected

---

[7]https://sites.google.com/view/clef2020-checkthat/

[8]https://en.wikipedia.org/wiki/Trump_peace_plan

[9]crawling had stopped only for three weeks in July 2019

[10]www.bbc.com/news/world-europe-47764393

[11]https://en.wikipedia.org/wiki/2019_Istanbul_earthquake

[12]www.aa.com.tr/en/operation-peace-spring/operation-peace-spring-starts-in-n-syria-erdogan/1607147

between January and June is much higher than other months because local elections were hold on 31st March and 24th of June (repeated elections for Istanbul) and Twitter was one of the main platforms for political discussions.

4 Tweet Selection

As we have collected tweets more than we can annotate, we have to select a sample among them. A random sampling could cause many not-check-worthy tweets. Inspired by test collection construction methodology in the field of information retrieval (Voorhees, 2001), we first collected claims fact-checked by fact-checking websites (Section 4.1) and then used each claim as a search query to retrieve tweets which are similar to claims we collected (Section 4.2). Using tweets similar to claims also allow us to seek answer for our research question RQ-2. Now we explain our tweet selection process in detail.

4.1 Claim Crawling

In order to ensure the quality of our collection, we focused on fact-checking websites certified by International Fact Checking Network (IFCN)[13] which investigates fact-checking websites on various issues such as nonpartisanship and transparency of fact-checking methodology. Thus, we gathered claims fact-checked by Teyit[14] and Doğruluk Payı[15] (DP) which are the only Turkish fact-checking websites certified by IFCN. Teyit usually focuses on claims spread on social media platforms while DP investigates veracity of claims made by politicians. We crawled all claims fact-checked by Teyit and DP between February 2015 and January 2020. While tweets we crawled have been posted in 2019, we did not filter claims based on their date. This is because people might make the same claim multiple times. For instance, many people believe that the moon landing in 1969 was fake and this claim circulates for decades.

We eliminated claims about pictures or videos because we focus on claims that can be analyzed linguistically. In total, we collected 573 claims from DP and 192 from Teyit, yielding 765 claims in total.

Algorithm 1 Tweet Selection
Input: Tweets T, Claims C
Output: Selected Tweets ST

```
 1: Build an index for T
 2: ST ← []
 3: for each claim in C do
 4:     ranked ← BM25(index, claim)
 5:     ST ← ST ∩ ranked[0]
 6:     i ← 1
 7:     count ← 0
 8:     while i < ranked.size() do
 9:         S ← LDF(ranked[i], ranked[i − 1])
10:         if score < threshold then
11:             ST ← ST ∩ ranked[i]
12:             count ← count + 1
13:             if count == 3 then
14:                 break
15:         i ← i + 1
16: return ST
```

4.2 Selecting Tweets to be Labeled

In selection of tweets to be labeled, we have three main goals: 1) building a balanced test collection in term of label distribution, 2) having a diverse set of tweets in terms of topic and linguistics features, and 3) ensuring that some of tweets contain claims fact-checked by experts for our research question RQ-2.

Our tweet selection algorithm is presented at **Algorithm 1**. We first index all tweets without stemming using Lucene search engine library [Line 1]. This process also eliminates exactly same tweets, which exist a lot in tweet collections due to retweets. Subsequently, for each claim, we use the claim itself as a search query and rank the tweets using BM25 ranking function [Line 4]. However, instead of getting the top ranked tweets, we apply a two-step process to find tweets related to our crawled claims but different each other. This is because we observed that many tweets are not exactly same but are quite similar. For instance, two tweets might have the same message but one of them has an additional URL, hashtag, and/or emoji. In particular, we first select the top ranked tweet to be labeled [Line 5]. Then, starting from the top ranked tweets, we calculate textual similarity of tweets ranked consecutively [Line 9]. If similarity of tweets are lower than a pre-defined threshold value, we add the respective tweet (i.e., tweet with a lower rank) to our selected tweet list [Lines 13-

14]. In order to calculate textual similarity between two tweets, we first remove mentions, URLs and non-alphanumerical characters, and then calculate the approximate similarity based on Levenshtein Distance[16]. Empirically, we set the similarity score threshold to 0.80. We select three tweets for each claim using this method [Lines 12-14].

Using the algorithm explained above, we selected 1714 tweets for claims crawled from DP, and 573 tweets for claims crawled from Teyit, yielding 2287 tweets in total[17].

5 Annotation Process

Two authors of this paper and 7 volunteers annotated the tweets we selected. All annotators are native speakers of Turkish language and have degrees at various disciplines including law, computer science, dentistry, history, and business administration. Their ages are between 22 and 35. We believe that having annotators with diverse backgrounds allows us to capture different thoughts and perspectives about check-worthy claims.

Before starting the annotation process, we explained the dataset and the annotation task to each volunteer. In the annotation interface, annotators are able to see tweets to be labeled and also respective claims used to retrieve them. Annotators are asked the following three questions in the annotation task.

- Is the tweet relevant to the claim?

- Do you think that the tweet contains a check-worthy claim?

- If you think the tweet has a check-worthy claim, why do you think it is check-worthy?

We did not put any restrictions to define their rationale not to induce any bias. Annotators used a free-style text form to type their rationale behind their check-worthiness judgment. We only requested annotators to do their best to be consistent in their rationale definition and use the same text for the same rationale to better analyze their rationales in the post-process of the data.

Each tweet has been annotated by three annotators separately. We divided the participants into 3

groups. Then each annotator group labeled a separate set of tweets. The sizes of tweet sets were determined based on availability of each annotator group because they did this annotation task voluntarily. In particular, the number of tweets assigned to each group are, 384, 427, and 1476. In order to prevent bias in the annotations, the annotators have not seen labels of others until the labelling process ends. In total, we collected 2287x3=6861 relevance and check-worthiness judgments.

6 Analysis of TrClaim-19

Table 2 presents statistics about TrClaim-19. Aggregating each tweet's relevance and check-worthiness judgments based on majority voting yields 974 (=78+267+387+242) relevant (i.e., 42% of our collection) and 875 (=387+242+211+35) check-worthy claims (i.e., 38% of our collection) in total.

RQ-1 What is the agreement level between non-experts on check-worthiness of claims? The annotations we collected show that non-expert fact-checkers (i.e., annotators in our study) highly disagree on check-worthiness of claims. In Table 2, we observe that annotators fully agree on check-worthiness of 1033 (=78+242+678+35) tweets (i.e., 45% of all collection) but not for the remaining 1254 tweets (i.e., 55% of all collection). Fleiss' kappa score for check worthiness judgments is 0.23, which accounts for 'fair agreement' according to Fleiss et al. (1971). As a reference point, Fleiss' Kappa score for relevance judgments is 0.61 which accounts for 'substantial agreement'. This suggests that judging check-worthiness of claims is a more subjective task than relevance judging.

As we mention before, we had grouped annotators into three groups. In order to see whether there is any difference in annotation agreement levels among groups, we also calculated Fleiss' kappa score for each group separately. Fleiss' Kappa scores for each group's check-worthiness judgments are between 0.17 and 0.32, suggesting that there is no notable difference among groups.

Overall, regarding our research question, our results suggest that non-expert people do disagree on check-worthiness of claims. Therefore, instead of using binary judgments as in existing datasets, we believe that graded judgments are more suitable for this task. Note that TrClaim-19's judgments can be easily converted to graded judgments using check worthy ratios for each tweet.

---

[16]https://github.com/seatgeek/fuzzywuzzy

[17]for some claims, the search engine returned less than three tweets

Table 2: Label Distribution. Relevance judgments are aggregated based on majority voting. Check Worthy Ratio shows the ratio of "check worthy" annotations among three annotations for each tweet.

Relevance	Check Worthy Ratio	The Number of Tweets		
		Teyit	DP	Total
Relevant	0/3	32	46	78
	1/3	85	182	267
	2/3	141	246	387
	3/3	142	100	242
Non-Relevant	0/3	84	594	678
	1/3	52	337	389
	2/3	29	182	211
	3/3	8	27	35

Table 3: Sample Tweets Relevant to the Respective Claims Fact-Checked by Experts with Varying Check Worthy Judgment Ratios

Original	Translation	CW Ratio
Yüksek teknolojili ürünlerin imalattaki payı yüzde 3'e geriledi	The share of high-tech products in production fell to 3 percent	0/3
Bugüne kadar Suriyeli sığınmacılar için harcanan para 40 milyar Dolar	The total amount of money spent for Syrian refugees are 40 billions dollars.	1/3
Trafik kazalarında son on yılda 52 bin 95 kişi yaşamını yitirdi	52,095 people have died due to traffic accidents in the last ten years	2/3
Avrupa'da genç işsizliği yükselen iki ülkeden biri Türkiye	Turkey is one of the two countries in Europe in which youth unemployment increases.	3/3

RQ-2 Do non-experts have different opinion about check-worthiness of claims than experts? Relevant tweets in TrClaim-19 might be useful to seek an answer for this research question. Claims we crawled from Teyit and DP have been fact-checked by experts. Thus, we can safely assume that expert fact-checkers considered these claims as check-worthy. In Table 2, we see that check-worthy ratio of 78 relevant tweets is 0/3 (i.e., all annotators disagreed with experts). Furthermore, in 267 tweets, two-third of annotators considered the tweets as not check-worthy in contrast to experts. Overall, in 36% ($= \frac{78+267}{78+267+387+242}$) cases, annotators disagreed with expert fact-checkers.

In order to shed light this disagreement between experts and non-experts, **Table 3** shows sample relevant tweets (original Turkish tweets and their translations) for varying check-worthy ratios. We selected tweets that all annotators judged as relevant to the respective claim. In the table, we observe that none of the annotators considered the claim about the share of high-tech products in production. This might be because their life is not directly affected by this claim about economics. On the other hand, all annotators considered the claim about youth unemployment as check-worthy. This might be because the annotators are young and, therefore, interested in youth unemployment.

During our annotation process, annotators knew that the respective claims are fact-checked by experts. This might potentially affect their judgments. We leave the analysis of this potential bias as future work. However, regarding RQ-2, it is noteworthy that annotators disagreed with experts in many cases despite they knew that experts fact-checked those claims.

RQ-3: What are the main reasons to label a claim as check-worthy? Annotators judged tweets as check-worthy 2683 times (i.e., without aggregation) and provided rationales for these cases. As we did not put any restriction on how they should define rationales, they provided 71 different texts as their rationales in total. We observed that annotators used different texts for same or similar rationales (e.g., "refugee rights", "refugees", and "refugee problems"). Therefore, we manually in-

Table 4: The Most Common Rationale Groups in TrClaim-19 and a Sample Tweet for Each Group. Rationales and tweets are manually translated to English. The numbers in parantheses represent how many times rationales in the respective group appear in Tr-Claim-19.

Rationale Group	Actual Rationales Provided by Annotators	A Sample Tweet
Economics (508)	"economy", "assessment of economical status", "the impact of governmental decisions on economics"	In Turkey, 70% of the population is in debt, the poorest people get only 6.1% of GDP
Politics (376)	"security of voting", "impact on society after elections", "election time and its impacts", "politics and its impact on society", "political", "It can negatively impact governmental institutions and politicians", "political propaganda", "It might affect people's political stance", "about a political party", "municipality services"	"Republican People's Party's investigation proposal about attacking Kılıçdaroğlu has been rejected"
Society (287)	"Social problems", "gender inequality in society", "It is about an important topic for the society", "Assessment of people's psychosocial status", "About the society", "national"	"We increased women's labor force participation to 34.1%"
General (187)	"The assessment of an existing issue"	"With its 82 million population, Turkey is 18th most crowded country. In addition. It has the 19th largest economy in the world."
International (58)	"International Politics", "Foreign agenda", "Universal", "The impact of events happened in Turkey on other issues", "International Comparison"	United States Secretary of State Mike Pompeo: "Trump is ready to use military force against Turkey if needed."
Interesting (41)	"The claim is interesting", "strange"	"Europe Central Bank has printed Euro souvenir banknotes featuring Ataturk for collectors."
Security (35)	"Security", "military", "terror"	Yesterday it was a dream that Turkey would produce its own national tank, rifle, helicopter, submarine and UAV. Now it became a reality with Erdogan. The ratio of national defense systems (used by the army) increased from 15% to 75%.
Unclear & Suspicious Claims (33)	"Suspicious", "Checking a partial information about something"	It is said that President Erdogan spent 1,006,621 Turkish Liras of the discretionary fund in the first five months of 2019
Education (33)	"Education"	The number of unemployed people with a university degree exceeded one million
Health (28)	"health", "accident", "work accident"	Carefulness increased, work accidents decreased

vestigated all rationales and grouped them under 26 categories[18]. We observe that some of the rationales are just a few words (e.g., "human rights", "health"), suggesting that the claim is check-worthy because it is about an important topic. On the other hand, some annotators provided clear rationales

---

[18] We share both original rationales and our rationale groups

such as "The claim is interesting", "People might make an important decision about their life because of this claim", and "It can negatively affect the perception towards people or institutions".

Table 4 shows the most frequently stated 10 rationale groups, the actual rationale texts provided by annotators and a sample tweet for each group. The rest of the rationales groups are as follows[19]: ecology (23), refugees (21), agriculture (17), national values (16), scandals (13), historical events (12), denials (12), human rights (11), science (10), tourism (8), media (7), infrastructure (7), influential on non-political issues" (6), violence (2), and culture (1).

Rationales provide useful insight for check-worthy claim detection task. Our main observations are as follows. Firstly, topic of a claim is an important factor to make it check-worthy. In particular, economics, politics and social issues are the most common topics in check-worthy claims. Secondly, people might have different rationales to consider a claim as check-worthy. For instance, three annotators considered the following tweet as check-worthy but provided rationales at different groups (namely, health, politics, and social issues): "The copays for medical examination and drugs will increase by 60% and 70%, respectively, on Monday". While the claim is clearly about health, other annotators considered it check-worthy for its impact on politics and social life. Thirdly, annotators frequently expressed negative outcomes or problems in their rationales (e.g., "ecological problems", "infraction of rules on a important topic", "illegal action", "problems of refugees", and "injustice"). This suggests that claims about negative issues are more likely to be check-worthy than claims about positive issues. Fourthly, many rationales we collected are about possible impacts of claims such as "it might affect people's political stance", "it can change the perception towards an influential person in the history", and "people might make an important decision based on this claim". Therefore, impact of claims should be also considered in detecting check-worthy claims. Lastly, rationales like "national values" and "about a topic important for the society" suggest that check-worthiness of some claims are not universal but they are check-worthy for just a particular nation/country. Therefore, check-worthy claim detection models should

also consider national issues of each country.

7 Baseline Results

In this section, we provide performance results of four models on our dataset in order to provide reference baselines for future studies. We first randomly selected 635 claims (out of 765) gathered from Teyit and DP, and used 1900 tweets retrieved using these selected claims for training. The remaining 387 tweets are used for testing. The baseline models we use are as follows.

- **M-BERT:** As the best performing models in CLEF 2020 Check That! Lab (Barrón-Cedeno et al., 2020) used variants of BERT model (Devlin et al., 2019), we fine tune multiligual cased version of BERT (i.e., M-BERT) using traning data.

- **BERTurk:** Pires et al. (2019) report that M-BERT's performance might decrease for the languages with different word orders in sentences. Turkish language has also different word ordering than English. Therefore, we fine tune BERTurk (Schweter, 2020) which is a monolingual BERT model pre-trained using only Turkish texts.

- **Logistic Regression with Bag-of-Words (LR-BOW):** We train a logistic regression model with bag-of-words features. In particular, we first apply the following preprocessing techniques: case folding, removing non-alphabetic characters, eliminating stopwords with NLTK[20], and stemming[21]. We tokenize using NLTK and eventually, have 6157 distinct words to be used as the bag-of-words features.

- **Support Vector Machines with Bag-of-Words (SVM-BOW):** We use the same bag-of-words features and train an SVM model with the training data.

We use Scikit toolkit[22] for both SVM-BOW and LR-BOW models with default parameters. We adjust all models in two settings: binary and multiclass classification. In binary classification we use aggregated labels (i.e., "check-worthy" and "not check-worthy") based on majority voting for

---

[19]The numbers in parentheses represent how many times a rationale from the respective group appears in TrClaim-19.

[20]`www.nltk.org/`
[21]`https://snowballstem.org`
[22]`https://scikit-learn.org`

Table 5: Evaluation results for baseline models on TrClaim-19. The best result for each metric is **boldfaced**.

Model	AP	P@1	P@5	P@10	P@30	R-P	nDCG
M-BERT	**.3825**	**1.0000**	**.8000**	**.4000**	.3000	.3510	.8708
BERTurk	.3687	0.0000	.6000	.4000	.3000	**.3709**	**.8895**
BOW-LR	.3609	**1.0000**	.2000	.2000	.2667	.3245	.8815
BOW-SVM	.3716	**1.0000**	.2000	.2000	**.3333**	.3444	.8372

each tweet. In multiclass classification, we use total number of check-worthy labels for each tweet, yielding a quaternary (4-point) scale of labels (i.e., 0, 1, 2, and 3). We rank tweets based on their check-worthiness using our baseline models. We report average precision (AP), R-Precision (R-P), and precision with different cutoff values (P@k) for binary classification. For multiclass classification, we report nDCG scores. **Table 5** shows the evaluation results for the baseline models.

Based on AP, P@1, P@5, and P@10, M-BERT yields the highest scores. BERTurk model outperforms others based on R-P and nDCG metrics. As expected, BERT based models outperform LR-BOW and SVM-BOW models in most of the cases. However, their scores are close in many cases, and SVM-BOW and LR-BOW slightly outperform M-BERT and BERTurk models in various cases. This might be because of the size of the training dataset. Future studies might explore weak supervision or cross lingual transfer learning to better fine tune BERT models.

8 Conclusion

In this work, we introduce TrClaim-19, which is the first annotated dataset for Turkish check-worthy claims. We first crawled 225M Turkish tweets in 2019 by tracking keywords about important events happened in Turkey. In order to select the tweets to be annotated, we first crawled 765 claims fact-checked by two Turkish fact-checking websites. Then we used these claims as search queries to select 3 tweets to be annotated for each claim. In total, we collected annotations for 2287 Turkish tweets. In addition to check-worthy annotations, we also collected rationales behind their judgments. Furthermore, we provide performance results of baseline models on TrClaim-19 for future studies.

In our analysis of TrClaim-19, we have the following observations. Firstly, annotators have low agreement on check-worthiness of claims, suggesting that we need graded judgments, instead of bi-nary judgments. Secondly, in many cases, non-experts disagree with experts on check-worthiness of claims even though they knew that they have been fact-checked by experts. Thirdly, annotators might have different rationales for labeling a claim as check-worthy. Fourthly, the rationales we collect suggest that topics of claims are the main factors affecting their check-worthiness. In particular, claims about economics, politics, and society are likely to be check-worthy. Lastly, the rationales suggest that claims about negative events are more likely to be check-worthy than claims about positive events.

In the future, we plan to extend to our work covering other languages. Besides being useful data resources, they will also allow us to compare rationales across different languages and cultures. In addition, we plan to apply a think-aloud methodology to collect rationales, allowing us to better understand the thought process of annotators. Furthermore, collecting rationales for not-check-worthy claims might be useful to understand disagreement between annotators.

References

Pepa Atanasova, Preslav Nakov, Georgi Karadzhov, Mitra Mohtarami, and Giovanni Da San Martino. 2019. Overview of the clef-2019 checkthat! lab: Automatic identification and verification of claims. task 1: Check-worthiness. In *CLEF (Working Notes)*.

Alberto Barrón-Cedeno, Tamer Elsayed, Preslav Nakov, Giovanni Da San Martino, Maram Hasanain, Reem Suwaileh, Fatima Haouari, Nikolay Babulkov, Bayan Hamdan, Alex Nikolov, et al. 2020. Overview of checkthat! 2020: Automatic identification and verification of claims in social media. In *International Conference of the Cross-Language Evaluation Forum for European Languages*, pages 215–236. Springer.

Federica Cherubini and Lucas Graves. 2016. The rise of fact-checking sites in europe. *Reuters Institute for the Study of Journalism, University of Oxford*.

Jacob Devlin, Ming-Wei Chang, Kenton Lee, and

Kristina Toutanova. 2019. Bert: Pre-training of deep bidirectional transformers for language understanding. In *Proceedings of the 2019 Conference of the North American Chapter of the Association for Computational Linguistics: Human Language Technologies, Volume 1 (Long and Short Papers)*, pages 4171–4186.

Tamer Elsayed, Reem Suwaileh, Wajdi Zaghouani, Spas Kyuchukov, Giovanni Da San Martino, and Preslav Nakov. 2018. Overview of the clef-2018 checkthat! lab on automatic identification and verification of political claims. task 1: Check-worthiness.

J.L. Fleiss et al. 1971. Measuring nominal scale agreement among many raters. *Psychological Bulletin*, 76(5):378–382.

Richard Fletcher, Alessio Cornia, Lucas Graves, and Rasmus Kleis Nielsen. 2018. Measuring the reach of "fake news" and online disinformation in europe. *Reuters institute factsheet*.

Pepa Gencheva, Preslav Nakov, Lluís Màrquez i Villodre, Alberto Barrón-Cedeño, and Ivan Koychev. 2017. A context-aware approach for detecting worth-checking claims in political debates. In *RANLP*.

Naeemul Hassan, Chengkai Li, and Mark Tremayne. 2015. Detecting check-worthy factual claims in presidential debates. In *CIKM '15*.

Naeemul Hassan, Gensheng Zhang, Fatma Arslan, Josue Caraballo, Damian Jimenez, Siddhant Gawsane, Shohedul Hasan, Minumol Joseph, Aaditya Kulkarni, Anil Kumar Nayak, Vikas Sable, Chengkai Li, and Mark Tremayne. 2017. Claimbuster: The first-ever end-to-end fact-checking system. *PVLDB*, 10:1945–1948.

Israa Jaradat, Pepa Gencheva, Alberto Barrón-Cedeño, Lluís Màrquez, and Preslav Nakov. 2018. Claimrank: Detecting check-worthy claims in arabic and english. In *Proceedings of the 2018 Conference of the North American Chapter of the Association for Computational Linguistics: Demonstrations*, pages 26–30.

Cédric Lespagnol, Josiane Mothe, and Md Zia Ullah. 2019. Information nutritional label and word embedding to estimate information check-worthiness. In *Proceedings of the 42nd International ACM SIGIR Conference on Research and Development in Information Retrieval*, pages 941–944. ACM.

Tyler McDonnell, Matthew Lease, Mucahid Kutlu, and Tamer Elsayed. 2016. Why is that relevant? collecting annotator rationales for relevance judgments. *HCOMP*, 16:139–148.

Preslav Nakov, Alberto Barrón-Cedeño, Tamer Elsayed, Reem Suwaileh, Lluís Màrquez, Wajdi Zaghouani, Pepa Atanasova, Spas Kyuchukov, and Giovanni Da San Martino. 2018. Overview of the clef-2018 checkthat! lab on automatic identification and verification of political claims. In *International Conference of the Cross-Language Evaluation Forum for European Languages*, pages 372–387.

Ayush Patwari, Dan Goldwasser, and Saurabh Bagchi. 2017. Tathya: A multi-classifier system for detecting check-worthy statements in political debates. *Proceedings of the 2017 ACM on Conference on Information and Knowledge Management*.

Telmo Pires, Eva Schlinger, and Dan Garrette. 2019. How multilingual is multilingual bert? In *Proceedings of the 57th Annual Meeting of the Association for Computational Linguistics*, pages 4996–5001.

Stefan Schweter. 2020. Berturk - bert models for turkish.

Ellen M Voorhees. 2001. The philosophy of information retrieval evaluation. In *Workshop of the cross-language evaluation forum for european languages*, pages 355–370. Springer.

Soroush Vosoughi, Deb Roy, and Sinan Aral. 2018. The spread of true and false news online. *Science*, 359(6380):1146–1151.

Discourse structure interacts with reference but not syntax in neural language models

Forrest Davis and **Marten van Schijndel**
Department of Linguistics
Cornell University
{fd252|mv443}@cornell.edu

Abstract

Language models (LMs) trained on large quantities of text have been claimed to acquire abstract linguistic representations. Our work tests the robustness of these abstractions by focusing on the ability of LMs to learn interactions between different linguistic representations. In particular, we utilized stimuli from psycholinguistic studies showing that humans can condition reference (i.e. coreference resolution) and syntactic processing on the same discourse structure (implicit causality). We compared both transformer and long short-term memory LMs to find that, contrary to humans, implicit causality only influences LM behavior for reference, not syntax, despite model representations that encode the necessary discourse information. Our results further suggest that LM behavior can contradict not only learned representations of discourse but also syntactic agreement, pointing to shortcomings of standard language modeling.

1 Introduction

Neural network language models (LMs), pretrained on vast amounts of raw text, have become the dominant input to downstream tasks (Peters et al., 2018; Radford et al., 2018; Devlin et al., 2019). Commonly, these tasks involve aspects of language comprehension (or understanding). One explicit example is coreference resolution, wherein anaphora (e.g., pronouns) are linked to antecedents (e.g., nouns) requiring knowledge of syntax, semantics, and world-knowledge to match human-like comprehension.

Recent work has suggested that LMs acquire abstract, often human-like, knowledge of syntax (e.g., Gulordava et al., 2018; Futrell et al., 2018; Hu et al., 2020). Additionally, knowledge of grammatical and referential aspects linking a pronoun to its antecedent noun (reference) have been demonstrated for both transformer and long short-term

memory architectures (Sorodoc et al., 2020). Humans are able to modulate both referential and syntactic comprehension given abstract linguistic knowledge (e.g., discourse structure). Contrary to humans, we find that discourse structure (at least as it pertains to implicit causality) only influences LM behavior for reference, not syntax, despite model representations that encode the necessary discourse information.

The particular discourse structure we examined is governed by implicit causality (IC) verbs (Garvey and Caramazza, 1974). Such verbs influence pronoun comprehension:

(1)   a.   Sally frightened Mary because she was so terrifying.
      b.   Sally feared Mary because she was so terrifying.

In (1), *she* agrees in gender with both *Sally* and *Mary*, so both are possible antecedents. However, English speakers overwhelmingly interpret *she* as referring to *Sally* in (1-a) and *Mary* in (1-b), despite the semantic overlap between the verbs. Verbs that have a subject preference (e.g., *frightened*) are called subject-biased IC verbs, and verbs with an object preference (e.g., *feared*) are called object-biased IC verbs.

In addition to pronoun resolution, IC verbs also interact with relative clause (RC) attachment:

(2)   a.   John babysits the children of the musician who...
      (i)   ...lives in La Jolla.
      (ii)   ...are students at a private school.
      b.   John detests the children of the musician who...
      (i)   ...lives in La Jolla.
      (ii)   ...are arrogant and rude.

(from Rohde et al., 2011)

Proceedings of the 24th Conference on Computational Natural Language Learning, pages 396–407
Online, November 19-20, 2020. ©2020 Association for Computational Linguistics
https://doi.org/10.18653/v1/P17

In (2), (2-a) and (2-b) are sentence fragments with possible continuations modifying *the musician* in (2-a-i) and (2-b-i) and continuations modifying *the children* in (2-a-ii) and (2-b-ii). We might expect human continuation preferences to be the same in (2-a) and (2-b). However, the use of an object-biased IC verb (*detests*) in (2-b) increases the proportion of continuations given by human participants that refer to the *children* (i.e. (2-b-ii) vs. (2-b-i)). Without an object-biased IC verb the majority of continuations refer to the more recent noun (i.e. *musician*).

Effects of IC have received renewed interest in the field of psycholinguistics in recent years (e.g., Kehler et al., 2008; Ferstl et al., 2011; Hartshorne and Snedeker, 2013; Hartshorne, 2014; Williams, 2020). Current accounts of IC claim that the phenomenon is inherently a linguistic process, which does not rely on additional pragmatic inferences by comprehenders (e.g., Rohde et al., 2011; Hartshorne and Snedeker, 2013). Thus, IC is argued to be contained within the linguistic signal, analogous to evidence of syntactic agreement and verb argument structure within corpora. We hypothesize that if these claims are correct, then current LMs will be able to condition reference and syntactic attachment by IC verbs with just language data (i.e. without grounding).

We tested this hypothesis using unidirectional transformer and long short-term memory network (LSTM; Hochreiter and Schmidhuber, 1997) language models. We find that LSTM LMs fail to acquire a subject/object-biased IC distinction that influences reference or RC attachment. In contrast, transformers learned a representational distinction between subject-biased and object-biased IC verbs that interacts with both reference and RC attachment, but the distinction only influenced model output for reference. The apparent failure of model syntactic behavior to exhibit an IC contrast that is present in model representations raises questions about the broader capacity of LMs to display human-like linguistic knowledge.

2   Related Work

The ability of LMs to encode referential knowledge has largely been explored in the domain of coreference resolution. Prior work has suggested that LMs can learn coreference resolution to some extent (e.g., Peters et al., 2018; Sorodoc et al., 2020). In the present study, we focus on within-sentence resolution rather than the ability of LMs to track entities over larger spans of text (cf. Sorodoc et al., 2020). Previous work at this granularity of coreference resolution has shown LSTM LMs strongly favor reference to male entities (Jumelet et al., 2019), for which the present study finds additional support. Rather than utilizing a more limited modeling objective such as coreference resolution (cf. Cheng and Erk, 2020), we followed Sorodoc et al. (2020) in focusing on the representation of referential knowledge by models trained with a general language modeling objective.

With regards to linguistic representations, a growing body of literature suggests that LSTM LMs are able to acquire syntactic knowledge. In particular, subject-verb agreement has been explored extensively (e.g., Linzen et al., 2016; Bernardy and Lappin, 2017; Enguehard et al., 2017) with results at human level performance in some cases (Gulordava et al., 2018). Additionally, work has shown human-like behavior when processing reflexive pronouns, negative polarity items (Futrell et al., 2018), center embedding, and syntactic islands (Wilcox et al., 2018, 2019). This literature generally suggests that LMs encode some type of abstract syntactic representation (e.g., Prasad et al., 2019). Additionally, recent work has shown LMs learn linguistic representations beyond syntax, such as pragmatics and discourse structure (Jeretic et al., 2020; Schuster et al., 2020; Davis and van Schijndel, 2020a).

The robustness of these abstract linguistic representations, however, have been questioned in recent work, suggesting that learned abstractions are weaker than standardly assumed (e.g., Trask et al., 2018; van Schijndel et al., 2019; Kodner and Gupta, 2020; Davis and van Schijndel, 2020b). The present study builds on these recent developments by demonstrating the inability of LMs to utilize discourse structure in syntactic processing.

3   Language Models

We trained 25 LSTM LMs on the Wikitext-103 corpus (Merity et al., 2016) with a vocabulary constrained to the most frequent 50K words.[1] We used

---

[1]The models had two LSTM layers with 400 hidden units each, 400-dimensional word embeddings, a dropout rate of 0.2 and batchsize 20, and were trained for 40 epochs (with early stopping) using PyTorch. The mean perplexity for the models on the validation data was 40.6 with a standard deviation of 2.05. The LSTMs and code for the experiments in this paper can be found at `https://github.com/forrestdavis/ImplicitCausality`.

two pretrained unidirectional transformer LMs: TransformerXL (Dai et al., 2019) and GPT-2 XL (Radford et al., 2019).[2]

TransformerXL was trained on Wikitext-103, like our LSTM LMs, but has more parameters and a larger vocabulary. GPT-2 XL differs from the other models in lacking recurrence (instead utilizing non-recurrent self-attention) and in amount and diversity of training data (1 billion words compared to the 103 million in Wikitext-103). As such, we caution against extracting explicit, mechanistic claims from the present study concerning the relationship between learned linguistic knowledge and model configurations and training data. Instead, our work points to apparent differences between transformers and LSTMs with regard to use and acquisition of discourse structure, leaving explanatory principles to further work.

4   Interactions with Reference

The results of Sorodoc et al. (2020) suggested that referential contrasts based in grammatical features (e.g., gender) would be easier for models to discern then those purely focused on referential selection (e.g., antecedents with the same gender but differing in preference). To evaluate this claim, we analyzed the degree to which IC verb type (i.e. subject vs. object biased) influenced i) model pronoun preferences when the possible referents differed in gender (e.g., *Sally feared Bob because...*), and ii) similarity of model representations between the pronoun and possible referents when they share the same gender (e.g., *Fred feared Bob because he...*). Our prediction was that IC would have a weaker influence in (ii) than (i).

4.1   Referential Stimuli

Our data consisted of the stimuli from a human experiment conducted in Ferstl et al. (2011), which asked participants to give continuations to sentence fragments of the following form:

(3)   Kate accused Bill because ...

Continuations were coded across 305 verbs for whether participants referenced the subject (i.e. *she*) or the object (i.e. *he*).[3] The results of this coding were then converted into a bias score for each

verb, ranging from 100 for verbs whose valid continuations uniquely refer to the subject (i.e. subject-biased) to -100 for verbs whose valid continuations uniquely refer to the object (i.e. object-biased). In the present study, we took 246 of these verbs[4] and generated stimuli as in (3) using 14 pairs of stereotypical male and female nouns (e.g., *man* vs. *woman*, *king* vs. *queen*), rather than rely on proper names as was done in Ferstl et al. (2011).[5] We created two categories of stimuli, those with differing gender[6] and those with the same gender resulting in 6888 sentences per category.

4.2   Measures

We evaluated our models independently for external behavior (e.g., predicted next-words) and internal representations (e.g., hidden states). Ideally, model behavior should condition on an abstracted representation that distinguishes subject-biased IC verbs from object-biased IC verbs. Similarly, a representational distinction between subject and object-biased IC verbs should have some influence on model behavior. We find that this is not the case for the LMs under investigation; a representational distinction between subject vs. object-biased IC verbs does not condition model behavioral differences.

To evaluate behavior, we appended a pronoun to (3) and calculated information-theoretic surprisal (Shannon, 1948; Hale, 2001; Levy, 2008). Surprisal is defined as the inverse log probability assigned to each word (w_i) in a sentence given the preceding context:

$$\text{surprisal}(w_i) = -\log p(w_i|w_1...w_{i-1}) \quad (1)$$

The probability of a word was calculated by applying the softmax function to a LM's output layer. Surprisal has been correlated with human processing difficulty (Smith and Levy, 2013; Frank et al., 2015) allowing us to compare model behavior to human behavior. We predicted that IC verbs would influence surprisal, with subject-biased ICs lowering the surprisal of pronouns agreeing with the subject, and object-biased ICs lowering the surprisal of the prounouns agreeing with the object. This methodology follows subject-verb agreement experiments, where verbs that agree in number with

---

[2]We used HuggingFace's implementation of these models (Wolf et al., 2019).

[3]An additional category, other, was included for ambiguous (i.e. *they hate each other*) or non-referential continuations (i.e. *it was a rough day*).

[4]59 verbs were outside of our LSTM LM vocabulary, so they were excluded.

[5]See Appendix A for all the pairs.

[6]We balanced our stimuli by gender, so we had the same number of female subjects as male subjects and vice versa.

the subject are less surprising than those that do not (e.g., *Cats are* vs. **Cats is*; Linzen et al., 2016; Mueller et al., 2020)

To evaluate model representations, we followed work in representational similarity analysis and used Pearson's r[7] to measure the similarity between model representations (see Kriegeskorte et al., 2008; Chrupała and Alishahi, 2019).[8]

We build on work that has looked at the propagation of information across time within a layer (as in Giulianelli et al., 2018; Jumelet et al., 2019). In such work, model behavior for subject-verb agreement and coreference is linked to model representations, and in particular, stronger model representations of previous time steps that relate to the model's current prediction.

In the present study, we focused on the similarity between the pronoun and possible antecedents when they shared the same gender:

(4)   a.   The mother amused the girl because she ...

        b.   The mother applauded the girl because she ...

Specifically, for (4) we computed the layer-wise similarity between the hidden representation of *she* with *mother* and *girl*.[9] The bias score found in Ferstl et al. (2011) for *amused* in (4-a) was 67 (i.e. the verb is subject-biased) and for *applauded* in (4-b) it was -84 (i.e. the verb is object-biased). Thus, we predicted that a layer that encodes a human-like IC distinction should have greater similarity between *she* and *mother* in the case of *amused* than between *she* and *girl*, and vice versa for *applauded*.

---

[7]Specifically, corrcoef from numpy.

[8]There exist a number of other measures of representational similarity (e.g., Morcos et al., 2018). In the present study, our use of experimental materials from psycholinguistic studies resulted in far fewer data than is needed for these methods, where one wants much more data than the dimensions of the representations. This is particularly stark for the syntactic stimuli where the embedding size for GPT-2 XL is roughly 13 times larger than the number of stimuli. These techniques may ultimately provide stronger evidence for representations of implicit causality in these language models, particularly for the LSTM LMs where no representational trace of implicit causality was found. It is worth noting that the LSTM behavior does not show an influence of implicity causality, so if we were to find such a representation with a better measure of similarity it would further the disconnect between model representations and behavior we found for the transformers. We hope to explore this in future work.

[9]Given the BPE tokenizer for GPT-2 XL, if a noun was broken into components, we used the hidden representation of the final component.

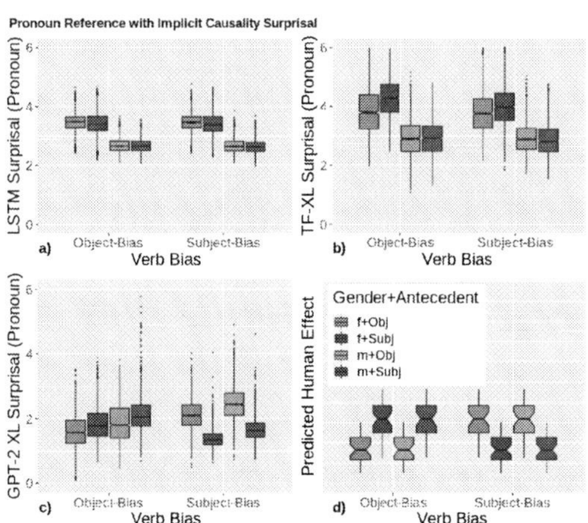

Figure 1: Model surprisal (in **a)** LSTM LMs, **b)** TransformerXL, and **c)** GPT-2 XL) at the pronoun and **d)** the predicted qualitative human-like pattern; stimuli from Ferstl et al. (2011) (e.g., *the man accused the woman because she*). Broken into antecedent (subject vs. object) and gender of pronoun (male vs. female). Lower surprisal corresponds to greater model preference.

4.3   Influence of IC on Referential Behavior

We calculated the surprisal for our LMs at the pronoun in our experimental stimuli, with the prediction that IC bias would modulate surprisal. Results for each LM type (LSTMs, TransformerXL, GPT-2 XL) are given in Figure 1. Statistical analyses[10] were conducted via linear-mixed effects models.[11] Post-hoc t-tests were conducted to assess effects.[12]

As is visually apparent in Figure 1, all three models showed some gender bias (male for TransformerXL and LSTM LMs and female for GPT-2 XL), in line with existing findings of gender preferences in LSTMs (see Jumelet et al., 2019).

The effect of IC bias was mixed across the LMs. For the LSTMs, the influence of IC was marginal ($p = 0.02$) being driven by an extremely small dif-

---

[10]We used lmer (version 1.1.23; Bates et al., 2015) and lmerTest (version 3.1.2; Kuznetsova et al., 2017) in R.

[11]We fit a model to predict surprisal at the pronoun with a three way interaction between IC bias, position of gender matching noun, and gender of pronoun and a random intercept for item. We ran a model with the continuous bias score from Ferstl et al. (2011) and another with a categorical bias effect derived from the bias score in Ferstl et al. (2011), with positive bias scores corresponding to a subject-biased verb and negative bias scores corresponding to a object-biased verb. These models had comparable results and are reported in the supplemental materials.

[12]The threshold for statistical significance was p = 0.005. Full output from the statistical models are given in the supplemental materials, and all R code to recreate the tests and figures is on Github.

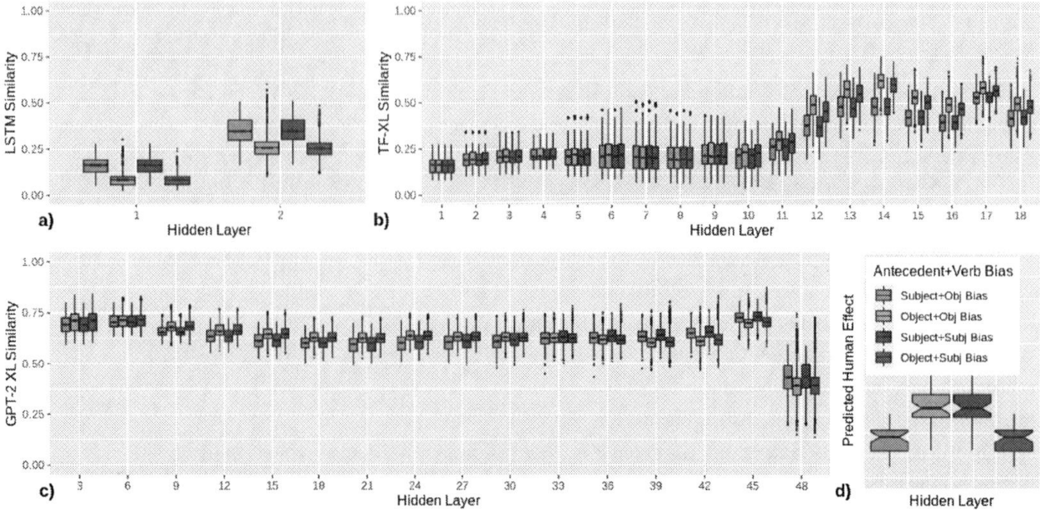

Figure 2: Layer-wise representational similarity (in **a)** LSTM LMs, **b)** TransformerXL, and **c)** GPT-2 XL) between pronoun and subject/object and **d)** the predicted qualitative human-like pattern); stimuli from Ferstl et al. (2011) (e.g., *the man accused the boy because he*). Broken into antecedent (subject vs. object) and IC bias type (subject-bias vs. object-bias). We include every third layer for GPT-2 XL (48 layers total). Greater similarity corresponds to greater relationship between pronoun and antecedent.

ference (0.02 bits) in surprisal centered on male pronouns agreeing in gender with the subject. There was neither a significant effect for object pronouns or for female pronouns referring to subjects. We concluded that the LSTM IC effect was spurious and that LSTM LMs acquired no IC-conditioned expectation about reference.

For TransformerXL, there was a slight lowering in surprisal for reference to male subjects with subject-biased verbs, and a larger lowering in surprisal for reference to female subjects after subject-biased verbs. That is to say, subject-biased IC verbs did lower the surprisal of pronouns referring to subjects, as predicted. However, there was no influence of IC when pronouns referred to the object. This suggests that preferences for local agreement in TransformerXL are much stronger than the influence of IC-bias, which only appears with subject-biased verbs.

The behavior of GPT-2 XL was in line with the human findings from Ferstl et al. (2011). Subject-biased verbs lowered the surprisal of pronouns referring to the subject, and object-biased verbs lowered the surprisal of pronouns referring to the object, regardless of gender. This suggests that GPT-2 XL has acquired a robust IC representation that influences expectations for pronominal reference.

4.4 Influence of IC on Referential Representation

We turn now to the ability of the models to distinguish the correct referent when both the subject and object have the same gender. Previous literature has suggested that this effect would be weaker than in the mismatching gender case above (see Sorodoc et al., 2020). We relied on a representational analysis (detailed in Section 4.2) to evaluate the preferences of the LMs. Results for each LM type are given in Figure 2.

Statistical significance was determined via linear-mixed effects models with post-hoc t-tests assessing the effects.[13] As predicted, IC bias had a weaker effect when choosing between competing nouns with the same gender for reference (e.g., *the woman admires the queen because she*).

For LSTM LMs, IC bias did not influence model representations, at least as measured in the present study. For TransformerXL there was a small difference in degree of similarity from layers 12 to

---

[13] We fit models predicting similarity from a four way interaction of IC bias, noun comparison (subject or object), model layer, and gender and a random intercept for item. Two IC bias effects were considered: the gradient value given in Ferstl et al. (2011) and a categorical value where positive bias corresponds to a subject-biased verb and negative bias corresponds to a object-biased verb. Similar results were found with both effects with both models given in the supplemental materials.

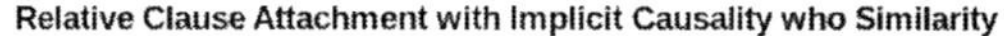

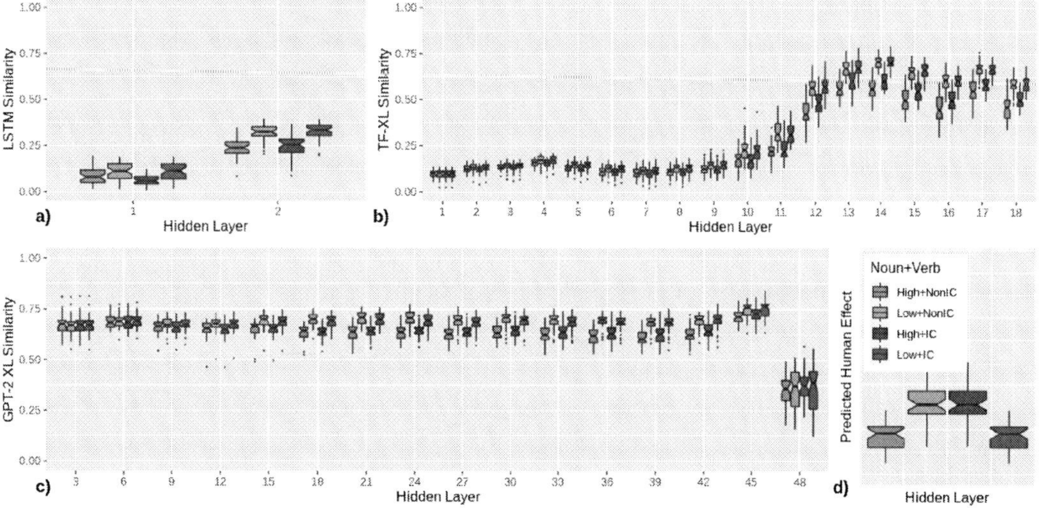

Figure 3: Layer-wise representational similarity (in **a)** LSTM LMs, **b)** TransformerXL, and **c)** GPT-2 XL) between *who* and the higher/lower noun, and **d)** the qualitative predicted human-like pattern); stimuli from Rohde et al. (2011) (e.g., *the man admired the agent of the rockers who*). Broken into attachment location (higher noun vs. lower noun) and verb type (object-biased IC verb vs. non-IC verb). We include every third layer for GPT-2 XL (48 layers total). Greater similarity corresponds to greater relationship between attachment location and *who*.

18. The pronoun was more similar to the object when the verb was object-biased. In contrast, there was no significant effect for subject-biased verbs, despite the reverse effect in behavior when antecedents had mismatched gender (i.e. subject-bias, not object-bias, influenced pronoun surprisal in our behavioral analysis).

For GPT-2 XL we found a small, yet significant, difference in degree of similarity with the subject antecedent starting in layer 15 and continuing through layer 47. That is, there was greater similarity between the pronoun and the subject when the verb was subject-biased. There was no effect for pronouns referring to the object. These results suggest that the influence of IC is only weakly present when both the subject and object are possible antecedents (i.e. they are the same gender). It therefore seems that models were only able to fully leverage an IC contrast to resolve reference when gender differences unambiguously distinguished between subject and object.

5 Interactions with Syntactic Attachment

We turn now to the relationship between IC verbs and syntax. Recall the prediction that object-biased IC verbs should interact with RC attachment to license more cases of syntactic attachment to the higher noun compared to lower noun (i.e. *chef*

in *Anna scolded the chef of the aristocrats who was/were...*).

5.1 Syntactic Stimuli

We used stimuli from Rohde et al. (2011), which consisted of two experiments: a sentence completion task and a self-paced reading task. The sentence completion task consisted of 21 prompts like:

(5) a. Carl admires the agent of the rockstars who...

    b. Carl works with the agent of the rockstars who...

The key manipulation lies with the main verb. In (5-a), *admires* is an object-biased IC verb, and in (5-b), *works with* is a non-IC verb. In the present study, we took 14 of these prompts[14] and generated stimuli balanced for number (i.e. we added *Carl admires the agents of the rockstar who...*), for a total of 112 sentences.

The self-paced reading time study in Rohde et al. (2011) consisted of 20 pairs of sentences, as in:

(6) a. Anna scolded the chef of the aristocrats who was/were routinely letting

---

[14]7 prompts were excluded because either the non-IC or the IC verb was not in the vocabulary of our LSTM LMs. For the remaining prompts, we replaced ceo(s) with boss(es), supermodel(s) with superstar(s), and rockstar(s) with rocker(s).

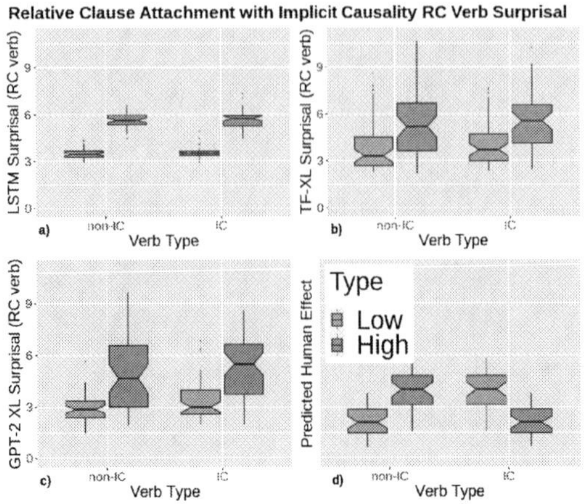

Figure 4: Model surprisal (in **a)** LSTM LMs, **b)** TransformerXL, **c)** GPT-2 XL, and **d)** qualitative predicted human-like pattern) at the RC verb (*was/were*); stimuli from Rohde et al. (2011) (e.g., *the man admired the agent of the rockers who was/were*). Broken into location of agreement (High vs. Low). Lower surprisal corresponds to greater model preference.

   food go to waste.

 b. Anna studied with the chef of the aristocrats who was/were routinely letting food go to waste.

As with the completion study, the central manipulation in the self-paced reading study lies with whether the verb is an object-biased IC verb (*scolded*) or not (*studied with*). Rather than give completions, though, human participants read sentences where the RC verb (e.g., *was* or *were*) either agreed with the higher noun (e.g., *chef*) or the lower noun (e.g., *aristocrats*). Rohde et al. (2011) reported decreased reading times for agreement with the higher noun when the verb was object-biased compared to when the verb was not object-biased. In other words, an object-biased IC verb facilitated attachment to the higher noun. In evaluating our models on these stimuli, we again balanced them by number, so that the higher and lower noun were equally frequent as singular or plural in our test data. This resulted in 192 test sentences generated from 12 pairs.[15]

5.2   Measures

For the sentence completion stimuli, we conducted a cloze task. Specifically, given the sentence fragment *the man admires the agent of the rockstars who*, we calculated the top 100 most likely next words for the LMs. These were then tagged for part-of-speech using spaCy and a score was assigned based on the weighted probability of a continuation using a singular verb (i.e. probability mass assigned to singular verbs divided by probability mass assigned to all verbs).[16] Our prediction is that object-biased IC main verbs will lead to more continuations agreeing with the higher noun (e.g., *agent*).

As detailed in Section 4.2, we calculated information-theoretic surprisal and layer-wise similarity. With the self-paced reading time stimuli (e.g., 6), we calculated surprisal at the RC verb and calculated similarity between *who* (and *was/were*) and the higher and lower nouns (e.g., *chef* and *aristocrats* for (6)). We predicted that with object-biased IC verbs like *scolded* in (6) there would be greater similarity between *who* and *chef* than for *who* and *aristocrats* in layers that have an IC distinction (vice versa for non-IC verbs like *studied*).

5.3   Influence of IC on Syntactic Behavior

To test the influence of IC verbs on model behavior for RC attachment, we followed the experiments in Rohde et al. (2011). The results are given in Figure 4. We evaluated statistical significance with linear-mixed effects models.[17] Post-hoc t-tests were conducted to assess any effects. None of the LM architectures showed any influence of IC on model behavior, either for the cloze task or the self-paced reading stimuli. Rather, they all had a strong preference for agreeing with the lower noun.[18]

---

[15]We excluded pairs where either of the main verbs was not in the vocabulary of our LSTM LMs. There was one noun substitution, florist(s) with clerk(s). Given that all our LMs were unidirectional, we ignored the material after the RC verb. Additionally, for both the completion and self-paced reading stimuli, we substituted male names with *the man* and female names with *the woman*.

[16]We excluded verbs that were ambiguous (e.g., *ate*).

[17]We fit models predicting surprisal at the RC verb from a three way interaction of agreement location, main verb type (object-biased IC or not), and number and a random intercept for item. For the cloze task, we fit models predicting percent singular continuation from an interaction between location of singular agreement (higher or lower noun) and main verb type and a random intercept for item.

[18]With regard to categorical preferences (i.e. numerically lower surprisal for one attachment location over another for a given stimulus), all the LMs have overwhelming preferences for attachment to the lower noun. The LSTM LMs favored attachment to the higher noun in 0% of stimuli (across both IC and non-IC stimuli). For TransformerXL, attachment to the higher noun was preferred in 25% of the stimuli with an object-biased IC verb (i.e. where we expect a preference for attachment to the higher noun) and attachment to the higher noun in 27% of the stimuli without an object-biased IC verb

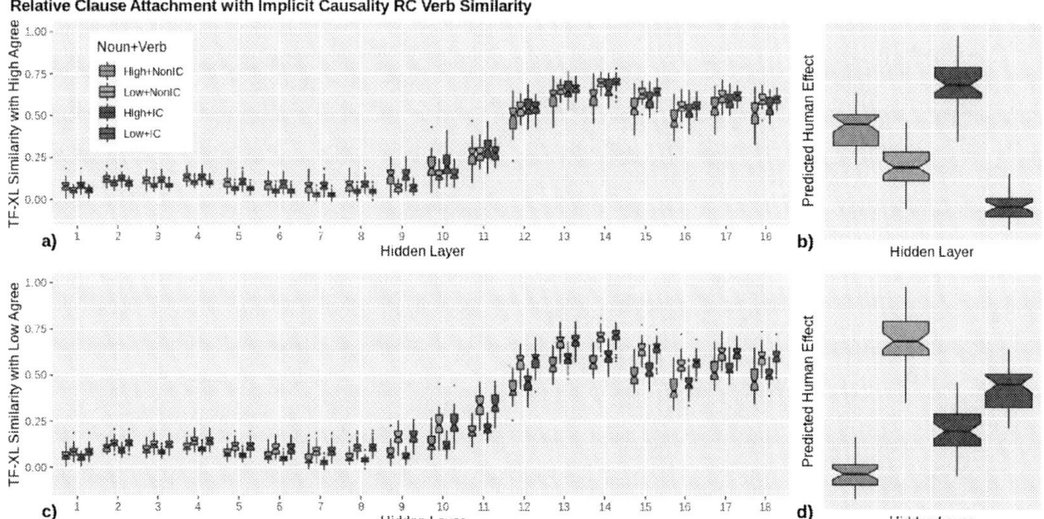

Figure 5: Layer-wise representational similarity between the RC verb (*was/were*) and the higher/lower noun; stimuli from Rohde et al. (2011) (e.g., *the man admired the agent of the rockers who was/were*). Results broken into attachment location (higher noun vs. lower noun) and verb type (object-biased IC verb vs. non-IC verb) are given in **a)**, for stimuli where the RC verb agrees with the higher noun (e.g., *agent of the rockers who was*), and in **c)**, for stimuli where the RC verb agrees with the lower noun (e.g., *rockers who were*). The explicit agreement should force a particular attachment location to be preferred, with verb IC bias dampening this effect (the predicted qualitative human-like pattern is depicted in **b)** and **d)**). Greater similarity corresponds to greater relationship between attachment location and *was/were*.

5.4 Influence of IC on Syntactic Representations

We examined the representational similarity between *who* and the possible attachment points (i.e. higher or lower noun) and the RC verb (*was/were*) and the possible attachment points. Results for all three LM architectures for *who* are given in Figure 3, and results for the RC verb are given for TransformerXL in Figure 5. Statistical significance was determined via linear-mixed effects models.[19] Post-hoc t-tests were conducted to assess effects.

The LSTM LMs had no representational effect of IC on either *who* or the RC verb, similar to the lack of an effect in pronouns. Instead, the LSTM LMs

representations always had greater similarity to the lower noun, in line with the robust preference for attaching to the lower noun in behavior (i.e. model surprisal).

For TransformerXL, object-biased IC verbs increased the similarity between the higher noun and both *who* and the RC verb (regardless of agreement). That is, the presence of an object-biased IC verb increased the similarity of the RC verb and the higher noun both when the RC verb agreed in number with the higher noun (e.g., *chef...was*) and when the RC verb did not agree in number (e.g., *chef...were*). There was no effect of IC on the similarity between the lower noun and *who* or the RC verb.

For GPT-2, object-biased IC verbs increased the similarity between the higher noun and *who*, but only increased the similarity between the RC verb and the higher noun when they agreed in number (i.e. increased similarity between *chef* and *was* not *chef* and *were*). As with TransformerXL, there was no analogous effect on the similarity between the lower noun and *who* or the RC verb (i.e. no change in similarity based on the main verb).

We found TransformerXL had greater similar-

(i.e. where we do not expect attachment to the higher noun). Finally, for GPT-2 XL, for the stimuli with an object-biased IC verb attachment to the higher noun was preferred in 23% of the stimuli, and for stimuli without an object-biased IC verbs 9% of the time.

[19] Specifically, we fit a model predicting the similarity between *who* and the possible nouns with a three way interaction of main verb type (object-biased IC verb or not), noun (higher or lower), and layer with a random intercept for item. Additionally, we fit a model predicting the similarity between *was/were* and the possible nouns with a four way interaction of main verb type (object-biased IC verb or not), noun (higher or lower), agreement location, and layer with a random intercept for item.

ity between the RC verb and the lower noun in the final layer, regardless of verbal agreement (i.e. even in cases of ungrammatical attachment, TransformerXL preferred local attachment). Similarly, GPT-2 XL showed no preference for attachment location in the final layers despite unambiguous agreement with only one of the nouns. Strikingly, both transformer LMs showed greater similarity with the agreeing noun (i.e. similarity conditioned on syntax) in their earlier layers, with the final layers obscuring this distinction.

These results suggest that a preference for local agreement is robust in both LSTMs and transformer LMs. The transformers showed representations that encoded the IC contrast, as with the referential experiments. However, this knowledge did not propagate to the final layers, in line with the absent behavioral effects detailed above. Moreover, unambiguous syntactic knowledge about RC attachment was discarded in the final layers of TransformerXL and GPT-2. These results suggest that non-linguistic locality preferences dominate model representations and behavior.

6 Discussion

The present study examined the extent to which discourse structure, determined by implicit causality verbs, could be acquired by transformer and LSTM language models (cf. *Sally frightened Mary because she...* and *Sally feared Mary because she...*). Specifically, we evaluated, via comparison to human experiments, whether IC verb biases could influence reference and syntactic attachment in LMs. Analyses were conducted at two levels of granularity: model behavior (e.g., probability assigned to possible next words) and model representation (e.g., similarity between hidden representations). Given the claims in recent literature that implicit causality arises without extra pragmatic inference on the part of human comprehenders, we hypothesized that LMs would be able to acquire such contrasts (analogous to their ability to acquire syntactic agreement).

We found that LSTM LMs were unable to demonstrate knowledge of IC either in influencing reference or syntax. However, a transformer (TransformerXL) trained on the exact same data as the LSTM LMs was able to partially represent an IC distinction, but model output was only influenced by IC bias when resolving reference, not syntactic attachment. In evaluating a transformer model trained on vastly more data (GPT-2 XL), we found a more robust, human-like sensitivity to IC bias when resolving reference: subject-biased IC verbs increased model preference for subject pronouns and object-biased IC verbs increased model preferences for object pronouns. However, the same mismatch as TransformerXL between model representation and model behavior arose in processing syntactic attachment.

In contrast to our results, Davis and van Schijndel (2020a) showed syntactic predictions for LSTM LMs are influenced by some aspects of discourse structure. A simple explanation for these conflicting results may be that the LMs we examined here are unable to learn the syntactic operation of attachment, and thus no influence of discourse can surface. The erasure of number agreement in the final layers of the transformer LMs (see Section 5.4) provides compelling evidence towards this conclusion.[20]

From a theoretical perspective, the present study provides additional support for the centering of implicit causality within the linguistic signal proper. That is, IC bias is learnable, to some degree, without pragmatic inference as hypothesized in Section 1 (see also Hartshorne, 2014). The mismatches in syntactic representations and behavior suggest, however, that models ignore the abstract categories that are learned, contrary to human findings (cf. Rohde et al., 2011).

We believe a solution may lie in changing model training objectives (i.e. what linguistic unit should be predicted). Psycholinguistic studies focusing on the interaction of discourse and syntax have suggested that coherence relations may be the unit of linguistic prediction, in contrast to the next-word prediction used in most language modeling work (see Rohde et al., 2011). We leave to future work an investigation of this suggestion as well as teasing apart the exact role that training data and model architecture play in the interaction between types of linguistic representation.

Acknowledgments

Thank you to members of the C.Psyd lab at Cornell, who gave feedback on an earlier form of this work. We would also like to thank the three anonymous reviewers for their comments and suggestions.

---

[20]Further cross-linguistic evidence bearing on the inability of LSTM LMs, specifically, to learn relative clause attachment is given in Davis and van Schijndel (2020b).

References

Douglas Bates, Martin Mächler, Ben Bolker, and Steve Walker. 2015. Fitting linear mixed-effects models using lme4. *Journal of Statistical Software*, 67(1):1–48.

Jean-Philippe Bernardy and Shalom Lappin. 2017. Using deep neural networks to learn syntactic agreement. *Linguistic Issues in Language Technology*, 15.

Pengxiang Cheng and Katrin Erk. 2020. Attending to Entities for Better Text Understanding. In *Proceedings of the AAAI Conference on Artificial Intelligence*, volume 34.

Grzegorz Chrupała and Afra Alishahi. 2019. Correlating neural and symbolic representations of language. In *Proceedings of the 57th Annual Meeting of the Association for Computational Linguistics*, pages 2952–2962, Florence, Italy. Association for Computational Linguistics.

Zihang Dai, Zhilin Yang, Yiming Yang, Jaime Carbonell, Quoc Le, and Ruslan Salakhutdinov. 2019. Transformer-XL: Attentive Language Models beyond a Fixed-Length Context. In *Proceedings of the 57th Annual Meeting of the Association for Computational Linguistics*, pages 2978–2988, Florence, Italy. Association for Computational Linguistics.

Forrest Davis and Marten van Schijndel. 2020a. Interaction with Context During Recurrent Neural Network Sentence Processing. In *Proceedings of the 42nd Annual Meeting of the Cognitive Science Society*.

Forrest Davis and Marten van Schijndel. 2020b. Recurrent Neural Network Language Models Always Learn English-Like Relative Clause Attachment. In *Proceedings of the 58th Annual Meeting of the Association for Computational Linguistics*, pages 1979–1990, Online. Association for Computational Linguistics.

Jacob Devlin, Ming-Wei Chang, Kenton Lee, and Kristina Toutanova. 2019. BERT: Pre-training of Deep Bidirectional Transformers for Language Understanding. In *Proceedings of the 2019 Annual Conference of the North American Chapter of the Association for Computational Linguistics*. Association for Computational Linguistics.

Émile Enguehard, Yoav Goldberg, and Tal Linzen. 2017. Exploring the Syntactic Abilities of RNNs with Multi-task Learning. In *Proceedings of the 21st Conference on Computational Natural Language Learning (CoNLL 2017)*, pages 3–14. Association for Computational Linguistics.

Evelyn C Ferstl, Alan Garnham, and Christina Manouilidou. 2011. Implicit causality bias in English: A corpus of 300 verbs. *Behavior Research Methods*, 43(1):124–135.

Stefan L. Frank, Leun J. Otten, Giulia Galli, and Gabriella Vigliocco. 2015. The ERP response to the amount of information conveyed by words in sentences. *Brain & Language*, 140:1–11.

Richard Futrell, Ethan Wilcox, Takashi Morita, and Roger Levy. 2018. RNNs as psycholinguistic subjects: Syntactic state and grammatical dependency. *arXiv preprint arXiv:1809.01329*.

Catherine Garvey and Alfonso Caramazza. 1974. Implicit causality in verbs. *Linguistic inquiry*, 5(3):459–464.

Mario Giulianelli, Jack Harding, Florian Mohnert, Dieuwke Hupkes, and Willem Zuidema. 2018. Under the hood: Using diagnostic classifiers to investigate and improve how language models track agreement information. In *Proceedings of the 2018 EMNLP Workshop BlackboxNLP: Analyzing and Interpreting Neural Networks for NLP*, pages 240–248, Brussels, Belgium. Association for Computational Linguistics.

Kristina Gulordava, Piotr Bojanowski, Edouard Grave, Tal Linzen, and Marco Baroni. 2018. Colorless green recurrent networks dream hierarchically. In *Proceedings of the 2018 Annual Conference of the North American Chapter of the Association for Computational Linguistics*. Association for Computational Linguistics.

John Hale. 2001. A probabilistic Earley parser as a psycholinguistic model. In *Proceedings of the second meeting of the North American Chapter of the Association for Computational Linguistics on Language technologies*, pages 1–8. Association for Computational Linguistics.

Joshua K Hartshorne. 2014. What is implicit causality? *Language, Cognition and Neuroscience*, 29(7):804–824.

Joshua K Hartshorne and Jesse Snedeker. 2013. Verb argument structure predicts implicit causality: The advantages of finer-grained semantics. *Language and Cognitive Processes*, 28(10):1474–1508.

Sepp Hochreiter and Jürgen Schmidhuber. 1997. Long short-term memory. *Neural Computation*, 9(8):1735–1780.

Jennifer Hu, Jon Gauthier, Peng Qian, Ethan Wilcox, and Roger Levy. 2020. A Systematic Assessment of Syntactic Generalization in Neural Language Models. In *Proceedings of the 58th Annual Meeting of the Association for Computational Linguistics*, pages 1725–1744, Online. Association for Computational Linguistics.

Paloma Jeretic, Alex Warstadt, Suvrat Bhooshan, and Adina Williams. 2020. Are natural language inference models IMPPRESsive? Learning IMPlicature and PRESupposition. In *Proceedings of the 58th Annual Meeting of the Association for Computational Linguistics*, pages 8690–8705, Online. Association for Computational Linguistics.

Jaap Jumelet, Willem Zuidema, and Dieuwke Hupkes. 2019. Analysing Neural Language Models: Contextual Decomposition Reveals Default Reasoning in Number and Gender Assignment. In *Proceedings of the 23rd Conference on Computational Natural Language Learning*, pages 1–11, Hong Kong, China. Association for Computational Linguistics.

Andrew Kehler, Laura Kertz, Hannah Rohde, and Jeffrey L Elman. 2008. Coherence and coreference revisited. *Journal of semantics*, 25(1):1–44.

Jordan Kodner and Nitish Gupta. 2020. Overestimation of Syntactic Representation in Neural Language Models. In *Proceedings of the 58th Annual Meeting of the Association for Computational Linguistics*, pages 1757–1762, Online. Association for Computational Linguistics.

Nikolaus Kriegeskorte, Marieke Mur, and Peter A Bandettini. 2008. Representational similarity analysis-connecting the branches of systems neuroscience. *Frontiers in Systems Neuroscience*, 2:4.

Alexandra Kuznetsova, Per B. Brockhoff, and Rune H. B. Christensen. 2017. lmerTest package: Tests in linear mixed effects models. *Journal of Statistical Software*, 82(13):1–26.

Roger Levy. 2008. Expectation-based syntactic comprehension. *Cognition*, 106(3):1126–1177.

Tal Linzen, Emmanuel Dupoux, and Yoav Goldberg. 2016. Assessing the ability of LSTMs to learn syntax-sensitive dependencies. *Transactions of the Association for Computational Linguistics*, 4:521–535.

Stephen Merity, Caiming Xiong, James Bradbury, and Richard Socher. 2016. Wikitext-103. Technical report, Salesforce.

Ari Morcos, Maithra Raghu, and Samy Bengio. 2018. Insights on representational similarity in neural networks with canonical correlation. In S. Bengio, H. Wallach, H. Larochelle, K. Grauman, N. Cesa-Bianchi, and R. Garnett, editors, *Advances in Neural Information Processing Systems 31*, pages 5727–5736. Curran Associates, Inc.

Aaron Mueller, Garrett Nicolai, Panayiota Petrou-Zeniou, Natalia Talmina, and Tal Linzen. 2020. Cross-Linguistic Syntactic Evaluation of Word Prediction Models. In *Proceedings of the 58th Annual Meeting of the Association for Computational Linguistics*, pages 5523–5539, Online. Association for Computational Linguistics.

Matthew E. Peters, Mark Neumann, Mohit Iyyer, Matt Gardner, Christopher Clark, Kenton Lee, and Luke Zettlemoyer. 2018. Deep contextualized word representations. In *Proceedings of the 2018 Annual Conference of the North American Chapter of the Association for Computational Linguistics*. Association for Computational Linguistics.

Grusha Prasad, Marten van Schijndel, and Tal Linzen. 2019. Using Priming to Uncover the Organization of Syntactic Representations in Neural Language Models. In *Proceedings of the 23rd Conference on Computational Natural Language Learning*.

Alec Radford, Karthik Narasimhan, Tim Salimans, and Ilya Sutskever. 2018. Improving Language Understanding by Generative Pre-Training. Technical report, OpenAI.

Alec Radford, Jeffrey Wu, Rewon Child, David Luan, Dario Amodei, and Ilya Sutskever. 2019. Language Models are Unsupervised Multitask Learners. Technical report, OpenAI.

Hannah Rohde, Roger Levy, and Andrew Kehler. 2011. Anticipating explanations in relative clause processing. *Cognition*, 118(3):339–358.

Sebastian Schuster, Yuxing Chen, and Judith Degen. 2020. Harnessing the linguistic signal to predict scalar inferences. In *Proceedings of the 58th Annual Meeting of the Association for Computational Linguistics*, pages 5387–5403, Online. Association for Computational Linguistics.

Claude Shannon. 1948. A mathematical theory of communication. *Bell System Technical Journal*, 27:379–423, 623–656.

Nathaniel J Smith and Roger Levy. 2013. The effect of word predictability on reading time is logarithmic. *Cognition*, 128(3):302–319.

Ionut-Teodor Sorodoc, Kristina Gulordava, and Gemma Boleda. 2020. Probing for Referential Information in Language Models. In *Proceedings of the 58th Annual Meeting of the Association for Computational Linguistics*, pages 4177–4189, Online. Association for Computational Linguistics.

Andrew Trask, Felix Hill, Scott E Reed, Jack Rae, Chris Dyer, and Phil Blunsom. 2018. Neural arithmetic logic units. In *Advances in Neural Information Processing Systems*, pages 8035–8044.

Marten van Schijndel, Aaron Mueller, and Tal Linzen. 2019. Quantity doesn't buy quality syntax with neural language models. In *Proceedings of the 2019 Conference on Empirical Methods in Natural Language Processing*. Association for Computational Linguistics.

Ethan Wilcox, Roger Levy, and Richard Futrell. 2018. What Syntactic Structures block Dependencies in RNN Language Models? In *Proceedings of the 41st Annual Meeting of the Cognitive Science Society*.

Ethan Wilcox, Roger Levy, and Richard Futrell. 2019. Hierarchical Representation in Neural Language Models: Suppression and Recovery of Expectations. In *Proceedings of the 2019 ACL Workshop BlackboxNLP: Analyzing and Interpreting Neural Networks for NLP*.

Elyce Dominique Williams. 2020. Language Experience Predicts Pronoun Comprehension in Implicit Causality Sentences. Master's thesis, University of North Carolina at Chapel Hill.

Thomas Wolf, Lysandre Debut, Victor Sanh, Julien Chaumond, Clement Delangue, Anthony Moi, Pierric Cistac, Tim Rault, R'emi Louf, Morgan Funtowicz, and Jamie Brew. 2019. HuggingFace's Transformers: State-of-the-art Natural Language Processing. *ArXiv*, abs/1910.03771.

A Stereotypically gendered nouns used in referential experiments

male	female
man	woman
boy	girl
father	mother
uncle	aunt
husband	wife
actor	actress
prince	princess
waiter	waitress
lord	lady
king	queen
son	daughter
nephew	niece
brother	sister
grandfather	grandmother

Continual Adaptation for Efficient Machine Communication

Robert D. Hawkins[1], Minae Kwon[2], Dorsa Sadigh[2,3], Noah D. Goodman[1,2]
Departments of [1]Psychology, [2]Computer Science, and [3]Electrical Engineering
Stanford University, Stanford, CA 94305
{rxdh, mnkwon, ngoodman}@stanford.edu, dorsa@cs.stanford.edu

Abstract

To communicate with new partners in new contexts, humans rapidly form new linguistic conventions. Recent neural language models are able to comprehend and produce the existing conventions present in their training data, but are not able to flexibly and interactively adapt those conventions on the fly as humans do. We introduce an interactive repeated reference task as a benchmark for models of adaptation in communication and propose a regularized continual learning framework that allows an artificial agent initialized with a generic language model to more accurately and efficiently communicate with a partner over time. We evaluate this framework through simulations on COCO and in real-time reference game experiments with human partners.

1 Introduction

Communication depends on shared conventions about the meanings of words (Lewis, 1969), but the real-world demands of language use often require agents to go *beyond* fixed conventional meanings (Grice, 1975; Davidson, 1986). Recent work on *pragmatic* and *context-aware* models has approached this problem by equipping speaker and listener agents with the ability to explicitly reason about one another. Pragmatic reasoning allows listeners to infer richer intended meanings by considering counterfactual alternatives, and allows speakers to be appropriately informative, not merely truthful (Goodman and Frank, 2016; Andreas and Klein, 2016; Fried et al., 2018; Monroe et al., 2017; Vedantam et al., 2017).

These models have largely focused on one-shot settings, where the context is the immediate visual environment. In common interactive settings, however, the relevant context for pragmatic competence also includes the history of previous interactions with the same communication partner. Human in-

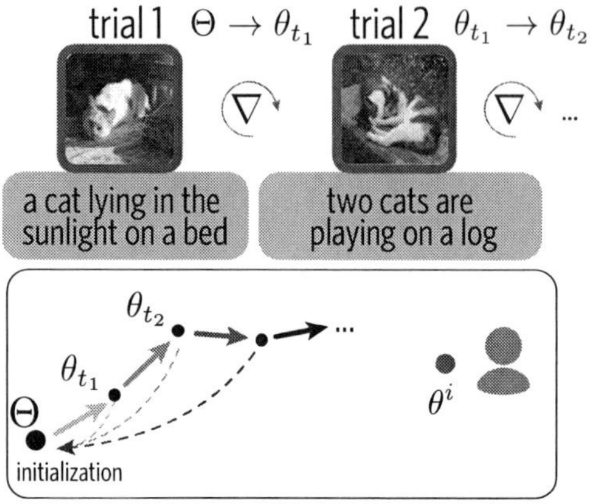

Figure 1: We introduce a regularized continual learning approach allowing agents initialized with a pretrained language model Θ to iteratively infer the language model θ^i used by a partner, over repeated interactions $\{t_1, t_2 \dots\}$ in an online reference game.

terlocutors are able to establish *ad hoc* conventions based on this history (Clark and Wilkes-Gibbs, 1986; Clark, 1996), allowing for increasingly *accurate* and *efficient* communication. Speakers can remain understandable while expending significantly fewer words (Krauss and Weinheimer, 1964; Orita et al., 2015; Staliūnaitė et al., 2018; Hawkins et al., 2020a; Stewart et al., 2020).

For example, consider a nurse visiting a bedridden patient at their home. The first time the patient asks the nurse to retrieve a particular medication, they must painstakingly identify a specific bottle, e.g. "the medicine for my back pain in a small blue medicine bottle labeled Flexeril in my bathroom." But after a week of care, they may just ask for the "back meds" and expect the nurse to know which bottle they mean. Such flexibility poses a challenge for current pragmatic models. For an artificial agent to establish new conventions, as humans do, it must go beyond pragmatic reasoning at the single-utterance timescale to *learn* about

Proceedings of the 24th Conference on Computational Natural Language Learning, pages 408–419
Online, November 19-20, 2020. ©2020 Association for Computational Linguistics
https://doi.org/10.18653/v1/P17

its partners over longer timescales.

Here, we propose that the problem of *ad hoc* convention formation can be usefully re-formulated as an inference problem amenable to online domain adaptation. Our approach is motivated by a growing body of evidence in cognitive science that humans quickly re-calibrate their expectations about how language is used by different partners (Grodner and Sedivy, 2011; Yildirim et al., 2016). This empirical work highlights three key challenges facing a scalable adaptation approach. First, because the target data comes from intentional agents, *pragmatic reasoning* must be deployed throughout adaptation to strengthen inferences (Frank et al., 2009). Second, because the data is sparse, strong adaptation risks catastrophic forgetting; yet, human speakers are able to revert to their background expectations for the next interlocutor (Wilkes-Gibbs and Clark, 1992; Metzing and Brennan, 2003). Third, the ability to ground the meanings of later, shorter utterances (e.g. "back meds") in the use of earlier, longer utterances requires a *compositional* representation; otherwise the connection between the utterances is not clear (Hawkins et al., 2020a).

Our primary contribution is an online continual learning framework for transforming pragmatic agents into *adaptive* agents that can be deployed in real-time interactions. This framework is shown schematically in Fig. 1: after each trial, we take a small number of gradient steps to update beliefs about the language model used by the current partner. To evaluate our framework, we first introduce a benchmark *interactive* repeated reference task (Fig. 2) using contexts of natural images. In Sec. 3, we introduce the three core components of our algorithm: (i) a contrastive loss objective incorporating explicit pragmatic reasoning, (ii) a KL regularization objective to prevent overfitting or catastrophic forgetting, and (iii) a data augmentation step for compositionally assigning credit to sub-utterances. In Sec. 4, we report experiments demonstrating that this algorithm enables more effective communication with naive human partners over repeated interactions. Finally, in Sec. 5 we report a series of ablation studies showing that each component plays a necessary role, and close with a discussion of important areas for future research in Sec. 6

2   Related work

Personalizing language models. Adapting or personalizing language models is a classic problem of practical interest for NLP, where shifts in the data distribution are often found across test contexts (Kneser and Steinbiss, 1993; Riccardi and Gorin, 2000; Bellegarda, 2004; Ben-David et al., 2010). Our approach draws upon the idea of dynamically fine-tuning RNNs (Mikolov et al., 2010; Krause et al., 2017), which has successfully explained key patterns of human behavior in self-paced reading tasks (Van Schijndel and Linzen, 2018). We also draw on the regularization objectives proposed in this literatures (Li and Bilmes, 2007; Liu et al., 2016). However, the interactive communicative setting we consider poses several distinct challenges from traditional speech recognition (Miao and Metze, 2015) or text classification settings (Blitzer et al., 2007; Glorot et al., 2011) for which adaptation is typically considered. Partner-specific observations of language use are sparser, must be incorporated online, and are generated by intentional agents.

Incorporating discourse history. Previous work has incorporated discourse history in reference games using explicit co-reference detection (Roy et al., 2019) or contribution tracking (DeVault and Stone, 2009) techniques. An alternative approach is to include embeddings of the history as conditional input to the model at test time (Haber et al., 2019). Similar approaches have been proposed for sequential visual question answering (Ohsugi et al., 2019; Choi et al., 2018). Rather than pre-training a fixed, monolithic language model and incorporating shared history on top of this model at test time, we suggest that the underlying language model itself ought to be continually adapted over the course of an interaction.

Bayesian models of adaptation. Models of adaptation in cognitive science are typically formulated in terms of (hierarchical) Bayesian belief-updating based on evidence of language use (Kleinschmidt and Jaeger, 2015; Roettger and Franke, 2019; Delaney-Busch et al., 2019; Hawkins et al., 2017; Schuster and Degen, 2020). In these models, each new observation is taken as statistical evidence about the partner's language model, allowing pairs to coordinate on shared expectations and ground new conventions in their partner's previous behavior (see Sec. 3.2). While these models capture key theoretical properties of human adaptation, they do not scale well to natural-language applications, where neural networks are dominant.

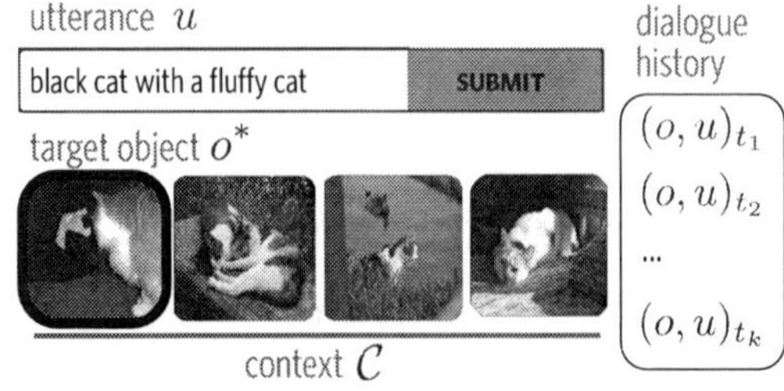

Figure 2: In a repeated reference game, a speaker agent must repeatedly communicate the identity of the same objects in context to a listener agent.

3 Approach

We begin by recasting convention formation as an online domain adaptation problem. As in previous computational approaches to pragmatics (e.g. Goodman and Frank, 2016; Andreas and Klein, 2016), we formulate this problem as an inference about another agent. The key theoretical idea is to expand the scope of pragmatic inference from the single-utterance timescale to evidence accumulated over longer timescales of an interaction. In addition to inferring a partner's intended meaning (or interpretation) for each individual utterance, an adaptive agent pools across previous utterances to infer the distinct but stable way their partner uses language. Under this inference framework, an agent must both (1) begin with background expectations about language shared across many partners, and (2) have a mechanism to rapidly learn the specific language model used by the current partner. Our work assumes a conventional neural language model as the starting point and focuses on the partner-specific inference problem. In this section, we describe our repeated reference game benchmark task (3.1), review the underlying problem as it has been previously formulated in a Bayesian framework (3.2), and finally describe our algorithm for adapting neural language models (3.3).

3.1 Repeated reference game task

As a benchmark for studying domain adaptation in communication, we use the *repeated reference game* task (Fig. 2), which has been widely used in cognitive science to study partner-specific adaptation in communication (Krauss and Weinheimer, 1964; Clark and Wilkes-Gibbs, 1986; Wilkes-Gibbs and Clark, 1992). In this task, a speaker agent and a listener agent are shown a context of images, $\mathcal{C}$ (e.g. four images of cats). On each trial, one of

these images is privately designated as the *target object*, o^*, for the speaker (e.g. the image with the thick border shown on the left). The speaker agent thus takes the pair $(o^*, \mathcal{C})$ as input and returns an utterance u (e.g. "black cat with a fluffy cat") that will allow the listener to select the target from $\mathcal{C}$. The listener agent takes $(u, \mathcal{C})$ as input and returns a softmax probability for each image, which it uses to make a selection. Both agents then receive feedback about the listener's selection and the identity of the target. Critically, the sequence of trials is constructed so that each image appears as the target several times. For example, our evaluations loop through each target six times, allowing us to observe how communication about each image changes as a function of dialogue history (see Fig. S1 in Supplementary Materials for examples).

3.2 The inference problem

We begin by assuming that agents represent the semantics of their language as a function relating natural language utterances u to actual states of the world o (here, images). We further assume that this function belongs to a family parameterized by θ, and denote the parameter used by a particular agent i with θ^i (see Fig. 1). If an artificial agent knows the true value of θ^i – their current partner's semantics[1] – they are in a better position to understand them, and to be understood in turn. However, because θ^i is not directly observable and θ varies across partners and contexts, it must be inferred (Bergen et al., 2016). Furthermore, it is in the agent's best interest to use its updated beliefs about its partner's θ to guide its own production and interpretation. An important consequence of this formulation is that conventionalization, the process by which parties converge on an efficient way to refer to something, emerges naturally as a consequence of mutual adaptation, the process by which each party independently tries to infer their interlocutor's language model (Smith et al., 2013; Hawkins et al., 2020b).

This is the central computational problem of adaptation, which we formalize as follows. Following Bayes Rule, the adaptive agent's beliefs about θ^i, conditioning on observations D^i from the shared history of interactions in that context, are:

$$P(\theta^i|D^i, \Theta) \propto P(D^i|\theta^i)P(\theta^i|\Theta) \qquad (1)$$

---

[1]Traditionally, this semantic function is truth-conditional, mapping utterance-state pairs to Boolean values, but recent approaches have shifted to more graded, real-valued functions such as those implemented by neural networks.

This formulation decomposes the inference into two terms, a prior term $P(\theta^i|\Theta)$ and a likelihood term $P(D^i|\theta^i)$.[2] The prior captures the idea that different partners share some general features of the semantics, represented by Θ, since they speak the same language; in the absence of partner-specific information, the agent ought to be regularized toward this background knowledge.

The likelihood term, on the other hand, accounts for direct evidence of language use. It represents an explicit forward model of an agent: different latent values of θ generate different observable actions. In other words, the standard single-utterance pragmatic inference problem is nested within the longer-timescale inference about θ. While explicit reasoning about the other agent is typically considered at the time of action selection (i.e. when the speaker is choosing an utterance, or when the listener is choosing a referent; Goodman and Frank, 2016; Andreas and Klein, 2016), this likelihood term importantly incorporates such reasoning at the time of *adaptation* (i.e. when updating beliefs about θ based on previous actions; Frank et al., 2009; Smith et al., 2013).

3.3 Continual adaptation for neural models

If we let θ be the weights of an image-captioning network, then the background knowledge shared across partners, Θ, corresponds to a pre-trained initialization, and conditioning on partner-specific data under a Bayesian prior corresponds to regularized gradient descent on θ. We exploit this connection to derive an online continual learning scheme that addresses the challenges of adapting to a human partner in a repeated reference game task.

Architecture and algorithm overview. Concretely, we consider an architecture that combines a convolutional visual encoder (ResNet-152) with an LSTM decoder (Vinyals et al., 2015). The LSTM takes a 300-dimensional embedding as input for each word in an utterance and its output is linearly projected back to a softmax distribution over the vocabulary size. To pass the visual feature vector computed by the encoder into the decoder, the final layer of ResNet was replaced by a fully-connected adapter layer. This layer was jointly pre-trained with the decoder on the COCO training corpus (Lin et al., 2014) and frozen. The COCO corpus con-

---

Algorithm 1 Update step for adaptive model

1: **Input**: θ_t: weights at time t
2: **Output**: θ_{t+1}: updated weights
3: **Data**: (u_t, o_t): observed utterance and object
4: **for** step **do**
5:     sample augmented batch $\mathbf{u} \sim \mathcal{P}(u_t)$
6:     let $f_{\theta_t} = \log P_{\theta_t}(\mathbf{u}|o_t) + \log P_{\theta_t}(o_t|\mathbf{u}) -$
           $\text{reg}(o_{1:t-1}, u_{1:t-1})$
7:     update $\theta_t \leftarrow \theta_t + \beta \nabla f_{\theta_t}$
8: **end for**

---

tains images of common objects, each annotated with multiple human captions. The CNN-LSTM architecture allows an agent to select utterances, by using beam search over captions given a target image as input, and also to select objects from the context, by evaluating the likelihood of the caption for each image in context and taking the most likely one.

Critically, we assume the agent will select actions on each trial using the value of θ it believes its partner to be using, so updating its own model is equivalent to updating expectations about its partner's model. Using the pre-trained model as our initialization, we can fine-tune the decoder weights (i.e. word embeddings, LSTM, and linear output layer) within a particular communicative interaction. Our algorithm is specified in Algorithm 1. Upon observing the utterance-object pair produced on each trial of the repeated reference game (Line 3), we take a small number of gradient steps updating the model weights to reflect the usage observed so far (Lines 4-7). Our adaptation objective function (Line 6) is built from combining a standard cross-entropy term with a KL-based regularization term to prevent catastrophic forgetting and a contrastive term to incorporate pragmatic reasoning about the visual context. In the following sections, we explain these terms and also introduce a final component of our approach: compositional data augmentation.

Utterance likelihood. For our benchmark repeated reference game, the data obtained on trial t is a paired observation of an utterance u and an intended object of reference o. The simplest learning objective for θ is the standard cross-entropy loss: the likelihood of this utterance being produced to convey the intended target in isolation: $P_\theta(u|o)$. This likelihood can be computed directly from the neural captioning model, where the probability of each word in $u = \{w_0, \ldots, w_\ell\}$ is given

---

[2]For the rest of this paper, we only consider the case of adapting to one partner, so we will drop the partner index i.

by the softmax decoder output conditioned on the sentence so far, $P_{\theta_t}(w_i|o, w_{-i})$, so:

$$P_{\theta_t}(u|o) \propto \prod_{i < \ell} P_{\theta_t}(w_i|o, w_{-i}) \qquad (2)$$

Contrastive likelihood. The same object-utterance pairs can be viewed as being generated by a listener agent selecting o *relative to the other distractors* in the immediate context $\mathcal{C}$ of other objects. This reasoning requires inverting the captioning model to evaluate how well the utterance u describes each object in $\mathcal{C}$, and then normalizing:

$$P_{\theta_t}(o|u, \mathcal{C}, \theta_t) \propto P_{\theta_t}(u|o)P(o) \qquad (3)$$

This inversion is based on models of one-shot pragmatic inference in reference games (Goodman and Frank, 2016; Andreas and Klein, 2016; Vedantam et al., 2017; Cohn-Gordon et al., 2018). While optimizing the utterance likelihood serves to make the observed utterance more likely for the target in *isolation*, optimizing the contrastive likelihood allows the agent to make a stronger inference that it does *not* apply to the distractors.

KL Regularization. Fine-tuning repeatedly on a small number of data points presents a clear risk of catastrophic forgetting (Robins, 1995), losing our ability to produce or understand utterances for other images. While limiting the number of gradient steps keeps the adapted model somewhat close to the prior, we will show that this is not sufficient (see Sec. 5.1). Because small differences in weights can lead to large differences in behavior for neural models, we also consider a regularization that tethers the *behavior* of the adapted model close to the behavior at initialization. Specifically, we consider a *KL regularization* term that explicitly minimizes the divergence between the captioning model's output probabilities before and after fine-tuning for unseen images (Yu et al., 2013; Galashov et al., 2018). It is not tractable to take the KL divergence over the (nearly infinite) space of all possible natural-language utterances. Hence, we approximate the divergence incrementally by expanding from the maximum a posteriori (MAP) word denoted w^* at each step according to the initial model P_Θ (see Appendix A):

$$\sum_{i < \ell} D_{\mathrm{KL}}\left[P_\Theta(w_i|o, w^*_{-i}) \,\|\, P_{\theta_t}(w_i|o, w^*_{-i})\right] \qquad (4)$$

where ℓ is the length of the MAP caption. This loss is then averaged across random images sampled from the full domain $\mathcal{O}$, not just those in context.

Compositional data augmentation. Agents should be able to infer previous successes on a longer utterance (e.g. "two men are sitting on a bench"), that the component parts of this utterance (e.g. "two men", "a bench") are also likely to convey the intended meaning. In the absence of a (weakly) compositional representation, a speaker has no way of doing credit assignment: observing that a listener successfully chose the target upon hearing a long utterance only provides further evidence for the full utterance. Fine-tuning an LSTM architecture will increase the likelihood of sub-strings to some extent after a successful selection, but this is insufficient for two reasons. First, not all sub-strings are syntactically well-formed referring expressions (e.g. "two men are"), and the LSTM lacks a syntactic representation to represent such coherence. Second, the likelihood of the full utterance will always be increased by more than any sub-utterance.

To address these problems, we explored a data augmentation step that introduces a stronger compositionality bias via referential entailments (Young et al., 2014). After each trial, we augmented the speaker's utterance u with a small denotation graph $D(u)$ containing the set of all noun phrases found in the syntactic dependency parse of u, and optimize our objective function on batches of these entailments. By independently updating expectations about well-formed entailments alongside the longer utterances that were actually produced, we hypothesized that our model could more naturally ground shorter, conventionalized labels in the shared history of successful understanding.

Local rehearsal. A second form of augmentation we explore is *local rehearsal*: at each step we include data from the history of interaction $D = \{(u, o)\}_{1:t}$ up to the current time t, to prevent overfitting to the most recent observation. In practice we subsample batches from the interaction history in a separate loss term with its own weighting coefficient, ensuring the new data point and a batch of its subphrase augmentations are used in every gradient step. We initialize D with the utterance the model generates for each object.

4 Interactive human evaluations

In this section, we evaluate our model's performance in *real-time interactions* with human speakers. Our artificial agent was paired with human partners to play a repeated reference game using

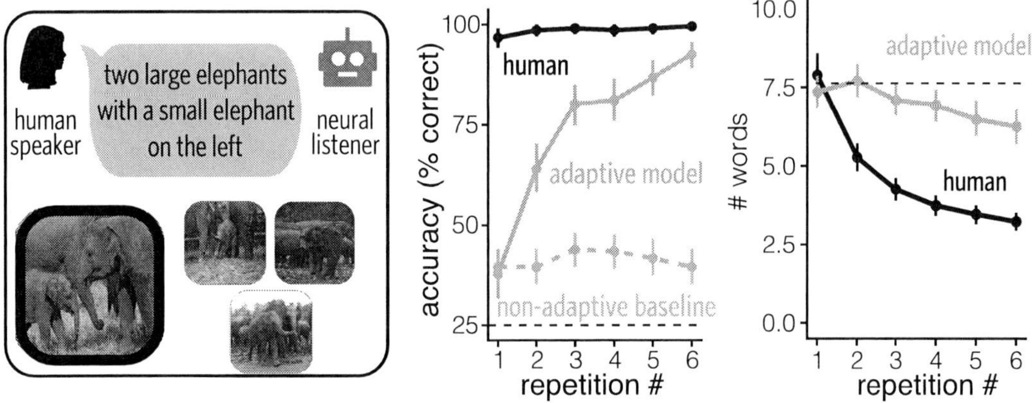

Figure 3: Communication becomes more efficient and accurate as our model adapts to a human speaker. Example contexts and utterances are shown. Error bars are bootstrapped 95% CIs.

images from the validation set of the COCO corpus (Lin et al., 2014; Chen et al., 2015) as the targets of reference. Critically, we constructed contexts to create a diagnostic mismatch between the COCO pre-training regime and the referential test regime. Specifically, we chose contexts such that the model's *accuracy* — the probability of identifying the target — would be poor at the outset.

To obtain appropriately challenging contexts, we used our pre-trained model's own visual encoder to find sets of highly similar images within the same category. We first extracted 256-dimensional feature vectors for each image from the final, fully-connected layer of the encoder. We then used these features to partition the images into 100 groups using a k-means algorithm, sampled one image from each cluster, and took its 3 nearest neighbors in feature space, yielding 100 unique contexts of 4 images each. This adversarial process explicitly identified contexts that our pre-trained captioning model would be poorly equipped to distinguish.

Human baselines. We first investigated the baseline performance of human speakers and listeners. We recruited 108 participants (54 pairs) from Amazon Mechanical Turk and automatically paired them into an interactive environment with a chatbox. For each pair, we sampled a context and constructed a sequence of 24 trials structured into 6 repetition blocks, where each of the 4 images appeared as the target once per block. We prevented the same target appearing twice in a row and scrambled the order of the images on each player's screen on each trial. We found that pairs of humans were highly accurate, with performance consistently near ceil-

ing (Fig. 3, black lines). At the same time, their utterances grew increasingly efficient: their utterances reduced in length across repeated interaction ($t = 25.8$, $p < 0.001$).[3]

4.1 Model performance

Next, we evaluated the performance of our adaptive model in the listener role (for a similar analysis of our model in the speaker role, see Appendix D). We recruited 57 additional participants from Amazon Mechanical Turk who were told they would be paired with an artificial agent learning how they talk. This task was identical to the one performed by pairs of humans, except we allowed only a single message to be sent through the chatbox on each trial. This message was sent to a server where the model weights from the previous trial were loaded to the GPU, used to generate a response, and updated for the next round. The approximate latency for the model to respond was 5-10s depending on how many games were running simultaneously.

For our adaptation objective function, we used a linear combination of the utterance and contrastive losses and the KL-regularization (see Appendix B for hyper-parameter settings). We also used local rehearsal and compositional data augmentation. While the pre-trained model initially performs much less accurately than humans, as expected, our adaptive listener shows rapid improvement in accuracy over the course of interaction (Fig. 3).

---

[3] Note that our contexts were selected to be challenging under the impoverished language prior of our pre-trained listener model, but were not expected to require any adaptation for human listeners to achieve high accuracy; see Hawkins et al. (2020a) for a more challenging stimulus domain used to elicit strong human adaptation.

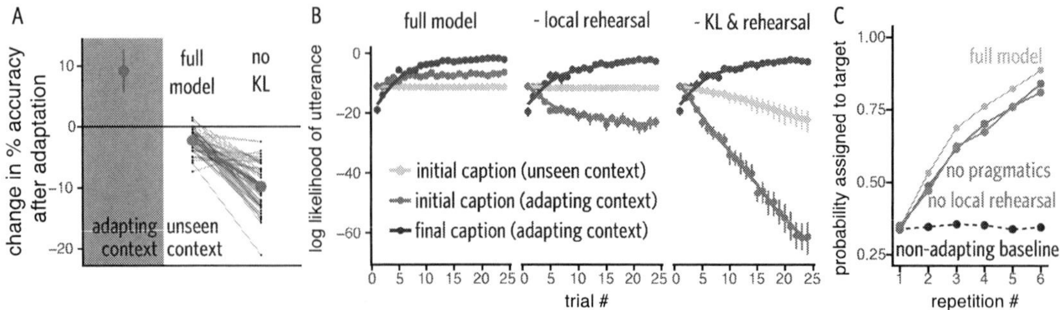

Figure 4: Ablation studies of the listener model. (A-B) KL regularization prevents catastrophic forgetting over the course of adaptation. (C) Local rehearsal and pragmatic reasoning independently contribute to successful listener adaptation. Error bars are bootstrapped 95% CIs.

In a mixed-effects logistic regression predicting trial-level accuracy, including pair- and image-level random effects, we found a significant increase in the probability of a correct response with successive repetitions, $z = 12.6$, $p < 0.001$, from 37% correct (slightly above chance levels of 25%) to 93% at the end. To test whether this success can be attributed to the initial quality of the listener model, or to *humans* adapting to a relatively unchanging model, we examined the performance of a non-adapting baseline (i.e. a model using the pre-trained model weights on every trial). We evaluated this baseline offline, using the utterances we recorded from the online games. This baseline showed no improvement, staying only slightly above chance accuracy over the course of the task.

5 Analysis

We now proceed to a series of ablation analyses that analyze the role played by each component of our approach. These analyses involve offline simulations conducted on the data we collected in the previous section.

5.1 KL regularization prevents catastrophic forgetting

We begin by testing the effectiveness of our KL regularization term (Eq. 4) for preventing catastrophic forgetting. We reasoned that changing expectations in the adaptation context should not interfere with expectations in other, unseen contexts. To directly analyze such interference, we adapted an ablated variant of our listener model over the course of a game with one context of images, and then measured its average accuracy identifying the target given the initial utterances produced by different speakers on different (unseen) contexts. We then compared this test accuracy with the baseline accuracy achieved by an *unadapted* listener model.

We cross-validated these estimates over many adaptation contexts. Specifically, because the baseline was already close to chance on 'challenging' contexts (Fig. 3), we used an additional set of 52 human-human interactions we collected in easier contexts (where images belonged to different COCO categories) to better expose degradations in performance. While accuracy significantly increased compared to baseline in the adapting context for both variants, we found a 10% drop in accuracy on unseen contexts for the ablated variant with no KL term, compared to only a 2% drop in the model using the full loss ($t(51) = 12.2, p < 0.001$ in a paired t test; see Fig. 4A).

Next, to more thoroughly probe the *progression* of interference, we conducted a second analysis examining the likelihood assigned to different captions by the listener model over the course of adaptation. We tracked both the initial captions produced by the pre-trained initialization in the adapting context and in unseen contexts. To obtain unseen contexts, we sampled a set of images from COCO that were not used in our experiment, and generated a caption for each. We also generated initial captions for the *target* objects in the adapting context. We recorded the likelihood of all of these sampled captions under the model at the beginning and at each step of adaptation until the final round. Finally, we greedily generated an utterance for each target at the *end* and retrospectively evaluated its likelihood at earlier points during adaptation.

These three likelihood curves are compared for ablated models in Fig. 4B. By definition, the final caption in the adapting context becomes more likely in all cases (brown line). Without the local rehearsal mechanism, the initial caption the model expected in the adapting context becomes less likely as it is replaced by the human partner's preferred caption (red line). Only when the KL term is removed, however, do we find interference with the model's expectations for unseen contexts (yellow line). Thus, we find that KL regularization plays a critical role in preventing catastrophic forgetting.

5.2 Pragmatics and local rehearsal improve listener performance

Next, we consider the contributions of other key components for success. Specifically, we constructed ablated variants of our model with no pragmatics (i.e. no contrastive loss term during adaption), and with no local rehearsal (i.e. no ability to keep training on batches from the history of the interaction). We simulated adaptation for these ablated variants on the 57 games where human speakers produced utterances for our listener model, and examined the probability assigned to the target after hearing each utterance (Fig. 4C). We found in a mixed-effects regression that each of these components independently contributes to success, as the ablated variants perform significantly worse than the full model ($z = 2.1$, $p = 0.03$ and $z = 3.6$, $p < 0.001$ for variants with no local rehearsal and no pragmatics, respectively; see Appendix C for regression details). Compared to an entirely non-adapting baseline, however, even these ablated variants improved over time.

6 Discussion

Relationship to human adaptation The theoretical ties between our approach and proposed cognitive models of human adaptation raises several questions. First, it is possible that improved performance could be driven by human *speakers* adapting in response to our listener agent's successes and errors rather than the other way around. While some degree of human adaptation is inevitable – for example, humans only seemed to shorten their utterances once our models' accuracy began to rise – human adaptation alone is insufficient to explain gains in accuracy. If these gains were due to human speakers gradually discovering utterances that a pre-trained (non-adapting) model could understand, we would expect some gains in the accuracy of our baseline non-adapting model over time. Furthermore, we found that the handful of human speakers that dramatically changed their descriptions across rounds actually performed worse than those who adhered to consistent descriptions.

With this said, the extent of adaptation in human-computer dialogue is known to be affected by human participants' expectations about the artificial agent (Branigan et al., 2011; Koulouri et al., 2016), potentially including expectations about whether it will be adaptive or not. Bi-directional adaptation effects may be more pronounced in other dialogue settings where the human and model both speak, giving the human an opportunity to re-use utterances produced by the model. It will be important for future work to evaluate non-adaptive baselines *online* rather than offline, as we did, in order to observe exactly how humans respond to, or compensate for, non-adaptive agents.

Second, it is natural to ask how our model would perform in the *speaker* role with a human *listener*, using their (sparse) response success as feedback rather than their utterances. In ongoing work, we have found that the same approach allows a (pragmatic) model to converge to more efficient conventions in the speaker role (see Appendix D in supplemental), such that the same language model can flexibly switch between speaker and listener roles with the same human partner. Still, it is unlikely that this speaker model reduces in the same way as human speakers do (see Supplemental Fig. S1 for examples). Differences may reflect additional accessibility, grammaticality, or compositionality biases in humans; direct comparisons remain an open question for cognitive science.

Third, scaling the principles of computational-level Bayesian cognitive models to neural networks capable of adapting to natural language in practice required several algorithmic-level innovations which are not yet plausible proposals for human cognition (Marr, 2010). While our local rehearsal mechanism may be consistent with replay mechanisms in human memory, our KL regularization mechanism implausibly requires earlier parameter values of the model to be held in memory. Our data augmentation mechanism was introduced specifically to compensate for the inability of the LSTM architecture to propagate the use of a referring expression to its entailments, but we expect that human language processing mechanisms achieve this effect by different means. We expect further work to refine these algorithmic components as neural language models continue to advance.

Relationship to language learning Our work is also related to broader efforts to ground language learning and emergent communication in usage, where artificial agents are trained to use language *from scratch* by playing interactive reference games (Wang et al., 2016; Lazaridou et al., 2016; Wang et al., 2017; Chevalier-Boisvert et al., 2019). Rather than starting our agents from scratch, we have emphasized the need for continual, partner-specific learning even among mature language users with existing priors. This raises another question: how are these different timescales of learning related to one another? One possibility is that the need to quickly adapt one's language to new partners and contexts over short timescales may serve as a functional pressure shaping languages more broadly.

Recent theories in cognitive science have formalized this hypothesis in a *hierarchical* Bayesian model (Hawkins et al., 2020b). In this model, the prior Θ that an agent brings into subsequent interactions is updated to reflect the overall distribution of partner-specific models θ^i, thus balancing general and idiosyncratic language knowledge in a principled way. For neural language models, however, there is an apparent tension between the strong KL regularization required to *prevent* unwanted interference with background knowledge during partner-specific adaptation, leading to catastrophic forgetting, and the flexibility to generalize or transfer conventions to new communicative settings as required for language learning. We do not want to regularize so strongly that agents memorize conventions only applying to a single image that is completely reset after each interaction; instead, we wish to obtain a gradient of generalization across both referents and partners as a function of similarity (Markman and Makin, 1998).

One promising solution to this problem, motivated by connections between hierarchical Bayes and algorithms like MAML (Finn et al., 2017; Grant et al., 2018; Nagabandi et al., 2019), is to perform a meta-learning 'outer loop' updating the initialization Θ, taking into account the regularized, partner-specific 'inner loop' of adaptation for each θ^i. In principle, a meta-learning approach for neural language learning would distill abstract, shared aspects of language into a unified Θ, while still allowing for rapid *ad hoc* conventionalization. Still, cognitively plausible and scalable meta-learning algorithms remain an open area of research.

Limitations and future work While our evaluations were limited to a canonical CNN-RNN image captioning architecture, a key open question for future work is how our continual adaptation approach ought to be implemented for more complex, state-of-the-art architectures. One possibility, following the approach recently proposed by Jaech and Ostendorf (2018a), is to allow context (e.g. partner identity) to control a low-rank transformation of the weight matrix such that online fine-tuning can take place in a more compact context embedding space (Jaech and Ostendorf, 2018b).

Furthermore, while we adapted the entire parameterized RNN module end-to-end, future work should explore the effect of limiting adaption to subcomponents (e.g. only word embeddings) or expanding adaptation to additional model components such as attention weights or high-level visual representations. Beyond possible consequences for engineering better adaptive models, each of these variants corresponds to a distinct cognitive hypothesis about exactly *which* representations are being adapted on the fly in human communication.

A final area for future work is generalizing the forms of social feedback that can be used as data D^i for updating representations beyond the sparse choices in a reference game. In particular, forms of *repair* through question-asking or other non-referential dialogue acts may license stronger inferences about a partner's language model and allow misunderstandings to be resolved more quickly in challenging contexts (Drew, 1997; Dingemanse et al., 2015; Li et al., 2016). These forms of feedback may be particularly important for extending our approach beyond the benchmark task of repeated reference games to the more complex domains of real-world conversational tasks.

Conclusion Human language use is remarkably flexible, continuously adapting to the needs of the current situation. In this paper, we introduced a challenging repeated reference game benchmark for artificial agents, which requires such adaptability to succeed. We proposed a continual learning approach allowing agents to form context-specific conventions by fine-tuning general-purpose representations. Even when pre-trained models initially perform inaccurately or inefficiently, our approach allows such models to quickly adapt to their partner's language in the given context and thus become more accurate and more efficient using common ground.

Acknowledgments

This research was supported in part by a Stanford HAI Hoffman-Yee Research Grant, Office of Naval Research grant ONR MURI N00014-16-1-2007 and DARPA agreement FA8650-19-C-7923, as well as NSF award #1911835 to RDH, and NSF award #1941722 to DS. We are grateful to audiences at the 2019 ICML Workshop on Adaptive and Multi-Task Learning, where an early version of this work was presented, and to three anonymous reviewers for their insightful comments.

> All code and materials available at:
> https://github.com/hawkrobe/
> continual-adaptation

References

Jacob Andreas and Dan Klein. 2016. Reasoning about pragmatics with neural listeners and speakers. In *Proceedings of EMNLP*, pages 1173–1182.

Jerome R Bellegarda. 2004. Statistical language model adaptation: review and perspectives. *Speech Communication*, 42(1):93–108.

Shai Ben-David, John Blitzer, Koby Crammer, Alex Kulesza, Fernando Pereira, and Jennifer Wortman Vaughan. 2010. A theory of learning from different domains. *Machine learning*, 79(1-2):151–175.

Leon Bergen, Roger Levy, and Noah Goodman. 2016. Pragmatic reasoning through semantic inference. *Semantics and Pragmatics*, 9(20).

John Blitzer, Mark Dredze, and Fernando Pereira. 2007. Biographies, bollywood, boom-boxes and blenders: Domain adaptation for sentiment classification. In *Proceedings of ACL*, pages 440–447.

Holly P Branigan, Martin J Pickering, Jamie Pearson, Janet F McLean, and Ash Brown. 2011. The role of beliefs in lexical alignment: Evidence from dialogs with humans and computers. *Cognition*, 121(1):41–57.

Xinlei Chen, Hao Fang, Tsung-Yi Lin, Ramakrishna Vedantam, Saurabh Gupta, Piotr Dollár, and C Lawrence Zitnick. 2015. Microsoft COCO captions: Data collection and evaluation server. *arXiv preprint arXiv:1504.00325*.

Maxime Chevalier-Boisvert, Dzmitry Bahdanau, Salem Lahlou, Lucas Willems, Chitwan Saharia, Thien Huu Nguyen, and Yoshua Bengio. 2019. BabyAI: First steps towards grounded language learning with a human in the loop. In *Proceedings of the 7th International Conference on Learning Representations*.

Eunsol Choi, He He, Mohit Iyyer, Mark Yatskar, Wentau Yih, Yejin Choi, Percy Liang, and Luke Zettlemoyer. 2018. QUAC: Question answering in context. In *Proceedings of EMNLP*, pages 2174–2184.

Herbert H Clark. 1996. *Using language*. Cambridge University Press.

Herbert H Clark and Deanna Wilkes-Gibbs. 1986. Referring as a collaborative process. *Cognition*, 22(1):1–39.

Reuben Cohn-Gordon, Noah Goodman, and Chris Potts. 2018. Pragmatically informative image captioning with character-level reference. In *Proceedings of NAACL*, pages 439–443.

Donald Davidson. 1986. A nice derangement of epitaphs. *Philosophical grounds of rationality: Intentions, categories, ends*, 4:157–174.

Nathaniel Delaney-Busch, Emily Morgan, Ellen Lau, and Gina R Kuperberg. 2019. Neural evidence for bayesian trial-by-trial adaptation on the N400 during semantic priming. *Cognition*, 187:10–20.

David DeVault and Matthew Stone. 2009. Learning to interpret utterances using dialogue history. In *Proceedings of EACL*, pages 184–192.

Mark Dingemanse, Seán G Roberts, Julija Baranova, Joe Blythe, Paul Drew, Simeon Floyd, Rosa S Gisladottir, Kobin H Kendrick, Stephen C Levinson, Elizabeth Manrique, Giovanni Rossi, and N. J. Enfield. 2015. Universal principles in the repair of communication problems. *PloS one*, 10(9):e0136100.

Paul Drew. 1997. 'Open' class repair initiators in response to sequential sources of troubles in conversation. *Journal of Pragmatics*, 28(1):69–101.

Chelsea Finn, Pieter Abbeel, and Sergey Levine. 2017. Model-agnostic meta-learning for fast adaptation of deep networks. In *Proceedings of the 34th International Conference on Machine Learning*, pages 1126–1135.

Michael C Frank, Noah D Goodman, and Joshua B Tenenbaum. 2009. Using speakers' referential intentions to model early cross-situational word learning. *Psychological Science*, 20(5):578–585.

Daniel Fried, Jacob Andreas, and Dan Klein. 2018. Unified pragmatic models for generating and following instructions. In *Proceedings of NAACL*, pages 1951–1963.

Alexandre Galashov, Siddhant M Jayakumar, Leonard Hasenclever, Dhruva Tirumala, Jonathan Schwarz, Guillaume Desjardins, Wojciech M Czarnecki, Yee Whye Teh, Razvan Pascanu, and Nicolas Heess. 2018. Information asymmetry in KL-regularized RL. In *Proceedings of the 7th International Conference on Learning Representations*.

Xavier Glorot, Antoine Bordes, and Yoshua Bengio. 2011. Domain adaptation for large-scale sentiment classification: A deep learning approach. In *Proceedings of the 28th International Conference on Machine Learning*, pages 513–520.

Noah D Goodman and Michael C Frank. 2016. Pragmatic language interpretation as probabilistic inference. *Trends in Cognitive Sciences*, 20(11):818 – 829.

Erin Grant, Chelsea Finn, Sergey Levine, Trevor Darrell, and Thomas Griffiths. 2018. Recasting gradient-based meta-learning as hierarchical bayes. In *Proceedings of the 6th International Conference on Learning Representations*.

H. P. Grice. 1975. Logic and conversation. In P. Cole and J. Morgan, editors, *Syntax and Semantics*, pages 43–58. Academic Press, New York.

Daniel Grodner and Julie C Sedivy. 2011. The effect of speaker-specific information on pragmatic inferences. In *The processing and acquisition of reference*, volume 2327, pages 239–272. MIT Press.

Janosch Haber, Tim Baumgärtner, Ece Takmaz, Lieke Gelderloos, Elia Bruni, and Raquel Fernández. 2019. The PhotoBook dataset: Building common ground through visually-grounded dialogue. In *Proceedings of ACL*, pages 1895–1910.

Robert D Hawkins, Michael C Frank, and Noah D Goodman. 2017. Convention-formation in iterated reference games. In *Proceedings of the 39th annual meeting of the Cognitive Science Society*.

Robert D Hawkins, Michael C Frank, and Noah D Goodman. 2020a. Characterizing the dynamics of learning in repeated reference games. *Cognitive Science*, 44(6):e12845.

Robert D Hawkins, Noah D Goodman, Adele E Goldberg, and Thomas L Griffiths. 2020b. Generalizing meanings from partners to populations: Hierarchical inference supports convention formation on networks. In *Proceedings of the 42nd annual meeting of the Cognitive Science Society*.

Aaron Jaech and Mari Ostendorf. 2018a. Low-rank RNN adaptation for context-aware language modeling. *Transactions of the Association for Computational Linguistics*, 6:497–510.

Aaron Jaech and Mari Ostendorf. 2018b. Personalized language model for query auto-completion. In *Proceedings of ACL*, pages 700–705.

Dave F Kleinschmidt and T Florian Jaeger. 2015. Robust speech perception: Recognize the familiar, generalize to the similar, and adapt to the novel. *Psychological Review*, 122(2):148.

Reinhard Kneser and Volker Steinbiss. 1993. On the dynamic adaptation of stochastic language models. In *IEEE International Conference on Acoustics, Speech, and Signal Processing*, pages 586–589.

Theodora Koulouri, Stanislao Lauria, and Robert D Macredie. 2016. Do (and say) as I say: Linguistic adaptation in human–computer dialogs. *Human–Computer Interaction*, 31(1):59–95.

Ben Krause, Emmanuel Kahembwe, Iain Murray, and Steve Renals. 2017. Dynamic evaluation of neural sequence models. In *Proceedings of the 35th International Conference on Machine Learning*, pages 2771–2780.

Robert M Krauss and Sidney Weinheimer. 1964. Changes in reference phrases as a function of frequency of usage in social interaction: A preliminary study. *Psychonomic Science*, 1(1-12):113–114.

Angeliki Lazaridou, Alexander Peysakhovich, and Marco Baroni. 2016. Multi-agent cooperation and the emergence of (natural) language. In *Proceedings of the 5th International Conference on Learning Representations*.

David Lewis. 1969. *Convention: A philosophical study*. Harvard University Press.

Jiwei Li, Alexander H Miller, Sumit Chopra, Marc'Aurelio Ranzato, and Jason Weston. 2016. Learning through dialogue interactions by asking questions. In *Proceedings of the 5th International Conference on Learning Representations*.

Xiao Li and Jeff Bilmes. 2007. A Bayesian divergence prior for classifier adaptation. In *Artificial Intelligence and Statistics*, pages 275–282.

Tsung-Yi Lin, Michael Maire, Serge Belongie, James Hays, Pietro Perona, Deva Ramanan, Piotr Dollár, and C Lawrence Zitnick. 2014. Microsoft COCO: Common objects in context. In *Proceedings of ECCV*, pages 740–755. Springer.

Chaojun Liu, Yongqiang Wang, Kshitiz Kumar, and Yifan Gong. 2016. Investigations on speaker adaptation of LSTM RNN models for speech recognition. In *Proceedings of the IEEE International Conference on Acoustics, Speech and Signal Processing*, pages 5020–5024.

Arthur B Markman and Valerie S Makin. 1998. Referential communication and category acquisition. *Journal of Experimental Psychology: General*, 127(4):331.

David Marr. 2010. *Vision: A computational investigation into the human representation and processing of visual information*. MIT press.

Charles Metzing and Susan E Brennan. 2003. When conceptual pacts are broken: Partner-specific effects on the comprehension of referring expressions. *Journal of Memory and Language*, 49(2):201–213.

Yajie Miao and Florian Metze. 2015. On speaker adaptation of long short-term memory recurrent neural networks. In *Proceedings of the 16th Annual Conference of the International Speech Communication Association*, pages 1101–1105.

Tomáš Mikolov, Martin Karafiát, Lukáš Burget, Jan Černocký, and Sanjeev Khudanpur. 2010. Recurrent neural network based language model. In *Proceedings of the 11th annual conference of the International Speech Communication Association*, pages 1045–1048.

Will Monroe, Robert D. Hawkins, Noah D. Goodman, and Christopher Potts. 2017. Colors in context: A pragmatic neural model for grounded language understanding. *Transactions of the Association for Computational Linguistics*, 5:325–338.

Anusha Nagabandi, Chelsea Finn, and Sergey Levine. 2019. Deep online learning via meta-learning: Continual adaptation for model-based RL. In *Proceedings of the 7th International Conference on Learning Representations*.

Yasuhito Ohsugi, Itsumi Saito, Kyosuke Nishida, Hisako Asano, and Junji Tomita. 2019. A simple but effective method to incorporate multi-turn context with BERT for conversational machine comprehension. In *Proceedings of the First Workshop on NLP for Conversational AI*, pages 11–17.

Naho Orita, Eliana Vornov, Naomi Feldman, and Hal Daumé III. 2015. Why discourse affects speakers' choice of referring expressions. In *Proceedings of ACL*, pages 1639–1649.

Giuseppe Riccardi and Allen L Gorin. 2000. Stochastic language adaptation over time and state in natural spoken dialog systems. *IEEE Transactions on Speech and Audio Processing*, 8(1):3–10.

Anthony Robins. 1995. Catastrophic forgetting, rehearsal and pseudorehearsal. *Connection Science*, 7(2):123–146.

Timo B Roettger and Michael Franke. 2019. Evidential strength of intonational cues and rational adaptation to (un-) reliable intonation. *Cognitive Science*, 43(7):e12745.

Subhro Roy, Michael Noseworthy, Rohan Paul, Daehyung Park, and Nicholas Roy. 2019. Leveraging past references for robust language grounding. In *Proceedings of CoNLL*, pages 430–440.

Sebastian Schuster and Judith Degen. 2020. I know what you're probably going to say: Listener adaptation to variable use of uncertainty expressions. *Cognition*, 203:104285.

Nathaniel J Smith, Noah Goodman, and Michael Frank. 2013. Learning and using language via recursive pragmatic reasoning about other agents. In *Advances in Neural Information Processing Systems*, pages 3039–3047.

Ieva Staliūnaitė, Hannah Rohde, Bonnie Webber, and Annie Louis. 2018. Getting to "Hearer-old": Charting referring expressions across time. In *Proceedings of EMNLP*, pages 4350–4359.

Ian Stewart, Diyi Yang, and Jacob Eisenstein. 2020. Characterizing collective attention via descriptor context: A case study of public discussions of crisis events. In *Proceedings of the 14th International AAAI Conference on Web and Social Media*, pages 650–660.

Marten Van Schijndel and Tal Linzen. 2018. A neural model of adaptation in reading. In *Proceedings of EMNLP*, pages 4704–4710.

Ramakrishna Vedantam, Samy Bengio, Kevin Murphy, Devi Parikh, and Gal Chechik. 2017. Context-aware captions from context-agnostic supervision. In *Proceedings of the IEEE Conference on Computer Vision and Pattern Recognition*, pages 1070–1079.

Oriol Vinyals, Alexander Toshev, Samy Bengio, and Dumitru Erhan. 2015. Show and tell: A neural image caption generator. In *Proceedings of the IEEE Conference on Computer Vision and Pattern Recognition*, pages 3156–3164.

Sida I Wang, Samuel Ginn, Percy Liang, and Christoper D Manning. 2017. Naturalizing a programming language via interactive learning. In *Proceedings of ACL*, pages 929–938.

Sida I Wang, Percy Liang, and Christopher D Manning. 2016. Learning language games through interaction. In *Proceedings of ACL*, page 2368–2378.

Deanna Wilkes-Gibbs and Herbert H Clark. 1992. Coordinating beliefs in conversation. *Journal of Memory and Language*, 31(2):183–194.

Ilker Yildirim, Judith Degen, Michael K Tanenhaus, and T Florian Jaeger. 2016. Talker-specificity and adaptation in quantifier interpretation. *Journal of Memory and Language*, 87:128–143.

Peter Young, Alice Lai, Micah Hodosh, and Julia Hockenmaier. 2014. From image descriptions to visual denotations: New similarity metrics for semantic inference over event descriptions. *Transactions of the Association for Computational Linguistics*, 2:67–78.

Dong Yu, Kaisheng Yao, Hang Su, Gang Li, and Frank Seide. 2013. KL-divergence regularized deep neural network adaptation for improved large vocabulary speech recognition. In *Proceedings of the IEEE International Conference on Acoustics, Speech and Signal Processing*, pages 7893–7897.

Diverse and Relevant Visual Storytelling with Scene Graph Embeddings

Xudong Hong[12], Rakshith Shetty[1], Asad Sayeed[3],
Khushboo Mehra[2], Vera Demberg[2] and Bernt Schiele[1]

[1]Dept. of Computer Vision and Machine Learning, MPI Informatics
[2]Dept. of Language Science and Technology, Saarland University
[3]Dept. of Philosophy, Linguistics, and Theory of Science, University of Gothenburg

{xhong,kmehra,vera}@coli.uni-saarland.de
{rshetty,schiele}@mpg.mpi-inf.de, asad.sayeed@gu.se

Abstract

A problem in automatically generated stories for image sequences is that they use overly generic vocabulary and phrase structure and fail to match the distributional characteristics of human-generated text. We address this problem by introducing explicit representations for objects and their relations by extracting scene graphs from the images. Utilizing an embedding of this scene graph enables our model to more explicitly reason over objects and their relations during story generation, compared to the global features from an object classifier used in previous work. We apply metrics that account for the diversity of words and phrases of generated stories as well as for reference to narratively-salient image features and show that our approach outperforms previous systems. Our experiments also indicate that our models obtain competitive results on reference-based metrics.

1 Introduction

Visual storytelling is the generation of a coherent narrative from a series of images (Huang et al., 2016). In this paper, we address a particular challenge in visual storytelling: reflecting human preferences in narrative structure, especially the choice of content words and phrases that comprise a readable story. Humans prefer to use diverse words and phrases to construct the storyline to avoid repetitions within or across sentences. For example, in the human-written story in Fig. 1, very few content words are repeated. However, Modi and Parde (2019) have found that recent work often generate repetitive words and phrases which leads to repetitions across sentences and makes stories less diverse. For example, in the first story of Fig. 1, the model generates a verb phrase *had a great time* and then repeats it in the fifth sentence. These words

---

[1] *Typo generated by human: "have" instead of "gave".*

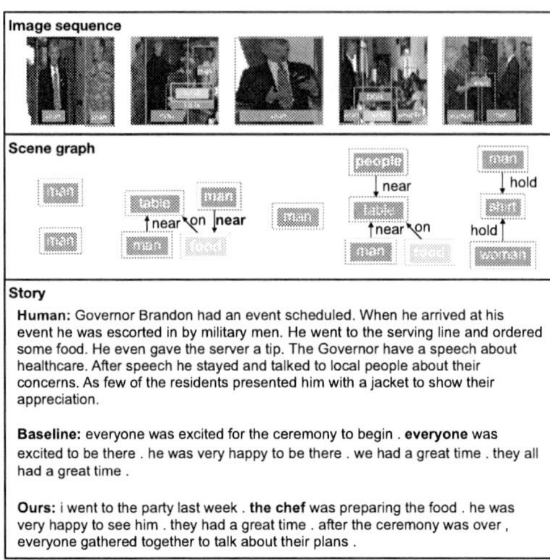

Figure 1: Example of extracting scene graphs from images and their relationship to content words and phrases in the stories. The first story (**Baseline**) is generated by AREL (Wang et al., 2018b). The second story (**Ours**) is generated by our proposed model. The **Human** story comes from the VIST dataset (Huang et al., 2016)[1].

and phrases are usually overly generic. We argue that this is because relations between objects in the last image are not well-represented in the image embedding, forcing the model to produce generic alternatives.

We address this problem by employing a more explicit and structured representation of objects and their relations in form of *scene graphs* (Johnson et al., 2015). Scene graphs encode both spatial and predicate relations between objects in the images as well as semantic event relations (actions and their participants). Relations like *(man, near, food)* in the scene graph in Fig. 1 are essential to generate more specific noun phrases (e.g., *the chef*) instead of generic ones (e.g., *everyone*).

In our approach, we extract scene graphs from the images and then learn *scene graph embeddings*

Proceedings of the 24th Conference on Computational Natural Language Learning, pages 420–430
Online, November 19-20, 2020. ©2020 Association for Computational Linguistics
https://doi.org/10.18653/v1/P17

using graph neural networks (Marcheggiani and Perez-Beltrachini, 2018) for each image, which combine the visual features and the discrete semantic information from the scene graphs. A combination of story-wide and individual-image scene graph features is then decoded in the form of a story; parameter-sharing in the decoder encourages narrative coherence.

One difficulty in learning scene graph embeddings together with an end-to-end visual storytelling model is that they introduce a large number of parameters, increasing both computational and learning complexity and making them more difficult to integrate into larger, computationally-expensive learning approaches. We therefore break down the problem into a pipeline with three steps designed to be parameter-efficient and trained independently (Fig. 2): (1) the extraction and augmentation of scene graphs with an existing automatic tool; (2) the training of a graph encoder to obtain scene graph embeddings; and (3) the application of an attention-based visual storytelling model to these embeddings to generate stories. The first two steps establish that we can achieve competitive results without an end-to-end model that requires both story and image to be paired at all steps of training. The third step uses an attention mechanism to supplant a complex graph encoder in the second step, reducing the number of parameters in the story generation model.

Our results show that not only is this approach competitive with other recent work in terms of standard reference-based measures (e.g., BLEU), it has an addtional advantage: the distributional properties of the generated text are closer to human-generated stories than the output of competing systems. The improved quality of the stories and the finer control over the bias of the captioning model afforded by our approach is thus reflected in the outcome of our implementation and experiments.

The main contributions of this paper are:

(a) we introduce a pipeline method for visual storytelling that uses a graph-to-sequence model to learn embeddings for augmented scene graphs and an attention mechanism to combine the scene graph embeddings; (b) we perform the first fine-grained analysis of the diversity of visual stories by inspecting word and phrase distributions and show that machine generated stories from previous models are far less diverse than human-written stories; and (c) we show that the generated stories from our pipeline are not only more diverse than previous work but also more relevant to the images.

2   Related Work

Visual storytelling. Extracting a good representation of the information in the visual input is a key part of the visual storytelling task. Prior work in visual storytelling has typically opted for global features extracted from a pre-trained convolutional neural network (Liu et al., 2017; Yu et al., 2017; Wang et al., 2018a,b; Huang et al., 2019) and has focused on improving the language generation model. Wang et al. (2017) show that introducing regional features and implicit coreference relations of entities leads to more human-realistic word usage in generated stories. Only few prior works employ an intermediate structured representation on story telling task. Yang et al. (2019a) use an external database of knowledge graphs to enchance the visual representation and improve story telling performance. We use scene graphs extracted from images, which does not require an external knowledgebase. Wang et al. (2020) extract scene graphs from images and train an end-to-end model with a graph convolutional encoder directly on visual stories. We propose a pipeline method which first obtains scene graph embeddings from images then applies them to visual storytelling in order to reduce the difficulty of learning both the scene graph embeddings and the story generation model together. Our attention-based story generation model has less parameters while obtaining competitive results.

Scene graph representation. A scene graph is a symbolic representation of structural information where entities are nodes and their relations are edges (Johnson et al., 2015). The large scene-graph annotated Visual Genome (Krishna et al., 2017) dataset has enabled the development of models to extract scene graph representations from images (Zellers et al., 2018; Chen et al., 2019). These scene graph represenations have proven effective on various tasks like image retrieval (Johnson et al., 2015) and image generation (Johnson et al., 2018).

Scene graph based image captioning. A sequential scene graph representation is used to encode images in Gao et al. (2018) to improve image captioning. Yang et al. (2019b) propose auto-encoding text-based scene graphs to learn a shared dictionary between visual and text based graphs, achieving state-of-the-art image captioning performance. Wang et al. (2019b) show that image scene graphs extracted using a trained model can match the captioning performance of an oracle with access to ground-truth graphs. Aligning text- and image-based scene graphs has also been used to generate image captions without paired data (Gu et al., 2019).

3 Model Design

The task of visual storytelling can be decomposed into two distinct parts: (1) extracting relevant information from input images I into compact features and (2) generating stories using these visual features. We improve the visual feature representation by switching from commonly-used global feature vectors to a scene graph-based representation which explicitly encodes objects and their relations. We also reduce the number of parameters by taking a modular approach that separates learning scene graph embeddings from images and generating visual stories. This allows us to independently train the scene graph embedding model and to design a visual storytelling model with fewer parameters yet competitive performance.

Our full pipeline is shown in Fig. 2. We first apply a scene graph generator to extract scene graphs containing vertices for objects and edges for relations between two objects. We then augment the scene graph for each image by adding regional features (see section 3.1). A graph neural network embeds each graph node by aggregating information from across the graph. We propose a pre-training step to independently learn this graph embedding. To do this, we obtain the confidence of the object detector for each object in each image, termed as *visual saliency*, and construct a sequence of object labels ordered by their visual saliency for each image. Then we train a graph-to-sequence model to predict this object sequence given the scene graph embedding of the corresponding image (see section 3.2). To generate stories, we extract both global and regional features from the scene graph embedding for each image and feed them to an attention-based story generation model (see section 3.3).

3.1 Scene Graph Augmentation

Scene graphs can be extracted with the Knowledge-embedded Routing Network (KERN), a state-of-the-art scene graph generator (Chen et al., 2019) built on top of a Faster R-CNN object detector (Ren et al., 2015). KERN generates scene graphs $G = (G_1, G_2, ..., G_N)$ for all images, where each scene graph $G'_j = \{V_j, E_j\}$ contains a set of nodes V_j representing recognised entities with node labels $v_1, v_2, ..., v_M$ and a set of edges E_j with edge labels representing relations between entities.

An issue here is that scene graphs are not always connected, but graph neural encoders require connected graphs as input (see the first scene graph in Fig. 2). To obtain a single connected graph for each image, we augment the scene graphs by introducing a *global* node in each graph G'_j, and connect it to all other nodes in the graph.

At this stage, the augmented scene graph contains discrete categorical triplets like *(man, near, table)* (see Fig. 2 for examples). It does not contain detailed visual appearance or shape information: e.g., the color of the man's suit. We address this by augmenting each node in the graph with a corresponding visual feature vector. This is done by extracting Regions of Interest (RoIs) of each object from the backbone Faster R-CNN model of KERN. Then we apply the RoI align algorithm (He et al., 2017) to extract visual features corresponding to each node. The *global* node is assigned the mean features of all the nodes in the graph.

3.2 Scene Graph Embedding

We employ graph convolution networks (GCN; Kipf and Welling, 2017) to encode our augmented scene graph, since they have been effective in learning representations with graph-like structures like parse trees (Du and Black, 2019) and knowledge graphs (Song et al., 2020).

When it comes to the learning of the scene graph encoders, we are inspired by human behaviours in image description task. Objects that appear earlier in image captions usually attract more human attention and are more visually salient to humans (Griffin and Bock, 2000; He et al., 2019). There is a large agreement between human attended regions and activation maps of the last convolutional layer of a VGG-16 network, even though the VGG-16 network is not fine-tuned for captioning (He et al., 2019). If a region of the feature maps is highly activated, it is very likely to be classified as an object with higher confidence. Therefore, we conclude that objects that appear earlier in captions should have a higher confidence when they are passed through a VGG-16 network. We make an assumption that it is the same in visual storytelling and leave the proof for future work due to space limitations.

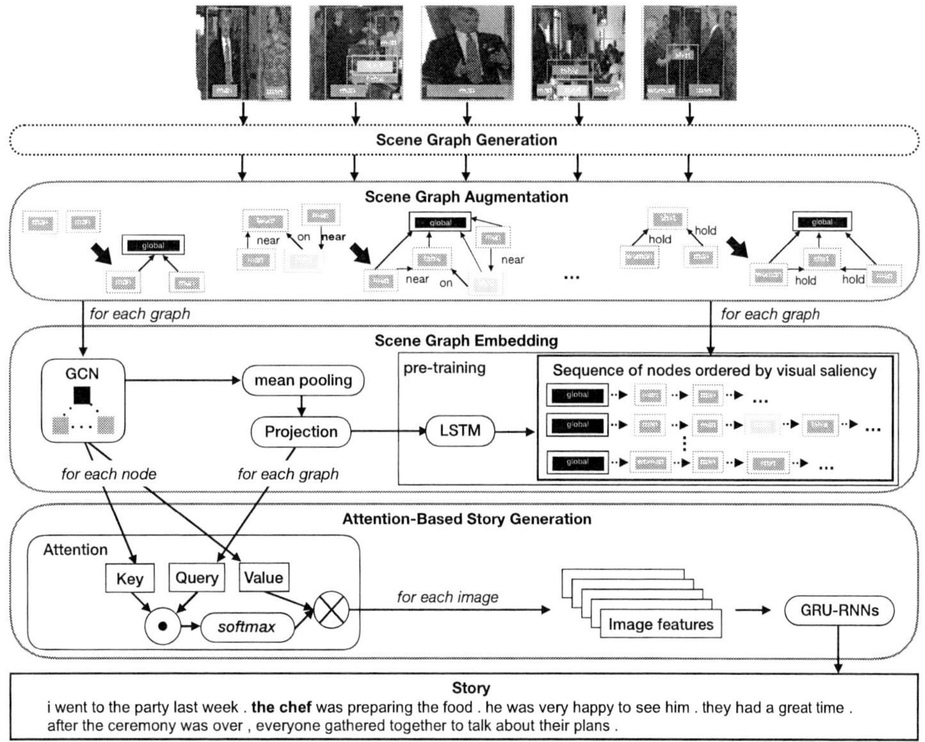

Figure 2: Our pipeline for visual storytelling.

To simulate this phenomenon, we order the object labels in the scene graph of each image with their confidence and design a graph-to-sequence model to predict this sequence. The model contains two major components, a GCN which encodes the augmented scene graph and a recurrent neural network decoder which generates the sequence of object labels $(v_1, v_2, ..., v_M)$ ordered by their visual saliency, i.e. confidence from the object detector. This allows us to train the GCN in in a self-supervised manner without needing additional labels and keeps objects that tend to be more salient in similar sequence positions across images, giving them an advantage in training.

Graph encoder. We use a multiplicative Relational Graph Convolutional Network (mRGCN; Hong et al., 2019), a variant of GCN assigning parameters not only for nodes but also for edges in a graph, as the graph encoder to introduce explicit representations for edge labels. Given the augmented scene graph G, each node is represented with an regional visual feature vector $\mathbf{x}_v \in \mathbb{R}^d$ extracted from the object detector. For the first layer of the encoder, the hidden representation of the node $\mathbf{h}_v^1 = \mathbf{x}_v$. Then the l-th mRGCN layer

computes the hidden representation for node v in $(l+1)$-th layer as follows:

$$\mathbf{h}_v^{l+1} = f(\mathbf{W}\mathbf{h}_v^l + \sum_{u \in N(v)} \mathbf{W}_{dir(e)}\mathbf{h}_u^l \circ \mathbf{r}_e) \quad (1)$$

where $\mathbf{W} \in \mathbb{R}^{d \times h}$ is a trainable parameter. $N(v)$ is the set of all neighbours of node v. f is the ReLU non-linearity. "$\circ$" is the Hadamard product, $\mathbf{W}_{dir(e)} \in \mathbb{R}^{d \times h}$, $dir(e) \in \{in, out\}$ is the direction of the edge $e_{u,v}$ connecting u and v. $\mathbf{r}_e \in \mathbb{R}^h$ is an embedding of the label of the edge $e_{u,v}$. Each layer aggregates the direct neighbours of each node. We stack L GCN layers to encode the full graph.

Object label generator. We use a two-layer LSTM (Hochreiter and Schmidhuber, 1997) to merge the node representations and generate the sequence of object labels. We apply global attention (Luong et al., 2015) to re-weight the hidden representations from the first layer and merge them into a global hidden vector $\mathbf{h}'_G$. The we feed the global hidden vector into two-layer feed-forward networks to get the global encoder output $\mathbf{h}_G$. The probability of node label y_t conditioned on input G and previous node label $y_{1:t-1}$ is obtained by applying a softmax layer on the decoder output as $P(y_t|y_{1:t-1}, G) = softmax(g(\mathbf{h}_G, \mathbf{h}_C))$, where g is a perceptron.

Pre-training. The graph-to-sequence model is trained to maximize the likelihood function $ll = \prod_{|Y|}^{t=1} P(y_t|y_{1:t-1}, G)$. We use extracted visual features as node embeddings and randomly initialise edge embeddings in the encoder. We tune three hyper-parameters on a validation set to minimise the loss, namely the number of hidden units in mRGCN encoder, the number of hidden units in LSTM, and the number of GCN layers. Then we extract augmented scene graph embeddings for the target dataset. After the pre-training of the graph embeddings, each node representation should contain not only node-specific information but also the information from neighbours up to a distance of L.

3.3 Attention-Based Story Generation

The pre-trained graph embeddings serve as input to the story generation model. Instead of using a full graph encoder as Wang et al. (2020), we use the global representations of each image and the local representations of each entity extracted from the pre-trained mRGCN scene graph encoder. This allows us to encode both object-specific information and the relations between each object and the whole image.

We use a dot product attention mechanism to merge all the entities into one hidden vector for each image as follows:

$$\mathbf{a} = \frac{exp(\mathbf{Kq})}{\sum_{j=1}^{M} exp(\mathbf{K}_j \mathbf{q})} \tag{2}$$

$$\mathbf{h} = \mathbf{V}^T \mathbf{a} \tag{3}$$

where we use the global image representations as the query $\mathbf{q} \in \mathbb{R}^d$ and local object representations as the keys $\mathbf{K} \in \mathbb{R}^{M \times d}$ and values $\mathbf{V} \in \mathbb{R}^{M \times d}$.

We follow Wang et al. (2018b) in using a GRU to encode the hidden vectors of all images in a sequential manner and to generate the story. The model is optimised using maximum likelihood estimation with backpropagation.

4 Experiment and Evaluation

Now we show that using pre-trained scene graph embeddings yields competitive results as compared to state-of-the-art approaches on reference-based metrics while using fewer parameters in the image encoder. We also perform an ablation study to show

that all proposed components contribute to the performance of the full model and that scene graph embeddings are effective across different attention mechanisms. While the reference-based metrics are useful, they do not always correlate with better story quality as perceived by humans (Wang et al., 2018b). Hence, we also evaluate our model in terms of diversity of word and phrase structure and propose metrics to explicity measure the correctness of object references in section 5. Results show that our scene graph-based model uses more diverse/relevant words and phrases compared to prior work.

4.1 Experiment Design

We train and evaluate our storytelling model on the VIST dataset (Huang et al., 2016), containing 50K visual stories of 10K Flickr albums with 210K images. Each story is based on a 5-image sequence. We follow Wang et al. (2018b) and split the data into 40K training, 10K validation, and 10K test set. We extract scene graphs (including node and edge labels) with the state-of-the-art scene graph generator, KERN, mentioned above.

For neural architecture like GCN in scene graph embeddings, we need to select one important hyperparameter, the number of layers in the GCN encoder. We therefore perform a grid seach from 1 to the maximal diameter in all augmented scene graph. The number of GCN layers is also bounded by the memory size of our GPU cards. So we choose a maximum of 6. We train the scene graph embedding on the VIST dataset and select the optimal setting by validation loss.

We compare our models with previous baselines: **Contextual Attention** (CA; Wang et al., 2017) uses local features from an object detector and a contexual attention layer to intergrate features from different images.

Hierarchically Structured Reinforcement Learning (HSRL; Huang et al., 2019) proposed a hierarchical RNN trained to generate stories by reinforcement learning, with two critics including a multi-modal and a language-style discriminator.

Adversarial Reward Learning (AREL; Wang et al., 2018b) is an Adversarial REward Learning framework to learn an implicit reward function from human demonstrations and then optimize policy search with the learned reward.

Hierarchical Photo-Scene Encoder (HPSR; Wang et al., 2019a) applied hierarchically struc-

Models	# para	B-1	B-2	B-3	B-4	M	R-L	C
CA (Wang et al., 2017)	3.36 M	-	-	-	-	31.73	-	-
HSRL (Huang et al., 2019)	1.05 M	-	-	-	12.3	35.2	30.8	10.7
AREL (Wang et al., 2018b)	1.05 M	63.7	39	23.1	14	35	29.6	9.5
HPSR (Wang et al., 2019a)	1.05 M	61.9	37.8	21.5	12.2	34.4	**31.2**	8
KS (Yang et al., 2019a)	1.05 M	**66.4**	39.2	23.1	12.8	35.2	29.9	**12.1**
SGVST (Wang et al., 2020)	3.41 M	65.1	**40.1**	**23.8**	14.7	**35.8**	29.9	9.8
Ours: SGEmb, attn	2.10 M	62.2	38.7	23.5	**14.8**	35.6	30.2	8.6

Table 1: Results of proposed model on test set compared to previous work using reference-based metrics including BLEU (B), METEOR (M), ROUGE-L (R-L), and CIDEr-D (C). # para is the number of parameters in the image encoder to obtain one vector representation for each image. Parameters in pre-trained components are not counted.

Model variations	B-4	M	R-L
Visual features			
VGG global	13	34.4	29.7
ResNet global	13.6	34.9	29.5
SGEmb global	12	33.8	28.8
VGG, attn	13.5	35.5	30.1
Attention types			
VGG, add attn	12.6	34.2	29.5
VGG, location attn	13.8	35.1	29.8
VGG, simple attn	13.9	35.1	29.7
SGEmb, add attn	13.6	35.5	30.1
SGEmb, location attn	14.1	35.5	30.1
SGEmb, simple attn	14	35.5	**30.2**
Our full model			
SGEmb, attn	**14.8**	**35.6**	**30.2**

Table 2: Ablation study of our full model versus different variants using reference-based metrics including BLEU-4 (B-4), METEOR (M), and ROUGE-L (R-L).

tured reinforcement learning to generate topically coherent multi-sentence stories.

Knowledgeable Storyteller (KS; Yang et al., 2019a) extract objects with an object detector, infer relations between objects with an external knowledge base, and train a knowledge-augmented story generation model.

SGVST (Wang et al., 2020) extract scene graphs from the image sequence and use GCN with temporal convolutionals to merge features across images.

The ablation study we performed over our full model is intended to demonstrate whether the scene graph embedding and the attention mechanism contribute to the final results. We compare the full model with the following simplified models:
VGG global is an seq2seq model using VGG16 (Simonyan and Zisserman, 2015) global features.
ResNet global is a seq2seq model using ResNet-152 (He et al., 2016) global features.
SGEmb global is a seq2seq model which uses only global features from the scene graph embedding.
VGG, attn is an attention-based model which uses regional features directly from the object detector instead of the scene graph embedding.
SGEmb, attn is our full model with scene graph embedding and attention mechanism.

4.2 Reference-Based Evaluation

We first evaluate our model and ablations using automatic reference-based metrics on the test set to quantify the similarity between the generated stories w.r.t. human-written ones. We use metrics including unigram (B-1), bigram (B-2), trigram (B-3), and 4-gram (B-4) BLEU scores (Papineni et al., 2002), METEOR (M; Banerjee and Lavie, 2005), ROUGE-L (R; Lin, 2004), and CIDEr (C; Vedantam et al., 2015), based on Wang et al. (2018b)'s evaluation code.

Comparison with baselines. We compare our model with baselines on reference-based metrics in table 1. Our model outperforms all previous methods which do not utilize scene graphs (except SGVST) on BLEU-4 and METEOR. Compared to the recent work using scene graphs, SGVST, we obtain a better score on BLEU-4 and competitive results on BLEU-3, METEOR, and ROUGE-L, although we perform with lower scores on BLEU-1, BLEU-2, and CIDEr. This indicates that the relations between objects in scene graph embeddings empower our model to generate long phrases that are more similar to human text. However, the similarity of shorter grammatical units is sacrificed.

Ablation study. We also report the results of our ablated models to show the importance of the scene graph embedding and the attention mechanism in table 1. Removing the scene graph embedding from our final model and using VGG features in-

       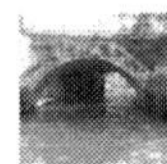

Human: It's great being the bookstore cat, I feel so literate! Oh yeah? It's way better being the liquor store cat! I feel sooo meow lol fft Who do you think you are? I'm Catman, who the hell are you? Would you two shut up and help me knit a sweater?

AREL: i went to the store last week . the cat was so excited to see him . i bought a lot of books . i bought a lot of stuff . the cat was very happy to see the cat .

Ours: i went to the store to buy some books . the cat was very excited to see the dog . i had a lot of food . i had a great time **at the restaurant** . the cat was **on the bed** .

Human: My family was taking a trip in another country. We decided to try the local river cruise to see the sites. It dropped us off deep in the jungle Me and dad were able to get alot of good photos. We ended up back in town at the end of the day.

AREL: a group of friends went on a trip to the lake . we had a lot of fun . they were able to take a swim in the water . we had a great time . the river was very beautiful and beautiful .

Ours: the family went on a trip to the lake . we went to the park to take a **boat ride** . the kids enjoyed the water and the water . we had a great time at the beach . it was a beautiful day .

Human: James would be retiring this year and everyone decided to get him a cake at work. The cake was the most delicious part of the lunch! Everyone was really excited to wish him luck and get in line for some cake. It was great because everyone got to talk and remember the great times with their co-worker. James decides to wave goodbye for the final picture. Everyone will miss him.

AREL: today , we had a cake . he was very excited . everyone was having a great time . all of my friends were there to celebrate . he was very happy to be there .

Ours: it was a birthday cake for the party . i had a great time at the party . my friends and family were there to celebrate . i had a great time at the party . **[male]** was very happy to be there .

Human: There was a good variety of costumes at this Halloween party. There was a pirate. There was a balloon man. There was even a Shrinner. The diversity of the outfits added color to this Halloween party. It also reminded us how different each of us are as individuals.

AREL: the party was a lot of fun . we had a lot of fun at the party . we all had a lot of fun . we had a lot of fun playing games . at the end of the day , they all had a great time .

Ours: it was time for the **halloween party** . there were a lot of people there . the man was dressed up as a man . the men are having a great time at the party . the whole family was there to **celebrate the occasion** .

Figure 3: Qualitative results of our model versus AREL and human-written stories.

stead (VGG, attn) decreases BLEU-4 by 1.3 (-8.8%). Using global features from the object detector (VGG global, ResNet global) or global scene graph embeddings (SGEmb global) without the attention mechanism harms performance across all metrics significantly. We further compare models using regional features from scene graph embeddings and from the VGG object detector across different attention mechanisms, like additive attention (add attn; Bahdanau et al., 2014), location-based attention (location attn; Luong et al., 2015), simple attention (simple attn, computing coefficient with keys only) and dot product attention (attn, i.e., the one we use in the full model). Results show that scene graph embeddings boost performance of models across all types of attention mechanisms on all three metrics.

4.3 Qualitative Results

We perform a qualitative comparison to identify what is different in generated stories when we introduce scene graph embeddings and the attention mechanism, as in Figure 1. AREL generates *everyone*, a very generic expression referring to all *man* objects in the image. After introducing scene

graph embeddings, our model generates a more specific term *chef* which can be inferred from the sub-graph *(man, near, food)* of the second image. More examples can be found in Figure 3.

5 Evaluating Diversity and Relevance

To get an in-depth understanding of the diversity of different types of words or phrases in generated stories, we perform the first fine-grained analysis of the distributions of words by different Part-of-Speech (POS) tags and phrases by different constituent tags. We first process the generated stories with a state-of-the-art POS tagger and constituency parser (Joshi et al., 2018). Then we plot the frequency vs. rank distributions following Zipf's Law for each POS tag and each constituent tag. We follow Holtzman et al. (2019) to compute the Zipf's coefficient to check how similar the distributions of generated stories are to human-written stories. Using this metric, we compare the diversity of output stories from our model to the baselines and to the best-available prior work, AREL[2].

Baselines	Noun	Verb	Adj.	Adv.	Pronoun	all
VGG global	1.141	1.592	1.67	2.06	2.186	1.195
ResNet global	1.107	**1.428**	1.461	**1.843**	**1.545**	1.172
AREL**	1.101	1.433	**1.367**	1.928	1.791	1.185
SGEmb global	1.14	1.505	1.645	2.127	1.859	1.185
VGG, attn	1.193	1.541	1.669	2.032	2.055	1.203
Ours: SGEmb, attn	**1.092**	1.439	1.495	1.995	1.617	**1.165**
Human	0.795	1.088	0.965	1.083	1.118	1.011

Table 3: Zipf's coefficient of the word distribution on test set compared to baselines. The score of generated stories should be as close to the human scores as possible, so the **smaller** numbers are better.

Baselines	NP	VP	PP	Adj. P	Adv. P	all
VGG global	1.191	1.208	1.148	**1.023**	3.043	1.067
ResNet global	1.128	1.054	1.087	1.215	2.424	1.013
AREL**	1.117	1.043	1.035	1.11	2.953	1
SGEmb global	1.164	1.137	1.119	1.309	3.456	1.046
VGG, attn	1.23	1.245	1.183	1.227	3.273	1.093
Ours: SGEmb, attn	**1.101**	**1.037**	**1.007**	1.057	**1.959**	**0.987**
Human	0.794	0.563	0.583	0.703	0.983	0.723

Table 4: Zipf's coefficient of the phrase distribution on test set compared to baselines. The score of generated stories should be as close to the human scores as possible, so the **smaller** numbers are better.

5.1 Word Diversity

In table 3, our model obtains the lowest Zipf's coefficient, closest to the human score, which shows that our model generates more diverse words than the baselines. By POS tag, our model generates the most diverse nouns. The ResNet global baseline generate more diverse verbs, adverbs and pronouns by using a stronger image feature extraction backbone. Generating diverse adjectives requires accurate visual features. The performance of our model is bounded by the VGG object detector. Producing pronouns requires cross-image coreference resolutions for objects. Handling this implicitly leads to sub-optimal results of our model diversity in pronouns. However, our proposed architecture is independent of the backbone network and can be upgraded to the stronger ResNet backbone in future work.

5.2 Phrase Diversity

From Table 4, we see that the phrase diversity scores are similar to word diversity, with our model achieving lowest Zipf's coefficient overall and across all tags except on adjective phrases. This indicates that our stories are also more diverse on the phrase level than the baselines. Suprisingly, the VGG global obtains the lowest score on adjective phrases. We thus counted the unique adjective phrases generated by VGG global (31) and by our model (65). We can conclude that the VGG global model generates less unique adjective phrases but with a distribution closer to that of humans.

5.3 Relevance

Models	match/story	# matches
VGG global	1.62	1579
ResNet global	1.90	1859
AREL**	1.94	1896
SGEmb global	1.58	1542
VGG, attn	1.65	1613
Ours: SGEmb, attn	**1.99**	**1946**
Human	3.01	2939

Table 5: Relevance metric evaluation on the test set.

We show in previous sections that our model generates more diverse nouns and noun phrases. However, do these diverse nouns actually appear in the corresponding images? To explicitly measure this, we utilize the ground truth image captions also available in VIST. Since human written captions refer to salient objects appearing the image, we posit that a relevant story should also refer to these objects as much as possible. Based on this we can quantify the relevance of the generated stories. First, we automatically match the noun phrases in the generated stories with the noun phrases in the corresponding human image captions. The matching is based on the head noun in the noun phrase. We experimented with Lin's similarity on Word-Net synsets (Lin, 1998) and cosine similarity using GloVe and BERT embeddings (Pennington et al., 2014; Devlin et al., 2019). The threshold value for counting a match was optimised to minimise false positives on a set of human annotated matches (number=194) from 10 stories in the validation set. We obtained the highest precision using GloVe embeddings, with a threshold of 0.85 (precision=0.82, recall=0.11). This metric is then computed on our model as well as the baselines. The results in table 5 show that the stories generated by our model have higher matches with entities in human-generated captions. Our scene graph embedding model also outperforms the model using the stronger ResNet features, showing that explicitly representing objects and relations in the form of scene graphs helps the model correctly refer to salient objects.

6 Conclusions

We show that introducing scene graph embeddings into visual storytelling with a pipeline method can obtain competitive results while reducing the number of parameters in the storytelling model. We also perform the first fine-grained analysis on the distributions of words and phrases in generated stories which shows that scene graph embeddings increase word and phrase diversities and bring the distributions closer to that of humans. We finally show that the diverse noun phrases we generate are more relevant to the objects in the images.

Future work One benefit of this work is that it provides a baseline for the pre-training of images in visual storytelling, allowing for any images to be used to augment the model without requiring story text; in future work, we will show that this mitigates the limitation of data size. We are currently working on how to merge regional representations for each graph effectively in pre-training and storytelling. GCN is a powerful method for pre-training, but the number of layers is strongly related to the diameter of the graph which is highly variable. A solution is to use Graph Transformer (Cai and Lam, 2020) which learns global attentions across the whole graph.

Moreover, we would like to explore how to extract features from images more accurately for storytelling. The edges of scene graphs in the Visual Genome dataset only contain spatio-temporal relations and limited numbers of general actions like 'holding' as in Fig. 1. We need to extract more common-sense directed events like 'giving' from a sub-graph of the scene graph. This requires implicit graph induction in the current model; we will test an explicit component.

Acknowledgement This research was funded in part by the German Research Foundation (DFG) as part of SFB 1102 "Information Density and Linguistic Encoding" and a Swedish Research Council (VR) grant (2014-39) for the Centre for Linguistic Theory and Studies in Probability (CLASP). Xudong Hong is supported by International Max Planck Research School for Computer Science (IMPRS-CS) of Max-Planck Institute for Informatics (MPI-INF). We sincerely thank the anonymous reviewers for their insightful comments that helped us to improve this paper.

References

Dzmitry Bahdanau, Kyunghyun Cho, and Yoshua Bengio. 2014. Neural machine translation by jointly learning to align and translate. *arXiv preprint arXiv:1409.0473*.

Satanjeev Banerjee and Alon Lavie. 2005. METEOR: An automatic metric for MT evaluation with improved correlation with human judgments. In *Proceedings of the ACL Workshop on Intrinsic and Extrinsic Evaluation Measures for Machine Translation and/or Summarization*, pages 65–72, Ann Arbor, Michigan. Association for Computational Linguistics.

Deng Cai and Wai Lam. 2020. Graph transformer for graph-to-sequence learning. In *The Thirty-Fourth AAAI Conference on Artificial Intelligence, AAAI 2020, The Thirty-Second Innovative Applications of Artificial Intelligence Conference, IAAI 2020, The Tenth AAAI Symposium on Educational Advances in Artificial Intelligence, EAAI 2020, New York, NY, USA, February 7-12, 2020*, pages 7464–7471. AAAI Press.

Tianshui Chen, Weihao Yu, Riquan Chen, and Liang Lin. 2019. Knowledge-embedded routing network for scene graph generation. In *Proceedings of the IEEE Conference on Computer Vision and Pattern Recognition*, pages 6163–6171.

Jacob Devlin, Ming-Wei Chang, Kenton Lee, and Kristina Toutanova. 2019. Bert: Pre-training of deep bidirectional transformers for language understanding. In *Proceedings of the 2019 Conference of the North American Chapter of the Association for*

Computational Linguistics: Human Language Technologies, Volume 1 (Long and Short Papers), pages 4171–4186.

Wenchao Du and Alan W Black. 2019. Learning to order graph elements with application to multilingual surface realization. In *Proceedings of the 2nd Workshop on Multilingual Surface Realisation (MSR 2019)*, pages 18–24.

Lizhao Gao, Bo Wang, and Wenmin Wang. 2018. Image captioning with scene-graph based semantic concepts. In *Proceedings of the 2018 10th International Conference on Machine Learning and Computing*, pages 225–229.

Zenzi M Griffin and Kathryn Bock. 2000. What the eyes say about speaking. *Psychological science*, 11(4):274–279.

Jiuxiang Gu, Shafiq Joty, Jianfei Cai, Handong Zhao, Xu Yang, and Gang Wang. 2019. Unpaired image captioning via scene graph alignments. In *Proceedings of the IEEE International Conference on Computer Vision*, pages 10323–10332.

Kaiming He, Georgia Gkioxari, Piotr Dollár, and Ross Girshick. 2017. Mask r-cnn. In *Proceedings of the IEEE international conference on computer vision*, pages 2961–2969.

Kaiming He, Xiangyu Zhang, Shaoqing Ren, and Jian Sun. 2016. Deep residual learning for image recognition. In *Proceedings of the IEEE conference on computer vision and pattern recognition*, pages 770–778.

Sen He, Hamed R Tavakoli, Ali Borji, and Nicolas Pugeault. 2019. Human attention in image captioning: Dataset and analysis. In *Proceedings of the IEEE International Conference on Computer Vision*, pages 8529–8538.

Sepp Hochreiter and Jürgen Schmidhuber. 1997. Long short-term memory. *Neural computation*, 9(8):1735–1780.

Ari Holtzman, Jan Buys, Li Du, Maxwell Forbes, and Yejin Choi. 2019. The curious case of neural text degeneration. In *International Conference on Learning Representations*.

Xudong Hong, Ernie Chang, and Vera Demberg. 2019. Improving language generation from feature-rich tree-structured data with relational graph convolutional encoders. In *Proceedings of the 2nd Workshop on Multilingual Surface Realisation (MSR 2019)*, pages 75–80.

Qiuyuan Huang, Zhe Gan, Asli Celikyilmaz, Dapeng Wu, Jianfeng Wang, and Xiaodong He. 2019. Hierarchically structured reinforcement learning for topically coherent visual story generation. In *Proceedings of the AAAI Conference on Artificial Intelligence*, volume 33, pages 8465–8472.

Ting-Hao Huang, Francis Ferraro, Nasrin Mostafazadeh, Ishan Misra, Aishwarya Agrawal, Jacob Devlin, Ross Girshick, Xiaodong He, Pushmeet Kohli, Dhruv Batra, et al. 2016. Visual storytelling. In *Proceedings of the 2016 Conference of the North American Chapter of the Association for Computational Linguistics: Human Language Technologies*, pages 1233–1239.

Justin Johnson, Agrim Gupta, and Li Fei-Fei. 2018. Image generation from scene graphs. In *Proceedings of the IEEE conference on computer vision and pattern recognition*, pages 1219–1228.

Justin Johnson, Ranjay Krishna, Michael Stark, Li-Jia Li, David Shamma, Michael Bernstein, and Li Fei-Fei. 2015. Image retrieval using scene graphs. In *Proceedings of the IEEE conference on computer vision and pattern recognition*, pages 3668–3678.

Vidur Joshi, Matthew Peters, and Mark Hopkins. 2018. Extending a parser to distant domains using a few dozen partially annotated examples. In *Proceedings of the 56th Annual Meeting of the Association for Computational Linguistics (Volume 1: Long Papers)*, pages 1190–1199.

Thomas N. Kipf and Max Welling. 2017. Semi-supervised classification with graph convolutional networks. In *5th International Conference on Learning Representations, ICLR 2017, Toulon, France, April 24-26, 2017, Conference Track Proceedings*. OpenReview.net.

Ranjay Krishna, Yuke Zhu, Oliver Groth, Justin Johnson, Kenji Hata, Joshua Kravitz, Stephanie Chen, Yannis Kalantidis, Li Jia Li, David A. Shamma, Michael S. Bernstein, and Li Fei-Fei. 2017. Visual Genome: Connecting Language and Vision Using Crowdsourced Dense Image Annotations. *International Journal of Computer Vision*, 123(1):32–73.

Chin-Yew Lin. 2004. ROUGE: A package for automatic evaluation of summaries. In *Text Summarization Branches Out*, pages 74–81, Barcelona, Spain. Association for Computational Linguistics.

Dekang Lin. 1998. An information-theoretic definition of similarity. In *Proceedings of the Fifteenth International Conference on Machine Learning*, pages 296–304.

Yu Liu, Jianlong Fu, Tao Mei, and Chang Wen Chen. 2017. Let your photos talk: Generating narrative paragraph for photo stream via bidirectional attention recurrent neural networks. In *Proceedings of the Thirty-First AAAI Conference on Artificial Intelligence*, pages 1445–1452.

Thang Luong, Hieu Pham, and Christopher D. Manning. 2015. Effective approaches to attention-based neural machine translation. In *Proceedings of the 2015 Conference on Empirical Methods in Natural Language Processing*, pages 1412–1421, Lisbon, Portugal. Association for Computational Linguistics.

Diego Marcheggiani and Laura Perez-Beltrachini. 2018. Deep graph convolutional encoders for structured data to text generation. In *Proceedings of the 11th International Conference on Natural Language Generation*, pages 1–9, Tilburg University, The Netherlands. Association for Computational Linguistics.

Yatri Modi and Natalie Parde. 2019. The steep road to happily ever after: an analysis of current visual storytelling models. In *Proceedings of the Second Workshop on Shortcomings in Vision and Language*, pages 47–57, Minneapolis, Minnesota. Association for Computational Linguistics.

Kishore Papineni, Salim Roukos, Todd Ward, and Wei-Jing Zhu. 2002. Bleu: a method for automatic evaluation of machine translation. In *Proceedings of the 40th Annual Meeting of the Association for Computational Linguistics*, pages 311–318, Philadelphia, Pennsylvania, USA. Association for Computational Linguistics.

Jeffrey Pennington, Richard Socher, and Christopher Manning. 2014. Glove: Global vectors for word representation. In *Proceedings of the 2014 conference on empirical methods in natural language processing (EMNLP)*, pages 1532–1543.

Shaoqing Ren, Kaiming He, Ross Girshick, and Jian Sun. 2015. Faster r-cnn: Towards real-time object detection with region proposal networks. In *Advances in neural information processing systems*, pages 91–99.

Karen Simonyan and Andrew Zisserman. 2015. Very deep convolutional networks for large-scale image recognition. In *3rd International Conference on Learning Representations, ICLR 2015, San Diego, CA, USA*.

Linfeng Song, Ante Wang, Jinsong Su, Yue Zhang, Kun Xu, Yubin Ge, and Dong Yu. 2020. Structural information preserving for graph-to-text generation. In *Proceedings of the 58th Annual Meeting of the Association for Computational Linguistics*, pages 7987–7998.

Ramakrishna Vedantam, C Lawrence Zitnick, and Devi Parikh. 2015. Cider: Consensus-based image description evaluation. In *Proceedings of the IEEE Conference on Computer Vision and Pattern Recognition*, pages 4566–4575.

Bairui Wang, Lin Ma, Wei Zhang, Wenhao Jiang, and Feng Zhang. 2019a. Hierarchical Photo-Scene Encoder for Album Storytelling. *Proceedings of the AAAI Conference on Artificial Intelligence*, 33:8909–8916.

Dalin Wang, Daniel Beck, and Trevor Cohn. 2019b. On the role of scene graphs in image captioning. In *Proceedings of the Beyond Vision and LANguage: inTEgrating Real-world kNowledge (LANTERN)*, pages 29–34, Hong Kong, China. Association for Computational Linguistics.

Hanqi Wang, Siliang Tang, Yin Zhang, Tao Mei, Yueting Zhuang, and Fei Wu. 2017. Learning deep contextual attention network for narrative photo stream captioning. In *Proceedings of the on Thematic Workshops of ACM Multimedia 2017*, pages 271–279.

Jing Wang, Jianlong Fu, Jinhui Tang, Zechao Li, and Tao Mei. 2018a. Show, Reward and Tell: Automatic Generation of Narrative Paragraph from Photo Stream by Adversarial Training. *The AAAI Conference on Artificial Intelligence (AAAI), 2018.*, pages 7396–7403.

Ruize Wang, Zhongyu Wei, Piji Li, Qi Zhang, and Xuanjing Huang. 2020. Storytelling from an image stream using scene graphs. In *The Thirty-Fourth AAAI Conference on Artificial Intelligence, AAAI 2020, New York, NY, USA, February 7-12, 2020*, pages 9185–9192. AAAI Press.

Xin Wang, Wenhu Chen, Yuan-Fang Wang, and William Yang Wang. 2018b. No metrics are perfect: Adversarial reward learning for visual storytelling. In *Proceedings of the 56th Annual Meeting of the Association for Computational Linguistics (Volume 1: Long Papers)*, pages 899–909, Melbourne, Australia. Association for Computational Linguistics.

Pengcheng Yang, Fuli Luo, Peng Chen, Lei Li, Zhiyi Yin, Xiaodong He, and Xu Sun. 2019a. Knowledgeable storyteller: A commonsense-driven generative model for visual storytelling. *IJCAI International Joint Conference on Artificial Intelligence*, 2019-Augus:5356–5362.

Xu Yang, Kaihua Tang, Hanwang Zhang, and Jianfei Cai. 2019b. Auto-encoding scene graphs for image captioning. In *Proceedings of the IEEE Conference on Computer Vision and Pattern Recognition*, pages 10685–10694.

Licheng Yu, Mohit Bansal, and Tamara Berg. 2017. Hierarchically-attentive RNN for album summarization and storytelling. In *Proceedings of the 2017 Conference on Empirical Methods in Natural Language Processing*, pages 966–971, Copenhagen, Denmark. Association for Computational Linguistics.

Rowan Zellers, Mark Yatskar, Sam Thomson, and Yejin Choi. 2018. Neural Motifs: Scene Graph Parsing with Global Context. *Proceedings of the IEEE Computer Society Conference on Computer Vision and Pattern Recognition*, pages 5831–5840.

Alleviating Digitization Errors in Named Entity Recognition for Historical Documents

Emanuela Boros[1], **Ahmed Hamdi**[1], **Elvys Linhares Pontes**[1], **Luis Adrián Cabrera-Diego**[1],
Jose G. Moreno[1,2], **Nicolas Sidere**[1], and **Antoine Doucet**[1]

[1] University of La Rochelle, L3i, F-17000, La Rochelle, France
{emanuela.boros,ahmed.hamdi,elvys.linhares_pontes,luis.cabrera_diego}@univ-lr.fr
{nicolas.sidere,antoine.doucet}@univ-lr.fr
[2] University of Toulouse, IRIT, UMR 5505 CNRS, F-31000, Toulouse, France
jose.moreno@irit.fr

Abstract

This paper tackles the task of named entity recognition (NER) applied to digitized historical texts obtained from processing digital images of newspapers using optical character recognition (OCR) techniques. We argue that the main challenge for this task is that the OCR process leads to misspellings and linguistic errors in the output text. Moreover, historical variations can be present in aged documents, which can impact the performance of the NER process. We conduct a comparative evaluation on two historical datasets in German and French against previous state-of-the-art models, and we propose a model based on a hierarchical stack of Transformers to approach the NER task for historical data. Our findings show that the proposed model clearly improves the results on both historical datasets, and does not degrade the results for modern datasets.

1   Introduction

With the emergence of large scale archives of digitized contents, the need for efficient preservation and accessibility of historical documents through appropriate technologies increased exponentially. At the same time, there is a growing interest in extracting relevant information from historical sources. In this paper, we address the named entity recognition (NER) task which aims at identifying real-world entities, such as names of people, organizations, and locations within historical documents.

Since most of the state-of-the-art research focuses on NER for modern available datasets, the performance of the NER systems grew at a fast pace, enabled by the representational capacity of neural networks and off-the-shelf pre-trained word embeddings (Ma and Hovy, 2016; Lample et al., 2016; Yadav and Bethard, 2018). More recently,

NER models based on contextual word and subword representations provided by ELMo (Peters et al., 2018), Flair (Akbik et al., 2018), or BERT (Devlin et al., 2019), achieved impressive improvements. The Transformer-based (Vaswani et al., 2017) architectures for NER became popular since the release of the BERT (Bidirectional Encoder Representations from Transformers) model.

However, while most NER systems have been developed to generally address contemporary data, NER systems for processing historical documents are less common. To extract entities from historical documents, NER tools face additional challenges. As the majority of these documents are hardcover, they are scanned and processed by an OCR to transcribe the text. However, an OCR tool can occasionally misrecognize letters and improperly identify its textual content. This can be due to the level of degradation of the actual document being scanned, to the digitization artifacts and also to the quality of the OCR tool. This leads to digitization errors in the transcribed text, such as misspelled locations or person names.

Languages evolve through time and certain words can have a different meaning depending on the period of time analyzed (Hamilton et al., 2016). The spelling of words can also change due to new orthographic conventions or cultural tendencies (Scheible et al., 2011). This high level of spelling differences can be incompatible with modern orthography and the produced noise can severely affect modern NLP systems (Lopresti, 2009).

To address these challenges of NER on historical documents, we propose a robust NER model based on a stack of Transformers that includes fine-tuned BERT encoders. We study the impact of such a model, and we conclude that this type of model is suited for the extraction of entities from historical documents.

431

Proceedings of the 24th Conference on Computational Natural Language Learning, pages 431–441
Online, November 19-20, 2020. ©2020 Association for Computational Linguistics
https://doi.org/10.18653/v1/P17

The remainder of this paper is organized as follows. In Section 2, we present and discuss a selection of works concerning NER in modern and historical documents. Then, in Section 3, the datasets explored in this work are presented. The proposed model is detailed in Section 4. The experiments are described in Section 5. We present and discuss the obtained results in Section 6. Finally, Section 7 concludes this paper and hints at future work.

2 Related Work

NER for modern documents The first end-to-end systems for sequence labeling tasks are based on pre-trained word and character embeddings encoded either by a bidirectional Long Short Term Memory (BiLSTM) network or a Convolutional Neural Network (CNN) (Collobert et al., 2011; Lample et al., 2016; Ma and Hovy, 2016; Aguilar et al., 2017; Chiu and Nichols, 2016), along with a Conditional Random Fields (CRF) decoder. One shortcoming of this type of model is that they were based on a single context-independent representation for each word. This problem has been further attenuated by methods based on language model pre-training that produced context-dependent word representations. These recent large-scale language models methods such as BERT (Devlin et al., 2019) and ELMo (Peters et al., 2018) further enhanced the performance of NER, yielding state-of-the-art performances (Peters et al., 2017, 2018; Baevski et al., 2019).

NER for historical documents Historical documents pose multiple challenges that either depend on the quality of digitization or the historical variations of a language. Studies on how the NER models can be impacted by the digitization process (Miller et al., 2000; Rodriquez et al., 2012; Hamdi et al., 2019; van Strien et al., 2020) have clearly shown that the performance scores of a NER model can significantly decrease when applied on historical documents.

The increased interest in contributing to historical language resources is driven forward by the creation of new gold standards for historical document processing. For example, Hubková (2019) created and annotated a corpus using scanned Czech historical newspapers, and Ahmed et al. (2019) proposed a German gold standard for NER in historical biodiversity literature.

A recent competition organized by the *Identifying Historical People, Places, and other Entities* (HIPE) lab at CLEF 2020[1], not only that it created a gold standard for German and French historical texts, but also encouraged researchers to participate in two sub-tasks, named entity recognition and classification and entity linking.

Considering the high level of spelling differences between modern and historical documents, variance (inconsistency), and uncertainty (digitization errors) found in historical documents, the recent methods assess these shortcomings differently.

Erdmann et al. (2016) presented a CRF-based model with handcrafted features for Latin historical texts and motivated the choice of Part-of-Speech (POS) tagger by the fact that this NLP tool leverages the highly informative morphological complexity of Latin. The BiLSTM-based model proposed by Hubková (2019) applied a character-based CNN to encode the different spellings of words.

Similar to the latter approach, we also consider that the NER model itself can help in alleviating the historical documents issues, without the use of language-specific engineered features. Differently, we introduce the NER for historical documents to the language model methods based on the Transformer architecture (Vaswani et al., 2017) and BERT (Devlin et al., 2019) methods, that, to our knowledge, have not been approached in previous research, with regard to processing historical documents.

With new needs and resources in the context of historical NER processing, we evaluate our proposed model on the dataset proposed by the HIPE competition, and we also propose a new gold standard for German and French, to assess our assumptions.

3 Datasets

We conduct experiments on two datasets that comprise digitized historical newspapers, HIPE and NEWSEYE datasets in French and German. Additionally, we study how the proposed methods behave in the case of contemporary data, by experimenting on the English CoNLL 2003 dataset (Tjong Kim Sang and De Meulder, 2003).

The HIPE dataset was created by the CLEF 2020 Evaluation Lab HIPE challenge (Ehrmann et al., 2020a). It is composed of articles from several Swiss, Luxembourgish, and American historical newspapers from 1790 to 2010 (Ehrmann et al.,

---

[1]impresso.github.io/CLEF-HIPE-2020/

2020b). More concisely, the German articles were collected from 1790 to 1940, and the French articles, from 1790 to 2010. The corpus was manually annotated by natives following the annotation guidelines derived from the Quaero annotation guide[2].

We also present the NEWSEYE dataset, composed of historical newspapers in French (1814-1944) and German (1845-1945). The documents were collected through the national libraries of France[3] (BnF) and Austria[4] (ONB), respectively. This dataset was annotated following guidelines derived from the Quaero annotation guide[5]. The annotation process was made by native speakers for each language using the Transkribus tool[6]. In order to compute the inter-annotator agreement (IAA), we used the Kappa coefficient introduced by Cohen (1960). Several pages from each corpus (German and French) have been annotated twice by two groups of annotators. Satisfactory IAA scores were reached for the two corpora (0.90 for French and 0.91 for German). The NewsEye corpus is split into 80% for training and 20% for both validation and testing.

The CoNLL 2003 dataset consists of newswire from the Reuters RCV1 corpus and it includes standard train, development, and test sets.

Table 1 presents the statistics regarding the number and type of entities in the aforementioned datasets. The statistics are divided according to the training, development, and test sets.

4 Model

We based our NER model on the pre-trained model BERT proposed by Devlin et al. (2019). Although original recommendations suggest that unsupervised pre-training of BERT encoders are expected to be sufficiently powerful on modern datasets, we consider that adding extra Transformer layers could contribute to the alleviation of word errors or misspellings.

First, we use a pre-trained BERT model, and second, we stack n Transformer blocks on top, finalized with a CRF prediction layer. We refer to this model as BERT+$n\times$Transf where n is a hyper-

	Type	train	dev	test	train	dev	test
		FR			DE		
HIPE	LOC	3,067	664	854	1,747	771	595
HIPE	ORG	833	172	130	358	158	130
HIPE	PERS	2,513	428	502	1,170	677	311
HIPE	PROD	198	53	61	112	48	62
HIPE	TIME	273	73	53	118	69	49
NEWSEYE	LOC	4,878	522	698	4,024	525	894
NEWSEYE	ORG	1,602	142	229	3,171	307	252
NEWSEYE	PERS	5,023	853	788	2,346	424	461
NEWSEYE	PROD	185	57	23	43	12	16

	Type	train	dev	test
		EN		
CoNLL-03	LOC	7,140	1,837	1,668
CoNLL-03	ORG	6,321	1,341	1,661
CoNLL-03	PERS	6,600	1,842	1,617
CoNLL-03	MISC	3,438	922	702

Table 1: Overview of the HIPE, NEWSEYE, and CoNLL 2003 datasets statistics. LOC = Location, ORG = Organization, PERS = Person, PROD = Product, TIME = Time and MISC = Miscellaneous.

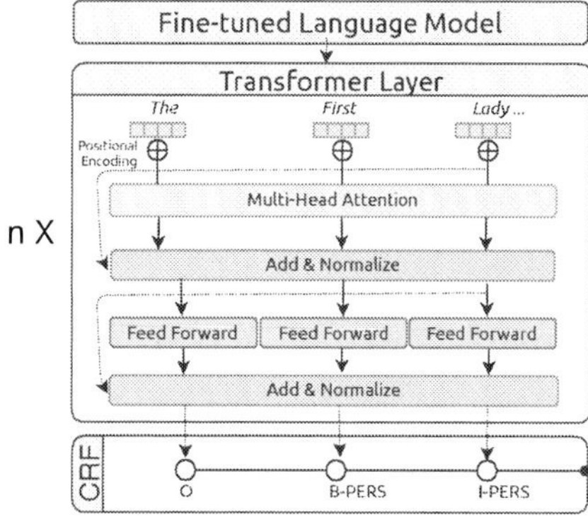

Figure 1: Main architecture of the BERT+$n\times$Transf.

parameter referring to the number of Transformer layers. The global architecture of our model is depicted in Figure 1. We used Transformer blocks with parameters that we chose empirically similar to the configuration of the blocks in the fine-tuned model[7].

The reasons for using BERT models are that they can easily be fine-tuned for a wide range of tasks, but also that they produce high-performing systems (Devlin et al., 2019; Conneau and Lample, 2019; Radford et al., 2018). Nonetheless, despite the major impact of BERT in the NLP community, re-

---

[2]Quaero guidelines

[3]https://www.bnf.fr

[4]https://www.onb.ac.at/

[5]The main difference is that several named entities subtypes were ignored. In addition, the TIME type was not included in the annotation of the NEWSEYE dataset.

[6]https://transkribus.eu/Transkribus/

[7]Note that they can vary as multiple BERT-based models are available for different languages.

searchers question the ability of this model to deal with noisy text (Sun et al., 2020) unless complementary techniques are used (Muller et al., 2019; Pruthi et al., 2019).

More specifically, the built-in tokenizer of BERT first performs simple white-space tokenization, then applies a Byte Pair Encoding (BPE) based tokenization, WordPiece (Wu et al., 2016). For example, word can be split into character n-grams (e.g. compatibility $\rightarrow$ 'com', '##pa', '##ti', '##bility'), where ## is a special symbol for representing the presence of a sub-word that was recognized.

Between the types of OCR errors that can be encountered in historical documents, the character insertion modification has the minimum influence (Sun et al., 2020), because the tokenization at the sub-word level of BERT would not change much in some cases, such as 'practically' $\rightarrow$ 'practicaally'. Meanwhile, the substitution and deletion errors can hurt the performance of the tokenizer the most due to the generation of uncommon samples, such as 'professionalism' $\rightarrow$ 'pr9fessi9nalism' that is tokenized as 'pr', '##9', '##fes', '##si', '##9', '##nal', '##sm'. BERT has been demonstrated to have a sensitivity to its sub-word segmentation when it comes to such words, as the meaning of the sub-words can diminish the initial meaning of the correctly spelled word (Sun et al., 2020). Thus, these new noisy tokens could influence the performance of BERT-based models[8].

On top of BERT, we add a stack of Transformer blocks (encoders). A Transformer block (encoder), as proposed in (Vaswani et al., 2017), is a deep learning architecture based on multi-head attention mechanisms with sinusoidal position embeddings. It is composed of a stack of identical layers. Each layer has two sub-layers. The first is a multi-head self-attention mechanism, and the second is a simple, position-wise fully connected feed-forward network. A residual connection is around each of the two sub-layers, followed by layer normalization. All sub-layers in the model, as well as the embedding layers, produce outputs of dimension 512. In our implementation, we used learned absolute positional embeddings (Gehring et al., 2017) instead, as it is a common practice[9]. Vaswani et al.

(2017) found that the two versions produced nearly identical results.

We assume that the additional Transformer layers can alleviate the sensitivity of the built-in tokenizer of BERT towards OOV, OCR errors, or misspellings, and contribute to the learning or finding the proper informative words around entities.

5 Experiments

5.1 Baseline

We chose as a baseline the model proposed by Ma and Hovy (2016), an end-to-end model combining a BiLSTM and a CNN character encoding, in order to take advantage of the word and character features. The character-level features are known to capture morphological and shape information (Kanaris et al., 2007; Santos and Zadrozny, 2014; dos Santos and Guimarães, 2015) that can also offer the possibility of obtaining a representation for misspelled, custom, or abnormal words. For the baseline, we used the FastText[10] pre-trained word embedding models (Grave et al., 2018)[11].

Additionally, we analyze the aid that can be brought by an available larger dataset by training the baseline model in two stages in a transfer learning setting, similar to the setting in which the BERT encoder is used in our model:

1. *pre-training*, where the network is trained on a larger-scale available contemporary dataset

2. *fine-tuning*, where the pre-trained network is further trained on the historical datasets

The modern datasets are the following:

- For French, we use the fr-WikiNER[12] dataset that is extracted from Wikipedia articles. It contains about 500k tokens from which around 31k are named entities.

- For German, we use the de-GermEval[13] dataset generated from German Wikipedia and News Corpora as a collection of citations. The dataset covers over 31k sentences corresponding to over 590k tokens from which around 33k are named entities.

---

[8]To increase the chances for misspelled, non-canonical, or new words to be recognized, we enrich the vocabulary of the tokenizer with these tokens, while allowing not only the BERT encoder but also the added Transformer layers to learn them from scratch.

[9]https://huggingface.co/

[10]https://fasttext.cc/docs/en/crawl-vectors.html

[11]For a more detailed description of the model and of the hyperparameters can be found in Ma and Hovy (2016).

[12]https://figshare.com/articles/Learning_multilingual_named_entity_recognition_from_Wikipedia/5462500

[13]https://sites.google.com/site/germeval2014ner/data

5.2 Metrics

The evaluation of the NER task is done in a coarse-grained manner, with the entity (not token) as the unit of reference (Makhoul et al., 1999). We compute precision (P), recall (R), and F1 measure (F1) at micro-level, i.e. error types are considered over all documents. Two evaluation scenarios were considered: *micro-strict*, which looks for an exact boundary matching, and *micro-fuzzy*, where a prediction is correct when there is at least one token overlap (Ehrmann et al., 2020a). Further, statistical significance is measured through a two-tailed t-test, with an estimated p-value between 0.01 and 0.05.

5.3 Data Pre-processing

The HIPE dataset was initially segmented at the article-level. Since BERT is able to consume only a limited context of tokens as their input (512), we segment the articles at sentence-level. We also reconstruct the original text, including hyphenated words. The reconstructed text was passed through Freeling 4.1 (Padró and Stanilovsky, 2012) to obtain a segmentation based on sentences. We made use of the same segmentation for the baseline model. Moreover, for the BERT$+n\times$Transf, we feed the model with batches of same sized inputs.

5.4 Hyperarameters

The hyperparameters used for both models are depicted as follows.

For the German NER, we chose as a pre-trained encoder the `bert-base-german-europeana`. This BERT model has been used in other NER tasks for processing contemporary and historical German documents (Schweter and Baiter, 2019; Riedl and Padó, 2018). It was trained using a large collection of newspapers provided by the Europeana Library.[14]

For the French NER, we rely on the large version of the pre-trained CamemBERT (Martin et al., 2020) model, i.e. (`camembert-large`). This model was trained on a large French corpus. Camem-BERT proposes some differences with respect to other BERT models. For instance, it uses whole-word masking and SentencePiece tokenization (Kudo and Richardson, 2018) instead of Word-Piece tokenization (Wu et al., 2016) as the original BERT.

For the English dataset CoNLL, we experimented with both `bert-base-cased` and

---

[14]`http://www.europeana-newspapers.eu/`

`bert-large-cased`, pre-trained models presented in (Devlin et al., 2019).

We denote the number of layers (i.e., Transformer blocks) as L, the hidden size as H, and the number of self-attention heads as A. `bert-base-cased` has L=12, H=768, A=12, `bert-large-cased` and `camembert-large`, L=24, H=1024, A=16. In all the cases, the top Transformer blocks have L=1 for $1\times$Transf and L=2 for $2\times$Transf, H=128, A=12, chosen empirically. The BERT-based encoders are fine-tuned on the task during training.

For training, we followed the selection of parameters presented in (Devlin et al., 2019). We found that 2×10^{-5} learning rate and a mini-batch of dimension 4 for German and English, and 2 for French, provide the most stable and consistent convergence across all experiments as evaluated on the development set.

6 Results

In this section, we provide experimental results of the baseline model and the proposed method. In order to assess the ability of both models with regard to the presence of errors provided by an OCR, we present several experiments:

- In Table 2, the first two experiments are performed with the baseline model, with and without the pre-training proposed by the transfer learning method on larger contemporary datasets.

- It is necessary to analyze how sensitive the proposed model is to the number of Transformer layers, the hyper-parameter n. Therefore, we conduct two experiments for ablation study with the n value $\in \{0, 1, 2\}$. The values > 2 obtained lower performance results and had a tendency to overfit. Therefore, in the same Table 2, we present next these experiments.

- In Table 3, the results for the baseline model without any transfer learning (as it was unnecessary) are presented, along with the same ablation study for the BERT$+n\times$Transf.

From the results in the Table 2, we can see the evidence that the BERT-based models with $n\times$Transf achieve, for both datasets and languages, higher *micro-fuzzy* and *micro-strict* performance values than the BERT model stand-alone and the baseline

	HIPE						NEWSEYE					
	DE			FR			DE			FR		
	P	R	F1	P	R	F1	P	R	F1	P	R	F1
BiLSTM-CNN												
fuzzy	83.3	70.1	76.1	89.9	83.9	86.8	81.2	42.4	55.7	82.2	77.2	79.6
strict	69.4	58.4	63.4	77.7	72.5	75.0	54.8	28.6	37.6	65.5	61.4	63.4
BiLSTM-CNN (transfer learning)[†]												
fuzzy	81.1	75.0	77.9**	87.8	88.8	88.3	76.4	49.4	60.0**	83.6	77.8	80.6*
strict	67.4	62.2	64.7**	77.3	78.2	77.7	48.6	31.4	38.1**	66.9	62.3	64.5*
BERT												
fuzzy	83.4	88.3	85.8**	89.5	91.9	90.7*	60.1	67.0	63.4**	86.1	81.8	83.9**
strict	74.1	78.5	76.2**	81.1	83.3	82.1*	46.8	52.2	49.4**	70.1	66.6	68.3**
BERT+1×Transf												
fuzzy	85.8	87.3	86.5**	91.3	92.9	**92.1**	82.3	66.4	**73.5**	88.7	82.1	**85.3**
strict	77.2	78.6	77.9**	83.5	84.9	**84.2**	62.7	50.6	56.0**	74.4	68.9	**71.5**
BERT+2×Transf												
fuzzy	87.0	87.2	**87.1**	91.5	92.4	91.9**	83.3	64.4	72.6**	89.7	80.1	84.7 **
strict	78.6	78.7	**78.7**	83.4	84.2	83.8**	64.9	50.2	**56.6**	75.0	67.0	70.8**

Table 2: NER test results for the HIPE and NEWSEYE datasets in French and German. All models have as a decoder layer a CRF. [†]= with pre-training on larger modern datasets. All metrics are micro. Statistical significance is measured through a two-tailed t-test. * denotes a significant improvement over the BiLSTM model at p $\leq$ 0.05, ** denotes p $\leq$ 0.01.

models. All models have a statistical significance < 0.01, thus, adding $n \times$Transf can improve model generalizability for NER on historical documents.

Moreover, they generally manage to maintain a balance between recall and precision, while the baseline models vary, depending on the language. We also notice that, while in general, both models obtain a more or less precision-recall balance, there are two cases where there is a large imbalance, more specifically in the NEWSEYE German dataset. Comparing with the baseline models, the BERT+$n \times$Transf only achieves a 20 percentage points difference between precision and recall, while the baseline suffers from 40 points difference.

In the context of transfer learning applied for the baseline models, two performance results, for NEWSEYE in German, and for HIPE in French are higher due to the fine-tuning on these datasets, while the others are not degraded by the pre-training on larger contemporary datasets. This observation confirms the previous studies done on this type of model regarding their robustness to misspellings (Sun et al., 2020; Pruthi et al., 2019). We also notice that for German both datasets, the results for transfer learning from contemporary German datasets are statistically significant ($< 0.01\%$), while contemporary datasets the performance difference for both French datasets was minimal (either < 0.5 for French NEWSEYE or < 0.9 for French HIPE).

	CoNLL-03 EN		
	P	R	F1
BiLSTM-CNN			
micro-fuzzy	91.0	89.7	90.4
micro-strict	89.2	87.9	88.5

	P	R	F1	P	R	F1
	`bert-base-cased`			`bert-large-cased`		
BERT						
micro-fuzzy	91.7	93.0	92.3	92.4	93.5	92.9
micro-strict	90.3	91.6	90.9	91.1	92.2	91.6
BERT+1×Transf						
micro-fuzzy	92.5	93.2	**92.8**	92.7	93.4	**93.1**
micro-strict	91.1	91.8	**91.4**	91.4	92.1	**91.8**
BERT+2×Transf						
micro-fuzzy	92.0	93.2	92.6	92.9	93.4	**93.1**
micro-strict	90.6	91.8	91.2	91.6	92.1	**91.8**

Table 3: NER test results for the CoNLL 2003 dataset. All models have as a decoder layer a CRF.

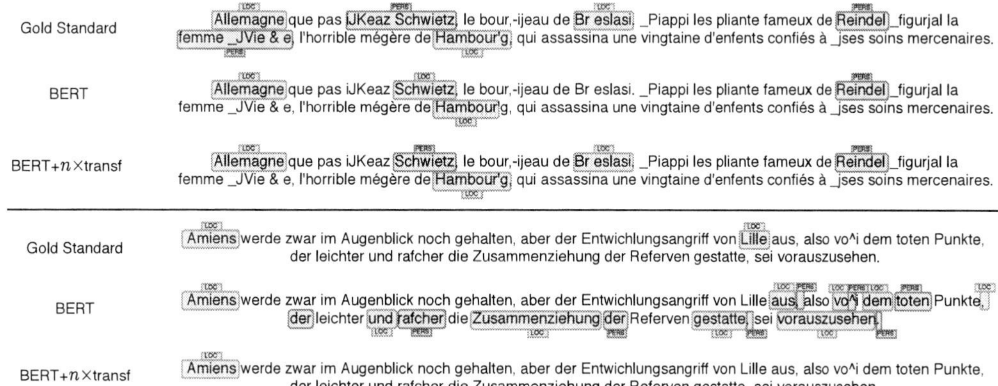

Figure 2: An example of NER predictions on the HIPE dataset in French (top part) and German (bottom part).

In the context of modern data, in the Table 3, the F1 values of the stand-alone BERT model applied on the CoNLL 2003 dataset fairly correspond to the ones reported in (Devlin et al., 2019) (the authors report a F1 of 92.4% for `bert-base-cased` and 92.8% for `bert-large-cased`). While the F1 value has a very small margin difference from the (Devlin et al., 2019), the performance results for the BERT+n×Transf slightly increased for both proposed models. We assume that one reason would be that the capacity of representation of extra Transformer layers, even in a context where no misspelling errors are present, can contribute to a modest improvement. While this improvement is more visible for the BERT `bert-base-cased`+1×Transf (a difference of a half of percentage point), and 0.3 percentage points for `bert-base-cased`+2×Transf, for the `bert-large-cased` BERT+n×Transf, the values remain unchanged (with a difference of 0.2 percentage points from BERT).

6.1 Discussion

For more qualitative analysis, we examine the number of unrecognized words by the pre-trained BERT-based models that were added to the specific tokenizers (WordPiece for BERT and Sentence-Piece for CamemBERT). For NEWSEYE German, 8.84% of the total number of words in the vocabulary needed to be fully trained, while only 0.14% were unknown in the HIPE dataset. Following this observation, we notice that there is a large F1 margin between BERT+CRF and BERT+n×Transf (63.4% in comparison with 73.5% and 72.6%, respectively), a fact that could be motivated by the large percentage of unknown words.

Moreover, for German, even though the BERT encoder was pre-trained on a digitized historical dataset (`bert-base-german-europeana`), the proposed model contributed greatly to the coverage of the misspelled or abnormal words present in the NEWSEYE. For French, the results vary of around $1 - 2$ percentage F1 points between the stand-alone BERT and the BERT+n×Transf models.

Between the two datasets, only HIPE was also annotated with the Levenshtein Ratio between the gold standard entities and the transcribed ones. In Figure 3, we compare BERT and BERT+n×Transf by analyzing the number of correct predicted entities with respect to the Levenshtein distance. For the French predictions, for 56.25% of the different values of the distance, the stacked models had relatively more correct predictions. A French example of a misspelled entity that is recognized by both BERT+n×Transf but not by BERT is presented in Figure 2, in the upper part. For German, only in 18.75% of the cases, the stacked models have more correctly identified entities that are misrecognized.

We also presume that the introduction by the stacked Transformers of additional hyperparameters can increase the ability of the architecture to better model long-range contexts. Thus, we analyzed the correctly predicted German and French HIPE entities by their length. We noticed that BERT+n×Transf is better than BERT at predicting entities composed of multiple tokens (large entities). For example, for French HIPE, from 170 entities with a length equal or higher than five tokens[15], the stand-alone BERT managed to correctly detect 70% of them, while both BERT+n×Transf models

---

[15]The length of French HIPE entities ranges from one to 21 tokens.

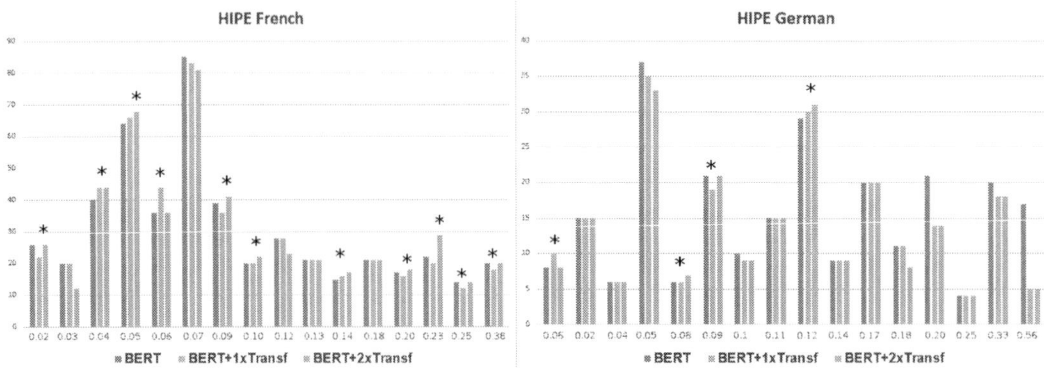

Figure 3: Correct predictions of misspelled entities based on the Levenshtein Ratio.

correctly identified 72.94% of them. German HIPE has less entities longer than five tokens[16], more exactly 97, and while the stand-alone BERT detected 50.51% of them, the BERT+$n \times$Transf models correctly detected and classified 55.67% for $n = 1$ and 54.63% for $n = 2$. In the following examples from Table 4, our method correctly predicted the full entity frequently while the stand-alone BERT only predicted a part of it.

Analyzing the French predictions for BERT and BERT+$n \times$Transf, we observed that BERT detects on average 75.04% of the entities of size 1 to 10, with other models performing slightly better. However, for entities with more than 10 tokens, there is clear a difference, since BERT detects 55.54% of the entities, while BERT+$1 \times$Transf detects 57.13%, and BERT+$2 \times$Transf reaches 82.52%. Examples are given in Table 4.

Gold standard	Predicted by	
	BERT	**BERT**+$n \times$**Transf**
signéKocH, avocat	, avocat	signéKocH, **avocat**
district de Gumbinnen	Gumbinnen	district de **Gumbinnen**
Armel Guerne. son adaptateur	Armel Guerne	**Armel Guerne.** son adaptateur
M. Javits, sénateur de New York juif et pro- israèlien	M. Javits, sénateur de New York	**M. Javits, sénateur de New York** juif et pro- israèlien

Table 4: Examples of long entities predicted by all models (the entity parts detected by BERT alone are highlighted in bold font under BERT+$n \times$Transf).

In the lower part of Figure 2, we present a German example where BERT becomes confused and

predicts multiple partial spurious entities in a sentence. One can also observe that these entities are of two of the most common types in the dataset, persons (PERS) and locations (LOC). In this case, there is an overprediction of these types, which leads us to the interpretation that BERT is sensitive to misspellings and might overfit on OCR-related patterns. This observation proves that BERT has unbalanced attention to misspelled or corrupted words when the most informative words contain such errors (Sun et al., 2020).

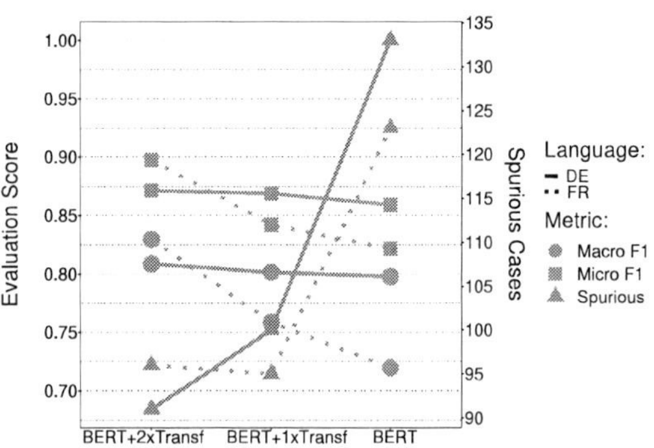

Figure 4: Number of spurious entities with respect to *micro-fuzzy* and *macro-fuzzy* F1 regarding the HIPE corpus.

To assess these assumptions, in Figure 4, we compare, per model and language, the values of *micro-fuzzy* F1 and *macro-fuzzy* F1 in the HIPE corpus. We include, as well, the number of spurious cases, i.e. tokens that were considered as an entity, despite not belonging to one, such as 'Zusammenziehung' in Figure 2.[17] Due to the difference between *micro* and *macro* metrics, we can

---

[16]The length of German HIPE entities ranges from one to 16 tokens.

[17]We obtained the spurious cases by searching for predicted named entities that did not correspond, partially or totally, to one in the gold standard.

ascertain that the three presented models focused on predicting the most frequent entity types, i.e. PERS and LOC. Moreover, we can see that BERT achieved its result by creating more spurious cases in comparison to BERT+$n\times$Transf. This could mean that BERT learned that overpredicting was a straightforward solution to achieve better results. In the case of BERT+$n\times$Transf, we can see that the Transformer layers made the models to be more conservative and at the same time more accurate in their predictions.

7 Conclusions and Future Work

We presented a deep learning architecture for NER based on stacked Transformer layers that includes a fine-tuned BERT encoder and several Transformer blocks. Results on two historical datasets in French and German showed the fitness of the proposed model to process noisy digitized text corpora in distinct languages. At the same time, the approach did not degrade the performance over modern data. Thus, this type of model appears to be adapted for the NER of historical document collections.

While the improvements brought by the proposed NER model are clear, our analysis of the results highlighted several factors that could influence the results. Further analysis remains to be done. Thus, hereafter, we will investigate detailed variations of our architecture. In addition, we intend to explore data augmentation techniques, simulating digitized data by adding noise to digitally-born documents. This could be a solution to increase the size and expand the diversity of training datasets for performing NLP tasks over historical documents.

Acknowledgments

This work has been supported by the European Union's Horizon 2020 research and innovation program under grants 770299 (NewsEye) and 825153 (Embeddia).

References

Gustavo Aguilar, Suraj Maharjan, Adrian Pastor López-Monroy, and Thamar Solorio. 2017. A multi-task approach for named entity recognition in social media data. In *Proceedings of the 3rd Workshop on Noisy User-generated Text*, pages 148–153, Copenhagen, Denmark. Association for Computational Linguistics.

Sajawel Ahmed, Manuel Stoeckel, Christine Driller, Adrian Pachzelt, and Alexander Mehler. 2019. BIOfid Dataset: Publishing a German Gold Standard for Named Entity Recognition in Historical Biodiversity Literature. In *Proceedings of the 23rd Conference on Computational Natural Language Learning (CoNLL)*, pages 871–880, Hong Kong, China. Association for Computational Linguistics.

Alan Akbik, Duncan Blythe, and Roland Vollgraf. 2018. Contextual string embeddings for sequence labeling. In *Proceedings of the 27th International Conference on Computational Linguistics*, pages 1638–1649.

Alexei Baevski, Sergey Edunov, Yinhan Liu, Luke Zettlemoyer, and Michael Auli. 2019. Cloze-driven pretraining of self-attention networks. In *Proceedings of the 2019 Conference on Empirical Methods in Natural Language Processing and the 9th International Joint Conference on Natural Language Processing (EMNLP-IJCNLP)*, pages 5360–5369, Hong Kong, China. Association for Computational Linguistics.

Jason PC Chiu and Eric Nichols. 2016. Named entity recognition with bidirectional lstm-cnns. *Transactions of the Association for Computational Linguistics*, 4:357–370.

Jacob Cohen. 1960. A coefficient of agreement for nominal scales. *Educational and psychological measurement*, 20(1):37–46.

Ronan Collobert, Jason Weston, Léon Bottou, Michael Karlen, Koray Kavukcuoglu, and Pavel Kuksa. 2011. Natural language processing (almost) from scratch. *Journal of machine learning research*, 12(ARTICLE):2493–2537.

Alexis Conneau and Guillaume Lample. 2019. Cross-lingual language model pretraining. In H. Wallach, H. Larochelle, A. Beygelzimer, F. dAlché-Buc, E. Fox, and R. Garnett, editors, *Advances in Neural Information Processing Systems 32*, pages 7059–7069. Curran Associates, Inc.

Jacob Devlin, Ming-Wei Chang, Kenton Lee, and Kristina Toutanova. 2019. BERT: Pre-training of deep bidirectional transformers for language understanding. In *Proceedings of the 2019 Conference of the North American Chapter of the Association for Computational Linguistics: Human Language Technologies, Volume 1 (Long and Short Papers)*, pages 4171–4186, Minneapolis, Minnesota. Association for Computational Linguistics.

Maud Ehrmann, Matteo Romanello, Stefan Bircher, and Simon Clematide. 2020a. Introducing the clef 2020 hipe shared task: Named entity recognition and linking on historical newspapers. In *European Conference on Information Retrieval*, pages 524–532. Springer.

Maud Ehrmann, Matteo Romanello, Simon Clematide, Phillip Benjamin Ströbel, and Raphaël Barman. 2020b. Language resources for historical newspapers: the impresso collection. In *Proceedings of The 12th Language Resources and Evaluation Conference*, pages 958–968.

Alex Erdmann, Christopher Brown, Brian D Joseph, Mark Janse, Petra Ajaka, Micha Elsner, and Marie-Catherine de Marneffe. 2016. Challenges and solutions for Latin named entity recognition. In *COLING 2016: 26th International Conference on Computational Linguistics*, pages 85–93. Association for Computational Linguistics.

Jonas Gehring, Michael Auli, David Grangier, Denis Yarats, and Yann N. Dauphin. 2017. Convolutional sequence to sequence learning. In *Proceedings of the 34th International Conference on Machine Learning - Volume 70*, ICML'17, page 1243–1252. JMLR.org.

Edouard Grave, Piotr Bojanowski, Prakhar Gupta, Armand Joulin, and Tomas Mikolov. 2018. Learning word vectors for 157 languages. In *Proceedings of the International Conference on Language Resources and Evaluation (LREC 2018)*.

Ahmed Hamdi, Axel Jean-Caurant, Nicolas Sidere, Mickaël Coustaty, and Antoine Doucet. 2019. An analysis of the performance of named entity recognition over ocred documents. In *2019 ACM/IEEE Joint Conference on Digital Libraries (JCDL)*, pages 333–334. IEEE.

William L. Hamilton, Jure Leskovec, and Dan Jurafsky. 2016. Diachronic word embeddings reveal statistical laws of semantic change. In *Proceedings of the 54th Annual Meeting of the Association for Computational Linguistics (Volume 1: Long Papers)*, pages 1489–1501, Berlin, Germany. Association for Computational Linguistics.

Helena Hubková. 2019. *Named-entity recognition in Czech historical texts: Using a CNN-BiLSTM neural network model.* Ph.D. thesis.

Ioannis Kanaris, Konstantinos Kanaris, Ioannis Houvardas, and Efstathios Stamatatos. 2007. Words versus character n-grams for anti-spam filtering. *International Journal on Artificial Intelligence Tools*, 16(06):1047–1067.

Taku Kudo and John Richardson. 2018. SentencePiece: A simple and language independent subword tokenizer and detokenizer for neural text processing. In *Proceedings of the 2018 Conference on Empirical Methods in Natural Language Processing: System Demonstrations*, pages 66–71, Brussels, Belgium. Association for Computational Linguistics.

Guillaume Lample, Miguel Ballesteros, Sandeep Subramanian, Kazuya Kawakami, and Chris Dyer. 2016. Neural architectures for named entity recognition. In *Proceedings of the 2016 Conference of the North*

American Chapter of the Association for Computational Linguistics: Human Language Technologies, pages 260–270, San Diego, California. Association for Computational Linguistics.

Daniel Lopresti. 2009. Optical character recognition errors and their effects on natural language processing. *International Journal on Document Analysis and Recognition (IJDAR)*, 12(3):141–151.

Xuezhe Ma and Eduard Hovy. 2016. End-to-end sequence labeling via bi-directional LSTM-CNNs-CRF. In *Proceedings of the 54th Annual Meeting of the Association for Computational Linguistics (Volume 1: Long Papers)*, pages 1064–1074, Berlin, Germany. Association for Computational Linguistics.

John Makhoul, Francis Kubala, Richard Schwartz, Ralph Weischedel, et al. 1999. Performance measures for information extraction. In *Proceedings of DARPA broadcast news workshop*, pages 249–252. Herndon, VA.

Louis Martin, Benjamin Muller, Pedro Javier Ortiz Suárez, Yoann Dupont, Laurent Romary, Éric de la Clergerie, Djamé Seddah, and Benoît Sagot. 2020. CamemBERT: a tasty French language model. In *Proceedings of the 58th Annual Meeting of the Association for Computational Linguistics*, pages 7203–7219, Online. Association for Computational Linguistics.

David Miller, Sean Boisen, Richard Schwartz, Rebecca Stone, and Ralph Weischedel. 2000. Named entity extraction from noisy input: speech and ocr. In *Proceedings of the sixth conference on Applied natural language processing*, pages 316–324. Association for Computational Linguistics.

Benjamin Muller, Benoît Sagot, and Djamé Seddah. 2019. Enhancing bert for lexical normalization. In *Proceedings of the 5th Workshop on Noisy User-generated Text (W-NUT 2019)*, pages 297–306.

Lluís Padró and Evgeny Stanilovsky. 2012. FreeLing 3.0: Towards Wider Multilinguality. In *Proceedings of the Eight International Conference on Language Resources and Evaluation (LREC'12)*, pages 2473–2479, Istanbul, Turkey. ELRA.

Matthew Peters, Mark Neumann, Mohit Iyyer, Matt Gardner, Christopher Clark, Kenton Lee, and Luke Zettlemoyer. 2018. Deep contextualized word representations. In *2018 Conference of the North American Chapter of the Association for Computational Linguistics: Human Language Technologies (NAACL-HLT 2018)*, pages 2227–2237, New Orleans, Louisiana. Association for Computational Linguistics.

Matthew E Peters, Waleed Ammar, Chandra Bhagavatula, and Russell Power. 2017. Semi-supervised sequence tagging with bidirectional language models. *arXiv preprint arXiv:1705.00108*.

Danish Pruthi, Bhuwan Dhingra, and Zachary C. Lipton. 2019. Combating adversarial misspellings with robust word recognition. In *57th Annual Meeting of the Association for Computational Linguistics (ACL 2019)*, pages 5582–5591, Florence, Italy.

Alec Radford, Karthik Narasimhan, Tim Salimans, and Ilya Sutskever. 2018. Improving language understanding by generative pre-training.

Martin Riedl and Sebastian Padó. 2018. A named entity recognition shootout for german. In *Proceedings of the 56th Annual Meeting of the Association for Computational Linguistics (Volume 2: Short Papers)*, pages 120–125.

Kepa Joseba Rodriquez, Mike Bryant, Tobias Blanke, and Magdalena Luszczynska. 2012. Comparison of named entity recognition tools for raw OCR text. In *11th Conference on Natural Language Processing, KONVENS 2012, Empirical Methods in Natural Language Processing, Vienna, Austria, September 19-21, 2012*, volume 5 of *Scientific series of the ÖGAI*, pages 410–414. ÖGAI, Wien, Österreich.

Cícero dos Santos and Victor Guimarães. 2015. Boosting named entity recognition with neural character embeddings. In *Proceedings of the Fifth Named Entity Workshop*, pages 25–33, Beijing, China. Association for Computational Linguistics.

Cícero dos Santos and Bianca Zadrozny. 2014. Learning character-level representations for part-of-speech tagging. In *Proceedings of the 31st International Conference on Machine Learning (ICML-14)*, pages 1818–1826.

Silke Scheible, Richard J. Whitt, Martin Durrell, and Paul Bennett. 2011. Evaluating an 'off-the-shelf' POS-tagger on early modern German text. In *Proceedings of the 5th ACL-HLT Workshop on Language Technology for Cultural Heritage, Social Sciences, and Humanities*, pages 19–23, Portland, OR, USA. Association for Computational Linguistics.

Stefan Schweter and Johannes Baiter. 2019. Towards robust named entity recognition for historic German. In *Proceedings of the 4th Workshop on Representation Learning for NLP (RepL4NLP-2019)*, pages 96–103, Florence, Italy. Association for Computational Linguistics.

Daniel van Strien, Kaspar Beelen, Mariona Coll Ardanuy, Kasra Hosseini, Barbara McGillivray, and Giovanni Colavizza. 2020. Assessing the impact of ocr quality on downstream nlp tasks.

Lichao Sun, Kazuma Hashimoto, Wenpeng Yin, Akari Asai, Jia Li, Philip Yu, and Caiming Xiong. 2020. Adv-bert: Bert is not robust on misspellings! generating nature adversarial samples on bert. *arXiv preprint arXiv:2003.04985*.

Erik F. Tjong Kim Sang and Fien De Meulder. 2003. Introduction to the CoNLL-2003 shared task: Language-independent named entity recognition. In *Proceedings of the Seventh Conference on Natural Language Learning at HLT-NAACL 2003*, pages 142–147.

Ashish Vaswani, Noam Shazeer, Niki Parmar, Jakob Uszkoreit, Llion Jones, Aidan N Gomez, Łukasz Kaiser, and Illia Polosukhin. 2017. Attention is all you need. In *Advances in neural information processing systems*, pages 5998–6008.

Yonghui Wu, Mike Schuster, Zhifeng Chen, Quoc V Le, Mohammad Norouzi, Wolfgang Macherey, Maxim Krikun, Yuan Cao, Qin Gao, Klaus Macherey, et al. 2016. Google's neural machine translation system: Bridging the gap between human and machine translation. *arXiv preprint arXiv:1609.08144*.

Vikas Yadav and Steven Bethard. 2018. A survey on recent advances in named entity recognition from deep learning models. In *Proceedings of the 27th International Conference on Computational Linguistics*, pages 2145–2158, Santa Fe, New Mexico, USA. Association for Computational Linguistics.

Analysing Word Representation in the Input and Output Layers of Neural Language Models

Steven Derby   Paul Miller   Barry Devereux
Queen's University Belfast, Belfast, United Kingdom
{sderby02, p.miller, b.devereux}@qub.ac.uk

Abstract

Researchers have recently demonstrated that tying the neural weights between the input look-up table and the output classification layer can improve training and lower perplexity on sequence learning tasks such as language modelling. Such a procedure is possible due to the design of the softmax classification layer, which previous work has shown to comprise a viable set of semantic representations for the model vocabulary, and these these output embeddings are known to perform well on word similarity benchmarks. In this paper, we make meaningful comparisons between the input and output embeddings and other SOTA distributional models to gain a better understanding of the types of information they represent. We also construct a new set of word embeddings using the output embeddings to create locally-optimal approximations for the intermediate representations from the language model. These locally-optimal embeddings demonstrate excellent performance across all our evaluations.

1 Introduction

Neural Language Modelling has recently gained popularity in NLP. A Neural Network Language Model (NNLM) is tasked with learning a conditional probability distribution over the occurrences of words in text (Mikolov et al., 2011). This language modelling objective requires a neural network with sufficient capacity to learn meaningful linguistic information such as semantic knowledge and syntactic structure. Due to their ability to learn these important linguistic phenomena, NNLMs have been successfully employed as an effective method for generative pretraining (Dai and Le, 2015) and transfer learning to other natural language tasks (Peters et al., 2018a; Howard and Ruder, 2018; Radford et al., 2018). As previously suggested by Bengio et al. (2003), Mnih

and Hinton (2007) and Mnih and Teh (2012), the weights of the final fully-connected output layer, or output embeddings, which compute the conditional probability distribution over the lexicon, also constitute a legitimate set of embedding vectors representing word meaning, as is the case for the input embeddings. This commonality between the input and output layers of the NNLM has motivated researchers to tie these representations together during training, improving performance on language modelling tasks (Inan et al., 2016; Press and Wolf, 2017). Furthermore, such a procedure is intuitive, since both the input and output embeddings of the network would appear to be performing a similar task of encoding information about lexical content. As described by Inan et al. (2016), they clearly live in an identical semantic space in language models, unlike other machine learning models were the input and output embeddings have no direct link.

On the other hand, it would also be reasonable to assume that the output representations require highly task-specific features (Peters et al., 2018a,b; Devlin et al., 2019). Despite their utility in language modelling, in-depth analysis of these input and output vector representations remains limited. The goal of this work is to gain a deeper understanding of the aspects of language captured in these contrasting representations. Our two main contributions[1] are as follows:

1. We perform an investigation to uncover both the broad types of semantic knowledge and fine-grained linguistic phenomena encoded within each set of word representations.

2. We propose a simple method for constructing locally-optimal approximations that we use to extend our analysis to the intermediate representations from the network.

---

[1]Code available at https://github.com/stevend94/CoNLL2020

442

Proceedings of the 24th Conference on Computational Natural Language Learning, pages 442–454
Online, November 19-20, 2020. ©2020 Association for Computational Linguistics
https://doi.org/10.18653/v1/P17

Though generally considered task-agnostic, by making extensive comparisons between these neural representations we may reason about the type of information most salient in the representations in each semantic space. Our results demonstrate that the input and output embeddings share little in common with respect to their strength and weaknesses, while the locally-optimal embeddings generally perform the best on most downstream tasks.

2   Related Work

Recent trends in NLP has seen a focus towards building generative pretraining models, which have achieved state-of-the-art performance on downstream tasks (Peters et al., 2018a; Radford et al., 2018; Devlin et al., 2019; Lan et al., 2019; Liu et al., 2019; Yang et al., 2019). These sequence-based autoencoder models have almost universally adopted the convention of weight tying in their input and output layers, which has been shown to improve training and decrease perplexity scores on language modelling tasks (Inan et al., 2016; Press and Wolf, 2017). Motivated by these results, researchers have proposed a number of modifications to these networks in relation to the output classification layers. For example, Gulordava et al. (2018a) combine weight-tying with a linear projection layer in the penultimate stage of the network to both decouple hidden state representations from the output embeddings and control the size of the embedding vectors. Takase et al. (2017) suggest modifying the architecture of the network by adding a gating mechanism between the input layer and the final classification layer of NNLMs. Focusing solely on the final classification layer, Yang et al. (2017) propose using a number of weighted softmax distributions, called a *Mixture of Softmaxes*, to overcome the bottleneck formed by their limited capacity. Takase et al. (2018) extend this approach by adding what they call a *Direct Output Connection*, which computes the probability distribution at all layers of the NNLM. Other work has focused on weight tying such as with the *Structural Aware* output layer (Pappas et al., 2018; Pappas and Henderson, 2019). Despite their importance, there is limited work which attempts to further analyse these output embeddings beyond the work of Press and Wolf (2017), who show that these representations outperform the input embeddings on word similarity benchmarks. In recent years, such analyses has gained popularity in the NLP community as

researchers have shifted their focus towards interpretability in neural networks (Alishahi et al., 2019; Linzen et al., 2019). Examples include probing tasks, which are supervised machine learning problems that look to decode salient linguistic features from embedding vectors (Adi et al., 2016; Wallace et al., 2019; Tenney et al., 2019). Other work has focused on determining whether more cognitive aspects of meaning are adequately encoded within these representations, through probing (Collell and Moens, 2016; Li and Gauthier, 2017; Derby et al., 2020) or using cross-modal mappings (Rubinstein et al., 2015; Fagarasan et al., 2015; Bulat et al., 2016; Derby et al., 2019; Li and Summers-Stay, 2019). Moving beyond basic linguistic phenomena, researchers have also investigated more complex aspects of language such as syntactical structure using probing methods (Linzen et al., 2016; Bernardy and Lappin, 2017; Gulordava et al., 2018b; Marvin and Linzen, 2018).

3   Research Context and Motivation

In this section, we first discuss some background about the input and output embeddings in NNLMs. Then, we briefly discuss how to compute new representations that are locally-optimal to the prediction step from the fully-connected softmax layer of the NNLM, by using stochastic gradient descent.

3.1   Neural Network Language Model

Consider a sequence of text $(y_1, y_2, \ldots y_N)$ represented as a list of one-hot token vectors. The goal of a neural network language model is to maximize the conditional probability of the next word based on the previous context. For a vocabulary V, at the time step $t - 1$ the network computes the probability distribution y_t^* of possible target words as follows:

$$\begin{aligned}
e_t &= E y_{t-1} \\
h_t &= f(e_t, h_{t-1}) \\
a_t &= W h_t + b \\
y_t^* &= \text{Softmax}(a_t)
\end{aligned} \tag{3.1}$$

where f consists of one or many temporally compatible layers, such as LSTMs (Hochreiter and Schmidhuber, 1997) or masked transformers (Vaswani et al., 2017). The function f takes in a previous state as contextual information $h_{t-1} \in \mathbb{R}^{d_f}$ and embeddings e_t from the look-up table $E \in \mathbb{R}^{d_e \times |V|}$, and produces a new hidden state h_t which the fully-connected output layer uses to compute the probability distribution y_t^*. We then compute the cross-entropy loss $\mathcal{L}(y_t, y_t^*)$ between the predicted distribution and the actual distribution, and minimize the loss with gradient descent.

To consider the case of weight-tying, we first note the fact that the size of the predicted probability distribution must span the length of the lexicon V. Then, disregarding the bias term, as $W \in \mathbb{R}^{|V| \times d_f}$ it is easy to see how we can set $E = W^T$ if we set $d_f = d_e$. Weight tying has several advantages, including less training parameters and improved perplexity scores on language modelling objectives (Inan et al., 2016; Press and Wolf, 2017). However, the information that both the input and output embeddings must individually learn in order to predict the correct target concept may be entirely different.

3.2 Hidden State Word Representations

While these output embeddings can function as a set of semantic representations, their real goal is to instead compute the conditional probability distribution over the lexicon using context information from the hidden layers of the network. As such, the output embeddings may contain certain features that are specific to the language modelling objective, allowing them to identify information from the hidden layers that is relevant to predicting the target word. In addition to considering the input and output embeddings, we also consider the activation vectors from the latent layers of the language model in order to extend the scope of our analysis. From the perspective of how these layers represent lexical information, we are interested in the activation vectors in the hidden layers that lead to high prediction probabilities for the target words.

Intuitively, in order to find some activation vector from the latent layers that best represents a particular word, we would like to generate a sentence fragment that is optimal with respect to predicting that word (i.e. the hidden state h_t for the sentence fragment yields the highest possible probability value for the target word being the next word in the sequence, given the calculations in Eqn. 3.1). We could then use these hidden state activations for each word as an additional embedding space, similar to Bommasani et al. (2020). However, we lack an efficient generative process for finding such optimal sentence fragments. We could sample a large number of sentence fragments from a corpus and record which sentence fragments give the high-

est output probability for each word in our lexicon, but this will be highly inefficient and moreover will not guarantee that we have found the *best* hidden state activation vector for each word.

In the next section, we present a procedure to identify such optimal hidden states, which we refer to as *locally-optimal vectors*.

3.3 Locally-optimal Vectors

To find a latent representation that maximally predicts the target word from the final classification layer of the NNLM, we build a gradient-based approximation for each word. To achieve this, we employ a similar technique to *Activation Maximization* in computer vision (Simonyan et al., 2013). For a pretrained NNLM, let $W \in \mathbb{R}^{d_f \times |V|}$ be the weight matrix (i.e. output embeddings) and let $b \in \mathbb{R}^{|V|}$ be the bias vector of the final prediction layer of the network. For each word in $w \in V$, we want to find the corresponding input $I \in \mathbb{R}^{d_f}$ that maximizes the probability of the word w. Let S_w be the score function for the word $w \in V$, which takes an input and gives the probability output of the target class w. We can then formulate the problem as

$$\underset{I \in \mathbb{R}^{d_f}}{\arg \max} \, S_w(I) - \lambda ||I||_2^2 \qquad (3.2)$$

where

$$S_w(I) = \text{Softmax}(W^T I + b)_w \qquad (3.3)$$

where λ is a regularisation parameter. As described by Simonyan et al. (2013), maximizing the class probability can be achieved by minimizing the score for incorrect classes. This is undesirable for visualization purposes (see Simonyan et al., 2013), which is the reason why softmax normalization is usually omitted, though in our case, finding the most probable class is desirable. The regularisation term stops the magnitude of the vectors growing too large and instead focuses on the angular information between representations. We refer to these representations as *AM Embeddings*. Although these embeddings have the same dimensionality as the hidden states h_t in the NNLM and play the same role in the softmax calculation, we note that they are not derived from any particular text sequence input to the NNLM and indeed there may not exist any sentence fragment that produces these hidden state activations.

4   Methodology

For our research, we require a NNLM that provides good performance without weight tying, so that

Models	Semantic Similarity		Semantic Relatedness			Hybrid		BrainBench	
	WordSim-S	SimLex999	WordSim-R	MEN	MTurk	WordSim	RW	fMRI	MEG
Distributional Semantic Models									
Word2Vec	0.759	0.400	0.555	0.725	0.660	0.645	0.637	0.687	0.677
GloVe	0.680	0.352	0.475	0.727	0.604	0.546	0.530	0.657	0.623
FastText	0.782	0.391	0.585	**0.742**	0.678	0.668	0.647	0.680	0.682
Pretrained NNLM Representations									
Input Embs.	0.734	0.420	0.361	0.640	0.556	0.527	**0.694**	0.661	0.683
Output Embs.	0.771	0.417	0.543	0.677	0.642	0.635	0.541	0.699	0.709
AM Embs.	**0.793**	**0.486**	**0.614**	0.741	**0.685**	**0.692**	0.649	**0.705**	**0.710**

Table 1: Results (accuracy % for BrainBench; Spearman's ρ for the other evaluations) for the three JLM-derived embedding spaces, along with three other state-of-the-art distributional semantic models.

we may analyse the input and output embeddings as separate entities. We use the freely-available language model of Jozefowicz et al. (2016), which we refer to as **JLM**. The JLM network consists of a character level embedding input and two LSTM layers of size 8192, which both incorporate a projection layer to reduce the hidden state dimensionality down to 1024. The softmax output of the model has a word-level vocabulary of 800K word classes, and the model is trained on the one billion word news dataset (Chelba et al., 2013).

4.1 Pretrained NNLM Embeddings

We first acquire the input and output embeddings by extracting the appropriate matrices from their respective locations in the JLM network, with the input embeddings generated using the character-level layers. We then construct the AM embeddings, first by randomly initialising a set of $|V|$ vectors before optimising using the Adam optimiser with a learning rate of 0.001 and regularisation term $\lambda=10^{-5}$. We train for 100 epochs, with a batch size of 1024 using *Keras*. Due to the enormous size of the lexicon of the JLM language model, we downsample the 800K word vocabulary by taking the first 20K most frequently occurring words, which gives good coverage over the evaluation datasets.

4.2 Distributional Semantic Models

We also want to compare these embeddings with state-of-the-art distributional semantic models in order to make meaningful comparisons. For this, we use the skip-gram implementation of *Word2Vec* (Mikolov et al., 2013) and *FastText* (Bojanowski et al., 2017) using the *gensim* package[2] and the Python implementation of Facebook's *FastText*[3] re-

spectively. *Word2Vec* was trained with embeddings of size 300 and a context window of 5, while *FastText* uses the default settings with embedding size 100, window size 5, and ngrams of sizes from 3 to 6. We also train a Python implementation of *GloVe* (Pennington et al., 2014) for 100 epochs with a learning rate of 0.05 to construct word embeddings of size 300. For a fair comparison, all models are trained on the same billion-word dataset (Chelba et al., 2013) as JLM.

5 Experiments

To assess these representations for both task-specific effectiveness and fine-grained linguistic knowledge, we perform a broad range of experiments. These assessments include comparison with human understanding on word relations (Intrinsic Evaluations), analysing performance on supervised machine learning tasks (Extrinsic Evaluations), and using probing tasks to isolate linguistic phenomena. We hypothesise that the input and output embeddings should perform quite well on the intrinsic benchmarks, while the AM embeddings should give the best results on downstream prediction tasks, which we would similarly expect with the hidden representations from the intermediate layers of the network (Peters et al., 2018a).

5.1 Intrinsic Evaluations

We first compare the word embeddings with human semantic judgements of word pair similarity. The rationale is that a good semantic model should correlate with semantic ground-truth information elicited from humans, either from conscious judgments, or from patterns of brain activation as people process the words (Bakarov, 2018).

[2]https://radimrehurek.com/gensim/
[3]https://pypi.org/project/fasttext/

Models	Binary Classification					Multiclass		Entailment	Paraphrase
	MR	CR	MPQA	Subj.	SST2	SST5	TREC	SICK-E	MRPC
Distributional Semantic Models									
Word2Vec	70.76	71.18	85.88	86.34	75.78	38.82	79.20	71.38	66.49 / 79.87
Glove	68.22	69.59	84.58	86.94	73.86	36.15	78.60	70.83	69.57 / 80.97
FastText	70.64	67.87	85.77	87.59	77.59	38.87	73.20	70.57	66.49 / 79.87
Pretrained NNLM Representations									
Input Embs.	71.32	**76.56**	87.04	88.45	76.39	40.05	85.6	**79.58**	**73.22 / 81.51**
Output Embs.	72.10	67.13	87.57	88.37	79.24	39.37	81.60	75.44	68.58 / 80.82
AM Embs.	**72.76**	75.15	**87.76**	**89.20**	79.85	**41.27**	**86.00**	75.14	66.49 / 79.87

Table 2: Results on the *SentEval* transfer learning tasks measured in % accuracy for all six of our embeddings. Each task is grouped into four categories, *Binary Classification, Multiclass Classification, Entailment/Relatedness* and *Paraphrase Detection*. For the *MRPC* dataset, the results are % accuracy and F1 $\times$ 100.

Similarity Benchmarks   A traditional method for evaluating word embeddings uses the intuition of human raters about word semantic similarity. Word similarity benchmarks can, in general, be partitioned into two types: *semantic similarity* and *semantic relatedness*. Here, semantic relatedness refers to the strength of association between words (e.g. COFFEE and CUP), while semantic similarity reflects shared semantic properties (e.g. COFFEE and TEA). For benchmarks focusing on semantic relatedness/association, we use **MEN** (Bruni et al., 2012), **MTurk** (Radinsky et al., 2011) and **WordSim353-Rel** (Agirre et al., 2009), and for semantic similarity we use **SimLex-999** (Hill et al., 2015), and **WordSim353-Sim** (Agirre et al., 2009). We also include two datasets whose judgement scores do not fall into either category, **WordSim353** (Finkelstein et al., 2002) and **RareWords** (Luong et al., 2013). For the embedding vectors, similarity is computed using the cosine between pairs of word vectors, with Spearman's ρ used to measure the correlation between human scores and the cosine similarities. We perform our analysis using the *Vecto* python package (Rogers et al., 2018)[4].

Predicting Brain Data   We also evaluate these embeddings on another intrinsic evaluation task that does not directly employ human semantic judgement. Instead, this evaluation asks whether the embedding models can reliably predict activation patterns in human brain imaging data as participants processed the meanings of words. For this, we use **BrainBench** (Xu et al., 2016)[5], a semantic evaluation platform that includes two separate neu-

roimaging datasets (fMRI and MEG) from humans for 60 concept words. This benchmark evaluates how well the embeddings can make predictions about the neuroimaging data using a 2 vs. 2 test, with 50% indicating chance accuracy.

Intrinsic evaluation results   In general, the output embeddings perform better than the input embeddings (Table 1), similar to (Press and Wolf, 2017). The only case where the input embeddings yield higher correlations than the output embeddings are on *Rare Words*. We can attribute this to the fact that the input embeddings are constructed from character-level representations. In comparison to the SOTA distributional models, the output embeddings tend to only beat *FastText* on *SimLex999* and *BrainBench*, while also struggling in comparison to *Word2Vec* on semantic relatedness and hybrid tasks. On the other hand, our AM embeddings perform very well in all evaluations, being the top-preforming model in most evaluations and performing quite similarly to *FastText* on MEN and *Rare Words*. While we hypothesised that the AM embeddings should perform quite well on downstream tasks, the ability of these novel word embeddings to explain human semantic judgement and reliably decode brain imaging data is surprising and interesting.

5.2 Extrinsic Evaluations

Next, we evaluate these representations by analysing their performance on a number of downstream tasks. Each task may demand a certain set of features relevant to the task, requiring these representations to encode a wide range of linguistic knowledge. We expect the output embeddings to perform better than the input embeddings and other

---

[4]`https://vecto.readthedocs.io`
[5]`http://www.langlearnlab.cs.uvic.ca/brainbench/`

Models	SICK-R	STS B
Distributional Semantic Models		
Word2Vec	75.32	57.93
Glove	71.64	56.03
FastText	75.95	58.52
Pretrained NNLM Representaitons		
Input Embs.	**79.49**	**62.23**
Output Embs.	78.86	61.72
AM Embs.	78.69	61.13

Table 3: Pearson correlation results on SICK-R and STS B semantic relatedness benchmarks.

SOTA semantic models based on previous research, which demonstrates that representations from the upper layers of the NNLM tend to perform better at prediction tasks (Peters et al., 2018a,b; Devlin et al., 2019). Since the AM embeddings represent a locally-optimal instance for the penultimate layer of the network, we also expect them to perform well.

Transfer Learning Tasks We make use of *SentEval* (Conneau et al., 2017), an evaluation suite for analysing the performance of sentence representations. Though we are working with word embeddings, applications rarely require words in isolation. To build sentence embeddings, we take the average embedding vector of all words in the sentence. *SentEval* includes a number of binary classification datasets, including two movie review sentiment datasets (**MR**) (Pang and Lee, 2005) and (**SST2**) (Socher et al., 2013), a product review dataset (**CR**) (Hu and Liu, 2004), subjectivity dataset (**Subj.**) (Pang and Lee, 2004) and an opinion polarity dataset (**MPQA**) (Wiebe et al., 2005). It also includes two multiclass classifications tasks, a question type classification dataset (**TREC**) (Voorhees and Tice, 2000) and a movie review dataset with five sentiment classes (Socher et al., 2013), as well as an entailment dataset (**SICK-E**) (Marelli et al., 2014) and paraphrase detection dataset (**MRPC**) (Dolan et al., 2004). For classification, we use a one-layer PyTorch GPU model with default parameters and Adam optimisation.

The results (Table 2) show that, on binary classification tasks, the input and output embeddings perform quite similarly, while both provide better results than the distributional models in almost all cases. Taking a closer look, we can see that the out-

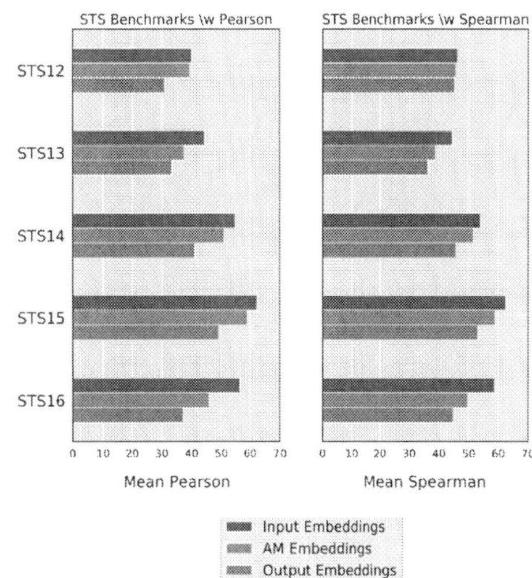

Figure 1: Results on STS benchmarks from *SentEval* toolkit. Here we report average *Pearson* and *Spearman* correlation scores on each benchmark.

put embeddings perform best at predicting movie review sentiment (**MR, SST2**) and opinion polarity (**MPQA**), while the input embeddings provide the highest scores when predicting product review sentiment (**CR**) and subjectivity (**Subj.**). When predicting multiple classes (**TREC, SST5**), the input embeddings perform marginally better than the output embeddings, though the AM embeddings perform best overall on both binary and multiclass datasets. Interestingly, the input embeddings are much better at both predicting entailment (**SICK-E**) and paraphrase detection (**MRPC**) than all other models.

Semantic Text Similarity To further evaluate how well these embeddings perform at judging sentence relations, we also employ transfer learning to the semantic relatedness tasks from *SemEval*, in particular **SICK-R** (Marelli et al., 2014) and **STS B** (Cer et al., 2017). The task consists of sentence pairs with scores ranging from 0 to 5, indicating the level of similarity between the sentences. We see from the results (Table 3) that the input embeddings again give the highest correlation with semantic relatedness scores, similar to the previous results. Furthermore, the AM embeddings perform worse at judging relatedness than the output embeddings, though the differences are quite small. Our AM embeddings still outperform all SOTA distributional models.

We also perform transfer learning on a set of Semantic Textual Similarity (**STS**) benchmarks,

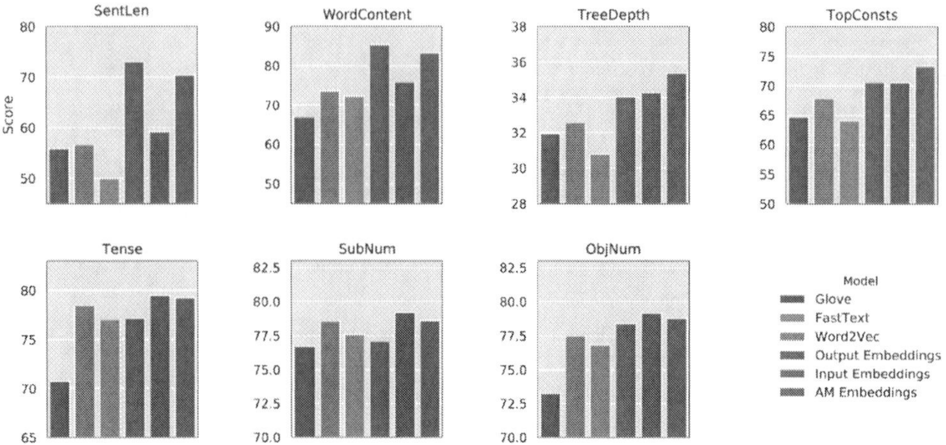

Figure 2: Results on each probing task, divided into three categories of task; **Surface Information**, **Syntactic Structure** and **Semantic Information**.

which include the 2012 (Agirre et al., 2012), 2013 (Agirre et al., 2013), 2014 (Agirre et al., 2014), 2015 (Agirre et al., 2014) and 2016 (Agirre et al., 2016) semantic similarity tasks. Each dataset contains sentence pairs similar to the relatedness tasks, though each is taken from different sources such as news articles or forums. Here, we record performance using the average *Pearson* and *Spearman* correlation for each *STS* dataset, with results displayed in Figure 1. The input embeddings again give the best performance on all datasets, similar to previous results on sentence relatedness. Furthermore, the AM embeddings perform better than the output embeddings on all datasets, in contrast to the previous findings. The results demonstrate that the input embeddings are much more suited to sentence comparison tasks than the other pretrained NNLM embeddings.

5.3 Probing Tasks

We next examine whether the embedding vectors capture certain linguistic properties when utilised as sentence representations. These probing tasks are formulated as a supervised classification problem, with strong performance indicating the presence of an isolated characteristic such as sentence length. Similar to the transfer learning tasks, we take the average embedding vector of all words to generate the sentence embedding. These tasks are taken from Conneau et al. (2018), which includes probing tasks partitioned into three separate categories.

- **Surface Information**: The tasks include sen-

tence length prediction (**SentLen**) and deciding whether a word is present in the representations (**WordContent**).

- **Syntactical Information**: Focusing on grammatical structure, these include tasks for predicting the maximum length of a node to the root (**TreeDepth**) and predicting the top constituent below the $<$S$>$ node (**TopConsts**).

- **Semantic Information**: Focusing on dependency knowledge, these include tasks for predicting the tense of the main verb (**Tense**), the number of subjects of the main clause (**SubjNum**) and the number of objects of the main clause (**ObjNum**).

We exclude other probing tasks that rely on word position in the sentence, since these averaged word embeddings are invariant with respect to word order[6]. The results are displayed in Figure 2. The SOTA distributional models tend to perform worse than the pretrained NNLM representations when predicting **SentLen** and **WordContent**, though the output models perform poorly compared to the input and AM embeddings. The AM embeddings perform well, perhaps because of their training objective which incentivises linear separability. When predicting syntactic information, the input and output embeddings perform similarly at classifying **TreeDepth** and **TopConsts**, with the AM embeddings performing best. Finally, when predicting

---

[6]Results on these tasks confirm this, with accuracy at chance levels.

Models	NNLM$_{Input}$			NNLM$_{Output}$			NNLM$_{Tied}$		
	Train	Validation	Test	Train	Validation	Test	Train	Validation	Test
Distributional Semantic Models									
Word2Vec	57.0	58.9	59.3	59.0	67.2	67.4	74.9	64.9	65.3
Glove	61.8	62.5	63.1	66.3	74.4	74.5	90.5	76.8	77.4
FastText	58.0	59.7	60.2	60.6	68.9	69.0	77.9	67.6	68.0
Pretrained NNLM Representaitons									
Inputs Embs.	51.1	57.0	57.2	58.6	66.0	66.23	72.4	64.9	65.2
Output Embs.	52.4	57.6	58.1	**47.9**	**56.1**	**56.0**	55.5	53.3	53.3
AM Embs.	**48.7**	**55.8**	**56.40**	48.5	56.50	56.7	**52.7**	**52.0**	**52.4**

Table 4: Perplexity scores on the Penn Treebank for language models trained using each embedding model as fixed vector inputs, fixed weight outputs or both tied together.

Tense, **SubjNum** and **ObjNum**, the output embeddings are superior, which may be due to the output embeddings heavily encoding dependency information that is relevant to predicting the upcoming word during language modelling. Indeed, LSTMs are particularly good at learning dependency information such as subject-verb agreement (Linzen et al., 2016).

6   Neural Language Modelling

We have demonstrated that the linguistic knowledge captured by the input and output embeddings are moderately distinct. These results may imply that the input and output embeddings of the NNLM require a particular set of non-overlapping characteristics that are important to their respective roles in the NNLM. To further understand whether and how these representations are distinctive to their particular functions in the input and output layers, we perform domain transfer on the language modelling objective. For our evaluation, we test each set of embedding vectors when fixed as certain weights in the network:

1. **NNLM$_{In}$**: Fixing our embedding vectors as the lookup table input to the language model.
2. **NNLM$_{Out}$**: Fixing the softmax output layer by using the transpose of the stacked embedding vectors as the matrix of dense weights, without a bias vector.
3. **NNLM$_{Tied}$**: Fixing the embedding inputs and softmax output by using our embeddings as the tied weights.

Here we expect the input embeddings and output embeddings to perform well in the case of **NNLM$_{In}$** and **NNLM$_{Out}$** respectively, since in these cases their role is congruent with their origi-

nal role in JLM. We also expect the other distributional models to perform well as input embeddings based on previous research. It will also be interesting to see how the AM representations perform since they are trained using output embeddings and thus should share a lot of their linguistic knowledge. If the input and output embeddings perform similarly, we can infer that these representations contain considerable overlap in lexical information. However, if they perform poorly when their roles are switched, we can conclude that these representations must learn some role-specific features not encoded in the other semantic spaces. See the appendix for training details, which closely follow the medium-sized LSTM model presented by Zaremba et al. (2014) with the Penn Treebank dataset (Marcus et al., 1993).

6.1   Perplexity Results

Results are displayed in Table 4. In the **NNLM$_{In}$** models, we see that the AM embeddings provide the best performance, even outperforming the input embeddings, with the output embeddings and SOTA distributional models performing quite well. We also note that the input embeddings still provide slightly better performance than the output embeddings in this analysis. In the case of the **NNLM$_{Out}$** networks, most of the distributional models perform poorly. The NNLM struggles when the distributional models are utilised as fully-connected classification weights, while the output embeddings, which were trained for this task, perform best, though the AM embeddings also perform well. The input embeddings perform poorly in the **NNLM$_{Out}$** model, indicating that the output embeddings do encode role-specific knowledge not captured by the other distributional models. Finally, when we tie and fix the weights, the SOTA distributional models and input embeddings do not improve the performance much in the **NNLM$_{\text{Tied}}$** model. Both the output embeddings and AM embeddings have good performance, and our AM embeddings surprisingly give the best results.

7 Discussion

We can draw several conclusions from these results. As expected, the type of semantic knowledge these representations capture is dependent on their position in the network.

7.1 Semantic Knowledge

The input embeddings struggle with representing word-level semantic relationships though perform well at estimating relatedness between sentences and paraphrase detection. The input embeddings also seem to encode several aspects of surface-level information such as sentence length, which is behavior more expected of contextualised representations of meaning. Indeed, the input embeddings seem to contain at least some qualities that make them suitable for building sentence-level representations. On the other hand, the output embeddings struggle as sentence-level representations. This is not so surprising, since these embeddings are the input components used to construct contextual representations in the intermediate layers, unlike the output embeddings.

The output embeddings seem to correlate more closely with human judgment on the word-level association and neuroimaging data for isolated concept words than the input embeddings. Furthermore, the output embeddings are highly task-specific to language modelling. Though other distributional semantic models estimate representations of meaning through somewhat similar language modelling objectives, they fail to learn any meaningful knowledge that is transferable to the output classification layer of the language modelling task.

7.2 Weight Tying

There are a number of characteristics that each set of representations seem to capture quite well given their position in the architecture of the NNLM. In a tied representation, we would expect the network to learn a set of embedding vectors that encode all such knowledge, though the contribution from each layer may not be entirely equal. Press and Wolf (2017) noted that, due to the update rules that occur when using weight tying between these layers, the output embeddings get updated at each row after every iteration, unlike the input embeddings. This implies a greater degree of similarity of the tied embedding to the untied model's output embedding than to its input embedding. From the perspective of this work, we would also add that a tied representation would be more similar to the output embeddings since the information they capture is more important to the overall learning objective. Based on our results, while the output embedding knowledge is quite transferable to the input embeddings, the converse is false.

7.3 Transfer Learning

In recent years, representations from pretrained neural language models have become a popular choice for transfer learning to other tasks. Generally, the intermediate representations from the layers of the network are preferred, since they are contextualised over the sentence and generally perform better in downstream tasks. In our work, we use the AM embeddings to behave as a stand-in for the intermediate layers' hidden states that are locally-optimal to each particular target word. Similar to these intermediate representations, our AM embeddings perform quite well on downstream NLP tasks. While this is to be expected, the results on the intrinsic evaluations and language modelling tasks are surprising. We would expect these embeddings to learn quite a bit of knowledge from the output embeddings, though the increase in performance on some tasks is striking. This may be due to the activation maximisation training objective that we employ, which forces linear separability between words in the lexicon whilst preserving the semantic information about each word (see Appendix).

8 Conclusion

We perform an in-depth analysis of the input and output embeddings of neural network language models to investigate what linguistic features are encoded in each semantic space. We also extend our analysis by constructing locally-optimal vectors from the output embeddings, which seem to provide overall better performance on both intrinsic and extrinsic evaluation tasks, beating well-established distributional semantic models in almost all evaluations.

References

Yossi Adi, Einat Kermany, Yonatan Belinkov, Ofer Lavi, and Yoav Goldberg. 2016. Fine-grained analysis of sentence embeddings using auxiliary prediction tasks. *arXiv preprint arXiv:1608.04207.*

Eneko Agirre, Enrique Alfonseca, Keith Hall, Jana Kravalova, Marius Paşca, and Aitor Soroa. 2009. A study on similarity and relatedness using distributional and WordNet-based approaches. In *Proceedings of Human Language Technologies: The 2009 Annual Conference of the North American Chapter of the Association for Computational Linguistics*, pages 19–27, Boulder, Colorado. Association for Computational Linguistics.

Eneko Agirre, Carmen Banea, Claire Cardie, Daniel Cer, Mona Diab, Aitor Gonzalez-Agirre, Weiwei Guo, Rada Mihalcea, German Rigau, and Janyce Wiebe. 2014. SemEval-2014 task 10: Multilingual semantic textual similarity. In *Proceedings of the 8th International Workshop on Semantic Evaluation (SemEval 2014)*, pages 81–91, Dublin, Ireland. Association for Computational Linguistics.

Eneko Agirre, Carmen Banea, Daniel Cer, Mona Diab, Aitor Gonzalez-Agirre, Rada Mihalcea, German Rigau, and Janyce Wiebe. 2016. SemEval-2016 task 1: Semantic textual similarity, monolingual and cross-lingual evaluation. In *Proceedings of the 10th International Workshop on Semantic Evaluation (SemEval-2016)*, pages 497–511, San Diego, California. Association for Computational Linguistics.

Eneko Agirre, Daniel Cer, Mona Diab, and Aitor Gonzalez-Agirre. 2012. SemEval-2012 task 6: A pilot on semantic textual similarity. In **SEM 2012: The First Joint Conference on Lexical and Computational Semantics – Volume 1: Proceedings of the main conference and the shared task, and Volume 2: Proceedings of the Sixth International Workshop on Semantic Evaluation (SemEval 2012)*, pages 385–393, Montréal, Canada. Association for Computational Linguistics.

Eneko Agirre, Daniel Cer, Mona Diab, Aitor Gonzalez-Agirre, and Weiwei Guo. 2013. *SEM 2013 shared task: Semantic textual similarity. In *Second Joint Conference on Lexical and Computational Semantics (*SEM), Volume 1: Proceedings of the Main Conference and the Shared Task: Semantic Textual Similarity*, pages 32–43, Atlanta, Georgia, USA. Association for Computational Linguistics.

Afra Alishahi, Grzegorz Chrupała, and Tal Linzen. 2019. Analyzing and interpreting neural networks for NLP: A report on the first blackboxnlp workshop. *Natural Language Engineering*, 25(4):543–557.

Amir Bakarov. 2018. A survey of word embeddings evaluation methods. *arXiv preprint arXiv:1801.09536.*

Yoshua Bengio, Réjean Ducharme, Pascal Vincent, and Christian Jauvin. 2003. A neural probabilistic language model. *Journal of machine learning research*, 3(Feb):1137–1155.

Jean-Philippe Bernardy and Shalom Lappin. 2017. Using deep neural networks to learn syntactic agreement. *LiLT (Linguistic Issues in Language Technology)*, 15.

Piotr Bojanowski, Edouard Grave, Armand Joulin, and Tomas Mikolov. 2017. Enriching word vectors with subword information. *Transactions of the Association for Computational Linguistics*, 5:135–146.

Rishi Bommasani, Kelly Davis, and Claire Cardie. 2020. Interpreting Pretrained Contextualized Representations via Reductions to Static Embeddings. In *Proceedings of the 58th Annual Meeting of the Association for Computational Linguistics*, pages 4758–4781, Online. Association for Computational Linguistics.

Elia Bruni, Gemma Boleda, Marco Baroni, and Nam-Khanh Tran. 2012. Distributional semantics in technicolor. In *Proceedings of the 50th Annual Meeting of the Association for Computational Linguistics (Volume 1: Long Papers)*, pages 136–145, Jeju Island, Korea. Association for Computational Linguistics.

Luana Bulat, Douwe Kiela, and Stephen Clark. 2016. Vision and feature norms: Improving automatic feature norm learning through cross-modal maps. In *Proceedings of the 2016 Conference of the North American Chapter of the Association for Computational Linguistics: Human Language Technologies*, pages 579–588.

Daniel Cer, Mona Diab, Eneko Agirre, Iñigo Lopez-Gazpio, and Lucia Specia. 2017. SemEval-2017 task 1: Semantic textual similarity multilingual and crosslingual focused evaluation. In *Proceedings of the 11th International Workshop on Semantic Evaluation (SemEval-2017)*, pages 1–14, Vancouver, Canada. Association for Computational Linguistics.

Ciprian Chelba, Tomas Mikolov, Mike Schuster, Qi Ge, Thorsten Brants, Phillipp Koehn, and Tony Robinson. 2013. One billion word benchmark for measuring progress in statistical language modeling. *arXiv preprint arXiv:1312.3005.*

Guillem Collell and Marie-Francine Moens. 2016. Is an image worth more than a thousand words? on the fine-grain semantic differences between visual and linguistic representations. In *Proceedings of COLING 2016, the 26th International Conference on Computational Linguistics: Technical Papers*, pages 2807–2817. The COLING 2016 Organizing Committee.

Alexis Conneau, Douwe Kiela, Holger Schwenk, Loïc Barrault, and Antoine Bordes. 2017. Supervised learning of universal sentence representations from natural language inference data. In *Proceedings of the 2017 Conference on Empirical Methods in Natural Language Processing*, pages 670–680, Copenhagen, Denmark. Association for Computational Linguistics.

Alexis Conneau, German Kruszewski, Guillaume Lample, Loïc Barrault, and Marco Baroni. 2018. What you can cram into a single $&!#* vector: Probing sentence embeddings for linguistic properties. In *Proceedings of the 56th Annual Meeting of the Association for Computational Linguistics (Volume 1: Long Papers)*, pages 2126–2136, Melbourne, Australia. Association for Computational Linguistics.

Andrew M Dai and Quoc V Le. 2015. Semi-supervised sequence learning. In C. Cortes, N. D. Lawrence, D. D. Lee, M. Sugiyama, and R. Garnett, editors, *Advances in neural information processing systems 28*, pages 3079–3087. Curran Associates, Inc.

Steven Derby, Paul Miller, and Barry Devereux. 2019. Feature2Vec: Distributional semantic modelling of human property knowledge. In *Proceedings of the 2019 Conference on Empirical Methods in Natural Language Processing and the 9th International Joint Conference on Natural Language Processing (EMNLP-IJCNLP)*, pages 5853–5859, Hong Kong, China. Association for Computational Linguistics.

Steven Derby, Paul Miller, and Barry Devereux. 2020. Encoding lexico-semantic knowledge using ensembles of feature maps from deep convolutional neural networks. In *Proceedings of the 28th International Conference on Computational Linguistics*. Association for Computational Linguistics.

Jacob Devlin, Ming-Wei Chang, Kenton Lee, and Kristina Toutanova. 2019. BERT: Pre-training of deep bidirectional transformers for language understanding. In *Proceedings of the 2019 Conference of the North American Chapter of the Association for Computational Linguistics: Human Language Technologies, Volume 1 (Long and Short Papers)*, pages 4171–4186, Minneapolis, Minnesota. Association for Computational Linguistics.

Bill Dolan, Chris Quirk, and Chris Brockett. 2004. Unsupervised construction of large paraphrase corpora: Exploiting massively parallel news sources. In *COLING 2004: Proceedings of the 20th International Conference on Computational Linguistics*, pages 350–356, Geneva, Switzerland. COLING.

Luana Fagarasan, Eva Maria Vecchi, and Stephen Clark. 2015. From distributional semantics to feature norms: grounding semantic models in human perceptual data. In *Proceedings of the 11th International Conference on Computational Semantics*, pages 52–57, London, UK. Association for Computational Linguistics.

Lev Finkelstein, Evgeniy Gabrilovich, Yossi Matias, Ehud Rivlin, Zach Solan, Gadi Wolfman, and Eytan Ruppin. 2002. Placing search in context: The concept revisited. *ACM Trans. Inf. Syst.*, 20(1):116–131.

Kristina Gulordava, Laura Aina, and Gemma Boleda. 2018a. How to represent a word and predict it, too: Improving tied architectures for language modelling. In *Proceedings of the 2018 Conference on Empirical Methods in Natural Language Processing*, pages 2936–2941, Brussels, Belgium. Association for Computational Linguistics.

Kristina Gulordava, Piotr Bojanowski, Edouard Grave, Tal Linzen, and Marco Baroni. 2018b. Colorless green recurrent networks dream hierarchically. In *Proceedings of the 2018 Conference of the North American Chapter of the Association for Computational Linguistics: Human Language Technologies, Volume 1 (Long Papers)*, pages 1195–1205, New Orleans, Louisiana. Association for Computational Linguistics.

Felix Hill, Roi Reichart, and Anna Korhonen. 2015. SimLex-999: Evaluating semantic models with (genuine) similarity estimation. *Computational Linguistics*, 41(4):665–695.

Sepp Hochreiter and Jürgen Schmidhuber. 1997. Long short-term memory. *Neural Computation*, 9(8):1735–1780.

Jeremy Howard and Sebastian Ruder. 2018. Universal language model fine-tuning for text classification. In *Proceedings of the 56th Annual Meeting of the Association for Computational Linguistics (Volume 1: Long Papers)*, pages 328–339, Melbourne, Australia. Association for Computational Linguistics.

Minqing Hu and Bing Liu. 2004. Mining and summarizing customer reviews. In *Proceedings of the Tenth ACM SIGKDD International Conference on Knowledge Discovery and Data Mining*, KDD '04, page 168–177, New York, NY, USA. Association for Computing Machinery.

Hakan Inan, Khashayar Khosravi, and Richard Socher. 2016. Tying word vectors and word classifiers: A loss framework for language modeling. *arXiv preprint arXiv:1611.01462*.

Rafal Jozefowicz, Oriol Vinyals, Mike Schuster, Noam Shazeer, and Yonghui Wu. 2016. Exploring the limits of language modeling. *arXiv preprint arXiv:1602.02410*.

Zhenzhong Lan, Mingda Chen, Sebastian Goodman, Kevin Gimpel, Piyush Sharma, and Radu Soricut. 2019. ALBERT: A lite BERT for self-supervised learning of language representations. *arXiv preprint arXiv:1909.11942*.

Dandan Li and Douglas Summers-Stay. 2019. Mapping distributional semantics to property norms with deep neural networks. *Big Data and Cognitive Computing*, 3(2):30.

Lucy Li and Jon Gauthier. 2017. Are distributional representations ready for the real world? Evaluating word vectors for grounded perceptual meaning. In *Proceedings of the First Workshop on Language Grounding for Robotics*, pages 76–85, Vancouver, Canada. Association for Computational Linguistics.

Tal Linzen, Grzegorz Chrupała, Yonatan Belinkov, and Dieuwke Hupkes, editors. 2019. *Proceedings of the 2019 ACL Workshop BlackboxNLP: Analyzing and Interpreting Neural Networks for NLP*. Association for Computational Linguistics, Florence, Italy.

Tal Linzen, Emmanuel Dupoux, and Yoav Goldberg. 2016. Assessing the ability of LSTMs to learn syntax-sensitive dependencies. *Transactions of the Association for Computational Linguistics*, 4:521–535.

Yinhan Liu, Myle Ott, Naman Goyal, Jingfei Du, Mandar Joshi, Danqi Chen, Omer Levy, Mike Lewis, Luke Zettlemoyer, and Veselin Stoyanov. 2019. Roberta: A robustly optimized bert pretraining approach. *arXiv preprint arXiv:1907.11692*.

Thang Luong, Richard Socher, and Christopher Manning. 2013. Better word representations with recursive neural networks for morphology. In *Proceedings of the Seventeenth Conference on Computational Natural Language Learning*, pages 104–113, Sofia, Bulgaria. Association for Computational Linguistics.

Mitchell Marcus, Beatrice Santorini, and Mary Ann Marcinkiewicz. 1993. Building a large annotated corpus of English: The Penn Treebank.

Marco Marelli, Stefano Menini, Marco Baroni, Luisa Bentivogli, Raffaella Bernardi, and Roberto Zamparelli. 2014. A SICK cure for the evaluation of compositional distributional semantic models. In *Proceedings of the Ninth International Conference on Language Resources and Evaluation (LREC'14)*, pages 216–223, Reykjavik, Iceland. European Language Resources Association (ELRA).

Rebecca Marvin and Tal Linzen. 2018. Targeted syntactic evaluation of language models. In *Proceedings of the 2018 Conference on Empirical Methods in Natural Language Processing*, pages 1192–1202, Brussels, Belgium. Association for Computational Linguistics.

T. Mikolov, S. Kombrink, L. Burget, J. Černocký, and S. Khudanpur. 2011. Extensions of recurrent neural network language model. In *2011 IEEE International Conference on Acoustics, Speech and Signal Processing (ICASSP)*, pages 5528–5531.

Tomas Mikolov, Ilya Sutskever, Kai Chen, Greg S Corrado, and Jeff Dean. 2013. Distributed representations of words and phrases and their compositionality. In C. J. C. Burges, L. Bottou, M. Welling, Z. Ghahramani, and K. Q. Weinberger, editors, *Advances in Neural Information Processing Systems 26*, pages 3111–3119. Curran Associates, Inc.

Andriy Mnih and Geoffrey Hinton. 2007. Three new graphical models for statistical language modelling. In *Proceedings of the 24th International Conference on Machine Learning*, ICML '07, page 641–648, New York, NY, USA. Association for Computing Machinery.

Andriy Mnih and Yee Whye Teh. 2012. A fast and simple algorithm for training neural probabilistic language models. In *Proceedings of the 29th International Coference on International Conference on Machine Learning*, ICML'12, page 419–426, Madison, WI, USA. Omnipress.

Bo Pang and Lillian Lee. 2004. A sentimental education: Sentiment analysis using subjectivity summarization based on minimum cuts. In *Proceedings of the 42nd Annual Meeting of the Association for Computational Linguistics (ACL-04)*, pages 271–278, Barcelona, Spain.

Bo Pang and Lillian Lee. 2005. Seeing stars: Exploiting class relationships for sentiment categorization with respect to rating scales. In *Proceedings of the 43rd Annual Meeting of the Association for Computational Linguistics (ACL'05)*, pages 115–124, Ann Arbor, Michigan. Association for Computational Linguistics.

Nikolaos Pappas and James Henderson. 2019. Deep residual output layers for neural language generation. volume 97 of *Proceedings of Machine Learning Research*, pages 5000–5011, Long Beach, California, USA. PMLR.

Nikolaos Pappas, Lesly Miculicich, and James Henderson. 2018. Beyond weight tying: Learning joint input-output embeddings for neural machine translation. In *Proceedings of the Third Conference on Machine Translation: Research Papers*, pages 73–83, Brussels, Belgium. Association for Computational Linguistics.

Jeffrey Pennington, Richard Socher, and Christopher Manning. 2014. GloVe: Global vectors for word representation. In *Proceedings of the 2014 Conference on Empirical Methods in Natural Language Processing (EMNLP)*, pages 1532–1543, Doha, Qatar. Association for Computational Linguistics.

Matthew Peters, Mark Neumann, Mohit Iyyer, Matt Gardner, Christopher Clark, Kenton Lee, and Luke Zettlemoyer. 2018a. Deep contextualized word representations. In *Proceedings of the 2018 Conference of the North American Chapter of the Association for Computational Linguistics: Human Language Technologies, Volume 1 (Long Papers)*, pages 2227–2237, New Orleans, Louisiana. Association for Computational Linguistics.

Matthew Peters, Mark Neumann, Luke Zettlemoyer, and Wen-tau Yih. 2018b. Dissecting contextual word embeddings: Architecture and representation. In *Proceedings of the 2018 Conference on Empirical Methods in Natural Language Processing,* pages 1499–1509, Brussels, Belgium. Association for Computational Linguistics.

Ofir Press and Lior Wolf. 2017. Using the output embedding to improve language models. In *Proceedings of the 15th Conference of the European Chapter of the Association for Computational Linguistics: Volume 2, Short Papers*, pages 157–163, Valencia, Spain. Association for Computational Linguistics.

Alec Radford, Karthik Narasimhan, Tim Salimans, and Ilya Sutskever. 2018. Improving language understanding by generative pre-training.

Kira Radinsky, Eugene Agichtein, Evgeniy Gabrilovich, and Shaul Markovitch. 2011. A word at a time: Computing word relatedness using temporal semantic analysis. In *Proceedings of the 20th International Conference on World Wide Web*, WWW '11, page 337–346, New York, NY, USA. Association for Computing Machinery.

Anna Rogers, Shashwath Hosur Ananthakrishna, and Anna Rumshisky. 2018. What's in your embedding, and how it predicts task performance. In *Proceedings of the 27th International Conference on Computational Linguistics*, pages 2690–2703, Santa Fe, New Mexico, USA. Association for Computational Linguistics.

Dana Rubinstein, Effi Levi, Roy Schwartz, and Ari Rappoport. 2015. How well do distributional models capture different types of semantic knowledge? In *Proceedings of the 53rd Annual Meeting of the Association for Computational Linguistics and the 7th International Joint Conference on Natural Language Processing (Volume 2: Short Papers)*, pages 726–730, Beijing, China. Association for Computational Linguistics.

Karen Simonyan, Andrea Vedaldi, and Andrew Zisserman. 2013. Deep inside convolutional networks: Visualising image classification models and saliency maps. *arXiv preprint arXiv:1312.6034*.

Richard Socher, Alex Perelygin, Jean Wu, Jason Chuang, Christopher D. Manning, Andrew Ng, and Christopher Potts. 2013. Recursive deep models for semantic compositionality over a sentiment treebank. In *Proceedings of the 2013 Conference on Empirical Methods in Natural Language Processing*, pages 1631–1642, Seattle, Washington, USA. Association for Computational Linguistics.

Sho Takase, Jun Suzuki, and Masaaki Nagata. 2017. Input-to-output gate to improve RNN language models. In *Proceedings of the Eighth International Joint Conference on Natural Language Processing (Volume 2: Short Papers)*, pages 43–48, Taipei, Taiwan. Asian Federation of Natural Language Processing.

Sho Takase, Jun Suzuki, and Masaaki Nagata. 2018. Direct output connection for a high-rank language model. In *Proceedings of the 2018 Conference on Empirical Methods in Natural Language Processing*,

pages 4599–4609, Brussels, Belgium. Association for Computational Linguistics.

Ian Tenney, Patrick Xia, Berlin Chen, Alex Wang, Adam Poliak, R Thomas McCoy, Najoung Kim, Benjamin Van Durme, Samuel R Bowman, Dipanjan Das, et al. 2019. What do you learn from context? probing for sentence structure in contextualized word representations. *arXiv preprint arXiv:1905.06316*.

Ashish Vaswani, Noam Shazeer, Niki Parmar, Jakob Uszkoreit, Llion Jones, Aidan N. Gomez, undefinedukasz Kaiser, and Illia Polosukhin. 2017. Attention is all you need. In *Proceedings of the 31st International Conference on Neural Information Processing Systems*, NIPS'17, page 6000–6010, Red Hook, NY, USA. Curran Associates Inc.

Ellen M. Voorhees and Dawn M. Tice. 2000. Building a question answering test collection. In *Proceedings of the 23rd Annual International ACM SIGIR Conference on Research and Development in Information Retrieval*, SIGIR '00, page 200–207, New York, NY, USA. Association for Computing Machinery.

Eric Wallace, Yizhong Wang, Sujian Li, Sameer Singh, and Matt Gardner. 2019. Do NLP models know numbers? probing numeracy in embeddings. In *Proceedings of the 2019 Conference on Empirical Methods in Natural Language Processing and the 9th International Joint Conference on Natural Language Processing (EMNLP-IJCNLP)*, pages 5307–5315, Hong Kong, China. Association for Computational Linguistics.

Janyce Wiebe, Theresa Wilson, and Claire Cardie. 2005. Annotating expressions of opinions and emotions in language. *Language resources and evaluation*, 39(2-3):165–210.

Haoyan Xu, Brian Murphy, and Alona Fyshe. 2016. BrainBench: A brain-image test suite for distributional semantic models. In *Proceedings of the 2016 Conference on Empirical Methods in Natural Language Processing*, pages 2017–2021, Austin, Texas. Association for Computational Linguistics.

Zhilin Yang, Zihang Dai, Ruslan Salakhutdinov, and William W Cohen. 2017. Breaking the softmax bottleneck: A high-rank rnn language model. *arXiv preprint arXiv:1711.03953*.

Zhilin Yang, Zihang Dai, Yiming Yang, Jaime Carbonell, Russ R Salakhutdinov, and Quoc V Le. 2019. Xlnet: Generalized autoregressive pretraining for language understanding. In H. Wallach, H. Larochelle, A. Beygelzimer, F. d'Alché-Buc, E. Fox, and R. Garnett, editors, *Advances in Neural Information Processing Systems 32*, pages 5753–5763. Curran Associates, Inc.

Wojciech Zaremba, Ilya Sutskever, and Oriol Vinyals. 2014. Recurrent neural network regularization. *arXiv preprint arXiv:1409.2329*.

On the Computational Power of Transformers and its Implications in Sequence Modeling

Satwik Bhattamishra   **Arkil Patel**   **Navin Goyal**
Microsoft Research India
{t-satbh,t-arkpat,navingo}@microsoft.com

Abstract

Transformers are being used extensively across several sequence modeling tasks. Significant research effort has been devoted to experimentally probe the inner workings of Transformers. However, our conceptual and theoretical understanding of their power and inherent limitations is still nascent. In particular, the roles of various components in Transformers such as positional encodings, attention heads, residual connections, and feedforward networks, are not clear. In this paper, we take a step towards answering these questions. We analyze the computational power as captured by Turing-completeness. We first provide an alternate and simpler proof to show that vanilla Transformers are Turing-complete and then we prove that Transformers with only positional masking and without any positional encoding are also Turing-complete. We further analyze the necessity of each component for the Turing-completeness of the network; interestingly, we find that a particular type of residual connection is necessary. We demonstrate the practical implications of our results via experiments on machine translation and synthetic tasks.

1 Introduction

Transformer (Vaswani et al., 2017) is a recent self-attention based sequence-to-sequence architecture which has led to state of the art results across various NLP tasks including machine translation (Ott et al., 2018), language modeling (Radford et al., 2018) and question answering (Devlin et al., 2019). Although a number of variants of Transformers have been proposed, the original architecture still underlies these variants.

While the training and generalization of machine learning models such as Transformers are the central goals in their analysis, an essential prerequisite to this end is characterization of the computational

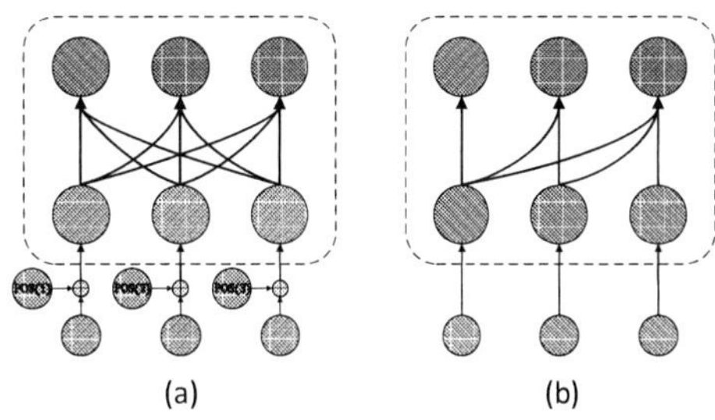

Figure 1: (a) Self-Attention Network with positional encoding, (b) Self-Attention Network with positional masking without any positional encoding

power of the model: training a model for a certain task cannot succeed if the model is computationally incapable of carrying out the task. While the computational capabilities of recurrent networks (RNNs) have been studied for decades (Kolen and Kremer, 2001; Siegelmann, 2012), for Transformers we are still in the early stages.

The celebrated work of Siegelmann and Sontag (1992) showed, assuming arbitrary precision, that RNNs are *Turing-complete*, meaning that they are capable of carrying out any algorithmic task formalized by Turing machines. Recently, Pérez et al. (2019) have shown that vanilla Transformers with hard-attention can also simulate Turing machines given arbitrary precision. However, in contrast to RNNs, Transformers consist of several components and it is unclear which components are necessary for its Turing-completeness and thereby crucial to its computational expressiveness.

The role of various components of the Transformer in its efficacy is an important question for further improvements. Since the Transformer does not process the input sequentially, it requires some form of positional information. Various positional encoding schemes have been proposed to capture order information (Shaw et al., 2018; Dai et al., 2019; Huang et al., 2018). At the same time, on

455

Proceedings of the 24th Conference on Computational Natural Language Learning, pages 455–475
Online, November 19-20, 2020. ©2020 Association for Computational Linguistics
https://doi.org/10.18653/v1/P17

machine translation, Yang et al. (2019) showed that the performance of Transformers with only positional masking (Shen et al., 2018) is comparable to that with positional encodings. In case of positional masking (Fig. 1), as opposed to explicit encodings, the model is only allowed to attend over preceding inputs and no additional positional encoding vector is combined with the input vector. Tsai et al. (2019) raised the question of whether explicit encoding is necessary if positional masking is used. Additionally, since Pérez et al. (2019)'s Turing-completeness proof relied heavily on residual connections, they asked whether these connections are essential for Turing-completeness. In this paper, we take a step towards answering such questions. Below, we list the main contributions of the paper,

- We provide an alternate and arguably simpler proof to show that Transformers are Turing-complete by directly relating them to RNNs.

- More importantly, we prove that Transformers with positional masking and without positional encoding are also Turing-complete.

- We analyze the necessity of various components such as self-attention blocks, residual connections and feedforward networks for Turing-completeness. Figure 2 provides an overview.

- We explore implications of our results on machine translation and synthetic tasks.[1]

2   Related Work

Computational Power of neural networks has been studied since the foundational paper McCulloch and Pitts (1943); in particular, among sequence-to-sequence models, this aspect of RNNs has long been studied (Kolen and Kremer, 2001). The seminal work by Siegelmann and Sontag (1992) showed that RNNs can simulate a Turing machine by using unbounded precision. Chen et al. (2018) showed that RNNs with ReLU activations are also Turing-complete. Many recent works have explored the computational power of RNNs in practical settings. Several works (Merrill et al., 2020), (Weiss et al., 2018) recently studied the ability of RNNs to recognize counter-like languages. The capability of RNNs to recognize strings of balanced

parantheses has also been studied (Sennhauser and Berwick, 2018; Skachkova et al., 2018). However, such analysis on Transformers has been scarce.

Theoretical work on Transformers was initiated by Pérez et al. (2019) who formalized the notion of Transformers and showed that it can simulate a Turing machine given arbitrary precision. Concurrent to our work, there have been several efforts to understand self-attention based models (Levine et al., 2020; Kim et al., 2020). Hron et al. (2020) show that Transformers behave as Gaussian processes when the number of heads tend to infinity. Hahn (2020) showed some limitations of Transformer encoders in modeling regular and context-free languages. It has been recently shown that Transformers are universal approximators of sequence-to-sequence functions given arbitrary precision (Yun et al., 2020). However, these are not applicable[2] to the complete Transformer architecture. With a goal similar to ours, Tsai et al. (2019) attempted to study the attention mechanism via a kernel formulation. However, a systematic study of various components of Transformers has not been done.

3   Definitions and Preliminaries

All the numbers used in our computations will be from the set of rational numbers denoted $\mathbb{Q}$. For a sequence $X = (x_1, \ldots, x_n)$, we set $X_j := (x_1, \ldots, x_j)$ for $1 \leq j \leq n$. We will work with an alphabet Σ of size m, with special symbols $\#$ and $\$$ signifying the beginning and end of the input sequence, respectively. The symbols are mapped to vectors via a given 'base' embedding $f_b : \Sigma \to \mathbb{Q}^{d_b}$, where d_b is the dimension of the embedding. E.g., this embedding could be the one used for processing the symbols by the RNN.

We set $f_b(\#) = \mathbf{0}_{d_b}$ and $f_b(\$) = \mathbf{0}_{d_b}$. *Positional encoding* is a function $\mathrm{pos} : \mathbb{N} \to \mathbb{Q}^{d_b}$. Together, these provide embedding for a symbol s at position i given by $f(f_b(s), \mathrm{pos}(i))$, often taken to be simply $f_b(s) + \mathrm{pos}(i)$. Vector $[\![s]\!] \in \mathbb{Q}^m$ denotes one-hot encoding of a symbol $s \in \Sigma$.

3.1   RNNs

We follow Siegelmann and Sontag (1992) in our definition of RNNs. To feed the sequences

---

[1] We have made our source code available at https://github.com/satwik77/Transformer-Computation-Analysis.

[2] Hahn (2020) and Yun et al. (2020) study encoder-only seq-to-seq models with fixed length outputs in which the computation halts as soon as the last symbol of the input is processed. Our work is about the full Transformer (encoder and decoder) which is a seq-to-seq model with variable length sequence output in which the decoder starts operating sequentially after the encoder.

$s_1 s_2 \ldots s_n \in \Sigma^*$ to the RNN, these are converted to the vectors $\boldsymbol{x}_1, \boldsymbol{x}_2, \ldots, \boldsymbol{x}_n$ where $\boldsymbol{x}_i = f_b(s_i)$. The RNN is given by the recurrence $\boldsymbol{h}_t = g(\boldsymbol{W}_h \boldsymbol{h}_{t-1} + \boldsymbol{W}_x \boldsymbol{x}_t + \boldsymbol{b})$, where $t \geq 1$, function $g(\cdot)$ is a multilayer feedforward network (FFN) with activation σ, bias vector $\boldsymbol{b} \in \mathbb{Q}^{d_h}$, matrices $\boldsymbol{W}_h \in \mathbb{Q}^{d_h \times d_h}$ and $\boldsymbol{W}_x \in \mathbb{Q}^{d_h \times d_b}$, and $\boldsymbol{h}_t \in \mathbb{Q}^{d_h}$ is the hidden state with given initial hidden state $\boldsymbol{h}_0$; d_h is the hidden state dimension.

After the last symbol s_n has been fed, we continue to feed the RNN with the terminal symbol $f_b(\$)$ until it halts. This allows the RNN to carry out computation after having read the input.

A class of seq-to-seq neural networks is Turing-complete if the class of languages recognized by the networks is exactly the class of languages recognized by Turing machines.

Theorem 3.1. *(Siegelmann and Sontag, 1992) Any seq-to-seq function $\Sigma^* \to \Sigma^*$ computable by a Turing machine can also be computed by an RNN.*

For details please see section B.1 in appendix.

3.2 Transformer Architecture

Vanilla Transformer. We describe the original Transformer architecture with positional encoding (Vaswani et al., 2017) as formalized by Pérez et al. (2019), with some modifications. All vectors in this subsection are from $\mathbb{Q}^d$.

The transformer, denoted Trans, is a seq-to-seq architecture. Its input consists of (i) a sequence $\boldsymbol{X} = (\boldsymbol{x}_1, \ldots, \boldsymbol{x}_n)$ of vectors, (ii) a seed vector $\boldsymbol{y}_0$. The output is a sequence $\boldsymbol{Y} = (\boldsymbol{y}_1, \ldots, \boldsymbol{y}_r)$ of vectors. The sequence $\boldsymbol{X}$ is obtained from the sequence $(s_1, \ldots, s_n) \in \Sigma^n$ of symbols by using the embedding mentioned earlier: $\boldsymbol{x}_i = f(f_b(s_i), \mathrm{pos}(i))$.

The transformer consists of composition of *transformer encoder* and *transformer decoder*. For the feedforward networks in the transformer layers we use the activation as in Siegelmann and Sontag (1992), namely the saturated linear activation function $\sigma(x)$ which takes value 0 for $x < 0$, value x for $0 < x < 1$ and value 1 for $x > 1$. This activation can be easily replaced by the standard ReLU activation via $\sigma(x) = \mathrm{ReLU}(x) - \mathrm{ReLU}(x - 1)$.

Self-attention. The self-attention mechanism takes as input (i) a *query* vector $\boldsymbol{q}$, (ii) a sequence of *key* vectors $\boldsymbol{K} = (\boldsymbol{k}_1, \ldots, \boldsymbol{k}_n)$, and (iii) a sequence of *value* vectors $\boldsymbol{V} = (\boldsymbol{v}_1, \ldots, \boldsymbol{v}_n)$. The $\boldsymbol{q}$-attention over $\boldsymbol{K}$ and $\boldsymbol{V}$, denoted $\mathrm{Att}(\boldsymbol{q}, \boldsymbol{K}, \boldsymbol{V})$, is a vector $\boldsymbol{a} = \alpha_1 \boldsymbol{v}_1 + \alpha_2 \boldsymbol{v}_2 + \cdots + \alpha_n \boldsymbol{v}_n$, where (i)

$(\alpha_1, \ldots, \alpha_n) = \rho(f^{\mathrm{att}}(\boldsymbol{q}, \boldsymbol{k}_1), \ldots, f^{\mathrm{att}}(\boldsymbol{q}, \boldsymbol{k}_n))$.
(ii) The normalization function $\rho : \mathbb{Q}^n \to \mathbb{Q}^n_{\geq 0}$ is hardmax: for $\boldsymbol{x} = (x_1, \ldots, x_n) \in \mathbb{Q}^n$, if the maximum value occurs r times among $x_1, \ldots, x_n$, then $\mathrm{hardmax}(\boldsymbol{x})_i := 1/r$ if x_i is a maximum value and $\mathrm{hardmax}(\boldsymbol{x})_i := 0$ otherwise. In practice, the softmax is often used but its output values are in general not rational.

(iii) For vanilla transformers, the scoring function f^{att} used is a combination of multiplicative attention (Vaswani et al., 2017) and a non-linear function: $f^{\mathrm{att}}(\boldsymbol{q}, \boldsymbol{k}_i) = -\big|\langle \boldsymbol{q}, \boldsymbol{k}_i \rangle\big|$. This was also used by Pérez et al. (2019).

Transformer encoder. A *single-layer encoder* is a function $\mathrm{Enc}(\boldsymbol{X}; \boldsymbol{\theta})$, with input $\boldsymbol{X} = (\boldsymbol{x}_1, \ldots, \boldsymbol{x}_n)$ a sequence of vectors in $\mathbb{Q}^d$, and parameters $\boldsymbol{\theta}$. The output is another sequence $\boldsymbol{Z} = (\boldsymbol{z}_1, \ldots, \boldsymbol{z}_n)$ of vectors in $\mathbb{Q}^d$. The parameters $\boldsymbol{\theta}$ specify functions $Q(\cdot), K(\cdot), V(\cdot)$, and $O(\cdot)$, all of type $\mathbb{Q}^d \to \mathbb{Q}^d$. The functions $Q(\cdot), K(\cdot)$, and $V(\cdot)$ are linear transformations and $O(\cdot)$ an FFN. For $1 \leq i \leq n$, the output of the self-attention block is produced by

$$\boldsymbol{a}_i = \mathrm{Att}(Q(\boldsymbol{x}_i), K(\boldsymbol{X}), V(\boldsymbol{X})) + \boldsymbol{x}_i \quad (1)$$

This operation is also referred to as the encoder-encoder attention block. The output $\boldsymbol{Z}$ is computed by $\boldsymbol{z}_i = O(\boldsymbol{a}_i) + \boldsymbol{a}_i$ for $1 \leq i \leq n$. The addition operations $+\boldsymbol{x}_i$ and $+\boldsymbol{a}_i$ are the residual connections. The complete L-layer transformer encoder $\mathrm{TEnc}^{(L)}(\boldsymbol{X}; \boldsymbol{\theta}) = (\boldsymbol{K}^e, \boldsymbol{V}^e)$ has the same input $\boldsymbol{X} = (\boldsymbol{x}_1, \ldots, \boldsymbol{x}_n)$ as the single-layer encoder. In contrast, its output $\boldsymbol{K}^e = (\boldsymbol{k}_1^e, \ldots, \boldsymbol{k}_n^e)$ and $\boldsymbol{V}^e = (\boldsymbol{v}_1^e, \ldots \boldsymbol{v}_n^e)$ contains two sequences. $\mathrm{TEnc}^{(L)}$ is obtained by composition of L single-layer encoders: let $\boldsymbol{X}^{(0)} := \boldsymbol{X}$, and for $0 \leq \ell \leq L - 1$, let $\boldsymbol{X}^{(\ell+1)} = \mathrm{Enc}(\boldsymbol{X}^{(\ell)}; \boldsymbol{\theta}_\ell)$ and finally, $\boldsymbol{K}^e = K^{(L)}(\boldsymbol{X}^{(L)}), \quad \boldsymbol{V}^e = V^{(L)}(\boldsymbol{X}^{(L)})$.

Transformer decoder. The input to a *single-layer decoder* is (i) $(\boldsymbol{K}^e, \boldsymbol{V}^e)$ output by the encoder, and (ii) sequence $\boldsymbol{Y} = (\boldsymbol{y}_1, \ldots, \boldsymbol{y}_k)$ of vectors for $k \geq 1$. The output is another sequence $\boldsymbol{Z} = (\boldsymbol{z}_1, \ldots, \boldsymbol{z}_k)$.

Similar to the single-layer encoder, a single-layer decoder is parameterized by functions $Q(\cdot), K(\cdot), V(\cdot)$ and $O(\cdot)$ and is defined by

$$
\begin{aligned}
\boldsymbol{p}_t &= \mathrm{Att}(Q(\boldsymbol{y}_t), K(\boldsymbol{Y}_t), V(\boldsymbol{Y}_t)) + \boldsymbol{y}_t, & (2)\\
\boldsymbol{a}_t &= \mathrm{Att}(\boldsymbol{p}_t, \boldsymbol{K}^e, \boldsymbol{V}^e) + \boldsymbol{p}_t, & (3)\\
\boldsymbol{z}_t &= O(\boldsymbol{a}_t) + \boldsymbol{a}_t,
\end{aligned}
$$

where $1 \leq t \leq k$. The operation in (2) will be

referred to as the *decoder-decoder attention* block and the operation in (3) as the *decoder-encoder attention* block. In (2), positional masking is applied to prevent the network from attending over symbols which are ahead of them.

An L-layer Transformer decoder $\text{TDec}^L((\boldsymbol{K}^e, \boldsymbol{V}^e), \boldsymbol{Y}; \boldsymbol{\theta}) = z$ is obtained by repeated application of L single-layer decoders each with its own parameters, and a transformation function $F : \mathbb{Q}^d \to \mathbb{Q}^d$ applied to the last vector in the sequence of vectors output by the final decoder. Formally, for $0 \leq \ell \leq L-1$ and $\boldsymbol{Y}^0 := \boldsymbol{Y}$ we have $\boldsymbol{Y}^{\ell+1} = \text{Dec}((\boldsymbol{K}^e, \boldsymbol{V}^e), \boldsymbol{Y}^\ell; \boldsymbol{\theta}_\ell), \quad z = F(\boldsymbol{y}_k^L).$ Note that while the output of a single-layer decoder is a sequence of vectors, the output of an L-layer Transformer decoder is a single vector.

The complete Transformer. The output $\text{Trans}(\boldsymbol{X}, \boldsymbol{y}_0) = \boldsymbol{Y}$ is computed by the recurrence $\tilde{\boldsymbol{y}}_{t+1} = \text{TDec}(\text{TEnc}(\boldsymbol{X}), (\boldsymbol{y}_0, \boldsymbol{y}_1, \dots, \boldsymbol{y}_t))$, for $0 \leq t \leq r - 1$. We get $\boldsymbol{y}_{t+1}$ by adding positional encoding: $\boldsymbol{y}_{t+1} = \tilde{\boldsymbol{y}}_{t+1} + \text{pos}(t + 1)$.

Directional Transformer. We denote the Transformer with only positional masking and no positional encodings as Directional Transformer and use them interchangeably. In this case, we use standard multiplicative attention as the scoring function in our construction, i.e. $f^{\text{att}}(\boldsymbol{q}, \boldsymbol{k}_i) = \langle \boldsymbol{q}, \boldsymbol{k}_i \rangle$. The general architecture is the same as for the vanilla case; the differences due to positional masking are the following.

There are no positional encodings. So the input vectors $\boldsymbol{x}_i$ only involve $f_b(s_i)$. Similarly, $\boldsymbol{y}_t = \tilde{\boldsymbol{y}}_t$. In (1), $\text{Att}(\cdot)$ is replaced by $\text{Att}(Q(\boldsymbol{x}_i), K(\boldsymbol{X}_i), V(\boldsymbol{X}_i))$ where $\boldsymbol{X}_i := (\boldsymbol{x}_1, \dots, \boldsymbol{x}_i)$ for $1 \leq i \leq n$. Similarly, in (3), $\text{Att}(\cdot)$ is replaced by $\text{Att}(\boldsymbol{p}_t, \boldsymbol{K}_t^e, \boldsymbol{V}_t^e)$.

Remark 1. Our definitions deviate slightly from practice, hard-attention being the main one since hardmax keeps the values rational whereas softmax takes the values to irrational space. Previous studies have shown that soft-attention behaves like hard-attention in practice and Hahn (2020) discusses its practical relevance.

Remark 2. Transformer Networks with positional encodings are not necessarily equivalent in terms of their computational expressiveness (Yun et al., 2020) to those with only positional masking when considering the encoder only model (as used in BERT and GPT-2). Our results in Section 4.1 show their equivalence in terms of expressiveness for the complete seq-to-seq architecture.

4 Primary Results

4.1 Turing-Completeness Results

In light of Theorem 3.1, to prove that Transformers are Turing-complete, it suffices to show that they can *simulate* RNNs. We say that a Transformer simulates an RNN (as defined in Sec. 3.1) if on every input $s \in \Sigma^*$, at each step t, the vector $\boldsymbol{y}_t$ contains the hidden state $\boldsymbol{h}_t$ as a subvector, i.e. $\boldsymbol{y}_t = [\boldsymbol{h}_t, \cdot]$, and halts at the same step as the RNN.

Theorem 4.1. *The class of Transformers with positional encodings is Turing-complete.*

Proof Sketch. The input $s_0, \dots, s_n \in \Sigma^*$ is provided to the transformer as the sequence of vectors $\boldsymbol{x}_0, \dots, \boldsymbol{x}_n$, where $\boldsymbol{x}_i = [\boldsymbol{0}_{d_h}, f_b(s_i), \boldsymbol{0}_{d_h}, i, 1]$, which has as sub-vector the given base embedding $f_b(s_i)$ and the positional encoding i, along with extra coordinates set to constant values and will be used later.

The basic observation behind our construction of the simulating Transformer is that the transformer decoder can naturally implement the recurrence operations of the type used by RNNs. To this end, the FFN $O^{\text{dec}}(\cdot)$ of the decoder, which plays the same role as the FFN component of the RNN, needs sequential access to the input in the same way as RNN. But the Transformer receives the whole input at the same time. We utilize positional encoding along with the attention mechanism to isolate $\boldsymbol{x}_t$ at time t and feed it to $O^{\text{dec}}(\cdot)$, thereby simulating the RNN.

As stated earlier, we append the input $s_1, \dots, s_n$ of the RNN with \$'s until it halts. Since the Transformer takes its input all at once, appending by \$'s is not possible (in particular, we do not know how long the computation would take). Instead, we append the input with a single \$. After encountering a \$ once, the Transformer will feed (encoding of) \$ to $O^{\text{dec}}(\cdot)$ in subsequent steps until termination. Here we confine our discussion to the case $t \leq n$; the $t > n$ case is slightly different but simpler.

The construction is straightforward: it has only one head, one encoder layer and one decoder layer; moreover, the attention mechanisms in the encoder and the decoder-decoder attention block of the decoder are trivial as described below.

The encoder attention layer does trivial computation in that it merely computes the identity function: $\boldsymbol{z}_i = \boldsymbol{x}_i$, which can be easily achieved, e.g. by using the residual connection and setting the value vectors to $\boldsymbol{0}$. The fi-

$t < n$ and at $i = n$ for $t \geq n$. This use of scoring function is similar to Pérez et al. (2019).

At this point, $O^{\text{dec}}(\cdot)$ has at its disposal the hidden state $\boldsymbol{h}_t$ (coming from $\boldsymbol{y}_t$ via $\boldsymbol{p}_t$ and the residual connection) and the input symbol $\boldsymbol{x}_t$ (coming via the attention mechanism and the residual connection). Hence $O(\cdot)$ can act just like the FFN (Lemma C.4) underlying the RNN to compute $\boldsymbol{h}_{t+1}$ and thus $\boldsymbol{y}_{t+1}$, proving the induction hypothesis. The complete construction can be found in Sec. C.2 in the appendix.

$\square$

Theorem 4.2. *The class of Transformers with positional masking and no explicit positional encodings is Turing-complete.*

Proof Sketch. As before, by Theorem 3.1 it suffices to show that Transformers can simulate RNNs. The input $s_0, \ldots, s_n$ is provided to the transformer as the sequence of vectors $\boldsymbol{x}_0, \ldots, \boldsymbol{x}_n$, where $\boldsymbol{x}_i = [\mathbf{0}_{d_h}, \mathbf{0}_{d_h}, f_b(s_i), [\![s_i]\!], 0, \mathbf{0}_m, \mathbf{0}_m, \mathbf{0}_m]$. The general goal for the directional case is similar to the vanilla case, namely we would like the FFN $O^{\text{dec}}(\cdot)$ of the decoder to directly simulate the computation in the underlying RNN. In the vanilla case, positional encoding and the attention mechanism helped us feed input $\boldsymbol{x}_t$ at the t-th iteration of the decoder to $O^{\text{dec}}(\cdot)$. However, we no longer have explicit positional information in the input $\boldsymbol{x}_t$ such as a coordinate with value t. The key insight is that we do not need the positional information explicitly to recover $\boldsymbol{x}_t$ at step t: in our construction, the attention mechanism with masking will recover $\boldsymbol{x}_t$ in an indirect manner even though it's not able to "zero in" on the t-th position.

Let us first explain this without details of the construction. We maintain in vector $\boldsymbol{\omega}_t \in \mathbb{Q}^m$, with a coordinate each for symbols in Σ, the fraction of times the symbol has occurred up to step t. Now, at a step $t \leq n$, for the difference $\boldsymbol{\omega}_t - \boldsymbol{\omega}_{t-1}$ (which is part of the query vector), it can be shown easily that only the coordinate corresponding to s_t is positive. Thus after applying the linearized sigmoid $\sigma(\boldsymbol{\omega}_t - \boldsymbol{\omega}_{t-1})$, we can isolate the coordinate corresponding to s_t. Now using this query vector, the (hard) attention mechanism will be able to retrieve the value vectors for all indices j such that $s_j = s_t$ and output their average. Crucially, the value vector for an index j is essentially $\boldsymbol{x}_j$ which depends only on s_j. Thus, all these vectors are equal to $\boldsymbol{x}_t$, and so is their average. This recovers $\boldsymbol{x}_t$, which

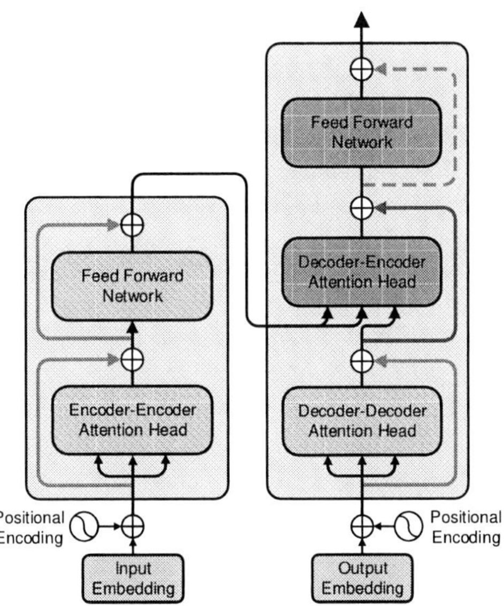

Figure 2: Transformer network with various components highlighted. The components marked red are essential for the Turing-completeness whereas for the pairs of blocks and residual connections marked green, either one of the component is enough. The dashed residual connection is not necessary for Turing-completeness of the network.

nal $K^{(1)}(\cdot)$ and $V^{(1)}(\cdot)$ functions bring $(\boldsymbol{K}^e, \boldsymbol{V}^e)$ into useful forms by appropriate linear transformations: $\boldsymbol{k}_i = [\mathbf{0}_{d_b}, \mathbf{0}_{d_b}, \mathbf{0}_{d_b}, -1, i]$ and $\boldsymbol{v}_i = [\mathbf{0}_{d_b}, f_b(s_i), \mathbf{0}_{d_b}, 0, 0]$. Thus, the key vectors only encode the positional information and the value vectors only encode the input symbols.

The output sequence of the decoder is $\boldsymbol{y}_1, \boldsymbol{y}_2, \ldots$. Our construction will ensure, by induction on t, that $\boldsymbol{y}_t$ contains the hidden states $\boldsymbol{h}_t$ of the RNN as a sub-vector along with positional information: $\boldsymbol{y}_t = [\boldsymbol{h}_t, \mathbf{0}_{d_b}, \mathbf{0}_{d_b}, t+1, 1]$. This is easy to arrange for $t = 0$, and assuming it for t we prove it for $t+1$. As for the encoder, the decoder-decoder attention block acts as the identity: $\boldsymbol{p}_t = \boldsymbol{y}_t$. Now, using the last but one coordinate in $\boldsymbol{y}_t$ representing the time $t + 1$, the attention mechanism $\text{Att}(\boldsymbol{p}_t, \boldsymbol{K}^e, \boldsymbol{V}^e)$ can retrieve the embedding of the t-th input symbol $\boldsymbol{x}_t$. This is possible because in the key vector $\boldsymbol{k}_i$ mentioned above, almost all coordinates other than the one representing the position i are set to 0, allowing the mechanism to only focus on the positional information and not be distracted by the other contents of $\boldsymbol{p}_t = \boldsymbol{y}_t$: the scoring function has value $f^{\text{att}}(\boldsymbol{p}_t, \boldsymbol{k}_i) = -|\langle \boldsymbol{p}_t, \boldsymbol{k}_i \rangle| = -|i - (t+1)|$. For a given t, it is maximized at $i = t + 1$ for

459

can now be fed to $O^{\text{dec}}(\cdot)$, simulating the RNN.

We now outline the construction and relate it to the above discussion. As before, for simplicity we restrict to the case $t \leq n$. We use only one head, one layer encoder and two layer decoder. The encoder, as in the vanilla case, does very little other than pass information along. The vectors in $(\boldsymbol{K}^e, \boldsymbol{V}^e)$ are obtained by the trivial attention mechanism followed by simple linear transformations: $\boldsymbol{k}_i^e = [\mathbf{0}_{d_h}, \mathbf{0}_{d_h}, \mathbf{0}_{d_b}, [\![s_i]\!], 0, \mathbf{0}_m, \mathbf{0}_m, \mathbf{0}_m]$ and $\boldsymbol{v}_i^e = [\mathbf{0}_{d_h}, \mathbf{0}_{d_h}, f_b(s_i), \mathbf{0}_m, 0, \mathbf{0}_m, [\![s_i]\!], \mathbf{0}_m]$.

Our construction ensures that at step t we have $\boldsymbol{y}_t = [\boldsymbol{h}_{t-1}, \mathbf{0}_{d_h}, \mathbf{0}_{d_b}, \mathbf{0}_m, \frac{1}{2^t}, \mathbf{0}_m, \mathbf{0}_m, \omega_{t-1}]$. As before, the proof is by induction on t.

In the first layer of decoder, the decoder-decoder attention block is trivial: $\boldsymbol{p}_t^{(1)} = \boldsymbol{y}_t$. In the decoder-encoder attention block, we give equal attention to all the $t + 1$ values, which along with $O^{\text{enc}}(\cdot)$, leads to $\boldsymbol{z}_t^{(1)} = [\boldsymbol{h}_{t-1}, \ \mathbf{0}_{d_h}, \ \mathbf{0}_{d_b}, \boldsymbol{\delta}_t, \ \frac{1}{2^{t+1}}, \mathbf{0}_m, \mathbf{0}_m, \ \omega_t]$, where essentially $\boldsymbol{\delta}_t = \sigma(\omega_t - \omega_{t-1})$, except with a change for the last coordinate due to special status of the last symbol \$ in the processing of RNN.

In the second layer, the decoder-decoder attention block is again trivial with $\boldsymbol{p}_t^{(2)} = \boldsymbol{z}_t^{(1)}$. We remark that in this construction, the scoring function is the standard multiplicative attention [3]. Now $\langle \boldsymbol{p}_t^{(2)}, \boldsymbol{k}_j^e \rangle = \langle \boldsymbol{\delta}_t, [\![s_j]\!] \rangle = \delta_{t,j}$, which is positive if and only if $s_j = s_t$, as mentioned earlier. Thus attention weights in $\text{Att}(\boldsymbol{p}_t^{(2)}, \boldsymbol{K}_t^e, \boldsymbol{V}_t^e)$ satisfy $\text{hardmax}(\langle \boldsymbol{p}_t^{(2)}, \boldsymbol{k}_1^e \rangle, \ldots, \langle \boldsymbol{p}_t^{(2)}, \boldsymbol{k}_t^e \rangle) = \frac{1}{\lambda_t}(\mathbb{I}(s_0 = s_t), \mathbb{I}(s_1 = s_t), \ldots, \mathbb{I}(s_t = s_t))$, where λ_t is a normalization constant and $\mathbb{I}(\cdot)$ is the indicator. See Lemma D.3 for more details.

At this point, $O^{\text{dec}}(\cdot)$ has at its disposal the hidden state $\boldsymbol{h}_t$ (coming from $\boldsymbol{z}_t^{(1)}$ via $\boldsymbol{p}_t^{(2)}$ and the residual connection) and the input symbol $\boldsymbol{x}_t$ (coming via the attention mechanism and the residual connection). Hence $O^{\text{dec}}(\cdot)$ can act just like the FFN underlying the RNN to compute $\boldsymbol{h}_{t+1}$ and thus $\boldsymbol{y}_{t+1}$, proving the induction hypothesis.

The complete construction can be found in Sec. D in the Appendix.

$\square$

In practice, Yang et al. (2019) found that for NMT, Transformers with only positional masking achieve comparable performance compared to the ones with positional encodings. Similar evidence

---

[3] Note that it is closer to practice than the scoring function $-|\langle \boldsymbol{q}, \boldsymbol{k} \rangle|$ used in Pérez et al. (2019) and Theorem 4.1

was found by Tsai et al. (2019). Our proof for directional transformers entails that there is no loss of order information if positional information is only provided in the form of masking. However, we do not recommend using masking as a replacement for explicit encodings. The computational equivalence of encoding and masking given by our results implies that any differences in their performance must come from differences in learning dynamics.

4.2 Analysis of Components

The results for various components follow from our construction in Theorem 4.1. Note that in both the encoder and decoder attention blocks, we need to compute the identity function. We can nullify the role of the attention heads by setting the value vectors to zero and making use of only the residual connections to implement the identity function. Thus, even if we remove those attention heads, the model is still Turing-complete. On the other hand, we can remove the residual connections around the attention blocks and make use of the attention heads to implement the identity function by using positional encodings. Hence, either the attention head or the residual connection is sufficient to achieve Turing-completeness. A similar argument can be made for the FFN in the encoder layer: either the residual connection or the FFN is sufficient for Turing-completeness. For the decoder-encoder attention head, since it is the only way for the decoder to obtain information about the input, it is necessary for the completeness. The FFN is the only component that can perform computations based on the input and the computations performed earlier via recurrence and hence, the model is not Turing-complete without it. Figure 2 summarizes the role of different components with respect to the computational expressiveness of the network.

Proposition 4.3. *The class of Transformers without residual connection around the decoder-encoder attention block is not Turing-complete.*

Proof Sketch. We confine our discussion to single-layer decoder; the case of multilayer decoder is similar. Without the residual connection, the decoder-encoder attention block produces $\boldsymbol{a}_t = \text{Att}(\boldsymbol{p}_t, \boldsymbol{K}^e, \boldsymbol{V}^e) = \sum_{i=1}^n \alpha_i \boldsymbol{v}_i^e$ for some α_i's such that $\sum_i^n \alpha_i = 1$. Note that, without residual connection $\boldsymbol{a}_t$ can take on at most $2^n - 1$ values. This is because by the definition of hard attention the vector $(\alpha_1, \ldots, \alpha_n)$ is characterized by the set of zero coordinates and there are at most $2^n - 1$

such sets (all coordinates cannot be zero). This restriction on the number of values on a_t holds regardless of the value of p_t. If the task requires the network to produce values of a_t that come from a set with size at least 2^n, then the network will not be able to perform the task. Here's an example task: given a number $\Delta \in (0, 1)$, the network must produce numbers $0, \Delta, 2\Delta, \ldots, k\Delta$, where k is the maximum integer such that $k\Delta \leq 1$. If the network receives a single input Δ, then it is easy to see that the vector a_t will be a constant (v_1^e) at any step and hence the output of the network will also be constant at all steps. Thus, the model cannot perform such a task. If the input is combined with $n - 1$ auxiliary symbols (such as $\#$ and $\$$), then in the network, each a_t takes on at most $2^n - 1$ values. Hence, the model will be incapable of performing the task if $\Delta < 1/2^n$. Such a limitation does not exist with a residual connection since the vector $a_t = \sum_{i=1}^{n} \alpha_i v_i^e + p_t$ can take arbitrary number of values depending on its prior computations in p_t. For further details, see Sec. C.1 in the Appendix.

$\square$

Discussion. It is perhaps surprising that residual connection, originally proposed to assist in the learning ability of very deep networks, plays a vital role in the computational expressiveness of the network. Without it, the model is limited in its capability to make decisions based on predictions in the previous steps. We explore practical implications of this result in section 5.

5 Experiments

In this section, we explore the practical implications of our results. Our experiments are geared towards answering the following questions:
Q1. Are there any practical implications of the limitation of Transformers without decoder-encoder residual connections? What tasks can they do or not do compared to vanilla Transformers?
Q2. Is there any additional benefit of using positional masking as opposed to absolute positional encoding (Vaswani et al., 2017)?

Although we showed that Transformers without decoder-encoder residual connection are not Turing complete, it does not imply that they are incapable of performing all the tasks. Our results suggest that they are limited in their capability to make inferences based on their previous computations, which is required for tasks such as counting and language modeling. However, it can be shown that the model

is capable of performing tasks which rely only on information provided at a given step such as copying and mapping. For such tasks, given positional information at a particular step, the model can look up the corresponding input and map it via the FFN. We evaluate these hypotheses via our experiments.

Model	Copy Task	Counting
Vanilla Transformers	100.0	100.0
- Dec-Enc Residual	99.7	0.0
- Dec-Dec Residual	99.7	99.8

Table 1: BLEU scores ($\uparrow$) for copy and counting task. Please see Section 5 for details

For our experiments on synthetic data, we consider two tasks, namely the *copy task* and the *counting task*. For the copy task, the goal of a model is to reproduce the input sequence. We sample sentences of lengths between 5-12 words from Penn Treebank and create a train-test split of 40k-1k with all sentences belonging to the same range of length. In the counting task, we create a very simple dataset where the model is given one number between 0 and 100 as input and its goal is to predict the next five numbers. Since only a single input is provided to the encoder, it is necessary for the decoder to be able to make inferences based on its previous predictions to perform this task. The benefit of conducting these experiments on synthetic data is that they isolate the phenomena we wish to evaluate. For both these tasks, we compare vanilla Transformer with the one without decoder-encoder residual connection. As a baseline we also consider the model without decoder-decoder residual connection, since according to our results, that connection does not influence the computational power of the model. We implement a single layer encoder-decoder network with only a single attention head in each block.

We then assess the influence of the limitation on Machine Translation which requires a model to do a combination of both mapping and inferring from computations in previous timesteps. We evaluate the models on IWSLT'14 German-English dataset and IWSLT'15 English-Vietnamese dataset. We again compare vanilla Transformer with the ones without decoder-encoder and decoder-decoder residual connection. While tuning the models, we vary the number of layers from 1 to 4, the learning rate, warmup steps and the number of heads. Specifications of the models, experimental setup, datasets and sample outputs can be found in Sec. E

Model	De-En	En-Vi
Vanilla Transformers	32.9	28.8
- Dec-Enc Residual	24.1	21.8
- Dec-Dec Residual	30.6	27.2

Table 2: BLEU scores ($\uparrow$) for translation task. Please see Section 5 for details.

in the Appendix.

Results on the effect of residual connections on synthetic tasks can be found in Table 1. As per our hypothesis, all the variants are able to perfectly perform the copy task. For the counting task, the one without decoder-encoder residual connection is incapable of performing it. However, the other two including the one without decoder-decoder residual connection are able to accomplish the task by learning to make decisions based on their prior predictions. Table 3 provides some illustrative sample outputs of the models. For the MT task, results can be found in Table 2. While the drop from removing decoder-encoder residual connection is significant, it is still able to perform reasonably well since the task can be largely fulfilled by mapping different words from one sentence to another.

For positional masking, our proof technique suggests that due to lack of positional encodings, the model must come up with its own mechanism to make order related decisions. Our hypothesis is that, if it is able to develop such a mechanism, it should be able to generalize to higher lengths and not overfit on the data it is provided. To evaluate this claim, we simply extend the copy task upto higher lengths. The training set remains the same as before, containing sentences of length 5-12 words. We create 5 different validation sets each containing 1k sentences each. The first set contains sentences within the same length as seen in training (5-12 words), the second set contains sentences of length 13-15 words while the third, fourth and fifth sets contain sentences of lengths 15-20, 21-25 and 26-30 words respectively. We consider two models, one which is provided absolute positional encodings and one where only positional masking is applied. Figure 3 shows the performance of these models across various lengths. The model with positional masking clearly generalizes up to higher lengths although its performance too degrades at extreme lengths. We found that the model with absolute positional encodings during training overfits on the fact that the 13th token is always the terminal symbol. Hence, when evalu-

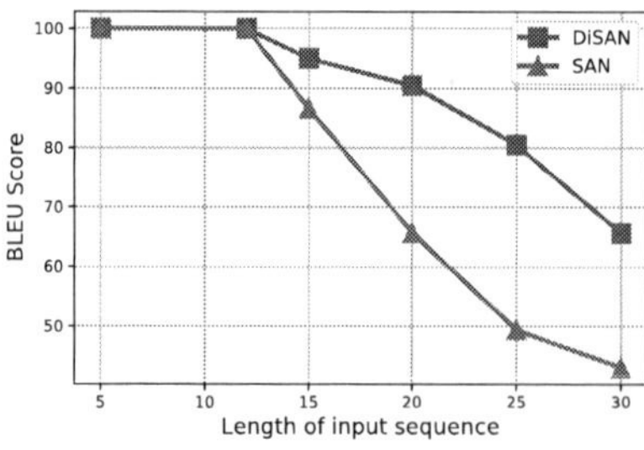

Figure 3: Performance of the two models on the copy task across varying lengths of test inputs. DiSAN refers to Transformer with only positional masking. SAN refers to vanilla Transformers.

ated on higher lengths it never produces a sentence of length greater than 12. Other encoding schemes such as relative positional encodings (Shaw et al., 2018; Dai et al., 2019) can generalize better, since they are inherently designed to address this particular issue. However, our goal is not to propose masking as a replacement of positional encodings, rather it is to determine whether the mechanism that the model develops during training is helpful in generalizing to higher lengths. Note that, positional masking was not devised by keeping generalization or any other benefit in mind. Our claim is only that, the use of masking does not limit the model's expressiveness and it may benefit in other ways, but during practice one should explore each of the mechanisms and even a combination of both. Yang et al. (2019) showed that a combination of both masking and encodings is better able to learn order information as compared to explicit encodings.

Source	– 42
Reference	– 43 44 45 46 47
Vanilla Transformer	– 43 44 45 46 47
- Dec-Enc Residual	– 27 27 27 27 27
- Dec-Dec Residual	– 43 44 45 46 47

Table 3: Sample outputs by the models on the counting task. Without the residual connection around Decoder-Encoder block, the model is incapable of predicting more than one distinct output.

6 Discussion and Final Remarks

We showed that the class of languages recognized by Transformers and RNNs are exactly the same. This implies that the difference in performance of both the networks across different tasks can be attributed only to their learning abilities. In contrast to RNNs, Transformers are composed of multiple components which are not essential for their computational expressiveness. However, in practice they may play a crucial role. Recently, Voita et al. (2019) showed that the decoder-decoder attention heads in the lower layers of the decoder do play a significant role in the NMT task and suggest that they may be helping in language modeling. This indicates that components which are not essential for the computational power may play a vital role in improving the learning and generalization ability.

Take-Home Messages. We showed that the order information can be provided either in the form of explicit encodings or masking without affecting computational power of Transformers. The decoder-encoder attention block plays a necessary role in conditioning the computation on the input sequence while the residual connection around it is necessary to keep track of previous computations. The feedforward network in the decoder is the only component capable of performing computations based on the input and prior computations. Our experimental results show that removing components essential for computational power inhibit the model's ability to perform certain tasks. At the same time, the components which do not play a role in the computational power may be vital to the learning ability of the network.

Although our proofs rely on arbitrary precision, which is common practice while studying the computational power of neural networks in theory (Siegelmann and Sontag, 1992; Pérez et al., 2019; Hahn, 2020; Yun et al., 2020), implementations in practice work over fixed precision settings. However, our construction provides a starting point to analyze Transformers under finite precision. Since RNNs can recognize all regular languages in finite precision (Korsky and Berwick, 2019), it follows from our construction that Transformer can also recognize a large class of regular languages in finite precision. At the same time, it does not imply that it can recognize all regular languages given the limitation due to the precision required to encode positional information. We leave the study of Transformers in finite precision for future work.

Acknowledgements

We thank the anonymous reviewers for their constructive comments and suggestions. We would also like to thank our colleagues at Microsoft Research and Michael Hahn for their valuable feedback and helpful discussions.

References

Yining Chen, Sorcha Gilroy, Andreas Maletti, Jonathan May, and Kevin Knight. 2018. Recurrent neural networks as weighted language recognizers. In *Proceedings of the 2018 Conference of the North American Chapter of the Association for Computational Linguistics: Human Language Technologies, Volume 1 (Long Papers)*, pages 2261–2271, New Orleans, Louisiana. Association for Computational Linguistics.

Zihang Dai, Zhilin Yang, Yiming Yang, Jaime Carbonell, Quoc Le, and Ruslan Salakhutdinov. 2019. Transformer-XL: Attentive language models beyond a fixed-length context. In *Proceedings of the 57th Annual Meeting of the Association for Computational Linguistics*, pages 2978–2988, Florence, Italy. Association for Computational Linguistics.

Jacob Devlin, Ming-Wei Chang, Kenton Lee, and Kristina Toutanova. 2019. BERT: Pre-training of deep bidirectional transformers for language understanding. In *Proceedings of the 2019 Conference of the North American Chapter of the Association for Computational Linguistics: Human Language Technologies, Volume 1 (Long and Short Papers)*, pages 4171–4186, Minneapolis, Minnesota. Association for Computational Linguistics.

Michael Hahn. 2020. Theoretical limitations of self-attention in neural sequence models. *Transactions of the Association for Computational Linguistics*, 8:156–171.

Jiri Hron, Yasaman Bahri, Jascha Sohl-Dickstein, and Roman Novak. 2020. Infinite attention: Nngp and ntk for deep attention networks. *arXiv preprint arXiv:2006.10540*.

Cheng-Zhi Anna Huang, Ashish Vaswani, Jakob Uszkoreit, Noam Shazeer, Curtis Hawthorne, Andrew M. Dai, Matthew D. Hoffman, and Douglas Eck. 2018. An improved relative self-attention mechanism for transformer with application to music generation. *ArXiv*, abs/1809.04281.

Hyunjik Kim, George Papamakarios, and Andriy Mnih. 2020. The lipschitz constant of self-attention. *arXiv preprint arXiv:2006.04710*.

Guillaume Klein, Yoon Kim, Yuntian Deng, Jean Senellart, and Alexander Rush. 2017. OpenNMT: Open-source toolkit for neural machine translation. In *Proceedings of ACL 2017, System Demonstrations*, pages 67–72, Vancouver, Canada. Association for Computational Linguistics.

John F Kolen and Stefan C Kremer. 2001. *A field guide to dynamical recurrent networks*. John Wiley & Sons.

Samuel A Korsky and Robert C Berwick. 2019. On the computational power of rnns. *arXiv preprint arXiv:1906.06349*.

Yoav Levine, Noam Wies, Or Sharir, Hofit Bata, and Amnon Shashua. 2020. Limits to depth efficiencies of self-attention. *arXiv preprint arXiv:2006.12467*.

Minh-Thang Luong and Christopher D Manning. 2015. Stanford neural machine translation systems for spoken language domains. In *Proceedings of the International Workshop on Spoken Language Translation*, pages 76–79.

Warren S McCulloch and Walter Pitts. 1943. A logical calculus of the ideas immanent in nervous activity. *The bulletin of mathematical biophysics*, 5(4):115–133.

William Merrill, Gail Weiss, Yoav Goldberg, Roy Schwartz, Noah A. Smith, and Eran Yahav. 2020. A formal hierarchy of RNN architectures. In *Proceedings of the 58th Annual Meeting of the Association for Computational Linguistics*, pages 443–459, Online. Association for Computational Linguistics.

Myle Ott, Sergey Edunov, David Grangier, and Michael Auli. 2018. Scaling neural machine translation. In *Proceedings of the Third Conference on Machine Translation: Research Papers*, pages 1–9, Brussels, Belgium. Association for Computational Linguistics.

Jorge Pérez, Javier Marinković, and Pablo Barceló. 2019. On the turing completeness of modern neural network architectures. In *International Conference on Learning Representations*.

Alec Radford, Karthik Narasimhan, Tim Salimans, and Ilya Sutskever. 2018. Improving language understanding by generative pre-training. *URL https://s3-us-west-2. amazonaws. com/openai-assets/researchcovers/languageunsupervised/language understanding paper. pdf*.

Alexander Rush. 2018. The annotated transformer. In *Proceedings of Workshop for NLP Open Source Software (NLP-OSS)*, pages 52–60, Melbourne, Australia. Association for Computational Linguistics.

Luzi Sennhauser and Robert Berwick. 2018. Evaluating the ability of LSTMs to learn context-free grammars. In *Proceedings of the 2018 EMNLP Workshop BlackboxNLP: Analyzing and Interpreting Neural Networks for NLP*, pages 115–124, Brussels, Belgium. Association for Computational Linguistics.

Peter Shaw, Jakob Uszkoreit, and Ashish Vaswani. 2018. Self-attention with relative position representations. In *Proceedings of the 2018 Conference of the North American Chapter of the Association for Computational Linguistics: Human Language Technologies, Volume 2 (Short Papers)*, pages 464–468, New Orleans, Louisiana. Association for Computational Linguistics.

Tao Shen, Tianyi Zhou, Guodong Long, Jing Jiang, Shirui Pan, and Chengqi Zhang. 2018. Disan: Directional self-attention network for rnn/cnn-free language understanding. In *Thirty-Second AAAI Conference on Artificial Intelligence*.

Hava T Siegelmann. 2012. *Neural networks and analog computation: beyond the Turing limit*. Springer Science & Business Media.

Hava T Siegelmann and Eduardo D Sontag. 1992. On the computational power of neural nets. In *Proceedings of the fifth annual workshop on Computational learning theory*, pages 440–449. ACM.

Natalia Skachkova, Thomas Trost, and Dietrich Klakow. 2018. Closing brackets with recurrent neural networks. In *Proceedings of the 2018 EMNLP Workshop BlackboxNLP: Analyzing and Interpreting Neural Networks for NLP*, pages 232–239, Brussels, Belgium. Association for Computational Linguistics.

Yao-Hung Hubert Tsai, Shaojie Bai, Makoto Yamada, Louis-Philippe Morency, and Ruslan Salakhutdinov. 2019. Transformer dissection: An unified understanding for transformer's attention via the lens of kernel. In *Proceedings of the 2019 Conference on Empirical Methods in Natural Language Processing and the 9th International Joint Conference on Natural Language Processing (EMNLP-IJCNLP)*, pages 4344–4353, Hong Kong, China. Association for Computational Linguistics.

Ashish Vaswani, Noam Shazeer, Niki Parmar, Jakob Uszkoreit, Llion Jones, Aidan N Gomez, Łukasz Kaiser, and Illia Polosukhin. 2017. Attention is all you need. In *Advances in neural information processing systems*, pages 5998–6008.

Elena Voita, David Talbot, Fedor Moiseev, Rico Sennrich, and Ivan Titov. 2019. Analyzing multi-head self-attention: Specialized heads do the heavy lifting, the rest can be pruned. In *Proceedings of the 57th Annual Meeting of the Association for Computational Linguistics*, pages 5797–5808, Florence, Italy. Association for Computational Linguistics.

Gail Weiss, Yoav Goldberg, and Eran Yahav. 2018. On the practical computational power of finite precision RNNs for language recognition. In *Proceedings of the 56th Annual Meeting of the Association for Computational Linguistics (Volume 2: Short Papers)*, pages 740–745, Melbourne, Australia. Association for Computational Linguistics.

Baosong Yang, Longyue Wang, Derek F. Wong, Lidia S. Chao, and Zhaopeng Tu. 2019. Assessing the ability of self-attention networks to learn word order. In *Proceedings of the 57th Annual Meeting of the Association for Computational Linguistics*, pages 3635–3644, Florence, Italy. Association for Computational Linguistics.

Chulhee Yun, Srinadh Bhojanapalli, Ankit Singh Rawat, Sashank Reddi, and Sanjiv Kumar. 2020. Are transformers universal approximators of sequence-to-sequence functions? In *International Conference on Learning Representations*.

A Roadmap

We begin with various definitions and results. We define simulation of Turing machines by RNNs and state the Turing-completeness result for RNNs. We define vanilla and directional Transformers and what it means for Transformers to simulate RNNs. Many of the definitions from the main paper are reproduced here, but in more detail. In Sec. C.1 we discuss the effect of removing a residual connection on computational power of Transformers. Sec. C.2 contains the proof of Turing completeness of vanilla Transformers and Sec. D the corresponding proof for directional Transformers. Finally, Sec. 5 has further details of experiments.

B Definitions

Denote the set $\{1, 2, \ldots, n\}$ by $[n]$. Functions defined for scalars are extended to vectors in the natural way: for a function F defined on a set A, for a sequence $(a_1, \ldots, a_n)$ of elements in A, we set $F(a_1, \ldots, a_n) := (F(a_1), \ldots, F(a_n))$. Indicator $\mathbb{I}(P)$ is 1, if predicate P is true and is 0 otherwise. For a sequence $X = (x_{n'}, \ldots, x_n)$ for some $n' \geq 0$, we set $X_j := (x_{n'}, \ldots, x_j)$ for $j \in \{n', i+1, \ldots, n\}$. We will work with an alphabet $\Sigma = \{\beta_1, \ldots, \beta_m\}$, with $\beta_1 = \#$ and $\beta_m = \$$. The special symbols $\#$ and $\$$ correspond to the beginning and end of the input sequence, resp. For a vector v, by 0_v we mean the all-0 vector of the same dimension as v. Let $\bar{t} := \min\{t, n\}$

B.1 RNNs and Turing-completeness

Here we summarize, somewhat informally, the Turing-completeness result for RNNs due to (Siegelmann and Sontag, 1992). We recall basic notions from computability theory. In the main paper, for simplicity we stated the results for *total recursive* functions $\phi : \{0, 1\}^* \to \{0, 1\}^*$, i.e. a function that is defined on every $s \in \{0, 1\}^*$ and whose values can be computed by a Turing machine. While total recursive functions form a satisfactory formalization of seq-to-seq tasks, here we state the more general result for *partial recursive functions*. Let $\phi : \{0, 1\}^* \to \{0, 1\}^*$ be partial recursive. A partial recursive function is one that need not be defined for every $s \in \{0, 1\}^*$, and there exists a Turing Machine $\mathcal{M}$ with the following property. The input s is initially written on the tape of the Turing Machine $\mathcal{M}$ and the output $\phi(s)$ is the content of the tape upon acceptance which

is indicated by halting in a designated accept state. On s for which ϕ is undefined, $\mathcal{M}$ does not halt.

We now specify how Turing machine $\mathcal{M}$ is simulated by RNN $R(\mathcal{M})$. In the RNNs in (Siegelmann and Sontag, 1992) the hidden state h_t has the form

$$h_t \quad = \quad [q_t, \Psi_1, \Psi_2],$$

where $q_t = [q_1, \ldots, q_s]$ denotes the state of $\mathcal{M}$ one-hot form. Numbers $\Psi_1, \Psi_2 \in \mathbb{Q}$, called stacks, store the contents of the tape in a certain Cantor set like encoding (which is similar to, but slightly more involved, than binary representation) at each step. The simulating RNN $R(\mathcal{M})$, gets as input encodings of $s_1 s_2 \ldots s_n$ in the first n steps, and from then on receives the vector 0 as input in each step. If ϕ is defined on s, then $\mathcal{M}$ halts and accepts with the output $\phi(s)$ the content of the tape. In this case, $R(\mathcal{M})$ enters a special accept state, and Ψ_1 encodes $\phi(s)$ and $\Psi_2 = 0$. If $\mathcal{M}$ does not halt then $R(\mathcal{M})$ also does not enter the accept state.

Siegelmann and Sontag (1992) further show that from $R(\mathcal{M})$ one can further explicitly produce the $\phi(s)$ as its output. In the present paper, we will not deal with explicit production of the output but rather work with the definition of simulation in the previous paragraph. This is for simplicity of exposition, and the main ideas are already contained in our results. If the Turing machine computes $\phi(s)$ in time $T(s)$, the simulation takes $O(|s|)$ time to encode the input sequence s and $4T(s)$ to compute $\phi(s)$.

Theorem B.1 ((Siegelmann and Sontag, 1992)). *Given any partial recursive function* $\phi : \{0, 1\}^* \to \{0, 1\}^*$ *computed by Turing machine* $\mathcal{M}_\phi$, *there exists a simulating RNN* $R(\mathcal{M}_\phi)$.

In view of the above theorem, for establishing Turing-completeness of Transformers, it suffices to show that RNNs can be simulated by Transformers. Thus, in the sequel we will only talk about simulating RNNs.

B.2 Vanilla Transformer Architecture

Here we describe the original transformer architecture due to (Vaswani et al., 2017) as formalized by (Pérez et al., 2019). While our notation and definitions largely follow (Pérez et al., 2019), they are not identical. The transformer here makes use of positional encoding; later we will discuss the transformer variant using directional attention but without using positional encoding.

The transformer, denoted Trans, is a sequence-to-sequence architecture. Its input consists of (i) a sequence $X = (x_1, \ldots, x_n)$ of vectors in $\mathbb{Q}^d$, (ii) a seed vector $y_0 \in \mathbb{Q}^d$. The output is a sequence $Y = (y_1, \ldots, y_r)$ of vectors in $\mathbb{Q}^d$. The sequence X is obtained from the sequence $(s_0, \ldots, s_n) \in \Sigma^{n+1}$ of symbols by using the embedding mentioned earlier: $x_i = f(f_b(s_i), \text{pos}(i))$ for $0 \leq i \leq n$. The transformer consists of composition of *transformer encoder* and a *transformer decoder*. The transformer encoder is obtained by composing one or more *single-layer encoders* and similarly the transformer decoder is obtained by composing one or more *single-layer decoders*. For the feed-forward networks in the transformer layers we use the activation as in (Siegelmann and Sontag, 1992), namely the saturated linear activation function:

$$\sigma(x) = \begin{cases} 0 & \text{if } x < 0, \\ x & \text{if } 0 \leq x \leq 1, \\ 1 & \text{if } x > 1. \end{cases} \quad (4)$$

As mentioned in the main paper, we can easily work with the standard ReLU activation via $\sigma(x) = \text{ReLU}(x) - \text{ReLU}(x-1)$. In the following, after defining these components, we will put them together to specify the full transformer architecture. But we begin with self-attention mechanism which is the central feature of the transformer.

Self-attention. The self-attention mechanism takes as input (i) a *query* vector q, (ii) a sequence of *key* vectors $K = (k_1, \ldots, k_n)$, and (iii) a sequence of *value* vectors $V = (v_1, \ldots, v_n)$. All vectors are in $\mathbb{Q}^d$.

The q-attention over keys K and values V, denoted by $\text{Att}(q, K, V)$, is a vector a given by

$$(\alpha_1, \ldots, \alpha_n) = \rho(f^{\text{att}}(q, k_1), \ldots, f^{\text{att}}(q, k_n)),$$
$$a = \alpha_1 v_1 + \alpha_2 v_2 + \cdots + \alpha_n v_n.$$

The above definition uses two functions ρ and f^{att} which we now describe. For the normalization function $\rho : \mathbb{Q}^n \to \mathbb{Q}^n_{\geq 0}$ we will use hardmax: for $x = (x_1, \ldots, x_n) \in \mathbb{Q}^n$, if the maximum value occurs r times among $x_1, \ldots, x_n$, then hardmax$(x)_i := 1/r$ if x_i is a maximum value and hardmax$(x)_i := 0$ otherwise. In practice, the softmax is often used but its output values are in general not rational. The names soft-attention and

hard-attention are used for the attention mechanism depending on which normalization function is used.

For the Turing-completeness proof of vanilla transformers, the scoring function f^{att} used is a combination of multiplicative attention (Vaswani et al., 2017) and a non-linear function: $f^{\text{att}}(q, k_i) = -\left|\langle q, k_i \rangle\right|$. For directional transformers, the standard multiplicative attention is used, that is, $f^{\text{att}}(q, k_i) = \langle q, k_i \rangle$.

Transformer encoder. A *single-layer encoder* is a function $\text{Enc}(X; \theta)$, where θ is the parameter vector and the input $X = (x_1, \ldots, x_n)$ is a sequence of vector in $\mathbb{Q}^d$. The output is another sequence $Z = (z_1, \ldots, z_n)$ of vectors in $\mathbb{Q}^d$. The parameters θ specify functions $Q(\cdot), K(\cdot), V(\cdot)$, and $O(\cdot)$, all of type $\mathbb{Q}^d \to \mathbb{Q}^d$. The functions $Q(\cdot), K(\cdot)$, and $V(\cdot)$ are usually linear transformations and this will be the case in our constructions:

$$Q(x_i) = x_i^T W_Q,$$
$$K(x_i) = x_i^T W_K,$$
$$V(x_i) = x_i^T W_V,$$

where $W_Q, W_K, W_V \in \mathbb{Q}^{d \times d}$. The function $O(\cdot)$ is a feed-forward network. The single-layer encoder is then defined by

$$a_i = \text{Att}(Q(x_i), K(X), V(X)) + x_i, \quad (5)$$
$$z_i = O(a_i) + a_i.$$

The addition operations $+x_i$ and $+a_i$ are the residual connections. The operation in (5) is called the encoder-encoder attention block.

The complete L-layer transformer encoder $\text{TEnc}^{(L)}(X; \theta)$ has the same input $X = (x_1, \ldots, x_n)$ as the single-layer encoder. By contrast, its output consists of two sequences (K^e, V^e), each a sequence of n vectors in $\mathbb{Q}^d$. The encoder $\text{TEnc}^{(L)}(\cdot)$ is obtained by repeated application of single-layer encoders, each with its own parameters; and at the end, two trasformation functions $K^L(\cdot)$ and $V^L(\cdot)$ are applied to the sequence of output vectors at the last layer. Functions $K^{(L)}(\cdot)$ and $V^{(L)}(\cdot)$ are linear transformations in our constructions. Formally, for $1 \leq \ell \leq L - 1$ and $X^1 := X$, we have

$$X^{\ell+1} = \text{Enc}(X^\ell; \theta_\ell),$$
$$K^e = K^{(L)}(X^L),$$
$$V^e = V^{(L)}(X^L).$$

The output of the L-layer Transformer encoder $(\boldsymbol{K}^e, \boldsymbol{V}^e) = \text{TEnc}^{(L)}(\boldsymbol{X})$ is fed to the Transformer decoder which we describe next.

Transformer decoder. The input to a *single-layer decoder* is (i) $(\boldsymbol{K}^e, \boldsymbol{V}^e)$, the sequences of key and value vectors output by the encoder, and (ii) a sequence $\boldsymbol{Y} = (\boldsymbol{y}_1, \ldots, \boldsymbol{y}_k)$ of vectors in $\mathbb{Q}^d$. The output is another sequence $\boldsymbol{Z} = (\boldsymbol{z}_1, \ldots, \boldsymbol{z}_k)$ of vectors in $\mathbb{Q}^d$.

Similar to the single-layer encoder, a single-layer decoder is parameterized by functions $Q(\cdot), K(\cdot), V(\cdot)$ and $O(\cdot)$ and is defined by

$$
\begin{aligned}
\boldsymbol{p}_t &= \text{Att}(Q(\boldsymbol{y}_t), K(\boldsymbol{Y}_t), V(\boldsymbol{Y}_t)) + \boldsymbol{y}_t, &(6)\\
\boldsymbol{a}_t &= \text{Att}(\boldsymbol{p}_t, \boldsymbol{K}^e, \boldsymbol{V}^e) + \boldsymbol{p}_t, &(7)\\
\boldsymbol{z}_t &= O(\boldsymbol{a}_t) + \boldsymbol{a}_t.
\end{aligned}
$$

The operation in (6) will be referred to as the *decoder-decoder attention* block and the operation in (7) as the *decoder-encoder attention* block. In the decoder-decoder attention block, positional masking is applied to prevent the network from attending over symbols which are ahead of them.

An L-layer Transformer decoder is obtained by repeated application of L single-layer decoders each with its own parameters and a transformation function $F : \mathbb{Q}^d \to \mathbb{Q}^d$ applied to the last vector in the sequence of vectors output by the final decoder. Formally, for $1 \leq \ell \leq L-1$ and $\boldsymbol{Y}^1 = \boldsymbol{Y}$ we have

$$
\begin{aligned}
\boldsymbol{Y}^{\ell+1} &= \text{Dec}((\boldsymbol{K}^e, \boldsymbol{V}^e), \boldsymbol{Y}^\ell; \theta_\ell),\\
\boldsymbol{z} &= F(\boldsymbol{y}_t^L).
\end{aligned}
$$

We use $\boldsymbol{z} = \text{TDec}^L((\boldsymbol{K}^e, \boldsymbol{V}^e), \boldsymbol{Y}; \theta)$ to denote an L-layer Transformer decoder. Note that while the output of a single-layer decoder is a sequence of vectors, the output of an L-layer Transformer decoder is a single vector.

The complete Transformer. A *Transformer network* receives an input sequence $\boldsymbol{X}$, a seed vector $\boldsymbol{y}_0$, and $r \in \mathbb{N}$. For $t \geq 0$ its output is a sequence $\boldsymbol{Y} = (\boldsymbol{y}_1, \ldots, \boldsymbol{y}_r)$ defined by

$$
\tilde{\boldsymbol{y}}_{t+1} = \text{TDec}\left(\text{TEnc}(\boldsymbol{X}), (\boldsymbol{y}_0, \boldsymbol{y}_1, \ldots, \boldsymbol{y}_t)\right).
$$

We get $\boldsymbol{y}_{t+1}$ by adding positional encoding: $\boldsymbol{y}_{t+1} = \tilde{\boldsymbol{y}}_{t+1} + \text{pos}(t+1)$. We denote the complete Transformer by $\text{Trans}(\boldsymbol{X}, \boldsymbol{y}_0) = \boldsymbol{Y}$. The Transformer "halts" when $\boldsymbol{y}_T \in H$, where H is a prespecified halting set.

Simulation of RNNs by Transformers. We say that a Transformer simulates an RNN (as defined in Sec. B.1) if on input $s \in \Sigma^*$, at each step t, the vector $\boldsymbol{y}_t$ contains the hidden state $\boldsymbol{h}_t$ as a subvector: $\boldsymbol{y}_t = [\boldsymbol{h}_t, \cdot]$, and halts at the same step as RNN.

C Results on Vanilla Transformers

C.1 Residual Connections

Proposition C.1. *The Transformer without residual connection around the Decoder-Encoder Attention block in the Decoder is not Turing Complete*

Proof. Recall that the vectors $\boldsymbol{a}_t$ is produced from the Encoder-Decoder Attention block in the following way,

$$
\boldsymbol{a}_t = \text{Att}(\boldsymbol{p}_t, \boldsymbol{K}^e, \boldsymbol{V}^e) + \boldsymbol{p}_t
$$

The result follows from the observation that without the residual connections, $\boldsymbol{a}_t = \text{Att}(\boldsymbol{p}_t, \boldsymbol{K}^e, \boldsymbol{V}^e)$, which leads to $\boldsymbol{a}_t = \sum_{i=1}^n \alpha_i \boldsymbol{v}_i^e$ for some α_is such that $\sum_i^n \alpha_i = 1$. Since $\boldsymbol{v}_i^e$ is produced from the encoder, the vector $\boldsymbol{a}_t$ will have no information about its previous hidden state values. Since the previous hidden state information was computed and stored in $\boldsymbol{p}_t$, without the residual connection, the information in $\boldsymbol{a}_t$ depends solely on the output of the encoder.

One could argue that since the attention weights α_is depend on the query vector $\boldsymbol{p}_t$, it could still use it gain the necessary information from the vectors $\boldsymbol{v}_i^e$s. However, note that by definition of hard attention, the attention weights α_i in $\boldsymbol{a}_t = \sum_{i=1}^n \alpha_i \boldsymbol{v}_i^e$ can either be zero or some nonzero value depending on the attention logits. Since the attention weights α_i are such that $\sum_i^n \alpha_i = 1$ and all the nonzero weights are equal to each other. Thus given the constraints there are $2^n - 1$ ways to attend over n inputs excluding the case where no input is attended over. Hence, the network without decoder-encoder residual connection with n inputs can have at most $2^n - 1$ distinct $\boldsymbol{a}_t$ values. This implies that the model will be unable to perform a task that takes n inputs and has to produce more than $2^n - 1$ outputs. Note that, such a limitation will not exist with a residual connection since the vector $\boldsymbol{a}_t = \sum_{i=1}^n \alpha_i \boldsymbol{v}_i^e + \boldsymbol{p}_t$ can take arbitrary number of values depending on its prior computations in $\boldsymbol{p}_t$.

As an example to illustrate the limitation, consider the following simple problem, given a value Δ, where $0 \leq \Delta \leq 1$, the network must produce the values $0, \Delta, 2\Delta, \ldots, k\Delta$, where k is the maximum integer such that $k\Delta \leq 1$. If the network receives a single input Δ, the encoder will produce only one particular output vector and regardless of what the value of the query vector p_t is, the vector a_t will be constant at every timestep. Since a_t is fed to feedforward network which maps it to z_t, the output of the decoder will remain the same at every timestep and it cannot produce distinct values. If the input is combined with $n-1$ auxiliary symbols (such as # and $), then the network can only produce $2^n - 1$ outputs. Hence, the model will be incapable of performing the task if $\Delta < 1/2^n$.

Thus the model cannot perform the task defined above which RNNs and Vanilla Transformers can easily do with a simple counting mechanism via their recurrent connection.

For the case of **multilayer decoder**, consider any L layer decoder model. If the residual connection is removed, the output of decoder-encoder attention block at each layer is $a_t^{(\ell)} = \sum_{i=1}^n \alpha_i^{(\ell)} v_i^e$ for $1 \leq \ell \leq L$. Observe, that since output of the decoder-encoder attention block in the last (L-th) layer of the decoder is $a_t^{(L)} = \sum_{i=1}^n \alpha_i^{(L)} v_i^e$. Since the output of the L layer decoder will be a feedforward network over $a_t^{(L)}$, the computation reduces to the single layer decoder case. Hence, similar to the single layer case, if the task requires the network to produce values of a_t that come from a set with size at least 2^n, then the network will not be able to perform the task.

This implies that the model without decoder-encoder residual connection is limited in its capability to perform tasks which requires it to make inferences based on previously generated outputs. $\square$

C.2 Simulation of RNNs by Transformers with positional encoding

Theorem C.2. *RNNs can be simulated by vanilla Transformers and hence the class of vanilla Transformers is Turing-complete.*

Proof. The construction of the simulating transformer is simple: it uses a single head and both the encoder and decoder have one layer. Moreover, the encoder does very little and most of the action happens in the decoder. The main task for the simulation is to design the input embedding (building on the given base embedding f_b), the feedforward network $O(\cdot)$ and the matrices corresponding to functions $Q(\cdot), K(\cdot), V(\cdot)$.

Input embedding. The input embedding is obtained by summing the symbol and positional encodings which we next describe. These encodings have dimension $d = 2d_h + d_b + 2$, where d_h is the dimension of the hidden state of the RNN and d_b is the dimension of the given encoding f_b of the input symbols. We will use the symbol encoding $f^{\mathrm{symb}} : \Sigma \to \mathbb{Q}^d$ which is essentially the same as f_b except that the dimension is now larger:

$$f^{\mathrm{symb}}(s) = [\mathbf{0}_{d_h}, f_e(s); \ \mathbf{0}_{d_h}, 0, 0].$$

The positional encoding $\mathrm{pos} : \mathbb{N} \to \mathbb{Q}^d$ is simply

$$\mathrm{pos}(i) = [\mathbf{0}_{d_h}, \mathbf{0}_{d_b}, \mathbf{0}_{d_h}, i, 1].$$

Together, these define the combined embedding f for a given input sequence $s_0 s_1 \cdots s_n \in \Sigma^*$ by

$$f(s_i) = f^{\mathrm{symb}}(s_i) + \mathrm{pos}(i) = [\mathbf{0}_{d_h}, f_b(s_i), \mathbf{0}_{d_h}, i, 1].$$

The vectors $v \in \mathbb{Q}^d$ used in the computation of our transformer are of the form

$$v = [h_1, s; \ h_2, x_1, x_2],$$

where $h_1, h_2 \in \mathbb{Q}^{d_h}, s \in \mathbb{Q}^{d_e}$, and $x_1, x_2 \in \mathbb{Q}$. The coordinates corresponding to the h_i's are reserved for computation related to hidden states of the RNN, the coordinates corresponding to s are reserved for base embeddings, and those for x_1 and x_2 are reserved for scalar values related to positional operations. The first two blocks, corresponding to h_1 and s are reserved for computation of the RNN.

During the computation of the Transformer, the underlying RNN will get the input $s_{\bar{t}}$ at step t for $t = 0, 1, \ldots$, where recall that $\bar{t} = \min\{t, n\}$. This sequence leads to the RNN getting the embedding of the input sequence $s_0, \ldots, s_n$ in the first $n + 1$ steps followed by the embedding of the symbol $ for the subsequent steps, which is in accordance with the requirements of (Siegelmann and Sontag, 1992). Similar to (Pérez et al., 2019) we use the following scoring function in the attention mechanism in our construction,

$$f^{\mathrm{att}}(q_i, k_j) = -|\langle q_i, k_j \rangle| \tag{8}$$

Construction of TEnc. As previously mentioned, our transformer encoder has only one layer, and the computation in the encoder is very simple: the attention mechanism is not utilized, only the residual connections are. This is done by setting the matrix for $V(\cdot)$ to the all-zeros matrix, and the feedforward networks to always output $\mathbf{0}$. The application of appropriately chosen linear transformations for the final $K(\cdot)$ and $V(\cdot)$ give the following lemma about the output of the encoder.

Lemma C.3. *There exists a single layer encoder denoted by* TEnc *that takes as input the sequence* $(\boldsymbol{x}_1, \ldots, \boldsymbol{x}_n, \$)$ *and generates the tuple* $(\boldsymbol{K}^e, \boldsymbol{V}^e)$ *where* $\boldsymbol{K}^e = (\boldsymbol{k}_1, \ldots, \boldsymbol{k}_n)$ *and* $\boldsymbol{V}^e = (\boldsymbol{v}_1, \ldots, \boldsymbol{v}_n)$ *such that,*

$$
\begin{aligned}
\boldsymbol{k}_i &= [\mathbf{0}_h, \mathbf{0}_s;\ \mathbf{0}_h, -1, i], \\
\boldsymbol{v}_i &= [\mathbf{0}_h, \boldsymbol{s}_i;\ \mathbf{0}_h, 0, 0].
\end{aligned}
$$

Construction of TDec**.** As in the construction of TEnc, our TDec has only one layer. Also like TEnc, the decoder-decoder attention block just computes the identity: we set $V^{(1)}(\cdot) = \mathbf{0}$ identically, and use the residual connection so that $\boldsymbol{p}_t = \boldsymbol{y}_t$.

For $t \geq 0$, at the t-th step we denote the input to the decoder as $\boldsymbol{y}_t = \tilde{\boldsymbol{y}}_t + \mathrm{pos}(t)$. Let $\boldsymbol{h}_0 = \mathbf{0}_h$ and $\tilde{\boldsymbol{y}}_0 = \mathbf{0}$. We will show by induction that at the t-th timestep we have

$$
\boldsymbol{y}_t = [\boldsymbol{h}_t, \mathbf{0}_s;\ \mathbf{0}_h, t+1, 1]. \tag{9}
$$

By construction, this is true for $t = 0$:

$$
\boldsymbol{y}_0 = [\mathbf{0}_h, \mathbf{0}_s;\ \mathbf{0}_h, 1, 1].
$$

Assuming that it holds for t, we show it for $t+1$.
By Lemma C.5

$$
\mathrm{Att}(\boldsymbol{p}_t, \boldsymbol{K}^e, \boldsymbol{V}^e) = [\mathbf{0}_h, \boldsymbol{v}_{\overline{t+1}};\ \mathbf{0}_h, 0, 0]. \tag{10}
$$

Lemma C.5 basically shows how we retrieve the input $\boldsymbol{s}_{\overline{t+1}}$ at the relevant step for further computation in the decoder. It follows that

$$
\begin{aligned}
\boldsymbol{a}_t &= \mathrm{Att}(\boldsymbol{p}_t, \boldsymbol{K}^e, \boldsymbol{V}^e) + \boldsymbol{p}_t \\
&= [\boldsymbol{h}_t, \boldsymbol{s}_{\overline{t+1}}, \mathbf{0}_h, t+1, 1].
\end{aligned}
$$

In the final block of the decoder, the computation for RNN takes place:

Lemma C.4. *There exists a function $O(\cdot)$ defined by feed-forward network such that,*

$$
O(\boldsymbol{a}_t) = [(\boldsymbol{h}_{t+1} - \boldsymbol{h}_t), -\boldsymbol{s}_{\overline{t+1}}, \mathbf{0}_h, -(t+1), -1],
$$

where $\boldsymbol{W}_h, \boldsymbol{W}_x$ and $\boldsymbol{b}$ denote the parameters of the RNN under consideration.

This leads to

$$
\boldsymbol{z}_t = O(\boldsymbol{a}_t) + \boldsymbol{a}_t = [\boldsymbol{h}_{t+1}, \mathbf{0}_s;\ \mathbf{0}_h, 0, 0].
$$

$\square$

We choose the function F for our decoder to be the identity function, therefore $\tilde{\boldsymbol{y}}_{t+1} = [\boldsymbol{h}_{t+1}, \mathbf{0}_s;\ \mathbf{0}_h, 0, 0]$, which means $\boldsymbol{y}_{t+1} = \tilde{\boldsymbol{y}}_{t+1} + \mathrm{pos}(i+1) = [\boldsymbol{h}_{t+1}, \mathbf{0}_s;\ \mathbf{0}_h, t+2, 1]$, proving our induction hypothesis.

C.3 Technical Lemmas

Proof of Lemma C.3. We construct a single-layer encoder achieving the desired $\boldsymbol{K}^e$ and $\boldsymbol{V}^e$. We make use of the residual connections and via trivial self-attention we get that $\boldsymbol{z}_i = \boldsymbol{x}_i$. More specifically for $i \in [n]$ we have

$$
\begin{aligned}
V^{(1)}(\boldsymbol{x}_i) &= \mathbf{0}, \\
\boldsymbol{a}_i &= \mathbf{0} + \boldsymbol{x}_i, \\
O(\boldsymbol{a}_i) &= \mathbf{0}, \\
\boldsymbol{z}_i &= \mathbf{0} + \boldsymbol{a}_i = \boldsymbol{x}_i.
\end{aligned}
$$

$V^{(1)}(\boldsymbol{x}_i) = \mathbf{0}$ can be achieved by setting the weight matrix as the all-0 matrix. Recall that $\boldsymbol{x}_i$ is defined as

$$
\boldsymbol{x}_i = [\ \mathbf{0}_h, \boldsymbol{s}_i, \\
\mathbf{0}_h, i, 1\ ].
$$

We then apply linear transformations in $K(\boldsymbol{z}_i) = \boldsymbol{z}_i \boldsymbol{W}_k$ and $V(\boldsymbol{z}_i) = \boldsymbol{z}_i \boldsymbol{W}_v$, where

$$
\boldsymbol{W}_k^T = \left[
\begin{array}{ccccc}
0 & 0 & \cdots & 0 & 0 \\
\vdots & & \ddots & \vdots & \vdots \\
0 & 0 & \cdots & 0 & 0 \\
\hline
0 & 0 & \cdots & 0 & 1 \\
0 & 0 & \cdots & -1 & 0
\end{array}
\right],
$$

and $\boldsymbol{W}_k \in \mathbb{Q}^{d \times d}$, and similarly one can obtain $\boldsymbol{v}_i$ by setting the submatrix of $\boldsymbol{W}_v \in \mathbb{Q}^{d \times d}$ formed by the first $d-2$ rows and columns to the identity matrix, and the rest of the entries to zeros.

$\square$

Lemma C.5. *Let $\boldsymbol{q}_t \in \mathbb{Q}^d$ be a query vector such that $\boldsymbol{q} = [\cdot, \ldots, \cdot, t+1, 1]$ where $t \in \mathbb{N}$ and '$\cdot$' denotes an arbitrary value. Then we have*

$$
\mathrm{Att}(\boldsymbol{q}_t, \boldsymbol{K}^e, \boldsymbol{V}^e) = [\mathbf{0}_h, \boldsymbol{s}_{\overline{t+1}}, \mathbf{0}_h, 0, 0]. \tag{11}
$$

Proof. Recall that $p_t = y_t = [h_t, 0, \ldots, 0, t + 1, 1]$ and $k_i = [0, 0, \ldots, 0, -1, i]$ and hence

$$\langle p_t, k_i \rangle = i - (t + 1),$$

$$f^{\text{att}}(p_t, k_i) = -|i - (t + 1)|.$$

Thus, for $i \in [n]$, the scoring function $f^{\text{att}}(p_t, k_i)$ has the maximum value 0 at index $i = t + 1$ if $t < n$; for $t \geq n$, the maximum value $t + 1 - n$ is achieved for $i = n$. Therefore

$$\text{Att}(p_t, K^e, V^e) = s_{\overline{t+1}}.$$

$\square$

Proof of Lemma C.4. Recall that

$$a_t = [\quad h_t, s_{\overline{t+1}}, \\ 0_h, t + 1, 1 \quad]$$

Network $O(a_t)$ is of the form

$$O(a_t) = W_2 \sigma(W_1 a_t + b_1),$$

where $\mathbf{W}_i \in \mathbb{Q}^{d \times d}$ and $b \in \mathbb{Q}^d$ and

$$\mathbf{W}_1 = \begin{array}{c} \\ d_h \\ d_e \\ d_h \\ 2 \end{array} \begin{array}{cccc} d_h & d_e & d_h & 2 \\ \left[\begin{array}{c|c|c|c} \mathbf{W}_h & \mathbf{W}_x & 0 & 0 \\ \hline 0 & \mathbf{I} & 0 & 0 \\ \hline \mathbf{I} & 0 & 0 & 0 \\ \hline 0 & 0 & 0 & \mathbf{I} \end{array}\right] \end{array}$$

and $b_1 = [b_h, 0_s, 0_h, 0, 0]$. Hence

$$\sigma(\mathbf{W}_1 a_t + b_1) = [\sigma(\mathbf{W}_h h_t + \mathbf{W}_x s_{\overline{t+1}} + b), \\ s_{\overline{t+1}}, h_t, t + 1, 1]$$

Next we define $\mathbf{W}_2$ by

$$\mathbf{W}_2 = \begin{array}{c} \\ d_h \\ d_e \\ d_h \\ 2 \end{array} \begin{array}{cccc} d_h & d_e & d_h & 2 \\ \left[\begin{array}{c|c|c|c} \mathbf{I} & 0 & -\mathbf{I} & 0 \\ \hline 0 & -\mathbf{I} & 0 & 0 \\ \hline 0 & 0 & 0 & 0 \\ \hline 0 & 0 & 0 & -\mathbf{I} \end{array}\right] \end{array}.$$

This leads to

$$O(a_t) = \mathbf{W}_2 \sigma(\mathbf{W}_1 a_t + b_1) \\ = [\sigma(\mathbf{W}_h h_t + \mathbf{W}_x s_{\overline{t+1}} + b) - h_t, -s_{\overline{t+1}}, \\ 0_h, -(t + 1), -1],$$

which is what we wanted to prove. $\square$

D Completeness of Directional Transformers

There are a few changes in the architecture of the Transformer to obtain directional Transformer. The first change is that there are no positional encodings and thus the input vector x_i only consists of s_i. Similarly, there are no positional encodings in the decoder inputs and hence $y_t = \tilde{y}_t$. The vector $\tilde{y}$ is the output representation produced at the previous step and the first input vector to the decoder $\tilde{y}_0 = 0$. Instead of using positional encodings, we apply positional masking to the inputs and outputs of the encoder.

Thus the encoder-encoder attention in (5) is redefined as

$$a_i^{(\ell+1)} = \text{Att}(Q(z_i^{(\ell)}), K(Z_i^{(\ell)}), V(Z_i^{(\ell)})) + z_i^{(\ell)},$$

where $Z^{(0)} = X$. Similarly the decoder-encoder attention in (7) is redefined by

$$a_t^{(\ell)} = \text{Att}(p_t^{(\ell)}, K_t^e, V_t^e) + p_t^{(\ell)},$$

where ℓ in $a_t^{(\ell)}$ denotes the layer ℓ and we use $v^{(\ell,b)}$ to denote any intermediate vector being used in ℓ-th layer and b-th block in cases where the same symbol is used in multiple blocks in the same layer.

Theorem D.1. *RNNs can be simulated by vanilla Transformers and hence the class of vanilla Transformers is Turing-complete.*

Proof. The Transformer network in this case will be more complex than the construction for the vanilla case. The encoder remains very similar, but the decoder is different and has two layers.

Embedding. We will construct our Transformer to simulate an RNN of the form given in the definition with the recurrence

$$h_t = g(W_h h_{t-1} + W_x x_t + b).$$

The vectors used in the Transformer layers are of dimension $d = 2d_h + d_e + 4|\Sigma| + 1$. Where d_h is the dimension of the hidden state of the RNN and d_e is the dimension of the input embedding.

All vector $v \in \mathbb{Q}^d$ used during the computation of the network are of the form

$$v = [h_1, h_2, s_1, [\![s_1]\!], x_1, [\![s_2]\!][\![s_3]\!], [\![s_4]\!]]$$

where $h_i \in \mathbb{Q}^{d_h}, s \in \mathbb{Q}^{d_e}$ and $x_i \in \mathbb{Q}$. These blocks reserved for different types of objects. The vectors $\boldsymbol{h}_i$s are reserved for computation related to hidden states of RNNs, $\boldsymbol{s}_i$s are reserved for input embeddings and $\boldsymbol{x}_i$s are reserved for scalar values related to positional operations.

Given an input sequence $s_0 s_1 s_2 \cdots s_n \in \Sigma^*$ where $s_0 = \#$ and $s_n = \$$, we use an embedding function $f : \Sigma \to \mathbb{Q}^d$ defined as

$$
f(s_i) = \boldsymbol{x}_i = [\quad \boldsymbol{0}_h, \boldsymbol{0}_h, \boldsymbol{s}_i,
$$
$$
[\![s_i]\!], 0, \boldsymbol{0}_\omega, \boldsymbol{0}_\omega, \boldsymbol{0}_\omega \quad]
$$

Unlike (Pérez et al., 2019), we use the dot product as our scoring function as used in Vaswani et al. (2017) in the attention mechanism in our construction,

$$
f^{\mathrm{att}}(\boldsymbol{q}_i, \boldsymbol{k}_j) = \langle \boldsymbol{q}_i, \boldsymbol{k}_j \rangle.
$$

For the computation of the Transformer, we also use a vector sequence in $\mathbb{Q}^{|\Sigma|}$ defined by

$$
\boldsymbol{\omega}_t = \frac{1}{t+1} \sum_{j=0}^{t} [\![s_t]\!],
$$

where $0 \leq t \leq n$. The vector $\boldsymbol{\omega}_t = (\omega_{t,1}, \dots, \omega_{t,|\Sigma|})$ contains the proportion of each input symbol till step t for $0 \leq t \leq n$. Set $\boldsymbol{\omega}_{-1} = \boldsymbol{0}$. From the defintion of $\boldsymbol{\omega}_t$, it follows that at any step $1 \leq k \leq |\Sigma|$ we have

$$
\omega_{t,k} = \frac{\phi_{t,k}}{t+1}, \tag{12}
$$

where $\phi_{t,k}$ denotes the number of times the k-th symbol β_k in Σ has appeared till the t-th step. Note that $\omega_{t,0} = \frac{1}{t+1}$ since the first coordinate corresponds to the proportion of the start symbol $\#$ which appears only once at $t = 0$. Similarly, $\omega_{t,|\Sigma|} = 0$ for $0 \leq t < n$ and $\omega_{t,|\Sigma|} = 1/(t+1)$ for $t \geq n$, since the end symbol $\$$ doesn't appear till the end of the input and it appears only once at $t = n$.

We define two more sequences of vectors in $\mathbb{Q}^{|\Sigma|}$ for $0 \leq t \leq n$:

$$
\boldsymbol{\Delta}_t = \sigma(\boldsymbol{\omega}_t - \boldsymbol{\omega}_{t-1}),
$$
$$
\boldsymbol{\delta}_t = (\Delta_{t,1}, \dots, \Delta_{t,|\Sigma|-1}, 1/2^{t+1}).
$$

Here $\boldsymbol{\Delta}_t$ denotes the difference in the proportion of symbols between the t-th and $(t-1)$-th steps, with the applicatin of sigmoid activation. In vector $\boldsymbol{\delta}_t$, the last coordinate of $\boldsymbol{\Delta}_t$ has been replaced with $1/2^{t+1}$. The last coordinate in $\boldsymbol{\omega}_t$ indicates the proportion of the terminal symbol $\$$ and hence the last value in $\boldsymbol{\Delta}_t$ denotes the change in proportion of $\$$.

We set the last coordinate in $\boldsymbol{\delta}_t$ to an exponentially decreasing sequence so that after n steps we always have a nonzero score for the terminal symbol and it is taken as input in the underlying RNN. Different and perhaps simpler choices for the last coordinate of $\boldsymbol{\delta}_t$ may be possible. Note that $0 \leq \Delta_{t,k} \leq 1$ and $0 \leq \delta_{t,k} \leq 1$ for $0 \leq t \leq n$ and $1 \leq k \leq |\Sigma|$.

Construction of TEnc. The input to the network DTrans_M is the sequence $(s_0, s_1, \dots, s_{n-1}, s_n)$ where $s_0 = \#$ and $s_n = \$$. Our encoder is a simple single layer network such that $\mathrm{TEnc}(\boldsymbol{x}_0, \boldsymbol{x}_1, \dots, \boldsymbol{x}_n) = (\boldsymbol{K}^e, \boldsymbol{V}^e)$ where $\boldsymbol{K}^e = (\boldsymbol{k}_0^e, \dots, \boldsymbol{k}_n^e)$ and $\boldsymbol{V}^e = (\boldsymbol{v}_0^e, \dots, \boldsymbol{v}_n^e)$ such that,

$$
\boldsymbol{k}_i^e = [\quad \boldsymbol{0}_h, \boldsymbol{0}_h, \boldsymbol{0}_s,
$$
$$
[\![s_i]\!], 0, \boldsymbol{0}_\omega, \boldsymbol{0}_\omega, \boldsymbol{0}_\omega \quad], \tag{13}
$$

$$
\boldsymbol{v}_i^e = [\quad \boldsymbol{0}_h, \boldsymbol{0}_h, \boldsymbol{s}_i,
$$
$$
\boldsymbol{0}_\omega, 0, \boldsymbol{0}_\omega, [\![s_i]\!], \boldsymbol{0}_\omega \quad].
$$

Similar to our construction of the encoder for vanilla transformer (Lemma C.3), the above $\boldsymbol{K}^e$ and $\boldsymbol{V}^e$ can be obtained by making the output of $\mathrm{Att}(\cdot) = 0$ by choosing the $V(\cdot)$ to always evaluate to 0 and similarly for $O(\cdot)$, and using residual connections. Then one can produce $\boldsymbol{K}^e$ and $\boldsymbol{V}^e$ via simple linear transformations using $K(\cdot)$ and $V(\cdot)$.

Construction of TDec. At the t-th step we denote the input to the decoder as $\boldsymbol{y}_t = \tilde{\boldsymbol{y}}_t$, where $0 \leq t \leq r$, where r is the step where the decoder halts. Let $\boldsymbol{h}_{-1} = \boldsymbol{0}_h$ and $\boldsymbol{h}_0 = \boldsymbol{0}_h$. We will prove by induction on t that for $0 \leq t \leq r$ we have

$$
\boldsymbol{y}_t = [\quad \boldsymbol{h}_{t-1}, \boldsymbol{0}_h, \boldsymbol{0}_s,
$$
$$
\boldsymbol{0}_\omega, \tfrac{1}{2^t}, \boldsymbol{0}_\omega, \boldsymbol{0}_\omega, \boldsymbol{\omega}_{\overline{t-1}} \quad]. \tag{14}
$$

This is true for $t = 0$ by the choice of seed vector:

$$
\boldsymbol{y}_0 = [\quad \boldsymbol{0}_h, \boldsymbol{0}_h, \boldsymbol{0}_s,
$$
$$
\boldsymbol{0}_\omega, 1, \boldsymbol{0}_\omega, \boldsymbol{0}_\omega, \boldsymbol{0}_\omega \quad].
$$

Assuming the truth of (14) for t, we show it for $t + 1$.

Layer 1. Similar to the construction in Lemma C.3, in the decoder-decoder attention block we set $V^{(1)}(\cdot) = \boldsymbol{0}_d$ and use the residual connections to set $\boldsymbol{p}_t^{(1)} = \boldsymbol{y}_t$. At the t-th step in the decoder-encoder attention block of layer 1 we have

$$
\mathrm{Att}(\boldsymbol{p}_t^{(1)}, \boldsymbol{K}_{\bar{t}}^e, \boldsymbol{V}_{\bar{t}}^e) = \sum_{j=0}^{\bar{t}} \hat{\alpha}_{t,j}^{(1,2)} \boldsymbol{v}_j^e,
$$

where

$$(\hat{\alpha}_{t,1}^{(2,2)}, \ldots, \hat{\alpha}_{t,\bar{t}}^{(2,2)})$$
$$= \mathsf{hardmax}\left(\langle p_t^{(1)}, k_1^e\rangle, \ldots, \langle p_t^{(1)}, k_{\bar{t}}^e\rangle\right)$$
$$= \mathsf{hardmax}(0, \ldots, 0)$$
$$= \left(\frac{1}{\bar{t}+1}, \ldots, \frac{1}{\bar{t}+1}\right).$$

Therefore

$$\sum_{j=0}^{\bar{t}} \hat{\alpha}_{t,j}^{(1,2)} v_j^e = \begin{bmatrix} \mathbf{0}_h, \mathbf{0}_h, s_{0:t}, \\ \mathbf{0}_\omega, 0, \mathbf{0}_\omega, \omega_{\bar{t}}, \mathbf{0}_\omega \end{bmatrix}$$

where

$$s_{0:t} = \frac{1}{\bar{t}+1} \sum_{j=0}^{\bar{t}} s_j.$$

Thus,

$$a_t^{(1)} = \mathsf{Att}(p_t^{(1)}, K_{\bar{t}}^e, V_{\bar{t}}^e) + p_t^{(1)}$$
$$= [h_{t-1}, \mathbf{0}_h, s_{0:t}, \mathbf{0}_\omega, \frac{1}{2^t}, \mathbf{0}_\omega, \omega_{\bar{t}}, \omega_{\overline{t-1}}].$$

In Lemma D.2 we construct feed-forward network $O^{(1)}(\cdot)$ such that

$$O^{(1)}(a_t^{(1)}) = [\mathbf{0}_h, \mathbf{0}_h, -s_{0:t}, \delta_{\bar{t}}, -\frac{1}{2^t} + \frac{1}{2^{t+1}},$$
$$\mathbf{0}_\omega, -\omega_{\bar{t}}, -\omega_{\overline{t-1}} + \omega_{\bar{t}}].$$

Hence

$$z_t^{(1)} = O^{(1)}(a_t^{(1)}) + a_t^{(1)} \tag{15}$$
$$= [h_{t-1}, \mathbf{0}_h, \mathbf{0}_s, \delta_{\bar{t}}, \frac{1}{2^{t+1}}, \mathbf{0}_\omega, \mathbf{0}_\omega, \omega_{\bar{t}}].$$

Layer 2. In the first block of layer 2, we set the value transformation function to identically zero similar to Lemma C.3, i.e. $V^{(2)}(\cdot) = \mathbf{0}$ which leads to the output of $\mathsf{Att}(\cdot)$ to be $\mathbf{0}$ and then using the residual connection we get $p_t^{(2)} = z_t^{(1)}$. It follows by Lemma D.3 that

$$\mathsf{Att}(p_t^{(2)}, K_{\bar{t}}^e, V_{\bar{t}}^e)$$
$$= [\mathbf{0}_h, \mathbf{0}_h, s_{\bar{t}}, \mathbf{0}_\omega, 0, \mathbf{0}_\omega, [\![s_t]\!], \mathbf{0}_\omega].$$

Thus,

$$a_t^{(2)} = \mathsf{Att}(p_t^{(2)}, K_{\bar{t}}^e, V_{\bar{t}}^e) + p_t^{(2)}$$
$$= [h_{t-1}, \mathbf{0}_h, s_{\bar{t}}, \delta_{\bar{t}}, \frac{1}{2^{t+1}}, \mathbf{0}_\omega, [\![s_t]\!], \omega_{\bar{t}}].$$

In the final block of the decoder in the second layer, the computation for RNN takes place. In

Lemma D.4 below we construct the feed-forward network $O^{(2)}(\cdot)$ such that

$$O^{(2)}(a_t^{(2)}) = [\sigma(\mathbf{W}_h h_{t-1} + \mathbf{W}_x s_{\bar{t}} + b) - h_{t-1}$$
$$\mathbf{0}_h, -s_{\bar{t}}, -\delta_t, 0, \mathbf{0}_\omega, -[\![s_t]\!], \mathbf{0}_\omega]$$

and hence

$$z_t^{(2)} = O^{(2)}(a_t^{(2)}) + a_t^{(2)}$$
$$= [\sigma(\mathbf{W}_h h_{t-1} + \mathbf{W}_x s_{\bar{t}} + b), \mathbf{0}_h, \mathbf{0}_s,$$
$$\mathbf{0}_\omega, \frac{1}{2^{t+1}}, \mathbf{0}_\omega, \mathbf{0}_\omega, \omega_{\bar{t}}],$$

which gives

$$y_{t+1} = \begin{bmatrix} h_t, \mathbf{0}_h, \mathbf{0}_s, \\ \mathbf{0}_\omega, \frac{1}{2^{t+1}}, \mathbf{0}_\omega, \mathbf{0}_\omega, \omega_{\bar{t}} \end{bmatrix},$$

proving the induction hypothesis (14) for $t+1$, and completing the simulation of RNN. $\qquad\square$

D.1 Technical Lemmas

Lemma D.2. *There exists a function $O^{(1)}(.)$ defined by feed-forward network such that,*

$$O^{(1)}(a_t^{(1)}) = [\mathbf{0}_h, \mathbf{0}_h, -s_{0:t}, \delta_t,$$
$$-\frac{1}{2^t} + \frac{1}{2^{t+1}}, \mathbf{0}_\omega, -\omega_t, -\omega_{t-1} + \omega_t]$$

Proof. We define the feed-forward network $O^{(1)}(.)$ such that

$$O^{(1)}(a_t^{(1)}) = [\mathbf{0}_h, \mathbf{0}_h, -s_{0:t}, \delta_t - \omega_t,$$
$$-\frac{1}{2^t} + \frac{1}{2^{t+1}}, \mathbf{0}_\omega, \mathbf{0}_\omega, -\omega_{t-1} + \omega_t]$$

where

$$\delta_t = (\mathbf{\Delta}_{t,1}, \ldots, \mathbf{\Delta}_{t,n-1}, 1/2^{t+1}), \quad 0 \leq \delta_t \leq 1$$

Recall that,

$$a_t^{(1)} = \begin{bmatrix} h_{t-1}, \mathbf{0}_h, s_{0:t}, \\ \omega_t, \frac{1}{2^t}, \mathbf{0}_\omega, \mathbf{0}_\omega, \omega_{t-1} \end{bmatrix}$$

We define the feed-forward network $O(a_t)$ as follows,

$$O^{(1)}(a_t) = \mathbf{W}_2 \sigma(\mathbf{W}_1 a_t^{(1)} + b_1)$$

where $\boldsymbol{W}_i \in \mathbb{Q}^{d \times d}$ and $\boldsymbol{b}_1 \in \mathbb{Q}^d$. Define $\boldsymbol{W}_1$ as

$$
\begin{array}{c c}
 & \begin{array}{c c c c c c c} 2d_h & d_e & d_\omega & 1 & d_\omega & d_\omega & d_\omega \end{array} \\
\begin{array}{c} 2d_h \\ d_e \\ d_\omega - 1 \\ 1 \\ 1 \\ d_\omega \\ d_\omega \\ d_\omega \end{array} &
\left[\begin{array}{c|c|c|c|c|c|c}
\mathbf{0} & \mathbf{0} & \mathbf{0} & \mathbf{0} & \mathbf{0} & \mathbf{0} & \mathbf{0} \\ \hline
\mathbf{0} & \mathbf{I} & \mathbf{0} & \mathbf{0} & \mathbf{0} & \mathbf{0} & \mathbf{0} \\ \hline
\mathbf{0} & \mathbf{0} & \mathbf{0} & \mathbf{0} & \mathbf{0} & \mathbf{I} & -\mathbf{I} \\ \hline
\mathbf{0} & \mathbf{0} & \mathbf{0} & \frac{1}{2} & \mathbf{0} & \mathbf{0} & \mathbf{0} \\ \hline
\mathbf{0} & \mathbf{0} & \mathbf{0} & \frac{1}{2} & \mathbf{0} & \mathbf{0} & \mathbf{0} \\ \hline
\mathbf{0} & \mathbf{0} & \mathbf{I} & \mathbf{0} & \mathbf{0} & \mathbf{0} & \mathbf{0} \\ \hline
\mathbf{0} & \mathbf{0} & \mathbf{0} & \mathbf{0} & \mathbf{0} & \mathbf{I} & \mathbf{0} \\ \hline
\mathbf{0} & \mathbf{0} & \mathbf{0} & \mathbf{0} & \mathbf{0} & \mathbf{0} & \mathbf{I}
\end{array} \right]
\end{array}
$$

and $\boldsymbol{b}_1 = \mathbf{0}$, then

$$
\sigma(\boldsymbol{W}_1 \boldsymbol{a}_t^{(1)} + \boldsymbol{b}_1) = [\mathbf{0}_h, \mathbf{0}_h, \boldsymbol{s}_{0:t}, \boldsymbol{\Delta}_t, \frac{1}{2^{t+1}},
$$
$$
\boldsymbol{\omega}_t, \ \boldsymbol{\omega}_{t-1}, \ \boldsymbol{\omega}_{t-1}]
$$

We define $\boldsymbol{W}_2$ as

$$
\begin{array}{c c}
 & \begin{array}{c c c c c c c} 2d_h & d_e & d_{\omega-1} & 2 & d_\omega & d_\omega & d_\omega \end{array} \\
\begin{array}{c} 2d_h \\ d_e \\ d_\omega - 1 \\ 1 \\ 1 \\ d_\omega \\ d_\omega \\ d_\omega \end{array} &
\left[\begin{array}{c|c|c|c|c|c|c}
\mathbf{0} & \mathbf{0} & \mathbf{0} & \mathbf{0} & \mathbf{0} & \mathbf{0} & \mathbf{0} \\ \hline
\mathbf{0} & -\mathbf{I} & \mathbf{0} & \mathbf{0} & \mathbf{0} & \mathbf{0} & \mathbf{0} \\ \hline
\mathbf{0} & \mathbf{0} & \mathbf{I} & \mathbf{0} & \mathbf{0} & \mathbf{0} & \mathbf{0} \\ \hline
\mathbf{0} & \mathbf{0} & \mathbf{0} & 1,0 & \mathbf{0} & \mathbf{0} & \mathbf{0} \\ \hline
\mathbf{0} & \mathbf{0} & \mathbf{0} & -2,1 & \mathbf{0} & \mathbf{0} & \mathbf{0} \\ \hline
\mathbf{0} & \mathbf{0} & \mathbf{I} & \mathbf{0} & \mathbf{0} & \mathbf{0} & \mathbf{0} \\ \hline
\mathbf{0} & \mathbf{0} & \mathbf{0} & \mathbf{0} & \mathbf{0} & -\mathbf{I} & \mathbf{0} \\ \hline
\mathbf{0} & \mathbf{0} & \mathbf{0} & \mathbf{0} & \mathbf{0} & \mathbf{I} & -\mathbf{I}
\end{array} \right]
\end{array}
$$

This leads to

$$
O^{(1)}(\boldsymbol{a}_t^{(1)}) = [\mathbf{0}_h, \mathbf{0}_h, \boldsymbol{s}_{0:t}, \boldsymbol{\delta}_t,
$$
$$
-\frac{1}{2^t} + \frac{1}{2^{t+1}}, \ \mathbf{0}_\omega, \ -\boldsymbol{\omega}_t, \ -\boldsymbol{\omega}_{t-1} + \boldsymbol{\omega}_t]
$$

which is what we wanted to prove.

$\square$

Lemma D.3. *Let $\boldsymbol{p}_t^{(2)} \in \mathbb{Q}^d$ be a query vector such that*

$$
\boldsymbol{p}_t^{(2)} = [\ \cdot, \ \cdot, \ \cdot,
$$
$$
\boldsymbol{\delta}_t, \ \cdot, \cdot, \cdot, \cdot \ ]
$$

where $t \geq 0$ and '$\cdot$' denotes an arbitrary value. Then we have

$$
\mathrm{Att}(\boldsymbol{p}_t^{(2)}, \boldsymbol{K}_{\bar{t}}^e, \boldsymbol{V}_{\bar{t}}^e) = [\ \mathbf{0}_h, \mathbf{0}_h, \boldsymbol{s}_{\bar{t}},
$$
$$
\mathbf{0}_\omega, 0, \mathbf{0}_\omega, [\![s_t]\!], \mathbf{0}_\omega \ ]. \tag{16}
$$

Proof. Let

$$
(\hat{\alpha}_{t,1}^{(2,2)}, \ldots, \hat{\alpha}_{t,\bar{t}}^{(2,2)})
$$
$$
= \mathsf{hardmax}\left(\langle \boldsymbol{p}_t^{(2)}, \boldsymbol{k}_1^e \rangle, \ldots, \langle \boldsymbol{p}_t^{(2)}, \boldsymbol{k}_{\bar{t}}^e \rangle \right)
$$

be the vector of normalized attention scores in the decoder-encoder attention block of layer 2 at time t. Then

$$
\mathrm{Att}(\boldsymbol{p}_t^{(2)}, \boldsymbol{K}_{\bar{t}}^e, \boldsymbol{V}_{\bar{t}}^e) = \sum_{j=0}^{\bar{t}} \hat{\alpha}_{t,j}^{(2,2)} \boldsymbol{v}_j^e.
$$

We claim that

Claim 1. *For $t \geq 0$ we have*

$$
(\hat{\alpha}_{t,1}^{(2,2)}, \ldots, \hat{\alpha}_{t,\bar{t}}^{(2,2)})
$$
$$
= \frac{1}{\lambda_{\bar{t}}} \left(\mathbb{I}(s_0 = s_t), \mathbb{I}(s_1 = s_t), \ldots, \mathbb{I}(s_{\bar{t}} = s_t) \right),
$$

where λ_t is a normalization factor given by $\lambda_t = \sum_{j=0}^{n-1} \mathbb{I}(s_j = s_t)$.

We now prove the lemma assuming the claim above. Denote the L.H.S. in (16) by $\boldsymbol{\gamma}_t$. Note that if $s_j = s_t$, then $\boldsymbol{v}_j^e = \boldsymbol{\gamma}_t$. Now we have

$$
\begin{aligned}
\sum_{j=0}^{\bar{t}} \hat{\alpha}_{t,j}^{(2,2)} \boldsymbol{v}_j^e &= \frac{1}{\lambda_t} \sum_{j=0}^{\bar{t}} \mathbb{I}(s_j = s_t) \, \boldsymbol{v}_j^e \\
&= \frac{1}{\lambda_t} \left(\sum_{j=0}^{\bar{t}} \mathbb{I}(s_j = s_t) \right) \boldsymbol{\gamma}_t \\
&= \boldsymbol{\gamma}_t,
\end{aligned}
$$

completing the proof of the lemma modulo the proof of the claim, which we prove next. $\square$

Proof. (of Claim 1) For $0 < t \leq n$, the vector $\boldsymbol{\omega}_t - \boldsymbol{\omega}_{t-1}$ has the form

$$
\left(\left(\frac{1}{t+1} - \frac{1}{t} \right), \ldots, \left(\frac{\phi_{t,k}}{t+1} - \frac{\phi_{t-1,k}}{t} \right), \ldots, 0 \right).
$$

If $s_t = \beta_k$, then

$$
\begin{aligned}
(\boldsymbol{\omega}_t &- \boldsymbol{\omega}_{t-1})_k & (17) \\
&= \left(\frac{\phi_{t,k}}{t+1} - \frac{\phi_{t-1,k}}{t} \right) & (18) \\
&= \left(\frac{\phi_{t-1,k} + 1}{t+1} - \frac{\phi_{t-1,k}}{t} \right) & (19) \\
&= \frac{t - \phi_{t-1,k}}{t(t+1)} & (20) \\
&\geq \frac{1}{t(t+1)}. & (21)
\end{aligned}
$$

The last inequality used our assumption that $s_0 = \#$ and that $\#$ does not occur at any later time and therefore $\phi_{t-1,j} < t$. On the other hand, if $s_t \neq \beta_k$, then

$$
\begin{aligned}
(\boldsymbol{\omega}_t - \boldsymbol{\omega}_{t-1})_k &= \left(\frac{\phi_{t,k}}{t+1} - \frac{\phi_{t-1,k}}{t} \right) \\
&= \left(\frac{\phi_{t-1,k}}{t+1} - \frac{\phi_{t-1,k}}{t} \right) \\
&= -\frac{\phi_{t-1,j}}{t(t+1)} \qquad (22) \\
&\leq 0.
\end{aligned}
$$

This leads to,

$$
\begin{aligned}
(\boldsymbol{\omega}_t - \boldsymbol{\omega}_{t-1})_k &> 0 \qquad \text{if } s_t = \beta_k, \\
(\boldsymbol{\omega}_t - \boldsymbol{\omega}_{t-1})_k &\leq 0 \qquad \text{otherwise.}
\end{aligned}
$$

In words, the change in the proportion of a symbol is positive from step $t-1$ to t if and only if it is the input symbol at the t-th step. For $0 \leq t \leq n$ and $1 \leq k \leq |\Sigma|$, this leads to

$$
\begin{aligned}
\boldsymbol{\Delta}_{t,k} = \sigma(\boldsymbol{\omega}_t - \boldsymbol{\omega}_{t-1})_k &> 0 \qquad \text{if } s_t = \beta_k, \\
\boldsymbol{\Delta}_{t,k} = \sigma(\boldsymbol{\omega}_t - \boldsymbol{\omega}_{t-1})_k &= 0 \qquad \text{otherwise,}
\end{aligned}
$$

For $t > n$,

$$
\boldsymbol{\Delta}_t = 0.
$$

Recall that $\boldsymbol{p}_t^{(2)} = \boldsymbol{z}_t^{(1)}$ which comes from (15), and $\boldsymbol{k}_j^e$ is defined in (13). We reproduce these for convenience:

$$
\begin{aligned}
\boldsymbol{p}_t^{(2)} &= [\; \boldsymbol{h}_{t-1}, \; \boldsymbol{0}_h, \; \boldsymbol{0}_s, \\
&\qquad \boldsymbol{\delta}_{\bar{t}}, \; \tfrac{1}{2^{t+1}}, \boldsymbol{0}_\omega, \boldsymbol{0}_\omega, \; \boldsymbol{\omega}_{\bar{t}} \;], \\
\boldsymbol{k}_j^e &= [\; \boldsymbol{0}_h, \boldsymbol{0}_h, \boldsymbol{0}_s, \\
&\qquad [\![s_j]\!], 0, \boldsymbol{0}_\omega, \boldsymbol{0}_\omega, \boldsymbol{0}_\omega \;].
\end{aligned}
$$

It now follows that for $0 < t < n$, if $0 \leq j \leq t$ is such that $s_j \neq s_t$, then

$$
\langle \boldsymbol{p}_t^{(2)}, \boldsymbol{k}_j^e \rangle = \langle \boldsymbol{\delta}_t, [\![s_j]\!] \rangle = \delta_{t,i} = 0.
$$

And for $0 < t < n$, if $0 \leq j \leq t$ is such that $s_j = s_t = \beta_i$, then

$$
\langle \boldsymbol{p}_t^{(2)}, \boldsymbol{k}_j^e \rangle = \langle \boldsymbol{\delta}_t, [\![s_j]\!] \rangle = \delta_{t,i} \qquad (23)
$$

$$
= \frac{t - \phi_{t-1,j}}{t(t+1)} \geq \frac{1}{t(t+1)}. \qquad (24)
$$

Thus, for $0 \leq t < n$, in the vector $\left(\langle \boldsymbol{p}_t^{(2)}, \boldsymbol{k}_0^e \rangle, \ldots, \langle \boldsymbol{p}_t^{(2)}, \boldsymbol{k}_t^e \rangle \right)$, the largest coordinates are the ones indexed by j with $s_j = s_t$ and they all equal $\frac{t - \phi_{t-1,i}}{t(t+1)}$. All other coordinates are 0. For $t \geq n$, only the last coordinate $\langle \boldsymbol{p}_t^{(2)}, \boldsymbol{k}_n^e \rangle = \langle \boldsymbol{\delta}_t, [\![\$]\!] \rangle = \frac{1}{2^{t+1}}$ is non-zero. Now the claim follows immediately by the definition of hardmax. $\qquad \square$

Lemma D.4. *There exists a function $O^{(2)}(.)$ defined by feed-forward network such that, for $t \geq 0$,*

$$
\begin{aligned}
O^{(2)}(\boldsymbol{a}_t^{(2)}) = [\sigma(\boldsymbol{W}_h \boldsymbol{h}_{t-1} + \boldsymbol{W}_x \boldsymbol{s}_{\bar{t}} + \boldsymbol{b}) - \boldsymbol{h}_{t-1}, \\
\boldsymbol{0}_h, -\boldsymbol{s}_{\bar{t}}, -\boldsymbol{\delta}_t, 0, \boldsymbol{0}_\omega, -[\![s_t]\!], \boldsymbol{0}_\omega]
\end{aligned}
$$

where $\boldsymbol{W}_h, \boldsymbol{W}_x$ and $\boldsymbol{b}$ denote the parameters of the RNN under consideration.

Proof. Proof is very similar to proof of lemma C.4. $\qquad \square$

E Details of Experiments

In this section, we describe the specifics of our experimental setup. This includes details about the dataset, models, setup and some sample outputs.

E.1 Impact of Residual Connections

The models under consideration are the vanilla Transformer, the one without decoder-encoder residual connection and the one without decoder-decoder residual connection. For the synthetic tasks, we implement a single layer encoder-decoder network with only a single attention head in each block. Our implementation of the Transformer is adapted from the implementation of (Rush, 2018). Table 4 provides some illustrative sample outputs of the models for the copy task.

SOURCE & REFERENCE	– there was no problem at all says douglas ford chief executive officer of the futures exchange
DIRECTIONAL TRANSFORMER	– there was no problem at all says douglas ford chief executive officer of the futures exchange
VANILLA TRANSFORMER	– there was no problem at all says douglas ford chief executive officer

Table 4: Sample outputs by the models on the copy task on length 16. With absolute positional encodings the model overfits on terminal symbol at position 13 and generates sequence of length 12.

For the machine translation task, we use Open-NMT (Klein et al., 2017) for our implementation. For preprocessing the German-English dataset we used the script from fairseq. The dataset contains about 153k training sentences, 7k development sentences and 7k test sentences. The hyperparameters to train the vanilla Transformer were obtained from fairseq's guidelines. We tuned the parameters on the validation set for the two baseline model. To preprocess the English-Vietnamese dataset, we follow Luong and Manning (2015). The dataset contains about 133k training sentences. We use

the tst2012 dataset containing 1.5k sentences for
validation and tst2013 containing 1.3k sentences
as test set. We use noam optimizer in all our experiments. While tuning the network, we vary the
number of layer from 1 to 4, the learning rate, the
number of heads, the warmup steps, embedding
size and feedforward embedding size.

E.2   Masking and Encodings

Our implementation for directional transformer is
based on (Yang et al., 2019) but we use only unidirectional masking as opposed to bidirectional used
in their setup. While tuning the models, we vary
the layers from 1 to 4, the learning rate, warmup
steps and the number of heads.

An Expectation Maximisation Algorithm for Automated Cognate Detection

Roddy MacSween
Homerton College & Computer Laboratory
University of Cambridge
rlm72@cantab.ac.uk

Andrew Caines   **Paula Buttery**
Computer Laboratory
University of Cambridge
{apc38|pjb48}@cam.ac.uk

Abstract

In historical linguistics, cognate detection is the task of determining whether sets of words have common etymological roots. Inspired by the comparative method used by human linguists, we develop a system for automated cognate detection that frames the task as an inference problem for a general statistical model consisting of observed data (potentially cognate pairs of words), latent variables (the cognacy status of pairs) and unknown global parameters (which sounds correspond between languages). We then give a specific instance of such a model along with an expectation-maximisation algorithm to infer its parameters. We evaluate our system on a dataset of 8140 cognate sets, finding its performance of our method to be comparable to the state of the art. We additionally carry out qualitative analysis demonstrating various advantages it has over existing systems. We also suggest several ways our work could be extended within the general theoretical framework we propose.

1 Introduction

In historical linguistics, two words are deemed cognate if they share a root in a parent language, for example German 'Nacht' and English 'night' which both originate from Proto-Indo-European *$nók^wts$. The task of cognate detection is interesting in its own right, but is also an important part of the larger task of proto-language reconstruction.

As described in Campbell (2013), the *comparative method* used by historical linguists to reconstruct an ancestral language from a set of potentially cognate words in daughter languages consists of three steps: assembling cognates, establishing sound correspondences and reconstructing proto-sounds. Automation of this method is made challenging by the fact that "the comparative linguist typically jumps back and forth among these steps" because of a mutual dependence between

cognacy judgements and hypothesised sound correspondences. Whether two words should be deemed cognate depends on whether the sounds in them correspond according to known rules for the languages. For instance, the *t* and *ts* sounds in English and German are known to correspond, which is evidence for "tooth" and "Zahn" being cognate. But sound correspondence rules are themselves theorised based on which sounds coincide in known cognate pairs. Therefore a linguist must iteratively adapt their hypotheses about which words are cognate and which sounds correspond until they can reach a definite conclusion.

Existing approaches to automated cognate detection (ACD) fail to fully capture this idea of dealing with mutual dependence using an iterative method. Some early approaches are not iterative at all, while several more recent methods are iterative to some extent but either only carry out a small fixed number of iterations or use incomplete and ad hoc methods to update sound correspondences based on tentative cognacy judgements. In this paper we design and implement an iterative algorithm that uses the method of *expectation maximisation* for statistical inference, which is close to historical linguists' method of updating sound correspondences in one iteration based on cognacy judgements from the previous iteration.

This probabilistic approach is the main novel feature of our work, but we also build on existing approaches in other ways. Other than the work of List (2012), previous computational methods generally use little linguistic theory as a basis for making cognate judgements; in contrast, our model uses *phonological features* as a factor in determining how likely phones are to correspond. We also use a new method of clustering to turn cognate judgements between pairs of words into sets of cognates from multiple languages. We evaluate our system on a dataset consisting of 8140 cognate sets

476

Proceedings of the 24th Conference on Computational Natural Language Learning, pages 476–485
Online, November 19-20, 2020. ©2020 Association for Computational Linguistics
https://doi.org/10.18653/v1/P17

partitioned into 10 typological groups originated by List (2012).

2 Related work

Several approaches to ACD exist, with a review of the majority given in Rama et al. (2018). Most of these have the same overall structure: given a list of sets of possible cognates, they align words using some metric (typically based on the phones that make up the words) and use some function of scores of alignments to judge cognacy. The alignment process generally uses methods from bioinformatics such as the Needleman-Wunsch algorithm (Needleman and Wunsch, 1970).

Normalised Edit Distance (Nerbonne and Heeringa, 1997) (NED) performs alignment using a manually specified distance matrix for phones. It has been used with a simple binary measure (distance only depends on whether or not two phones are the same) and more complex measures. This was a relatively early method and is not iterative.

Rama et al. (2018) discuss two methods that do not use alignment. Consonant Class Matching (CCM) (Turchin et al., 2010) is a very simple approach: it determines whether words are cognate based on whether their first consonants fall into the same sound classes. On the other hand, the system of Jäger et al. (2017) is more complex; it uses similarity as measured by other methods such as those below as a feature source for classification of cognacy using Support Vector Machines (SVMs).

The online Pointwise Mutual Information method (Rama et al., 2017) (PMI) is similar to ours in that it performs alignment with a distance matrix for pairs of phones which is adjusted iteratively. However, they do not update weights in a probabilistic way based on tentative cognacy probabilities at each iteration in the same way as us. We take into account all pairs of possible cognates in the dataset weighted by their estimated cognacy probability; in comparison they use a fixed set of cognate words deemed to be probably cognate, and these are treated uniformly. They also do not set weights in a linguistically motivated way. The system of Steiner et al. (2011) is similar to PMI, but using the LZ78 algorithm (Ziv and Lempel, 1978) to produce weights instead of PMI scores. Gilman (2012) describes another similar algorithm.

We use the LexStat algorithm (List, 2012) as a baseline in evaluation of our system. LexStat is partially iterative: it uses a simple heuristic to determine which pairs of words are definitely cognate and then sets weights for an alignment step based on those. In contrast, our system can iterate indefinitely rather than just twice. Unlike methods such as PMI, LexStat does use linguistic theory in judging cognacy of word pairs. Rather than computing distance between individual phones, it groups phones into sound classes (by place and manner of articulation) and then considers combinations of sound classes and prosodic contexts as the segments used for alignment. The use of sound classes is similar to our framework with phonological features, although ours is in some ways more general. Prosodic context is not taken into account by our system and could be a future extension.

Overall, the primary difference between our system and previous work is the way in which we adjust parameters for how likely two sounds are to correspond based on intermediate estimates of cognacy probabilities. Producing theories about which sounds correspond based on cognacy judgements is a key part of the method followed by human linguists, but many existing automated methods do not do this at all. Those that do often only make a limited number of adjustments, or lack theoretical justification for the approach used. In contrast, in our system this process has equal status to the inference step in the opposite direction, and has a rigorous probabilistic interpretation within the expectation-maximisation framework. The probabilistic framework used also has the benefit of allowing easier identification of limitations of the system, such as cases where unrealistic assumptions of independence are made. A key element of our system that enables this approach is the fact that we separately model the processes of generating two cognate words from a common ancestor and two non-cognates from different ancestors. In comparison, previous work implicitly models only the former.

2.1 PanPhon

We initialise our parameters using weights derived from the PanPhon database (Mortensen et al., 2016) of phonological features with the standard categorisation of Chomsky and Halle (1968). These are binary or ternary variables representing possible axes of variation of phones. For example, the [+/- voice] feature distinguishes between sounds such as b, d and z where the vocal folds vibrate during articulation and those such as p, t and k where they do not. This is relevant to our cognate detection because phones with similar feature sets are more likely to correspond in cognate pairs. Not all features have equal status for this, for instance the [+/-syllabic] feature is especially useful.

Human historical linguists form theories about evolution of languages involving complex relationships between multiple features (for example, the change of certain stops from voiced to voiceless between Proto-Indo-European and Proto-Germanic). Our system currently uses phonological features in a simple language-independent way, however one advantage it has is the fact that these sophisticated linguistic theories could in principle be integrated into it simply by altering the initialisation code, without changing the overall framework. This lowers the barrier for linguists to experiment with adding their domain knowledge into an automated cognate detection system, since a wide variety of linguistic models could be implemented with changes to only a small section of the codebase.

3 Model

3.1 General framework

We can formulate cognate detection as a probabilistic inference task, where for a dataset of n pairs of words we have a sequence X of n random variables representing the generation of the pairs, a sequence Z of n indicator variables for the event of each pair being cognate, and some global parameters θ that $P(X, Z)$ depends on. Then cognate detection can be done by finding values for θ maximising the likelihood of the observed words

$$\sum_{z \in \{0,1\}^n} P(X, Z = z \mid \theta) \tag{1}$$

then using the probability distribution these give over Z to judge cognacy.

It is difficult to do this maximisation directly. Instead, we can use an expectation-maximisation (EM) algorithm (Dempster et al., 1977):

- Initialise $\theta = \theta^{(0)}$

- Find the distribution of Z for $\theta = \theta^{(t)}$ (expectation step)

- Update $\theta^{(t+1)}$ to take the values maximising the expectation with respect to the above distribution of the log likelihood of the observed data (maximisation step)

v   oː   ɣ   ə   l

f   ɣ   k   -   l

Figure 1: Generation of *voːɣəl* and *fɣkl* (Dutch and Icelandic words for 'bird') as cognates

- Repeat expectation and maximisation steps until $\theta^{(t)}$ converges

3.2 Cognacy model

3.2.1 Definition

A model must be chosen that makes the maximisation step computationally feasible. Here, we use two separate models for the case where a pair of words are cognate and the case where they are not. For two words w and w' we model $P(X_i = (w, w') \mid Z_i = 1)$ by assuming the words have been generated on a phone-by-phone basis from some word in the parent language as shown in Figure 1. Each pair of arrows is associated with a parameter, for instance θ_{vf} is the probability that a random phone in the parent language would generate v in Dutch and f in Icelandic. Then we have

$$P(X_n = (w, w') \mid Z_n = 1) = \prod_i \theta_{\texttt{align}(w,w')_i} \tag{2}$$

where $\texttt{align}(w, w')$ is the sequence of pairs of aligned phones in the two words,

Figure 2 shows the similar model for $P(X_i = (w, w') \mid Z_i = 0)$. Here each individual arrow is associated with a parameter α_x. Formally we have

p   t   a   k   w   a   z   o

Figure 2: Generation of *ptak* and *wazo* (Polish and French words for "bird") from separate etymons

$$P(X_n = (w, w') \mid Z_n = 0) =$$
$$\prod_i \alpha_{\texttt{first}(\texttt{align}(w,w')_i)}$$
$$\prod_j \alpha_{\texttt{second}(\texttt{align}(w,w')_j)} \tag{3}$$

where $\texttt{first}$ and $\texttt{second}$ are the first and second components of pairs of the alignment of the words. We use alignments rather than the words themselves even in the non-cognate case[1] because if we used the words directly this would imply a model where deletions only occur for words which are cognate, which is not realistic.

4 Algorithm

4.1 E-step

The expectation step of our algorithm involves for each pair of words $X_n = (w, w')$ computing the probability under some set of parameters θ, α, α' that they are cognate. By Bayes' rule we have

$$P(Z_n = c \mid X_n = (w, w')) =$$
$$\frac{P(X_n = (w, w') \mid Z_n = c)P(Z_n = 1)}{\substack{P(X_n = (w, w') \mid Z_n = 0)P(Z_n = 0)+ \\ P(X_n = (w, w') \mid Z_n = 1)P(Z_n = 1)}} \quad (4)$$

We compute $P(X_n = (w, w') \mid Z_n = 0)$ and $P(X_n = (w, w') \mid Z_n = 1)$ using Equation 2 and Equation 3. $P(\text{cognate})$ and $P(\neg\text{cognate})$ can be either fixed values, or vary during the iteration.

Calculating $P(X_n = (w, w') \mid Z_n)$ requires an alignment of w and w'. We produce a new alignment at each iteration by using the Needleman-Wunsch algorithm (Needleman and Wunsch, 1970) with the logarithms of θ values as weights. This gives an alignment with the maximum likelihood of cognacy according to the model, since the Needleman-Wunsch algorithm involves summing weights (which is equivalent to multiplying the original probabilities). If there are multiple best alignments, one is chosen arbitrarily.

4.1.1 M-step

The maximisation step takes probabilities of cognacy for all pairs of words and infers the best fitting parameters. For the α parameters the process for this is analogous to simple maximum likelihood estimation with known values for $\mathbf{Z}$. In that case, for a phone x we would estimate α_x as the frequency of x across all words in non-cognate pairs in the relevant taxon. Here we instead have a distribution over $\mathbf{Z}$ so we use the expected frequency:

$$\alpha_x = \frac{E(\#x)}{\sum_y E(\#y)} \quad (5)$$

where $E(\#x)$ is the number of occurrences of phone x in words of the relevant taxon, with the

count for each occurrence weighted by the probability that the containing word is not part of a cognate pair.

The equivalent formula could be used to estimate θ parameters, however this might cause problems because some pairs of corresponding phones may not occur in the dataset but still be modelled as having non-zero probability.

To deal with this, we use *additive smoothing* (Manning et al., 2008) for estimation of θ parameters. In general, given a random variable X with d discrete values and n trials, a smoothed estimator for each parameter of X is

$$P(X = x) = \frac{\#(X = x) + \beta}{n + \beta d} \quad (6)$$

where $\#(X = x)$ is the number of times x occurred and β is a smoothing parameter.

Additive smoothing typically uses the same β value for each parameter. This is appropriate when there is no relevant prior information. However, in this case there is some information that should be taken into account: frequent pairs are on average made up of frequent individual phones. Therefore rather than using a constant smoothing parameter, we weight it for each pair by the frequencies of its component phones, giving an estimation of

$$\theta_{xy} = \frac{E(\#(x, y)) + \beta\frac{E(\#x)E(\#y)}{\#\text{pairs}}}{\sum_{(z, w)} E(\#(z, w)) + \beta\#\text{pairs}} \quad (7)$$

where $E(\#(x, y))$ is the count of alignments of phones x and y weighted by probabilities of containing words being cognate, $E(\#x)$ is the same for individual phones, and $\#\text{pairs}$ is the total number of possible pairs of phones (the product of the number of phones for each taxon). Note that $E(\#x)$ here is weighted by the probability of cognacy whereas in Equation 5 it was weighted by probability of *non*-cognacy.

4.1.2 Initialisation

Expectation maximisation is guaranteed to find a locally optimal set of parameters, however depending on the initial values they may not be globally optimal. Often this is dealt with by running the algorithm multiple times from a variety of initial parameters. However, this will not work in our case as our algorithm is very general; it can infer completely arbitrary phone-level relationships between taxons and therefore most possible sets of initial parameters will lead to poor local optima.

---

[1] The difference being that the aligned words may contain -, indicating insertion/deletion

Therefore we must initialise the parameters in a linguistically motivated way.

The α parameters are straightforward to set using the proportions of phones in the whole dataset (i.e. in the same way as in the maximisation step but taking the whole dataset to be noncognate).

The θ parameters must be initialised in a more complex way. Each pair of phones is assigned a weight based on the category it falls into. These categories depend on phonological features of phones, as given by PanPhon. The categories we use are as follows:

1. Two identical phones

2. Two phones that differ in one phonological feature, for instance t and d

3. Two phones that differ in two features

4. Two phones that differ in more than two features, but have the same value for the syllabic feature (are either both consonants or both vowels[2])

5. A phone and a gap (representing a deletion)

6. All other pairs

Then weights for the pairs are normalised to give valid probabilities.

4.1.3 Clustering

Using the expectation-maximisation algorithm described above gives probabilities of cognacy for one pair of taxons, but the dataset we use has multiple taxons. Therefore some method is needed to turn scored pairs of words into clusters of cognates. Previous approaches use clustering algorithms from bioinformatics such as UPGMA (Sokal, 1958) for this (e.g. (List, 2012)) which produce clusters of cognates with low *average* distances.

We use a method that is instead concerned with the *maximum* distance between pairs in a cluster. This seems more similar to the approach a human linguist would take: when trying to determine whether a language is part of some family, they would not consider on average how close it is to each member, but rather try to find a single member that is inarguably related to it.

Our method is to create a graph where nodes are words and there is an edge between two words if

their computed cognacy probability exceeds some threshold. Then the clusters of cognates are the connected components of this graph. We find these clusters using the well-known algorithm described in Hopcroft and Tarjan (1973).

5 Evaluation

5.1 Dataset

To evaluate our system we use a dataset compiled by List (2012) for use with LexStat. The dataset consists of several partitions, containing words from different taxon families. Each partition contains a list of words, with their corresponding taxons, glosses (meanings), IPA transcriptions and gold-standard cognate-set annotations. Two words are considered to be potentially cognate if they have the same gloss (and do not belong to the same taxon). Table 1 gives details about the number of glosses, cognate sets and words in each partition of the dataset we use. The original dataset has two additional partitions, but these did not have transcriptions in a suitable form and therefore were not used. The BAI partition contains tone numerals, but our system is unable to use the information they provide so they are discarded in the preprocessing step. Other than this we follow the same procedure for all partitions. Further details about the dataset are given in Section 4.3.4 of List (2012).

5.2 Method

The source code for our system is available at `https://github.com/roddyyaga/cognates/` and can be used to reproduce these results.

Our system has several hyperparameters that must be set: the weights used to produce initial θ values, the smoothing parameter β, the number of iterations, and the threshold used in clustering. We set these by testing on the PIE section of the dataset. This did not cause overfitting, since the system does not perform better either in absolute terms or relative to other sections on that subset.

For the weights for the initial θ values, we used the following values: 25,000, 5000, 50, 20, 10, 1 for the categories in subsubsection 4.1.2.

For the smoothing parameter β we used 0.0001. We found that the sections of this dataset each contained enough datapoints that smoothing did not improve classification performance. However, a small level of smoothing did make the system more efficient, since with zero smoothing there were some cases where all alignments of a pair of words had

---

[2]This feature specifies whether a phone can be the nucleus of a syllable (Chomsky and Halle, 1968, 354). Vowels are [+syllabic] and (unless they are syllabic) consonants are [−syllabic].

Partition	Description	Glosses	Cognate sets	Words
BAI	Bai dialects	110	205	1028
IEL	Indo-European languages	207	1778	4393
JAP	Japanese dialects	200	458	1985
OUG	Uralic languages	110	239	2055
PAN	Austronesian languages	210	2730	4358
GER	Germanic languages and dialects	110	182	814
KSL	various languages	200	1179	1400
PIE	Indo-European languages	110	615	2172
ROM	Romance languages	110	177	589
SLV	Slavic languages	110	165	454

Table 1: Overview of the dataset used

zero probability, meaning there was a large number of highest scoring alignments which took significant time to iterate through.

For the threshold value we used 0.1. However, for most sections of the dataset using these hyperparameters the estimated cognacy probabilities for most pairs of words became very close to 0 or 1 after several iterations, therefore many threshold values would have given similar performance. Compared with an even spread of output probabilities across the range $(0, 1)$, this bimodal distribution has the drawback that it prevents interpretation of the probabilities as degrees of certainty. However, it has the advantage that it makes performance relatively independent of the choice of threshold.

Additionally, our system has a baseline probability of cognacy that must be set for each pair of taxon. We evaluated the system both using a fixed baseline (set to 0.005) and using a dynamic baseline where the value for each pair of taxons was updated after each iteration. Updates were made using the estimated cognacy probabilities for each pair of words produced in the expectation step. For each pair of taxons, we estimated a new baseline probability from these probabilities by taking the arithmetic mean across all word pairs for that taxon pair. The principle behind this dynamic adjustment is that the system can learn to behave differently for pairs of related taxons and unrelated pairs, based on how related the words in each pair appear to be at each iteration. We used a value of 0.005 as an initial baseline probability for all taxon pairs. The number of iterations was five for the fixed baseline and four for the method with updates.

Subset	LexStat	Fixed	Dynamic
PIE	**0.83**	**0.83**	**0.83**
SLV	0.94	**0.96**	**0.96**
OUG	0.92	**0.94**	**0.94**
GER	0.94	0.95	**0.96**
JAP	**0.93**	**0.93**	**0.93**
ROM	**0.94**	0.90	0.90
BAI	**0.89**	0.88	**0.89**
KSL	**0.94**	0.90	0.93
IEL	**0.81**	0.77	**0.81**
PAN	0.81	0.80	**0.83**

Table 2: Comparison of F-scores achieved by LexStat and this system (using both a fixed and dynamic baseline).

5.3 Results

We evaluated the cognacy judgements of our system using *B-cubed F-score* (List, 2012) with the LingPy library (List et al., 2019). These results are summarised in Table 2.

Overall our system performs very similarly to LexStat, and our results did not differ by a large amount depending on the method for setting the baseline. The results in List (2012) show LexStat outperforms previous systems on this dataset, and the more recent work of Rama et al. (2018) confirms that LexStat is still the best performing system (at least for the language families under consideration here). Therefore we can conclude our system performs approximately as well as the current state of the art.

The results of our system vary between partitions in a way that is not illustrated by the summary in Table 2. Figure 3 shows the F-score achieved at each iteration by our system (using the dynamic baseline). For some partitions of the dataset, the F-score

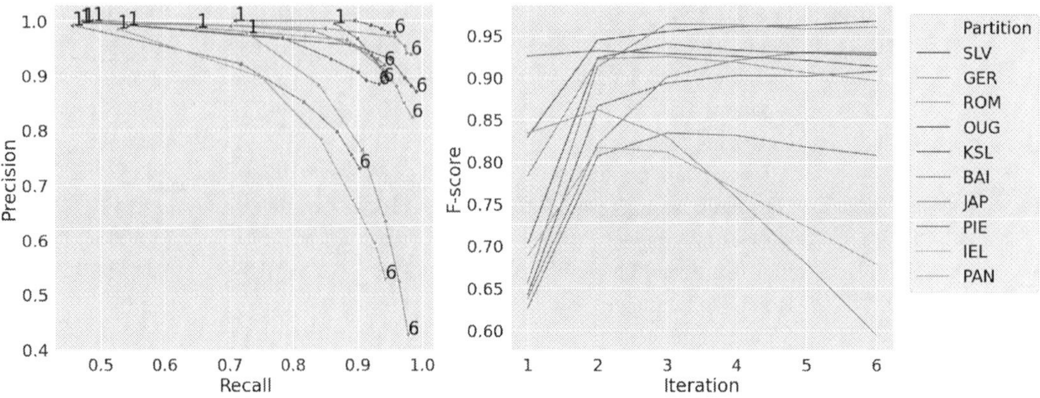

Figure 3: B-cubed precision and recall at each iteration, and B-cubed F-score at each iteration

converges and plateaus after the first few iterations, or continues to increase at every iteration. But for other partitions such as IEL and PAN it peaks after a couple of iterations and then decreases.

The root cause of this behaviour is unclear; IEL and PIE have very different results after the third iteration even though they behave similarly up to that point and cover the same language families. However from Figure 3 we can see that the cause is not that the system get worse overall at judging cognacy for the IEL and PAN partitions but rather that it is trading decreased precision for increased recall, because the distribution of estimated cognate probabilities is shifting relative to the threshold.

5.4 Error analysis

We also perform a qualitative analysis of some individual errors made by our system and LexStat on the PIE partition, and patterns among these errors.

In general, both systems tend to make the same kinds of errors. They both judge pairs of cognates with dissimilar forms as noncognate, for instance French *wazo* and Italian *utʃːɛllo* ('bird'). Likewise, they incorrectly judge noncognate pairs that are coincidentally similar, such as Bulgarian *kutʃɛ* and Hindi *kʊttaː* ('dog'). In these cases, it seems likely that a human without prior knowledge of historical sound changes in the relevant languages would make the same errors. In other cases, both systems make errors that a human (even without linguistic knowledge) would be unlikely to make. For example, they both judge Bulgarian *vsitʃki* and Czech *fʃɪxnⁱɪ* ('all') as noncognate, when intuitively it seems clear that those words plus Polish *fʃistsi* and Russian *fsʲe* form a cognate set.

The converse tendency – incorrectly grouping to-gether sets of words that intuitively appear noncognate – is only observed in our system and not Lex-Stat. For instance, our system groups the Romance words for "all" (French *tu*, Portuguese *todu* etc.) with the Germanic words (Dutch *alə*, English *ɔːl* etc.) while LexStat correctly distinguishes the two. However, weaker relative performance in this regard by our system is compensated for by better performance for glosses where there are only one or two cognate sets. For example, LexStat produces 5 cognate sets for the word "salt": one each for the families of Slavic, Germanic and Romance languages (except French), one with Armenian and French, and one with just Greek. In comparison, apart from Armenian (which is incorrectly put in its own set) our system correctly reaches the natural conclusion[3] that all the words are cognate.

While LexStat does not incorrectly merge large distinct cognate sets, both systems do incorrectly judge individual noncognate pairs even when they have dissimilar forms. This most frequently occurs for short words, where chance resemblance between one or two pairs of phones has a large overall effect (for instance *f* and *v* in Greek *fiði* and Polish *vɔ̃ʒ* ('snake')).

One interesting error that reveals a shortcoming of our system's clustering method is its judgement of Italian *vɛntre* as cognate with Italian *textipa-pantʃa*. By definition it is not possible for two words from the same taxon to be cognate with itself, and our system will not judge them as such directly. But it is possible for the clustering algorithm to produce these judgements indirectly since cognacy is transitive. In this case, one word in

---

[3]Given their phonetic similarity, e.g. Bulgarian *sol*, English *soːlt*, French *sɛl* and Italian *sale*

the set of French *vã tʁ*, Portuguese *vẽtrə*, Spanish *bjentre* and Italian *ventre* has been (incorrectly) judged as cognate with one of Italian *pantʃa* and Romanian *pəntetse*. However, it is not obvious how to resolve this, since some alternative clusterings that avoid this impossibility (for instance in this case putting *ventre* in its own cognate set) would be strictly worse. One possible approach might be considering all sets of edges in the cognacy probability graph where removing them would give a possible clustering and removing the set with the lowest total probability.

There are several patterns in the "obvious" errors produced by both systems. Firstly, relationships between more than two words with the same gloss are often ignored. For instance, the errors described above with *vsitʃki* and cognates could be avoided by taking into account the fact that those words form part of a mutually similar set rather than considering their relationships with other words in that set in isolation. Similarly, the fact that the taxons under consideration form families is ignored. For example, there are several cases where the words from Romance languages form one cognate set, but one or both systems group them as two sets: one with the French word by itself and another containing all the others. Finally, both systems treat the sequences of phones that form words uniformly. But there are many cases where cognate pairs of words are more similar at the start than the end, and in particular where one word is shorter than the other. Several examples of this occur for French, for instance *sẽ* is cognate with Italian *seno* ('blood'). One way to adapt our cognacy model to deal with this would be placing a greater emphasis on phone correspondence probabilities at the start of the word.

5.5 Analysis of sound correspondence parameters

We can examine the behaviour of the system by looking at how the θ parameters change at each iteration. For instance, after the first iteration on the PIE subset the 15 pairs with the highest probabilities for English and German are (-, ə), (s, z), (ə, ə), (a, a), (t, t), (b, b), (s, s), (ɪ, ɪ), (h, h), (æ, a), (f, f), (l, l), (d, t), (r, r) and (n, n) – predominantly pairs of identical phones. This is unsurprising given the high initial weights given to these.

After five iterations the pairs with the probabilities are quite different, the top 15 being (t, t), (s, z),

(t, ts), (h, h), (ɪ, ɪ), (t, s), (v, v), (f, f), (m, m), (l, l), (d, t), (-, n), (-, ə), (n, n) and (r, r). Many of these such as (v, v) and (t, ts) are well-known sound correspondences, validating our method. Similar results are observed for other pairs of taxons.

5.6 Armenian-Greek case study

We also tested our system on a subset of the PIE partition containing only Armenian and Greek words. Many of the sound changes between Proto-Indo-European and Armenian are unusually dramatic, for instance the change from **dw* to *erk*. This makes detecting cognates between these languages considerably more challenging task. We also use this case study to demonstrate how initialisation of the model's parameters can be done in in linguistically motivated and language specific ways.

This new dataset consists of 24 cognate pairs of words and 75 noncognate pairs. It was produced by dropping words from taxons other than Armenian and Greek from the PIE partition, and also dropping words from those taxons when only one taxon had words for a gloss.

This dataset contains much smaller cognate sets than the overall dataset (each has either 1 or 2 elements) and is skewed towards noncognate pairs, while our focus in this analysis is more on achieving correct detection of cognates rather than correctly avoiding false claims of cognacy. These factors make B-cubed F-score an unsuitable metric to use, as high scores for this can be achieved by judging all pairs of words as noncognate. Therefore instead we consider accuracy among cognate and noncognate pairs separately.

As a baseline, we evaluated LexStat on this dataset. We found that regardless of the threshold used, it judged all pairs of words as noncognate, since there were no obvious patterns of sound correspondence.

We then tested our system using three methods for setting initial parameters. First we used the same weights as before ("original weights"). Second, we used that method except with the weights for identical phones being reduced from 25,000 to 8500 ("lowered identical weights"). Third, we used a variation of the second method where the weights for several individual pairs of phones increased to 8500 ("increased reflex weights"). Proto-Indo-European **d* has reflexes *ð* and *t* in Greek and Armenian respectively. Similarly, the consonant cluster **dw* has reflex *ð* in Greek and *erk* in Arme-

483

Method	Cog.	Noncog.	Overall
LexStat	0.00	**1.00**	**0.75**
Original	0.13	0.96	**0.75**
Lowered identical	0.29	0.83	0.69
Increased reflex	**0.54**	0.83	**0.75**

Table 3: Accuracies for all pairs plus cognate and noncognate subsets on the Armenian-Greek data. Results for our system were produced after 3 iterations.

nian. Reflecting these correspondences, we set the weights for the pairs $(ð, t)$, $(ɛ, \text{-})$, $(ɾ, ð)$ and $(k, \text{-})$ to 8500.

We experimented with increasing the weights for corresponding reflexes with a weight of 25,000 for identical phones, but found this gave the same results as just using the original weights. The reason for this is that assigning such a high weight to identical phones causes the initial probabilities for other categories of correspondence to be very low, and so only words with a high proportion of exactly matching phones will be given a high probability of cognacy. This is not an issue when the system is evaluated on the original partitions of the dataset, as these have many cognate pairs that are almost identical. But the Armenian and Greek words generally differ more, and in particular the pairs with the corresponding reflexes mentioned above do not contain matching identical phones. Therefore it is necessary to relax the emphasis on identical phones in order to judge these words as cognate.

Table 3 shows the accuracies produced by Lex-Stat and these three methods. LexStat judges all pairs as noncognate, which achieves a relatively high overall accuracy since the dataset is skewed towards noncognates. In comparison, our system does judge a minority of pairs as cognate, achieving positive accuracy for cognate pairs at the cost of reduced accuracy for noncognates. The combined effect for our "original weights" and "increased reflex weights" parameter settings is an overall accuracy that is marginally higher than that of LexStat, but the more meaningful advantage of our system for challenging data such as this is that its parameters can be varied to allow cognates to be detected at all. Increasing the weights for corresponding reflexes caused a significant[4] increase in accuracy for cognate pairs while leaving accuracy for noncognate pairs unchanged. This increase comes from pairs of words containing the sound correspondences men-

tioned such as Armenian *tal* and Greek *ðino* ('to give') and Armenian *jɛrku* and Greek *ðjo* ('two') being correctly judged as cognate when they were not previously. This positive effect from setting initial weights based on known linguistic relationships between languages demonstrates how our system could be used for joint human-computer cognate detection.

6 Conclusions

In this paper, we formalised the task of cognate detection as inference in a general statistical model, defined a specific example of such a model, and then designed and implemented an expectation-maximisation algorithm for that model. We evaluated its performance on an existing dataset, finding it to be comparable with the current state of the art. We also evaluated it qualitatively to demonstrate advantages it has over existing systems, such as greater flexibility on challenging datasets.

There are many ways this system could be extended by future work. The word-level model of cognacy could be made more sophisticated in various regards; one that appears especially promising from our qualitative evaluation would be to give different weights to pairs of aligned phones depending on the position they come in the word or on neighbouring phones, which would improve the system's ability to capture conditioned sound changes (Campbell, 2013, 15). A larger change would be to modify the system to perform cognate detection and phylogenetic reconstruction of taxon families simultaneously. This could significantly increase the performance of the system, since many of the errors observed here could be avoided by using information about taxon families. It would also build on our approach of mimicking the method of a human linguist by going from iteratively alternating between making cognate judgements and determining sound correspondences to iteratively alternating between those steps and reconstruction of language family trees.

Acknowledgements

This second and third authors are supported by Cambridge Assessment, University of Cambridge. We thank the anonymous reviewers for their helpful feedback.

---

[4]One-sided t-test, $p < 0.05$

References

Lyle Campbell. 2013. *Historical Linguistics: An Introduction*, 3rd edition. Edinburgh University Press.

Noam Chomsky and Morris Halle. 1968. *The sound pattern of English*. Harper & Row New York.

A. P. Dempster, N. M. Laird, and D. B. Rubin. 1977. Maximum likelihood from incomplete data via the em algorithm. *Journal of the Royal Statistical Society. Series B (Methodological)*, 39(1):1–38.

Sophia Gilman. 2012. Comparative method algorithm. *Cambridge Occasional Papers in Linguistics*, 6.

John Hopcroft and Robert Tarjan. 1973. Algorithm 447: Efficient algorithms for graph manipulation. *Commun. ACM*, 16(6):372–378.

Gerhard Jäger, Johann-Mattis List, and Pavel Sofroniev. 2017. Using support vector machines and state-of-the-art algorithms for phonetic alignment to identify cognates in multi-lingual wordlists. In *Proceedings of the 15th Conference of the European Chapter of the Association for Computational Linguistics: Volume 1, Long Papers*, pages 1205–1216.

Johann-Mattis List. 2012. Lexstat: Automatic detection of cognates in multilingual wordlists. In *Proceedings of the EACL 2012 Joint Workshop of LINGVIS & UNCLH*, EACL 2012, pages 117–125, Stroudsburg, PA, USA. Association for Computational Linguistics.

Johann-Mattis List, Simon J Greenhill, Tiago Tresoldi, and Robert Forkel. 2019. LingPy. A Python library for quantitative tasks in historical linguistics.

Christopher D Manning, Prabhakar Raghavan, and Hinrich Schütze. 2008. *Introduction to information retrieval*. Cambridge University Press.

David R. Mortensen, Patrick Littell, Akash Bharadwaj, Kartik Goyal, Chris Dyer, and Lori S. Levin. 2016. Panphon: A resource for mapping IPA segments to articulatory feature vectors. In *Proceedings of COLING 2016, the 26th International Conference on Computational Linguistics: Technical Papers*, pages 3475–3484. ACL.

Saul B Needleman and Christian D Wunsch. 1970. A general method applicable to the search for similarities in the amino acid sequence of two proteins. *Journal of Molecular Biology*, 48(3):443–453.

John Nerbonne and Wilbert Heeringa. 1997. Measuring dialect distance phonetically. In *Computational Phonology: Third Meeting of the ACL Special Interest Group in Computational Phonology*.

Taraka Rama, Johann-Mattis List, Johannes Wahle, and Gerhard Jäger. 2018. Are automatic methods for cognate detection good enough for phylogenetic reconstruction in historical linguistics? In *Proceedings of the 2018 Conference of the North American Chapter of the Association for Computational Linguistics: Human Language Technologies, Volume 2 (Short Papers)*, pages 393–400, New Orleans, Louisiana. Association for Computational Linguistics.

Taraka Rama, Johannes Wahle, Pavel Sofroniev, and Gerhard Jäger. 2017. Fast and unsupervised methods for multilingual cognate clustering. *CoRR*, abs/1702.04938.

Robert R Sokal. 1958. A statistical method for evaluating systematic relationships. *Univ. Kansas, Sci. Bull.*, 38:1409–1438.

Lydia Steiner, Michael Cysouw, and Peter Stadler. 2011. A pipeline for computational historical linguistics. *Language Dynamics and Change*, 1(1):89–127.

Peter Turchin, Ilia Peiros, and Murray Gell-Mann. 2010. Analyzing genetic connections between languages by matching consonant classes. *Journal of Language Relationship*, 5:117–126.

Jacob Ziv and Abraham Lempel. 1978. Compression of individual sequences via variable-rate coding. *IEEE transactions on Information Theory*, 24(5):530–536.

Filler-gaps that neural networks fail to generalize

Debasmita Bhattacharya and **Marten van Schijndel**
Department of Linguistics
Cornell University
{db758|mv443}@cornell.edu

Abstract

It can be difficult to separate abstract linguistic knowledge in recurrent neural networks (RNNs) from surface heuristics. In this work, we probe for highly abstract syntactic constraints that have been claimed to govern the behavior of filler-gap dependencies across different surface constructions. For models to generalize abstract patterns in expected ways to unseen data, they must share representational features in predictable ways. We use cumulative priming to test for representational overlap between disparate filler-gap constructions in English and find evidence that the models learn a general representation for the existence of filler-gap dependencies. However, we find no evidence that the models learn any of the shared underlying grammatical constraints we tested. Our work raises questions about the degree to which RNN language models learn abstract linguistic representations.

1 Introduction

While sentences appear highly variable on the surface, many syntactic constructions share the same underlying constraints, which determine their acceptability or grammaticality, i.e. the extent to which they are considered "well formed" through adherence to the rules of grammar. One of the strongest pieces of evidence for the existence of these shared underlying constraints are filler-gap constructions such as:

(1)   What does Leslie like __?

Filler-gap constructions contain a dependency between an overt filler (*what* in (1)) and a gap site (underlined above). The filler is bound to a referent (e.g., *Robin's painting*) that can fill the gap:

(2)   Leslie likes Robin's painting.

There are well-known restrictions (*islands*; Ross, 1967) that prevent certain words from participating in a filler-gap dependency. For example, it isn't possible to form a filler-gap dependency with prenominal (left-branch) noun modifiers:[1]

(3)   *Whose does Leslie like __ painting?

Further, very different filler-gap constructions obey shared underlying principles (e.g., *subjacency*; Chomsky, 1973). In this work, we probe recurrent neural network (RNN) language model understanding[2] of these underlying principles in English.

Recent work has claimed that recurrent neural network language models understand filler-gap dependencies (Chowdhury and Zamparelli, 2018; Wilcox et al., 2018, 2019). However, behavioral probing has suggested that this understanding is relatively superficial and doesn't reflect the underlying constraints that govern filler-gap acceptability (Chaves, 2020). An intermediate possibility, which we explore in this paper, is that RNNs do acquire a basic understanding of the underlying constraints but that the learned representations of the constraints are too weak to correctly drive behavior in behavioral probing tasks.

We use cumulative priming (van Schijndel and Linzen, 2018; Prasad et al., 2019) to test for representational overlap between disparate constructions. While we find some evidence that RNNs learn a general representation for the existence of filler-gap dependencies (in keeping with Wilcox et al., 2018, 2019), we find no evidence that RNNs

---

[1]Throughout this paper we adopt notational conventions from the syntax literature. * indicates an ungrammatical or unacceptable sentence, and ?? indicates a sentence whose acceptability is between wholly acceptable and wholly unacceptable.

[2]We use terms such as 'understand' and 'represent' to refer to the ability of RNN models to process language successfully. We do not mean to imply that models have true, deep understanding of linguistic phenomena as humans do. We simply use these terms for convenience.

Proceedings of the 24th Conference on Computational Natural Language Learning, pages 486–495
Online, November 19-20, 2020. ©2020 Association for Computational Linguistics
https://doi.org/10.18653/v1/P17

learn shared representation of the associated governing constraints (in keeping with Chaves, 2020).

Several recent papers have highlighted ways in which RNN behavior actually reflects shallow surface heuristics (McCoy et al., 2019; Chaves, 2020; Davis and van Schijndel, 2020). Note that the representational overlap we seek in the present study is actually a requirement for appropriate generalization of abstract knowledge to unseen data. This is what differentiates abstract knowledge from the surface heuristics that make RNN behavior fragile to adversarial methods. Therefore, our finding that RNNs fail to learn any shared abstract constraints across filler-gap constructions despite being sensitive to the existence of filler-gap dependencies raises questions about the ability of these models to learn abstract generalizable linguistic patterns.

2 Background

There are a number of different kinds of filler-gap constructions whose behavior is governed by a variety of different underlying constraints (see Table 1). Previous work has probed model understanding of filler-gap dependencies by testing model performance on individual construction types rather than the underlying constraints that might govern them (Chowdhury and Zamparelli, 2018; Wilcox et al., 2018, 2019, c.f. Chaves 2020). These studies have followed the logic of the subject-verb agreement probing literature (e.g., Linzen et al., 2016): a model that understands filler-gap dependencies should assign greater probability to grammatical filler-gap dependencies than to ungrammatical filler-gap dependencies. However, certain properties are shared across a variety of filler-gap constructions, giving rise to the hypothesis in the syntax literature that there are shared constraints that underlie multiple different filler-gap constructions. Chaves (2020) identifies failure cases where neural language models incorrectly rank sentences containing acceptable and unacceptable filler-gap dependencies, possibly because they have overlearned the individual filler-gap constructions without understanding the broader underlying constraints. In this paper, we test whether models understand four underlying filler-gap constraints that have been widely studied in the syntax literature. Specifically, we test whether multiple constructions that are governed by a single constraint share any representational features that are not present in other constructions. If such selec-

tive representational overlap exists, it could be an indication that the models do understand the underlying constraints but that their representation is too weak to correctly rank acceptable/unacceptable sentence pairs.

Cumulative priming has been introduced as a method for probing the linguistic representations encoded in RNNs (van Schijndel and Linzen, 2018; Prasad et al., 2019; Lepori et al., 2020).[3] This approach involves fine-tuning pretrained models for a single epoch with a small amount of additional training data. The pretrained model acts as a filter on the linguistic features learned during fine-tuning. More salient features will be affected by the fine-tuning to a larger degree than less salient features. By measuring the responsiveness of the model to linguistic input before and after priming (fine-tuning), researchers can identify which linguistic features are salient for the pretrained model. Importantly, if one construction primes a different construction, there is representational overlap between the two constructions within the model. Therefore, this approach provides a direct method of separating abstract linguistic knowledge from surface heuristics.

3 Constructions

We analyze eight types of syntactic constructions involving filler-gap dependencies in English. Syntacticians often refer to these dependencies as extractions, which alludes to the linguistic theory that filler phrases originate at the gap site before being *extracted* to the filler site during language production.

3.1 Adjunct islands

An adjunct island is formed from an adjunct clause, out of which wh-extraction is not possible. Adjunct clauses are introduced by *because*, *if*, and *when*, as well as by relative clauses.

(4)   a.   She ate her hat because they announced the plan.

      b.   **What** did she eat her hat because they announced __?

---

[3]For example, Prasad et al. (2019) use cumulative priming to show that RNN language models cluster multiple different kinds of relative clauses together in representation space (suggesting an abstract relative clause representation), and that simple syntactic features (passivity, relative clause reduction) are similarly clustered. However, the syntactic abstractions probed by Prasad et al. (2019) are still tied to surface cues.

Construction	Examples	L	S	E	D
Adjunct island	*What did you go home because you needed to do __?	-		-	
Wh- island	*Whom did Susan ask why Sam was waiting for __?		-		(+)
Subject island	*Who is that __ went home likely?	-	-	-	
Left branch island	*Whose does Susan like __ account?		-		(+)
Coordinate structure island	*What did Sam eat __ and broccoli?			+	
Complex NP island	*What did you hear the claim that Fred solved __?		-		
Object extraction	Who is it probable that Bill likes __?	+		+	(+)
Non-bridge verb island	*How did she whisper that he had died __?	?	?		

Table 1: Island constructions (rows) and the associated underlying constraints (L-marking, Subjacency, and the Empty Category Principle) that govern their behavior. We only examine constraints that are hypothesized to apply to multiple of our construction types. For constraints that are thought to be particularly influential of a construction, we denote the influence with +/-. For example, subject island extractions are unacceptable because they violate L-marking, while object extractions are acceptable because they adhere to L-marking. Discourse-Linking (D-linking) is an optional shared feature that can make some unacceptable constructions more acceptable.

3.2 Wh-islands

A wh-island is created by an embedded sentence which is introduced by a wh-word. Extraction out of a wh-island results in an unacceptable sentence.

(5)   a.   Sam wonders who solved the problem.
       b.   ***What** does Sam wonder who solved __?

3.3 Subject islands

A subject island is formed from a subject clause or a subject phrase, out of which wh-movement is not possible.

(6)   a.   That he has met Julia Roberts is unlikely.
       b.   ***Who** is that __ has met Julia Roberts unlikely?

(7)   a.   The rumour about Susan was circulating.
       b.   ***Whom** was the rumour about __ circulating?

3.4 Left branch islands

Left branch islands consist of noun phrases with modifiers, such as possessive determiners and attributive adjectives, that appear on a left branch under the noun. These preceding modifiers of a noun cannot be extracted from a noun phrase.

(8)   a.   Eric likes John's boat.
       b.   ***Whose** does Eric like __ boat?

(9)   a.   You failed the difficult test.
       b.   ***How difficult** did you fail the __ test?

3.5 Coordinate structure islands

Coordinate structure islands allow extraction out of a conjunct of a coordinate structure only if the extraction affects all the conjuncts of the coordinate structure equally, i.e. if the extraction occurs across the board.

(10)   a.   They ordered [tiramisu] and [espresso].
       b.   ***What** did they order [tiramisu] and __?
       c.   ***What** did they order __ and [espresso]?

(11)   a.   Alicia [gave a guitar to me] and [loaned a trumpet to you].
       b.   **What** did Alicia [give __ to me] and [loan __ to you]?

3.6 Complex noun phrase islands

Complex noun phrase islands ban extraction from the clausal complement of a noun, and from a relative clause modifying a noun.

(12)   a.   You heard the rumour that Bill speaks a Balkan language.
       b.   ***What** did you hear the rumour that Bill speaks __?

(13)   a.   They hired someone who cleans a dirty surface.
       b.   ***What dirty surface** did they hire someone who cleans __?

3.7 Object extraction

Object extraction is when a filler-gap dependency involves an object clause or phrase. In contrast to subject islands, object extraction produces acceptable sentences.

(14)   a.   She told me <u>that her mother</u> is a teacher.
       b.   **Her mother**, she told me __, is a teacher.

(15)   a.   It is important to invite <u>Will</u> to our party.
       b.   **Who** is it important to invite __ to our party?

3.8 Non-bridge verb islands

Non-bridge verb islands ban extraction out of that-clause verb complements when the matrix verb is a non-bridge verb. Non-bridge verbs include manner-of-speaking verbs, such as whisper or shout.

(16)   a.   She thinks that he died <u>in his sleep</u>.
       b.   **How** does she think that he died __?

(17)   a.   She whispered that he had died <u>in his sleep</u>.
       b.   *__How__ did she whisper that he had died __?

The unacceptability of non-bridge verb islands hinges on the frequency of the verb (Liu et al., 2019). Therefore, the degree to which different constraints govern its behavior is hotly debated. As such, we do not use this construction when probing for underlying contraint knowledge. However, we do include grammatical variants of this construction (16-b) as acceptable stimuli in our general filler-gap analysis (Section 7.2).

4 Constraints

We analyze four underlying syntactic principles that have been hypothesized to govern the behavior of the above constructions.

4.1 Subjacency

Subjacency (Chomsky, 1973) is defined in terms of the notion of extraction mentioned in the previous section. Syntacticians theorize that a filler is iteratively extracted from its gap site to particular possible landing sites during language production. The subjacency principle states that extraction is only permitted if all landing site positions that intervene between the filler and the gap are unfilled during the extraction process. If the possible structural positions are unavailable because they are filled with another lexical item, extraction is blocked and the resulting filler-gap dependency is deemed ungrammatical. The effect of the subjacency constraint can be observed in the above examples of Wh-islands, subject islands, left branch islands, and complex noun phrase islands.

4.2 Empty Category Principle

The Empty Category Principle (ECP; Kayne, 1980; Chomsky, 1981) is a syntactic constraint that requires a gap be properly governed. To be properly governed, gaps must be identifiable as empty positions in the surface structure of a sentence, which allows a tree structure to "remember" what has happened at earlier stages of a sentence's derivation. Adherence to this constraint makes extraction of a wh-word from a subject or adjunct position ungrammatical, while extraction from an object position or from a coordinate structure island is grammatical.

4.3 L-marking

L-Marking (Chomsky, 1986) is a process that defines the types of categories that act as barriers to movement, including extraction. A category is L-marked if and only if it gets its theta role from a lexical head. A theta role specifies the number and type of arguments that are syntactically required by a particular verb. For example, direct objects in English receive theta roles from the main verb, while adjuncts and subjects do not. Movement is grammatical only when it occurs out of an L-marked phrase, as in object extraction but not in adjunct or subject islands.

4.4 D-linking

Discourse-linking or D-linking (Pesetsky, 1987) indicates that there is a pre-existing contextual relationship between a filler and its associated noun phrase (e.g., *which man*). D-linked phrases contrast with non-discourse linked interrogative pronouns such as *who*, which do not necessarily imply familiar discourse entities. Left branch island extractions and wh-island extractions become more acceptable with a D-linked wh-phrase (Pesetsky, 1987; Atkinson et al., 2015). For example:

(18)   a.   ??**Which book** did Will ask why John read __?

b. *__What__ did Will ask why John read
___?

Since D-linking is an optional feature that can be added to filler-gap constructions, it isn't something that can be violated, per se. Therefore, in our analyses to probe for D-linking knowledge we only test constructions that adhere to D-linking (18-a).

5 Models

We focused in this work on recurrent neural language models with long short-term memory units (LSTMs; Hochreiter and Schmidhuber, 1997). We analyzed five of the highest performing models released by van Schijndel et al. (2019),[4] who showed that these models perform comparably to state-of-the-art transformers GPT and BERT on many simple syntactic agreement tasks. The models are 2-layer LSTMs with 400 hidden units per layer, each with a unique random initialization, trained on 80 million training tokens of English Wikipedia data. Analyzing multiple similar models with different random seeds helps ensure that our results are more representative of a class of models rather than simply revealing how a single exceptional model behaves (e.g., BERT; Devlin et al., 2019). This is very important given the speed with which new individual models supplant each other in the literature. Our results are averaged across all five of our models.

6 Method

We generated 40 sentences per construction type, partitioned into a prime set (15 sentences) and a test set (25 sentences). Sentences are available in the supplementary materials.

We measured model performance as the average surprisal (negative log-probability; Shannon, 1948; Hale, 2001) experienced by a model M when processing each word w_i of each sentence s_j in a set S:

$$\text{perf}(M, S) =$$
$$-\frac{1}{|S|} \sum_{j=1}^{|S|} \frac{1}{|s_j|} \sum_{i=1}^{|s_j|} \log \text{P}_M(w_i \mid w_{0..i-1}) \quad (1)$$

Priming is achieved by giving the model a single training epoch on the set of priming stimuli

<hr>

[4] https://zenodo.org/record/3559340

S_P. This process produces a modified model M'_P whose performance on a test set S_T differs from the original model in a way that gives insight into the representations of the original model. One way to think about this is that pretraining provides a certain kind of model initialization. Priming the model moves the model representations along gradients which are characterized by an interaction of the priming stimuli and the initial pre-trained model state. If a set of priming stimuli has a consistent set of features, the initial state's sensitivity to that set of features can be probed with those stimuli. Following Prasad et al. (2019), we denote this raw effect of priming (also known as adaptation) as:

$$\mathbb{A}(S_T \mid S_P, M) =$$
$$\text{perf}(M, S_T) - \text{perf}(M'_P, S_T) \quad (2)$$

We are actually interested in the interaction between the original model and the priming set, but the above measure also includes the interaction between the original model and the test set. Less expected (more surprising) test constructions can produce larger measures of priming simply because the original model has more room for improvement (Prasad et al., 2019). Therefore, we used linear regression to predict the size of the priming effect using the original model's performance on the test set:

$$\mathbb{A}(S_T \mid S_P, M) \sim \beta_0 + \beta_1 \text{perf}(M, S_T) + \epsilon \quad (3)$$

To obtain a more appropriate *adaptation effect* (AE) for analysis, we subtracted out the predicted linear relation between the original model's test performance and the size of the final priming effect:

$$AE(S_T \mid S_P, M) =$$
$$\mathbb{A}(S_T \mid S_P, M) - \beta_1 \text{perf}(M, S_T) \quad (4)$$

This measure of priming more directly reflects the interaction of the original model with the priming set, normalizing the adaptation effect by each model and prime construction, and producing a comparable measure to that studied by Prasad et al. (2019). Across all analyses, greater values of the adaptation effect indicate greater similarity between adaptation and test structures.

Recently, Kodner and Gupta (2020) have raised concerns about the efficacy of this technique in probing model representations. Specifically, they showed that non-syntactic models can produce qualitative patterns that appear to mimic the effects of syntactic priming. However, their results demonstrate that while the qualitative patterns may be similar, syntactic priming produces much larger effects in syntactic models compared with non-syntactic models. Therefore, their results should not be taken as an indictment of this methodology but simply that reasonable baselines must be employed when using this probing method.

7   Probing for Filler-Gaps

7.1   Null-Prime Baseline

Adaptation effects are difficult to interpret on their own. A positive effect indicates that priming produced more accurate predictions in a given class, while a negative effect indicates the opposite, but the magnitude of the effect is tricky to interpret. Following Prasad et al. (2019), for each analysis we define a class of interest and then compare within-class adaptation effects to cross-class adaptation effects. However, as Kodner and Gupta (2020) point out, spurious correlations may be introduced during stimulus creation/selection. Therefore, we also compare to null-primed models, which use the same original models but we prime them on prime sets whose sentences are shuffled at the word level (as Example (19-b)):

(19)   a.   *__What__ does Sam wonder who solved
          __?

      b.   *Sam wonder What does solved who?

These shuffled null-prime stimuli do not contain any filler-gap dependencies, and so the adaptation effect from null-priming must represent phenomena in which we are not interested (e.g., lexical priming). Our effect-of-interest (filler-gap knowledge) is therefore reflected in any adaptation effect in excess of the null-prime effect.

7.2   Priming Filler-Gap Existence

First we ask whether the models have learned to represent the overall existence of a filler-gap dependency. To test this, we partition our stimuli into wholly acceptable constructions (involving object extraction, bridge verb extraction, and instances of left branch extraction and coordinate structure extraction) and wholly unacceptable constructions (the remaining constructions). We then test whether

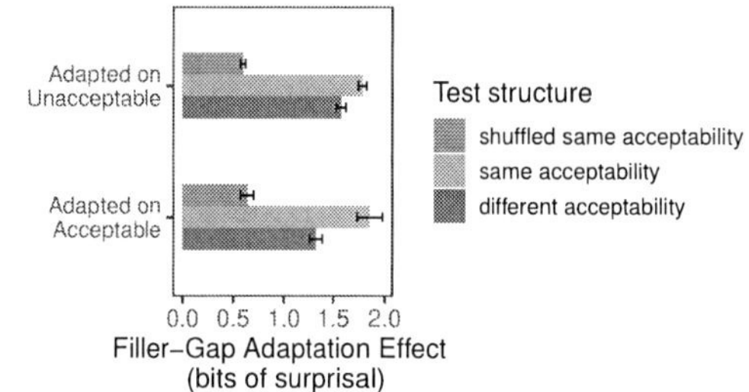

Figure 1: Adaptation effect produced by the existence of a filler-gap dependency. The green bars (top) represent priming a construction type from shuffled instances of similar acceptability. The gold bars (middle) represent the grammatical priming grammatical and ungrammatical priming ungrammatical effect. The pink bars (bottom) represent the acceptable priming unacceptable and vice versa effects.

grammatical constructions can prime ungrammatical constructions and vice versa.

Although at the sentence level, ungrammatical constructions do not have a resolvable filler-gap dependency, that unacceptability only manifests at or near the end of the sentence. From the perspective of our unidirectional models, both sets of sentences initially require the retention of an apparent "filler." We therefore hypothesize that if the models understand filler-gap, both of these sets should initially contain a shared unidirectional representation of filler-gap existence.

We find that grammatical constructions prime ungrammatical constructions beyond the baseline shuffled adaptation effect (Figure 1). In other words, fine-tuning on grammatical items teaches the models how to process ungrammatical items with apparent filler-gap dependencies. We also find that ungrammatical items prime grammatical items in a similar fashion. Since the single unifying feature present in both grammatical and ungrammatical constructions is the presence of an apparent filler-gap dependency, these results suggest that the models contain a representation of filler-gap existence that is shared across constructions.

8   Probing for Filler-Gap Constraints

We next consider constraint-specific priming in order to determine whether the aforementioned abstraction of filler-gap dependency has shared substructure that would indicate understanding of the filler-gap constraints described in Section 4.

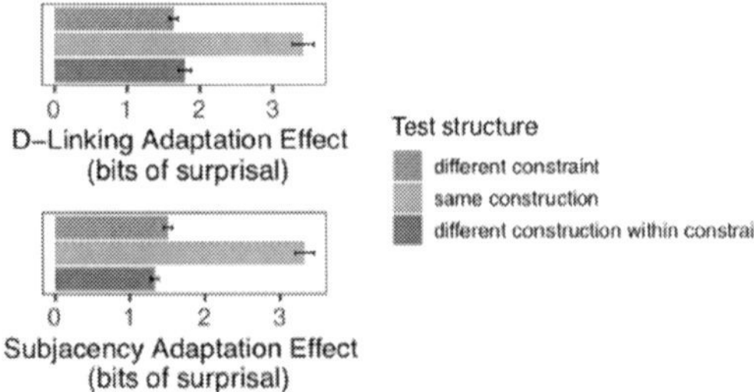

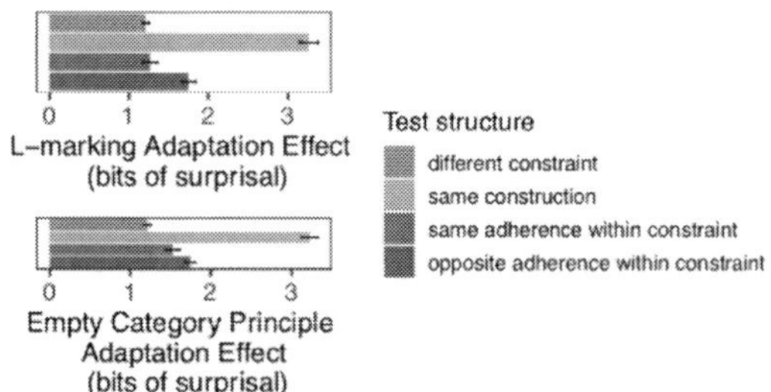

Figure 2: Adaptation effect due to D-linking adherence and Subjacency violation. Green bars (top) represent priming of a construction with constructions from other constraints (indicating general filler-gap priming). Gold bars (middle) represent priming of each construction with other constructions of the same type. Pink bars (bottom) represent priming of each construction with other constructions governed by the same constraint.

Figure 3: Adaptation effect due to L-marking and ECP. Some constructions adhered to these constraints and others violated them. Green bars (top) represent priming of a construction with constructions from other constraints (indicating general filler-gap priming). Gold bars (second from top) represent priming of each construction with other constructions of the same type. Pink bars (third from top) represent adherence priming adherence and violation priming violation. Purple bars (bottom) represent adherence priming violation and vice versa.

8.1 Filler-Gap Existence Baseline

In the previous section, we found that RNNs represent the existence of filler-gap dependencies similarly across construction types. We are therefore interested in whether the models systematically differentiate between filler-gap constructions that are governed by different constraints. If so, we would expect the shared representation of a constraint to produce greater priming within a constraint than across constraints. Therefore, rather than using shuffled sentences, our lower-bound baseline in this section consists of the adaptation effect from priming on sentences that do not share a constraint (green bars). We also use an upper-bound baseline adaptation effect from when models are tested and primed with the same syntactic construction (though the actual sentences differed; gold bars).

8.2 Priming Filler-Gap Constraints

Our results are presented in Figures 2 and 3. We divided our constructions based on those that consistently adhere to or violate particular constraints. If an abstract filler-gap constraint is learned by the model, then constraint adherence should prime adherence in the test set and constraint violation should prime violation in the test set (pink bars). Further, true understanding of a constraint would mean that constraint adherence would prime subsequent adherence more than subsequent violation and vice versa (purple bars reflect adherence priming violation and vice versa).

For subjacency, simple existence of filler-gap primed the model significantly more than other constructions involving subjacency.[5] Adherence to D-linking primed subsequent adherence to D-linking significantly more than simple filler-gap existence did, suggesting that perhaps the models do have an abstract representation of D-linking (but see Section 8.3).

Constructions involving L-marking and ECP produced significantly more priming in the mismatched adherence condition (adherence priming violation; violation priming adherence) than the matched adherence condition (adherence priming adherence; violation priming violation), suggesting that these constraints aren't learned by RNN language models. In fact, matched adherence in L-marking was not significantly different than priming with unrelated filler-gap sentences. Matched adherence in ECP did produce significantly greater priming than filler-gap existence, but since the priming effect was even greater for mismatched adherence, we can conclude that the model did not have an abstract representation of ECP that modulates filler-gap acceptability in a predictable way.

8.3 D-Linking Modulation

Our priming results in the previous subsection suggested that D-linked stimuli prime subsequent D-linking more than simple filler-gap existence does. However, D-linking also has an explicit surface

---

[5]Significance was determined by two-sample t-tests. See Supplementary Materials for details.

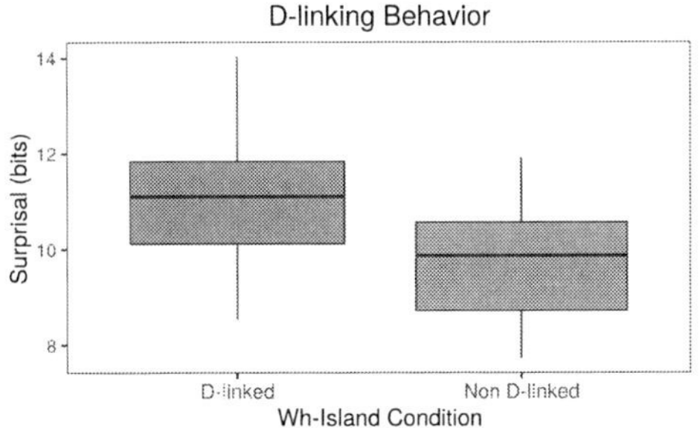

Figure 4: Pretrained model surprisal of D-linked wh-extractions (left) and non-D-linked wh-extractions (right). If the models learned to use D-linking to modulate the acceptability of filler-gap constructions, the surprisal of D-linked constructions should be lower.

cue, sentence-initial 'which', that could produce representational clustering even without an abstract linguistic concept of the constraint. Therefore, in this section, we use a behavioral probe to determine whether the models actually encode the underlying constraint.

As noted above, D-linking increases the acceptability of a filler-gap dependency.

(20)   a.   ??**Which book** did Will ask why John read __?

        b.   ***What** did Will ask why John read __?

At the filler, D-linking provides semantic clues to help predict the gap site (e.g., books will be bought or read but not eaten), and at the gap site D-linking greatly reduces the set of possible referents and eases retrieval of the correct referent both for syntactic attachment of the filler and for comprehension of the sentence (e.g., John did not read a sign or a scroll). We therefore expect that a model that understands D-linking will find D-linked sentences easier to process, similar to humans. We compared model performance (average surprisal; Equation 1) on each set of constructions. If a model uses D-linking in a human-like way, the D-linked sentences (like (20-a)) should produce better performance (be less surprising) than the non-D-linked sentences (like (20-b)).

In contrast to humans, RNNs find D-linked sentences more surprising than non-D-linked ones (Figure 4). In other words, the models prefer the less acceptable filler-gap constructions. These results suggest that the underlying D-linking feature is not learned even in a construction-specific way, let alone in a way that is shared across multiple constructions.

Based on the findings in the current and preceding sections, we conclude that RNN language models do not go beyond representing the existence of filler-gap dependencies to representing any of the shared underlying constraints we studied here.

9   Discussion

Our results support previous behavioral findings that recurrent neural language models acquire some abstract concept of "filler-gap dependency" (Chowdhury and Zamparelli, 2018; Wilcox et al., 2018, 2019), but go farther than those findings by indicating that this concept is representationally shared across different constructions. However, our findings also indicate that RNNs do not encode any of the syntactic filler-gap constraints we studied.

Both grammatical and ungrammatical sentences involving apparent filler-gap dependencies cause models to anticipate the existence of subsequent filler-gap dependencies. However, in two of four cases, the baseline adaptation effect from priming on unrelated filler-gap constructions was comparable to or greater than that from priming on other constructions governed by the same constraint. Constructions that violated ECP and L-marking were represented similarly to constructions that adhered to those same constraints. And models assigned lower probability to sentences involving D-linking than sentences without D-linking, which is the opposite of human results.

Overall, our results provide robust evidence that Chaves (2020) was correct that recurrent neural language models do not fully understand filler-gap constructions. While it is entirely possible that the constraints analyzed in this work do not actually govern filler-gap dependencies (i.e. these particular syntactic theories may be incorrect), we chose four constraints that have been very widely studied by syntacticians precisely because of their broad coverage. Therefore, even if the underlying syntactic theories are incorrect, it is conceivable that RNNs could induce these constraints as plausible abstractions to aid in filler-gap processing. It is therefore striking that RNNs learn none of them.

One might wonder whether our priming sets simply needed to be larger to observe the desired priming effects. Our priming sets consisted of 15 items, which is comparable to the number of priming stimuli used by Prasad et al. (2019) and Kodner and Gupta (2020). Since the constraints we study involve fewer surface cues, they could require more priming data to produce noticable effects. However, our non-baseline adaptation effects were around 1.5 bits, which is much larger than the 0.5-1 bit priming effects seen in those previous studies. Since we are already seeing large priming effects with these constructions, it seems unlikely that increasing the amount of priming data would produce qualitatively different effects.

We selected four common, well-studied filler-gap influences from the syntax literature and tested whether RNNs shared representational features across filler-gap constructions in a way that would suggest they had learned those constraints. While we did find evidence that RNNs encode some general representation of the existence of filler-gap dependencies, we found no evidence for more abstract underlying shared constraints. That is, while we find that RNN language models can learn abstract representations that are shared across constructions, our work raises questions about the depth of such abstractions.

Acknowledgements

We would like to thank Miloje Despić for feedback on the theoretical syntax discussion in this work. We would also like to thank the C.Psyd lab at Cornell for feedback on earlier versions of this work.

References

Emily Atkinson, Aaron Apple, Kyle Rawlins, and Akira Omaki. 2015. Similarity of wh-phrases and acceptability variation in wh-islands. *Frontiers in Psychology*, 6(2048).

Rui Chaves. 2020. What don't RNN language models learn about filler-gap dependencies? In *Proceedings of the Society for Computation in Linguistics (SCiL) 2020*, pages 20–30.

Noam Chomsky. 1973. Conditions on transformations. In S. Anderson and P. Kiparsky, editors, *A Festschrift for Morris Halle*, pages 232–286. Holt, Rinehart & Winston, New York.

Noam Chomsky. 1981. *Lectures on Binding and Government: The Pisa Lectures*. Foris Publications.

Noam Chomsky. 1986. *Barriers*. MIT Press.

Shammur Absar Chowdhury and Roberto Zamparelli. 2018. RNN simulations of grammaticality judg-ments on long-distance dependencies. In *Proceedings of the 27th International Conference on Computational Linguistics*, pages 133–144, Santa Fe, New Mexico, USA. Association for Computational Linguistics.

Forrest Davis and Marten van Schijndel. 2020. Recurrent neural network language models always learn English-like relative clause attachment. In *Proceedings of the 58th Annual Meeting of the Association for Computational Linguistics*, pages 1979–1990, Online. Association for Computational Linguistics.

Jacob Devlin, Ming-Wei Chang, Kenton Lee, and Kristina Toutanova. 2019. BERT: Pre-training of deep bidirectional transformers for language understanding. In *Proceedings of the 2019 Conference of the North American Chapter of the Association for Computational Linguistics: Human Language Technologies, Volume 1 (Long and Short Papers)*, pages 4171–4186, Minneapolis, Minnesota. Association for Computational Linguistics.

John Hale. 2001. A probabilistic Earley parser as a psycholinguistic model. In *Second Meeting of the North American Chapter of the Association for Computational Linguistics*.

Sepp Hochreiter and Jürgen Schmidhuber. 1997. Long short-term memory. *Neural Comput.*, 9(8):1735–1780.

Richard Kayne. 1980. ECP extensions. *Linguistic Inquiry*.

Jordan Kodner and Nitish Gupta. 2020. Overestimation of syntactic representation in neural language models. In *Proceedings of the 58th Annual Meeting of the Association for Computational Linguistics*, pages 1757–1762, Online. Association for Computational Linguistics.

Michael Lepori, Tal Linzen, and R. Thomas McCoy. 2020. Representations of syntax [MASK] useful: Effects of constituency and dependency structure in recursive LSTMs. In *Proceedings of the 58th Annual Meeting of the Association for Computational Linguistics*, pages 3306–3316, Online. Association for Computational Linguistics.

Tal Linzen, Emmanuel Dupoux, and Yoav Goldberg. 2016. Assessing the ability of LSTMs to learn syntax-sensitive dependencies. *Transactions of the Association for Computational Linguistics*, 4:521–535.

Yingtong Liu, Rachel Ryskin, Richard Futrell, and Edward Gibson. 2019. Factive and manner-of-speaking islands are an artifact of nonlinearity in the acceptability judgment task. In *Proceedings of the 32nd Annual CUNY Conference on Human Sentence Processing (CUNY 2019)*.

Tom McCoy, Ellie Pavlick, and Tal Linzen. 2019. Right for the wrong reasons: Diagnosing syntactic heuristics in natural language inference. In *Proceedings of the 57th Annual Meeting of the Association for Computational Linguistics*, pages 3428–3448, Florence, Italy. Association for Computational Linguistics.

David Pesetsky. 1987. Wh-in-situ: movement and unselective binding. *The representation of (in) definiteness*, pages 98–129.

Grusha Prasad, Marten van Schijndel, and Tal Linzen. 2019. Using priming to uncover the organization of syntactic representations in neural language models. In *Proceedings of the 23rd Conference on Computational Natural Language Learning (CoNLL)*, pages 66–76, Hong Kong, China. Association for Computational Linguistics.

John Ross. 1967. *Constraints on variables in syntax.* Ph.D. thesis, Massachusetts Institute of Technology.

Marten van Schijndel and Tal Linzen. 2018. A neural model of adaptation in reading. In *Proceedings of the 2018 Conference on Empirical Methods in Natural Language Processing*, pages 4704–4710, Brussels, Belgium. Association for Computational Linguistics.

Marten van Schijndel, Aaron Mueller, and Tal Linzen. 2019. Quantity doesn't buy quality syntax with neural language models. In *Proceedings of the 2019 Conference on Empirical Methods in Natural Language Processing and the 9th International Joint Conference on Natural Language Processing (EMNLP-IJCNLP)*, pages 5831–5837, Hong Kong, China. Association for Computational Linguistics.

Claude E. Shannon. 1948. The mathematical theory of communication. *Bell Systems Technical Journal*, 27:379–423.

Ethan Wilcox, Roger Levy, and Richard Futrell. 2019. What syntactic structures block dependencies in RNN language models? In *Proceedings of the 41st Annual Meeting of the Cognitive Science Society (CogSci)*, pages 1199–1205.

Ethan Wilcox, Roger Levy, Takashi Morita, and Richard Futrell. 2018. What do RNN language models learn about filler–gap dependencies? In *Proceedings of the 2018 EMNLP Workshop BlackboxNLP: Analyzing and Interpreting Neural Networks for NLP*, pages 211–221, Brussels, Belgium. Association for Computational Linguistics.

Don't Parse, Insert: Multilingual Semantic Parsing with Insertion Based Decoding

Qile Zhu[1]*, Haidar Khan[2], Saleh Soltan[2], Stephen Rawls[2], and Wael Hamza[2]
[1]University of Florida, [2]Amazon Alexa AI
valder@ufl.edu
{khhaida,ssoltan,sterawls,waelhamz}@amazon.com

Abstract

Semantic parsing is one of the key components of natural language understanding systems. A successful parse transforms an input utterance to an action that is easily understood by the system. Many algorithms have been proposed to solve this problem, from conventional rule-based or statistical slot-filling systems to shift-reduce based neural parsers. For complex parsing tasks, the state-of-the-art method is based on autoregressive sequence to sequence models to generate the parse directly. This model is slow at inference time, generating parses in $O(n)$ decoding steps (n is the length of the target sequence). In addition, we demonstrate that this method performs poorly in zero-shot cross-lingual transfer learning settings. In this paper, we propose a non-autoregressive parser which is based on the insertion transformer to overcome these two issues. Our approach 1) speeds up decoding by 3x while outperforming the autoregressive model and 2) significantly improves cross-lingual transfer in the low-resource setting by 37% compared to autoregressive baseline. We test our approach on three well-known monolingual datasets: ATIS, SNIPS and TOP. For cross lingual semantic parsing, we use the MultiATIS++ and the multilingual TOP datasets.

1 Introduction

Given a query, a semantic parsing module identifies not only the *intent* (play music, book a flight) of the query but also extracts necessary *slots* (entities) that further refines the action to perform (which song to play? Where or when to go?). A traditional rule-based or slot-filling system classifies a query with one intent and tags each input token (Mesnil et al., 2013). However, supporting more complex queries that are composed of multiple intents and nested slots is a challenging problem (Gupta et al., 2018).

Gupta et al. (2018) and Einolghozati et al. (2019) propose to use a Shift-Reduce parser based on Recurrent Neural Network for these complex queries. Recently, Rongali et al. (2020) propose directly generating the parse as a formatted sequence and design a unified model based on sequence to sequence generation and pointer networks. Their approach formulates the tagging problem into a generation task in which the target is constructed by combining all the necessary intents and slots in a flat sequence with no restriction on the semantic parse schema.

A relatively unexplored direction is the cross-lingual transfer problem (Duong et al., 2017; Susanto and Lu, 2017), where the parsing system is trained in a high-resource language and transfered directly to a low-resource language (zero-shot).

The state-of-the-art model leverages the autoregressive decoder such as Transformer (Vaswani et al., 2017) and Long-Short-Term Memory (LSTM) (Hochreiter and Schmidhuber, 1997) to generate the target sequence (representing the parse) from left to right. The left to right autoregressive generation constraint has two drawbacks: 1) generating a parse takes $O(n)$ decoding time, where n is the length of the target sequence. This is further exacerbated when paired with standard search algorithms such as beam search. 2) In the cross-lingual setting, autoregressive parsers have difficulty transferring between languages.

A recent direction in machine translation and natural language generation to speed up sequence to sequence models is non-autoregressive decoding (Stern et al., 2019; Gu et al., 2018, 2019). Since the parsing task in the sequence to sequence framework only requires inserting tags rather than generating the whole sequence, an insertion based parser is both faster and more natural for language transfer than an autoregressive parser.

In this paper, we leverage insertion based se-

---

*Work done while interning at Amazon Alexa

Proceedings of the 24th Conference on Computational Natural Language Learning, pages 496–506
Online, November 19-20, 2020. ©2020 Association for Computational Linguistics
https://doi.org/10.18653/v1/P17

quence to sequence models for the semantic parsing problem that require only O(log(n)) decoding time to generate a parse. We enhance the insertion transformer (Stern et al., 2019) with the pointer mechanism, since the entities in the source sequence are ensured to appear in the target sequence. Our non-autoregressive based model can also boost the performance on the zero-shot and few-shot cross-lingual setting, in which the model is trained on a high-resource language and tested on low-resource languages. We also introduce a copy source mechanism for the decoder to further improve the cross lingual transfer performance. In this way, the pointer embedding will be replaced by the corresponding outputs from the encoder. We test our proposed model on several well known datasets, TOP (Gupta et al., 2018), ATIS (Price, 1990), SNIPS (Coucke et al., 2018), MultiATIS++ (Xu et al., 2020) and multilingual TOP (Xia and Monti, 2021).

In summary, the main contributions of our work include:

- To our knowledge, we are the first to apply the non-autoregressive framework to the semantic parsing task. Experiments show that our approach can reduce the decoding steps by 66.7%. By starting generation with the whole source sequence, we can further reduce the number of decoding steps by 82.4%.

- We achieve new state-of-the-art Exact Match (EM) scores on ATIS (89.14), SNIPS (91.00) and TOP (86.74, single model) datasets.

- We introduce a copy encoder outputs mechanism and achieve a significant improvement compared to the autoregressive decoder and sequence labeling on the zero-shot and few-shot setting in cross lingual transfer semantic parsing. Our approach surpasses the autoregressive baseline by 9 EM points on average over both simple (MultiATIS++) and complex (multilingual TOP) queries and matches the performance of the sequence labeling baseline on MultiATIS++.

2 Background

In this section, we introduce the sequence generation via insertion operations and the pretrained models we leverage in our work.

2.1 Sequence Generation Via Insertion

We begin by briefly describing sequence generation via insertion, for a more complete description see (Stern et al., 2019).

Let $x_1, x_2, ..., x_m$ be the source sequence with length m and $y_1, y_2, ..., y_n$ denotes the target sequence with length n. We define the generated sequence h_t at decoding step t. In the autoregressive setting, $h_t = y_{1,2,...,t-1}$. In insertion based decoding, h_t is a subsequence of the target sequence y that preserves order. For example, if the final sequence $y = [A, B, C, D, E]$, then $h_t = [B, E]$ is a valid intermediate subsequence while $h_t = [C, A]$ is an invalid intermediate subsequence.

During decoding step $t + 1$, we insert tokens into h_t. In the previous example, there are three available insertion slots: before token B, between B and E and after E. We always add special tokens such as bos (begin of the sequence) and eos (end of the sequence) to the subsequences. The number of available insertion slots will be $T - 1$ where T is the length of h_t including bos and eos. If we insert one token in all available slots, multiple tokens can be generated in one time step.

In order to predict the token to insert in a slot, we form the representation for each insertion slot by pooling the representations of adjacent tokens. We have $T - 1$ slots for a sequence with length T. Let $r \in \mathbb{R}^{T \times d}$, where T is the sequence length and d denotes the hidden size of the transformer decoder layer. All slots $s \in \mathbb{R}^{(T-1) \times d}$ can be computed as:

$$s = concat(r[1 :], r[: -1]) \cdot W_s, \quad (1)$$

where $r[1 :]$ is the entire sequence representation excluding the first token, $r[: -1]$ is the entire sequence representation excluding the last token and $W_s \in \mathbb{R}^{2d \times d}$ is a trainable projection matrix. We apply $softmax$ to the slot representations to obtain the token probabilities to insert at each slot.

2.2 Pretrained Models

Pretrained language models (Devlin et al., 2019; Liu et al., 2019; Lan et al., 2020; Dong et al., 2019; Peters et al., 2018) have sparked significant progress in a wide variety of natural language processing tasks. The basic idea of these models is to leverage the knowledge from large-scale corpora by using a language modeling objective to learn a representation for tokens and sentences. For downstream tasks, the learned representations are

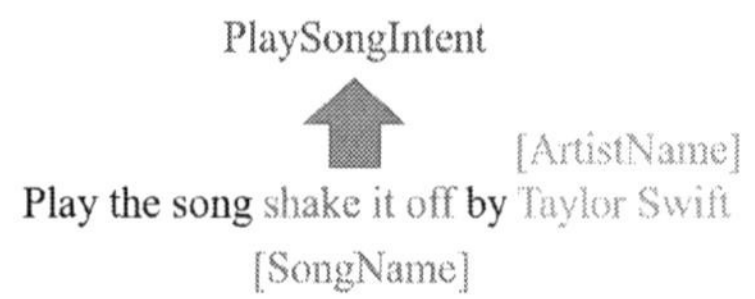

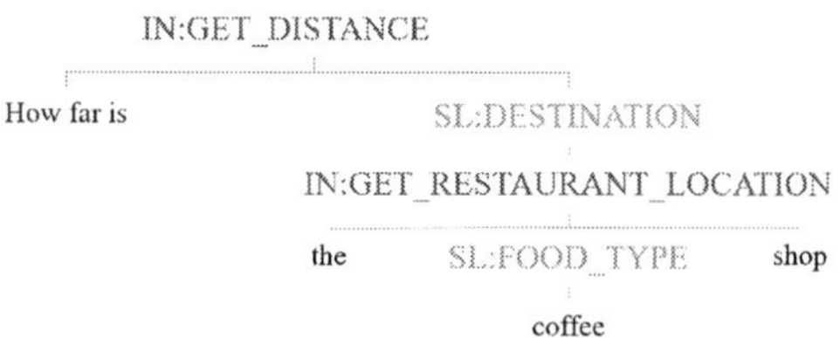

Left: [IN:PS @0 @1 @2 [SL:SName @3 @4 @5 SL:SName] @6 [SL:AName @7 @8 SL:ArName] IN:PS]
Right: [IN:GD @0 @1 @2 [SL:DEST [IN:GRL @3 [SL:FT @4 SL:FT] @5 IN:GRL] SL:DEST] IN:GD]

Figure 1: Example of a simple query (left) and complex query (right). The complex query contains multiple intents and nested slots and can be represented as a tree structure. The two queries are represented as formatted sequences that are treated as the target sequence in the parsing task. IN is the intent, SL is the slot. Source tokens that appear in the target sequence are replaced by pointers with the form @*n* where *n* denotes its location in the source sequence. For complex queries, we can build the parse from top to bottom and left to right.

fine-tuned for the task. This improvement is even more significant when the downstream task has few labeled examples.

We also follow this trend, and use the Transformer (Vaswani et al., 2017) based pretrained language model. We use the RoBERTa base (Liu et al., 2019) (we refer to this model as RoBERTa) as our query encoder to fairly compare with the previous method. This model has the same architecture as BERT base (Devlin et al., 2019) with several modifications during pretraining. It uses a dynamic masking scheme and removes the next sentence prediction task. RoBERTa is also trained with longer sentences and larger batch sizes with more training samples. For the multilingual zero-shot and few-shot semantic parsing task, we use XLM-R (Conneau et al., 2020) and multilingual BERT (Devlin et al., 2019) which are trained on text for more than 100 languages.

3 Methodology

In this section, we introduce our non-autoregressive sequence to sequence model for the semantic parsing problem.

3.1 Query Formulation

To train a sequence to sequence model, we prepare a source sequence and a target sequence. For the task of semantic parsing, the source sequence is the query in natural language. We construct the target sequence following Rongali et al. (2020) and Einolghozati et al. (2019). Tokens in the source sequence that are present in the target sequence are replaced with the special pointer token *ptr-n*, where *n* is the position of that token in the source sequence. By using pointers in the decoder, we can drastically reduce the vocabulary size. We follow previous work and use symmetrical tags for *intents* and *slots*. Fig. 1 shows two examples, a simple query and a complex query with the corresponding target sequences. This formulation is also able to express other tagging problems like named entity recognition (NER).

3.2 Insertion Transformer

We use the insertion transformer (Stern et al., 2019) as the base framework for the decoder. The insertion transformer is a modification of the original transformer decoder architecture (Vaswani et al., 2017). The original transformer decoder predicts the next token based on the previously generated sequence while the insertion transformer can predict tokens for all the available slots. In this setup, tokens in the decoder side can attend to the entire sequence instead of only their left side. This means we remove the causal self-attention mask in the original decoder.

3.2.1 Pointer Network with Copy

Pointer Network: In the normal sequence to sequence model, target tokens are generated by feeding the final representations (decoder hidden states) through a feed-forward layer and applying a softmax function over the whole target vocabulary. This is slow when the vocabulary size is large (Yang et al., 2018). In parsing, the entities in the source sequence will always appear in the target sequence. We can leverage the pointer mechanism (Vinyals et al., 2015) to reduce the target vocabulary size by dividing the vocabulary into two types: *tokens* that are the parsing symbols like intent and slot names, and *pointers* to words in the source sequence.

Since we have two kinds of target tokens, we use

two slightly different ways to obtain unnormalized probabilities for each type. For the tokens in the tagging vocabulary, we feed the hidden states generated by the insertion transformer and slot pooling to a dense layer to produce the logits of size V (tagging vocabulary). The tagging vocabulary contains only the parse symbols like intents and slots together with several special tokens such as *bos*, *eos*, the padding and unknown token. For the pointers, we compute the scaled dot product attention scores between the slot representation and the encoder output. The attention scores will be computed as

$$a(Q, K) = \frac{QK^T}{\sqrt{h}}, \tag{2}$$

where query (Q) is the slot representation, the encoder outputs would be the key (K) and h is the hidden size of the query. Since the hidden size of encoder and decoder may be different, we also do a projection of query and key to the same dimension with two dense layers. Notice that the length of attention scores follows the length of the source sequence. Concatenating the attention scores with size n and the logits for the tagging vocabulary (V), we get the unnormalized distribution over $V + n$ tokens. We apply the $softmax$ function to obtain the final distribution over these tokens.

Copy Mechanism: Rongali et al. (2020) use a set of special embeddings to represent pointer tokens. This is a problem because the pointer embedding cannot encode semantic information since it points to different words across examples. Instead, we reuse the encoder output that the pointer token points to. Without copying, the special pointer embedding would learn a special position based representation for the source language that is hard to transfer to other languages.

3.3 Training and Loss

Training the insertion decoder requires sampling source and target sequences from the training data. We randomly sample valid subsequences from the target sequence to mimic intermediate insertion steps. We first sample a length $k \in [0, n]$ for the subsequence, where n is the length of the target sequence (here n excludes the *bos* and *eos* tokens). We select k tokens from the target sequence and maintain the original ordering. This sampling helps the model learn to insert tokens from the initial generation state as well as intermediate generation.

The insertion transformer can do parallel decoding since we can insert tokens in all available insertion slots. However, for each insertion slot, there may be multiple candidate tokens that can be inserted. For example, given a target sequence $[A, B, C, D, E]$ and a valid subsequence $[A, E]$, the candidates for the slot between token A and E are B, C, D. We use the two different weighting schemes proposed in Stern et al. (2019): uniform weights and balanced binary tree weights.

Binary Tree Weights: The motivation for applying binary tree weighting is to make the decoding time nearly O(log(n)). Consider the example of sequence A, B, C, D, E again, the desired order of generation would be $[bos, eos] \rightarrow [bos, C, eos] \rightarrow [bos, A, C, E, eos] \rightarrow [bos, A, B, C, D, E, eos]$. To achieve this goal, we weight the candidates according to their positions. For the sequence above, candidates in the span of $[bos, eos]$ are A, B, C, D, E. We assign token C the highest weight, then lower weights for B, D and the lowest weights for A, E.

Given a sampled subsequence with length $k + 1$, we have k insertion slots at location $l = (0, 1, ..., k - 1)$. Let $c_{l_0}, ... c_{l_i}$ be the candidates for one location l. We can define a distance function d_j for each token j in the candidates of l:

$$d_l(j) = |j - \frac{i}{2}|, \tag{3}$$

where i is the number of candidates in the location l. We then use the negative distance to compute the softmax based weighting (Rusu et al., 2016; Norouzi et al., 2016):

$$w_l(j) = \frac{exp(-d_l(j)/\tau)}{\sum_{m=0}^{i} exp(-d_l(m)/\tau)}. \tag{4}$$

Where τ is the temperature hyperparameter which allows us to control the sharpness of the weight distribution.

Uniform Weights: Instead of encouraging the model to follow a tree structure generation order, we can also treat the candidates equally. This performs better than the binary tree weights when we input the whole source sequence to the decoder as the initial sequence. In this case, we only need to insert the tagging tokens; the number of candidates is not as large as from scratch ($[bos, eos]$). This uniform weighting can be easily done by taking $\tau \rightarrow \infty$.

Loss Function: The autoregressive sequence to sequence model uses the negative log-likelihood loss since in each decoding step, there is only one ground-truth label. However, in our approach, we have multiple candidates for each insertion slot. Therefore, we use the KL-divergence between the predicted token distribution and the ground truth distribution. Then the loss for insertion slot l is:

$$L_{slot}(x, h_t, l) = D_{KL}((p_l|(x, h_t))\|g_l), \quad (5)$$

where p_l is the distribution output by the decoder and g_l is the target distribution where we set the probability to 0 for tokens that are not candidates. Note that the ground truth distribution depends on the weighting scheme for generation.

Finally, we have the complete loss averaged over all the insertion slots:

$$L(x, h_t) = \frac{1}{k+1} \sum_{l=0}^{k} L_{slot}(x, h_t, l) \quad (6)$$

3.4 Termination Strategy

Terminating generation for insertion based decoding is not as straightforward as autoregressive decoding, which only needs the no-insertion token to be predicted. Insertion decoding requires a similar mechanism for every insertion slot. When computing the slot-loss above, if there are no candidates for the slot we set the ground truth label as the no-insertion token. At inference time, we can stop decoding when all available slots predict the no-insertion token. However, there is a problem when combining the sampling method and this termination strategy. The no-insertion token is more frequent compared with other tokens. The same situation is also encountered in (Stern et al., 2019). This is solved by adding a penalty hyperparameter to control the sequence length generated by the decoder. The hyperparameter is simply a scalar subtracted from the log probability of the no-insertion token for each insertion slot during inference. By doing this, we set a threshold for the difference between the no-insertion token and the second-best choice.

4 Experiments

In this section, we introduce the datasets and baseline models we experiment with. Then we report the results of monolingual experiments and cross lingual transfer learning experiments.

4.1 Datasets

4.1.1 SNIPS

The SNIPS dataset (Coucke et al., 2018) is a public dataset aimed to improve the semantic parsing models. It contains seven different intents: SearchCreativeWork, GetWeather, BookRestaurant, PlayMusic, AddToPlaylist, RateBook, and SearchScreeningEvent. For each intent, there are about 2000 training samples and 100 test samples. The SNIPS dataset consists of only simple queries.

4.1.2 ATIS

The Airline Travel Information System (ATIS) (Price, 1990) dataset was originally collected in the early 90s. The utterances are transcribed from the audio recordings of flight reservation calls. Similar to SNIPS, it consists of only simple queries. ATIS contains seventeen different intents. However, nearly 70% of the queries are the FLIGHT intent.

Recently, a multilingual version of ATIS called MultiATIS++ is introduced by Xu (2020). It is an extension of the Multilingual ATIS (Upadhyay et al., 2018). Besides the original three languages (English, Hindi and Turkish), MultiATIS++ adds six new languages including Spanish, German, Chinese, Japanese, Portuguese and French annotated by human experts and consists of a total of 37,084 training samples and 7,859 test samples. We exclude Turkish in our experiments as the test set size is limited.

4.1.3 TOP

Since ATIS and SNIPS contain only simple queries, the Facebook Task Oriented Parsing (TOP) dataset (Gupta et al., 2018) was introduced for complex hierarchical and nested queries that are more challenging. The dataset contains around 45,000 annotated queries with 25 intents and 36 slots. They further split them into training (31,000), validation (5,000) and test (9,000). As shown in Fig. 1, the nested slots make it harder to parse using a simple sequence tagging model. We also do experiments on multilingual TOP (Xia and Monti, 2021) with Italian and Japanese data. In this dataset, the training and validation set is machine translated while the test set is annotated by human experts.

4.2 Baseline Models

Monolingual Baselines: For monolingual experiments, we select the algorithms reported in Rongali et al. (2020) as baselines for ATIS and SNIPS.

Method	TOP		ATIS		SNIPS	
	EM	IC	EM	IC	EM	IC
Joint BiRNN (Hakkani-Tür et al., 2016)	-	-	80.70	92.60	73.20	96.90
Attention BiRNN (Liu and Lane, 2016)	-	-	78.90	91.10	74.10	96.70
Slot Gated Full Attention (Goo et al., 2018)	-	-	82.20	93.60	75.50	97.00
CapsuleNlU (Zhang et al., 2019)	-	-	83.40	95.00	80.90	97.30
SR(S)+ELMO+SVMRank (Gupta et al., 2018)	83.93	-	-	-	-	-
SR(E)+ELMO+SVMRank (Gupta et al., 2018)	**87.25**	-	-	-	-	-
AR-S2S-PTR (paper) (Rongali et al., 2020)	86.67	98.13	87.12	**97.42**	87.14	98.00
AR-S2S-PTR (reproduce) (Rongali et al., 2020)	85.67	98.17	88.91	97.09	90.71	**98.43**
IT-S2S-PTR ($\tau = 1$)	**86.74**	98.47	**89.14**	97.31	**91.00**	**98.43**
IT-S2S-PTR (input-src, uniform)	85.41	**98.71**	-	-	-	-

Table 1: Exact Match and Intent Classification scores for on the test set. Input-src means the initial input of the decoder is the whole source sequence. For the shift reduce parsing models, E denotes the ensemble model and S is the single model.

Model	Avg. steps	# tokens generated per step								
		1	2	3	4	5	6	7	8	9
AR-S2S-PTR	17.7	1	1	1	1	1	1	1	1	1
IT-S2S-PTR	5.9	1.0	2.0	3.96	6.66	6.24	3.17	1.6	1.4	1.2
IT-S2S-PTR(input-src)	**3.1**	4.99	2.92	1.37	1.00	0.54	0.27	0.25	1.0	1.0

Table 2: Decoding statistics on the TOP dataset. Average target sequence length of TOP is 17.7 tokens, we see that the insertion based parser can fully utilize binary tree decoding. "input-src" means we set the whole source sequence as the initial decoder state.

Two of them leverage the power of RNNs: with attention (Liu and Lane, 2016) and without attention (Hakkani-Tür et al., 2016). Another model works completely with attention (Goo et al., 2018). A Capsule Networks based model is also included (Zhang et al., 2019). Finally, we compare with the autoregressive sequence to sequence with pointer model which is most recent (Rongali et al., 2020). Simple tagging based models cannot easily handle the complex queries in the TOP dataset. For the TOP dataset, we compare with two previous models, a shift reduce parsing model (Gupta et al., 2018) and the autoregressive sequence to sequence model (Rongali et al., 2020). For all monolingual experiments, we use RoBERTa as our pretrained encoder (Liu et al., 2019).

Cross lingual Baselines: For multilingual experiments (zero-shot and few-shot), we use a sequence labelling model based on multilingual BERT and an autoregressive sequence to sequence model (Rongali et al., 2020) as our baseline. To make fair comparasion, we also use the copy source mechanism in the AR model. For sequence labeling, instead of using F1 score, we also use the exact

match (EM) which requires all intents and slots are labeled correctly by the model.

4.3 Results

4.3.1 Model Configuration

We use the pretrained RoBERTa and mBERT as the encoder for our model. For the decoder side, we use 4 layers with 12 heads transformer decoder. The hidden size of the decoder is the same as the embedding size of the pretrained encoder. For optimization, we use Adam (Kingma and Ba, 2015) with $\beta_1 = 0.9$ and $\beta_2 = 0.98$, paired with the Noam learning rate (initialized with 0.15) scheduler (Vaswani et al., 2017) with 500 warmup steps. For cross-lingual experiments, we freeze the encoder's embedding layer.

4.3.2 Monolingual Results

We use the exact match (EM) accuracy as the main metric to measure the performance of different models. By using EM, the entire parsing sequence predicted by the model has to match the reference sequence, since it's not easy to apply the F1 score or semantic error rate (Thomson et al., 2012) to

	en	es	pt	de	fr	hi	zh	ja*	avg
IT-S2S-PTR	**87.23**	**50.06**	**39.30**	**39.46**	**46.78**	11.42	**28.72**	12.60	32.69
AR-S2S-PTR	86.83	40.72	33.38	34.00	17.22	7.45	23.74	10.04	23.77
mBERT	86.33	48.46	38.56	39.12	42.98	**15.22**	21.89	**23.29**	32.78

Table 3: Zero-shot cross lingual EM scores by our approach (IT), autoregressive baseline (AR) and sequence labeling baseline (mBERT). Results are averaged over four random seeds. For our approach, we initialize the decoder with source sequences. * indicates that the data format for the language is not consistent with the S2S model tokenizer.

	en	it	ja
IT-S2S-PTR	84.61	50.07	3.64
AR-S2S-PTR	**85.4**	41.06	0.64

Table 4: Zero-shot EM scores on multilingual TOP dataset. Model is trained on English only.

complex queries. It's better to use the EM here for both simple and complex queries. We also report the intent classification accuracy for our models.

Main Result: Table 1 shows the results from monolingual experiments on three datasets: TOP, ATIS and SNIPS. Our insertion transformer with pointer achieves new state-of-the-art performance on ATIS and SNIPS under EM metric. For TOP dataset, our model matches the best performance reported for single models (AR-S2S-PTR) despite being 3x faster.

We also experiment with starting generation with the entire source sequence as the initial state of the decoder. The performance degrades slightly in this case, possibly due to a training/inference mismatch in this setting. This degradation is likely due to training the model to generate the entire target sequence but only asking the model to generate tags during inference.

Decoding Steps: Since our approach can do parallel decoding, the number of decoding steps is only $O(\log(n))$. Table 2 shows the statistics for the average decoding steps for the TOP dataset and the number of generated tokens per step. The insertion transformer with pointer only needs 5.9 steps while the autoregressive needs 17.7, resulting in a 3x speedup with insertion decoding. The decoding steps can be further reduced to 3.1 when we start decoding with the source sequence as the initial sequence for the decoder. Theoretically, a perfect binary tree based insertion model should generate 2^{n-1} tokens for the n_{th} decoding step. We can see

that our approach can make full use of the parallel decoding during the first three steps, since the average length of TOP's test samples is only 17.7.

Weighting Strategy: We do experiments on both binary tree weighting and uniform weighting for the TOP dataset. We set $\tau \in [0.5, 1.0, 1.5, 2.0]$ and find 1.0 performs best. Binary tree weights are better than uniform in the setting of decoding from scratch. However, uniform performs better when we decode from the whole source sequence.

4.3.3 Cross Lingual Transfer Results

For MultiATIS++, we train on English training data and test on all languages. Table 3 shows the results of our approach compared to the autoregressive and sequence labeling baselines. We find that:

- Our approach outperforms the baseline on most of the languages except Hindi and Japanese. For Japanese, we found inconsistencies in the tokenizer that is the likely cause of the degradation [1].

- The autoregressive baseline performs poorly on cross lingual experiments. For example, it only achieves 17.22 EM on the French test set while the other two systems achieve > 40 EM. This highlights the weakness of autoregressive parsers that cannot produce parses directly from the encoded representations of the source sequence.

- The order of the sentence in Hindi and Japanese is different from others, this may limit the performance of transfer learning for S2S parsers.

We also test on the multilingual TOP dataset (Xia and Monti, 2021), which extends the TOP datasets

---

[1] Chinese is tokenized at the character level in mBERT, while Katakana/Hiragana are tokenized with whitespace. Data in MultiATIS++ is mixed in these two fashions.

# samples	IT-S2S-PTR				AR-S2S-PTR			
	0	10	50	100	0	10	50	100
it	**50.07**	50.13	52.69	**56.42**	41.06	42.23	44.98	46.96
ja	**3.64**	4.7	18.01	**18.96**	0.64	1.73	10.78	18.56

Table 5: Few-shot EM scores on multilingual TOP dataset with model pretrained on English. Training samples used in few-shot are sampled from the test set and excluded during testing.

to other languages providing human annotated Italian and Japanese test sets. TOP contains a much larger test set compared to ATIS. Table 4 shows the zero-shot results and Table 5 shows the few-shot results.

In the zero-shot setting, our approach achieves 50.07 EM score for Italian while AR only achieves 41.06. Both models are unable to achieve good performance in the zero-shot setting for Japanese. We speculate on this behavior in the few-shot experiment results.

In the few shot setting, we finetune the model in two stages, first on the entire English data and then with 10, 50, 100 training samples from other languages. Our approach outperforms the AR baseline in all few shot settings. For Italian, increasing training samples from 10 to 100 does not result in much gain, since the knowledge from English can readily be transferred to Italian, probably due to the similarity of the languages. To further improve the performance on Italian, the model may need many more training samples. However, for Japanese little knowledge (like word order) can be transferred from English so both models can perform as if training from scratch. There may be two reasons here: 1) the order of a sentence is different from English. 2) the annotated target is aligned with the original words in the multilingual TOP so the order of pointers are mixed. Thus, we see the EM scores improves drastically as the number of training samples increases.

4.4 Ablation Study

For ablation study, we separate the experiments to monolingual and multilingual as above. For multilingual experiments, we use the Italian from multilingual TOP dataset.

From Table 6, we observe that the copy mechanism improves performance in the monolingual setting. For the hyperparameter τ, recall that a higher value for τ would result in flatter (more uniform) weights for the candidates. $\tau = 1.0$ provides

	EM
IT-S2S-PTR	86.74
$\tau = 0.1$	74.84
$\tau = 0.5$	85.47
$\tau = 1.0$	**86.74**
$\tau = 1.5$	86.33
no copy	86.09

Table 6: The ablation study for the τ parameter and copy source embedding vector vs. no copy in the monolingual setting. Results on the TOP dataset show the importance of copying source embeddings. We also observe that small values of τ (i.e. weighting the central token for insertion heavily) degrade performance.

Models	EM
IT-S2S-PTR-Best	50.07
- copy	47.00
- input-src	42.03
AR-S2S-PTR-BEST	41.06
- copy	30.87

Table 7: The ablation study for source embedding copying and starting generation from source tokens in the cross-lingual setting. Results are zero-shot in Italian. For the IT-S2S model, both copying and starting generation with source tokens contribute to zero-shot performance

the best balance between equally weighting the candidates and weighting the next token to be inserted heavily. However, we find that when initializing the decoder with source sequences, uniform weights performs better than binary tree weights.

For cross-lingual experiments, we introduce two components to improve the performance. Table 7 shows that both of them help in the zero-shot transfer setting. From the results, we can observe that initializing the decoder with the source sequence plays an important role in zero-shot transfer, which is impossible for the autoregressive based models. The copy mechanism is again beneficial for both the sequence to sequence models, improving the performance of even the autoregressive model from 30.87 EM to 41.06 EM in the zero-shot Italian experiment.

5   Related Work

Monolingual Semantic Parsing: The task oriented semantic parsing for intent classification and slot detection is usually achieved by sequence labeling. Normally, the system will first classify the query based on the sentence level semantic and then label each word in the query. Conditional Random Fields (CRFs) (Peters et al., 2018; Lan et al., 2020; Jiao et al., 2006) is one of the most successful algorithms applied to this task before deep learning dominated the area. Deep learning algorithms boost the performance of semantic parsing, especially using recurrent neural networks (Liu and Lane, 2016; Hakkani-Tür et al., 2016). Other architectures are also explored, such as convolutional neural networks (Kim, 2014) and capsule networks (Zhang et al., 2019).

Cross Lingual Transfer Semantic Parsing: Multilingual natural language understanding has been studied in a variety of tasks including part-of-speech (POS) tagging (Plank and Agić, 2018; Yarowsky et al., 2001; Täckström et al., 2013), named entity recognition (Zirikly and Hagiwara, 2015; Tsai et al., 2016; Xie et al., 2018) and semantic parsing (Xu et al., 2020). Before the advent of pretrained cross-lingual language models, researchers leveraged the representations learned by multilingual neural machine translation (NMT). Another approach is to use NMT to translate between the source language and the target language. However, it is challenging for the sequence tagging tasks: labels on the source language need to be projected on the translated sentences (Xu et al., 2020). Pretrained cross-lingual language models (Devlin et al., 2019; CONNEAU and Lample, 2019) achieve great success in various multilingual natural language tasks.

6   Conclusion

In this paper, we tackle two shortcomings of the autoregressive sequence to sequence semantic parsing models: 1) expensive decoding and 2) poor cross-lingual performance.

We propose 1) insertion transformer with pointers and 2) a copy mechanism which replaces the pointer embeding with corresponding encoder out-puts, to mitigate these two problems. Our model can achieve O(log(n)) decoding time with parallel decoding. For the specific task of semantic parsing, we can further reduce the decoding steps by initializing the decoder sequence with the whole source sequence. Our model achieves new state-of-the-art performance on both simple queries (ATIS and SNIPS) and complex queries (TOP). In cross-lingual transfer, our approach surpasses the baselines in the zero-shot setting by 9 EM points on average across 9 languages.

Acknowledgements

We thank the reviewers for their excellent feedback. Special thanks also to Emilio Monti and Menglin Xia for their help with the multilingual TOP dataset.

References

Alexis Conneau, Kartikay Khandelwal, Naman Goyal, Vishrav Chaudhary, Guillaume Wenzek, Francisco Guzmán, Edouard Grave, Myle Ott, Luke Zettlemoyer, and Veselin Stoyanov. 2020. Unsupervised cross-lingual representation learning at scale. In *Proceedings of the 58th Annual Meeting of the Association for Computational Linguistics*, pages 8440–8451, Online. Association for Computational Linguistics.

Alexis CONNEAU and Guillaume Lample. 2019. Cross-lingual language model pretraining. In H. Wallach, H. Larochelle, A. Beygelzimer, F. d'Alché-Buc, E. Fox, and R. Garnett, editors, *Advances in Neural Information Processing Systems 32*, pages 7059–7069. Curran Associates, Inc.

Alice Coucke, Alaa Saade, Adrien Ball, Théodore Bluche, Alexandre Caulier, David Leroy, Clément Doumouro, Thibault Gisselbrecht, Francesco Caltagirone, Thibaut Lavril, Maël Primet, and Joseph Dureau. 2018. Snips voice platform: an embedded spoken language understanding system for private-by-design voice interfaces. *CoRR*, abs/1805.10190.

Jacob Devlin, Ming-Wei Chang, Kenton Lee, and Kristina Toutanova. 2019. BERT: pre-training of deep bidirectional transformers for language understanding. In *Proceedings of the 2019 Conference of the North American Chapter of the Association for Computational Linguistics: Human Language Technologies, NAACL-HLT 2019, Minneapolis, MN, USA, June 2-7, 2019, Volume 1 (Long and Short Papers)*, pages 4171–4186. Association for Computational Linguistics.

Li Dong, Nan Yang, Wenhui Wang, Furu Wei, Xiaodong Liu, Yu Wang, Jianfeng Gao, Ming Zhou, and Hsiao-Wuen Hon. 2019. Unified language model pre-training for natural language understanding and generation. In *Advances in Neural Information Processing Systems*, pages 13042–13054.

Long Duong, Hadi Afshar, Dominique Estival, Glen Pink, Philip R Cohen, and Mark Johnson. 2017. Multilingual semantic parsing and code-switching. In *Proceedings of the 21st Conference on Computational Natural Language Learning (CoNLL 2017)*, pages 379–389.

Arash Einolghozati, Panupong Pasupat, Sonal Gupta, Rushin Shah, Mrinal Mohit, Mike Lewis, and Luke Zettlemoyer. 2019. Improving semantic parsing for task oriented dialog. *CoRR*, abs/1902.06000.

Chih-Wen Goo, Guang Gao, Yun-Kai Hsu, Chih-Li Huo, Tsung-Chieh Chen, Keng-Wei Hsu, and Yun-Nung Chen. 2018. Slot-gated modeling for joint slot filling and intent prediction. In *Proceedings of the 2018 Conference of the North American Chapter of the Association for Computational Linguistics: Human Language Technologies, Volume 2 (Short Papers)*, pages 753–757.

Jiatao Gu, James Bradbury, Caiming Xiong, Victor O.K. Li, and Richard Socher. 2018. Non-autoregressive neural machine translation. In *International Conference on Learning Representations*.

Jiatao Gu, Changhan Wang, and Junbo Zhao. 2019. Levenshtein transformer. In *Advances in Neural Information Processing Systems*, pages 11181–11191.

Sonal Gupta, Rushin Shah, Mrinal Mohit, Anuj Kumar, and Mike Lewis. 2018. Semantic parsing for task oriented dialog using hierarchical representations. In *Proceedings of the 2018 Conference on Empirical Methods in Natural Language Processing*, pages 2787–2792.

D. Hakkani-Tür, G. Tür, A. Çelikyilmaz, Yun-Nung Chen, Jianfeng Gao, L. Deng, and Ye-Yi Wang. 2016. Multi-domain joint semantic frame parsing using bi-directional rnn-lstm. In *INTERSPEECH*.

Sepp Hochreiter and Jürgen Schmidhuber. 1997. Long short-term memory. *Neural computation*, 9(8):1735–1780.

Feng Jiao, Shaojun Wang, Chi-Hoon Lee, Russell Greiner, and Dale Schuurmans. 2006. Semi-supervised conditional random fields for improved sequence segmentation and labeling. In *Proceedings of the 21st International Conference on Computational Linguistics and 44th Annual Meeting of the Association for Computational Linguistics*, pages 209–216, Sydney, Australia. Association for Computational Linguistics.

Yoon Kim. 2014. Convolutional neural networks for sentence classification. In *Proceedings of the 2014 Conference on Empirical Methods in Natural Language Processing (EMNLP)*, pages 1746–1751, Doha, Qatar. Association for Computational Linguistics.

Diederik P. Kingma and Jimmy Ba. 2015. Adam: A method for stochastic optimization. In *3rd International Conference on Learning Representations, ICLR 2015, San Diego, CA, USA, May 7-9, 2015, Conference Track Proceedings*.

Zhenzhong Lan, Mingda Chen, Sebastian Goodman, Kevin Gimpel, Piyush Sharma, and Radu Soricut. 2020. ALBERT: a lite BERT for self-supervised learning of language representations. In *International Conference on Learning Representations*.

Bing Liu and Ian Lane. 2016. Attention-based recurrent neural network models for joint intent detection and slot filling. In *Interspeech 2016, 17th Annual Conference of the International Speech Communication Association, San Francisco, CA, USA, September 8-12, 2016*, pages 685–689. ISCA.

Yinhan Liu, Myle Ott, Naman Goyal, Jingfei Du, Mandar Joshi, Danqi Chen, Omer Levy, Mike Lewis, Luke Zettlemoyer, and Veselin Stoyanov. 2019. RoBERTa: A robustly optimized BERT pretraining approach. *CoRR*, abs/1907.11692.

Grégoire Mesnil, Xiaodong He, Li Deng, and Yoshua Bengio. 2013. Investigation of recurrent-neural-network architectures and learning methods for spoken language understanding. In *Interspeech*, pages 3771–3775.

Mohammad Norouzi, Samy Bengio, Navdeep Jaitly, Mike Schuster, Yonghui Wu, Dale Schuurmans, et al. 2016. Reward augmented maximum likelihood for neural structured prediction. In *Advances In Neural Information Processing Systems*, pages 1723–1731.

Matthew Peters, Mark Neumann, Mohit Iyyer, Matt Gardner, Christopher Clark, Kenton Lee, and Luke Zettlemoyer. 2018. Deep contextualized word representations. In *Proceedings of the 2018 Conference of the North American Chapter of the Association for Computational Linguistics: Human Language Technologies, Volume 1 (Long Papers)*, pages 2227–2237, New Orleans, Louisiana. Association for Computational Linguistics.

Barbara Plank and Željko Agić. 2018. Distant supervision from disparate sources for low-resource part-of-speech tagging. In *Proceedings of the 2018 Conference on Empirical Methods in Natural Language Processing*, pages 614–620, Brussels, Belgium. Association for Computational Linguistics.

Patti Price. 1990. Evaluation of spoken language systems: The ATIS domain. In *Speech and Natural Language: Proceedings of a Workshop Held at Hidden Valley, Pennsylvania, June 24-27, 1990*.

Subendhu Rongali, Luca Soldaini, Emilio Monti, and Wael Hamza. 2020. Don't parse, generate! a sequence to sequence architecture for task-oriented semantic parsing. In *Proceedings of The Web Conference 2020*, pages 2962–2968.

Andrei A. Rusu, Sergio Gomez Colmenarejo, Çaglar Gülçehre, Guillaume Desjardins, James Kirkpatrick, Razvan Pascanu, Volodymyr Mnih, Koray Kavukcuoglu, and Raia Hadsell. 2016. Policy distillation. In *4th International Conference on Learning Representations, ICLR 2016, San Juan, Puerto Rico, May 2-4, 2016, Conference Track Proceedings*.

Mitchell Stern, William Chan, Jamie Kiros, and Jakob Uszkoreit. 2019. Insertion transformer: Flexible sequence generation via insertion operations. In *ICML*.

Raymond Hendy Susanto and Wei Lu. 2017. Neural architectures for multilingual semantic parsing. In *Proceedings of the 55th Annual Meeting of the Association for Computational Linguistics (Volume 2: Short Papers)*, pages 38–44.

Oscar Täckström, Dipanjan Das, Slav Petrov, Ryan McDonald, and Joakim Nivre. 2013. Token and type constraints for cross-lingual part-of-speech tagging. *Transactions of the Association for Computational Linguistics*, 1:1–12.

Blaise Thomson, Milica Gasic, Matthew Henderson, Pirros Tsiakoulis, and Steve Young. 2012. N-best error simulation for training spoken dialogue systems. In *2012 IEEE Spoken Language Technology Workshop (SLT)*, pages 37–42. IEEE.

Chen-Tse Tsai, Stephen Mayhew, and Dan Roth. 2016. Cross-lingual named entity recognition via wikification. In *Proceedings of The 20th SIGNLL Conference on Computational Natural Language Learning*, pages 219–228, Berlin, Germany. Association for Computational Linguistics.

Shyam Upadhyay, Manaal Faruqui, Gokhan Tür, Hakkani-Tür Dilek, and Larry Heck. 2018. (almost) zero-shot cross-lingual spoken language understanding. In *2018 IEEE International Conference on Acoustics, Speech and Signal Processing (ICASSP)*, pages 6034–6038. IEEE.

Ashish Vaswani, Noam Shazeer, Niki Parmar, Jakob Uszkoreit, Llion Jones, Aidan N Gomez, Łukasz Kaiser, and Illia Polosukhin. 2017. Attention is all you need. In *Advances in neural information processing systems*, pages 5998–6008.

Oriol Vinyals, Meire Fortunato, and Navdeep Jaitly. 2015. Pointer networks. In *Advances in neural information processing systems*, pages 2692–2700.

Menglin Xia and Emilio Monti. 2021. Multilingual neural semantic parsing with pretrained encoders. In *Proceedings of the 16th European Chapter of the Association for Computational Linguistics*. Submitted.

Jiateng Xie, Zhilin Yang, Graham Neubig, Noah A. Smith, and Jaime Carbonell. 2018. Neural cross-lingual named entity recognition with minimal resources. In *Proceedings of the 2018 Conference on Empirical Methods in Natural Language Processing*, pages 369–379, Brussels, Belgium. Association for Computational Linguistics.

Weijia Xu, Batool Haider, and Saab Mansour. 2020. End-to-end slot alignment and recognition for crosslingual NLU. *CoRR*, abs/2004.14353.

Zhilin Yang, Zihang Dai, Ruslan Salakhutdinov, and William W. Cohen. 2018. Breaking the softmax bottleneck: A high-rank RNN language model. In *International Conference on Learning Representations*.

David Yarowsky, Grace Ngai, and Richard Wicentowski. 2001. Inducing multilingual text analysis tools via robust projection across aligned corpora. In *Proceedings of the First International Conference on Human Language Technology Research*.

Chenwei Zhang, Yaliang Li, Nan Du, Wei Fan, and Philip Yu. 2019. Joint slot filling and intent detection via capsule neural networks. In *Proceedings of the 57th Annual Meeting of the Association for Computational Linguistics*, pages 5259–5267, Florence, Italy. Association for Computational Linguistics.

Ayah Zirikly and Masato Hagiwara. 2015. Cross-lingual transfer of named entity recognizers without parallel corpora. In *Proceedings of the 53rd Annual Meeting of the Association for Computational Linguistics and the 7th International Joint Conference on Natural Language Processing (Volume 2: Short Papers)*, pages 390–396, Beijing, China. Association for Computational Linguistics.

Learning Context-Free Languages with Nondeterministic Stack RNNs

Brian DuSell
University of Notre Dame
bdusell1@nd.edu

David Chiang
University of Notre Dame
dchiang@nd.edu

Abstract

We present a differentiable stack data structure that simultaneously and tractably encodes an exponential number of stack configurations, based on Lang's algorithm for simulating nondeterministic pushdown automata. We call the combination of this data structure with a recurrent neural network (RNN) controller a Nondeterministic Stack RNN. We compare our model against existing stack RNNs on various formal languages, demonstrating that our model converges more reliably to algorithmic behavior on deterministic tasks, and achieves lower cross-entropy on inherently nondeterministic tasks.

1 Introduction

Although recent neural models of language have made advances in learning syntactic behavior, research continues to suggest that inductive bias plays a key role in data efficiency and human-like syntactic generalization (van Schijndel et al., 2019; Hu et al., 2020). Based on the long-held observation that language exhibits hierarchical structure, previous work has proposed coupling recurrent neural networks (RNNs) with differentiable stack data structures (Joulin and Mikolov, 2015; Grefenstette et al., 2015) to give them some of the computational power of pushdown automata (PDAs), the class of automata that recognize context-free languages (CFLs). However, previously proposed differentiable stack data structures only model deterministic stacks, which store only one version of the stack contents at a time, theoretically limiting the power of these stack RNNs to the deterministic CFLs.

A sentence's syntactic structure often cannot be fully resolved until its conclusion (if ever), requiring a human listener to track multiple possibilities while hearing the sentence. Past work in psycholinguistics has suggested that models that keep multiple candidate parses in memory at once can explain human reading times better than models which assume harsher computational constraints. This ability also plays an important role in calculating expectations that facilitate more efficient language processing (Levy, 2008). Current neural language models do not track multiple parses, if they learn syntax generalizations at all (Futrell et al., 2019; Wilcox et al., 2019; McCoy et al., 2020).

We propose a new differentiable stack data structure that explicitly models a nondeterministic PDA, adapting an algorithm by Lang (1974) and reformulating it in terms of tensor operations. The algorithm is able to represent an exponential number of stack configurations at once using cubic time and quadratic space complexity. As with existing stack RNN architectures, we combine this data structure with an RNN controller, and we call the resulting model a Nondeterministic Stack RNN (NS-RNN).

We predict that nondeterminism can help language processing in two ways. First, it will improve trainability, since all possible sequences of stack operations contribute to the objective function, not just the sequence used by the current model. Second, it will improve expressivity, as it is able to model concurrent parses in ways that a deterministic stack cannot. We demonstrate these claims by comparing the NS-RNN to deterministic stack RNNs on formal language modeling tasks of varying complexity. To show that nondeterminism aids training, we show that the NS-RNN achieves lower cross-entropy, in fewer parameter updates, on some deterministic CFLs. To show that nondeterminism improves expressivity, we show that the NS-RNN achieves lower cross-entropy on nondeterministic CFLs, including the "hardest context-free language" (Greibach, 1973), a language which is at least as difficult to parse as any other CFL and inherently requires nondeterminism. Our code is available at `https://github.com/bdusell/nondeterministic-stack-rnn`.

Proceedings of the 24th Conference on Computational Natural Language Learning, pages 507–519
Online, November 19-20, 2020. ©2020 Association for Computational Linguistics
https://doi.org/10.18653/v1/P17

2 Background and Motivation

In all differentiable stack-augmented networks that we are aware of (including ours), a network called the *controller*, which is some kind of RNN (typically an LSTM), is augmented with a differentiable stack, which has no parameters of its own. At each time step, the controller emits weights for various stack operations, which at minimum include push and pop. To maintain differentiability, the weights need to be continuous; different designs for the stack interpret fractionally-weighted operations differently. The stack then executes the fractional operations and produces a stack *reading*, which is a vector that represents the top of the updated stack. The stack reading is used as an extra input to the next hidden state update.

Designs for differentiable stacks have proceeded generally along two lines. One approach, which we call *superposition* (Joulin and Mikolov, 2015), treats fractional weights as probabilities. The other, which we call *stratification* (Sun et al., 1995; Grefenstette et al., 2015), treats fractional weights as "thicknesses."

Superposition In the model of Joulin and Mikolov (2015), the controller emits at each time step a probability distribution over three stack operations: push a new vector, pop the top vector, and no-op. The stack simulates all three operations at once, setting each stack element to the weighted interpolation of the elements above, at, and below it in the previous time step, weighted by push, no-op, and pop probabilities respectively. Thus, each stack element is a superposition of possible values for that element. Because stack elements depend only on a fixed number of elements from the previous time step, the stack update can largely be parallelized. Yogatama et al. (2018) developed an extension to this model that allows a variable number of pops per time step, up to a fixed limit K. Suzgun et al. (2019) also proposed a modification of the controller parameterization.

Stratification The model proposed by Sun et al. (1995) and later studied by Grefenstette et al. (2015) takes a different approach, assigning a *strength* between 0 and 1 to each stack element. If the stack elements were the layers of a cake, then the strengths would represent the thickness of each layer. At each time step, the controller emits a push weight between 0 and 1 which determines the strength of a new vector pushed onto the stack, and a pop weight between 0 and 1 which determines how much to slice off the top of the stack. The stack reading is computed by examining the top layer of unit thickness and interpolating the vectors proportional to their strengths. This relies on min and max operations, which can have zero gradients. In practice, the model can get trapped in local optima and requires random restarts (Hao et al., 2018). This model also affords less opportunity for parallelization because of the interdependence of stack elements within the same time step. Hao et al. (2018) proposed an extension that uses memory buffers to allow variable-length transductions.

Nondeterminism In all the above models, the stack is essentially deterministic in design. In order to recognize a nondeterministic CFL like $\{ww^{\mathrm{R}}\}$ from left to right, it must be possible, at each time step, for the stack to track all prefixes of the input string read so far. None of the foregoing models, to our knowledge, can represent a set of possiblities like this. Even for deterministic CFLs, this has consequences for trainability; at each time step, training can only update the model from the vantage point of a single stack configuration, making the model prone to getting stuck in local minima.

To overcome this weakness, we propose incorporating a nondeterministic stack, which affords the model a global view of the space of possible ways to use the stack. Our controller emits a probability distribution over stack operations, as in the superposition approach. However, whereas superposition only maintains the per-element marginal distributions over the stack elements, we propose to maintain the full distribution over the whole stack contents. We marginalize the distribution as late as possible, when the controller queries the stack for the current top stack symbol.

In the following sections, we explain our model and compare it against those of Joulin and Mikolov (2015) and Grefenstette et al. (2015). Despite taking longer in wall-clock time to train, our model learns to solve the tasks optimally with a higher rate of success.

3 Pushdown Automata

In this section, we give a definition of nondeterministic PDAs (§3.2), describe how to process strings with nondeterministic PDAs in cubic time (§3.3), and reformulate this algorithm in terms of tensor operations (§3.4).

3.1 Notation

Let ϵ be the empty string. Let $\mathbb{1}[\phi]$ be 1 when proposition ϕ is true, 0 otherwise. If A is a matrix, let $A_{i:}$ and $A_{:j}$ be the ith row and jth column, respectively, and define analogous notation for tensors.

3.2 Definition

A *weighted pushdown automaton (PDA)* is a tuple $M = (Q, \Sigma, \Gamma, \delta, q_0, \bot)$, where:

- Q is a finite set of states.
- Σ is a finite input alphabet.
- Γ is a finite stack alphabet.
- $\delta \colon Q \times \Gamma \times \Sigma \times Q \times \Gamma^* \to \mathbb{R}_{\geq 0}$ maps transitions, which we write as $q, x \xrightarrow{a} r, y$, to weights.
- $q_0 \in Q$ is the start state.
- $\bot \in \Gamma$ is the initial stack symbol.

In this paper, we do not allow non-scanning transitions (that is, those where $a = \epsilon$). Although this does not reduce the weak generative capacity of PDAs (Autebert et al., 1997), it could affect their ability to learn; we leave exploration of non-scanning transitions for future work.

For simplicity, we will assume that all transitions have one of the three forms:

$$q, x \xrightarrow{a} r, xy \qquad \text{push } y \text{ on top of } x$$
$$q, x \xrightarrow{a} r, y \qquad \text{replace } x \text{ with } y$$
$$q, x \xrightarrow{a} r, \epsilon \qquad \text{pop } x.$$

This also does not reduce the weak generative capacity of PDAs.

Given an input string $w \in \Sigma^*$ of length n, a *configuration* is a triple (i, q, β), where $i \in [0, n]$ is an input position indicating that all symbols up to and including w_i have been scanned, $q \in Q$ is a state, and $\beta \in \Gamma^*$ is the content of the stack (written bottom to top). For all i, q, r, β, x, y, we say that $(i-1, q, \beta x)$ *yields* $(i, r, \beta y)$ if $\delta(q, x \xrightarrow{w_i} r, y) > 0$. A *run* is a sequence of configurations starting with $(0, q_0, \bot)$ where each configuration (except the last) yields the next configuration.

Because our model does not use the PDA to accept or reject strings, we omit the usual definitions for the language accepted by a PDA. This is also why our definition lacks accept states.

As an example, consider the following PDA, for the language $\{ww^{\mathrm{R}} \mid w \in \{0, 1\}^* \}$:

$$M = (Q, \Sigma, \Gamma, \delta, q_1, \bot)$$
$$Q = \{q_1, q_2\}$$
$$\Sigma = \{0, 1\}$$
$$\Gamma = \{0, 1, \bot\}$$

where δ contains the transitions

$$q_1, x \xrightarrow{a} q_1, xa \qquad x \in \Gamma, a \in \Sigma$$
$$q_1, a \xrightarrow{a} q_2, \epsilon \qquad a \in \Sigma$$
$$q_2, a \xrightarrow{a} q_2, \epsilon \qquad a \in \Sigma.$$

This PDA has a possible configuration with an empty stack ($\bot$) iff the input string read so far is of the form ww^{R}.

To make a weighted PDA probabilistic, we require that all transition weights be nonnegative and, for all a, q, x:

$$\sum_{r \in Q} \sum_{y \in \Gamma^*} \delta(q, x \xrightarrow{a} r, y) = 1.$$

Whereas many definitions make the model generate symbols (Abney et al., 1999), our definition makes the PDA operations conditional on the input symbol a. The difference is not very important, because the RNN controller will eventually assume responsibility for reading and writing symbols, but our definition makes the shift to an RNN controller below slightly simpler.

3.3 Recognition

Lang (1974) gives an algorithm for simulating all runs of a nondeterministic PDA, related to Earley's algorithm (Earley, 1970). At any point in time, there can be exponentially many possibilities for the contents of the stack. In spite of this, Lang's algorithm is able to represent the set of all possibilities using only quadratic space. As this set is regular, its representation can be thought of as a weighted finite automaton, which we call the *stack WFA*, similar to the graph-structured stack used in GLR parsing (Tomita, 1987).

Figure 1 depicts Lang's algorithm as a set of inference rules, similar to a deductive parser (Shieber et al., 1995; Goodman, 1999), although the visual presentation is rather different. Each inference rule is drawn as a fragment of the stack WFA. If the transitions drawn with solid lines are present in the stack WFA, and the side conditions in the right column are met, then the transition drawn with a dashed line can be added to the stack WFA. The algorithm repeatedly applies inference rules to add states and transitions to the stack WFA; no states or transitions are ever deleted.

Each state of the stack WFA is of the form (i, q, x), where i is a position in the input string, q is a PDA state, and x is the top stack symbol. We briefly explain each of the inference rules:

Axiom creates an initial state and pushes $\perp$ onto the stack.

Push pushes a y on top of an x. Unlike Lang's original algorithm, this inference rule applies whether or not state $(j{-}1, q, x)$ is reachable.

Replace pops a z and pushes a y, by backing up the z transition (without deleting it) and adding a new y transition.

Pop pops a z, by backing up the z transition as well as the preceding y transition (without deleting them) and adding a new y transition.

The set of accept states of the stack WFA changes from time step to time step; at step j, the accept states are $\{(j, q, x) \mid q \in Q, x \in \Gamma\}$. The language recognized by the stack WFA at time j is the set of possible stack contents at time j.

An example run of the algorithm is shown in Figure 2, using our example PDA and the string 0110. At time step $j = 3$, the PDA reads 1 and either pushes a 1 (path ending in state $(3, q_1, 1)$) or pops a 1 (path ending in state $(3, q_2, 0)$). Similarly at time step $j = 4$, and the existence of a state with top stack symbol $\perp$ indicates that the string is of the form ww^R.

The total running time of the algorithm is proportional to the number of ways that the inference rules can be instantiated. Since the Pop rule contains three string positions (i, j, and k), the time complexity is $O(n^3)$. The total space requirement is characterized by the number of possible WFA transitions. Since transitions connect two states, each with a string position (i and j), the space complexity is $O(n^2)$.

3.4 Inner and Forward Weights

To implement this algorithm in a typical neural-network framework, we reformulate it in terms of tensor operations. We use the assumption that all transitions are scanning, although it would be possible to extend the model to handle non-scanning transitions using matrix inversions (Stolcke, 1995).

Define $\text{Act}(\Gamma) = \bullet\Gamma \cup \Gamma \cup \{\epsilon\}$ to be a set of possible stack actions: if $y \in \Gamma$, then $\bullet y$ means "push y," y means "replace with y," and ϵ means "pop."

Given an input string w, we pack the transition weights of the PDA into a tensor Δ with dimensions $n \times |Q| \times |\Gamma| \times |Q| \times |\text{Act}(\Gamma)|$:

$$\Delta[j][q, x \to r, \bullet y] = \delta(q, x \xrightarrow{w_j} r, xy)$$
$$\Delta[j][s, z \to r, y] = \delta(s, z \xrightarrow{w_j} r, y) \qquad (1)$$
$$\Delta[j][s, z \to r, \epsilon] = \delta(s, z \xrightarrow{w_j} r, \epsilon).$$

We compute the transition weights of the stack WFA (except for the initial transition) as a tensor of *inner weights* γ, with dimensions $n \times n \times |Q| \times |\Gamma| \times |Q| \times |\Gamma|$. Each element, which we write as $\gamma[i \to j][q, x \to r, y]$, is the weight of the stack WFA transition

$$\boxed{i, q, x} \xrightarrow{\quad y \quad} \boxed{j, r, y}$$

The equations defining γ are shown in Figure 3. Because these equations are a recurrence relation, we cannot compute γ all at once, but (for example) in order of increasing j.

Additionally, we compute a tensor α of *forward weights* of the stack WFA. This tensor has dimensions $n \times |Q| \times |\Gamma|$, and its elements are defined by the recurrence

$$\alpha[1][r, y] = \mathbb{1}[r = q_0 \wedge y = \perp]$$
$$\alpha[j][r, y] = \sum_{i=1}^{j-1} \sum_{q, x} \alpha[i][q, x]\, \gamma[i \to j][q, x \to r, y]$$
$$(2 \leq j \leq n).$$

The weight $\alpha[j][r, y]$ is the total weight of reaching a configuration $(r, j, \beta y)$ for any β from the initial configuration, and we can use α to compute the probability distribution over top stack symbols at time step j:

$$\tau^{(j)}(y) = \frac{\sum_r \alpha[j][r, y]}{\sum_{y'} \sum_r \alpha[j][r, y']}.$$

4 Neural Pushdown Automata

Now we couple the tensor formulation of Lang's algorithm for nondeterministic PDAs with an RNN controller.

4.1 Model

The controller can be any type of RNN; in our experiments, we used a LSTM RNN. At each time step, it computes a hidden vector $\mathbf{h}^{(j)}$ with d dimensions from the previous hidden vector, an input

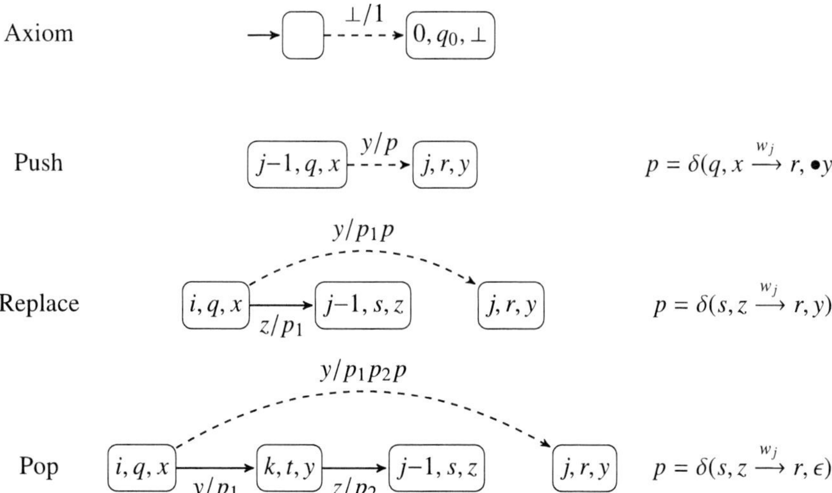

Figure 1: Lang's algorithm drawn as operations on the stack WFA. Solid edges indicate existing transitions; dashed edges indicate transitions that are added as a result of the stack operation.

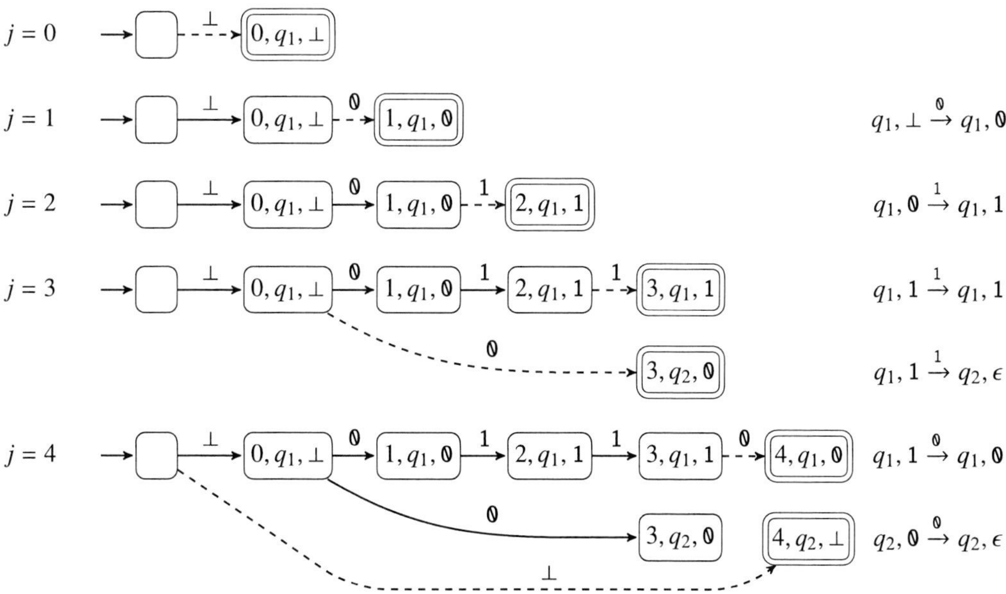

Figure 2: Run of Lang's algorithm on our example PDA and the string 0110. The PDA transitions used are shown at right.

For $1 \leq i < j \leq n$,

$$\gamma[i \to j][q, x \to r, y] =$$

$$\mathbb{1}[i = j{-}1] \, \Delta[j][q, x \to r, \bullet y] \qquad\qquad \text{Push}$$

$$+ \sum_{s,z} \gamma[i \to j{-}1][q, x \to s, z] \, \Delta[j][s, z \to r, y] \qquad\qquad \text{Replace}$$

$$+ \sum_{k=i+1}^{j-2} \sum_{t} \sum_{s,z} \gamma[i \to k][q, x \to t, y] \, \gamma[k \to j{-}1][t, y \to s, z] \, \Delta[j][s, z \to r, \epsilon] \quad \text{Pop}$$

Figure 3: Equations for computing inner weights.

vector $\mathbf{x}^{(j)}$, and the distribution over current top stack symbols, $\tau^{(j)}$, defined above:

$$\mathbf{h}^{(j)} = R\left(\mathbf{h}^{(j-1)}, \begin{bmatrix} \mathbf{x}^{(j)} \\ \tau^{(j)} \end{bmatrix}\right)$$

where R can be any RNN unit. This state is used to compute an output vector $\mathbf{y}^{(j)}$ as usual:

$$\mathbf{y}^{(j)} = \mathrm{softmax}\left(\mathbf{A}\mathbf{h}^{(j)} + \mathbf{b}\right)$$

where $\mathbf{A}$ and $\mathbf{b}$ are parameters with dimensions $|\Sigma| \times d$ and $|\Sigma|$, respectively. In addition, the state is used to compute a conditional distribution over actions, $\Delta[j]$:

$$\mathbf{z}_{qxry}^{(j)} = \exp\left(\mathbf{C}_{qxry\cdot}\mathbf{h}^{(j)} + \mathbf{D}_{qxry}\right)$$

$$\Delta[j][q, x \to r, y] = \frac{\mathbf{z}_{qxry}^{(j)}}{\sum_{r',y'} \mathbf{z}_{qxr'y'}^{(j)}}$$

where $\mathbf{C}$ and $\mathbf{D}$ are tensors of parameters with dimensions $|Q| \times |\Gamma| \times |Q| \times |\mathrm{Act}(\Gamma)| \times d$ and $|Q| \times |\Gamma| \times |Q| \times |\mathrm{Act}(\Gamma)|$, respectively. (This is just an affine transformation followed by a softmax over r and y.) These equations replace equations (1).

4.2 Implementation

We implemented the NS-RNN using PyTorch (Paszke et al., 2019), and doing so efficiently required a few crucial tricks. The first was a workaround to update the γ and α tensors in-place in a way that was compatible with PyTorch's automatic differentiation; this was necessary to achieve the theoretical quadratic space complexity. The second was an efficient implementation of a differentiable einsum operation[1] that supports the log semiring (as well as other semirings), which allowed us to implement the equations of Figure 3 in

a reasonably fast, memory-efficient way that avoids underflow. Our einsum implementation splits the operation into fixed-size blocks where the multiplication and summation of terms can be fully parallelized. This enforces a reasonable upper bound on memory usage while suffering only a slight decrease in speed compared to fully parallelizing the entire einsum operation.

5 Experiments

In this section, we describe our experiments comparing our NS-RNN and three baseline language models on several formal languages.

5.1 Tasks

Marked reversal The language of palindromes with an explicit middle marker, with strings of the form $w\#w^{\mathrm{R}}$, where $w \in \{0, 1\}^*$. This task should be easily solvable by a model with a deterministic stack, as the model can push the string w to the stack, change states upon reading $\#$, and predict w^{R} by popping w from the stack in reverse.

Unmarked reversal The language of (even-length) palindromes without a middle marker, with strings of the form ww^{R}, where $w \in \{0, 1\}^*$. When the length of w can vary, a language model reading the string from left to right must use nondeterminism to guess where the boundary between w and w^{R} lies. At each position, it must either push the input symbol to the stack, or else guess that the middle point has been reached and start popping symbols from the stack. An optimal language model will interpolate among all possible split points to produce a final prediction.

Padded reversal Like the unmarked reversal language, but with a long stretch of repeated symbols in the middle, with strings of the form $wa^p w^{\mathrm{R}}$, where $w \in \{0, 1\}^*$, $a \in \{0, 1\}$, and $p \geq 0$. The

---

[1] https://github.com/bdusell/semiring-einsum

512

purpose of the padding is to confuse a language model attempting to guess where the middle of the palindrome is based on the content of the string. In the general case of unmarked reversal, a language model can disregard split points where a valid palindrome does not occur locally. Since all substrings of a^p are palindromes, the language model must deal with a larger number of candidates simultaneously.

Dyck language The language D_2 of strings with two kinds of balanced brackets.

Hardest CFL Designed by Greibach (1973) to be at least as difficult to parse as any other CFL:

$$L_0 = \{x_1, y_1, z_1; \cdots x_n, y_n, z_n; \mid$$
$$n \geq 0,$$
$$y_1 \cdots y_n \in \$D_2,$$
$$x_i, z_i \in \{, , \$, (,), [,]\}^*\}.$$

Intuitively, L_0 contains strings formed by dividing a member of $\$D_2$ into pieces (y_i) and interleaving them with "decoy" pieces (substrings of x_i and z_i). While processing the string, the machine has to nondeterministically guess whether each piece is genuine or a decoy. Greibach shows that for any CFL L, there is a string homomorphism h such that a parser for L_0 can be run on $h(w)$ to find a parse for w. See Appendix A for more information.

5.2 Data

For each task, we construct a probabilistic context-free grammar (PCFG) for the language (see Appendix B for the full grammars and their parameters). We then randomly sample a training set of 10,000 examples from the PCFG, filtering samples so that the length of a string is in the interval [40, 80] (see Appendix C for our sampling method). The training set remains the same throughout the training process and is not re-sampled from epoch to epoch, since we want to test how well the model can infer the probability distribution from a finite sample.

We sample a validation set of 1,000 examples from the same distribution and a test set with string lengths varying from 40 to 100, with 100 examples per length. The validation set is randomized in each experiment, but for each task, the test set remains the same across all models and random restarts. For simplicity, we do not filter training samples from the validation or test sets, assuming that the chance of overlap is very small.

5.3 Evaluation

Since, in these languages, the next symbol cannot always be predicted deterministically from previous symbols, we do not use prediction accuracy as in previous work. Instead, we compute per-symbol cross-entropy on a set of strings S. Let p be any distribution over strings; then:

$$H(S, p) = \frac{\sum_{w \in S} -\log p(s)}{\sum_{w \in S} |w|}.$$

We compute the cross-entropy for both the stack RNN and the distribution from which S is sampled and report the difference. This can be seen as an approximation of the KL divergence of the stack RNN from the true distribution.

Technically, because the RNN models do not predict the end of the string, they estimate $p(w \mid |w|)$, not $p(w)$. However, they do not actually use any knowledge of the length, so it seems reasonable to compare the RNN's estimate of $p(w \mid |w|)$ with the true $p(w)$. (This is why, when we bin by length in Figure 5, some of the differences are negative.)

A benefit of using cross-entropy instead of prediction accuracy is that we can easily incorporate new tasks as long as they are expressed as a PCFG. We do not, for example, need to define a language-dependent subsequence of symbols to evaluate on.

5.4 Baselines

We compare our NS-RNN against three baselines: an LSTM, the Stack LSTM of Joulin and Mikolov (2015) ("JM"), and the Stack LSTM of Grefenstette et al. (2015) ("Gref"). We deviate slightly from the original definitions of these models in order to standardize the controller-stack interface to the one defined in Section 4.1, and to isolate the effects of differences in the stack data structure, rather than the controller mechanism. For all three stack models, we use an LSTM controller whose initial hidden state is fixed to 0, and we use only one stack for the JM and Gref models. (In early experiments, we found that using multiple stacks did not make a meaningful difference in performance.) For JM, we include a bias term in the layers that compute the stack actions and network output. We do allow the no-op operation, and the stack reading consists of only the top stack cell. For Gref, we set the controller output $\mathbf{o}'_t$ equal to the hidden state $\mathbf{h}_t$, so we compute the stack actions, pushed vector, and network output directly from the hidden state. We encode all input symbols as one-hot vectors; there are no embedding layers.

5.5 Hyperparameters

For all models, we use a single-layer LSTM with 20 hidden units. We selected this number because we found that an LSTM of this size could not completely solve the marked reversal task, indicating that the hidden state is a memory bottleneck. For each task, we perform a hyperparameter grid search for each model. We search for the initial learning rate, which has a large impact on performance, from the set $\{0.01, 0.005, 0.001, 0.0005\}$. For JM and Gref, we search for stack embedding sizes in $\{2, 20, 40\}$. We manually choose a small number of PDA states and stack symbol types for the NS-RNN for each task. For marked reversal, unmarked reversal, and Dyck, we use 2 states and 2 stack symbol types. For padded reversal, we use 3 states and 2 stack symbol types. For the hardest CFL, we use 3 states and 3 stack symbol types.

As noted by Grefenstette et al. (2015), initialization can play a large role in whether a Stack LSTM converges on algorithmic behavior or becomes trapped in a local optimum. To mitigate this, for each hyperparameter setting in the grid search, we run five random restarts and select the hyperparameter setting with the lowest average difference in cross entropy on the validation set. This gives us a picture not only of the model's performance, but of its rate of success. We initialize all fully-connected layers except for the recurrent LSTM layer with Xavier uniform initialization (Glorot and Bengio, 2010), and all other parameters uniformly from $[-0.1, 0.1]$.

We train all models with Adam (Kingma and Ba, 2015) and clip gradients whose magnitude is above 5. We use mini-batches of size 10; to generate a batch, we first select a length and then sample 10 strings of that length. We train models until convergence, multiplying the learning rate by 0.9 after 5 epochs of no improvement in cross-entropy on the validation set, and stopping after 10 epochs of no improvement.

6 Results

We show plots of the difference in cross entropy on the validation set between each model and the source distribution in Figure 4. For all tasks, stack-based models outperform the LSTM baseline, indicating that the tasks are effective benchmarks for differentiable stacks. For the marked reversal, unmarked reversal, and hardest CFL tasks, our model consistently achieves cross-entropy closer to the source distribution than any other model. Even for the marked reversal task, which can be solved deterministically, the NS-RNN, besides achieving lower cross-entropy on average, learns to solve the task in fewer updates and with much higher reliability across random restarts. In the case of the mildly nondeterministic unmarked reversal and highly nondeterministic hardest CFL tasks, the NS-RNN converges on the lowest validation cross-entropy. On the Dyck language, which is a deterministic task, all stack models converge quickly on the source distribution. We hypothesize that this is because the Dyck language represents a case where stack usage is locally advantageous everywhere, so it is particularly conducive for learning stack-like behavior. On the other hand, we note that our model struggles on padded reversal, in which stack-friendly signals are intentionally made very distant. Although the NS-RNN outperforms the LSTM baseline, the JM model solves the task most effectively, though still imperfectly.

In order to show how each model performs when evaluated on strings longer than those seen during training, in Figure 5, we show cross-entropy on separately sampled test data as a function of string length. All test sets are identical across models and random restarts, and there are 100 samples per length. The NS-RNN consistently does well on string lengths it was trained on, but it is sometimes surpassed by other stack models on strings that are outside the distribution of lengths it was trained on. This suggests that the NS-RNN conforms more tightly to the real distribution seen during training.

7 Conclusion

We presented the NS-RNN, a neural language model with a differentiable stack that explicitly models nondeterminism. We showed that it offers improved trainability and modeling power over previous stack-based neural language models; the NS-RNN learns to solve some deterministic tasks more effectively than other stack-LSTMs, and achieves the best results on a challenging nondeterministic context-free language. However, we note that the NS-RNN struggled on a task where signals in the data were distant, and did not generalize to longer lengths as well as other stack-LSTMs; we hope to address these shortcomings in future work. We believe that the NS-RNN will prove to be a powerful tool for learning and modeling ambiguous syntax in natural language.

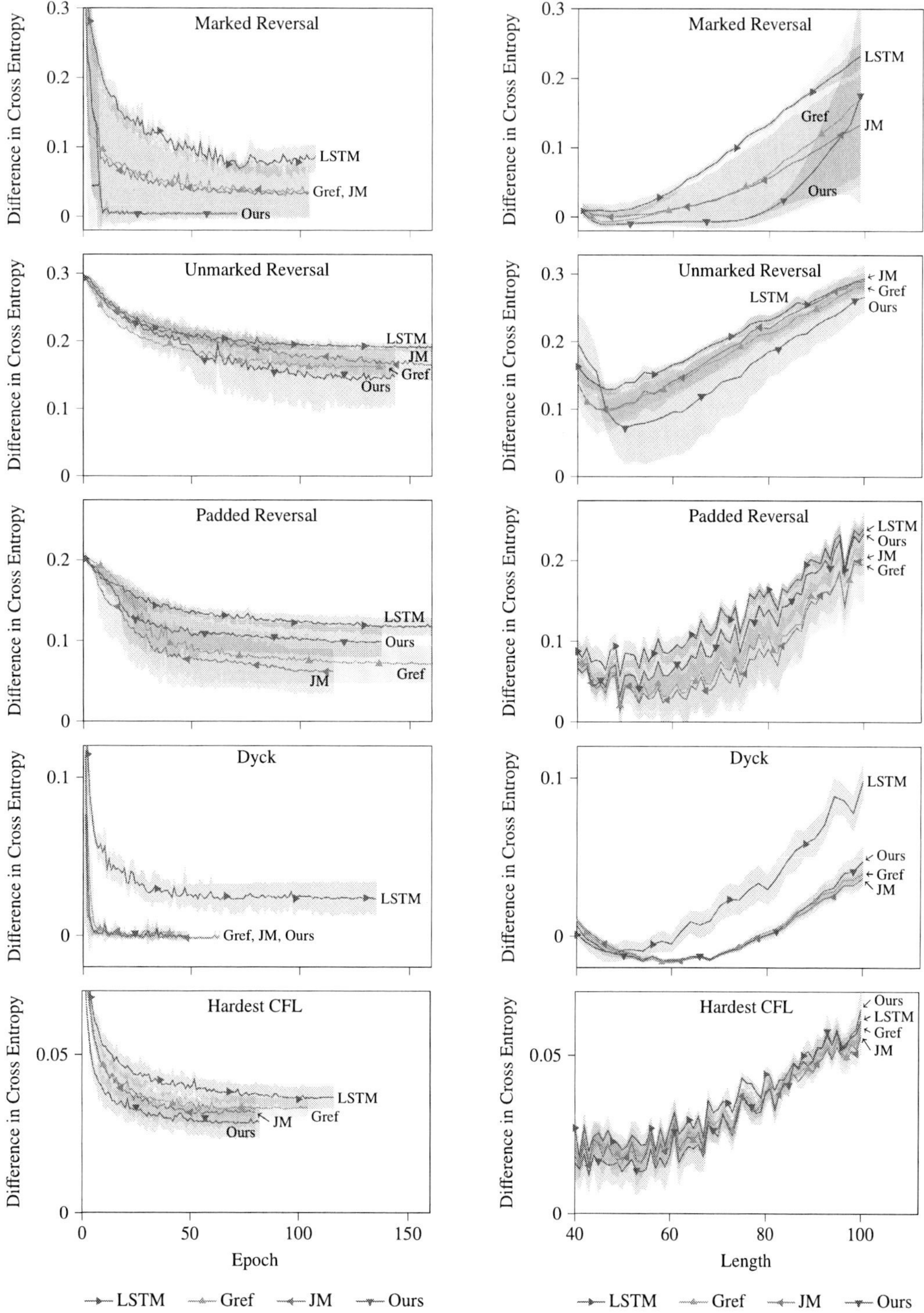

Figure 4: Cross-entropy difference in nats between model and source distribution on validation set, as a function of training time. Lines are averages of five random restarts, and shaded regions are standard deviations. After a random restart converges, the value of its last epoch is used in the average for later epochs.

Figure 5: Cross-entropy difference in nats on the test set, binned by string length. Some models achieve a negative difference, for reasons explained in §5.3. Each line is the average of the same five random restarts shown in Figure 4.

Acknowledgements

This research was supported in part by a Google Faculty Research Award. We would like to thank Justin DeBenedetto and Darcey Riley for their helpful comments, and the Center for Research Computing at the University of Notre Dame for providing the computing infrastructure for our experiments.

References

Steven Abney, David McAllester, and Fernando Pereira. 1999. Relating probabilistic grammars and automata. In *Proc. ACL*, pages 542–549.

Salvador Aguinaga, David Chiang, and Tim Weninger. 2019. Learning hyperedge replacement grammars for graph generation. *IEEE Trans. Pattern Analysis and Machine Intelligence*, 41(3):625–638.

Jean-Michel Autebert, Jean Berstel, and Luc Boasson. 1997. Context-free languages and pushdown automata. In Grzegorz Rozenberg and Arto Salomaa, editors, *Handbook of Formal Languages*, pages 111–174. Springer.

Jay Earley. 1970. An efficient context-free parsing algorithm. *Comm. ACM*, 13(2):94–102.

Richard Futrell, Ethan Wilcox, Takashi Morita, Peng Qian, Miguel Ballesteros, and Roger Levy. 2019. Neural language models as psycholinguistic subjects: Representations of syntactic state. In *Proc. NAACL HLT*, pages 32–42.

Xavier Glorot and Yoshua Bengio. 2010. Understanding the difficulty of training deep feedforward neural networks. In *Proc. AISTATS*, pages 249–256.

Joshua Goodman. 1999. Semiring parsing. *Computational Linguistics*, 25(4):573–605.

Edward Grefenstette, Karl Moritz Hermann, Mustafa Suleyman, and Phil Blunsom. 2015. Learning to transduce with unbounded memory. In *Proc. NeurIPS*, volume 2, pages 1828–1836.

Sheila A. Greibach. 1973. The hardest context-free language. *SIAM J. Comput.*, 2(4):304–310.

Yiding Hao, William Merrill, Dana Angluin, Robert Frank, Noah Amsel, Andrew Benz, and Simon Mendelsohn. 2018. Context-free transductions with neural stacks. In *Proc. BlackboxNLP*, pages 306–315.

Jennifer Hu, Jon Gauthier, Peng Qian, Ethan Wilcox, and Roger Levy. 2020. A systematic assessment of syntactic generalization in neural language models. In *Proc. ACL*, pages 1725–1744.

Armand Joulin and Tomas Mikolov. 2015. Inferring algorithmic patterns with stack-augmented recurrent nets. In *Proc. NeurIPS*, volume 1, pages 190–198.

Diederik P. Kingma and Jimmy Lei Ba. 2015. Adam: A method for stochastic optimization. In *Proc. ICLR*.

Bernard Lang. 1974. Deterministic techniques for efficient non-deterministic parsers. In *Proc. Colloquium on Automata, Languages, and Programming*, pages 255–269.

Roger Levy. 2008. Expectation-based syntactic comprehension. *Cognition*, 106:1126–77.

Richard McCoy, Robert H. Frank, and Tal Linzen. 2020. Does syntax need to grow on trees? Sources of hierarchical inductive bias in sequence-to-sequence networks. *Trans. ACL*, 8:125–140.

Adam Paszke, Sam Gross, Francisco Massa, Adam Lerer, James Bradbury, Gregory Chanan, Trevor Killeen, Zeming Lin, Natalia Gimelshein, Luca Antiga, Alban Desmaison, Andreas Kopf, Edward Yang, Zachary DeVito, Martin Raison, Alykhan Tejani, Sasank Chilamkurthy, Benoit Steiner, Lu Fang, Junjie Bai, and Soumith Chintala. 2019. PyTorch: An imperative style, high-performance deep learning library. In *Proc. NeurIPS*, pages 8024–8035.

Marten van Schijndel, Aaron Mueller, and Tal Linzen. 2019. Quantity doesn't buy quality syntax with neural language models. In *Proc. EMNLP-IJCNLP*, pages 5831–5837.

Stuart M. Shieber, Yves Schabes, and Fernando C. N. Pereira. 1995. Principles and implementation of deductive parsing. *Journal of Logic Programming*, 24(1):3–36.

Andreas Stolcke. 1995. An efficient probabilistic context-free parsing algorithm that computes prefix probabilities. *Computational Linguistics*, 21(2):165–201.

G. Z. Sun, C. Lee Giles, H. H. Chen, and Y. C. Lee. 1995. The neural network pushdown automaton: Model, stack, and learning simulations. Technical Report UMIACS-TR-93-77 and CS-TR-3118, University of Maryland. Revised version.

Mirac Suzgun, Sebastian Gehrmann, Yonatan Belinkov, and Stuart M. Shieber. 2019. Memory-augmented recurrent neural networks can learn generalized Dyck languages. arXiv:1922.03329.

Masaru Tomita. 1987. An efficient augmented context-free parsing algorithm. *Computational Linguistics*, 13(1–2):31–46.

Ethan Wilcox, Roger Levy, and Richard Futrell. 2019. Hierarchical representation in neural language models: Suppression and recovery of expectations. In *Proc. BlackboxNLP*, pages 181–190.

Dani Yogatama, Yishu Miao, Gábor Melis, Wang Ling, Adhiguna Kuncoro, Chris Dyer, and Phil Blunsom. 2018. Memory architectures in recurrent neural network language models. In *Proc. ICLR*.

A The Hardest CFL

Greibach (1973) describes a CFL, L_0, which is the "hardest" CFL in the sense that an efficient parser for L_0 is also an efficient parser for any other CFL L. It is defined as follows. (We deviate from Greibach's original notation for the sake of clarity.) Every string in L_0 is of the following form:

$$\alpha_1 ; \alpha_2 ; \cdots \alpha_n ; \; \in L_0$$

that is, a sequence of strings α_i, each terminated by $;$. No α_i can contain $;$. Each α_i, in turn, is divided into three parts, separated by commas:

$$\alpha_i = x_i , y_i , z_i$$

The middle part, y_i, is a substring of a string in D_2. The brackets in y_i do not need to be balanced, but all of the y_i's concatenated must form a string in D_2, prefixed by \$. The catch is that x_i and z_i can be any sequence of bracket, comma, and \$ symbols, so it is impossible to tell, in a single α_i, where y_i begins and ends. A parser must nondeterministically guess where each y_i is, and cannot verify a guess until the end of the string is reached.

The design of L_0 is justified as follows. Suppose we have a parser for L_0 which, as part of its output, identifies the start and end of each y_i. Given a CFG G in Greibach normal form (GNF), we can adapt the parser for L_0 to parse $\mathcal{L}(G)$ by constructing a string homomorphism h, such that $w \in \mathcal{L}(G)$ iff $h(w) \in L_0$, and the concatenated y_i's encode a leftmost derivation of w under G.

The homomorphism h always exists and can be constructed from G as follows. Let the nonterminals of G be $V = \{A_1, \ldots, A_{|V|}\}$. Recall that in GNF, every rule is of the form $A_i \to a A_{j_1} \cdots A_{j_m}$ and S does not appear on any right-hand side. Define

$$\mathrm{push}(A_i) = ([^i ($$

$$\mathrm{pop}(A_i) = \begin{cases})]^i) & A_i \neq S \\ \$ & A_i = S. \end{cases}$$

We encode each rule of G as

$$\mathrm{rule}(A_i \to a A_{j_1} \cdots A_{j_m}) =$$
$$\mathrm{pop}(A_i)\, \mathrm{push}(A_{j_1}) \cdots \mathrm{push}(A_{j_m}).$$

Finally, we can define h as

$$h(b) = \left(\bigodot_{(A \to b\gamma) \in G} \mathrm{rule}(A \to b\gamma) \right) ;$$

where $\odot$ concatenates strings together delimited by commas. Then there is a valid string of y_i's iff there is a valid derivation of w with respect to G.

B PCFGs for Generating Data

We list here the production rules and weights for the PCFG used for each of our tasks. Let $f(\mu) = 1 - \frac{1}{\mu+1}$, which is the probability of failure associated with a negative binomial distribution with a mean of μ failures before one success. For a recursive PCFG rule, a probability of $f(\mu)$ results in an average of μ applications of the recursive rule.

B.1 Marked reversal

We set $\mu = 60$.

$$S \to 0S0 \; / \; \tfrac{1}{2} f(\mu)$$
$$S \to 1S1 \; / \; \tfrac{1}{2} f(\mu)$$
$$S \to \# \quad / \; 1 - f(\mu)$$

B.2 Unmarked reversal

We set $\mu = 60$.

$$S \to 0S0 \; / \; \tfrac{1}{2} f(\mu)$$
$$S \to 1S1 \; / \; \tfrac{1}{2} f(\mu)$$
$$S \to \epsilon \quad / \; 1 - f(\mu)$$

B.3 Padded reversal

Let μ_c be the mean length of the reversed content, and let μ_p be the mean padding length. We set $\mu_c = 60$ and $\mu_p = 30$.

$$S \to 0S0 \; / \; \tfrac{1}{2} f(\mu_c)$$
$$S \to 1S1 \; / \; \tfrac{1}{2} f(\mu_c)$$
$$S \to T_0 \quad / \; \tfrac{1}{2}(1 - f(\mu_c))$$
$$S \to T_1 \quad / \; \tfrac{1}{2}(1 - f(\mu_c))$$
$$T_0 \to 0T_0 \; / \; f(\mu_p)$$
$$T_0 \to \epsilon \quad / \; 1 - f(\mu_p)$$
$$T_1 \to 1T_1 \; / \; f(\mu_p)$$
$$T_1 \to \epsilon \quad / \; 1 - f(\mu_p)$$

B.4 Dyck language

Let μ_s be the mean number of splits, and let μ_n be the mean nesting depth. We set $\mu_s = 1$ and $\mu_n = 40$.

$$S \to ST \; / \; f(\mu_s)$$
$$S \to T \quad / \; 1 - f(\mu_s)$$
$$T \to (S) \; / \; \tfrac{1}{2} f(\mu_n)$$
$$T \to [S] \; / \; \tfrac{1}{2} f(\mu_n)$$
$$T \to () \quad / \; \tfrac{1}{2}(1 - f(\mu_n))$$
$$T \to [] \quad / \; \tfrac{1}{2}(1 - f(\mu_n))$$

B.5 Hardest CFL

Let μ_c be the mean number of commas, μ_{sf} be the mean short filler length, μ_{lf} be the mean long filler length, p_s be the probability of a semicolon, μ_s be the mean number of bracket splits, and μ_n be the mean bracket nesting depth. We set $\mu_c = 0.5$, $\mu_{sf} = 0.5$, $\mu_{lf} = 2$, $p_s = 0.25$, $\mu_s = 1.5$, and $\mu_n = 3$.

$$
\begin{aligned}
S' &\to R\$QSL; &&/\ 1 \\
L &\to L',U &&/\ 1 \\
L' &\to ,VL' &&/\ f(\mu_c) \\
L' &\to \epsilon &&/\ 1 - f(\mu_c) \\
R &\to U,R' &&/\ 1 \\
R' &\to R'V, &&/\ f(\mu_c) \\
R' &\to \epsilon &&/\ 1 - f(\mu_c) \\
U &\to WU &&/\ f(\mu_{sf}) \\
U &\to \epsilon &&/\ 1 - f(\mu_{sf}) \\
V &\to WV &&/\ f(\mu_{lf} - 1) \\
V &\to W &&/\ 1 - f(\mu_{lf} - 1) \\
W &\to (&&/\ 0.2 \\
W &\to) &&/\ 0.2 \\
W &\to [&&/\ 0.2 \\
W &\to] &&/\ 0.2 \\
W &\to \$ &&/\ 0.2 \\
Q &\to L;R &&/\ p_s \\
Q &\to \epsilon &&/\ 1 - p_s \\
S &\to SQT &&/\ f(\mu_s) \\
S &\to T &&/\ 1 - f(\mu_s) \\
T &\to (QSQ) &&/\ \tfrac{1}{2}f(\mu_n) \\
T &\to [QSQ] &&/\ \tfrac{1}{2}f(\mu_n) \\
T &\to (Q) &&/\ \tfrac{1}{2}(1 - f(\mu_n)) \\
T &\to [Q] &&/\ \tfrac{1}{2}(1 - f(\mu_n))
\end{aligned}
$$

C Sampling Strings with Fixed Length from a PCFG

For practical reasons, we restrict strings we sample from PCFGs to those whose lengths lie within a certain interval, say $[\ell_{\min}, \ell_{\max}]$. The lengths of strings sampled randomly from PCFGs tend to have high variance, and we often want data sets to consist of strings of a certain length (e.g. longer strings in the test set than in the training set).

To do this, we first sample a length ℓ uniformly from $[\ell_{\min}, \ell_{\max}]$. Then we use an efficient dynamic programming algorithm to sample strings directly from the distribution of strings in the PCFG with length ℓ. This algorithm is adapted from an algorithm presented by Aguinaga et al. (2019) for sampling graphs of a specific size from a hyperedge replacement grammar.

The algorithm operates in two phases. The first (Algorithm 1) computes a table T such that every entry $T[A, \ell]$ contains the total probability of sampling a string from the PCFG with length ℓ. The second (Algorithm 2) uses T to randomly sample a string from the PCFG (using S as the nonterminal parameter X), restricted to those with a length of exactly ℓ.

Let nonterminals(β) be an ordered sequence consisting of the nonterminals in β. Let Compositions(ℓ, n) be a function that returns a (possibly empty) list of all compositions of ℓ that are of length n (that is, all ordered sequences of n positive integers that add up to ℓ).

Algorithm 1 Computing the probability table T

Require: G has no ϵ-rules or unary rules

1: **function** COMPUTEWEIGHTS(G, T, X, ℓ)
2:     **for all** rules $X \to \beta\ /\ p$ in G **do**
3:         $N \leftarrow$ nonterminals(β)
4:         $\ell' = \ell - |\beta| + |N|$
5:         **for** C in Compositions($\ell', |N|$) **do**
6:             $t[\beta, C] \leftarrow p \times \prod_{i=1}^{|N|} T[N_i, C_i]$
7:     **return** t
8: **function** COMPUTETABLE(G, n)
9:     **for** ℓ from 1 to n **do**
10:         **for all** nonterminals X **do**
11:             $t \leftarrow$ COMPUTEWEIGHTS(G, T, X, ℓ)
12:             $T[X, \ell] = \sum_{\beta, C} t[\beta, C]$
13:     **return** T

Because this algorithm only works on PCFGs that are free of ϵ-rules and unary rules, we automatically refactor our PCFGs to remove them before providing them to the algorithm.

Some of our PCFGs do not generate any strings for certain lengths, which is detected at line 3 of Algorithm 2. In this case, we restart the sampling procedure from the beginning. This means that the distribution we are effectively sampling from is as follows. Let $G(w)$ be the probability of w under PCFG G, and let $G(\ell)$ be the probability of all strings of length ℓ, that is,

$$
G(\ell) = \sum_{w \text{ s.t. } |w| = \ell} G(w).
$$

Algorithm 2 Sampling a string using T

Require: T is the output of COMPUTETABLE(G, ℓ)
 1: **function** SAMPLESIZED(G, T, X, ℓ)
 2:     **if** $T[X, \ell] = 0$ **then**
 3:         **error**
 4:     $t \leftarrow$ COMPUTEWEIGHTS(G, T, X, ℓ)
 5:     sample (β, C) with probability $\dfrac{t[\beta, C]}{T[X, \ell]}$
 6:     $s \leftarrow \epsilon$
 7:     $i \leftarrow 1$
 8:     **for** j from 1 to $|\beta|$ **do**
 9:         **if** β_j is a terminal **then**
10:             append β_j to s
11:         **else**
12:             $s' \leftarrow$ SAMPLESIZED(G, T, β_j, C_i)
13:             append s' to s
14:             $i \leftarrow i + 1$
15:     **return** s

Then the distribution we are sampling from is

$$p_{\text{sample}}(w) = \frac{1}{|\{\ell \mid G(\ell) > 0\}|} \frac{G(w)}{G(|w|)}.$$

When computing the lower-bound cross-entropy of the validation and test sets, we must compute $p_{\text{sample}}(w)$ for each string w. Finding $G(w)$ requires re-parsing w with respect to G and summing the probabilities of all valid parses using the Inside algorithm. We can look up the value of $G(|w|)$ in the table entry $T[S, |w|]$ produced in the sampling algorithm.

Generating Narrative Text in a Switching Dynamical System

Noah Weber [3,1], Leena Shekhar [1*], Heeyoung Kwon[1]
Niranjan Balasubramanian[1], Nathanael Chambers [2]
[1]Stony Brook University
{lshekhar,heekwon,niranjan}@cs.stonybrook.edu
[2]United States Naval Academy
nchamber@usna.edu
[3]Johns Hopkins University
nweber6@jhu.edu

Abstract

Early work on narrative modeling used explicit plans and goals to generate stories, but the language generation itself was restricted and inflexible. Modern methods use language models for more robust generation, but often lack an explicit representation of the scaffolding and dynamics that guide a coherent narrative. This paper introduces a new model that integrates explicit narrative structure with neural language models, formalizing narrative modeling as a *Switching Linear Dynamical System* (SLDS). A SLDS is a dynamical system in which the latent dynamics of the system (i.e. how the state vector transforms over time) is controlled by top-level discrete *switching* variables. The switching variables represent narrative structure (e.g., sentiment or discourse states), while the latent state vector encodes information on the current state of the narrative. This probabilistic formulation allows us to control generation, and can be learned in a semi-supervised fashion using both labeled and unlabeled data. Additionally, we derive a Gibbs sampler for our model that can "fill in" arbitrary parts of the narrative, guided by the switching variables. Our filled-in (English language) narratives outperform several baselines on both automatic and human evaluations.

1 Introduction

A narrative is a textualized sequence of events that serves as a coherent outline for an actual story (Prince, 2003). Effective narratives are typically built on top of higher level *narrative scaffolds*[1] which specify at an abstract level how the story should evolve along different dimensions. Example scaffolds include descriptions of the emotional trajectory of a story (Vonnegut, 1981; Reagan et al., 2016), the goals of characters throughout

---

*Author now at Microsoft

[1]We use the term scaffold as an umbrella term to cover many types of plans and structures that underlie stories.

Tom didn't know why his internet speed was so slow.
Tom wasn't sure what to do with his computer.
He thought he would fix it himself.
Tom was surprisingly good.
Tom was happy to be surfing the internet again

Table 1: A sample filled in narrative generated by our SLDS model given the first and last sentences as input (grayed out), the middle 3 sentences are imputed by our model (bold).

the story (Meehan, 1977; Turner, 1993), or the abstract types of events that may occur (Martin et al., 2018). The parts of a scaffold are generic, and like Propp's originally proposed narrative functions (Propp, 1928), can be reused across stories. To be fully reusable, one needs to go beyond just identifying *what* the elements of the narrative scaffold are, and also indicate *how* each scaffold element changes the properties of the current story state. We refer to the explication of these transformation/transitions as the *narrative dynamics*.

Prior work on automatic narrative generation has a rich history of modeling both *narrative scaffolds* and *narrative dynamics* (Meehan, 1977; Lebowitz, 1985; Turner, 1993; Riedl and Young, 2006, 2010a). The modeling of both narrative scaffold and dynamics often imbued these systems with a greater degree of control for the user in generating stories, allowing users to flexibly specify desired outcomes or plot points (or more generally, the state of the narrative) that should be achieved at certain sections of the story. Constrained generation (for example, constraining the story to start and end with particular sentences, such as that given in Table 1), is an ability these systems often gained for free through the modeling of dynamics.

Though successful in this regard, this success has only been realized in closed domains, where

Proceedings of the 24th Conference on Computational Natural Language Learning, pages 520–530
Online, November 19-20, 2020. ©2020 Association for Computational Linguistics
https://doi.org/10.18653/v1/P17

the narrative scaffolds can be specified in a limited ontology and the dynamics operations can be written by hand (such as e.g. the action schemata of Riedl and Young (2010a)). Neural generation has since helped scale to open domains (Roemmele and Gordon, 2015; Khalifa et al., 2017) but not with the same level of control over the narrative. Several recent works have looked at adding the narrative scaffolding component back into neural text generating systems (Fan et al.; Martin et al., 2018; Yao et al., 2019; Xu et al., 2018; Fan et al., 2019). These systems however still do not utilize an explicit model of narrative dynamics, and are thus restricted in the controllability aspect.

In this work, we show how the insight of modeling the structure of a narrative along with general purpose dynamics can be combined with modern neural network based language models. We do this by explicitly modeling the narrative state with a latent vector, and modeling how this state transforms over time as a *Switching Linear Dynamical System* (SLDS). We show how this formulation captures the concepts of narrative dynamics and scaffolds in a way compatible with current neural generation systems. Finally we show that, by explicitly modeling these dynamics, our models obtain the ability to "fill in" narratives; all without being explicitly trained to do so and with no further training required. We evaluate our model with both human evaluation and several automatic measures[2] and show that our model outperforms several strong baselines.

2 A Switching Dynamical System for Narrative Generation

In this section, we give a brief overview of Switching Dynamical systems and how they can be used to capture both a scaffold of the narrative as well as the narrative dynamics. We then describe in detail the components of our model and its relation to existing models.

2.1 Narrative Dynamics in a Dynamical System

The specifics of the narrative (characters, setting, etc.), will differ between stories, but as Propp (1928) notes, the way they transition to the next point in the narrative (what we refer to as "narrative dynamics") is often shared. Let's say that, as done often, we represent the 'narrative specifics' at time

step[3] i with a latent vector Z_i. A natural way to explicitly model how this state evolves over time that fits with the above observation is as a *Linear Dynamical System*:

$$Z_{i+1} = A Z_i + \epsilon \; ; \; \epsilon \sim \mathcal{N}(0, \Sigma)$$

Where A is a matrix, shared across all narratives, and Σ is a noise term that takes into consideration idiosyncrasies different narratives will have[4]. The fact that the shared transition matrix A is linear means that narratives will have linearly analogous trajectories through time, despite having different details (comparable to stories with different settings but matching structures such as *Ran/King Lear*, *Ulysses/Odyssey*, etc). Of course, the fatal flaw of the model is that it assumes there exists only one transition matrix, and thus only one possible way to transition through a narrative!

2.2 Narrative Scaffolds as Switching Variables

A more fitting model would thus be a *Switching Linear Dynamical System* (Ackerson and Fu, 1970; Chang and Athans, 1978; Murphy, 1998). In an SLDS, we assume there exists a set of K different sets of dynamics, $\{(A_1, \Sigma_1), ...(A_K, \Sigma_K)\}$. At time step $i + 1$, *one* of these sets of dynamics is used. The one used depends on the value of a discrete variable at time step $i+1$ called the switching variable, $S_{i+1} \in \{1, ...K\}$:

$$Z_{i+1} = A_{S_{i+1}} Z_i + \epsilon \; ; \; \epsilon \sim \mathcal{N}(0, \Sigma_{S_{i+1}})$$

There is a switching variable S_i associated with each time step. The switching variable value itself evolves over time by a prior Markov process, $P(S_{i+1}|S_i)$[5]. This top level chain of switching variables thus forms our *narrative scaffold*, indicating *what* transitions we must go through in the narrative, with the dynamics matrices indicating *how* they transition.

2.3 Narrative Scaffold - Emotional Trajectory

What the switching variables actually represent can be chosen by the user. Straightforward narrative

---

[2]Evaluation in this paper is done on English text data

[3]In our case, we take each sentence in the narrative to be a different timestep. Different levels of granularity for a timestep may be more befitting for other domains.

[4]Note that a bias term may also be added here (we do this in our implementation). We leave the bias off here for clarity

[5]Other ways to formulate this transformation are also possible (Barber, 2006; Linderman et al., 2016). The Markov assumption is a common one and we use it here for simplicity.

scaffolds include event sequences (Martin et al., 2018), keywords (Yao et al., 2019), or latent template ids (Wiseman et al., 2018). More complex but potentially more informative scaffolds may be created using concepts such as story grammar non-terminals (Lakoff, 1972; Thorndyke, 1977), or character action taken throughout a story (Riedl and Young, 2010b).

In our work, we use the sentiment trajectory of the narrative as the scaffold. That is, each S_i for a sentence indicates the overall coarse sentiment of the sentence (Positive, Negative, or Neutral). Though simple, the overall sentiment trajectory of a narrative is important in defining the high level 'shape' of a narrative often shared among different narratives (Vonnegut, 1981; Reagan et al., 2016). Furthermore, sentiment trajectory has been shown to be fairly useful in story understanding tasks (Chaturvedi et al., 2017; Liu et al., 2018). We discuss in the conclusion future directions for using different types of scaffolds.

2.4 The Full Model

The final component of the model is a conditional language model that generates sentence i conditioned on the current Z_i, and all previous sentences, $X_{:i}$. Generation continues until an `<eos>` is reached. This conditional language model may be parameterized as desired, but in this work, we parameterize it as an RNN neural network language model.

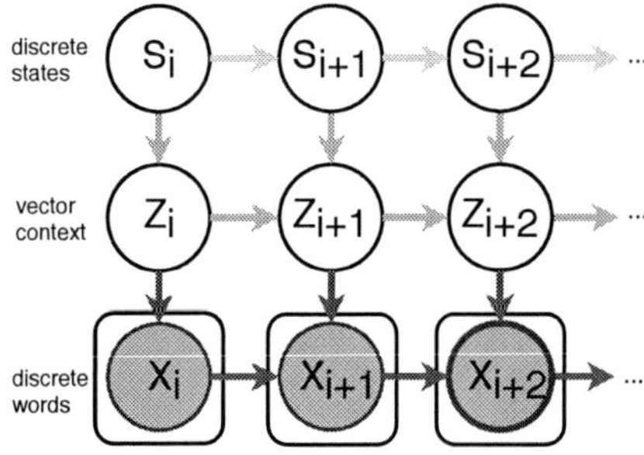

Figure 1: SLDS Generative model-S_i is a discrete state (sentiment of a sentence in a multi-sentence narrative). Z_i is a continuous latent vector that is conditioned on to generate the ith sentence in the narrative , X_i. The dynamics of the narrative are completely captured in the dynamical system controlling the latent vector Z. How to transition from Z_i to Z_{i+1} is determined by the state variable S_{i+1}. Arrows from X_i to X_{i+2} have been left out for clarity.

The graphical model for our SLDS is pictured in Figure 1. The model consists of three sets of variables: (1) Switching variables $S_1, ..., S_N$, (2) Latent state variables $Z_1, ..., Z_N$ capturing the details of the narrative at sentence i, (3) The sentences themselves $X_1, ...X_N$, where each sentence X_i has n_i words, $x_1^i, ...x_{n_i}^i$. The joint over all variables factorizes as below into the following components ($X_{:i}$ stands for all sentences before X_i):

$$P(\mathbf{S}, \mathbf{Z}, \mathbf{X}) = (\prod_i^N \underbrace{P(X_i|Z_i, X_{:i})}_{❸})$$

$$(\prod_i^N \underbrace{P(Z_i|Z_{i-1}, S_i)}_{❷})(\prod_i^N \underbrace{P(S_i|S_{i-1})}_{❶})$$

❶ **Narrative Scaffold Planner**: The factor $P(S_i|S_{i-1})$ is a transition matrix, which we calculate via count based statistics from training. It is fed in as prior knowledge and fixed.

❷ **Narrative Dynamics Network**: The factor $P(Z_i|Z_{i-1}, S_i)$ is determined like a switching linear dynamical system:

$$Z_i = A_{S_i}Z_{i-1} + B_{S_i}\epsilon, \; ; \epsilon \sim \mathcal{N}(0, I)$$

which is equivalent to drawing Z_i from a Normal distribution with mean $A_{S_i}Z_{i-1}$ and variance $B_{S_i}B_{S_i}^T$.

❸ **Conditional Language model**: The factor $P(X_i|Z_i, X_{:i})$ is parameterized by an RNN language model conditioned on the latent Z_i.

3 Learning and Posterior Inference

Due to the conditionals parameterized by neural networks we use amortized variational inference in a manner similar to Variational AutoEncoders (Kingma and Welling, 2013), both to learn an approximate posterior $q(S, Z|X)$ and to learn the generative model parameters by maximizing a lower bound on the data likelihood (ELBO). We assume that the approximate posterior factorizes as follows:

$$q(\mathbf{S}, \mathbf{Z}|\mathbf{X}) =$$

$$(\prod_i^N q(S_i|\mathbf{X}))(\prod_i^N q(Z_i|Z_{i-1}, S_i, X_{:i}, X_i))$$

Like in VAEs, computing these individual factors is done through a parameterized function called the *inference* or *recognition* network whose parameters are trained jointly with the generative model.

In our case there are two forms for the factors in our posterior: (1) The first form, $q(S_i|\mathbf{X}) = q_{S_i}$ is parameterized by a classifier that takes in the set of sentences $\mathbf{X}$ and outputs a categorical distribution over the switching variables. (2) The second form, $q(Z_i|Z_{i-1}, S_i, X_{:i}, X_i) = q_{Z_i}$ is realized by functions $f_\mu(Z_{i-1}, S_i, X_{:i}, X_i)$ and $f_\sigma(Z_{i-1}, S_i, X_{:i}, X_i)$ that output the mean and variance, respectively, of a Gaussian over Z_i.

Borrowing terminology from VAEs, the approximate posterior (the factors given above) act as an 'encoder', while the generative model from the previous section can be seen as the 'decoder'. This type of training has been previously used in (Krishnan et al., 2015, 2017; Fraccaro et al., 2016, 2017; Karl et al., 2017).

3.1 Lower bound formula & exact training algorithm

As mentioned previously, we optimize all parameters (including the variational factor functions) by optimizing a lower bound on the data likelihood. The model may be trained either with supervision labels for the switching states (in our case, sentiment labels) or without supervised labels.

If one is training *without the sentiment labels*, then the lower bound on the marginal likelihood (and thus our optimization objective) may be written as follows:

$$L = \mathbb{E}_{S_1, \ldots S_N \sim q_{S_i}}\left[M - \sum_i^N KL(q_{S_i}||p(S_i|S_{i-1}))\right]$$

$$\text{where, } M = \mathbb{E}_{Z_1, \ldots Z_N \sim q_{Z_i}}\left[\sum_i^N (\log p(X_i|Z_i) - KL(q_{Z_i}||p(Z_i|Z_{i-1}, S_i)))\right]$$

The derivation for this objective is identical to that found in (Krishnan et al., 2017; Fraccaro et al., 2016), and simply relies on using properties of iterated expectations. All expectations are estimated with Monte Carlo samples.

If training *with the sentiment labels $S_1, \ldots, S_N$*, then the objective is similar (but without the sampling of the switching states), and is augmented with an additional supervision objective as done in Kingma et al. (2014):

$$L_S = M + \sum_i^N q_{S_i}$$

The final training procedure for a single narrative is: (1) For each sentence (starting from the first), sample the switching state S_i from $q(S_i|\mathbf{X})$. (2) For each sentence (starting from the first), sample the latent Z_i from $q(Z_i|S_i, Z_{i-1}, X)$. (3) Evaluate the data likelihood and KL term(s) with these samples. (4) Take the gradients of objective w.r.t. all parameters, using the reparameterization trick for q_{Z_i} (Kingma and Welling, 2013) or the Gumbel-Softmax[6] trick for q_{S_i} (Jang et al., 2017), and optimize.

4 Interpolations via Gibbs Sampling

One of the benefits of probabilistic formulation is the possibility (if an inference procedure can be found) of generating narratives with specific constraints, where the constraints may be specified as clamped variables in the model. In this section, we show how narratives may be generated conditioned on arbitrary bits and pieces of the narrative already filled in, using approximate Gibbs sampling. This allows one to, for example, interpolate a narrative given the first and the last sentence (similar to how earlier story generation systems were able to generate with a given end goal in mind). Some examples of these interpolations generated by our system can be found in Table 3. We give the equations and summarize the algorithm in the next sections.

4.1 Conditionals for Gibbs Sampling

For our Gibbs sampling algorithm we give the narrative scaffold (switching variables), $S_1, \ldots, S_T \in \mathbf{S}$ and a set of observed sentences, $\mathbf{X}^+$. This may be any set of sentences (the first and last, just the second sentence, etc) as inputs to the system. We wish to find values for the unobserved sentences in set $\mathbf{X}^-$ by sampling from $P(\mathbf{X}^-, Z_1, \ldots, Z_T|\mathbf{S}, \mathbf{X}^+)$. We perform this sampling via Gibbs sampling. Two different forms of conditionals need to be derived to do this. One over Z_i conditioned on everything else, and one over X_i conditioned on everything else.

---

[6]We use the soft variant of Gumbel-Softmax. Rather than forcing a hard choice for S_i, we directly use the Gumbel-Softmax output and combine the transition matrices via a convex combination

One can show[7] that the distribution over Z_i conditioned on everything else will be approximately proportional to the following Gaussian:

$$\mathcal{N}_{Z_{i+1}}(A_{S_{i+1}} Z_i, \Sigma_{S_{i+1}}) \mathcal{N}_{Z_i}(f_\mu(\cdot), f_\sigma(\cdot)) \quad (1)$$
$$\propto \mathcal{N}_{Z_i}(\mu_*, \Sigma_*) \text{ where,}$$
$$\Sigma_* = \left(A_{S_{i+1}}^T \Sigma_{S_{i+1}}^{-1} A_{S_{i+1}} + f_\sigma(\cdot)^{-1}\right)^{-1}$$
$$\mu_* = \Sigma_*^T \left(Z_{i+1} \Sigma_{S_{i+1}}^{-1} A_{S_{i+1}} + f_\mu(\cdot)^T f_\sigma(\cdot)^{-1}\right)^T$$

To find the second conditional, one can use the d-separation properties of the graph to find that it is proportional to:

$$P(X_i | Z_i, Z_{i+1}, S_i, S_{i+1}, X_{:i}, X_{i+1})$$
$$\propto P(X_{i+1} | X_{:i}, X_i, Z_{i+1}) P(X_i | X_{:i}, Z_i)$$

These two distributions are simply factors of our conditional language model, and both terms can thus be evaluated easily. In theory, one could use this fact to sample the original conditional via Metropolis-Hastings. Unfortunately, we found this approach to be too slow in practice. We observed that the simple heuristic of deterministically assigning X_i to be the greedy decoded output of the conditional language model $P(X_i | X_{:i}, Z_i)$ works well, as evidenced by the empirical results. We leave it for future work to research different conditional language model parameterizations allowing easy sampling from this conditional[8]

4.2 Gibbs Sampling Interpolation Overview

The variables in the Gibbs sampler are first initialized using some heuristics (see Supplemental). After initialization, performing interpolations with Gibbs sampling follows a two step process: First, for each Z_i, sample a value Z' from equation (1) and set Z_i to Z'. Then, for each X_i in $\mathbf{X}^-$, find a new value for X_i by running greedy decoding using the conditional language model.

5 Training Details

5.1 Dataset and Preprocessing

We use the ROCStories corpora introduced in Mostafazadeh et al. (2016). It contains 98,159 short commonsense stories in English as training, and 1,570 stories for validation and test each. Each

story in the dataset has five-sentences and captures causal and temporal commonsense relations. We limit our vocabulary size to 16,983 based on a per-word frequency cutoff set to 5. For sentiment tags, we automatically tag the entirety of the corpus with the rule based sentiment tagger, Vader (Hutto and Gilbert, 2014), and bucket the polarity scores of Vader into three tags: neutral, negative, and positive. These tags form the label set of the S variables in our SLDS model. We tokenize the stories with Spacy tokenizer (Honnibal and Montani, 2017). Each sentences in the input narrative has an <eos> tag except for the S2S model discussed below.

5.2 Switching Linear Dynamical System (SLDS)

The SLDS has RNN encoder and decoder networks with single layer GRU cells of hidden size 1024 and an input embedding size of 300. We train the model using Adam with the defaults used by PyTorch. We stop training when the validation loss does not decrease for 3 consecutive epochs. Training details for all models and baselines remain same as above unless otherwise mentioned.

5.3 Baselines

Language Model (LM) : We train a two layer recurrent neural language model with GRU cells of hidden size 512.

Sequence-to-Sequence Attention Model (S2S) We train a two layer neural sequence to sequence model equipped with bi-linear attention function with GRU cells of hidden size 512. Sentiments tags for a narrative (1 for each sentence) are given as input to the model and the corresponding sentences are concatenated together as the output with only one <eos> tag at the end. This model is trained with a 0.1 dropout. This model is comparable to the static model of (Yao et al., 2019), and other recent works employing a notion of scaffolding into neural generation (albeit adapted for our setting).

Linear Dynamical System (LDS) We also train a linear dynamical system as discussed in Section 2.1 as one of our baselines for fair comparisons. Apart from having just a *single* transition matrix this model has the same architectural details as SLDS.

Semi-Supervised SLDS (SLDS-X%) To gauge the usability of semi-supervision, we also train semi-supervised SLDS models with varying

---

[7]See Supplemental for derivation

[8]One possibility is take advantage of 'orderless' pretrained models through sampling (Wang and Cho, 2019). Approaches such as the one recently proposed in Donahue et al. (2020) may also be useful for this purpose.

amount of labelled sentiment tags unlike the original model which uses 100% tagged data. We refer to these as SLDS-X%, where X is the % labelled data used for training: 1%, 10%, 25%, and 50%.

6   Evaluations

As described above, our model is able to perform narrative interpolations via an approximate Gibbs sampling procedure. At the core of our evaluations is thus a fill-in-the-sentences task. We provide 1 or 2 sentences, and require the model to generate the rest of the narrative . We evaluate this via automatic evaluations as well as with crowd-sourced human evaluations. We also report perplexity to evaluate the models' ability to fit the data. Lastly, we look at whether the transitions learned by the SLDS models capture what they are intended to capture: does using the transition matrix associated with a sentiment tag (positive/negative/neutral) lead to a generated sentence with that sentiment?

6.1   Generating the Interpolations

For the SLDS models, the interpolations are generated via the Gibbs sampling algorithm described earlier. In all experiments for the SLDS models we draw **50** samples (including burn in samples) and output the interpolation that maximizes the probability of the given sentence(s). Since the baselines do not have the means for doing interpolations, we simulate 'interpolations' for the baselines; we draw **1000** samples using top k (with k=15) truncated sampling (conditioned on the given initial sentences, if available). We then output the sample that maximizes the probability of the clamped sentences around which we are interpolating the others. We allow the S2S access to the gold sentiment tags. To give a lower bound on the performance of the SLDS model, we do not provide it with gold tags. We instead provide the SLDS model with the semi-noisy[9] tags that are output from $q(S_i|X)$.[10]

6.2   Automatic Evaluation of Interpolations

We automatically evaluate on four different types of interpolations (where different combinations of sentences are removed and the model is forced to regenerate them), We evaluate the generations with the ROUGE (Lin, 2004) and METEOR (Banerjee and Lavie, 2005) metrics using the true sentences as targets. Table 2 shows the automatic evaluation results from interpolations using our proposed models and baselines. The #Sent(s) column indicates which sentence(s) were removed, and then regenerated by the model. We gave the baselines a slight edge over SLDS because they pick the best out of 1000 samples while SLDS is only out of 50. The SLDS models see their largest gain over the baseline models when at least the first sentence is given as an input. The baseline models do better when the first and second sentence need to be imputed. This is likely due to the fact that having access to the earlier sentences allows a better initialization for the Gibbs sampler. Surprisingly, the semi-supervised variants of the SLDS models achieve higher scores. The reasons for this is discussed below in the Perplexity section.

6.3   Human Evaluation of Interpolations

6.3.1   Annotation Scheme

As automatic evaluation metrics are not sufficient to assess the quality of any creative task such as narrative generation, we measure the quality of the generations through human evaluation of 200 stories on the Amazon Mechanical Turk platform. We provided Turkers with two generated narratives from two different models, each with five sentences. The first and last sentences were fed to each model as input, and the middle three sentences were generated. Each pair of narratives is graded by 3 users each with two tasks: (1) to rank on a scale of 0-3 each of the sentences except the first one on the basis of its coherency with the previous sentence(s) and (2) compare and rank the two narratives based on their overall coherency, ie how well the story connects the starting/ending sentences.

6.3.2   Human Evaluation Results

Table 4 reports the result of human evaluations of SLDS and baseline generations. We can observe that people preferred narratives generated by SLDS over the ones generated by baseline models (LM and S2S) as they found the former model more coherent, which is an important criteria for narrative generation. **51.3%** of the time SLDS generates better narratives than the LM model while LM in turn does it only **35.0%** of the times. 13.7% of the generations end up in tie. The mean sentence level coherence score for SLDS is around 12.5% larger than that of the LM, with a slightly lower standard

---

[9]To confirm that these tags are noisier, we repeat the experiments in Table 2, but feed gold tags to our models. We find that the gold tags lead to a sizable increase in performance for our model. See Appendix for more detail.

[10]Note that missing sentences, X, are used *only* for computing these noisy tags.

# Sent(s)	Metric	SLDS	SLDS-1	SLDS-10	SLDS-25	SLDS-50	S2S	LM	LDS
2nd	R1	17.60	19.36	20.46	**20.92**	19.55	18.79	18.30	17.33
	R2	2.43	3.46	3.86	**4.10**	3.43	3.14	2.83	2.31
	RL	16.43	17.76	19.03	**19.45**	17.87	17.39	16.68	15.97
	M	6.35	6.84	6.98	**7.15**	6.94	7.11	6.76	6.13
4th	R1	16.98	17.90	18.64	18.14	**19.39**	15.38	14.03	17.06
	R2	2.20	2.61	2.74	2.29	**3.23**	1.97	1.40	2.31
	RL	15.20	16.21	16.69	16.08	**17.43**	13.90	12.64	15.24
	M	6.33	7.11	6.92	6.53	**7.18**	5.84	5.61	6.89
$1^{st} + 2^{nd}$	R1	15.40	16.04	16.11	16.33	16.27	**18.91**	17.38	14.32
	R2	1.79	1.65	1.97	2.17	1.83	**2.62**	2.03	1.47
	RL	14.63	15.15	15.23	15.47	15.27	**17.89**	16.48	13.41
	M	5.34	5.27	5.40	5.44	5.42	**6.81**	6.07	4.80
$3^{rd} + 4^{th}$	R1	23.35	23.59	23.57	**23.65**	23.60	20.68	20.01	21.66
	R2	3.77	3.35	3.76	3.58	**3.93**	2.51	1.91	2.94
	RL	21.56	21.49	21.87	**21.88**	21.67	18.87	18.28	20.04
	M	8.28	8.26	8.22	8.12	**8.29**	7.51	7.26	7.87

Table 2: F1 scores for ROUGE-1, 2, and L and METEOR (M) (default mode score) for randomly sampled 500 stories from the test set. #Sents(s) column represents the "fill in" sentence(s) that the models generated using Gibbs sampling. Our SLDS models pick the best of **50** samples, the baselines models pick the best of **1000** samples

Ed was playing baseball in his yard.	Last week I had an idea.
He was running down the hill.	**I was so nervous that I decided to make a presentation.**
His ball was coming towards him.	I soon found it hard to come up with new ideas.
It was very scary!	I didn't think it would be so hard.
Ed was scared.	But then, an idea came to me and I was back on track.
Ben has always wanted to learn how to play the piano	Tim was always on his bike during the summer.
His parent bought him one.	**He had a lot of fun.**
Ben enrolls in a piano class with a local tutor.	**One day he decided to cut his bike down.**
Ben practiced every day.	**He hit a rock and fell off the bike and hit a tree.**
He gets better with every lesson.	He broke his arm.

Table 3: Sample interpolations from Gibbs sampling. Grayed out lines are provided as input and bold sentences are generated by SLDS.

deviation. We see similar results when compared against the S2S model.

System	Sent Coh. (0-3)	Best Story
LM	1.68 ± 1.01	35.0%
SLDS	$\mathbf{1.89 \pm 0.96}$	**51.3%**
S2S	1.67 ± 1.00	35.1%
SLDS	$\mathbf{1.87 \pm 0.97}$	**51.9%**

Table 4: Human evaluation scores for filled-in narrative generation. Humans judged sentence coherence and chose which model filled in the *most* coherent narrative overall (13.7% and 13% tie for LM and S2S).

6.4 Language Modeling Perplexity Score

As our models are essentially language models, we evaluated their per-sentence negative log-likelihood and per-word perplexity scores[11], which can be viewed as an indirect measure of how well a system works as a generative model of narrative text. For the SLDS and LDS models these scores are approximations, an upper bound (the negative of the ELBO) to the actual values. For the other two models the scores are exact. A good model should assign low perplexity scores to its test set. In Table 5 SLDS achieves the lowest scores, implying that it is able to model the data distribution well. In Table 6

---

[11]Note that since S2S appends the `eos` token only at the end, its per-sentence NLL is slightly lower than that of LM.

we also calculate the perplexity scores for the semi-supervised SLDS models to assess the effectiveness of semi-supervised training. Surprisingly, the models with less supervision scored better in terms of perplexity. One possibility for this might be the use of the soft Gumbel-Softmax in the semi-supervised models. The soft Gumbel-Softmax variant does not commit to using a single transition matrix at each time step (instead linearly combining them, weighted by the Softmax weights). This fact may permit the model greater flexibility in fitting the training data. While this leads to better scores in metrics such as perplexity or BLEU, it does leads to transitions that are worse in capturing the properties they should be capturing, as we shall see in the next section.

System	NLL	PPL
LM	196.30	35.41
S2S	192.25	43.36
LDS	≤186.24	29.49
SLDS	**≤182.17**	**27.39**

Table 5: NLL and PPL scores on the test set. Lower is better for both the metrics. Variance in NLL calculation is in the order of 10^{-3}.

System	NLL	PPL
SLDS-1%	**≤177.60**	**25.19**
SLDS-10%	≤178.81	25.77
SLDS-25%	≤181.11	26.87
SLDS-50%	≤185.07	28.88
SLDS	≤182.17	27.39

Table 6: Approximate NLL and PPL scores for SLDS and semi-supervised SLDS on the test set.

6.5 Evaluation of Transition Dynamics

One matter of interest is whether or not the transitions are capturing what they are supposed to capture, appropriate sentiment. Since we used the sentiment tagger Vader for training tags, we again utilize it to evaluate whether using transitions of a certain sentiment actually leads the model to produce outputs with the given sentiment. To perform this evaluation, we give as input to our models (and the S2S baseline) the sentiment tags for a sentence and allow it to generate a sentence conditioned on these sentiment tags. We then tag the generated sentences with Vader and see if the sentiment tags match the originals. We calculate the

F1 score across all sentiment tags and report the macro average. In Table 7 we see that having labels is incredibly important for meaningful transitions. There is a large drop in F1 as the amount of labels given to the model is decreased. The SLDS model that is trained with 100% of the labels performs a little better than even S2S, despite not having direct access to the sentiment labels (SLDS only uses the sentiment labels to decide which transition to use while the S2S model uses attention directly on the sentiment labels).

System	Macro F1
S2S	95.8
SLDS-1%	50.2 ± 1.1
SLDS-10%	51.4 ± 1.1
SLDS-25%	58.7 ± 0.4
SLDS-50%	74.6 ± 0.1
SLDS	**96.1 ± 0.0**

Table 7: Macro F1 scores on sentiment classification task. Results for SLDS and SLDS-X% are averaged over 5 runs.

7   Related Work

Story/narrative generation has a rich history in the field of AI. Many early systems were based on structured formalisms for describing common narrative structures (Lakoff, 1972; Thorndyke, 1977; Meehan, 1977), many being inspired by the initial work of (Propp, 1928). There has been a swath of recent work that has looked to add some semblance of a 'narrative scaffold' back into generation methods (Fan et al.; Martin et al., 2018; Yao et al., 2019; Xu et al., 2018). Many of these methods work as conditional LMs (conditioned directly on the scaffold). This line of work may be combined with our formalization as well, by conditioning the generation on the switching state as well, as done in the model of Barber (2006). Recent work by Tambwekar et al. (2019) has similar goals to ours in permitting more controlability in generation systems, developing a RL-based system that allows users to specify an end goal for a story (by specifying the event class that is desired to appear at the end). Their work differs from ours in that it does not deal with text directly, modeling only the sequences of events in the narrative. It may be possible to utilize this model as the scaffolding component in our model (utilizing their RL policy for the scaffold planner, rather than the simple

Markovian distribution used here).

8 Conclusion and Future Work

In this paper, we formulated the problem of narrative generation as a switching dynamical system. We showed how this formulation captures notions important in narrative generation, such as narrative dynamics and scaffolds. We developed an approximate Gibbs sampling algorithm for the model that permits the system to generate interpolations conditioned on arbitrary parts of the narrative, and evaluated these interpolations using both human and automatic evaluations. Though in this work we used sentiment tags for our scaffolds/switching variables, future work may look at utilizing different kinds of information to guide the generation of narratives. Utilizing the main predicate of a sentence as a scaffold would be a logical next step, and may prove more informative than the sentiment trajectory. A scaffold such as this can take on many more possible values than a sentiment tag, and as such, it may prove difficult to assign a set of dynamics to each value. Another avenue for future work would deal with this possible problem. One potential solution could be to associate each switching variable value with a (learned) vector in a probability simplex, and use this vector to combine a small set of "primitive" dynamics matrices in order to get that value's associated set of dynamics.

References

G Ackerson and K Fu. 1970. On state estimation in switching environments. *IEEE Transactions on Automatic Control*, 15(1):10–17.

Satanjeev Banerjee and Alon Lavie. 2005. METEOR: An automatic metric for MT evaluation with improved correlation with human judgments. In *Proceedings of the ACL Workshop on Intrinsic and Extrinsic Evaluation Measures for Machine Translation and/or Summarization*, pages 65–72, Ann Arbor, Michigan. Association for Computational Linguistics.

David Barber. 2006. Expectation correction for smoothed inference in switching linear dynamical systems. *Journal of Machine Learning Research*, 7(Nov):2515–2540.

C. B. Chang and M. Athans. 1978. State estimation for discrete systems with switching parameters. *IEEE Transactions on Aerospace and Electronic Systems*, AES-14(3):418–425.

Snigdha Chaturvedi, Haoruo Peng, and Dan Roth. 2017. Story comprehension for predicting what happens next. In *Proceedings of the 2017 Conference on Empirical Methods in Natural Language Processing*, pages 1603–1614, Copenhagen, Denmark. Association for Computational Linguistics.

Chris Donahue, Mina Lee, and Percy Liang. 2020. Enabling language models to fill in the blanks. In *Proceedings of the 58th Annual Meeting of the Association for Computational Linguistics*, pages 2492–2501, Online. Association for Computational Linguistics.

Angela Fan, Mike Lewis, and Yann Dauphin. Hierarchical neural story generation. In *Proceedings of the 56th Annual Meeting of the Association for Computational Linguistics (Volume 1: Long Papers)*.

Angela Fan, Mike Lewis, and Yann Dauphin. 2019. Strategies for structuring story generation. In *Proceedings of the 57th Annual Meeting of the Association for Computational Linguistics*, pages 2650–2660.

Marco Fraccaro, Simon Kamronn, Ulrich Paquet, and Ole Winther. 2017. A disentangled recognition and nonlinear dynamics model for unsupervised learning. In *NeurIPS 2017*.

Marco Fraccaro, Søren Kaae Sønderby, Ulrich Paquet, and Ole Winther. 2016. Sequential neural models with stochastic layers. In *NeurIPS 2016*.

Matthew Honnibal and Ines Montani. 2017. spaCy 2: Natural language understanding with Bloom embeddings, convolutional neural networks and incremental parsing. To appear.

Clayton J Hutto and Eric Gilbert. 2014. Vader: A parsimonious rule-based model for sentiment analysis of social media text. In *AAAI conference on weblogs and social media*.

Eric Jang, Shixiang Gu, and Ben Poole. 2017. Categorical reparameterization with gumbel-softmax. In *ICLR*.

Maximilian Karl, Maximilian Sölch, Justin Bayer, and Patrick van der Smagt. 2017. Deep variational bayes filters: Unsupervised learning of state space models from raw data. *ICLR*.

Ahmed Khalifa, Gabriella AB Barros, and Julian Togelius. 2017. Deeptingle. *ICCC*.

Diederik P Kingma and Max Welling. 2013. Auto-encoding variational bayes. *arXiv preprint arXiv:1312.6114*.

Durk P Kingma, Shakir Mohamed, Danilo Jimenez Rezende, and Max Welling. 2014. Semi-supervised learning with deep generative models. In *NeurIPS 2014*.

Rahul G. Krishnan, Uri Shalit, and David Sontag. 2015. Deep kalman filters. *CoRR*.

Rahul G. Krishnan, Uri Shalit, and David Sontag. 2017. Structured inference networks for nonlinear state space models. In *AAAI 2017*.

George Lakoff. 1972. Structural complexity in fairy tales.

Michael Lebowitz. 1985. Story-telling as planning and learning. *Poetics*, 14(6):483–502.

Chin-Yew Lin. 2004. Rouge: A package for automatic evaluation of summaries. In *ACL 2004*.

Scott W Linderman, Andrew C Miller, Ryan P Adams, David M Blei, Liam Paninski, and Matthew J Johnson. 2016. Recurrent switching linear dynamical systems. *AISTATS*.

Fei Liu, Trevor Cohn, and Timothy Baldwin. 2018. Narrative modeling with memory chains and semantic supervision. In *Proceedings of the 56th Annual Meeting of the Association for Computational Linguistics (Volume 2: Short Papers)*, pages 278–284, Melbourne, Australia. Association for Computational Linguistics.

Lara J. Martin, Prithviraj Ammanabrolu, William Hancock, Shruti Singh, Brent Harrison, and Mark O. Riedl. 2018. Event representations for automated story generation with deep neural nets. *AAAI*.

James R. Meehan. 1977. Tale-spin, an interactive program that writes stories. In *IJCAI*, pages 91–98.

Nasrin Mostafazadeh, Nathanael Chambers, Xiaodong He, Devi Parikh, Dhruv Batra, Lucy Vanderwende, Pushmeet Kohli, and James F. Allen. 2016. In *Proceedings of the 2016 Conference of the North American Chapter of the Association for Computational Linguistics: Human Language Technologies*, pages 839–849, San Diego, California. Association for Computational Linguistics. [link].

Kevin P Murphy. 1998. Switching kalman filters.

Gerald Prince. 2003. *A dictionary of narratology*.

Vladimir Propp. 1928. *Morphology of the Folktale*.

Andrew J Reagan, Lewis Mitchell, Dilan Kiley, Christopher M Danforth, and Peter Sheridan Dodds. 2016. The emotional arcs of stories are dominated by six basic shapes. *EPJ Data Science*, 5(1):31.

Mark O. Riedl and R. Michael Young. 2006. Story planning as exploratory creativity: Techniques for expanding the narrative search space. *New Generation Computing*, 24(3):303–323.

Mark O. Riedl and Robert Michael Young. 2010a. Narrative planning: Balancing plot and character. *J. Artif. Intell. Res.*, 39:217–268.

Mark O. Riedl and Robert Michael Young. 2010b. Narrative planning: Balancing plot and character. *J. Artif. Intell. Res.*, 39:217–268.

Melissa Roemmele and Andrew S Gordon. 2015. Creative help: a story writing assistant. In *International Conference on Interactive Digital Storytelling*, pages 81–92. Springer.

Pradyumna Tambwekar, Murtaza Dhuliawala, Animesh Mehta, Lara J Martin, Brent Harrison, and Mark O Riedl. 2019. Controllable neural story generation via reinforcement learning. *IJCAI*.

Perry W Thorndyke. 1977. Cognitive structures in comprehension and memory of narrative discourse. *Cognitive psychology*, 9(1):77–110.

Scott R. Turner. 1993. *Minstrel: A Computer Model of Creativity and Storytelling*. Ph.D. thesis.

Kurt Vonnegut. 1981. *Palm Sunday*. Rosetta Books.

Alex Wang and Kyunghyun Cho. 2019. BERT has a mouth, and it must speak: BERT as a Markov random field language model. In *Proceedings of the Workshop on Methods for Optimizing and Evaluating Neural Language Generation*, pages 30–36, Minneapolis, Minnesota. Association for Computational Linguistics.

Sam Wiseman, Stuart M Shieber, and Alexander M Rush. 2018. Learning neural templates for text generation. In *Proceedings of the 2018 Conference on Empirical Methods in Natural Language Processing*, pages 3174–3187, Brussels, Belgium. Association for Computational Linguistics.

Jingjing Xu, Yi Zhang, Qi Zeng, Xuancheng Ren, Xiaoyan Cai, and Xu Sun. 2018. A skeleton-based model for promoting coherence among sentences in narrative story generation. In *Proceedings of the 2018 Conference on Empirical Methods in Natural Language Processing*, pages 4306–4315, Brussels, Belgium. Association for Computational Linguistics.

Lili Yao, Nanyun Peng, Ralph M. Weischedel, Kevin Knight, Dongyan Zhao, and Rui Yan. 2019. Plan-and-write: Towards better automatic storytelling. *AAAI*, abs/1811.05701.

Appendix

9 Gibbs Sampling Derivation

With the d-separation properties of the graph (and substituting in our variational posterior approximation Q), we can write the conditional distribution

# Sent(s)	Metric	SLDS	SLDS-1	SLDS-10	SLDS-25	SLDS-50	S2S	LM	LDS
$1^{st} + 2^{nd}$	R1	17.89	17.93	18.06	18.51	18.44	**18.91**	17.38	14.32
	R2	2.30	1.98	2.35	2.57	2.21	**2.62**	2.03	1.47
	RL	15.01	15.96	16.41	16.73	16.31	**17.89**	16.48	13.41
	M	6.06	5.83	6.21	6.49	6.37	**6.81**	6.07	4.80
$3^{rd} + 4^{th}$	R1	23.41	23.78	24.03	**24.08**	23.60	20.68	20.01	21.66
	R2	3.79	3.51	3.88	3.62	**3.93**	2.51	1.91	2.94
	RL	21.97	21.86	22.00	**22.10**	21.67	18.87	18.28	20.04
	M	8.32	8.27	8.32	8.30	**8.33**	7.51	7.26	7.87

Table 8: F1 scores for ROUGE-1, 2, and L and METEOR (M) (default mode score) for randomly sampled 500 stories from the test set. #Sents(s) column represents the "fill in" sentence(s) that the models generated using Gibbs sampling. Our SLDS models pick the best of **50** samples, the baselines models pick the best of **1000** samples

of some Z_i given everything else as follows:

$$P(Z_i|Z_{i-1}, Z_{i+1}, S_i, S_{i+1}, X_i, X_{i-1})$$
$$\propto P(Z_{i+1}, S_{i+1}|Z_{i-1}, Z_{i+1}, S_i, S_{i+1}, X_i, X_{i-1}, Z_i)$$
$$* P(Z_i|Z_{i-1}, S_i, X_i, X_{i-1})$$
$$\approx P(Z_{i+1}, S_{i+1}|Z_{i-1}, S_i, S_{i+1}, X_i, X_{i-1}, Z_i)$$
$$* Q(Z_i|Z_{i-1}, S_i, X_i, X_{i-1})$$
$$= P(Z_{i+1}|S_{i+1}, Z_{i-1}, S_i, S_{i+1}, X_i, X_{i-1}, Z_i)$$
$$* P(S_{i+1}|S_i)Q(Z_i|Z_{i-1}, S_i, X_i, X_{i-1})$$
$$\propto P(Z_{i+1}|S_{i+1}, Z_{i-1}, S_i, S_{i+1}, X_i, X_{i-1}, Z_i)$$
$$* Q(Z_i|Z_{i-1}, S_i, X_i, X_{i-1})$$
$$= P(Z_{i+1}|S_{i+1}, Z_i)Q(Z_i|Z_{i-1}, S_i, X_i, X_{i-1})$$
$$= \mathcal{N}_{Z_{i+1}}(A_{S_{i+1}}Z_i, \Sigma_{S_{i+1}})\mathcal{N}_{Z_i}(f_\mu(\cdot), f_\sigma(\cdot))$$

The rest can be derived by taking the PDFs of the two Gaussian densities above, getting rid of constants that don't depend on Z_i, multiplying them together, and completing the square to obtain the numerator of a Gaussian over Z_i (such that Z_i appears nowhere else in the equation). This numerator can then be multiplied by the normalizing constant (that does not depend on Z_i) to obtain exactly a Gaussian pdf with the mean and variance as given below:

$$\mathcal{N}_{Z_{i+1}}(A_{S_{i+1}}Z_i, \Sigma_{S_{i+1}})\mathcal{N}_{Z_i}(f_\mu(\cdot), f_\sigma(\cdot))$$
$$\propto \mathcal{N}_{Z_i}(\mu_*, \Sigma_*) \text{ where,}$$
$$\Sigma_* = \left(A_{S_{i+1}}^T \Sigma_{S_{i+1}}^{-1} A_{S_{i+1}} + f_\sigma(\cdot)^{-1}\right)^{-1}$$
$$\mu_* = \Sigma_*^T \left(Z_{i+1}\Sigma_{S_{i+1}}^{-1} A_{S_{i+1}} + f_\mu(\cdot)^T f_\sigma(\cdot)^{-1}\right)^T$$

10 Manual Error Analysis of Generations

We evaluate the quality of sentences of 20 generated narratives are not considered coherent by Turkers. We find that, in a broader context, 16 stories out of 20 are not good enough in terms of connecting the ending with the previous sentences. Also, in 14 out of 20 stories, *mild* off-topic sentences are introduced, which are aligned with the main topic of the story but not along with local coherency (i.e. the previous and the next sentences). When considering a narrower context, or sentence level, we confirm that only 9 out of 60 generated sentences are ungrammatical, so they fail to deliver their meaning.

11 Initializing the Gibbs Sampler

Initializing Z : We first initialize the Z variables in the sampler. This is done as follows: The Z variables are initialized in increasing order. If sentence X_i is provided as input, then we sample from the approximate posterior q_Z in order to initialize Z_i. If X_i is missing, then we sample using the dynamics distribution, $P(Z_i|Z_{i-1}, S_i)$. Since we initialize in increasing order, we are guaranteed to have Z_{i-1}.

Initializing X : We next initialize the missing text. Initializing the missing text X_i is simply done by greedy decoding from the language model conditioned on Z_i, and previous sentences.

12 Automatic Evaluation Results with Gold Labels

Below in Table 8 we provide the results for the automatic experiments with gold labels fed to our method. We find a sizable increase in performance by providing the gold labels, and thus use the automatic labels as noisy proxies in order to establish a lower bound on performance.

"What Are You Trying to Do?"
Semantic Typing of Event Processes

Muhao Chen[1,2], Hongming Zhang[3]*, Haoyu Wang[1], Dan Roth[1]
[1]Department of Computer and Information Science, UPenn
[2]Information Sciences Institute, USC
[3]Department of Computer Science and Engineering, HKUST
muhaoche@usc.edu; hzhangal@cse.ust.hk;
{why16gzi, danroth}@seas.upenn.edu

Abstract

This paper studies a new cognitively motivated semantic typing task, *multi-axis event process typing*, that, given an event process, attempts to infer free-form type labels describing (i) the type of action made by the process and (ii) the type of object the process seeks to affect. This task is inspired by computational and cognitive studies of event understanding, which suggest that understanding processes of events is often directed by recognizing the goals, plans or intentions of the protagonist(s). We develop a large dataset containing over 60k event processes, featuring ultra fine-grained typing on both the action and object type axes with very large ($10^3 \sim 10^4$) label vocabularies. We then propose a hybrid learning framework, P2GT, which addresses the challenging typing problem with indirect supervision from glosses[1] and a joint learning-to-rank framework. As our experiments indicate, P2GT supports identifying the intent of processes, as well as the fine semantic type of the affected object. It also demonstrates the capability of handling few-shot cases, and strong generalizability on out-of-domain processes.[2]

1 Introduction

Events are the fundamental building blocks of natural languages. To help machines understand events, extensive research effort has been devoted to inducing how events described in text are procedurally connected (Ning et al., 2017; Radinsky et al., 2012), and how they form *event processes*[3] (Pichotta and Mooney, 2014; Berant et al., 2014; Jindal and Roth, 2013). Consequently, such prototypical schematic sequences of events have found

important use cases including storyline construction (Do et al., 2012; Radinsky and Horvitz, 2013), narrative cloze (Chaturvedi et al., 2017; Lee and Goldwasser, 2019), biological process comprehension (Berant et al., 2014) and diagnostic prediction (Zhang et al., 2020b).

Nonetheless, understanding an event process is not just about inducing temporal relations between events or inferring missing steps in an event sequence. As suggested by cognitive studies (Zacks et al., 2001; Zacks and Tversky, 2001; Kurby and Zacks, 2008), a process of events is defined more by the goals, plans, intentions, or traits of its performer, rather than by physical characteristics. For example, a series of events *digging a hole*, *putting in some seeds*, *filling with soil* and *watering the soil*, occurs in a specific sequence since these steps are directed towards the central goal of *planting a plant* by the performer. Similarly, we can tell that *making a dough*, *adding toppings*, *preheating the oven* and *baking the dough* is likely a chain of actions aimed at *cooking pizza*. Indeed, aforementioned studies show that humans understand a plausible event process by hypothesizing the objectives those co-occurring events aim for, or the ultimate consequence the process seeks to accomplish. Accordingly, we suggest that computational methods for event understanding would benefit from conceptualizing the intentions behind the processes. Moreover, inducing intentions is crucial to rich understanding of text (Rashkin et al., 2018), and could potentially support other applications such as commonsense reasoning (Sap et al., 2019), summarization (Daumé III and Marcu, 2006), reading comprehension (Berant et al., 2014) and schema induction (Huang et al., 2016).

To understand the intentions of event processes, the *first* contribution of this paper is to propose a new semantic typing task. The *event process typing* task seeks to retrieve ultra fine-grained type

---

* This work was done when the author was visiting the University of Pennsylvania.

[1]A gloss provides a sense definition for a lexeme.

[2]The contributed learning resources, software and a system demonstration are available at http://cogcomp.org/page/publication_view/915.

[3]A.k.a. event chains (Chambers and Jurafsky, 2008).

Proceedings of the 24th Conference on Computational Natural Language Learning, pages 531–542
Online, November 19-20, 2020. ©2020 Association for Computational Linguistics
https://doi.org/10.18653/v1/P17

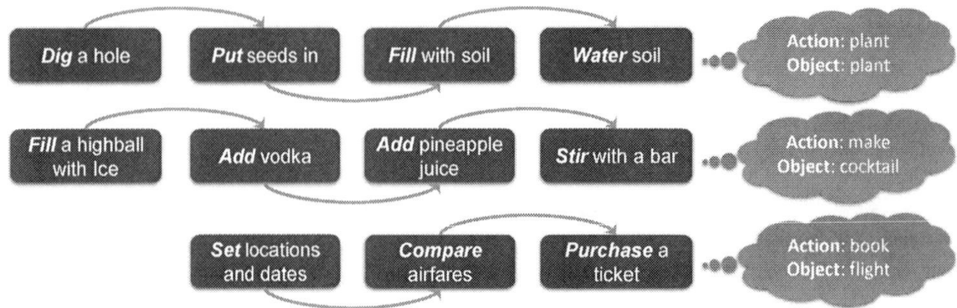

Figure 1: Examples of type inference for event processes.

information to summarize the goal and intention of the associated events. Specifically, each event process is typed along two axes: the *action type* that describes the type of action the process takes, and the *object type* that semantically types the object(s) that the process seeks to affect. Figure 1 shows several accordingly typed event processes. Motivated by recent works on entity typing (Choi et al., 2018; Zhou et al., 2018), our task employs large type vocabularies supporting diverse free-form semantic labels for both axes.

To facilitate related research, we developed a large dataset extracted from wikiHow[4], as the *second* contribution of this paper. This dataset contains over 60,000 processes of primitive events, and features fine-grained action and object type labels for each process. While the dataset aims at creating rich examples of event process intentions, it is also a challenging dataset from two perspectives. First, vocabularies on both type axes are remarkably diverse, giving over 1,000 action type labels and over 10,000 object type labels. And, these fine-grained type vocabularies occur quite sparsely – around 68% of action types and 88% of object types occur fewer than 10 times. This leads to a few-shot learning scenario and, in nearly half of the cases, one-shot. Second, the free-form type labels are generally external to the lexical content of the associated events appearing in a process. Hence, this typing task could not be easily handled with an extractive method (Nenkova and McKeown, 2012).

While the task and dataset pose a non-trivial learning problem, the free-form type system allows for a practical form of indirect supervision based on gloss knowledge. As the *third* contribution, we propose a hybrid learning framework, P2GT (i.e., process-to-gloss based typing), to leverage such in-

direct supervision for event process typing. Instead of directly inferring the multi-axis type labels, we find it to be much easier to seize on the semantic relatedness between the process-gloss pair, as the gloss provides richer semantic information than the label itself. For few-shot cases, gloss definitions also represent useful side information to jump-start inducing labels that are rarely seen or completely unseen in training.

The proposed framework fine-tunes a pre-trained language model to capture the relatedness of an event process and the gloss of types with a ranking task objective. To incorporate more precise gloss information, the training process deploys a word sense disambiguation (WSD) module for both verbs and nouns. Joint learning for both action and object types is enforced to further complement scarce supervision signals. Based on extensive experimental evaluation, the proposed framework exhibits promising performance of inferring the fine-grained multi-axis type information. Specifically, it outperforms a strong RoBERTa-based baseline by 2.4-3.0 folds in *recall@1*. We also show that the incorporated gloss knowledge supports few-shot case prediction, and benefits our model's generalization to out-of-domain event processes.

2 Task and Dataset

We hereby formulate the task of multi-axis event process typing, and introduce the contributed dataset.

2.1 Task Definition

Following Chambers and Jurafsky (2008), we define a process as a sequence of primitive events $P = [e_1, e_2, ..., e_l]$ performed by one common protagonist (or performer). Since the protagonist is shared among the events, each event e_i thereof contains a *predicate* a_i mentioning an action performed

---

[4]https://www.wikihow.com/

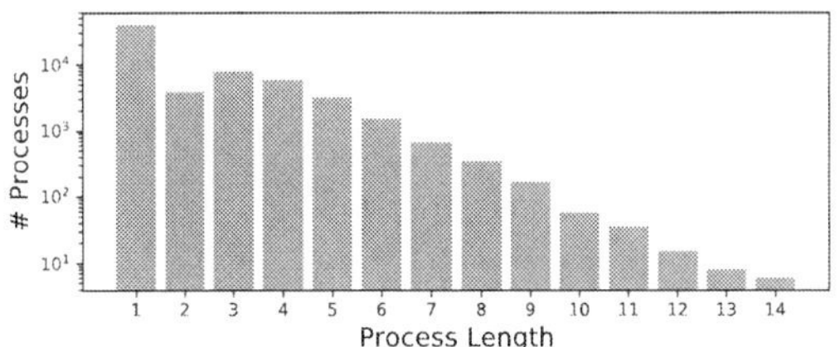

Figure 2: Distribution of process lengths.

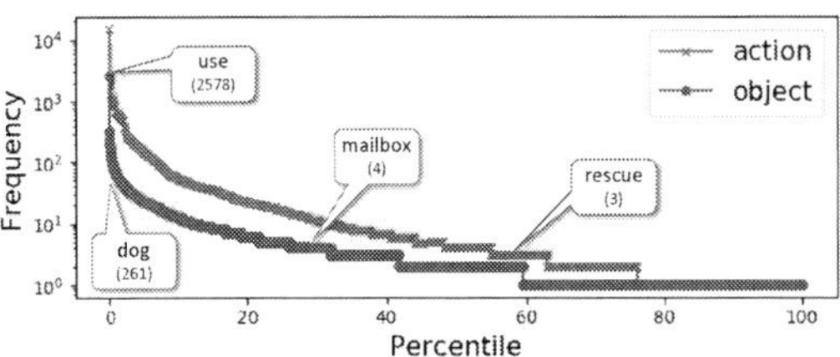

Figure 3: Distribution of action and object types. Number of frequencies are shown in the brackets.

by the protagonist, and an object o_i describing the object(s) that the action is taken upon. The goal is to conceptualize the overall intention behind the process P into two labels, i.e. A from the verb vocabulary that describes the overall action of P, and O from the noun vocabulary that describes what object(s) the process is most likely to affect. Such type inference is important to applications that require commonsense reasoning based on chains of activities, including event-based summarization, narrative prediction and open-domain QA.

2.2 Dataset

We construct a large corpus of typed event processes based on wikiHow – an online wiki-style community containing a collection of professionally edited how-to guideline articles.

Construction A set of the articles are crawled from wikiHow, where each included article describes ordered steps of activities to complete a central goal (e.g. the article "How to book a flight" describes necessary steps to complete an airline booking). Each described step of an article forms a standalone section, which provides an easy-to-consume format for obtaining event processes with clear intentions. We use AllenNLP (Gardner et al., 2018) to perform SRL on section titles of a goal-step article, and extract the VERB (predicate a_i) and ARG1 (object o_i) outputs from the section titles to form the corresponding sequence of (primitive) events. Note that some articles may contain multiple step sequences for the same goal, e.g. booking

a flight can be separated to two alternatives, either about booking online or via phone call. In such cases, each alternative is extracted as a separate process. Moreover, we only preserve processes where every primitive event contains both VERB and ARG1. Any ARG0's are however omitted, since all events in a process share the same protagonist.

To obtain the type information, we first run SRL on the clause after "how to" in the article titles, from which the VERB term is seized as the action type label. Then on the ARG1 output of SRL, we fetch only the lemmatized head word based on dependency parsing and lemmatization (Bird and Loper, 2004). This typically gives us the non-plural noun that represents the object type, whereas other dependents including modifiers are dropped. Consider the clause in "How to make a birthday cake", after *make* is fetched with SRL, the head word *cake* will be preserved from the ARG1 "a birthday cake", providing an adequately abstracted label for object typing while being consistent to task definition.

Statistics The above effort obtains 62,277 clean event processes, each of which is labeled with both action and object types. Lengths of the processes are varied, for which the distribution is plotted in Figure 2. While the dataset gives a rich variety of instances for processes and intentions, it features a challenging type system for several reasons:

- *Diversity.* The fine-grained type vocabularies consist of 1,336 action types and 10,441 object types. As shown in Figure 3, both sets of labels generally form long-tail distributions.

- *Few-shot cases.* There are 68.3% of action type labels and 88.2% of object type labels occuring fewer than 10 times across all processes. This fact indicates extreme few-shot cases that are challenging to learning and inference.

- *External labels.* In around 91.2% processes, the action type labels are different from the predicates of associated events, while 84.2% of processes have object type labels that do not appear as event objects. Such generally external labels easily cause extractive or sequence-to-label prediction methods to fall short.

3 Process Typing with Gloss Knowledge

In this section, we present our method for the multi-axis event process typing task. The proposed P2GT framework conducts learning in three steps. A pre-trained language model is first used to produce the representations of processes. Then, the gloss information of type vocabularies is encoded as intermediate representations for type labels using the same language model, for which WSD is performed to refine the gloss information of polysemous labels during training. Finally, the language model is fine-tuned with a ranking task objective to capture the association of process-gloss pairs. In the last step thereof, joint learning is performed for typing on both axes to complement the scarce supervision signals, where a process representation is separately projected and handled for action and object types in the latent space. Figure 4 displays the overall model architecture.

In the rest of this section, we introduce the technical details of each step for learning and inference.

3.1 Process Representation

We use the officially released *RoBERTa-base* (Liu et al., 2019) for representations of event processes. RoBERTa improves the original BERT (Devlin et al., 2019) with a modified training procedure. It is considered one of the SOTA models for semantic representation of lexical sequences.

To encode a process P, we concatenate the predicate and object (a_i and o_i) of each event (e_i). Then those contents of all primitive events in P are sequentially concatenated, while the separator token of RoBERTa </s> is added between the contents of every consecutive two events. The entire lexical sequence is enclosed between tokens <s> and </s> to denote the beginning and end of the sequence. Following convention (Bommasani et al., 2020), mean-pooling of hidden states produces the encoded representation of the process, denoted $\mathbf{P}$.

3.2 Label Representation

In our problem setting, directly capturing the association between a process and a free-form type label can be difficult. Hence, we propose a way of indirect supervision by using gloss knowledge as intermediate representations of type labels. The sense definitions in the glosses contain much richer semantic information of the labels themselves. Therefore, leveraging intermediate representations seeks to better characterize the semantic relatedness of processes and labels, especially when the labels are often external to the event content. Glosses also adequately provide side information to jump-start few-shot label representations.

Given a label L for either type axis, we use the same RoBERTa model (with shared parameters)

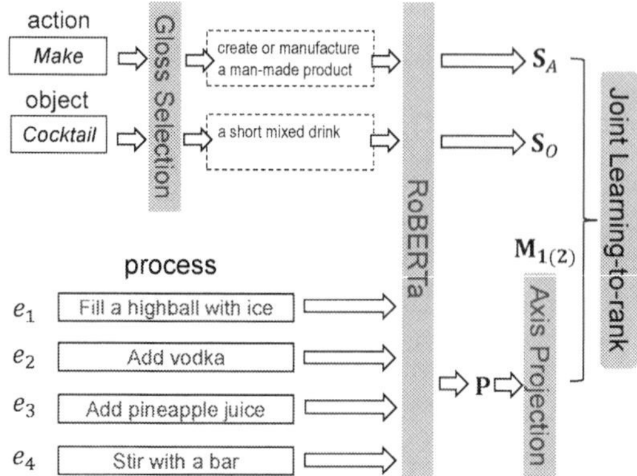

Figure 4: A gloss selection module selects the proper glosses of the training labels. Then a RoBERTa language model captures the event process, and separately generates gloss-based representations for positive and negative sampled labels. The entire learning process conducts joint learning-to-rank on both type axes.

for process representation to encode its gloss sense definition. The mean-pooling result produces the gloss-based label representation denoted $\mathbf{S}_L$. Consider that the verb and noun terms in label vocabularies can be polysemous, we employ either of the following two techniques to select the glosses in the learning phase:

- *Pre-trained WSD models.* One technique is to employ off-the-shelf WSD models that handle both verb and noun senses (Hadiwinoto et al., 2019; Huang et al., 2019). This could more precisely find the right definition for each label given the specific context of a process, and allows each (polysemous) label to have varied representations when typing different processes. During training P2GT, we run WSD on the concatenation of type labels $[A, O]$ to select the glosses of A and O for each training case.

- *Most frequent senses (MFS).* Suppose a WSD model is not available, then the default way is to match a label only to its most frequent (or predominant) sense in sense-annotated corpora (Langone et al., 2004; Camacho-Collados et al., 2016). The MFS method has been a very strong baseline for unsupervised WSD (Tripodi and Navigli, 2019), as it is natural in language text that words generally express their predominant senses in most cases (McCarthy et al., 2007). Specifically for our task, the purpose is not to infer the exact sense, but rather generating a semantically rich (and allowably noisy) representation for type labels. In practice, we find this simple technique to perform reasonably well as we type the event processes (§4.3).

Besides these two techniques, we also tried others to represent a label, including concatenating all its gloss sense definitions, or concatenating most frequent two or more senses. They however do not perform as well as the aforementioned two techniques, hypothetically due to the noise introduced to label representations. More technical details about WSD and the source inventory of glosses are to be described in Experiments (§4.1).

3.3 Learning Objective

Let (P, A, O) be a process P denoted by action and object labels A and O, our model captures the semantic associations between a RoBERTa encoded process $\mathbf{P}$ and label glosses $\mathbf{S}_A$ and $\mathbf{S}_O$ by optimizing a ranking task objective. In detail, we define the margin ranking loss for action typing as

$$L_1^P = [s\left(\mathbf{M}_1 \cdot \mathbf{P}, \mathbf{S}_{A'}\right) - s\left(\mathbf{M}_1 \cdot \mathbf{P}, \mathbf{S}_A\right) + \gamma_1]_+ ,$$

and that for object typing as

$$L_2^P = [s\left(\mathbf{M}_2 \cdot \mathbf{P}, \mathbf{S}_{O'}\right) - s\left(\mathbf{M}_2 \cdot \mathbf{P}, \mathbf{S}_O\right) + \gamma_2]_+ .$$

$[x]_+$ thereof denotes the positive part of the input x (i.e. $\max(x, 0)$). γ_1 and γ_2 are two positive constant margins. $\mathbf{M}_1$ and $\mathbf{M}_2$ correspond to two learnable linear projections dedicated to the two type axes respectively. $s(\cdot)$ is the cosine similarity measure. $A' \in V$ and $O' \in N$ are negative-sample labels. In the setting with WSD deployed in training, negative sampling randomly fetches from all glosses of labels that appear in the training data, except for the gloss(es) of the positive label. This allows chances for different glosses of a polysemous label to serve as negative samples. Otherwise, the only gloss of every negative-sample label is utilized in the MFS setting.

The eventual learning objective is to optimize the following joint loss, where D denotes the dataset:

$$L = \frac{1}{|D|} \sum_{P \in D} L_1^P + L_2^P.$$

Note that we have incorporated different margins that can trade-off between L_1^P and L_2^P, hence we do not use weight coefficients to combine these two terms of ranking losses.

3.4 Inference

The inference phase of P2GT performs a nearest neighbor search to type a process P. Let $\mathbf{M}$ refer to either $\mathbf{M}_1$ for the action type or $\mathbf{M}_2$ for the object type, our framework finds the gloss-based label representation that is closest to $\mathbf{M} \cdot \mathbf{P}$ from the corresponding vocabulary. Specifically for the setting with polysemous label representations, it is sufficient to consider for each label only its gloss that is embedded most closely to $\mathbf{M} \cdot \mathbf{P}$, so as to not redundantly consider candidate labels.

4 Experiments

To evaluate the proposed P2GT framework for event process typing, we conduct several experiments on the contributed dataset, and compare with a wide selection of baseline methods (§4.1-§4.3). A case study is also provided on typing processes from an external dataset (§4.4).

4.1 Experimental Settings

Similar to Rashkin et al. (2018), we randomly separate the 62,277 processes into a training/dev./test set using an 80/10/10% split. We report three ranking metrics, i.e. *MRR* (mean reciprocal rank), *recall@1* and *recall@10*. All metrics are preferred to be higher to indicate better performance.

We compare our framework with a number of its variants by performing the following modification: (i) Simplifying the framework by separately learning for the two type axes, instead of performing joint training; (ii) Different settings of gloss selection in training, using either WSD or FSM; (iii) Different information used to represent each primitive event e_i, e.g., only using either a_i or o_i (marked with *partial event*) according to the type axis, instead of using both. Besides, we compare with sequence-to-label (S2L) generators (Rashkin et al., 2018). A method of such is an encoder-decoder architecture trained to directly map from sequences to unigrams of the type vocabulary, which is originally used by recent work (Rashkin et al., 2018) to infer intentions from a single-clause description of a primitive event. Specifically, we employ three variants of S2L using different encoders. Besides one based on RoBERTa (marked as S2L-RoBERTa), the two others are the BiGRU encoder (S2L-BiGRU) and mean-pooling encoder (S2L-mean) with Skip-Gram word embeddings used by Rashkin et al. (2018). Note that to train S2L models, the original paper uses an cross-entropy loss

Type axes		Action			Object	
Metrics	*MRR*	*recall@1*	*recall@10*	*MRR*	*recall@1*	*recall@10*
S2L-mean-pool	3.72	1.96	5.95	1.01	0.80	1.66
S2L-BiGRU	7.94	4.40	12.71	4.20	2.72	6.19
S2L-RoBERTa	8.36	5.31	14.69	4.88	3.24	8.10
Single P2GT-MFS (partial event)	18.03	14.36	17.16	10.36	6.37	17.64
Single P2GT-WSD (partial event)	18.07	14.05	17.82	10.72	6.68	18.03
Single P2GT-MFS	24.10	19.67	32.40	13.71	8.86	23.09
Single P2GT-WSD	25.83	19.93	37.50	14.19	9.32	24.84
Joint P2GT-MFS	28.57	20.63	**43.14**	15.26	10.62	25.01
Joint P2GT-WSD	**29.11**	**21.21**	42.84	**15.70**	**11.07**	**25.51**

Table 1: Results (in percentage) for multi-axis event process typing. S2L methods with different encoding techniques are original or adopted from Event2Mind (Rashkin et al., 2018). *partial event* marks the cases where only a_i (or o_i) is encoded for each event e_i in the process to infer the action (or object) type. *Joint* or *Single* denotes whether to use joint training for both type axes or not. MFS and WSD marks ways of gloss selection in training.

Event processes	Predictions
Position yourself ⇒ Trim your eyebrows ⇒ Use the eyebrow pencil	A: strop, **highlight**, **_thread_**, blunt, *sharpen* O: unibrow, **eyebrow**, straightener, **eyelash**, razor
Learn how to strum ⇒ Use a metronome ⇒ Play to recorded songs ⇒ Grow skills	A: **play**, **practice**, *strum*, *tune*, box O: cymbal, **_mandolin_**, **guitar**, **dulcimer**, flute
Get a referral ⇒ Verify the specialist 's qualifications ⇒ Ask questions ⇒ Assess whether treatment is working	A: **find**, **_choose_**, use, apply, drink O: therapist, *physician*, **specialist**, *surgeon*, *psychiatrist*
Go to DMV ⇒ Take photos ⇒ Take vision test ⇒ Take permit test ⇒ Take road test	A: **obtain**, *verify*, explore, drive, polish O: **license**, check, visa, carfax, toll
Create your clan ⇒ Maintain your clan ⇒ Add another clan ⇒ Defend the borders ⇒ Do the hunting	A: **adopt**, **_create_**, **spawn**, *homestead*, become O: **clan**, **_warrior_**, *headhunter*, skirmish, *necrons*
Prepare the jack ⇒ Locate the filler hole ⇒ Fill the oil ⇒ Close the filler hole	A: *bleed*, *grease*, **_add_**, **fill**, inflate O: **oil**, pump, *biodiesel*, blowing, choke

Table 2: Top 5 predictions on examples of test cases by Joint-P2GT-WSD. Ground truths are underscored, reasonably correct labels are boldfaced, and close ones are italic. Few-shot labels appearing ≤ 10 times are in blue.

to model the distribution of unigrams. We instead train the process encoder to directly fit the embeddings of label surface forms similar to a reverse dictionary (Hill et al., 2016; Chen et al., 2019), which offers notably better performance.

4.2 Model Configuration

We use sense definitions from WordNet (Miller, 1995) to define the labels. While such glosses cover all verbs in the action type vocabularies, there are 7.92% of processes where object type labels do not find WordNet senses. For each such case, we select from WordNet the lexeme that is embedded most closely to the label, and use the predominant sense of that lexeme to generate the label representation. For the training setting with WSD, we use the BERT-NN model (Hadiwinoto et al., 2019), which is one of the SOTA WSD methods that is trained on the SemCor corpus (Langone et al., 2004). In fact, despite the ones that are dedicated to nouns

(Scarlini et al., 2020; Pasini and Navigli, 2017), other SOTA methods for WSD (Huang et al., 2019; Maru et al., 2019; Tripodi and Navigli, 2019) may also apply to our framework, for which we leave the investigation to future work.

We use AMSGrad (Reddi et al., 2018) to optimize the learning objective, with the learning rate set to 0.0001. The batch size is set to 64 to fit the memory of one Titan RTX 6000 GPU. Training is limited to 50 epochs that is enough for all models to converge. Margins are chosen from 0.0 to 0.4 with a step of 0.1, based on *recall@1* performance on the dev. set. Accordingly, $\gamma_1 = 0.2$ and $\gamma_2 = 0.1$ are selected for Single P2GT methods, while both margins are set to 0.1 for the joint-learning P2GT.

4.3 Results

We report the results of event process typing on both axes in Table 1, whereof the results for typing actions are generally better than those for the object

Event processes	Predictions
Make explosive materials ⇒ Obtain a container ⇒ Obtain shrapnel ⇒ Install a trigger	*A*: **detonate**, **assemble**, blacken *O*: **grenade**, **blaster**, **mine**
Ignore order ⇒ Enter area ⇒ Enforce blockade ⇒ Force to retreat from area	*A*: **conquer**, *disarm*, **invade** *O*: *barrier*, **soldier**, **fortress**
Capture two opposition posts ⇒ Kill many fighters ⇒ Destroy three armed trucks ⇒ Confiscate artillery guns	*A*: *kill*, **demolish**, **fight** *O*: *melee*, **conflict**, **stronghold**
Cooperate with the counsel investigation ⇒ Open his remarks ⇒ Apologize many times ⇒ Try to restore public trust	*A*: *respond*, disagree, **accept** *O*: *apology*, *disagreement*, **slander**
Travel in a presidential motorcade ⇒ Be shot once in the back ⇒ Be taken to hospital ⇒ Be pronounced dead	*A*: *survive*, **die**, tackle *O*: **assassin**, crash, *roadkill*
Give advance notice ⇒ Give notice ⇒ Issue dividends	*A*: **honor**, **pay**, reward *O*: *finance*, **equity**, **subsidy**
Target quotes ⇒ Target shares quotes ⇒ Ask to clarify offer ⇒ Challenge to merge agreement ⇒ Challenge to merge businesses	*A*: **compare**, **maximize**, **negotiate** *O*: *prospectus*, **quote**, **settlement**
Clean windows ⇒ Buy plants ⇒ Hang pictures ⇒ Paint walls ⇒ Carpet floors	*A*: **redecorate**, **decorate**, *refurbish* *O*: **room**, **bedroom**, *makeover*

Table 3: Case study for typing event processes in the news domain. The predictions are given by Joint P2GT-WSD trained on our full dataset. Each case is given top 3 predictions on both axes, whereof reasonably correct ones are boldfaced, and relevant ones are italic. Few-shot labels appearing up to 10 times in our dataset are in blue.

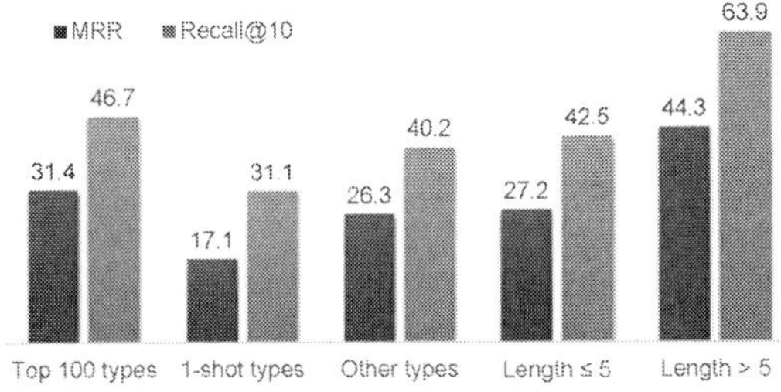

Figure 5: Comparison of action typing on different portions of the test set. We compare results by Joint P2GT-MFS for top 100 frequent types, one-shot types and the rest, as well as results on processes of different lengths. 5 is the median length of processes in the dataset.

axis due to different sizes of candidate spaces.

The results by the S2L baseline methods show that incorporating pre-trained RoBERTa offers noticeably better performance than other encoding techniques. However, it is drastically superseded by the Single P2GT setting without WSD-based gloss selection. When typing the action, with the same representation of event processes, P2GT supercedes S2L-RoBERTa with an absolute increase of *MRR* by 15.47% (ca. 1.88× relative increase), and that of *recall@1* by 14.36% (ca. 2.7× relative increase). For object typing, the absolute increments are 8.83% in *MRR* (ca. 1.82× relatively) and 5.62% in *recall@1* (ca. 1.72× relatively). This also indicates that incorporating gloss knowledge for label representations brings along

the most substantial improvement to the task, inasmuch as glosses attain rich semantic information to jump-start type labels and realistically support sequence-level learning-to-rank.

On the other hand, incorporating WSD for gloss selection in training slightly causes absolute increment of up to 1.73% in *MRR* for action typing and 0.48% in *MRR* for object typing. This is partly due to that the predominant sense definitions can generally seize precise or close definitions to represent the labels in most cases. Hence, sense selection provides lesser improvement, especially when the candidate space is large. It is noteworthy that, partially giving the predicate or object information of associated events is not enough to infer the type information. In fact, the performance drop is in accordance with human cognition, as giving a chain of predicates only or objects only is not enough to predict the intentions of the event process. Consider the first example in Figure 1, observing only a chain of the protagonist's actions *dig*, *put*, *fill* and *water*, or only the participating objects *hole*, *seed* and *soil* are clearly not enough to infer the overall action and the objective that directs the entire process. Accordingly, the partial event representation causes significant performance drop of 3.35-7.76% in terms of *MRR*, and 2.49-5.86% in terms of *recall@1*. Lastly, joint learning brings along performance gain by 1.51-4.47% in *MRR* and 0.96-1.76% in *recall@1*, indicating the effectiveness of leveraging complementary supervision signals. Note that the evaluation strictly enforces *exact match* in large candidate spaces, thus underestimating the system performance. While it is difficult for the model to always rank the ground-truth labels on the top, it can often infer reasonably close labels as top predictions, for which a couple of examples are shown in Table 2.

To understand how differently our method performs on processes of different characteristics, we additionally perform an error analysis. In Figure 5, we compare action prediction by P2GT with joint learning and MFS-based gloss selection on different proportions of the test set. It is expected that the performance on more frequent labels are better than on infrequent ones due to ampler training cases. Nonetheless, on the extremely challenging one-shot cases, our method still performs reasonably well, and drastically excels the overall results by baseline methods. Additionally, we observe that typing longer event processes is easier, as they provide more contextual information of associated events to help inferring the central goal. In contrast, as short processes are less informative, *MRR* scores for those sized 2 and 3 are 24.17% and 25.41%.

4.4 Case Study

We conduct a case study using a subset of the NYT narrative cloze dataset provided by Lee and Goldwasser (2019). This dataset includes a series of event processes extracted from news reports, and we use those processes to showcase the prediction of P2GT on out-of-domain processes. According to Table 3, although the content and concepts of processes in military and political news are mostly irrelevant to the intentional goals in our dataset, P2GT is able to infer reasonably correct type information on both axes. Particularly, many of the top predictions give few-shot labels. This further exhibits that gloss knowledge is effective to improve the generalization of the typing model, both in terms of handling domain shifting and few-shot cases. Specifically, the case study also points out the direction of our further study on how well gloss-based label representations can generally benefit domain adaptation and few-shot learning in natural language understanding tasks.

5   Related Work

Prediction tasks on event processes have attracted much attention recently, while many ex-

isting works focus on extraction and completion of event processes. For example, Radinsky et al. (2012; 2013) mine sequences of frequently co-ocurring events from multiple temporally connected documents, and use the sequence knowledge to predict the future event(s) of a process. Berant et al. (2014) propose to extract biological processes with SRL, and help machine reading comprehension for biological articles. A series of other works learn for sequential event prediction using language models (Chaturvedi et al., 2017; Peng et al., 2019) or association rules (Letham et al., 2013), and further cope with downstream tasks such as narrative cloze tests. On the contrary, fewer efforts have been made for inferring the intentions or central goals behind a composite of events. A recent work by Rashkin et al. (2018) is particularly relevant to this topic, which learns a sequence-to-label generator to predict the intention of one primitive event based on a single-clause description. This is however essentially different from our focus on processes of multiple events.

Semantic typing has been investigated for language components other than events, such as entities and word senses. Due to the large body of work in this line of research, we can only provide a highly selected summary for most recent outcomes. For entity typing, recent research has coped with highly challenging problem settings. Those include few-shot or zero-shot typing with contextual distant supervision (Zhou et al., 2018) and description-based label embeddings (Obeidat et al., 2019). Others realize ultra-fine type systems with the help of head-word supervision (Choi et al., 2018), hierarchical learning-to-rank (Chen et al., 2020) and structured label representations (Xiong et al., 2019; Hao et al., 2019). Several aforementioned techniques are also employed to supersense typing (Levine et al., 2020; Peters et al., 2019) and POS tagging (Owoputi et al., 2013). In terms of type labeling, our work is inspired by Choi et al. (2018)'s way of leveraging free-form lexemes for ultra-fine entity types. Nevertheless, besides typing on a different modality, our work is also distinguished in the multi-axis typing system, and the way of leveraging gloss-based indirect supervision.

Representation learning of gloss knowledge has been incorporated in various tasks. A number of works encode gloss definitions for monolingual (Hill et al., 2016; Noraset et al., 2017; Pilehvar, 2019; Hedderich et al., 2019) and cross-lingual

(Chen et al., 2019; Zhang et al., 2020a) reverse dictionary prediction, as well as out-of-vocabulary lexical representation (Kumar et al., 2019; Prokhorov et al., 2019; Bahdanau et al., 2017). Definitions have also been leveraged to generate zero-shot entity representations in knowledge graphs (Kartsaklis et al., 2018; Chen et al., 2018; Long et al., 2017). Some other works inject gloss representations to improve WSD (Huang et al., 2019; Luo et al., 2018; Blevins and Zettlemoyer, 2020). Gloss-BERT (Huang et al., 2019) thereof formalizes the WSD problem as classifying context-gloss pairs. Our learning approach on process-gloss pairs is connected to that approach, whereas we handle a learning-to-rank objective, and make inference in a much larger candidate space than the sense space of a single word.

6 Conclusion

We propose a new task of event process understanding, by semantically typing the intended action of an event process and the object(s) it seeks to affect. To facilitate research in this direction, we develop a new dataset, gathering over 60 thousand event processes with ultra fine-grained type vocabularies. We further propose a hybrid learning framework, which leverages indirect supervision from gloss knowledge. The proposed P2GT framework fine-tunes RoBERTa to capture the association of process-gloss pairs. Label gloss selection mechanisms and joint training are incorporated to further improve the performance. Experiments show that P2GT offers promising performance on inferring the fine-grained type information, and exhibits satisfactory generalizability on out-of-domain event processes.

For future work, we are interested in identifying salient events in processes, i.e., those that most significantly define the central goals. Incorporating process typing into downstream tasks such as summarization and commonsense QA is also an important direction.

Acknowledgement

We appreciate the anonymous reviewers for their insightful comments. Also, we would like thank Jennifer Sheffield and other members of the UPenn Cognitive Computation Group for giving suggestions that improved the manuscript.

This research is supported by the Office of the Director of National Intelligence (ODNI), Intelligence Advanced Research Projects Activity (IARPA), via IARPA Contract No. 2019-19051600006 under the BETTER Program, and by Contract FA8750-19-2-1004 with the US Defense Advanced Research Projects Agency (DARPA). The views expressed are those of the authors and do not reflect the official policy or position of the Department of Defense or the U.S. Government.

References

Dzmitry Bahdanau, Tom Bosc, Stanislaw Jastrzebski, Edward Grefenstette, Pascal Vincent, and Yoshua Bengio. 2017. Learning to compute word embeddings on the fly. *CoRR*, abs/1706.00286.

Jonathan Berant, Vivek Srikumar, Pei-Chun Chen, Abby Vander Linden, Brittany Harding, Brad Huang, Peter Clark, and Christopher D. Manning. 2014. Modeling biological processes for reading comprehension. In *Proceedings of the 2014 Conference on Empirical Methods in Natural Language Processing (EMNLP)*, pages 1499–1510, Doha, Qatar. Association for Computational Linguistics.

Steven Bird and Edward Loper. 2004. NLTK: The natural language toolkit. In *Proceedings of the ACL Interactive Poster and Demonstration Sessions*, pages 214–217, Barcelona, Spain. Association for Computational Linguistics.

Terra Blevins and Luke Zettlemoyer. 2020. Moving down the long tail of word sense disambiguation with gloss informed bi-encoders. In *Proceedings of the 58th Annual Meeting of the Association for Computational Linguistics*, pages 1006–1017, Online. Association for Computational Linguistics.

Rishi Bommasani, Kelly Davis, and Claire Cardie. 2020. Interpreting Pretrained Contextualized Representations via Reductions to Static Embeddings. In *Proceedings of the 58th Annual Meeting of the Association for Computational Linguistics*, pages 4758–4781, Online. Association for Computational Linguistics.

José Camacho-Collados, Mohammad Taher Pilehvar, and Roberto Navigli. 2016. Nasari: Integrating explicit knowledge and corpus statistics for a multilingual representation of concepts and entities. *Artificial Intelligence*, 240:36–64.

Nathanael Chambers and Dan Jurafsky. 2008. Unsupervised learning of narrative event chains. In *Proceedings of ACL-08: HLT*, pages 789–797, Columbus, Ohio. Association for Computational Linguistics.

Snigdha Chaturvedi, Haoruo Peng, and Dan Roth. 2017. Story Comprehension for Predicting What Happens Next. In *In proceedings of the Conference on Empirical Methods in Natural Language Processing*.

Muhao Chen, Yingtao Tian, Kai-Wei Chang, Steven Skiena, and Carlo Zaniolo. 2018. Co-training embeddings of knowledge graphs and entity descriptions for cross-lingual entity alignment. In *Proceedings of the 27th International Joint Conference on Artificial Intelligence*, pages 3998–4004.

Muhao Chen, Yingtao Tian, Haochen Chen, Kai-Wei Chang, Steven Skiena, and Carlo Zaniolo. 2019. Learning to represent bilingual dictionaries. In *Proceedings of the 23rd Conference on Computational Natural Language Learning (CoNLL)*, pages 152–162, Hong Kong, China. Association for Computational Linguistics.

Tongfei Chen, Yunmo Chen, and Benjamin Van Durme. 2020. Hierarchical entity typing via multi-level learning to rank. In *Proceedings of the 58th Annual Meeting of the Association for Computational Linguistics*, pages 8465–8475, Online. Association for Computational Linguistics.

Eunsol Choi, Omer Levy, Yejin Choi, and Luke Zettlemoyer. 2018. Ultra-fine entity typing. In *Proceedings of the 56th Annual Meeting of the Association for Computational Linguistics (Volume 1: Long Papers)*, pages 87–96, Melbourne, Australia. Association for Computational Linguistics.

Hal Daumé III and Daniel Marcu. 2006. Bayesian query-focused summarization. In *Proceedings of the 21st International Conference on Computational Linguistics and 44th Annual Meeting of the Association for Computational Linguistics*, pages 305–312, Sydney, Australia. Association for Computational Linguistics.

Jacob Devlin, Ming-Wei Chang, Kenton Lee, and Kristina Toutanova. 2019. BERT: Pre-training of deep bidirectional transformers for language understanding. In *Proceedings of the 2019 Conference of the North American Chapter of the Association for Computational Linguistics: Human Language Technologies, Volume 1 (Long and Short Papers)*, pages 4171–4186, Minneapolis, Minnesota. Association for Computational Linguistics.

Quang Do, Wei Lu, and Dan Roth. 2012. Joint Inference for Event Timeline Construction. In *Proc. of the Conference on Empirical Methods in Natural Language Processing (EMNLP)*.

Matt Gardner, Joel Grus, Mark Neumann, Oyvind Tafjord, Pradeep Dasigi, Nelson F. Liu, Matthew Peters, Michael Schmitz, and Luke Zettlemoyer. 2018. AllenNLP: A deep semantic natural language processing platform. In *Proceedings of Workshop for NLP Open Source Software (NLP-OSS)*, pages 1–6, Melbourne, Australia. Association for Computational Linguistics.

Christian Hadiwinoto, Hwee Tou Ng, and Wee Chung Gan. 2019. Improved word sense disambiguation using pre-trained contextualized word representations. In *Proceedings of the 2019 Conference on Empirical Methods in Natural Language Processing and the 9th International Joint Conference on Natural Language Processing (EMNLP-IJCNLP)*, pages 5297–5306, Hong Kong, China. Association for Computational Linguistics.

Junheng Hao, Muhao Chen, Wenchao Yu, Yizhou Sun, and Wei Wang. 2019. Universal representation learning of knowledge bases by jointly embedding instances and ontological concepts. In *Proceedings of the 25th ACM SIGKDD International Conference on Knowledge Discovery & Data Mining*, pages 1709–1719.

Michael A. Hedderich, Andrew Yates, Dietrich Klakow, and Gerard de Melo. 2019. Using multisense vector embeddings for reverse dictionaries. In *Proceedings of the 13th International Conference on Computational Semantics - Long Papers*, pages 247–258, Gothenburg, Sweden. Association for Computational Linguistics.

Felix Hill, Kyunghyun Cho, Anna Korhonen, and Yoshua Bengio. 2016. Learning to understand phrases by embedding the dictionary. *Transactions of the Association for Computational Linguistics*, 4:17–30.

Lifu Huang, Taylor Cassidy, Xiaocheng Feng, Heng Ji, Clare R. Voss, Jiawei Han, and Avirup Sil. 2016. Liberal event extraction and event schema induction. In *Proceedings of the 54th Annual Meeting of the Association for Computational Linguistics (Volume 1: Long Papers)*, pages 258–268, Berlin, Germany. Association for Computational Linguistics.

Luyao Huang, Chi Sun, Xipeng Qiu, and Xuanjing Huang. 2019. GlossBERT: BERT for word sense disambiguation with gloss knowledge. In *Proceedings of the 2019 Conference on Empirical Methods in Natural Language Processing and the 9th International Joint Conference on Natural Language Processing (EMNLP-IJCNLP)*, pages 3509–3514, Hong Kong, China. Association for Computational Linguistics.

Prateek Jindal and Dan Roth. 2013. Extraction of Events and Temporal Expressions from Clinical Narratives. *Journal of Biomedical Informatics (JBI)*.

Dimitri Kartsaklis, Mohammad Taher Pilehvar, and Nigel Collier. 2018. Mapping text to knowledge graph entities using multi-sense LSTMs. In *Proceedings of the 2018 Conference on Empirical Methods in Natural Language Processing*, pages 1959–1970, Brussels, Belgium. Association for Computational Linguistics.

Sawan Kumar, Sharmistha Jat, Karan Saxena, and Partha Talukdar. 2019. Zero-shot word sense disambiguation using sense definition embeddings. In *Proceedings of the 57th Annual Meeting of the Association for Computational Linguistics*, pages 5670–5681, Florence, Italy. Association for Computational Linguistics.

Christopher A Kurby and Jeffrey M Zacks. 2008. Segmentation in the perception and memory of events. *Trends in cognitive sciences*, 12(2):72–79.

Helen Langone, Benjamin R. Haskell, and George A. Miller. 2004. Annotating WordNet. In *Proceedings of the Workshop Frontiers in Corpus Annotation at HLT-NAACL 2004*, pages 63–69, Boston, Massachusetts, USA. Association for Computational Linguistics.

I-Ta Lee and Dan Goldwasser. 2019. Multi-relational script learning for discourse relations. In *Proceedings of the 57th Annual Meeting of the Association for Computational Linguistics*, pages 4214–4226, Florence, Italy. Association for Computational Linguistics.

Benjamin Letham, Cynthia Rudin, and David Madigan. 2013. Sequential event prediction. *Machine learning*, 93(2-3):357–380.

Yoav Levine, Barak Lenz, Or Dagan, Ori Ram, Dan Padnos, Or Sharir, Shai Shalev-Shwartz, Amnon Shashua, and Yoav Shoham. 2020. SenseBERT: Driving some sense into BERT. In *Proceedings of the 58th Annual Meeting of the Association for Computational Linguistics*, pages 4656–4667, Online. Association for Computational Linguistics.

Yinhan Liu, Myle Ott, Naman Goyal, Jingfei Du, Mandar Joshi, Danqi Chen, Omer Levy, Mike Lewis, Luke Zettlemoyer, and Veselin Stoyanov. 2019. Roberta: A robustly optimized bert pretraining approach. *arXiv preprint arXiv:1907.11692*.

Teng Long, Emmanuel Bengio, Ryan Lowe, Jackie Chi Kit Cheung, and Doina Precup. 2017. World knowledge for reading comprehension: Rare entity prediction with hierarchical LSTMs using external descriptions. In *Proceedings of the 2017 Conference on Empirical Methods in Natural Language Processing*, pages 825–834, Copenhagen, Denmark. Association for Computational Linguistics.

Fuli Luo, Tianyu Liu, Zexue He, Qiaolin Xia, Zhifang Sui, and Baobao Chang. 2018. Leveraging gloss knowledge in neural word sense disambiguation by hierarchical co-attention. In *Proceedings of the 2018 Conference on Empirical Methods in Natural Language Processing*, pages 1402–1411, Brussels, Belgium. Association for Computational Linguistics.

Marco Maru, Federico Scozzafava, Federico Martelli, and Roberto Navigli. 2019. SyntagNet: Challenging supervised word sense disambiguation with lexical-semantic combinations. In *Proceedings of the 2019 Conference on Empirical Methods in Natural Language Processing and the 9th International Joint Conference on Natural Language Processing (EMNLP-IJCNLP)*, pages 3534–3540, Hong Kong, China. Association for Computational Linguistics.

Diana McCarthy, Rob Koeling, Julie Weeds, and John Carroll. 2007. Unsupervised acquisition of predominant word senses. *Computational Linguistics*, 33(4):553–590.

George A Miller. 1995. Wordnet: a lexical database for english. *Communications of the ACM*, 38(11):39–41.

Ani Nenkova and Kathleen McKeown. 2012. A survey of text summarization techniques. In *Mining text data*, pages 43–76. Springer.

Qiang Ning, Zhili Feng, and Dan Roth. 2017. A structured learning approach to temporal relation extraction. In *Proceedings of the 2017 Conference on Empirical Methods in Natural Language Processing*, pages 1027–1037, Copenhagen, Denmark. Association for Computational Linguistics.

Thanapon Noraset, Chen Liang, Larry Birnbaum, and Doug Downey. 2017. Definition modeling: Learning to define word embeddings in natural language. In *Thirty-First AAAI Conference on Artificial Intelligence*.

Rasha Obeidat, Xiaoli Fern, Hamed Shahbazi, and Prasad Tadepalli. 2019. Description-based zero-shot fine-grained entity typing. In *Proceedings of the 2019 Conference of the North American Chapter of the Association for Computational Linguistics: Human Language Technologies, Volume 1 (Long and Short Papers)*, pages 807–814, Minneapolis, Minnesota. Association for Computational Linguistics.

Olutobi Owoputi, Brendan O'Connor, Chris Dyer, Kevin Gimpel, Nathan Schneider, and Noah A. Smith. 2013. Improved part-of-speech tagging for online conversational text with word clusters. In *Proceedings of the 2013 Conference of the North American Chapter of the Association for Computational Linguistics: Human Language Technologies*, pages 380–390, Atlanta, Georgia. Association for Computational Linguistics.

Tommaso Pasini and Roberto Navigli. 2017. Train-o-Matic: Large-scale supervised word sense disambiguation in multiple languages without manual training data. In *Proceedings of the 2017 Conference on Empirical Methods in Natural Language Processing*, pages 78–88, Copenhagen, Denmark. Association for Computational Linguistics.

Haoruo Peng, Qiang Ning, and Dan Roth. 2019. KnowSemLM: A knowledge infused semantic language model. In *Proceedings of the 23rd Conference on Computational Natural Language Learning (CoNLL)*, pages 550–562, Hong Kong, China. Association for Computational Linguistics.

Matthew E. Peters, Mark Neumann, Robert Logan, Roy Schwartz, Vidur Joshi, Sameer Singh, and Noah A. Smith. 2019. Knowledge enhanced contextual word representations. In *Proceedings of the 2019 Conference on Empirical Methods in Natural Language*

Processing and the 9th International Joint Conference on Natural Language Processing (EMNLP-IJCNLP), pages 43–54, Hong Kong, China. Association for Computational Linguistics.

Karl Pichotta and Raymond Mooney. 2014. Statistical script learning with multi-argument events. In *Proceedings of the 14th Conference of the European Chapter of the Association for Computational Linguistics*, pages 220–229, Gothenburg, Sweden. Association for Computational Linguistics.

Mohammad Taher Pilehvar. 2019. On the importance of distinguishing word meaning representations: A case study on reverse dictionary mapping. In *Proceedings of the 2019 Conference of the North American Chapter of the Association for Computational Linguistics: Human Language Technologies, Volume 1 (Long and Short Papers)*, pages 2151–2156, Minneapolis, Minnesota. Association for Computational Linguistics.

Victor Prokhorov, Mohammad Taher Pilehvar, Dimitri Kartsaklis, Pietro Lio, and Nigel Collier. 2019. Unseen word representation by aligning heterogeneous lexical semantic spaces. In *Proceedings of the AAAI Conference on Artificial Intelligence*, volume 33, pages 6900–6907.

Kira Radinsky, Sagie Davidovich, and Shaul Markovitch. 2012. Learning causality for news events prediction. In *Proceedings of the 21st international conference on World Wide Web*, pages 909–918. ACM.

Kira Radinsky and Eric Horvitz. 2013. Mining the web to predict future events. In *Proceedings of the sixth ACM international conference on Web search and data mining*, pages 255–264. ACM.

Hannah Rashkin, Maarten Sap, Emily Allaway, Noah A. Smith, and Yejin Choi. 2018. Event2Mind: Commonsense inference on events, intents, and reactions. In *Proceedings of the 56th Annual Meeting of the Association for Computational Linguistics (Volume 1: Long Papers)*, pages 463–473, Melbourne, Australia. Association for Computational Linguistics.

Sashank J Reddi, Satyen Kale, and Sanjiv Kumar. 2018. On the convergence of adam and beyond. In *International Conference on Learning Representations (ICLR)*.

Maarten Sap, Ronan Le Bras, Emily Allaway, Chandra Bhagavatula, Nicholas Lourie, Hannah Rashkin, Brendan Roof, Noah A Smith, and Yejin Choi. 2019. Atomic: An atlas of machine commonsense for if-then reasoning. In *Proceedings of the AAAI Conference on Artificial Intelligence*, volume 33, pages 3027–3035.

Bianca Scarlini, Tommaso Pasini, and Roberto Navigli. 2020. Sensembert: Context-enhanced sense embeddings for multilingual word sense disambigua-tion. In *The Thirty-Fourth AAAI Conference on Artificial Intelligence, (AAAI)*, pages 8758–8765. AAAI Press.

Rocco Tripodi and Roberto Navigli. 2019. Game theory meets embeddings: a unified framework for word sense disambiguation. In *Proceedings of the 2019 Conference on Empirical Methods in Natural Language Processing and the 9th International Joint Conference on Natural Language Processing (EMNLP-IJCNLP)*, pages 88–99, Hong Kong, China. Association for Computational Linguistics.

Wenhan Xiong, Jiawei Wu, Deren Lei, Mo Yu, Shiyu Chang, Xiaoxiao Guo, and William Yang Wang. 2019. Imposing label-relational inductive bias for extremely fine-grained entity typing. In *Proceedings of the 2019 Conference of the North American Chapter of the Association for Computational Linguistics: Human Language Technologies, Volume 1 (Long and Short Papers)*, pages 773–784, Minneapolis, Minnesota. Association for Computational Linguistics.

Jeffrey M Zacks, Todd S Braver, Margaret A Sheridan, David I Donaldson, Abraham Z Snyder, John M Ollinger, Randy L Buckner, and Marcus E Raichle. 2001. Human brain activity time-locked to perceptual event boundaries. *Nature neuroscience*, 4(6):651–655.

Jeffrey M Zacks and Barbara Tversky. 2001. Event structure in perception and conception. *Psychological bulletin*, 127(1):3.

Lei Zhang, Fanchao Qi, Zhiyuan Liu, Yasheng Wang, Qun Liu, and Maosong Sun. 2020a. Multi-channel reverse dictionary model. In *Proceedings of the AAAI Conference on Artificial Intelligence*, pages 312–319.

Tianran Zhang, Muhao Chen, and Alex Bui. 2020b. Diagnostic prediction with sequence-of-sets representation learning for clinical event. In *Proceedings of the 18th International Conference on Artificial Intelligence in Medicine (AIME)*.

Ben Zhou, Daniel Khashabi, Chen-Tse Tsai, and Dan Roth. 2018. Zero-shot open entity typing as type-compatible grounding. In *Proceedings of the 2018 Conference on Empirical Methods in Natural Language Processing*, pages 2065–2076, Brussels, Belgium. Association for Computational Linguistics.

A Corpus for Outbreak Detection of Diseases Prevalent in Latin America

Antonella Dellanzo
Dept. of Computer Science
FCEyN
Universidad de Buenos Aires,
Argentina
antodellanzo@gmail.com

Viviana Cotik
Dept. of Computer Science
FCEyN
Universidad de Buenos Aires,
Argentina
vcotik@dc.uba.ar

José Ochoa-Luna
Dept. of Computer Science
Universidad Católica San Pablo,
Arequipa, Peru
jeochoa@ucsp.edu.pe

Abstract

In this paper we present an annotated corpus which can be used for training and testing algorithms to automatically extract information about diseases outbreaks from news and health reports. We also propose initial approaches to extract information from it. The corpus has been constructed with two main tasks in mind. The first one, to extract entities about outbreaks such as disease, host, location among others. The second one, to retrieve relations among entities, for instance, in such geographic location fifteen cases of a given disease were reported. Overall, our goal is to offer resources and tools to perform an automated analysis so as to support early detection of disease outbreaks and therefore diminish their spreading.

1 Introduction

In recent years, several contagious diseases have aroused. Many of them, such as dengue, Guillain-Barré, Zika and microcephaly, occur in tropical regions of the world as in Latin America. There are also other diseases such as Chagas, also referred to as American trypanosomiasis, which have existed for many decades, but not many resources are used to treat them, probably because they do not appear in densely populated areas and their usual hosts belong to populations of scarce socioeconomic resources. On the other hand, there are endemic diseases, such as hantavirus, which appear recurrently in some regions of Argentina and Chile, among other countries. Finally, we are facing nowadays the COVID-19 pandemics.

Those illnesses have many issues in common: 1) they are dangerous in terms of number of losses of human life or lifelong consequences to those who carried them, 2) their economic impact can be very important (as in loss of tourism incomes with hantavirus, and loss in almost all economic areas with the isolation imposed by different governments due to the COVID-19 pandemics), and 3) when an outbreak occurs there is few available data that can support for data-driven decision making policies.

In this work we attack the third issue, we argue that information including number of cases, host and location of the host, among others, is crucial in order to understand the propagation of the illness and diminish its spreading. When available, the information usually is of poor quality (incomplete, incorrect, inconsistent, not publicly available, and it lacks the timeliness attribute, among others).

Thus, our goal is to contribute with automated tools and resources that allow to alert and inform about possible outbreak diseases and some illnesses prevalent in Latin America. To do so, we have constructed an annotated corpus based on ProMED-mail (Carrion and Madoff, 2017), a reporting system dedicated to the dissemination of information on epidemics of infectious diseases. We have also implemented an initial baseline, whose results will allow us to answer the following questions a) are there in the articles any mention to a disease?, b) in case there is: to which?, c) how many cases are reported in the article, d) in which geographic location is the disease located?, e) if there are causes or possible causes mentioned, which are they? and f) what is the date of the report?.

In the paper, we also emphasize the process followed to build the corpus which can serve as guide for future developments. In addition, we also present results on information extraction techniques applied over the corpus (namely, a named entity recognition (NER) rule-based technique). Although preliminary, the algorithm shows promising results that can be further extended to analyze news and social media.

The rest of the paper is organized as follows. Section 2 presents previous work in digital surveillance

Proceedings of the 24th Conference on Computational Natural Language Learning, pages 543–551
Online, November 19-20, 2020. ©2020 Association for Computational Linguistics
https://doi.org/10.18653/v1/P17

in public health. In Section 3 we describe the creation of an annotated corpus. Section 4 describes the implemented methods for doing named entity recognition. Section 5 shows preliminary results obtained from the baseline method proposed. Finally, Section 6 describes the conclusions reached so far and the future directions we are planning.

2 Related Works

Digital surveillance has been an important topic in public health. A large number of the papers published in Public Health informatics is about the epidemiological surveillance based on the new data generated in the current digital era (Thiebaut and Cossin, 2019). Research studies show that social media may be valuable tools in the disease surveillance toolkit used to detect disease outbreaks due to could be faster than traditional methods and to enhance outbreak response (Charles-Smith et al., 2015). Thus, social media constitutes a source of information for the surveillance of various public health outcomes on a real-time basis (Thiebaut and Cossin, 2019). For instance, we see that Twitter data has been used to aid in public health efforts concerned with surveillance, event detection, pharmacovigilance, forecasting, disease tracking and geographic identification, demonstrating positive results (Edo-Osagie et al., 2020). Public health surveillance is therefore a natural application for artificial intelligence techniques, the use of web-based data requires Natural Language Processing approaches to extract the information.

In this context, when national surveillance data are lacking, informal disease surveillance systems provide an opportunity to understand epidemiological trends (Desai et al., 2019). In this paper we have focused on building a corpus from ProMED (Carrion and Madoff, 2017). ProMED (The Program for Monitoring Emerging Diseases) is an internet-based reporting system for emerging infectious. Regions and countries could benefit from complementing their undiagnosed disease surveillance systems with ProMED-mail tool (Rolland et al., 2020). It is worth noting the effectiveness of ProMED as an epidemiological data source by focusing on coronaviruses (Bonilla-Aldana et al., 2020).

While ProMED is a reliable source of information, it is not currently equipped to provide detailed epidemiological data. For example, ProMED often does not report case or death counts beyond what is included in the text of a post. In order to extract this information from ProMED posts in a systematic way further analysis is required (Carrion and Madoff, 2017). One important work in this direction has been the Platform for Automated extraction of Disease Information from the web (PADI-web) (Arsevska et al., 2018). This tool generates epidemiological information on diseases, locations, dates, hosts and number of cases for outbreaks mentioned in news and social media articles. To do so, it combines Information extraction based on rule-based systems and data mining techniques. There is also a machine learning algorithm trained to better classify or identify information on diseases. This proposal is the most related to ours, however, unlike PADI-web, we focus on building a corpus from proMED-mail articles on diseases prevalent in Latin America.

3 Creating the Corpus

In this section we present the process involved to construct the corpus based on proMED-mail news articles (NPA). First, we present the dataset. Then, we explain the data cleansing processed followed, the annotation schema and criteria developed, a summary of the annotation guidelines and how we have been performing the annotation process. After, we show the statistics of our dataset and we explain the results of our inter annotator agreement. Finally, we present the data statements of our data (Bender and Friedman, 2018).

3.1 Corpus

In order to construct the corpus we downloaded articles from ProMED-mail, a reporting system dedicated to the rapid dissemination of information on epidemics of infectious diseases, among others (Arsevska et al., 2018).[1] The articles published on ProMED-mail have been edited based on journalistic notes from different media by an interdisciplinary staff.

We retrieved 811 articles written in Spanish and focused on reported issues in Latin America that mention the appearance of certain pathologies (measles, hantavirus, Guillain-barre, zika, microcephaly and Chagas). The retrieved articles were written between 11/5/2018 and 10/5/2019. Articles are formed by a title, a date and the main text. They also contain metadata, that had to be removed, as we explain in the next section.

---

[1] ProMED-mail `https://promedmail.org/about-promed/`

3.2 Data cleansing

We removed ProMED-Mail articles metadata with the use of regular expressions (regex). We keep only the article title, date and article note. The three components constitute what we call the article or NPA. An example of a ProMed-Mail article with its metadata is shown bellow.

Article title
Date
****
Un comunicado de ProMED-mail *(a communication of ProMED-mail)*
http://www.promedmail.org
... (7 lines of metadata in this case: date, source, etc.)
[Editado por *$name*] *([edited by $name])*
Article note
Comunicado por: *$name* <*$mailaddress*>
(Communicated by: $name <$mail address>)
– ProMED-ESP
...............................jt

Freeling (Padró and Stanilovsky, 2012) was chosen as the language analyzer in order to do some natural language processing (NLP) tasks such as tokenization, sentence splitting and as an aid to our named entity (NE) recognition algorithm. We had to perform some normalization over the text to meet some criteria required by Freeling. The main normalization tasks are listed next.

- in our notes dates are sometimes written using a slash (eg. *10/03/2018*) and sometimes using a dash (eg. *10-03-2018*). We used regex in order to transform dates written with dashes to dates written with slashes,

- some articles use comma and others use dot as a thousand symbol separator. We used regex in order transform all thousand symbol separators to dots,

- in the articles, some countries are written by their acronym instead of by their entire name (eg. *EE.UU.* -USA- for *Estados Unidos - United States-*). We replaced acronyms by their complete name so that Freeling would recognize them as a location when we use its NER functionality.

3.3 Annotation schema and criteria

Named entities as well as binary and ternary relations between named entities have been annotated.

To do so, we are using the brat rapid annotation tool (Stenetorp et al., 2012).

In the remainder of this subsection, we describe entities, concepts and relations that have been annotated.

The following entities and characteristics are being annotated:

disease (DS): entity corresponding to a pathological finding or diagnosis, eg. zika and Chagas,

date (DT): mention to a date, eg. 28 de febrero, 2019 (02/28/19), and 30 de abril (April 30),

location (LOC): geographic location, eg. MÉXICO: (JAL), Capiatá and Montevideo,

number of cases (NoC): mentions to the number of cases of a disease,

origin (OR): entities corresponding to the cause of a disease, eg. in *The transmission of the disease occurred through the consumption of contaminated Açai, consumption of contaminated Açai* is annotated as origin.

transmission form (TF): refers to the form of transmission of a disease. It is only annotated when there is an origin in the same sentence. eg. in *the virus is transmitted by a mosquito bite, virus* is annotated as DS, *mosquito* as OR and *bite* as TF.

host (Hst): mention to the person or animal who contracted the disease, eg. dog, infant, pregnant woman, immigrant.

Other annotated concepts (called modifiers) have also been considered:

negation (NT) and uncertainty terms (UT): terms that indicate negation or lack of certainty, eg. *negative, absence, no, nonexistence* (for negations), *suspected cases, may cause, under observation* (for uncertainties).

past terms (PT): terms that mention a fact that happened in the past, eg. in the past, in 2014, back in 2019,

conditional (COND): terms corresponding to a fact that may happen in the future, eg. in *if dengue persists, then actions should be taken in order to (...), if* is a conditional modifier.

The binary relations that have been annotated are:

disease occurs in (DsOccIn): relation among a disease and the geographic location where it occurs, eg. in *eleven cases of chagas in the state of Mérida, chagas* would be annotated as the disease and *Mérida* as a location. Also, a *DsOcIn* relation would be annotated among chagas and Mérida,

origin occurs in (OrOccIn): relation among cause of infection (origin) and geographic location, eg. in *an oral outbreak of the disease in the neighborhood of Belén is under investigation*, *oral outbreak* would be annotated as origin and *neighborhood of Belén* as a location. Also, a *OrOccIn* relation would be annotated among both entities,

cases of disease (NoCDs): relation among number of cases of a disease eg. a total of 391 cases of Zika were detected. Here, *391* would be annotated as number of cases and *Zika* as disease. Also, a *NoCDis* relation would be annotated among 391 and Zika,

cases in location (NoCLoc): relation among number of cases in a location, eg. in *there are already 100 patients with Guillain-Barré syndrome in Peru*, *100* would be annotated as NoC and *Peru* as a location. A *NoCHt* relation would be annotated among both entities.

cases of host (NoCHt): relation among number of cases affecting a particular host, eg. in *(...) a group of 32 newborns with microcephaly in Brazil*, *32* would be annotated as NoC and *newborns* as host. A *NoCHt* relation would be annotated among both entities.

date of disease (DtDs): date in which a disease occurred eg. *so far in 2013, 4 persons died (...) from chagas*. Here, *2013* would be annotated as date and *chagas* as disease. Also, a *DtDs* relation would be annotated among 2013 and chagas,

cause of disease (OrDs): cause of a disease (eg. zika (cause -and also disease-) in pregnant women is the cause of Guillain-Barré syndrome in their babies. In this case zika would be annotated as cause (origin entity) and as disease and Guillain-Barré as disease. Also a *OrDs* relation would be annotated among zika and Buillain-Barré,

negates disease, location, number of cases or cause (NegDs, NegLoc, NegNoC, NegOr, NegTf): relations among a negation term and: a disease, a location, a number of cases, a cause or a transmission form, eg. *10 of the cases didn't present microcephaly*. Here, *microcephaly* would be annotated as disease and *didn't* as a negation. Also, a *NegDs* relation would be annotated among microcephaly and didn't.

speculates disease, origin or transmission form (UcDs, UcOr, UcTf, UcNoC): relations among a speculation term and: a disease, an origin, a number of cases or a transmission form, eg. in *the transmission form is suspected to be through ingestion or orally (...)*, *suspected* would be annotated as uncertainty, and *ingestion* and *orally* as origin. Also, an *UcOr* relation would be annotated among suspected and ingestion, and another among suspected and orally,

occurs to (OccTo): relation among a disease and a host (who suffered from the disease), eg. in *chagas prevalence in donors (blood donors) has decreased*, *chagas* would be annotated as disease and *donors* as host. Also, an *OccTo* relation would be annotated among chagas and donors,

transmission cause (TfOr): relation among a transmission form and a cause, eg. *there was an oral transmission through food contaminated by chipo feces*. Here, *oral* would be annotated as transmission form and *food contaminated by chipo feces* as origin. Also, a *TfOr* relation would be annotated among them,

temporal conditional or past (TempCond, TempNt): relations among a conditional or past term and a disease, or among a past term and number of cases, eg. in *last week the appearance of cases of chagas disease has been reported (...)*, *last week* would be annotated as past and *chagas* as disease. Also, a *TempNt* relation would be annotated between *last week* and *chagas*. Finally, the

following ternary relations have been annotated:

speculates relation (UcOrDs): relation among an uncertainty term and the cause of a disease, eg. in *a significant number of virus strains (OR) circulate in the country and all of them can cause hantavirus pulmonary syndrome*, *virus strains* would be annotated as OR, *can cause* as uncertainty and *hantavirus pulmonary syndrome* as a disease. Also *can cause* should be related to *virus strains* and also to *hantavirus pulmonary syndrome* with a Uc-NoCDs relation,

speculates number of cases of disease (Uc-NoCDs): allows relations among an UT, NoC and a disease, eg. in *283 cases of people are suspected of having zika (...)*, *283* would be annotated as NoC, *zika* as Ds and *suspected* as Uncertainty. A ternary *SUcNoCDs* relation would be annotated among 283, zika and suspected.

3.4 Annotation guidelines

Next, we present a summary of the annotation guidelines:

- **diseases** will be annotated as such, only if they appear in the same sentence as NoC or other complementary information.

- **hosts** are annotated only if they have a special characteristic (eg. pregnant, infant and dog). If a person without further description of its characteristics contracted a disease, *person* is not annotated as host. Hosts are the carriers of the disease (not those of a secondary virus that causes the disease).

- **negations and speculations** that are not related to a NE or to a RE have not been annotated.

- the **largest possible term** has to be annotated in the case there is one entity embedded in a bigger one, eg. "mosquito aedes aegipty" (*aedes aegipty mosquito*) should be annotated rather than *mosquito*.

- **relations between sentences** have not been annotated.

- **Other:**

    - terms corresponding to a NE, that are misspelled must be annotated.
    - only NPAs, whose title refers to a Latin American country will be annotated. Nevertheless, if the note mentions other countries outside Latin America, these countries or cities will be annotated as locations.

3.5 Annotation process

The annotation was carried out by Spanish native speakers from Peru and Argentina. Some of them are computer science master students, others are linguists, and others are computer scientists that do research in NLP and with a background on annotation in different areas (from now on, *the experts*).

A document with the annotation schema and criteria was written and many meetings were held with the annotators in order to solve doubts. After having annotated a first dataset doubts and differences in criteria were reviewed and the annotation guidelines (described in Subsection 3.4) were written by the experts with more detail. After two annotation-revision iterations, the final guidelines were defined and annotations were performed (in what we call iteration 3). Now we are on working in iteration number 3.

Disagreements were solved by the experts.

3.6 Dataset Analysis

Since the title of the notes already contain a lot of information, we will work with 1) only the title and the date of the article (reduced article), and 2) the entire NPA (title, date and article note -body of the article-).

Once the annotation was performed by all the annotators, the final dataset was evaluated to know how many entities, relations and events of each type were found.

Overall 170 different newspaper articles have been annotated. Average number of sentences: 11, average number of words per article 367. Average length of titles 11 words.

The average number of sentences per article was 11, the average number of words per article was 367, and the average number of words in titles was 11.

Tables 1 and 2 show the number of annotated entities and modifiers (eg. negations) and the number of different entities and modifiers for the entire article and for the reduced article.

type	total	different
Date	245	213
Disease	1087	143
Host	283	134
Location	759	315
Number of cases	606	264
Origin	417	217
Transmission form	106	80
Negation	22	14
Past	154	118
Uncertainty	108	68

Table 1: Type and amount of entities, modifiers and other characteristics with more than five occurrences for NPA.

It may seem strange that there are 143 different diseases. That is for many reasons: some diseases that are not of interest for our study (eg. hypertension and diabetes) have also been annotated. Also, some diseases are written with many variations (eg. Guillain-Barré is written in ten different ways).

Tables 3 and 4 show for NPAs and reduced articles relations, the entities related by them, and the total number of relations and the number of different relations appearing in the annotated texts.

3.7 Inter-annotator agreement

To evaluate the consistency among the annotations performed between pairs of annotators, the inter-annotator agreement (IAA) was calculated using the Cohen's Kappa coefficient (κ) (Cohen, 1960).

type	total	different
Date	156	149
Disease	183	26
Host	25	17
Location	160	59
Origin	51	18
Transmission form	13	10
Uncertainty	7	3

Table 2: Type and amount of entities, modifiers and other characteristics with more than five occurrences for article title and date.

relation	entities	total	different
DsOccIn	DS-LOC	551	330
DtDs	DT-DS	52	42
NegDs	NT-DS	9	7
NegOr	NT-CA	13	12
NoCDs	NoC-DS	340	291
NoCHt	NoC-HT	76	71
NoCLoc	NoC-LOC	144	139
OccTo	DS-HT	192	121
OrDs	CA-DS	288	182
OrOccIn	CA-LOC	38	33
PtDs	PT-DS	103	92
PtNoC	PT-NoC	50	49
TfOr	TF-CA	69	65
UcDs	UT-DS	14	14
UcNoC	UT-NoC	55	55
UcNoCDs	UC-NoC-DS	5	4
UcOr	UT-CA	28	25
UcOrDs	UC-CA-DS	7	6
UcOrDs	UC-DS-CA	7	7

Table 3: Relations with more than five occurrences annotated among entities in NPAs.

The Cohen Kappa Score was calculated with scikit-learn library,[2] which given two arrays (one corresponding to the annotation of each annotator), returns the score for that annotation.

In our implementation a token will be considered to have the same label (type of named entity or of relation) if and only if both annotators assigned the exact set of labels to it (or none).

For a set of 27 NPA annotated in common by both students and experts, we obtained a minimum κ value of 0.16 (obtained in the first iteration of annotations), a maximum of 0.73 (obtained in the second iteration) and an average value of 0.52 throughout the 27 annotated NPAs.

3.8 Data statements

Data statements were proposed by Bender and Friedman (2018) to address critical issues, such as biases, when working with natural language data.

[2] Sklearn Metrics Cohen Kappa Score. Available at: http://https://scikit-learn.org/stable/ modules/generated/sklearn.metrics.cohen_ kappa_score [Accessed June 2020].

relation	entities	total	different
DsOccIn	DS-LOC	162	89
OccTo	DS-HT	26	21
OrDs	CA-DS	42	17
OrOccIn	CA-LOC	17	15
TfOr	TF-CA	6	5

Table 4: Relations with more than five occurrences annotated among entities in reduced articles.

In following paragraphs we describe the data statements of our corpus, including some annotation decisions.

We selected texts from ProMed-mail written in Spanish that mention at least one of the following terms: chagas, measles, hantavirus, Guillain Barré, zika or microcephaly and that were written between 04/01/2001 and 10/5/2019.

From those, we selected only those that talk about Spanish speaking Latin American countries. Our goal was to obtain quality news about previously mentioned illnesses and their prevalence in Latin American countries. Therefore we selected ProMed-mail as source.

The language used is the usual in newspaper articles. Nevertheless, news are shorter than they usually are. Each country has its particularities in the use of Spanish (in what regards texts, different word choice). Nevertheless, in the articles, standard Spanish is used (it can not be identified to the variant used in a particular country).

Annotator guideline developers speak different variations of Spanish, so do the annotators. Nevertheless, we evaluate that this fact did not hinder an accurate understanding of the annotation criteria or the newspapers articles. We do not have information of ProMed-mail editors' demographics.

4 Approaches for Extracting Information

In this section we present a rule-based named entity recognizer applied to reduced NPAs and to whole NPAs. We also developed a connectionist state of the art method for doing NER. However, since we still do not have a sufficient amount of annotated texts as to train the neural network, we will only show preliminary results of our rule-based method for the titles of the notes and for the complete articles.

We used Freeling to perform named entity recognition and classification (NERC) of some entities and regular expressions to detect others. After, based on an analysis of a subset of our data we defined a rule-based method to detect named entities.

In next sections we present a summary of our rule-based and machine learning methods we are developing.

4.1 Rule-based method

Below we describe the defined rules.

Recognition of number of cases (NoC)

To detect NoC entities we used the following heuristic:

1) we PoS-tagged the NPAs with Freeling. Tokens tagged as numbers (*Z*) or as as ordinal adjectives (*A0*) are potential NoC candidates.

2) We kept those candidates containing only numbers and eventually dots or commas ([0-9.,]+) (eg. the token *D8*, tagged as *Z*, was eliminated).

3) Candidates that met following rules were also removed: i) those that are followed by any of the words *day*, *month*, *year*, *percentage* or *%*, since the detected number probably refers to a point in time or to a percentage and not to a NoC, ii) some ordinal adjectives, like *last*,[3] and

4) finally, from the remaining candidates, we picked only those that are at a maximum distance of 7 to some of the words belonging to a list of words that might be related to number of cases (eg. *cases* and *infected*).

Recognition of locations (LOC)

The process to detect LOC entities is as follows:

1) we created a Gazetteer with data downloaded from *GeoNames*[4] (cities,[5] regions, countries -and their official language- and continents were downloaded).

2) Freeling NER and NEC modules were ran and we kept only those tokens tagged as locations (*NP00G00*).

3) Almost all articles mention a location in their title. To collect the valid ones, we filtered those tagged as such (step 2) and eliminated those that do not belong to Latin America or those that belong, but whose inhabitants native language is not Spanish or Portuguese. [6]

4) We only keep those NPA entities tagged as locations by Freeling that are related to the location found in the article note title.[7]

5) If there exists some kind of ambiguity (eg. *El Salvador* is a country and a city in Mexico), we select the location with the highest population.

6) Finally, we keep only those locations that co-occur in the same sentence as a NoC entity.

Recognition of other named entities

The rest of the named entities (diseases, hosts, origin, transmission form, and negation, uncertainty, past and conditional terms) were detected by the use of regular expressions and lists of terms developed ad-hoc by us based on the subset of NPA analyzed. Dates were detected with the use of Freeling.

Dates and negation, uncertainty, past and conditional terms were recognized as NER only if they co-occurr in the same sentence and within a fixed distance to another entity to which they might be related.

4.2 Machine learning method

We are currently working on a machine learning method for NER based on the work from Akbik et al (2018).

Therefore, we are using the library provided by the authors. We initialized a set of stacked embeddings in Spanish. Then, we are going to train the sequence tagger with our annotated articles by adapting the proposed architecture. This process will be finished once we have a higher number of annotated articles.

5 Preliminary Results

In this Section we show preliminary results of our rule-based method. 20 % of our dataset, not used for doing the analysis was used to test the results. We show the usual Precision, Recall and F1 metrics for each entity and an overall average score that considers all named entities.

Therefore, the annotated files were transformed to coNLL format with the script *anntoconll.py* provided by brat. A normalization and transformation was performed and conlleval perl script[8] was ran.

---

[3]Others, as *first*, may refer to NoC, so they were not removed.

[4]GeoNames WebServices. Available at: `http://www.geonames.org/export` [Accessed April 2020].

[5]For Latin American cities, those with population over 5000 inhabitants were obtained, for other cities, those with more than 15.000.

[6]This information is taken from the information downloaded from GeoNames (step 1).

[7]Eg. cities belonging to the country, and country where the city or region belongs to.

[8]Available at: `https://www.clips.uantwerpen.`

Tables 5 and 6 show results for NPAs and for the reduced articles.

NE	P	R	F1
Date	0.63	0.44	0.52
Disease	0.74	0.67	0.70
Host	0.53	0.28	0.37
Location	0.31	0.61	0.41
Number of cases	0.63	0.43	0.51
Origin	0.07	0.13	0.09
Transmission form	0.03	0.15	0.05
Conditional	0.00	0.00	0.00
Negation	0.58	0.09	0.16
Past	0.07	0.17	0.10
Uncertainty	0.16	0.13	0.14
Total	0.48	0.46	0.47

Table 5: Performance of the rule-based method for NPAs.

NE	P	R	F1
Date	0.79	0.65	0.71
Disease	0.89	0.85	0.87
Host	0.64	0.64	0.64
Location	0.69	0.63	0.66
Origin	0.18	0.50	0.26
Transmission form	0.08	0.14	0.10
Negation	1.00	0.33	0.50
Uncertainty	0.00	0.00	0.00
Total	0.72	0.69	0.70

Table 6: Performance of the rule-based method for reduced NPAs. Only those entities and modifiers that appear in the title are shown.

Next, we do a brief analysis of our results. 1) For NPAs, generally those NE detected only by regex and lists of terms have the worst results (Hst, OR, TF, NT, UT, PT and COND). This is mainly due to differences with the annotation criteria and to the fact that lists of terms were not comprehensive enough. 2) Nevertheless, in both cases (NPAs and partial notes) diseases had much better results. We assume that it is because there is a reduced number of diseases we are looking for. 3) For NPAs, those NE that were based on the use of Freeling and of more elaborated rules had better results. 4) The main differences among the algorithm and the annotation criteria are between i) what is considered past, ii) the difference among OR and TF (it occurrs in partial NPAs and NPAs), and iii) the dates. 5) the algorithm does not detect zika as a cause of microcephaly. This is due to the fact that zika is not in the list of possible causes (entity origin). 6) We also notice a difference among the annotation criteria and the development of the algorithm when seeing the results for LOC NE. That, together with

the fact that mainly in the title, countries are usually mentioned together with the abbreviation of a city (eg. *BRASIL: (SP)*) made that LOC results are not good. With our gazetteers, we don't have a way to know the expansion of the abbreviations.

Furthermore, those abbreviations are usually non-standard. 7) Normalizing dates, would enhance results of Freeling date detection. 8) Finally, uncertainty has bad results in reduced NPAs. It only appears in eight titles and there was a mismatch among those detected by the algorithm and those annotated by the annotators.

Overall, as we imagined, NER worked better for the title than for the NPAs. Those results that are low are mainly associated with the lack of normalization and the difference with the annotation criteria (eg. OR and TF). Finally, even though the results do not seem encouraging, there are entities that were recognized correctly by the algorithm but no by the annotators (eg. in *the Ministry reported that there are 24.011 suspected cases of (...)*), the algorithm correctly recognized *24.011* as NoC and *suspected cases* as UT, but the annotator did not. This shows that the annotation and annotation criteria still have to be improved.

6 Conclusion

We have just presented an initial annotated corpus based on ProMED-mail which can be used for early detection systems of outbreak diseases prevalent in Latin America. While there are several social media sources for disease surveillance, there is a lack of tools that can automatically provide detailed epidemiological data. Thus, the whole process of building the corpus was oriented to aid the extraction of useful health facts. With this corpus, it is possible to analyze medium/long articles from reliable sources such as ProMED-mail and answer queries regarding detailed and direct diseases incidences. This can be useful for understanding epidemiological trends.

We have also proposed an initial baseline rule based algorithm that automatically extract diseases related entities. The results reported are promising and we also plan to work on relation extraction. We are developing a baseline based on co-occurrence of named entities. The analysis of the preliminary results shows different criteria between the algorithm rules and the annotation criteria. This analysis will help us review and enhance our corpus. Finally, the rule-based method is very laborious

be/conll2000/chunking/conlleval.txt [Accessed July 2020].

and is not always useful to detect entities without understanding the contexts in which they appear.

Acknowledgements

This work was funded by CONCYTEC-FONDECYT under the call E041-01 [contract number 34-2018-FONDECYT-BM-IADT-SE].

References

Alan Akbik, Duncan Blythe, and Roland Vollgraf. 2018. Contextual string embeddings for sequence labeling. In *COLING 2018, 27th International Conference on Computational Linguistics*, pages 1638–1649.

Elena Arsevska, Sarah Valentin, Julien Rabatel, Jocelyn de Goër de Hervé, Sylvain Falala, Renaud Lancelot, and Mathieu Roche. 2018. Web monitoring of emerging animal infectious diseases integrated in the french animal health epidemic intelligence system. *PloS one*, 13(8).

Emily M Bender and Batya Friedman. 2018. Data statements for natural language processing: Toward mitigating system bias and enabling better science. *Transactions of the Association for Computational Linguistics*, 6:587–604.

D. K. Bonilla-Aldana, Y. Holguin-Rivera, I. Cortes-Bonilla, M. C. Cardona-Trujillo, A. García-Barco, H. A. Bedoya-Arias, A. A. Rabaan, R. Sah, and A. J. Rodriguez-Morales. 2020. Coronavirus infections reported by promed, february 2000-january 2020. *Travel medicine and infectious disease*, 35(101575).

M. Carrion and L. C. Madoff. 2017. Promed-mail: 22 years of digital surveillance of emerging infectious diseases. *International health*, 9(3):177—-183.

L. E. Charles-Smith, T. L. Reynolds, M. A. Cameron, M. Conway, E. H. Lau, J. M. Olsen, J. A. Pavlin, M. Shigematsu, L. C. Streichert, K. J. Suda, and C. D. Corley. 2015. Using social media for actionable disease surveillance and outbreak management: A systematic literature review. *PloS one*, 10(10).

Jacob Cohen. 1960. A coefficient of agreement for nominal scales. *Educational and psychological measurement*, 20(1):37–46.

A. N. Desai, A. Anyoha, L. C. Madoff, and B. Lassmann. 2019. Changing epidemiology of listeria monocytogenes outbreaks, sporadic cases, and recalls globally: A review of promed reports from 1996 to 2018. *International journal of infectious diseases*, 84:48—-53.

O. Edo-Osagie, B. De La Iglesia, I. Lake, and O. Edeghere. 2020. A scoping review of the use of twitter for public health research. *Computers in biology and medicine*, 122(103770).

Lluís Padró and Evgeny Stanilovsky. 2012. Freeling 3.0: Towards wider multilinguality. In *Proceedings of the Language Resources and Evaluation Conference (LREC 2012)*, Istanbul, Turkey. ELRA.

C. Rolland, C. Lazarus, C. Giese, B. Monate, A. S. Travert, and J. Salomon. 2020. Early detection of public health emergencies of international concern through undiagnosed disease reports in promed-mail. *Emerging infectious diseases*, 26(2):336—-339.

Pontus Stenetorp, Sampo Pyysalo, Goran Topić, Tomoko Ohta, Sophia Ananiadou, and Jun'ichi Tsujii. 2012. brat: a web-based tool for NLP-assisted text annotation. In *Proceedings of the Demonstrations Session at EACL 2012*, Avignon, France. Association for Computational Linguistics.

R. Thiebaut and S. Cossin. 2019. Artificial intelligence for surveillance in public health. *Yearbook of medical informatics*, 28(1):232—-234.

Are Pretrained Language Models Symbolic Reasoners Over Knowledge?

Nora Kassner*, Benno Krojer*, Hinrich Schütze
Center for Information and Language Processing (CIS)
LMU Munich, Germany
`kassner@cis.lmu.de`

Abstract

How can pretrained language models (PLMs) learn factual knowledge from the training set? We investigate the two most important mechanisms: reasoning and memorization. Prior work has attempted to quantify the number of facts PLMs learn, but we present, using synthetic data, the first study that investigates the causal relation between facts present in training and facts learned by the PLM. For reasoning, we show that PLMs seem to learn to apply some symbolic reasoning rules correctly but struggle with others, including two-hop reasoning. Further analysis suggests that even the application of learned reasoning rules is flawed. For memorization, we identify schema conformity (facts systematically supported by other facts) and frequency as key factors for its success.

1 Introduction

Pretrained language models (PLMs) like BERT (Devlin et al., 2019), GPT-2 (Radford et al., 2019) and RoBERTa (Liu et al., 2019) have emerged as universal tools that capture a diverse range of linguistic and – as more and more evidence suggests – factual knowledge (Petroni et al., 2019; Radford et al., 2019).

Recent work on knowledge captured by PLMs is focused on probing, a methodology that identifies the set of facts a PLM has command of. But little is understood about how this knowledge is acquired during pretraining and why. We analyze the ability of PLMs to acquire factual knowledge focusing on two mechanisms: reasoning and memorization. We pose the following two questions:
a) Symbolic reasoning: Are PLMs able to infer knowledge not seen explicitly during pretraining?
b) Memorization: Which factors result in successful memorization of a fact by PLMs?

We conduct our study by pretraining BERT from scratch on synthetic corpora. The corpora are composed of short knowledge-graph like facts: subject-relation-object triples. To test whether BERT has learned a fact, we mask the object, thereby generating a cloze-style query, and then evaluate predictions.

Symbolic reasoning. We create synthetic corpora to investigate six symbolic rules (equivalence, symmetry, inversion, composition, implication, negation); see Table 1. For each rule, we create a corpus that contains facts from which the rule can be learned. We test BERT's ability to use the rule to infer unseen facts by holding out some facts in a test set. For example, for composition, BERT should infer, after having seen that leopards are faster than sheep and sheep are faster than snails, that leopards are faster than snails.

Our setup is similar to link prediction in the knowledge base domain and therefore can be seen as a natural extension of the question: "Language models as knowledge bases?" (Petroni et al., 2019). In the knowledge base domain, prior work (Sun et al., 2019; Zhang et al., 2020) has shown that models that are able to learn symbolic rules are superior to ones that are not.

Talmor et al. (2019) also investigate symbolic reasoning in BERT using cloze-style queries. However, in their setup, there are two possible reasons for BERT having answered a cloze-style query correctly: (i) the underlying fact was correctly inferred or (ii) it was seen during training. In contrast, since we pretrain BERT from scratch, we have full control over the training setup and can distinguish cases (i) and (ii).

A unique feature of our approach compared to prior work (Sinha et al., 2019; Richardson et al., 2020; Weston et al., 2016; Clark et al., 2020) is that we do not gather all relevant facts and present them to the model at inference time. This is a crucial

---

*equal contribution

Proceedings of the 24th Conference on Computational Natural Language Learning, pages 552–564
Online, November 19-20, 2020. ©2020 Association for Computational Linguistics
https://doi.org/10.18653/v1/P17

Rule		Definition	Example
EQUI	Equivalence	$(e, r, a) \iff (e, s, a)$	(bird, can, fly) $\iff$ (bird, is able to, fly)
SYM	Symmetry	$(e, r, f) \iff (f, r, e)$	(barack, married, michelle) $\iff$ (michelle, married, barack)
INV	Inversion	$(e, r, f) \iff (f, s, e)$	(john, loves, soccer) $\iff$ (soccer, thrills, john)
NEG	Negation	$(e, r, a) \iff (e, \text{not } r, b)$	(jupiter, is, big) $\iff$ (jupiter, is not, small)
IMP	Implication	$(e, r, a) \Rightarrow (e, s, b), (e, s, c),...$	(dog, is, mammal) $\Rightarrow$ (dog, has, hair), (dog, has, neocortex), ...
COMP	Composition	$(e, r, f) \wedge (f, s, g) \Rightarrow (e, t, g)$	(tiger, faster than, sheep) $\wedge$ (sheep, faster than, snail) $\Rightarrow$ (leopard, faster than, snail) with $r = s = t$

Table 1: The six symbolic rules we investigate (cf. (Nayyeri et al., 2019)) with an example in natural language for entities $e, f, g \in E$, relations $r, s, t \in R$ and attributes $a, b, c \in A$.

difference – note that human inference similarly does not require that all relevant facts are explicitly repeated at inference time.

We find that i) BERT is capable of learning some one-hop rules (equivalence and implication). ii) For others, even though high test precision suggests successful learning, the rules were not in fact learned correctly (symmetry, inversion and negation). iii) BERT struggles with two-hop rules (composition). However, by providing richer semantic context, even two-hop rules can be learned.

Given that BERT can in principle learn some reasoning rules, the question arises whether it does so for standard training corpora. We find that BERT-large has only partially learned the types of rules we investigate here. For example, BERT has some notion of "X shares borders with Y" being symmetric, but it fails to understand rules like symmetry in other cases.

Memorization. During the course of pretraining, BERT sees more data than any human could read in a lifetime, an amount of knowledge that surpasses its storage capacity. We simulate this with a scaled-down version of BERT and a training set that ensures that BERT cannot memorize all facts in training. We identify two important factors that lead to successful memorization. (i) Frequency: Other things being equal, low-frequency facts are not learned whereas frequent facts are. (ii) Schema conformity: Facts that conform with the overall schema of their entities (e.g., "sparrows can fly" in a corpus with many similar facts about birds) are easier to memorize than exceptions (e.g., "penguins can dive").

We publish our code for training and data generation. [1]

[1] https://github.com/BennoKrojer/reasoning-over-facts

2 Data

To test PLMs' reasoning capabilities, natural corpora like Wikipedia are limited since it is difficult to control what the model sees during training. Synthetic corpora provide an effective way of investigating reasoning by giving full control over what knowledge is seen and which rules are employed in generating the data.

In our investigation of PLMs as knowledge bases, it is natural to use (subject, relation, object) triples as basic units of knowledge; we refer to them as *facts*. The underlying vocabulary consists of a set of entities $e, f, g, ... \in E$, relations $r, s, t, ... \in R$ and attributes $a, b, c, ... \in A$, all represented by artificial strings such as e_{14}, r_3 or a_{35}. Two types of facts are generated. (i) **Attribute facts**: relations linking entities to attributes, e.g., (e, r, a) = (leopard, is, fast). (ii) **Entity facts**: relations linking entities, e.g., (e, r, f) = (Paris, is the capital of, France).

In the test set, we mask the objects and generate cloze-style queries of the form "$e \; r$ [MASK]". The model's task is then to predict the correct object.

2.1 Symbolic Reasoning

Table 1 gives definitions and examples for the six rules (EQUI, SYM, INV, COMP, IMP, NEG) we investigate. The definitions are the basis for our corpus generation algorithms, shown in Figure 1. SYM, INV, COMP generate entity facts and EQUI, IMP, NEG attribute facts. We create a separate corpus for each symbolic rule. Facts are generated by sampling from the underlying vocabulary. For §2.1, this vocabulary consists of 5000 entities, 500 relations and 1000 attributes. Half of the relations follow the rule, the other half is used to generate random facts of entity or attribute type.

We can most easily think of the corpus generation as template filling. For example, looking at SYM in Table 1, the template is $(e, r, f) \iff (f, r, e)$. We first sample a relation r from R and

```
EQUI                         SYM                          INV                          COMP                             IMP                          NEG
C = ∅, D = ∅                 C = ∅, D = ∅                 C = ∅, D = ∅                 C = ∅, D = ∅                     C = ∅, D = ∅                 C = ∅, D = ∅
for i ∈ 1 . . . n do         for i ∈ 1 . . . n do         for i ∈ 1 . . . n do         for i ∈ 1 . . . n do             for i ∈ 1 . . . n do         for i ∈ 1 . . . n do
  (r, s) ∼ R × R               r ∼ R                        (r, s) ∼ R × R               (r, s, t) ∼ R × R × R             (r, s) ∼ R × R               r ∼ R
  a ∼ A                        for j ∈ 1 . . . m do         for j ∈ 1 . . . m do         for j ∈ 1 . . . m do             for k ∈ 1 . . . l do         for j ∈ 1 . . . m do
  for j ∈ 1 . . . m do           (e, f) ∼ E × E               (e, f) ∼ E × E               (e, f, g) ∼ E × E × E            b ∼ A                          e ∼ E
    e ∼ E                        C = C ∪ {(e, r, f)}          C = C ∪ {(e, r, f)}          C = C ∪ {(e, r, f)}              α ∼ A × . . . × A              a ∼ A
    addC=Bernoulli(0.5)          D = D ∪ {(f, r, e)}          D = D ∪ {(f, s, e)}          C = C ∪ {(f, s, g)}              for j ∈ 1 . . . m do           b = antonym(a)
    if addC then                                                                          D = D ∪ {(e, t, g)}                e ∼ E                        negated=Bernoulli(0.5)
      C = C ∪ {(e, r, a)}                                                                                                    C = C ∪ {(e, r, b)}          if negated then
      D = D ∪ {(e, s, a)}                                                                                                    for a ∈ α do                   C = C ∪ {(e, not r, a)}
    else                                                                                                                       D = D ∪ {(e, s, a)}           D = D ∪ {(e, r, b)}
      C = C ∪ {(e, s, a)}                                                                                                                                 else
      D = D ∪ {(e, r, a)}                                                                                                                                    C = C ∪ {(e, r, a)}
                                                                                                                                                            D = D ∪ {(e, not r, b)}
```

Figure 1: Pseudocode for symbolic reasoning corpus generation. "$a \sim A$" stands for: a is randomly sampled from A. ("$\alpha \sim A \times \ldots \times A$": a tuple of 4 attributes is sampled.) The vocabulary consists of entities $e, f, g \in E$, relations $r, s, t \in R$ and attributes $a, b, c \in A$. Train/test corpora are formed from C and D. $n = 20$, $m = 800$, $l = 2$. See §2.1 for details.

```
FREQ                            SCHEMA
C = ∅                           C = ∅
m = 1                           for i ∈ 1 . . . k do
for i ∈ 1 . . . n do              δ ∼ E × . . . × E
  (e, f) ∼ E × E                  for r in R do
  r ∼ R                             schema = Bernoulli(0.5)
  for j ∈ 1 . . . m do              if schema then
    C = C ∪ {(e, r, f)}               α ∼ A × . . . × A
  if i%(n/100) == 0 then             for e ∈ δ do
    m+ = 1                             for a ∈ α do
                                          add = Bernoulli(0.5)
                                          if add then
                                            C = C ∪ {(e, r, a)}
                                          else
                                            exception = Bernoulli(0.5)
                                            if exception then
                                              a ∼ A
                                              C = C ∪ {(e, r, a)}
                                    else
                                      for e ∈ δ do
                                        add = Bernoulli(0.5)
                                        if add then
                                          a ∼ A
                                          C = C ∪ {(e, r, a)}
```

Figure 2: Pseudocode for memorization corpus generation. "$a \sim A$" stands for: a is randomly sampled from A. ("$\delta \sim E \times \ldots \times E$": a tuple of 250 entities is sampled. "$\alpha \sim A \times \ldots \times A$": a tuple of 10 attributes is sampled.) The vocabulary consists of entities $e \in E$, relations $r \in R$ and attributes $a \in A$. C is both training set and test set. $n = 800{,}000$, $k = 250$. See §2.2 for details.

then two entities e and f from E. We then add (e, r, f) and (f, r, e) to the corpus – this is one *instance* of applying the SYM rule from which symmetry can be learned. Similarly, the other rules also generate instances.

For each of the other rules, the template filling is modified to conform with its definition in Table 1. INV corresponds directly to SYM. COMP is a two-hop rule whereas the other five are one-hop rules. EQUI generates instances from which one can learn that the relations r and s are equivalent. IMP generates implication instances, e.g., (e, r, b) (= (dog, is, mammal)) implies (e, s, a_1) (= (dog, has, hair)), (e, s, a_2) (= (dog, has, neocortex)) etc. Per premise we create four implied facts.

For NEG, we generate pairs of facts (e, r, a) (=

(jupiter, is, big)) and $(e, \text{not } r, b)$ (= (jupiter, is, not, small)). We define the antonym function in Figure 1 (NEG) as returning for each attribute its antonym, i.e., attributes are paired, each pair consisting of a positive and a negative attribute.

Each of the six generation algorithms has the outer loop "for $i \in 1 \ldots n$" (where $n = 20$) that samples one, two or three relations (and potentially attributes) and generates a subcorpus for these relations; and the inner loop "for $j \in 1 \ldots m$" (where $m = 800$) that generates the subcorpus of instances for the sampled relations.

Train/test split. The data generation algorithms generate two subsets of facts C and D, see Figure 1. For each rule, we merge all of C with 90% of D (randomly sampled) to create the training set. The rest of D (i.e., the other 10%) serves as the test set.

For some of the cloze queries "$e \, r \, [\text{MASK}]$", there are multiple correct objects that can be substituted for MASK. Thus, we rank predictions and compute precision at m, i.e., precision in the top m where m is the number of correct objects. We average precision at m for all cloze queries.

This experimental setup allows us to test to what extent BERT learns the six rules, i.e., to what extent the facts in the test set are correctly inferred from their premises in the training set.

2.2 Memorization

For memorization, the vocabulary consists of 125,000 entities, 20 relations and 2250 attributes.

Effect of frequency on memorization. Our first experiment tests how the frequency of a fact influences its successful memorization by the model. Figure 2 (left, FREQ) gives the corpus generation algorithm. The outer loop generates 800,000 random facts. These are divided up in groups of 8000. A fact in the first group of 8000 is added once to the corpus, a fact from the second group is added twice and so on. A fact from the last group is added 100 times to the corpus. The resulting corpus C is both the training set and the test set.

Effect of schema conformity. In this experiment, we investigate the hypothesis that a fact can be memorized more easily if it is schema conformant.

Figure 2 (right, SCHEMA) gives the corpus generation algorithm. We first sample an entity group: $\delta \sim E \times \ldots \times E$. For each group, relations are either related to the schema ("if schema") or are not (else clause). For example, for the schema "primate" the relations "eat" (eats fruit) and "climb" (climbs trees) are related to the schema, the relation "build" is not since some primates build nests and treehouses, but others do not.

For non-schema relations, facts with random attributes are added to the corpus. In Figure 4, we refer to these facts as (facts with) **unique attributes**. For relations related to the schema, we sample the attributes that are part of the schema: $\alpha \sim A \times \ldots \times A$ (e.g., ("paranut",...,"banana") for "eat"). Facts are then generated involving these attributes and added to the corpus. In Figure 4, we refer to these facts as (facts with) **group attributes**. We also generate exceptions (e.g., "eats tubers") since schemas generally have **exceptions**.

Similarly, the two lines "add = Bernoulli(0.5)" are intended to make the data more realistic: for a group of entities, its relations and its attributes, the complete cross product of all facts is not available to the human learner. For example, a corpus may contain sentences stating that chimpanzees and baboons eat fruit, but none that states that gorillas eat fruit.

For this second memorization experiment, training set and test set are again identical (i.e., $= C$).

In a final experiment, we modify SCHEMA as follows: exceptions are added 10 times to the corpus (instead of once). This tests the interaction between schema conformity and frequency.

3   BERT Model

BERT uses a deep bidirectional Transformer (Vaswani et al., 2017) encoder to perform masked language modeling. During pretraining, BERT randomly masks positions and learns to predict fillers. We use source code provided by Wolf et al. (2019). Following (Liu et al., 2019), we perform dynamic masking and no next sequence prediction.

rule	train	test
EQUI	99.95	98.28
SYM	99.97	98.40
INV	99.99	87.21
IMP	100.00	80.53
NEG	99.98	20.54
COMP	99.98	0.01
ANTI	100.00	14.85

Table 2:   Precision in % of completing facts for symbolic rules. Training corpora generated as specified in Figure 1. See §4.1 for detailed discussion.

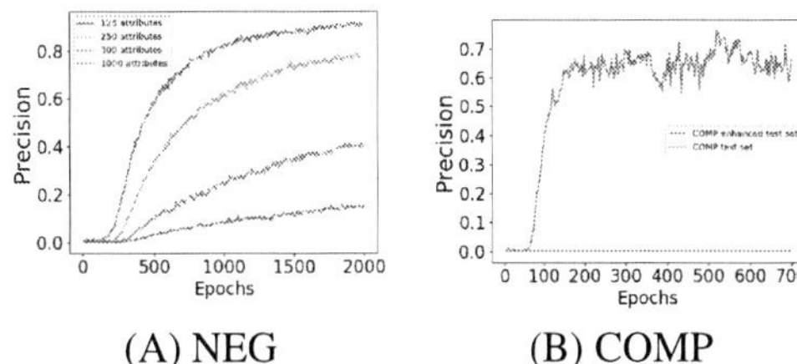

(A) NEG   (B) COMP

Figure 3:   Learning curves for symbolic reasoning. (A) shows precision for NEG with a varying number of attributes. A reduction to 125 attributes enables BERT to successfully apply antonym negation to the test set. (B) shows test set precision for COMP following the standard setup (orange) and an enhanced version (blue). Only in enhanced, i.e., with the introduction of additional facts adding more semantic information, is COMP generalized.

For symbolic rules, we start with BERT-base and tune hyperparameters. We vary the number of layers to avoid that rule learning fails due to over-parametrization, see appendix for details. We report precision based on optimal configuration.

In the memorization experiment, our goal is to investigate the effect of frequency on memorization. Due to a limited compute infrastructure, we scale down BERT to a single hidden layer with 3 attention heads, a hidden size of 192 and an intermediate size of 768.

4   Results, Analysis and Discussion

4.1   Symbolic Reasoning

Table 2 gives results for the symbolic reasoning experiments. BERT has high test set precision for EQUI, SYM, INV and IMP. As we see in Table 1, these rules share that they are "one-hop": The inference can be straightforwardly made from a single premise to a conclusion, e.g., "(barack married michelle)" implies "(michelle married barack)". The crucial difference to prior work is that the premise is not available at inference time. "(michelle married barack)" is correctly inferred by the model based on its memory of having seen the fact "(barack married michelle)" in the training set and based on the successful acquisition of the symmetry rule. Table 2 seems to suggest that BERT is able to learn one-hop rules and it can successively apply these rules in a natural setting in which the premise is not directly available.

In the rest of this section, we investigate these results further for SYM, INV, NEG and COMP.

4.1.1 Analysis of SYM and INV

Table 2 seems to indicate that BERT can learn that a relation r is symmetric (SYM) and that s and t are inverses (INV) – the evidence is that it generates facts based on the successfully acquired symmetry and inversion properties of the relations r, s and t. We now show that while BERT acquires SYM and INV partially, it also severely overgenerates. Our analysis points to the complexity of evaluating rule learning in PLMs and opens interesting avenues for future work.

Our first observation is that in the SYM experiment, BERT understands *all relations* to be symmetric. Recall that of the total of 500 relations, 250 are symmetric and 250 are used to generate random facts. If we take a fact with a random relation r, say (e, r, f), and prompt BERT with "$(f, r, [MASK])$", then e is predicted in close to 100% of cases. So BERT has simply learned that any relation is symmetric as opposed to distinguishing between symmetric and non-symmetric relations.

This analysis brings to light that our setup is unfair to BERT: it never sees evidence for non-symmetry. To address this, we define a new experiment, which we call ANTI because it includes an additional set of "anti" relations that are sampled from R^* with $R^* \cap R = \emptyset$ and $|R| = |R^*|$. ANTI facts take the following form: (e, r, f), (f, r, g) with $e \neq g$. Using this ANTI template we follow the standard data generation procedure. The corpus is now composed of symmetric, anti-symmetric and random facts. ANTI training data indicate to BERT that $r \in R^*$ is not symmetric since many instances of r facts are seen, with specific entities (f in the example) occurring in both slots, but there is never a symmetric example.

Table 2 (ANTI) shows that BERT memorizes ANTI facts seen during training but on test, BERT only recognizes 14.85% of ANTI facts as non-symmetric. So it still generalizes from the 250 symmetric relations to most other relations (85.15%),

even those without any "symmetric" evidence in training. So it is easy for BERT to learn the concept of symmetry, but it is hard to teach it to distinguish between symmetric and non-symmetric relations.

Similar considerations apply to INV. BERT successfully predicts correct facts once it has learned that s and t are inverses – but it overgeneralizes by also predicting many incorrect facts; e.g., for (e, s, f) in train, it may predict (f, t, e) (correct), but also (e, t, f) and (f, s, e) (incorrect).

In another INV experiment, we add, for each pair of (f, r, e) and (e, s, f) two facts that give evidence of non-symmetry: (f, r, g) and (e, s, h) with $e \neq g$ and $h \neq f$. We find that test set precision for INV (i.e., inferring (e, s, f) in test from (f, r, e) in train) drops to 17% in this scenario. As for SYM, this indicates how complex the evaluation of rule learning is.

In summary, we have found that SYM and INV are learned in the sense that BERT generates correct facts for symmetric and inverse relations. But it severely overgenerates. Our analysis points to a problem of neural language models that has not received sufficient attention: they can easily learn that the order of arguments is not important (as is the case for SYM relations), but it is hard for them to learn that this is the case *only for a subset of relations*. Future work will have to delineate the exact scope of this finding – e.g., it may not hold for much larger training sets with millions of occurrences of each relation. Note, however, that human learning is likely to have a bias against symmetry in relations since the vast majority of verbs[2] in English (and presumably relations in the world) is asymmetric. So unless we have explicit evidence for symmetry, we are likely to assume a relation is non-symmetric. Our results suggest that neural language models do not have this bias – which would be problematic when using them for learning from natural language text.

4.1.2 Analysis of NEG

NEG was the only rule for which parameter tuning improved performance. A reduction to four layers obtained optimal results.

In Table 2 we report a test set precision of 20.54%. Why is negation more challenging than implication? Implication allows the model to generalize over several entities all following the same rule (e.g., every animal that is a mammal has a

---

[2]For example, almost all of the verb classes in (Levin, 1993) are asymmetric.

neocortex). This does not hold for negation (e.g., a leopard is fast but a snail is not fast). BERT must learn antonym negation from a large number of possible combinations. By reducing the number of possible combinations (decreasing the number of attributes from 1000 to 500, 250 and 125) BERT's test set precision increases, see Figure 3 (A). With 125 attributes a precision of 91% is reached. A reduction of attributes makes antonym negation very similar to implication.

We investigate BERT's behavior concerning negation further by adding an additional attribute set A^*, with $A^* \cap A = \emptyset$ and $|A| = |A^*|$ to the vocabulary. A^* does not follow an antonym schema. We sample $a \in A^*, e \in E, r \in R$ to add additional random facts of the type (e, r, a) or $(e, \text{not } r, a)$ to NEG's training set. After training we test on the additional random facts seen during training by inserting or removing the negation marker. We see that BERT is prone to predict both (e, r, b) and $(e, \text{not } r, b)$ for b $\in A^*$ (for 38%). Antonym negation was still learned.

We conclude that antonym negation can be learned via co-occurrences but a general concept of negation is not understood.

This is in agreement with prior work (Ettinger, 2020; Kassner and Schütze, 2020) showing that BERT trained on natural language corpora is as likely to generate a true statement like "birds can fly" as a factually false negated statement like "birds cannot fly".

4.1.3 Analysis of COMP

Why does BERT not learn COMP? COMP differs from the other rules in that it involves two-hop reasoning. Recall that a novelty of our experimental setup is that premises are not presented at inference time – two-hop reasoning requires that two different facts have to be "remembered" to make the inference, which intuitively is harder than a one-hop inference. Figure 3 (B) shows that the problem is not undertraining (orange line).

Similar to the memorization experiment, we investigate whether stronger semantic structure in form of a schema can make COMP learnable. We refer to this new experiment as **COMP enhanced**. Data generation is defined as follows: Entities are divided into groups of 10. Relations are now defined between groups in the sense that the members of a group are "equivalent". More formally, we sample entity groups (groups of 10) E_1, E_2, E_3 and relations r, s, t. For all $e_1 \in E_1, e_2 \in$

$E_2, e_3 \in E_3$, we add (e_1, r, e_2) and (e_2, s, e_3) to C and (e_1, t, e_3) to D. In addition, we introduce a relation "samegroup" and add, for all $e_m, e_n \in E_i$, $(e_m, \text{samegroup}, e_n)$ to C – this makes it easy to learn group membership. As before, the training set is the merger of C and 90% of D and the test set is the rest of D.

Similar semantic structures occur in real data. The simplest case is a transitive example: (r) planes (group 1) are faster than cars (group 2), (s) cars (group 2) are faster than bikes (group 3), (t) planes (group 1) are faster than bikes (group 3).

Figure 3 (B) shows that BERT can learn COMP moderately well from this schema-enhanced corpus (blue curve): precision is clearly above 50% and peaks at 76%.

The takeaway from this experiment is that two-hop rules pose a challenge to BERT, but that they are learnable if entities and relations are embedded in a rich semantic structure. Prior work (Brown et al., 2020) has identified the absence of "domain models" (e.g., a domain model for common sense physics) as one shortcoming of PLMs. To the extent that PLMs lack such domain knowledge (which we simulate here with a schema), they may not be able to learn COMP.

4.2 Natural Language Corpora

In this section, we investigate to what extent the PLMs BERT and RoBERTa have learned SYM and INV from natural language corpora. See Table 3. For "smaller/larger" (INV), we follow Talmor et al. (2019) and test which of the two words is selected as the more likely filler in a pattern like "Jupiter is [MASK] than Mercury". For the other three relations ("shares borders with" (SYM), "is the opposite of" (SYM), "is the capital of" / "'s capital is" (INV)), we test whether the correct object is predicted in the pattern "e r [MASK]" (as in the rest of the paper). We give the number of (i) consistent ("cons."), (ii) correct and consistent ("correct") and (iii) inconsistent ("inc.") predictions. (A prediction is consistent and incorrect if it is consistent with the rule, but factually incorrect.)

In more detail, we take a set of entities (countries like "Indonesia", cities like "Jakarta") or adjectives like "low" that are appropriate for the relation and test which of the entities / adjectives is predicted. For each of the five relations, we run both BERT-large-cased and RoBERTa-large and report the more consistent result.

relation	rule	completions			examples
		cons.	correct	inc.	
shares borders with	SYM	152	152	2	(ecuador,peru) (togo,ghana), (ghana,nigeria)
is the opposite of	SYM	179	170	71	(demand,supply) (injustice,justice), (justice,truth)
is the capital of (C-of) *'s capital is (s-C-is)*	INV	59	59	1	(indonesia,s-C-is,jakarta) (canada,s-C-is,ottawa), (ottawa,C-of,ontario)
is smaller/larger than (countries)	INV	54	23	99	(russia,larger,canada), (canada,smaller,russia) (brazil,smaller,russia), (russia,smaller,brazil)
is smaller/larger than (planets)	INV	9	9	36	(jupiter,larger,mercury), (mercury,smaller,jupiter) (sun,bigger,earth), (earth,bigger,sun)

Table 3: Can PLMs (BERT and RoBERTa) learn SYM and INV from natural language corpora? For "smaller/larger", we follow Talmor et al. (2019) and test which of the two words is selected as a filler in a pattern like "Jupiter is [MASK] than Mercury". For the other three relations, we test whether the correct object is predicted (as in the rest of the paper). We give the number of (i) consistent ("cons."), (ii) correct and consistent ("correct") and (iii) inconsistent ("inc.") predictions. Blue: consistent examples. Red: inconsistent examples. (We make the simplifying assumption that "justice" can only have one opposite.)

Consistency and accuracy are high for "shares borders with" and "capital". However, this is most likely due to the fact that many of these facts occur verbatim in the training corpora of the two models. For example, Google shows 54,800 hits for "jakarta is the capital of indonesia" and 1,290 hits for "indonesia's capital is jakarta" (both as a phrase). It is not possible to determine which factor is decisive here: successful rule-based inference or memorization. The ultimate futility of this analysis is precisely the reason that we chose to work with synthetic data.

Consistency for "is the opposite of" is much lower than for the first two relations, but still decent. To investigate this relation further, we also tested the relation "is the same as". It turns out that many of the "opposite" objects are also predicted for "is the same as", e.g., "high is the same as *low*" and "low is the same as *high*" where the predicted word is in italics. This indicates that the models have not really learned that "is the opposite of" is symmetric, but rather know that antonyms are closely associated and often occur together in phrases like "X is the opposite of Y", "X and Y", "X noun, Y noun" (e.g., "good cop, bad cop") etc. Apparently, this is then incorrectly generalized to "is the same as".

Consistency and accuracy are worse for "smaller/larger". "smaller/larger" sentences of the sort considered here are probably rarer in genres like Wikipedia than "shares borders with" and "is the capital of". A Wikipedia article about a country will always say what its capital is and which countries it borders, but it will not enumerate the countries that are smaller or larger.

In summary, although we have shown that pre-trained language models have some ability to learn symbolic rules, there remains considerable doubt that they can do so based on natural corpora.

4.3 Memorization

Experimental results for the memorization experiments are shown in Figure 4.

(A) shows that frequent facts are memorized well (0.8 for frequency 100) and that rare facts are not (≈ 0.0 for frequencies < 15).

(B) shows that BERT memorizes schema conformant facts perfectly ("group attributes"). Accuracy for exceptions is clearly lower than those of schema conformant facts: about 80%. The frequency of each fact in the training corpus in this experiment is 1. Overall, the total amount of exceptions is much lower than the total amount of schema conformant facts.

(C) shows that exceptions are perfectly learned if 10 copies of each exception are added to the corpus – instead of 1 in (B). In this case, limited capacity affects memorization of schema-conformant facts: accuracy drops to ≈ 0.9.

In summary, we find that both frequency and schema conformity facilitate memorization. Schema conformant facts and exceptions compete for memory if memory capacity is limited – depending on frequency one or the other is preferentially learned by BERT.

5 Limitations

Our experimental design makes many simplifying assumptions: i) Variation in generated data is more

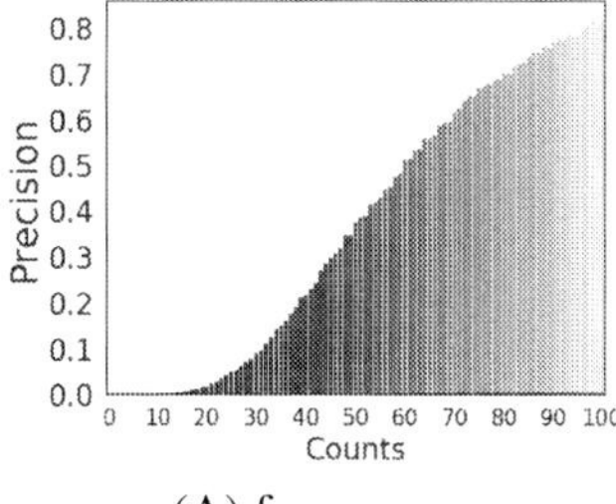
(A) frequency

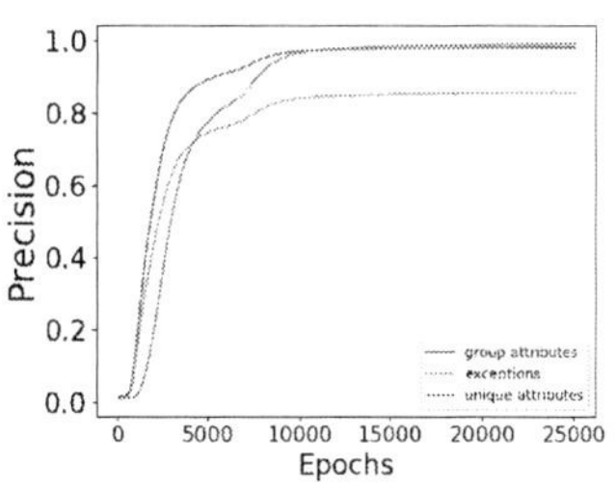
(B) schema conformity,
exceptions rare

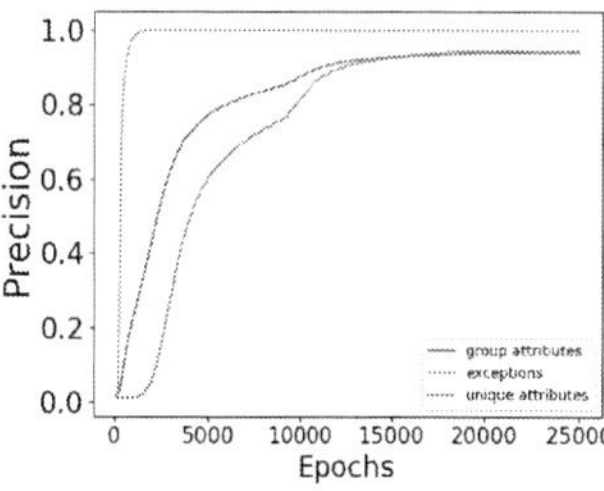
(C) schema conformity,
exceptions frequent

Figure 4: Memorization experiments. We investigate the effect of frequency and schema conformity on memorization. (A) Frequent facts are memorized well (0.8 for frequency 100), rare facts are not (≈ 0.0 for frequencies < 15). (B) BERT memorizes schema conformant facts perfectly ("group attributes"). Accuracy for rare exceptions is clearly lower (80%). (C) Exceptions are perfectly learned if 10 copies of each exception are added to the corpus – instead of 1 in (B). In this case, limited capacity affects memorization of schema-conformant facts ("group attributes" drops to ≈ 0.9).

limited than in naturally occurring data. ii) Semantics are deliberately restricted to one rule only per generated corpus. iii) We do not investigate effects of model and corpus size.

i) In natural corpora relations can have more than two arguments, entities can have several tokens, natural data are noisier than synthetic data etc. Also, we study each rule in isolation.

ii) While our simplified corpora make learning easier in some respects, they may make it harder in others. Each corpus is focused on providing training material for one symbolic rule, but it does not contain any other "semantic" signal that may be helpful in learning symbolic reasoning: distributional signals, entity groupings, hierarchies, rich context etc. The experimental results of "COMP enhanced" indicate that indeed such signals are beneficial to symbolic rule learning. The interplay of such additional sources of information for learning with symbolic rules is an interesting question for follow up work.

iii) Results are based on BERT-base and scaled-down versions of BERT-base only, just as training corpora are orders of magnitude smaller than natural training corpora. We varied model and corpus sizes within the limits of our compute infrastructure, but did not systematically study their effect on our findings.

Our work is an initial exploration of the question whether symbolic rules can be learned in principle, but we view it mainly as a starting point for future work.

6 Related Work

Radford et al. (2019) and Petroni et al. (2019) show in a zero-shot question answering setting that PLMs have factual knowledge. Our main question is: under what conditions do PLMs learn factual knowledge and do they do so through memorization or rule-based inference?

Sun et al. (2019) and Zhang et al. (2020) show in the knowledge graph domain that models that have the ability to capture symbolic rules like SYM, INV and COMP outperform ones that do not. We investigate this question for PLMs that are trained on language corpora.

Talmor et al. (2019) test PLMs' symbolic reasoning capabilities probing pretrained and finetuned models with cloze-style queries. Their setup makes it impossible to distinguish whether a fact was inferred or memorized during pretraining. Our synthetic corpora allow us to make this distinction.

Clark et al. (2020) test finetuned BERT's reasoning capabilities, but they always make premise and conclusion locally available to the model, during training and inference. This is arguably not the way much of human inference works; e.g., the fact F that X borders Y allows us to infer that Y borders X even if we were exposed to F a long time ago.

Richardson et al. (2020) introduce synthetic corpora testing logic and monotonicity reasoning. They show that BERT performs poorly on these new datasets, but can be quickly finetuned to good performance. The difference to our work again is that they make the premise available to the model at inference time.

For complex reasoning QA benchmarks (Yang

559

et al., 2018; Sinha et al., 2019), PLMs are finetuned to the downstream tasks. Their performance is difficult to analyze: it is not clear whether any reasoning capability is learned by the PLM or by the task specific component.

Another line of work (Gururangan et al., 2018; Kaushik and Lipton, 2018; Dua et al., 2019; Mc-Coy et al., 2019) shows that much of PLMs' performance on reasoning tasks is due to statistical artifacts in datasets and does not exhibit true reasoning and generalization capabilities. With the help of synthetic corpora, we can cleanly investigate PLMs' reasoning capabilities.

Hupkes et al. (2020) study the ability of neural models to capture compositionality. They do not investigate our six rules, nor do they consider the effects of fact frequency and schema conformity. Our work confirms their finding that transformers have the ability to capture both rules and exceptions.

A large body of research in psychology and cognitive science has investigated how some of our rules are processed in humans, e.g., Sloman (1996) for implication. There is also a lively debate in cognitive science as to how important rule-based reasoning is for human cognition (Politzer, 2007).

Yanaka et al. (2020); Goodwin et al. (2020) are concurrent studies of systematicity in PLMs. The first shows that monotonicity inference is feasible for syntactic structures close to the ones observed during training. The latter shows that PLMs can exhibit high over-all performance on natural language inference despite being non-systematic.

Roberts et al. (2020) show that the amount of knowledge captured by PLMs increases with model size. Our memorization experiments investigate the factors that determine successful acquisition of knowledge.

Guu et al. (2020) modify the PLM objective to incentivize knowledge acquisition. They do not consider symbolic rule learning nor do they analyze what factors influence successful memorization.

Based on perceptrons and convolutional neural networks, Arpit et al. (2017); Zhang et al. (2017) study the relation of generalizing from real structured data vs. memorizing random noise in the image domain, similar to our study of schema-conformant facts and outliers. They do not study transformer based models trained on natural language.

7 Conclusion

We studied BERT's ability to capture knowledge from its training corpus by investigating its reasoning and memorization capabilities. We identified factors influencing what makes successful memorization possible and what is learnable beyond knowledge explicitly seen during training. We saw that, to some extent, BERT is able to infer facts not explicitly seen during training via symbolic rules.

Overall, effective knowledge acquisition must combine both parts of this paper: memorization and symbolic reasoning. A PLM is not able to store an unlimited amount of knowledge. Through acquiring reasoning capabilities, knowledge gaps can be filled based on memorized facts. A schema-conformant fact ("pigeons can fly") need not be memorized if there are a few facts that indicate that birds fly and then the ability of flight can be filled in for the other birds. The schema conformity experiments suggest that this is happening. It is easier to capture knowledge that conforms with a schema instead of memorizing facts one by one.

There are several directions for future work. First, we made many simplifying assumptions that should be relaxed in future work. Second, how can we improve PLMs' ability to learn symbolic rules? We see two avenues here, either additional inductive biases could be imposed on PLMs' architectures or training corpora could be modified to promote learning of symbolic rules.

Acknowledgements

We thank Peter Clark for helpful discussions and our reviewers for constructive feedback.

This work was funded by the German Federal Ministry of Education and Research (BMBF, Grant No. 01IS18036A) and by Deutsche Forschungsgemeinschaft (DFG, Grant ReMLAV: Relational Machine Learning for Argument Validation). The authors of this work take full responsibility for its content.

References

Devansh Arpit, Stanisław Jastrzundefinedbski, Nicolas Ballas, David Krueger, Emmanuel Bengio, Maxinder S. Kanwal, Tegan Maharaj, Asja Fischer, Aaron Courville, Yoshua Bengio, and Simon Lacoste-Julien. 2017. A closer look at memorization in deep networks. In *Proceedings of the 34th International Conference on Machine Learning - Volume 70*, ICML'17, page 233242. JMLR.org.

Tom B. Brown, Benjamin Mann, Nick Ryder, Melanie Subbiah, Jared Kaplan, Prafulla Dhariwal, Arvind Neelakantan, Pranav Shyam, Girish Sastry, Amanda Askell, Sandhini Agarwal, Ariel Herbert-Voss, Gretchen Krueger, Tom Henighan, Rewon Child, Aditya Ramesh, Daniel M. Ziegler, Jeffrey Wu, Clemens Winter, Christopher Hesse, Mark Chen, Eric Sigler, Mateusz Litwin, Scott Gray, Benjamin Chess, Jack Clark, Christopher Berner, Sam Mc-Candlish, Alec Radford, Ilya Sutskever, and Dario Amodei. 2020. Language models are few-shot learners.

Peter Clark, Oyvind Tafjord, and Kyle Richardson. 2020. Transformers as soft reasoners over language. *IJCAI*.

Jacob Devlin, Ming-Wei Chang, Kenton Lee, and Kristina Toutanova. 2019. BERT: Pre-training of deep bidirectional transformers for language understanding. In *Proceedings of the 2019 Conference of the North American Chapter of the Association for Computational Linguistics: Human Language Technologies, Volume 1 (Long and Short Papers)*, pages 4171–4186, Minneapolis, Minnesota. Association for Computational Linguistics.

Dheeru Dua, Yizhong Wang, Pradeep Dasigi, Gabriel Stanovsky, Sameer Singh, and Matt Gardner. 2019. Drop: A reading comprehension benchmark requiring discrete reasoning over paragraphs. In *NAACL-HLT*.

Allyson Ettinger. 2020. What bert is not: Lessons from a new suite of psycholinguistic diagnostics for language models. *Transactions of the Association for Computational Linguistics*, 8:34–48.

Emily Goodwin, Koustuv Sinha, and Timothy J. O'Donnell. 2020. Probing linguistic systematicity. In *Proceedings of the 58th Annual Meeting of the Association for Computational Linguistics*, pages 1958–1969, Online. Association for Computational Linguistics.

Suchin Gururangan, Swabha Swayamdipta, Omer Levy, Roy Schwartz, Samuel Bowman, and Noah A. Smith. 2018. Annotation artifacts in natural language inference data. In *Proceedings of the 2018 Conference of the North American Chapter of the Association for Computational Linguistics: Human Language Technologies, Volume 2 (Short Papers)*, pages 107–112, New Orleans, Louisiana. Association for Computational Linguistics.

Kelvin Guu, Kenton Lee, Zora Tung, Panupong Pasupat, and Ming-Wei Chang. 2020. REALM: Retrieval-augmented language model pre-training. *ArXiv*, abs/2002.08909.

Dieuwke Hupkes, Verna Dankers, Mathijs Mul, and Elia Bruni. 2020. Compositionality decomposed: How do neural networks generalise? *J. Artif. Intell. Res.*, 67:757–795.

Nora Kassner and Hinrich Schütze. 2020. Negated and misprimed probes for pretrained language models: Birds can talk, but cannot fly. *ACL*.

Divyansh Kaushik and Zachary C. Lipton. 2018. How much reading does reading comprehension require? a critical investigation of popular benchmarks. In *Proceedings of the 2018 Conference on Empirical Methods in Natural Language Processing*, pages 5010–5015, Brussels, Belgium. Association for Computational Linguistics.

Beth Levin. 1993. *English Verb Classes and Alternations*. The University of Chicago Press, Chicago.

Yinhan Liu, Myle Ott, Naman Goyal, Jingfei Du, Mandar Joshi, Danqi Chen, Omer Levy, Mike Lewis, Luke Zettlemoyer, and Veselin Stoyanov. 2019. RoBERTa: A robustly optimized BERT pretraining approach. *CoRR*, abs/1907.11692.

Tom McCoy, Ellie Pavlick, and Tal Linzen. 2019. Right for the wrong reasons: Diagnosing syntactic heuristics in natural language inference. In *Proceedings of the 57th Annual Meeting of the Association for Computational Linguistics*, pages 3428–3448, Florence, Italy. Association for Computational Linguistics.

Mojtaba Nayyeri, Chengjin Xu, Jens Lehmann, and Hamed Shariat Yazdi. 2019. Logicenn: A neural based knowledge graphs embedding model with logical rules. *ArXiv*, abs/1908.07141.

Fabio Petroni, Tim Rocktäschel, Sebastian Riedel, Patrick Lewis, Anton Bakhtin, Yuxiang Wu, and Alexander Miller. 2019. Language models as knowledge bases? In *Proceedings of the 2019 Conference on Empirical Methods in Natural Language Processing and the 9th International Joint Conference on Natural Language Processing (EMNLP-IJCNLP)*, pages 2463–2473, Hong Kong, China. Association for Computational Linguistics.

Guy Politzer. 2007. Reasoning with conditionals. *Topoi*, 26(1):79–95.

Alec Radford, Jeff Wu, Rewon Child, David Luan, Dario Amodei, and Ilya Sutskever. 2019. Language models are unsupervised multitask learners.

Kyle Richardson, Hai Hu, Lawrence S. Moss, and Ashish Sabharwal. 2020. Probing natural language inference models through semantic fragments. In *Thirty-Fourth AAAI Conference on Artificial Intelligence*.

Adam Roberts, Colin Raffel, and Noam Shazeer. 2020. How much knowledge can you pack into the parameters of a language model? *ArXiv*, abs/2002.08910.

Koustuv Sinha, Shagun Sodhani, Jin Dong, Joelle Pineau, and William L. Hamilton. 2019. CLUTRR: A diagnostic benchmark for inductive reasoning from text. In *Proceedings of the 2019 Conference on Empirical Methods in Natural Language Processing and the 9th International Joint Conference on Natural Language Processing (EMNLP-IJCNLP)*, pages 4506–4515, Hong Kong, China. Association for Computational Linguistics.

Steven A. Sloman. 1996. The empirical case for two systems of reasoning. *Psychological Bulletin*, 119(1):3–22.

Zhiqing Sun, Zhi-Hong Deng, Jian-Yun Nie, and Jian Tang. 2019. Rotate: Knowledge graph embedding by relational rotation in complex space. In *International Conference on Learning Representations*.

Alon Talmor, Yanai Elazar, Yoav Goldberg, and Jonathan Berant. 2019. oLMpics - on what language model pre-training captures. *ArXiv*, abs/1912.13283.

Ashish Vaswani, Noam Shazeer, Niki Parmar, Jakob Uszkoreit, Llion Jones, Aidan N Gomez, Ł ukasz Kaiser, and Illia Polosukhin. 2017. Attention is all you need. In I. Guyon, U. V. Luxburg, S. Bengio, H. Wallach, R. Fergus, S. Vishwanathan, and R. Garnett, editors, *Advances in Neural Information Processing Systems 30*, pages 5998–6008. Curran Associates, Inc.

Jason Weston, Antoine Bordes, Sumit Chopra, and Tomas Mikolov. 2016. Towards ai-complete question answering: A set of prerequisite toy tasks. In *4th International Conference on Learning Representations, ICLR 2016, San Juan, Puerto Rico, May 2-4, 2016, Conference Track Proceedings*.

Thomas Wolf, Lysandre Debut, Victor Sanh, Julien Chaumond, Clement Delangue, Anthony Moi, Pierric Cistac, Tim Rault, R'emi Louf, Morgan Funtowicz, and Jamie Brew. 2019. Huggingface's transformers: State-of-the-art natural language processing. *ArXiv*, abs/1910.03771.

Hitomi Yanaka, Koji Mineshima, Daisuke Bekki, and Kentaro Inui. 2020. Do neural models learn systematicity of monotonicity inference in natural language? In *Proceedings of the 58th Annual Meeting of the Association for Computational Linguistics*, pages 6105–6117, Online. Association for Computational Linguistics.

Zhilin Yang, Peng Qi, Saizheng Zhang, Yoshua Bengio, William Cohen, Ruslan Salakhutdinov, and Christopher D. Manning. 2018. HotpotQA: A dataset for diverse, explainable multi-hop question answering. In *Proceedings of the 2018 Conference on Empirical Methods in Natural Language Processing*, pages 2369–2380, Brussels, Belgium. Association for Computational Linguistics.

Chiyuan Zhang, Samy Bengio, Moritz Hardt, Benjamin Recht, and Oriol Vinyals. 2017. Understanding deep learning requires rethinking generalization. In *5th International Conference on Learning Representations, ICLR 2017, Toulon, France, April 24 - 26, 2017, Conference Track Proceedings*.

Zhanqiu Zhang, Jianyu Cai, Yongdong Zhang, and Jie Wang. 2020. Learning hierarchy-aware knowledge graph embeddings for link prediction. In *Thirty-Fourth AAAI Conference on Artificial Intelligence*.

A   Hyperparameters

A.1   Model hyperparameters

For all reported results we trained with a batch-size of 1024 and a learning rate of 6e-5.

Our experiments for symbolic rules started with the BERT-base model with 12 layers, 12 attention heads, hidden size of 768 and intermediate size of 3072. For rules with a low test precision (NEG and COMP) we then conducted a restricted grid search (restricted due to limited compute infrastructure): We tried all possible numbers of layers from 1 to 12 and then only considered the best result. For NEG the best performance came from 4 layers, whereas COMP did not show improvements for any number of layers. For NEG with 3 layers (which had a very similar performance to 4 layers) we exemplarily tested whether changing the attention heads, hidden size or intermediate size improves precision. For this we trained with the following 4 settings:

- attention heads = 6, hidden size = 768, intermediate size = 3072

- attention heads = 12, hidden size = 384, intermediate size = 1536

- attention heads = 12, hidden size = 192, intermediate size = 768

- attention heads = 12, hidden size = 96, intermediate size = 192

However this did not further improve precision.

A.2   Data hyperparameters

In previous iterations of our experiments, we had used different settings for generating our data. For instance, we had varied the number of rules in our corpora: 50 or 100 instead of the presented 20 rules. Even the sampling process itself can be tweaked to allow for less overlaps between rules and between instances of one rule. However, we observed the same trends and similar numbers across these different settings.

B   Symbolic rules

In the following sections, we present illustrating corpora for **INV**, **IMP** and **COMP enhanced**. Each line is one datapoint. We also include the control group at the end of each corpus that does not follow any rule. In the case of composition enhanced, "{...}" indicates the sampled group which is not part of the actual dataset.

We illustrate our training corpora using real world entities and relations. Note that the actual corpora used for training are composed of an entirely synthetic vocabulary. For simplicity we show grouped composition with enhancement with groups of 4, instead of 10 as it is in the real data.

B.1   INV

Paris CapitalOf France
France HasCapital Paris

...

Egypt HasCapital Cairo (counterpart in test-set)

...

Apple Developed iOS
iOS DevelopedBy Apple

...

Germany RandomRelation China
Cairo RandomRelation Norway

B.2   IMP

{(Flu), (Cough, RunningNose, Headache, Fever)}
Kevin HasDisease Flu
Kevin HasSymptom Cough
Kevin HasSymptom RunningNose
Kevin HasSymptom Headache
Kevin HasSymptom Fever

...

Mariam HasDisease Flu

...

Peter RandomRelation Pain
Sarah RandomRelation Tooth

B.3 Comp enhanced

{e8, e2, e4, e5}
e8 ConnectedTo e2
e8 ConnectedTo e4
e8 ConnectedTo e5
e2 ConnectedTo e8

...
{e15, e13, e12, e19}
e15 ConnectedTo e13
e15 ConnectedTo e12

...
{e25, e24, e29, e20}
e25 ConnectedTo e24
e25 ConnectedTo e29

...
e8 r1 e15
e8 r1 e13
e8 r1 e12
e8 r1 e19
e2 r1 e15
e2 r1 e13

...
e5 r1 e19

...
e15 r2 e25
e15 r2 e24
e15 r2 e29
e15 r2 e20

...
e19 r2 e20

...
e8 r3 e25
e8 r3 e24
e8 r3 e29
e8 r3 e20

...

...
e133 r61 e23
e56 r61 e29

...

Understanding Linguistic Accommodation
in Code-Switched Human-Machine Dialogues

Tanmay Parekh
Language Technologies Institute
Carnegie Mellon University
tparekh@cs.cmu.edu

Emily P. Ahn
Department of Linguistics
University of Washington
eahn@uw.edu

Yulia Tsvetkov
Language Technologies Institute
Carnegie Mellon University
ytsvetko@cs.cmu.edu

Alan W Black
Language Technologies Institute
Carnegie Mellon University
awb@cs.cmu.edu

Abstract

Code-switching is a ubiquitous phenomenon in multilingual communities. Natural language technologies that wish to communicate like humans must therefore adaptively incorporate code-switching techniques when they are deployed in multilingual settings. To this end, we propose a Hindi-English human–machine dialogue system that elicits code-switching conversations in a controlled setting. It uses different code-switching agent strategies to understand how users respond and accommodate to the agent's language choice. Through this system, we collect and release a new dataset COMMONDOST, comprising of 439 human–machine multilingual conversations. We adapt pre-defined metrics to discover linguistic accommodation from users to agents. Finally, we compare these dialogues with Spanish-English dialogues collected in a similar setting, and analyze the impact of linguistic and socio-cultural factors on code-switching patterns across the two language pairs.[1]

1 Introduction

When interlocutors share more than one language, they nearly inevitably engage in *code-switching (CS)*: shifting from one language to another (Sankoff and Poplack, 1981; Muysken, 2000; Auer, 2013). Since most people in the world today are multilingual (Grosjean and Li, 2013), CS is a ubiquitous phenomenon in multilingual communities. It goes beyond simple lexical borrowing to blending of languages at syntactic, grammatical and morphological levels (Sitaram et al., 2019). Code-switching has been studied in linguistics and sociolinguistics for decades (Poplack, 1980; Gumperz, 1982; Milroy et al., 1995; Auer,

---

[1]The code and data is available at https://github.com/TanmayParekh/commonDost

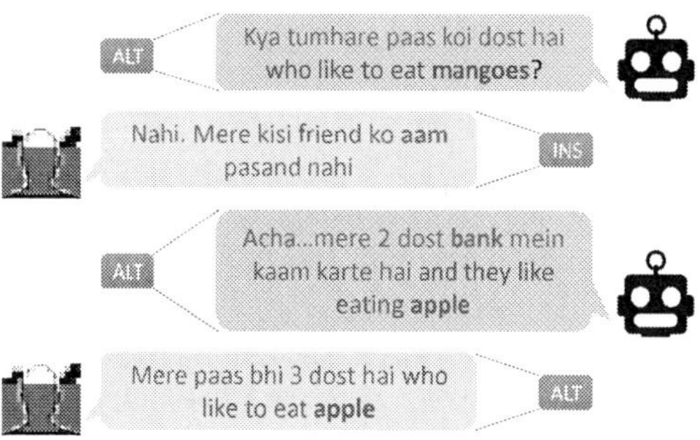

Figure 1: We present a bilingual dialogue system for human-machine conversations in Hindi-English (Red: Hindi, Blue: English). We discover that humans positively adopt the agent's code-switching style (ALT and INS) and the language choice for keywords (highlighted in bold).

2013; Gardner-Chloros and Weston, 2015) since it reveals various linguistic and socio-cultural behaviours (Heller, 1982). However, NLP studies of written CS are limited to social media texts, rather than natural conversation, and tend to focus on single sentences, rather than be contextualized in a dialogue (Rabinovich et al., 2019).

Advances in dialogue research (Vinyals and Le, 2015; Zhang et al., 2020; Serban et al., 2016) have enabled conversational AI technologies for human–machine interactions, like Alexa and Siri. Although these technologies are pervasive, they still have limited abilities to accommodate to the user, and they do not account for the ubiquity of multilingual communication. Due to the lack of code-switching abilities in existing language technologies, there has been limited work in studying linguistic accommodation in written CS dialogues.

With the ultimate goal to enable adaptive code-switching dialogue agents, in this paper we study user accommodation, i.e., *entrainment* (Brennan

565

Proceedings of the 24th Conference on Computational Natural Language Learning, pages 565–577
Online, November 19-20, 2020. ©2020 Association for Computational Linguistics
https://doi.org/10.18653/v1/P17

and Clark, 1996) in CS human–machine dialogues. Our exploratory analysis of user accommodation will facilitate better development of dialogue agents which can eventually accommodate to users in return. To this end, we adopt a collaborative dialogue framework of Ahn et al. (2020), which converses with Spanish–English (Spanglish) bilinguals. To facilitate a more general analysis, we extend this framework to Hindi–English (Hinglish), a language pair which is typologically distinct from Spanglish and is spoken by millions of people.

We begin by providing background on code-switching (§2) and linguistic accommodation (§3) We then introduce our generalized bilingual dialogue system (§4). In §5, we describe our experimental setup for Hinglish data collection and discuss the data statistics. We later provide our exploratory analysis of language accommodation and other socio-linguistic factors affecting the CS patterns in the user utterances (§6). A case-study comparing code-switching distributions across Hinglish and Spanglish is presented in §7. Finally, we discuss directions for future work in §8.

This paper's contributions include: (1) the development of a bilingual collaborative dialogue system easily generalizable to a new CS language pair, (2) a new dataset, COMMONDOST, comprising of 439 Hindi-English human–machine conversations, (3) adaptation of accommodation metrics and a corresponding analysis of accommodation of language style and choice in CS dialogues, and (4) an exploratory study of linguistic and socio-cultural factors on users' CS patterns across Spanglish and Hinglish.

2 Code-Switching Strategies

Given that CS is used in very nuanced ways, researchers have been studying *how people code-switch*, examining the switch-points of languages syntactically (Poplack, 1980; Solorio and Liu, 2008), prosodically (Fricke et al., 2016), lexically (Kootstra, 2012), pragmatically (Begum et al., 2016), and so forth. Many works have attempted to model code-switching text and speech from a statistical perspective (Garg et al., 2018a,b). Recent works and benchmarks such as Linguistic Code-switching Evaluation (LinCE) (Aguilar et al., 2020) and GLUECoS (Khanuja et al., 2020) have provided a unified platform to evaluate CS data for various NLP tasks across various language pairs. Our work is in line with these recent efforts to pro-vide NLP capabilities to users with diverse linguistic backgrounds. We extend the human–machine CS dialogue system by Ahn et al. (2020) to a new language pair of Hindi-English.

In order to better understand the style and usage of languages in a code-switched utterance, we cluster and characterize these utterances by a set of pre-defined CS strategies. Previous works have mainly identified two commonly used code-switching (CS) strategies: *Insertional* and *Alternational*, and these strategy distinctions are important in implementations of CS technology (Muysken, 2000; Bullock et al., 2018).

Insertional CS strategy involves one language to be the matrix language (MatL) with the other serving as the embedded language (EmbL). Words/phrases from EmbL are inserted in the sentence while maintaining the grammar and structure of MatL (Myers-Scotton, 1993). On the other hand, Alternational CS strategy involves alternating between separate independent clauses of the languages, switching from one MatL to another.

In our work, we focus on the Hindi-English language pair. We experiment with 4 CS strategies - (1) EN$\xrightarrow{ins}$HI (inserting English phrases into Hindi MatL), (2) HI$\xrightarrow{ins}$EN (inserting Hindi phrases into English MatL), (3) HI$\xrightarrow{alt}$EN (alternating from Hindi MatL to English MatL), and (4) EN$\xrightarrow{alt}$HI (alternating from English MatL to Hindi MatL).

CS is also observed more often in informal and casual settings than formal ones (Sitaram et al., 2019). We test this hypothesis by inducing informality in the agent's strategies. Although recent works (Madaan et al., 2020) have introduced neural methods to induce informality, we deploy a simple way to moderate formality by adding discourse markers (e.g. "so", "well") at the beginning and ending of sentences. These markers are independent of context and syntax (Schiffrin, 1988), and are often associated with informality (Jucker, 2002). Thus, we define four more agent strategies by infusing informality (+ *Informality*) in each of the previously described 4 CS strategies.

3 Measuring Accommodation in Dialogue

Communication Accommodation Theory posits that people adjust their behaviors or speech styles to their conversational partners' (Giles et al., 1973). Linguistic accommodation has proven to reduce interpersonal distance (Camilleri, 1996) and is correlated with dialogue success and engagement (Nenkova et al., 2008). Although well-studied in the monolingual dialogues (Brennan and Clark, 1996; Niederhoffer and Pennebaker, 2002), it is relatively new in the CS setting. Soto et al. (2018) found rate of code-switching to be accommodated in human–human Spanish-English dialogues. Choice of language when code-switching can also be adapted in dialogues (Bawa et al., 2018). Fricke et al. (2016) further discover that part-of-speech of a CS utterance may impact the following language choice. Our work adds to this field by studying accommodation of language choice for lexical classes. In terms of quantifying accommodation, we adapt a metric from Mizukami et al. (2016) to measure accommodation (we refer it to as *global* accommodation).

Global accommodation extends the score proposed in Nenkova et al. (2008) by aggregating a speaker's word usage across an entire dialogue and biases it relatively with other non-partners in the corpus. For two partners a and b, we denote $E_{a,b} = -\sum_{w \in V} |Pr_a(w) - Pr_b(w)|$ for a given word class V (where $Pr(w)$ is the empirical probability of word w). Denoting the set of non-partners for the speaker a by $\mathcal{N}_a$, we define *ratio* as

$$ratio(E_{(a,b)}, E_{(a,np)}) = \begin{cases} 1 & E_{(a,b)} > E_{(a,np)} \\ 0.5 & E_{(a,b)} = E_{(a,np)} \\ 0 & E_{(a,b)} < E_{(a,np)} \end{cases}$$

for all non-partners $np \in \mathcal{N}_a$. The *global* score for the speaker a is the average of *ratio* over all the non-partners. The final *global* score for the dataset is the average of the scores over all the speakers in the dataset. In context of human–machine conversations, we choose the set of non-partners for an agent to be the set of humans that did not interact with this agent. Since this metric is defined primarily for lexical accommodation, we redefine different styles as a lexical class to adapt it for measuring stylistic accommodation.

Danescu-Niculescu-Mizil et al. (2011) presented another interesting metric which measures accommodation *locally* across turns within a single dialogue. For two partners a and b, we can formulate this metric as

$$local_{(a,b)}(C) = Pr\left(T_b^C | T_a^C\right) - Pr\left(T_b^C\right)$$

where T_a and T_b denote the messages of a and b respectively. Here, T_b is the reply to T_a. T_b^C (and T_a^C) denote the prevalence of style C in T_b (and T_a). In essence, it attempts to measure an increase/decrese in the usage of a style C by b grounded on the usage of C by a. In our setting of human–machine conversations, since the agent's strategy is fixed, it's not as interesting to use this metric for our analysis. Thus, we focus our analysis only using *global* accommodation metric.

4 Bilingual Dialogue System

Our bilingual human–machine dialogue system mainly serves two important purposes: (1) collection of CS data and (2) experimentation of new agent strategies. Previous work (Ramanarayanan and Suendermann-Oeft, 2017) developed a rule-based CS dialogue system restricted to a fixed set of prompts. Ahn et al. (2020) proposed a more flexible bilingual system for English-Spanish as an extension of a monolingual goal-oriented collaborative dialogue framework (He et al., 2017), originally designed for the MUTUALFRIENDS task. This task provides the two conversational partners A and B individually with a knowledge base (KB) of friends, out of which there is exactly one friend common in both KBs. Each friend in the KB has several attributes such as hobby, location of work, etc. The goal of the task is to collaboratively find this mutual friend by text conversations between the two partners–which can be human or machine.

The modifications made by Ahn et al. (2020) for extending this monolingual system to support bilingual Spanish-English dialogues were mainly in three components: (1) Bilingual Readability: Supporting instructions and KB available to the users in Spanish as well as English, (2) Bilingual Response Generation: Procuring parallel Spanish sentences using a Machine Translation (MT) system and applying rule-based transformations for generating code-switched Spanglish, (3) Bilingual Response Understanding: Translating code-switched Spanish-English to monolingual English (using a MT system) and passing it to the pre-existing response understanding system for English.

Ahn et al. (2020)'s modified Spanish-English dialogue system cannot be directly applied across other language pairs due to three key reasons: (1) The dialogue system relies on a robust CS MT system[2] which is more readily available for resource-rich languages like Spanish and English. Such

---

[2] Translation from code-switched Spanish-English to monolingual English.

systems might not be accessible for languages like Tagalog and Swahili. (2) The linguistic rule-based adaptations for generation are simple in the case of Spanish-English as they are typologically closer. On the contrary, linguistically diverse pairs like Telugu-English might need further adaptations due to differences in word order and morphology. (3) Spanish and English are written using the same script. Many other language pairs within which CS is pervasive, like Hindi-English, are written in different scripts, and are typically romanized in the CS setting. Lack of normalization and robust transliteration models pose challenges to multiple system components for such pairs.

In our work, we build a more generalized dialogue system to tackle the challenges stated above. One highlight of this modified system is its simplicity, which helps in adapting to new language pairs easily. We briefly discuss these challenges and our enhancements to various components for our Hindi-English dialogue system below.

Language Bias in KB Due to social and cultural priors, certain domains and topics in the KB might not be equally represented in both languages. In order to avoid biasing the language usage in the dialogue and promote code-switching, it is necessary to carefully choose equilingual domains. In the case of Hinglish, we replace the domain of *college majors*, which is highly anglicized with respect to Hindi, with *favourite fruit* which is more equally represented in both languages.

Handling gender-markings Third person pronouns and verb forms in Hindi are usually gender-marked (eg. *karta/karti* [he/she does], *uska/uski* [his/her]). Since the Spanglish KB does not provide any information about the gender of friends, we consequently notice the dialogues using this system to be gender-skewed. In the COMMON-AMIGOS Spanglish data (Ahn et al., 2020), the ratio of masculine to feminine word usage was 3.9; whereas for Hinglish[3], this gender-ratio is 27.7. We mitigate this by simply adding a new "gender" attribute to the KB and correspondingly, notice a drastic drop of the gender-ratio to 3.4 for Hinglish.

Dialogue Generation The Spanglish dialogue system utilizes a MT system[4] to generate parallel Spanish-English sentences and leverages rule-based transformations (specific to Spanish) to gen-erate code-switched sentences. For language-pairs written in a non-native script (e.g. Hinglish written in English), there is a need of an additional transliteration model alongside a MT model for script-conversion. This agglomeration of the models leads to a cascade of errors that results in a poor overall translation. We circumvent this issue by building a simple phrase-based translation system. Despite its simplicity, the translation performance of the system is qualitatively better owing to the closed domain nature of the task.

Furthermore, the rule-based transformations need appropriate modifications to accommodate the new language pair. For Hinglish, we synthesize additional transformations to handle differences in word order and verb conjugations.

Natural Language Understanding (NLU) The Spanglish dialogue system relies on a robust MT system for converting CS user utterances to English and then exploits an English NLU component for entity extraction. Procuring such MT systems[5] for other language-pairs is not feasible. This issue is amplified for languages written in non-native script (Hinglish) due to lack of normalization in user sentences. We overcome this challenge by building a simple dictionary-based NLU component which can directly understand and extract entities from CS Hinglish text. Although it cannot handle complex inputs, this simple model still outperforms the translation-based NLU pipeline.

5 Data

We use the modified bilingual dialogue framework (§4) to collect romanized Hindi-English CS data for human–machine dialogues. Here, we first describe this data collection process and later discuss statistics for the collected data.

5.1 Data Collection

The majority of our data (80%) was collected by crowdsourcing our task on the Amazon Mechanical Turk[6] (AMT) platform, while the other 20% of the data was collected via participation from local Indian communities. A pre-requisite audio-based question-answering test is used to ensure the proficiency of the participants to chat in Hinglish. We limit three attempts per participant to boost diversity of the data.

---

[3]Tested on a set of 65 pilot dialogues.

[4]Google Translate API in the original implementation.

[5]Phrase-based translation systems perform poorly because user utterances are open-domain.

[6]https://www.mturk.com.

A: hey do you have any friends working at the zoo *ya dost hai jise sona pasand hai* [or friends who like sleeping] ?

H: *mere paas 2 dost hai jo* zoo *mei kaam karte hai aur unko* photography *ya* drawing *pasand hai* respectively [I have 2 friends who work in the zoo and they like photography and drawing respectively]

A: *toh* [so] i have some female friends *jinhe aam khana pasand hai* [who like eating mango]

H: *mere paas ek* female friend *hai jisko aam khana pasand hai aur usko* dancing *pasand hai* [I have 1 female friend who likes eating mango and likes dancing]

Table 1: Excerpt from a dialogue from our COMMON-DOST dataset. We highlight the Hindi content in *italics* along with its English translation in []. H: human and A: agent.

In order to draw direct comparisons between the collected Hinglish and Spanglish data, we closely follow the task setup as in Ahn et al. (2020). The instructions for the task are provided in Hinglish. We further use a post-task survey to gather sociolinguistic information about the participants. More details about the data collection process are described in the Appendix.

5.2 Data Processing

Owing to the lack of normalization of romanized Hindi, data processing and analysis is a non-trivial task. Further, due to paucity of CS data, there are fewer commercial systems available. To circumvent this issue, we develop simple custom tools and describe them below.

Language ID (LID) Tagger It is an important component to identify language usage (Hindi/English) by users in the dialogue data. We build a dictionary-based tagger using pre-populated lists of most common English words. We mark the remaining words with the Hindi LID[7]. This simple model achieves an accuracy of 94.5% on an unseen set of 84 human-annotated sentences. The tagged data is further corrected by human annotators.

CS Strategy Classifier We classify the user utterances into one of 7 strategies - 4 CS (see §2), 2 *monolingual* (Hindi and English), or *Neither*. We

develop a simple rule-based system utilizing the LIDs for detection of these strategies. Although this system uses simple heuristics, it achieves an F1 score of 0.85 on an unseen set of 84 CS sentences. Two independent human linguists achieve an average F1 score of 0.85 on this set, thus validating the performance of the classifier.

5.3 Data Statistics

We collect a total of 439 human–machine conversations (we provide an example dialogue in Table 1) across a pool of 164 unique people, wherein close to 85% participants attempted the task more than once. The distributions of the data collected via AMT and the local community are nearly the same except for age[8]. The self-reported survey further reveals that among unique users, 72% were male, 91% have a college degree, and 90% originate from the Indian subcontinent. Nearly 72% of users speak an additional regional Indian language other than Hindi or English.

	Hinglish	Spanglish
# Dialogues	439	587
# User Utterances	4,361	4,617
# User Tokens	29,117	28,452
% Task Success	59%	64%
Avg dialogue length	9.93	7.9
Avg utterance length	6.68	6.2
EN vocab size	539	571
HI/SP vocab size	1,280	846
% EN utterances	19%	16%
% HI/SP utterances	34%	44%
% CS utterances	47%	39%
% CS dialogues	92%	70%

Table 2: Data statistics for the Hinglish COMMON-DOST dataset and its comparison with the Spanglish COMMONAMIGOS dataset. EN: English, HI: Hindi and SP: Spanish.

We present the general statistics of our COMMONDOST data and compare it with the Spanglish COMMONAMIGOS dialogue dataset (Ahn et al., 2020) in Table 2. Although our absolute task success rate is not very high, we procure good quality code-switched dialogue data due to the agent's engagement. Notably, we observe longer chats (12.44 utterances per dialogue) for unsuccessful dialogues compared to successful ones (8.17). We

---

[7]Ambiguous words are handled with separate rules.

[8]The data collected from the local Indian community is skewed towards a younger age group.

Agent Strategy	# Dial	Task Success	Avg Utts	Avg Tok/Utt	% EN Utt	% HI Utt	% CS Utt
HI $\xrightarrow{alt}$ EN	39	64%	10.87	6.79	**14%**	**41%**	45%
+ Informal	42	60%	9.88	**7.51**	**13%**	33%	**54%**
EN $\xrightarrow{alt}$ HI	39	54%	9.36	**5.86**	**23%**	31%	46%
+ Informal	42	48%	10.38	6.95	**12%**	34%	**54%**
EN $\xrightarrow{ins}$ HI	41	**76%**	9.56	6.39	20%	**27%**	53%
+ Informal	35	57%	8.46	**8.2**	**5%**	25%	**69%**
HI $\xrightarrow{ins}$ EN	41	63%	8.66	**6.05**	**28%**	**24%**	47%
+ Informal	41	**73%**	11.12	6.39	19%	37%	44%
HI mono	40	**45%**	9.53	6.86	**9%**	**55%**	**36%**
EN mono	39	51%	10.41	6.08	**57%**	**19%**	**24%**
random	40	55%	10.88	6.63	**12%**	**41%**	46%

Table 3: General statistics of the CommonDost user dialogues filtered by agent strategy. We highlight the statistically significant (with $p < 0.05$) in **bold**. # Dial: Number of dialogues, Avg Utts: Average number of utterances per dialogue, Avg Tok/Utt: Average number of tokens per utterance, % EN Utt: Percentage of English utterances, % HI Utt: Percentage of Hindi utterances, % CS Utt: Percentage of code-switched utterances.

also observe that utterances in the Hinglish data are generally longer than that of their Spanglish counterparts. In terms of vocabulary sizes, we observe that CommonAmigos data has a smaller Spanish vocabulary size when compared to the Hindi vocabulary size in the CommonDost data. Overall, there is more CS in Hinglish data compared to Spanglish data.

6 Analysis of Hinglish Conversations

We study the impact of each of the agent strategies (4 CS strategies and their informal counterparts) on the user dialogues using various dialogue- and language-oriented dimensions, as shown in Table 3. We also introduce monolingual agent strategies (*HI mono* and *EN mono*) and a random CS strategy[9] as baselines for our analysis. We procure roughly 40 dialogues for each agent strategy for a principled comparison across these metrics.

6.1 Code-switching and Task Success

Our data substantiates the prevalence of CS in the language pair of Hindi-English. Although no explicit instructions were provided to exhibit code-switching, 92% of the dialogues and 47% of the user utterances are code-switched (Table 2). Furthermore, even when the agent converses com-

pletely in Hindi or English, we observe CS in nearly 30% of the user utterances (Table 3). Thus clearly, our dialogue system elicits code-switching.

In a goal-oriented framework like ours, task success is an essential metric to assess our agent (Column 3 in Table 3). We observe that task success is significantly better when the agent uses a CS strategy (62%) compared to agent's monolingual strategies (48%). Furthermore, when users were asked to rate the agent for how non-native the agent seemed (1-5, 5 is most non-native), agents using CS strategies were rated 2.62, which is much lower than 2.92 and 3.11 when agents used monolingual and random strategies respectively. Thus, CS aids in better communication and engagement between the agent and the user as suggested in Camilleri (1996), which eventually translates to better success rate.

6.2 Informality improves Dialogue Quality

Infusion of informality in the agent's CS strategies has two major observable effects on the user dialogue. First, we observe an increased user utterance length (column 5 in Table 3), which is in contrast to the finding in Ahn et al. (2020). We attribute this to the users being less curt[10] as they find the informal agent is relatively more friendly. The us-

---

[9]We randomly switch between languages at a phrase-level.

[10]1-2 word user utterances reduce by 7% when agent uses informal strategies.

age of discourse markers per dialogue by the users increases from 1.87 to 2.44 when conversing with an informal agent compared to a formal one. Second, we witness a higher CS and reduced English usage in the user utterances (column 6 and 8 in Table 3), similar to the finding in Spanglish (Ahn et al., 2020). Finally, when users were asked to rate the agent for how human-like it seemed, (1-5, 5 is most human-like), informal agents were rated 3.99, which is higher than 3.54 for an agent without informality. We conclude that informality helps the agent be perceived as friendlier. It induces longer and more code-switched user responses, improving the quality of the conversation.

6.3 Linguistic Accommodation in Dialogue

We focus our analysis of accommodation on the choice and style of language usage in the CS setting. We utilize the *global* accommodation metric (§3) to quantify our learnings.

Stylistic Dimension	Global score
Lexical Items (KB)	0.790
- English	0.648
- Hindi	0.700
CS Strategies	0.665

Table 4: Reporting the *global* accommodation metric for the word class of lexical items (KB) (row 1). We further report the accommodation score for the choice of language for these items (row 2 and 3). Finally we report the score for accommodation of CS strategies (row 4). Divergence is indicated by 0 while 1 indicates convergence, and 0.5 is no accommodation.

6.3.1 Language choice for lexical items

Lexical accommodation of a word class is a common and well-observed phenomenon in monolingual dialogues. In the CS setting, we study an additional dimension of language choice for the word class. For example, *if the agent uses the English word for mentioning fruits in its utterance, will the user also use the English word for referring fruits in their utterance*? We focus this analysis on the word class of all the lexical items in the knowledge base (in Hindi and English). First, we evaluate the overall language-independent score for the word class and then the language-dependent scores highlighting the accommodation of language choice for referring to the word class (first three rows in Table 4).

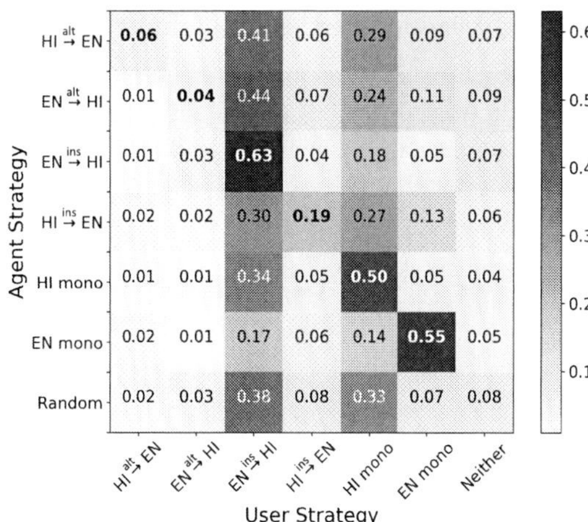

Figure 2: Probability distributions of the usage of CS strategies in user utterances (across the columns) for each agent strategy (across the rows). We highlight the statistically significant ($p < 0.05$) numbers in **bold**.

We notice a high accommodation score for the overall word class of lexical items, which is expected due to the nature of the task. We further witness a positive accommodation score for the usage of both languages (Hindi and English) while referring to this word class. This result is more motivating given there is an inherent user bias[11] to use Hindi words (60%) compared to English words (40%) while referring to lexical items in the dialogue. Thus, we conclude that the agent's language choice for lexical items positively influences the users' language choice too.

6.3.2 Accommodation of CS Strategy

In Table 3, we observe higher CS in user utterances when the agent is code-switching (51%) compared to when the agent is conversing monolingually (30%). This elicits the global accommodation of the phenomenon of code-switching by the users. Here, we focus on studying the accommodation of the style of CS between the user and the agent.

Using the rule-based CS strategy classifier (§5.2), we cluster the user utterances into one of the seven strategies - 4 CS, 2 monolingual, or neither. In Figure 2, we present a confusion matrix to study the impact of each agent's CS strategy[12] on the usage of the users' strategy. Each row in the matrix represents the normalized distribution[13] of the user

---

[11]Calculated by comparing usage on the *random* baseline.
[12]We do not maintain the distinction of informal strategies.
[13]We exclude sentences with length < 3 as they do not follow any particular CS strategy.

571

CS strategies for the given agent strategy.

The diagonal elements in the matrix represent the percentage when the user adopts the same strategy as the agent. In any column of the matrix, we observe that these elements are the highest (statistically significant with $p < 0.05$). This implies that the user's usage of any given CS strategy increases significantly when the agent is using the same strategy. Using the *global* accommodation metric to quantify this phenomenon (last row of Table 4), we observe a high positive accommodation score. Based on these observations, we conclude that users synchronize their style of language use with the agent in a CS setting.

6.4 Language Proficiency influences Hinglish CS

We cluster and analyze user dialogues based on the self-reported additional languages of proficiency in the post-task survey. Diving deeper into the usage of CS strategies filtered by their language of proficiency, we find a general peculiarity amongst speakers proficient in South Indian languages (Malayalam, Telugu, Tamil and Kannada). These speakers (specifically Telugu) have a higher usage of $HI \xrightarrow{ins} EN$ and $EN \xrightarrow{alt} HI$ and a relatively lower usage of $EN \xrightarrow{ins} HI$ CS strategies in their utterances. These strategies indicate that such speakers are using English as their MatL, or at least starting with it. Alternatively, we find a higher usage of $EN \xrightarrow{ins} HI$ and $HI \xrightarrow{alt} EN$ strategies for speakers proficient in North Indian languages (Gujarati, Marathi, Punjabi, Odia and Bengali). These two strategies indicate that such speakers are adopting Hindi as their MatL, or at least in the beginning (which is opposite as observed for South Indian speakers). This phenomenon can be attributed to a higher influence of English in the South Indian languages and correspondingly, Hindi in the North Indian languages as suggested in Baldridge (2002).

Overall, we believe that other languages of proficiency, as a proxy for geographical region and cultural factors, largely impact the dialogue and CS patterns, and are understudied in general. Studying such patterns in human–human dialogues (eg. when a North Indian speaker converses with a South Indian speaker in a CS setting) would reveal further various socio-cultural factors influencing code-switching.

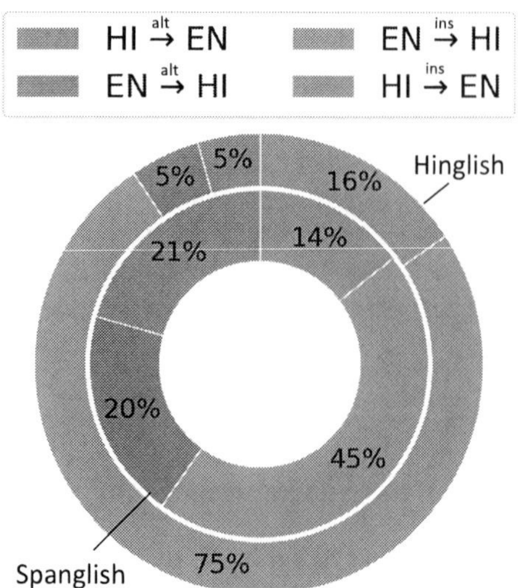

Figure 3: Comparing the distributions of users' usage of CS strategies in Hinglish and Spanglish. Alternational CS is relatively less frequent in Hinglish. Inner circle: Spanglish and Outer circle: Hinglish

7 Comparison of Spanglish and Hinglish

To gain better insights into how linguistic and socio-cultural factors influence code-switching patterns, we compare the distributions of the users' usage of various CS strategies in Hinglish and Spanglish in Figure 3. We observe that $EN \xrightarrow{ins} HI$ and $EN \xrightarrow{ins} SP$ are the most dominant CS strategies in Hinglish and Spanglish respectively. On the other hand, we notice a large difference in the usage of Alternational CS strategies in the language pairs. For Spanglish, it accounts to roughly 40% while it is merely 10% for Hinglish.

As attributed by the Equivalence Constraint, CS points tend to occur only if a syntactic rule is not violated in either of the two languages being mixed (Poplack, 1980). Given this requirement, a pair of languages that have differing word order could have more constraints on where switches can occur. We hypothesize that Alternational CS may not work within a verb clause in Hindi as it is a verb-final (SOV) language while English is verb-medial (SVO). Spanish is verb-medial like English, and their word order similarity may facilitate the use of Alternational CS.

Beyond structural differences, sociolinguistic factors may affect CS strategies of speakers. Backus (1998) describes a gradient of strategy usage across generations of immigrants. Earlier generations of immigrants would progress from simple to complex insertions, and later generations would alternate the two languages, eventually using reverse insertion. As the Spanglish dataset includes later generations of immigrants to the US, 90% of Hinglish speakers are 1st generation. This would highlight Hinglish speakers' affinity towards insertion into the Hindi matrix language.

Additionally, the status of English in the US (for Spanglish) and English in India (for Hinglish) is different. As found in §6.4, the status of English can vary within regions of India itself, and this can lead to varying uses of CS strategy. Attitudes towards language use have been shown to affect code choice in bilingual speakers (Redinger, 2010). It is likely that attitudes towards CS is not the same in the Spanglish and Hinglish populations, which can provide further variability in the speakers' language choice.

8   Conclusion and Future Work

In our work, we proposed a generalized bilingual dialogue system and procured human–machine dialogue data (COMMONDOST) for the language pair of Hindi-English using this system. Adaptation of this dialogue system for newer CS languages could promote collection of more bilingual dialogue data.

Analysis of the COMMONDOST conversations revealed how users positively adopt and accommodate the agent's style of using language in a CS utterance. We also studied how informality and cultural factors independently affect the users' CS patterns. This proves that our findings are extendable across two CS pairs of Hinglish and Spanglish (Ahn et al., 2020). Similar analysis can be done for new language pairs (such as Arabic-English) and datasets from different domains. Another area of potential research would be to compare our findings of the CS patterns and accommodation with human–human CS conversations.

Finally, we discussed how linguistic and sociopolitical factors affect the distribution of users' CS patterns across the language pairs of Hinglish and Spanglish. Despite their dissimilarities, the similarities across these language pairs is encouraging, as it open avenues to learn about how code-switching functions cross–linguistically. We pave the path for future research on comparisons of multiple CS language pairs.

Acknowledgments

The authors are grateful to the anonymous reviewers for their invaluable feedback. This material is based upon work supported by the National Science Foundation under Grant No. IIS2007960.

References

Gustavo Aguilar, Sudipta Kar, and Thamar Solorio. 2020. Lince: A centralized benchmark for linguistic code-switching evaluation. In *Proceedings of The 12th Language Resources and Evaluation Conference*, pages 1803–1813.

Emily Ahn, Cecilia Jimenez, Yulia Tsvetkov, and Alan Black. 2020. What code-switching strategies are effective in dialogue systems? *Proceedings of the Society for Computation in Linguistics*, 3(1):308–318.

Peter Auer. 2013. *Code-switching in conversation: Language, interaction and identity*. Routledge.

Albert Marie Backus. 1998. *Two in one: Bilingual speech of Turkish immigrants in The Netherlands*. Tilburg University Press.

Jason Baldridge. 2002. Linguistic and social characteristics of indian english. *Language in India*, 2(4).

Anshul Bawa, Monojit Choudhury, and Kalika Bali. 2018. Accommodation of conversational code-choice. In *Proceedings of the Third Workshop on Computational Approaches to Linguistic Code-Switching*, pages 82–91.

Rafiya Begum, Kalika Bali, Monojit Choudhury, Koustav Rudra, and Niloy Ganguly. 2016. Functions of code-switching in tweets: An annotation scheme and some initial experiments. *LREC. i*, pages 1644–1650.

Susan E Brennan and Herbert H Clark. 1996. Conceptual pacts and lexical choice in conversation. *Journal of Experimental Psychology: Learning, Memory, and Cognition*, 22(6):1482.

Barbara E Bullock, Gualberto Guzmán, Jacqueline Serigos, and Almeida Jacqueline Toribio. 2018. Should code-switching models be asymmetric? *Proc. Interspeech 2018*, pages 2534–2538.

Antoinette Camilleri. 1996. Language values and identities: Code switching in secondary classrooms in malta. *Linguistics and education*, 8(1):85–103.

Cristian Danescu-Niculescu-Mizil, Michael Gamon, and Susan Dumais. 2011. Mark my words!: linguistic style accommodation in social media. In *Proceedings of the 20th international conference on World wide web*, pages 745–754. ACM.

Melinda Fricke, Judith F Kroll, and Paola E Dussias. 2016. Phonetic variation in bilingual speech: A lens for studying the production-comprehension link. *Journal of Memory and Language*, 89:110–137.

Penelope Gardner-Chloros and Daniel Weston. 2015. Code-switching and multilingualism in literature. *Language and Literature*, 24(3):182–193.

Saurabh Garg, Tanmay Parekh, and Preethi Jyothi. 2018a. Code-switched language models using dual RNNs and same-source pretraining. In *Proceedings of the 2018 Conference on Empirical Methods in Natural Language Processing*, pages 3078–3083, Brussels, Belgium. Association for Computational Linguistics.

Saurabh Garg, Tanmay Parekh, and Preethi Jyothi. 2018b. Dual language models for code switched speech recognition. In *Proceedings of the 19th Annual Conference of the International Speech Communication Association (INTERSPEECH)*.

Howard Giles, Donald M Taylor, and Richard Bourhis. 1973. Towards a theory of interpersonal accommodation through language: Some canadian data. *Language in society*, 2(2):177–192.

François Grosjean and Ping Li. 2013. *The Psycholinguistics of Bilingualism*. Wiley-Blackwell.

John J Gumperz. 1982. *Discourse strategies*, volume 1. Cambridge University Press.

He He, Anusha Balakrishnan, Mihail Eric, and Percy Liang. 2017. Learning symmetric collaborative dialogue agents with dynamic knowledge graph embeddings. In *Proceedings of the 55th Association for Computational Linguistics (ACL)*.

Monica Heller. 1982. Negotiations of language choice in montreal. *Language and social identity*, pages 108–118.

Andreas H Jucker. 2002. *Discourse markers in Early Modern English*. Routledge.

Simran Khanuja, Sandipan Dandapat, Anirudh Srinivasan, Sunayana Sitaram, and Monojit Choudhury. 2020. GLUECoS: An evaluation benchmark for code-switched NLP. In *Proceedings of the 58th Annual Meeting of the Association for Computational Linguistics*, pages 3575–3585, Online. Association for Computational Linguistics.

Gerrit Jan Kootstra. 2012. *Code-switching in monologue and dialogue: Activation and alignment in bilingual language production*. [Sl: sn].

Aman Madaan, Amrith Setlur, Tanmay Parekh, Barnabas Poczos, Graham Neubig, Yiming Yang, Ruslan Salakhutdinov, Alan W Black, and Shrimai Prabhumoye. 2020. Politeness transfer: A tag and generate approach. In *Proceedings of the 58th Annual Meeting of the Association for Computational Linguistics*, pages 1869–1881, Online. Association for Computational Linguistics.

James Milroy et al. 1995. *One speaker, two languages: Cross-disciplinary perspectives on code-switching*. Cambridge University Press.

Masahiro Mizukami, Koichiro Yoshino, Graham Neubig, David Traum, and Satoshi Nakamura. 2016. Analyzing the effect of entrainment on dialogue acts. In *Proceedings of the 17th Annual Meeting of the Special Interest Group on Discourse and Dialogue*, pages 310–318.

Pieter Muysken. 2000. Bilingual speech: a typology of code-mixing.

Carol Myers-Scotton. 1993. Common and uncommon ground: Social and structural factors in codeswitching. *Language in society*, 22(4):475–503.

Ani Nenkova, Agustin Gravano, and Julia Hirschberg. 2008. High frequency word entrainment in spoken dialogue. In *Proceedings of 46th Annual Meeting of the Association for Computational Linguistics ACL-08: HLT, Short Papers*, pages 169–172.

Kate G Niederhoffer and James W Pennebaker. 2002. Linguistic style matching in social interaction. *Journal of Language and Social Psychology*, 21(4):337–360.

Shana Poplack. 1980. Sometimes i'll start a sentence in english y termino en español. *Linguistics*, 18:581–618.

Ella Rabinovich, Masih Sultani, and Suzanne Stevenson. 2019. Codeswitch-reddit: Exploration of written multilingual discourse in online discussion forums. In *Proc. of EMNLP*.

Vikram Ramanarayanan and David Suendermann-Oeft. 2017. Jee haan, i'd like both, por favor: Elicitation of a code-switched corpus of hindi–english and spanish–english human–machine dialog. In *Proc. Interspeech 2017*, pages 47–51.

Daniel Redinger. 2010. *Language attitudes and code-switching behaviour in a multilingual educational context: the case of Luxembourg*. Ph.D. thesis, University of York.

David Sankoff and Shana Poplack. 1981. A formal grammar for code-switching. *Research on Language & Social Interaction*, 14(1):3–45.

Deborah Schiffrin. 1988. *Discourse markers*. 5. Cambridge University Press.

Iulian V Serban, Alessandro Sordoni, Yoshua Bengio, Aaron Courville, and Joelle Pineau. 2016. Building end-to-end dialogue systems using generative hierarchical neural network models. In *Proceedings of the 30th AAAI Conference on Artificial Intelligence*.

Sunayana Sitaram, Khyathi Raghavi Chandu, Sai Krishna Rallabandi, and Alan W Black. 2019. A survey of code-switched speech and language processing. *arXiv preprint arXiv:1904.00784*.

Thamar Solorio and Yang Liu. 2008. Learning to predict code-switching points. *Proceedings of the 2008 Conference on Empirical Methods in Natural Language Processing*, (October):973–981.

Victor Soto, Nishmar Cestero, and Julia Hirschberg. 2018. The role of cognate words, POS tags, and entrainment in code-switching. *Proc. Interspeech 2018*, pages 1938–1942.

Oriol Vinyals and Quoc V. Le. 2015. A neural conversational model. In *Proceedings of the 31st International Conference on Machine Learning*.

Yizhe Zhang, Siqi Sun, Michel Galley, Yen-Chun Chen, Chris Brockett, Xiang Gao, Jianfeng Gao, Jingjing Liu, and Bill Dolan. 2020. DIALOGPT : Large-scale generative pre-training for conversational response generation. In *Proceedings of the 58th Annual Meeting of the Association for Computational Linguistics: System Demonstrations*, pages 270–278, Online. Association for Computational Linguistics.

A   Task Illustration

We present the user interface for the MTurk task in Figure 4. The users are shown the task-related information and instructions at all points in time for quick reference. We present the knowledge-base (KB) of the friends in a tabular format on the right. The information in the table has both the English and Hindi translations of the entities and items in the KB. At the bottom of the page, we have the main chat interface. It comprises of a running timer (maximum of 8 mins), a chat history window showing the user and agent's responses and finally a text input box for writing responses. The user can chat with the agent using the chat window or guess the mutual friend using *Select* button corresponding to that friend in the table on the right.

B   Example Dialogues

In addition to Table 1, we present additional samples of dialogues from the collected COMMON-DOST dataset (Table 5, 6, 7). Table 5 elicits a case of style accommodation by the user to the agent's CS strategy. Initially the user conversed in monolingual English, but later used a HI$\xrightarrow{alt}$EN CS strategy following the agent.

H:	dont you have any friends who works in zoo in and like photography
A:	*mere paas ek dost hai* [I have one friend] working at the factory
H:	*kya tere pass* [Do you have] any friend works in the office
A:	*mere paas do dost hai* [I have two friends] working at the office

---

Table 5: Excerpt from a dialogue from our COMMON-DOST dataset. We highlight the Hindi content in *italics* along with its English translation in []. H: human and A: agent.

In Table 6, we observe that the user doesn't change its strategy with respect to the agent's CS strategy and continues conversing in monolingual Hindi. Further, this example also highlights the challenge of normalization of romanized Hindi as many words like *dosth* and *dho* are spelt differently owing to the language proficiency of the user.

A few dialogues in our dataset are extremely short as well if the user is able to guess the common friend early enough. One example of such a dialogue is presented in Table 7. The "SELECT"

A:	i have two *dost* [friends] working at the *machalighar* [aquarium].
H:	*haaa* [yes]
H:	*eek dosth hai* [there is one friend]
A:	i have one *dost* [friend] who likes *sona* [sleeping], one *dost* [friend] who likes *machali pakadna* [fishing] . . *aur tere* [and yours] ?
H:	*machali pakadna dho hai* [two for fishing]

Table 6: Excerpt from a dialogue from our COMMON-DOST dataset. We highlight the Hindi content in *italics* along with its English translation in []. H: human and A: agent.

notation denotes the selection of the mutual friend. The conversation comprised of just a single user utterance (which was a greeting). Such dialogues are usually very sparse as guessing the common friend without any information is a low probability event.

A:	*suprabhat* [Good morning]
H:	*namaste* [Hello]
A:	oh do you have any *dost* [friend] who like eating *santra* [orange] ?
H:	SELECT {"fruits": "orange", "hobbies": "traveling", "loc": "the office", "gender": "female"}
A:	SELECT {"fruits": "orange", "hobbies": "traveling", "loc": "the office", "gender": "female"}

Table 7: Excerpt from a dialogue from our COMMON-DOST dataset. We highlight the Hindi content in *italics* along with its English translation in []. H: human and A: agent.

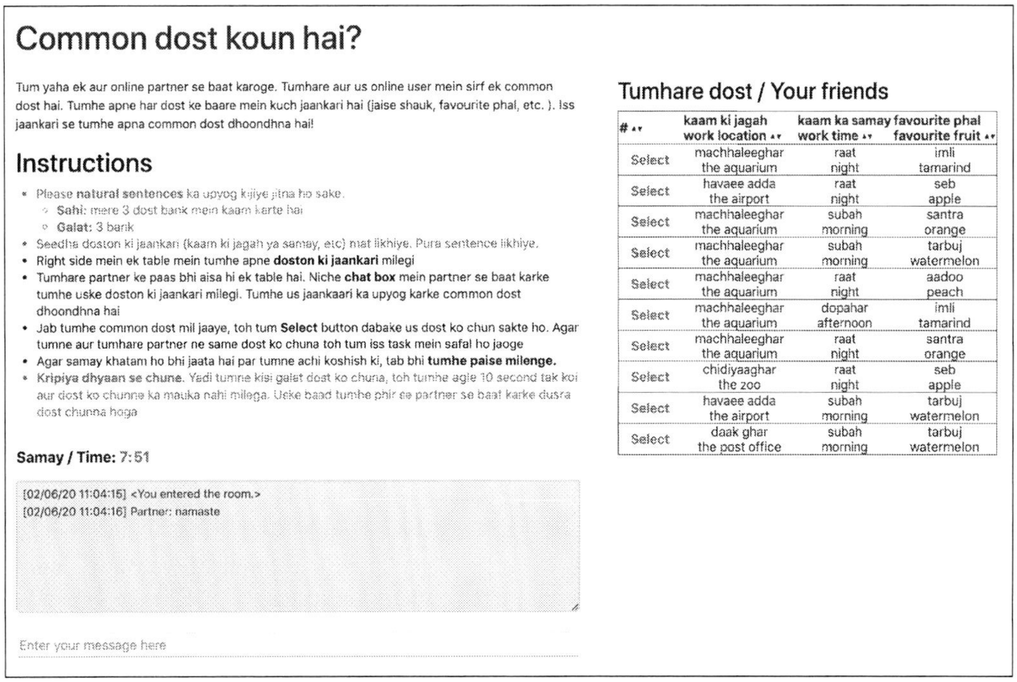

Common dost koun hai?

Tum yaha ek aur online partner se baat karoge. Tumhare aur us online user mein sirf ek common dost hai. Tumhe apne har dost ke baare mein kuch jaankari hai (jaise shauk, favourite phal, etc.). Iss jaankari se tumhe apna common dost dhoondhna hai!

Instructions

* Please **natural sentences** ka upyog kijiye jitna ho sake.
  * **Sahi**: mere 3 dost bank mein kaam karte hai
  * **Galat**: 3 bank
* Seedha doston ki jaankari (kaam ki jagah ya samay, etc) mat likhiye. Pura sentence likhiye.
* Right side mein ek table mein tumhe apne **doston ki jaankari** milegi
* Tumhare partner ke paas bhi aisa hi ek table hai. Niche **chat box** mein partner se baat karke tumhe uske doston ki jaankari milegi. Tumhe us jaankaari ka upyog karke common dost dhoondhna hai
* Jab tumhe common dost mil jaaye, toh tum **Select** button dabake us dost ko chun sakte ho. Agar tumne aur tumhare partner ne same dost ko chuna toh tum iss task mein safal ho jaoge
* Agar samay khatam ho bhi jaata hai par tumne achi koshish ki, tab bhi **tumhe paise milenge.**
* **Kripiya dhyaan se chune.** Yadi tumne kisi galat dost ko chuna, toh tumhe agle 10 second tak koi aur dost ko chunne ka mauka nahi milega. Uske baad tumhe phir se partner se baat karke dusra dost chunna hoga

Samay / Time: 7:51

```
[02/06/20 11:04:15] <You entered the room.>
[02/06/20 11:04:16] Partner: namaste
```

Enter your message here

Tumhare dost / Your friends

# ▲▼	kaam ki jagah work location ▲▼	kaam ka samay work time ▲▼	favourite phal favourite fruit ▲▼
Select	machhaleeghar the aquarium	raat night	imli tamarind
Select	havaee adda the airport	raat night	seb apple
Select	machhaleeghar the aquarium	subah morning	santra orange
Select	machhaleeghar the aquarium	subah morning	tarbuj watermelon
Select	machhaleeghar the aquarium	raat night	aadoo peach
Select	machhaleeghar the aquarium	dopahar afternoon	imli tamarind
Select	machhaleeghar the aquarium	raat night	santra orange
Select	chidiyaaghar the zoo	raat night	seb apple
Select	havaee adda the airport	subah morning	tarbuj watermelon
Select	daak ghar the post office	subah morning	tarbuj watermelon

Figure 4: Illustration of the chat screen shown/used by the MTurk users for attempting the task - *Common dost koun hai?*[Who's the mutual friend?]. We collected the CommonDost using this setup.

Identifying Robust Markers of Parkinson's Disease in Typing Behaviour Using a CNN-LSTM Network

Neil Dhir[12†], Mathias Edman[1†], Álvaro Sánchez Ferro[3], Tom Stafford[4], Colin Bannard[5]

[1]Kamin AI, [2]Alan Turing Institute, [3]HM CINAC,
[4]University of Sheffield, [5]University of Liverpool
{neil,mathias}@kamin.ai, alvarosferro@hotmail.com
t.stafford@sheffield.ac.uk, cbannard@liverpool.ac.uk

Abstract

There is urgent need for non-intrusive tests that can detect early signs of Parkinson's disease (PD), a debilitating neurodegenerative disorder that affects motor control. Recent promising research has focused on disease markers evident in the fine-motor behaviour of typing. Most work to date has focused solely on the timing of keypresses without reference to the linguistic content. In this paper we argue that the identity of the key combinations being produced should impact how they are handled by people with PD, and provide evidence that natural language processing methods can thus be of help in identifying signs of disease. We test the performance of a bi-directional LSTM with convolutional features in distinguishing people with PD from age-matched controls typing in English and Spanish, both in clinics and online.[1]

1 Introduction

Parkinson's disease is a neurodegenerative disease that affects approximately 1% of people over the age of 60 (De Lau and Breteler, 2006). Its cardinal manifestations include bradykinesia (slowness of movement), tremor and rigidity. These result from the degeneration of dopaminergic neurons in the basal ganglia (an area of the brain responsible for action selection). A particular challenge in the treatment of PD is that by the time such motor signs are present, over 50% of neurons in the affected area of the basal ganglia (the substantia nigra) have been lost (Fearnley and Lees, 1991). While neuroimaging can pick up on these changes (Barber et al., 2017), such procedures are prohibitively expensive and cannot be performed on whole populations. There is thus an urgent need for cheap and easy-to-administer measures that can be used for the identification of at-risk individuals.

A long-used simple motor test for PD is the alternating finger tapping test (Burns and DeJong, 1960). This test involves asking a person to alternately tap an index finger in two locations a set distance apart on a surface or on a keyboard (Giovannoni et al., 1999). People with PD are typically able to perform fewer taps over a 30 second period than people with no diagnosis. While such measures have proved useful, they suffer from a clear lack of specificity – slowing of movement is also a strong predictor of other neurodegenerative disorders, such as Alzeimer's disease (Roalf et al., 2018). Furthermore, neural degeneration is unlikely to be detected by as coarse-grained a measure as tapping rate until the disease is relatively advanced. If specificity and earlier detection is to be achieved more targeted tests will be required.

There is good theoretical reason to think that more PD-specific markers will be present in recordings of learned serial order behaviours, such as making a cup of tea, driving or typing. Analysis of the production of such frequently-performed behaviours, and their underlying neurobiology, often distinguishes between habit (the automatic production of routinised movements) and goal-directed responses (behaviours that involve top-down planning; Dolan and Dayan 2013). There is substantial evidence that the degeneration of the basal ganglia in PD primarily affects areas responsible for automatic behaviours (Sharman et al., 2013), and results in a shift in the balance of habitual and goal-directed control (Hadj-Bouziane et al., 2013). Redgrave et al. (2010) predict that people with early-stage or prodromal PD will have a problem initiating their automatic behaviours.

This paper focuses on the detection of markers of PD in one such behaviour – that of typing. It is motivated by the prediction that people with PD

[†]Equal contribution.
[1]Code, models and data used in this paper can be found at:
http://typingresearch.com/conll2020/

Proceedings of the 24th Conference on Computational Natural Language Learning, pages 578–595
Online, November 19-20, 2020. ©2020 Association for Computational Linguistics
https://doi.org/10.18653/v1/P17

will, from very early on and potentially prodromally (before the emergence of the acute symptoms that allow conventional diagnosis), change the way that they type, as they lose capacity for automatic control. Natural language processing provides us with techniques that we can use to pick up on those changes. As a motor behaviour, typing has been the focus of previous work on detecting or monitoring PD (see related work section). Some such work has focused on coarse-grained measures such as typing speed. These suffer from the lack of specificity associated with tapping measures. Other promising work has looked at more detailed timing measures. However this has continued to ignore the identity of the sequences being typed. Different sequences of keys present different motor challenges due to the position of the keys on the keyboard and the hand used. The extent to which typing these will be facilitated by prior automatisation depends on the relative frequency with which they have been typed (Behmer and Crump, 2016). We therefore expect consideration of the content of typing to be critical in picking up on PD-related changes.

We describe a method for using a convolutional neural network (CNN) long short term memory (LSTM) network to distinguish people with PD from age-matched people with no diagnosis. One motivation for this choice is that we want to pick up on the fine temporal details of the sequential data, in order to provide a measure that will be specific to PD. However the difficulty in picking up on such subtle information is that any typing dataset will also contain cruder information, such as the average differences in overall timing across participants. In order to tackle this, we normalise all temporal variables using robust scaling – subtracting each participant's median value from all their datapoints and dividing by their interquartile range. We thereby require our network to pick up on more subtle and potentially disease-specific information.

The contributions of this article are as follows:

- We introduce a new task and data type of urgent clinical importance.

- We show that when we remove coarse-grained differences between people with PD and controls we are able to detect a strong (and, we suggest, more disease-specific) signal.

- We provide evidence that adding character information to a CNN-LSTM that contains only timing information improves performance across datasets.

2   Related work

A simple motor test that we might consider a precursor to the use of typing is the alternating finger tapping test (Burns and DeJong, 1960). This test involves asking a person to alternately tap an index finger in two locations a set distance apart on a surface or on a keyboard (Giovannoni et al., 1999). Noyce et al. (2014) report that the number of key taps in 30 seconds (averaged across hands) can be used to distinguish patients from controls, identifying 50% of true positives with only 15% false positives. Using the same measure (selecting the worst performing limb in patients and comparing it with the best performing limb in controls), Hasan et al. (2019) report an AUC of 0.87.

While tapping tests are widely used they suffer from a lack of specificity to PD. While they distinguish people with PD from control participants with considerable success, there is good reason to think that they will struggle to distinguish PD from other neurodegenerative disorders. Roalf et al. (2018) report an AUC of 0.68 in distinguishing people with PD from people with Alzheimer's disease using a single tapping test.

In pursuit of an easier-to-gather alternative to finger-tapping tests, Austin et al. (2011) examine the interkey intervals (IKIs) of people typing usernames while logging-in to a website. They found a moderate-to-strong correlation between the participants' median IKIs during typing and the mean time between taps finger taps in a 10 second period. Building on this, Giancardo et al. (2016) used key-hold times during transcription typing in order to distinguish 42 people with recently-diagnosed PD (off medication) from 43 controls. Properties of the distribution of hold times for each patient was used in an ϵ-support regression to generate a unique score. In a two-fold cross-validation this achieved a combined AUC of 0.81, comparable to an AUC of 0.75 achieved with an alternating finger tapping test on the same sample. Adams (2017) logged key events during regular computer use over an extended period by 20 patients and 33 controls. Information about hold times and IKIs, including measures of variance and of asymmetry between hands was used in a classification ensemble of eight different classification methods. This ensemble, trained on the new data, achieved an AUC of 0.97 on the 85 participants from Giancardo et al. (2016).

All of the work described above has represented typing behaviour with summary statistics rather than as sequences. Furthermore they have analysed the timing of keystrokes without considering what is being typed. The one exception to this latter point is the work of Bannard et al. (2019) who look at the accuracy of typing while copying text using engineered features. They predict that people with PD, while making more errors in general, should make fewer 'habit slips'. This is when a well-learned sequence of key presses is produced in an inappropriate context, such as typing t-h-i-n-g when the intended word is t-h-i-n because -i-n-g is a frequent sequence. They find that is the case, and that adding this information to a generalised additive regression model predicting disease progression gives an improvement in fit relative to a model just including timing information.

3 Datasets

We perform analyses of the following three datasets, representing two different usage contexts (recruited and tested in a clinic, and recruited and tested remotely online) and two different languages: English and Spanish. All participants were tested via a browser-based app which presents a series of sentences to be copy-typed, and collects the identity and timing of each key-press. All datasets contain information about key down timing (when the typist pressed each key), and the online-recruited dataset additionally contains information about about key up timing (when they released each key). Summary statistics are found in table 1.

Table 1: Summary statistics of the datasets under investigation. Here N_p^+ refers to the number of PD patients (unmedicated and medicated) with N_p^- referring to the number of control participants. N_s^+ is the number of sentences typed by PD positive patients.

Collection	Language	N_p^+/N_p^-	N_s^+/N_s^-
In-clinic	English	16/25	426/739
In-clinic	Spanish	11/9	310/265
Online	English	99/130	1415/1862

3.1 In-clinic English copy-typing

Sixteen patients and 25 age-matched controls were recruited and tested during a visit to a hospital clinic in the UK (see Bannard et al. 2019). Patients were recruited to be in the early stages of PD (Hoehn-Yahr stages $0 - 2.5$, UPDRS < 20 in the medicated state), with normal cognitive function and < 5 years from a confirmed diagnosis. All patients were asked to type 15 sentences, all of which

were taken from English-language Wikipedia articles, and ranged from 10 to 25 words (average of $\mu = 19$ words) in length. The experimental protocol was approved by NHS Health Research Authority (no. STH18662TK). All participants were tested twice – once before taking their morning medication and once after for patients. On a five point self assessment of their typing ability, ranging from none to secretarial proficiency, control participants reported an average 3.1 (4% no experience) and patients reported an average 2.7 (12% no experience).

3.2 In-clinic Spanish copy-typing

Eleven patients and nine age-matched controls were tested during a visit to a hospital clinic in Spain (see Bannard et al. 2019). The inclusion criteria for patients was the same as for the clinic-tested English sample. All patients were asked to type 30 sentences, all of which were taken from Spanish language Wikipedia articles, and ranged from 12 to 25 words (average of $\mu = 18$ words) in length. The experimental protocol was approved by HM Hospitales, Spain (no. 14.11.710-GHM). Participants were tested only once. Six of the patients were tested prior to taking their morning medication and five after. On a five point self assessment of their typing ability, ranging from none to secretarial proficiency, control participants reported an average 3.9 (0 had no experience) and patients reported an average 3.7 (0 had no experience).

3.3 Online English copy-typing

For this newly-collected dataset, 130 controls and 100 people with PD were recruited and tested online. The people with PD were recruited via the recruitment service of a major US-based Parkinson's charity. The control participants were recruited via a participant recruitment service. All participants were aged between 50 and 90 and identified as resident in the US. Patients were recruited to be self-reportedly in the early stages of PD (Hoehn-Yahr stages $0 - 3$ as indicated by responses to a questionnaire), and within five years of a diagnosis. The sentences typed were the same as those typed by the in-clinic English sample. The experimental protocol was approved by the University of Liverpool Ethics Committee (no. 4572). Of the 100 people with PD, 24 reported that they either do not take medication or had not taken any medication yet that day. On a five point self assessment of their typing ability, ranging from novice to expert, control participants reported an average 2.6 (13% novices), medicated people with PD an average 3 (4% novices), and unmedicated people with PD an average 3.1 (8% novices). Note that in contrast to what we see in the clinic-collected datasets, the people with PD here rate their typing ability more highly than the controls. Unlike the in-clinic samples, this dataset contains information about both key down timing and key up timing.

4 Method

We implement a neural language model (NLM) which receives two different types of information in variety of combinations: (1) *Character identity information*: one-hot encoded character sequences; continuous bag-of-words model (Mikolov et al., 2013) encoded character sequences; (2) *Keypress timing information*: inter-key interval (IKI), time elapsed between consecutive key down events; hold-time, time elapsed between key down and key up events for a specific character; pause, time difference between key up and key down events for consecutive key presses. The temporal information is shown pictorially in fig. 1.

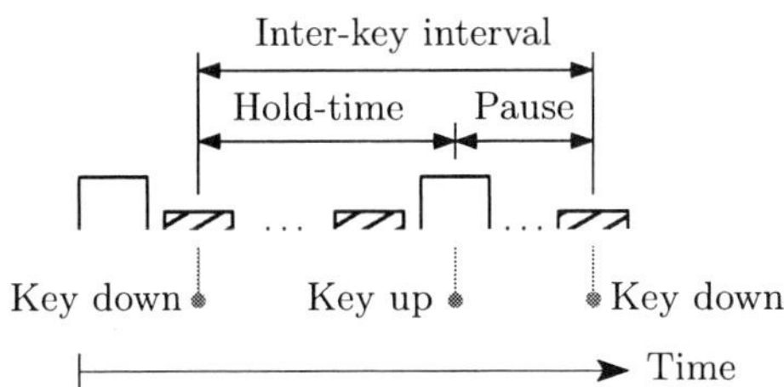

Figure 1: Pictorial description of the compression and release of keyboard keys and the temporal information that results from those actions.

Different timing information is available in different datasets as reported in §3. We adapt our data representation accordingly. We are interested here in the value of character information over timing, and examine its utility by building models with just timing and then with timing and character.

Our approach is inspired by the recent work of Kim (2014); Kim et al. (2016); Zhang et al. (2015). The main component is the temporal convolutional module (Zhang et al., 2015), which computes a one-dimensional (1D) convolution over characters. Convolutional neural networks (CNN) employ layers with convolving filters (Kim, 2014) which are applied to local features (derived in our case from the above information list of textual information).

Diverging from their approach, we use a smaller number of convolutional layers followed by a bidirectional long short-term memory (LSTM) layer (Schuster and Paliwal, 1997). As such, our architecture is able to extract both local and global features as described in the work by Zhou et al. (2015) who utilise a similar architecture. For a detailed description of the model architecture see fig. 2 and appendix B.

4.1 Data representation

Our model takes sentences (as sequence of characters and/or key press timing information) as input. Before introducing the construction process of sentence sequences we shall give a detailed description of its elements.

First, for the sake of comparison, we conduct experiments with two different character-identity representations. The default representation is one-hot encoding of characters where each unique character is associated with an index i such that the representation of a character is a binary vector $\mathbf{c}$ where $c_i = 1$ and $c_j = 0$, $\forall j \neq i$. We also evaluate using a continuous vector representation of characters, which is an adaptation of the commonly-used continuous bag-of-words (CBOW) embedding (Mikolov et al., 2013). While for word embeddings the CBOW algorithm learns the representation by predicting words from the surrounding context, our character level adaptation utilises the same algorithm but for the task of predicting characters from their context. We learn the character embeddings from a corpus of 100,000 Wikipedia articles[2], such that we obtain a character dictionary where each character is associated with a unique continuous vector representation of 50 dimensions.

The datasets in §3 contain, in addition to the characters used, a timestamp for each character key-down press t^d. However only for the online English copy-typing dataset in §3.3 are timestamps for key-up events denoted t^{up}, available. We define the order of a character sequence as the order of the associated key-down timestamps indexed by k such that $t^d_{k-1} \leq t^d_k$, $\forall k \in 1, \ldots, K$. For most end-to-end deep learning one typically omits feature engineering and let the networks learn feature representations from large datasets. Here however we are dealing with relatively small (in the context of deep learning) datasets. In particular the

---

[2] https://blog.lateral.io/2015/06/the-unknown-perils-of-mining-wikipedia/

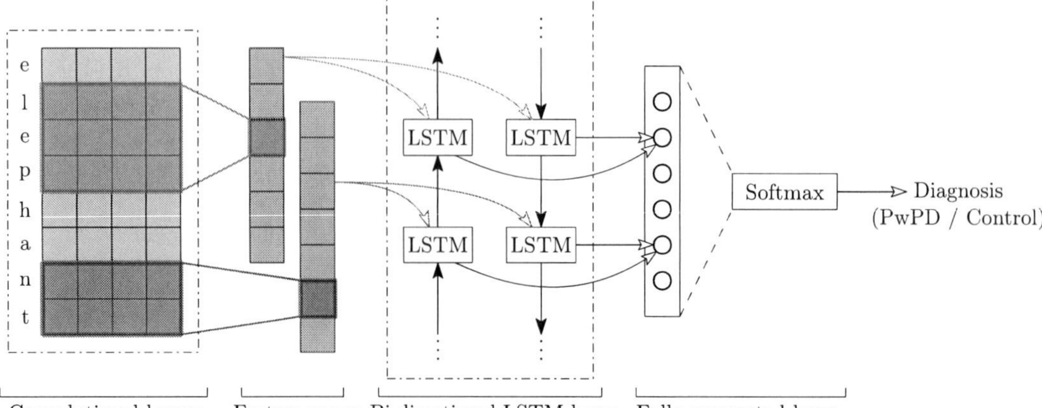

Figure 2: Architecture of the neural language model applied to the example word: elephant. On the left is shown the encoding matrix $\mathbf{X}^n$ where each row, as shown, corresponds to a character. From left to right, we see the elements of the NLM including convolutional layers, a bi-directional LSTM layer and finally a fully connected output layer with Softmax activation.

In-clinic English and Spanish datasets contain just 1165 and 575 sentences respectively (see table 1 for further details). To aid learning we thus engineer a set of three features from the key press timestamps.

As discussed in section §1 and §2 we expect the effects of bradykinesia among people with PD (PwPD) to result in differences in the average timings of keystrokes. However the goal of our experiments is not to maximise performance on any one dataset, but rather to find evidence of more robust PD-specific typing characteristics that can help improve the specificity of PD detection systems. To this end we attempt to mute the coarse-grained, between-group differences in our data by employing participant-level standardisation of all timing related features. This is done by computing the median and interquartile range of all key press timing features for each participant, and then robustly scaling their corresponding sentences by subtracting the median and dividing by the interquartile range.

Finally a sentence is represented as

$$\mathbf{x}^n_{1:K} = x_1 \oplus x_2 \oplus \cdots \oplus x_k \oplus \cdots \oplus x_K \quad (1)$$

where $\oplus$ is the concatenation operator, where n indexes each sentence, k indexes each character within each sentence and x is the character identity encoding vector (one-hot or CBOW) appended with the timing features associated with the key press of that character keypress. The longest sentence in any dataset has length $K_{\max}$, and any encoded sentence $K_n < K_{\max}$, $\forall n \in \{1, \ldots, N\}$ is padded with $|K_{\max} - K_n|$ all-zero vectors so that all encoded sentences $\mathbf{X}^n$, have the same size: $\mathbf{X}^n \in [0, 1]^{K_{\max} \times m}$.

4.2 Text pre-processing

Here we will briefly discuss the most important preprocessing steps. The complete procedure, with detailed description, can be found in appendix A. First, following the recommendation of Zhang et al. (2015), all sentences are converted to lower-case. Second, in this study we partially 'implement' the error correction employed by the participant. While we are interested in the errors that participants make, and indeed Bannard et al. (2019) show that the error types made can be indicative of disease status, we assume that the process by which they notice and correct those errors will be idiosyncratic and not informative regarding our classification goals. Consider the following example sentence, taken from the dataset described in §3.1:

```
Books include Penguin
Island, a satire on the
F✗Dreyfus afffair✗✗✗✗air.
```

Here the user has employed five corrective actions (backspaces) which we indicate with ✗. For each sentence we implement and then delete all but one of these backspace actions leaving only the first errorfully pressed key (the first f in the fff) and a single backspace symbol. Thus the text becomes:

```
Books include Penguin
Island, a satire on the
F✗Dreyfus afff✗air.
```

The single correction character ✗ is left in the text to be used as indicators for the NLM in the downstream classification task. When only a single corrective action occurs it is simply left unamended as shown above. For an example see fig. 5 where the correction character passed to the NLM is ω.

5 Experimental setup

The purpose of our experiments is to understand the effect of including character information in the classification of PD patients, when employing copy-typing as a diagnosis medium. Using the model discussed in §4 we conduct multiple binary-classification experiments to distinguish sentences written by people with PD (PwPD), from those written by age-matched controls. The same exercise is undertaken to classify participants themselves.

We evaluate performance by measuring the area under the receiver operating characteristic curve (AUC). This is a common approach when dealing with a two-class prediction problem (binary classification), in which the outcomes are labelled either as positive (PwPD) or negative (control). The AUC scores reported in §6 are calculated on the test sets. For sentence classification we use participant level five-fold cross-validation ensuring that sentences from any one participant do not exist in both the train and test set. We report the mean and standard deviation over folds. For participant classification we aggregate the sentence classification probabilities using logistic regression with leave-one-out cross validation and employ bootstrapping to report mean and standard deviation. The model is applied to the datasets described in detail in §3 with summary statistics given in table 1.

We conduct hyperparameter search, model introspection and ablation studies. Each dataset is preprocessed according to the procedures outlined in §4.1 and §4.2, and split into train, test and validation sets. This partitioning reduces the number of samples which can be used for learning the model. Our datasets are small compared to those typically used for deep learning. We deal with this in multiple ways, as detailed in appendix C.

6 Results

Our main experiments, as outlined above, involve the use of timing information that has been robustly scaled at the participant level in order to remove coarse-grained differences between groups. To aid understanding of the data, however, we will first report the performance of a classifier that uses the information that we have removed - the median and interquartile range of keypresses - as the sole features. The AUCs for logistic regressions using

these features as predictors can be seen in table 3.

Table 3: Results from logistic regression models with median and interquartile range for interkey intervals as features. We report mean AUC (and SDs) for both medicated PwPD vs. controls in the On columns and unmedicated PwPD vs. controls in the Off column. The Spanish PwPD are mixed in medication status but treated as a single group due to the small sample size.

	Sentence classification	
Dataset	Off	On
In-clinic English	0.76 (0.14)	0.76 (0.11)
Online English	0.64 (0.11)	0.53 (0.04)
In-clinic Spanish	0.91 (0.13)	N/A
	Participant classification	
Dataset	Off	On
In-clinic English	0.77 (0.08)	0.76 (0.08)
Online English	0.56 (0.07)	0.56 (0.04)
In-clinic Spanish	0.91 (0.09)	N/A

As can be seen the performance of these classifiers is good in some cases, particularly for the in-clinic Spanish dataset. However performance is variable, being poorest for the online dataset. This pattern of results is to be expected and our goal here is not to surpass their performance but to see how we can perform with more PD-specific features. The results for our main models, using the robust-scaled data, are reported in table 2 and fig. 3. For all datasets, the addition of character information gives an improvement in performance over timing-only models. The dataset on which the simple IKI summary-statistic models reported above do worst (the online English dataset) is the dataset on which the best performance is reported here. This is likely because it is the largest dataset and thus the best suited to deep learning methods. This suggests that performance improvements will be possible for the network models with larger datasets.

6.1 Model interpretation

Deep learning models are often criticised for being black box machines and the interpretation of deep learning techniques is a growing area of interest (Buhrmester et al., 2019). We apply one such technique – Gradient-weighted Class Activation Mapping (Grad-CAM; Selvaraju et al. 2017) – to our model. Grad-CAM is commonly used to analyse how CNN-based computer vision models make decisions and highlight regions in the image that the

Table 2: Results from NLM experiments showing improved performance for inclusion of character identity information across all datasets. We report mean AUC (and SDs) for both medicated PwPD vs. controls in the *On* columns and unmedicated PwPD vs. controls in the *Off* column. The Spanish PwPD are mixed in medication status but treated as a single group due to the small sample size.

Dataset	Sentence classification		Participant classification	
	Off	On	Off	On
In-clinic English				
Time Only	0.56 (0.09)	0.59 (0.07)	0.47 (0.09)	0.58 (0.09)
Time and Character (one-hot)	**0.64 (0.03)**	**0.66 (0.07)**	**0.65 (0.09)**	**0.80 (0.07)**
Time and Character (CBOW)	0.62 (0.05)	0.65 (0.11)	0.64 (0.09)	0.70 (0.08)
Online English				
Time Only	0.68 (0.16)	0.64 (0.10)	0.73 (0.06)	0.65 (0.04)
Time and Character (one-hot)	**0.78 (0.14)**	**0.70 (0.04)**	0.79 (0.06)	0.70 (0.04)
Time and Character (CBOW)	0.77 (0.13)	0.67 (0.08)	**0.84 (0.05)**	**0.75 (0.04)**
In-clinic Spanish				
Time Only	0.51 (0.13)	N/A	0.68 (0.13)	N/A
Time and Character (one-hot)	**0.68 (0.11)**	N/A	**0.77 (0.12)**	N/A

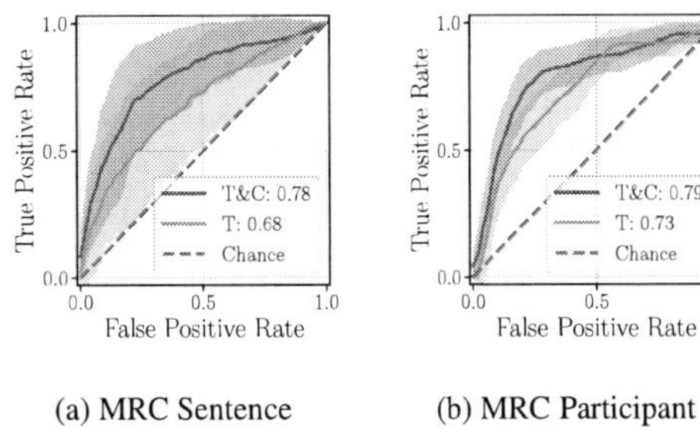

(a) MRC Sentence   (b) MRC Participant

Figure 3: ROC curves for sentence-level (a) and participant (b) classification for the (one-hot) online English *Off*-medication datasets are included.

model deems important. We repurpose Grad-CAM to analyse which part of a sentence a CNN-based NLM deems important for classification. For illustration we have included an example visualisation where we have applied our model to a sentiment analysis task where Grad-CAM highlights the parts of the sentence that indicate it should be classified as having positive sentiment – see fig. 4. We use the same approach to produce visualisations that highlight the parts of a sentence that our model uses to make a distinction between PwPD and Controls.

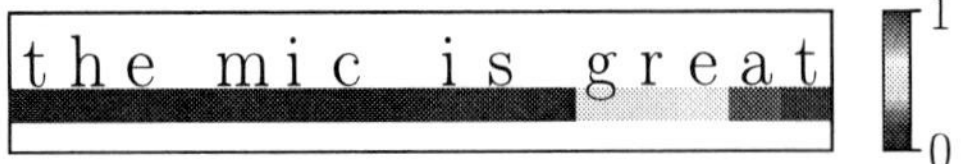

Figure 4: Example of Grad-CAM visualisation where we apply our network to a sentiment analysis task. Here we see the Grad-CAM highlighting the word "great" as important for determining that the sentence has positive sentiment.

Grad-CAM plots for example PwPD and control participants from the online English dataset for each of our sentences can be found in appendix D. These images show the gradients of the second and final convolutional layer for the positive diagnosis ("typist has PD") classification class. Grad-CAM visualisations for all participants and sentences, all convolutional layers and all classification classes, can be accessed at `http://typingresearch.com/conll2020/`. An illustrative two-word excerpt from one of our sentences typed by a single PwPD can be seen in figure fig. 5. The first word `different` (typed with a single corrected error on the second character by this typist) is mostly blue indicating that there is little in the sequence of keystrokes that the model takes as indicating that it was typed by a PwPD, while the second word `pronunciation` spans more colours indicating that it contains keystrokes that are indicative of its being typed by a PwPD.

Looking across participants we see that certain parts of the sentences are consistently more important for classification than others, as indicated by their having gradients that diverge between PwPD and controls. The first thing that this illustrates is that key identity matters, confirming the conclusions of our ablation study. It also allows us to look at what properties the most discriminative key sequences have in common. While no single property can be identified as the clearest marker of PD, we can identify suggestive patterns that are useful in understanding typing in this population. This

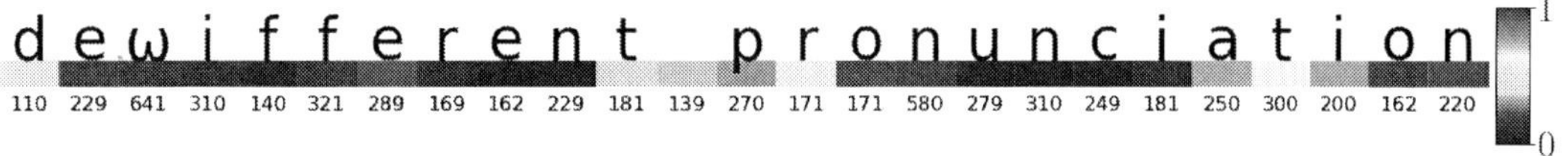

Figure 5: Grad-CAM visualisation of our network applied to a sentence typed by one participant, here ω stands in for a correction to the text. The colours represent the importance of the different parts of the string for determining that the typist has PD. The bottom numbers are the inter-key intervals between typed characters.

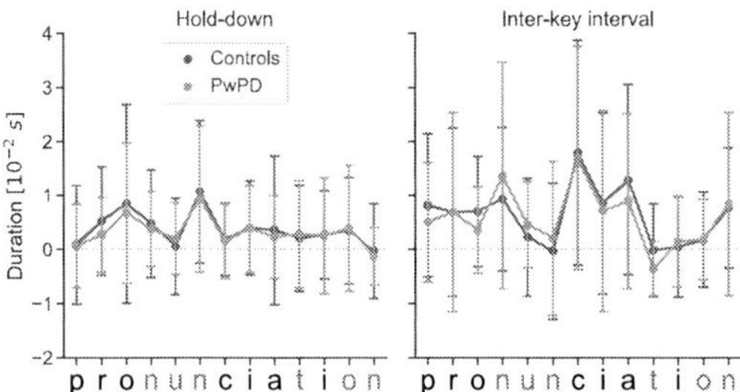

Figure 6: Plot showing the mean and standard deviations for the participant-scaled key hold and inter-key intervals for each character in the word. The black (left) and red (right) colouring indicates which hand typed that character.

exploration serves as an illustration of how model interpretation can provide potential mechanistic hypotheses to be tested in future work.

One pattern that the network seems to pick up on can be seen in fig. 5 by observing the changes in gradients for the keys with respect to the interkey intervals seen below the sequence. There is a sequence of keys with high gradients at the end of the first word and beginning of the second that have relatively low IKIs. A notable property of this subsequence is that each of the keys is typically typed with a different hand from the previous key. Figure 6 shows the mean and standard deviations for (robustly-scaled) key hold times and inter-key intervals for the word pronunciation. The letters are colour coded according to whether the character is typed with the same hand (red) as the preceding character or the other hand (black). This is based on the approximation that the leftmost 5 columns of the keyboard (from Q, A and Z to T, G and B) are typed with the left hand and the rightmost 5 columns are typed with the right (Feit et al., 2016). Moving between keys when switching hands is fairly straightforward to perform while switching between keys with the same hand requires considerable agility. We observe in our data that the typing speed of PwPD is differentially affected by this more than that of the controls. The network picks up on this and has a tendency toward higher gradients at between-hand transitions where the typing

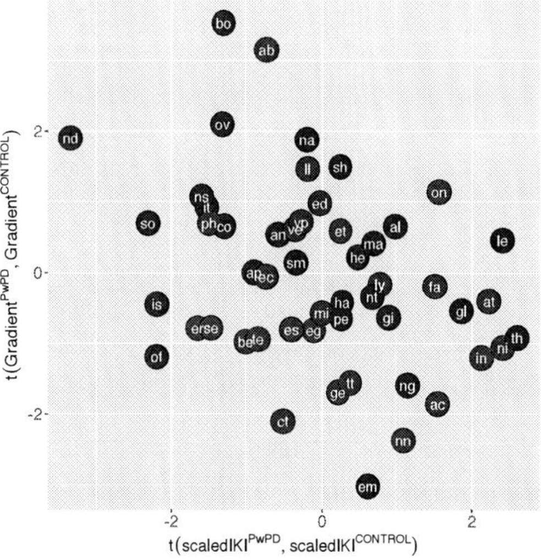

Figure 7: Key transitions for a single example sentence plotted along three dimensions. The $y-$axis indicates the discriminative ability of each key transition, indicated by the t-value for a comparison of the gradients for that keypress in patients and controls, such that a high value indicates that patients have consistently higher gradients than controls. The $x-$axis represents the extent to which the distribution of scaled IKIs for each keystroke are differ between patients and controls, again using a $t-$test (so that a high value indicates that patients have more consistently higher scaled IKIs than controls). The circles containing bigrams that involve a within-hand transition are shown in red and the circles containing across-hand-transition bigrams are shown in blue. The bigrams that have highest values on the y scale (that have gradients that are most consistently higher in patients in controls) are those that have a lower a value on the $x-$scale (they are associated with a relative dip in IKI in patients that is consistently more pronounced than anything seen in patients) and are shown in blue (involve a between key transition). This is apparent from the high ratio of blue to red circles in the top left quadrant and indicates that the model takes a dip in inter-key intervals for between-hand-transition bigrams as a marker of PD.

speed has a relative dip for a participant. Figure 7 provides further illustration of this widespread pattern.

A second property of key sequences that appears to be important is their transitional probability. There is good reason to think that PwPD will have difficulty deploying learned habits in typing. We know that the timing of keystrokes in typists is sensitive to the transitional probabilities between keys (Behmer and Crump, 2016), and we can take this as a marker of acquired habits. We would expect this relationship to be altered in PwPD. Mixed effects modelling with by-participant random intercepts and slopes confirms that this is the case in our data with an increase of a 26% of an IKI interquartile range for each unit of standard deviation in bigram surprisal (inverse log probability of each character given the previous character) for controls, and a significant 3% lower increase in PwPD ($p < 0.01$) across all participants. This indicates a reduced sensitivity to decreases in key transition probabilities in pwPD relative to controls. It is also the case that gradients are significantly higher for keys with high surprisal. Figure 8 displays the three-way relationship between gradient divergence, IKI divergence and surprisal and suggests that the model is picking up on the reduced effect of transitional probabilities on interkey intervals for PwPD relative to controls.

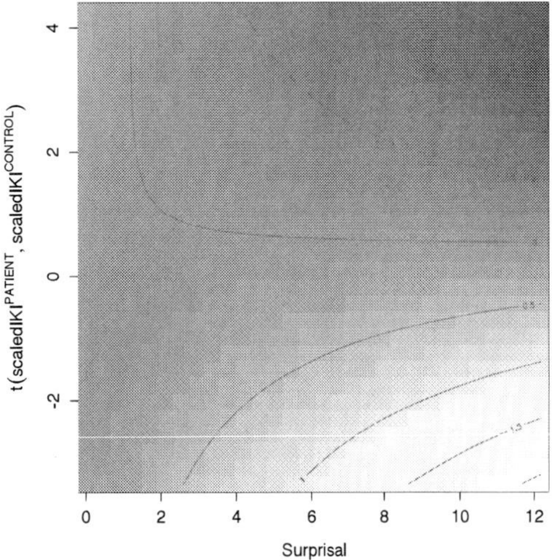

Figure 8: Contour – red (low) to yellow (high) – of gradient divergence (t-value for PwPD-Control comparison) for different values of scaled IKI divergence (t-value for PwPD-Control comparison again) and bigram surprisal. Gradient divergence is greatest for key transitions with high surprisal for which PwPD have low scaled IKI relative to controls. The model appears to pick up on the dampening of surprisal-related IKI spikes for PwPD relative to controls.

7 Conclusion

In this paper we have provided evidence that natural language processing techniques and in particular CNN-LSTM networks can identify markers of Parkinson's disease in logged typing behaviour. Critically there is good reason to think that the markers identified will have high specificity with regards to Parkinson's disease. While simple motor tests like the finger tapping test, and summary timing statistics from typing data, are widely used to distinguish PwPD from people without the disease, they rely on disease signs that PD has in common with other disorders - namely general slowing. In this work we first remove this disease sign from the data and then use a CNN-LSTM to pick up on more subtle changes in performance. We report very promising performance using this approach. We further report on an analysis of the gradients in our model which suggests that it is picking up on plausible effects of PD seen in the data.

Previous work has sought to distinguish PwPD from controls by observing how rapidly and consistently they press keys when typing. However, such work begins by discarding potentially valuable information - the identity of the keys pressed. We found that including key identify in our data/model provided a performance improvement relative to timing-only models. We found an improvement in performance (increased AUC) in identifying patients among participants tested in clinics in both English and Spanish. Furthermore we found a substantial leap in performance on the more difficult task of discriminating PD patients from controls in a new large dataset recruited and tested online.

These results suggest that NLP techniques allows us to identify theoretically-motivated markers of PD (Redgrave et al., 2010) in typing data. These incorporate both speed and character information, and so may be more robust than currently-used markers. Future work will of course require that we test this directly, by collecting typing data from people with other neurological disorders and using these markers for multi-class classification. This work is only the tip of the iceberg in terms of the contribution that NLP can make to the task of detecting signs of Parkinson's disease, and potentially other movement disorders, in typing data.

Acknowledgements

This work was supported by an MRC Confidence in Concept Award to the University of Liverpool.

References

Warwick R Adams. 2017. High-accuracy detection of early Parkinson's Disease using multiple characteristics of finger movement while typing. *PLOS ONE*, 12(11):e0188226.

Daniel Austin, Holly Jimison, Tamara Hayes, Nora Mattek, Jeffrey Kaye, and Misha Pavel. 2011. Measuring motor speed through typing: a surrogate for the finger tapping test. *Behavior Research Methods*, 43(4):903–909.

Colin Bannard, Mariana Leriche, Oliver Bandmann, Christopher H Brown, Elisa Ferracane, Alvaro Sánchez-Ferro, José Obeso, Peter Redgrave, and Tom Stafford. 2019. Reduced habit-driven errors in Parkinson's Disease. *Scientific Reports*, 9(1):3423.

Thomas R Barber, Johannes C Klein, Clare E Mackay, and Michele TM Hu. 2017. Neuroimaging in premotor Parkinson's disease. *NeuroImage: Clinical*, 15:215–227.

Lawrence P Behmer and Matthew JC Crump. 2016. Crunching big data with fingertips: How typists tune their performance toward the statistics of natural language. In *Big Data in Cognitive Science*, pages 329–345. Psychology Press.

Vanessa Buhrmester, David Münch, and Michael Arens. 2019. Analysis of explainers of black box deep neural networks for computer vision: A survey. *arXiv preprint arXiv:1911.12116*.

B Delisle Burns and J David DeJong. 1960. A preliminary report on the measurement of Parkinson's disease. *Neurology*, 10(12):1096–1096.

Francois Chollet. 2017. *Deep Learning with Python*, 1st edition. Manning Publications Co., USA.

Lonneke ML De Lau and Monique MB Breteler. 2006. Epidemiology of Parkinson's disease. *The Lancet Neurology*, 5(6):525–535.

Ray J Dolan and Peter Dayan. 2013. Goals and Habits in the Brain. *Neuron*, 80(2):312–325.

Julian M Fearnley and Andrew J Lees. 1991. Ageing and Parkinson's disease: substantia nigra regional selectivity. *Brain*, 114(5):2283–2301.

Anna Maria Feit, Daryl Weir, and Antti Oulasvirta. 2016. How we type: Movement strategies and performance in everyday typing. In *Proceedings of the 2016 CHI Conference on Human Factors in Computing Systems*, pages 4262–4273.

Luca Giancardo, Alvaro Sanchez-Ferro, Teresa Arroyo-Gallego, Ian Butterworth, Carlos S Mendoza, Paloma Montero, Michele Matarazzo, José A Obeso, Martha L Gray, and R San José Estépar. 2016. Computer keyboard interaction as an indicator of early Parkinson's disease. *Scientific Reports*, 6:34468.

G Giovannoni, J Van Schalkwyk, VU Fritz, and AJ Lees. 1999. Bradykinesia akinesia incoordination test (BRAIN TEST): an objective computerised assessment of upper limb motor function. *Journal of Neurology, Neurosurgery & Psychiatry*, 67(5):624–629.

Ian Goodfellow, Yoshua Bengio, and Aaron Courville. 2016. *Deep Learning*. MIT Press. http://www.deeplearningbook.org.

Fadila Hadj-Bouziane, Isabelle Benatru, Andrea Brovelli, Hélène Klinger, Stéphane Thobois, Emmanuel Broussolle, Driss Boussaoud, and Martine Meunier. 2013. Advanced Parkinson's disease effect on goal-directed and habitual processes involved in visuomotor associative learning. *Frontiers in Human Neuroscience*, 6:351.

Hasan Hasan, Maggie Burrows, Dilan S Athauda, Bruce Hellman, Ben James, Tom Warner, Thomas Foltynie, Gavin Giovannoni, Andrew J Lees, and Alastair J Noyce. 2019. The BRadykinesia Akinesia INcoordination (BRAIN) tap test: capturing the sequence effect. *Movement Disorders Clinical Practice*.

Yoon Kim. 2014. Convolutional neural networks for sentence classification. In *Proceedings of the 2014 Conference on Empirical Methods in Natural Language Processing (EMNLP)*, pages 1746–1751, Doha, Qatar. Association for Computational Linguistics.

Yoon Kim, Yacine Jernite, David Sontag, and Alexander M Rush. 2016. Character-aware neural language models. In *Thirtieth AAAI Conference on Artificial Intelligence*.

Diederik P Kingma and Jimmy Ba. 2014. Adam: A method for stochastic optimization. *arXiv preprint arXiv:1412.6980*.

Tomas Mikolov, Kai Chen, Greg Corrado, and Jeffrey Dean. 2013. Efficient estimation of word representations in vector space. *arXiv preprint arXiv:1301.3781*.

Alastair J Noyce, Anna Nagy, Shami Acharya, Shahrzad Hadavi, Jonathan P Bestwick, Julian Fearnley, Andrew J Lees, and Gavin Giovannoni. 2014. Bradykinesia-Akinesia Incoordination Test: Validating an Online Keyboard Test of Upper Limb Function. *PLOS ONE*, 9(4):e96260.

Peter Redgrave, Manuel Rodriguez, Yoland Smith, Maria C Rodriguez-Oroz, Stephane Lehericy, Hagai Bergman, Yves Agid, Mahlon R DeLong, and Jose A Obeso. 2010. Goal-directed and habitual control in the basal ganglia: implications for Parkinson's disease. *Nature Reviews Neuroscience*, 11(11):760.

David R Roalf, Petra Rupert, Dawn Mechanic-Hamilton, Laura Brennan, John E Duda, Daniel Weintraub, John Q Trojanowski, David Wolk, and

Paul J Moberg. 2018. Quantitative assessment of finger tapping characteristics in mild cognitive impairment, Alzheimer's disease, and Parkinson's disease. *Journal of Neurology*, 265(6):1365–1375.

Mike Schuster and Kuldip Paliwal. 1997. Bidirectional recurrent neural networks. *IEEE Transactions on Signal Processing*, 45:2673 – 2681.

Ramprasaath R Selvaraju, Michael Cogswell, Abhishek Das, Ramakrishna Vedantam, Devi Parikh, and Dhruv Batra. 2017. Grad-cam: Visual explanations from deep networks via gradient-based localization. In *Proceedings of the IEEE international conference on computer vision*, pages 618–626.

Michael Sharman, Romain Valabregue, Vincent Perlbarg, Linda Marrakchi-Kacem, Marie Vidailhet, Habib Benali, Alexis Brice, and Stephane Lehéricy. 2013. Parkinson's disease patients show reduced cortical-subcortical sensorimotor connectivity. *Movement Disorders*, 28(4):447–454.

Nitish Srivastava, Geoffrey Hinton, Alex Krizhevsky, Ilya Sutskever, and Ruslan Salakhutdinov. 2014. Dropout: A simple way to prevent neural networks from overfitting. *Journal of Machine Learning Research*, 15(1):1929–1958.

Xiang Zhang, Junbo Zhao, and Yann LeCun. 2015. Character-level convolutional networks for text classification. In *Advances in Neural Information Processing Systems*, pages 649–657.

Chunting Zhou, Chonglin Sun, Zhiyuan Liu, and Francis Lau. 2015. A C-LSTM neural network for text classification. *arXiv preprint arXiv:1511.08630*.

A   Preprocessing copy-typing data

In this section we outline the detailed steps that were taken in the preparation of the data for this study. As noted in the body, the datasets under consideration are those in table 1 which reproduce here for completeness.

Collection	Language	N_p^+/N_p^-	N_s^+/N_s^-
In-clinic	English	16/25	426/739
In-clinic	Spanish	11/9	310/265
Online	English	99/130	1415/1862

The following data-cleaning and data-wrangling steps were taken, to prepare the data for preprocessing:

1. Remove duplicate responses.

2. Calculate Levenshtein distance (edit distance) and remove sentences which have a measured value[3] above 75. This is done on the *typed* sentences (i.e. the ones seen by the user during the experiment, not the concatenated logged keys).

3. Remove all sentences where participants have employed ←, →, ↑ and ↓ keys. As the error-corrective behaviour becomes too-complex with their inclusion, they were removed to simplify the problem space.

4. Replace [Space] (spacebar) with a blank key to homogenise the dataset.

5. Make all sentences lower-case (to facilitate better inference in the modelling stage) – see (Zhang et al., 2015).

6. To create a homogeneous key corpus for all participants, the following keys (all were extracted from the dataset itself) were mapped to <unk>:

   - [ContextMenu]
   - [Delete]
   - [End]
   - [Enter]
   - [F11]
   - [F16]
   - [\n]
   - [Home]
   - [Insert]
   - [MediaPreviousTrack]
   - [None]
   - [NumLock]
   - [PageDown]
   - [Process]
   - [Unidentified]

This is necessary because all participants took part in the data collection, used their own personal computer, and thus by extension their own keyboard. We use a US English keyboard which has a grid size of 5×14.

7. Remaining keys with a character length of more than one, are mapped to Greek letters so as to not corrupt the character encoding downstream in the NLM:

   - [backspace] $\rightarrow \alpha$
   - [shift] $\rightarrow \beta$
   - [control] $\rightarrow \gamma$
   - [capslock] $\rightarrow \delta$
   - [meta] $\rightarrow \epsilon$
   - [tab] $\rightarrow \zeta$
   - [alt] $\rightarrow \eta$

8. We set an option which allows for the [shift] key to be completely dropped. We do this owing to its use for capitalising letters. As this is not of interest to us in this study we typically remove it.

9. Hold-time and inter-key interval outliers are removed and replaced with the first moment of a kernel density estimate of those timings, for all sentences typed by a given participant.

10. Backspace implementation is the next step, as described in §4.2.

---

[3] A cut-off value was selected by inspection, and it was found that any sentence which had a value below this was not informative enough to warrant inclusion.

B Model architecture

Table 4: Detailed description of NLM architecture

Layer	Details	
1D Convolution	#filters	16
	filter size	3
	stride	1
	L2 regularisation	1e-6
	Activation	ReLU
Dropout	probability	0.5
1D Convolution	#filters	8
	filter size	3
	stride	1
	L2 regularisation	1e-6
	Activation	ReLU
Dropout	probability	0.5
Bidirectional LSTM	#hidden units	64
	Activation	tanh
Fully connected	input size	64
	output size	2
	Activation	Softmax

C Model training

To counter act over-fitting we use an array of standard techniques including dropout (Srivastava et al., 2014), weight regularisation and early stopping(Goodfellow et al., 2016, §7). Additionally we employ a task specific training schedule to aid feature learning in the convolutional layers. We first split our sentences into word pairs such that we effectively increase the number of samples, e.g. `Books include Penguin Island...` $\rightarrow$ `[Books include, Penguin Island,...]`. Given that the convolutional layers operate locally on the sentence we can then pre-train the filters on this augmented dataset in a more stochastic optimisation process. We then use the standard protocol (Chollet, 2017, §5.3) for transfer learning by freezing the convolutional filter weights before training ensues on the sentence datasets until performance on the validation set stops improving. Finally we unlock the convolutional filters and re-start training on the sentence dataset with a lower learning-rate and larger batch size.

The models are trained via Adam optimisation (Kingma and Ba, 2014) over shuffled mini-batches with early stopping terminating training if validation loss does not improve for 16 epochs. The initial learning rate is set to 0.001 and is decreased by a factor 0.5 if the validation loss does not improve for 10 epochs. We use a batch size of 16 for the word-pair convolutional filter pre-training and the first round of training on the sentence datasets, for second tuning round we increase the batch size to 32 and start with a learning rate of 10^{-4}. For regularisation we use dropout with probability 0.5 on and L2 regularisation with factor 10^{-6} on all convolutional layers.

D Additional Grad-CAM visualisations

Shown in this section are additional examples of the 1D Grad-CAM, applied to all sentences, with positive and negative examples shown for each in the pages overleaf. The gradient and timing visualisations (the Grad-CAMs) can be understood by consulting the legend in fig. 9.

Character	Ω	c o n s o n a n t
Gradient intensity		
Inter-key interval	α	11 23 14 20 45 31 25 44 22
Hold time	β	10 17 9 16 40 23 21 32 20
Pause time	γ	1 5 5 4 5 8 4 12 2

Figure 9: Grad-CAM legend. The *left panel* contains the keys and the respective magnitudes they measure. The *right panel* contains a small example of the 1D Grad-CAM applied to the word `consonant`.

Additional Grad-CAM figures are shown overleaf.

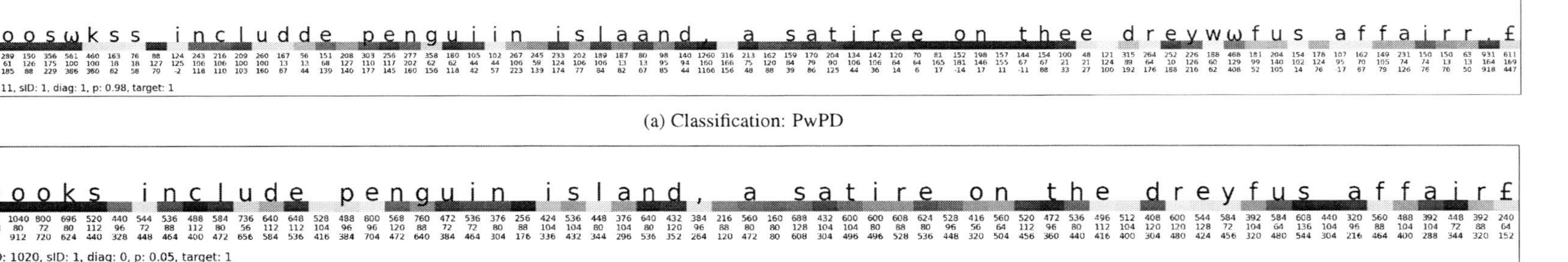

(a) Classification: PwPD

(b) Classification: Control

Figure 10: Sentence 1 classification using the proposed approach. Positive and negative example shown.

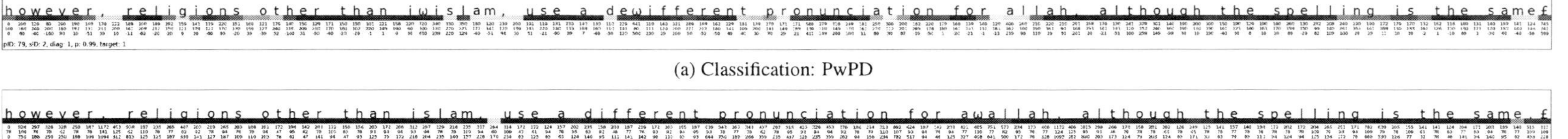

(a) Classification: PwPD

(b) Classification: Control

Figure 11: Sentence 2 classification using the proposed approach. Positive and negative example shown.

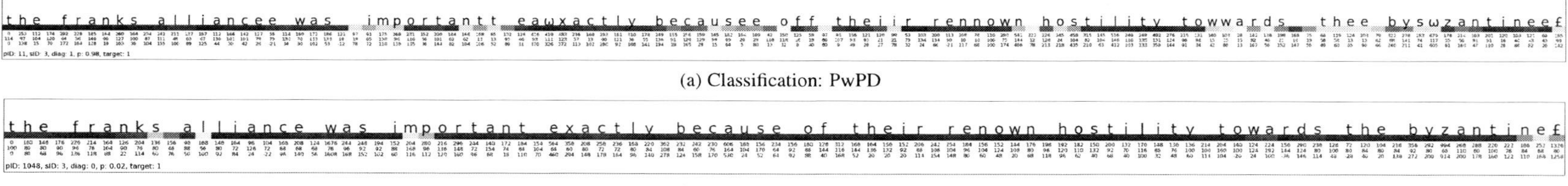

(a) Classification: PwPD

(b) Classification: Control

Figure 12: Sentence 3 classification using the proposed approach. Positive and negative example shown.

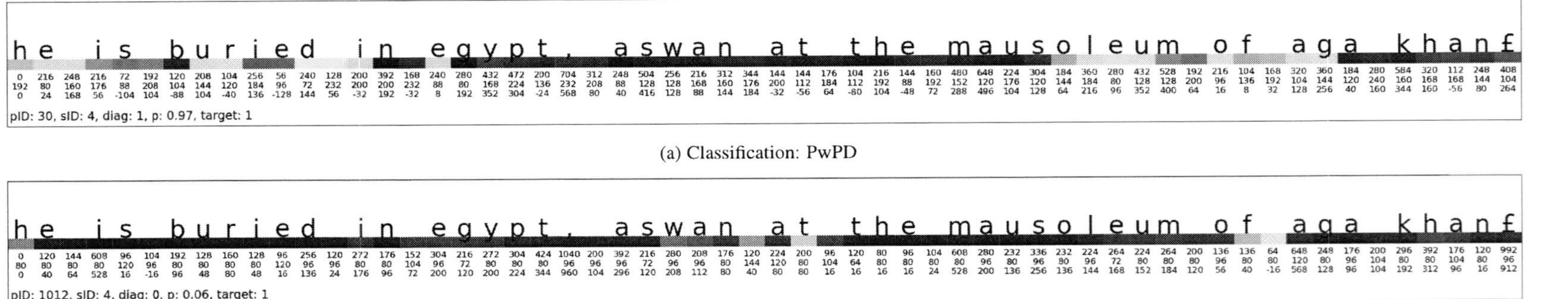

(a) Classification: PwPD

(b) Classification: Control

Figure 13: Sentence 4 classification using the proposed approach. Positive and negative example shown.

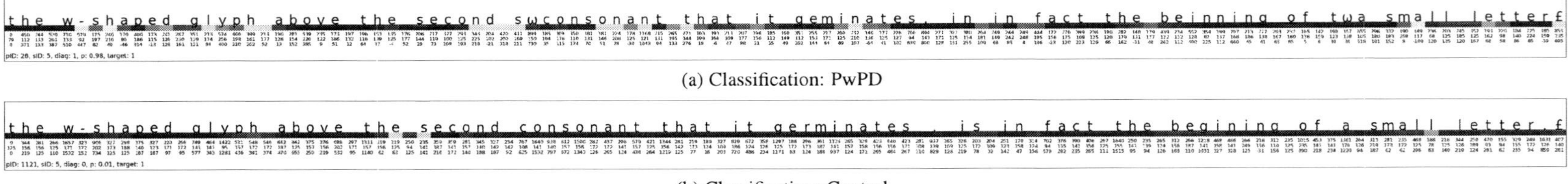

(a) Classification: PwPD

(b) Classification: Control

Figure 14: Sentence 5 classification using the proposed approach. Positive and negative example shown.

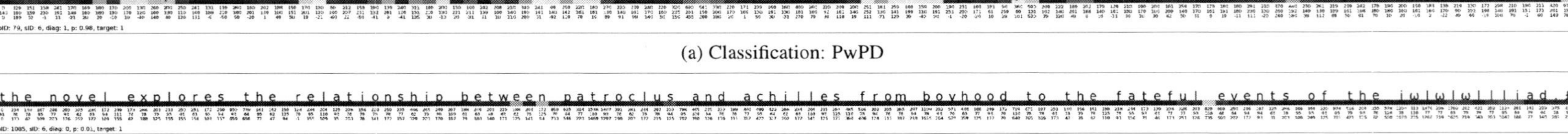

(a) Classification: PwPD

(b) Classification: Control

Figure 15: Sentence 6 classification using the proposed approach. Positive and negative example shown.

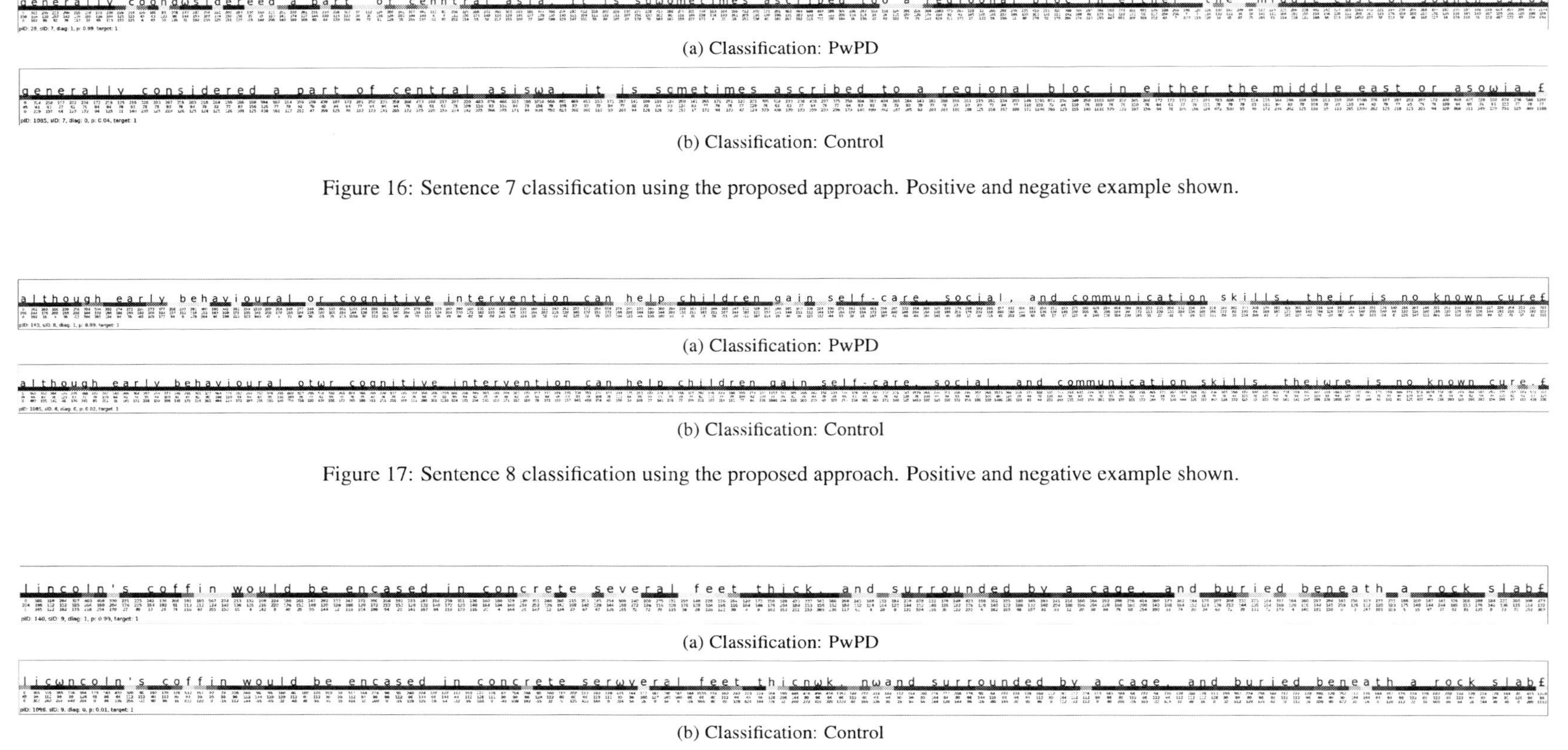

(a) Classification: PwPD

(b) Classification: Control

Figure 16: Sentence 7 classification using the proposed approach. Positive and negative example shown.

(a) Classification: PwPD

(b) Classification: Control

Figure 17: Sentence 8 classification using the proposed approach. Positive and negative example shown.

(a) Classification: PwPD

(b) Classification: Control

Figure 18: Sentence 9 classification using the proposed approach. Positive and negative example shown.

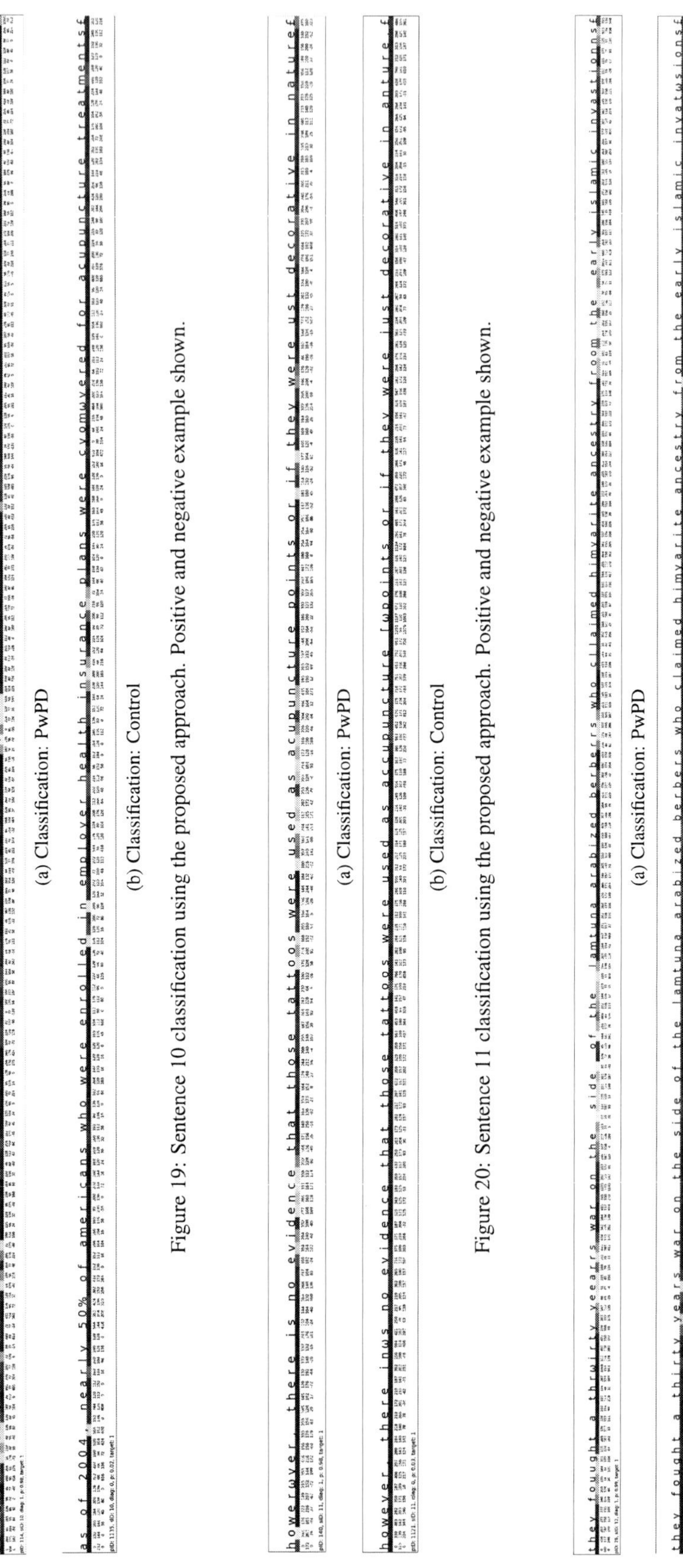

(a) Classification: PwPD

(b) Classification: Control

Figure 19: Sentence 10 classification using the proposed approach. Positive and negative example shown.

(a) Classification: PwPD

(b) Classification: Control

Figure 20: Sentence 11 classification using the proposed approach. Positive and negative example shown.

(a) Classification: PwPD

(b) Classification: Control

Figure 21: Sentence 12 classification using the proposed approach. Positive and negative example shown.

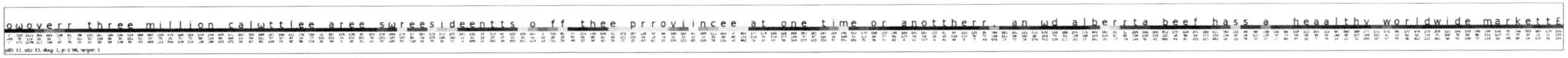

(a) Classification: PwPD

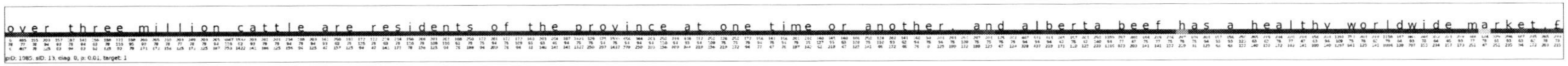

(b) Classification: Control

Figure 22: Sentence 13 classification using the proposed approach. Positive and negative example shown.

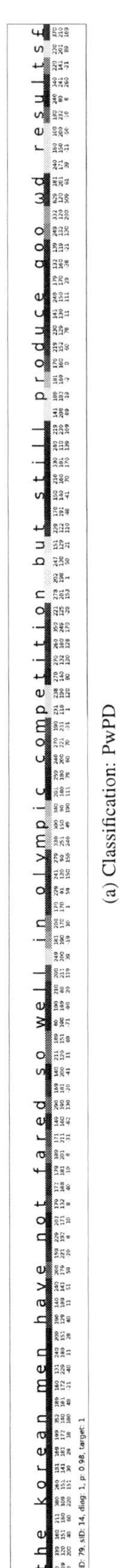

(a) Classification: PwPD

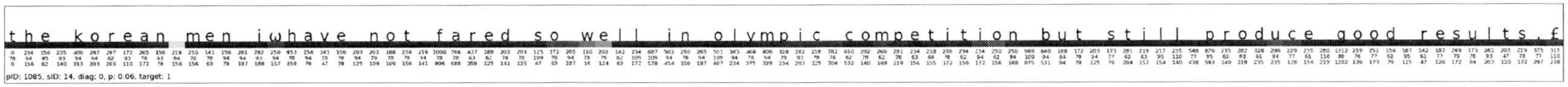

(b) Classification: Control

Figure 23: Sentence 14 classification using the proposed approach. Positive and negative example shown.

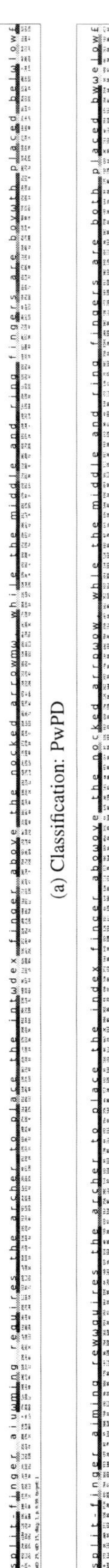

(a) Classification: PwPD

(b) Classification: Control

Figure 24: Sentence 15 classification using the proposed approach. Positive and negative example shown.

An Empirical Study on Model-agnostic Debiasing Strategies
for Robust Natural Language Inference

Tianyu Liu[1] *   **Xin Zheng**[3] *   **Xiaoan Ding**[4]   **Baobao Chang**[1][2]   **Zhifang Sui**[1][2]

[1] Peking University, Beijing, China   [2] Peng Cheng Laboratory, Shenzhen, China
[3] Beijing University of Posts and Telecommunications, Beijing, China
[4] University of Chicago, IL, USA

{tianyu0421, chbb, szf}@pku.edu.cn, zheng_xin@bupt.edu.cn
xiaoanding@uchicago.edu

Abstract

The prior work on natural language inference (NLI) debiasing mainly targets at one or few known biases while not necessarily making the models more robust. In this paper, we focus on the model-agnostic debiasing strategies and explore how to (or is it possible to) make the NLI models robust to multiple distinct adversarial attacks while keeping or even strengthening the models' generalization power. We firstly benchmark prevailing neural NLI models including pretrained ones on various adversarial datasets. We then try to combat distinct known biases by modifying a mixture of experts (MoE) ensemble method (Clark et al., 2019) and show that it's nontrivial to mitigate multiple NLI biases at the same time, and that model-level ensemble method outperforms MoE ensemble method. We also perform data augmentation including text swap, word substitution and paraphrase and prove its efficiency in combating various (though not all) adversarial attacks at the same time. Finally, we investigate several methods to merge heterogeneous training data (1.35M) and perform model ensembling, which are straightforward but effective to strengthen NLI models.

1 Introduction

Natural language inference (NLI) (also known as recognizing textual entailment) is a widely studied task which aims to infer the relationship (e.g., *entailment, contradiction, neutral*) between two fragments of text, known as *premise* and *hypothesis* (Dagan et al., 2005, 2013). Recent works have found that NLI models are sensitive to the compositional features (Nie et al., 2019), syntactic heuristics (McCoy et al., 2019), stress test (Geiger et al., 2018; Naik et al., 2018) and human artifacts in the data collection phase (Gururangan et al., 2018; Poliak et al., 2018b; Tsuchiya, 2018).

Accordingly, several adversarial datasets are proposed for these known biases[1].

Through our preliminary trials on specific adversarial datasets, we find that although the model specific or dataset specific debiasing methods could increase the model performance on the paired adversarial dataset, they might hinder the model performance on other adversarial datasets, as well as hurt the model generalization power, i.e. deficient scores on cross-datasets or cross-domain settings. These phenomena motivate us to investigate if it exists a unified model-agnostic debiasing strategy which can mitigate distinct (or even all) known biases while keeping or strengthening the model generalization power.

We begin with NLI debiasing models. To make our trials more generic, we adopt a mixture of experts (MoE) strategy (Clark et al., 2019), which is known for being model-agnostic and is adaptable to various kinds of known biases, as backbone. Specifically we treat three known biases, namely word overlap, length mismatch and partial input heuristics as independent experts and train corresponding debiasing models. Our results show that the debiasing methods tied to one particular known bias may not be sufficient to build a generalized, robust model. This motivates us to investigate a better solution to integrate the advantages of distinct debiasing models. We find model-level ensemble is more effective than other MoE ensemble methods. Although our findings are based on the MoE backbone due to the prohibitive exhaustive studies on the all existing debiasing strategies, we provide actionable insights on combining distinct NLI debiasing methods to the practitioners.

---

[1] In this paper, we use the term 'bias' to refer to these known dataset biases in NLI following Clark et al. (2019). In other context, 'bias' may refer to systematic mishandling of gender or evidences of racial stereotypes (Rudinger et al., 2017) in NLI datasets or models.

*Equal contribution.

Proceedings of the 24th Conference on Computational Natural Language Learning, pages 596–608
Online, November 19-20, 2020. ©2020 Association for Computational Linguistics
https://doi.org/10.18653/v1/P17

Datasets	Paper	Categories	Labels	Size
PI-CD	(a)	1‖3‖7	(E,N,C)	3.2k
PI-SP	(b)	1‖3‖7	(E,N,C)	.37k
IS-SD	(c)	2‖5‖8	(¬E, E)	30k
IS-CS	(d)	2‖3‖7	(E,N,C)	.65k
LI-LI	(e)(f)	2‖4‖9	(E,C)	9.9K
LI-TS	(g)(h)	2‖6‖10	(¬C, C)	9.8K
ST-WO	(e)	2‖4‖11	(E,N,C)	9.8K
ST-NE	(e)	2‖4‖11	(E,N,C)	9.8K
ST-LM	(e)	2‖4‖11	(E,N,C)	9.8K
ST-SE	(e)	2‖4‖12	(E,N,C)	31K

(a) Gururangan et al. (2018) (b) Liu et al. (2020)
(c) McCoy et al. (2019) (d) Nie et al. (2019)
(e) Naik et al. (2018) (f) Glockner et al. (2018)
(g) Wang et al. (2019c) (h) Minervini and Riedel

Category	First-level	Second-level
1	(I)	Partial input heuristics
2	(I)	Inter-sentence heuristics
3	(II)	Instance selection
4	(II)	Single Sentence Modification
5	(II)	Sentence Pair Modification
6	(II)	Sentence Pair Swapping
7	(III)	Lexical Statistical Irregularity
8	(III)	Syntactic Statistical Irregularity
9	(III)	Lexical Inference
10	(III)	First Order Logic
11	(III)	Stress Test - Distraction Test
12	(III)	Stress Test - Noise Test

(I) Where are the heuristics?
(II) How did the dataset constructed?
(III) Which aspect did the dataset detect?

Table 1: The information of adversarial datasets (Sec 2) we use in this paper. We categorize and rename these datasets as discussed in Sec 2.1.

Then we explore model agnostic and generic data augmentation methods in NLI, including text swap, word substitution and paraphrase. We find these methods could help NLI models combat multiple (though not all) adversarial attacks, e.g. augmenting training data by swapping hypothesis and premise could boost the model performance on stress tests and lexical inference test, and data augmentation by paraphrasing the hypothesis sentences could help the models resist the superficial patterns from syntactic and partial input heuristics. We also observe that increasing training size by incorporating heterogeneous training resources is a simple but effective method to build robust and generalized models. Specifically we investigate how to incorporate different training data with different sizes and annotation processes, as well as the best way to perform model ensembling.

2 Benchmark Datasets

Our benchmark datasets include the adversarial datasets[2] and some widely used general-purpose

NLI datasets which test the generalization power of NLI models. [3]

2.1 Adversarial Datasets

Categorization: to provide more insights on how the adversarial datasets attack the models, we roughly categorize them in Table 1 according to their characteristics and elaborate the categorization in this section. To facilitate the narrative of following sections, we rename the adversarial datasets according to their prominent features.

Comparability: all the following datasets are collected based on the public available resources proposed by their authors, thus the experimental results in this paper are comparable to the numbers reported in the original papers and the other papers that use these datasets[4].

2.1.1 Partial-input (PI) Heuristics

Partial-input heuristics refer to the hypothesis-only bias (Poliak et al., 2018b) in NLI.

Classifier Detected Datasets (PI-CD): Gururangan et al. (2018) trained a neural classifier (fastText[5]) on the hypothesis sentences and then treated those instances in the SNLI test sets which can not be correctly classified as 'hard' instances.

Surface Pattern Datasets (PI-SP): Liu et al. (2020) recognized surface patterns which are highly correlated to the specific labels and correspondingly proposed adversarial test sets which are against surface patterns' indications. We use their 'hard' instances for MultiNLI mismatched dev set as adversarial datasets.

2.1.2 Inter-sentences (IS) Heuristics

Syntactic Diagnostic Datasets (IS-SD): The HANS dataset (McCoy et al., 2019) includes lexical overlap, subsequence and constituent heuristics between the hypothesis and premises sentences, e.g. the model might incorrectly predict '*entailment*' for instance like 'The actor was paid by the judge' and 'The actor paid the judge'.

Compositionality-sensitivity Datasets (IS-CS): Nie et al. (2019) trained a softmax regression

---

datasets in the sense that the NLI models can not reach the same performance on these datasets as the in-domain test sets.

[3] The datasets used in this paper can be found in the following github repository https://github.com/tyliupku/nli-debiasing-datasets

[4] The ownership of these datasets belong to their authors. We encourage the readers to acknowledge and cite the original papers listed in Table 1 when using them.

[5] https://fasttext.cc/

---

[2] Some datasets listed in Table 1 were originally proposed to probe for systematicity. Here we call them 'adversarial'

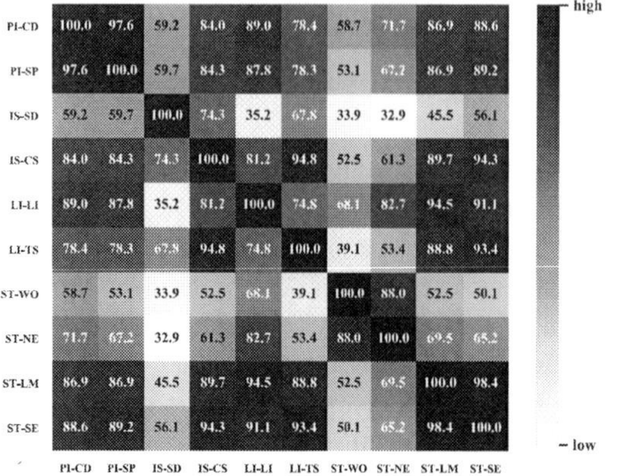

Figure 1: The surrogate correlations between different adversarial datasets. We show the Pearson's correlation coefficients of model performance on different adversarial datasets in different runs (Sec 2.1.5).

model using unigram pattern pair features across two sentences as well as unigram features in hypothesis and premise sentences to obtain the 'lexically misleading scores (LMS)' for each instance in the test sets. We use $CS_{0.7}$ in their paper which denotes the subsets whose LMS are larger that 0.7.

2.1.3 Logical Inference Ability (LI)

Lexical Inference Test (LI-LI): A proper NLI system should recognize hypernyms and hyponyms; synonym and antonyms. We merge the "antonym" category in Naik et al. (2018) and Glockner et al. (2018) to assess the models' capability to model lexical inference.

Text-fragment Swap Test (LI-TS): NLI system should also follow the first-order logic constraints (Wang et al., 2019c; Minervini and Riedel, 2018). For example, if the premise sentence s_p entails the hypothesis sentence s_h, then s_h must not be contradicted by s_p. We then swap the two sentences in the original MultiNLI mismatched dev sets. If the gold label is '*contradiction*', the corresponding label in the swapped instance remains unchanged, otherwise it becomes '*non-contradicted*'.

2.1.4 Stress Test (ST)

We also include the "word overlap" (**ST-WO**), "negation" (**ST-NE**), "length mismatch" (**ST-LM**) and "spelling errors" (**ST-SE**) in Naik et al. (2018), in which ST-WO aims at detecting lexical overlap heuristics described in McCoy et al. (2019) (IS-SD in Sec 2.1.2); ST-NE aims at detecting strong negative lexical cues in partial-input sentences like PI-SP in Sec 2.1.2.

	SNLI	MNLI	DNLI	ANLI
Train	549362	392702	249947	162765
Valid	9842	9832	31696	2200
Test	9824	9815	31232	2200

Table 2: Statistics for datasets used in Sec 5. For MNLI, we utlize the matched dev and mismatched dev sets as valid and test sets respectively.

2.1.5 Insights within Adversarial Tests

To provide actionable insights to NLP practitioners, we list how these adversarial instances constructed and why they might fail NLI models in Table 1. Those adversarial datasets are potentially correlated with each other due to similar constructing process or constructing goals. For example, 'PI-CD', 'PI-SP' and 'IS-CS' are all created with instance selection from original test sets in order to attack the models which improperly rely on the superficial lexical patterns, thus they might be potentially correlated. Although we could analytically assess the correlation between adversarial datasets, it is hard to demonstrate their underlying relationships from a quantitative perspective. We instead try to utilize the model performances on these adversarial datasets as surrogates to visualize their correlations. Concretely, we first collect the model accuracy scores on each adversarial dataset according to 30 runs of 10 baseline models (3 runs each) listed in Table 3. Then we show the pearson correlation coefficients of the model scores on any two distinct adversarial datasets in Fig 1. According to Fig 1, 'IS-SD' (HANS) has higher correlation with 'IS-CS' and 'LI-TS' compared with other adversarial datasets, we assume this is because they are constructed based on cross sentence heuristics in the natural occurring settings, as opposed to stress test datasets which add tautology like 'and true is true' to the end of hypothesis sentences (Naik et al., 2018). 'LI-LI' instances are created by few lexical changes on premise sentence which would easily fall into 'word overlap' heuristics as elaborated in the 'IS-SD' dataset, thus 'LI-LI' has low correlation with 'IS-SD'.

2.2 Other Data Resources

Generalization Power Test: we test the models on several general purpose datasets, including NLI diagnostic dataset (Diag) (Wang et al., 2019b), for which we use 'Matthews correlation coefficient' (Matthews, 1975) as the evaluation metric. We also incorporate RTE (Dagan et al., 2005), SICK (Marelli et al., 2014) and SciTail (Khot et al.,

	Adversarial Test								Generalization Power Test					MNLI
	PI-CD	PI-SP	IS-SD	IS-CS	LI-LI	LI-TS	ST	Avg.	RTE	DIAG	SICK	SciTail	Avg.	MNLI
InferSent	52.1	55.3	53.9	33.5	43.6	70.5	53.3	51.7	61.8	10.6	25.4	24.7	30.6	70.5
+ELMO	48.6	59.8	_55.2_	42.1	38.5	72.4	52.7	52.8	62.5	9.8	24.6	18.5	28.9	72.5
DAM	55.0	54.4	50.2	35.7	62.7	74.3	53.0	55.0	62.7	10.3	_27.0_	_30.0_	32.5	70.3
ESIM	_55.1_	_66.3_	49.8	_52.7_	_63.2_	_79.6_	_53.8_	60.1	_66.2_	_11.3_	25.1	27.5	32.5	_77.3_
BERT_B	72.2	73.9	63.8	65.4	85.6	82.6	63.5	72.4	75.4	36.2	54.2	66.1	58.0	83.5
BERT_L	74.7	75.5	70.4	70.6	87.9	83.8	67.3	75.7	77.6	39.4	55.5	68.3	60.2	85.7
XLNet_B	73.1	77.9	71.2	70.4	85.5	84.8	68.5	75.9	78.0	39.2	55.8	66.7	59.9	86.6
XLNet_L	78.8	**81.7**	76.7	77.3	**93.4**	88.5	72.4	81.3	83.4	45.9	**57.6**	**73.0**	65.0	89.3
RoBERTa_B	76.6	80.9	72.0	74.1	89.6	85.3	66.4	77.8	80.9	42.1	55.9	69.0	62.0	87.4
RoBERTa_L	**80.0**	79.2	**80.0**	**77.0**	92.4	**88.6**	**73.4**	81.5	**84.4**	**50.5**	57.3	72.2	66.1	**89.9**

Table 3: The performance of models on adversarial and generalization power tests (Sec 2) trained on MultiNLI. B and L in the subscript denote base and large versions of pretrained models. We use **bold** and underlined numbers to represent the highest scores in each column/block. Same marks are also used in Table 4, 5 and 6.

2018) in our testing.

Training Resources: apart from SNLI (Bowman et al., 2015), and MultiNLI (Williams et al., 2018), we also incorporate Diverse NLI (DNLI) (Poliak et al., 2018a) and Adversarial NLI (ANLI) (Nie et al., 2020) datasets for training. For DNLI, we merge the subsets to form unified train/valid/test sets. Dataset Statistics are shown in Table 2.

2.3 Model Performance on the Benchmark

We show the performance of different models trained on MultiNLI in Table 3. The general trend is that more powerful model which has higher performance on the original (in-domain) test sets (RoBERTa (large)) outperforms most models in both adversarial and general purpose settings.

In the following sections, we investigate several model agnostic methods for debiasing NLI models. Specifically, we are interested in: 1) how to (or is it possible to) make the NLI models robust to multiple distinct adversarial attacks using a unified debiasing method and 2) how the debiasing methods influence model generalization power of NLI.

3 Mixture of Experts (MoE) Debiasing

We utilize the MoE ensemble model Clark et al. (2019) as the backbone to mitigate three known biases in NLI. Concretely, we implement the 'instance reweighting' and 'bias product' methods in Clark et al. (2019). Based on these methods, we perform several trials on combating several distinct NLI biases at the same time.

3.1 Debiasing Methods

Notations: for a known NLI bias, they firstly train a bias-only model B and then use its output b as a

guidance to train the prime model. In the context of three-way NLI training, $\mathbf{b_i}$ is a normalized 3-element vector which represents the predicted possibility of each NLI label for i-th training example. Suppose $\mathbf{p_i}$ is output of the prime model which has the same meaning as $\mathbf{b_i}$.

Instance Reweighting: suppose $b_i^{y_i}$ is the possibility that the bias-only model assigns to the correct label y_i for i-th training example. They trained the models in a weighted version of the data, where the weight α_i for the i-th training example is $(1\text{-}b_i^{y_i})$. The loss function for a training batch with k examples is a weighted sum of instance-level loss l_i: $\mathbf{L}_{batch} = \alpha_i * l_i / (\sum_{i=1}^{k} \alpha_i)$.

Bias Product Ensemble: an ensemble method that is a product of experts $\hat{\mathbf{p_i}} = softmax(log(\mathbf{p_i}) + log(\mathbf{b_i}))$.

By doing so, the prime model would be encouraged to learn all the information except the specific bias. An intuitive justification from the probabilistic view can be found in Clark et al. (2019). Note that while training, only the prime model is updated while the bias-only model remains unchanged.

3.2 Known Biases in NLI

Word overlap heuristics: To combat the word overlap heuristics (HANS (McCoy et al., 2019), renamed as IS-SD in Sec 2.1.2), Clark et al. (2019) used the following features to train a bias-only model: (1) whether the hypothesis is a subsequence of the premise, (2) whether all words in the hypothesis appear in the premise, (3) the percent of words from the hypothesis that appear in the premise, (4) the average and the max of the minimum distance between each premise word with each hypothesis word. We use their trained

| | Baseline | Word Overlap | | Partial Input | | Sentence Length | | Debiasing Combination | | |
	(BERT_{base})	ReW	BiasProd	ReW	BiasProd	ReW	BiasProd	MixW	AddProd	BestEn
PI-CD	72.2	70.9	71.4	**72.6**	71.8	**72.6**	72.3	71.9	71.3	**72.6**
PI-SP	73.9	70.6	70.1	74.7	73.0	**75.2**	73.3	71.7	70.4	73.9
IS-SD	63.8	69.2	71.0	65.7	63.8	56.9	59.5	54.6	61.5	**72.5**
IS-CS	65.4	64.8	64.2	67.1	**68.9**	64.9	66.9	65.4	**68.9**	64.9
LI-LI	85.6	87.0	87.8	86.0	85.0	85.7	85.5	86.8	**88.4**	87.7
LI-TS	82.6	81.8	81.7	82.0	82.3	81.3	83.7	82.3	81.9	**84.5**
ST-LM	82.2	82.3	81.7	81.6	81.1	82.6	82.7	82.6	79.9	**83.1**
Gen. Avg.	58.0	56.8	56.6	57.5	56.7	57.9	57.5	57.1	55.9	**58.1**
MNLI	83.5	84.2	82.8	84.3	83.3	80.3	80.9	84.0	81.2	**84.5**

Table 4: The performance of debiasing methods (Sec 3) based on BERT base model (baseline) trained on MultiNLI. ReW, BiasProd refer to instance reweighting and bias product ensemble methods in Sec 3.1. Word overlap, partial input and sentence length are the known biases in NLI (Sec 3.2). MixW, AddProd, BestEn are our trials to combine distinct debiasing methods (Sec 3.3). 'Gen. Avg' is the average score of test sets in generalization power test. **Bold** numbers mark the highest score (besting debiasing model) *in each row*.

bias-only model output for experiments.

Partial input heuristics: To combat the hypothesis-only bias in NLI (PI-CD and PI-SP in Sec 2.1.1), we use RoBERTa (base) model to train a bias-only model by taking only hypothesis sentences as inputs. Our hypothesis-only model gets 60.4% accuracy on the mismatched dev set of MultiNLI, which is higher than the reported numbers in Gururangan et al. (2018) (52.3%) and Poliak et al. (2018b) (55.18%).

Sentence length heuristics: Gururangan et al. (2018) shows that the length of hypothesis and premise over different labels is not evenly distributed (ST-LM in Sec 2.1.4). So we trained a bias-only classifier based on the following sentence length related features: 1) the sentence lengths of hypothesis and premise sentences, 2) the mean and difference of these lengths. Our classifier achieves 41.3% accuracy on the mismatched dev set of MultiNLI, which outperforms the majority class baseline by 6.1%.

3.3 Combating Distinct Biases

Suppose we already have m bias-only models $\{B^1, B^2, \cdots, B^m\}$ and the corresponding output $\{\mathbf{b^1}, \mathbf{b^2}, \cdots, \mathbf{b^m}\}$ at hand, we test three different approaches to integrate these models.

MixWeight: Using the product of weights from different debiasing models while performing instance reweighting. We replace the weight for the i-th training example (α_i in Sec 3.1) with $\prod_{j=1}^{m}(1 - b_i^{y_i})$ and utilize the same loss function as 'instance reweighting' in Sec 3.1).

AddProduct: We view different bias-only models as multiple independent experts and then apply the bias product ensemble as 'bias product en-

semble' in Sec 3.2: $\hat{\mathbf{p_i}} = softmax(log(\mathbf{p_i}) + \sum_{j=1}^{m} log(\mathbf{b_i^j}))$.

BestEnsemble: We also try to ensemble the best single debiasing models. In our experiments (Table 4), we ensemble the three reweighting models ('ReW' models in column 2,4 and 6) for each bias to form the BestEnsemble model.

3.4 Discussions for MoE Methods

For **mixture of experts model**, we summarize our findings from Table 4 below:

1) For all three known biases in Sec 3.2, we find that the debiasing methods targeting at specific known biases increase the model performance on the corresponding adversarial datasets, e.g. for the word overlap heuristics, BiasProd model gets 71.0% accuracy on IS-SD (HANS) test set, 7.2% higher than baseline.

2) The bias-specific methods might not make the NLI models more robust and generalized. For example, the methods designed for word overlap heuristics get lower scores on PI-CD, PI-SP, IC-CS, LI-TS test sets than the baseline model.

3) The proposed debiasing merging methods BestEn (Sec 3.3) inherits the advantages of the 4 bias-specific methods on PI-CD, IS-SD, LI-TS and ST-LM compared with other MoE debiasing models.

4 Data Augmentation

In this section, we explore 3 automatic augmentation ways without collecting new data. For fair comparison, in all the following settings, we double the training size by automatically generating the same number of augmented instances as the original training sets as shown in Table 5.

| | Adversarial Test | | | | | | | Generalization Power Test | | | | | |
	PI-CD	PI-SP	IS-SD	IS-CS	LI-LI	LI-TS	ST	Avg.	RTE	DIAG	SICK	SciTail	Avg.	MNLI
Baseline	**72.2**	73.9	63.8	65.4	85.6	82.6	63.5	72.4	75.4	**36.2**	54.2	66.1	**58.0**	83.5
Text Swap	71.7	72.8	63.5	**67.4**	**86.3**	**86.8**	**66.5**	**73.6**	73.3	35.3	54.7	**66.8**	57.6	**83.7**
Sub (synonym)	69.8	72.0	62.4	65.8	85.2	82.8	64.3	71.8	74.4	34.2	55.1	65.8	57.4	83.5
Sub (MLM)	71.0	72.8	64.4	65.9	85.6	83.3	64.9	72.6	74.8	34.7	**55.4**	65.7	57.7	83.6
Paraphrase	72.1	**74.6**	**66.5**	66.4	85.7	83.1	64.8	73.3	**75.8**	35.1	55.0	65.0	57.7	**83.7**

Table 5: The performance of BERT base model under different data augmentation strategies (Sec 4).

4.1 Methods

Text Swap: It is an easy-to-implement method which swaps the premise p and hypothesis h sentences in the original datasets. It might be an potential solution to combat the partial-input heuristics (Sec 2.1.1) as the superficial patterns are not observed in the premise sentences. According to the first-order logic rules (LI-TS in Sec 2.1.3), we can only determine the gold labels for the swapped sentence pairs whose original labels are *contradiction*. For the *entailment* and *neutral* instances, we using the ensembled RoBERTa large model trained on 'all4' training set (Table 6) to label the swapped sentence pairs.

Word Substitution: We also tried to create new training instances by flipping the words in the hypothesis sentences. We try two ways to perform substitution: 1) **synonym**: We use NLTK (Bird and Loper, 2004) to firstly find the synonym candidates of the content words (including nouns, verbs and adjectives) in the hypothesis sentences, and then we replace the content words with their synonyms if the cosine similarity ([-1,1]) between the original window and the window after replacement is larger than 0. The window contains at most 3 words including the replaced word and its neighbours. We represent that window by max-pooling over the 300d Glove (Pennington et al., 2014) embedding of the words in that window. 2) **Masked LM**: we randomly select 30% content words and then load the pretrained BERT large model to perform masked LM task. We uniformly sample from top-100 ranking candidate words (excluding the original word) and then replace the original content word with the sampled one.

Paraphrase: We create the paraphrases for the original hypothesis sentences by back translation (Wieting and Gimpel, 2018; Hu et al., 2019) using the pretrained English-German and German-English machine translation models (Ng et al., 2019). To increase the diversity, we use beam search (size=5) for German-English translation and get the paraphrase by sampling from the candidate sentences.

4.2 Quality Analysis

To assess the quality of augmented data, we conduct both automatic and human evaluation. For automatic evaluation, we use the best NLI model (RoBERTa(large) model with 'All4+SinEN' in Table 6) in this paper to judge if the labels of augmented data are consistent with the predictions of our best NLI model. For human evaluation, we firstly sample 50 instances from each augmented training data and then hire 3 human annotators to decide the relation for the sentences pairs. We shuffle the 200 instances without showing the annotators the augmentation method for certain instances. We also ask the annotators to be objective and not to guess the augmentation methods and then use the majority vote for final annotation. The accuracy of text swap, word substitution (synonym), word substitution (MLM) and paraphrase are 84.0%, 82.0%, 88.1% and 92.9% respectively based on human-annotated gold labels. Correspondingly, word substitution (synonym), word substitution (MLM) and paraphrase get 76.9 %, 83.5% and 94.5% accuracy on the automatic evaluation. Paraphrase augmentation is shown to have the highest quality among the four methods.

4.3 Discussions for Data Augmentations

For **Data Augmentation**, we show the performance of a BERT base model using different data augmentation methods in Table 5.

Text swap method increases the model performance on IS-CS, LI-LI, LI-TS and ST test sets, as it can make the data distribution in the premises and hypotheses more balanced. It is also an easy-to-implement method which could serve as a baseline to evaluate other automatic data augmentation methods. For the other two methods, the fragility of NLI models to partial input and inter-sentence heuristics is partially due to the rigid word-label concurrence (PI-SP in Sec 2.1.1) or word-to-word mapping (IS-SD, IS-CS in Sec 2.1.2). More di-

	\multicolumn{8}{c}{Adversarial Test}	\multicolumn{5}{c}{Generalization Power Test}	\multicolumn{4}{c}{Original Test Sets}
	PI-CD	PI-SP	IS-SD	IS-CS	LI-LI	LI-TS	ST	Avg.	RTE	DIAG	SICK	SciTail	Avg.	DNLI	ANLI	SNLI	MNLI
\multicolumn{18}{c}{**RoBERTa (base) Model**}
D(only)	38.5	48.2	55.6	40.9	12.6	72.9	40.9	44.2	54.9	9.1	40.9	39.4	36.1	92.9	32.6	42.1	47.0
A(only)	64.6	60.6	57.9	66.9	92.6	80.8	68.1	70.2	80.6	33.8	51.2	63.7	57.3	58.9	49.1	73.6	78.5
S(only)	82.2	64.4	67.4	62.2	93.2	80.7	64.6	73.5	72.5	36.0	_57.8_	49.6	54.0	58.8	31.3	91.3	79.9
M(only)	76.6	80.9	72.0	74.1	89.6	85.3	66.4	77.8	80.9	42.1	55.9	69.0	62.0	59.3	29.4	84.2	87.4
M+S	_82.8_	80.1	73.3	74.4	91.8	85.6	67.8	79.4	81.2	40.7	57.5	67.4	61.7	60.5	28.3	91.7	87.4
M+S+D	82.7	79.8	75.1	72.9	92.1	84.7	68.1	79.3	80.4	40.9	57.1	68.3	61.8	92.8	30.3	91.7	87.7
All4	82.6	_81.7_	_77.0_	_74.7_	94.7	85.3	_69.1_	80.7	83.7	41.9	57.3	_70.5_	63.4	_93.0_	49.2	_91.9_	87.7
All4+SR	82.6	82.5	74.7	73.8	_95.2_	_86.0_	69.0	80.5	_83.9_	41.3	57.3	69.6	63.0	92.8	49.1	91.7	_87.8_
All4+PR	83.4	79.5	75.5	73.8	94.6	85.5	_69.1_	80.2	83.8	_44.0_	57.5	_70.5_	64.0	92.9	_51.2_	_91.9_	87.6
\multicolumn{18}{c}{**RoBERTa (large) Model**}
All4	84.6	**83.8**	79.6	**79.3**	94.9	88.6	71.6	83.2	87.6	**50.2**	57.9	73.1	67.2	93.2	55.5	92.7	90.4
All4+ME	**85.0**	81.4	**80.1**	77.7	**95.7**	88.7	72.2	83.0	87.2	47.4	**58.0**	73.7	66.6	**93.3**	54.8	**93.0**	90.2
All4+SE	**85.0**	81.9	77.5	77.9	95.4	**89.2**	**72.5**	82.8	**88.5**	49.3	57.9	**73.9**	67.4	**93.3**	**55.7**	**93.0**	**90.6**

Table 6: Performance of RoBERTa model trained on different datasets using multiple reweighting and ensemble strategies (Sec 5). 'D', 'A', 'S', 'M', 'All4' denotes DNLI, ANLI, SNLI, MNLI and the merge of all 4 datasets respectively. 'M+S' is created by merging MNLI and SNLI datasets, same principle in other settings. 'ME' and 'SE' denote the ensemble strategies in Sec 5.2: the ensemble of 3 distinct models: BERT(large), XLNet(large) and RoBERTa(large) and the ensemble of 3 RoBERTa(large) models. 'SR' and 'PR' refer to the size-based and performance-based reweighting in Sec 5.1. Here for 'PR' we use the average score of all the listed tests in 'D(only)', 'A(only)', 'S(only)' and 'M(only)' rows as their corresponding performance.

verse lexical choices via word substitution or paraphrase might help to relieve the biases caused by these heuristics. We see that 'word sub' in Table 5 outperforms baseline on IS-CS, LI-TS and ST; 'paraphrase' outperforms the baseline on IS-SD, LI-TS. However, these two methods get lower scores on other adversarial and general purpose datasets as these debiasing techniques bias the model towards being robust to a specific bias, so it compensates by trading off performance.

5 Dataset Merging and Model Ensemble

In this section we explore 1) to what extend larger dataset and ensemble would make the NLI models more robust to distinct adverserial datasets. 2) what is the best way to combine the large-scale NLI training sets in very different domains.

5.1 Merging Heterogeneous Datasets

To set up more diverse and stronger baselines for the proposed benchmark datasets, we use 4 large-scale training datasets: SNLI, MNLI, DNLI and ANLI for the following experiments. Those training sets are created using different strategies. Specifically, SNLI and MNLI are created in a human elicited way (Poliak et al., 2018b): the human annotators are asked to write a hypothesis sentence according to the given premise and label. DNLI recasts other NLP tasks to fit in the form of NLI. ANLI is created as hard datasets that may fail the

models. Since those datasets vary in sizes, domains and collection processes, they might have different contribution to the final predictions. Here we investigate two instance reweighting methods accordingly.

Notations: suppose we have k training sets $\{T_i\}_{i=1}^k$ whose sizes are $\{n_i\}_{i=1}^k$. The accuracies of a baseline model trained on $\{T_i\}_{i=1}^k$ are $\{p_i\}_{i=1}^k$ respectively. p_i can be the average scores of multiple test sets or the score on an single in-domain/ out-of-domain/ adversarial test set.

Size-based reweighting (SR): Smaller training sets might have less influence on the models than larger ones. In this setting, we try to increase the weight of smaller datasets so that each dataset contributes more equally to the final predictions. We implement this reweighting method by replacing the α_i in Sec 3.1 with $(\sum_k n_k)/n_i (i \in T_i)$.

Performance-based reweighting (PR): Different training sets may vary in annotation quality and collection process thus have distinct model performance. In this setting, we reweight the training instances with the performance of a baseline model on the specific training sets. We still use the instance weights in Sec 3.1 with $\alpha_i = p_i/(\sum_k p_k)(i \in T_i)$.

5.2 Model Ensemble

We try two modes for model ensemble: **mixed** and **single** mode. In the mixed mode, we ensemble three different models (BERT, XLNet, RoBERTa)

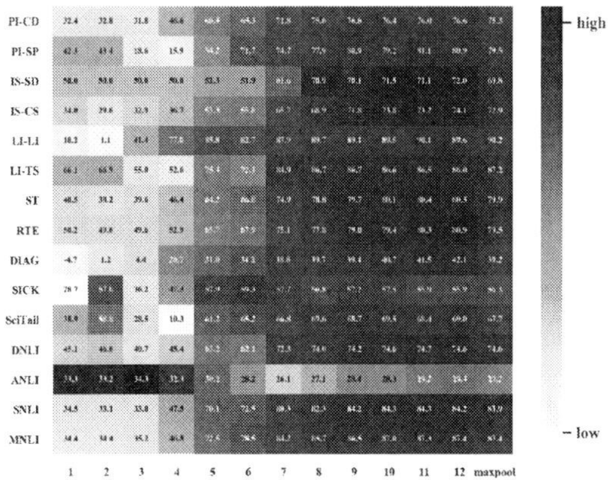

Figure 2: Per-layer analysis for RoBERTa(base) model trained on MultiNLI. Darker blue denotes higher score. 'max' represents the maxpooled vector across all layers. Nearly all test sets except ANLI get higher scores by using higher layers. On ANLI, the performance of the first 4 layers are close to random guess while that of higher layers is about 4 point lower than random guess.

while in the single mode, we ensemble three same models (RoBERTa*3). More details in appendix.

5.3 Discussions

For **Dataset merging and model ensemble**, according to Table 6, We find that:

1) Incorporating heterogeneous training data is a straightforward method to enhance the robustness of NLI models. Empirically we see incorporating datasets with adversarial human-in-the-loop annotating (e.g. ANLI) is more efficient that incorporating automatically constructed dataset without human curation (e.g. DNLI).

2) In RoBERTa base model, the 'All4+PR' model get higher scores on diagnostic and ANLI test sets than 'All4' baseline, which shows that increasing the weight of higher quality dataset may help to increase accuracy on certain test sets. Notably, performance based reweighting helps the model gain 2 points (49.2 vs 51.2) on ANLI compared with baseline model while keeping the inference ability on DNLI, SNLI and MNLI test sets.

3) In RoBERTa large model, we see that on some datasets, like IS-SD, the mixed ensemble model may even outperform the single ensemble model even if its two components (XLNet and BERT) are less powerful than those (RoBERTa) in single ensemble mode.

Labels	Transformation	Datasets
($\neg$E, E)	C$\Rightarrow$ $\neg$E, N$\Rightarrow$ $\neg$E	IS-SD, RTE, DNLI
($\neg$C, C)	E$\Rightarrow$ $\neg$C, N$\Rightarrow$ $\neg$C	LI-TS
(E, C)	-	LI-LI
(N, E)	-	SciTail

Table 7: How we evaluate the test sets with only two labels in 3-way NLI classification. E,C,N,$\neg$ means *entailment, contradiction, neutral* and *not* respectively. $\Rightarrow$ means changing the left-hand side model prediction with the right-hand side label while evaluation.

	RTE	SICK	SciTail	DNLI	ANLI	SNLI	MNLI
Origin	75.4	54.2	66.1	54.2	27.7	80.0	**83.5**
Mixed	**75.5**	54.3	**67.3**	54.8	27.4	79.9	83.4
Oracle	**75.5**	**55.2**	**67.3**	**56.7**	**28.0**	**80.3**	**83.5**

Table 8: The performance of BERT base model under different model selection strategies.

6 Experimental Settings

6.1 Implementation Details

We set up both pretrained and non-pretrained model baselines for the proposed evaluation bechmarks. We rerun their public available codebases (Wolf et al., 2019), including InferSent (Conneau et al., 2017) [6] (w/ and w/o Elmo (Peters et al., 2018)), DAM (Parikh et al., 2016) [7], ESIM (Chen et al., 2017)[8], BERT (uncased) (Devlin et al., 2019), XLNet (cased) (Yang et al., 2019) and RoBERTa (Liu et al., 2019), [9]. we map the vector at the position of the '[CLS]' token in the pretrained models to three-way NLI classification via linear transformation. We show the per-layer analyses for RoBERTa model in Table 2. We try to reduce the randomness of our experiments by 3 runs using different random seeds. We report the median of the 3 runs for all the tables except the ensemble-related (Sec 5.2) experiments in Table 6. Table 7 shows how we evaluate the test sets with only two labels in 3-way NLI classification.

6.2 Model Selection Strategy

Since we test the NLI models on multiple general-purpose dataset. it is an important question how we choose the dev set. We explore 3 different model selection settings:

[6] https://github.com/facebookresearch/InferSent
[7] https://github.com/harvardnlp/decomp-attn
[8] https://github.com/coetaur0/ESIM
[9] https://github.com/huggingface/transformers

1) **Origin**: using the original in-domain dev set.
2) **Mixed**: using the merged dev sets which include all the instances in the in-domain and extra dev sets in generalization power tests.
3) **Oracle**: tuning the model for each generalization power test using its own dev set.

We show the performance of a BERT base model trained on MultiNLI utilizing the above mentioned model selection strategies in Table 8. In this paper we use the 'origin' mode, as it is too expensive to use the 'oracle' strategy in all experiments, besides we did not see much difference between the 'mixed' and 'origin' modes. Notably when we merge different training sets, we also merge their dev sets correspondingly to form a unified in-domain dev set in Table 6.

7   Related Work

Bias in NLI: The bias in the data annotation exists in many tasks, e.g. lexical inference (Levy et al., 2015), visual question answering (Goyal et al., 2017), ROC story cloze (Cai et al., 2017; Schwartz et al., 2017) etc. The NLI models are shown to be sensitive to the compositional features in premises and hypotheses(Nie et al., 2019; Dasgupta et al., 2018), data permutations (Schluter and Varab, 2018; Wang et al., 2019c) and vulnerable to adversarial examples (Iyyer et al., 2018; Minervini and Riedel, 2018; Glockner et al., 2018) and crafted stress test (Geiger et al., 2018; Naik et al., 2018). Other evidences of artifacts include sentence occurrence (Zhang et al., 2019), syntactic heuristics between hypotheses and premises (McCoy et al., 2019) and black-box clues derived from neural models (Gururangan et al., 2018; Poliak et al., 2018b; He et al., 2019). Rudinger et al. (2017) showed hypotheses in SNLI has the evidence of gender, racial stereotypes, etc. Sanchez et al. (2018) analysed the behaviour of NLI models and the factors to be more robust. Feng et al. (2019) discussed how to use partial-input baseline in future dataset creation. Belinkov et al. (2019); Clark et al. (2019); He et al. (2019); Yaghoobzadeh et al. (2019); Ding et al. (2020) proposed efficient methods to mitigate a particular known bias in NLI.

Benchmark collection in NLI: GLUE (Wang et al., 2019b,a) benchmark contains several NLI-related benchmark datasets. However it does not include adversarial test sets, domain specific test (Romanov and Shivade, 2018; Ravichander et al.,

2019). Researchers create NLI datasets using different collection criteria, such as recasting other NLP tasks to NLI (Poliak et al., 2018a), iteratively filtering adversarial training data by model decisions (Bras et al., 2020) (model-in-the-loop), counterfactually augmenting training data by human editing examples to break the model (Kaushik et al., 2020) (human-in-the-loop) and multi-round annotating depending on both human and model decisions (Nie et al., 2020).

8   Conclusions

We try to investigate how to build robust and generalized NLI models by model-agnostic debiasing strategies, including mixture of experts ensemble (MoE), data augmentation (DA), dataset merging and model ensemble, and benchmark these methods on various adversarial and general purpose datasets. Our findings suggest model-level MoE ensemble, text swap DA and performance based dataset merging would effectively combat multiple (though not all) distinct biases.

Although we haven't found a debiasing strategy that can guarantee the NLI models to be more robust on every adversarial dataset used in this paper, we leave the question of whether such a debiasing method exists for future research.

Acknowledgments

We would like to thank Sam Wiseman and Kevin Gimpel for very thoughtful discussions, and the anonymous reviewers for their helpful feedback. This project is supported by NSFC (No. 61876004, No. U19A2065) and Beijing Academy of Artificial Intelligence (BAAI).

References

Yonatan Belinkov, Adam Poliak, Stuart Shieber, Benjamin Van Durme, and Alexander Rush. 2019. On adversarial removal of hypothesis-only bias in natural language inference. pages 256–262, Minneapolis, Minnesota. Association for Computational Linguistics.

Steven Bird and Edward Loper. 2004. NLTK: The natural language toolkit. In *Proceedings of the ACL Interactive Poster and Demonstration Sessions*, pages 214–217, Barcelona, Spain. Association for Computational Linguistics.

Samuel R. Bowman, Gabor Angeli, Christopher Potts, and Christopher D. Manning. 2015. A large annotated corpus for learning natural language inference.

In *Proceedings of the 2015 Conference on Empirical Methods in Natural Language Processing*, pages 632–642, Lisbon, Portugal. Association for Computational Linguistics.

Ronan Le Bras, Swabha Swayamdipta, Chandra Bhagavatula, Rowan Zellers, Matthew E. Peters, Ashish Sabharwal, and Yejin Choi. 2020. Adversarial filters of dataset biases. *CoRR*, abs/2002.04108.

Zheng Cai, Lifu Tu, and Kevin Gimpel. 2017. Pay attention to the ending:strong neural baselines for the ROC story cloze task. In *Proceedings of the 55th Annual Meeting of the Association for Computational Linguistics (Volume 2: Short Papers)*, pages 616–622, Vancouver, Canada. Association for Computational Linguistics.

Qian Chen, Xiaodan Zhu, Zhen-Hua Ling, Si Wei, Hui Jiang, and Diana Inkpen. 2017. Enhanced LSTM for natural language inference. In *Proceedings of the 55th Annual Meeting of the Association for Computational Linguistics (Volume 1: Long Papers)*, pages 1657–1668, Vancouver, Canada. Association for Computational Linguistics.

Christopher Clark, Mark Yatskar, and Luke Zettlemoyer. 2019. Don't take the easy way out: Ensemble based methods for avoiding known dataset biases. In *Proceedings of the 2019 Conference on Empirical Methods in Natural Language Processing and the 9th International Joint Conference on Natural Language Processing (EMNLP-IJCNLP)*, pages 4069–4082, Hong Kong, China. Association for Computational Linguistics.

Alexis Conneau, Douwe Kiela, Holger Schwenk, Loïc Barrault, and Antoine Bordes. 2017. Supervised learning of universal sentence representations from natural language inference data. In *Proceedings of the 2017 Conference on Empirical Methods in Natural Language Processing*, pages 670–680, Copenhagen, Denmark. Association for Computational Linguistics.

Ido Dagan, Oren Glickman, and Bernardo Magnini. 2005. The PASCAL recognising textual entailment challenge. In *Machine Learning Challenges, Evaluating Predictive Uncertainty, Visual Object Classification and Recognizing Textual Entailment, First PASCAL Machine Learning Challenges Workshop, MLCW 2005, Southampton, UK, April 11-13, 2005, Revised Selected Papers*, volume 3944 of *Lecture Notes in Computer Science*, pages 177–190. Springer.

Ido Dagan, Dan Roth, Mark Sammons, and Fabio Massimo Zanzotto. 2013. *Recognizing Textual Entailment: Models and Applications*. Synthesis Lectures on Human Language Technologies. Morgan & Claypool Publishers.

Ishita Dasgupta, Demi Guo, Andreas Stuhlmüller, Samuel Gershman, and Noah D. Goodman. 2018. Evaluating compositionality in sentence embeddings. In *Proceedings of the 40th Annual Meeting of the Cognitive Science Society, CogSci 2018, Madison, WI, USA, July 25-28, 2018.* cognitivesciencesociety.org.

Jacob Devlin, Ming-Wei Chang, Kenton Lee, and Kristina Toutanova. 2019. BERT: Pre-training of deep bidirectional transformers for language understanding. In *Proceedings of the 2019 Conference of the North American Chapter of the Association for Computational Linguistics: Human Language Technologies, Volume 1 (Long and Short Papers)*, pages 4171–4186, Minneapolis, Minnesota. Association for Computational Linguistics.

Xiaoan Ding, Tianyu Liu, Baobao Chang, Zhifang Sui, and Kevin Gimpel. 2020. Discriminatively-tuned generative classifiers for robust natural language inference. *CoRR*, abs/2010.03760.

Shi Feng, Eric Wallace, and Jordan Boyd-Graber. 2019. Misleading failures of partial-input baselines. In *Proceedings of the 57th Annual Meeting of the Association for Computational Linguistics*, pages 5533–5538, Florence, Italy. Association for Computational Linguistics.

Atticus Geiger, Ignacio Cases, Lauri Karttunen, and Christopher Potts. 2018. Stress-testing neural models of natural language inference with multiply-quantified sentences. *CoRR*, abs/1810.13033.

Max Glockner, Vered Shwartz, and Yoav Goldberg. 2018. Breaking NLI systems with sentences that require simple lexical inferences. In *Proceedings of the 56th Annual Meeting of the Association for Computational Linguistics (Volume 2: Short Papers)*, pages 650–655, Melbourne, Australia. Association for Computational Linguistics.

Yash Goyal, Tejas Khot, Douglas Summers-Stay, Dhruv Batra, and Devi Parikh. 2017. Making the V in VQA matter: Elevating the role of image understanding in visual question answering. In *2017 IEEE Conference on Computer Vision and Pattern Recognition, CVPR 2017, Honolulu, HI, USA, July 21-26, 2017*, pages 6325–6334. IEEE Computer Society.

Suchin Gururangan, Swabha Swayamdipta, Omer Levy, Roy Schwartz, Samuel Bowman, and Noah A. Smith. 2018. Annotation artifacts in natural language inference data. In *Proceedings of the 2018 Conference of the North American Chapter of the Association for Computational Linguistics: Human Language Technologies, Volume 2 (Short Papers)*, pages 107–112, New Orleans, Louisiana. Association for Computational Linguistics.

He He, Sheng Zha, and Haohan Wang. 2019. Unlearn dataset bias in natural language inference by fitting the residual. In *Proceedings of the 2nd Workshop on Deep Learning Approaches for Low-Resource NLP (DeepLo 2019)*, pages 132–142, Hong Kong, China. Association for Computational Linguistics.

J. Edward Hu, Huda Khayrallah, Ryan Culkin, Patrick Xia, Tongfei Chen, Matt Post, and Benjamin Van Durme. 2019. Improved lexically constrained decoding for translation and monolingual rewriting. In *Proceedings of the 2019 Conference of the North American Chapter of the Association for Computational Linguistics: Human Language Technologies, Volume 1 (Long and Short Papers)*, pages 839–850, Minneapolis, Minnesota. Association for Computational Linguistics.

Mohit Iyyer, John Wieting, Kevin Gimpel, and Luke Zettlemoyer. 2018. Adversarial example generation with syntactically controlled paraphrase networks. In *Proceedings of the 2018 Conference of the North American Chapter of the Association for Computational Linguistics: Human Language Technologies, Volume 1 (Long Papers)*, pages 1875–1885, New Orleans, Louisiana. Association for Computational Linguistics.

Divyansh Kaushik, Eduard H. Hovy, and Zachary Chase Lipton. 2020. Learning the difference that makes A difference with counterfactually-augmented data. In *8th International Conference on Learning Representations, ICLR 2020, Addis Ababa, Ethiopia, April 26-30, 2020*. OpenReview.net.

Tushar Khot, Ashish Sabharwal, and Peter Clark. 2018. Scitail: A textual entailment dataset from science question answering. In *Proceedings of the Thirty-Second AAAI Conference on Artificial Intelligence, (AAAI-18), the 30th innovative Applications of Artificial Intelligence (IAAI-18), and the 8th AAAI Symposium on Educational Advances in Artificial Intelligence (EAAI-18), New Orleans, Louisiana, USA, February 2-7, 2018*, pages 5189–5197. AAAI Press.

Omer Levy, Steffen Remus, Chris Biemann, and Ido Dagan. 2015. Do supervised distributional methods really learn lexical inference relations? In *Proceedings of the 2015 Conference of the North American Chapter of the Association for Computational Linguistics: Human Language Technologies*, pages 970–976, Denver, Colorado. Association for Computational Linguistics.

Tianyu Liu, Zheng Xin, Baobao Chang, and Zhifang Sui. 2020. HypoNLI: Exploring the artificial patterns of hypothesis-only bias in natural language inference. In *Proceedings of the 12th Language Resources and Evaluation Conference*, pages 6852–6860, Marseille, France. European Language Resources Association.

Yinhan Liu, Myle Ott, Naman Goyal, Jingfei Du, Mandar Joshi, Danqi Chen, Omer Levy, Mike Lewis, Luke Zettlemoyer, and Veselin Stoyanov. 2019. RoBERTa: A robustly optimized BERT pretraining approach. *CoRR*, abs/1907.11692.

Marco Marelli, Luisa Bentivogli, Marco Baroni, Raffaella Bernardi, Stefano Menini, and Roberto Zamparelli. 2014. SemEval-2014 task 1: Evaluation of compositional distributional semantic models on full sentences through semantic relatedness and textual entailment. In *Proceedings of the 8th International Workshop on Semantic Evaluation (SemEval 2014)*, pages 1–8, Dublin, Ireland. Association for Computational Linguistics.

Brian W Matthews. 1975. Comparison of the predicted and observed secondary structure of t4 phage lysozyme. *Biochimica et Biophysica Acta (BBA)-Protein Structure*, 405(2):442–451.

Tom McCoy, Ellie Pavlick, and Tal Linzen. 2019. Right for the wrong reasons: Diagnosing syntactic heuristics in natural language inference. In *Proceedings of the 57th Annual Meeting of the Association for Computational Linguistics*, pages 3428–3448, Florence, Italy. Association for Computational Linguistics.

Pasquale Minervini and Sebastian Riedel. 2018. Adversarially regularising neural NLI models to integrate logical background knowledge. In *Proceedings of the 22nd Conference on Computational Natural Language Learning*, pages 65–74, Brussels, Belgium. Association for Computational Linguistics.

Aakanksha Naik, Abhilasha Ravichander, Norman Sadeh, Carolyn Rose, and Graham Neubig. 2018. Stress test evaluation for natural language inference. In *Proceedings of the 27th International Conference on Computational Linguistics*, pages 2340–2353, Santa Fe, New Mexico, USA. Association for Computational Linguistics.

Nathan Ng, Kyra Yee, Alexei Baevski, Myle Ott, Michael Auli, and Sergey Edunov. 2019. Facebook FAIR's WMT19 news translation task submission. In *Proceedings of the Fourth Conference on Machine Translation (Volume 2: Shared Task Papers, Day 1)*, pages 314–319, Florence, Italy. Association for Computational Linguistics.

Yixin Nie, Yicheng Wang, and Mohit Bansal. 2019. Analyzing compositionality-sensitivity of NLI models. In *The Thirty-Third AAAI Conference on Artificial Intelligence, AAAI 2019, The Thirty-First Innovative Applications of Artificial Intelligence Conference, IAAI 2019, The Ninth AAAI Symposium on Educational Advances in Artificial Intelligence, EAAI 2019, Honolulu, Hawaii, USA, January 27 - February 1, 2019*, pages 6867–6874. AAAI Press.

Yixin Nie, Adina Williams, Emily Dinan, Mohit Bansal, Jason Weston, and Douwe Kiela. 2020. Adversarial NLI: A new benchmark for natural language understanding. In *Proceedings of the 58th Annual Meeting of the Association for Computational Linguistics*, pages 4885–4901, Online. Association for Computational Linguistics.

Ankur Parikh, Oscar Täckström, Dipanjan Das, and Jakob Uszkoreit. 2016. A decomposable attention model for natural language inference. In *Proceedings of the 2016 Conference on Empirical Methods in Natural Language Processing*, pages 2249–2255, Austin, Texas. Association for Computational Linguistics.

Jeffrey Pennington, Richard Socher, and Christopher Manning. 2014. GloVe: Global vectors for word representation. In *Proceedings of the 2014 Conference on Empirical Methods in Natural Language Processing (EMNLP)*, pages 1532–1543, Doha, Qatar. Association for Computational Linguistics.

Matthew Peters, Mark Neumann, Mohit Iyyer, Matt Gardner, Christopher Clark, Kenton Lee, and Luke Zettlemoyer. 2018. Deep contextualized word representations. In *Proceedings of the 2018 Conference of the North American Chapter of the Association for Computational Linguistics: Human Language Technologies, Volume 1 (Long Papers)*, pages 2227–2237, New Orleans, Louisiana. Association for Computational Linguistics.

Adam Poliak, Aparajita Haldar, Rachel Rudinger, J. Edward Hu, Ellie Pavlick, Aaron Steven White, and Benjamin Van Durme. 2018a. Collecting diverse natural language inference problems for sentence representation evaluation. In *Proceedings of the 2018 Conference on Empirical Methods in Natural Language Processing*, pages 67–81, Brussels, Belgium. Association for Computational Linguistics.

Adam Poliak, Jason Naradowsky, Aparajita Haldar, Rachel Rudinger, and Benjamin Van Durme. 2018b. Hypothesis only baselines in natural language inference. In *Proceedings of the Seventh Joint Conference on Lexical and Computational Semantics*, pages 180–191, New Orleans, Louisiana. Association for Computational Linguistics.

Abhilasha Ravichander, Aakanksha Naik, Carolyn Rose, and Eduard Hovy. 2019. EQUATE: A benchmark evaluation framework for quantitative reasoning in natural language inference. In *Proceedings of the 23rd Conference on Computational Natural Language Learning (CoNLL)*, pages 349–361, Hong Kong, China. Association for Computational Linguistics.

Alexey Romanov and Chaitanya Shivade. 2018. Lessons from natural language inference in the clinical domain. In *Proceedings of the 2018 Conference on Empirical Methods in Natural Language Processing*, pages 1586–1596, Brussels, Belgium. Association for Computational Linguistics.

Rachel Rudinger, Chandler May, and Benjamin Van Durme. 2017. Social bias in elicited natural language inferences. In *Proceedings of the First ACL Workshop on Ethics in Natural Language Processing*, pages 74–79, Valencia, Spain. Association for Computational Linguistics.

Ivan Sanchez, Jeff Mitchell, and Sebastian Riedel. 2018. Behavior analysis of NLI models: Uncovering the influence of three factors on robustness.

In *Proceedings of the 2018 Conference of the North American Chapter of the Association for Computational Linguistics: Human Language Technologies, Volume 1 (Long Papers)*, pages 1975–1985, New Orleans, Louisiana. Association for Computational Linguistics.

Natalie Schluter and Daniel Varab. 2018. When data permutations are pathological: the case of neural natural language inference. In *Proceedings of the 2018 Conference on Empirical Methods in Natural Language Processing*, pages 4935–4939, Brussels, Belgium. Association for Computational Linguistics.

Roy Schwartz, Maarten Sap, Ioannis Konstas, Leila Zilles, Yejin Choi, and Noah A. Smith. 2017. The effect of different writing tasks on linguistic style: A case study of the ROC story cloze task. In *Proceedings of the 21st Conference on Computational Natural Language Learning (CoNLL 2017)*, pages 15–25, Vancouver, Canada. Association for Computational Linguistics.

Masatoshi Tsuchiya. 2018. Performance impact caused by hidden bias of training data for recognizing textual entailment. In *Proceedings of the Eleventh International Conference on Language Resources and Evaluation (LREC 2018)*, Miyazaki, Japan. European Language Resources Association (ELRA).

Alex Wang, Yada Pruksachatkun, Nikita Nangia, Amanpreet Singh, Julian Michael, Felix Hill, Omer Levy, and Samuel R. Bowman. 2019a. Superglue: A stickier benchmark for general-purpose language understanding systems. In *Advances in Neural Information Processing Systems 32: Annual Conference on Neural Information Processing Systems 2019, NeurIPS 2019, 8-14 December 2019, Vancouver, BC, Canada*, pages 3261–3275.

Alex Wang, Amanpreet Singh, Julian Michael, Felix Hill, Omer Levy, and Samuel R. Bowman. 2019b. GLUE: A multi-task benchmark and analysis platform for natural language understanding. In *7th International Conference on Learning Representations, ICLR 2019, New Orleans, LA, USA, May 6-9, 2019*. OpenReview.net.

Haohan Wang, Da Sun, and Eric P. Xing. 2019c. What if we simply swap the two text fragments? A straightforward yet effective way to test the robustness of methods to confounding signals in nature language inference tasks. In *The Thirty-Third AAAI Conference on Artificial Intelligence, AAAI 2019, The Thirty-First Innovative Applications of Artificial Intelligence Conference, IAAI 2019, The Ninth AAAI Symposium on Educational Advances in Artificial Intelligence, EAAI 2019, Honolulu, Hawaii, USA, January 27 - February 1, 2019*, pages 7136–7143. AAAI Press.

John Wieting and Kevin Gimpel. 2018. ParaNMT-50M: Pushing the limits of paraphrastic sentence embeddings with millions of machine translations. In *Proceedings of the 56th Annual Meeting of the Association for Computational Linguistics (Volume 1: Long Papers)*, pages 451–462, Melbourne, Australia. Association for Computational Linguistics.

Adina Williams, Nikita Nangia, and Samuel Bowman. 2018. A broad-coverage challenge corpus for sentence understanding through inference. In *Proceedings of the 2018 Conference of the North American Chapter of the Association for Computational Linguistics: Human Language Technologies, Volume 1 (Long Papers)*, pages 1112–1122, New Orleans, Louisiana. Association for Computational Linguistics.

Thomas Wolf, Lysandre Debut, Victor Sanh, Julien Chaumond, Clement Delangue, Anthony Moi, Pierric Cistac, Tim Rault, Rémi Louf, Morgan Funtowicz, and Jamie Brew. 2019. Huggingface's transformers: State-of-the-art natural language processing. *CoRR*, abs/1910.03771.

Yadollah Yaghoobzadeh, Remi Tachet des Combes, Timothy J. Hazen, and Alessandro Sordoni. 2019. Robust natural language inference models with example forgetting. *CoRR*, abs/1911.03861.

Zhilin Yang, Zihang Dai, Yiming Yang, Jaime G. Carbonell, Ruslan Salakhutdinov, and Quoc V. Le. 2019. XLNet: Generalized autoregressive pretraining for language understanding. In *Advances in Neural Information Processing Systems 32: Annual Conference on Neural Information Processing Systems 2019, NeurIPS 2019, 8-14 December 2019, Vancouver, BC, Canada*, pages 5754–5764.

Guanhua Zhang, Bing Bai, Jian Liang, Kun Bai, Shiyu Chang, Mo Yu, Conghui Zhu, and Tiejun Zhao. 2019. Selection bias explorations and debias methods for natural language sentence matching datasets. In *Proceedings of the 57th Annual Meeting of the Association for Computational Linguistics*, pages 4418–4429, Florence, Italy. Association for Computational Linguistics.

Cloze Distillation: Improving Neural Language Models with Human Next-Word Predictions

Tiwalayo N. Eisape[1]   Noga Zaslavsky[1,2]   Roger P. Levy[1]

[1]Department of Brain and Cognitive Sciences, [2]Center for Brains Minds and Machines

Massachusetts Institute of Technology

{eisape, nogazs, rplevy}@mit.edu

Abstract

Contemporary autoregressive language models (LMs) trained purely on corpus data have been shown to capture numerous features of human incremental processing. However, past work has also suggested dissociations between corpus probabilities and human next-word predictions. Here we evaluate several state-of-the-art language models for their match to human next-word predictions and to reading time behavior from eye movements. We then propose a novel method for distilling the linguistic information implicit in human linguistic predictions into pre-trained LMs: Cloze Distillation. We apply this method to a baseline neural LM and show potential improvement in reading time prediction and generalization to held-out human cloze data.

1 Introduction

Modern language models (LMs) demonstrate outstanding general-purpose command over language. The majority of these models acquire language by maximizing the in-context probability of each word in their training corpus (Figure 1), typically with a self-supervised objective. This simple corpus probability matching has resulted in models that learn impressive powers of both psychometric prediction (Frank and Bod, 2011; Fossum and Levy, 2012; Frank et al., 2015; Goodkind and Bicknell, 2018; Hale et al., 2018; van Schijndel and Linzen, 2018; Warstadt and Bowman, 2020; Wilcox et al., 2020) and language more generally (Devlin et al., 2019; Radford et al., 2019).

In humans, prediction may underlie both learning (Kuhl, 2004; Huang and Snedeker, 2013) and processing (Ryskin et al., 2020; Levy, 2008; Clark, 2013). Human linguistic prediction can be understood as not only lexical but also as taking place both above and below the word level (Federmeier and Kutas, 1999; Federmeier et al., 2002); parallel,

i.e., predictive commitments are maintained over several linguistic units at once (Levy, 2008); and graded, i.e., commitment is licensed to varying degrees based on features of the linguistic unit being predicted. Rather than placing bets (Jackendoff, 1987) on which single word will come next, humans make many diffuse bets at multiple linguistic levels (e.g., syntactic, orthographic, lexical, etc.).

Surprisal theory (Hale, 2001; Levy, 2008) describes the utility of the approach taken by the human language processor, as lexical prediction is often an ill-constrained classification problem — for agents with very large vocabularies (LMs, humans), context is often not sufficiently constraining for high accuracy multiple, thousand-way classification decisions, but is typically constraining enough to accurately infer next-word features (such as part of speech, and semantic category). A large body of evidence demonstrates that these graded next-word predictions are reflected in human processing times (Ehrlich and Rayner, 1981; Demberg and Keller, 2008; Smith and Levy, 2013; Luke and Christianson, 2016) as well as neural responses (Kutas and Hillyard, 1980; Frank et al., 2015).

Corpus data are (imperfect) samples from the linguistic environment of a native speaker, and psycholinguistic data indicate that accurate prediction is important to efficient language comprehension. Under the principle of rational analysis (Anderson, 1990), it is thus to be expected that artificial language models trained on corpus data would correlate with human linguistic predictions and thus have good psychometric predictive accuracy. Nevertheless, past work (Smith and Levy, 2011) has suggested dissociations between corpus probabilities and human next-word estimates. Here, we further investigate this relationship using artificial language models and the most extensive corpus of sequential cloze completions that we are aware of: the Provo Corpus (Provo henceforth; Luke and

609

Proceedings of the 24th Conference on Computational Natural Language Learning, pages 609–619

Online, November 19-20, 2020. ©2020 Association for Computational Linguistics

https://doi.org/10.18653/v1/P17

Christianson, 2018).

First, we use Provo to test the psychometric performance of three state-of-the-art Transformer-based (Vaswani et al., 2017) LMs — XLNet (Yang et al., 2019), Transformer-XL (Dai et al., 2019), and GPT-2 (Radford et al., 2019) — alongside a smaller 2-layer LSTM (Hochreiter and Schmidhuber, 1997) trained on wikitext-103 (Merity et al., 2016), and a 5-gram LM baseline (Stolcke, 2002). We find that, while the Transformer models achieve the lowest perplexity on Provo and the best fit to the cloze data, the LSTM model provides the best account of reading times in terms of raw correlation. These findings show a dissociation between recapitulating corpus statistics and mimicking human language processing, operationalized here with reading times. That is, models that minimize perplexity on next-word prediction do not necessarily provide the best account of reading times. Second, based on these findings, we propose Cloze Distillation: a novel method for distilling linguistic information implicit in human cloze completions into pre-trained LMs. We apply this method to the LSTM model and show substantial improvement in reading time prediction and word frequency estimation, in addition to generalization to held-out human cloze data.

2 Human Cloze Predictions

The objective for most modern LMs is to compute a probability distribution over the model's vocabulary V for the likely next-word $x \in V$ at position i given the context $\mathbf{x}_{<i}$ consisting of the sequence of preceding words in the document. Similarly, as humans process language, they make constant and implicit linguistic predictions.

One commonly used measure of these predictions in humans is the Cloze task. In its original form (Taylor, 1953), the task involved masking a word or words in a source text passage and asking participants to provide words for the masked elements that would make the passage "whole again", a task structure adopted by contemporary masked language models (Devlin et al., 2019). In experimental psycholinguistics, however, the most common version of the Cloze task has involved presenting the beginning, or *prefix*, of a passage and having participants either complete it or provide the word that they think comes next (Figure 1), a task more closely matching that of autoregressive language models (Radford et al., 2019). In this paper, we focus on this latter type of Cloze task, which elicits samples from comprehenders' subjective next-word probability distributions (DeLong et al., 2005; Staub et al., 2015). For any given prefix, we can estimate the cloze distribution of a typical native speaker from pooled cloze responses across a large number of participants (Luke and Christianson, 2018), similar to how the fundamental output of an autoregressive language model is a vector of next-word probabilities.

2.1 The Provo Corpus

We use the Provo Corpus (Luke and Christianson, 2018) as our source of paired cloze completion and reading time data. The Provo Corpus derives from 55 paragraphs of text taken from sources including online news articles, popular science, and fiction. For each paragraph p, next-word cloze completions were elicited for each prefix $\mathbf{x}_{<i}$ for $i = 2, \dots |p|$ (2,689 sentence prefixes total). Prefixes were presented to participants ($N = 470$) as a continuous multi-line text (Figure 1). This resulted in an average of 40 cloze responses with 15 unique continuations per prefix.

Additionally, Luke and Christianson (2018) collected eye movement data from eighty-four native speakers of American English as they read these 55 text passages, using a high-resolution SR Research EyeLink 1000 eye tracker.

The Provo cloze data, eye movement data, and the relationship between them are analyzed in detail in (Luke and Christianson, 2016). Luke and Christianson (2016) point out that while context is rarely constraining enough to facilitate exact next-word prediction, modal cloze responses often constitute *partial* matches to the target words. For example, given the prefix *With schools still closed, cars still buried and streets still ...*, the true continuation, *blocked*, has a cloze probability of only 0.07. But the overwhelming majority of cloze responses are partial fits to the correct word: 79% of the responses are verbs, and 72% are inflectional matches (ended with -ed), with the two most frequent responses being *closed* and *covered* (example from Luke and Christianson, 2018). In addition, they showed that cloze probabilities are highly predictive of reading times, adding to prior work showing a word's reading time is a function of its predictability in context (e.g., Smith and Levy, 2013).

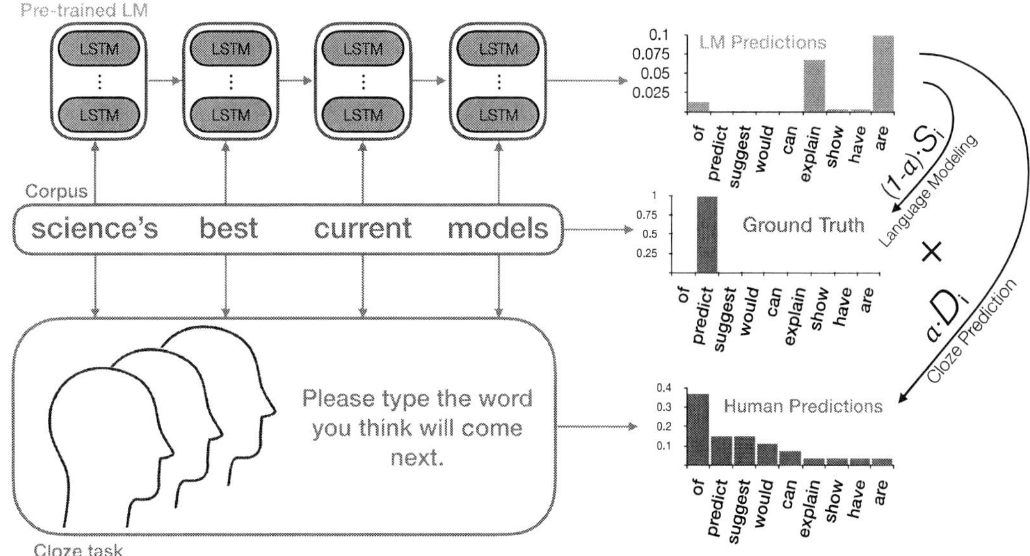

Figure 1: Illustration of the Cloze task and the Cloze Distillation objective. Given one of Provo's prefixes — in this example, one that ends in ... *science's best current models*, where the true next word (ground truth) is *predict* — human subjects were prompted, as shown in the Cloze task box, to predict the word they thought was likely to follow. The Cloze Distillation loss is constructed by combining (1) the KL divergence D_i between the human cloze distribution and the LM's next-word distribution, and (2) the LM's predicted surprisal S_i of the true next word given the prefix.

3 Testing Language Models on Provo

The findings of Luke and Christianson (2016) highlight cloze as a useful test-bed for LMs. Specifically, a LM that employs predictions similar to those that underlie human language processing is expected to be a good model of human cloze responses. Therefore, we evaluate here a suite of LMs on their ability to match human cloze distributions. Additionally, we use the LMs' ability to predict reading times as a second measure of fit to human expectations, extending past work using LMs to predict reading times (Frank and Bod, 2011; Wilcox et al., 2020).

3.1 Models

We consider in our analysis the following LMs:

1. **5-gram**: N-gram model using a window size of 5 with Kneser-Ney smoothing, obtained via the SRILM language modeling toolkit (Stolcke, 2002).

2. **LSTM**: A standard 2-layer LSTM RNN implemented in PyTorch (Paszke et al., 2017), used here with 256 hidden units and word embedding size of 256, and trained on the wikitext-103 corpus (Merity et al., 2016) via a next-word prediction task (40 epochs, batch size = 40, learning rate = 20).

3. **GPT-2**: A Transformer-based LM trained on the WebText corpus (Radford et al., 2019).

4. **Transformer-XL** (TXL; Dai et al., 2019): A Transformer-based LM with a segment level recurrence mechanism and relative positional embeddings trained on wikitext-103.

5. **XLNet** (Yang et al., 2019): A Transformer-based LM trained with a permutation language modeling objective as well as a segment level recurrence mechanism and relative positional embeddings. Training data consists of ~30 billion tokens across 6 different copora.

We use the LMzoo python package (Gauthier et al., 2020) to access the 5-gram model, and the HuggingFace transformers python package (Wolf et al., 2019) for accessing Transformer models (gpt2-large, transfo-xl-wt103, and xlnet-large-cased respectively). These Transformer models use subword tokens (Sennrich et al., 2016); we defined word probabilities for these models as the joint probability of the subword tokens comprising the word given the context.

Model	$\langle D_i \rangle$	$\langle \tau_i \rangle$	$\langle S_i \rangle$	F_{intr}	F_{base}	ρ_{gaze}	ρ_{freq}
Cloze	NA	NA	3.99 ± 2.60	198.10	30.90	0.36	-0.43
GPT-2	2.30 ± 1.57	-0.57 ± 0.004	6.11 ± 5.00	252.70	46.11	0.40	-0.46
XLNet	2.39 ± 1.68	-0.58 ± 0.005	6.39 ± 5.70	260.50	46.08	0.41	-0.48
TXL	3.27 ± 1.92	-0.47 ± 0.005	8.09 ± 5.50	238.30	30.54	0.39	-0.50
LSTM	3.74 ± 1.86	-0.39 ± 0.006	8.58 ± 4.90	361.20	41.47	0.47	-0.63
5-gram	3.89 ± 1.84	-0.20 ± 0.007	12.48 ± 7.00	161.00	16.72	0.31	-0.41

Table 1: Evaluation of LMs on Provo reveals a dissociation between performance on next-word prediction and psychometric measures that reflect human language processing. F_{intr} and F_{base} show the F-test statistics (Section 3.2.2) against various baseline predictors. ρ_{gaze} and ρ_{freq} show correlation with gaze and frequency respectively (Pearson's ρ). $\langle D_i \rangle$ is average KL-divergence between the empirical cloze distribution and the LM's distributions; $\langle \tau_i \rangle$ is rank correlation between down-sampled model surprisals and surprisal values based on the empirical cloze probabilities; $\langle S_i \rangle$ is average surprisal over the text in Provo; all standard deviations are computed by paragraph.

3.2 Metrics

We use several metrics to evaluate the fit of our models to human reading times and cloze responses. We discuss and motivate them in the following section.

3.2.1 Cloze Responses

We use two measures to evaluate the performance of each model on human cloze data. First, we measure the deviation between the empirically estimated cloze distribution, $P_{\text{cloze}}(x|\mathbf{x}_{<i})$, where x is a potential next-word at position i in a document[1] and the model's next-word distribution, $P_{\text{model}}(x|\mathbf{x}_{<i})$, using the Kullback-Leibler (KL) divergence:

$$D_i \equiv D\left[P_{\text{cloze}}(x|\mathbf{x}_{<i})\|P_{\text{model}}(x|\mathbf{x}_{<i})\right] \quad (1)$$

$$= \sum_{x \in V} P_{\text{cloze}}(x|\mathbf{x}_{<i}) \log \frac{P_{\text{cloze}}(x|\mathbf{x}_{<i})}{P_{\text{model}}(x|\mathbf{x}_{<i})} \ .$$

While the KL divergence is a natural measure for comparing distributions, it is potentially limited for our purposes due to the sparsity of the cloze data. To address this, we also consider Kendall's Tau correlation coefficient, which may be more robust to estimation errors resulting from small sample effects. Specifically, we consider Kendall's Tau correlation between LM surprisals and surprisals estimated form human cloze data, denoted here by $\tau_i \equiv \tau\left[P_{\text{cloze}}(x|\mathbf{x}_{<i}), P_{\text{model}}(x|\mathbf{x}_{<i})\right]$.

To further evaluate the models' ability to mimic cloze responses and to control for the sparsity of the human cloze data, we simulated a cloze task

experiment with our LMs. For each LM, we generated 40 cloze responses[2] per prefix $\mathbf{x}_{<i}$ in Provo by sampling from $P_{\text{model}}(x|\mathbf{x}_{<i})$. We repeated this experiment 50 times for each model. The results were similar in both the down-sampling and without-down-sampling conditions, and we report only the down-sampling condition in Table 1.

3.2.2 Reading Times

We use *gaze duration* during first-pass reading as our measure of reading times, which is the amount of time a reader's eyes spend on a word the first time they fixate it (Rayner, 1998; if a reader fixates a word to the right before fixating the word in question, the word has been "skipped" and there is no valid gaze duration). It is well established that gaze duration captures a wide variety of cognitive processes during real-time language-comprehension, including the relationship between a word and the context in which it appears (Staub, 2011).

We evaluate the ability of a LM to account for human reading times based on their predicted surprisal values,

$$S_i \equiv -\log_2 P_{\text{model}}(x_i|\mathbf{x}_{<i}) \,, \quad (2)$$

as it has been previously shown to capture several characteristics of human language comprehension and pattern with reading times (Smith and Levy, 2013; Wilcox et al., 2020). Similarly, we define cloze surprisals by taking the negative log of the empirical cloze probabilities[3], i.e.,

---

[1] As participants in Luke and Christianson (2018) were given only within-paragraph context when prompted for each cloze response, each paragraph constitutes a unique document in our analysis.

[2] We generated 40 responses because most prefixes in Provo had at least 40 responses provided by participants.

[3] We use the cloze probability estimates from Luke and Christianson (2018)'s 'Orthographic Match Model' – a logit mixed-effects model including only random by-word intercepts. These estimates are nearly perfectly correlated with the relative frequency estimate of cloze ($\rho = .999$), but crucially

$-\log_2 P_{\text{cloze}}(x_i|\mathbf{x}_{<i})$. We then measure Pearson's correlation ρ between reading times and surprisal values. In addition, we use ANOVA tests to measure the models' predictive capacities beyond standard baseline predictors of reading time (Howes and Solomon, 1951; Kliegl et al., 2006; Leyland et al., 2013) — log word frequency and word length. That is, for each model (either an LM or the cloze distribution), we enter its surprisal values into a linear mixed-effects model (LME) along with the baseline predictors, and measure their contribution by computing the F-test statistic between the full LME and an LME where model surprisals are ablated out. In the case of F_{base} the baseline predictors were frequency, length, and their interaction. In the case of F_{intr} the baseline predictors were simply random by-word intercepts. We use both word frequencies estimated from the Corpus of Contemporary American English (COCA; Davies, 2010) and from wikitext-103 (Merity et al., 2016) in our analysis. As the results of our analyses were qualitatively the same in both conditions we report only results from COCA in the analyses to follow.

3.3 Results

The main results of evaluating the LMs on Provo are summarized in Table 1. First, averaging the KL divergence and suprisals values over word positions i in Provo (that is, $\langle D_i \rangle$ and $\langle S_i \rangle$ respectively), shows that the ability of LMs to predict human cloze responses tracks with their language modeling performance. This pattern is also reflected in Kendall's τ correlation between model surprisals and surprisals constructed from the human cloze distribution. At the same time, Table 1 reveals a dissociation between next-word prediction, reflected by $\langle S_i \rangle$, and human language processing, as reflected in reading times. Specifically, the LSTM model, which does not perform as well as the Transformer-based LMs in next-word prediction on Provo, as reflected in its higher $\langle S_i \rangle$, exhibits superior ability in predicting reading times, as measured in ρ_{gaze} and F_{intr}. This result is similar to that of Merkx and Frank (2020), who found that Gated Recurrent Unit networks outperformed Transformer models with lower perplexity in predicting gaze duration.

We note that when predicting reading times not only from the model's surprisal values, but also using the baseline predictors (word frequency and

---

do not include cloze probabilities of zero (which would yield infinite surprisal).

length), the LSTM model no longer outperforms the Transformer-based models (Table 1, F_{base}). Nonetheless, it is striking that the LSTM model, which is much smaller than the Transformer-based models and was trained on much less data, achieves the best performance in predicting reading times without the baseline predictors.

3.4 Intermediate Conclusions

Past work shows that human predictions systematically diverge from corpus probabilities (Smith and Levy, 2011). Our analysis extends these findings by testing current state-of-the-art LMs trained on much larger datasets, and showing that, while better estimates of corpus probabilities may yield better models of human next-word predictions, there does not seem to be a strict positive correlation between the ability to approximate corpus probabilities and the ability to predict human reading times, as evidenced by models with higher $\langle S_i \rangle$ being on-par and even better at predicting reading times compared to models with lower $\langle S_i \rangle$.

Recent studies (Ettinger, 2020; Hao et al., 2020; Jacobs and McCarthy, 2020) have found similar trends when comparing LMs to cloze data. Hu et al. (2020) also found only a loose relationship between perplexity (a monotonic function of $\langle S_i \rangle$) and syntactic generalization, adding to a growing body of evidence suggesting that while optimizing for corpus probabilities can create somewhat psycholinguistically-enabled language models (Linzen et al., 2016; Futrell et al., 2019; Hu et al., 2020), there may be a dissociation between corpus probabilities and human expectations.

4 Cloze Distillation

Here, we show how to leverage these findings to improve the ability of LMs to match human expectations, providing more appealing neural language models for human language processing. To this end, we propose Cloze Distillation: a method for using human next-word predictions as learning targets together with corpus statistics within a knowledge distillation framework.

4.1 Knowledge Distillation

Knowledge distillation (Buciluundefined et al., 2006; Ba and Caruana, 2014; Hinton et al., 2015) is a technique of imbuing knowledge from a teacher model into a student model by training the student to make the same predictions as the teacher. Typically deployed as a form of model compression, knowledge distillation is useful for those looking to deploy insights from one or more complicated models into a single smaller model. Recently, knowledge distillation has also proven useful to cognitive scientists in creating low-dimensional neural network cognitive models (Schaeffer et al., 2020). When humans are used as the 'teacher' this can be seen as a specific case of a more general cognitive modeling strategy, task-based modeling.

4.2 The Cloze Distillation Objective

Knowledge distillation has proven its usefulness in NLP where researchers have distilled knowledge from very large and/or syntactically aware language models into naive models showing it is possible to transfer even subtle linguistic preferences from teacher to student (Kim and Rush, 2016; Kuncoro et al., 2019; Sanh et al., 2020; Kuncoro et al., 2020).

We take inspiration from this work and leverage the general framework both as a method for distilling knowledge from a 'teacher' with desirable linguistic biases (humans in our case) and as a tool for cognitive modeling by using empirical cloze distributions P_{cloze} as target distributions in a knowledge distillation framework.

We follow this approach to arrive at the following loss function for Cloze Distillation (CD):

$$L_i = \alpha D_i - (1 - \alpha) S_i. \qquad (3)$$

That is, for each context $\mathbf{x}_{<i}$ we compute the CD loss by linearly interpolating D_i, the KL divergence between the distributions of the human teacher and the student model as defined in equation (1), with an autoregressive language modeling objective that places unit probability mass on the true next-word, formally defined by S_i in equation (2). Thus, CD fine-tunes LMs to predict the next word in the document while simultaneously producing a distribution over next-words that mirrors the empirical human cloze distribution for that context. This process is illustrated in Figure 1.

To evaluate the utility of the human cloze data, we vary the values of α from $\alpha = 0$, which corresponds to pure next-word prediction driven fine-tuning, to $\alpha = 1$, which corresponds to pure cloze-prediction based fine-tuning.

4.3 Cloze-Distilled LSTM

To begin to evaluate the CD paradigm, we apply it to the LSTM from Section 3 by fine-tuning this model using the CD objective over Provo. To test generalization and utilize the full corpus, we use a k-fold cross-validation scheme with $k = 55$, the number of paragraphs in Provo where humans are provided the full preceding paragraph as context. That is, each fold consists of data from one paragraph in the Provo dataset. We use 100 epochs for training. We provide our LM with the same context as humans, up to the beginning of the current paragraph.

Additionally, we vary α to test the utility of our cloze data and cross-validated separately for each value of α in the range $[0, 1]$, sampled at intervals of 0.05. This resulted in 1,155 unique models for testing. We wish to emphasize that even utilizing the entire Provo corpus via cross-validation, we are left with only 2685 training samples, which is minuscule with respect to the model's pre-training data (roughly 100 million samples). We refer to the resultant model as cloze-distilled LSTM (CD-LSTM).

4.4 Results

After fine-tuning on the CD objective, we note several interesting adaptions in model behavior. These mainly include significant improvement over the standard LSTM baseline in predicting human reading times and cloze distributions (Figure 2). We also discuss improvements in next-word prediction performance over Provo (Figure 3).

4.4.1 Reading times

Psychometric predictive capacity is starkly improved with Cloze Distillation, and the strength of the effect scales with α. This can be seen in Figure 2, which shows the statistical comparison of the CD-LSTM for varying levels of α. We add another model comparison designed to isolate the ability of CD-LSTM to predict reading times above the standard LSTM (Figure 2a). Specifically, we enter CD-LSTM's surprisals into an LME along with baseline predictors and surprisals from the standard LSTM and compute the F-test statistic against a LME with CD-LSTM surprisal ablated out.

CD-LSTM exhibits a significant improvement with α in its ability to predict reading times above the non-fine-tuned model (Figure 2a), as well as

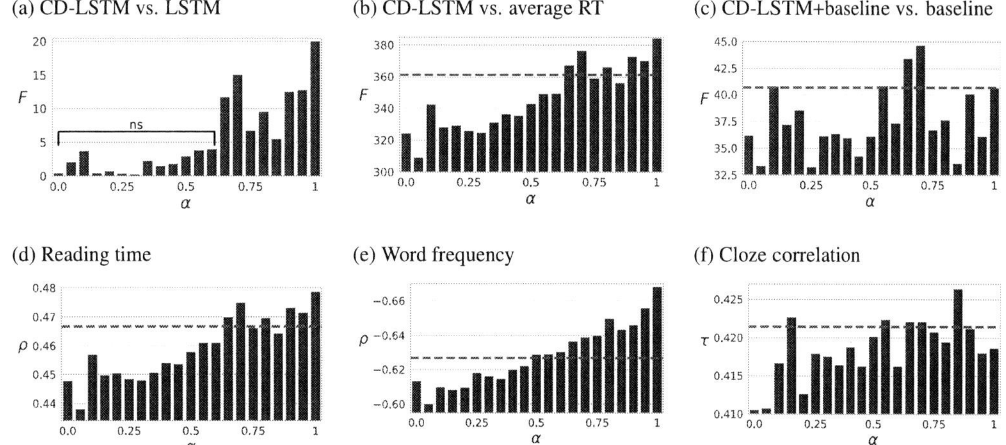

Figure 2: Results for CD-LSTM and the LSTM model (without any fine tuning) show that Cloze Distillation yields substantial improvement across several psychometric measures. Panels (a)-(c) show changes in F statistics as a function of α for three LME comparisons, and panels (d)-(f) show changes in three correlational measures. Dashed lines in panels (b)-(f) show the performance of the LSTM model. (a) LME based on CD-LSTM's surprisals outperforms the LME based on the LSTM's surprisals for most values of α (not significant for $\alpha < 0.65$). (b) LME based on CD-LSTM's surprisals outperforms the null (intercept only) model, and this performance generally improves with α. (c) LME based on CD-LSTM's surprisals with the baseline factors (word frequency and length) outperforms the baseline-only LME for several values of α. (d) Pearson's correlation between CD-LSTM's surprisals and reading times. (e) Pearson's correlation between CD-LSTM's surprisals and word frequencies. (f) Kendall's τ correlation between CD-LSTM's surprisals and human cloze surprisals.

improvements over an intercept-only model (Figure 2b) and baseline-only (Figure 2c). Correlation with reading time and CD-LSTM's surprisal also steadily increases with α (Figure 2d). These findings suggest that, as we postulate, Cloze Distillation is a useful paradigm for extracting the information about human linguistic expectations that is implicit in human cloze predictions and incorporating it into LMs.

4.4.2 Cloze

We report improvements in predicting held out cloze data, where $\langle D_i \rangle$ is decreased from 3.8 (at $\alpha = 0$) to 3.6 (at $\alpha = 0.65$) (Figure 3). τ correlation also exceeds that of the baseline model for several values of α (though there does not seem to be a consistent trend across α-s).

This result is intriguing as it implies that the requisite information for computing cloze distributions is learned over fine-tuning. Furthermore, we see a peak at $\alpha = 0.65$ and not at $\alpha = 1$, which suggests that in training LMs to predict cloze data, some signal from next-word prediction remains vital.

4.4.3 Language modeling

In addition to improved performance on our human language processing benchmarks, we see a robust increase in language modeling performance for most values of α, as evidenced by average surprisal over Provo (Figure 3). We note, the standard deviation in $\langle S_i \rangle$ for our LSTM over Provo was 1.86 bits (Table 1). The improvements we see are less than this deviation, and are thusly below the level of significance, though we do see a consistent trend in α. This effect is most substantial for intermediate values of α, suggesting that a combination of human knowledge and next-word prediction improves relative to either one of these factors on its own. This indicates that both parts of the loss function (ground truth next-words, human cloze) provide useful information for predicting text that is not entirely overlapping.

This is interesting given the low $\langle S_i \rangle$ of human cloze data. The fact that humans can contend with large language models trained explicitly on next-word prediction even on subsets of text, together with our Cloze Distillation results suggests there is linguistic information in human cloze that can be harnessed by LMs to subserve general language

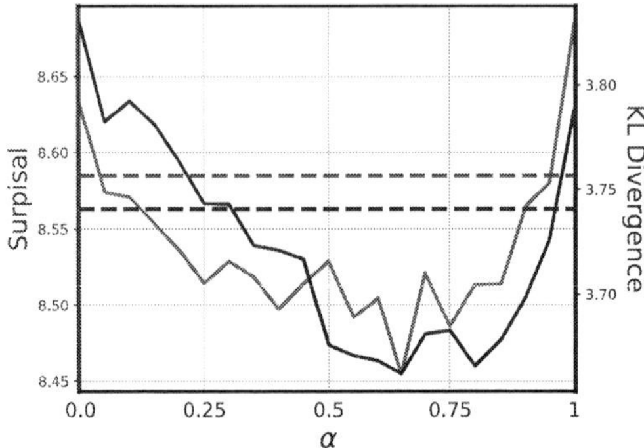

Figure 3: Average Surprisal (left) and KL divergence (right) over Provo as a function of the distillation interpolation coefficient α. Dashed lines show LSTM performance before fine-tuning.

modeling and is disjoint from the information accessible in corpus probability (Smith and Levy, 2011).

4.4.4 Frequency

We also note that as α increases, the CD-LSTM next-word predictions exhibit increased correlation with frequency (Figure 2e), suggesting that cloze distilled LMs may learn to better predict frequent words. This is interesting as a proof of concept that Cloze Distillation distills information implicit in cloze into language models as previous work (Smith and Levy, 2011) has shown human cloze is skewed toward more frequent words, relative to corpus probability.

5 Conclusion

Our analyses provide further evidence of a misalignment between language model estimates and human expectations. The method we provide: Cloze Distillation, demonstrates that shifting training incentives away from corpus probability toward psycholinguistic task-based modeling can result in better cognitive models and better language models. Still, given several of our models predict reading times beyond the cloze data collected in Provo (Table 1) there are several possible explanations for the effect Cloze Distillation has on language model performance.

One is that the Cloze task produces data that are a more faithful reflection of the expectations deployed in human reading and are thus able to guide the models toward a fundamentally more human-like set of expectations – despite being under-sampled. If this is true and human subjec-

tive next-word estimates also provide signal about next-word probabilities across corpora (reflecting the implicit knowledge speakers have learned about the statistics of their language), this would explain why Cloze Distillation improves next-word prediction accuracy on a new corpus (Provo).

Another possibility is that the models we survey are fundamentally better than the cloze data at capturing the human expectations deployed in reading. Though this would not explain the boost in performance we see in reading time prediction with Cloze Distillation, because several of our models predict reading times better than the cloze data itself, this can not yet be ruled out. We leave the further exploration of this to future work as larger-scale collection of human cloze data allows.

That said, the fact that we were able to induce appreciable adaptions in model behavior with such little data highlights the richly orienting information available in even noisy human predictions. Though it is unclear how language users learn to make such sophisticated predictions (we provided this information to our model with direct supervision), our model's ability to learn from such small scale data highlights the potential utility of such predictions in a language acquisition setting — it seems that human predictions are strong enough to significantly bolster the signal in raw linguistic input abetting extensive adaption from relatively little data.

As of now, the current dataset's scale restricts Cloze Distillation to use as a fine-tuning method. Furthermore, we use simple LSTMs to perform a detailed analysis of Cloze Distillation with dense sampling in α and thorough cross-validation. It is possible that deploying Cloze Distillation during pre-training in large models (e.g., Transformers) could result in models better able to learn the word features humans demonstrate knowledge of in their cloze responses and we leave the exploration of this to future work as well.

Methods such as Cloze Distillation provide an avenue forward for psycholinguists interested in taking LMs seriously as candidate models of human language processing and to natural language processing researchers interested in reverse engineering and deploying insights from human sentence processing. Cloze Distillation highlights these goals as potentially mutually-reinforcing.

6 Acknowledgements

TNE was supported by the GEM consortium and the MIT Dean of Sciences Fellowship. NZ was supported by an MIT BCS Fellowship in Computation. RPL was supported by NSF grant IIS1815529, a Google Faculty Research Award, and a Newton Brain Science Award. We thank Robert Chen for helping collect model surprisals, as well as Peng Qian and Jon Gauthier for helpful discussions.

References

John R. Anderson. 1990. *The Adaptive Character of Human Thought*. Hillsdale, NJ: Lawrence Erlbaum.

Jimmy Ba and Rich Caruana. 2014. Do Deep Nets Really Need to be Deep? In *Advances in Neural Information Processing Systems 27*, pages 2654–2662.

Cristian Buciluundefined, Rich Caruana, and Alexandru Niculescu-Mizil. 2006. Model Compression. In *Proceedings of the 12th ACM SIGKDD International Conference on Knowledge Discovery and Data Mining*, KDD, page 535–541, New York, NY, USA. Association for Computing Machinery.

Andy Clark. 2013. Whatever Next? Predictive Brains, Situated Agents, and the Future of Cognitive Science. *Brain and Behavioral Sciences*, 36(3):181–204.

Zihang Dai, Zhilin Yang, Yiming Yang, Jaime Carbonell, Quoc Le, and Ruslan Salakhutdinov. 2019. Transformer-XL: Attentive language models beyond a fixed-length context. In *Proceedings of the 57th Annual Meeting of the Association for Computational Linguistics*, pages 2978–2988, Florence, Italy. Association for Computational Linguistics.

Mark Davies. 2010. The Corpus of Contemporary American English as the First Reliable Monitor Corpus of English. *Literary and Linguistic Computing*, 25(4):447–464.

Katherine A DeLong, Thomas P Urbach, and Marta Kutas. 2005. Probabilistic Word Pre-Activation During Language Comprehension Inferred from Electrical Brain Activity. *Nature Neuroscience*, 8(8):1117–1121.

Vera Demberg and Frank Keller. 2008. Data from Eye-tracking Corpora as Evidence for Theories of Syntactic Processing Complexity. *Cognition*, 109(2):193–210.

Jacob Devlin, Ming-Wei Chang, Kenton Lee, and Kristina Toutanova. 2019. BERT: Pre-training of deep bidirectional transformers for language understanding. In *Proceedings of the 2019 Conference of the North American Chapter of the Association for Computational Linguistics: Human Language Technologies, Volume 1 (Long and Short Papers)*, pages 4171–4186, Minneapolis, Minnesota. Association for Computational Linguistics.

Susan F. Ehrlich and Keith Rayner. 1981. Contextual Effects on Word Perception and Eye Movements During Reading. *Journal of Verbal Learning and Verbal Behavior*, 20(6):641 – 655.

Allyson Ettinger. 2020. What BERT is not: Lessons from a New Suite of Psycholinguistic Diagnostics for Language Models. *Transactions of the Association for Computational Linguistics*, 8:34–48.

Kara D Federmeier and Marta Kutas. 1999. A Rose by Any Other Name: Long-Term Memory Structure and Sentence Processing. *Journal of Memory and Language*, 41(4):469–495.

Kara D Federmeier, Devon B McLennan, Esmeralda De Ochoa, and Marta Kutas. 2002. The Impact of Semantic Memory Organization and Sentence Context Information on Spoken Language Processing by Younger and Older Adults: an ERP Study. *Psychophysiology*, 39(2):133–146.

Victoria Fossum and Roger Levy. 2012. Sequential vs. Hierarchical Syntactic Models of Human Incremental Sentence Processing. In *Proceedings of the 3rd Workshop on Cognitive Modeling and Computational Linguistics (CMCL 2012)*, pages 61–69, Montréal, Canada. Association for Computational Linguistics.

Stefan L Frank and Rens Bod. 2011. Insensitivity of the Human Sentence-processing System to Hierarchical Structure. *Psychological Science*, 22(6):829–834.

Stefan L Frank, Leun J Otten, Giulia Galli, and Gabriella Vigliocco. 2015. The ERP Response to the Amount of Information Conveyed by Words in Sentences. *Brain and Language*, 140:1–11.

Richard Futrell, Ethan Wilcox, Takashi Morita, Peng Qian, Miguel Ballesteros, and Roger Levy. 2019. Neural Language Models as Psycholinguistic Subjects: Representations of Syntactic State. In *Proceedings of the 2019 Conference of the North American Chapter of the Association for Computational Linguistics: Human Language Technologies, Volume 1 (Long and Short Papers)*, pages 32–42, Minneapolis, Minnesota. Association for Computational Linguistics.

Jon Gauthier, Jennifer Hu, Ethan Wilcox, Peng Qian, and Roger Levy. 2020. SyntaxGym: An Online Platform for Targeted Evaluation of Language Models. In *Proceedings of the 58th Annual Meeting of the Association for Computational Linguistics: System Demonstrations*, pages 70–76, Online. Association for Computational Linguistics.

Adam Goodkind and Klinton Bicknell. 2018. Predictive Power of Word Surprisal for Reading Times is a Linear Function of Language Model Quality. In

Proceedings of the 8th Workshop on Cognitive Modeling and Computational Linguistics (CMCL 2018), pages 10–18, Salt Lake City, Utah. Association for Computational Linguistics.

John Hale. 2001. A Probabilistic Earley Parser as a Psycholinguistic Model. In *Second Meeting of the North American Chapter of the Association for Computational Linguistics*.

John Hale, Chris Dyer, Adhiguna Kuncoro, and Jonathan Brennan. 2018. Finding Syntax in Human Encephalography with Beam Search. In *Proceedings of the 56th Annual Meeting of the Association for Computational Linguistics (Volume 1: Long Papers)*, pages 2727–2736, Melbourne, Australia. Association for Computational Linguistics.

Yiding Hao, Simon Mendelsohn, Rachel Sterneck, Randi Martinez, and Robert Frank. 2020. Probabilistic Predictions of People Perusing: Evaluating Metrics of Language Model Performance for Psycholinguistic Modeling. *arXiv preprint arXiv:2009.03954*.

Geoffrey Hinton, Oriol Vinyals, and Jeffrey Dean. 2015. Distilling the Knowledge in a Keural Network. In *Deep Learning and Representation Learning Workshop at NuerIPS*.

Sepp Hochreiter and Jürgen Schmidhuber. 1997. Long Short-Term Memory. *Neural Computation*, 9(8):1735–1780.

D.H. Howes and R.L. Solomon. 1951. Visual duration threshold as a function of word-probability. *Journal of Experimental Psychology*, 41(6):401—410.

Jennifer Hu, Jon Gauthier, Peng Qian, Ethan Wilcox, and Roger Levy. 2020. A Systematic Assessment of Syntactic Generalization in Neural Language Models. In *Proceedings of the 58th Annual Meeting of the Association for Computational Linguistics*, pages 1725–1744, Online. Association for Computational Linguistics.

Yi Ting Huang and Jesse Snedeker. 2013. The Use of Lexical and Referential Cues in Children's Online Interpretation of Adjectives. *Developmental Psychology*, 49(6):1090–1102.

Ray Jackendoff. 1987. *Consciousness and the Computational Mind*, volume 356. The MIT Press, Cambridge, MA.

Cassandra L. Jacobs and Arya D. McCarthy. 2020. The Human Unlikeness of Neural Language Models in Next-word Prediction. In *Proceedings of the The Fourth Widening Natural Language Processing Workshop*, page 115, Seattle, USA. Association for Computational Linguistics.

Yoon Kim and Alexander M. Rush. 2016. Sequence-Level Knowledge Distillation. In *Proceedings of the 2016 Conference on Empirical Methods in Natural Language Processing*, pages 1317–1327, Austin, Texas. Association for Computational Linguistics.

Reinhold Kliegl, Antje Nuthmann, and Ralf Engbert. 2006. Tracking the Mind During Reading: The Influence of Past, Present, and Future Words on Fixation Durations. *Journal of Experimental Psychology*, 135:12–35.

Patricia K Kuhl. 2004. Early Language Acquisition: Cracking the Speech Code. *Nature Reviews Neuroscience*, 5(11):831–843.

Adhiguna Kuncoro, Chris Dyer, Laura Rimell, Stephen Clark, and Phil Blunsom. 2019. Scalable Syntax-Aware Language Models Using Knowledge Distillation. In *Proceedings of the 57th Annual Meeting of the Association for Computational Linguistics*, pages 3472–3484, Florence, Italy. Association for Computational Linguistics.

Adhiguna Kuncoro, Lingpeng Kong, Daniel Fried, Dani Yogatama, Laura Rimell, Chris Dyer, and Phil Blunsom. 2020. Syntactic Structure Distillation Pretraining for Bidirectional Encoders. *arXiv preprint arXiv:2005.13482*.

Marta Kutas and Steven A. Hillyard. 1980. Reading senseless sentences: Brain potentials reflect semantic incongruity. *Science*, 207(4427):203–205.

Roger Levy. 2008. Expectation-based syntactic comprehension. *Cognition*, 106(3):1126–1177.

Louise-Ann Leyland, Julie A. Kirkby, Barbara J. Juhasz, Alexander Pollatsek, and Simon P. Liversedge. 2013. The Influence of Word Shading and Word Length on Eye Movements During Reading. *Quarterly Journal of Experimental Psychology*, 66(3):471–486. PMID: 21988376.

Tal Linzen, Emmanuel Dupoux, and Yoav Goldberg. 2016. Assessing the ability of LSTMs to Learn Syntax-Sensitive Dependencies. *Transactions of the Association for Computational Linguistics*, 4:521–535.

Steven G. Luke and Kiel Christianson. 2016. Limits on Lexical Prediction During Reading. *Cognitive Psychology*, 88:22 – 60.

Steven G. Luke and Kiel Christianson. 2018. The Provo Corpus: A Large Eye-Tracking Corpus with Predictability Norms. *Behavior Research Methods*, 50(2):826–833.

Stephen Merity, Caiming Xiong, James Bradbury, and Richard Socher. 2016. Pointer Sentinel Mixture Models. *arXiv preprint arXiv:1609.07843*.

Danny Merkx and Stefan L Frank. 2020. Comparing Transformers and RNNs on Predicting Human Sentence Processing Data. *arXiv preprint arXiv:2005.09471*.

Adam Paszke, Sam Gross, Soumith Chintala, Gregory Chanan, Edward Yang, Zachary DeVito, Zeming Lin, Alban Desmaison, Luca Antiga, and Adam

Lerer. 2017. Automatic Differentiation in Py-Torch. *Neural Information Processing Systems Autodiff Workshop.*

Alec Radford, Jeffrey Wu, Rewon Child, David Luan, Dario Amodei, and Ilya Sutskever. 2019. Language Models are Unsupervised Multitask Learners. *OpenAI Blog*, 1(8):9.

Keith Rayner. 1998. Eye Movements in Reading and Information Processing: 20 Years of Research. *Psychological Bulletin*, 124(3):372–422.

Rachel Ryskin, Roger P Levy, and Evelina Fedorenko. 2020. Do Domain-General Executive Resources Play a Role in Linguistic Prediction? Re-evaluation of the Evidence and a Path Forward. *Neuropsychologia*, 136:107258.

Victor Sanh, Lysandre Debut, Julien Chaumond, and Thomas Wolf. 2020. DistilBert, a Distilled Version of BERT:Smaller, Faster, Cheaper and Lighter. *arXiv preprint arXiv:1910.01108.*

Rylan Schaeffer, Mikail Khona, Leenoy Meshulam, and Ila Rani Fiete. 2020. Reverse-engineering Recurrent Neural Network Solutions to a Hierarchical Inference Task for Mice. *bioRxiv.*

Marten van Schijndel and Tal Linzen. 2018. Modeling Garden Path Effects without Explicit Hierarchical Syntax. In *Proceedings of the 40th Annual Meeting of the Cognitive Science Society*, pages 2600–2605, Austin, Texas. Cognitive Science.

Rico Sennrich, Barry Haddow, and Alexandra Birch. 2016. Improving neural machine translation models with monolingual data. In *Proceedings of the 54th Annual Meeting of the Association for Computational Linguistics (Volume 1: Long Papers)*, pages 86–96, Berlin, Germany. Association for Computational Linguistics.

Nathaniel Smith and Roger Levy. 2011. Cloze but no Cigar: The Complex Relationship between Cloze, Corpus, and Subjective Probabilities in Language Processing. *Proceedings of the Annual Meeting of the Cognitive Science Society*, 33(33).

Nathaniel J Smith and Roger Levy. 2013. The Effect of Word Predictability on Reading Time is Logarithmic. *Cognition*, 128(3):302–319.

Adrian Staub. 2011. Word Recognition and Syntactic Attachment in Reading: Evidence for a Staged Architecture. *Journal of Experimental Psychology. General*, 140(3):407.

Adrian Staub, Margaret Grant, Lori Astheimer, and Andrew Cohen. 2015. The Influence of Cloze Probability and Item Constraint on Cloze Task Response Time. *Journal of Memory and Language*, 82:1 – 17.

Andreas Stolcke. 2002. SRILM - an Extensible Language Modeling Toolkit. In *Seventh international conference on spoken language processing.*

W. L. Taylor. 1953. "Cloze Procedure": A New tool for Measuring Readability. *Journalism Quarterly*, 30:415.

Ashish Vaswani, Noam Shazeer, Niki Parmar, Jakob Uszkoreit, Llion Jones, Aidan N Gomez, Ł ukasz Kaiser, and Illia Polosukhin. 2017. Attention is All You Need. In I. Guyon, U. V. Luxburg, S. Bengio, H. Wallach, R. Fergus, S. Vishwanathan, and R. Garnett, editors, *Advances in Neural Information Processing Systems 30*, pages 5998–6008. Curran Associates, Inc.

Alex Warstadt and Samuel R Bowman. 2020. Can Neural Networks Acquire a Structural Bias from Raw Linguistic Data? In *Proceedings of the 2020 Conference of the Cognitive Science Society*, pages 1737–1743.

Ethan Gotlieb Wilcox, Jon Gauthier, Jennifer Hu, Peng Qian, and Roger P. Levy. 2020. On the Predictive Power of Neural Language Models for Human Real-Time Comprehension Behavior. In *Proceedings of the 2020 Conference of the Cognitive Science Society*, pages 1707–1713.

Thomas Wolf, Lysandre Debut, Victor Sanh, Julien Chaumond, Clement Delangue, Anthony Moi, Pierric Cistac, Tim Rault, Rémi Louf, Morgan Funtowicz, Joe Davison, Sam Shleifer, Patrick von Platen, Clara Ma, Yacine Jernite, Julien Plu, Canwen Xu, Teven Le Scao, Sylvain Gugger, Mariama Drame, Quentin Lhoest, and Alexander M Rush. 2019. HuggingFace's Transformers: State-of-the-Art Natural Language Processing. *arXiv e-prints*, page arXiv:1910.03771.

Zhilin Yang, Zihang Dai, Yiming Yang, Jaime Carbonell, Russ R Salakhutdinov, and Quoc V Le. 2019. XLNet: Generalized Autoregressive Pretraining for Language Understanding. In *Advances in neural information processing systems*, pages 5753–5763.

Disentangling dialects: a neural approach to Indo-Aryan historical phonology and subgrouping

Chundra A. Cathcart[1,2] **and Taraka Rama**[3]

[1]Department of Comparative Language Science, University of Zurich
[2]Center for the Interdisciplinary Study of Language Evolution, University of Zurich
[3]Department of Linguistics, University of North Texas
`chundra.cathcart@uzh.ch`, `taraka.kasicheyanula@unt.edu`

Abstract

This paper seeks to uncover patterns of sound change across Indo-Aryan languages using an LSTM encoder-decoder architecture. We augment our models with embeddings representing language ID, part of speech, and other features such as word embeddings. We find that a highly augmented model shows highest accuracy in predicting held-out forms, and investigate other properties of interest learned by our models' representations. We outline extensions to this architecture that can better capture variation in Indo-Aryan sound change.

1 Introduction

The Indo-Aryan languages, comprising Sanskrit (otherwise known as Old Indo-Aryan, or OIA) and its descendant languages, including medieval languages like Pāli and modern languages such as Hindi/Urdu, Panjabi, and Bangla, form a well-studied subgroup of the Indo-European language family. At the same time, many aspects of the Indo-Aryan languages' history remain poorly understood. One reason is that there are large historical gaps in the attestation of Indo-Aryan languages, making it challenging to document when certain shared innovations took place. Additionally, while the operation of sound changes are a diagnostic for subgrouping that historical linguistic often employ, Indo-Aryan languages have remained in close contact for millennia, borrowing words from each other and making it difficult to establish subgroup-defining sound laws using the traditional comparative method of historical linguistics.

While a number of large digitized multilingual resources pertaining to the Indo-Aryan languages exist, these data sets have not been widely used in studies, and our understanding of Indo-Aryan dialectology stands to benefit greatly from the application of deep learning techniques. This paper

seeks to move further towards closing this gap. We use an LSTM-based encoder-decoder architecture to analyze a large data set of OIA etyma (ancestral forms) and medieval/modern Indo-Aryan reflexes (descendant forms) extracted from a digitized etymological dictionary, with the goal of inferring patterns of sound change from input/output string pairs. We use language embeddings with the goal of capturing individual languages' historical phonological behavior. We augment this basic model with additional embeddings that may help in capturing irregular patterns of sound change not captured by language embeddings; additionally, we compare the performance of these models against a baseline model that is embedding-free.

We evaluate the performance of models with different embeddings by assessing the accuracy with which held-out forms in medieval/modern Indo-Aryan languages are predicted on the basis of the OIA etyma from which they descend, and carry out a linguistically informed error analysis. We provide a quantitative evaluation of the degree of agreement between the genetic signal of each model's embeddings and a reference taxonomy of the Indo-Aryan languages. We find that a model with embeddings representing data points' language ID, part of speech, semantic profile and etymon ID predicts held-out forms that are closest to the ground truth forms, but that a tree constructed from language embeddings learned by this model shows lower agreement with a reference taxonomy of Indo-Aryan than a tree constructed on the basis of a model with only language embeddings, and that in general, the ability of our models to recapitulate uncontroversial genetic signal is mixed. Finally, we carry out experiments designed to investigate the information captured by specific embeddings used in our models; we find that our models learn meaningful information from augmented representations, and outline directions for future research.

Proceedings of the 24th Conference on Computational Natural Language Learning, pages 620–630
Online, November 19-20, 2020. ©2020 Association for Computational Linguistics
https://doi.org/10.18653/v1/P17

2 Background: Indo-Aryan dialectology

Despite a long history of scholarship, there is no general consensus regarding the subgrouping of Indo-Aryan languages comparable to that regarding other branches of Indo-European, such as Slavic or Germanic. Scholars argue for a core-periphery (Hoernle, 1880; Grierson, 1967 [1903-28]; Southworth, 2005; Zoller, 2016) or East-West split between the languages (Montaut, 2009, 2017), or are agnostic to the higher-order subgrouping of Indo-Aryan, given the many challenges involved in establishing such groups (for discussion, see Southworth 1964; Jeffers 1976; Masica 1991; Toulmin 2009). Disagreement between these groups stems largely from the fact that the different hypotheses are based on different linguistic features, and there is no agreed upon way in which to establish that individual features shared across languages are inherited from a common ancestor rather than due to parallel innovation. The traditional comparative method of historical linguistics (Hoenigswald, 1960; Weiss, 2015) tends to establish linguistic subgroups on the basis of innovations in morphology as well as shared sound changes, some of which are thought to be unlikely to operate independently. Indeed, many scholars have agreed that Indo-Aryan subgrouping should be established according to sound change; however, the establishment of regular sound changes has proved challenging given the high degree of irregularity in the data (Masica, 1991). Our method has the potential to detect regularities and bear on the questions described above.

3 Related work

Traditional computational dialectology (Kessler, 1995; Nerbonne and Heeringa, 2001) identifies dialect clusters using edit distance; more recent work uses neural architectures for dialect classification based on social media data for languages such as English (Rahimi et al., 2017b,a) and German (Hovy and Purschke, 2018). Computational methods have been applied to the related field of historical linguistics to identify cognates (words that go back to a common ancestor) and infer relationships between languages (Rama et al., 2018) as well as the reconstruction of ancestral words through Bayesian methods (Bouchard-Côté et al., 2013), gated neural networks (Meloni et al., 2019) and non-neural sequence labeling methods (Ciobanu and Dinu, 2020).

Other recent work infers language embeddings from large parallel corpora using different neural architectures (Östling and Tiedemann, 2017; Johnson et al., 2017; Tiedemann, 2018; Rabinovich et al., 2017). These embeddings tend to produce hierarchical clustering configurations that are close to the language classification trees inferred from historical linguistic research. These claims have been tested by Bjerva et al. (2019) who find that the distances between learned language representations may not be reflective of genetic relationship but of structural similarity. It is not always straightforward to interpret the sources of differentiation among these embeddings; typically, embeddings based on synchronic patterns of language use in corpora may be due to word order patterns, phonotactic patterns, or a number of other interrelated language-specific distributions. Cathcart and Wandl (2020) investigate the patterns of sound change captured by a neural encoder-decoder architecture trained on Proto-Slavic and contemporary Slavic word forms, and find that embeddings dispay at least partial genetic signal, but also note a negative relationship between overall model accuracy and the degree to which embeddings reflect the *communis opinio* subgrouping of Slavic.

4 Data and rationale for model design

We use data from an etymological dictionary of the Indo-Aryan languages (Turner, 1962–1966).[1] We extract OIA etyma and their corresponding reflexes in medieval and modern Indo-Aryan languages (e.g., OIA *vākya* 'speech, words' develops to Pāli *vākya*, Kashmiri *wākh*, etc.). As the traditional Indological orthography used to transcribe forms in the dictionary is phonemic, we retain this representation and convert characters with diacritics to a Normalization Form Canonical Decomposition (NFD) Unicode representation in order to reduce the number of input and output character types. Additionally, we extract glosses provided for OIA etyma (at the time of writing, the extraction of reflex glosses cannot be straightforwardly automated due to the unstructured nature of the markup language, plus the absence of glosses for certain reflexes). We match languages in the dictionary with the closest matching glottocode from the Glottolog database (Hammarström et al., 2017), and omit languages with fewer than 100 entries. This results in a data set of 82431 forms in 61 languages; the number of

---

[1] Online at `https://dsalsrv04.uchicago.edu/dictionaries/soas/`

forms in each language can be seen in Table 1. The most frequent language is the medieval language Prakrit, followed by Hindi, the medieval language Pāli, Marathi, and Panjabi.

As mentioned above, a goal of this study is to employ language embeddings in a neural model in order to capture language-level regularities in sound change from which genetic information can be extracted. However, there are many factors in our data set that lead to irregularity in sound change. Some irregularity is due to contact between Indo-Aryan languages (Turner, 1975 [1967]) as well as analogical change; other instances of irregularity are due to artifacts of the way that data are presented in the etymological dictionary. A key source of systematic morphological non-congruence is the fact that for verbal forms, the OIA third-person present singular is often paired with modern Indo-Aryan infinitives. For instance, OIA *vaśati* 'wishes, wills' is paired with reflexes such as Assamese *bahāiba* (non-cognate verbal endings are in bold), whereas a non-verbal form with a similar ending, OIA *ūnaviṁśati* 'nineteen', is paired with reflexes such as Assamese *unaix*, which does not contain a morphological mismatch. We do not wish for our our system to learn that the first pattern is a sound change. For this reason we code OIA etyma according to whether or not they are verbal, potentially allowing our system to disentangle morphological mismatches from legitimate sound changes.

A more interesting and poorly understood point (that is not merely an artifact of the data) is that etyma with certain semantic profiles may be more prone to certain analogical changes. For instance, nouns of certain semantic fields may be more likely to receive a diminutive suffix, which may then be reanalyzed as part of the noun stem; additionally, semantically related nouns are known to undergo analogical contamination (Malkiel, 1962) or develop specific patterns of sound symbolism (Carling and Johansson, 2014; Blasi et al., 2016). Finally, particular etyma may favor a particular "prototype" showing specific patterns of sound change. An example of this phenomenon can be seen in reflexes of OIA *vismarati* 'forgets'. OIA *sm* usually changes to *m(h)* or *s(s)* in descendant languages; however, only one reflex of *vismarati* shows *m(h)* (Prakrit *vimharai*), while the rest show *s(s)*. It is possible that an early variant *visarati* was diffused among neighboring dialects and an early date. All in all, while we do not explicitly model contact,

accounting for the factors described above can improve model accuracy and allow us to tease apart legitimate patterns of sound change from orthogonal factors.

In order to achieve this goal, we augment a basic model using language embeddings with different embedding types designed to account for idiosyncrasies of data collection as well as potential real-world sources of irregularity like those described above. We make use of embeddings that represent the part of speech (POS) of the OIA etymon. Additionally, we represent the semantic profile of each OIA etymon by generating embeddings of each etymon's English language gloss using a pretrained BERT model (Devlin et al., 2019; Wolf et al., 2019), though this approach does not fully encapsulate the OIA word's semantics. Finally, we wish to take into account idiosyncratic patterns displayed by individual etyma (such as *vismarati*, as discussed above). A one-hot encoding of etymon IDs is costly, as there are 13580 unique etyma in our dataset; instead, we combine information from BERT embeddings and the input string in order to produce a unique embedding for each etymon in the data set. In sum, these augmentations provide a way for our model to disentangle the orthogonal forces of sound change and other factors.

5 Model

Our experiments use an LSTM Encoder-Decoder with 0th-order nonmonotonic hard attention (Wu and Cotterell, 2019). The authors' architecture works as follows: for each input x (for our purposes an OIA etymon), a latent representation $h_j^{\text{enc}} \in \mathbb{R}^{2D}$ is learned for each time step $j \in \{1, ..., |x|\}$ via a bidirectional LSTM on the basis of the input symbol at time step j. For each output y (for our purposes a medieval/modern Indo-Aryan reflex), a latent representation $h_i^{\text{dec}} \in \mathbb{R}^D$ is learned via a forward LSTM for each time step $i \in \{1, ..., |y|\}$ on the basis of the output symbol at time step $i - 1$. The probability that the output is aligned with the jth input symbol at time i is equal to softmax($h_i^{\text{dec}\top} T h_j^{\text{enc}}$), where $T \in \mathbb{R}^{D \times 2D}$ is a learned parameter. The emission probability of the output symbol at time i given such an alignment is proportional to $\exp(W \tanh(S[h_i^{\text{dec}}; h_j^{\text{enc}}]))$, and is hence also dependent on the previous output symbols ($W \in \mathbb{R}^{\Sigma_y \times 3D}$ and $S \in \mathbb{R}^{3D \times 3D}$ are learned parameters). Structural zeros are used in order to ensure that the alignment between the input and

Language	Glottocode	N
Prakrit(Maharashtri)	maha1305	8118
Hindi	hind1269	5948
Pali	pali1273	5225
Marathi	mara1378	4895
EasternPanjabi	panj1256	4622
Gujarati	guja1252	4490
Sindhi	sind1272	4020
Odia	oriy1255	3925
Nepali	nepa1254	3807
Sinhala	sinh1246	3791
Bengali	beng1280	3109
WesternPanjabi	west2386	3060
Kumaoni	kuma1273	2857
Kashmiri	kash1277	2659
Assamese	assa1263	2543
Maithili	mait1250	1466
Shina	shin1264	1152
Bagheli	bagh1251	1086
Bhadrawahi	bhal1244	814
Khowar	khow1242	797
Kachchi	kach1277	789
Dhivehi	dhiv1236	775
Bhojpuri	bhoj1244	750
Konkani	konk1267	672
Garhwali	garh1243	672
Phalura	phal1254	648
Awadhi	gang1265	607
Dameli	dame1241	607
Bhadrawahi	bhad1241	602
NortheastPashayi	nort2666	525
Gawar-Bati	gawa1247	520
Kalami	kala1373	488
Kalasha	kala1372	407
VlaxRomani	vlax1238	397
MahasuPahari	maha1287	381
Torwali	torw1241	374
Kalasha	sout2669	329
Shumashti	shum1235	316
NorthwestPashayi	laur1248	292
Jaunsari	jaun1243	269
Wotapuri-Katarqalai	wota1240	258
Domari	nawa1257	245
NortheastPashayi	aret1240	243
Domaaki	doma1260	239
IndusKohistani	indu1241	224
Savi	savi1242	207
Tirahi	tira1253	186
KohistaniShina	kohi1248	186
Churahi	chur1258	181
Marwari(India)	marw1260	166
NorthwestPashayi	nort2665	148
NortheastPashayi	kura1247	147
Lomavren	loma1235	146
WesternPanjabi	mult1243	143
Chambeali	cham1307	142
NortheastPashayi	wega1238	140
WelshRomani	wels1246	138
Braj	braj1242	135
SoutheastPashayi	sout2672	130
Khetrani	khet1238	120
Pangwali	pang1282	103

Table 1: Number of reflexes for languages in the data

output string is strictly monotonically increasing.[2]

In our experiments, we concatenate embeddings encoding the features described in the previous section to our input at each time step, namely (L)anguage ID, (P)art of speech, (S)emantic profile, and (E)tymon. We use a one-hot encoding of language ID and POS ID, and employ BERT embeddings (reduced from 768 to 128 dimensions using principal component analysis) to represent an etymon's semantic profile. Embeddings for etyma are represented by contatenating the first and last states of a Bidirectional LSTM encoding of the etymon string to the BERT-based semantic embedding (denoted by $e(\mathsf{gloss}_i)$)). Formally, these embeddings consist of the following, for a given data point index $i \in \{1, ..., |\mathsf{data}|\}$:

- L: $z_i^{\mathsf{lang}} = \mathrm{MLP}(\mathsf{lang}_i)$
- P: $z_i^{\mathsf{POS}} = \mathrm{MLP}(\mathsf{POS}_i)$
- S: $z_i^{\mathsf{sem}} = \mathrm{MLP}(e(\mathsf{gloss}_i))$
- E: $z_i^{\mathsf{etym}} = \mathrm{MLP}([\mathrm{MLP}([\mathrm{LSTM}(x_{i,1:|x_i|})_{|x_i|}; \mathrm{LSTM}(x_{i,|x_i|:1})_{|x_i|}]); z_i^{\mathsf{sem}}])$

After one or more of these embeddings are concatenated to an input token, the resulting concatenation is passed to another MLP layer, which is then fed to the encoder-decoder architecture. We increment our models by concatenating embeddings to the input in a stepwise fashion, yielding four models (L, LP, LPS, LPSE). Additionally, we compare our models against a baseline that does not use any embeddings.

We set the embedding and hidden layer dimension size to 128. We carry out K-fold ($K = 8$) cross-validation to assess model accuracy, training our models on mini-batches of 64 data points for a maximum of 200 epochs, validating on 10% of the training data and stopping early if the validation loss does not decrease over twenty consecutive epochs. We use the Adam optimizer (Kingma and Ba, 2015) with a learning rate of .001. We greedily decode test data using the fitted models, generating each output token on the basis of the previous generated token.[3]

---

[2] Although Wu and Cotterell (2019) report superior performance of a 1st-order hard monotonic model that penalizes alignments which jump more than w time steps; we did not implement this model since we could not make a principled decision regarding the value of w.

[3] Code and results are available at `https://github.com/chundrac/ia-conll-2020`

6 Results

We assess the accuracy with which our models predict held-out medieval/modern Indo-Aryan forms on the basis of the corresponding OIA etymon input by measuring the phoneme error rate (PER), which we define as the Levenshtein distance between the predicted and true form divided by the length of the longer string (normalized Levenshtein distance), and the word error rate (WER), or the proportion of held-out forms where one or more errors occurs in the predicted form. Mean PER and WER values are found for each model in Table 2.

As expected, the baseline model performs the worst according to these metrics. Of the non-baseline models, the model with language and POS embeddings shows the worst overall performance; highly augmented models such as the model which uses language, POS, semantic and etymon embeddings shows the best performance in terms of PER. However, the model with only language embeddings shows the best performance in terms of WER, indicating that the LPSE model introduces errors in a higher number of individual predicted words even if it produces fewer errors overall. We carry out pairwise Wilcoxon signed-rank tests to assess the significance of differences in PER between models, using the Bonferroni correction for multiple comparisons; all between-model differences are highly significant or significant, with the exception of the difference between the L and LPS models.

Figure 1 displays the relationship between language-level PER and the number of training examples for a given language. The correlation between these two variables is negative and significant (Spearman's ρ is between $-.39$ and $-.54$ for all models. However, as shown by the lines of best fit plotted in the figure, this correlation is considerably weaker for the baseline model than for the other models. Interestingly, the omission of language embeddings seems to have resulted in higher error rates for languages with larger numbers of training examples; if no information regarding language ID is fed to the encoder-decoder, there seems to be no way to keep highly influential languages from interfering in the patterns learned for other highly influential languages.

7 Error analysis

PER based on unweighted Levenshtein distance is agnostic to error type. In a task such as ours, some error types will indicate strongly that our models

Model	PER	WER
L	.257	**.808**
LP	.262	.818
LPS	.256	.813
LPSE	**.255**	.809
Baseline	.346	.940

Table 2: Phoneme error rates and word error rates for each model. All pairwise PER comparisons between models are highly significant ($p < 0.001$) according to a Wilcoxon signed-rank test with Bonferroni correction, with the exception of L–LPS ($p = 1$) and LPS–LPSE ($p = 0.02$).

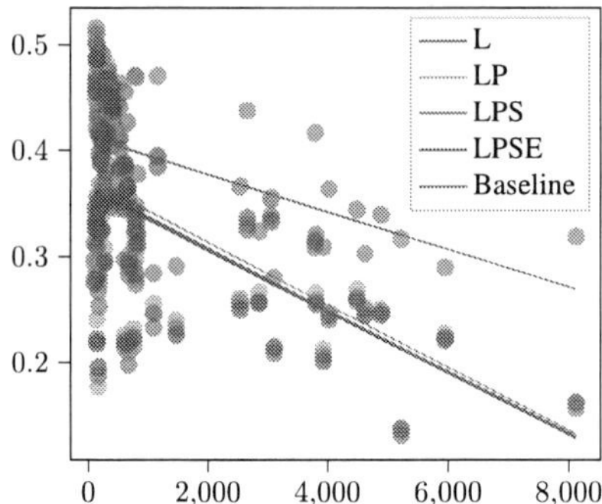

Figure 1: Language-level PER plotted by the number of training examples for each language, for each model.

have failed to learn meaningful generalizations regarding sound change. Additionally, certain errors produced by a model may be due to errors in the data when the model has in fact learned a meaningful pattern of change.

With this in mind we turn to a quantitative but linguistically informed error analysis designed to investigate the types of errors made by each model and assess the degree to which each model makes certain errors. One error type consists of errors in vowel quality or quantity: the LPS model erroneously generates Kashmiri *muhun* (< OIA *mōháyati* 'bewilders') as *mŏhun*. Errors of this sort affect consonants as well: the Pāli form *addana* (< OIA *ardana* 'tormenting') is erroneously generated as *aḍḍana* by the LP model. Errors of this sort, particularly vowel type errors, often occur at the right word edge, perhaps due to confusion resulting from the restructuring of the OIA case and gender systems in many Indo-Aryan languages; e.g., Sindhi *vali* (< OIA *vallī* 'creeper') is generated as *vala*

Language	Glottocode	True	L	LP	LPS	LPSE	Baseline
Bagheli	bagh1251	machlī	machilā	mãs	machā	māchī	macch
Jaunsari	jaun1243	māchā	māch	māś	bhēċū	māchā	macch
Khowar	khow1242	maċí	muċh	maċ	máċu	muċh	macch
VlaxRomani	vlax1238	maċo	māch	machar	māċh	maċhi	macch
Bhadrawahi	bhal1244	maċhli	maċh	machli	maċhi	machli	māchā
Bhadrawahi	bhad1241	machlī	meċhlī	meċhl	machlī	meċhlī	mācho
Kachchi	kach1277	macch	machī	machi	machi	machī	mācho
Odia	oriy1255	mācha	mācha	mācha	macha	mācha	mācho
Pali	pali1273	maccha	maccha	maccha	maccha	maccha	mācho
EasternPanjabi	panj1256	macch	masch	macch	macchā	macchā	mācho
Dhivehi	dhiv1236	mas	mais	mais	mahi	mati	māch
Hindi	hind1269	machlī	māch	māch	māch	māch	māch
Konkani	konk1267	māslī	māsi	māċ	māċa	māċu	māch
Sindhi	sind1272	machu	machu	machu	machu	machu	māch
NortheastPashayi	aret1240	māċ	mõċ	māċī	mõċ	maċot	māch
Hindi	hind1269	māch	machlī	māch	machlī	māchī	māch
Marathi	mara1378	māsā	māch	mās	mās	mās	māch
Bengali	beng1280	māch	māchlā	meċā	māch	māchā	macha
Gawar-Bati	gawa1247	maċotá	māċh	māċ	māċ	maċ	macha
Prakrit(Maharashtri)	maha1305	maccha	maccha	maccha	maccha	maccha	macha
Sinhala	sinh1246	masā	mas	masa	mas	masā	macha
Bhadrawahi	bhad1241	machli	machlī	maċhlī	machlī	machlī	machī
Garhwali	garh1243	māchu	māchu	maċhlu	māchī	māchu	machī

Table 3: Selected held-out forms generated on the basis of OIA *mátsya* 'fish' for several languages. The true held-out form is presented alongside forms generated by the L, LP, LPS, LPSE and baseline models.

by the LP and LPS models. Some errors involve excrescence or insertion, where extra phonological information is erroneously produced in the predicted form, e.g., LPS *kiriruvalana* for Sinhala *kirivāla* (< OIA *kṣīravallī* 'Batatus paniculata'). Elsewhere, we find erroneous deletion of phonological material, e.g. LPS *lūṛh* in place of Bagheli *loṛhnihār* (< OIA *luṭháti* 'rolls, wallows'). Some errors involve the generation of output that is phonemically analyzable as the ground truth form, e.g., L *kachwā* for Hindi *kachuā* (< OIA *kacchapa* 'turtle, tortoise'). Along with source errors or morphological mismatches that simply cannot be detected by our model architecture, the errors mentioned above make up the bulk of errors produced by models.

We align tokens in held-out forms with tokens in predicted forms using the Needleman-Wunsch algorithm (Needleman and Wunsch, 1970), allowing us to automatically extract errors made by each model (e.g., instances where *ḷ* was generated instead of *l*). We classify mismatches between held-out and predicted tokens according to whether they involve an insertion, a deletion, a change affecting a vowel (other than deletion), or a change affecting a consonant (other than deletion). Proportions of these changes across models are given in Table 4. As can be observed, error type rates are similar across models; however, the baseline model has lower rates of erroneous deletion than other

models, and higher rates of incorrect substitutions affecting consonants. A possible reason for this behavior is that the baseline model, which lacks language embeddings, likely comes under influence from Prakrit, which contains the most training examples in the data set (well-attested languages like Hindi contain fewer training examples due to partial replacement of vocabulary inherited from OIA by Persian and Arabic loanwords). Prakrit did not undergo vowel or consonant deletion to the extent that later-attested Indo-Aryan languages did; hence, the overwhelming influence of this language on the model would make deletion a less likely change overall. Prakrit did however undergo drastic changes to consonants, such as full assimilation of clusters other than nasal-plosive sequences; if the model is influenced by this behavior, it may account for some of the instances of incorrect consonant substitution not seen in the other models. As an example, Marathi *khābārī* (< OIA *kārṣmaryā* 'the tree Gmelina arborea') is incorrectly predicted to be *khãvarī* by the LP model, but the baseline model produces the more conservative *kāmbhārī*.

Selected held-out reflexes of OIA *mátsya* 'fish' are provided in Table 3 along with their predicted counterparts for each model, illustrating the challenges that our models face when predicting held-out forms. The reflexes provided all descend from *mátsya*, but some have gained extra morphology during their development, most frequently the suffix *-la*, a morpheme added to a number of medieval/modern Indo-Aryan nouns. For morphological irregularities of this type, models endowed with semantic information have the potential to infer that certain semantically related nouns acquire the suffix *-la* during their development; at the same time, the L model, which lack semantic information, generates forms reflecting a *-la* suffix, which may indicate that it has learned certain phonotactic patterns from the target-side language model, which is shared across all languages. The baseline model consistently produces a limited number of reflex types, likely informed by the most frequent languages in the sample (i.e., Prakrit and Hindi).

	I	D	V	C
L	0.19	0.24	0.35	0.22
LP	0.20	0.22	0.35	0.22
LPS	0.20	0.23	0.35	0.22
LPSE	0.20	0.23	0.35	0.22
B	0.20	0.19	0.36	0.26

Table 4: Proportions of error types (erroneous insertion [I], deletion [D], vowel substitution [V], consonant substitution [C]) produced by each model.

8   Genetic signal

We investigate the degree to which the language-level embeddings learned by our models represent the genetic relatedness of Indo-Aryan languages in our sample. For the language embeddings produced by each model, we compute the cosine distances between each pair of embeddings, and use these distances to construct language trees using neighbor joining (NJ, Saitou and Nei, 1987). We compare each tree to a reference taxonomy of the Indo-Aryan languages taken from Glottolog (Hammarström et al., 2017), which contains relatively uncontroversial language groupings but does not resolve all subgroupings, and hence contains numerous polytomies (i.e., non-binary branchings).

We measure the distance between two language trees is measured using Generalized Quartet Distance (GQD, Pompei et al., 2011; Rama et al., 2018). A quartet in a phylogenetic language tree consists of four languages and can either be resolved ("butterfly") or unresolved ("star"). The generalized quartet distance is the ratio of the number of butterfly quartets which differ across trees to

the total number of butterfly quartets in the reference tree. While our reference tree is non-binary, the trees inferred from our models' embeddings are binary. Accordingly, the GQD measure does not penalize the inferred tree, ignoring the star quartets found in the reference tree. The GQD scores for all our models are given in Table 5, along with scores for a baseline tree constructed using averaging the normalized Levenshtein distance (LDN) between cognate forms for pairs of languages (lower values indicate greater agreement).

Model	GQD
L	0.509
LP	0.559
LPS	0.514
LPSE	0.569
LDN	**0.304**

Table 5: GQD between the inferred tree and the reference tree for each model

Notably, despite its good performance according to the PER metric, the embeddings produced by the LPSE model show the lowest agreement with a reference taxonomy of Indo-Aryan out of all of the models used in our experiments, particularly when compared with the model that uses only language embeddings. A possible explanation is that by including additional embeddings in our models designed to capture different patterns of sound change in different morphological, semantic and etymological scenarios, we have filtered out critical information relevant to subgrouping, removing valuable genetic signal displayed by morphological traits, which may explain why the model with language embeddings outperforms the other models. A similar negative relationship between model accuracy and genetic signal displayed by embeddings was found by Cathcart and Wandl (2020).

At the same time, all models are significantly outperformed by the LDN tree, indicating that string distances between contemporary forms capture inter-language relationships at more levels of granularity than the distances computed from the embeddings learned by our models. All models, including the LPSE model, are successful at learning patterns of change within individual lineages and recapitulating shallow subgroups. For visualization, we map LPSE embeddings to three-dimensional space using multidimensional scaling

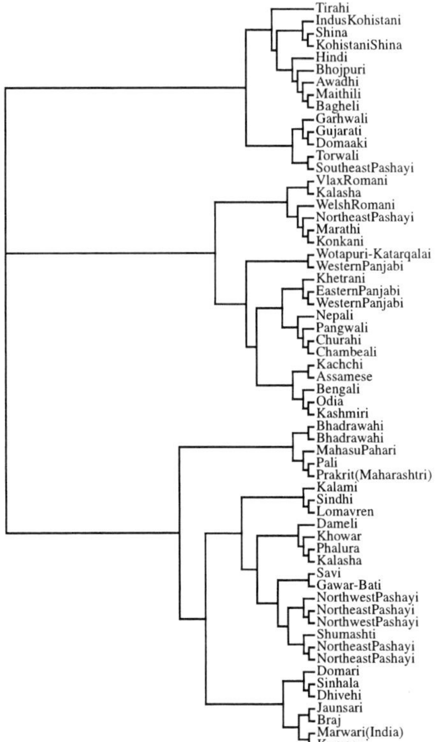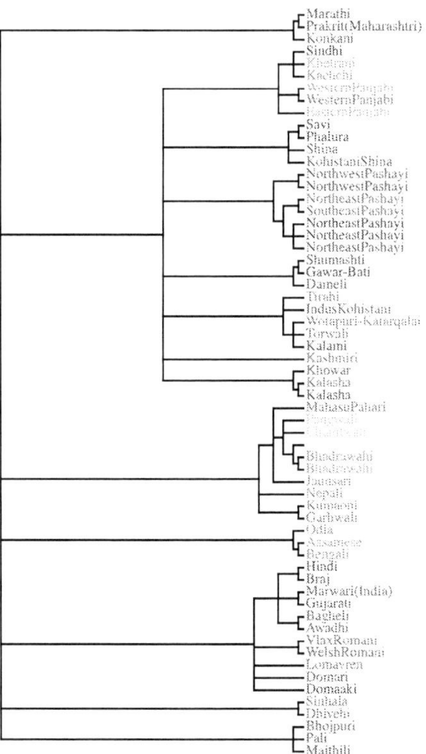

Figure 2: Tree constructed from LPSE model embeddings using neighbor joining (left) and reference taxonomy of the Indo-Aryan languages in our sample, taken from Glottolog (right). Colors of languages represent the positions of their respective language embeddings from the LPSE model in three-dimensional space.

and color the taxa of the reference tree using RGB color vectors produced by these normalized values, as shown in Figure 2. Similarly colored taxa are close to each other in embedding space. In general, very close relatives appear to occupy the same region of embedding space, but small groups within large taxa may be distant from each other in the same space, indicating premature but not altogether unpromising results for our attempt to capture genetic signal in the data we analyze.

9 Representations learned by embeddings

Here, we investigate whether our architecture has learned properties of the different patterns displayed by verbal and non-verbal forms. OIA verbs end in *-ti* and *-tē*; virtually no OIA nouns end in *-tē*, and while some OIA nouns end in *-ti*, they tend to have a different phonotactic profile from OIA verb forms. Hence, it is entirely possible that encoder-decoder models with embeddings that encode part of speech ignore this information and can simply

learn mappings such as OIA *-ati* > Assamese *-iba* (e.g., from OIA *vaśati* : Assamese *bahāiba*), since *-iba* is a suffix that freqently co-occurs with the OIA sequence *-ati*. The fact that a model with only language embeddings outperforms a model with language embeddings and part-of-speech embeddings provides a reason to suspect that our architecture does not learn anything about the morphological mismatches found between OIA verb citation forms and medieval/modern Indo-Aryan forms, simply because it does not need to — surface patterns in phonology may be sufficient to learn the correct mapping between input and output.

To investigate whether our models have learned anything from part-of-speech embeddings, we carry out an experiment where we feed held-out data to the LP, LPS, and LPSE models, holding the language ID and semantic and etymological information constant but perturbing the POS ID (i.e., changing it to VERB for non-verbal data and changing it to NON-VERB for verbal data). We measure the normalized Levenshtein distance between forms decoded with true POS IDs and forms decoded with perturbed POS IDs, and average these PER values for verbal and non-verbal forms. As shown in Table 6, changing a verbal POS ID to a non-verbal one results in a more dissimilar form, whereas the opposite change has less of an effect (all differences are highly significant according to a Mann-Whitney test, $p < .001$), since our system never encounters certain noun suffixes with a verbal POS ID and hence doesn't learn variable patterns for these suffixes. Differences are most pronounced for the LP model, but when more information is concatenated to the input, the effect of using an embedding for POS ID appears to be absorbed by the other embeddings, and the disparity levels out. This indicates that our augmented models do learn meaningful information from the POS ID, but that models endowed with semantic information learn more fine-grained patterns and produce more accurate results than the LP model.

	LDN		Match	
Model	N→V	V→N	N→V	V→N
LP	0.226	0.291	0.604	0.535
LPS	0.189	0.204	0.668	0.619
LPSE	0.170	0.220	0.700	0.628

Table 6: Average normalized Levenshtein distance between predicted held-out forms with unperturbed and perturbed POS IDs ([N]on-verb and [V]erb), grouped by model and POS (left); average proportion of leftmost matching segments found between these pairs of forms.

In the majority of Indo-Aryan languages, verbal morphology (such as the infinitive ending) consists of suffixes with straightforwardly affixal behavior (Masica, 1991, 321ff.); stem alternations are rare outside of valency changing processes. It is therefore worthwhile to know the extent to which our perturbations reflect this quality: do the differences in output caused by perturbing the POS ID accumulate at the right word edge, or are they distributed throughout the word? In order to investigate this question, we tabulate the length of the leftmost matching substring across each output string and its perturbed counterpart, and divide this number by the mean of the two strings; higher values indicate that the two strings differ only according to a suffix. As shown in the right half of Table 6, mean values for this quantity tend to be greater than .5, indicating that perturbing the POS ID tends to result in different suffixation. Further investigation of these distributions and metrics designed to capture this quality is outside the scope of this paper but will provide stimulating future research.

10 Discussion and Outlook

In this paper, we investigated the ability of LSTM-based encoder-decoder architectures to capture recurrent patterns of sound change between OIA and medieval/modern Indo-Aryan languages, as well as encode information regarding the genetic relationships between languages. We found that a model augmented with information regarding forms' language ID, POS ID, semantic profile, and etymon ID showed the lowest phoneme error rate out of all models, but that language embeddings learned by this model showed low agreement with a reference taxonomy of Indo-Aryan, and that in general, our models struggled to capture uncontroversial genetic signal. This issue may be in part due to architectural choices we made, along with challenging aspects of the data set we used, drawn from a diverse group of languages.

Our experiments show that the use of different embeddings appears to allow our models to learn deviations from regular sound change that are found in words with certain parts of speech, semantic profiles, or that reflect particular etyma. At the same time, there are many avenues for improving the performance of models on this highly challenging data set. In future work, we plan to obtain glosses for reflex forms in the dictionary in order to determine whether the semantic distance between an etymon and a reflex can capture vagaries of analogical change that we were unable to model in this paper. Additionally, our models learned embeddings for POS IDs that did not vary across languages, rather than language-specific ones, and we built our models incrementally in a stepwise function rather than considering all possible subsets of predictors of interest, decisions that may have influenced our results. Greater flexibility will play an important role in future deep learning approaches that hope to capture the multifaceted diachronic processes that yield synchronic linguistic similarity and dissimilarity.

Acknowledgements

We thank anonymous CoNLL reviewers for helpful comments, and Sidaarth Sabhnani for assistance with data extraction.

References

Johannes Bjerva, Robert Östling, Maria Han Veiga, Jörg Tiedemann, and Isabelle Augenstein. 2019. What do language representations really represent? *Computational Linguistics*, 45(2):381–389.

Damián E. Blasi, Søren Wichmann, Harald Hammarström, Peter F. Stadler, and Morten H. Christiansen. 2016. Sound–meaning association biases evidenced across thousands of languages. *Proceedings of the National Academy of Sciences*, 10.1073/pnas.1605782113.

Alexandre Bouchard-Côté, David Hall, Thomas L. Griffiths, and Dan Klein. 2013. Automated reconstruction of ancient languages using probabilistic models of sound change. *Proceedings of the National Academy of Sciences*, 110:4224–4229.

Gerd Carling and Niklas Johansson. 2014. Motivated language change: processes involved in the growth and conventionalization of onomatopoeia and sound symbolism. *Acta Linguistica Hafniensia*, 46(2):199–217.

Chundra Cathcart and Florian Wandl. 2020. In search of isoglosses: continuous and discrete language embeddings in Slavic historical phonology. In *Proceedings of the 17th SIGMORPHON Workshop on Computational Research in Phonetics, Phonology, and Morphology*, pages 233–244, Online. Association for Computational Linguistics.

Alina Maria Ciobanu and Liviu P Dinu. 2020. Automatic identification and production of related words for historical linguistics. *Computational Linguistics*, 45(4):667–704.

Jacob Devlin, Ming-Wei Chang, Kenton Lee, and Kristina Toutanova. 2019. BERT: Pre-training of deep bidirectional transformers for language understanding. In *Proceedings of the 2019 Conference of the North American Chapter of the Association for Computational Linguistics: Human Language Technologies, Volume 1 (Long and Short Papers)*, pages 4171–4186, Minneapolis, Minnesota. Association for Computational Linguistics.

George A. Grierson. 1967 [1903-28]. *Linguistic Survey of India*. Motilal Banarsidass, Delhi.

Harald Hammarström, Robert Forkel, and Martin Haspelmath. 2017. Glottolog 3.3. Max Planck Institute for the Science of Human History.

Henry M. Hoenigswald. 1960. *Language change and linguistic reconstruction*. University of Chicago Press, Chicago.

A. F. Rudolf Hoernle. 1880. *A comparative grammar of the Gaudian languages*. Trübner and Co., London.

Dirk Hovy and Christoph Purschke. 2018. Capturing regional variation with distributed place representations and geographic retrofitting. In *Proceedings of the 2018 Conference on Empirical Methods in Natural Language Processing*, pages 4383–4394, Brussels, Belgium. Association for Computational Linguistics.

Robert J Jeffers. 1976. The position of the Bihārī dialects in Indo-Aryan. *Indo-Iranian Journal*, 18(3-4):215–225.

Melvin Johnson, Mike Schuster, Quoc V Le, Maxim Krikun, Yonghui Wu, Zhifeng Chen, Nikhil Thorat, Fernanda Viégas, Martin Wattenberg, Greg Corrado, et al. 2017. Google's multilingual neural machine translation system: Enabling zero-shot translation. *Transactions of the Association for Computational Linguistics*, 5:339–351.

Brett Kessler. 1995. Computational dialectology in Irish Gaelic. In *Proceedings of the 7th Conference of the European Chapter of the Association for Computational Linguistics*, pages 60–67, Dublin. EACL.

Diederik P. Kingma and Jimmy Ba. 2015. Adam: A method for stochastic optimization. In *International Conference on Learning Representations (ICLR)*.

Yakov Malkiel. 1962. Weak phonetic change, spontaneous sound shift, lexical contamination. *Lingua*, 11:263–275.

Colin P. Masica. 1991. *The Indo-Aryan languages*. Cambridge University Press, Cambridge.

Carlo Meloni, Shauli Ravfogel, and Yoav Goldberg. 2019. Ab antiquo: Proto-language reconstruction with rnns. *arXiv preprint arXiv:1908.02477*.

Annie Montaut. 2009. Ergative and pre-ergative patterns in Indo-Aryan as predications of localization.

Annie Montaut. 2017. Grammaticalization of participles and gerunds in Indo-Aryan: Preterite, future, infinitive. *Unity and diversity in grammaticalization scenarios*, 16:97.

Saul B. Needleman and Christian D. Wunsch. 1970. A general method applicable to the search for similarities in the amino acid sequence of two proteins. *Journal of Molecular Biology*, 48:443–53.

John Nerbonne and Wilbert Heeringa. 2001. Computational comparison and classification of dialects. *Dialectologia et Geolinguistica*, 9:69–83.

Robert Östling and Jörg Tiedemann. 2017. Continuous multilinguality with language vectors. In *Conference of the European Chapter of the Association for Computational Linguistics*, pages 644–649. Association for Computational Linguistics.

Simone Pompei, Vittorio Loreto, and Francesca Tria. 2011. On the accuracy of language trees. *PloS one*, 6(6):e20109.

Ella Rabinovich, Noam Ordan, and Shuly Wintner. 2017. Found in translation: Reconstructing phylogenetic language trees from translations. In *Proceedings of the 55th Annual Meeting of the Association for Computational Linguistics (Volume 1: Long Papers)*, pages 530–540, Vancouver, Canada. Association for Computational Linguistics.

Afshin Rahimi, Timothy Baldwin, and Trevor Cohn. 2017a. Continuous representation of location for geolocation and lexical dialectology using mixture density networks. In *Proceedings of the 2017 Conference on Empirical Methods in Natural Language Processing*, pages 167–176.

Afshin Rahimi, Trevor Cohn, and Timothy Baldwin. 2017b. A neural model for user geolocation and lexical dialectology. In *Proceedings of the 55th Annual Meeting of the Association for Computational Linguistics (Volume 2: Short Papers)*, pages 209–216.

Taraka Rama, Johann-Mattis List, Johannes Wahle, and Gerhard Jäger. 2018. Are automatic methods for cognate detection good enough for phylogenetic reconstruction in historical linguistics? In *Proceedings of the 2018 Conference of the North American Chapter of the Association for Computational Linguistics: Human Language Technologies, Volume 2 (Short Papers)*, pages 393–400.

N. Saitou and M. Nei. 1987. The neighbor-joining method: a new method for reconstructing phylogenetic trees. *Molecular Biology and Evolution*, 4(4):406–425.

Franklin Southworth. 1964. Family-tree diagrams. *Language*, 40(4):557–565.

Franklin C. Southworth. 2005. *Linguistic Archaeology of South Asia*. Routledge, London.

Jörg Tiedemann. 2018. Emerging language spaces learned from massively multilingual corpora. In Eetu Mäkelä, Mikko Tolonen, and Jouni Tuominen, editors, *Proceedings of the Digital Humanities in the Nordic Countries 3rd Conference (DHN 2018)*, pages 188–197.

Matthew Toulmin. 2009. *From linguistic to sociolinguistic reconstruction: the Kamta historical subgroup of Indo-Aryan*. Pacific Linguistics, Research School of Pacific and Asian Studies, The Australian National University, Canberra.

Ralph L. Turner. 1962–1966. *A comparative dictionary of Indo-Aryan languages*. Oxford University Press, London.

Ralph L. Turner. 1975 [1967]. Geminates after long vowel in Indo-aryan. In *R.L. Turner: Collected Papers 1912–1973*, pages 405–415. Oxford University Press, London.

Michael Weiss. 2015. The comparative method. In Claire Bowern and Bethwyn Evans, editors, *The Routledge handbook of historical linguistics*, pages 127–145. Routledge, London.

Thomas Wolf, Lysandre Debut, Victor Sanh, Julien Chaumond, Clement Delangue, Anthony Moi, Pierric Cistac, Tim Rault, Rémi Louf, Morgan Funtowicz, et al. 2019. Huggingface's transformers: State-of-the-art natural language processing. *ArXiv*, pages arXiv–1910.

Shijie Wu and Ryan Cotterell. 2019. Exact hard monotonic attention for character-level transduction. In *Proceedings of the 57th Annual Meeting of the Association for Computational Linguistics*, pages 1530–1537, Florence, Italy. Association for Computational Linguistics.

Claus-Peter Zoller. 2016. Outer and Inner Indo-Aryan, and northern India as an ancient linguistic area. *Acta Orientalia*, 77:71–132.

K-RSL: a Corpus for Linguistic Understanding, Visual Evaluation, and Recognition of Sign Languages

Alfarabi Imashev, Medet Mukushev, Vadim Kimmelman[†], Anara Sandygulova
Department of Robotics and Mechatronics, School of Engineering and Digital Sciences,
Nazarbayev University, Kazakhstan
[†]Department of Linguistic, Literary and Aesthetic Studies,
University of Bergen, Norway
alfarabi.imashev@nu.edu.kz, mmukushev@nu.edu.kz,
vadim.kimmelman@uib.no, anara.sandygulova@nu.edu.kz

Abstract

The paper presents the first dataset that aims to serve interdisciplinary purposes for the utility of computer vision community and sign language linguistics. To date, a majority of Sign Language Recognition (SLR) approaches focus on recognising sign language as a manual gesture recognition problem. However, signers use other articulators: facial expressions, head and body position and movement to convey linguistic information. Given the important role of non-manual markers, this paper proposes a dataset and presents a use case to stress the importance of including non-manual features to improve the recognition accuracy of signs. To the best of our knowledge no prior publicly available dataset exists that explicitly focuses on non-manual components responsible for the grammar of sign languages. To this end, the proposed dataset contains 28250 videos of signs of high resolution and quality, with annotation of manual and non-manual components. We conducted a series of evaluations in order to investigate whether non-manual components would improve signs' recognition accuracy. We release the dataset to encourage SLR researchers and help advance current progress in this area toward real-time sign language interpretation. Our dataset will be made publicly available at https://krslproject.github.io/krsl-corpus

1 Introduction

There exist over 300 sign languages around the world that are native to 70 million deaf people (Bragg et al., 2019). Sign languages are comprised of hand gestures, arms and body movements, head position, facial expressions, and lip patterns (Sandler and Lillo-Martin, 2006). While automatic speech recognition has progressed to being commercially available, automatic Sign Language Recognition (SLR) is still in its infancy (Cooper et al., 2011).

To date, more than half of published vision-based research utilizes isolated sign language data with a vocabulary size of less than 50 signs (Koller, 2020). But the real-world utility of SLR solutions requires continuous recognition, which is significantly more challenging than recognising individual signs due to co-articulation (the ending of one sign affecting the start of the next), depiction (visually representing or enacting content), epenthesis effects (insertion of extra features into signs), generalization, and so on (Bragg et al., 2019). As a result, realistic, generalisable, and large datasets are necessary to advance SLR.

Current efforts in SLR do not address the complexities of sign language linguistics, and thus have a limited real-world value (Bragg et al., 2019). Chatzis et al. (2020) highlight the importance of non-manual components of sign languages. For example, they can change meaning of a verb, or differentiate between objects and people. According to Koller (2020), there is an overall lack of non-manual parameters that are included in medium and larger vocabulary recognition systems. For example, many computer vision approaches focus on the signers' hands only and tend to ignore the rich channel of information conveyed by non-manual articulators: facial expressions, mouthing, movement and position of the head and body conveying important grammatical and lexical information. In addition, many datasets allowed novice or non-native contributions (i.e. students) in addition to slower signing and simplifying the style and the vocabulary to make the computer vision problem easier but of no real value (Bragg et al., 2019). For the progress in SLR, interdisciplinary efforts are required with an involvement of native signers and sign language linguists.

Beyond targeting the local need of creating the first corpus within CIS (Commonwealth of Independent States) region suitable for machine learn-

Proceedings of the 24th Conference on Computational Natural Language Learning, pages 631–640
Online, November 19-20, 2020. ©2020 Association for Computational Linguistics
https://doi.org/10.18653/v1/P17

Datasets	Signers	Vocabulary	Videos
Purdue RVL-SLLL ASL (2002) (Martínez et al., 2002)	14	104	2,576
GSL Lemmas (2007) (Efthimiou and Fotinea, 2007)	2	1046	2,100
RWTH-BOSTON (2008) (Athitsos et al., 2008)	5	483	7,768
SIGNUM (2008) (Von Agris et al., 2008)	25	780	3,703
Finish S-pot (2014) (Viitaniemi et al., 2014)	5	1211	4,328
RWTH-PHOENIX-Weather 2014 T(Cihan Camgoz et al., 2018)	9	1231	45,760
Video-Based CSL (2018) (Huang et al., 2018)	50	178	25,000
KETI (2019) (Ko et al., 2019)	12	419	11,578
GSL SI (2019) (Chatzis et al., 2020)	7	310	10,290
K-RSL	**10**	**600**	**28,250**

Table 1: Datasets used for sign language recognition

ing, the motivation behind the proposed dataset is in the need to stress the importance of non-manual components present in many signs. The proposed dataset contains continuous sign language data with a focus on specifically selected cases where non-manual markers play a vital role in differentiating between similar signs or sentences. This approach of corpus creation allows researchers from different fields to conduct experiments utilising this dataset. To date, SL linguists and ML researchers were rarely able to utilize the same datasets due to limitations of both kinds. Thus, we make the following contributions:

- we release the first Kazakh-Russian Sign Language (KRSL) corpus consisting of 10 signers, 28250 continuous sentences, and vocabulary size 600 signs appropriate for ML research;

- we release raw videos appropriate for linguists and general population;

- we release isolated signs, extracted frames and features for easy and fast experiments aiming at compatibility with the formats of other SL datasets;

- we evaluate pose estimation and action recognition approaches to setup baselines on the K-RSL dataset.

Section 2 presents the background on sign languages and non-manual components followed by a brief description of other SL datasets. Section 3 outlines the proposed dataset. Section 4 details a series of baseline evaluations conducted in order to investigate whether non-manual components would improve recognition accuracy. Section 5 details our use case evaluation. Section 6 concludes the paper.

2 Related work

This section discusses related work on sign language datasets, state of the art in SLR, and the importance of non-manual features for sign languages.

2.1 Sign Language Datasets

Sign language datasets consist of videos of either isolated or continuous signing. Table 1 presents a comparison of the continuous sign language datasets commonly utilized for sign language recognition with an inclusion of the proposed K-RSL ordered by date. Bragg et al. (2019) specify that the size of the datasets, continuous signing, involvement of native signers, and signers' variety are the main concerns related to current datasets. These challenges put a limitation on the accuracy and robustness of the models developed for SLR to be deployed in the real-world applications.

2.2 Sign Language Recognition

Latest works in the area of SLR are focused on vision-based continuous sign language recognition. All the evaluations are performed on the RWTH-PHOENIX-Weather 2014 dataset (Cihan Camgoz et al., 2018). There are various approaches offering recognition frameworks utilizing deep neural networks, reinforcement learning or recurrent neural networks. For example, Zhang et al. (2019) proposed an approach that apply encoder-decoder structure to the reinforcement learning. Their method achieved competitive results when compared with other methods and has a Word Error Rate (WER) of 38.3%. Temporal segmentation creates additional challenges for continuous SLR. To address this issue, Huang et al. (2018) proposed the Hierarchical Attention Network with Latent

Phrases type	Signers	Phrases	Repetitions	Videos	Glosses
Question-Statement	5	200	10	10000	150
Emotions	5	60	10	3000	140
Emotional Question-Statement	10	30	10	9000	20
Minimal pairs	5	125	10	6250	360
K-RSL total	**10**	**415**	**10**	**28250**	**600**

Table 2: Kazakh-Russian Sign Language dataset

Space (LS-HAN). This proposed framework eliminated the preprocessing of temporal segmentation and achieved the accuracy of 0.617. Zhou et al. (2019) proposed I3D-TEM-CTC framework with iterative optimization for continuous sign language recognition. By increasing the quality of pseudo labels, the final performance of the system was improved and achieved a WER of 34.5%. However, the most promising results were achieved by combining different modalities. Cui et al. (2019) proposed recurrent convolutional neural network on the multi-modal fusion data of RGB images along with the optical flow data and achieved WER of 22.86%. Koller et al. (2019) presented approaches where they focused on the sequential parallelism to learn a sign language, mouth shape and handshape classifier. They have improved the WER to 26.0%. This clearly shows that combination of manual and non-manual features such as mouth shape could significantly improve performance of the recognition systems.

2.3 Importance of Non-manual Features

Sign languages are natural languages existing in the visual modality (Sandler and Lillo-Martin, 2006). Signs in sign languages are produced not only by using the manual articulators (the hands), but also by non-manual articulators (the body, head, facial features). The importance of the non-manual features is evidenced e.g. by the fact that signers focus their attention not on the hands of the interlocutor, but on the face (Pfau and Quer, 2010).

It has been shown that non-manual markers function at different levels in sign languages (Pfau and Quer, 2010). On the lexical level, signs which are manually identical can be distinguished by facial expression or specifically by mouthing (silent articulation of a word from a spoken language) (Crasborn et al., 2008). Signs referring to emotions are obligatorily accompanied by lexicalized facial expressions related to the corresponding emotion. Non-manual markers are especially important

on the level of sentence and beyond. Specifically, negation in many sign languages is expressed by head movements (Zeshan, 2004a), and questions are distinguished from statements by eyebrow and head position almost universally (Zeshan, 2004b). Of course, signers also use the face to express their emotions, so emotional and linguistic non-manual markers can interact in complex ways (De Vos et al., 2009).

Antonakos et al. (2015) presented an overview of non-manual parameter employment for SLR and conclude that a limited number of works focused on employing non-manual features in SLR. There have been works that focused on combining both manual and non-manual features (Freitas et al., 2017; Liu et al., 2014; Yang and Lee, 2013; Mukushev et al., 2020) or non-manual features only (Kumar et al., 2017). While the importance of non-manual markers has been thoroughly demonstrated in linguistic research, their role in sign language recognition has not been investigated in detail yet.

3 The Proposed K-RSL Corpus

Given the important role of non-manual markers, in this paper we present a corpus which is motivated by the importance of both manual and non-manual features. We focus on specific cases where non-manual markers play a vital role in differentiating between similar signs or similar sentences.

3.1 Kazakh-Russian Sign Language (KRSL)

KRSL is the sign language used in the Republic of Kazakhstan. KRSL is closely related to Russian Sign Language (RSL) as centralized language policy of Soviet Union led to the spread of RSL in the Soviet republics. According to Kimmelman et al. (2020) both KRSL and RSL show a substantial lexical overlap, and are completely mutually intelligible. At the same time, it cannot be concluded that the same applies to the grammar of the two languages.

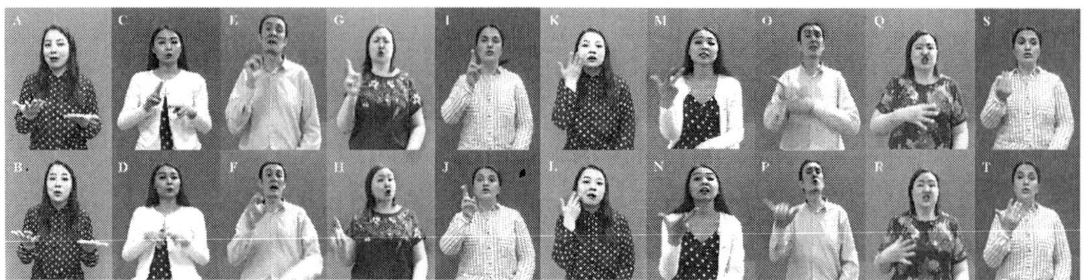

Figure 1: Examples of each sign from our dataset: A) "which one" statement, B) "which one" question, C) "which" statement, D) "which" question, E) "how" statement, F) "how" question, G) "what" statement, H) "what" question, I) "who" statement, J) "who" question, K) "when" statement, L) "when" question, M) "where(location)" statement, N) "where(location)" question, O) "where(direction)" statement, P) "where(direction)" question, Q) "where(direction)" statement, R) "where(direction)" question, S) "how much" statement, T) "how much" question.

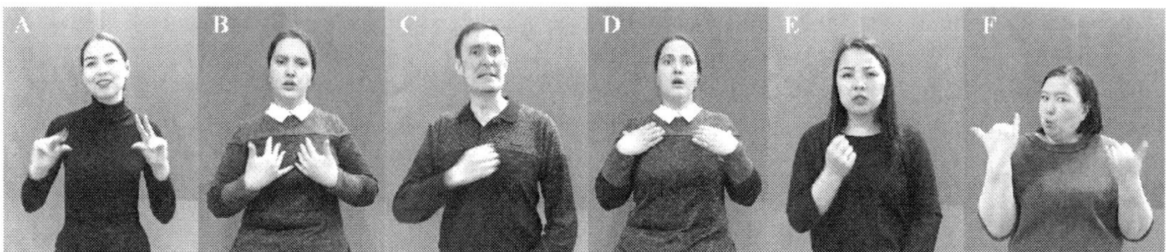

Figure 2: Emotions: A) "happy", B) "sad", C) "anger", D) "scared", E) "pity", F) "surprised".

3.2 The Data

K-RSL dataset consists of videos of phrases, recorded by five professional sign language interpreters and one subset was additionally recorded by five deaf participants who are also native signers. Dataset can be divided into four subsets from the linguistic point of view: question-statement pairs, signs of emotion, emotional question-statement pairs, and phonologically similar signs (minimal pairs). They have been asked to sign 200 phrases for the first subset, 60 phrases for the second subset, 30 phrase with 3 emotional characteristics for the third subset, and 125 phrases for the fourth subset accordingly. Each phrase was repeated at least ten times in a row by each signer.

The five hearing participants are hearing native signers of KRSL, as they grew up with parents using KRSL at home. Four of them are employed as news interpreters at the national television. The setup had a green background and a LOGITECH C920 HD PRO WEBCAM. The shooting was performed in an office space without professional lighting sources. The summary of the K-RSL dataset is presented in Table 2.

3.2.1 Question vs Statement

Similar to question words in many spoken languages, question signs in KRSL can be used not only in questions (*Who came?*) but also in statements (*I know who came*). Thus, each question sign can occur either with non-manual question marking (eyebrow raise, sideward or backward head tilt), or without it. In addition, question signs are usually accompanied by mouthing of the corresponding Russian/Kazakh word (e.g. *kto/kim* for 'who', and *chto/ne* for 'what'). While question signs are also distinguished from each other by manual features, mouthing provides extra information, which can be used in recognition. Thus, the two types of non-manual markers (eyebrow and head position vs. mouthing) can play a different role in recognition: the former can be used to distinguish statements from questions, and the latter can be used to help distinguish different question signs from each other. To this end, we selected ten words and composed twenty phrases with each word (ten statements and ten questions): 'what', 'who', 'which', 'which one', 'when', 'where (direction)', 'where (location)', 'why', 'how', and 'how much'. We distinguish them to twenty classes (as ten words have a pair in both statement and question form).

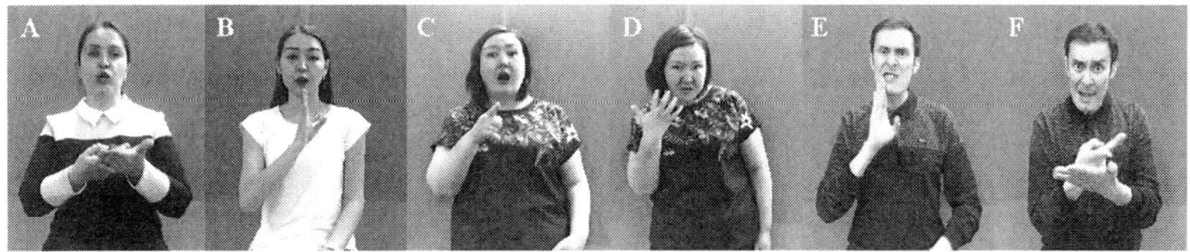

Figure 3: Examples of facial expressions in neutral, surprised and angry state of mind: A) neutral statements, B) neutral question, C) surprised statement, D) surprised question, E) angry statement, E) angry question.

Figure 4: Examples of three phonological minimal pairs: A) "tea", B) "Thursday", C) "orange", D) "October", E) "Moscow" F) "old".

3.2.2 Emotion signs

In KRSL, as in other sign languages, the signs for emotions, such as ANGRY, SAD, SURPRISED, SCARED, PITY, HAPPY are accompanied with facial expressions corresponding to the emotion named by the sign. Therefore, we collected phrases containing the six signs for basic emotions. We hypothesized that, since facial expressions in this signs are lexically associated with them, inclusion of non-manual components can improve recognition of these signs.

3.2.3 Emotional questions vs. emotional statements

De Vos et al. (2009) analyzed interaction of emotional facial expressions and grammatical non-manual markers in Sign Language of the Netherlands (NGT). They elicited polar and content questions in NGT, as well as sentences with topic marking signed neutrally, with anger, or with surprise. Polar questions and topics are normally accompanied with raised eyebrows, while content questions with furrowed eyebrows; the emotion of anger causes eyebrow furrowing, and the emotion of surprise causes eyebrow raise. Therefore, in some of the contexts emotions and grammar were in agreement (e.g. surprised polar questions), while in others in competition (e.g. angry polar questions). The researchers found that emotional and grammatical non-manuals interact in complex ways.

We created a similar dataset for KRSL. The signers were asked to sign ten sentences as either a statement (no eyebrow movement expected), a polar questions (eyebrow raise expected) or wh-questions (adding single question sing), and with three different emotions: neutral, surprise (eyebrow raise expected), and anger (eyebrow furrowing expected). We hypothesized that emotions and grammatical markers would interact in complex ways, and that these interactions might negatively influence recognition accuracy when recognizing sentence types (questions vs statements).

3.2.4 Minimal pairs

Similar to words in spoken languages, signs can form minimal pairs: one can find signs that are minimally different in their manual component (Sandler and Lillo-Martin, 2006). For instance, the KRSL signs "Moscow", "old", and "grandmother" all have the same handshape (the fist) and location (the cheek), but different movements. It is possible to find signs which are distinguished by handshape only or by location only as well.

We hypothesized that minimal pairs of signs are potentially difficult for recognition, as they are quite similar in shape. However, these signs are additionally distinguished by mouthing (see above). Therefore, including non-manual components can improve sign recognition for such pairs of signs. We thus created a dataset with 15 minimal pairs of signs signed as parts of phrases.

3.3 Openpose Feature Extraction

We utilized OpenPose library (Cao et al., 2017; Wei et al., 2016) in order to extract the keypoints of the person in the videos. OpenPose is the real-time multi-person keypoint detection library for body, face, hands, and foot estimation provided by Carnegie Mellon University (Simon et al., 2017). It detects 2D information of 25 keypoints (joints) on the body and feet, 2x21 keypoints on both hands and 70 keypoints on the face. It also provides a 3D single-person keypoint detection in real time on multi-camera videos. OpenPose provides the values for each keyframe as an output in JSON format. Since the dataset we use consists of RGB videos, we only consider 2D keypoints in this work.

4 Baseline methods

Signing recognition can be considered as a variation of action recognition or human pose estimation tasks. Keypoint detection library OpenPose (Cao et al., 2017; Wei et al., 2016) enables us to evaluate both manual (hand keypoints) and non-manual features (face and pose keypoints). One of the latest works in action recognition (Tran et al., 2018) introduces a new spatiotemporal convolutional block R(2+1)D that achieves state-of-the-art results. In order to analyze and classify collected dataset we employ both approaches as a baseline models for isolated sign recognition. We have extracted isolated clips from the statement-question subset of following signs: 'what', 'who', 'which', 'which one', 'when', 'where (direction)', 'where (location)', 'why', 'how', and 'how much'. We distinguish them to twenty classes (as ten words have a pair in both statement and question form).

4.1 Pose estimation baseline

Our subsets mainly imply classification problems and have sequential features. Generally, we extract features in each frame of videos using OpenPose (Cao et al., 2017; Wei et al., 2016) library and then feed it to the classification algorithm. Therefore, we exploit classical machine learning techniques, namely Logistic regression by concatenating sequences of keypoints into one sample. The sequence of keyframes holds the frames of each sign video. Since we aim to compare performances of non-manual features, we prepared two conditions: **manual only** and **manual and non-manual fea-**

tures combined. Consequentially, in the first case, one datapoint consists of concatenated keypoints of each video and has a maximum of 30 frames * 84 keypoints = 2520 **manual only** features, while in the second case, one datapoint consists of 30 frames * 274 keypoints = 8220 **manual and non-manual features** for each of the twenty classes. We used the *scikit-learn* library for Python as the keypoints classification method for the experiments presented in this paper.

4.2 Action recognition baseline

Latest works in action recognition either employ Two-Stream Inflated 3D ConvNet (I3D) (Carreira and Zisserman, 2017) or spatiotemporal convolutional block R(2+1)D (Tran et al., 2018). Both architectures are usually trained on ImageNet (Russakovsky et al., 2015) and fine-tuned on Kinetics dataset (Kay et al., 2017).

In this paper, we employ R(2+1)D (Ghadiyaram et al., 2019) model which is highly accurate and significantly faster than other approaches. It is additionally pre-trained on over 65 million videos. Also, it uses as input only video frames, which makes it faster comparing to other approached that require optical flow fields as additional input. In order to recognize signs from our dataset we fine-tuned R(2+1)D on the statement-questions subset. Since we have a different number of classes in our subset, only the last fully connected of the model is re-trained.

4.3 Implementation details

The action recognition baseline is implemented in PyTorch (Paszke et al., 2019) and uses a R(2+1)D pre-trained model (Ghadiyaram et al., 2019). Model input size (number of consecutive frames) is set to 8 and batch size is 16. We train the model for 20 epochs with a starting learning rate of 0.0001. All frames are scaled to a resolution of 112 112 and keeping original ratio. Also, during the training process frames are randomly cropped with scale between 0.6 and 1. The pose estimation baseline is implemented using scikit-learn library (Pedregosa et al., 2011) and takes as an input sequence of keypoints extracted using the OpenPose library (Cao et al., 2017; Wei et al., 2016). We train Logistic Regression classifier using the 'lbfgs' solver and L2 penalty.

4.4 Suggested Train-Test Splits

As stated in Table 2, each subset has 5 signers, which were assigned an approximately equal number of videos. The only exception is the Emotional Question-Statement subset which has 10 signers. We assign all videos performed by 4 signers in the train set and videos with the remaining signer into the test set. In addition, we choose the remaining signer for each class randomly, to diversify train and test data. Validation set is randomly chosen from the train set and has 20% length of the train set.

4.5 Data augmentation

The main problem of developing sign language recognition algorithm is that data is usually not big and/or diverse enough for generalization. Thus, we suggest a simple method to augment image sequences of fixed length from videos with a variable amount of frames. The only constraint is that a video has to be longer than a chosen fixed length.

Given a sign video $V = (f_1, f_2, ..., f_m)$ that contains m frames, which satisfies condition $m \geq n$, where n is the chosen fixed sequence length, we pick equally distanced frames from videos with a random initial frame. By distance between the frames, we mean the difference between their indexes, let's call it s.

$$s = \left\lfloor \frac{m}{n} \right\rfloor$$

The initial frame is picked among all possible candidates which are first s frames with k left-over frames after them. Here, $k = m \bmod n$. Therefore, the augmented fixed sized sequence is $S = (f_i, f_{i+s}, f_{i+2s}, ..., f_{i+ns})$, where i is a random integer from 1 to $s + k$.

5 Experimental Results

A series of experiments was conducted in order to investigate whether non-manual features would improve recognition accuracy. All experiments were performed on isolated signs extracted from the Question-Statement subset and divided into 20 classes (10 signs as statement and questions). The first experiment was the classification of 20 classes. For this reason we trained two baseline models: a logistic regression model using only manual features and with non-manual features as an input, and a R(2+1)D model on full frames as an input. Evaluation of each model was repeated 10 times with random train/test splits to avoid extreme cases. Table 3 presents the mean scores and standard deviations for the first experiment. The second experiment used the same dataset with 20 classes to compare and contrast the accuracy in terms of its improvement with different combinations of non-manual components. Table 4 presents the accuracy scores for each combination of features.

	R(2+1)D	Logistic regression	
Features	Full frame	Manual	Non-manual
Mean	86%	73.4%	77%
Std Dev	1	0.45	0.57

Table 3: Mean scores of accuracy for the question-statement subset after 10 iterations with random train/test splits

5.1 Question vs. Statement

Our first experiment used the Question-Statement subset divided into 20 classes (10 signs used in statements and questions). We have extracted manual and non-manual features for the isolated signs of the Question-Statement subset. The highest accuracy was achieved by the R(2+1)D model and was 86%, which is 9% higher comparing to the Logistic regression model. For the Logistic regression model trained on sequence of keypoints testing mean accuracy scores are 73.4% and 77% on manual-only and both manual and non-manual features respectively. As expected, non-manual features improved the results by 3.6% on average (from 73.4% accuracy to 77% accuracy). At the same time, improvement was not very high. The reason for that could be that the number of non-manual features is bigger than the number of manual features.

5.2 A case of combining different modalities

In this experiment different combinations of non-manual markers (eyebrow and head position vs. mouthing) were compared and their role in recognition was analyzed.

The lowest testing accuracy was 73.25% for the combination of manual features and eyebrows keypoints. Eyebrows without any other non-manual feature did not provide valuable information for recognition. Only when they were used in combination with other features, the accuracy was improved. The highest testing accuracy was 78.2% for the combination of manual features and faceline, eyebrows, and mouth keypoints. When only mouth keypoints were used in combination with the manual features, the accuracy also increased by 0.5% compared to the baseline of 77%. Thus, we see that mouthing provides extra information, which can be used in recognition, because signers usually articulate words while performing corresponding signs. Eyebrows and head position provide additional grammatical markers to differentiate statements from questions.

Features combination	Accuracy
Manual only	73.4%
Manual & Non-manual all	77%
Manual & Face, eyebrows, mouth	**78.2%**
Manual & Eyebrows, mouth	77.2%
Manual & Only mouth	77.5%
Manual & Only eyebrows	73.25%

Table 4: Comparison of results of features combinations

6 Conclusion

This paper presents the K-RSL dataset motivated by the need to create SL datasets for interdisciplinary purposes e.g. for computer vision and computational linguistics research. Due to the challenging nature of SLR, the proposed dataset aims to attract the attention of the computer vision community with the K-RSL dataset being linguistically rich. The data was carefully selected to find various cases when manual gestures will not provide good performance and will stress the need to include non-manual components into consideration. In addition to computer vision community, this dataset can be utilized by the linguistics community to explore research questions and computationally prove their hypotheses. Future work will include expanding the vocabulary of the corpus in addition to diversifying and increasing the number of signers recorded in noisy environmental conditions (e.g. outside of the office environment).

Acknowledgment

This work was supported by the Nazarbayev University Faculty Development Competitive Research Grant Program 2019-2021 "Kazakh Sign Language Automatic Recognition System (K-SLARS)". Award number is 110119FD4545.

References

Epameinondas Antonakos, Anastasios Roussos, and Stefanos Zafeiriou. 2015. A survey on mouth modeling and analysis for sign language recognition. *11th IEEE International Conference and Workshops on Automatic Face and Gesture Recognition (FG)*, 1:1–7.

Vassilis Athitsos, Carol Neidle, Stan Sclaroff, Joan Nash, Alexandra Stefan, Quan Yuan, and Ashwin Thangali. 2008. The american sign language lexicon video dataset. *2008 IEEE Computer Society Conference on Computer Vision and Pattern Recognition Workshops*, pages 1–8.

Danielle Bragg, Oscar Koller, Mary Bellard, Larwan Berke, Patrick Boudreault, Annelies Braffort, Naomi Caselli, Matt Huenerfauth, Hernisa Kacorri, Tessa Verhoef, et al. 2019. Sign language recognition, generation, and translation: An interdisciplinary perspective. In *The 21st International ACM SIGACCESS Conference on Computers and Accessibility*, pages 16–31. ACM.

Zhe Cao, Tomas Simon, Shih-En Wei, and Yaser Sheikh. 2017. Realtime multi-person 2d pose estimation using part affinity fields. In *Proceedings of the IEEE Conference on Computer Vision and Pattern Recognition*, pages 7291–7299.

Joao Carreira and Andrew Zisserman. 2017. Quo vadis, action recognition? a new model and the kinetics dataset. In *proceedings of the IEEE Conference on Computer Vision and Pattern Recognition*, pages 6299–6308.

Theocharis Chatzis, Andreas Stergioulas, Dimitrios Konstantinidis, Kosmas Dimitropoulos, and Petros Daras. 2020. A comprehensive study on deep learning-based 3d hand pose estimation methods. *Applied Sciences*, 10(19):6850.

Necati Cihan Camgoz, Simon Hadfield, Oscar Koller, Hermann Ney, and Richard Bowden. 2018. Neural sign language translation. pages 7784–7793.

Helen Cooper, Brian Holt, and Richard Bowden. 2011. Sign language recognition. *Visual Analysis of Humans*, pages 539–562.

Onno A Crasborn, Els Van Der Kooij, Dafydd Waters, Bencie Woll, and Johanna Mesch. 2008. Frequency distribution and spreading behavior of different types of mouth actions in three sign languages. *Sign Language & Linguistics*, 11(1):45–67.

Runpeng Cui, Hu Liu, and Changshui Zhang. 2019. A Deep Neural Framework for Continuous Sign Language Recognition by Iterative Training. *IEEE Transactions on Multimedia*, 21(7):1880–1891.

Connie De Vos, Els Van der Kooij, and Onno Crasborn. 2009. Mixed signals: Combining linguistic and affective functions of eyebrows in questions in sign language of the netherlands. *Language and speech*, 52(2-3):315–339.

Eleni Efthimiou and Stavroula-Evita Fotinea. 2007. Gslc: creation and annotation of a greek sign language corpus for hci. *International Conference on Universal Access in Human-Computer Interaction*, pages 657–666.

Fernando A Freitas, Sarajane M Peres, Clodoaldo AM Lima, and Felipe V Barbosa. 2017. Grammatical facial expression recognition in sign language discourse: a study at the syntax level. *Information Systems Frontiers*, 19(6):1243–1259.

Deepti Ghadiyaram, Du Tran, and Dhruv Mahajan. 2019. Large-scale weakly-supervised pre-training for video action recognition. In *Proceedings of the IEEE Conference on Computer Vision and Pattern Recognition*, pages 12046–12055.

Jie Huang, Wengang Zhou, Qilin Zhang, Houqiang Li, and Weiping Li. 2018. Video-based sign language recognition without temporal segmentation. In *32nd AAAI Conference on Artificial Intelligence, AAAI 2018*, pages 2257–2264. AAAI press.

Will Kay, Joao Carreira, Karen Simonyan, Brian Zhang, Chloe Hillier, Sudheendra Vijaya-narasimhan, Fabio Viola, Tim Green, Trevor Back, Paul Natsev, et al. 2017. The kinetics human action video dataset. *arXiv preprint arXiv:1705.06950*.

Vadim Kimmelman, Alfarabi Imashev, Medet Muku-shev, and Anara Sandygulova. 2020. Eyebrow position in grammatical and emotional expressions in kazakh-russian sign language: A quantitative study. *PloS one*, 15(6):e0233731.

Sang-Ki Ko, Chang Jo Kim, Hyedong Jung, and Choongsang Cho. 2019. Neural sign language translation based on human keypoint estimation. *Applied Sciences*, 9(13):2683.

Oscar Koller. 2020. Quantitative survey of the state of the art in sign language recognition. *arXiv preprint arXiv:2008.09918*.

Oscar Koller, Cihan Camgoz, Hermann Ney, and Richard Bowden. 2019. Weakly Supervised Learning with Multi-Stream CNN-LSTM-HMMs to Discover Sequential Parallelism in Sign Language Videos. *IEEE Transactions on Pattern Analysis and Machine Intelligence*, pages 1–1.

Sunil Kumar, Manas Kamal Bhuyan, and Biplab Ketan Chakraborty. 2017. Extraction of texture and geometrical features from informative facial regions for sign language recognition. *Journal on Multimodal User Interfaces*, 11(2):227–239.

Jingjing Liu, Bo Liu, Shaoting Zhang, Fei Yang, Peng Yang, Dimitris N Metaxas, and Carol Neidle. 2014. Non-manual grammatical marker recognition based on multi-scale, spatio-temporal analysis of head pose and facial expressions. *Image and Vision Computing*, 32(10):671–681.

Aleix M Martínez, Ronnie B Wilbur, Robin Shay, and Avinash C Kak. 2002. Purdue rvl-slll asl database for automatic recognition of american sign language. *Proceedings. Fourth IEEE International Conference on Multimodal Interfaces*, pages 167–172.

Medet Mukushev, Arman Sabyrov, Alfarabi Imashev, Kenessary Koishybay, Vadim Kimmelman, and Anara Sandygulova. 2020. Evaluation of manual and non-manual components for sign language recognition. In *Proceedings of The 12th Language Resources and Evaluation Conference*, pages 6073–6078.

Adam Paszke, Sam Gross, Francisco Massa, Adam Lerer, James Bradbury, Gregory Chanan, Trevor Killeen, Zeming Lin, Natalia Gimelshein, Luca Antiga, Alban Desmaison, Andreas Kopf, Edward Yang, Zachary DeVito, Martin Raison, Alykhan Tejani, Sasank Chilamkurthy, Benoit Steiner, Lu Fang, Junjie Bai, and Soumith Chintala. 2019. Pytorch: An imperative style, high-performance deep learning library. In H. Wallach, H. Larochelle, A. Beygelzimer, F. dAlché-Buc, E. Fox, and R. Garnett, editors, *Advances in Neural Information Processing Systems 32*, pages 8024–8035. Curran Associates, Inc.

F. Pedregosa, G. Varoquaux, A. Gramfort, V. Michel, B. Thirion, O. Grisel, M. Blondel, P. Prettenhofer, R. Weiss, V. Dubourg, J. Vanderplas, A. Passos, D. Cournapeau, M. Brucher, M. Perrot, and E. Duchesnay. 2011. Scikit-learn: Machine learning in Python. *Journal of Machine Learning Research*, 12:2825–2830.

Roland Pfau and Josep Quer. 2010. Nonmanuals: Their prosodic and grammatical roles. *Sign languages*, pages 381–402.

Olga Russakovsky, Jia Deng, Hao Su, Jonathan Krause, Sanjeev Satheesh, Sean Ma, Zhiheng Huang, Andrej Karpathy, Aditya Khosla, Michael Bernstein, Alexander C. Berg, and Li Fei-Fei. 2015. ImageNet Large Scale Visual Recognition Challenge. *International Journal of Computer Vision (IJCV)*, 115(3):211–252.

Wendy Sandler and Diane Lillo-Martin. 2006. *Sign language and linguistic universals*. Cambridge University Press.

Tomas Simon, Hanbyul Joo, Iain Matthews, and Yaser Sheikh. 2017. Hand keypoint detection in single images using multiview bootstrapping. In *Proceedings of the IEEE conference on Computer Vision and Pattern Recognition*, pages 1145–1153.

Du Tran, Heng Wang, Lorenzo Torresani, Jamie Ray, Yann LeCun, and Manohar Paluri. 2018. A closer look at spatiotemporal convolutions for action recognition. In *Proceedings of the IEEE conference on Computer Vision and Pattern Recognition*, pages 6450–6459.

Ville Viitaniemi, Tommi Jantunen, Leena Savolainen, Matti Karppa, and Jorma Laaksonen. 2014. S-pot–a benchmark in spotting signs within continuous signing. European Language Resources Association (LREC).

Ulrich Von Agris, Moritz Knorr, and Karl-Friedrich Kraiss. 2008. The significance of facial features for automatic sign language recognition. *8th IEEE International Conference on Automatic Face & Gesture Recognition*, pages 1–6.

Shih-En Wei, Varun Ramakrishna, Takeo Kanade, and Yaser Sheikh. 2016. Convolutional pose machines. In *Proceedings of the IEEE Conference on Computer Vision and Pattern Recognition*, pages 4724–4732.

Hee-Deok Yang and Seong-Whan Lee. 2013. Robust sign language recognition by combining manual and non-manual features based on conditional random field and support vector machine. *Pattern Recognition Letters*, 34(16):2051–2056.

Ulrike Zeshan. 2004a. Hand, head and face-negative constructions in sign languages. *Linguistic Typology*, 8(1):1–58.

Ulrike Zeshan. 2004b. Interrogative constructions in signed languages: Crosslinguistic perspectives. *Language*, pages 7–39.

Zhihao Zhang, Junfu Pu, Liansheng Zhuang, Wengang Zhou, and Houqiang Li. 2019. Continuous Sign Language Recognition via Reinforcement Learning. pages 285–289. Institute of Electrical and Electronics Engineers (IEEE).

Hao Zhou, Wengang Zhou, and Houqiang Li. 2019. Dynamic Pseudo Label Decoding for Continuous Sign Language Recognition. pages 1282–1287. Institute of Electrical and Electronics Engineers (IEEE).

From Dataset Recycling to Multi-Property Extraction and Beyond

Tomasz Dwojak[1,2]**, Michał Pietruszka**[1,3]**, Łukasz Borchmann**[1,4]**,
Jakub Chłędowski**[1,3]**, and Filip Graliński**[1,2]

[1]Applica.ai
[2]Faculty of Mathematics and Computer Science, Adam Mickiewicz University in Poznan
[3]Faculty of Mathematics and Computer Science, Jagiellonian University
[4]Institute of Computing Science, Poznan University of Technology

`tomasz.dwojak@applica.ai`

Abstract

This paper investigates various Transformer architectures on the WikiReading Information Extraction and Machine Reading Comprehension dataset. The proposed dual-source model outperforms the current state-of-the-art by a large margin. Next, we introduce WikiReading Recycled—a newly developed public dataset, and the task of multiple-property extraction. It uses the same data as WikiReading but does not inherit its predecessor's identified disadvantages. In addition, we provide a human-annotated test set with diagnostic subsets for a detailed analysis of model performance.

1 Introduction

The emergence of attention-based models has revolutionized Natural Language Processing (Young et al., 2018). Pretraining these models on large corpora like BookCorpus (Zhu et al., 2015) has been shown to yield a reliable and robust base for downstream tasks. These include Natural Language Inference (Bowman et al., 2015), Question Answering (Rajpurkar et al., 2016), Named Entity Recognition (Yadav and Bethard, 2018; Goyal et al., 2018; Li et al., 2020), and Property Extraction (Hewlett et al., 2016).

The creation of large supervised datasets often comes with trade-offs, such as one between the quality and quantity of data. For instance, the WikiReading dataset (Hewlett et al., 2016) has been created in such a way that WikiData annotations were treated as the expected answers for related Wikipedia articles. However, the above datasets were created separately, and the information content of both sources overlaps only partially. Hence, the resulting dataset may contain noise.

The best models can achieve results better than the human baseline across many NLP datasets such as MSCQAs (Wang et al., 2018), STS-B, QNLI (Raffel et al., 2020), CoLA or MRPC (Wang et al., 2020). However, as a consequence of different kinds of noise in the data, they rarely maximize the score metric (Stanislawek et al., 2019). While current work in NLP is focused on preparing new datasets, we regard recycling the current ones as equally important as creating a new one. Thus, after outperforming previous state-of-the-art on WikiReading, we investigated the dataset's weaknesses and created an entirely new, more challenging Multi-Property Extraction task with improved data splits and a reliable, human-annotated test set.

Contribution. The specific contributions of this work are the following. We analyzed the WikiReading dataset and pointed out its weaknesses. We introduced a Multi-Property Extraction task by creating a new dataset: WikiReading Recycled. Our dataset contains a human-annotated test set, with multiple subsets aimed to benchmark qualities such as generalization on unseen properties. We introduced a Mean-Multi-Property-F_1 score suited for the new Multi-Property Extraction task. We evaluated previously used architectures on both datasets. Furthermore, we showed that pretrained transformer models (Dual-Source RoBERTa and T5) beat all other baselines. The new dataset and all the models mentioned in the present paper were made publicly available on GitHub.[1]

2 Related Work

Early work in relation extraction revolves around problems crafted using distant supervision methods, which are semi-supervised methods that automatically label pools of unlabeled data (Craven and Kumlien, 1999). In contrast, many QA datasets were created through crowd-sourcing, where annotators were asked to formulate questions with

---

[1]`https://github.com/applicaai/multi-property-extraction`

Proceedings of the 24th Conference on Computational Natural Language Learning, pages 641–651
Online, November 19-20, 2020. ©2020 Association for Computational Linguistics
https://doi.org/10.18653/v1/P17

Dataset	Task	Input	Output
SNLI	Natural Language Inference	two sentences	relation between the sentences
SQUAD	Question Answering	article, question	answer to the question
WiNER	Named Entity Recognition	article	annotated named entities
WR	Property Extraction	article, property	value of the property
WRR (ours)	Multi-Property Extraction	article, properties	values of the properties

Table 1: Comparison of NLP tasks on text comprehension and information extraction. More differences between WR and WRR were outlined in Table 3.

answers that require knowledge retrieval and information synthesis. One of the most popular QA datasets is Wikipedia-based SQUAD, where an instance consists of a human-formulated question, and an encyclopedic reading passage used to base the answer on (Rajpurkar et al., 2018). Another crowd-sourced dataset that profoundly influenced Natural Language Inference research is SNLI (Bowman et al., 2015)—a three-way semantics-based classification of a relation between two different sentences.

Both SQUAD and SNLI are large-scale Machine Reading Comprehension (MRC) tasks, but they cannot be treated as Property Extraction as defined in Section 3; hence they are not considered in this paper. Similarly, some MRC problems framed in TREC tracks, such as Conversational Assistance or Question Answering, are beyond the scope of this paper (Dalton et al., 2020; Dang et al., 2007).

Hewlett et al. (2016) proposed the WikiReading dataset that consists of a Wikipedia article and related WikiData statement. No additional annotation work was performed, yet the resulting dataset was of presumably high reliability. Nevertheless, we consider an additional human annotation to be desired (Section 4.3). Alongside the dataset, a property extraction task was introduced. The idea behind it is to read an article given a property name and to infer the associated value from the article. The property extraction paradigm is described in detail in Section 3, whereas a brief comparison to related datasets is presented in Table 1.

Initially, the best-performing model used placeholders to allow rewriting out-of-vocabulary words to the output. Next, Choi et al. (2017) presented a reinforcement learning approach that improved results on a challenging subset of the 10% longest articles. This framework was extended by Wang and Jin (2019) with a self-correcting action that removes the inaccurate answer from the answer generation module and continues to read.

Data split	Size	In train	%
Validation set	1,452,591	1,374,820	94.65
Test set	821,409	780,639	95.04

Table 2: The size of WikiReading splits (*Size*) and number of articles leaked from the train set as an absolute value or percentage.

Hewlett et al. (2017) hold the state-of-the-art on WikiReading with their proposition of SWEAR that attends over a sliding window's representations to reduce documents to one vector from which another GRU network generates the answer (Chung et al., 2014). Additionally, they evaluated a strong semi-supervised solution on a randomly sampled 1% subset of WikiReading.

To the best of our knowledge, no authors validated Transformer-based models on WikiReading and pretrained encoders.

3 Property Extraction

Let a *property* denote any query for which a system is expected to return an answer from given text. Examples include *country of citizenship* for a biography provided as an input text, or *architect name* for an article regarding the opening of a new building. Contrary to QA problems, a query is not formulated as a question in natural language but rather as a phrase or keyword. We use the term *value* when referring to a valid answer for the stated query. Some properties have multiple valid answers; thus, multiple values are expected. Examine the case of Johann Sebastian Bach's biography for which property *sister* has eight values. We will refer to any task consisting of a tuple (properties, text) for which values are to be provided as a property extraction task.

The biggest publicly available dataset for property extraction is WikiReading (Hewlett et al., 2016). The dataset combines articles from

Wikipedia with Wikidata information. The dataset is of great value; however, several flaws can be identified. First, more than 95% of articles in the test set appeared in the train set (Table 2). Second, the unjustifiably large size of the test set is a substantial obstacle for running experiments. For instance, it takes 50 hours to process the test set using a Transformer model such as $T5_{SMALL}$ on a single NVidia V100 GPU. Finally, WikiReading assumes that every value in the test set can be determined on the basis of a given article. As shown later, this is not the case for 28% of values.

3.1 Towards Multi-Property Extraction

In the Multi-Property Extraction (MPE) scenario we propose, the system is expected to return values for multiple properties at once. Hence, can be considered a generalization of a single-property extraction task as it can be easily formulated as such. Thus, MPE is reverse-compatible with the single-property extraction, and it is still possible to evaluate models trained in the single-property setting.

Many arguments can be considered in favor of framing the problem as MPE. In a typical business scenario, multiple properties are expected to be extracted from a given document. The bulk inference requires a lower computational budget by a factor proportional to the mean number of properties per article, which makes MPE preferable. Moreover, one can expect that systems trained in such a way will manifest emergent properties resulting from the interaction between properties themselves. Consider the set of property-value pairs:

> date of birth: 1915-01-12, date of death: 1979-05-02, place of birth: Saint Petersburg

already predicted by an autoregressive model. It is in principle possible to answer:

> country of citizenship: Russian Empire, country of citizenship: Soviet Union

using the earlier predicted pairs only. This phenomenon emerges if the model (or person) learned the relationships between years, administrative boundaries of the city, and the transformation of the Russian Empire into a communist state that occurred in the meantime. Although no such reasoning is required and the problem can be solved by memorizing related co-occurrence patterns, we intend to achieve the mentioned emergent properties.

Feature	WR	WRR
Base unit	property	article
Examples	18.6M	4.1M
Properties/example	1	4.5
Metric	$M\text{-}F_1$	$MMP\text{-}F_1$
Human-annotated test	−	+
Dataset split	random	controlled
Unseen in evaluation	−	+
Article appears in	few splits	one split

Table 3: Selected differences between WR and WRR. Both metrics are described in Section 6.

4 WikiReading Recycled: Novel Dataset for Multi-Property Extraction

The comparison to existing datasets and shared tasks is briefly presented in Table 1, whereas Table 3 focuses on selected differences between WikiReading Recycled and WikiReading.

4.1 Desiderata

Our set of desiderata is based on the following intentions. We wished to introduce the problem of Multi-Property Extraction to evaluate systems that extract any number of given properties at once from the same source text. Our second objective was to ensure that an article may appear in precisely one data split. The third core intention was to introduce an article-centered data objective instead of a property-centric one. Note that an instance of data should be an article with multiple properties. The fourth objective was to ensure that all properties in the test set can be extracted or inferred. The fifth was to keep the validation and test sets within a reasonable size. Moreover, we aim to provide a test set of the highest quality, lacking noise that could arise from automatic processing. Finally, we intended to benchmark the model generalization abilities – the test set contains properties not seen during training, posing a challenge for current state-of-the-art systems.

4.2 Data Collection and Split

The WikiReading Recycled and WikiReading are based on the same data, yet differ in how they are arranged. Instances from the original WikiReading dataset were merged to produce over 4M samples in the MPE paradigm. Instead of performing a random split, we carefully divide the data assuming that 20% of properties should appear solely in the

Subset	Dev	Test-A	Test-B
rare	4.40	5.12	3.16
unseen	5.53	5.34	2.05
categorical	46.63	44.49	66.51
relational	53.36	55.50	33.49
exact match	20.20	20.16	33.67
long articles	50.39	56.15	30.45

Table 4: An average per-article size of the corresponding subsets as a percent of a total number of properties.

test set (more precisely, not seen before in train and validation sets). Around one thousand articles containing properties not seen in the remaining subsets were drafted to achieve the mentioned objective. Similarly, properties unique for the validation set were introduced to enable approximation of the test set performance without disclosing particular labels. Additionally, test and validation sets share 10% of the properties that do not appear in the train set, increasing the size of these subsets by 2,000 articles each. Another 2,000 articles containing the same properties as the train set were added to each of the validation and test sets. All the remaining articles were used to produce the training set.

To sum up, we achieved a design where as much as 50% of the properties cannot be seen in the training split, while the remaining 50% of the properties can appear in any split. We chose these properties carefully so that the size of the test and validation sets does not exceed 5,000 articles.

4.3 Human Annotation

The quality of test sets plays a pivotal role in reasoning about a system's performance. Therefore, a group of annotators went through the instances of the test set and assessed whether the value either appeared in the article or can be inferred from it. To make further analysis possible, we provide both datasets, before (test-A) and after (test-B) annotation.

The annotation process was non-trivial due to vagueness of the inferability definition, and the scientific character of the considered text. It was required to understand advanced encyclopedic articles e.g., about chemistry, biology, or astronomy, to answer domain-specific properties (scientific classifications or biological taxonomy), which are only possible with deep knowledge about the world and with the ability to learn during the process. Moreover, linguistic skills were required to transliterate

and transcribe first and last names. Note that we consider the value which appears in a different writing script as inferable. Due to the stated issues, we decided to rely on highly trained linguists as annotators.

The process was supported by several heuristics. In particular, the approximate string matching was used to highlight fragments of presumably high importance. Nevertheless, it took seven linguists more than 100 hours in total to complete. On average, two minutes and thirty second were required to verify data assigned to one Wikipedia article.

The relevance of annotation mentioned above can be demonstrated by the fact that 28% of the property-value pairs were marked as unanswerable and removed. As it will be shown later, the Mean-Multi-Property-F_1 on a pre-verified test-A was approximately 20 points lower, and 8% of articles were removed entirely from the test-B during the annotation process.

4.4 Diagnostic Subsets

We determined auxiliary validation subsets with specific qualities, not only to help improve data analysis but also to provide additional information at different stages of development of a system. The qualities we measure and the definition is provided below.

Rare, unseen. *Rare* and *unseen* properties were distinguished depending on their frequency. The number of occurrences in the train set was below a threshold of 4000 for each in *rare* and was precisely 0 for the *unseen* category.

Categorical, relational. We denote a property as *categorical* if its value set contains a limited number of values; otherwise, it is *relational*. We apply normalized entropy with a threshold of 0.7 to obtain properties that belong to the *categorical* subset. For instance, the *continent* property occurs 20060 times, but with 13 possible values, its normalized entropy equals 0.43; hence it is marked as *categorical*. This splitting method is not ideal, but we wanted to use the same method as in (Hewlett et al., 2016). For example, if the distribution of continents was uniform, the property would have been classified as relational. However, in practice, it almost never happens.

Exact match. The *exact match* category applies to cases where expected value is mentioned directly in the source text.

Long articles. Instances with articles longer than 695 words (threshold qualifying to the top 15% longest articles in the train set) constitute the *long articles* diagnostic set.

Characteristics of different systems can be compared qualitatively by evaluating on these subsets. For instance, the *long articles* subset is challenging for systems that consume truncated inputs. *Unseen* is precisely constructed to assess systems' ability to extract previously not seen properties. On the other hand, *rare* can be viewed as an approximation of the system's performance on a lower-resource downstream extraction task. The *categorical* subset is useful in assessing approaches featuring a classifier, whereas it is suboptimal to use such systems for *relational* due to richer output space. Similarly, the *exact match* can be approached with sequence tagging solutions. The share of each diagnostic subset is presented in Table 4.

5 Model Architectures

We evaluate different model architectures on the WikiReading Recycled dataset. We re-implemented the previously best performing WikiReading model, finetuned pretrained Transformer models, and applied a dual-source model. Their competitiveness can be demonstrated by the fact that we were able to outperform the previous state-of-the-art on the WikiReading by a far margin.

Basic seq2seq. A straightforward approach to single-property extraction is to use an LSTM sequence-to-sequence model where the input consists of a property name concatenated with the considered input text. To compare with the previous results, we reproduced the basic sequence-to-sequence model proposed by Hewlett et al. (2016).

Vanilla Transformer. A more up-to-date solution is to use the Transformer architecture (Vaswani et al., 2017) instead of an RNN, and a subword tokenization method, such as unigram LM tokenization (Kudo, 2018). We use the term *vanilla* to denote a model trained from scratch.

Vanilla Dual-Source Transformer. The Transformer architecture was extended to support two inputs and successfully applied in Automatic Post-Editing (Junczys-Dowmunt and Grundkiewicz, 2018). We propose to reuse this Dual-Source Transformer architecture in the property extraction tasks.

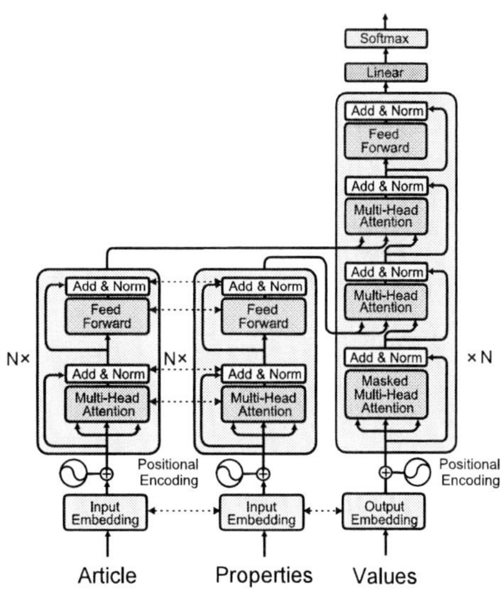

Figure 1: The architecture of Dual-Source Transformer as proposed by Junczys-Dowmunt and Grundkiewicz (2018) for Automatic Post-Editing. In the case of WikiReading Recycled and WikiReading, the encoder transforms an article and the corresponding properties separately.

The architecture consists of two encoders that share parameters and a single decoder. Moreover, the encoders and decoder share embeddings and vocabulary. In our approach, the first encoder is fed with the text of an article, and the second one takes the names of properties (Figure 1). The model is trained to generate a sequence of pairs: (*property*, *value*) separated with a special symbol.

Dual-Source RoBERTa. Recent research shows that pretrained language models can improve performance on downstream tasks (Radford et al., 2018). Therefore, we experimented with the pretrained RoBERTa language model as an encoder. RoBERTa models were developed as a hyper-optimized version of BERT with a byte-level BPE and a considerably larger dictionary (Liu et al., 2019; Devlin et al., 2019). All the model parameters, including the RoBERTa weights, were further optimized on the WikiReading Recycled task.

T5. Recently proposed T5 model (Raffel et al., 2020) is a Transformer model pretrained on a cleaned version of CommonCrawl. T5 is famous for achieving excellent performance on the Super-GLUE benchmark (Wang et al., 2019).

To create a model input, we concatenate a property name and an article. In the case of MPE, we reduce the dataset to the single property setting, as

	Basic seq2seq	Vanilla Transformer	Vanilla Dual-Source	Dual-Source RoBERTa	T5
Numer of inputs	1	1	2	2	1
Pretrained encoder	−	−	−	+	+
Pretrained decoder	−	−	−	−	+
Number of parameters	32M	46M	25M	234M	60M

Table 5: Comparison of evaluated models. The T5 model can be considered as a pretrained equivalent of Vanilla Transformer, and our RoBERTa-based model can be viewed as a partially-pretrained Vanilla Dual-Source Transformer. Basic seq2seq is an RNN counterpart of both T5 and Vanilla Transformer.

used by the T5 model's authors.

6 Evaluation

In this section, we describe the evaluation of previously proposed architectures on both WikiReading and WikiReading Recycled datasets. We would like to highlight that the results are not comparable between the two datasets, as they are based on different train/validation/test splits.

6.1 Metrics

The performance of systems is evaluated using the F1 metric, adapted for the WikiReading Recycled format. For WikiReading, Mean-F_1 follows the originally proposed micro-averaged metric and assesses F1 scores for each property instance, averaged over the whole test set.

Let E denote a set of expected property-value pairs and O model-generated property-value pairs. Assuming $|\cdot|$ stands for set cardinality, precision and recall can be formulated as follows:

$$P(E,O) = \frac{|E \cap O|}{|O|}, \; R(E,O) = \frac{|E \cap O|}{|E|}$$

Then F_1 is computed as a harmonic mean:

$$F_1(E,O) = 2 \cdot \frac{P(E,O) \cdot R(E,O)}{P(E,O) + R(E,O)}$$

Given a sequence $\mathcal{E} = \{E_1, E_2, .., E_n\}$ of expected answers for n test instances, and associated sequence of predictions $\mathcal{O} = \{O_1, O_2, .., O_n\}$, we calculate Mean-$F_1$ as:

$$\text{Mean-}F_1(\mathcal{E}, \mathcal{O}) = \frac{1}{n} \cdot \sum_{i \in [1,n]} F_1(E_i, O_i)$$

In WikiReading Recycled, we adjust the metric to handle many properties in a single test instance. To do that, the E_i and O_i sets contain values from many properties at once and n is equal to the number of articles. Note that in the case of the M-F_1 properties are considered as instances. We call our article-centric metric Mean-Multi-Property-F_1 or in short MMP-F_1.

6.2 Training Details

Since the basic seq2seq model description missed some essential details, they had to be assumed before model training. For example, we supposed that the model consisted of unidirectional LSTMs and truecasing was applied to the output. The rest of the parameters followed the description provided by the authors.

An extensive hyperparameter search was conducted for both Dual-Source Transformers on the WikiReading Recycled task. In the case of the Dual-Source Transformer evaluated on WikiReading we restricted ourselves to hyperparameters following the default values specified in the Marian NMT Toolkit (Junczys-Dowmunt et al., 2018). The only difference was the reduction of encoder and decoder depths to 4.

For the Vanilla Dual-Source Transformer evaluation, both WikiReading and WikiReading Recycled datasets were processed with a SentencePiece model (Kudo, 2018) trained on a concatenated corpus of inputs and outputs with a vocabulary size of 32,000. Dual-Source RoBERTa model is initialized with RoBERTa$_{\text{BASE}}$ (consisting of 12 encoder layers and a dictionary of 50,000 subword units).

In the case of the T5 model, we keep hyperparameters as close as possible to those used during pretraining. The training continues with restored AdaFactor parameters. We finetuned the *small* version of the model in a supervised-only manner.

We truncate the input to the first 512 tokens for all our models.

Hyperparameter Optimization. Hyperparameters for WikiReading Recycled were optimized

Model	Mean-F_1
Basic s2s (Hewlett et al., 2016)	70.8
Placeholder s2s (Choi et al., 2017)	75.6
SWEAR (Hewlett et al., 2017)	76.8
Basic s2s (our run)	74.8
Vanilla Transformer	79.3
Vanilla Dual-Source Transformer	**82.4**

Table 6: Results on WikiReading (test set). *Basic s2s* denotes the re-implemented model described in Section 6.2.

using the Tree-structured Parzen Estimator algorithm (Bergstra et al., 2011) with additional heuristics and Gaussian priors resulting from the default settings proposed for this sampler in the Optuna framework (Akiba et al., 2019). An evaluation was performed every 8,000 steps, and the validation-based early stopping was applied when no progress was achieved in 3 consecutive validations. The total number of 250 trials was performed for each architecture. Intermediate results of each trial were monitored and used to ensure only the top 10% trials were allowed to continue. Details of the hyperparameter optimization are presented in Appendix A.

6.3 Results on WikiReading

Although the main focus of our evaluation is the WikiReading Recycled dataset; we additionally evaluate whether the Vanilla Dual-Source Transformer can improve the state-of-the-art on WikiReading.

We reproduced the *Basic seq2seq* model. It achieved a Mean-F_1 score of 74.8, which is 4 points higher than reported by Hewlett et al. (2016). The difference may be caused by poor optimization in the original work. Our dual-source solution achieves 82.4 and outperforms the previous state-of-the-art model by 5.6 Mean-F_1 points. To measure the impact of using two encoders instead of one, we evaluated the Vanilla Single-source Transformer, which takes a concatenated pair of article and property as its input. Our dual-source model outperformed its single-source counterpart by 3.1 points. Table 6 presents the final results.

6.4 Results on WikiReading Recycled

The results on WikiReading show that the Dual-Source Transformer is beneficial to the Property Extraction task. On WikiReading Recycled, we supplement the evaluation with pretrained models: Dual-Source RoBERTa and T5.

Table 7 presents Mean-Multi-Property-F_1 scores on the annotated test set (test-B). All the transformer-based models outperform the *Basic seq2seq*. The Dual-Source Transformer achieved 77.5 Mean-Multi-Property-F_1. Its pretrained version, Dual-Source RoBERTa, improves the result by 1.4 points. As the T5 model beats the Vanilla Dual-Source Transformer, we may conclude that even though the WikiReading Recycled dataset is very large, the pretraining is crucial for this MPE task. It is worth remembering that the results on WikiReading and WikiReading Recycled are not comparable due to the dissimilarities in metrics and datasets. We will elaborate on that in section 7.

7 Discussion and Analysis

The final scores of transformer-based models differ slightly on WikiReading Recycled. In order to get more insight, we analyze the models on diagnostic sets described in Section 4.4.

Impact of Property Frequency. We provide two diagnostic sets related to property frequency: *unseen* and *rare*. Both dual-source models failed on the *unseen* subset. These models ignored the *unseen* properties from the input and did not generate any answer. The best result was achieved by the T5 model (10.9 points), albeit it still does not meet expectations.

The results on the *rare* subset show that the pretraining makes a difference if properties are infrequent in the train set (Figure 2).

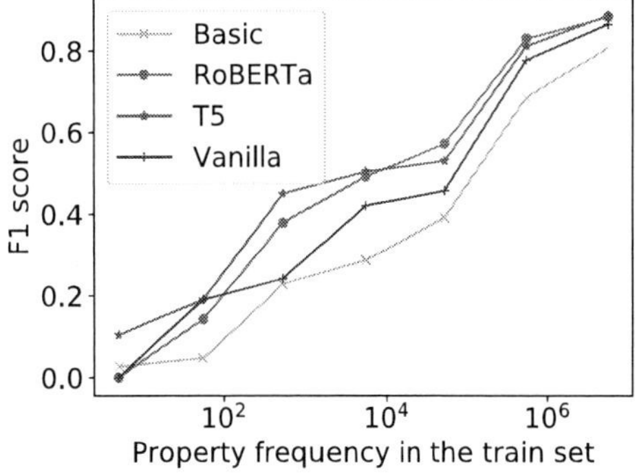

Figure 2: The relation of property frequency and Mean-Multi-Property-F_1. Both RoBERTa and Vanilla refer to Dual-Source Transformers.

Model	unseen	rare	categorical	relational	exact match	long	test-B
Basic seq2seq	2.0	30.2	84.9	50.2	71.1	56.4	75.2
Vanilla Dual-Source	0.0	40.7	83.9	70.8	80.5	63.1	77.5
Dual-Source RoBERTa	0.0	50.7	86.0	76.8	84.3	68.2	80.9
Finetuned T5	10.9	53.8	86.3	73.4	83.4	65.9	80.3

Table 7: Results on WikiReading Recycled human-annotated test set supplemented with scores on diagnostics subsets. All scores are Mean-Multi-Property-F_1.

Impact of Property Type. The extraction of some properties may be treated as a classification task since the set of their valid values is limited. In this case, all models perform similarly and achieve approximately 85 Mean-Multi-Property-F_1. The difficulty of the task increases proportionally to the normalized entropy value, which may lead to the divergence of model performances. This phenomenon is visible in the case of our Basic seq2seq, where the weakness is evident above the 0.5 threshold. The details are presented in Figure 3.

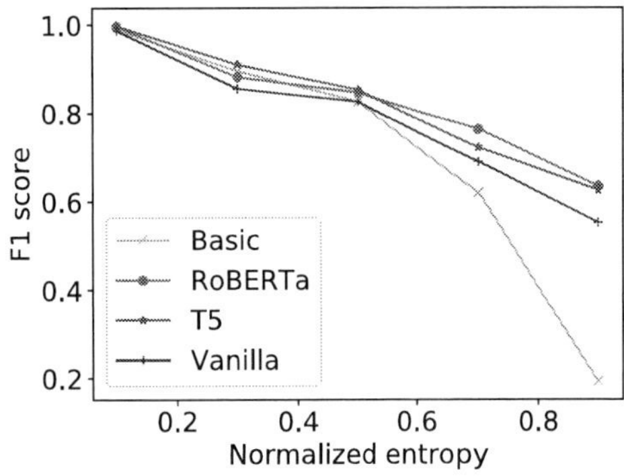

Figure 3: The relation of property normalized entropy and Mean-Multi-Property-F_1. Both RoBERTa and Vanilla refer to Dual-Source Transformers.

Exact Match and Long Articles. The results from the exact match and long articles subsets are correlated with the scores attained on the test-B set; however, the absolute values achieved differ substantially. This is because the long article subset is more challenging, as the chance of an answer appearing in the constant-length prefix decreases with the length of the article. The use of recently introduced models like LongFormer (Beltagy et al., 2020) and BigBird (Zaheer et al., 2020) might decrease the gap in scores between long and average-length articles. On the other hand, system performance should increase when the answer is provided directly in the text, as can be found in the exact match subset.

Difficulty of Test Sets. To compare the difficulty of the WikiReading and WikiReading Recycled test sets, we converted the outputs from the non-annotated WikiReading Recycled test set (test-A) to WikiReading format, and calculated the Mean-F_1. With the Vanilla Dual-Source Transformer, we obtained 54.0 Mean-F_1, 28.4 points less than on WikiReading. This considerable decrease in score shows that the WikiReading Recycled test-A set is more difficult than WikiReading. The reason behind this is that we removed leakage of articles between splits, and we also added more infrequent properties that are harder to answer.

Impact of Human Annotation. The Vanilla Dual-Source Transformer was evaluated on both WikiReading Recycled test sets. It obtained Mean-Multi-Property-F_1 of 62.6 on the non annotated test-A set, while achieving 77.5 on the annotated test-B. This discrepancy suggests that the linguists indeed succeeded to remove non-inferable properties. We anticipate that cleaning the train set in a similar fashion could improve the stability of the training and the overall results.

8 Summary

We introduced WikiReading Recycled—the first Multi-Property Extraction dataset with a human-annotated test set. We provided strong baselines that improved the current state-of-the-art on WikiReading by a large margin. The best-performing architecture was successfully adapted from Automatic Post-Editing systems. We show that using pretrained language models increases the performance on the WikiReading Recycled dataset significantly, despite its large size.

Additionally, we created diagnostic subsets to qualitatively assess model performance. The results on a challenging subset of *unseen* properties reveal that despite high overall scores, the evaluated systems fail to provide satisfactory performance.

Low scores indicate an opportunity to improve, as these properties were verified by annotators and are expected to be answerable. We look forward to seeing models closing this gap and leading to remarkable progress in Machine Reading Comprehension.

The dataset and models, as well as their detailed configurations required for reproducibility, are publicly available.

Acknowledgements

The Smart Growth Operational Programme supported this research under project no. POIR.01.01.01-00-0877/19 (A universal platform for robotic automation of processes requiring text comprehension, with a unique level of implementation and service automation).

References

Takuya Akiba, Shotaro Sano, Toshihiko Yanase, Takeru Ohta, and Masanori Koyama. 2019. Optuna: A next-generation hyperparameter optimization framework. In *Proceedings of the 25th ACM SIGKDD International Conference on Knowledge Discovery & Data Mining*, KDD '19, pages 2623–2631, New York, NY, USA. Association for Computing Machinery.

Iz Beltagy, Matthew E. Peters, and Arman Cohan. 2020. Longformer: The long-document transformer. *Computing Research Repository*, arXiv:2004.05150.

James S. Bergstra, Rémi Bardenet, Yoshua Bengio, and Balázs Kégl. 2011. Algorithms for hyper-parameter optimization. In J. Shawe-Taylor, R. S. Zemel, P. L. Bartlett, F. Pereira, and K. Q. Weinberger, editors, *Advances in Neural Information Processing Systems 24*, pages 2546–2554. Curran Associates, Inc.

Samuel R. Bowman, Gabor Angeli, Christopher Potts, and Christopher D. Manning. 2015. A large annotated corpus for learning natural language inference. In *Proceedings of the 2015 Conference on Empirical Methods in Natural Language Processing*, pages 632–642, Lisbon, Portugal. Association for Computational Linguistics.

Eunsol Choi, Daniel Hewlett, Jakob Uszkoreit, Illia Polosukhin, Alexandre Lacoste, and Jonathan Berant. 2017. Coarse-to-Fine Question Answering for Long Documents. In *Proceedings of the 55th Annual Meeting of the Association for Computational Linguistics (Volume 1: Long Papers)*, pages 209–220, Vancouver, Canada. Association for Computational Linguistics.

Junyoung Chung, Caglar Gulcehre, Kyunghyun Cho, and Yoshua Bengio. 2014. Empirical evaluation of gated recurrent neural networks on sequence modeling. In *NIPS 2014 Workshop on Deep Learning*.

Mark Craven and Johan Kumlien. 1999. Constructing biological knowledge bases by extracting information from text sources. In *Proceedings of the Seventh International Conference on Intelligent Systems for Molecular Biology*, pages 77–86. AAAI Press.

Jeffrey Dalton, Chenyan Xiong, and Jamie Callan. 2020. TREC CAsT 2019: The conversational assistance track overview. *Computing Research Repository*, Arxiv:2003.13624.

Hoa Trang Dang, Diane Kelly, and Jimmy J Lin. 2007. Overview of the TREC 2007 question answering track. In *Trec*, volume 7.

Jacob Devlin, Ming-Wei Chang, Kenton Lee, and Kristina Toutanova. 2019. BERT: Pre-training of deep bidirectional transformers for language understanding. In *Proceedings of the 2019 Conference of the North American Chapter of the Association for Computational Linguistics: Human Language Technologies, Volume 1 (Long and Short Papers)*, pages 4171–4186, Minneapolis, Minnesota. Association for Computational Linguistics.

Archana Goyal, Vishal Gupta, and Manish Kumar. 2018. Recent named entity recognition and classification techniques: A systematic review. *Computer Science Review*, 29:21–43.

Daniel Hewlett, Llion Jones, Alexandre Lacoste, and Izzeddin Gur. 2017. Accurate supervised and semi-supervised machine reading for long documents. In *Proceedings of the 2017 Conference on Empirical Methods in Natural Language Processing*, pages 2011–2020, Copenhagen, Denmark. Association for Computational Linguistics.

Daniel Hewlett, Alexandre Lacoste, Llion Jones, Illia Polosukhin, Andrew Fandrianto, Jay Han, Matthew Kelcey, and David Berthelot. 2016. WikiReading: A novel large-scale language understanding task over Wikipedia. In *Proceedings of the 54th Annual Meeting of the Association for Computational Linguistics (Volume 1: Long Papers)*, pages 1535–1545, Berlin, Germany. Association for Computational Linguistics.

Marcin Junczys-Dowmunt and Roman Grundkiewicz. 2018. MS-UEdin submission to the WMT2018 APE shared task: Dual-source transformer for automatic post-editing. In *Proceedings of the Third Conference on Machine Translation: Shared Task Papers*, pages 822–826, Belgium, Brussels. Association for Computational Linguistics.

Marcin Junczys-Dowmunt, Roman Grundkiewicz, Tomasz Dwojak, Hieu Hoang, Kenneth Heafield, Tom Neckermann, Frank Seide, Ulrich Germann, Alham Fikri Aji, Nikolay Bogoychev, André F. T. Martins, and Alexandra Birch. 2018. Marian: Fast neural machine translation in C++. In *Proceedings of ACL 2018, System Demonstrations*, pages 116–121, Melbourne, Australia. Association for Computational Linguistics.

Taku Kudo. 2018. Subword regularization: Improving neural network translation models with multiple subword candidates. In *Proceedings of the 56th Annual Meeting of the Association for Computational Linguistics (Volume 1: Long Papers)*, pages 66–75, Melbourne, Australia. Association for Computational Linguistics.

J. Li, A. Sun, J. Han, and C. Li. 2020. A survey on deep learning for named entity recognition. *IEEE Transactions on Knowledge and Data Engineering*, pages 1–1.

Yinhan Liu, Myle Ott, Naman Goyal, Jingfei Du, Mandar Joshi, Danqi Chen, Omer Levy, Mike Lewis, Luke Zettlemoyer, and Veselin Stoyanov. 2019. RoBERTa: A robustly optimized BERT pre-training approach. *Computing Research Repository*, arXiv:1907.11692.

Alec Radford, Karthik Narasimhan, Tim Salimans, and Ilya Sutskever. 2018. Improving language understanding by generative pre-training. Technical report, OpenAI.

Colin Raffel, Noam Shazeer, Adam Roberts, Katherine Lee, Sharan Narang, Michael Matena, Yanqi Zhou, Wei Li, and Peter J. Liu. 2020. Exploring the limits of transfer learning with a unified text-to-text transformer. *Journal of Machine Learning Research*, 21(140):1–67.

Pranav Rajpurkar, Robin Jia, and Percy Liang. 2018. Know what you don't know: Unanswerable questions for SQuAD. In *Proceedings of the 56th Annual Meeting of the Association for Computational Linguistics (Volume 2: Short Papers)*, pages 784–789, Melbourne, Australia. Association for Computational Linguistics.

Pranav Rajpurkar, Jian Zhang, Konstantin Lopyrev, and Percy Liang. 2016. SQuAD: 100,000+ questions for machine comprehension of text. In *Proceedings of the 2016 Conference on Empirical Methods in Natural Language Processing*, pages 2383–2392, Austin, Texas. Association for Computational Linguistics.

Tomasz Stanislawek, Anna Wróblewska, Alicja Wójcicka, Daniel Ziembicki, and Przemyslaw Biecek. 2019. Named entity recognition - is there a glass ceiling? In *Proceedings of the 23rd Conference on Computational Natural Language Learning (CoNLL)*, pages 624–633, Hong Kong, China. Association for Computational Linguistics.

Raymond Hendy Susanto, Hai Leong Chieu, and Wei Lu. 2016. Learning to capitalize with character-level recurrent neural networks: An empirical study. In *Proceedings of the 2016 Conference on Empirical Methods in Natural Language Processing*, pages 2090–2095, Austin, Texas. Association for Computational Linguistics.

Ashish Vaswani, Noam Shazeer, Niki Parmar, Jakob Uszkoreit, Llion Jones, Aidan N Gomez, Ł ukasz Kaiser, and Illia Polosukhin. 2017. Attention is all you need. In *Advances in Neural Information Processing Systems 30*, pages 5998–6008. Curran Associates, Inc.

Alex Wang, Yada Pruksachatkun, Nikita Nangia, Amanpreet Singh, Julian Michael, Felix Hill, Omer Levy, and Samuel Bowman. 2019. SuperGLUE: A stickier benchmark for general-purpose language understanding systems. In *Advances in Neural Information Processing Systems 32*, pages 3266–3280. Curran Associates, Inc.

Alex Wang, Amanpreet Singh, Julian Michael, Felix Hill, Omer Levy, and Samuel Bowman. 2018. GLUE: A multi-task benchmark and analysis platform for natural language understanding. In *Proceedings of the 2018 EMNLP Workshop BlackboxNLP: Analyzing and Interpreting Neural Networks for NLP*, pages 353–355, Brussels, Belgium. Association for Computational Linguistics.

Wei Wang, Bin Bi, Ming Yan, Chen Wu, Jiangnan Xia, Zuyi Bao, Liwei Peng, and Luo Si. 2020. StructBERT: Incorporating language structures into pretraining for deep language understanding. In *8th International Conference on Learning Representations, ICLR 2020, Addis Ababa, Ethiopia, April 26-30, 2020*.

Yu Wang and Hongxia Jin. 2019. A deep reinforcement learning based multi-step coarse to fine question answering (MSCQA) system. In *Proceedings of the AAAI Conference on Artificial Intelligence*, volume 33, pages 7224–7232.

Vikas Yadav and Steven Bethard. 2018. A survey on recent advances in named entity recognition from deep learning models. In *Proceedings of the 27th International Conference on Computational Linguistics*, pages 2145–2158, Santa Fe, New Mexico, USA. Association for Computational Linguistics.

T. Young, D. Hazarika, S. Poria, and E. Cambria. 2018. Recent trends in deep learning based natural language processing [review article]. *IEEE Computational Intelligence Magazine*, 13(3):55–75.

Manzil Zaheer, Guru Guruganesh, Avinava Dubey, Joshua Ainslie, Chris Alberti, Santiago Ontanon, Philip Pham, Anirudh Ravula, Qifan Wang, Li Yang, and Amr Ahmed. 2020. Big Bird: Transformers for longer sequences. *Computing Research Repository*, arXiv:2007.14062.

Yukun Zhu, Ryan Kiros, Rich Zemel, Ruslan Salakhutdinov, Raquel Urtasun, Antonio Torralba, and Sanja Fidler. 2015. Aligning books and movies: Towards story-like visual explanations by watching movies and reading books. In *Proceedings of the 2015 IEEE International Conference on Computer Vision (ICCV)*, ICCV '15, pages 19–27, USA. IEEE Computer Society.

Parameter	Search space	Vanilla Dual-source	RoBERTa
batch size	$2^{\{6,7,8,9\}}$	2^9	2^9
learning rate	1e-5, 5e-5,.., 1e-2	5e-4	5e-5
lr scheduler	inverse sqrt, linear decay	linear	linear
hidden dropout		0	0.1
attention dropout	0, 0.1	0	0.1
activation dropout		0	0
weight decay		0	0.1
encoder layers	1, .., 6	2	–
decoder layers		2	6
embedding dim*	$2^{\{5,6,..,9\}}$	2^9	–
ffn embedding dim*	$2^{\{6,7,..,11\}}$	2^7	–
attention heads*	$2^{\{2,3,4,5\}}$	2^3	–
activation function*	ReLU, GELU	ReLU	GELU
learned positional emb*	true, false	false	–
share all emb	true, false	false	–

Table 8: Search space considered and hyperparameters determined as optimal when the validation set of WRR is considered. The * symbol denotes tied hyperparameters set to the same values for both encoder and decoder where applicable. The use of pretrained RoBERTa model resulted in the necessity to stick with several architectural choices signalized by – character.

A Hyperparameter Search

Table 8 summarizes search space considered and hyperparameters determined as optimal when the validation set of WRR is considered.

Hyperparameters for WRR were optimized using the Tree-structured Parzen Estimator with additional heuristics and Gaussian priors resulting from the default settings proposed for this sampler in the Optuna framework. An evaluation was performed every 8,000 steps, and the validation-based early stopping was applied when no progress was achieved in three consecutive validations. Intermediate results of each trial (results from every validation) were monitored and used to stop unpromising training earlier.

The trial was pruned in the case its best intermediate value was in the bottom 90 percentiles among trials at the same step (only the top 10% of trials were allowed to continue the training). This process was disabled until five trials finished.

The total number of 250 trials was performed for each architecture.

B Basic seq2seq Replication Details

Since the basic seq2seq model description missed some essential details, they had to be assumed before model training. For example, we supposed that the model consisted of unidirectional LSTMs. It was trained with mean (per word) cross-entropy loss until no progress was observed for 10 consecutive validations occurring every 10,000 updates. Input and output sequences were tokenized and lowercased. Besides, and truecasing was applied to the output. We use syntok[2] tokenizer and a simple RNN-based truecaser proposed by Susanto et al. (2016). During inference, we used a beam size of 8. The rest of the parameters followed the description provided by the authors.

[2] https://github.com/fnl/syntok

How well does surprisal explain N400 amplitude under different experimental conditions?

James A. Michaelov
Deparmtment of Cognitive Science
University of California, San Diego
j1michae@ucsd.edu

Benjamin K. Bergen
Deparmtment of Cognitive Science
University of California, San Diego
bkbergen@ucsd.edu

Abstract

We investigate the extent to which word surprisal can be used to predict a neural measure of human language processing difficulty—the N400. To do this, we use recurrent neural networks to calculate the surprisal of stimuli from previously published neurolinguistic studies of the N400. We find that surprisal can predict N400 amplitude in a wide range of cases, and the cases where it cannot do so provide valuable insight into the neurocognitive processes underlying the response.

1 Introduction

The N400 component of the event-related brain potential is generally understood to be a neural signal of processing difficulty (Kutas and Federmeier, 2011). After over 1,000 articles published on the topic, we know that all else being equal, an upcoming word that is supported by the semantics of the context will elicit a lower-amplitude N400 than a word that is not (Kutas and Federmeier, 2011; Kuperberg et al., 2020). However, despite the great amount of experimental research on the topic, many aspects of the N400 are still not well understood.

In addition to 'long-standing and recent linguistic [...] inputs' (Kutas and Federmeier, 2011, p. 641), the context that impacts N400 amplitude is thought to include factors such as world experience, attentional state, and mood (Kutas and Federmeier, 2011). Over the last decade, there have been a number of attempts to use computational modeling to test hypotheses about the neurocognitive processes underlying the N400 and how the aforementioned factors may impact its amplitude (Parviz et al., 2011; Laszlo and Plaut, 2012; Laszlo and Armstrong, 2014; Rabovsky and McRae, 2014; Frank et al., 2015; Ettinger et al., 2016; Cheyette and Plaut, 2017; Brouwer et al., 2017; Delaney-Busch et al., 2017; Rabovsky et al., 2018; Venhuizen et al., 2018; Fitz and Chang, 2019).

As the majority of experimental research on the N400 involves manipulating the relationship between the stimulus and the preceding linguistic context (Kutas and Federmeier, 2011), a computational account of how linguistic inputs impact N400 amplitude is a logical starting point. Language models are inherently models of linguistic prediction based only on language input. Since N400 amplitude reflects how unexpected an upcoming word is based on context, the predictions of a language model can be used to model how expected a word is based on the linguistic input, and thereby investigate the extent to which N400 amplitude is explainable by linguistic input alone.

Recent research has shown that *surprisal*, a measure of how unlikely a language model predicts the next word in sequence to be, correlates overall with N400 amplitude (Frank et al., 2015; Aurnhammer and Frank, 2019). Thus, to investigate the extent to which N400 amplitude is explained by linguistic input alone, we ask to what extent surprisal can explain the variance observed in N400 amplitude.

In order to investigate this, we run experimental stimuli from eleven experiments from six papers (Urbach and Kutas, 2010; Kutas, 1993; Ito et al., 2016; Osterhout and Mobley, 1995; Ainsworth-Darnell et al., 1998; Kim and Osterhout, 2005) through two recurrent neural network language models (Jozefowicz et al., 2016; Gulordava et al., 2018), systematically comparing the significant predictors of N400 amplitude and surprisal. We find that in the majority of cases, significant differences in surprisal predict significant differences in N400 amplitude, and discuss the implications of the cases where it does not.

2 Background

2.1 The N400

The N400 is a negative deflection in the event-related brain potential (ERP) that peaks roughly

652

Proceedings of the 24th Conference on Computational Natural Language Learning, pages 652–663
Online, November 19-20, 2020. ©2020 Association for Computational Linguistics
https://doi.org/10.18653/v1/P17

400ms after the presentation of a stimulus (Kutas and Hillyard, 1980; Kutas and Federmeier, 2011). Most current accounts agree that N400 amplitude reflects processing difficulty for a specific lexical item, where a lower amplitude reflects prior activation of some of the semantic content associated with the word (Kutas and Federmeier, 2011; Kuperberg, 2016; Kuperberg et al., 2020).

Recent research has found that N400 amplitude '*decreases* with supportive context, but does not *increase* when predictions are violated' (DeLong and Kutas, 2020, p. 2, emphasis in original; see Kutas and Federmeier, 2011; Van Petten and Luka, 2012; Luke and Christianson, 2016; Kuperberg et al., 2020, for discussion). Crucially, therefore, we should not think of N400 amplitude as a general measure of prediction error. It is not the case that the N400 elicited by a word increases when the word is more semantically anomalous or unexpected based on the preceding context; rather, it is the case that N400 amplitude is reduced when the word is semantically congruous or predictable because it is facilitated by the preceding context.

This facilitation can occur in a large number of ways. All else being equal, words that are more semantically congruous, typical, or plausible completions of a sentence elicit lower N400 amplitudes than words that are more semantically incongruous, atypical, and implausible completions, respectively (e.g. Kutas and Hillyard, 1980; Urbach and Kutas, 2010; Ito et al., 2016; Osterhout and Mobley, 1995; Ainsworth-Darnell et al., 1998; Kim and Osterhout, 2005; Kutas and Federmeier, 2011).

One well-known correlate of N400 amplitude is the cloze probability (Taylor, 1953; Bloom and Fischler, 1980) of a word—the probability that it will be offered to fill a specific gap in a sentence by a given sample of individuals in a norming study. All else being equal, higher-cloze completions elicit lower N400 amplitudes (Kutas and Hillyard, 1984; Kutas and Federmeier, 2011). Additionally, even when matched for cloze, words semantically related to the highest-cloze completion elicit lower-amplitude N400s than unrelated words (Kutas, 1993; Federmeier and Kutas, 1999; Ito et al., 2016).

2.2 Cognitive Plausibility of RNN-LMs in N400 modeling

To disentangle the effect of linguistic input from other factors affecting N400 amplitude, a valid model of such linguistic input is needed. Recurrent Neural Network Language Models (RNN-LMs) are, in many ways, perfect models of the 'long-standing and recent linguistic [...] inputs' (Kutas and Federmeier, 2011, p. 641) thought to impact N400 amplitude. Long-standing linguistic inputs in humans are made up of previous language experience, which is analogous to a model's training data; and recent linguistic input is the linguistic context that impacts how humans understand the current utterance, which is analogous to the word sequence preceding the word to be predicted in the model's test data.

Beyond being largely developed as models of human language comprehension (Elman, 1990), recurrent neural network language models (RNN-LMs) have certain properties that make them reasonable models of human cognition. Keller (2010) identifies five features of the human language processing system that he argues are vital for a language model to be cognitively plausible. Three of these are exemplified by unidirectional RNN-LMs—like humans, they can make *predictions* about upcoming words, have a distance-based *memory cost*, and process language word-by-word in order in an *incremental* fashion (unlike bidirectional RNN-LMs and most transformer networks). The two remaining features, *efficiency and robustness* and *broad coverage* are determined more by the model's specific architecture and training than general architecture.

2.3 Surprisal and N400 amplitude

As discussed in Section 2.1, the neurolinguistic evidence suggests that the N400 is a measure of lexical processing difficulty. Recent work, both theoretical and experimental (e.g. Hale, 2001; Levy, 2008; Boston et al., 2008; Demberg and Keller, 2008; Smith and Levy, 2008; Roark et al., 2009; Brouwer et al., 2010; Mitchell et al., 2010; Monsalve et al., 2012; Fossum and Levy, 2012; Frank and Thompson, 2012; Smith and Levy, 2013; Frank, 2014; Willems et al., 2016; Delaney-Busch et al., 2017), has argued that surprisal, the negative logarithm of the probability of a word w_i given its preceding context $w_1...w_{i-1}$, as shown in Equation (1), is a good predictor of lexical processing difficulty.

$$S(w_i) = -\log P(w_i|w_1...w_{i-1}) \qquad (1)$$

Several researchers (Frank et al., 2015; Delaney-Busch et al., 2017; Aurnhammer and Frank, 2019) have directly demonstrated that surprisal is correlated with N400 amplitude. In their study, Delaney-Busch et al. (2017) use a Bayesian approach to calculate the surprisal associated with a target word given a related or unrelated prime (using word association norms and word frequency), and find that this is correlated with N400 amplitude. Frank et al. (2015) and Aurnhammer and Frank (2019) used a number of language models (including RNN-LMs) to calculate the surprisal of words in a natural language text, and compared this to the N400 elicited by these words in human participants, finding a statistically significant correlation.

Frank et al. (2015) and Aurnhammer and Frank (2019) also find that surprisal is a better predictor of N400 amplitude than a number of RNN-LM-derived metrics based on the full probability distributions predicted by the model such as entropy. We suggest that this may be explained by the aforementioned finding that while the N400 amplitude for a word decreases when its semantic content has been pre-activated, it does not increase when a specific prediction is violated. In other words, N400 amplitude is a kind of positive prediction error—a measure of how not-predicted the target word was. This is what surprisal is by definition—it only takes into account how much the actual target word was predicted and is not affected by the rest of the probability distribution. The other metrics, on the other hand, also take into account the rest of the predicted probability distribution, which does not appear to be reflected in N400 amplitude. Thus, there is a theoretical reason for using surprisal to predict N400 amplitude based on previous neurolinguistics research.

2.4 Predicting N400 effects

An alternative approach, that taken by Ettinger et al. (2016), is to use a language-model-derived metric as an analogue of the N400 and investigate whether experimental manipulations in the stimuli that result in statistically significant differences in N400 amplitude also result in statistically significant differences in the chosen metric. This approach allows researchers to investigate whether the reason for the correlation between the metric and N400 amplitude is in fact the experimental manipulation or some other factor.

This is the general approach that we take in this study; however, rather than focusing on the cosine similarity between the word embedding of target word and the combined embeddings of the previous words in the sentence (Ettinger et al., 2016), we model N400 amplitude as surprisal (following Frank et al., 2015; Delaney-Busch et al., 2017; Aurnhammer and Frank, 2019). Additionally, whereas Ettinger et al.'s (2016) proof-of-concept paper is based on 40 sample sentences from a single study investigating one phenomenon, we use stimuli from eleven experiments (with over 100 sentences each) covering a wide range of phenomena.

2.5 Other Models of N400 amplitude

While a number of other researchers have used neural networks to model specific N400 findings this way (Laszlo and Plaut, 2012; Laszlo and Armstrong, 2014; Rabovsky and McRae, 2014; Cheyette and Plaut, 2017; Brouwer et al., 2017; Rabovsky et al., 2018; Venhuizen et al., 2018; Fitz and Chang, 2019), these studies differ in that these models all have semantic representations as part of their input or are trained to learn to output some form of semantic representation. Thus, these models are also limited to the experiments for which they were trained.

For the same reason, these models can also not be used on their own to disentangle the effects of linguistic input from the semantic knowledge provided to them—this can only be done by comparison to models without this. While two of the studies compare their models to simple recurrent networks (SRNs) trained on the same data (Rabovsky et al., 2018; Fitz and Chang, 2019), these SRNs are not representations of the extent of what is possible with linguisitic input alone—these models are simple (for example, they do not use long short-term memory), and much of the power of RNNs comes from large training datasets (see, e.g., the discussion in Chelba et al., 2013).

Finally, it should be noted that while all of the studies discussed in this section aim to model real N400 effects, only two (Laszlo and Armstrong, 2014; Rabovsky and McRae, 2014) use stimuli from real N400 experiments; in the remaining studies, stimuli are chosen to represent manipulations that studies have found to influence N400 amplitude. Given that the N400 is still not fully understood, it is important to verify that the experimental manipulations investigated actually do elicit the expected N400 effect. For this reason, we only use experimental stimuli provided for published N400 experiments, and compare the effect on surprisal directly to the reported effects on N400 amplitude.

3 Approach, Motivations, and Hypotheses

The aim of this study is to investigate the boundary conditions of using surprisal to model N400 amplitude. While there is evidence that surprisal and N400 amplitude are correlated overall (Frank et al., 2015; Aurnhammer and Frank, 2019), it is unclear what variance in N400 amplitude is actually being explained by surprisal. While it is tempting to assume that surprisal is correlated with the N400 because the same factors that lead to reduced N400 amplitudes lead to reduced surprisal, this has thus far not been shown empirically.

This is the question that we investigate in this paper: which experimental manipulations that elicit a difference in N400 amplitude elicit the same difference in surprisal, and which do not?

We do this by running the (English language) stimuli from previously published N400 studies through two neural networks that have been used extensively to model human language processing (e.g., in Wilcox et al., 2018; Futrell et al., 2019; Wilcox et al., 2019; An et al., 2019; Costa and Chaves, 2020). The two models used are the the best English LSTM from Gulordava et al. (2018) and BIG LSTM+CNN INPUTS from Jozefowicz et al. (2016), henceforth (following Futrell et al., 2019) GRNN and JRNN, respectively. These models are both LSTM-RNN-LMs, but differ most notably in size and training data: The JRNN has two hidden layers (8192 and 1024 units), a 793471-word vocabulary, and was trained on 1 billion tokens (Chelba et al., 2013); while the GRNN has two hidden layers (both 650 units), a 50000-word vocabulary, and was trained on 90 million tokens.

In addition to answering questions about the nature of the neurocognitive systems underlying the N400, the results of this study also serve as a baseline for future research—they represent the best that current cognitively plausible neural network language models can do at predicting N400 amplitude using surprisal. Thus, future research that argues for additional sources of information or neurocognitive processes being involved in the N400 on the basis of modeling success should demonstrate that the inclusion of such components in the model improves upon the results presented here.

This aim of establishing a useful baseline is another reason for our choice of models—both are provided pre-trained by the authors, allowing for our results to be replicated and expanded upon. We also only use sets of stimuli that have been made available in papers or their supplementary materials. The stimuli from these papers (Urbach and Kutas, 2010; Kutas, 1993; Ito et al., 2016; Osterhout and Mobley, 1995; Ainsworth-Darnell et al., 1998; Kim and Osterhout, 2005), which cover a range of experimental manipulations that are discussed in Section 4, are included in text format in our supplementary materials[1].

4 Experiments

Figure 1 is a visualization of the findings of the original N400 studies and the results of the simulations. Given the differences in measurements, there is no scale—the heights of the bars indicate which conditions elicited higher or lower N400 amplitudes or surprisals relative to the others in the same experiment or simulation. All and only the significant differences between conditions for significant predictors of the N400 or surprisal are shown, not including significant interactions with recording locations on the scalp (which are beyond the scope of the present study). Black bars represent successful modeling of the differences in N400 amplitude, red bars represent unsuccessful or partially unsuccessful modeling, and purple bars indicate that the results are more complex than can be represented in this way. Only stimuli sets with over 100 stimulus sentences were run through the models (GRNN and JRNN); and while the models were not able to predict the surprisal of all target words (due to limited vocabularies or being unable to process certain characters in sentences), both models successfully calculated the surprisals of over 100 target words in each study. Stimuli, target word surprisals, and the code used to run the models are all included in our supplementary materials.

Where possible, the significant predictors of the surprisal of the GRNN and JRNN models were selected via backwards model selection using likelihood ratio tests of linear-mixed effects models (R Core Team, 2018; Bates et al., 2015) with and without the predictor under investigation as a main effect. When this was not possible, the significance of predictors were evaluated using a Type III ANOVA with Satterthwaite's method for estimating degrees of freedom (Kuznetsova et al., 2017). Significant differences between experimental conditions (i.e. between the levels of a predictor) were

---

[1] https://github.com/jmichaelov/does-surprisal-explain-n400

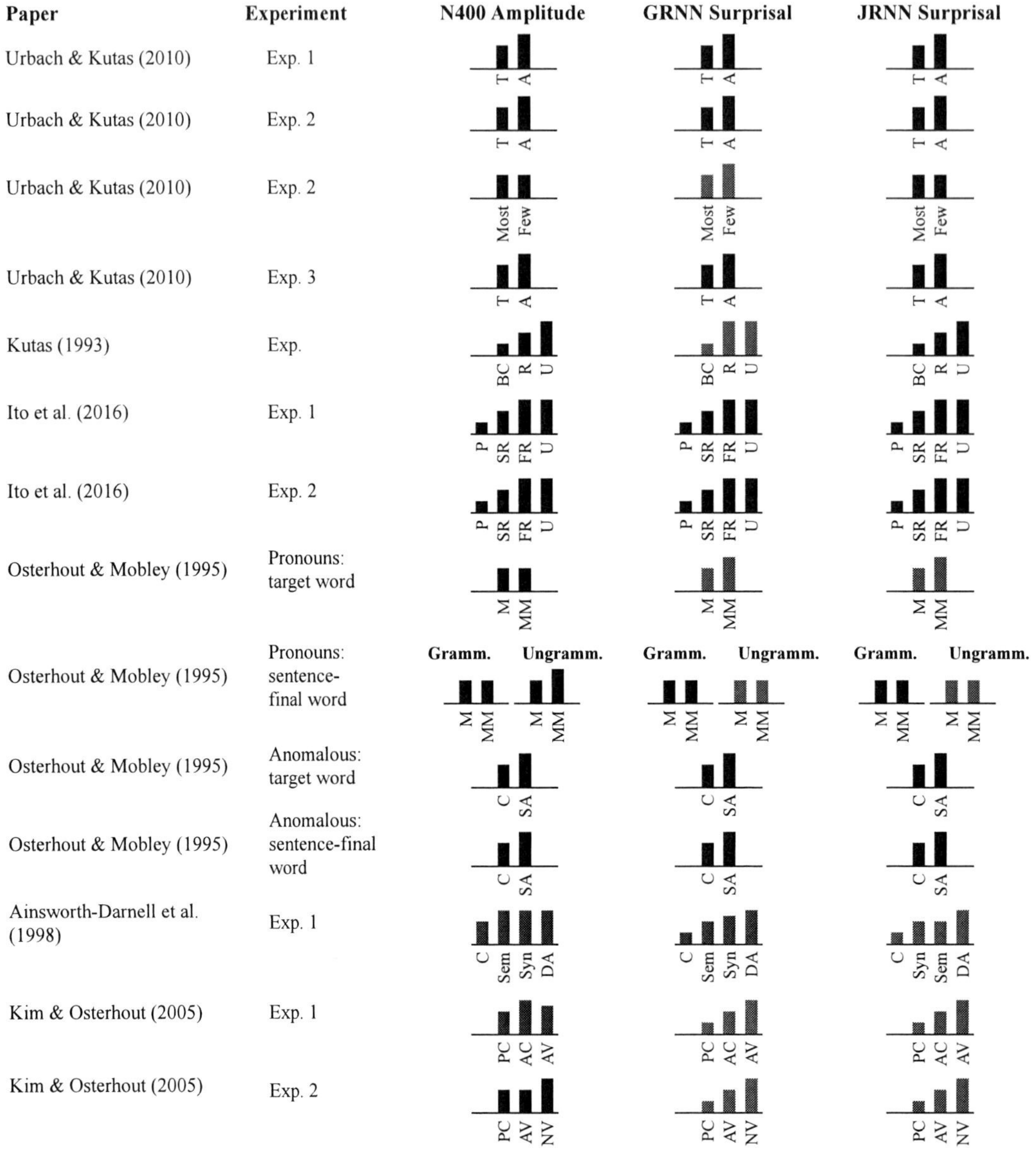

Paper	Experiment	N400 Amplitude	GRNN Surprisal	JRNN Surprisal
Urbach & Kutas (2010)	Exp. 1	T / A	T / A	T / A
Urbach & Kutas (2010)	Exp. 2	T / A	T / A	T / A
Urbach & Kutas (2010)	Exp. 2	Most / Few	Most / Few	Most / Few
Urbach & Kutas (2010)	Exp. 3	T / A	T / A	T / A
Kutas (1993)	Exp.	BC / R / U	BC / R / U	BC / R / U
Ito et al. (2016)	Exp. 1	P / SR / FR / U	P / SR / FR / U	P / SR / FR / U
Ito et al. (2016)	Exp. 2	P / SR / FR / U	P / SR / FR / U	P / SR / FR / U
Osterhout & Mobley (1995)	Pronouns: target word	M / MM	M / MM	M / MM
Osterhout & Mobley (1995)	Pronouns: sentence-final word	Gramm. (M / MM) Ungramm. (M / MM)	Gramm. (M / MM) Ungramm. (M / MM)	Gramm. (M / MM) Ungramm. (M / MM)
Osterhout & Mobley (1995)	Anomalous: target word	C / SA	C / SA	C / SA
Osterhout & Mobley (1995)	Anomalous: sentence-final word	C / SA	C / SA	C / SA
Ainsworth-Darnell et al. (1998)	Exp. 1	C / Sem / Syn / DA	C / Sem / Syn / DA	C / Syn / Sem / DA
Kim & Osterhout (2005)	Exp. 1	PC / AC / AV	PC / AC / AV	PC / AC / AV
Kim & Osterhout (2005)	Exp. 2	PC / AV / NV	PC / AV / NV	PC / AV / NV

Figure 1: The significant differences between all conditions of significant predictors of N400 amplitude in the original studies and the surprisal of the GRNN and JRNN models. **Black** bars indicate successful modeling of the differences in N400 amplitude, red bars indicate unsuccessful or partially unsuccessful modeling, and **purple** bars indicate that the results are more complex than shown.

calculated via t-test based on the selected linear-mixed effects model, using Satterthwaite's method to estimate degrees of freedom (Kuznetsova et al., 2017). In this paper, significant predictors and significant differences between conditions are considered those where $p < 0.05$ in the relevant statistical test. All code for the statistical analyses is included in our supplementary materials.

The remainder of this section discusses the experiments (and the original N400 studies on which they are based) in more detail.

4.1 Urbach and Kutas (2010): Experiment 1

Experiment 1 of Urbach and Kutas (2010) investigates the N400's sensitivity to the typicality of a patient of a described event. There were two kinds of sentences in this experiment exemplified by the following stimulus pair: *prosecutors accuse defendants* (TYPICAL; T in Figure 1) / *sheriffs*

(ATYPICAL; A) *of committing a crime.* As expected, the N400 elicited by TYPICAL object nouns is significantly lower in amplitude than that elicited by ATYPICAL object nouns.

Typicality was also a significant predictor of the surprisal of both the GRNN and JRNN models (GRNN: $p < 0.001$; JRNN: $p < 0.001$), with TYPICAL object nouns eliciting a lower surprisal than ATYPICAL ones (GRNN: $p < 0.001$; JRNN: $p < 0.001$).

4.2 Urbach and Kutas (2010): Experiment 2

Expanding on Experiment 1, Urbach and Kutas (2010) ask whether the results are affected by whether the sentences begin with the word *most* or *few* (or synonymous expressions), e.g. ***most prosecutors accuse defendants.*** The main effect of typicality remained. In addition, while the main effect of quantifier type was not significant overall (nor was there an interaction with typicality without an interacting electrode location variable), Urbach and Kutas (2010) found that FEW-type quantifiers reduced the N400 amplitude of ATYPICAL patients and reduced the extent to which N400 amplitude was lowered for TYPICAL patients, with this latter effect being found to be statistically significant via t-test.

Typicality predicted the surprisals of both RNNs in the same direction as in Experiemnt 1 ($p < 0.001$ for all statistical tests). The surprisal of the GRNN was also significantly predicted by quantifier type ($p < 0.001$), with FEW-type quantifiers eliciting significantly higher surprisals ($p < 0.001$). As this pattern is limited only to the GRNN (and the analogous main effect does not appear in Experiment 3 for either model), this finding is not considered further. The t-test comparing the N400 of TYPICAL objects under the FEW and MOST quantifiers does not replicate with surprisal—there is no significant difference (GRNN: $p = 0.107$; JRNN: $p = 0.249$).

4.3 Urbach and Kutas (2010): Experiment 3

Experiment 3 of Urbach and Kutas (2010) is a variant of Experiment 2. Instead of MOST or FEW sentence beginnings, the words *often* or *rarely* appear after the subject (agent) noun, e.g. *prosecutors **often** accuse defendants of committing a crime.* The aim of this was to investigate whether proximity of the quantifier to the target noun had an effect. Urbach and Kutas (2010) again found the same result—only typicality was a significant predictor of N400 amplitude overall; and a t-test found that

the N400 reduction for TYPICAL nouns was attenuated by the word *rarely.*

GRNN and JRNN surprisals were only significantly predicted by typicality, with typical nouns eliciting a lower surprisal than atypical nouns ($p < 0.001$ for all tests). The t-test comparing the N400 of TYPICAL objects under the FEW and MOST quantifiers does not replicate with surprisal—there is no significant difference (GRNN: $p = 0.367$; JRNN: $p = 0.283$).

4.4 Kutas (1993)

Kutas (1993) examines the effect of relatedness to the BEST COMPLETION (the highest-cloze completion). An example of a BEST COMPLETION (BC) and RELATED completion can be demonstrated by the following stimulus pair: *The pizza was too hot to **chew*** (RELATED; R) / ***eat*** (BC). An example of a BC and UNRELATED pair is the following sentence: *The paint turned out to be the wrong **consistency*** (UNRELATED; U)/ ***color*** (BC). BC nouns were found to elicit the lowest N400 amplitude, followed by RELATED nouns, followed by UNRELATED nouns.

Experimental condition is a significant predictor of both GRNN and JRNN surprisal. However, while the surprisals in the GRNN are different between the BC and other nouns ($p < 0.001$ for both RELATED and UNRELATED), there is no significant difference between RELATED and UNRELATED ($p = 0.820$). On the other hand, the surprisals of the JRNN are lowest for BC nouns, followed by RELATED nouns, followed by UNRELATED nouns ($p < 0.001$ for all pairwise comparisons).

4.5 Ito et al. (2016): Experiments 1 and 2

Ito et al. (2016) further investigate the relatedness effect by investigating whether a word that is related in form to the most PREDICTABLE word (i.e. the best completion) has a similar effect on N400 amplitude as being semantically related. The conditions can be illustrated with the following example sentence: *The student is going to the library to borrow a **book*** (PREDICTABLE; P)/ ***hook*** (FORM-RELATED; FR)/ ***page*** (SEMANTICALLY RELATED; SR)/ ***sofa*** (UNRELATED; U) *tomorrow.* In both Experiments 1 and 2, where the difference was in the amount of time that the stimuli were presented, Ito et al. (2016) found that experimental condition was a significant predictor, and specifically that PREDICTABLE words elicited the lowest N400 amplitude, followed by SEMANTICALLY RE-

LATED words, followed by the FORM-RELATED and UNRELATED completions, which did not differ in N400 amplitude.

We found the same pattern in the surprisal of both models ($p < 0.001$ for condition as a predictor; $p < 0.001$ for all significant pairwise comparisons; FR vs. U with GRNN surprisal: $p = 0.080$; FR vs. U with JRNN surprisal: $p = 0.399$).

4.6 Osterhout and Mobley: Experiment 2

4.6.1 Pronoun Matching

Osterhout and Mobley (1995) investigate the effect on the amplitude of the N400 elicited by words in sentences where pronouns either do or do not match a preceding noun, as illustrated in the following example: *The aunt heard that she* (MATCH; M) / *he* (MISMATCH; MM) *had won the lottery.* The MISMATCH sentences can be interpreted as grammatical sentences where the pronoun refers to a different person than that denoted by the sentence subject; or ungrammatical sentences, where the pronoun refers back to the sentence subject with the wrong gender. Osterhout and Mobley (1995) ask whether there is a difference in N400 amplitude between the two conditions, and whether this is affected by which interpretation is taken by participants.

Target Words First, Osterhout and Mobley (1995) look at the N400 measured at the pronoun itself, finding no significant effect of condition.

For both RNN-LMs, however, experimental condition is a significant predictor of surprisal, with matched pronouns eliciting a significantly lower surprisal ($p < 0.001$ for all tests).

Sentence-Final Words The N400 was also measured at the last word in the sentence. Under this condition, it was found that there was a reduced N400 for matching compared to mismatching pronouns, but only for participants who interpreted mismatching sentences to be ungrammatical.

In both models, condition was not found to be a significant predictor of surprisal (GRNN:$p = 0.775$; JRNN: $p = 0.112$). However, whether this is a successful replication of the responses of the participants who found the sentence to be grammatical ('Gramm.' in Figure 1) or a failure to replicate the results of those who found the sentence ungrammatical ('Ungramm.' in Figure 1) is unclear without further research, and thus this result is not discussed further in this paper.

4.6.2 Semantic Anomaly

In parallel to the pronoun stimuli, Osterhout and Mobley (1995) also compared N400 responses to sentences under the following experimental conditions: *The boat sailed down the river and sank* (CONTROL; C) / *coughed* (SEMANTICALLY ANOMALOUS; SA) *during the storm.*

Target Words N400 amplitude was significantly lower in response to the experimentally manipulated CONTROL words compared to SEMANTICALLY ANOMALOUS words. This effect was replicated in the surprisals of both models ($p < 0.001$ for all tests).

Sentence-Final Words The N400 and surprisals to sentence-final words followed the same pattern as target words ($p < 0.001$ for all tests).

4.7 Ainsworth-Darnell et al. (1998)

Ainsworth-Darnell et al. (1998) investigate the difference in N400 amplitude in response to syntactic and semantic anomaly, operationalized in the following way: *The chef entrusted the recipe **to relatives** before he left Italy* (CONTROL; C) / *The chef entrusted the recipe **to carrots** before he left Italy* (SEMANTIC ANOMALY; SEM) / *The chef entrusted the recipe **relatives** before he left Italy* (SYNTACTIC ANOMALY; SYN) / *The chef entrusted the recipe **carrots** before he left Italy* (DOUBLE ANOMALY; DA). While previous research argued that the N400 does not respond to SYNTACTIC ANOMALY, they found that the CONTROL nouns elicited lower N400 amplitudes than nouns in other conditions, but they did not find a significant difference between the SYNTACTIC ANOMALY and SEMANTIC ANOMALY conditions or between the SEMANTIC ANOMALY and DOUBLE ANOMALY conditions. Ainsworth-Darnell et al. (1998) do not report a test comparing the SYNTACTIC ANOMALY and DOUBLE ANOMALY conditions, but it should be noted that SYNTACTIC ANOMALY has a lower amplitude (based on the graphs) than SEMANTIC ANOMALY, so an unreported significant difference between these should not be ruled out.

Experimental condition is a significant predictor of both GRNN and JRNN surprisal ($p < 0.001$). For both models, the surprisal is lower for words in the CONTROL condition compared to other conditions ($p < 0.001$ for all pairwise comparisons), and there is no significant difference between word in the SYNTACTIC ANOMALY and SEMAN-

TIC ANOMALY conditions (GRNN: $p = 0.274$; JRNN: $p = 0.056$). The surprisals of the two models differ in that while DOUBLE ANOMALY words differ from SEMANTIC ANOMALY words in both models (GRNN: $p < 0.001$; JRNN: $p < 0.001$), they do not differ from the SYNTACTIC ANOMALY in GRNN surprisal but they do in JRNN surprisal (GRNN: $p = 0.059$; JRNN: $p < 0.001$). Based on these findings and inspection of the graphs in Ainsworth-Darnell et al. (1998), it appears that syntactic anomaly of this kind has a larger relative effect on surprisal than N400 amplitude.

4.8 Kim and Osterhout (2005): Experiment 1

Experiment 1 Kim and Osterhout (2005) investigate whether words that violate the event-structure of the described event are still facilitated if they are related to the event being described. The stimuli were of the following form: *The murder had been **witnessed** in the dark* (PASSIVE CONTROL; PC) / *The bystanders had been **witnessing** the crime* (ACTIVE CONTROL; AC) / *The murder had been **witnessing** by the three bystanders* (ATTRACTION VIOLATION; AV). General analysis found that condition only marginally predicted N400 amplitude, but pairwise comparison found one significant difference bwetween conditions: PC completions elicited lower-amplitude N400s than AC completions.

In both models, condition was a significant predictor of surprisal, and PCs elicited the lowest surprisals, followed ACs, followed by AVs ($p < 0.001$ for all tests).

4.9 Kim and Osterhout (2005): Experiment 2

Experiment 2 added the NO-ATTRACTION VIOLATION (NV) condition to the study, which is exemplified by the following sentence: *The unpleasant cough syrup was **witnessing** in the dark.* These were compared to results of the PC and AV conditions in Experiment 1. There was a significant main effect of condition, with PCs and AVs eliciting significantly lower-amplitude N400s than NVs.

Condition was a significant predictor the surprisals of both RNNs, with PCs eliciting a lower surprisal than AVs, followed by NVs with the highest surprisals ($p < 0.001$ for all tests).

5 General Discussion

We compared human N400 responses with surprisal in two RNN-LMs presented with the same stimuli, in the interest of determining the extent to which exposure to linguistic input alone can account for this particular component of human language processing. The results confirmed previous findings that surprisal is generally a good predictor of N400 amplitude, while also clearly demonstrating limitations of the models at capturing the human behavior.

5.1 Successful Predictions

The models effectively predicted certain kinds of contrast that the N400 is sensitive to.

Cloze The surprisals of both models for the Kutas (1993) and Ito et al. (2016) studies show that the surprisal of a language model is sensitive to cloze probability in the same direction as N400 amplitude—higher-cloze words elicit lower N400 amplitudes than lower-cloze words, and the same is true of surprisal.

Relatedness The results of the Kutas (1993) and Ito et al. (2016) experiments also show that surprisal matches N400 amplitude in that words that are related to the highest-cloze completion in terms of semantics, but not form, elicit a lower surprisal than semantically unrelated words, even controlling for these words' cloze.

Semantic typicality The surprisals of both models to the stimuli from Urbach and Kutas's (2010) three experiments demonstrate that the surprisal of a language model patterns in the same way as N400 amplitude in that more typical words (in a given context) elicit a lower surprisal than atypical words in the same context.

Semantic anomaly While the results are framed in the opposite direction in the original studies, the results from the Anomaly stimuli from Osterhout and Mobley (1995) and Experiment 1 of Ainsworth-Darnell et al. (1998) show that, all else being equal, completions that are not semantically anomalous (labeled 'controls' in these experiments) elicit a lower surprisal from language models than semantically anomalous completions, which is the result reported for N400 amplitude in the original studies.

Event structure violations The results for Experiment 2 of Kim and Osterhout (2005) show that both surprisal and N400 amplitude are reduced when a word is in line with event-structure norms, compared to a word that is not and is semantically unrelated to the preceding context.

5.2 Limitations and further directions

At the same time, there are areas where the predictive capabilities of the models are limited.

Quantifiers While the surprisal of the models matched the significant differences in Experiments 2 and 3 of Urbach and Kutas (2010) based on typicality overall, it did not replicate the finding that N400 amplitude was less reduced for TYPICAL nouns when they appeared with FEW or RARELY quantifiers. Thus, it may be the case that some more explicit (or at least more specific) representation of quantification is involved in the neurocognitive processes underlying the N400 than can be modeled by surprisal alone.

Event structure violations Overall, the surprisal of both models is more sensitive to morphosyntactic or event structure violations than N400 amplitude is (for a discussion on the extent to which these can be considered separate in the context of ERPs, see Kuperberg, 2016). For the stimuli from both Kim and Osterhout (2005) experiments, despite the ATTRACTION VIOLATION stimuli eliciting both a significantly reduced N400 amplitude and surprisal compared to the NO-ATTRACTION VIOLATION stimuli, surprisal remained significantly higher for ATTRACTION VIOLATION stimuli than either of the control stimuli, which is not the case with N400 amplitude. Thus, by contrast with the case of quantifiers discussed above (Urbach and Kutas, 2010), which seems to require a more detailed semantic representation, shallower or broader semantic representation might be needed to capture responses to the kinds of stimuli presented in Kim and Osterhout (2005). If the goal is to improve the extent to which models capture human behavior, then there might be ways to accomplish this. Frank and Willems (2017), for example, use cosine distance between the sum of the vectors of all the preceding words in the sentence and the target word to predict the BOLD response (using fMRI) in N400 areas. Given the collateral facilitation of words semantically related to the highest-cloze completions of sentences, it is not unreasonable to assume that a similar process of spreading activation may occur for the preceding as well as the predicted upcoming word in the sentence. One way to implement this could be to weight the RNN model's predictions of the next word by each word's similarity to a general sentence-vector such as that used by Frank and Willems (2017) before the probabilities are transformed into surprisal[2].

Morphosyntactic Anomaly While there has been some discussion about the extent to which event structure violation and morphosyntactic anomalies can be considered separate in the context of ERPs (see, e.g. Kuperberg, 2016), there are clear cases where the surprisal of the language models appear to be more sensitive to morphosyntactic anomaly than N400 amplitude is. This can be seen in humans in the results of Experiment 1 of Ainsworth-Darnell et al. (1998), where words that exhibit either semantic or syntactic anomalies elicit equally reduced surprisal. By contrast, the models predict grammatical continuations to a sentence over ungrammatical ones. This leads to lower surprisals for semantically anomalous words that are syntactically acceptable than those that are both syntactically and semantically anomalous. This difference between humans and the models supports the idea that there needs to be some way to weight predictions by semantic relatedness to the preceding context.

6 Conclusions

Previous work has found that surprisal is a good predictor of N400 amplitude overall. Comparisons of surprisal in RNN-LMs to human N400 responses to the same input sentences showed for the first time that suprisal manages to account for a wide range of phenomena found in human N400 experiments. But at the same time, there are linguistic phenomena where it overpredicts, and others where it underpredicts a significant difference in the human N400 response. From the perspective of human language processing, this suggests that the activation of semantic and lexical features indexed by the N400 cannot be entirely captured by exposure to linguistic input alone. Specifically, quantification, aspects of event structure, and morphosyntactic anomalies seem to require some other learning architecture than the bottom-up statistical learning represented by standard recurrent neural networks. From the perspective of model-building, in order to improve a language-model based cognitive model of the N400, we need to allow for the addition of more shallow semantic processing (independent of syntax and event structure) such as an implementation of spreading activation.

---

[2]See Kuperberg's (2016) discussion on bag-of-word approaches to the N400.

References

Kim Ainsworth-Darnell, Harvey G Shulman, and Julie E Boland. 1998. Dissociating brain responses to syntactic and semantic anomalies: Evidence from event-related potentials. *Journal of Memory and Language*, 38(1):112–130.

Aixiu An, Peng Qian, Ethan Wilcox, and Roger Levy. 2019. Representation of Constituents in Neural Language Models: Coordination Phrase as a Case Study. In *Proceedings of the 2019 Conference on Empirical Methods in Natural Language Processing and the 9th International Joint Conference on Natural Language Processing (EMNLP-IJCNLP)*, pages 2888–2899, Hong Kong, China. Association for Computational Linguistics.

Christoph Aurnhammer and Stefan L Frank. 2019. Evaluating information-theoretic measures of word prediction in naturalistic sentence reading. *Neuropsychologia*, 134:107198.

Douglas Bates, Martin Mächler, Ben Bolker, and Steve Walker. 2015. Fitting linear mixed-effects models using lme4. *Journal of Statistical Software*, 67(1):1–48.

Paul A Bloom and Ira Fischler. 1980. Completion norms for 329 sentence contexts. *Memory & cognition*, 8(6):631–642.

Marisa Ferrara Boston, John Hale, Reinhold Kliegl, Umesh Patil, and Shravan Vasishth. 2008. Parsing costs as predictors of reading difficulty: An evaluation using the potsdam sentence corpus. *Journal of Eye Movement Research.-ISSN*, 2(1):1–12.

Harm Brouwer, Matthew W. Crocker, Noortje J. Venhuizen, and John C. J. Hoeks. 2017. A Neurocomputational Model of the N400 and the P600 in Language Processing. *Cognitive science*, 41:1318–1352.

Harm Brouwer, Hartmut Fitz, and John CJ Hoeks. 2010. Modeling the noun phrase versus sentence coordination ambiguity in dutch: evidence from surprisal theory. In *Proceedings of the 2010 Workshop on Cognitive Modeling and Computational Linguistics*, pages 72–80. Association for Computational Linguistics.

Ciprian Chelba, Tomas Mikolov, Mike Schuster, Qi Ge, Thorsten Brants, Phillipp Koehn, and Tony Robinson. 2013. One billion word benchmark for measuring progress in statistical language modeling. *arXiv preprint arXiv:1312.3005*.

Samuel J Cheyette and David C Plaut. 2017. Modeling the N400 ERP component as transient semantic overactivation within a neural network model of word comprehension. *Cognition*, 162:153–166.

Jillian K Da Costa and Rui P Chaves. 2020. Assessing the ability of Transformer-based Neural Models to represent structurally unbounded dependencies. In *Proceedings of the Society for Computation in Linguistics (SCiL)*, volume 3, page 10.

Nathaniel Delaney-Busch, Emily Morgan, Ellen F Lau, and Gina R Kuperberg. 2017. Comprehenders rationally adapt semantic predictions to the statistics of the local environment: a bayesian model of trial-by-trial N400 amplitudes. In *Proceedings of the 39th Annual Conference of the Cognitive Science Society*.

Katherine A DeLong and Marta Kutas. 2020. Comprehending surprising sentences: sensitivity of post-N400 positivities to contextual congruity and semantic relatedness. *Language, Cognition and Neuroscience*, pages 1–20.

Vera Demberg and Frank Keller. 2008. Data from eye-tracking corpora as evidence for theories of syntactic processing complexity. *Cognition*, 109(2):193–210.

Jeffrey L Elman. 1990. Finding structure in time. *Cognitive Science*, 14(2):179–211.

Allyson Ettinger, Naomi Feldman, Philip Resnik, and Colin Phillips. 2016. Modeling N400 amplitude using vector space models of word representation. In *Proceedings of the 38th Annual Conference of the Cognitive Science Society*, Philadelphia, USA.

Kara D. Federmeier and Marta Kutas. 1999. A Rose by Any Other Name: Long-Term Memory Structure and Sentence Processing. *Journal of Memory and Language*, 41(4):469–495.

Hartmut Fitz and Franklin Chang. 2019. Language ERPs reflect learning through prediction error propagation. *Cognitive Psychology*, 111:15 – 52.

Victoria Fossum and Roger Levy. 2012. Sequential vs. hierarchical syntactic models of human incremental sentence processing. In *Proceedings of the 3rd workshop on cognitive modeling and computational linguistics*, pages 61–69. Association for Computational Linguistics.

Stefan Frank and Robin Thompson. 2012. Early effects of word surprisal on pupil size during reading. In *Proceedings of the Annual Meeting of the Cognitive Science Society*, volume 34.

Stefan L. Frank. 2014. Modelling reading times in bilingual sentence comprehension. In *Proceedings of the Annual Meeting of the Cognitive Science Society*, volume 36.

Stefan L. Frank, Leun J. Otten, Giulia Galli, and Gabriella Vigliocco. 2015. The ERP response to the amount of information conveyed by words in sentences. *Brain and Language*, 140:1–11.

Stefan L Frank and Roel M Willems. 2017. Word predictability and semantic similarity show distinct patterns of brain activity during language comprehension. *Language, Cognition and Neuroscience*, 32(9):1192–1203.

Richard Futrell, Ethan Wilcox, Takashi Morita, Peng Qian, Miguel Ballesteros, and Roger Levy. 2019. Neural language models as psycholinguistic subjects: Representations of syntactic state. In *Proceedings of the 2019 Conference of the North American Chapter of the Association for Computational Linguistics: Human Language Technologies, Volume 1 (Long and Short Papers)*, pages 32–42, Minneapolis, Minnesota. Association for Computational Linguistics.

Kristina Gulordava, Piotr Bojanowski, Edouard Grave, Tal Linzen, and Marco Baroni. 2018. Colorless green recurrent networks dream hierarchically. *arXiv:1803.11138 [cs]*. ArXiv: 1803.11138.

John Hale. 2001. A probabilistic Earley parser as a psycholinguistic model. In *Proceedings of the second meeting of the North American Chapter of the Association for Computational Linguistics on Language technologies*, pages 1–8. Association for Computational Linguistics.

Aine Ito, Martin Corley, Martin J Pickering, Andrea E Martin, and Mante S Nieuwland. 2016. Predicting form and meaning: Evidence from brain potentials. *Journal of Memory and Language*, 86:157–171.

Rafal Jozefowicz, Oriol Vinyals, Mike Schuster, Noam Shazeer, and Yonghui Wu. 2016. Exploring the Limits of Language Modeling. *arXiv:1602.02410 [cs]*.

Frank Keller. 2010. Cognitively plausible models of human language processing. In *Proceedings of the ACL 2010 Conference Short Papers*, pages 60–67, Uppsala, Sweden. Association for Computational Linguistics.

Albert Kim and Lee Osterhout. 2005. The independence of combinatory semantic processing: Evidence from event-related potentials. *Journal of Memory and Language*, 52(2):205–225.

Gina R. Kuperberg. 2016. Separate streams or probabilistic inference? What the N400 can tell us about the comprehension of events. *Language, Cognition and Neuroscience*, 31(5):602–616.

Gina R Kuperberg, Trevor Brothers, and Edward W Wlotko. 2020. A tale of two positivities and the N400: Distinct neural signatures are evoked by confirmed and violated predictions at different levels of representation. *Journal of Cognitive Neuroscience*, 32(1):12–35.

Marta Kutas. 1993. In the company of other words: Electrophysiological evidence for single-word and sentence context effects. *Language and cognitive processes*, 8(4):533–572.

Marta Kutas and Kara D. Federmeier. 2011. Thirty Years and Counting: Finding Meaning in the N400 Component of the Event-Related Brain Potential (ERP). *Annual Review of Psychology*, 62(1):621–647.

Marta Kutas and Steven A. Hillyard. 1980. Reading Senseless Sentences: Brain Potentials Reflect Semantic Incongruity. *Science*, 207(4427):203–205.

Marta Kutas and Steven A. Hillyard. 1984. Brain potentials during reading reflect word expectancy and semantic association. *Nature*, 307(5947):161–163.

Alexandra Kuznetsova, Per B Brockhoff, and Rune Haubo Bojesen Christensen. 2017. lmertest package: tests in linear mixed effects models. *Journal of Statistical Software*, 82(13).

Sarah Laszlo and Blair C Armstrong. 2014. PSPs and ERPs: Applying the dynamics of post-synaptic potentials to individual units in simulation of temporally extended Event-Related Potential reading data. *Brain and language*, 132:22–27.

Sarah Laszlo and David C Plaut. 2012. A neurally plausible parallel distributed processing model of event-related potential word reading data. *Brain and language*, 120(3):271–281.

Roger Levy. 2008. Expectation-based syntactic comprehension. *Cognition*, 106(3):1126–1177.

Steven G. Luke and Kiel Christianson. 2016. Limits on lexical prediction during reading. *Cognitive Psychology*, 88:22–60.

Jeff Mitchell, Mirella Lapata, Vera Demberg, and Frank Keller. 2010. Syntactic and semantic factors in processing difficulty: An integrated measure. In *Proceedings of the 48th annual meeting of the Association for Computational Linguistics*, pages 196–206. Association for Computational Linguistics.

Irene Fernandez Monsalve, Stefan L Frank, and Gabriella Vigliocco. 2012. Lexical surprisal as a general predictor of reading time. In *Proceedings of the 13th Conference of the European Chapter of the Association for Computational Linguistics*, pages 398–408. Association for Computational Linguistics.

Lee Osterhout and Linda A Mobley. 1995. Event-related brain potentials elicited by failure to agree. *Journal of Memory and Language*, 34(6):739–773.

Mehdi Parviz, Mark Johnson, Blake Johnson, and Jon Brock. 2011. Using language models and latent semantic analysis to characterise the N400m neural response. In *Proceedings of the Australasian Language Technology Association Workshop 2011*, pages 38–46.

R Core Team. 2018. *R: A Language and Environment for Statistical Computing*. R Foundation for Statistical Computing, Vienna, Austria.

Milena Rabovsky, Steven S. Hansen, and James L. McClelland. 2018. Modelling the N400 brain potential as change in a probabilistic representation of meaning. *Nature Human Behaviour*, 2(9):693–705.

Milena Rabovsky and Ken McRae. 2014. Simulating the N400 ERP component as semantic network error: Insights from a feature-based connectionist attractor model of word meaning. *Cognition*, 132(1):68–89.

Brian Roark, Asaf Bachrach, Carlos Cardenas, and Christophe Pallier. 2009. Deriving lexical and syntactic expectation-based measures for psycholinguistic modeling via incremental top-down parsing. In *Proceedings of the 2009 Conference on Empirical Methods in Natural Language Processing: Volume 1-Volume 1*, pages 324–333. Association for Computational Linguistics.

Nathaniel J Smith and Roger Levy. 2008. Optimal processing times in reading: a formal model and empirical investigation. In *Proceedings of the Annual Meeting of the Cognitive Science Society*, volume 30.

Nathaniel J Smith and Roger Levy. 2013. The effect of word predictability on reading time is logarithmic. *Cognition*, 128(3):302–319.

Wilson L Taylor. 1953. "cloze procedure": A new tool for measuring readability. *Journalism Bulletin*, 30(4):415–433.

Thomas P. Urbach and Marta Kutas. 2010. Quantifiers more or less quantify on-line: ERP evidence for partial incremental interpretation. *Journal of Memory and Language*, 63(2):158–179.

Cyma Van Petten and Barbara J. Luka. 2012. Prediction during language comprehension: Benefits, costs, and ERP components. *International Journal of Psychophysiology*, 83(2):176–190.

Noortje J. Venhuizen, Matthew W. Crocker, and Harm Brouwer. 2018. Expectation-based Comprehension: Modeling the Interaction of World Knowledge and Linguistic Experience. *Discourse Processes*, 0(0):1–27.

Ethan Wilcox, Roger Levy, Takashi Morita, and Richard Futrell. 2018. What do RNN Language Models Learn about Filler–Gap Dependencies? In *Proceedings of the 2018 EMNLP Workshop BlackboxNLP: Analyzing and Interpreting Neural Networks for NLP*, pages 211–221, Brussels, Belgium. Association for Computational Linguistics.

Ethan Wilcox, Peng Qian, Richard Futrell, Miguel Ballesteros, and Roger Levy. 2019. Structural Supervision Improves Learning of Non-Local Grammatical Dependencies. In *Proceedings of the 2019 Conference of the North American Chapter of the Association for Computational Linguistics: Human Language Technologies, Volume 1 (Long and Short Papers)*, pages 3302–3312, Minneapolis, Minnesota. Association for Computational Linguistics.

Roel M Willems, Stefan L Frank, Annabel D Nijhof, Peter Hagoort, and Antal Van den Bosch. 2016. Prediction during natural language comprehension. *Cerebral Cortex*, 26(6):2506–2516.